LAROUSSE GARDENING AND GARDENS

LAROUSSE GARDENING AND GARDENS

Larousse Gardening and Gardens. Published by The Hamlyn Publishing Group Limited, a division of the Octopus Publishing Group Limited, Michelin House, 81 Fulham Road, London SW3 6RB, from the French language edition Larousse Jardins et Jardinage published by Libraire Larousse/Mon Jardin Ma Maison.

Facts on File, Inc.
460 Park Avenue South
New York NY 10016
USA

Library of Congress Cataloging-in-Publication Data

Larousse gardening and gardens / Pierre Anglade. editor.
p. cm.
ISBN 0-8160-2242-9
1. Gardens. 2. Gardening. I. Anglade, Pierre.
SB450.97.L37 1990
635.9—dc 20 89-45612
CIP

Facts On File books are available at special discounts when purchased in bulk quantities for businesses, associations, institutions or sales promotion. Please contact the Special Sales Department of our New York office at 212/683-2244 (dial 800/322-8755 except in NY, AK or HI).

Composition by Servis Filmsetting Ltd
Produced by Mandarin Offset—printed in Hong Kong

10 9 8 7 6 5 4 3 2 1

CONTENTS

Chapter 1:
The History of the Garden **6**
The Gardens of Antiquity 8
The Gardens of Islam 11
The Medieval Garden 13
The Gardens of the Renaissance 16
The French Garden 20
The King's Gardens 23
The English Landscape Garden 30
The Garden – an Autobiography 36
The European Quest for Plants 41
The Japanese Garden 44
The Flower Garden 51
Tradition and the American Garden 55
Gardens Old and New 59

Chapter 2:
Types of Garden **66**
The Ornamental Garden 66
The Flower Garden 70
Raised Flowerbeds 85
The Rock Garden 88
Climbing Plants 96
Flowers for Cutting 102
The Water Garden 106
The Vegetable Garden 111
The Orchard 124
Hedges 132
Lawns 135
Ground-cover Plants 141
Greenhouses 143
Patio and Balcony Gardens 147
Paths and Steps 155
Walls and Fences 159
Special Corners 161

Chapter 3:
Gardening Techniques **164**
Growing Conditions 164
Pests, Diseases and Physiological Disorders 202
Planting 210
Propagating plants 226
Pruning 260

Chapter 4:
A–Z of Garden Plants **289**
Guidelines for Plant Hardiness 583

Chapter 5:
A Passion for Plants **586**
The Creators 586
The Botanists 594
Botanic Gardens 599
Plant Hunters 603
Artists and Illustrators 613
Writers 616

Index **618**

THE HISTORY OF THE GARDEN

Jean Cotelle's painting of this sumptuous feature at Versailles (the Marais) gives Louis XIV's garden divine associations.

From prehistoric times, the plant cycle of birth, growth, flowering and fruiting, followed by death and rebirth, was considered a manifestation of divine will. It was from the mysteries and bounty of the soil that every civilisation drew its most potent forces and symbols. The cycle of the seasons, mirroring life itself, was associated with the gods. Throughout the ages, this unchanging natural order was revered.

For millenia, man was a gatherer of wild fruit, of seeds and roots. As soon as he settled, agricultural life began, and the first signs of social organization were seen in the clearing of ground for vegetable plots. It was in this way that the first gardens emerged and were dedicated to the gods of Egypt, Babylonia, Persia and Greece, the innumerable deities, givers and protectors of life,who had the power to create the fruits and flowers.

The garden or paradise recreated

Sources of nourishment, and homes for gods and demi-gods, guardian spirits of wood and water, these first gardens provided the models for Eden, for paradise or for those mythical islands of happiness evoked in the oldest texts of Chinese civilisation.

Food requirements, improved agricultural techniques, improvement of plants by natural and artificial hybridization, the introduction and disappearance of species through such factors as war or pilgrimage, voyages of discovery, the work of botanists, or even simply the migration of birds, are all influences that have gradually transformed the character and nature of the garden plants.

Plants came to be grown not just for food but for their beauty and for their medicinal or magical properties. The choice of plants and organisation of a garden often expressed this duality of purpose.

In the course of centuries, nature was tamed and brought under control. Attitudes to nature ranged from the formally trained and pruned trees in the Roman *topia* to the formal gardens of France and to the naturalistic English parks of the eighteenth century.

Man, the 'creator' of gardens

The desire to impose man's will on nature lies behind all the gardens that have been created over the past three thousand years. This desire provides the key to an understanding of styles, fashions and revolutionary changes. Gardens faithfully reflect their creators and the civilisation from which they arise.

Once we learn how to 'read' the famous gardens of history, they have as much to teach us as any book about the architecture, philosophy, botany, sculpture, painting and hydraulics of the times.

Each type of garden requires a certain ideal space. Some are more discreet and intimate than others, with the warmth that comes from a modest scale. A tiny Japanese garden with a few stones, a patch of water to catch the sky and some carefully selected plants may well be as moving and effective as a costly display. It is for each gardener to define his own objectives, his own ideal, so the garden becomes a natural extension of the gardener's personality.

Middleton Place, South Carolina is based on seventeenth-century Anglo-Dutch garden design.

THE GARDENS OF ANTIQUITY

Two thousand years ago, the influences of Egypt, Persia and Greece converged in Rome to produce remarkable gardens, such as that of Hadrian's villa, and the gardens of the Emperor Tiberius.

Egyptian gardens

In Egypt, all vegetation and human culture became concentrated in the valley of the Nile beyond which, as today, the burning desert extends for miles. In the valley, however, the annual flood brought fertile silt and water to renew the soil.

Osiris, a god of many forms and ruler of the plant world was especially celebrated at the moment when, each year, the waters of the Nile began to recede and tilling the soil could recommence.

At this time, effigies would be made of Osiris, using moist clay to which a few seeds were added. These would then germinate and the statues, covered in young shoots, would predict good harvests. Carried out every year at the same time, this rite celebrated the renewal of life.

Less is known about the organization of Egyptian gardens than about their arable farming. However, tomb paintings suggest that the choice and arrangement of plants combined aesthetic and utilitarian concerns.

Water played an important role, and was conducted for irrigation purposes through canals and channels. (It was one of these canals – the Canopus, in the Nile Delta – that the Emperor Hadrian copied when he had his villa built near Tivoli during the first century AD.) The smaller channels had stone or cement edges, to prevent water loss, and were necessarily more formal than a 'natural' stream. Pools were laid out within the gardens, usually of a rectangular kind, surrounded by shady trees. These provided relief from the heat as well as serving as fish ponds and havens for water birds. Thus the garden supplied flowers, fruit and vegetables, and also a reasonable variety of meat for the table.

Persian gardens

From Persia, the Romans inherited luxury and refinement in the art of garden design. Persian gardens were enclosed by walls, to divide them from the wild, desert country outside, and to give shade and coolness. Tall evergreens and leafy plane trees also provided shade, while contrasting colours came in spring from the peach, almond and apricot blossom, and from spring bulbs. The centre of every garden was its scheme of water channels, either flowing down from a sequence of four terraces, or, most often, arranged in a cross-shaped pattern, radiating from a central spring. As in Judaeo-Christian and later Muslim writings this was linked to the idea of God's first creation, an ideal garden where 'four rivers' flow from the abode of the blessed. Pavilions were built either centrally, as an 'island' in the pool, or in a dominant position overlooking the pool or the sequence of terraces.

The word 'paradise' is itself of Persian origin, coming from *pairidaeza*, meaning an enclosure, and was applied to the enclosed hunting parks of the Persian kings. Taken into Greek as *paradeisos*, a rich and kingly park, the word came to mean both the Hebrew idea of the original garden of Eden – the peaceful home of the first man in his innocent state – and the heavenly kingdom, or 'celestial paradise'.

The Greek influence

Greece, whose influence on Rome was immense left a different heritage: history, heroes and gods. Roman gardens, whether in the regions of Rome or Tuscany, or on the hills around Naples, reflected this influence. Roman gardens were often given features in Latin, *topia* – which recalled the famous scenes or landscape of Greece, or commemorated some aspect of Greek mythology. In smaller gardens these scenes were achieved by frescoes, with rustic or mythological subjects. Many of these frescoes, and indeed gardens, have been amazingly preserved in the ruins of Pompeii and Herculaneum, two towns which lie on the lower slopes of Vesuvius, and were buried by volcanic ash in the eruption of AD 97.

Much of our knowledge of Roman gardens comes from these sites, scores of which have been excavated since their re-discovery in the eighteenth century. There are remains of villa gardens in Italy, and in many parts of the Roman empire – in Spain, south Germany, Austria, and

A hypothetical reconstruction of the gardens of the Emperor Tiberius, on the island of Capri, off the coast of Italy.

HADRIAN'S VILLA

Between AD 118 and 138 the Emperor Hadrian created a vast country estate, at Tibur – the modern Tivoli – a few miles east of Rome. The ruins which remain bear witness to an extraordinary and extravagant scheme of buildings and gardens – and are particularly intriguing, since there is little in the way of contemporary written comment. One of the few descriptions is by the Roman writer, Spartian, who records:

> *Hadrian's villa at Tibur was marvellously constructed, and he actually gave to parts of it names of provinces and places of the greatest renown, calling them for instance, Lyceum, Academia . . . Canopus, Pecile and Tempe. And in order not to omit anything, he even made a Hades.*

'Lyceum' and 'Academia' represented the great educational institutions of Greece; 'Canopus' was a luxurious city on a small branch of the Nile; 'Pecile' was the Stoa poikile *or 'painted colonnade' at Athens, used as a promenade by philosophers, and 'Tempe' was the rural valley in northern Greece celebrated by many Greek poets. Among the many sizeable ruins, and the different garden areas which cover some 160 acres (64.7 hectares) at Tibur, we still do not know what all the different features were meant to be. The Pecile has been identified – a gigantic wall 250yd (232m) long, 30ft (9m) high, so aligned that one can walk either on the sunny or the shady side, according to the season and the time of day. The Canopus is also known – a long, serene canal, with a curving colonnade and statuary at one end, with a version of the Erechtheum (from the Acropolis) on one side, and a half-domed building (possibly a temple of Serapis – or a dining chamber!) at the other end. What, or where representation of Hades was, we do not know, while one of the most beautiful of the many remaining structures in Hadrian's vast 'villa', is still a mystery – a circular island in a circular pool, surrounded by a colonnade. Generally called the 'marine theatre', it may have been a library or, a tempting theory, a quiet and private retreat for the emperor, to which he could retire, pulling up the drawbridge, for moments of repose.*

Later gardens were to echo Hadrian's extravagance – not least Versailles – and also repeat his use of buildings, monuments or motifs intended to recall the glories of the past, or of other parts of the world. In the sixteenth century the great Villa d'Este, a few miles uphill from Hadrian's villa, included the Rometta, a feature with miniature buildings recalling ancient Rome, like a model village in our own day; the Boboli gardens in Florence featured a circular island, the Isolotto, *recalling the 'marine theatre'; and in the eighteenth century, the landscape gardens of England consciously recalled scenes from Greece and Italy, with temples, grottoes, monuments, and whole landscapes designed to bring back the vale of Tempe, or Arcadia, or the Elysian Fields . . . Later still, at Malibu in California came the 'Roman gardens' of the J. Paul Getty Museum, of which Hadrian himself would have been proud!*

France. In Britain, the villa garden at Fishbourne, in West Sussex, England, has recently been meticulously excavated and restored. On a far grander scale are the remains of the emperor Hadrian's villa, at Tibur (the modern Tivoli), some 15 miles (24km) east of Rome.

Roman literature has rich and detailed references to the agriculture, gardens and botanic knowledge of the age. In particular, we may read of agriculture and gardens in the writings of Columella; of botany in the encyclopaedic *Natural History* of Pliny the Elder; and of two large villa gardens, in the letters of Pliny the Younger, who writes proudly to friends describing his properties. These are just three examples of the wealth of available material.

THE GARDENS OF ISLAM

As the Roman empire crumbled slowly away, instability grew. Throughout Europe, people shut themselves away in castles and behind the solid walls of fortified towns. It was a world of stone in which there was little place for gardens. Then, suddenly, the whole Mediterranean from the Levant to Spain was over-run.

Like conquerors everywhere, the Muslims were influenced by the cultures that they now ruled. Advancing into Persia, they discovered undreamed of luxury and refinement enjoyed by the conquered princes. The desert warriors, accustomed to frugal lives, were dazzled by this world of marble palaces and perfumed gardens.

The enchanting garden illustrated in this fifteenth-century Persian miniature depicts a wide variety of stylized plants, trees, shrubs and flowers, secluded from the world at large by a high wall.

The gardens of the south of Spain

When, at the beginning of the eighth century, the Muslims became established in southern Spain, they built cities and sought peace and repose in the shade of their gardens. They remained in Andalusia for more than eight centuries and the gardens that they left behind in Seville and, above all, in Granada, reflect the highest degree of beauty and refinement. It is from these oases of peace created a thousand years ago that the modern patio evolved.

The source of Islamic garden design lies in the Muslim idea of Paradise, as expressed in the Koran. The same inspiration was to govern the gardens of Muslim lands in the east: Persia, Mughul India and Turkey. But from Spain, above all, the influence of such gardens was to spread into the culture of Christian Europe – up into northern Spain, and, slowly, to Italy and France, affecting to some extent the development of the cloister gardens of the Middle Ages.

According to the Koran, paradise was the abode of the blessed. After their death, the faithful enter gardens which are enclosed, and contain unfailing fountains. There, 'they shall feel neither the scorching heat nor the biting cold. Trees will spread their shade around them, and fruits will hang in clusters over them'.

In this celestial garden flow the four rivers of Paradise – according to the Koran, 'there shall flow . . . rivers of unpolluted water, and rivers of milk for ever fresh; rivers of delectable wine and rivers of clearest honey'.

Here, then, is the source of the garden design of southern Spain. In a limited space, cool fountains, shady pavilions and the subtle fragrance of a few flowers provide the perfect contrast to the strain, heat and violence of years of warfare.

Enclosed gardens

The Islamic garden is secret and enclosed. The master of the house rules and shields family life and his wives from outside eyes. Pots of flowers provide bright colours throughout the year. However stifling the summer heat, the air is cooled by small fountain-jets, and the atmosphere is made more tranquil by the sound of gently trickling water, falling from one level to another.

The richer the household, the more elaborate the garden. In the gardens of the Alcazar, in Seville, are several garden courtyards – the most famous being built in 1364–6 for the Spanish ruler Pedro the Cruel, using Moorish craftsmen. In Granada, the gardens of the Generalife and the Alhambra were built over many years, and contain many variations on the four-part div-

Islamic garden design is at its most beautiful and refined in the gardens of the Alhambra, Granada.

ision of Paradise: well watered, cool and shaded, tranquil and enclosed.

Garden carpets

Garden carpets, of Persian origin, have been made in Muslim countries for many centuries. The carpets served both as a substitute for 'real' gardens, when the terrain was too dry and barren for a watered enclosure, and as an additional adornment of a courtyard (or even of an orchard, for an open-air celebration). On a desert campaign, a warrior king might take such a carpet to lay out on the floor of his tent, to remind him of a gentler, cooler scene; and in times of peace, a patterned, flowery carpet might be spread among fruit trees in the spring, to create an ordered 'garden' as the centre for a party, a gathering of poets or even a lovers' meeting.

These carpets, square or rectangular in shape, were commonly divided by streams, ornamented with fish, and shaded by lines of cypress trees. There was everlasting colour from flowering fruit trees, and sound and movement was intimated by singing birds and leaping, prancing and scampering animals – all woven with bright colours and convincing realism, and set in a composition which had the order and perfection of Paradise.

THE COURTYARD GARDEN

At the heart of the Islamic house, shut off from the world, lies the courtyard garden, a marvel of coolness and shade, a place for peace and tranquillity. Its calm has justly been compared with that of tea-gardens in Japan, where the trembling of a single bamboo represents the only sign of life.

The walls are painted in light colours, often white, and the courtyard garden is enclosed by columns and vaults, behind which lie the main rooms. Under the surrounding arcade, the floor is brick, tiled or paved, often in traditional Moorish patterns. Within the central space, open to the sky – an area of a few square yards – there may be elaborate designs in tilework or paving slabs and plants such as shrubs, flowers in pots and sometimes a palm tree.

At the centre is a small fountain or a basin from which runs a fine stream of water; its barely perceptible movement and sound preserve the old dream of the cool gardens of paradise promised to faithful Muslims as their final reward.

In this peaceful retreat, the family would assemble away from prying eyes. A heavy wooden door or shutter would be drawn against the wrought-iron grille so that passers-by could not see this enchanted area and its riches.

THE MEDIEVAL GARDEN

As time passed, arable land and pasturage spread out around the fortified towns, the high castle walls and the solidly defended abbeys and convents. The countryside, however, was still far from secure, and at the first sign of war the inhabitants had to fall back within their defences.

Within walls, town, abbey, castle or manor house, gardens were necessarily small. Every scrap of ground under cultivation was precious. Most important were herbs grown for everyday culinary, medicinal and, where necessary, magical, use.

While there are few pictures of medieval gardens before the late fifteenth century, written descriptions, a few plans, and many lists of plants needed for medicines exist from earlier times. From around AD 800, there are lists of plants which the emperor Charlemagne ordered to be grown in the towns of his empire. There is *Hortulus*, a poem in Latin by the monk, Walafrid Strabo, describing the plants grown in his small monastery garden, with a little about their cultivation and much about their uses! A highly detailed plan of an ideal monastery, drawn up around 816, and kept at the Abbey of St Gall in Switzerland, shows several enclosed rectangular garden areas, divided into rectangular beds, each inscribed with the name of a separate plant. The vegetable garden had 18 different beds, and plants, while the physic (or medicinal) garden had 16. In the monks' graveyard there were symmetrical plantings of fruit trees and nuts. In Charlemagne's list, in Walafrid's poem, and in the blueprint for a great monastery, every plant was useful. Even roses and lilies, grown by Walafrid, are praised not only for their beauty but also for their practical values: the lily cures snake-bite, and the rose has innumerable uses, its petals often being strewn on floors, for example, to ward off odours and illness.

The rose – a symbolic flower

Many flowers, particularly the rose, also had important symbolic meaning. In Christian imagery the white rose signified purity – that of Christ and the Virgin Mary – while the red rose represented the blood of his sacrifice and that of

This illustration – c.1500 – to the medieval French poem, Romance of the Rose *shows the hero twice: first, as he stands outside the garden wall, and then, delighted by the joyous scene, once inside the garden.*

the Christian martyrs. In secular works, the white and red rose meant innocence and passion, in that order. The long and complex French poem, *The Romance of the Rose*, begun by Guillaume de Lorris in the 1220s, continued by Jean de Meung, and partly translated into English a century later by Geoffrey Chaucer, has as its subject the lover's symbolic quest for the 'rose'. This search takes place within a huge, four-square garden. The lover first sees the rose when he peers into a reflecting pool; he falls in love with it, the emblem of feminine beauty, and reaches it, after 20,000 lines, at the end of the poem. The 'lady' whom this rose symbolises is never described. Like the rose, she too is a symbol, an ideal.

Medieval Plants

The range of plants cultivated in medieval times was limited in some areas but extensive in others compared to the balance today. Until the

TOPIARY AND CARPENTER'S WORK

An illustration of Brockenhurst Park Garden by Walter Tyndale shows topiary hedges dividing the garden.

In their simpler forms, clipped hedges and woven wattle fences were used to enclose or separate the garden, or a part of it, in preference to a costly wall. In Roman times topiary quickly attained a degree of complexity in European gardens. Woody plants, usually box or yew were clipped into ornamental shapes: giants, animals, letters forming the owner's name. In the Middle Ages, the topiarist's art did not go much beyond training bushes into a series of circular stages or platforms, looking rather like an ornamental cake-stand.

Pergolas, in contrast, and wattle work were often complex in Roman and medieval gardens. They varied from simple structures for supporting grape vines, to long, shady walkways round the sides of the garden, archways and arbours.

Pergolas, called 'carpenter's work' in medieval England, were made from trellis, or woven wattles, and often supported climbing roses, jessamine, vines or honeysuckle. In the early 1300s, the Italian writer Pietro de' Crescenzi recommended 'trellis work and tunnels in the shape of houses, tents or pavilions' for the gardens of reasonably well-off persons, while noble and royal gardens might include 'a palace with rooms and towers made uniquely from trees'. From the late fifteenth century both topiary and carpenter's work became fantastically elaborate, and were notable elements in a number of Renaissance gardens.

Woven wattles were used to keep earth from sliding down, as fences, and as the vertical edges of garden seats, built against a wall or round the trunk of a tree. These seats, which might also be faced with planks or bricks, were filled in with earth and given a top surface of turf. One of the first references to turf seats is in the gardening book De Vegetabilibus *of Albertus Magnus (c.1260). He writes, 'Between the beds and the grass a raised turf section must be set up, with delightful flowers and suitable for sitting on.'*

sixteenth century or later, there were no tomatoes, no potatoes, no maize, no tobacco; no sunflowers, no passion flower or magnolia or Virginia creeper. Thousands of species were added to general cultivation in Europe between about 1500 and the present day. These came not only from the Americas, but from China, Japan, Turkey, Persia, southern Africa and Australasia.

On the other hand, in medieval times many native field and hedgerow plants, or weeds, were keenly cultivated for medicinal or culinary purposes: agrimony, for example, pennyroyal, tansy, dandelion, betony and cow parsley are among the many.

Experiments with grafting

The Romans had long practised grafting: joining together pieces of two different plants, a stock, or growing root, and a scion, or aboveground portion, so that they are eventually united. In the Middle Ages complex experiments were undertaken to raise 'mixed' or 'composite' plants. This was recommended in the 1300s by Pietro de' Crescenzi, who admired 'trees variously and marvellously grafted', with 'many different fruit growing on a single tree'. In the *Ménagier de Paris* of 1393 (a work on domestic economy, translated into English as *The Goodman of Paris)*, there is advice for the production of seedless grapes:

> If you would have grapes without pips, take at the waxing of the moon . . . a vine plant with its root, and slit the stock right through the midst unto the root, and draw out the pith from each side. . .

Raised beds

In the miniatures which illustrate the later manuscripts of Pietro de' Crescenzi's work, the medieval garden appears as a space hemmed in by the walls of the house, the streets, and neighbouring houses. The garden is divided up into many square beds, usually raised up a few inches above the dividing paths, by planks pinned into place with short stakes.

These slightly 'raised beds' occur today in tidy vegetable or ornamental gardens, lined with planks, bricks or ornamental tiles. Their use, to drain surplus moisture from beds into sand or gravel paths, goes back to Roman times. Walafrid Strabo, the poet monk who wrote about his garden in the ninth century, is the first to state that planks were used in this way, and the custom was one that was much used throughout Europe until well into the seventeenth century.

In Europe, no medieval gardens have survived, cultivated continuously until the present day. Walls, yes, but not the gardens within them. Imaginative and exciting recreations of 'cloister' gardens have been attempted,such as the Cloisters, in Fort Tryon Park, New York City, but it is not until the sixteenth century, and the gardens of the Renaissance, that we may truly say 'These gardens still exist much as they did when they were first created.'

The White Garden at Sissinghurst in Kent, England, created in 1946, combines a formal pattern of paths and hedges with exuberant planting in white, palest silver and cream.

THE GARDENS OF THE RENAISSANCE

The Renaissance was a period in history when the art of the garden perfectly expressed the deeper significance of the age, with all its aspirations, challenges and rejections of outmoded ideas.

It is above all the age of discovery – the European re-discovery of the classical past, incorporating the literature, culture, and philosophy of ancient Greece and Rome; the discovery of the New World, and the ardent exploration of many hitherto unknown parts of the globe; and the discovery of Man himself, liberated from many centuries of ignorance, and entering a new age of intellectual and spiritual adventure.

True, these 'discoveries' were enjoyed and experienced by the privileged few the rich, the educated, the fortunate – while the vast mass of Europeans continued with lives only slightly affected and slowly changed by the new excitement of the Renaissance. Thus gardens of a humbler kind (like agriculture generally) may not at first seem to have altered much between, say, the fifteenth and the sixteenth centuries. But for the wealthy and the cultured in Italy, and subsequently for those in France and northern Europe, gardens were profoundly affected by the Renaissance – both through the *re-discovery* of information regarding the gardens of ancient Rome, and through the *discovery* of the New World, bringing new plants to enrich the European stock – a process which ran parallel to the introduction of new species from parts of the Old World, notably tulips and hyacinths.

Classical statuary animates and embellishes the seventeenth-century garden of the Palazzo Pfanner, at Lucca.

The Decameron and garden design

Around 1350, a young Florentine, Giovanni Boccaccio, put together the tales that have become famous as the *Decameron*. The framework involves a group of aristocratic men and women who leave Florence for a while to avoid the plague, and who, during their ten days' stay in various country retreats, tell each other stories to while away the time.

The *Decameron* occupies an important place in the history of the garden. The garden that Boccaccio describes is blessed by nature and, for the most part, the trees and flowers grow with little restraint. Around the house, however, the paths are straight and the plants are formally trained. There is even a monumental fountain foreshadowing those of the Renaissance. This valuable description of a fourteenth-century garden illustrates the subtle but profound change that was beginning to take place in Italy and, more particularly, Tuscany.

The cradle of Renaissance thought

The renaissance of the arts which preceded the religious and philosophical developments of the age emerged first in Tuscany, a region of Italy famed for the beauty of its scenery, its mild climate and rich soil. At the centre was the city of Florence. Here, men discussed the meaning of life, a new world order, the nature of man's relationship to the divine. And they turned to the wisdom of antiquity, seeking to understand the world, to affirm the preeminence and freedom of reason, without neglecting the mysteries of creation.

At the same time, rich families, dynasties of merchants and bankers, including the Medicis, became established in Florence and, from there, spread out over the whole of Italy and Europe. Up to the end of the sixteenth century, thanks to the generous patronage of princes and merchants, sumptuous gardens were created, round the magnificent palaces and villages which the owners had built for themselves, in town and in the country.

Many of these buildings and their gardens survive, for example: the Boboli gardens, Florence; the Villa Medici at Castello; the Villa Medici at Pratolino; and the Villa Gamberaia. In Rome, there is yet another Villa Medici, and not far from Rome are the Villa Lante at Viterbo, the Villa Farnese, Caprarola, the Villa d'Este at Tivoli and the Villa Aldobrandini at Frascati.

The 'river' or step cascade at the villa Aldobrandini at Frascati flows into the water theatre, or nymphaeum, containing grottoes and various ornamental water features.

The spirit of the garden

The renaissance of architecture which began in Florence also spread in its influence to gardens, which were themselves seen as architectural objects.

From the mid-fifteenth century a transformation took place in garden design. Water was cunningly channelled through fountains. Trees were clipped to precise shapes. The terrain, often steep and hilly, chosen for its fine views, was given regularity by staircases and terraces. Basins and channels were fed from streams gushing from the hills.

Leon Battista Alberti (1404–72), architect, poet, musician and philosopher, was to be one of the principal figures of the neo-platonist school that had such a great influence on the arts of the Renaissance. For Alberti and the other writers and poets in the circle of Lorenzo de Medici, the observation of nature necessarily entailed reflection on the garden, a small universe where natural forces were tamed. The cultured excitement of the Italian Renaissance was quickly noted and admired by foreigners, particularly the French, present in Italy for military and political reasons. René of Anjou, Charles VII, Charles VIII and François I all brought back to France the revelation of the marvellous gardens they had seen. Under an almost eternally blue sky, the garden formed a natural extension to the palace or villa, as if it were 'a residence but for walls and roof'.

Carpenter's work

The news of the Italian Renaissance spread northwards, across the Alps to the German states, and north-west to the Low Countries and to the British Isles. In these countries, far fewer gardens survived from the Renaissance, often because their features were constructed not in brick or stone, but in the elaborate but short-lived form of 'carpenter's work'. Books, illustrated by wood engravings, paintings and tapestries record these fantastic structures, which were quickly and cheaply erected to celebrate a victory, or a dynastic marriage, or – in England – the numerous visits or 'progresses' made through the country by Queen Elizabeth I.

In 1583 the Flemish artist and architect Vredeman de Vries published his *Hortorum viridiarumque formae* ('The forms of gardens and orchards') which illustrated gardens embellished by these elegant carpentry constructions, often on a monumental scale. They were to enjoy great favour during the seventeenth century. Salomon de Caus, in his *Hortus Palatinus* published in 1620, included these 'covered rooms' of shade. This book illustrated the gardens of the Elector Palatine, on the steeply sloping ground at Heidelberg overlooking the River Neckar. While the structures in carpenter's work have all gone, the great terrace outlines of his gardens remain.

Trellis work, in the form of pergolas, bowers and arbours, that supported climbing plants, was often combined with fencing to keep animals, domestic and wild, from intruding. (In France, the early twentieth-century recreation of a Renaissance garden at Villandry shows how varied and useful carpenter's work can be.) The screen of climbing plants also served to protect the delicate skin of the ladies of the house from the ravages of the sun. At Het Loo in Holland, created in the 1690s, the queen's garden has densely covered trellis walks.

By the middle of the seventeenth century, trellis structures had become a permanent feature of French gardens and served as a backdrop for open-air theatre.

André Mollet's *Le Jardin de Plaisir*, published in 1651, reserves a place within its groves for a four-chambered bower to be constructed from trellis work. Together with smaller arbours, 'walls' of trellis also provided temporary screening and cover while newly planted trees grew. The high hedgerows at Versailles seen in the engravings by Perelle and Silvestre, for example, did not reach maturity for some years after planting. To give shape and order to the gardens in the meantime, it was necessary to resort to trellis and latticework.

Finally, 'trompe l'oeil' trellis structures were useful for creating visual surprises, accentuating the perspective of an avenue, focusing the eye on a statue or effectively disguising the entry to a grove.

The Italian landscape garden

The Villa d'Este was begun at Tivoli around 1550 and was quickly noted as one of the marvels of garden design. Visitors from France, England and Germany sang its praises. The Villa Lante, near Viterbo, was created in the 1580s, as was the *giardino segreto* or 'private garden' at Caprarola, the Villa Farnese. Whereas in France and northern Europe, gardens were relatively modest, in Italy they dominated the landscape and were filled with works of art, antique and contemporary sculptures, architectural extravagances, and curious 'scientific' devices, such as joke-fountains and other hydraulic toys, rediscovered from the study of classical treatises. The garden became a triumphant hymn to the glory of its creator, man.

The symbolism of the garden

Some elements of Renaissance gardens were richly symbolic. (The statues and sculptures of stone, marble, bronze or plaster in today's gardens are an echo of Renaissance gardens, themselves the reflection of the gardens of antiquity, places that celebrated gods and heroes of the visible and invisible world.) In Italy, the humanists, both clerics and laymen, eagerly studied the rediscovered texts of Greek and Roman literature. Today, the allegories and symbols of these texts have become remote again, as knowledge of the classics is less central to our culture. But for the cultured élite in the Renaissance, the significance of a statue, a basin or the ornamental features of a fountain might

The Ovato fountain at the Villa d'Este was designed by Pirro Ligorio in the 1550s, its egg shape symbolizing the origin of life. Statues of river gods look down from the wooded slopes to the controlled exuberance of the fountains.

refer to classical mythology, to Virgil's *Aeneid* or to Ovid's *Metamorphoses*.

Nature itself was pressed into symbolic service. The pine cone that often decorated gateways was a symbol of welcome as it held out, through its wealth of seed, the promise of numerous progeny.

The Villa d'Este

The Villa d'Este is one of the greatest Renaissance gardens. To escape the summer heat of the 'eternal city', wealthy Roman citizens had already begun building villas on the Tiburtine hills fifteen hundred years earlier. Here, a mountain torrent, the Anio, provided cool and plentiful water before flowing down to supply the immense villa-estate that the emperor Hadrian had constructed in the plain around AD 130. At Tivoli, Cardinal Ippolito d'Este, a cultivated churchman devoted to the arts and letters, had his palace and gardens built between 1550 and 1580. The main designer was Pirro Ligorio.

Beneath the palace, the first terrace leads to the grotto of Diana where the decoration recalls the *Metamorphoses* of Ovid, in which the transformation of mythological gods into the first plants and animals is described. Further down, water spurts from the breasts of sphinxes, symbolizing the milk on which the life of the garden depends. Immediately below, dragons guard the terrace of the Hundred Fountains where the story of the *Metamorphoses* is told in bas-relief. At the end of the path, the Ovato fountain is dominated by an immense arch of water under which it is possible to walk and remain dry. Behind the oval fountain basin, the hillside rises steeply, and statues of river gods survey the scene. Nearby, the great Organ Fountain still provides one of the world's most spectacular water displays. It used to boast many hydraulic delights as well – a water-organ, blown by air compressed by water-pressure; trumpets; bird-song; noises of cannon, and the sound of a volley from arquebuses.

At the far end of the Hundred Fountains is the Rometta, representing in miniature the monuments of ancient Rome. As in Hadrian's villa, this feature was intended to recall the glories of the past, and intimate that the garden of the Villa d'Este, built in the 1550s, is comparable in its magnificence to that of the Emperor Hadrian. The Villa d'Este's gardens were one example of many which were to repeat Hadrian's extravagant use of buildings, statues and motifs to recall past glories.

The gardens at Villandry, near Tours, were restored early in the twentieth century, based on Renaissance designs.

North of the Alps

Though grand gardens were certainly created in northern Europe in the sixteenth century, there was none of note until the gardens at Heidelberg in Germany, made by 1619, and the gardens at Schloss Hellbrunn, near Salzburg in Austria, created in 1613–15. At Heidelberg, the vast L-shaped terrace framework remains beside the castle, and at Schloss Hellbrunn are the rare and intriguing series of joke fountains, the best preserved in Europe. These include a stone dining table and seats, where jets of water shoot up through the seats, drenching the diners – all, that is, except the host, whose seat, at the head of the table, is solid.

Two important recreations of gardens in the Renaissance manner have been made in this century: at Villandry, near Tours in France, where a spacious and complex series of formal gardens based on patterns from the 1570s was laid out after 1910; and, on a far smaller scale, in the garden of the Tudor Museum at Southampton in England. Here the garden has been laid out with scrupulous attention to planting of species appropriate to the Tudor period.

THE FRENCH GARDEN

In 1570, Jacques Mollet was head gardener to the Duc d'Aumale at Anet, the magnificent estate that had been created around 1550 by Philibert Delorme for the beautiful Diane de Poitiers. His son, Claude Mollet, who worked with him, was to become famous for his layouts at Saint-Germain and Fontainebleau. In a work, *Théâtres des plans et jardinages*, published in 1631 after his death, he remarked interestingly: 'When my father was working at Anet, they used only to make small knots or compartments with various sorts of designs in each square, because gardeners merely went on in the old way to which they had become accustomed.'

Then an architect of repute, Etienne Du Pérac, arrived at Anet on his return from Italy... 'He made sketches of garden designs to show the young Claude how beautiful gardens were made; in such a way that one garden was no more than a single design, divided in two by principal paths... These were the first parterres in France to be laid out using the "broderie" (embroidery pattern) technique . . . I was no longer content to make knots or compartments in little squares, one of one sort and the next of another . . . This is why, since then, I have always worked on the grand scale . . . All that remains to be done in this case is to treat them in an original way.'

These quotations perfectly illustrate the spirit underlying the French garden which, from the beginning of the seventeenth century, would start to dominate and direct European fashion. Its most complete expression would be seen in the art of Le Nôtre, which blended three essential elements: space, order and movement.

The first box edging

In the sixteenth century, well-defined squares of flowers linked with colour had been bordered by thyme or santolina. This type of plant soon grew untidy, was difficult to maintain, and needed frequent replacing. From around 1600, it began to be replaced by elegant arabesques of slow-growing, long-lived dwarf box 'embroidered' on a ground of coloured sands and gravel. It was on one such 'Turkish carpet' that La Fontaine set his fable of the meal of the town rat and the country rat.

Claude Mollet relates how his father began, at the end of the sixteenth century, 'to make the first edgings of box. This was most unusual as few persons of quality wanted box to be planted

'Embroidery' in box and coloured gravels in the great parterre at Vaux-le-Vicomte, designed by Le Nôtre in the seventeenth century.

in their gardens'. (They disliked its pungent scent.) Santolina and thyme, being often sensitive to frost, 'could not survive for long in the extremes of our French climate. It was the great labour of expense of remaking and replanting the edgings every three years that led me to experiment with box so as not to have the trouble of replanting it so often'.

Gradually, box came to be accepted on the royal estates and served as the basis for complex arabesques that could be laid out easily. To eliminate the problems that arose with ephemeral flowers, the ground in these 'broderie' patterns was covered with coloured sands or crushed brick or gravel. Thus, maintenance was considerably reduced and weeds could easily be removed. A few compartments, however, continued to be reserved for flowers.

Le Jardin du Roi

The Jardin du Roi, now the Jardin des Plantes in Paris, had been created by Jean Robin, whose name would be immortalised in the tree Robinia – *Robinia pseudoacacia* or 'false acacia'. He kept a garden on the Ile de la Cité in Paris where he cultivated medicinal plants and flowers used as models in the design and embroidery of clothing for both men and women. In order to develop his experimental nursery, he succeeded in persuading Vallet, Henry IV's embroiderer, to suggest to the king that he be granted a subsidy for the import of new species: bulbs, cuttings and seed, in many cases from Holland.

In this way, the embroiderers would find new sources of inspiration, richer motifs, more fashionable ones, and the credit, of course, would go to Vallet. Thus, the wily supplier of simples and medicinal herbs to the king succeeded in his enterprise. Eventually the Jardin du Roi was to be run by Guy de la Brosse, but in France Vallet's name remained attached to the development of embroidery both in clothing and in the garden!

The arrival of new plants

Towards the middle of the sixteenth century, with the development of botanic gardens and collections, plants began to arrive in France from all over Europe and the Mediterranean basin, and new flowers were grown in gardens. Thus, in Pierre Vallet's *La Fritillaire ou Couronne impériale*, published in 1608, there are illustrations not only of tulip, cyclamen, martagon lily, anemone and ranunculus but also poppy, canna and geranium. The last-named were 'true' geraniums, not pelargoniums, which were introduced much later from Africa. Many wild flowers were also used in gardens and they included primulas and violets. Crocus, columbine, hellebore and aconite were grown both for their beauty and for their medicinal properties.

In his *Theatre des plans et jardinages*, Claude Mollet stresses that 'all flowers, tall or short, will be an embellishment for every kind of garden – so long as they are planted to order'. To ensure that the beds are never bare, he insists on knowing the exact flowering season and development of the plants. Three centuries later, this will also be the main concern of the gardeners who established the herbaceous border in England.

Great gardeners

Jacques Boyceau de la Barauderie, gentleman-in-waiting to Louis XIII, drew up the first plans for the gardens at Versailles and, in 1638, published his *Traité de jardinage* which served as a guide for many later gardeners and architects.

The du Cerceau family provided four designers of palaces and gardens, flourishing between 1530 and 1620. Jacques Androuet du Cerceau wrote *Les plus excellents batiments de France*, published in 1576–79. From 1600 to 1720, the Francini or Francine, a family of Italian descent, provided hydraulic specialists for the royal gardens.

Jacques Boyceau de la Barauderie (died c.1633) influenced the great French gardeners of the seventeenth century.

The colourful 'embroidered' parterres at Het Loo in Holland were laid out for William of Orange in the 1690s, and have been completely restored in the twentieth century.

Jacques and Claude Mollet were to have brilliant descendants. André Mollet, the son of Claude, designed gardens all over Europe, from England to Sweden, for the famous Queen Christina. In 1651, he published *Le Jardin de plaisir*, a book which had great influence on later formal garden design.

Het Loo, symbol of the spirit of the seventeenth century

Daniel Marot, architect, gardener and designer, was a French Protestant who was forced into exile by the revocation of the Edict of Nantes. In the service of the stadtholders of Holland, he supervised the construction of the palace and gardens of Het Loo, Netherlands in 1695.

Totally restored in the 1980s, Het Loo is a perfect example of the style that had been in favour in Europe from the 1650s. When it was built, Vaux-le-Vicomte had already been in existence for thirty years and Versailles was at the height of its magnificence.

With a relatively smaller, level site, Marot had to seek a compromise between Dutch tradition and the space and broad perspectives of France. This was the basis on which Het Loo was originally built. True to this, Het Loo has now been restored from the winding paths, streams and weeping willows which, from 1810, had transformed it into an English park.

Het Loo is constructed on a long perspective. From the raised path that encloses the parterres and ends in a semi-circular colonnade, 'broderics' of box can be seen laid out on coloured sand.

The four main compartments are square and cleverly punctuated with statues and fountains. The species of hardy plants that surround them were in use during the seventeenth century. So that they don't clash with the strict outlines of the 'broderies', these plants are used as background, and are not an essential aesthetic component.

In the small Queen's Garden, a sort of *giardino segreto*, orange and lemon trees in tubs nestle in the shelter of the palace, appearing in summer alongside pots of agapanthus and lantana.

Elaborate tunnels in trellis work are covered with climbing plants. In hot weather, they protected fair complexions from the sun.

Garden masterpieces

From 1650 onwards, for something like a century, masterpieces of formal garden design were created in many parts of France, but especially round Paris: Vaux-le-Vicomte, the Tuileries, Saint-Cloud, Versailles and Trianon, Chantilly, Marly, Rambouillet, Sceaux, Meudon. These, and others like them, were deeply admired – and devoutly imitated – in Sweden, Spain, Italy, Germany, the Netherlands, England and Russia.

In the perfection of many of these great gardens in France, the work of one particular garden designer was decisive – André Le Nôtre.

THE KING'S GARDENS

'To succeed in any profession, it is certainly a great advantage to be born of parents who have practised it successfully.' Charles Perrault, (who also wrote the *Tales of Mother Goose*!), wrote this in connection with J.-B. de La Quintinie (1626–88), the creator of the great Potager du Roi, the royal vegetable garden at Versailles. He had trained as a lawyer, and his studies in botany and

The 'Bon Chrétien' pear, one of the many varieties cultivated by La Quintinie in the vast Potager du Roi *at Versailles.*

in practical gardening were made as a result of passionate personal interest.

Unlike La Quintinie, Le Nôtre came from a gardening family, and he was to embark on his career with an infinitely easier start, thoroughly justifying the second part of Perrault's commentary: 'In such a case, principle becomes practice almost effortlessly and, if new knowledge is added to what has been inherited, one cannot fail to surpass others.'

The glory of Le Nôtre

André Le Nôtre (1613–1700) was the son and godson of eminent gardeners. His father, Jean Le Nôtre (d.1655), was the chief gardener at the Tuileries and appointed designer of parterres for all the royal gardens. His superior was Claude Mollet who would be responsible for the royal gardens until 1650. His godfather, André Bernard, was the Controller General of the royal gardens and his godmother was Claude Mollet's wife. Could a professional gardener hope for a better start in life?

In his youth, André Le Nôtre had added a further important dimension to his outlook. He had entered the studio of Louis XIII's chief painter, Simon Vouet, who had brought back many drawings and etchings from a long period of residence in Italy. Vouet, moreover, was the teacher of the painter Le Brun who was to share in the glories of Vaux-le-Vicomte and Versailles. Le Nôtre was never to forget these lessons and in the royal warrant of 1643 in which Louis XIII named him 'designer of all gardens' his 'great skill and experience in drawing' was also remarked upon. He also studied architecture with Lemercier and Mansart. His interests extended to optics, which was then in fashion, and to hydraulics, a science in which the Italian family of Francini (or Francine) excelled – the brothers Thomas and Alexandre, and Thomas's son François, who was responsible for the great fountains at Versailles.

André Le Nôtre (1613–1700), gardener to Louis XIV, painted by Lefèvre.

The garden of Vaux-le-Vicomte was laid out by Le Nôtre between 1656 and 1661. His first great creation, it was thoroughly restored in the late nineteenth century.

In his early forties, and by now master of his profession, Le Nôtre was introduced by Mansart to the Minister of Finance, Nicolas Fouquet, who was gathering together a brilliant array of talent for the creation of a sumptuous domain at Vaux-le-Vicomte, the work on which lasted from 1656 to 1661. The three principal professionals involved were the architect Le Vau, the painter Le Brun and the garden designer Le Nôtre. They worked together to produce a unified, and glorious ensemble comprising the château itself, with its glorious interior decoration, and the magnificent surrounding gardens, with their statues, fountains, parterres and canal.

On 17 August 1661, Fouquet held a celebration to mark the completion of this masterpiece; the château and gardens of Vaux-le-Vicomte. There were over 2000 guests, including the young king, Louis XIV (he was 23), and most of his courtiers. The festivities, a most sumptuous 'house-warming', lasted for hours, with two separate meals, a ballet and theatrical performances in the gardens, and fireworks at the end. The guests were dazzled, enchanted with the scene, with the courtesy and generosity of Fouquet, their host, and with the gallantry of the principal guest, Louis XIV.

Among all the guests, the king himself was the only one to be discontented. He was enraged. Fouquet's 'fairy palace' was, by far, more sumptuous and more elegant than any of the king's residences. In political terms, it was a statement of superiority, and Louis could not tolerate a rival. Within three weeks, Fouquet was arrested, imprisoned and remained in prison for the rest of his life.

For André Le Nôtre, this was an opening to glory. When Fouquet was incarcerated, the creators of Vaux-le-Vicomte were employed to work on the construction of Versailles. Under their hands, the little château and its modest gardens, built before 1630 for Louis XIII, would grow to its present heroic dimensions. For Le Nôtre, it was to be a lifetime's work and he would be engaged on the gardens until his death in 1700.

Le Nôtre's conception of a garden

At Vaux-le-Vicomte, Le Nôtre was able to apply principles that had matured out of a long tradition, deeply influenced by the Italian Renaissance. For two centuries, the French court had established ties with the great Italian families, the Estes and the Medicis. Through commerce, art, travel, marriage, the attractions of Rome and Italy and, above all, the common cultural heritage of Greece and Rome, there was a continuing inspiration for all kinds of creative activity. This was the cultural background that Le Nôtre expressed in his work. To this he brought certain principles from which he would never deviate.

The house or palace must stand in a roughly level setting, surrounded by a carpet of embroidery parterres, pools and paths. The great central parterres must be set at a slight distance from the building, and should be best seen from an elevated viewpoint, such as the principal rooms on the residence's first floor, or *piano nobile*. It is precisely this arrangement which we find at Vaux, Versailles and Chantilly.

The garden should be dominated by a principal axis, or *allée*, usually aligned on the garden front, and thus overlooked by the principal rooms of the building. Depending on the size of the domain, the axis might be cut at right angles by two or three lesser paths or *allées*.

Within the divisions of the garden, there should be a regular arrangement of ornamental features, some open, and others enclosed by tall hedges clipped into smooth, green 'walls', each feature being geometrically linked to the central axis. Each will have its own theme: here a maze, there an open-air room for banquets or concerts, there again an elaborate fountain.

Le Nôtre would never tolerate constricted views. The result is clear at Vaux, Versailles and Chantilly, gardens where he carried out his best work. At Versailles, one's eye is firmly led towards the lines of the *Tapis vert*, the green slope which leads away from the château towards the mile-long Grand Canal. At Chantilly and Vaux, the visitor's gaze is drawn inexorably towards the highest, most distant

GARDENS OF POWER

Louis XIV was passionately interested in his gardens, at Versailles, Trianon and Marly in particular, and spent much time and thought in planning, discussing and supervising their development and improvement. From the early 1660s, when the château and grounds of Versailles were converted from a relatively modest residence to one of the biggest palaces and gardens in the world, to the year of his death in 1715, gardens were one of his great passions.

He himself wrote a brief text, or guide, with instructions on how the gardens should be seen. Called the Manière de montrer les jardins de Versailles, *'How to show the gardens of Versailles', it is an itinerary, proceeding from point to point round the gardens, in numbered paragraphs. At each point, the features he wants visitors to appreciate are the fountains and their sculptured settings. The fountains at Versailles, as in all such great formal gardens, were a vital part of the composition, and Louis wanted, indeed demanded, ever more and ever bigger fountains. 'Full-throated fountains' was his repeated instruction.*

Fountains, soaring high into the air in a controlled geometry of jet, arc and spray, are an expression of man's power over nature. Here, the king could impress and overawe his ministers, subjects and visitors with the triumphant and arrogant extravagance of his garden. In addition to these disciplined but marvellous fountains, other elements of unruly nature were likewise 'tamed' and brought into a huge scheme of order and symmetry. Shrubs and trees were trimmed into massive, regular displays of 'green architecture', stone was carved into sweeping steps and balustrades, with elegant statues as focal points, and rough gravel and sand were spread and raked smoothly along paths and avenues stretching into the distance.

In this way the king's authority, extending from the immense château along the western axis of gardens, stretched out to include, seemingly, the whole of nature. 'These gardens are a country', wrote Martin Lister, an admiring English visitor, in 1698. Their vastness was something which he thought, could never be afforded in England.

Several hundred statues, many integrated into the sculpture of the fountains, were another dimension of the gardens of Versailles. The wealth required for their creation was obvious at once, but their choice conveyed an additional message, different from that of the Renaissance *gardens of the previous century. Then, the statuary in* Italian *gardens normally illustrated the owner's wealth and his culture, recalling varied and fascinating aspects of the Greco–Roman past. At Versailles, however, Louis' garden statuary illustrated the many facets of a single theme, the supreme power of the sun god Apollo. Louis had gladly allowed himself to be called* Le Roi Soleil, *'The Sun King', and the message of Apollo's supremacy and all-pervading influence in the gardens was a direct and vigorous assertion of the king's own authority.*

point and the sky by a series of gradual transitions.

In Le Nôtre's gardens, the slightest shifts in level are exploited to create rhythm and movement. The natural slope may be broken or accentuated to establish separate levels. Slightly raised promenades to the side of the central path may overlook the beds or the whole garden, and lend an architectural firmness and symmetry to the layout. Often, however, symmetry is achieved by optical illusion, and walks that appear the same are, in fact, at slightly different heights.

At Vaux, for example, the 'Crown' pool and fountain are visually balanced by a small, semicircular 'theatre', yet the surrounding walk on the east is quite a bit higher than the one on the western side. Le Nôtre has cunningly disguised the slight slope of the ground.

At the Tuileries, sited beside the River Seine, the terrace beside the river is actually higher than the one on the inland side of the garden. His long terraces at St Germain are again most cunningly angled, and given a midway bastion, so that their length appears neither monotonous nor too daunting.

In many of his gardens a basin, or canal, sometimes as large as a lake, is set in the lower part of the garden to collect the waters of the streams or springs flowing through the property. At Vaux-le-Vicomte, and at Chantilly (seat of the Prince de Condé), these waters were used to create vast canals.

Ironically, both Versailles and Marly lacked copious supplies of water, and so water had to be brought in. By far the most striking solution to this problem was the huge Machine de Marly, an enormous complex of waterwheels and pumps built beside the River Seine and powered by the river itself, like a millwheel. This forced water uphill to a great aqueduct, leading it to the gardens of Marly nearby, and to Versailles a few miles further on. Though the Machine has gone, sections of the aqueduct remain, standing like Roman ruins in the countryside near Paris.

At Versailles, the water was fed into tanks and reservoirs, released to power the galaxy of fountains and water effects throughout the gardens, and channelled at last into the cross-shaped canal, a mile in length and two thirds of a mile across the arms. Half a mile from the château, the mile-long 'stem' of the canal was aligned on the west front of the building. The 'arms', stretching to north and south, led to the palace of Trianon on the north side and to the Menagerie on the south.

In all these gardens, large or small, fountains played a vital part. Since the clear vistas from the building required a low garden profile along the main axes (for which the extensive embroidery parterres were admirably suited), fountains, set at the crucial junctions of paths and avenues, and at the ends of vistas, provided perfect vertical components. They were visible yet insubstantial, eye-catching since they were always moving, and essentially in contrast to the plants, stone and gravel forming the rest of the gardens. Their gleaming and variable colours, from white to darkest silver, and iridescent rainbow shades, and the comparable variety of their sound, contributed enormously to the gardens' delights.

At Marly the water, pumped up from the Machine, was first led to a reservoir high above the gardens (used for skating in the winter!), and from there into the Rivière, a step cascade of superb proportions. The tumbling water, aligned on the main axis of the gardens, fell at last into a pool facing the royal palace, and was then passed to the lower side of the building, to flow into a long, axial canal. Though the Rivière has long since been converted to a grassy slope, and the palace is marked only by the outline of its foundations, the pool, with a fountain, and the canal remain, watery reminders of vanished glory.

The golden age of the French garden

It is difficult to imagine the extent to which the glory of Louis XIV and France influenced garden designers in the years preceding the dark days that ended the reign. Invitations came from all over Europe to the French specialists, asking them to draw up plans similar to Versailles. At the same time, from the early 1680s, a stream of Huguenot architects and gardeners left France, because of religious persecution, and went to live and work in the Netherlands, England, and German states, such as Hanover or the Palatinate, where Protestants were tolerated.

All over Europe, gardens in the formal French style were laid out, and many still survive. The most ambitious were normally built for rulers and the most powerful noblemen, but smaller versions were common. In the German states, fine gardens in the French style remain at Herrenhausen, near Hanover; at

Charlottenburg, in Berlin; Ludwigsburg, near Stuttgart; Schwetzingen, in the Palatinate; Anspach, in Bavaria; Nymphenburg, in Munich; and in Austria, there are the great gardens of Schönbrunn and Belvedere in Vienna.

The making of these gardens spreads over a century. The garden at Herrenhausen was begun in the 1660s, and then vastly developed from the 1680s under the Electress Sophie of Hanover. She expressed passionate admiration for French gardens, and declared of her own garden, in French, not German, that it was 'le jardin de Herrenhausen, qui est ma vie'. She died, suddenly, in the garden in 1714. Schwetzingen, in contrast, was not begun until the 1740s, and its fine formal layout, aligned on the castle, was given a vastly different 'landscape' extension later in the century.

In the far north, in Sweden, the architect and garden designer Nicodemus Tessin had visited Versailles in 1687, and on his return to Stockholm laid out the immense formal garden of the royal palace of Drottningholm. This, like Schwetzingen, now boasts a fascinating extension, in the 'Chinese Style', added in the eighteenth century. Tessin also made a small and lovely parterre, a jewel of formal design, for his own house in the city. Other formal gardens made in Sweden include Sturefors, and Sandemar. In Russia, the French style was introduced by Peter the Great after his lengthy travels in western Europe. The grandiose layout at Peterhof on the Baltic, near Leningrad, was designed by the Frenchman Le Blond.

In southern Europe, there is La Granja, in Spain. La Granja, near Segovia, is more than a mere imitation of Versailles. It is the physical recreation of a childhood memory, a farewell to bygone days. Made for Philip V of Spain, the grandson of Louis XIV, this astonishing garden copies the works of Le Nôtre's craftsmen stone for stone, statue for statue, basin for basin.

In Italy, birthplace of the Renaissance garden, the French influence was strongly felt. On a scale as small as that of Tessin's private city garden in Stockholm, *part* of the garden of the Villa Lante was re-designed in the French style. In the lowest area of the garden, where a hollow square of 'knots' had surrounded the central pool and fountain sculpture, the pattern was altered in the early eighteenth century to contain two embroidery parterres, one on each side of the pool. In staggering contrast was the formal landscape at Caserta, near Naples. Here, in the 1750s, the Dutch architect and designer van Vittel (or, in Italian, Vanvitelli) laid out the largest formal garden of all, for King Charles III of Naples. Though some of the more elaborate and detailed features, such as plans for scroll-work parterres in front of the gigantic palace, were not fully realized, the principal feature, the stupendous step cascade, was built across the sloping landscape, for well over a mile. Patently

The immense gardens of Caserta, near Naples, created in the mid-eighteenth century, were intended to rival those of Versailles.

Allegrain's painting of La Salle des festins or 'Banquet Chamber' in the gardens of Versailles. It was designed by Le Nôtre in 1671.

The goddess Flora reigns over spring. At Versailles, each of the four seasons is celebrated by a separate fountain.

modelled on the Rivière at Marly, it remains as an astonishing and unique example of garden megalomania.

In addition to Het Loo in Holland, created for William of Orange in the 1690s, in Flanders, now Belgium, one of the last great formal gardens was created at Beloeil for the Prince de Ligne. It was completed in 1761, a century after the completion of Vaux-le-Vicomte.

In England, the French style was as powerful as in any country outside France. In the 1660s, Hampton Court was developed in formal style by Charles II, who had spent most of his exile in France. He had the fine semicircular garden in front of the palace and the Long Water beyond made in 1661–62. Superb embroidery parterres were added in the late 1680s by Daniel Marot, the Huguenot garden designer who created Het Loo for William of Orange.

Many formal gardens were made in England in the late seventeenth century. At Chatsworth, the great step cascade was made in the 1690s by Grillet, a Frenchman; and at Melbourne, in Derbyshire, a much smaller garden was laid out 'to suit with Versailles', designed by George London, who had spent some time in France studying the gardens. While these survive, many others, such as the gardens at Badminton and Longleat, have gone, drastically changed by later fashions. Two fine examples, begun well into the eighteenth century, may still be seen at St Paul's Walden Bury, in Hertfordshire, created in the early 1730s; and at Bicton, in Devonshire, begun around 1735.

Versailles and its gardens were an expression of royal power, in which the symbolic centre was the sun god Apollo, and the living, physical centre was the king himself, Louis XIV. The château and gardens were the vast and costly framework, almost temple, in which *Le Roi Soleil* resided and ruled, from where his decisions and his orders proceeded, and in which he could be seen. Here the most powerful ruler in Europe lived a life as 'public' as that of any human being before or since. Privileged and assorted groups of noblemen were present when he got up, was dressed, ate, held meetings of state, attended divine service, or balls, or musical or theatrical entertainments, went hunting in the park or made the lengthy tour of the gardens. This last occupation took place not hundreds, but thousands of times, sometimes on foot, or in a light carriage, or on horseback on the way to the hunt, or, in his old age, in a three-wheeled chair, the *roulotte*, which was pushed by favoured courtiers. These visits to different parts of the gardens, to inspect a new feature, examine changes to an older scheme, or watch a firework display on the great Canal, were made amid a throng of attendant and subservient nobles, ministers, diplomats and lesser beings. From a slight distance, suitably dressed visitors peered avidly at the glorious proceedings. At

Apollo the sun god is honoured everywhere at Versailles, the home of the Sun King, Louis XIV. Here a statue of Apollo leads his team of horses to the western ocean, to rest after their day's labour.

The château of La Roche-Courbon, near Saint-Porchaire, is surrounded by gardens laid out in the seventeenth-century manner. They were created in 1920–35 by Ferdinand Duprat.

each point, the Sun King could be seen, and his glory could be confirmed.

In the gardens, the entertainments were many and various: parties with food and music, fountains, fireworks and summer theatricals. These entertainments were often mobile festivals, beginning at the château of Versailles, and then migrating, by boat, along the Canal to Trianon. The royal vessel would be followed, or preceded, by another carrying the royal musicians.

Trianon, now called the Grand Trianon, to distinguish it from the Petit Trianon built in the eighteenth century, was first conceived as a retreat, a small residence for the king and his mistress Mme. de Montespan, away from the public gaze in the château at Versailles. When Mme. de Monstespan was replaced by Mme. de Maintenon, the building was also changed. It became bigger, and the sense of privacy was lessened, so Louis decided to make a slightly more distant retreat at Marly, some miles away from Versailles. He engagingly called it a 'hermitage' to his finance minister, to deflect accusations of extravagance.

Marly is most well known for the great hydraulic Machine which pumped up water from the River Seine, and for the Rivière, the imposing step cascade. Marly was to be at least as costly as Versailles, with an entire hillside dug away to give a view, while its marvels were to be enjoyed by a small and eminently select group of favourites. When Louis was planning to spend a few days at this 'hermitage', the bolder courtiers would approach him with the question 'Marly, sire?' His 'oui' or 'non', conveyed by a nod, might raise them to ecstasy, or plunge them into despair, according to whether they were invited or rejected as Louis' guests. The king's small central palace at Marly had twelve pavilions for his guests, and the décor at one time presented the palace as the sun, and the pavilions as the twelve different, and subordinate, signs of the Zodiac.

THE ENGLISH LANDSCAPE GARDEN

While the fame and influence of Versailles and its gardens were still at their highest, and while gardens imitating these glories were still being laid out by the rulers of every state in Europe, a reaction to this form of gardening was slowly developing.

The reaction started in England in the last years of the seventeenth, and in the first years of the eighteenth, century. Its origins cannot be attributed to one single fact, but to several political, cultural and social causes. In political terms, the British had come to resent the French supremacy in Europe. Long periods of warfare, culminating in Marlborough's military successes over the French in the early eighteenth century, had given the English the confident belief that they need not accept French 'superiority' in any form. Louis XIV was seen as a tyrant, while the English saw themselves as free men, militarily, politically and, by extension, culturally as well. So *why*, they asked, need they imitate the fashions of France so slavishly? Why need they imitate Versailles, with its autocratic atmosphere, when they were descendants of free Saxons, who had had their own form of elective government, from which the English Parliament was derived? The Saxons also had their own form of architecture, the Gothic style, completely different from the Classical architecture which reigned in France. If *freedom* was a keyword, then gardens should share this freedom, and resemble 'nature' rather than be tortured into 'unnatural' forms. By about 1710, the idea of straight lines in avenues or clipped hedges was proclaimed 'unnatural', and what was 'free' and 'natural' was praised as being good, true, and English.

The Italian influence

In this same period, it became a fairly common practice for wealthy young Englishmen to complete their education by going on The Grand Tour through Holland, France and Germany, often ending in Italy. Throughout the eighteenth century, their journals and travel

The gardens of Stourhead, in Wiltshire, England, were inspired in part by the paintings of Claude Lorrain and Gaspard Poussin.

Claude Lorrain's Landscape with the nymph Egeria *is characteristic of the paintings which helped to inspire English landscape gardens: 'natural' scenery, a lake, and ancient Classical buildings.*

writings illustrate their continuing delight and excitement in the discovery of Italy. Between 1700 and the 1790 Joseph Addison, Joseph Spence, James Boswell, Arthur Young, William Beckford and Richard Colt Hoare recorded, in different ways, their exhilarated reactions to this warm, cultured and welcoming country.

Italy was the home of a living past: classical antiquity around Rome and on the Via Appia to Tivoli; the Renaissance in Florence, where Lorenzo the Magnificent still seemed to be alive. Here was an enchantment of flowers and ruins, beautiful works of art and architecture in the shade of immemorial pines, that the English visitors would never forget.

The treasure of Italy's museums, churches and sumptuous villas attracted and often retained artists and writers from all over Europe. They were especially impressed and enchanted by the atmosphere of the Boboli, the Villa d'Este and the Villa Aldobrandini gardens, which had acquired a sweetly melancholy dilapidation in the century or more since their creation. This 'grandeur in decline' appealed to the English visitors all the more as it was in contrast to the arrogant perfection of the more recent gardens of France.

The road to Italy was taken by painters from Rubens to Poussin, from Simon Vouet to Fragonard and Hubert Robert, and from Richard Wilson to John Robert Cozens and J.M.W. Turner.

Ideal nature in an antique world

A French painter, Claude Gellée, known as 'Le Lorrain', was born in France near Nancy in 1600. He left for Italy in about 1613 and lived there until his death in 1682. Indirectly, and wholly unknown to him, Claude Lorrain was to play a role in the transformation of the great gardens of England. His paintings are steeped in dream-like poetry, and are, almost without exception, works of the imagination, not realistic depictions of a particular scene. His work is devoted to an ideal nature, to a perfect antique world, lulled by breezes and filled with ruins, visionary castles, ancient temples and ships embarking for far-off, unknown ports.

Claude, as he became known to the English, was one of the first and greatest landscape painters. His canvases, of antique and rural Italian scenes, are imbued with peace, with gods and men living side by side. These visions of paradise, brought to England as originals, carefully copied by other painters or reproduced in engravings, would profoundly influence garden design.

The philosophy of the landscape garden

Anthony Ashley Cooper, third Earl of Shaftesbury (1671–1713) and author of *The Moralists* (1709) was influenced philosophically by the discoveries of Newton and Leibniz, which showed the mathematical precision of the universe. These discoveries, exemplified in the formulation of the laws of gravity, and the understanding of how light is refracted to form the rainbow, encouraged the belief in a universe which was perfect in every respect. Nature's perfection must also be appreciated, and mankind should look at the immensely varied manifestations of the natural world with a new and more appreciative eye. If Nature was perfect, then there was not only no need for man to 'improve' on Nature, but man's interference was impertinence or even blasphemy.

This philosophy said in clearest tones, 'All attempts to "order" gardens are misguided. What we must do is "follow Nature".' Shaftesbury's *The Moralists*, declares, for example, that 'the wildness pleases' and that nature is found more truly in the 'original wilds' than in the 'artificial labyrinths' and 'feigned wildernesses' of royal gardens. He rejects 'the formal mockery of princely gardens' in favour of 'the rude rocks, the mossy caverns, the irregular unwrought grottoes and broken falls of waters'.

In 1709, these exhortations of Shaftesbury's were still in the realm of philosophy. Not until 1712 and 1713 did Addison, in the *Spectator*, and Pope, in the *Guardian*, put forward much gentler versions of these ideas in a popular form. Addison, for example, urged with persuasive mildness that one's country garden should be opened out to the landscape, so that, with a few alterations here and there, the garden itself might resemble a landscape painting: 'a man might make a pretty Landskip of his own possessions'. Pope turned his attention to the

FOLLIES

Most gardens have at least one or two man-made and generally architectural features, such as a seat, shelter, statue, terrace or flight of steps. In Roman times, springs, grottoes and sculptures of nymphs and fauns recreated dream landscapes inspired by Greece. In his villa at Tibur, Hadrian commemorated the Empire, while Renaissance princes incorporated the gods of Olympus from temples and tombs into the statuary of their sumptuous gardens.

In the Renaissance, the grotto was developed, a rocky cave, alcove or tunnel, built to commemorate the water-spirits of antiquity, such as river gods, or the sea god Neptune and his attendant Triton. These grottoes were also used to house the pneumatic and hydraulic toys, imitations of those described by Hero of Alexandria, a first-century scientist whose treatise, the Pneumatica, *was re-discovered in the sixteenth century.*

In the landscape gardens of the eighteenth century, features ranging from sculptures to temples, towers and grottoes, became ever more extravagant. So clearly lacking in any practical purpose, they were termed 'follies', built by people with 'more money than sense'.

These follies often disappeared soon after their construction, being flimsy as well as ridiculous. Hundreds of them, more sturdily built, remain to this day. At Hagley, in Worcestershire, stands the first 'ruined castle', deliberately built as a ruin in 1747–8. Around this time, a Gothic ruin resembling a fragment of a medieval abbey was built high up in the park overlooking Plymouth Sound, at Mount Edgcumbe. At Hawkstone, in Shropshire, a chain of grotto-tunnels runs along the crest of a sandstone cliff, which in the 1790s was the dwelling of a hired hermit.

Follies of equal eccentricity were built on the Continent. The wildest of all is the volcano built at Wörlitz, East Germany in about 1790. In France, there were follies galore. At Retz, the age of the Grecian Titans, is remembered with a gigantic ruined column. At Ermenonville, the darkness of prehistory is celebrated with a massive dolmen. Elsewhere gardens of a similar age are embellished with tombs and cenotaphs to heroes and great men of the past or, yet again, as at Méréville, Rambouillet, Chantilly or Trianon, with dairies. There were Egyptian pyramids, Gothic churches, Chinese pavilions, Turkish mosques, some built complete and large as life, some in miniature, some ruined. Some were spaced widely and separated from each other so that they did not 'clash', and others were crowded together hugger-mugger, as at the Parc Monceau in Paris.

monstrous artificialities of topiary. He felt that the clippings of trees, to turn them into walls of greenery, was a barbarous act. But this was still far from Shaftesbury's praise of 'wildness', which was put into practice nearly a century later.

A new garden art

The related debates and disputes over art, literature and philosophy which continued from the end of the seventeenth century and throughout the eighteenth century had a profound influence on garden styles. The styles of garden architecture became diversified to a fantastic extent. Beginning in the early 1720s with the re-discovery of 'Gothic' architecture as the original, native architecture of the Saxons, the builders of garden temples, summerhouses and viewing platforms quickly extended their range to include both Classical and Gothic ruined buildings. Oriental buildings were built, in Chinese, Indian and Moorish styles; Chambers' great Pagoda at Kew, built in 1761 is the most famous survivor. 'Primitive' structures were built of rough rocks, often resembling a mountain cave, or prehistoric monuments, including several small versions of Stonehenge! Untrimmed logs and tree roots were made into wild-looking shelters, which might be the dwellings of peasants or savages.

The Pagoda at the Royal Botanic Gardens, Kew, (1761) was designed by Sir William Chambers, together with several other 'exotic' buildings, now gone, including a mosque, a Chinese kiosk and an 'Alhambra'.

The gardeners of Stowe

In England, the eighteenth century was dominated by three great gardeners. They had, of course, many imitators, as had Le Nôtre in France. These three men – Bridgeman, Kent and Brown – found fame through their work on Lord Cobham's garden at Stowe in Buckinghamshire. This huge estate, which still survives as a major public school, encompasses the trends and developments of more than a century. The formal gardens were begun in the 1680s, to go with a relatively modest mansion. From the early eighteenth century, this building and its garden were repeatedly enlarged.

Charles Bridgeman

Around 1715, Lord Cobham entrusted his gardens to Charles Bridgeman. Bridgeman had already worked at Blenheim, and now began to lay out a vast formal garden with a large octagonal lake, fountains, straight walks, monuments and statues. Given the site of the existing house, however, it was impossible to produce a garden with the symmetry of Versailles. To overcome the obstacle created by the presence of a road, Bridgeman designed the gardens asymmetrically and surrounded them with a ha-ha, a ditch that eliminated the need for a boundary wall. In this way, it was possible to enjoy a view of the surrounding country from the rectilinear parterres, while the absence of a visible barrier between the garden and nature made the layout seem less artificial. From all over England, people came to admire Stowe.

William Kent

Bridgeman (1685–1748), was assisted from around 1730 by a new gardener, William Kent. This artist and architect, who had trained as a painter in Italy, was already well known as a

In the eighteenth century Stowe was the most talked-about and most visited garden in England. This monument, the Temple of British Worthies, is sited in a small, quiet valley named the 'Elysian Fields'.

garden designer, in a freer and more 'natural' style than Bridgeman's. At Stowe, he 'softened' the rigid lines of Bridgeman's formal scheme, and created, to the east of the main axis, the evocative and most lovely 'Elysian Fields', recalling the idealized Italian scenes painted by Claude and Gaspard Poussin. In the Elysian Fields are the Temple of British Worthies, the Temple of Ancient Virtue and the Shell Bridge, all designed by Kent.

Lancelot 'Capability' Brown

Brown, (1716–83), the third great gardener at Stowe, was appointed Head Gardener in 1741, aged twenty-four. He remained at Stowe until 1751, when he left to practice as a landscape gardener on his own. His contribution to the development of the gardens of Stowe is uncertain, but it is highly likely that he continued the process of 'softening' the earlier, formal layout. By the later eighteenth century, the main vista southwards from the house had been made to resemble a superb sweep of ideal but natural, countryside. Lawns were flanked by billowing trees, leading to a gleaming lake, with two small temples, the Lake Pavilions. Beyond, the carefully landscaped 'countryside' stretched for another half mile, and led to the view of a tall Corinthian archway on the horizon.

Other parts of the gardens have their own identities, carefully and brilliantly linked to the main axis. Today, over 30 monuments, including pillars, temples and bridges, remain spaced over some 400 acres.

By 1751 Brown's reputation was secure. He had already executed many private commissions while at Stowe. He was known as 'Capability' Brown for his way of saying that an estate had 'capabilities', and could be 'improved', when its owner asked for an assessment. By the time of his death, Brown had been involved in several hundred commissions, and had a greater hand in changing the English countryside than any other single person. Scores of his landscape gardens survive, most include a prominent area of water, such as a river, or a landscaped lake, as at Alnwick, Blenheim, Bowood, Longleat, Nuneham Courtenay, Petworth, Prior Park, Sheffield Park and Warwick Castle.

The Spirit of Stowe

When the English garden was at its height, there was but one tenet of faith: nature and cultivation must be set together. Fine trees and few flowers, as in nature; the beauty of the sky and of streams meandering through meadows, as in the happy legends of Arcady, must be crowned with cultured allusions to Rome and Greece. These might recall the pictures of Claude Lorrain or Gaspard Poussin, whose works were known to Kent, and to his educated patrons.

During the century which covered the evolution of Stowe, hundreds of other gardens were 'landscaped' by Kent, Brown and their imita-

The Temple of Apollo at Stourhead was built in 1765 on high ground overlooking the lake. It is modelled on the Temple of the Sun at Baalbec, which had been rediscovered a few years earlier.

tors. Some were small, like the poet Pope's garden beside the Thames at Twickenham. It was five acres in all, with a famous grotto-tunnel joining his house to the garden, on the other side of the road. Horace Walpole's garden at Strawberry Hill nearby was not much larger, though he added enough land to give him a clear view of the Thames. Beside these were the gigantic landscapes of Blenheim, Castle Howard, Chatsworth and Holkham, running to thousands of acres.

One of the intriguing aspects of this garden style – called *furor hortensis*, or 'garden mania' by Lord Chesterfield – was that, beside, and often in collaboration with, the professional designers, amateurs designed these gardens as well, both for themselves and for their friends; Pope designed his own, so did Walpole. Most famous among the amateurs was Charles Hamilton, who designed his own landscape garden at Painshill between about 1738 and 1770, and advised others, particularly Henry Hoare at Stourhead, Lord Shelbourne at Bowood, and the Beckfords, father and son, at Fonthill. Painshill is now in the course of restoration.

The garden of Stourhead

Stourhead is another memorable landscape garden, preserved almost exactly as it was in 1780. A wealthy banker, Henry Hoare, bought the Stourhead estate in 1718 and his son, also named Henry Hoare, transformed the valley to one side of his father's mansion. His work of garden creation went on from 1741 until the early 1780s, and then, from the end of the century, his nephew, Sir Richard Colt Hoare, made further developments to the scheme.

Thick belts of trees hide the mansion from the garden, so that, from every part of the garden, the house is invisible. It is a deliberate act, intended to separate the busy, 'worldly' life of the house from the Elysian and unworldly delights of the garden. Henry Hoare created a fine lake in the wooded valley, and, with the architect Henry Flitcroft, had several noble temples built round its shores: the Pantheon, the Temple of Flora and the Temple of Apollo, the latter raised up on higher ground. There is also a superb grotto, a bridge in 'Roman' style and, back from the lake, the medieval village church, and the Gothic tracery of the Bristol High Cross, brought here from Bristol in 1764.

The experience of going round this garden was intended by Henry Hoare to remind the visitor again and again of the glories of ancient Greece and Rome, with their architecture, mythology and literature. The impression was more subtle, however, as paintings of such scenes, by Claude or Gaspard Poussin, were also intended to be brought to mind. Of the view across the lake, towards the bridge, the High Cross and the church, Henry Hoare said ''tis a pretty Gaspard picture.'

THE GARDEN – AN AUTOBIOGRAPHY

In 1735, William Shenstone (1714–63) inherited a small grazing farm of around 150 acres near Sheffield, England called The Leasowes. He lived on this estate until his death, 'landscaping' the grounds and adorning the long walks round and through the property with modest monuments: urns, a statue, a ruin, a shelter or a seat with an inscription. These monuments were set at some 40 different points along the walks, and nearly all included a text, usually in English sometimes in Latin or French. These inscriptions encouraged the sensitive visitor to respond, to *feel* as Shenstone himself had felt in contemplating this or that aspect of nature, both within the garden itself or in the wider landscape.

Shenstone was one of the gifted amateurs, deeply read in literature, a tolerable poet and essayist himself, and much consulted by friends, who asked his advice on literary matters and on gardening. The Leasowes was visited by hundreds of garden enthusiasts in the eighteenth century, eager to experience delight in the beauties of nature which Shenstone had accentuated through his garden creation. His carefully placed monuments signposted what the emotional responses should be: beautiful, sublime, pensive, melancholic, dramatic or picturesque. Among the visitors was the American, Thomas Jefferson, whose fine landscape garden at Monticello in Virginia was much influenced by The Leasowes.

The Leasowes, near Sheffield, England.

FONTHILL AND 'ENGLAND'S WEALTHIEST SON'

Fonthill Abbey, Wiltshire – a gigantic Gothic folly.

When Alderman Beckford, Lord Mayor of London, died in 1770, he left his ten-year-old son William Beckford a fortune so great that the poet Byron called him 'England's wealthiest son'. Young William Beckford did not come of age until 1781. He had already travelled widely in Europe, and did so again until the 1790s, partly because of scandal which drove him out of England.

In 1793–94, he ordered a 12-ft (3.7m) wall to be built round much of his estate at Fonthill, in Wiltshire, and this wall eventually ran for some 15 miles (24km) round his wooded paradise. It was one of the sources of Coleridge's Kubla Khan *(1798),*

'So twice five miles of fertile ground
With walls and towers were girdled round'.

Within this enclosure, Beckford built the greatest Gothic folly of them all, the gigantic Fonthill Abbey. Designed by the architect James Wyatt, it was built between 1796 and 1816, its extent greater than that of Westminster Abbey, and its spire intended to be taller than that of Salisbury Cathedral. The spire fell down and was replaced by an octagonal tower, which collapsed in 1825, by which time Beckford had left, for lack of money.

Round this huge, Gothic building Beckford lived a solitary life, with hardly a visitor. But the gardens, the landscape, the woods, the lakes and the grottoes were developed with a passion which has rarely been equalled. His father had already created the mile-long Fonthill Lake, in the manner of Capability Brown, and beside it, near the water's edge, William Beckford built a winding chain of grottoes, and an Alpine garden with conifers in the quarry nearby. In the Abbey woods he made another lake, Bitham Lake, a large pool surrounded on most sides by rising slopes, which resembled 'the water-filled crater of an extinct volcano'.

Nearby was the American plantation, with species from the New World; elsewhere, a 'thornery' and a 'Norwegian Hut', described as 'a sort of log house, of very tasteful proportions', and said to be useful in wet weather. There was a 'Chinese garden', and, near the Abbey, a herb garden and a minute garden 'for a favourite dwarf'.

Turner painted the larger scenes at Fonthill in 1799, 'capturing' much of what has since gone. Today, only a fragment of the Abbey is left, set in dense woodland. The two lakes remain, but little else.

In the same period, and for a decade after Shenstone's time, the French writer and philosopher Jean-Jacques Rousseau (1712–78) was formulating a somewhat similar approach to nature, as a *personal* emotional experience between the viewer and the scene viewed. Far more than Shenstone, Rousseau rejected the rigid and formal garden style of the previous century, as being diametrically opposed to the supposed freedom of nature.

His thoughts on gardens are only part of his general philosophy, yet they are an important reflection of the powerful move towards appreciation of the wider landscape, and the deeply emotional approach this often involved. In his novel, *Nouvelle Héloïse* (1761), one section describes the garden which the heroine Julie has made, the 'Elysée'. This tree-ringed and secret area of three or four acres is entered only by the mistress, her maid and a few chosen and trusted friends. Otherwise, it is left to the birds, which are its 'owners', and to nature. It has no regular plan, and when the hero, St Preux, is allowed in, he exclaims that it has the quality of total remoteness found in a desert island, like the one on which Robinson Crusoe lived in the far Pacific.

Rousseau claimed that Nature, untouched by man, was essentially pure and perfect. Towards the end of his life, he had come to prefer the countryside to any garden, and his last, most pleasurable and most deeply-felt experiences were those of the naturalist, rather than the gardener, collecting flowers and plants in the woods and fields.

The Temple of Philosophy and Rousseau's tomb are set in the heart of the landscape garden at Ermenonville.

Ermenonville: A French Landscape Garden

The Marquis de Girardin (1735–1808) inherited his father's estate at Ermenonville in 1766, and transformed a small area of formal garden surrounded by farmland and woods into one of the most beautiful of all landscape gardens.

Girardin had travelled widely, both as a soldier, and as a private individual eager to visit other countries. His 'Grand Tour' took him to England in 1763, when he visited and was much impressed by The Leasowes; at the same time he was a passionate admirer of Rousseau. Settling at Ermenonville in 1766, the development of his estate into a garden landscape was governed above all by these two influences. He created scenes which are intended to evoke contemplative moods, with monuments chosen for their poetic associations, and surroundings of a gently 'natural' kind.

North of the château is a region of streams and pools, which once had a 'medieval' castle tower, a grove modelled on Julie's 'Elysée' in the *Nouvelle Héloïse* and a rougher area called the 'Wilderness' which included a rock and thatch hut for a rustic philosopher. In the southern half of the gardens is a lake, with a grotto and cascade dedicated to the water nymphs; a meadow called the 'Arcadian Fields'; a 'prehistoric' dolmen; an altar dedicated to 'revery'; and the ruined, or unfinished, Temple of Philosophy. An inscription reads 'Quis hoc perficiet?' – 'Who will complete this building', leaving the visitor to ponder on the as yet unsolved questions of philosophy. In the lake there is a small island, planted with poplar trees.

In 1778, Girardin invited Rousseau to stay at Ermenonville. Rousseau had experienced many difficulties in the 1770s, and had moved unhappily from place to place, believing that he was being persecuted. Coming to Ermenonville, he seems to have been happier, and certainly

The Temple of Philosophy was built, as a ruin, in the 1770s. Dedicated to the great philosophers, its stones bear the question 'Who will complete this building?'

enjoyed his botanical studies. After seven weeks, he died, and was buried on the little island with the poplar trees. His tomb is inscribed 'Here lies the man of nature and of truth'.

Chinoiserie and the Fantastic Garden

In the second half of the eighteenth century, there was a radical change in garden styles, at times approaching the fantastic. Already in the 1760s and 1770s two gardens, one in England and one in Germany, had been adorned with buildings of widely contrasting styles. At Kew, near Richmond on the outskirts of London, Princess Augusta employed Sir William

This Turkish mosque, at Schwetzingen in Germany, is one of the most elaborate of all late eighteenth-century 'follies'.

Chambers to landscape her ground, and to design several buildings. Some, like the Orangery and the Temples of Arethusa and Bellona, are in classical style, but there is also a Pagoda, built by Chambers in 1761, and originally accompanied by another building in Chinese style, a kiosk in a small lake. Not far away, were a Turkish mosque and a Moorish building, called the Alhambra.

In the 1770s, the mainly formal layout at Schwetzingen, in the Palatinate, was extended with a large 'English garden', in which, at a decent distance from each other, are a ruined Roman aqueduct, a Temple of Mercury, and a gigantic Turkish mosque. The architect, F.L. von Sckell, had been much impressed by Chambers' work at Kew!

In France, in the decade before the Revolution of 1789, many extravagant garden follies were built. Most have gone, including the Chinese House, built as a residence in the Désert de Retz. Beside it was a 'Chinese garden', and nearby was one of the wildest of all grottoes. Elsewhere there was a 'Turkish tent', and an ice-house built like an Egyptian pyramid. This last survives, along with a truly unique column, as one of the strangest of all garden follies. The bottom of a ruined column, some 45ft (13.5m) across, represents a fragment of the architecture of a race of giants. Had it been complete, as the visitor is expected to ponder, it might have been 300–400ft (90–120m) tall. It was hollow inside, and fitted out as a residence.

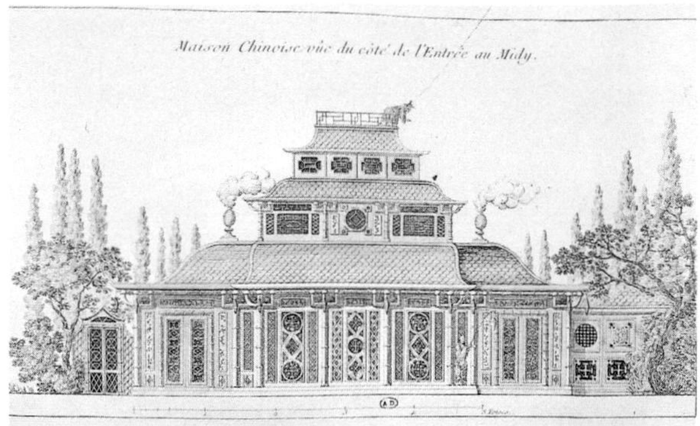

This 'Chinese house', now gone, was built as a garden residence in the 1780s, at Retz, near Saint-Germain.

If the Désert (or 'Wildness') de Retz was strange and gigantic, the Parc Monceau in Paris was strange, minute and grotesquely crowded. The designer, Carmontelle, and his patron, the Duc de Chartres, wanted a 'universe in miniature', and built within 45 acres (18 hectares) some 40 different follies. Today, there is still the tiny pyramid and a most lovely colonnade round an oval pool.

Chinoiserie and other exotic buildings continued to appear in gardens. In the early nineteenth century, the gardens of Sezincote, in Gloucestershire, England, were given monuments in Indian style, their design related to the magnificent onion-shaped domes of the Brighton Pavilion, built in 1815–21 for the Prince Regent.

One of the most extraordinary 'collections' of these follies to survive is at Alton Towers, in Staffordshire, England, where a variety of architects added buildings and monuments in every conceivable style to the gardens of the Earls of Shrewsbury, in 1814–35. Beside the great mansion in Gothic style, were a Roman bridge, a Swiss cottage (for a blind harper), a corkscrew fountain, a little Stonehenge, a Moorish conservatory, a Gothic look-out tower and much more. The most striking of all these was and indeed still is, the elegant Pagoda, built in 1827.

The Pagoda at Alton Towers, in Staffordshire, England. Built in 1827, it has a fountain jet at the top – a far cry from the original pagodas of China!

THE EUROPEAN QUEST FOR PLANTS

In gardens which harboured architecture inspired by the Renaissance, the role of flowers was secondary. In the seventeenth century, imported plants of particular interest, such as amaranth, lobelia, nasturtium, African marigold, anemone and narcissus, were used to border large beds and were often associated with native species. Until the dawn of the eighteenth century, the range available was not an especially wide one. Hedges of hornbeam, elm and lime were clipped into regular shapes, while arbours and bowers were developed to the perfection found in the 'green rooms' of Marly. Louis XIV was a lover of flowers, particularly bulbs, and Louis XV had large greenhouses built at the Petit Trianon to satisfy his botanical curiosity. For many years, travelling diplomats, traders, explorers and missionaries had been looking keenly for new seeds and cuttings to bring back to Europe. Gradually, the range of native and established trees, shrubs and herbaceous perennials, such as hollyhock, hawthorn, broom, lilac and philadelphus was increased to include magnolia, sophora and robinia. In the flower garden, Iceland poppies from Siberia came to England in 1730 and the South African ice plant, or mesembryanthemum, at about the same time. The dahlia, which came from Mexico, was not grown in Europe until 1789, and not in England until 1804.

In general, these new introductions did not gain immediate favour in the main garden of an estate, far less in the wider parkland. Instead, they were kept in 'conservatories' built for special collections of rare plants, or in an enclosed garden area separate from the main layout, often because it was thought that they were more tender than European species, and needed to be in a conservatory or in a sheltered area.

The new introductions, mostly from the Americas, southern Africa, China and Japan, arrived in different parts of Europe, depending on the links which the roving plant collectors had with their patrons or employers. Holland, France, England and Spain received particular plants, usually in the form of seed, before other countries, and it was often ten years before a new species from America was established in all the major European collections.

Here is a short list of a *few* introductions to Europe between 1700 and 1800, with dates for the arrival of the species in England: ivy-leaved pelargonium, 1701; red-hot poker, 1707; pelargonium, 1710; magnolia, c.1730; witch hazel, 1736; tree of heaven, 1751; maidenhair tree, 1754; tree paeony, 1789; hydrangea (*H. macrophylla*), 1789; chrysanthemum, c.1793; monkey puzzle tree, 1795. The Lombardy poplar, native to Italy, did not reach England until 1758.

The maidenhair tree, Ginkgo biloba, *was introduced to England in 1754, from Japan. The French botanist Michaux took it to America in 1784.*

THE EARLY TRAVELLERS

Perhaps more a traveller than a botanist, Sir Walter Raleigh nonetheless is thought to have brought both tobacco and the potato plant to England.

Over the centuries, conquerors, pilgrims, traders and adventurers in search of new horizons have all observed and collected the plants found in the course of their travels. It was desperately difficult to bring living plants, either with roots, or as cuttings, back to Europe from remote countries, since travel conditions and the length of the journey were so unfavourable. Often, plants discovered were familiar to people from a multitude of descriptions and drawings for many years before they were successfully introduced.

Plants satisfy many needs: as foods and spices, medicines and poisons, even ingredients of magic potions. As objects of trade, they have produced immense fortunes and to protect or procure them, wars have been fought, expeditions sent out and thousands of lives lost.

The mention of coffee, tobacco, rubber and quinine is enough to conjure up visions of past trading adventures, often with tragic aspects, while the illicit growth of Papaver somniferum, *the opium poppy, is a problem today.*

It would be impossible to draw up a full list of all the great pioneer herbalists and the botanists who succeeded them. Explorers came from every country and, for the most part, their names will never be known. Until the eighteenth century, these plant discoverers were mostly occupied with some other main task, as missionaries or traders. Although Sir Walter Raleigh, for example, brought back tobacco and the potato to England, we do not therefore think of him first and foremost as a botanist!

History gave us the name of Queen Hatshepsut of Egypt (fifteenth century BC) who is said to have brought home plants from a military campaign on the coast of Somalia. Herodotus makes frequent mention of plants encountered on his travels around the Mediterranean. Lucullus, who led his Roman armies as far as Cerasus on the shore of the Black Sea, noted a tree that bore delicious fruit and thus the cherry, cerasa *in Latin, was brought back to Italy. While among the plants introduced into Europe by the Crusaders was the crocus.*

The plant hunters

The men who went out in search of new plants did so in peril of their lives and were often rewarded by the association of their name with their discoveries. One mission, one voyage, one expedition, succeeded another: Kaempfer to Japan in the 1690s; La Condamine to Ecuador (1735–45); Hasselquist in the Levant (1750–52); Joseph de Jussieu to Peru, at first with La Condamine (1735); Pierre Poivre to China in 1745, and later to Java, and Mauritius; Bougainville and Commerson round the world (1766–69); Cook, Banks and Solander round the world (1768–71); Cook and the Forsters round the world (1772–75); Joseph Dombey in South America from the Andes to Peru (1777–81).

Raffeneau-Delile went in 1798 with Napoleon's expedition to Egypt. Finally, Aimé Bonpland returned from his travels in South America (1799–1804) with von Humboldt in order to direct the Empress Joséphine's collections at Malmaison.

P. J. Redouté painted many of the flowers grown at Malmaison, and is best known for his studies of roses.

The plants

Between 1800 and 1810, more than two thousand species were cultivated at Malmaison in France. Many had been established in Europe for some time, but their brilliant cultivation at Malmaison brought them extra fame. In 1802, the first dahlia seeds in France were germinated in the Empress's botanic garden, which rivalled the Jardin des Plantes in Paris. Above all, roses were accorded special attention and this fascination continues throughout the world today.

Books on the rose fill whole shelves in libraries and every year new cultivars emerge. There is a splendid collection at the modern French rosarium at l'Haÿ-les-Roses. Other fine collections of roses can be seen in France at Bagatelle, and in England at Castle Howard, Yorkshire; Mottisfont, Hampshire; Queen Mary's Garden, Regent's Park, in London; and at the Royal National Rose Society's grounds, St Albans, Hertfordshire. In Switzerland, there is the Parc de la Grange at Geneva.

In America, the Governor's Palace Gardens in Colonial Williamsburg contains a fine collection of roses found in eighteenth-century American Gardens, including *Rosa canina*, the dog rose; R. *centifolia*, the cabbage rose; R. *damascena*, the damask rose; R. *gallica*, the French rose; R. *gallica versicolor*, Rosamundi; R. *eglantaria*, the sweet briar; and R. *centifolia muscosa*, the moss rose. On a contemporary note, the All-America Rose Selections founded in 1938 to provide a trials system for testing and approving new rose cultivars, has demonstration and test gardens all over the country, including New York, Massachusetts, California, Louisiana, Minnesota and Missouri. Practically all are open to the public.

There are also 132 A.A.R.S. accredited public gardens in 41 states, where the general public can assess how the roses perform in local conditions. These include the Hershey Rose Gardens, Hershey, Pennsylvania; New York Botanical Gardens, Bronx; Warner Park Rose Garden, Chattanooga, Tennessee; Morcom Amphitheatre of Roses, Oakland, California; Houston Municipal Garden, Houston, Texas; and Kelleher Rose Garden, Boston, Massachusetts.

THE JAPANESE GARDEN

For a Westerner, there are few things more fascinating or disconcerting than the complexity of meaning that can be assumed by the Japanese garden. What significance underlies this composition of sand and stone, moss and bamboo, trees and ponds, elegant bridges and temples with smoothly curved roofs, the enigmatic austerity of a totally dry Zen 'space'? The eye hesitates, the mind is perplexed. Though Westerners may not be able to reach the deepest meaning of these creations, there are keys that allow them to decipher the main elements and to understand their sense and beauty.

The juxtaposition of elements is bound by strict rules, which often derive from Chinese traditions. In the sense that they, too, reflect civilisation and culture, legend and history, religion and philosophy, Oriental gardens are no different from their European counterparts. For almost 25 centuries, China has been impregnated with the spirit of Buddhism. In this age-old civilisation, sages, philosophers, monks, poets, calligraphers, painters and garden designers have evoked the deepest mysteries of nature and man's relations with the world, giving them a multitude of representations. The garden is a manifestation of man's place in the universe, a perfect and often magical link with the unknown and hidden forces that govern the world.

At the time of Buddha, Confucius and Lao-Tse, it was thought that the universe, both known and unknown, was subject to laws of eternal harmony and equilibrium. The gardens of the Italian Renaissance were, similarly, places where men might walk with confidence among the representations of their gods. In Europe, however, it was the creator of the garden who tended to impose his will and order on nature. In China, on the other hand, it was a universal order that was celebrated, in which every element had a unique and irreplaceable role, and man was but one element among many. The garden was soon identified with the ideal abode, the celestial paradise, the image of a state of perfection that was at once real and abstract, tangible and metaphysical.

The influence of China

By the eighth century AD, Chinese civilisation had already been in existence for well over a thousand years. In economics, politics and religion, relations were expanding with Korea and with Japan where, according to Chinese legend, the islands were borne on the backs of

Placed at the entrance to Japanese temples and gardens, 'tsukubai' are stone receptacles filled with water to allow the visitor to carry out ritual purification.

Set among the 'natural' forms of conifers and maples, the azaleas in this Kyoto garden are rigorously pruned, until they resemble blocks of green stone in the carpet of moss.

giant tortoises, spring was eternal and death unknown.

This enormous contribution from China, combined with the cult of ancestor worship, native to Japan and founded in Shintoism, which still thrives today, gave rise to highly varied forms of art, literature and philosophy. The four centuries of the Heian period (794–1185) were the golden age of Japan and of garden design. Nature was improved, to yield *paradise* – gardens which have, despite changes over the centuries, survived to the present day. Whether established on the site of Heian, today Kyoto, or, after 1600, in the tiny village of Edo that is now Tokyo, the subsequent gardens of Japan have all been inspired by those of the year 1000.

The Zen garden

Japanese garden design was influenced by three factors: the importance of religious communities in the social order, and their evolution towards forms that become ever more rigorous and austere; the call for a Japanese spiritual life in keeping with the Samurai code of chivalry; and the increasing importance of tea, the symbol and ceremony of exercises in concentration and meditation.

The proliferation of temples – there are still some 2,000 in the region of Kyoto and Nara, each with its own traditional garden, and often two or even three — led to more intensified study and to new creations. Each Buddhist sect followed its own rules in reaching out to the *universal*, through rock, sand and water; through growing plants; and through plants' symbolism, for they were considered perfect forms of life.

Around the thirteenth century, a Chinese branch of Buddhism known as *Chan* extended its influence to Japan where it is known as *Zen*. It aimed to eliminate from the temples and their gardens all manifestations of formal beauty which, through their seductions, might interfere with the discipline of meditation. On the other hand, everything was to be encouraged which helped man towards immersion in the perfect 'void' and thus, according to the Tao, 'to become concentrated in the One', 'to rise to heaven in the full light of day'. To this end, bright flowers, cool waters, shady trees and enervating or disturbing perfumes were banished. The Zen garden was a universe of sand, stone and moss, concentrated, immobile, and often directed or linked to key symbols: the tortoise, the terrestrial feminine element, *yin*; and the crane, the bird piercing the sky, the masculine conquering element, *yang*. These are the two principles of equilibrium whose union ensures the harmony of the world. Infinitely repeated under different guises, this is one of the main keys to the Japanese garden.

The temple garden should be considered as a feature of the monastery closely linked to the life of the community, a miniature and symbolic image of the universe. The sand out of which the

BONSAI, THE UNIVERSE OF MINIATURE

The art of the bonsai is beautifully displayed by this miniature Japanese White Pine.

For the Japanese, trees including dwarf maple, pine and apple, thriving in apparently intolerable growing conditions, have been a profoundly symbolic link between heaven and earth for centuries.

More than three centuries before Christ, the art of bonsai was already flourishing in the temples and palaces of T'sin China. These were adorned with pun-sai, *miniscule trees that grew naturally in the most inhospitable and unfavourable ground, where they triumphed over scorching wind and cold; arid soil and shade. These trees represented the indestructibility of life, the continuing rebirth of the universe through the seasons and an eternity indifferent to the forces of old age and death.*

Capable of living nearly two hundreds years, or three times a human life-span, these venerable trees were (and are) passed on from one generation to another in China and Japan. They were traditionally used as objects to aid meditation in Buddhist temples, helping both pilgrims and monks. A modest Bonsai plant in a pot attests to the power of nature and to the authority of man.

In Buddhism, size is of no significance: the smallest plant contains the mystery of the universe as powerfully and as completely as the largest garden. The forces that create a bonsai – the power of nature and the art of the gardener – are not opposites but harmonious and complementary. They may be represented by the duality, yin *– nature, and* yang *– man. This duality is repeated in two main styles of bonsai:* kengai, *in which the trunks are bent towards the ground, and* chokan, *in which they rise vertically.*

Introduced into Japan during the tenth century Heian period, the golden age of Nipponese civilisation, bonsai were cultivated by the nobility and the Buddhist communities. Today, however, it is a popular pastime. There are at least twenty methods of training the tiny trees, involving orientation of branches, sap restriction in certain areas, transplanting, repotting, root pruning, feeding and watering. All these operations require frequent attention. Bonsai is not a hobby to be taken up in an idle moment, but a lifetime's commitment.

rocks rise, these 'bones' of the earth, may be a distant echo of the Shinto enclosure where ancestral spirits could communicate with men. The introduction of tea added another dimension to gardens. Tea ceremonies have been strictly codified and studied for five centuries, and constitute a world rich in symbolism, in which the garden plays a direct part. Every element in the tea garden, every plant, every object, however decorative in appearance, is a sign and a reminder. The bamboo fence and gate are a symbolic boundary, a metaphor for the transition from the workaday world into another, more tranquil sphere. The tea garden is not merely a small enclosure around the tea room but a great 'elsewhere' in which the troubling constraints of ordinary existence may be forgotten.

The pathway, made from irregularly placed stepping stones, may be thought to represent a difficult mountain trail. At another level, this simple path may represent the way towards perfection. The stone lamp may perhaps enlighten judgement. The *tsukabai*, a trough-like basin, at which the 'traveller' or expected guest is welcomed with water, to wash away the dust of the road, is found outside temples, villas and even modest restaurants. Such garden features are common, indeed essential, in Japan. In Western gardens they have been familiar only since the present century, since Japan and its culture have become better known.

Shin, the life force

Japanese gardens were often designed according to an idealised image of famous sites in China or within the Japanese archipelago, and, in remoter times, they were subject to the complex rules of geomancy. Many different styles developed, and today, architects still find inspiration in historical examples, related to famous lakes in China, or to the volcanic peak of Mount Fuji in Japan. Certain themes, references and allusions persist, even though they continue to be intelligible to Western eyes. Faced with a few stones represesenting the sign *shin* (heart or life-force), the humblest Japanese visitor to a temple garden immediately understands the message. This symbol of *shin*, traced in sand, as on the margin of the pond at Saiho-ji, encapsulates the heart and life force of the Japanese garden.

The Daisen-in, a living picture

The monastery complex of Daitoku-ji on the outskirts of Kyoto contains around 30 temples belonging to the Zen Buddhist Rinzai sect. Founded in 1319, this town within a town has

The Daisen-in garden, in the Daitoku-ji temple in Kyoto, was made around 1513. This eighteenth-century woodcut shows the garden much as it was originally, and as it remains today.

been burnt down several times and then rebuilt. Several sub-temples of importance are still located there, the most famous being the Daisen-in, temple of the Great Hermit, with its much-admired east garden, laid out around 1513.

Established in 1509, when the Daitoku-ji was flourishing, the Daisen-in has one of the most celebrated dry gardens (*kare-sansui*) in Japan. Within an area of some 130sq yd (119sq m), its L-shaped scheme embraces a vast 'landscape' for dream and meditation. At the beginning of the sixteenth century, garden designers were almost invariably monks, poets and calligraphers. This garden was thought to be inspired by a Chinese wash painting of the Sung period (960–1279), corresponding to the Heian golden age in Japan.

The name of the designer remains unknown, but it may have been So-ami, a celebrated painter and master-gardener who painted landscapes within the building. He would certainly have used references to show that he was, like all cultured men of the time, thoroughly understanding of Chinese civilisation.

Japanese temple gardens may be interpreted in several complementary ways. At Daisen-in, for example, the garden may be viewed as a miniature landscape. In the background, there are mountains. The torrent that pours down from them passes under a bridge, flows past the islands and then spreads out into a great river, bearing a stone vessel loaded with the wisdom of the ages. One tradition suggests that this boat belonged to the shogun Ashikaga Yoshimasa, who would construct the Ginkaku-ji, or famous Silver Pavilion.

Other, less literal, interpretations are possible. Might not these high mountains be Mount Horai, abode of the blessed, and the torrent itself, the river of life? Again, the peaks of uneven height might evoke *yin* and *yang*, complementary terms associated with gardens. In the 'river' of sand are the islands of the tortoise and the crane. The unstated, the allusion and asymmetry are characteristics present in Japanese gardens of every epoch. Here, a small gallery, built in the eighteenth century and renewed in recent years, cuts across the landscape and obstructs the flow from left to right.

This garden is minute, compared even with the modern urban gardens and is not for active use. Visitors may view it from the wooden platform round the inner sides of the L-shaped garden. Ideally, it should be viewed slowly, as the play of light and shade varies this miniature yet universal scene.

The Kinkaku-ji, or Golden Pavilion, was first built in the late fourteenth century. The present building is a 1955 replica.

The Silver Pavilion

Begun in 1482, this elegant pavilion in the Chinese manner contains the key to many Japanese gardens. The shogun, Yoshimasa, grandson of Yoshimitsu, who had built the famous Golden Pavilion, intended the Silver Pavilion as a place of meditation. Situated outside the centre of Kyoto at the foot of wooded hills, it shared in the traditions of Zen and orthodox Buddhism. The place of honour was accorded to Kannon, the goddess of mercy in Chinese tradition. Yoshimasa, an enlightened and cultivated ruler, may have employed such famous gardeners as Soami and Zen'ami, and himself designed the traditional pond. It was modelled on the temple and garden of Saiho-ji, with the Koke-dera, or moss garden created in 1339. The rocks, islands, cascades and landscapes are recollections of the eleventh-century Heian period. The whole is a blend of religious culture, Chinese tradition and a vigorous affirmation of the Japanese character.

The Sea of Silver Sand

The feature which has made this Zen temple, once a country residence, so famous, is its Sea of Silver Sand. Beside the Silver Pavilion, and close to the classical pond, skirting the elegant pines and *karikomi* azaleas, a vast expanse of silver sand contrasts with the green foliage. As in all well tended Japanese gardens, this sand is regularly raked, and its deep, symmetrical ridges and furrows may represent the long, patient swell of the ocean. The function of this sea is to evoke the *niwa*, that pure space reserved for the spirits of the ancestors, and perhaps also to represent the *yin* part of the garden. To judge from the many wood cuts available, the sea of sand has been growing in size since the seventeenth century. The origin of the material used underlines a characteristically Japanese approach. The sand undoubtedly derives from the original excavation of the pond and its various modifications.

A garden of many symbols

Remarkable for its whiteness, the sand is also a product of the earth and, therefore, precious. Spread out before the temple, it becomes an instrument singularly adapted to meditation. The almost imperceptible texture and long perspective hold and entrance the eye. According to legend, the cone of sand rising on one shore of this immaculate sea was at first simply a load left by the workmen, but its formal perfection caught the eye of the shogun who saw it by moonlight. Hence its name, *Kogetsudai* (platform before the moon). Today it is thought to represent the cone of Mount Fuji.

In the temple of the Zuiho-in in Kyoto, sand, stone and moss compose an imaginary 'dry' landscape, inspired by Zen philosophy.

Katsura

Capturing a way of life that has gone forever, this garden best exemplifies seventeenth-century Japan. Other gardens would come later in Tokyo, 'the capital of the north', but Katsura represents the culmination of a thousand years in the development of garden design.

Continuously improved and extended between 1620 and 1639, this villa and its garden were created for Prince Toshihito and his son Toshidata. While Prince Toshihito may himself have had a major part in the design, he was guided by the great tea-master, Kobori Enshu (1579–1647). When Kobori Enshu was asked if

At the Imperial villa of Katsura in Kyoto, completed in 1659, this shingle promontory is thought to evoke the peninsula of Amanoshidate, while the pine tree on the right suggests the shell of a turtle symbolizing the feminine element of nature.

he would design the gardens, he replied that he would, on three conditions: that he be allowed unlimited time, unlimited money and freedom from interference. How many artists have longed for such conditions!

Prince Toshihito died in 1629, and it was his son Prince Toshidata who gave Katsura the refinement and elegance visible today and which make it one of the finest princely villas in Japan.

Originally, it was a small tea-house built close to the Katsura river, far from the political centre of Kyoto and intended for gatherings of cultivated art-lovers. The first light-weight structure was replaced in the 1630s by buildings whose purity and functional line are still much admired.

Though Katsura is termed an 'Imperial villa', is roughly contemporary with Vaux-le-Vicomte and Versailles, and is linked with patrons as important in Japan as Fouquet or Louis XIV were in France, the *scale* and the *style* of this villa and its gardens are deeply different. The area of the gardens is just 14 acres (5.6 hectares) while the buildings are essentially wooden, and deliberately simple. Yet they, and the gardens, are rich in subtlety.

A garden of transformations

The Imperial villa comprises a succession of tea-houses and rooms for music and intimate gatherings. *Shojis*, sliding walls, can be adjusted, according to the hour or season, to give a sense of the landscape corresponding exactly to the mood of the viewer. The views of the garden are not fixed but infinitely variable, by means of carefully chosen frames. This feature is central to the villa's design.

At Katsura, the tone is simple, rustic, pared down to essentials. The main entrance, for example, is a porch covered with the same thatch as that used for peasants' houses. The light bridges are covered with earth and moss. The paths are marked by thousands of stepping stones laid out in a complex code, their size, spacing, roughness or smoothness and accompanying moss all indicating to the visitor the pace of his walk, the scene he should appreciate, and the direction of his glance. A platform allows the rising of the moon top be seen from the best angle, when the bright orb is perfectly mirrored in the pool. To enrich the poetic sense of this garden, the placing of some features and the general design of the gardens are thought to allude to landscapes described in *The Tale of Genji*, the famous story written by Lady Murasaki in the eleventh century. Though its overall area is modest, the lake has a complex and sinuous shape. It is easy to imagine how moonlit boating parties could re-trace and recreate 'moments' from this courtly and poetic romance.

THE FLOWER GARDEN

During the long reign of Queen Victoria, from 1837 to 1901, the character of the English garden would change radically and, indeed, all of Europe was transformed by flowers.

The middle class rose to affluence and, as industry and transport developed, they had intimate pleasure gardens created for them, different from the vast landscapes designed by Kent and Brown. The middle class wanted gardens that were unassuming and colourful, not great landscape compositions highlighted with follies and evocations of antiquity.

By the beginning of the century, the United Kingdom had already begun to weave together a tight network of trading centres and colonies that would form a world commercial empire. From these territories in every latitude and climate came innumerable species of exotic plants. Horticulture progressed and the species that would adorn the gardens of England were hybridized, selected and distributed in Britain, throughout Europe, and in the United States.

New horticultural inventions

The lawnmower, patented by an Englishman, Edwin Beard Budding, in August, 1830, brought about a social revolution of a kind. No longer was there dependence on a large and increasingly costly team of gardeners, armed with scythes, as mowing could now be done neatly and easily by a single man. Thus, the lawn, that evident symbol of respectability, was no longer the monopoly of great landowners. Any gardener could now keep his own grass in perfect condition.

During the same period, another Briton, Dr Nathaniel Bagshaw Ward, perfected a sealed glass case in which plants could live in isolation from the surrounding environment, with the

Claude Monet's garden at Giverny, near Mantes, has been extensively restored, with plants which the painter would have grown here in the early twentieth century.

humidity remaining constant. From the mid-1830s the Wardian case enjoyed immense popularity and is used to this day in the form of jars and bottles for miniature gardens.

Ward's invention solved the problem of transporting exotic plants from their distant native land to England. The journey, by sailing ship, might last weeks or even months, and often the precious plants and cuttings taken in the East Indies, Japan, Australia or Chile would fail to survive the voyage. Before Ward's discovery, the contents of 19 out of 20 cases of plants brought to England from remote parts were dead by the end of the voyage. When his cases came into use, the survival rate rose to 19 out of 20! Along with the lawnmower and the ha-ha, a sunken ditch preventing animals straying onto lawns while allowing uninterrupted views, the Wardian case is one of the three great inventions to affect garden design.

The ease with which plants could now be propagated removed the barriers of rarity and allowed sales at affordable prices. New plants from all over the world appeared on balconies and gardens, in greenhouses and the great hothouses of public parks. These conservatories, whose climate could be easily controlled, underwent a prodigious development. As cast iron and sheet glass became more readily available, conservatories or hothouses were built in many private properties, and cathedral-sized hothouses went up in botanic gardens throughout Europe.

Garden fashion

In England, this was the great age of Kew, but Germany, France and the Netherlands did not lag behind in botanical enthusiasm. New, exciting and exotic plants were ready to be grown in abundance by all. The age of massed bedding had arrived. Round beds, raised beds, straight beds were filled with massed flowers of every colour, in geometric patterns which recalled the parterres of seventeenth-century France.

Mid-nineteenth century gardeners indulged in a welter of formal features: intricate geometry, patterns of letters, heraldry or animals, and complex topiary hedges. This in turn produced a reaction and, by the 1860s, the cult of the 'natural', a recurrent theme in English garden history, had won new support, opposing

THE AGE OF FLOWERS

The nineteenth century was the century of flowers, which were brought from all corners of the earth to adorn the gardens of Europe and America. The care, curiosity and attention devoted to them came almost to replace the interest formerly shown in the garden itself.

Intrepid and intelligent plant-hunters searched for, and brought back to Europe, trees, shrubs, and herbaceous plants in infinite variety. With the widespread use of the 'Wardian case', a sealed glass box invented by Nathaniel Bagshaw Ward, their successes were more dazzling and their failures fewer. Most of these plant-hunters were employed by the great botanic gardens, particularly Kew, and the treasures which they brought back were carefully nurtured, propagated and distributed to plant-lovers for their own collections.

While some plants were hardy, and could be safely grown out of doors, others needed shelter in the colder months, so the conservatory or hot-house came into its own. In Britain, the repeal of the glass tax, and improved techniques of making sheet glass and cast iron made such buildings less expensive. From the mid-nineteenth century, many middle-class Victorian houses boasted a conservatory, attached to the house, warmed by efficient central heating, and housing ferns, palms, and flowering shrubs.

*A list of the dozen most important and hardy introductions to Britain in the nineteenth century contains some surprises, and many plants taken for granted in Western gardens are revealed as relative newcomers. In 1804, the tiger lily arrived from China; in 1805, kerria, from Japan; in 1816, wistaria, from China; in the 1820s, eschscholzia, reintroduced from North America; in 1827, mahonia, from North America; in 1844, the Japanese anemone, from China (*via *Japan); in 1844, forsythia (*F.viridissima*), from China;* F.suspensa, *from Japan (*via *Holland) around 1850; in 1844, winter jasmine, from China; in 1849, berberis (*B.darwinii*), from Patagonia; in 1879, cotoneaster, from China; around 1890,* Russian vine, *from* Russia; *and in 1896, buddleja (*B.davidii*), from China.*

the formality and artificiality of early Victorian gardens. Massed or 'carpet' bedding did not die out, however. It survives in triumphant extravagance in many public gardens. From London to the seaside resorts of Europe and America, the hotel gardens of Cairo and Luxor, and even in Peking, massed formal bedding is still proudly displayed.

Gardening personalities

William Robinson, the Paris horticultural correspondent for *The Times*, was a lover of alpine plants in their natural habitat. In 1870, he published *The Wild Garden* and followed it with *The English Garden* in 1883. He collected plants that grew naturally in the countryside and added to these exotic plants brought from abroad. Plants of all kinds were venerated for their colour, form and foliage, these being the characteristics which he felt should govern the design of a garden. His 'revolutionary' attitude was to win many followers.

One of Robinson's admirers was Gertrude Jekyll, who met him in the 1880s, and came to know him well. She had trained as a painter, but when her eyesight weakened, she turned to gardening, a passion to which she devoted the remainder of her life. She did not share Robinson's total revulsion for the orderly display of cultivated plants, but sought to find ways of using them more freely than before. In general, annuals were of little interest to her, but bulbs, shrubs and, above all, perennials allowed her to compose scenes on the ground that were worthy of a painting. She arranged long borders with soft and subtle harmonies of colour, always taking into account the flowering season, the form and size of plants and the beauty and type of foliage.

Gertrude Jekyll, whose most important creations fall between 1890 and 1920, was not the inventor of the herbaceous border but she certainly advanced its popularity. This essentially English garden feature was developed in the 1840s, the oldest surviving example being at Arley Hall in Cheshire, laid out in 1846. Yet Jekyll's development of subtle 'tonal' planting schemes gave an extraordinary impetus to the concept of the herbaceous border, generating a popularity that continues today. Jekyll's influence has been felt most strongly at Hidcote Manor in Gloucestershire (laid out from 1908 onwards), Great Dixter in East Sussex (from 1911 onwards) and Sissinghurst in Kent (from 1930 onwards).

An English, turn-of-the-century garden designer and author, Gertrude Jekyll's great contribution to gardening was to develop and refine the concept of the herbaceous border.

Gertrude Jekyll worked on many gardens in collaboration with the architect Edwin Lutyens (1869–1944), and it was often his structural design which gave strength and firmness to the flowing, billowing drifts of her borders. The most important example of their partnership to survive is the great garden of Hestercombe, in Somerset, recently restored.

The influence of Robinson, Jekyll and Lutyens on modern gardens is incalculable and varied covering 'wild' water gardens to gardens of a formal, architectural character.

In the formal vein, there is Athelhampton in Dorset, created by Inigo Thomas in the 1890s. The landscape is a marvel of terraced enclosures, topiary and fountains, and rich with flowers. Iford Manor, in Wiltshire, was the home of the garden designer Harold Peto (1854–1933). His garden, built in terraces overlooking the River Avon and the fields beyond, is peopled with antique statues and sculpture, reminiscent of Renaissance gardens such as the Villa Medici, displaying the rediscovered masterpieces of the past. Equally formal, with firm hedge-lined terraces descending towards the Derbyshire countryside, is the garden at Renishaw, created by Sir George Sitwell from 1897 onwards. Deeply influenced by Italian Renaissance gardens, he re-created a second garden in Italy, at Montegufoni near Florence, later in the century. Even more 'Italian' in style is the elaborate water-side garden at Vizcaya in Florida, begun in 1912, with fountains, parterres, terraces and pavilions and a magnificent stone boat a few yards out to sea.

In France, a 'wild' garden was created by the painter Claude Monet (1840–1926). At Giverny,

Great Dixter, in East Sussex, England, combines areas of brilliant planting with complex topiary enclosures.

which he acquired in 1890, his garden is divided into two parts by a railway line. On one side, close to the house, the garden is formal and richly planted with flowers. On the other side is the water garden, an irregular pool ringed with weeping willows and cypresses, and crossed by small bridges wreathed in wisteria.

In the pool, mirroring the sky and the ever-moving clouds, are water lilies, the *nymphéas* which Monet painted again and again. A little later in the century, the 'wild' garden at Ninfa, south of Rome, was deeply influenced by Robinson and Jekyll. Set in the ruins of a medieval town, and crossed by a stream which flows from the towering, cliff-like hills rising in a semicircle round the garden, Ninfa is perfect for exotic plants such as bamboo, acer, gunnera, bougainvillea, and eschscholzia.

Great Dixter

The garden of Great Dixter, in East Sussex, is among the most successful in combining formal tradition with herbaceous and mixed borders and natural features.

The fifteenth-century house was acquired by Nathaniel Lloyd in 1910. He employed Lutyens to enlarge the house, and to lay out the 5 acres (2.2 hectares) of gardens. Lutyens' design, presented in 1911, was a series of 'garden rooms' round the house, divided by walls and archways, or by topiary hedges. This has survived, with the addition of a sunken garden and pool designed by Nathaniel Lloyd in 1923. But the rich planting, by Nathaniel Lloyd, his wife Mrs Daisy Lloyd, and their son Christopher Lloyd, the eminent English gardening author, has been continuously developed. There are over 100 varieties of clematis at Great Dixter; a magnificent enclosed rose garden; and the Long Border, with its astonishing combination of shrubs and herbaceous plants. The topiary is second to none, while 'natural' planting of bulbs such as crocus, narcissi and grape hyacinths, creates a sense of relaxed freedom among the orchard trees.

TRADITION AND THE AMERICAN GARDEN

The earliest American settlers had no time or energy for pleasure gardening; their main effort was geared towards survival. Nonetheless, the ground immediately outside settlers' homes was planted with useful species, which in those days included roses, paeonies, iris, hollyhocks, pinks, lilies, poppies and pot marigolds, as well as traditional culinary herbs, and a charming, cottage-garden effect resulted.

Even when life became more secure, the creation of magnificent gardens was not a high priority, perhaps because in a basically agricultural country, gardening becomes a 'busman's holiday'. Then, too, there was so much land, compared to that available in Europe, and the American flora was so varied and beautiful, that formal gardening may have seemed irrelevant.

The power of nostalgia

When ornamental gardens were made, they were largely nostalgic and traditional, harking back to Europe, ironic in view of the revolutionary birth of America, and its desire to shake free from European rule. These early gardens often copied the formal, rectilinear layout of Dutch, English and French gardens, and the underlying motive was probably the same: to show man's authority over the landscape and nature.

Long avenues of trees, mazes and knot gardens were especially popular in the South, and the formal style of gardening lasted longer there than in the North, indeed, longer than it did in Europe, possibly because Southern social

The gardens of Williamsburg, Virginia give an accurate picture of gardening in eighteenth-century America.

Two mirror-image lakes at Middleton Place, South Carolina form the wings of a butterfly in plan.

values were more rigidly hierarchical, and formal gardens had a particular social status.

One of the most famous examples of early eighteenth-century American gardens was Crowfield, near Charleston. It had spacious lawns with an ornamental lake in front of the house. To the back, a 1000ft (300m) long walk divided the garden in half, and it was further subdivided into parterres, canals, ponds, a lawn with a serpentine walk, and a small oak forest.

Other gardens of interest near Charleston include Magnolia Gardens of Drayton Hall and Middleton Place. Middleton Place was based on seventeenth-century Anglo-Dutch garden design, with huge *parterres de broderie*, stepped terraces, two mirror-image lakes, forming the wings of a 'butterfly' in plan, and broad avenues. Magnolia Gardens is a nineteenth-century design, similar to Repton's late work, with broad expanses of water and a rich variety of plants, though some formal avenues, lawns and shrubberies are included.

Williamsburg

The South, with its wealthy, tobacco-based economy, became settled and financially sound earlier than New England, and the gardens reflected this new-found wealth. The meticulous reconstruction of the gardens of Williamsburg, the capital of the colony of Virginia was based on original plant lists, plans, physical excavations and contemporary description; they give an accurate picture of gardening in eighteenth-century America.

Williamsburg is typical of Dutch-style English gardens of that time, with dense, intricate parterres of box; topiary; pleached *allées* and herb and vegetable gardens. Permanent evergreen planting was emphasised, with seasonal colour provided by flowers.

The compact, town gardens had central brick paths and smaller paths crossing at right angles; or a central circular, square or oval bed, with paths radiating from it. Between the paths were raised planting beds. These were often bordered in dwarf box, and contained flowers such as tulips, fritillaries and lilies; or vegetables. Flowering shrubs and small trees also featured, and huge trees and vast rolled lawns in the larger gardens, such as that of the Governor's Palace, which was built as an impressive symbol of Royal authority. Its garden also contained oval and diamond-shaped parterres, long flower borders, kitchen gardens, a canal and a holly maze equal to that at Hampton Court.

Similar reconstructions occur throughout the Eastern seaboard, including the lovely garden at the headquarters of the Pennsylvania Horticulture Society, in Philadelphia. The eighteenth-century garden at Mount Vernon, George Washington's home, was reconstructed and maintained by the Mount Vernon Ladies' Association, established during the Civil War for that purpose, and continuing to this day. Monticello, the home of Thomas Jefferson, with its Palladian style Mansion and gardens in the style of the great eighteenth-century English landscapes, has also been restored by a foundation set up for that purpose. Jefferson's garden notebooks, which recorded in great detail the development of his garden and the species included, proved of invaluable help in the restoration of both this and other Colonial gardens.

Central Park, New York City was planned by Calvert Vaux and Frederick Law Olmsted.

Private and public parks

The eighteenth-century 'natural' park landscapes of the great English estates provided a pattern for wealthy American landowners to follow. Examples, such as Hyde Park and De Vaux Park near the Hudson River, occur largely in the New England and Mid-Atlantic states, where the climate is conducive to fine lawn, a vital element in 'natural' landscape gardening. The origins of Hyde Park date back to 1700, but the principal improvements were carried out between 1824 and 1830 by Parmentier. De Vaux Park, Annondale, Duchesse County, was laid out in 1790 by Colonel André Vaux, a native of South Carolina. The gardens of Gore Place, in Massachusetts, were also inspired by Repton. The home of Massachusetts Governor Christopher Gore, the house and park-like gardens were begun in 1805, and continued to be developed over the next 20 years.

The Palladian style mansion of Monticello, home of Thomas Jefferson.

A.J. Downing (1815–1852) was the first American garden designer of note, and a follower of the 'gardenesque' style of Loudon. As well as the gardens surrounding his own home at Newburgh, he laid out Wodenethe, in Fishkill, New York. In 1851, Downing was engaged to lay the grounds around the Smithsonian Institute, the White House and the Capitol, in Washington, D.C. His life was tragically cut short when a Hudson River steamboat, on which he was a passenger, exploded.

Downing's partner was Calvert Vaux, an architectural painter by profession. Vaux planned Fairmount Park in Philadelphia and, together with Frederick Law Olmsted, Central

Victorian water-lily pads at Longwood Gardens, Chester, Pennsylvania.

Park in New York, the first and second public parks in America, respectively.

Twentieth-century eclecticism

The idea of combining many different styles in a single garden was immensely popular in Victorian Europe, and 'eclecticism' became equally popular in America. Notable among these 'composite' gardens is Longwood Gardens, in Chester, Pennsylvania. Created in 1909 by its owner, Pierre Samuel DuPont, it contains a topiary garden, a fountain garden in the style of Versailles, an Italian water garden, wilderness gardens, a lake, conservatory and plantings of botanical interest.

Filoli, in California, was created in 1915; over 700 acres (283 hectares), it contains a Dutch garden, wild garden, Japanese garden, walled garden and kitchen garden, among other styles. The framework is strongly geometric, in the Italian Renaissance style, with avenues of yew and stone pine, and hedges of myrtle and box.

Smaller but equally eclectic, is Vizcaya, near Miami, Florida. Designed in 1912, it is based on the architecture and landscape style of the Italian Renaissance, modified to include the exotic plants; parterres, for example, are made of jasmine, not box. As well as parterres, there are pools, formal lawns, fountains and water cascades. Stonework features as much as water, in the form of steps, balustrades, urns, statues and obelisks – even a stone boat!

Lastly, Dumbarton Oaks, in Washington, D.C., is created largely in the style of Gertrude Jekyll and Lutyens, with unique additions, such as the flooded cobbled garden, in which a heraldic pattern in cobbles is covered with a thin sheet of water; and a lavish, wisteria-covered pergola, in the style of sixteenth-century carpenter's work. It was designed between 1921 and 1947 by Beatrix Farrand in collaboration with Mildred Barnes Bliss, her client.

'Exotic' plants

Just as Europeans delighted in the discovery and distribution of 'exotic' plants from the New World, such as asters, magnolias and tulip trees, so the American settlers awaited ships carrying seeds, cuttings and plants from all over the world, but usually via England. Thus China asters, nasturtiums, globe amaranths, Oriental poppies, French and African marigolds and many spring-flowering bulbs made their way into American gardens.

GARDENS OLD AND NEW

It is intriguing that neither of the two most important garden designers, André Le Nôtre and Lancelot 'Capability' Brown, wrote any book or manual to describe the kinds of garden which they created with such success. Before and after them, are books in plenty, but the supreme masters of the French formal and the English landscape garden, respectively, left no text to summarise their achievement.

In contrast, garden writers are not always linked with a particular garden or gardens. This is true of Thomas Hill, the writer of the earliest English book on gardens to be printed. His *Most Briefe and Pleasant Treatyse* of 1563 is a mine of information (not always reliable) on gardening practice and design, but does not tell us whether he gardened, either for himself or for others.

As garden fashion changed, books were written to popularise new styles or defend the old, either in a general way, or with detailed instructions and illustrations. In 1641, André Mollet's *Le Jardin de Plaisir* gave detailed designs for parterres, and a century later, William and John Halfpenny produced *Rural Architecture in the Chinese Taste* (1750), followed by Thomas Wright a few years later, in his *Universal Architecture*, with designs for rustic arbours, grottoes and 'root houses'! Sir William Chambers, creator of the great Pagoda at Kew, produced a book on 'Chinese' buildings and furniture in 1757, and a *Dissertation on Oriental Gardening* in 1772. Horace Walpole had published his *History of the Modern Taste in Gardening* in 1771.

In Europe, similar volumes appeared. The Marquis de Girardin, creator of the gardens at Ermenonville, wrote *De la Composition des Paysages* (1777), and in 1819–20 Gabriel Thouin produced a work on garden design advocating 'natural' landscapes with curving, serpentine paths and streams. He proposed a drastic alteration to Versailles, with the addition of vast areas in 'sylvan, rustic, pastoral, Chinese-romantic and French-romantic' styles, connected by curving waterways. These fantasies were not put into practice!

By the early nineteenth century, the flow of books on gardens and gardening had become a river; today, it is a torrent. Humphry Repton's books in the 1800s were followed by J.C. Loudon's (between 1803 and 1845), and these by the writings of his wife, Jane Loudon. Her

Kew, near London, is the world's foremost botanic garden with a history extending over 250 years.

several books on gardening for ladies – notably *The Ladies' Companion to the Flower-Garden*, which first appeared in 1841, were immensely popular.

Later in the century came Shirley Hibberd, writing on ornamental aspects of the garden both plant and architectural (and indoors as well as outside); Dean Hole, writing on roses; the many volumes by William Robinson; and those of Gertrude Jekyll, advocating a more natural way of gardening, and subtlety of planting.

Plans for an imaginary 'picturesque' garden, with fantastic buildings, designed by Gabriel Thouin in the early nineteenth century.

From theory to practice

Often, sweeping changes in garden styles have led to the new fashion replacing and obliterating the old. Many old formal gardens in England were simply swept away in the eighteenth century, to be replaced by the new 'natural' landscape gardens of Capability Brown. Luckily, this is not always the case, and many famous historic gardens which survive today reveal several styles, curiously side by side, in different parts of the garden, or even one on top of another. At Kew, for example, there are several garden epochs represented: the landscape garden, with exotic follies by Sir William Chambers; the great Victorian botanic garden, with the Palm House and the Temperate House created in the 1840s and 1850s; and the *modern* botanic garden, with recently designed garden areas and the striking Princess of Wales Conservatory for tropical plants.

The clipped hedges of a maze at Fontainebleau, in winter.

At Hampton Court there is a similar, and even older, combination of garden styles. Many of the garden walls go back to the early sixteenth century, to the time of Cardinal Wolsey and Henry VIII. The Fountain Garden and the Long Water were begun by Charles II; Capability Brown is said to have planted the Great Vine. The massed bedding is triumphantly Victorian, and the long borders, among the best herbaceous borders in the world, are solidly of the present century.

Similar mixtures occur in France. At Fontainebleau, for example, there is a sixteenth-century grotto, a huge Le Nôtre parterre with fountain and canal, and a 'Jardin anglais', made in 1811–12, planted with exotic trees. Even Versailles, so strongly dominated by the autocratic spirit of Louis XIV, has a romantic grotto, created in the 1770s. At Trianon, a mile away, the formal gardens of the Grand Trianon, created in the 1670s, are in striking contrast with the little landscape garden, with lake, mill and dairy farm, created for Marie Antoinette a century later.

Looking back

Most of the history of garden design involves the gradual development of one style into another. Sometimes the new style grows out of a previous style, as the French formal garden grew out of the gardens of Renaissance Italy. At other times, the new style reacts against the

THE USES OF THE GARDEN

Napoleon with the Empress Joséphine at Malmaison. Though most of the huge garden has disappeared, a small park and her rose garden beside the château may still be enjoyed.

Just as garden style has changed over the ages, so have the uses to which gardens are put. While the earliest gardens may have been essentially for produce and medieval cloister gardens were designed for prayer and contemplation, many small modern gardens are multi-purpose, with features as diverse as a barbecue, a child's trampoline, a swimming pool, and a rockery for alpines.

In most periods, the garden has been an intensely social venue. Renaissance gardens were created for enjoyment of the present, enriched with allusions to the culture of the past. Stone dining tables were sited in shady corners, near the sight and sound of fountains, framed with classical sculptures, and enlivened with hydraulic toys, especially joke fountains. The display of sculpture eventually led to the garden as an exhibition-site, most noted in the Great Exhibition of 1851 in London's Hyde Park, and the funfare of the Festival of Britain, held in Battersea Park a century later.

Louis XIV's gardens at Versailles were designed to impress, even overawe, his visitors, but they were lavishly entertained in the process with theatrical displays, ballets and concerts; fireworks and excursions along the great Canal. The Canal at Versailles was large enough for a small fleet: a miniature man of war, galleys and gondolas. Two of the gondolas were the gift of the Republic of Venice, with a crew of gondoliers included. Their quarters beside the Canal were named Petite Venise, *or 'Little Venice'.*

At Trianon, flowers, rather than 'spectacles', were the central attraction. Huge hothouses were filled with hundreds of thousands of potted plants, ready for instant installation in the bedding areas. One region at Trianon, the 'King's Garden', could be given three different floral displays in a day.

The tradition of floral display, often involving passionate rivalries, has continued unabated. At Malmaison in the 1800s, the Empress Josephine created a centre for displays of roses, and today the extensive gardens of Keukenhof, in the Netherlands, are the world's greatest showcase for bulbs: tulips, narcissi, hyacinths, grape hyacinths and crown imperials. Yet Keukenhof is also a fine landscape garden, particularly admirable where the level ground has been excavated, or raised up in unobtrusive ridges, to create winding pools, divided by 'natural' slopes and belts of trees. Thousands upon thousands of visitors are hidden from each other by the gentle slopes, and discreetly absorbed into the flower-filled landscape.

At Vaux-le-Vicomte, Le Notre's scheme of avenues, hedges, sculpture and parterres is set round an elaborate pattern of water features: a moat, pools, canal and many fountains.

previous style, as the English landscape garden grew out of opposition to the gardens of France. The last century has also seen deliberate attempts to restore or recreate gardens in past styles.

Most notable, at the end of the nineteenth century, were Henri and Achille Duchêne (father and son), who restored the derelict gardens of Vaux-le-Vicomte to their present glory. Created in 1656–61 by Le Nôtre, the gardens of Vaux had been neglected for many decades, and the Duchênes were responsible for a scrupulous restoration of Le Nôtre's original scheme. Achille Duchêne later developed the garden of Courances in the style of Le Nôtre, and then laid out the 'water parterre' at Blenheim, in Oxfordshire, modelled on Le Nôtre's 1670s scheme at Versailles. This eminently formal garden scheme overlooks Capability Brown's lake, one of the most famous features of the English landscape garden.

As well as the great garden in the style of the Renaissance at Villandry in France, and the restoration of William of Orange's garden at Het Loo in the Netherlands, there is the unique project of restoration and recreation undertaken in the last half century at Colonial Williamsburg in Virginia. Here an entire complex of houses and gardens has been restored. Centred round the gardens of the Governor's palace, but with many smaller domestic gardens as well, it provides a unique insight into the gardens of a small but important Colonial town in the 1730s. The style of the gardens is firmly formal, with geometrical layouts aligned on the buildings, and with small, tidy beds outlined in box, and *allées* in hornbeam. Archaeological work at Colonial Williamsburg has uncovered a wealth of corroborative detail, down to the patterns of flowerpots, the placing of fence posts, and the deposits of box clippings in a sealed-off well! Box, is not native to America, and had to be imported from Europe for the gardens at Williamsburg in the 1730s.

The public park

While the great gardens of Versailles are visited daily by thousands of people, they did not begin as a 'public park', but as a royal domain. This is equally true of many fine gardens and parks in or near London, such as Hampton Court, St. James's Park, Hyde Park, Kensington Gardens and Greenwich Park.

In the first half of the nineteenth century, however, there was a movement to create *public* parks in the great cities, to alleviate the crowded, smoky, living conditions of the inhabitants. The forerunners were Victoria Park and Battersea Park in London, and Birkenhead Park on Merseyside. Birkenhead Park, laid out from 1843 onwards, and opened in 1847, was the first park in England to be established at public expense. Designed by Joseph Paxton, the head gardener of the Duke of Devonshire, at Chatsworth, the park was to be a permanently peaceful, 'rural' area, with pools, sweeping lawns, belts of trees, varied recreational features, and *freedom from traffic*, within the city confines.

Above all, it was to be for the use of the people.

A grand good thing

In 1850, only three years after it had been opened, Birkenhead Park was visited by a young American, Frederick Law Olmsted. He was immensely impressed by its quality and purpose. He wrote

> All this magnificent pleasure-ground is entirely, unreservedly and for ever the people's own. The poorest British peasant is as free to enjoy it . . . as the British queen . . . Is it not a grand good thing?

The long, gently descending water staircase at Courances, with its flat sheets of water, was created on a seventeenth-century model.

Olmsted's enthusiasm was translated into action. In 1857, in a competition for New York's proposed 'Central Park' his design was

The Pebble Garden at Dumbarton Oaks, Washington D.C.

Elliptical courtyard at Dumbarton Oaks, Washington D.C.

the winner, and much of the great expanse of Central Park today is derived from his initial plan and subsequent work as Landscape Architect for the project. (Olmsted and his colleague Calvert Vaux were the first to entitle themselves 'landscape architects'.)

In the following decades both Olmsted and Vaux were responsible for many important designs, from Prospect Park in Brooklyn, to parks in Boston, Massachusetts; California; Washington, D.C.; Illinois; as far south as Atlanta, Georgia; and north across the border to Mount Royal Park in Montreal, Canada.

Olmsted was not the only foreign visitor to be influenced by the growth of public parks in Victorian England. Louis Napoléon, exiled in England from 1846 to 1848, urged the transformation of many areas of Paris in the 1850s. His main designer was J.-C.-A. Alphand, who reshaped the Bois de Boulogne and the Bois de Vincennes, and designed the parks of Buttes-Chaumont and Montsouris, and the long garden areas flanking the Champs Elysées.

Private gardens

Centuries of garden design present a bewildering and inspiring variety of styles and sizes.

The wistaria over the bridge at Giverny was painted many times by Monet, as were the water lilies in the pond.

The swimming pool at William Randolph Hearst's gardens at San Simeon, California.

Private gardens are still created on a princely scale. William Randolph Hearst's gardens at San Simeon, and the Huntington Botanical Gardens in California each have several distinct and striking areas, as do the gardens of Dumbarton Oaks at Washington, D.C. At the same time, the relatively recent influence of Japanese gardens confirms that a garden masterpiece may be minute, just a few square yards, and therefore something which the tiniest city patch may achieve.

Modern designers have created fine gardens on these different scales. Sylvia Crowe, John Brookes and Derek Lovejoy are widely thought to have been Britain's foremost designers in recent years; in the United States, Thomas Church (1902–78), and in Brazil, Roberto Burle Marx (born in 1909) are equally renowned, and their work is found in several countries. But the private gardener now has at his disposal so great a selection of ideas, plants, materials and tools that the creation of one's own garden is intriguing, satisfying and eminently possible. Modern garden centres offer a wider range of equipment and plants than ever before. What would the feelings of early plant collectors have been, faced with the present choice of trees, shrubs, herbaceous plants and bulbs? What would Louis XIV, that lover of 'full-throated fountains', have thought, could he have used electric pumps for his water schemes?

The gardens of the past are there to study, enjoy, and even imitate. Today, vegetables, in utmost variety, can be grown; a small greenhouse can house cacti from New Mexico or the Kalahari; a sweep of lawn, and a few apple trees, underplanted with spring bulbs, can capture a rural scene. Topiary, formal or fantastic, can be created; as can knot gardens which Shakespeare would admire, or herbaceous borders as fine as Gertrude Jekyll's. A rockery no bigger than a table-top can be home to a collection of alpine plants, and a 'terrarium', the bottle garden descended from the 'Wardian case' invented in the 1830s, can house an indoor garden the size of a suitcase.

TYPES OF GARDEN

THE ORNAMENTAL GARDEN

Creating a garden is an exciting adventure. If you have a small patch, it is not too difficult to do, but where there is an area of 350 square yards (300 square metres) or more, you need to make a definite decision about its role. Is it to be functional or purely decorative? Is it for relaxation or to satisfy your passion for plants? Should the design be traditional and formal, or do you prefer tangled informality?

Planning becomes more complicated when you want to create a garden that is both ornamental and economic, especially if recreation is to have a role too. Vegetables and fruit may have to combine happily with a rock garden and maybe a greenhouse, play area and flower beds too.

Take your time and allow the garden to evolve. It is easy to adjust details as time goes on. However, you should start with an overall plan, so that areas for flowers and vegetables are clearly defined from the outset. In the first year, limit the work to making paths and controlling weeds so that the lie of the land can be seen and the areas of operation clearly defined. Work can begin on soil preparation: improving the structure and adding organic matter and nutrients.

Before planting, it is essential to consider the natural characteristics of the garden. If you only have a bare or sloping site, or maybe one or two trees, then it is important to make a note of likely exposure and protection. Knowing where these important areas are helps you decide where to place plants. If there is a slope, for example, surplus water will drain away. The slope will also govern how exposed various parts of the garden are; lower ground is colder. Decide which parts of the landscape you want to focus upon and which parts you want to conceal.

It is rare to have sufficient space available to include all the features of an ornamental garden. The idea, therefore, is to make the best possible use of the space there is. Here, the lawn gives an impression of depth, accentuated by the fact that the garden is planted right out to its edges. There is a small, secluded corner at the end of the garden.

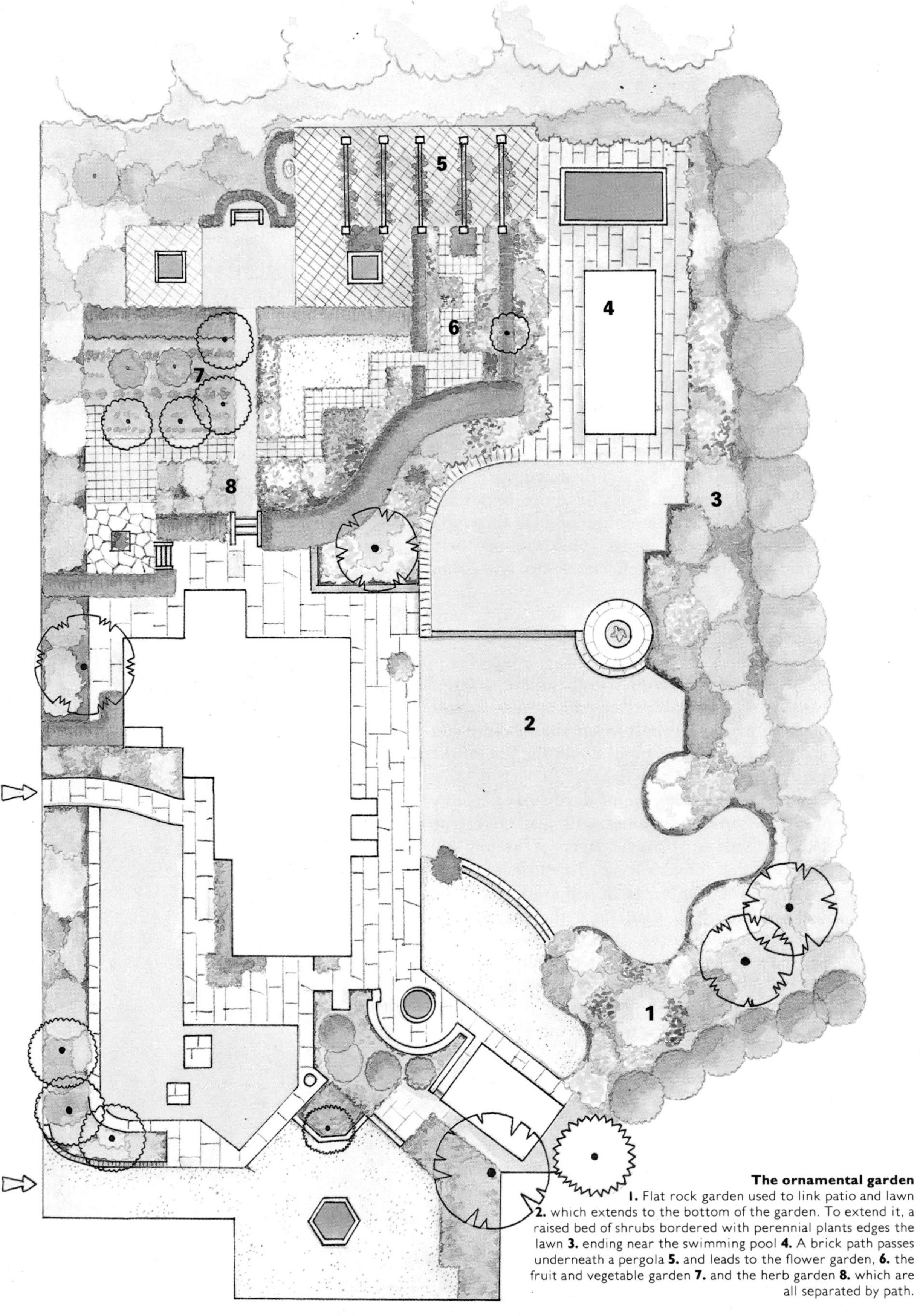

The ornamental garden
1. Flat rock garden used to link patio and lawn **2.** which extends to the bottom of the garden. To extend it, a raised bed of shrubs bordered with perennial plants edges the lawn **3.** ending near the swimming pool **4.** A brick path passes underneath a pergola **5.** and leads to the flower garden, **6.** the fruit and vegetable garden **7.** and the herb garden **8.** which are all separated by path.

Write down all these factors on a plan drawn to scale. Then make a sketch of the view you would like to see from the house and, if necessary, transfer this to a copy of the plan.

There are several options open for laying out your garden. You might employ a professional garden designer. This may be expensive, but could be a good idea if the area is large. Be sure to use a designer with a good reputation. Alternatively, you may decide to do all the work yourself, or to use specialists selectively, to create terracing, build stonework or handle large-scale planting, for example.

In any case, you need to know exactly what you want, and, perhaps even more importantly, what you do not want. Make this very clear to any specialists you use. If you do not, there is the risk that your garden will end up looking very different from the one you dreamed of.

Take photographs of the most important areas to give you a better idea of what they look like from different angles. This will also help you to explain yourself clearly to any other people involved.

The first work to be done is the hard landscaping: stonework, bricklaying and path construction.

Watering is a major consideration; a water point needs to be able to cover a radius of about 80 ft (25 m), so it is best to site these before you start planting. Take pipes down the line of the main paths where possible.

You need to be careful if you have to buy topsoil. Some companies will just cover the garden with a cosmetic layer of arable soil without first breaking up the surface of the ground. The two types of soil are likely to be very different, so that, once the plants have taken root in the new topsoil, the roots will be unable to penetrate the sub-soil. Only when the soil conditions are good and water and drainage laid on, should planting start.

It is sensible to start with the most permanent plants – trees. Remember that many trees grow much too large for the average garden, so be selective. Do not plant a tree without knowing its ultimate height. If there is room for only one tree, always site it away from the house. This gives it a number of advantages; the beauty of its outline, the quality of the shade it gives, and the flowers and fruit it bears. Small-fruited crab apple trees, cherry trees and mountain ash are good ones to choose. If you plant several trees, choose ones with different shapes, heights and breadths. The idea is to create a sense of depth and movement by using different sizes and shapes, just as you would in a flower-bed.

Organize each part of the garden individually around its layout, stamping it with your own particular taste. However, it is important to create links between the different areas in a logical, systematic way, based on the view from the house.

Imagine you are creating different types of garden around a typical family house: a small front garden, two narrow strips round the side of the house, and a larger plot at the back. The drive leading to the garage will partly determine how the garden is laid out, both because of where it is placed, and where it is in relation to the street. The front garden will therefore be regular, with a lawn, clumps of shrubs and straight paths.

Assuming the back of the house is the sunniest, this is the place for a terrace and a greenhouse to catch the winter sun. Put a sandpit and swing at the end of the terrace, attaching the swing to a tree, which also provides shade for part of the terrace. All these

A paved path. This is more expensive than a sand or grass path, but it lasts longer and is easier to maintain. It gives an elegant, neat but not too severe look to the garden.

are bordered by a lawn. This part of the garden also contains a mixed border placed against a neatly trimmed hedge. The same hedge continues into the front garden. The sides of the back garden are bordered by an informal, untrimmed hedge.

An opening in the hedge leads to the vegetable garden, ending in an informal hedge where you can pick bunches of flowers. Past that is a small orchard and, right at the very end, a small clump of trees.

Along the terrace, a low, dry stone wall functions as a rock garden with a small pond or a mixed border decorating one corner of the lawn. Near a side entrance or the garage, is a small lean-to for your gardening shoes and boots and perhaps a few tools as well. Alternatively, you might keep these in a discreet shed in the corner of the vegetable garden. Some herbs and spices are growing in a small area near the kitchen door.

As the final touch, part of the garden is illuminated. Only the approach to the house and the area immediately around it needs to be brightly lit. All that is needed elsewhere is the occasional small lamp in any areas that are often used at night or where there are hazards such as a pond or a flight of steps.

This imaginary garden has already become quite elaborate, and it may of course, be beyond your means financially. Equally, there is no reason why you should not simply make the whole thing into a lawn, or you could plant flowers and nothing else, or you could put in a mass of ground-cover plants. Whatever you do, it is important that you are happy with the result. This will be more likely if there is some sort of connecting thread running through the design. If you overdo the picturesque aspect, the garden will look incongruous, but if you create a harmony of colour and uniformity in the materials you use – the same stone and the same types of wood – the result will be an elegant garden which is full of variety.

Japanese garden. The red bridge goes well with the oriental design.

THE FLOWER GARDEN

Most gardens include some flowers. It is not necessary to have a large and elaborate display, for flowers can be integrated successfully with trees, shrubs and garden features.

A good flower garden will take account of the characteristics of each type of flowering plant; its height, colour, and flowering period, so that the overall effect is one of harmony with as long a period of interest as possible. The traditional flower garden consists mainly of herbaceous perennials, but it also includes flowering shrubs, annuals and bulbs.

The first flowerbeds

Flower gardens originated at the end of the nineteenth century. The art of creating flowerbeds was, for the most part, developed in England, but was also influenced by travellers' accounts of oriental gardens. At first only the affluent, with large houses and gardens and many gardeners, were able to afford such flowerbeds. Summer flowering plants were raised in a greenhouse and then bedded out as soon as they started to flower and the danger of frost had passed. These replaced fading spring flowering plants, which were removed and replaced the following autumn. This was labour intensive and in most cases very stiff and formal. Though such displays occasionally persist in gardens today, they are more frequently seen in parks or at flower shows.

The perennial or herbaceous flowerbed developed alongside the more traditional bedding and has now become popular and widespread because the plants persist from year to year without disturbance. This kind of flower gardening is equally satisfying and is much less expensive both in terms of time and money.

Double mixed borders, with a predominantly yellow colour, are effectively set off by spots of pink, orange, white and violet.

The mixed border: a year-round flowerbed

The main flowering period for herbaceous perennial plants is mid-spring to late summer. There may also be a second flowering period in early autumn. Not having a continual show of flowers does not matter in a large garden, where you can create other interesting and attractive features, but, if your garden is small, you cannot allow yourself such a luxury. Instead, you will have to turn your flowerbed into a kind of microcosm of the whole garden. Nowadays, it need not be restricted to perennials, but can also include shrubs, small trees, bulbs and annuals. This means that it looks attractive for a much longer period. Even during winter, the shapes of the plants and the bark of the trees and shrubs can be decorative.

This combination of different types of plants is called a mixed border. There are many different criteria for deciding how to make up your border: the colours and heights of the plants, their main season of flowering, how sheltered the area is and the type of soil. Most importantly, it depends on your own personal tastes. There is no ideal way of creating a mixed border but there are some simple rules to bear in mind when designing one.

A hedge for a mixed border

Mark out a long rectangle with a formal, trimmed hedge as a background. This should

Blue and orange mixed border
To give a flowerbed an undulating feel, it needs a variety of heights, shapes and volumes. If it is based on perennial plants, add a few shrubs, bulbs and annuals.

consist of a single variety of shrub and can be evergreen or deciduous. It should eventually attain a height of 8–10 ft (2.5–3 m). Instead of an evergreen species you could try a marcescent one, like beech, whose leaves die but do not fall off until the spring in some zones. The hedge should be uniform so that it contrasts with and acts as a foil to the diversity of flowering plants.

The best shrubs to use are yews, *Thujas* (arbor-vitae) and various *Cupressus* (cypresses). Hornbeam or beech may be tightly pruned to create a hedge. Avoid shrubs with light-coloured or gold and silver leaves, as these will not provide sufficient contrast to the flowers. Purple leaves, on the other hand, contrast too sharply, and can create gloom in the design.

Equally, you can place a mixed border against a wall or fence. If the wall is attractively weathered and neither too dark nor too light, leave it alone. Alternatively, plant a fast-growing climber, such as ampelopsis (porcelin berry) or actinidia (kiwi), to create a natural leafy covering for the wall. Some gardeners use decorative climbing plants, such as roses or clematis, to serve as a background for a mixed border, where they eventually form part of it.

Leave a gap of about 20 in (50 cm) between the flowerbed and the hedge; more if the flowerbed is a deep one. This will allow you access for trimming the hedge and maintaining the back of the flowerbed. In any case, the roots of the hedge will prevent anything from establishing successfully near by.

If a mixed border is fairly deep, leave a path between the hedge and the background plants so that all the plants are easily accessible.

The size of a mixed border

As long as all the plants can be easily seen, it does not matter too much what size mixed border you choose. However, a sense of depth is necessary in the form of different levels or layers between the eye of the observer and the back of the bed. You need at least three to five layers to create a satisfactory effect.

Siting the mixed border

Select the site for a mixed border carefully. Avoid hollows where frost can be trapped and damage spring flowers. The hedge should protect it from the prevailing winds. If not, the plants, even if properly staked, are likely to get blown around and end up looking bedraggled. The availability of light and the soil type are not such important considerations because by selecting plants carefully, you can create a very beautiful flowerbed irrespective of whether it is in the shade or bright sunlight, or whether the soil is dry, wet, acid or alkaline.

Obviously, it is best to start with a fairly rich, well-drained soil. It should be neutral or slightly acid and, preferably, in a sunny spot. This type of soil will grow the widest diversity of interesting plants. However, it is not usual for all these conditions to occur naturally. While it may be difficult to do anything about the available light, the soil can always be improved.

Preparing the soil

First, remove all weeds particularly perennial weeds, such as couch-grass (quack or witch-grass), bindweed, nettles and dandelions. Once the area is weed free, allow sufficient time for proper soil preparation before planting. If some areas are ready to accept plants early on, there is nothing to stop you sowing a selection of annuals to provide some early colour.

If the site you have selected consists of lawn, remove the turf with a spade. This can be composted for use elsewhere in the garden. In the meantime, add plenty of well-rotted organic matter to the newly prepared bed.

The soil needs thorough preparation during the autumn and winter as the bed is intended to become a long-lasting feature. The soil needs to be in the best possible condition if the plants are to grow well. Until recently, the only way of breaking up the soil was to use a spade; nowadays, the mechanical cultivator has made this task much easier. During digging or cultivating, incorporate plenty of well-rotted garden compost or other organic material and also add a general slow-acting fertilizer if necessary.

Planting the mixed border

Unless you take professional advice or are well informed about the behaviour of plants, you should proceed cautiously. If you make a mistake with annuals or bulbs, it does not matter much as you can remove the former at the end of the flowering period and transfer the latter when they are dormant. With perennials, this is more difficult; some die if they are moved, and others spread very rapidly or are almost indestructible. Many campanulas and some members of the poppy family, for example, are very persistent and, if you miss a single fragment of root, it will grow new plants.

Check the plants that you use very carefully; some that you thought were friends may turn out to be enemies. Even then, your problems may not be over, for the flowering season, height, speed of growth, or type of leaves of even the most carefully chosen plants may sometimes turn out to be different from what you expected. If so, keep these in the mixed border, but move them to a better position. An old gardener's trick is to place them in 2 gallon (10 litre) containers and bury these completely. If they grow the way they are supposed to, you can pull them up the following autumn and replant them again straight away without the container. If they do not grow the way you hoped, they will be easy to move.

In any event, to start off with, plant just a few specimens with plenty of space between them. A common mistake is to plant far too many at the outset. A mixed border will take four to five years to reach full maturity and, if it is closely planted, it will be unmanageable.

BACKGROUND SHRUBS FOR A MIXED BORDER
(check hardiness for your region)

	Recommended	**Not recommended**
Evergreen or semi-evergreen	Prunus laurocerasus Rhododendron ponticum (in acid soil) Viburnum tinus (laurustinus) Olearia (in a mild climate) Pittosporum (near the sea) Thuyas Yew Cupressocyparis Chamaecyparis lawsonia	Common ivy (sows itself everywhere) Ligustrum (too greedy) Box (too slow-growing) Lonicera nitida (too short) Flowering shrubs (too eye-catching) Bamboos (too invasive)
Deciduous	Acer campestre Corylus avellana Vitis Ampelopsis	Purple hazelnuts, purple beech, and other trees with purple foliage (too dark) Plane maple (sycamore in USA – too vigorous) Flowering shrubs (too eye-catching)

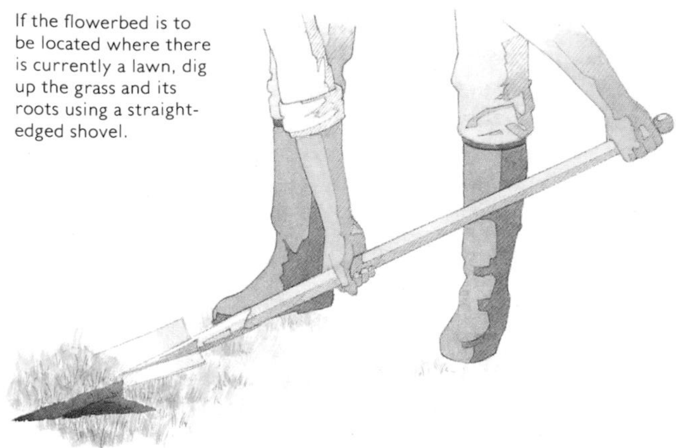

If the flowerbed is to be located where there is currently a lawn, dig up the grass and its roots using a straight-edged shovel.

Plant the bed in late autumn or early spring. Develop the garden as you would the house, starting with the major work, in this case the hedge which is the backbone and framework of the whole design. Follow with perennials, bulbs and, finally, annuals.

Colours

There are four basic types of colour scheme. The first is to plant a single colour. Another approach is to create a cameo effect by using all the different tones of one colour ranging into the colours closely allied to it. Thirdly, you can create harmony by using simple combinations such as pink and white. Finally, you might use contrasting colours, such as yellow and blue. If you simply use as many different colours as possible, the result will look unnatural. There are also some combinations of colours which simply do not go together, such as bluish pink

TRADITIONAL MIXED BORDER PLANTS

Plants	Sun	Shade	Cool soil	Dry soil	Alkaline soil	Acid soil
Acanthus mollis	X	X	X		X	X
Achillea filipend.	X			X	X	
Achillea millefol.	X		X	X		
Aconitum	X		X			X
Agapanthus	X		X		X	
Anchusa italica	X			X	X	
Anemone hupehensis	X	X	X		X	
Aquilegia	X		X		X	
Artemisia	X			X	X	
Asclepias	X		X		X	
Aster	X		X		X	
Astilbes	X		X			X
Aubrieta	X			X	X	
Brunnera macrophylla	X		X	X	X	
Campanula	X		X	X	X	X
Chrysanthemum maximum	X		X	X	X	
Coreopsis	X		X		X	
Crocosmia	X		X		X	
Cyclamen	X	X	X	X	X	X
Delphinium	X		X			X
Dianthus	X			X	X	
Euphorbia	X		X	X	X	
Filipendula	X		X			X
Gaillardia	X			X	X	
Geranium	X		X		X	X

and orange. Sometimes, however, if you make very careful use of jarring colours it can create an eye-catching effect.

Monochrome colour schemes

A white garden can be very effective indeed. One of the finest examples was created by Vita Sackville-West at Sissinghurst Castle, Kent in England. Although this type of border looks simple, it is actually very complex, for there is an infinite variety of whites: pure white, pinkish white, bluish white, silvery white, and cream. These do not always go well together, so you need to be careful when choosing them.

This is equally true of other colours, such as pink, blue and especially red. You could also experiment with more unusual colours, such as orange, violet or green.

The white garden at Sissinghurst in England. It uses Lilium regale 'Album', *Rosa filipes* 'Kiftsgate', *white eryngiums and arborescent lupins.*

TRADITIONAL MIXED BORDER PLANTS						
Plants	**Sun**	**Shade**	**Cool soil**	**Dry soil**	**Alkaline soil**	**Acid soil**
Geum	X		X		X	X
Gypsophila	X			X	X	
Helenium	X		X		X	X
Helianthemum	X			X	X	
Helianthus	X			X	X	
Helleborus	X	X	X		X	
Hemerocallis	X	X	X		X	X
Hosta		X	X		X	X
Iris	X			X	X	
Kniphofia	X			X	X	
Lavandula	X			X	X	
Ligularia	X		X		X	X
Lupinus	X		X			X
Macleaya	X	X	X		X	X
Monarda	X		X		X	X
Nepeta	X			X	X	
Paeonia	X		X		X	
Papaver	X			X	X	
Phlox	X		X			X
Primula	X		X		X	X
Rudbeckia	X		X		X	
Ruta	X			X	X	
Scabiosa	X		X		X	
Solidago	X		X	X	X	X
Stachys	X			X	X	
Trollius	X		X			X
Verbena	X		X		X	

A single-colour bed runs a strong risk of looking boring. A splash of bright colour will often create a welcome contrast to the basic colour. If you do this, make it a very small spot of colour – a single plant is enough – such as red in a white bed, or yellow in a blue one.

The cameo

Here, the choice of tones is rather easier. If you use pink as the overall colour, for example, choose either a bluish or a salmon pink. In the former case, all other types of pink will go well with it, and you can also use mauves and violets. In the latter, use colours tending towards orange.

Harmony through similarity

This is by far the easiest way of producing an attractive mixed border. If you are using pink and white, for example (though you could also use three, four or even five colours), you might alternate soft pinks with salmon pinks and separate them with white flowers. Creating contrast is a delicate matter but, if it is successful, it will be extremely attractive, and subtle differences of shade tend to be softened by the whole.

Pale colours are more suited to soft light, and vivid colours to bright light. Spring and autumn show off pastel shades to their best advantage, and summer brings out clear, bright colours. This also applies to the region in which you live; pastels for a northern sky, bright colours for places with a sunny climate.

Leaves are also very important, for their different shapes and colours form the link between the separate parts of a successful mixed border. About a third of the border should consist of greenery intermingled with the masses of colour. The greenery may come from plants grown solely for their foliage, or from plants flowering at different times.

Different tones of the same colour is the simplest combination for success in a mixed border.

A harmonious combination of pastel shades includes astilbes, monardas, matricarias, mallows and the white form of rose campion.

The leaves of annuals can serve to hide the gaps left by dormant bulbs or other leaves which have grown old and lost their attraction. This will happen naturally if you distribute plants with the same flowering period throughout the mixed border, instead of grouping them together. Even with 30 per cent or fewer plants actually in flower at any one time, the mixed border will look as though it is in full flower.

Types of mixed border

A mixed border needs harmonious shapes, as well as colours. In the past, the tendency was to make flowerbeds as regular and even as possible, with large clumps of plants. This mean that there was an even, rising slope of plants, with no gaps between them, from the path to the back of the mixed border. This not only looked totally artificial, but was monotonous, and the slightest blemish was very conspicuous.

Modern design is more elegant and simpler to create. Although the tallest plants are positioned at the back and the shortest at the front, they do not rise evenly. Rather, the tops of the plants gently rise and fall in turn, with small plants alternating with medium-sized ones and so on.

Suppose there are plants of six different heights (in practice, there will be many more), with no. 1 the shortest and no. 6 the tallest. Working from front to back, the sequence will be something like 1, 3, 2, 1, 4, 2, 3, 4, 5 and 6. Arranged like this, the flowerbed still looks very neat. However, the spread of each group of plants must also be taken into consideration. Small plants near the front are deliberately given a larger surface area than the taller ones. Gradually, as you go towards the back, this pattern is reversed. There is nothing wrong with placing a fairly tall plant, say 3½ ft (1 m) or more, at the very front, bordering the path, but it is important to choose a fine, slender one, such as an ornamental grass, so that the back of the flowerbed is easily visible.

To create unity in the overall design, make patches of colour balance each other. For example, if you have a large area of a particular plant on the left-hand side, place one or two specimens of the same plant on the right. Do not put them at exactly the same distance from the path; place them either slightly forward or slightly farther back.

You will need to create a 'frame' for your mixed border. This will mean that the plants at the ends are all medium-sized or tall. The shorter plants should feature only in the centre of the composition. If the bed is a long one, more than about 17 ft (5 m) in length, simply repeat the pattern.

Planting

The number of individual plants of each type will vary depending on the height of the fully grown plant. Work from the principle that for the same surface area, it will take twice as many 8 in (20 cm) plants as 16 in (40 cm) ones. Likewise, there will be twice as many 16 in (40 cm) as 32 in (80 cm) plants in the same area. This is not an unbreakable rule, but more of a guide which you can adapt yourself, to prevent any really glaring errors.

The distance between plants should be equal to their height when fully grown, but vary this rule slightly for the tallest and smallest plants. The rule applies even to tall plants if they have very large leaves, such as ornamental rhubarb. If they have small or medium-sized leaves, such as verbascums (mulleins), eremurus (foxtail lily) and delphiniums, plant them the equivalent of only half their height apart. For very short plants, less than 12 in (30 cm) high, base the distance on the diameter of the flower head, planting them twice this diameter apart.

After a while, the plants will be almost touching, at least when they are in flower. When they are dormant, there should be some space between them to allow access for routine cultivation. If dormant plants are touching, they should be moved further apart.

If you alternate the different heights, each plant will be easy to see but there will be no break in the overall continuity of the mixed

1. Ceanothus **2.** Macleaya **3.** Anchusa **4.** Ancolia **5.** Achillea **6.** Helianthemum. To obtain a natural effect, alternate the height of the plants, rising slowly towards the back. Then add the occasional taller plant at the front and in the middle as shown.

PROPORTION OF PLANTS IN A MIXED BORDER

Shrubs	***5%***
Perennials	***75%***
Bulbs	***10%***
Annuals	***10%***

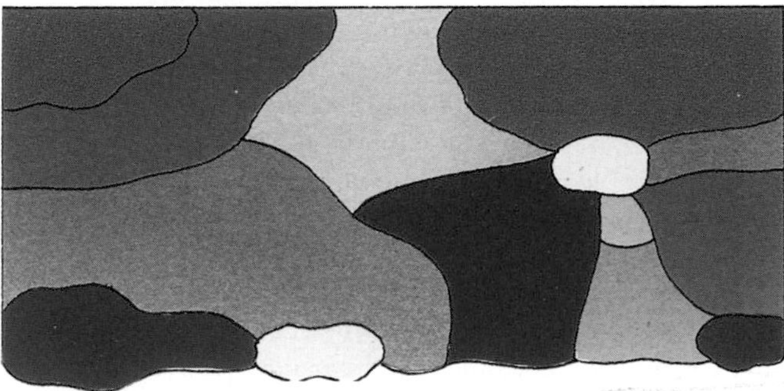

Distributing areas of colour
Each plant is represented by one colour in this example so that the organisation of the bed can be illustrated. The harmony of the design comes from the fact that the plants repeat in an apparently random fashion.

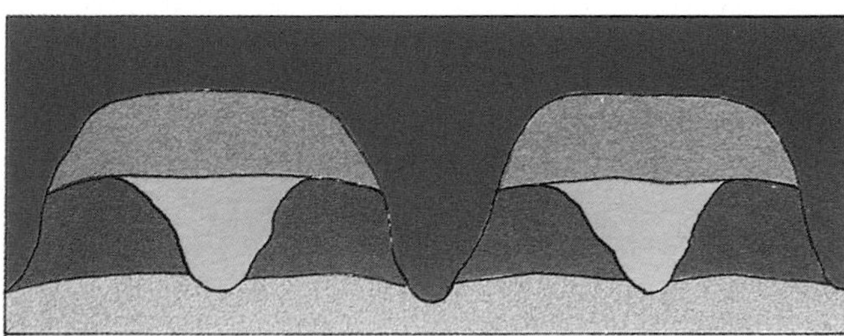

Framing a mixed border
In a large flowerbed where the sides and back are framed by a hedge, the same motif can be repeated several times.

border. There will be an even greater degree of harmony if you make use of the shapes of the plants.

Using shapes

There are three aspects of plant form which affect the design of the flowerbed: the overall shape of the plant, its opacity (i.e. whether it is light and airy or dense and does not let much light through), and the shape of its flowers.

Never put flowers of similar shape side by side, even if they are different colours. For example, do not juxtapose delphiniums and eremurus (foxtail lily), grasses and feathery ferns, or thyme and heather. Use contrasting shapes to create variety in the same way as different heights. Plant slender species beside dense ones; soft, woolly shapes beside clearly-defined ones, and spreading plants alongside those which are compact.

You should also alternate plants with different degrees of opacity. Put dense plants behind those which let plenty of light through, and even denser ones in front. For example, you might alternate large ornamental onions or alliums with geraniums.

The shapes of the flowers should be considered in the same way as the more general shapes of the plants. Do not juxtapose shapes which are too similar, such as agapanthus and ornamental onion, alstroemeria (Peruvian lily) and hemerocallis (day lily), colchicum and sternbergia, because both plants tend to lose their identities. This rule does not apply with plants of very different heights, such as hollyhocks and mallows, or when the flowers are different in size and in the way they are arranged

Informal flowerbed
The focus of this island bed is the tree. The plants decrease in height towards the ends of the bed, leaving the tallest ones grouped around the tree.

on the stem, such as rudbeckias (black-eyed susans) and asters.

Geometrical shapes

You may want to include geometric shapes, such as cones, spheres, and even cubes, in your mixed border. These will usually be evergreen shrubs, which either naturally take this form, such as some dwarf conifers, or are trimmed to shape, such as *Lonicera nitida* and box.

Evergreens can be used to make your mixed border interesting even in the middle of winter, but use them sparingly. The maximum number for a 23–26 ft (7–8 m) long flowerbed is five, and, even then, they should be of different heights and shapes. If you use more, they will be too dominant and the natural effect of the border will be lost in favour of the picturesque. This should never be the principle quality of a border. Similarly, inanimate ornaments, such as statues, fountains or rocks, spoil the overall effect. Features like these belong in other areas of a garden, not in a mixed border.

Climbing plants

In theory, plants should not overlap, as this creates a muddled effect. On the other hand, it is possible to link various parts of the layout in an attractive way using climbing plants.

Climbing plants may be annuals, such as nasturtiums and cobaea (cup-and-saucer vine), perennials, such as aconitum (monk's hood) and convolvulus (morning glory), or woody, such as clematis. Most creeping plants tend to be perennials with no fixed growing habits. They grow long, supple shoots from a fairly small rootstock and these work their way around the neighbouring plants. The best example of this is *Geranium endressii.* When you use plants like these, make sure they are not too heavy and are placed near plants which will be strong enough to support them.

Climbing plants, especially the very vigorous ones, such as the wistaria, ampelopsis (porcelin berry), and the *Clematis montana*, should not be used. Climbers which coil their stems around other plants for support, such as honeysuckle and convolvulus (morning glory), are also unsuitable as they tend to entangle the plants supporting them, making them jumbled and untidy. Try to use plants, like cobaea (cup-and-saucer vine), which attach themselves by tendrils, and those that use their flower stems, like some clematis. In the latter case, choose varieties which either need, or will tolerate, being cut back hard during the spring to give bushy foliage every year and support the neighbouring plants. You might also use clematis which grow annual herbaceous stems, such as *Clematis recta.*

It is a good idea to locate sharp outlines, such as neatly pruned box and conifers, alongside less formal shapes, such as this mixture of perennials, bulbs and annuals.

The environment

The sense of harmony created in the flowerbed should also extend to whatever adjoins it. It is important that the plants at the edge of a mixed border should spread on to the path, lawn or terrace in a fairly random way; otherwise the contrast between the flat, even shape of the lawn and the irregularity of the mixed border will make the border look as if it is being imprisoned. This consideration is often overlooked, particularly in the case of a lawn because grass will tend to invade the border and its edges need to be tidied up regularly, which is well-nigh

Just three plants – rose bushes, hosta and Geranium endressii *– have created a complete design which needs the minimum of upkeep.*

impossible if plants are growing out onto it. You still need to be able to cut the grass which is covered by the plants. A good way of overcoming this problem is to make a hard edge to the border using bricks or paving-stones. This edging should not be more than 8–12 in (20–30 cm) wide, and the same level as the soil. Do not plant fragile plants at the very edge. Avoid plants with runners at the edge, as they will take root anywhere that they touch the ground. It is not essential for the mixed border to overlap the path or lawn for its entire length; just a few plants spilling over here and there at random will give the sense of informality and flexibility that you need.

To prevent a mixed border looking hemmed in, let the plants spill over onto the lawn. To make the bed easier to look after, create a hard border between it and the lawn.

Island beds and parterres

You may not be able, or even want to create a traditional mixed border in the way just described, but you should always add colour to your garden with patches of mixed, mainly perennial plants. An alternative method is to make island beds or parterres.

Classical English design uses these to create a garden which is simply a series of long, irregularly-shaped flowerbeds separated by expanses of green lawn cut to look like a billiard-table. This can make the garden look very stiff and formal, as the plants are confined by the lawn instead of being allowed to wander on to it.

To make an attractive island bed, plan round existing features; trees, shrubs, and the rise and fall of the ground. If these features are not where you want them, you will need to create them yourself; shrubs and trees are the easiest to introduce.

Island beds can be any size, and sometimes consist of only five or six well-chosen plants. They can be any shape, depending on your own taste and the conspicuous features they are based around. As the island is visible from all directions, you should make sure that the highest plants are in the middle and the shorter ones are arranged round them in concentric circles. To

This attractive island of flowers has a lively, informal appearance.

get a natural effect, make it a long shape, with the tallest plants offset from one end. If the island is perpendicular to a slope, put the tallest plants at the lowest point.

If you dig too many island beds with paths running between them, the garden will look very artificial, so do not overdo them. Leave plenty of space in between and make sure they are as many different shapes and sizes as possible. As island beds contain fewer plants than a mixed border, they are easier to maintain. An additional advantage is that you can put one anywhere, even in a small garden.

The flexibility of island beds can be adapted to mixed borders. Although traditionally a mixed border is a rectangle, there is no reason why it should be totally regular; you could equally make it a zig-zag, a circle, or a long, winding strip. If you do this, you will probably not be able to see the whole border from one place, so it is possible to create different styles, depending on light and shade, or based on different seasons, or even using different dominant colours.

The vicarage garden

A third way of arranging masses of mixed plants is the vicarage garden. This developed during the nineteenth century in some countries of continental Europe and was designed to provide plenty of flowers for year-round decoration of the church altar. However, it almost certainly goes back to the garden of 'simples', that is medicinal and culinary herbs and spices, maintained by monasteries.

The original idea of a garden divided into squares of more or less the same size has remained, not because of its appearance, but for practical reasons. This regular layout can degenerate into a hopeless muddle, and successfully re-creating the old-fashioned quality of a vicarage garden depends on how much time people have, how good they are at gardening, and what it is to be used for. If you do manage to create an ornamental garden of this type, it is easier to manage than other kinds, and can create most attractive effects.

Organizing the vicarage garden

A traditional vicarage garden often includes an orchard and a vegetable garden, but only its ornamental function is considered here. In fact, the vicarage garden constitutes a halfway point between a mixed border and an island bed. As in a mixed border, each bed is either square or rectangular, and like an island bed, it can be viewed from all sides.

What you plant in each bed is entirely up to you, but, as a general rule, restrict each one to a specific plant or group of plants; the beds as a whole make up a mixture. Apart from rose bushes, do not use shrubs.

First, edge each bed with a low box hedge, and surround this with a pebble, brick or concrete border; do not use grass. This arrangement reduces maintenance and means that the plants do not spread on to the paths.

If you mix various types of flowers within each bed, make use of differences in their height by planting the tallest ones in the centre, as in an island bed. Alternatively, use plants of the same height. Square or rectangular beds are tra-

A typical vicarage garden, made up of neatly shaped beds with informal arrangements within.

ditional, but you can plant other geometric shapes, such as circles, ovals or lozenges. An elaborate compromise between a vicarage garden and a mixed border is to lay out the whole garden geometrically, separating the different parts with hedges that can also act as backdrops to traditional mixed borders. Make plenty of use of regularly-shaped shrubs, such as hybrid roses and trimmed bushes, with a trimmed plant border round the edges. If you do this, use grass paths. You can plant a wide variety of perennials, annuals and bulbs within this strict, regular framework, and so create a pleasing contrast between formality and informality. In addition, it is almost impossible to get it wrong.

The ideal vicarage garden

The natural edging surrounding the beds in a vicarage garden acts as a link between the plants in the flowerbed and the outside environment. You can use box, dwarf euonymus or *Lonicera nitida*. Box needs very careful trimming, and euonymus also requires careful maintenance. Both euonymus and *Lonicera nitida* are sensitive to heavy frosts, and the latter tends to be rather sparse. Probably the best edging plant, except in damp, shady situations, is *Santolina chamaecyparissus* (lavender cotton). This withstands temperatures as low as $-4°F$ ($-20°C$), grows to any height that you choose and tolerates being trimmed down to soil level in spring, if necessary. It requires only routine maintenance, cutting in early spring, and the removal of flower buds. It is an easy plant to propagate from cuttings at almost any time during spring and summer.

The flowerbeds in a vicarage garden should be accessible from all sides, and you will also need to be able to reach the centre. Make sure that the plants do not touch one another when they are dormant; keep about 8 in (20 cm) between them. Any that do touch, should be lifted and transplanted, allowing a little more space. Dig up the whole plant with a fork and then divide it. Replant the stronger, more vigorous, outside divisions. In any case this will be necessary every three or four years in order to keep herbaceous plants growing vigorously.

A decrease in the number of flowers indicates that it is time to lift and divide plants. Before

The vicarage garden
Groups of flowers are planted inside clearly defined raised flowerbeds. Here are: old roses and nepeta (catmint); lavender and pinks; cosmos and cornflowers; delphiniums and irises.

Santolina (lavender cotton) is an excellent border plant. It is very hardy, and needs little maintenance.

replanting, prepare the soil well, adding well-rotted organic matter and a liberal dressing of general fertilizer. Do this in autumn or early spring. Planting in autumn has the advantage of giving the plants time to re-establish themselves before the heat of summer.

Spring is the best time to make final adjustments to the positioning of adjoining plants; some are very unobtrusive while dormant. To avoid trampling the soil too much, stand on a thin plank of wood or a paving stone. This precaution is particularly useful near areas where plants require frequent attention, such as spring bulbs or annual plants.

Weeding

Even if you have completely cleared the site of weeds before planting, it will not be long before they start to reappear. Cultivate between the plants regularly, preferably at least once a week, especially during spring and autumn when weeds are likely to be most troublesome. There is no selective weedkiller which distinguishes between weeds and garden plants. Hoeing is the only successful method of weed control, and routine cultivation ensures that weed seedlings have no opportunity to become established.

Mulching inhibits the germination of weed seeds and makes hand weeding easier. A mulch

Flowerbeds and raised beds need regular weeding with a three-pronged hoe.

Staking up plants in a mixed border
To avoid disfiguring the mixed border, slide the stakes into plastic tubes buried in the earth.

of crushed pine bark decomposes slowly, retains warmth, is light and, most importantly, is sterile. Thus, weeds have great difficulty in germinating. However it is conspicuous and not considered to be particularly attractive. Chipped branches and brushwood are sometimes used instead; these are much more neutral in appearance and just as effective.

Use plastic mulch on new flowerbeds only; cover it up with a more attractive material. Remove it at the end of the first year when the plants are established, or it will make it harder to maintain the plants and slow down their development.

Straw is often difficult to obtain and is unsuitable because it is so conspicuous.

Partially rotted compost made from leaves is increasingly used. It is inconspicuous and provides somc nutrients for the flowerbed. Make sure that it is of good quality and does not contain weed seeds or roots. All mulches are good for maintaining warmth and a regular level of humidity.

As mulching reduces evaporation, the bed needs watering less frequently, although you must use plenty of water when you do. Hand watering the base of each plant is a tedious and time-consuming process, so it is a good idea to install a mechanical system. Sprinklers would flood the plants and damage them; a flat hose perforated on the underside is better. A variety of black and dark green plastic hoses are available. As they are inconspicuous, you can leave the hose in place for the whole summer, removing it as rainfall increases in autumn.

Staking plants

The main problem with mixed borders, island beds and squares is staking the plants. The alternatives are managing without staking the plants and risking their falling over and getting damaged, or having a mass of unattractive stakes which are visible for months although they are needed only for a few weeks.

Plants should be staked as soon as they begin to grow to avoid damaging them later. Insert lengths of plastic tubing, 6–8 in (15–20 cm) long, into the soil at the base of the plant, leaving 2 in (5 cm) protruding. Stakes can be inserted into the holes when they are needed. This trick does not solve the problem of staking plants, but it makes it a lot easier.

Tidying flowerbeds is sometimes neglected. Dead head flowers as soon as they start to fade or they will look bedraggled and the plants will put all their efforts into producing seeds instead of flowers. At the end of the season, just before winter sets in, cut back the plants as much as possible and remove any stems which have flagged or died. Cut back shrubs according to their flowering period. Prune during spring for summer flowering ones, and immediately after flowering for spring flowering varieties.

Treat diseases and pests as soon as they appear, and keep up a constant battle against slugs and snails by placing slug pellets beneath a tile, raised on a couple of stones.

RAISED FLOWERBEDS

Raised flowerbeds are mainly intended to contain shortlived plants. These are arranged to give the best possible impact and removed as soon as they start to lose their freshness, to be replaced by others. Raised flowerbeds are always geometrical shapes, and often found in formal gardens in public parks. However, there is no reason why you should not put one in your own garden if there is room.

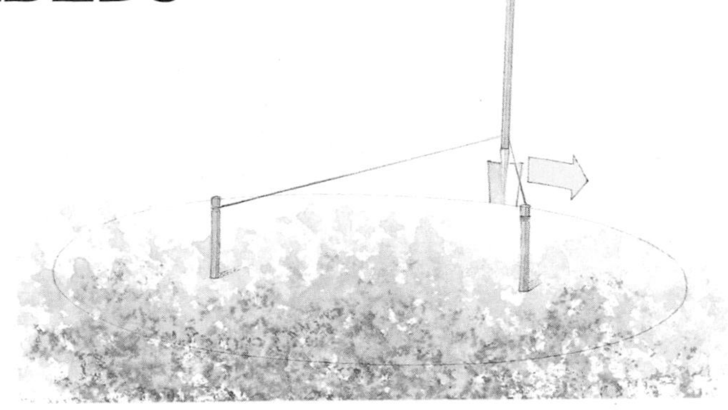

Designing an oval, raised bed

Shapes

Raised flowerbeds should be arranged symmetrically around a point taken as the centre of the garden or around a physical feature, such as a tree, a statue or a point where two paths cross. Use a piece of string to mark them out to avoid mistakes.

You need four pegs and four pieces of string to mark out a square or rectangular raised flowerbed. To make a circle, insert a sturdy stake where you want the centre to be. Tie one end of a piece of string the radius of the circle to it, and the other end to a spade. Stretch the string and mark a circle in the earth.

Ovals are more difficult. Insert two stakes and attach a long piece of string to them. Keeping the string taut with a spade, mark out an oval. You may need to adjust the spacing of the stakes and/or the length of the string several times before you get the right shape and size. If you want to create an identical flowerbed elsewhere, make sure you keep a note of these measurements.

Digging the flowerbed

Once you have marked the outline of the flowerbed, remove grass and weeds and turn

Raised beds should normally contain either one or two species, and just occasionally three. Arrange the plants in rows, with the tallest at the centre or the back. It is possible to use vibrant colours, like this grouping of zinnias and cosmos.

When finished, a traditional raised bed should be 16 in (40 cm) higher at its centre.

over the soil. As the soil should be slightly heaped, you may have to bring in some extra, besides improving the soil with sand, peat and well-rotted garden compost.

The finished flowerbed should be about 16 in–2 ft (40–60 cm) above the surrounding ground. This makes it easy to see all the plants in it. Use plants that are very close in height, perhaps occasionally punctuated by a few taller ones. Normally, a flowerbed will have a permanent border, a feature inherited from the French garden.

Plants

Space the plants at regular intervals. Mark the planting line with string and make a shallow drill with a hoe. Decide the planting positions and mark them with a rake with two short, hollow sticks fixed at the appropriate distance apart.

To arrange plants in an orderly way, dig a furrow with a toolhandle or the tip of a hoe.

Plant when the soil is freshly turned over, finely broken down and well raked. Arrange the plants so that they will cover the whole area of the soil within as short a time as possible. This means knowing your plants thoroughly and understanding how far you can expect them to spread.

Flowerbeds used to be used for up to four sets of plants in the course of a year. Nowadays, most people make do with two. One planting is made in autumn for spring-flowering plants, and the other in late spring to produce flowers from early summer until late autumn.

Planted in autumn, for spring bloom, the commonest plants to use are tulips, with a bed of pansies, daisies, primulas or forget-me-nots. Sow primulas in early spring, and the other plants by late spring or early summer.

The flowers you plant in summer might include a range of half-hardy plants with decorative foliage or flowers. The main ones are scarlet or red salvias, small-flowered begonias, impatiens, and geraniums, with perhaps a taller pattern provided by cannas and, in shady areas, tuberous begonias.

Replacing spring-flowering plants with summer-flowering ones requires careful planning. So too, does the planting of spring-flowering plants once the summer display has ended. You also need some extra space for raising plants before planting them in their permanent positions.

Sow spring-flowering plants in a frame, then prick them out into a seed bed. Allow them to grow on until they are big enough to plant out.

Sow summer-flowering plants in a greenhouse or on the window ledge from late winter onwards, so that they can be planted in early summer. Cannas and tuberous begonias should be started off in boxes of peat, kept in the warm, in early spring. Grow more plants than you need – say an extra five per cent – so that you can fill in any gaps. Delicate bulbous plants should be grown in pots buried in the earth so that they can be moved without damaging their roots. Some plants, such as coleus can be sown in mid-winter. Some gardeners start them in the greenhouse in late autumn and keep them there over winter. Pinch them out when necessary, so that, by the time you plant them out, they have developed plenty of stems and leaves and look bushy.

Mosaic gardening is only suitable for very formal gardens. The plants should be planted using a piece of string, and should be very regular in shape.

Mosaic (carpet bedding) designs

Mosaic design is difficult; it requires both very accurate design and dense beds of plants. They must be pinched out regularly, and often need to be trimmed with shears throughout the summer to maintain neat outlines. Plants with coloured foliage are used most often, and their lack of flowers is unimportant.

Sometimes, gardeners try to make this type of bed more informal by adding a sprinkling of less restrained annual flowers, but this is rarely satisfactory. This type of flowerbed is intended to be totally artificial. Its role in the garden is architectural; if you want something more natural looking, you should use mixed borders.

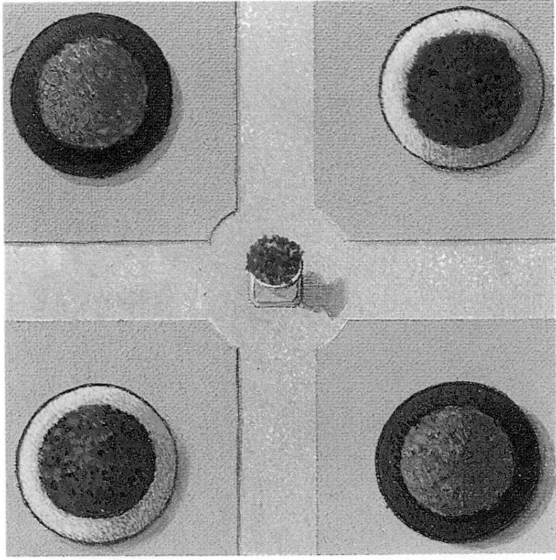

The art of mosaic design combines architectural and gardening techniques.

THE ROCK GARDEN

The rock garden originated in the Far East, where it was made up of deliberately placed rocks, planted in a haphazard manner. The plants were often quite sizeable bushes, or trees not noted for their blossoms. A rock garden can also be an imitation of a mountain environment; very rocky with small, brightly coloured plants and semi-shrubs. In this case, it is sometimes called an alpine garden.

A true alpine garden uses alpine plants and may include all the features of a mountain landscape: open grassland, with various grasses, rocks of all shapes and sizes, a pebbly topsoil and fresh, damp subsoil. This is not really practical unless you have a fairly large area of land to work on.

A successful rock garden may be based on the alpine garden, and, even though the plants grown may come from different altitudes and parts of the world, the result can be very attractive.

Whatever else it may be, a rock garden should not be a heap of earth scattered with random rocks. Nor should the stones be magnificent, neatly cut quarry stones. There is still a widespread belief that these are the ingredients of a successful rock garden but the difference between these and a real rock garden is striking, even to the untrained eye.

Even when the rock garden is constructed properly, it may be spoiled by planting too many ordinary, large, garden flowers; even three tulips, each with two flowers, can ruin the attraction. Other plants to avoid are giant pansies, French marigolds, and any of the varieties of salvia that look like red crepe paper.

A rock garden. Rock gardens are an excellent way of using soil which is naturally poor.

Building the rock garden

It is perfectly feasible to build a rock garden in a medium-sized garden, even on a very small area. The location should be open and sunny as most rock garden plants need lots of sunlight. You can always create slightly more shaded areas for plants which prefer shade.

A rock garden can take virtually any form you like, but do not use geometric shapes, as these do not exist in nature. Limit the height of the rock garden, unless your garden has a hillside or natural embankment where all you need to do is plant the flowers. On flat ground, a height of 20 in (50 cm) will be enough to create a good Alpine effect, provided that the rocks are firmly settled in the earth.

Use rocks of similar colour and texture to avoid an artificial, patchwork effect. Local stone is usually more economic but, if you have the choice, weathered grey or cream limestone create the best effect; they look warm and natural, and set off the plants well. Sandstone and granite are also suitable, providing that they are weathered, but shale and volcanic rock are too harsh in appearance.

Use fairly large rocks, at least for forming the main framework. The minimum size is about 16 × 24 in (40 × 60 cm) and 16 in (40 cm) thick. Rocks are too heavy to be tried out in different positions until they look right. Instead, make imitation stones of paper-covered wire netting,

Rock gardens make it possible to plant a large number of plants and bring out their individual features by means of careful selection. They have the additional advantage of allowing plants from very different environments to be placed close together.

Building a rock garden
A rock garden should not have too many ups and downs. The rocks can be quite large, and should just touch each other. Fill the gaps with a thin, light, growing medium.

about the size and shape of those available at your local garden centre. Try these out until you have the design you are looking for. Draw a plan, numbering each rock. At the garden centre, choose the stones and number them, according to your plan. When they have been delivered, you can easily set them up in your chosen design. This is a rather laborious but worthwhile process; once the rocks are in place and the flowers planted, nothing can be moved. By investing time at this stage, you can ensure that the rock garden will last a lifetime.

Do not use quarried stones, no matter how big they are. Normally, weathered rocks have a visible grain of strata and lines. Make sure the grain of each rock lies in the same direction, preferably horizontal or nearly horizontal. Once the large rocks are in place, you can add smaller ones which are easier to handle. Then fill in the gaps left.

The rock garden should be well drained. Use a mixture of one third peat, one third gravel or very coarse sand, and one third ordinary soil. This is not a very rich mixture, but it is more than adequate for the purpose. If the soil is very compact, place a layer of broken bricks or tiles beneath it.

To make them look natural, thc larger rocks should be partially embedded in the soil. They should give the impression of emerging from the ground, rather than lying on top of it. If there is room, you might build several layers of rocks, but this is difficult, as the rocks are heavy.

An effective, but less arduous approach is to construct irregularly shaped islands here and there; two blocks here, three there, and four somewhere else. Create 'valleys' in the gaps by digging them out, and use the excavated earth to supplement the growing medium.

Finally, cover the surface of the rock garden with gravel and pebbles. This enhances the appearance, and benefits the plants by keeping their roots cool and stopping them rotting around the collar. Use pebbles close in colour to the rocks: grey, beige and black for limestone; beige and brown for sandstone; grey and black for granite. Where possible, use weathered-looking granite, perhaps from the bottom of a stream. Do not use broken fragments of rock, and make sure the pebbles are different sizes. A good way to do this is to mix six buckets of fine gravel, four of course gravel, and one of pebbles; scatter the mixture at random.

You can also use this covering for paths to link the various parts of the rock garden rather than grass, which looks good but tends to spread to places where it is not wanted.

Gardeners are often advised to site a rock garden against a background for extra visual effect, but this rarely works. If the background is a wall, its inherent artificiality clashes with the rock garden. Trees would keep the sun off the rock garden and their roots would penetrate the porous material. A rock garden should show the plants to their best advantage, so site it wherever is most appropriate.

Planting the rock garden

The basic principle is very simple; limit your choice of plants for the rock garden to those that cannot be placed elsewhere in the garden. If you follow this guideline, you will avoid mistakes. Aubretia and golden alyssum, for example, might seem suitable plants because they are so short, but they are fast-growing and soon swamp the average rock garden. Keep them for mixed borders, where they fit in better.

Always bear in mind the size of fully grown plants. It should be in proportion to the size of the rock garden; for example, no more than 20 in (50 cm) for a rock garden about 160 sq ft (15 m^2). The only exception is very slow-growing plants, which you can always divide for propagation.

Shrubs are more of a problem. Consider whether they might not be better off somewhere else, and make sure they are not going to be too big. A young conifer, sold as a dwarf, can turn out to be comparatively huge ten years later. Mugo pines, for example, are described as dwarf even though they reach a height of 6–10 ft (2–3 m). A conifer grown in a rock garden should not be more than 4 ft (1.2 m) high and 2 ft (60 cm) in diameter.

The good thing about rock gardens is that you can mix flowers to create a medley of colours because the rocks pull together colours which would clash elsewhere.

Make sure you grow plants of different heights, but beware of putting tall, thin plants at the top and dwarf ones at the bottom. A good idea is to plant flowers to balance each other in the same way as in a mixed border. For example, put a large clump of a particular plant on one side of the rock garden and a couple of individual specimens of the same plant some distance away.

Rock garden plants can come from many different environments: acid or alkaline, damp or dry, mainly sunny, but sometimes also shady. It is easy to get these plants all living together in the same rock garden because it is a totally artificial environment. You can vary what you put in it entirely according to your own personal tastes. For example, instead of putting plants together because they thrive on similar soils, you could juxtapose plants from alkaline and clay soils.

Shade-loving plants should be grown at the northern end of the rock garden, or behind a rock or a bush.

Position plants which need high humidity in a mixture containing plenty of peat or leaf mould, towards the bottom of the rock garden. Another possibility, particularly in heavy soil, is to create

The differences in height, along with clumps of foliage and rocks, mean that clashing colours can be juxtaposed in a rock garden displayed the dwarf pinks and lime-green spurges in the foreground.

ROCKERY PLANTS				
Situation	**Sun**	**Shade**	**Damp soil**	**Well-drained soil**
Ancantho-limon	X			X
Achillea	X			X
Aciphylla	X			X
Adonis	X			X
Allium	X			X
Alyssum				X
Anacyclus	X			X
Anchusa	X			X
Andromeda		X		X
Androsace	X			X
Anemone	X			X
Antennaria	X			X
Antirrhinum	X			X
Aphyllanthes	X			X
Aquilegia	X			X
Arctostaphylos	X		X	
Arenaria	X			X
Arisæma		X		
Arisarum		X	X	
Asplenium		X	X	
Calceolaria	X		X	
Campanula	X			X
Carlina	X			X
Cassiope		X	X	
Celmisia	X			X
Codonopsis	X			X
Convolvulus	X			X
Cornus	X		X	
Corydalis	X		X	
Crocus	X			X
Cyananthus	X			X
Cyathodes		X	X	
Cyclamen	X	X	X	X
Daphne	X			X
Delphinium	X		X	
Dianthus	X			X
Diascia	X			X
Dodecatheon	X		X	
Dryas	X			X
Edrianthus	X			X

ROCKERY PLANTS				
Situation	**Sun**	**Shade**	**Damp soil**	**Well-drained soil**
Erigeron	X			X
Erinacea	X			X
Erinus	X			X
Euphorbia	X			X
Euryops	X			X
Genista	X			X
Gentiana	X			X
Haberlea	X		X	
Helichrysum	X			X
Hepatica		X	X	
Houstonia		X		X
Iris	X			X
Jeffersonia		X	X	
Leontopodium	X			X
Lewisia	X			X
Linaria	X			X
Lithodara	X			X
Meconopsis	X		X	
Mertensia	X			X
Narcissus	X		X	
Omphalodes	X			X
Onosma	X			X
Origanum	X			X
Oxalis	X			X
Papaver	X			X
Phlox	X			X
Phyteuma	X			X
Pleione		X	X	
Polygala	X		X	
Primula	X		X	
Ramonda	X		X	
Rhodohypoxis	X			X
Salix	X		X	
Sanguinaria		X	X	
Saxifraga	X			X
Semiaquilegia	X			X
Sempervivum	X			X
Soldanella	X		X	
Trillium		X	X	
Tulipa	X			X
Verbascum	X			X

a basin-shaped rock garden. Arrange the main rocks around the circumference and inclined towards the centre; dig the centre slightly deeper than the average level of the garden to make the water run towards the middle.

It is a good idea to mix plants which flower at different times of the year; tulip species and arenarias, or short growing lillies surrounded by dwarf rhododendrons (sandwort), for example. You may well end up with lots of plants in your rock garden and be hard put to remember exactly what is growing where. If this is the case, label them, though as the plants are small and close together, you may end up with a sea of labels. Use weatherproof zinc or flexible plastic labels, buried so that only ½ in (1 cm) is visible. You could also put them in weatherproof tubes, and bury the tubes at the bottom of each plant.

Maintenance

The soil used for the rock garden should be weed-free before it is distributed. The easiest way to ensure this is to spread it out in a corner of your garden several months in advance, water it so that the grass and weeds grow, then treat it with a contact weedkiller. Two or three treatments may be necessary. Mix the soil with peat and sand before placing it on the rock garden. Each time you plant something new, make sure the soil around the roots is free of anything undesirable. Weed the rock garden at least once a week during spring and autumn, the two main growing periods. Using a gravel mulch and packing the plants closely together, limits the number of weeds.

A flowering wall allows large numbers of plants to be used, without taking up too much space. Aubretias and wallflowers are among the plants thriving here.

The flowering wall

If you love rock plants but do not have the space to build a full-scale rock garden, a flowering wall is an alternative. This is not simply a case of restoring an existing wall, even a dry stone wall, because it will be almost impossible to plant anything in it. You need to build the wall specially so that it can be turned into a garden.

The different constituents of a flowering wall.

The height of the wall should not be more than one and a half times its width; for example, if it is 16 in (40 cm) wide, it should be no more than 2 ft (60 cm) high, and could be lower. Unlike the rock garden, it should be made up of relatively uniform stones, not rounded ones, so that they fit on top of one another.

It is fairly easy to build a wall, but might take quite a while. Make a double wall, and fill the cavity with a mixture of earth, peat and sand, the same way as in a rock garden. Put larger stones at the bottom, and smaller ones at the top. Although this is a dry stone wall, you may need to add a little mortar in places, making sure it is concealed, to provide strength. You might also create a trench at the base of the wall and fill it with a mixture containing plenty of peat and compost for plants which like coolness. Leave fairly large gaps between the stones so that there

Troughs can be used for growing very small or particularly delicate rock garden plants. A trough protects them better and can be shown off to best advantage, like a shop window.

is plenty of room for the plants. Do not create gaps by skipping a stone here and there, as these gaps will be too large and conspicuous. Plant as you build the wall, always placing plants between the vertical joints. Give them plenty of water during the two weeks following construction so that the soil filters down between the stones and becomes fairly tightly packed. Plant the cavity between the two walls in the same way as a window box, making sure the size of the plants is in proportion.

Flowering troughs

If you cannot build a rock garden or a flowering wall, a plant trough is worth considering. These are essentially gigantic window boxes made of stone or wood. Whatever size and material you choose, make sure the trough has at least one hole in the side for drainage; large troughs need two or even four holes.

Fill the trough two thirds full with drainage material, such as gravel or broken crocks. If you are going to grow rock plants, fill the trough with the same mixture as used for a rock garden. For other types of plants, add whatever material is appropriate. As you cannot create the surface undulations of a rock garden or a wall, make sure you alternate different shapes of flower, as in a mixed border.

If you cannot obtain a stone trough, you can make one yourself. A wooden box is used as a mould. Cover the outside of the box with expanded polystyrene (styrofoam) tiles. Make mortar of two parts sand, one part vermiculite, one part finely crumbled peat and two parts cement. Mix well with a shovel before adding sufficient water to give a sticky consistency. Coat three sides of the box with a thin, rough, uneven layer of mortar. Once you have applied the first layer, arrange a framework of wire netting and metal rods over it for additional strength. Continue to apply the mortar, until it is at least 2 in (5 cm) thick.

Bore drainage holes in the side, and leave the trough to dry for at least ten days, covered with a cloth if the weather is hot to prevent hair line cracks appearing. When it is dry, turn the trough over and remove the box from inside; the polystyrene (styrofoam) makes this easier.

A trough made in this way weathers quickly and soon looks natural. You can speed up the process by colouring it yourself. Before planting, sprinkle the trough with iron sulphate to give a pleasant beige colour. Start off with a mixture of one dessertspoon (teaspoon in USA) iron sulphate to a watering can of water. Repeat the process if the colour is not strong enough. As iron sulphate is slightly toxic to plants (it is used for burning moss off), leave the trough for at least two weeks before planting. If you do not like the effect, you can hose it off a couple of days beforehand.

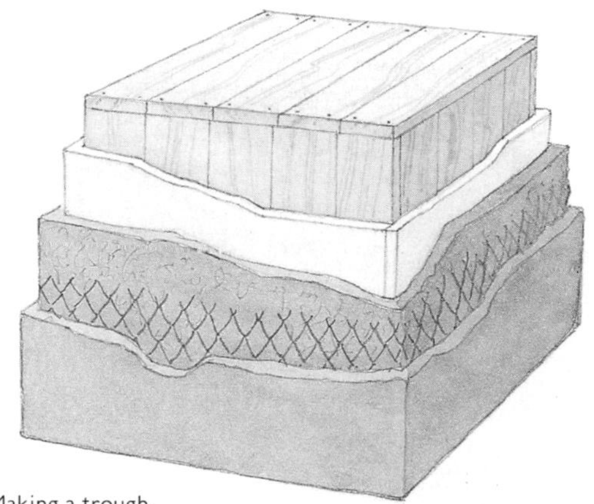

Making a trough.

Alpine greenhouses have no aesthetic pretensions. They simply serve to protect plants which are sensitive to cold winds or damp weather in winter.

The alpine greenhouse

Associated with the rock garden, the alpine greenhouse serves only one purpose: that of protecting the plants. It is solely a shelter for the collector of fragile rarities, all grown in pots.

Alpine greenhouses are not heated and should be well ventilated throughout the year. In their natural mountain habitat, plants experience very marked differences in the seasons; a short, hot summer, a severe winter, a damp spring and a non-existent autumn. This climate is very different from that of lower regions, so many alpine plants do not thrive in gardens. A greenhouse is not, therefore, an extravagance, as it shelters plants from the vagaries of the climate.

It is essentially similar to a traditional cold greenhouse. Cover the shelves with sheeting, and bury the pots in gravel. Gravel regulates the temperature and humidity. If you do not have sheeting full of gravel, you can use the double pot technique; one pot, with the plant growing in it, is placed inside another at least 2 in (5 cm) larger in diameter. Fill the space between the two, with gravel or coarse sand.

As the sole purpose is to keep the plants healthy and ensure that they flower, the appearance of the greenhouse is not important. There is no need to worry about making the labels as inconspicuous as possible.

Gravel serves to regulate the temperature and humidity surrounding plants.

CLIMBING PLANTS

Climbing plants have always been very popular, and deservedly so. Their popularity has increased even more with the growth of small city gardens. Because they take up less ground space, they have the effect of extending the garden by growing over areas which would not otherwise support plant life, such as walls and fences.

Walls not only support plants; they also protect them against the wind, and, because they tend to retain heat, help protect them against frost. This enables you to grow plants which might be damaged elsewhere in the same garden.

Climbing plants can be used to adorn greenhouses, arbours, pergolas and trees; they can be made into hedges, or serve as ground cover. There are plants which are particularly appropriate for each of these uses. They are planted and attached in different ways, depending on the effect required and the way they grow.

Preparing the soil

As these will be permanent plants, it is sensible to prepare a comfortable niche for them at the outset. This means making sure that the soil is well cultivated. Start by breaking up the top 16–20 in (40–50 cm) of soil over an area of 1 sq yd (1 m^2), regardless of the variety of plant. This is a good time to add a slow-release fertilizer and supplements, such as peat or compost. These are necessary for retaining moisture because the bottom of a wall is sheltered from rain. If you mix compost and peat, spread them over the surface and then integrate them into the soil.

If the soil is particularly poor, this is an opportunity to change it completely. The gar-

Climbing plants can be grown on vertical garden walls, and therefore increase the surface area of greenery and flowers. This patio wall is being used to grow a climbing vine, Vitis coignetia *(crimson glory vine), and* Carpenteria californica *(tree anemone).*

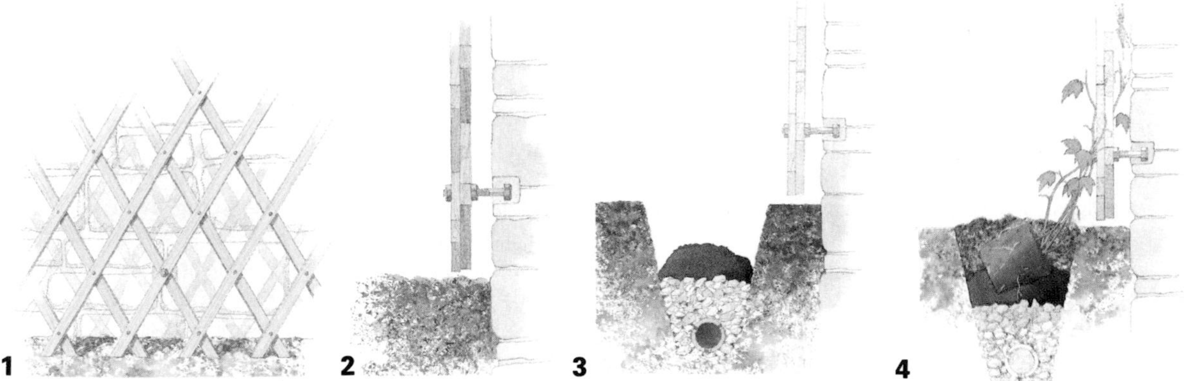

Planting climbing plants
1–2 Divide the wall into squares using a trellis fixed firmly to the wall. Leave a space of 1½–2 in (3–5 cm) between the trellis and the wall. **3.** Dig a hole 20 in (50 cm) away from the wall. Make sure the soil is well drained. **4.** Place the plant in the hole, tilt it towards the wall, then fix it to the support.

dens of newly built houses often contain pieces of broken plaster and brick at the bottom of a wall. You will also need to change the soil if it is alkaline and you want to plant climbers which require acid soils. In this case, you should also check the wall and if it is made of alkaline materials, separate from the soil with a sheet of thick polythene.

Some walls are situated along natural water flowlines with drains at the base. For these choose plants that do not have deep roots, or they may block the drains.

There are three types of plant suitable for growing on a wall:

(a) True *climbers*, which have a means of attaching themselves to the surface;

(b) *Rambling* plants, with long flexible stems, which need support;

(c) *Trellis* plants, which can support themselves. These are generally shrubs which simply need to be placed against the wall, depending upon their height.

Climbing plants have four different ways of attaching themselves; aerial roots (ivy, bignonia or trumpet vine), twining stems (wistaria, convolvulus or morning glory), tendrils (passion-flowers, cobaea or cup-and-saucer vine), and leaf petioles (nasturtiums, clematis).

Plants with aerial roots attach themselves to supports, even a smooth surface, without any help, and will grow in all directions without being trained.

Other climbing plants cannot do this and need support. Trellis is the traditional way of doing this. It is made of treated wooden laths, or plastic, and maybe flexible or rigid, square or diamond-shaped. Its thickness depends on the weight of the plant. Fix it securely at a minimum of points so that both trellis and plant can be moved, if need be. To cover a large surface, divide the trellis into easily handled sections which you can assemble. Leave a space of 1–2 in (3–5 cm) between the trellis and the wall.

The lightest plants need only plastic covered wire, or fine wire netting. Grey or beige is better than green which is usually very conspicuous.

The distance between the laths or the size of the mesh depends on how fast the plants grow; if they are slow growing it should be small, and if they are vigorous, they need a larger mesh.

Another method of support is to stretch strong wires in horizontal rows, 12 in (30 cm) apart for small plants and 20 in (50 cm) for larger ones. Fix these wires to strong vertical brackets using stretchers.

Rambling plants can be supported in the same way, but must be attached here and there with ties. As these plants do not attach themselves to a support, they need to be trained. Climbing

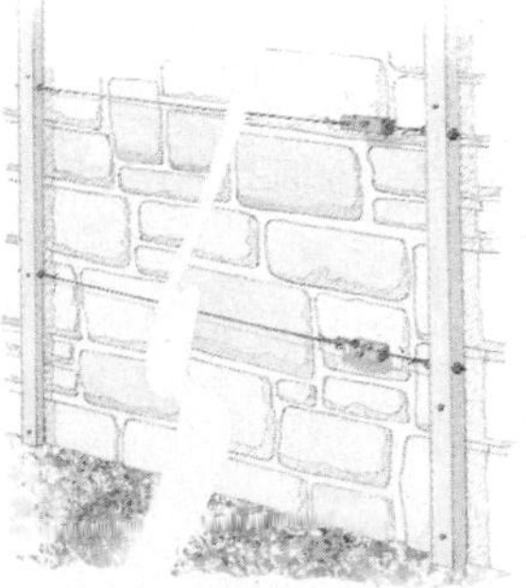

Climbing plants can also be trained along lengths of wire fixed to vertical battens using stretchers.

Plants which need staking can be fixed to eye bolts in the wall.

plants, on the other hand, tend to grow in all directions, sometimes not very attractively.

Trellis plants do not normally need any support, but, because they are fairly slender, they are at the mercy of gusts of wind. It is wise, therefore, to anchor each plant in four or five places, making sure that their supports are extremely solid.

Planting climbers

To make sure the plant has every chance of becoming established successfully, dig a hole large enough for the spread of roots. Once the plant is in place, fill in the hole, water the soil and firm it gently.

The closer the plant is to its support, the better it will attach itself. However, the further away the roots are, the more water will be available to them. The best compromise is to put the plant 20 in (50 cm) away from the wall, and to dig a channel from the foot of the plant to the support. If the stem is big enough (more than 3½ ft (1 m)), cover the horizontal part straight away. If not, leave it for a year. This method only works for plants, like honeysuckle and clematis, with flexible stems. Plant climbers with rigid stems sloping towards the wall, and tie them to a stake to guide the plant and stop the wind rubbing it against the wall.

The space between plants and the wall should be proportional to their rate of growth. For example, *Lonicera periclymenum* needs 12 in (30 cm). Make sure you do not plant anything close to corners, as these are constantly exposed to wind and draughts, which damage tender plants and young shoots.

The nature of the plants – hardy, tender etc. – will determine how exposed their planting positions should be. A north-facing wall is fairly well sheltered, and changes of temperature occur gradually. An east-facing wall can be harmful, as the plants will be exposed to frost on winter nights and to sunlight early in the morning, thawing them too quickly. West- and south-facing walls are milder, but they can get very hot, particularly as stone and brick heat up on sunny days. The plants here should be ones that thrive in the sun, rather than those, like ampelopsis (porcelin berry) and many roses, which may suffer from mildew.

Be careful that climbers planted against a house wall do not reach the roof or gutter; they would cause irreparable damage. Keep a distance of 3½ ft (1 m) between the top of the plant and the edge of the roof.

Plants which attach themselves directly on to a wall may damage it. Tendrils and aerial roots can penetrate a dry stone wall or old and crumbly mortar. Plants attached to old pebble-dashed walls may come away suddenly and take pieces of the wall with them. You should always repair and refinish old or damaged walls before you start planting against them. Alternatively, take the easier option of erecting a trellis.

Prickly plants are sometimes difficult to maintain and control. Never let them encroach upon areas where people are passing by.

Clematis montana *planted underneath a pine. This is a vigorous plant which is well suited to this size of tree.*

Planting around the base of a tree

It is essential to choose a climber which is suited to the situation, for a tree will not provide shelter in the same way as a wall. It should also be a plant which grows at a compatible speed with that of the tree. You might, for example, decorate a shrub with a clematis. A strong shrub or a small tree will take a fairly young vine, a large clematis, or perhaps an akebia. Only huge trees will be able to welcome giants like bignonia (trumpet vine) and ivy (to be used carefully) climbing hydrangeas and vines.

You should be also careful about using honeysuckle and wistaria, as they have a tendency to strangle trees. Honeysuckle will constrict young branches and slow down their growth. Wistaria is so strong that it can twist even the strongest metal, so you can imagine what it could do to a tree.

Climbing plants are a good way of decorating a dead or dying tree, especially if you do not want to cut the tree down. Climbers are easy to grow, and planting them with the support of a dead tree obviates the problem of digging and damaging the roots of a live tree. Live trees will also stop rainwater reaching the base of the climber. This is also the reason why it is not normally a good idea to plant climbers at the base of evergreen trees.

Plant the climber about 1–2 yd (1–2 m) from the tree trunk and guide it towards the tree using a long stake. Many people prefer to leave the plants to grow for a year or two before guiding them towards their host tree, providing they are not plants with tendrils. In either case, help the plant grow towards the trunk by a stretched wire. This will lead the climber up to the first branches of the tree, after which, in most cases it will develop very well on its own. Once it is doing so, you can remove the temporary support.

Prepare the soil carefully, in the same way as you would when planting at the base of a wall. Spread a mulch around the bottom of the plant, and make sure that plenty of peat and leaf mould have been incorporated into the soil. This prevents the roots of the tree absorbing some of the water which would otherwise benefit the climbing plant.

This intermingling of plant and tree is particularly attractive. The effect looks natural, as trees are what climbing plants most often use to grow on in the wild. It is possible to obtain unexpected effects of colour; a hornbeam may be covered in flowers, thanks to a *Clematis montana*, or an oak tree becomes eye-catching with vine leaves.

A tunnel of Laburnum *'Vossii', whose golden colour harmonises beautifully with the mauve of* Allium alfatuense*, an ornamental onion.*

A climber planted at the foot of a tree should be guided towards the tree using a stake.

Climbing plants will also allow you to create flowering bowers, pergolas or pathways. Plants climbing over a metal or wooden framework mingle into a mass of flowers and foliage. The elegance of the metalwork, often curved into beautiful shapes, will suit any garden, whether traditional, small, or very formal.

There are two types of wooden support: the traditional arbour of strong wooden uprights linked by trellis work; and the more rustic type, made up of horizontal and vertical poles or palings spaced fairly widely apart. There are also designs which consist of brick or stone pillars and a wooden roof.

In the first two cases, the uprights need to be firmly secured in the soil, as the plants covering them may be heavy and liable to catch the wind. The ideal solution, though not the only one, is to make a concrete foundation and fix the uprights in it with feet. Treat the wood with a suitable preservative, then wait for a month or two before you start putting plants in. Cover a metal framework with protective paint.

Use very hardy plants. Train them to cover the supports like a cloak; do not let them twist themselves around the supports. This allows you to remove the plants from the supports to carry out maintenance on them. Staked shrubs can also be used on supports like these. These occasionally appear in gardens, and avenues of laburnums (golden-chain tree) can be particularly striking.

Where wooden or metal trellises are exposed to the wind, you could use climbing plants to decorate pillars, obelisks, arches and other similar structures. This is most commonly seen in formal gardens, particularly in rose gardens. Often, the plant grows on the outside of the cage formed by the support.

Arbors and gates are simply other versions of the structures described above.

Topiary

Topiary is the name given to the technique of cutting shrubs into geometric shapes, such as cubes, spheres or cones, or into representational figures. It takes many years to achieve the full effect. Climbing plants can be shaped more quickly, over four or five years, perhaps. A light metal mesh is placed over a solid, soldered metal base in the shape of the topiary desired. Let the climbing plant grow naturally, training it occasionally, and clipping it once or twice a year. Although not the quickest way of producing topiary, evergreen plants, especially ivy, are best, particularly in winter, for obvious aesthetic reasons.

As well as disguising trees or shrubs with climbing plants, the reverse is possible; you can turn a climbing plant into a 'tree'. In fact, it is quite possible, using a strong stake as the only support, to transform fast-growing plants if not into 'trees', then at least into 'shrubs'.

For example if you plant ivy at the base of a post, it will adopt that shape of its own accord when it reaches the top. When wistaria has grown to a reasonable height, it forms sunshades of great beauty. Some slender and fine plants, such as honeysuckle and climbing hydrangeas, do the same thing. Choose specimens with plenty of stems, which can be tied on to the stake. They will not spill out until they reach the top of the stake, and will not be displayed in

Box cut into topiary designs in the famous gardens at Great Dixter, in Britain.

their true beauty until the main stake can be removed. This takes time, of course – sometimes 15 years – but the result is worth all the effort.

It is also possible to convert climbing plants into ground cover.

Climbers are outdoor plants, but a greenhouse, verandah or conservatory can make a good support. The back wall of a lean-to greenhouse or a veranda is the most appropriate place for climbing plants. Use the same methods for attaching them as for plants grown outdoors.

In a large or free-standing greenhouse climbers can be trained along the pillars or on a wide mesh. Once they have reached a reasonable height, the plants can be spread out to fill the roof. Do not allow them to touch the glass, which acts like a lens and focuses the sun's rays, causing scorching. They are also difficult to prune or treat. Do not let them touch central

Climbers in a greenhouse
Stretch solid wire parallel to the ridge of the roof, 3½ ft (1 m) apart and 20 in (50 cm) from the glass.

Wistaria pruned into a tree shape. The same result can be obtained with honeysuckle or akebias by training them onto a firm support.

heating pipes, as this will cause desiccation, and prevent them from obstructing vents and ventilation equipment.

For training plants up the side of a greenhouse, stretch plastic-coated metal wires about 20 in (50 cm) away from the glass, parallel to the ridge of the roof, and about $3\frac{1}{2}$ ft (1 m) apart. Set up a mesh of cross-wires on these basic supports. Climbing plants should not occupy more than a third of the total surface or they will reduce the light too severely.

Where possible, put the plants directly in the soil of the greenhouse, incorporating plenty of peat and general fertilizer, if necessary, before planting. Alternatively, use large containers placed beneath the staging.

Depending on the temperature of the greenhouse, you may be able to grow interesting fruit, such as out-of-season grapes (in a cold greenhouse), or passion fruit (in a temperate or warm greenhouse), as well as flowers.

Climbers in the greenhouse grow quite rapidly almost all year round. They should be carefully maintained; remove fading foliage regularly as it harbours all kinds of diseases and insect pests.

CLIMBING AND STAKED PLANTS
(check hardiness for your region)

Plants	Deciduous	Evergreen
Self-fixing	Campsis radicans, Hydrangea petiolaris, Parthenocissus tricuspidata, Schizophragma hydrangeoides and S. inteyrifoliam.	Hedera (various ivies), Lonicera (various honey-suckles)
Need support	Various actinidias, Akebia quinata, various Ampelopsis, Aristolochia macrophylla, Celastrus orbiculatus, various Clematises, Humulus lupulus, Parthenocissus henryana, Parthenocissus quinquefolia, Polygonum baldschuanicum, Roses, Rubus 'Benenden', various Schisandras, Solanum crispum, various Vitis, various wistarias. Annuals: Cobaea, Spanish beans, sweet peas, volubilis. Bulbs: Gloriosa rothschildiana.	Various Jasminiums, Lapageria rosea, Passiflora coerula.
Need staking	Chænomeles speciosa, various fuchsias, various laburnums, Ribes speciosum.	Ceanothus thyrsiflorus 'Repens', Fremonto-dendron californica, Magnolia grandiflora, Pyracantha, Taxus.

FLOWERS FOR CUTTING

Cut flowers are important to most gardeners. If you like having flowers in your garden, the chances are you will have them indoors too. If all you want is a fairly small arrangement once a week, you can pick the flowers from an ordinary ornamental garden. If your requirements are greater, it is wise to set up one particular corner of the garden solely for growing flowers for cutting.

Growing flowers rationally means that you can regularly obtain flowers for cutting more easily; you can cut as many as you like because the gaps left do not matter. You will be able to fill your house – and those of friends – with flowers.

Flowers for cutting are grown in rectangular beds, rather like vegetables. Indeed, the methods used to grow them resemble those of the vegetable garden in many ways, and the two often share the same corner of the garden. To obtain the best results, rationalize the layout, with the short-lived plants – annuals, bulbs – in the middle where the soil is most often cultivated. Put perennials around the edges and surround the whole bed with flowering shrubs.

Picking flowers for bouquets in summer.

The shrub hedge

Plant shrubs first. Choose them for their attractive flowers or foliage. They also act as a protective wind-barrier and screen the bed from the rest of the garden. The best place to site such a plot is at the end of an ornamental garden, where it acts as an area of transition between the ornamental garden and the vegetable garden or orchard. This was common in the nineteenth century.

Plant a range of shrubs to make up the hedge for a year-round supply of flowers and foliage. Shrubs with coloured foliage or decorative berries in autumn are useful. Apart from shrubs, such as cornus (dogwoods), with decorative bark, suitable varieties for winter flower arrangements include those which flower in spring, such as forsythias and *Chaenomeles speciosa* (Japanese quinces), as these can be gathered in bud. If you pick and take them indoors, they open, even in mid-winter.

This hedge is the ideal place for shrubs which flower too briefly to be an important feature in an ornamental garden. As the intention is not to create a dense hedge, but long stems for bunches of flowers, you keep them well pruned. Cut out branches which are too spindly or have too many shoots. If necessary, cut shrubs back quite drastically, as they send out new, fast-growing shoots.

Perennial plants

Plant herbaceous perennials around the edge of the bed, or at one end of it. Arrange them in rows by variety, and group them according to their height. Never mix varieties within a row, but you can mix groups with different flowering periods; early spring flowers, then spring, early summer, midsummer, and so on. This way, the flowerbeds are never empty of flowers.

Plant them in rows, leaving alternate rows empty. Vary the width of the row, depending on the size of the plant, and, therefore, the width of the gaps. You must be able to get between the plants easily.

Prepare the soil thoroughly. Incorporate plenty of well-rotted compost and dust liberally

The cut flower garden Flowers for cutting should be planted in narrow, evenly spaced rows so that they get plenty of sunlight.

with a slow-acting fertiliser. Do not start planting until the bed is weed-free and weed it regularly afterwards. Encourage steady growth for a continual supply of flowers. Water regularly as soon as the weather starts warming up, often as early as mid-spring.

After flowering, cut back the stems and start double-cropping the plants. Add small quantities of quick-acting fertilizers with a low nitrogen content until buds appear. Every four or five years, dig up the plants, divide them, and replant the outer young, vigorous divisions straight away.

To avoid gaps in the flowering season, transplant half a row one year, and the second half in the following year.

Roses, even rose bushes, can be planted in the same way as perennials, because of the way they grow and how they are used.

There are two groups of bulbous plants: those which last several years, and those which last only a season. The first type can be treated as perennials. The others should be planted formally and used exclusively for bedding purposes. Break up the soil well, and incorporate plenty of organic matter, and, if necessary, a balanced fertilizer.

Although perennials grow new foliage when existing leaves are cut off, because they have buds at the base, bulbs do not. Bulbs will either wilt or die if they lose their leaves during the growing season. This is why so few lilies produce good flowers for cutting after the first season.

You can circumvent this problem by growing only plants with leaves grouped at the base. This will allow you to cut the stems without

HEDGES OF FLOWERS FOR CUTTING	
Spring	Chænomeles superba, Choisya ternata, forsythias, Kolkitzia amabilis, Malus floribunda, various Prunus, Ribes sanguineum, Sorbus aucuparia, Syringa, Viburnum opulus
Summer	Buddleia davidii, Deutzia gracilis, Lavatera olbia 'Rosea', Philadelphus, roses, Weigelia florida
Autumn	Ceanothus 'Autumnal Blue', Choisya ternata, Cotinus coggygria, Euonymus europaens, Nyssa sylvatica, Pyracantha, Sorbus aucuparia, Viburnum opulus
Winter	Acacia, Cornus alba 'Sibirica', Carrya elliptica, Ilex, Lonicera fragrantissima, Mahonia japonica, Viburnum tinus

removing them altogether. In some cases, it is easier to buy bulbs such as gladioli, which are normally grown for a single season; after flowering you can simply throw them away.

Annual plants

In a garden of flowers intended for cutting, annual plants really come into their own. They have many advantages: they grow abundantly in a wide range of shapes and colours; they grow quickly and are easy to look after; and most of them flower profusely and produce flowers which last well in a vase.

The soil should be well-worked and raked smooth. Sow the seeds spaced well apart, especially those plants which do not like being transplanted. Remove the weakest ones two weeks after germination. It is better to sow them a little too far apart than too close together. If they get plenty of air and sunlight, they produce large quantities of flowers on strong stems.

Apart from tender annuals, such as tithonias (Mexican sunflower), which grow rather more slowly, you can make two sowings: the first in mid- to late spring, and the second two months later. Protect the second sowing from hot weather using a shade net or covering of fine material stretched over hoops. This will produce a superb harvest of flowers at the very end of the season.

In mild climates 'wintering' annuals, such as sweet peas, delphiniums, marigolds, red poppies and centaurias, are treated differently. Sow these outdoors in mid-autumn. They will germinate and over-winter as young plants, which will start flowering in mid-spring and continue until midsummer. Sow the second crop in mid- to late spring, and this will flower at the end of the season. Plants sown in autumn always grow much more quickly in the spring.

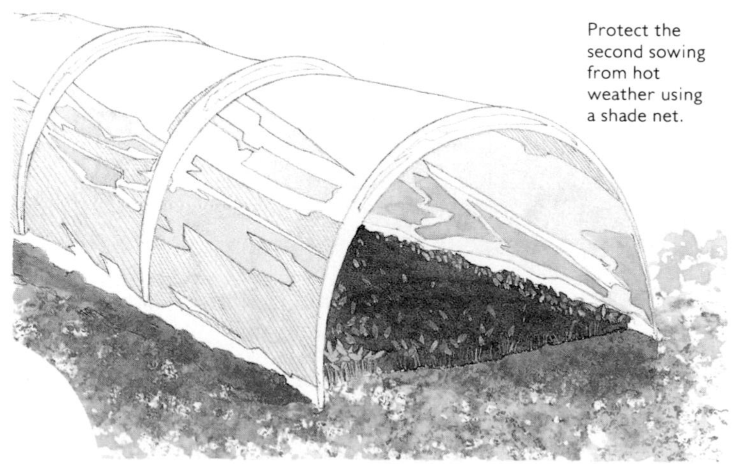
Protect the second sowing from hot weather using a shade net.

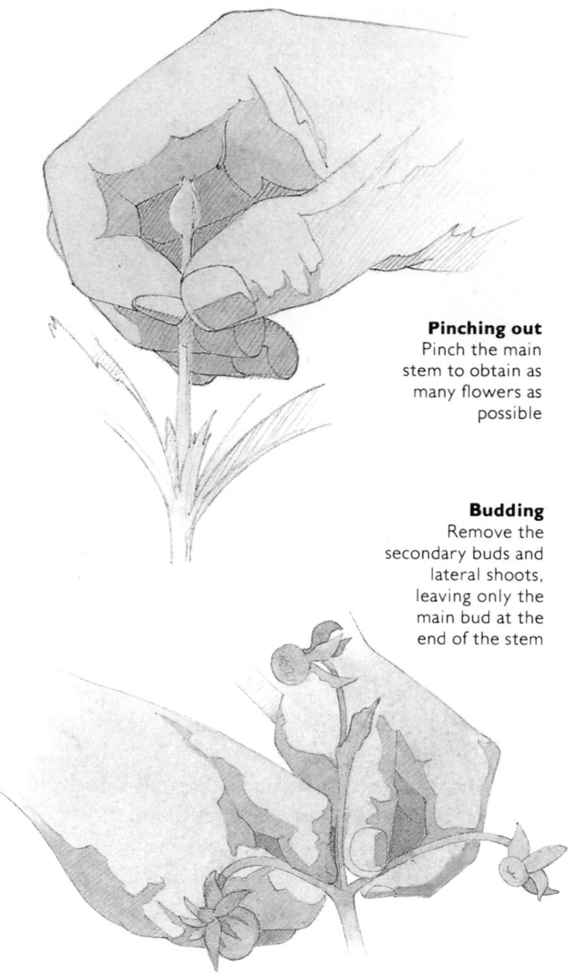
Pinching out Pinch the main stem to obtain as many flowers as possible

Budding Remove the secondary buds and lateral shoots, leaving only the main bud at the end of the stem

It is tempting to leave self-sown seedlings to grow. They always seem to grow well, but the bed will become chaotic. Self-sown seedlings are inferior to those raised from deliberately sown seed.

Looking after the garden

Weeding is the main maintenance operation in any garden. Most perennial plants, bulbs and annuals are easy to keep weed-free if the soil is in good condition and you attend to the task regularly.

Watering is very important in warm weather to maintain vigorous growth. Regular feeding is also essential.

Depending upon your requirements, it may be necessary to pinch out plants or to thin crowded buds. If you want a lot of flowers on each plant, pinch out the main growing point. This will then branch out into a number of secondary stems, and result in a bushy plant with flowers that are ideal for informal bouquets.

If you want long stems with very large individual flowers, be selective about pinching out. Remove all except the main bud at the end of each stem; remove all axillary buds and lateral shoots, as soon as they appear. Of course, this method does not work with plants, such as delphiniums, that have flower spikes. It is only suitable for sizeable flowers which grow on individual stems, such as scabious and dahlias.

Plants of this type must be staked so that they grow tall and straight. It does not matter if the stakes are fairly conspicuous, so you can insert as soon as the foliage starts to develop.

Individual stakes are suitable only for large plants with a reasonable number of uncrowded stems. Support smaller plants by stretching a nylon mesh with large holes over the bed at the beginning of the growing season. The stakes supporting the mesh should be about a third of the height of the full-grown plant. Stretching a length of string around the stakes helps keep the mesh rigid and the plants upright. In exposed areas where it is likely to be windy, it is also advisable to stretch wire between the stakes and stretch string across the middle of the mesh.

To prolong the flowering period, dead-head fading flowers regularly.

Low-growing plants benefit from a generous mulch of straw or plastic, not only to conserve moisture and suppress weeds, but to prevent the foliage and flowers being splashed by soil when it rains.

Picking the flowers

The best time to pick flowers is in the early morning when they are fresh. You will need a large flat basket and very sharp secateurs (hand pruners) and, if you are cutting roses, thick gloves. Make clean cuts, as these heal quickly.

Staking up flowers for cutting
Stretch a large-meshed net over the plants at the beginning of the season, and a piece of string around the edge of the net.

Make sure that you cut the stems of shrubs and rose bushes above the growing buds. When you are cutting bushes for their decorative autumn berries, do not remove more than a third of the stems on a single bush. The cut stems will grow again in spring, but they will not flower, and therefore not produce fruit, until the following year. If you only cut a third of the stems, there will always be fruiting wood on the bush.

Once you have taken the flowers indoors, remove the lower leaves and cut the stems to the length you want at an angle, so that as many of the water-conducting tissues as possible are in contact with the water. Stand the flowers in deep water. Crush the base of woody stems with a hammer or pliers. If the plants produce a sticky latex, such as poppies and euphorbias, cut the stems under water. Some gardeners advocate scalding the bottoms of hollow or pithy stems, such as hollyhocks. This is not always effective.

Cut the stems at an angle every three days or so. Renew the water in the vase before it becomes stagnant, and top it up regularly. Adding aspirin, sugar or charcoal to the water is said to maintain its clarity, although this is not proved. A drop of disinfectant containing potassium chloride will give good results, and specially prepared commercial cut flower preparations are recommended.

THE WATER GARDEN

Water is a delightful feature in a garden. Even if you have only a small pool, it adds a touch of magic, mystery and movement. Apart from looking attractive it enables you to grow plants that are impossible to cultivate elsewhere.

If you have a stream running through your garden, you will need to adapt it before you can grow plants alongside it, but there is no point in trying to change its course. The area next to a stream is often boggy. If it is narrow, you can create broader shallows by increasing the size of the natural curves. You could also take advantage of variations in the level of the land to make small pools. You can create little backwaters where the water is calm and popular pond plants can be grown.

It is important to ensure that nothing impedes the flow of water. Excessive shrubby growth can cause unwanted deposits of mud when the flow increases after heavy rain or a thaw.

The still water of a natural pond is also attractive and effective in a garden. Unfortunately, many natural ponds are not permanent features, and dry out in hot weather. Do not consider integrating a pond into the garden as a true water feature unless you are satisfied that it is reasonably permanent with a more or less stable water level.

Stream forming the centre of a garden. If the banks are well tended, they can be used for perennial plants of different heights and colours.

Artificial ponds

Most gardeners have to be content with an artificial pond. This is often a regular geometric shape, but sometimes approximates the shape of a natural pond.

Square or rectangular ponds are popular, as they are simple to build and fit in easily with the rest of the garden. A small pond can be made from concrete, but this is not suitable for a large pond, as it is difficult to make watertight and tends to crack. Ponds can be successfully constructed using a pool liner. The whole pond is lined with plastic sheeting on a 4 in (10 cm) base of sand, and attached to the corners and edges with tubular joints. An alternative method is to use a piece of sheeting 10 in (25 cm) larger than the depth of the pond and fold it back under the kerb-stones around the edge. Plastic liners last for about 10 years, and can be obtained moulded to the size you require.

Geometric ponds look attractive in a formal garden, sited near the house and near a neatly cut hedge or other solid, geometric feature.

To make a natural-looking pond, dig a hole the size and depth you require. Remove any sharp protrusions, such as roots or stones, from the sides and bottom. Spread a piece of plastic sheeting over the area. The pond should not slope too steeply. For an even more natural look, dig the pond 12 in (30 cm) deeper than you want it to be eventually, lay the plastic sheeting, and then cover the plastic with 12 in (30 cm) of earth. Pack the earth down well before filling the pond with water. It is a good idea to topdress the soil with a thin layer of pea gravel to prevent fish stirring it up.

Planting a water garden

1. Choose a natural hollow with no trees nearby. **2.** Dig the pond on two levels. **3.** Install plastic sheeting and cover it with earth. **4.** Plant out the banks. **5.** Cover the lower section in water and plant marginal aquatics and submerged plants. **6.** Fill the pond up to the top level two weeks later. **7.** Finally, put in floating plants.

This rectangular pond is compatible with the severe geometric style of the house nearby, the topiary hedges and the beds of irises.

Fibreglass ponds are widely available but avoid them if their colour is too bright or you cannot conceal their shape.

Whether artificial or natural, ponds and lakes can be constructed for still or flowing water. Flowing water is particularly attractive because, not only does its movement make it more eye-catching, it also reflects whatever is around it. However, many plants especially waterlilies, cannot tolerate constantly moving water.

The pond will occasionally need filling from a tap to compensate for evaporation. Where possible, use a recycling pump linked to a filter, with the pond filled from a fountain or waterfall if it is a geometric one, or from an imitation spring if it is a natural shape. Make sure you give a spring a natural look, and keep it in proportion to the size of the pond and the style of the surrounding garden. It is a good idea, particularly if the water is slow moving water, to accentuate its movement by placing a slight obstacle in the current. This creates eddies, bubbles and turbulence. It also disperses algae and other troublesome plant life. Fish devour insect larvae, and many of them graze on algae too.

The most natural site for a pond is at the lowest point of the garden. If your garden is flat, there are two possibilities: either create some undulations in the terrain – even small ones will do – converging upon the pond, or isolate it with plants. This creates a completely separate arca; a garden within a garden.

Plants

Aquatic plants grow in four different habitats: on damp banks; on the pool margins with the roots submerged, and the foliage and flowers above water; on the surface (floating plants); and underwater. You will not be able to grow moisture-loving plants around the edges, if the pond is artificial and separate from the surrounding ground. However, if water is allowed

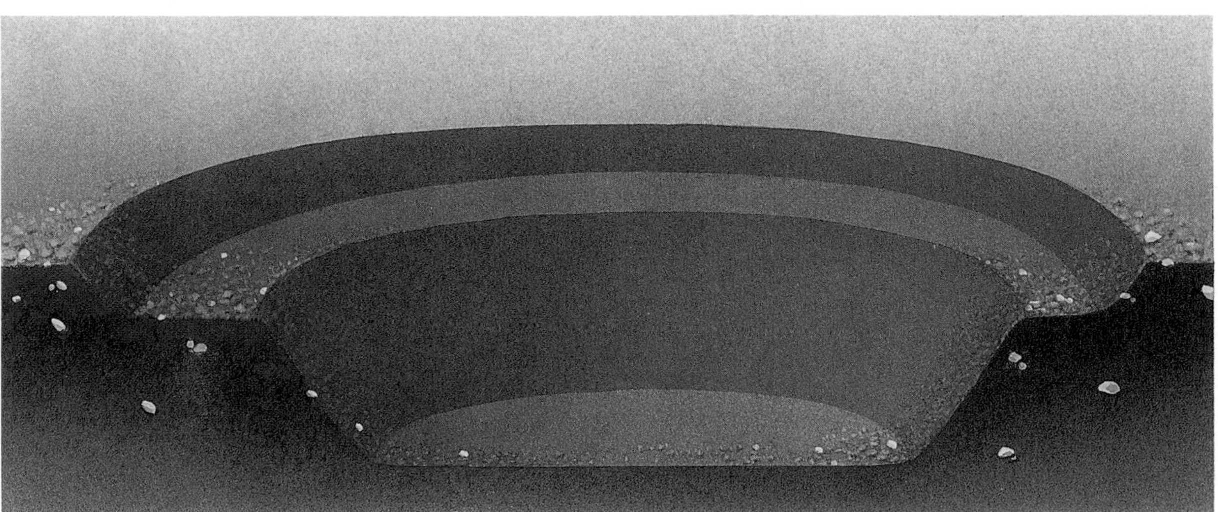

Dig the pond on two levels, for safety reasons and to allow the planting of aquatic plants at different depths. If there are large stones or rocks in the soil, fill in the gaps between them with a bed of sand before putting the plastic sheeting in place.

to seep out of the pond, either naturally or artificially, you will be able to grow plenty of luxuriant plants, including the huge, rhubarb-like gunnera (in mild climates), with its exciting sub-tropical appearance.

Grow as many plants as you like and have room for, but bear in mind that water has valuable reflective qualities which should not be wholly concealed. It is not advisable to plant trees near a pond. The roots may damage the lining of the pond, and the leaves fall into the water causing pollution.

It is generally better to grow plants in containers rather than planting them directly in the pond. This provides some control over their growth and makes routine maintenance easier. When you want to divide the plants, you can remove the containers and work in relative comfort. However, this is practical only in small or medium-sized garden pools. It is impractical in a large pond, especially a natural one, where it is more sensible to plant directly into the soil.

The ideal pond is constructed on two levels to accommodate different kinds of plants. Otherwise, some would have to be raised on bricks or stones. It is also more prudent from the point of view of safety.

Fill the pool before planting, but do not try to plant through water. If you are planting water-lilies and other deep water aquatics, remove the floating foliage and plant them at the desired depth. They will soon produce fresh leaves which will find their way to the surface. If you plant with the floating leaves intact, they tend to lift the plants out of the containers.

Plants which live totally submerged are usually sold as bundles of cuttings. These should be carefully planted in a container, with the lead weight that holds them together completely buried. If it is left exposed, the tops of the cuttings will rot off and float away. If you have a soil-bottomed pool, then the weighted bunches can be merely dropped into the water. They will sink to the floor and take root.

Fill a basket or other container with soil to within ½ in (1 cm) of the top, put the plant in as if you were potting it, and topdress the soil with pea gravel to prevent water discoloration. Use a heavy soil that is free of weeds, leaves or pieces of old turf which might decompose and pollute the water. Do not use soil collected from land which has recently been dressed with artificial fertilizer because this encourages the rapid development of algae.

A natural pond at the end of a garden. When surrounded by vegetation, it makes up a secluded, small habitat of its own.

When calculating the number of plants you need, bear in mind that the submerged plants contribute most to the balance of the pond by competing for mineral salts with green, water-discolouring algae. Floating and deep water plants shade the water and this also helps reduce algae. However no more than one third of the pond should be covered as open water is part of the attraction.

Bridges

In the case of a large pond or lake, a crossing point is worth considering. The choice is between stepping stones, a walkway or a bridge. A bridge can take any number of forms, provided it is in harmony with the surrounding landscape and in proportion to the sizes of the pond and the garden. Stone bridges are most attractive, but expensive and hard work to

Walkway mounted on small columns in a water garden.

build. Wooden bridges are easier. Dampness may make them slippery, so cover them in taut, triple-wound chicken wire, which is inconspicuous and relatively inexpensive. A more robust bridge can be sanded or encrusted with fine fragments of stone.

A walkway is really only another type of bridge. It consists of a series of planks running level with the water and mounted on piles for part of its length.

Stepping stones are made from large, flat stones with their tops just above the surface of the water. Use the roughest stones that you can find so that they are not too slippery. Stones like this may not be suitable if the water is moving, as they may seriously impede the flow and create eddies. In this case, cement very flat stones on to concrete piles. Attach the piles firmly to each other so that the stones do not rock to and fro, and then they will not have to be embedded in the bottom of the pond. This is particularly important in an artificial pond which could be easily damaged.

Ice

Ice is not a serious problem in natural ponds, or in artificial ponds designed to look natural.

The shape of the pond tends to restrict the formation of ice. The pressure of any ice that does form is normally absorbed quite adequately by the soil around the edges.

Geometric artificial ponds, particularly rectangular and square ones, can be protected in a number of ways:

place a soft material, such as expanded polystyrene, between the film of ice and the surface;

place upright stakes in the pond in winter;

use floating shapes to stop the ice covering the whole surface.

Wooden bridge in an informal garden. The arbour covering it bears a honeysuckle bush, which is reflected in the water.

THE VEGETABLE GARDEN

The vegetable garden is undoubtedly the earliest form of garden. It is still the most popular, especially in recent years with the increased interest in horticulture. Although it was originally a rural pursuit, dependent on having a natural source of water, the vegetable garden gradually crept into the fringes of towns, in the form of allotments, and even into the heart of the city, where in its simplest form it may be a single tomato or tarragon plant lovingly cultivated on a balcony or windowsill.

It has been estimated that to produce all the vegetables required to sustain one person for one year, it requires about 120 sq yds (100 m^2) of vegetable garden. If you wanted to produce vegetables for storing, such as potatoes or carrots, you would require up to 240 sq yds (200 m^2). If you do not have this amount of space available, or the time to cultivate it, you do not have to forego the pleasures of growing some of your own vegetables. They always taste better than commercially produced ones which often have to travel great distances and are kept for long periods of time before they reach the supermarket shelf.

Setting up a vegetable garden

You cannot set up a vegetable garden anywhere that takes your fancy. The area must be as sunny as possible. Keep away from tall walls or trees. Trees can also be troublesome because of their hungry probing roots. Although it should be sunny, the direction it faces will depend upon the gradient of the terrain. North- or east-facing slopes are not to be recommended. Vegetables much prefer a southerly or westerly aspect. One way of partially overcoming this problem is to grow the plants which need the most warmth across the slope.

The soil

Not all types of soil are suitable for vegetables. Acid soil or that which is very sticky or waterlogged is particularly difficult for vegetable growing. Most soils can be improved by installing good drainage or adding liberal quantities of well rotted manure or peat. The best soil for the vegetable garden is crumbly, neither acid nor alkaline, and contains clay, sand and humus in reasonably equal proportions. This is popularly referred to as loam. Soil like this is virtually non-existent in its natural state and has to be built up by the gardener over a period of years. It is always a good idea to analyze your soil to find out roughly what it contains and how rich it is. Adjustments can then be made if necessary. If your vegetable garden is in an area where other people are growing vegetables, it is worthwhile asking your neighbours for advice if their vegetables look as though they are doing well.

Spadework

You may be lucky enough to have an area which is already being gardened. It is also quite likely that all you may have is a piece of waste ground.

If you have the former, all you need to do is keep it maintained. If it is being used for purposes other than vegetable growing, you will need to remove the existing plants, then turn it over after carefully weeding it. If you wish to convert a lawn to a vegetable plot, you can easily remove the turf with a spade, stack it in a heap, leave it to rot and then make compost out of it. The soil beneath, although requiring plenty of organic matter incorporating into it, will be ready to use.

Waste ground will need more work done to it. Start by clearing the undergrowth and burning it. Cut down the weeds and wherever possible dig them out. Then turn the earth over thoroughly breaking up the clods. Alternatively you can use a chemical contact weedkiller to destroy the annual kinds. The perennial ones are more resistant and should be treated using systemic weedkillers which are absorbed by the foliage and enter the sap stream thereby killing the weeds completely.

Following weedkilling, the soil should be broken up to at least a spade depth, ideally two spades deep. This is called double digging. You can use a mechanical cultivator to do this, but a spade makes a much more satisfactory job. With a spade, you will need to break it up in two stages, each a spit deep. Each spit is the depth of a spade, so you work to two spits' depth, which is about 20 in (50 cm). If the soil is fairly soft and friable you will be able to work the soil to the

Before planting vegetables, turn the soil over thoroughly with a spade.

full depth during the first year. It is easier to work a small area of soil to this depth the first year, then another the following year and so on. If you make a proper job of breaking up the soil in this way, it will remain in good condition for many years.

Autumn is the best season in which to do this groundwork: tilling the soil, fertilizing and manuring it. This is the time when there will be the fewest vegetables in the garden, and the rain will probably have softened the earth and made it easier to work on. Later the frosts of winter will help break up the clods of earth, and by the spring it will be in perfect condition for preparing for a seed bed.

Laying out the garden

It is obviously easier to work the soil and to get around the vegetable garden if it is level. It will not lose water through downhill seepage, nor by furrowing if you get heavy rain. However, if it has a slight slope to it you are unlikely to have too many problems. If it slopes steeply, the best thing to do is arrange it so that the plantings run across the slope so that water is retained better. It is also best to site your vegetable garden as near to the house as possible so that you do not have to spend too much time and effort in fetching and carrying things to the house. Finally, the site must have at least one water point, ideally several.

The ideal vegetable garden
A well designed vegetable garden is easy to walk around and makes sensible use of the space available. Plants put in for several years should be placed around the outside of the area, and the sunniest wall should be used for a frame to keep delicate vegetables.

There is no need to surround it with a hedge, as its roots may absorb too much water from the soil and the foliage deprive the garden of sun. On the other hand, if you live in a windy area a hedge can make a useful windbreak. If you do plant a hedge, make sure it is only on the side from which the prevailing winds blow. What may be preferable is a wall or fence. Apart from the fact that it may be required by law, it also allows you to clearly show the boundaries of your property and discourages dogs and cats from being a nuisance. If part of the fence, say 8 –10 ft (2.5–3 m) is removable, it will allow a small lorry to get in if any materials, such as peat or manure, need to be delivered in large quantities.

Make the layout of your vegetable garden as simple as possible. Aim to make the best possible use of space and ensure that the vegetables are easy to get at. Start by laying a path down the middle of the garden, about 3 ft (1 m) wide. You may wish to use paving stones, gravel or even have a grass path: the main thing is to be able to get around it with a mechanical cultivator or a wheelbarrow whatever the weather. If you have a fairly large area of land available, put a second, narrower path 20 in (50 cm) wide at right angles to the first and starting from the middle of the plot. If it is a very large garden, you could also put a circular 20 in (50 cm) path around the edge. Each of the flowerbeds should have narrow gaps, 10 in (25 cm) of bare earth, in between them. If the earth is damp, put light planks along the paths so that you do not sink into them. These will also allow you to kneel down if necessary, without damaging the plants.

If all you have is a very small garden, simply put narrow paths around the main beds. Water points should also ideally be in the middle of the garden to avoid having to carry heavy hose pipes around. If the garden is very large, you may need several water points. You may find it useful to place a barrel or tank of water at the corners of each area served by a tap for emergency use. Cover these containers with lids, both for safety reasons and to minimize evaporation and keep mosquitoes away.

Even if the garden is near the house, keep your tools near the vegetables, in a shelter which is as watertight as possible. Do the same with weedkillers and similar products, making sure they are out of reach of children and pets, and locked securely in a cupboard.

One other thing you could set up in this type of garden is a south-facing frame for early sowings and for cultivating seedlings to be planted out.

Materials

The basic tools you need are fairly few in number: a planter, a transplanter, a hoe, a combined hoe and fork, a fork, a spade, a rake, a ball of string, a watering can and a dung fork (for straw and compost) are the minimum requirements. You may want to complete your equipment with some moveable frames or flexible tunnels with bow frames. There are of course many other tools and accessories which you may use occasionally and these can be added as the need arises.

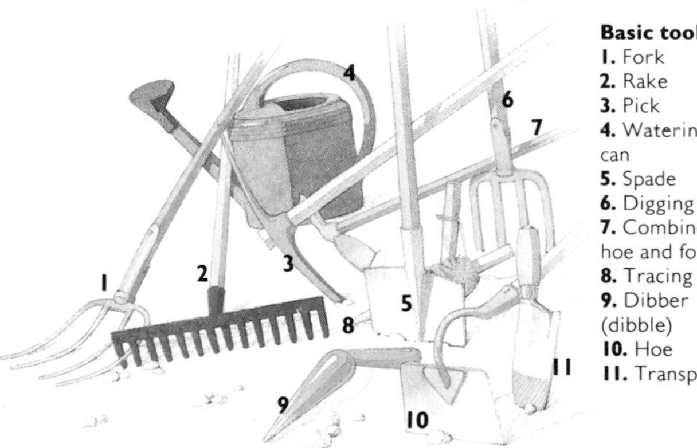

Basic tools
1. Fork
2. Rake
3. Pick
4. Watering can
5. Spade
6. Digging fork
7. Combined hoe and fork
8. Tracing line
9. Dibber (dibble)
10. Hoe
11. Transplanter

Arranging the vegetables

There are a number of specialised ways of arranging plants which are peculiar to vegetable gardening. The first of these is a single bed arrangement. This involves each bed containing one type of vegetable at any one time. The width of the bed should not be more than twice the length of your arm, because you need to be able to reach the centre easily. So that they benefit from the sun as much as possible and are easy to get around if you ever use a mechanical cultivator, align all the beds in the same direction. It does not matter how long they are, though if you are an ordinary amateur gardener you are unlikely to want them more than 23 ft (7 m) long. A market gardener will sometimes have beds which are 83 ft (25 m) or more in length.

Mark out where you are going to put the bed, then dig a trench along one side for the whole length of the bed, throwing the soil on to the path. Then remove this soil to the opposite path using a wheelbarrow. Next, dig a trench alongside the first one and fill the first with the soil from the second one. Dig a third and use the soil from it to fill the second, and so on. Fill the last trench with the soil from the first one. Once you have prepared the soil in this way, and broken down the lumps, the bed is ready for sowing.

When sowing seeds, drills need to be taken out using the edge of a hoe. Make them an appropriate depth and width for the size of the seeds you are going to plant. A good guide is to cover the seeds with approximately their own depth of soil.

Sow the seeds evenly along the drills, then cover them with soil and press down firmly. This is the method to use for all medium-sized or fairly small seeds. Some vegetables such as parsnips can also be sown in small clusters of three to five seeds at regular intervals along the line. The germinating seedlings are then thinned to the strongest individual.

Vegetables are divided into various categories depending on which part of the plant is harvested and also on how they reproduce. The main types are root vegetables, fruit, seed vegetables, bulbs and salad vegetables. Most of these vegetables have a vegetative cycle which takes less than twelve months up until harvesting. Perennial vegetables and herbs are often added to this list. Finally, there are the berries, which are similar to vegetables in the manner in which they are grown; traditionally the two are grown together.

For practical reasons, you should grow perennial vegetables and berries around the edges or at one end of the plot, to make it easier to cultivate the rest of the vegetable garden, where there is a higher turnover of plants. For the same reasons, it is best to group vegetables together by their growing season, so that when you are doing major work, all the plants currently growing are in the same corner of the garden.

Crop rotation

For centuries, market gardeners have been aware of the importance of rotating their crops.

Each plant has its own very specific requirements for nutrients like nitrogen, phosphorus and potassium, and trace elements such as iron, copper, manganese and so on.

If you grow the same plant in the same spot several seasons in a row, it will use up the same

Crop rotation
In this example an average of two plants a year are alternated in each bed. Crops will vary regionally.

Ist year.
1. Runner beans (leeks).
2. Tomatoes (lettuces).
3. Potatoes (cabbages).
4. Onions (turnips).
2nd year.
1. Peas (lettuce).
2. Cabbages (semi-dry French beans).
3. Broad beans (radishes). **4.** Leeks (spinach).
3rd year.
1. Beetroot (lamb's lettuce). **2.** Carrots (leeks). **3.** Garlic (chicory). **4.** Peas (cabbages).

nutrients, while another plant with different requirements will grow there quite happily. With the various fertilizers and supplements that are available it is possible to quickly restore any deficiency in the balance.

Plants are also subject to a number of diseases and pests. Crop rotation helps to prevent these from occurring, although good garden hygiene is very desirable.

It is best to grow your vegetables in a specific rotation. Grow brassicas following legumes, as the latter leave nitrogen in the soil which is much in demand by the leafy brassicas. Roots can be arranged either before or following, together with the general salad group including lettuce and spring onions.

If you are just starting a vegetable garden it is recommended to begin with those varieties which allegedly will 'clean up' the soil. These are useful for a garden where there is still a weed problem. The vegetables which do this need the soil to be turned over several times, a job which is easy to do and is also an opportunity to get rid of weeds. Potatoes fit the bill particularly well in this respect. With these, you turn the soil over when you prepare for the crop, again when you plant the seed tubers, then every time they are earthed up, and finally when you harvest them.

Dwarf French beans, beetroot, and tomatoes are plants which are easy to weed around. Lettuces and radishes, on the other hand, although they are very easy to grow, are not so suitable as they are very laborious to weed.

The easiest vegetables to grow are undoubtedly potatoes, tomatoes, peas, radishes, beetroot, courgettes, turnips, onions and leeks. French beans, garlic, shallots, salsify, cucumbers, gherkins, broad beans, spinach and fennel are also reasonably straightforward. Celery, asparagus, aubergines, peppers, and melons are really best grown by the more experienced gardener.

If you are unable to raise your own young plants, many varieties are available for purchase. These are usually sold in trays or pots. However, it is only those that transplant easily that should be treated this way. These include celery and courgettes.

Ornamental vegetable gardens

The vegetable garden of the French château of Villandry is a fine example of this type of garden. A garden like this takes a great deal of looking after, though, and may not repay all the effort you put into it. If you want to obtain the attractive effect of this garden all year round, you will have to grow more of some vegetables than you need. There are others, too, which may not be that appealing. It is better therefore to choose vegetables which look good and make them part of an ornamental garden.

The different types of vegetables

There are a great variety of vegetables you can grow in a vegetable garden. They can be divided into six main categories: roots, fruit, seeds, bulbs, leaves and perennials.

Root vegetables

As their name indicates, root vegetables have an expanded root full of nutrition. This is the major part of the vegetable. Although root crops belong to various botanical families, there are a certain number of requirements that they all have in common. If you want good roots, you need to prepare the soil meticulously. This means working it into a fine tilth and removing all the stones. If you add manure or compost, it should be very well rotted and incorporated during the previous autumn. If you have not been able to do this, use thoroughly sieved leaf mould or dried, powdered organic manure from the garden centre. Irrespective of the family that they belong to, you will need to water root vegetables frequently and generously. If they stop growing for any length of time, their quality is impaired. Carrots will go hard and radishes are likely to be very sharp.

Another thing you will need to do is weed the ground thoroughly before you plant, particularly for vegetables like carrots, for example, which grow very slowly and may get choked by weeds. Here again, if you add a little mulch it will work wonders.

With this type of vegetable, you should not add too much nitrogen. Potassium and phosphorus, on the other hand, will be welcomed by the plant.

Ornamental cabbage patch in a vegetable garden.

A bed of carrots, and oni[ons.] If carrots and onions are grown together it will help prevent their being attack[ed] by certain pests.

Carrots need to be thinned out, otherwise their roots are too close together and the carrots grow too thin. One traditional gardener's trick is to mix the seeds with radish seeds and sow the two together. As radishes grow very quickly, when you pick the radishes, the carrots are automatically thinned out.

Root vegetables get on perfectly well with other types of vegetable. One combination which is particularly recommended is carrots and onions: each of these repels the pests which attack the other. Turnips grow well in a slightly shaded position, as this makes them softer.

In general, root vegetables are very easy plants to grow, with the exception of root celery (celeriac), which needs a great deal of manure and water.

Fruit vegetables

Fruit vegetables consist of two families: the *Solanaceae* and the *Cucurbitaceae*. Although quite different botanically, the two families share a need for plenty of food and warmth.

These are fruits in the botanical sense of the word, in that they are the result of the fertilisation of flowers. They can either be picked when ripe or while still tender. You should restrict their numbers, as otherwise the plant will exhaust itself from having to produce large numbers of tiny fruit. With the exception of gherkins (small-growing *Cucumis sativus*), you should therefore pinch them out, though there are some varieties which do not grow or flower very much making pinching out unnecessary.

Sow all fruit vegetables very early on in the season. You can also gain time by buying young plants which you can plant straight away as soon as the frost has ended. Tomatoes are grown on stakes for practical reasons, though you can also grow them lying down with a layer of mulch to stop the plants getting dirty. Aubergines (egg plants) come in different colours and shapes: round, oval or long, black or white. Like potatoes, these two vegetables are vulnerable to attack by Colorado beetle.

The various cucurbitaceous vegetables, unlike other fruit vegetables, like manure and compost which has only slightly decomposed. Marrows and courgettes are one and the same plant. Always choose varieties which are suitable for the use to which you want to put them.

Tomatoes. Limiting fruit by pinching it out will allow it to ripen in the best conditions.

Seed vegetables

Seed vegetables consist mainly of legumes: French beans, peas and broad beans. These have the useful ability to fix and absorb nitrogen from the atmosphere using the bacteria which live on their roots. They also release this nitrogen into the soil. This means they enrich the soil they are growing in. Some are actually grown to serve as a green fertilizer.

Once you have harvested a legume crop, do not pull it up by the roots; it is better to cut the foliage down and leave as many nitrogen-rich roots as possible in the soil.

Peas and French beans (green beans), which used to be exclusively climbers, are now available in dwarf varieties. This means you do not have to spend time and energy staking them. You will still need to do this for some of the older kinds and exhibition varieties. Peas can be grown using either sticks or netting for support. Runner beans can be grown on simple stakes (which they will wind themselves around) or string or thread. The only problem with these is that they create shade. You can get round this problem by placing delicate vegetables, such as lettuces, close to the base of the beans, or

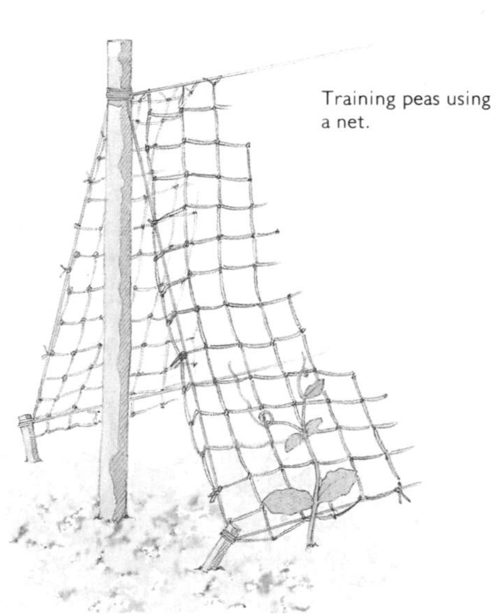

Training peas using a net.

Training runner beans using a frame.

Broad beans. This vegetable has been grown for centuries. It needs to be sheltered from cold winds.

alternatively plant vegetables which do not mind shade, such as turnips.

Legumes and garlic, onions, shallots and leeks have a reputation for not co-existing happily and you should therefore avoid planting any of these together. As for lentils, despite their delicious flavour, it is best not to grow them in a vegetable garden. They take up too much space, producing few pods in relation to the area they occupy, and each pod contains the princely number of two seeds! This point is better left to farmers and market gardeners who have the proper equipment to grow and harvest them on a large scale.

Shallots. This species is closely related to the onion; plant the bulbs in spring and pull them up in summer.

Bulbs

Bulbs in the vegetable garden are various species of the genus *Allium*. These mostly originate from the Mediterranean countries. They benefit from warmth and will not tolerate damp cold soil, which will encourage them to rot. There are some varieties of garlic and shallots which you can plant in spring or which do not mind fairly damp summers, but most gardeners agree that they do not taste as good. Garlic and shallots are grown by planting the bulbs.

Onions are sown as seeds, or you can also plant the onion sets. While onions are true vegetables, garlic and shallots are regarded more as herbs.

Leaf vegetables

Leaf vegetables are grown only for the green leafy portion above the soil. In some cases it is the leaves themselves which we enjoy eating, such as the salad vegetables. In others, it is the leaf-stalks or 'ribs' which are eaten, as in the case of cardoons, celery and leeks. The other leaf vegetable, the king of the vegetable garden, is the cabbage. Here it is the leaves which we eat with the white-heart cabbage, the stems of the kohlrabi, the young shoots of the Brussels sprout, and the buds of cauliflower and broccoli.

Different leaf vegetables have different requirements. Generally speaking, however, they get through large quantities of nitrogen, but you should never over-fertilize them as this promotes soft, disease-prone growth.

Perennial vegetables

The main representatives of the perennial vegetables are artichokes and asparagus. Rhubarb is sometimes also included in this group.

Artichokes are usually propagated from spring divisions. This plant likes warmth, but you should keep it well watered during the growing period, particularly while it is forming stems and buds. This ensures that they remain tender.

As artichokes remain in the same place for several years, you should cultivate and fertilize the soil thoroughly before planting. It is advisable to protect the base of each plant using plenty of straw and soil during the winter, as it may otherwise be harmed by the frost.

The artichoke reacts badly both to frost and to damp winters. Protect the roots using a mulch.

Every three years, in the spring, separate the best of the lateral shoots (the suckers) from the main stem, then throw the latter away. Replant the suckers straight away in a new area of soil.

Asparagus is without doubt the most demanding perennial vegetable there is, but one plant can last perhaps 15 years.

Depending on whether you want white or green asparagus, grow them either in a trench, covered with light soil, or level with the soil. But whichever type you choose, it is important to enrich the soil with plenty of well-rotted manure during the autumn before planting. After this, just mulch with a little more manure from time to time. Harvest the shoots as soon as they appear in the spring, and preferably eat them the same day that you pick them. If you do this, their flavour will be excellent. You should only go on picking them for two months after the first shoots have appeared. After that, leave the plant to grow, and produce fern. If you remove all the shoots the plant will die.

After 12 to 15 years, the plants will start to become a lot less productive. When this happens, discard them and start a new bed using two- to three-year-old crowns.

Berries

Although logic might suggest that berries should be included in the chapter on orchards, the amount of care they need, and also light, means it is normally best to grow them in a vegetable garden. Like perennial vegetables, they will last for several years in the same place, so you should start them off in soil which has been thoroughly cultivated.

Berries include strawberries, raspberries, blackberries, redcurrants, blackcurrants, and bilberries (blueberries).

Strawberries

The strawberries we grow today are derived from the European kind with small berries, and the large fruited American species. The small-fruited kinds are sold as perpetual strawberries. The plant produces large numbers of small, dark, highly scented berries. They are almost all dessert strawberries, and are occasionally also used to make wines and liqueurs.

To obtain white asparagus, plant fairly deep in light soil, and earth the shoots up regularly.

Green asparagus is obtained by planting at soil level.

Pick strawberries when the berries are shiny and red all over.

Harvest perpetuals when they are very ripe; they will come away from the plant by themselves. Eat the berries straight away. These strawberries do not produce stolons (runners), but instead form clumps which get thicker each year and which you can regularly divide to get more plants.

The large-fruited varieties of strawberries are better known and more widely cultivated. Originally, these strawberries gave only one crop a year. Later on mutations, two-crop varieties and ones with multiple flowering and fruiting, appeared. The single-crop forms give one very generous crop in a very short space of time, which is an advantage if you want plenty of strawberries all at the same time. They are perfect for jam-making, for example. They generally fruit earlier than the double-cropping variety. The latter give only a few more berries than the former, but spread over a longer period continuing until early to mid autumn. The fact that they give several, albeit smaller, crops means they are better suited to the needs of the average family.

Pick strawberries when the berries are a bright red colour all over. If you pick them with their stalks, you can wait a while before you eat them, though you should still eat them within twenty-four hours if you want to taste them at their best.

The large-berried variety produce wiry stems during the course of the growing season. These bear a series of young plants which take root when they touch the soil. Normally you should only allow the first plant that forms on each stolon to actually grow: this will prevent the parent plant from exhausting itself. You can either leave the young plants or runners to take root on the spot, or you can transplant them.

Make sure that the soil is well cultivated and of an alkaline persuasion. Plant the runners in the autumn or spring, 12–16 in (30–40 cm) apart, in three or four alternate rows. After they have finished flowering provide a layer of straw around the plants to stop the fruits touching each other or getting splashed with mud. A plastic mulch in the form of black sheeting is perfect, but put it there when you put the plants in and make cross-shaped cuts in it for planting through. This kind of mulch is often sold with the holes already in it at the right distance apart, and this makes it easier if you have not planted strawberries before.

After three or four years, the crop will start to deteriorate and you will then have to start another bed somewhere else. This will avoid exhausting the soil, and also help prevent diseases. Strawberries, unfortunately, are subject to several different viruses which greatly restrict fruiting. This is why you should not hesitate to get rid of old plants.

The young, fast-growing plants which come from your own runners will not always produce satisfactory results. Plants which you buy, on the other hand, are specially selected and will normally be virus-free.

Raspberries

Raspberries grow in the form of a creeping bush which can take over quite a large area, and you may need to limit the amount of space that they occupy. One way of doing this is to bury bricks upright below the surface of the soil.

The raspberry needs soil which is rich in humus, preferably in the form of well-rotted manure. But the raspberry does not mind very much what type of terrain it is grown in: the only things it dislikes are very cold or sticky soils and chalk. The fact that it grows stems and roots on the surface indicates that it dislikes dry weather.

As with strawberries, there are two types of raspberry: the single crop and multi-crop varieties. The former produce fast-growing shoots in spring which flower and bear fruit the following year. After this shoots die and are replaced by new ones. The multi-crop variety also produce shoots in spring, but these bear fruit the same year. The fruits appear on the ends of the stems in late summer or early autumn. They survive the winter, and then the lower part produces small bunches of flowers which fruit in early to mid summer and die afterwards. Whichever variety you plant, prune out the dead branches regularly and keep the soil well cultivated and weed-free. In the single-crop varieties, cut the stems which have fruited when you have finished harvesting. In the multi-crop varieties, cut the stems which are bearing fruit for the second time (they are distinguishable by their golden brown colour) in later summer. The young shoots will still be a pale green colour.

Plant the raspberries in autumn or in early spring, either in two rows 2 ft (60 cm) apart, or in a single row with the plants 16–20 in (40–50 cm) apart. It is not unusual for the plants to reach 6½ ft (2 m) in height if the soil is rich and has been well prepared. To make it easier to pick the berries and make sure they get plenty of light and water, create a support by stretching a piece of wire round four stakes situated one at each corner of the bed at a height of about 3½ ft (1 m).

Pick the raspberries when they are completely ripe. They will come away from the stalk cleanly. Then eat them as soon as possible.

The canes will start giving fewer fruit after 10 to 15 years. It is then time to start the bed again on a new area of soil, using young suckers from the base of the adult plants.

Like strawberries, raspberries are also vulnerable to viruses which severely damage the plant and prevent it from producing new fruit. If this happens, destroy the affected stems and start the new bed as far away from the old one as possible to avoid the virus spreading.

Blackberries

The blackberry bush, or bramble, belongs to the same genus as the raspberry. The plants you will find on sale in garden centres are the result of crosses between the common bramble and other plants of the same family.

One of the most popular varieties has long flexible branches with evergreen leaves with serrated edges. It bears fruit in early to mid autumn and has no prickles. The plant is very easy to grow. It rapidly forms large bushes with branches between 6½ and 13 ft (2 and 4 m) in length. It produces one crop a year, and should be cut in the same way as raspberry canes of the same type.

Blackberries multiply, not by producing suckers, but by spontaneous layering. As soon as a stem touches the ground, it takes root and gives birth to new plants which often become spiny again. To reduce this problem, fasten the stems along a wall, on a trellis or wire.

Picking blackberries. The garden varieties produce large quantities of fruit in autumn.

Unlike raspberries, blackberries do not detach themselves from the carpel, so they are generally less pleasant to eat. However they are full of flavour and are very good for making into jellies, sorbets, liqueurs and syrups.

Redcurrants

The several varieties of redcurrant which currently exist are more often the result of selection than hybridization. The berries ripen in early to mid summer, and sometimes not until late summer, which means they can be picked as needed if used for desserts.

Redcurrants grow into evenly-shaped bushes about 3 ft (1 m) in diameter and 3–4 ft (1–1.2 m) high. They are not very demanding as far as the type of soil on which they are grown is concerned. In fact, they are very easy, provided, as with all berry bushes, that they are given plenty of water while they are producing fruit. Otherwise the berries will become hard and dry or fall off before they are ripe. If they are to flower and grow berries properly, they need a climate with fairly sharp winters. They do not grow so well in mild climates.

Maintaining them is extremely simple: leave ten to twelve shoots per stem, and remove the oldest stems which have borne berries for the past four to five years. You can propagate them by taking cuttings from the most vigorous shoots in autumn. Leave them to root in some sand in a sheltered corner of your garden, and replant them in spring. A redcurrant bush will often last a good 20 years.

Although their pips and skins mean that they are not the ideal dessert fruit, redcurrants are, however, perfect for making jellies and syrups, and they freeze well.

Blackcurrants

Blackcurrants have almost the same requirements as redcurrants, except they need even more distinct seasons, with cold winters and hot summers. To ensure that they produce plenty of fruit, plant two different varieties, as blackcurrants are not always self-fertile.

The blackcurrant is a more vigorous plant than the redcurrant, reaching 5 ft (1.5 m) in height and diameter. Pick the berries before they are ripe, and use them straight away. They are not very good table fruits, but they go well in jellies, *crême de cassis* and syrups. They also have aromatic leaves which can be used to make infusions.

Bilberries (Blueberries)

Bilberries (blueberries) grow in large quantities in mountainous areas, but there are also American varieties which are grown in gardens.

The important thing to remember with these bushes is that they like quite acid, fairly poor soil with plenty of moisture. In some ways, they are moorland plants. They are very hardy, but do not like hot climates. They form low clusters with creeping stems and blue, very juicy berries during the summer.

They will grow for a long period in one place, so you should plant them so that they do not interfere with other garden activities. Put them at the far end of the garden, or alongside a path. Raspberry, redcurrant and blackcurrant bushes will also make an effective hedge between the vegetable garden and another part of the garden, orchard or ornamental garden.

Vines and actinidias

There are two other types of shrub which belong with the berries. The most important is the grapevine. This has been famous since time immemorial; the other, the actinidia, has only been grown widely during the past few years. The fruits of the latter are more commonly known as kiwi fruit.

Choose your vine according to your own personal tastes. The grapes are more or less musky, red or white, ripening between mid summer and mid autumn depending on the variety.

Blackcurrants are highly resistant to frost, and are quite happy in a northern climate.

The grape is full of sugar, and is a fruit which keeps well. If you pick the later varieties with a length of branch, soak the branch in water and store it in a cool, dark room you will have fresh grapes to eat even in the middle of winter.

Grow dessert grapes on a trellis against a wall, in a warm but not hot place. Alternatively, guide them across a pergola or up pieces of wire stretched out at various heights, starting quite low. In the latter case, they can be used as a border for a path. Do not plant them in a windy position.

Choose soil which is deep and free-draining, but not chalky. Cut the vines in two stages. Start by letting the vine grow unhindered simply removing any branches which develop where they are not wanted. Then, when the vine has reached the length or height you desire, stop it growing by cutting off the tips. Cut the many lateral branches back to two buds each winter. Pinch out new shoots while they are still tender, about 20 in (50 cm) above the second bunch. The vine resists frost very well, but the growing buds and flowers are very sensitive. It is therefore important not to plant your vine in an exposed position. The vine is easy to propagate by taking cuttings and layering.

Actinidias (kiwis) originally came from China, and they have become enormously popular recently as in a few years they will produce 220 lb (100 kg) of fruit per plant. Because they grow so well – they may exceed 50 ft (15 m) – and have such abundant foliage, you should plant them somewhere where it will be easy for them to grow, and not too hot. They have no particular enemies, and the only thing they dislike is a late frost. However, you will need a male and a female plant to produce fruit.

A single male plant will fertilize up to six or seven female ones. There are various types available, the main differences between them being the size of their fruit. The type species is the most productive, and its fruit has by far the highest vitamin content. Pick the fruit, with its attractive green colour, in mid to late autumn, when it is perfectly ripe, and it will last all winter in a store-room.

Although they are popular for making sorbets, jams and syrups, their very subtle perfume makes them more suitable for use in fruit salads and tarts.

Herbs

Herbs include plants which have a whole range of different requirements, habits and sizes. The annuals include chervil and basil.

Sow parsley in rectangular flowerbeds, in fairly light, aerated soil, and in a sunny position. The seed will germinate in a month. In areas where the climate is mild sow it at three different times between early spring and late summer so that you have some all year. It only requires well cultivated soil to grow in.

Chervil has an aniseedy flavour, and likes a moist and partly shaded, cool position. It germinates very quickly, in a week or so, but has a short lifespan. This means you will need to sow it about once a month. Alternatively, plant hardy chervil, a large, highly decorative plant; only use the tenderest leaves.

Basil is a very short-lived plant, lasting only one summer. Sow it in the warm in mid spring, and plant it in very rich, well watered soil.

Most other herbs are perennials, so they should be positioned so that they do not get in your way when working on your vegetable garden. They will not normally take up much room, so they are a good way of using up space which would otherwise remain unused, such as along the sides of paths, or in corners. Rosemary, bay, thyme, savory, sage and chives all like dry soil and a sunny position. Remove the flowers of chives as they appear to prevent them from exhausting themselves. Thyme, on the other hand, is said to be more aromatic if the stems bear flowers than if they are green.

Herb garden containing mint, hyssop and fennel. Herbs and spices often have delicate, highly decorative foliage.

Tarragon needs a very sunny, but not hot location, and deep, cool soil. Cut it frequently to encourage new shoots to grow. This will also help to prevent the mildew which it is prone to. If you pick the stems and dry or freeze them, they will still maintain their aroma. French tarragon is the most aromatic. It is propagated by division or cuttings.

THE ORCHARD

It is hard to resist the attraction of fruit grown yourself, particularly as for many people it evokes memories of childhood. In former times, the fruits sold in the shops were the same as those grown in people's gardens. Not only were they the same varieties, but the way they were grown and also their state of ripeness when picked were, if not identical, then at least comparable. Nowadays, the fruits we find have been selectively bred. Although they are attractively coloured, they are often less flavoursome, harder and woolly. It is no wonder that consumers and amateur gardeners are going back to the old varieties they once knew with as much enthusiasm as they once welcomed the mass-produced varieties. If you are a lover of fine black cherries, you may not find them readily available in the shops because some varieties are too fragile and do not travel well. The old cultivated home-grown varieties are gaining in appeal. It is easy to criticize modern varieties but they do have their positive elements. Recent techniques have allowed us to obtain stocks which are easy to grow – dwarf varieties, for example, – and varieties which are resistant to certain diseases.

Some modern-day fruit can be of a really excellent quality if grown properly: Golden Delicious, grown to a peak of ripeness is a really flavourful apple, whereas it can be quite bitter and uninspiring if it is picked while still green, a common practice if the fruit has to be transported some distance. The variety Granny Smith is not particularly special if grown in cool climates, but if given plenty of sun it is marvellous.

Napoleon white heart cherries. A crisp, slightly musky variety grown in Europe, which have the advantage of being immune to cherry worm.

Where to site your orchard

An orchard is a group of trees grown for their fruit. Where you plant fruit trees is extremely important. Some of them flower very early on in the year, and although they are hardy they will not bear fruit if they are affected by cold when they blossom. You should therefore avoid cold places at all costs. These will fall into two categories:

(a) Hillocks and humps which give no protection against the wind;

(b) Hollows, valley bottoms or depressions where cold air will sink whilst warm air rises.

On a slope, cold air behaves in the same way as water, flowing down to the lowest point, which obviously means it is not a good idea to plant fruit trees there.

The ideal place for a fruit tree is on a slight slope, facing west, southwest or south. The north is too likely to be affected by frost, and the east tends to be affected by alternate frosts and thaws which will kill off the flowers.

Whether they are on a slope or flat ground, you should make sure that as little cold air as possible reaches the trees and make it easy for it to escape from the orchard. If the ground is sloping, you could plant a windbreak of fairly tall, evergreen trees, or alternatively netting or fencing. Lower down the slope, be very careful to ensure that no obstacles (except the trunks of the fruit-trees, of course) obstruct the flow of cold air.

On a flat piece of ground, plant a windbreak to the north and east – in a garden, you might use ornamental varieties – and leave the west and south free. If these sides represent the boundaries of your garden, and you need to enclose it, do so using wire netting or an open fence to allow the cold wind to escape. These are general rules, and your garden may be a special case because of the way the land is laid out, or alternatively because of the prevailing winds. If you have a wall of trees, you can protect them by planting them near a wall or fence which they will grow up.

Another factor is how much sun the trees will get during the course of the growing season. They need plenty of sun if they are to produce abundant blossom, with large quantities of flavourful, sweet fruit, and also if they are to grow strongly and the wood is to mature properly. If the wood is solid, it will resist frost better and the tree will give a generous harvest. Of course, in a traditional garden there may not be any choice as to which way it is facing. Nor, if you have a restricted amount of space, will you want to give up part of that which you think is badly exposed. If this is the case, plant your fruit trees in the best possible position for their requirements and to make the best use of the area that you have available.

Which way fruit trees should face

You will need a south-facing area for apricot trees, cherries, peaches, pears, apples and plum trees.

Plant cherries with a westerly exposure and, in areas which have a mild climate choose a similar aspect for peaches, pears, apples and plums.

An east facing site is one of the harshest and you will only be able to plant cherries, apples and plums.

The north is a less favourable aspect, and it is best not to plant trees facing this direction, as you will get a less flavoursome fruit. Cooking apples and bitter cherries will grow reasonably well here, however.

Walls and fences will not only protect trees from the wind, but also create micro-climates which favour their growth. Not only is the temperature higher here, but the variations in temperature are less extreme. Walls act as storage heaters, accumulating heat during the day and releasing some of it during the night. In colder areas, they will often be essential if you want to grow fruit like peaches and apricots.

Pruning trees

A tree can simply be planted against a wall and left to grow at will. However, most gardeners want to control its size by pruning. Most often, however, they are grown in shapes: cordons, espalier or fan shapes, particularly if they are apples or pears. If they are to remain controlled, they need to be grafted on to 'dwarfing' rootstocks. These have a fairly restricted spread of branches and foliage and produce a large number of fruits from a small spread of tree.

You can also create shapes by pruning trees. Normally, as an amateur gardener you will not need to prune trees into shape, as the young trees are supplied ready trained by nurseries. You will need to attach them to the wall, either

Gum being given off by a cherry tree due to infestation by a pest.

using a wooden trellis or, more commonly, on wires stretched out at the right height. It is the branches which determine where they are to be placed for espaliers. For cordons and fan shapes, place them about 20 in (50 cm) apart. Note that you can also grow cordons, fans or espaliers away from the wall in rows in the garden.

The type of soil

You will not be able to establish an orchard on just any type of soil. The soil should be an average of about 2 ft (60 cm) deep, and well drained.

Cold, damp soil is not recommended for stone fruits such as peaches, cherries and apricots, as it will stunt the growth of the leaves and promote 'gumming' (oozing of sap), a bacterial infection which is very hard to control.

If the soil is rather heavy, improve it by adding plenty of organic matter.

If the soil is impermeable, you will need to create proper drainage using clay drainage pipes or those made from perforated plastic.

The chemistry of the soil is also an important factor in the quality of an orchard. It should be more or less neutral (pH_7), or slightly acid or alkaline. If it is too acidic (less than 5.8 pH), or too alkaline (more than 7), correct it appropriately, using alkaline supplements for acidic soil, and iron chelate or flowers of sulphur for alkaline soils.

Whichever type it is, you should prepare it well, as it will be occupied by the same trees for twenty to forty years if not longer. On a large area you can use a sub-soiler, a kind of plough with a special blade which breaks up a considerable depth of soil without turning it over, so that the sterile subsoil does not get mixed with the fertile topsoil. Always break up the soil well after removing all undergrowth and weeds.

If you only have a few trees on a small area of ground, all you need to do is break up the soil about one square yard (one square metre) around each tree. Also add a slow-release fertiliser containing nitrogen, phosphorus and potassium in roughly equal amounts. Then plant the trees, preferably in autumn.

Seed-fruit trees

Apple and quince trees need plenty of sun if they are to blossom well and produce tasty fruit.

Protecting the area from cold is very important with pear trees, as these blossom very early, from mid spring onwards. Alternatively, choose varieties which blossom late. Do not put the tree in a windy place, as wind is not an effective method of pollinating trees, and the insects, bees especially, which will pollinate the trees, do not like the wind.

Quinces are naturally small and should not cause any problems as far as space is concerned. Pear and apple trees, on the other hand, if they grow on their own roots, will become proper trees, sometimes very large ones. In a large garden, or if you plant certain varieties – cooking pears, or cider apples – where the fruit can fall to the ground and still be usable, this is less important. But eaters need to be picked before they fall off the tree and get bruised. The yield from a 'dwarf-tree' is proportionally much greater than from a full-size one. Also, jobs like thinning and pruning the tree are much easier if it is small. Apple trees are grafted on to selected rootstocks which have an identification number. This produces trees of varying vigour. So be careful when you buy from a nursery that the stock will give you the type of tree you want. Pear trees are grafted on to various selections of quinces; there are far fewer selections of pear rootstocks than apple rootstocks, but there are still enough of them.

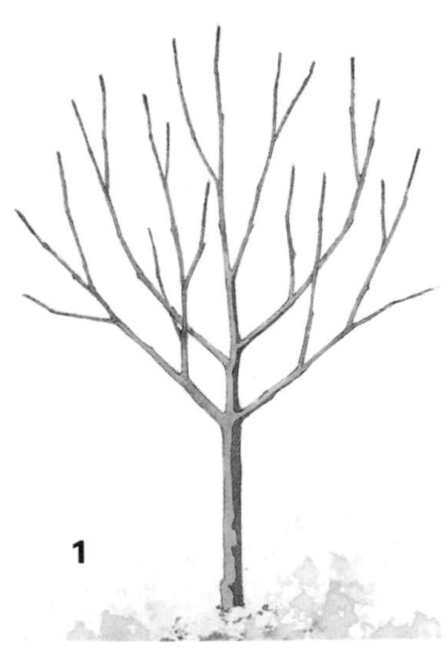

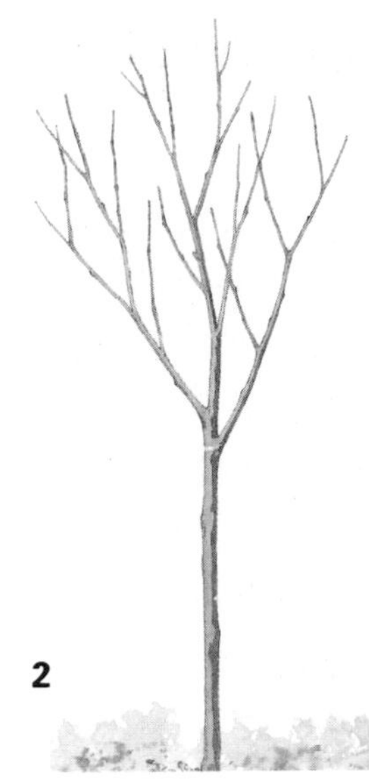

1. Half-stem
2. Goblet

You can obtain trees in various stages of development depending upon what you want. Different forms can be used for different purposes. Half-standards (semi-dwarfs) are best for large orchards: bushes of various sizes for large or medium-sized orchards, and fans, espaliers and cordons for small gardens.

If they are to bear plenty of fruit, you will need to prune them carefully, as this will make the tree put most of its energies into producing fruit instead of leaves and branches.

Recent rootstock developments and modern growing techniques have meant that very little pruning needs to be done. In some commercial orchards, the trees are planted as hedges and cut mechanically in the same way. However, they will almost certainly need regular spraying. If the fruits become too crowded they will need to be thinned out, so that you get regular crops which are of even size and quality. Ensure that they get plenty of water, particularly in spring when they blossom and the fruit starts to form.

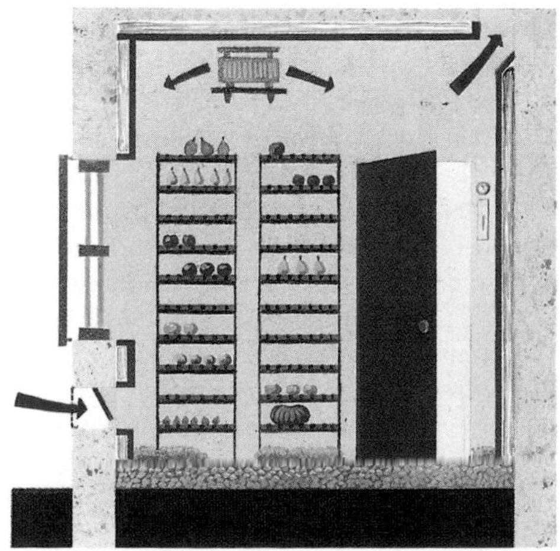

A good fruit store room needs to be well aired and healthy, with a constant room temperature of about 54°F (12°C).

The fruit will ripen at different times depending on where you are and what variety you have chosen; this may be anywhere between mid to late summer, and late autumn. The first fruits you pick should be eaten straight away, as they will not normally keep very long. Later maturing fruits will usually keep for several months, and some varieties will only fully ripen after they have been picked and stored. These will need a proper fruit store, which is cool but frost-free, dark and well ventilated. Place the fruit on a bed of straw or similar material for ventilation, but choose something which will not transfer its smell to the fruit. Make sure the fruit do not touch each other. Fruit trees will start producing crops after four years and, depending on how they are grown and how they are pruned they will last anything between fifteen and forty years.

Stone fruit trees

Cherry, peach and nectarine, plum and apricot trees all like plenty of sun, and should not be planted in heavy, wet soil as this tends to encourage 'gumming'.

Cherries are completely hardy trees, but although they blossom late, the blossom may be harmed by the cold. Depending on the variety,

The cherry tree is very popular because of its magnificent scented blossom, and also for the abundance of fruit it produces. These take only three months to ripen.

the amount of space you have and the size of the crop you want, plant one or more trees. Most cherry trees will grow very vigorously and very often an amateur gardener will only require one. Acid (sour or pie) cherries are small, but they look good almost anywhere, and their sumptuous, highly perfumed white blossom and brilliant autumn colours make them very good ornamental trees.

Cherries take relatively little looking after apart from pruning the young trees into the right shape. This involves removing the central leader and leaving only the crown of diverging branches. This makes the job of picking the cherries from the lower branches much easier. If you let the leader develop, it will be not you, but the birds who end up eating the cherries.

Cherry trees need ten years before they produce fruit in any significant quantity, but they make up for this by the fact that they last a very long time indeed: anything from 100 to 150 years. When picking cherries, only put the ladder against the strongest branches or the trunk, and never climb the tree if the wood breaks easily.

Cherries dislike stagnant water, but equally they do not like soil which is too light or thin. A good fibrous, but slightly acid or slightly alkaline soil is ideal.

White or pale pink cherries are succulent and strongly aromatic, with very good eating qualities. Red cherries are also good to eat, though these are less firm and ripen later in the year.

Black cherries are exceptional for their extraordinary 'stone' flavour which makes them very good eaters. They are fairly small and very soft which means they do not travel particularly well. So if they will grow in your area you may be best able to appreciate these by growing them yourself.

The translucent, bright red or pale red cherries known as acid (sour or pie) cherries grow on small trees. They are almost inedible raw, and they are usually used to make liqueurs or jam. Ordinary (sweet) cherries will come apart in alcohol and taste very unpleasant in jam.

Cherry trees produce ripe cherries within two and a half to three months, making them the fastest of all fruits to develop. But with the exception of acid (sour or pie) cherries, they are self-sterile and need to be grown near a proper pollinator. However, you are unlikely to be unlucky enough not to have a suitable one somewhere nearby.

Peaches and nectarines are both slight variants of one fruit. The differences lie in whether the stone adheres to the flesh and whether the skin is soft and downy or not. These trees have a reputation for being sensitive to cold, which is quite unjustified. Although it is true that their pink blossom appears very early and may be destroyed by frost, which means they are almost always grown in fairly southerly latitudes. Even there, they need to be grown in a sheltered position, and a wall or a hedge can often help a great deal.

Peach trees dislike alkaline soil, which causes chlorosis and turns them yellow. They are often grafted onto St Julien plum trees, which makes them fairly resistant. Various other rootstocks are used, giving the tree various degrees of vigorousness. This is unlikely to interest the amateur gardener, because peach trees and their relatives are small, and generally suitable for most types of garden.

The tree starts bearing fruit fairly soon in its life, but the tree itself is relatively short-lived. Keep its height under control and prune it when the sap is rising. Only cut the youngest branches: those which are less than two years old. Any more drastic pruning will tend to create 'gumming' (oozing of sap).

The disease which most often affects the peach tree is peach leaf curl. This makes the leaves puff up, then red spots appear and the leaves fall off. It can be controlled by spraying early in the season.

Depending on the variety and where they are grown, the peaches will ripen some time between mid summer and early autumn. The fruits with pale skin and green or white flesh are very popular, and they are the only ones which are scented.

The blood varieties have flesh streaked with red against a green background. They are soft and very sweet, and are perfect for eating, as well as using for sorbets, jams and tarts.

The yellow-fleshed varieties have been particularly popular in recent years, for they are very firm and eye-catching both to fruiterers and their suppliers. Although they can sometimes be quite bitter they can also be quite delicious. Another attraction is the firmness of their flesh, which can sometimes make them beautifully crisp and therefore keep well.

The grapevine peach is supposedly the most flavoursome peach of all. In fact, these are simply wild peach trees which have grown from peach stones thrown here and there by the owners of the vines. The result is a peach tree which might be an infinite variety of types. These peaches are often fairly small, about the size of a large plum, and thick-skinned. With luck, though, they can taste very good.

The almond tree is a very close relative of the peach, though it is taller and less resistant to cold. The difference is that in the almond, the flesh does not develop much, unlike the peach.

Plum trees blossom early, and although the blossom is slightly less sensitive to cold than that of peach trees, it is a good idea to put them in a sheltered location. Grow them on the same kind of soil as cherry trees: firm, fibrous and well drained, but not too acidic nor too alkaline. As they are not so deep rooted, they do not need such a deeply dug soil as cherry trees. Use a minimum of pruning, as the plum is one of the trees which is most sensitive to 'gumming' (oozing sap), a condition that is more likely if the tree has large pruning scars.

The harvest will be between mid summer and mid autumn, depending on the area and the variety. Mirabelles and Reine-Claudes are very popular in France, either for dessert or cooking use. But there are plenty of other varieties worth growing, some of which will be better adapted to suit your particular climate.

You can make prunes by drying plums with a tough skin on screens in a very low oven for several hours. In the past, the sun was used to dry them.

Plums also freeze extremely well, but when thawed they are only suitable for pies or jams. Plums often tend to alternate, meaning that one year they produce a large crop and little or none the following year. Pruning will go some of the way towards preventing this, but more importantly, they need thinning. In fact, this is a good idea for many varieties of fruit tree, such as apples, pears and peaches, and here it is essential.

Thinning means removing excess fruit when it has reached the size of a marble. Sometimes thinning is not enough, and the tree will still produce a huge crop. This can sometimes be heavy enough to break the branches. If this is likely you should support the tree and branches with poles. Cross-pollination is also necessary for most plum trees if they are to produce a healthy crop of fruit.

The apricot is a hardy tree, often grafted on to a St Julien plum tree, which keeps it small. Although it is undeniably a hardy tree, its drawback is that its blossom is particularly vulnerable to frost. For this reason, unless you live in a particularly mild climate, you will need to grow it against a wall or a fence. The sheltered

Almond tree. Because it flowers late and is sensitive to frost, the almond tree can only be grown in mild regions. It is content with poor, well-drained soil.

This ornamental hazelnut, Corylus avellana 'Contorta'*, produces round nuts with hard shells.*

position is also important for the fruit to ripen properly, as is plenty of sun. The fruit ripens in mid summer to early autumn, peaking in late summer.

All apricots are suitable for any use. Keep the best ones for desserts, especially as they look so attractive. The smaller ones often have a pitted skin and are better used for making jam.

The fruits you will see on a market stall often bear little relation to what a real apricot should be: juicy, very tender, and scented. Because of the time it takes to get them to market, they have to be picked when they are still green and not particularly pleasant to eat. Sometimes, though, green or slightly unripe apricots are useful in jam making, as they help it to set.

Apricots are self fertilizing and do not require another variety to help them set fruit. Like plums, they sometimes produce a big crop one year and a smaller one the next, but this is less marked than with plums. Also, the wood of the apricot tree is a little less fragile and less likely to break if overloaded.

Quinces are quite rare, but they have two particular merits: their blossom is very attractive, and their fruit can be used to make very good jelly.

Chestnut and walnut trees need plenty of space and are too large for the average garden. If you do grow them, it will probably be for their shade, rather than for their nuts.

The olive is also regarded as a fruit tree, but it is only suited to very warm southern climates. The same applies to citrus fruit.

The hazelnut is a relatively small tree, and apart from producing delicious nuts its foliage is very pleasant to look at. It is a temperate tree, and will make do with a fairly poor, even sandy soil. All the different species and varieties will bear fruit, including the ornamental forms with twisted branches, and those with purple leaves.

The bushes have male flowers (the catkins) and female ones separated on the same branches. They are fertilized by the wind. Although in theory the hazelnut is self fertilizing, the male and female flowers are not ready at the same time so it is better to have two varieties which flower at slightly different times. Hazelnuts are completely hardy, though if you can give them slight shelter from the worst of the wind, the conditions will be ideal for the pollen to drift and reach the female flowers.

Hazelnuts can be round and hard-shelled (avelines) or narrow and thin-shelled depending on the species (*Corylus avellana* or *Corylus maxima*) from which they come.

Another advantage of hazelnut trees is the fact that they are very good for growing truffles if they are 'sown' with the proper fungus (*Tuber melano sporum*). A final, additional merit is that the hazelnut requires no pruning.

The fig tree is the only more or less hardy representative of the genus *Ficus*. It is widely found in the tropics, and also common in people's homes. It is not a difficult tree to grow, but there are many misconceptions about it. It is a hardier plant than many believe it to be, and can be grown in quite northerly climes.

Fig tree growing in England. Despite their reputation, fig trees can grow in relatively cold climates.

If it is exposed to hard winters, they may seriously damage it, but it grows back easily and will fully recover in a year or two.

The fig is a very undemanding tree and will grow anywhere, provided the soil is not too wet. It is often found in the most unlikely and unwelcome places, such as holes in walls, which it particularly likes. It grows on its own roots and takes the shape of a large bush, which sometimes needs to be trimmed down to size. It can be increased by taking cuttings or shoots. A fig will grow almost anywhere, even in a fairly cool climate, and is sometimes grown simply for the delightful fresh smell of its leaves.

Figs have white, pink, yellow or violet flesh. They can be round or elongated. Most people agree that the yellow or violet ones, which ripen late, are the best. They can be eaten either fresh or in jam. The drawback of this tree is that, apart from the fact that it can spread and occupy a lot of space, its leaves can cause allergic reactions in people.

Pests

Apart from the pests which are specific to different types of fruit trees, the fact that they all produce sugar and starch in one form or another means they tend to be attacked by a variety of predators. Gnawing creatures can do a great deal of damage in the orchard and you should make sure trees are protected from these undesirable creatures by placing a zinc or plastic collar round the trunk a little way above the ground. The only other means of dealing with mice and voles is to use poisoned bait.

Strawberries and currant bushes protected against birds by a net.

An orchard which is not yet productive can be planted with bulbs such as daffodils.

Birds are a particular problem with cherry trees. Putting string over the trees to protect them is a difficult task, and removing it is even harder. Using noise to frighten them off is virtually useless, and a scarecrow will only have any effect for about quarter of an hour.

Wasps can be very useful in the spring in areas where greenfly are a pest because they prey on them, but they will often bore into pears, figs and grapes during late summer as they ripen. You can put pears and grapes into bags to protect them. Figs will attract bees if they become over-ripe, so if you pick them at the right time you will avoid this problem.

Bare earth or grass?

If you make a circle of bare earth at the bottom of each tree and provide a mulch, it will ensure that it prospers. The soil can be kept well aerated and this will improve the absorption of water when you water the tree. The size of the circle will depend on the diameter of the tree, though 7 ft (2 m) is a good rule of thumb. But grass down the rest of the area and keep it cut from time to time. The presence of grass is thought to give more flavoursome and colourful fruit. One traditional combination is to plant the orchard with hardy bulbs so that in spring the combination of blossom and flowering bulbs makes it into a beautiful ornamental garden.

HEDGES

A hedge needs to be pruned from the very outset. Seen in section, it should be trapezium shaped.

Hedges are often the most important feature of a garden, and yet they can also be the most neglected. Whether it is 20 in (50 cm) or 50 ft (15 m) tall, a hedge can set the whole style of the garden, hide it away from prying eyes and shelter it from the wind. It can serve to separate the various areas of the garden from one another and the garden from the outside world. It is often home to a whole array of animal life, some of which can be a positive benefit to the garden, for example, birds, hedgehogs and toads.

The type of hedge

The most traditional type of hedge consists of a single hardy species, kept regularly trimmed and about 8–10 ft (2.5–3 m) in height. Its main role is that of isolating the garden from the gaze of passers-by and from outside noise: it is a wall of vegetation.

As far as possible, try to use species which are suited to the general environment. In a wooded area, you may well want to use a deciduous hedge. Rows of fast-growing conifers are somewhat over-used at present. Other factors you will need to take into consideration are the climate, the amount of moisture in the soil, and whether it is alkaline or not.

A beech hedge. Beech is a hardy species and has the advantage of keeping most of its leaves during the winter.

Trimming

The main drawback to looking after a hedge is trimming it. The general shape of the hedge, viewed in section, should be a trapezium, not a rectangle, meaning it is wider at the base than at the top. This allows the whole of the hedge to get more light, particularly the shoots at the bottom which would otherwise lose their leaves. People often make the mistake of letting a young hedge grow to the height they finally want it before starting to trim it. This can have a devastating effect upon many coniferous hedges as they then have to be cut back to old wood which is no longer capable of putting out new shoots. Start trimming your hedge at a very early stage so that it produces branches and thickens out from the outset. Trim the hedge in summer and again in mid spring for fast-growing conifers.

Deciduous hedges are almost all able to regrow on old wood. This means that if you make a slip while cutting it, it will not do any lasting damage. If privacy is not so important, you may prefer to use trees with a very natural appearance, such as beech and hornbeam, which do not mind being pruned. Their leaves are described as marcescent, because, in mild climates, they stay on the branches after they have turned brown. These trees can be cut back quite drastically, even when they are only 6 in (15 cm) thick, or even down to ground level if necessary. They are also extremely good for separating one part of the garden from another and creating 'rooms' of greenery. Hedges which are very regular, whether they are evergreen or not, can also serve as a backdrop for more brightly coloured plants in raised beds or ordinary flower borders, as their neutral colours bring out those of the flowers.

Informal hedges are currently very popular. They combine unpruned shrubs and a few flowering ones to provide a splash of colour amid the greenery.

The informal hedge

In an informal hedge, the plants are left to grow of their own accord. An informal hedge can be made up of a single species or several mixed together. In an average garden, an informal hedge will be made up of trees no more than 6½–10 ft (2–3 m) in height. By definition, it is not trimmed at least not in the strict sense of the word. It is actually more of a question of cutting off old branches, shaping up bushes where they have become bedraggled or untidy and using pruning shears where they are simply too large.

An informal hedge might consist simply of one or two species, or you could mix several. If you do the latter, use bushes of different sizes and alternate tall, thin shapes with round ones. Some bushes might be very decorative, like rosebushes, while others might be simpler, like privet. To prevent the colours jarring, place neutral ones between the very spectacular ones to offset them. Likewise, do not combine eye-catching hedges, or create too many contrasts among bushes which peak at the same time. For example, a mixture of forsythia, flowering blackcurrant and Japanese quince is likely to look incongruous – use just one of them. If you surround the one you have chosen with lilacs, roses or privet, for example, it will be set off nicely. In fact, although there are fewer different species used to make it, an informal hedge follows the same rules of balance as a mixed border.

Perennial or annual climbing plants can also be used as part of a hedge: these will create an additional link to make the garden look larger.

The rustic hedge

A rustic hedge can be anything between 6½–50 ft (2–15 m) high, depending on the garden and the surrounding landscape. The plants it is made up of are very unsophisticated, because their role is first and foremost that of shielding the garden from the wind, though there is nothing to stop them serving an aesthetic purpose as well.

If you have a medium-sized or small garden, the hedge should not be more than 6½–10 ft (2–3 m) high.

If you have a very large area available, you might want to grow a wooded hedge of two layers: one layer is made up of tall trees (poplar,

Perennials grown against a hornbeam hedge. Behind this is a hedge of lime trees, itself situated in front of an informal hedge.

A rustic hedge of hawthorn, hornbeam and maple. In a hedge of this kind, made up of species which are not particularly eye catching, it is important to create an interplay of different shapes.

beech, maple, oak, ash and the like) between which are tall or medium-sized bushes in line with the trees.

If it is to be an authentic rustic hedge, it will probably contain mainly indigenous species. To make it a little more elegant, use forms and varieties which are more decorative. White ash (*Fraxinus americana*), for example, with its magnificent autumn colours, is a better choice than an ash which doesn't turn. If you choose hawthorn, make it white or pink, single or double. If you want to grow timber, make sure the tall trees have straight trunks with no low branches.

Gaps in the hedge

Whichever type of hedge you have, it will create more of an illusion of space if there are openings giving glimpses outside. If it is a formal hedge, these will be doorways or windows, either round or rectangular, cut out with shears. For informal hedges, create gradations of height and leave deliberate gaps which look natural.

You can also create other illusions. You can make a garden look longer by gradually decreasing the height of the hedge as it moves away from the house. You might use topiary. This can either be separate (animal figures, chess pieces etc), or incorporated into the hedge in the form of doors or archways. All of these will need constant care and attention. Topiary will also involve using a template so that it can be clipped without error.

The hedge as windbreak

The best windbreaks are ones which are not particularly solid. This is why trees are replaced by netting rather than solid material, if there are not enough of them or they are too small. Trees or shrubs which are set slightly apart or have branches with spaces between them will act as a filter for the wind, and for several yards past the hedge the strength of the wind may decrease by half or more. If, the trees are tightly packed together they will create eddy currents and at best will only protect a distance equal to the height of the hedge. In a particularly windy area, it is a good idea only to use deciduous trees and bushes. They will offer less resistance to the wind and there is less chance of their being uprooted or broken. The problem is more acute near the sea. Evergreens such as maritime pines (*Pinus pinaster*) and tamarisk (*Tamarix*) (in a mild climate) and Japanese black pine (*P. thunbergiana*), which are more resistant to salt, are particularly suitable for coastal regions.

The best shrubs for seaside areas apart from the tamarisk are olearia (daisy bush or tree aster), rose laurel and pittosporums (in a mild climate), atriplex or sea orach and elaeagnus (wild olive) and Pfitzer's juniper.

Planting the hedge

There may be legal requirements concerning the height of a hedge and the distance from the boundary of a property at which it may be planted. In some areas, the law states that the owner of the tree or bush is responsible for the branches which overhang a neighbouring property. Check requirements for your particular area with your local authority.

Planting the hedge should not be a problem if it is of average length. If it is unusually long, in the case of an informal hedge for example, it is worthwhile digging a trench, or having one dug, if the trees have large rootballs. Stake them up until they re-establish, which rarely happens for at least two years.

To plant small trees, stretch out a mulch made from plastic with holes in it and put the saplings through the holes. Fill the holes, water the saplings and cover the mulch with earth, gravel or bark.

LAWNS

Almost every garden nowadays has at least one area of lawn. It may be a manicured formal lawn, an informal play area or an uncultivated meadow, depending on the type of grass, what it is used for, and how much care is taken of it. A lawn sets off the rest of the garden, gives it depth, and provides a place for recreation if required.

A neatly trimmed, formal lawn is the most elegant, but it also requires the most care, both in planting and subsequent maintenance particularly cutting and watering. It wears out quickly if it is trodden on frequently, so it is no use as a recreation area especially for children.

Many amateur gardeners make do with a less ambitious lawn, using coarser varieties of grass, and without fussing if the odd dandelion grows here and there. This type of informal lawn requires a minimum of maintenance, stays fairly green, and is not harmed by garden chairs or children's feet.

A meadow, whether wild or grown from seed, is made up of very hardy species and needs very little maintenance: mowing two or three times a year and occasionally watering. It can also include flowering perennials and bulbs; the latter are very suitable as the lawn is not mown very often.

Choosing a site

Irrespective of the type of lawn, choose a sunny, well-drained, flat site. However, if this is not possible, there are seed mixes specially suited to shady or damp conditions.

The real problem with an uneven lawn is not so much the well-being of the grass as the fact that it is harder to look after. It is difficult to get a

A lawn is a restful, tranquil area. A garden breathes through a lawn, and the lawn in turn sets off the different colours, heights and depths of the garden. This pleasant feature of the garden can be designed in countless different ways. It is often a good idea to include areas specifically set aside for rest and relaxation, perhaps with benches to sit on.

A meadow-style lawn sown with daffodils. Lawns of this kind need particular care, as they have to fit around the life cycle of bulbs.

lawnmower to function properly on uneven ground or on a steep slope although modern hover mowers usually work satisfactorily. Grass has a tendency to dry out on rises and get drowned in hollows.

Working the soil

Soil type should be taken into consideration. Specialized seed merchants sell selections of grass seed suited to all types of soil.

Prepare the soil during the summer before sowing. Clear the area and weed it carefully. If you are using chemical weedkiller, choose a systemic type which enters the plants through the foliage and is transported in the sap. They break down quickly, leaving no trace behind.

One month before sowing, turn the soil over with a spade or a mechanical cultivator to aerate it. Any dormant weed seeds will germinate and can be easily removed.

This is also the time to get rid of stones and roots, and to incorporate well-rotted compost and a general fertilizer. Add either leaf mould or peat, at the rate of one or two buckets per sq yd (m^2). Double the amount for very sandy soils, as these act as a humidity regulator. Incorporate two buckets of coarse sand per sq yd (m^2) on heavy soil.

Once this work is done, break down the clods of soil and roll it, first in one direction and then at right angles. Repeat this a few days later and rake the soil to create a smooth surface.

A few days later, rake in a slow-release fertilizer, without firming the soil too hard. Pull up any weed seedlings as they appear and, in the meantime, about ten days later, sow the grass seed.

Sowing the seed

It does not matter when you sow grass seed, providing the weather is neither too hot nor too cold, but most gardeners prefer to sow in spring or autumn. The weather then should be warm enough for the seeds to germinate quickly and uniformly, but not so hot that the young shoots wither. Regular rain is most likely at these times of the year, so spring and autumn provide perfect conditions for the grass. It only needs watering if there is insufficient rain.

It is better to sow in spring in regions with early, cold winters. If grass seed is sown in the autumn, the lawn will not have time to establish itself before winter sets in. On the other hand, in very warm regions, with long, dry summers, it is better to sow grass seed in autumn. Elsewhere, it is often a good idea to sow half the lawn in autumn and the other half in spring. This avoids putting a very large area of the garden out of use for a prolonged period. This is a particularly

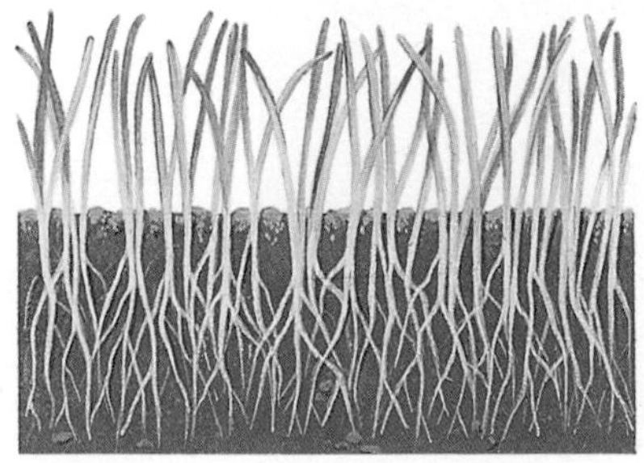

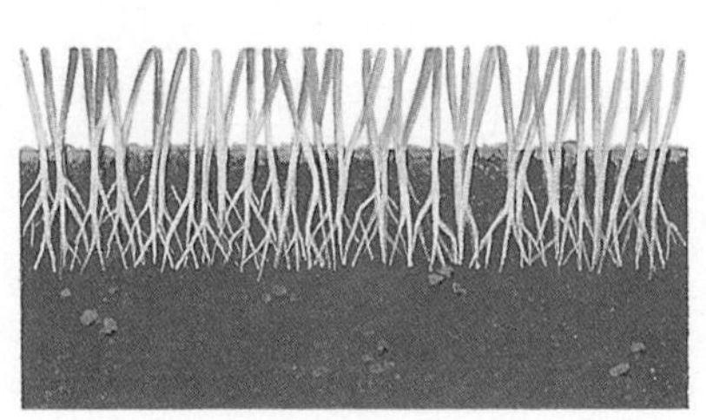

The depth of the roots is about equal to the height of a blade of grass. If grass is cut short, the roots will be short but densely packed.

useful approach if the lawn is the route to other parts of the garden.

Rake the soil once more before sowing. Divide the seeds into two equal quantities, and also set aside a small quantity to fill in the bare patches which will almost certainly appear when the grass starts growing. On average, it takes 300 to 400 seeds to sow 1 sq yd (m^2) of lawn.

Divide the area into strips with string. Sow the strips one by one with the first half of the seeds. Then mark out strips at right angles to the first set, and sow the other half of the seeds. Finish by rolling the ground and, if the weather is dry, water it using a very fine spray.

Within about three weeks, the grass grows to a height of 1–1½ in (3–4 cm). Roll it with a light roller to make sure it takes root properly. Mow for the first time about three to four weeks after this, with the blades at the highest setting.

Mowing

Mowing is the most important maintenance task, although lawns need attention in other ways too. Cut a good quality lawn once a week from early spring to late spring, at least once a week or as needed until late summer, and then once a week until late autumn. No more than ½ in (1 cm) should be trimmed at each cut. A blade of grass 1¼ in (3 cm) tall has roots which are 1¼ in (3 cm) long; a blade 2 in (5 cm) tall is likely to have roots the same length. This is why the grass should be mown on a higher setting in dry or cold weather. Lawns rarely need mowing in winter, as they hardly grow at all when the temperature is low.

If a lawn has not been mown for some time and has grown long, never try to put it right by cutting right down to ground level at one go. This causes the turf to dry out and leaves a yellow carpet for a least two weeks. Set the blades on their highest position and cut the grass a little shorter each time, until it has reached the desired height.

Mowers

A remarkably wide range of mowers is available today; in fact, there is a mower for every type of surface and every situation. Buy one suited to the size of the lawn. A petrol-driven mower with a seat will not be suitable for a 120 sq yd (100 m^2) lawn; similarly, a mechanical roller (push) mower is likely to be ineffective and exhausting anywhere but on a very small lawn. Self-driven mowers are ideal, especially for lawns with hills or mounds in them. Rotary mowers, either with wheels or a cushion of air, are also good.

After mowing, gather up the cuttings or they will suffocate the grass. Some mowers automatically collect them in a grass box. Use cuttings to make compost, preferably mixed with other vegetable waste. Always wear shoes with strong toecaps or boots when mowing, as accidents with lawnmowers, particularly electric mowers, still happen all too often.

For cutting the grass around obstacles, such as banks, rocks or trees, and for cutting along borders, use a light-weight electric strimmer with a nylon thread.

Looking after the lawn

Mowing the lawn in strips, rather than in a haphazard way, not only keeps it looking smart, it also saves time. If it is irregularly shaped, either follow the outlines, or divide it into imaginary squares or rectangles, and mow them one after the other.

A newly grown lawn is always a pleasure to see, but inevitably, weeds will eventually reappear. Apply a selective weedkiller in summer, a few days before, but never after, mowing the

For small or medium sized areas, use a traditional rotary-bladed motor mower.

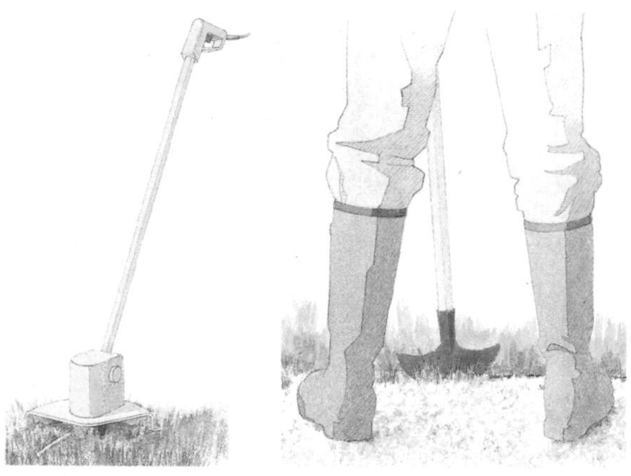

Cut around obstacles using an electric or hand lawn edger.

lawn. Tough, tap-rooted weeds can be pulled up by hand, using a small fork or an asparagus knife. The roots can be pulled out more easily after rain.

In theory, moss should never grow if the lawn is kept properly mown, rolled, fertilized, watered, drained, and aerated. If it does grow, destroy it in spring using iron sulphate, either neat or diluted with water, and sprinkled by hand. This turns the grass slightly brown, but it will soon recover, whereas the moss will be burned off. Afterwards, use a wheeled scarifier on the lawn. Burn the moss collected by the scarifier, as it is still capable of reproducing.

Use a hand scarifier, or, if the lawn is large, a wheeled one, in early autumn to cut the stolons of the grass and untangle them. This gives a thicker lawn. Use a de-thatcher to get rid of any dead material which is known as thatch.

To keep the lawn rooting well, roll it once or twice a month. Aerate it in autumn to prevent the soil compacting. Spike a small lawn with an ordinary garden fork. In some areas, you can buy long spikes which may be attached to a pair of shoes, so that all you need to do is to walk up and down a medium-sized lawn. For very large areas, use a roller aerator which also has spikes.

Lawns need regular feeding, as they exhaust the soil quickly. In autumn, sprinkle the surface with a lawn dressing taking care not to smother the grass completely. Go over it afterwards with a light raking or a broom.

Lawn dressing alone is not enough; the lawn will also need a quick-acting feed in the spring. Use fertilizers sparingly, and in the quantities recommended by the manufacturer. Applying too much burns the grass instead of feeding it. As a precaution, apply it in two stages, two weeks apart. Do not use fertilizer in autumn, except on an exhausted lawn.

Grass has a habit of taking over neighbouring areas, like paths and flower beds. This problem can be reducedor lawn edger by using a spade,

Aerate the soil in autumn using a fork.

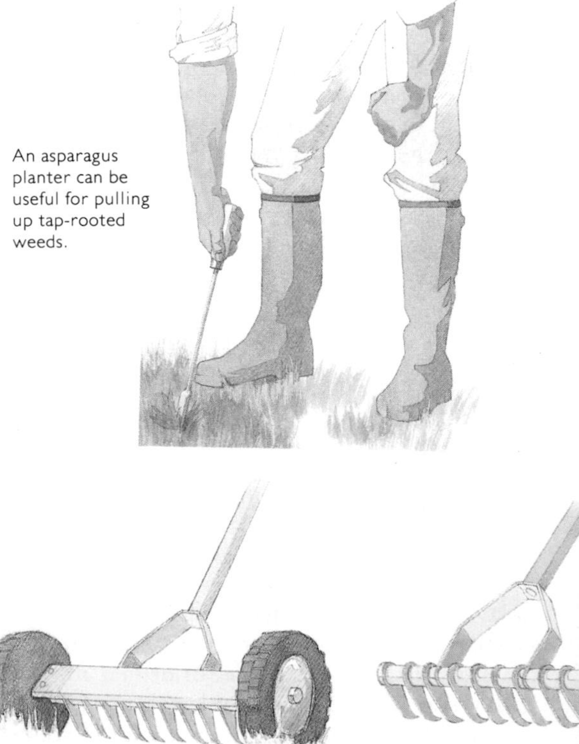

An asparagus planter can be useful for pulling up tap-rooted weeds.

Wheeled scarifier.

Scarifying rake.

or better still, an edging iron or lawn edger to redefine its outline once a year.

Also once a year, preferably in spring, put right any defects in the surface of the lawn. These may have been overlooked when the soil was prepared, or they may have appeared if the soil rose or sank during the winter. Irregularities show up more after the lawn has been mown. Flatten mounds with a spade, and fill in cracks or troughs with finely crumbled earth mixed with lawn dressing. Afterwards, re-sow the areas involved.

There may be patches where the grass has died because it has been stifled, or it has been compacted by being walked on, or simply because gaps are left when weeds were removed. Dig the soil over with a fork, feed it and then re-sow it. Do this in early spring because it must not be mown for at least six weeks, and the rest of the lawn will, therefore, be neglected during this time. If there are only a few, small patches, simply mow round them.

Even a well-maintained domestic lawn has a lifespan of only ten to 15 years. After this, the soil will have to be cultivated again and the lawn re-sown.

Using turf

This is a very practical way of creating a lawn, and the effect is one of a thick carpet made up of small squares rolled flat. It is a quick, but expensive way of establishing a lawn, and is best used for small areas. It is useful for filling in areas of lawn that have worn thin, as the rest of the lawn can still be tended and used.

The informal lawn

An informal lawn requires far less care and attention. Some gardeners do not even bother to mow or water them. There are seed mixes available suitable for this type of lawn, but always bear in mind that, whatever type, a lawn will only give back what has been put into it. This means that there will be periods when it is a bit yellow, when some areas are growing less strongly than others, or there are a number of weeds mixed in with the grass.

Informal lawns are often used as a kind of multi-purpose carpet for paddling pools, table tennis tables, and barbecues. Although it may be hardy, grass is not indestructible. It is a living material and will be more easily damaged if it is not given sufficient care and attention. When the paddling pool is put away it will leave a patch of dying grass which will never recover. People playing table tennis uproot the grass and dig holes in the soil, and a barbecue leaves scorch marks on the grass and makes the soil sterile.

A meadow-type lawn containing red poppies, daisies, knapweeds and grasses: all very hardy species which need little upkeep.

The meadow-type lawn

Natural meadows, where they still exist, are admired for their soft appearance, their variety of colour, created by the mixture of grasses and flowering plants, and the beautiful interplay of sunlight and shade. It is very tempting to create one in your own back garden, but a meadow is not beautiful all year round. The sheer size of a natural meadow gives it its rich appearance. It is at its best in early summer, when grasses, poppies and other annuals are in flower. To get the best out of this type of lawn in a garden, you will need to add decorative features for extra colour and variety.

It is not enough just to work over the soil and then wait for grass to grow on it. In fact, the soil requires as much preparation as a neatly tended lawn, and must be seeded with a variety of suitable grasses and hardy annual flowering plants, such as cornflowers and cosmos. Dot a few, undemanding perennials, such as meadowsweet (filipendula), around the lawn.

A combination of grass and bulbs is not always easy to get right. If cut three times a year at key times an attractive compromise can be obtained.

Bulbs can be particularly effective in meadows. Unfortunately, many gardeners confuse grasses and bulbs, and, as bulbs live from their leaves, they die if the leaves are cut down. Therefore, they are not really suitable for formal lawns which are mown frequently. In addition, some bulbs, including many types of crocuses, cannot grow in competition with fast-growing grasses. In a meadow, where the grass is deeper rooted and grows farther apart, crocuses grow well. A meadow is very well suited to many different types of bulbs, and these can withstand the thrice yearly mowings which the grass requires.

The early part of the year sees the flowering of snowdrops and aconites in late winter, crocus in early spring, daffodils in mid-spring, and English irises (*Iris xiphioides*) and camassias in late spring to early summer. These plants are adapted to the different heights of the grass as the seasons progress. The lower-growing plants flower when the grass is still fairly short, medium-height ones when it is growing, and taller ones when the grass is fully developed. There is regrowth in early to mid-autumn, with colchicums, autumn crocus and sternbergias, whose foliage appears in the following spring.

Mowing should follow the life cycles of these plants. Mow first in late summer, and then water the lawn well. Repeat a month later, before the autumn flowering bulbs grow. Mow the grass once more in late autumn, being especially careful not to cut off the short leaves of the bulb plants. If necessary simply mow round the areas where they are growing.

Any time you mow meadow grass, set the blades to their highest setting. Mow it again at a medium setting a week later. The late summer mowing will be difficult in a fast-growing meadow; use a brushwood cutter before doing the first round.

GROUND-COVER PLANTS

There is a wide range of plants suitable for ground cover. These plants smother large areas of bare soil with a carpet of greenery. A Pfitzer's juniper, for example, even though it may be 5 ft (1.5 m) tall, is a ground-cover plant, and even a weeping beech could be included in the same category. The normal definition of a ground-cover plant is that it is broader than it is high.

As these plants vary considerably in size, it is possible to balance their heights and shapes against each other, and even create a whole garden using them. They have many useful features. They conceal the soil; grow fairly vigorously and close together, leaving little room for weeds to develop; and they need a minimum of care and attention. These are plants for impatient gardeners who want quick results with a minimum of work.

Ground-cover plants offer the pleasant compromise of an attractive and varied garden without requiring too much maintenance. Ideally, they should be evergreen, but this is not essential and they can make the garden look rather fixed and unchanging. They need to be fast-growing, but not so invasive that they take over the whole garden. A number of climbing plants also fit the bill; ivy is one of the best. This will grow, even beneath conifers, and here it can serve as a good substitute for a lawn.

Clematis and wistaria make ideal cover for a concrete flagstone which is difficult to hide, a stony area, a slope where it is difficult to grow anything else, or a supporting spur of ground. In cases like these, the plants will need to be trained, or they will grow back on themselves and form unattractive hummocks. This is easily done by laying a trellis on the soil; a light one for clematis and a stronger one for wistaria. Creeping plants will also perform this function. A good example is the rosebush. More ground-covering varieties appear each year.

The gardener's dream is to have a lawn which requires no maintenance. In fact, there are lawn substitutes which do this. One (in moist climates) is the Treneague variety of chamomile, which has no flowers, and spreads rapidly. Another is an extraordinary juniper, *Juniperus horizontalis* 'Bar Harbor', with fine blue foliage, which can cover several square yards (m²) without growing more than 4 in (10 cm) high. Many nurseries sell it as ground cover, and it can be trampled underfoot without coming to any harm.

Ground-cover plants require the same preparations as any other plant: well-prepared soil and careful weeding. Although ground-cover plants stop weeds developing once they have become established, they will not get rid of weeds which are already well rooted.

Although the soil needs to be well cultivated, there is no point in swamping it with fertilizers as, with the exception of non-creeping shrubs, ground-covering plants are always taking over new areas of soil from which they can gain fresh

If ground-covering plants are suited to the nature of the terrain, they can form attractive gardens needing little maintenance, such as this carpet of Erica *(heather),* Sedum *and* Thymus *(thyme).*

Juniperus horizontalis. *These are coniferous shrubs which will carpet a large area of soil which would otherwise be difficult to fill.*

nutrients. Non-creeping shrubs can be planted surrounded with ground-cover plants, which are light and easy to pull up, until the shrub has filled out.

Plant creeping plants in small sprigs and clumps as far apart as possible within the area to be covered. They will smother the soil more rapidly than a single large clump of the same plant. Put down a mulch between the clumps to stop weeds growing during the first couple of years. After this, mulching is unnecessary. If you cannot plant out the whole area at one time, it is better to prepare and plant out one section so that you will not need to get back to it. Prepare and plant out subsequent sections each year. If you plant the entire area leaving gaps, or in a disorganized fashion, it will be a waste of time.

Choose the varieties of ground-cover plants carefully. They need to be fast-growing, but not ones which will destroy everything in their paths. Unless they are your favourites, avoid periwinkle and St. John's wort, which are virtually impossible to get rid of, and also try to avoid deep-rooting, creeping plants. These will look delightful for the first couple of years, untidy a year later, and a nightmare forever after that.

GROUND-COVERING PLANTS	
Perennial plants and sub-shrubs	**Shrubs**
Various Acaena, Achemilla mollis, Ajuga reptans, Arabis albida, Asperula odorata, Ballota pseudodictamnus, Brunnera macrophylla, Campanula poscharskyana, Centaurea montana, Cerastium tomentosum, Ceratostigma plumbaginoides, Convallaria majalis, Coronilla varia, Cyclamen hederifolium, Dianthus deltoides, Duchesnea indica, Geranium endressii, G. macrorrhizum, Helxine soleirolii, Hosta fortunei, Hypericum calycinum, Lamium galeobdolon, L. maculatum, Lithospermum purpureo-caruleum, Mentha, Nepeta faassenii, Petasites hybridus various Polygonums, Polypodium vulgare, Saxifraga umbrosa, Sedum spathulifolium, S. spectabile, S. spurium, Stachys olympica, Symphytum uplandicum, Thymus, Tiarella cordifolia, Vancuveria hexandra, Vinca major, V. minor, Viola labradorica, V. odorata, Waldsteinia ternata.	Berberis stenophyla 'Prostrata', B. thunbergii, Calluna vulgaris, Ceanothus thyrsiflorus 'Rupens', Convolvulus cneorum, Cornus canadensis, Cotoneaster horizontalis, Cytisus kewensis, various Erica, various Euonymus fortunei, various Hedera, Helianthumum hybrids, Hypericum moserianum, Juniperus chinensis 'Sargentii', J. saxatilis, J. horizontalis 'Bar Harbor', J. media 'Pfitzeriana', Lonicera pileata, Mahonia repens, Pachysandra terminalis, Picca abies 'Reflexa', Pernettya mucronata, Potentilla mandschurica, Prunus laurocerasus 'Otto Luyken', various rhododendrons, Romneya coulteri, various roses, Rubus calycinoides, R. tricolor, Salix lanata, Salvia officinalis, santolines, Senecio greyi, Spiraea japonica, Stephanandra incisa, Symphoricarpus, Tsuga canadensis 'Pendula'.

GREENHOUSES

Ever since exotic plants were first imported, every possible method has been tried to acclimatize them to more temperate regions. It soon became obvious that they would need to be sheltered, and this led to the appearance of the greenhouse. Later on, its use spread to the commercial growing of fruit and vegetables out of season.

Although the idea of the greenhouse is a very old one, dating back to the Middle Ages, it was not until the 19th century that it first started to appear. This was when all the criteria for building a successful greenhouse could be met: cheap, mass-produced glass, a high standard of construction – there are some very impressive 19th-century examples still in existence – power sources, low labour costs, and, not least, the availability of suitable plants. It is only relatively recently that so many plants have become available. However, wars, changing lifestyles, energy shortages, and rising prices have limited people's ambitions. Nevertheless, a greenhouse is the dream of almost every serious gardener, especially now, when modern techniques and materials have brought this dream within people's reach once again.

Types of greenhouse

Greenhouses are classified according to the temperature inside them. A warm greenhouse varies in temperature between 64° and 75°F (18° and 24°C) on average. It is rare nowadays because it is expensive to run. Some institutions, such as botanical gardens, and some orchid growers still have them. Interesting plants which need this kind of environment are fairly rare, and normally you can make do with a corner of a temperate or even a cold greenhouse with a mini-greenhouse inside it, during the winter.

Temperate greenhouses are much commoner. Here the minimum temperature is between 59° and 64°F (15° and 18°C). Most tropical plants adjust to this environment and, although growth may slow down in winter, they will generally grow well.

The cold greenhouse is the most widespread. Here the minimum winter temperature is between 41° and 59°F (5° and 15°C), and on a sunny day in the middle of winter artificial heating may well not be required because of the 'greenhouse effect'. A cold greenhouse fulfils the needs of most amateur gardeners, and can be used to overwinter plants such as orange trees, fuchsias, pelargoniums (geraniums) and cacti.

A huge variety of greenhouses is available. They can be divided into three main types: the tunnel, the span roof, and the lean-to.

The tunnel greenhouse is made up of large metal hoops with plastic film stretched over them, usually in a double layer for better insulation. They are unattractive, but are the cheapest type.

The span roof greenhouse looks like a miniature house; it may be covered with glass or rigid plastic. There are many standard models of this type.

The lean-to greenhouse is like a span roof type which has been cut in half lengthwise. It is

A greenhouse being used as a veranda. This forms a link between the house and the garden, and if it is turned into a conservatory means that there is an environment of greenery all year round.

A warm greenhouse creates the proper climate for rare plants from warmer climates, especially numerous beautiful exotics.

often sited against the wall of a house, and acts as an extension to the house.

The first two types are free-standing, so they lose more heat than a lean-to greenhouse, which is sheltered by the house. On the other hand, they get more sunlight, an important consideration because many greenhouse plants are more sensitive to a decrease in light than they are to a fall in temperature.

Materials

Greenhouses can be made from a variety of materials. The framework used to be made of iron, which took a great deal of looking after; they are now more usually made of galvanized tubing in the case of tunnel greenhouses, and wood or aluminium for span roof and lean-to greenhouses. Wood looks attractive, is rot-proof, and provides good insulation. But its weight and bulk are a drawback, and the uprights, joists and crossbeams can cut out a lot of light, especially in a glass-covered greenhouse. Aluminium is thinner and lighter, but it has a severe-look, is a poor insulator, and can create a lot of shade.

The transparent material used to cover the greenhouse – glass or plastic – is more important. Glass is expensive, heavy and fragile, but it is weather resistant, except in the case of hail, and is not damaged by the action of ultra-violet rays. It does not degenerate with age and allows the maximum heat to enter. This means that heat is retained in the greenhouse long after the sun has disappeared, or artificial heating has stopped.

Plastic is not permanent. Most plastics are broken down by the action of sunlight, so the covering must be renewed every three to ten years, depending on the exact type. Plastic becomes charged with static electricity so dust adheres to it. It allows less sunlight to pass through, and, because it melts, it can be dangerous in a fire. The advantages of plastic are that it is cheap, unbreakable, easily cut to size, strong but lightweight, and fairly good insulation, both by day and night, especially when used in a double layer.

Some plastics are now treated against static electricity and condensation. Their resistance to damage by ultra-violet rays is increasing, and some are even fireproof.

Because it is both strong and light, extensive sheets of plastic can be used without requiring support anywhere but round the edges. Glass may need up to ten times the number of wooden supports and frames, so plastic lets more light in. The initial building cost is much less, and, even if the plastic needs to be replaced after a few years, it is still more economical than glass.

Heat

A greenhouse retains a lot of the heat produced by the sun's rays. The rays pass through the walls of the greenhouse, but the energy, in the form of heat, remains trapped inside. This raises the temperature, so that it may be 86°F (30°C) or higher in the greenhouse, when it is only 50°F (10°C) outside. Better still, the temperature is likely to remain above freezing in the greenhouse, even when there is frost outside. But a greenhouse on its own is not enough in winter if temperatures are very low, the weather is cloudy, or during the night. Artificial heating is required.

There are many different methods of heating a greenhouse. It is not simply a matter of calorific value; keeping the temperature stable is essential, particularly with high temperatures. Solid fuel burning heaters are rarely used by amateur gardeners. Electric convectors are more flexible and easier to install, though it is wise to have this done by a specialist. He will know exactly what output is necessary, and the heater will conform to safety standards.

The greenhouse
Whatever it is used for, a greenhouse should be as attractive as it is functional. To serve its purpose, it needs easily controllable temperature and humidity.

A lean-to greenhouse can be heated by extending the domestic central heating system, but check that the boiler is able to support the extra load. A cold greenhouse heating system is the simplest type. An electric radiator with a thermostat is usually enough to prevent frost. Use a fan heater to keep the air moving and to distribute the heat evenly. Make sure that it is appropriate to the size of the greenhouse. Use gas-powered tubular fan heaters with electric ignition for larger greenhouses.

The greenhouse must also be properly insulated in winter. The best method is to fit transparent plastic film on the inside of the glass. The layer of air between this film and the glass creates a layer of insulation which can raise the temperature by 5°–11°F (3°–6°C). This gain in temperature more than outweighs the resulting slight loss of light.

Although providing adequate heat is the main concern in winter, too much heat can be a real problem in summer. The temperature inside a greenhouse can reach 113°F (45°C) or more, if it is not properly ventilated and shaded. Ventilation is also necessary to prevent the air becoming too humid or stagnant. If the greenhouse is well aired, it decreases the risk of disease.

Most greenhouses have louvres built into the walls for ventilation. Part of the roof may also open. There are also powered ventilators which are fitted at the top of a gable. These three methods are sometimes combined. They all include lower openings for the fresher, cooler air to come in, and higher ones for warm air to escape, to take advantage of convection. Some automatic ventilation systems are expensive and go wrong easily. Manual operation is more reliable. Whichever system you use, avoid draughts, as these harm the plants.

There are various methods of providing shade. One of the oldest ways is to brush whitewash over the outside of the greenhouse. This involves climbing on to the greenhouse, so mechanical shades are preferable. Blinds may be rigid, made of woven fabric or flexible. The first two are usually fitted outside the greenhouse, a short distance from the glass. Flexible blinds go inside, again away from the glass. This is to allow the air to circulate freely between the two layers.

Humidity and watering

The higher the temperature, the higher the humidity is likely to be, even when the greenhouse is well aired. When the temperature is low and the circulation of air poor, humidity is likely to be less of a problem. In summer, therefore, as well as watering the plants, water the ground and the shelves, to replace water lost in the air inside the greenhouse. In winter, on the other hand, only the plants need watering, and sparingly at that. Although most people remember to water well during summer, some forget to lower the humidity in winter. This encourages a number of diseases and plants die for no apparent reason. Plants tolerate a slight shortage of water better than they tolerate over-watering.

All-purpose greenhouse. This type of greenhouse is suitable for growing many s of plant, for taking cuttings and growing from seed, as well as for protecting delicate plants during winter.

PATIO AND BALCONY GARDENS

A town or city garden often develops into what amounts to an outdoor room, with a patio, balcony and window boxes. This environment is hostile to plants; not only is there stone or concrete instead of soil, but all the other climatic drawbacks are increased. The wind is stronger, the cold more intense, and the exposure to sunlight greater than any equivalent position in a garden.

Before creating a balcony garden, check with the local authority that putting plants on a balcony is permitted. The law sometimes imposes restrictions on height or on the distance between the edge of the balcony and the first plants. Some buildings are not allowed to have plants on them. Apart from common law, there are also laws on co-ownership of property which may prevent you creating a garden of this sort. You should check your lease for any relevant clauses. In any case, it is the owner who is liable if water, plants, or pots fall on to a public right of way. This is why you should never fix any object whatsoever to the outside of parapets and balustrades.

The area where plants will stand needs to be strong enough to support their weight. The architect's plans of recently constructed buildings may show the load bearing capacity. An architect may need to be consulted about older buildings.

The average load bearing capacity of a building is about 660 lb (300 kg) per 1.2 sq yd (m^2), which is actually quite low. For loggias, which are supported only around the edge, it is only 330 lb (150 g). A proper balcony, on the other hand, will bear nearly 880 lb (400 kg) per 1.2 sq yd (m^2). Modern window ledges have a capacity of 132 lb (60 kg) for every 39 in (1 m) of lateral thrust. It is very rare for a window-box to reach this kind of weight.

Waterproofing

A balcony, loggia, or patio will be normally waterproofed, but this is designed to deal only with short-term wetness, such as rain. Water may collect underneath tubs when they are watered, and can seep into cracks, causing structural damage. Overflowing or stagnant water must not be allowed to affect the surrounding area. This can be avoided by using an appropriate means of watering the plants and drip saucers and trays to collect surplus water.

Containers and their preparation

When creating a patio garden, the choice is between movable and fixed containers. Fixed containers may be made of concrete, brick, or wood, with a solid base. Insulating them is important, and there are two ways of doing it. You can paint on resin, tar, or some other liquid coating which hardens on contact with air. Make sure that it will not harm the plants once it has dried. Alternatively, you use durable plastic sheeting of the type used to line ponds. Cover the inside of the tub completely by one of these methods. This stops water seeping out and creating a nuisance, but still allows it to drain through a hole.

Paint the outside of a wooden tub with a protective coating to prevent it rotting. Use three coats of outdoor gloss varnish. Colours

A patio shaded by pruned planes and climbing plants with magnificent flowers.

Rhododendrons in earthenware pots. The ideal earthenware is thick, fine grained, and fired at a high temperature, which makes it resilient.

which reflect the light are likely to last longer. Linseed oil may also be used. It seeps into the wood and protects it, but still leaves it looking natural. Treat the tub with this every three to four years. Clean the surface well and simply apply another coat. Both paint and varnish need to be sanded down, and varnish, in particular, is very hard to remove when it is time to apply another layer. It also tends to blister in the sun. The outside of movable tubs should also be sealed.

Whether you choose permanent or movable containers, the selection is vast. Wood is fairly light, relatively inexpensive, easy to shape, pleasant to look at, and not harmed by frost. Its major disadvantages are that it reacts badly to heat and is easily damaged by damp, so that it may not last very long. This is why it is important to apply some sort of protective covering or preservative.

Plywood and other laminates are not suitable, as water makes them swell and come apart. The glue used in their manufacture is harmful to plants.

The traditional material for tubs and pots is terracotta. It is very attractive, especially once it has weathered. It is available either glazed or unglazed. The disadvantages of terracotta are that it is heavy, fragile, and has a low resistance to frost. But thick, fine-grained pottery, fired at a high temperature, is much stronger than other types. As most of the damp comes from the earth or compost in the pot, it is often a good idea to coat the inside with Norwegian tar or other waterproof glaze in the same way as wooden tubs. Then drill drainage holes in the sides with a slow-speed drill. Also, add some gritty materials to the compost (potting soil) to improve the drainage. Watertight pots can be painted on the outside.

Plastic has become immensely popular because it is light, weatherproof, smart but inconspicuous, and is often very cheap. Tubs with their own water reservoir are made from plastic. These need regular, but careful watering. Fill up the reserve supply before you go away from home. As soon as the cold weather starts, empty the reservoir by siphoning the water off, or it may freeze and split the pot.

These tubs do not break easily and water cannot seep through them. However, be careful when moving them around in winter, as low temperatures make them more fragile.

Expanded polystyrene (styrofoam) tubs are not particularly attractive, but they are cheap, very light and fairly durable. Most plants grow well in them. Polystyrene is an excellent insulator and protects the roots from both hot sun and cold weather.

Reconstituted stone is an agglomerate of powdered stone, moulded into various shapes. It is not a particularly attractive material and it is heavy. However, tubs made of this material can sometimes look very good. They are often porous, but frost-resistant.

All containers need drip trays beneath them. Alternatively, place them on blocks, bricks, or tiles to allow air to circulate and excess water to drain. These may also be necessary to keep containers horizontal if the balcony, patio or loggia is not level.

Choosing compost (potting soil)

Most compost (potting soil) is heavy; even a pot of a light growing medium can be a considerable weight by the time the plants have been added. Annuals do not weigh very much, but shrubs, of course, are a different matter. Bear in mind that, once plants have reached any size, they will tend to get caught by the wind.

Use the lightest compost (potting soil) available, and improve the drainage without impoverishing it. The mixture recommended is one part soilless potting compost, one part loam, and one part coarse peat.

You can add expanded polystyrene (styrofoam) balls, which are extremely lightweight. These allow the roots to become well established. However, they do not retain water or fertilizer, will eventually rot away and are difficult to work with. Static electricity makes them stick to the skin or to any plastic covering. They are conspicuous on the surface of the pot, and can make it look unattractive.

Expanded mica, or vermiculite, is fairly pleasant to handle, retains water and fertilizer, but permits the retention of air. However, it clings together, decomposes quickly, and sometimes clogs up the drainage holes of the pot.

Probably the best material to use is perlite. This is a kind of white, porous material, not unlike coarse sand. It is not so mobile in the mixture, and retains air, moisture, and nutrients. When mixed with compost, it is inconspicuous.

Do not buy these materials in bulk. Buy them by the bag, take it out on to the patio, and mix small quantities by placing equal amounts of the ingredients in a plastic bag and shaking it. It is best to work with manageable quantities each time.

If the containers are well drained and fairly small, put the mixture straight in on top of drainage crocks or a filter sheet. For the latter, you can use growing felt or polyester flannel, which is normally used to stretch wall fabrics.

The drainage mixture for the bottoms of large containers, including fixed tubs, is made up of fine gravel, expanded clay, or crocks. The latter should not be more than a fifth of the pot's depth. To prevent compost (potting soil) gradually sinking down into it and rendering it ineffective as a filter, place a sheet of growing felt or similar filtering material between. Put a layer of compost on top of the drainage, and then put in the rootball of the plant, which should just be flush with the edge of the pot. Fill the space around the rootball with compost, piling it up well. Finally, give the plant plenty of water.

The soil level should always be $\frac{3}{8}$–$\frac{3}{4}$ in (1–2 cm) below the rim of the pot so that water will not run off the top. If you are putting in a large number of plants, sowing annuals, or planting small plants around the base of larger ones in a large container, dig individual holes for them with a trowel.

Plants

There are no half measures on a patio; it is very warm when the sun is shining, and cold when it is not. It is possible to limit the effects of the sun with light, movable shades, but it is better to choose plants suitable for a patio.

Generally speaking, plants with silvery leaves, such as lavender, thick foliage, such as succulents, or leathery foliage, such as bay (laurel), are very resistant to the sun. Any Mediterranean plants thrive on a sunny patio, but be sure that they are not susceptible to frost,

1. Place a layer of growing medium on top of the drainage material.

2. Plant the soil ball of the plant so that it just touches the side of the pot.

3. Fill the gaps with the growing medium and press it down firmly.

4. Water copiously. The water should soak through the soil ball without forming pools.

or you will need to replant every year. Many annuals, such as geraniums and French marigolds to name just two of the wealth of colourful annuals available, are also suitable.

Shady positions are not necessarily cold. In a town or city, the houses opposite a shaded balcony may reflect light on to it. Cold is a killer because it comes irregularly. A plant exposed to freezing temperatures at night, followed by a rapid thaw when the sun comes up, is quite likely to die. In a shaded position, the plant still gets cold, but warms up slowly and there will be less risk of harm. Of course, this only applies to fairly hardy plants. It is possible to grow ferns and busy lizzies (impatiens), which are popular because of their wealth of flowers and bright colours. The begonia is the best tuberous plant for this position.

Do not plant tuberous or bulbous plants too close together in a tub, or they will not develop properly. They become undernourished if they have to compete with too many other plants, unless you take great care with feeding. When calculating the amount of space needed, reckon on annual plants trebling their height and diameter.

Plant bulbs and tubers at a distance equivalent to a third of their fully grown height. Bulbs and biennials, such as myosotis (forget-me-nots) and spring-flowering pansies, are planted in mid- to late autumn. Summer annuals are planted in late spring. Garden shops often suggest you plant them earlier, but a late spring frost can devastate an entire balcony.

It is possible to grow trees on a patio, providing the compost (soil) is properly prepared. The ideal ones are those with roots which are not too vigorous, but are densely fibrous so that they hold the tree in position. Avoid tap-rooted trees, they need to staked at first to stop them being knocked over by the wind, but they quickly settle. Young trees are cheaper, easier to get home, settle quickly, and offer little wind resistance. A large tree, unless it has a huge soil ball, needs to be guyed for at least three years before it can be left to its own devices.

A window box will not support anything

Rosemary and bay growing in pots on a rooftop. Aromatic plants with silvery foliage are very tolerant of strong sunlight.

A patio can be laid out to form a kind of garden in miniature, with climbing plants, shrubs and flowers.

bigger than a dwarf shrub, but it is possible to grow shrubs on a balcony. A loggia or patio allows even more scope.

The perfect shrub, with fine, evergreen leaves, sweet-smelling, multi-cropping flowers and stunning blossom, unfortunately does not exist. It is possible to approach this ideal; Mexican orange blossom, or *Choisya*, (in mild climates) has evergreen, scented foliage and two lots of scented flowers each year; bamboo, which is evergreen and often prettily coloured; viburnums, of which there are a number of suitable species, produce scented flowers in winter or spring, followed by attractive berries and fine autumnal foliage. Do not plant shrubs like syringas, for although they smell wonderful, they only last for two weeks in the year.

You can grow other plants, such as perennials, annuals or bulbs, as long as they are not too deep-rooted. Do not plant roses, which are prickly and can be an annoyance in a place where space is at a premium and people often rub against them.

Design

Designing a balcony or patio needs taste and respect for various rules. Do not block the passage. People need to move between the plants easily. Do not mix too many different shapes, or materials; otherwise the overall impression will be a muddle. The most harmonious design consists of two shapes and two materials, such as wood and soil. Resist the temptation to save space by putting window boxes along the balustrade. If you have children, these can be dangerous.

Planting out a balcony or patio allows a selection of all the best a garden has to offer. The small amount of space and the artificial environment mean that this mini-garden has to be designed in the same way as a bouquet of flowers, with results which are just as attractive. Vary shapes, sizes, and colours, following the same rules as for a herbaceous flower bed, though with fewer fine subtleties. Colours can go together and shapes be very prominent, as the rectangular structure is already imposed by the building and the containers. Some plants can be supple and drooping, but others should be regularly shaped, especially those forming the main framework of the design – most frequently the shrubs. In any case, no more than a third of the plants should be irregular.

You can place plants on the walls as well. Pots and window boxes can be attached to it. Make sure that they are securely fixed, so that the wind does not blow them down. Walls can also be used for climbing plants, using square or diamond-shaped trellises. Even if they are not covered with climbing plants, trellises can form an integral part of the design, giving the patio a more informal look. Some can also function as a

The Mexican orange, Choisya ternata, *has evergreen leaves and beautifully scented flowers, making it an ideal plant for patios and balconies in mild climates.*

An ideal patio
On a loggia-style patio, the weight should be evenly distributed round the edges, as close as possible to the load-bearing walls. This also makes it easier to get around the patio. The patio can then be turned into a kind of outdoor living room, an extention to the main body of the house.
This is a combination of a static and a mobile garden: very large troughs full of perennials and shrubs, smaller ones and pots being used to contain annual plants or bulbs. A pergola covered by a climbing plant can be an attractive way of cutting off a neighbouring building from view. The choice of plants on a patio should obviously be tailored to the amount of sunshine it receives.

kind of camouflage to make the area look bigger. Even a small one can transform a forbidding concrete wall into a landscape. A mirror placed against one wall makes the space look even larger. It must have plastic silvering, which is water-resistant. Do not place it in the sun because the reflection will be unbearable, fix it very firmly in a frame and do not put it directly against the wall. Surround its edge with tubular joints like those used in aquariums. The effect is improved if the mirror is surrounded by greenery, using a plant such as ampelopsis (porcelin vine).

Spread out plants in pots for a harmonious look, creating an interplay between the different sizes of pot and the sizes and shapes of the plants themselves. Try to cover as much of the surrounding urban landscape as possible, but avoid creating a complete curtain of greenery between the balcony and the outside. This would not be a garden, but a dark, gloomy grotto. Make sure at least two thirds of the balcony's width is open to the outside.

Block an undesirable view from a patio with a partly covered arbour sheltering an attractive feature, such as a fountain or a statue.

As they cannot seek water and nutrients from the depths of the soil, patio plants are at the mercy of their owners. They are also susceptible to many pests and diseases.

Enemies

The first enemy is air pollution. Its only favourable effect is to get rid of a few insect pests. More importantly, pollution stops some plants growing; sweet peas are a good example. It is harmful to plants with evergreen leaves because they become dirty and eventually suffocate. However, it is possible to counteract pollution to some extent. Sponge the largest leaves, and on rainy days, wash the others down with a hose. This helps overcome the problem of water flowing off and damaging neighbouring plants. Do this often and lightly rather than infrequently and generously. If dirt and dust are ignored for too long, they become caked on the leaves and hard to remove.

Although air pollution is harmful to many living creatures, some of the worst garden pests are unaffected by it. The commonest is greenfly, which are all the more prolific because some of their predators are killed off by urban pollution. Greenfly are so numerous in some areas that certain plants simply cannot be grown in cities. Many city gardeners have given up trying to grow nasturtiums, for example.

Systemic insecticides are the least hazardous. They are absorbed by the plants and carried in the sap. As soon as insects suck the sap they take in the poison. Some natural, plant-based insecticides need to be applied in the evening because they break down in sunlight. They are not effective for very long, and the treatment has to be repeated frequently. Apply insecticide on a calm, windless day and follow the manufacturer's instructions about wearing gloves and any other protection. If the plant is in a movable container, put it on the ground. This helps prevent the insecticide spreading. Leave the plant to dry before putting it back.

Oidium, or vine mildew, is a disease which appears in hot, dry weather in west or south-facing areas. If plants are affected by this once, they will almost certainly suffer from it the following year, so it is better to take preventative action in late spring. Some products are taken up by the sap of the plants. Not only do they make the leaves shiny, but also smell good.

Conditions on patios and balconies are extreme. When it is cold, it is really very cold, particularly as plants do not have the protection of a large body of soil as they would in an ordinary garden. Therefore, they heat up and cool down more quickly. However, the city is very slightly warmer in winter than open countryside because of the heat accumulated by buildings. As a result, less hardy plants have recently become popular in city gardens. Many plants previously regarded as being susceptible to frost are now being grown without any form of protection. But, in many parts of the world, past winters have shown that there are temperatures below which the protection provided by buildings in towns is illusory. It is therefore best to take precautions and to protect any plants that are not thoroughly hardy.

One way is to protect the roots with materials which allow air to circulate freely, but which are rotproof or which decompose very slowly. There are effective synthetic materials, but they are very ugly to look at; pulverised bark and leaf mould are better. Keep these materials in place by putting them between the stems or around the trunks of shrubs. Cover the roots of perennials after removing any dead leaves. A net stretched over the base of the plant stops the mulch blowing away.

Cold badly affects the roots of plants in small tubs and pots because they are surrounded by air. The containers can be covered with a layer of protection, but, apart from the huge amount of work this involves, the result is never going to look attractive. It is better to sacrifice a little room in the pot by insulating the inside before putting plants in. If it has straight edges, line it with sheets of expanded polystyrene ⅜ in (1 cm) thick. Cover the top edge of the polystyrene (styrofoam) with compost (soil) to conceal it. Use several layers of very thin polystyrene for round pots. Leave the drainage holes uncovered.

Although weeds may be a problem elsewhere in the garden, they are unlikely to be so here. The area to be weeded is small, and the light, friable compost in the tubs makes it easier to pull up any weeds. Wind-borne seeds are generally less numerous in urban areas.

Watering and feeding

Tubs with their own water reservoirs are easy. If you are not using these, water plants frequently, but sparingly. Water daily from mid-spring to late autumn, twice a day in summer, if necessary, once in the morning and once in the evening. In winter, water plants less often; be sure that the water will not freeze and that the plants have evergreen leaves. Plants on a patio exposed to the open air on a top floor balcony, benefit from the rain. In any other situation, even when it is pouring, the plants will receive little or no water.

A watering can is adequate for up to ten medium-sized pots or tubs. For larger numbers, use a hose pipe from the tap, or, better still, a drip system. This switches on automatically, and solves the problem of watering the garden when you are away.

The two main requirements for growing plants in containers are fertilizer and a good compost (potting soil). Plants growing in cramped conditions need careful attention in order to grow successfully. A reputable house plant fertilizer will do the job perfectly. Apply it often, but sparingly, as it is quickly washed away when the plant is watered.

The compost (soil) quickly becomes exhausted because of the demands the plants make upon it and because it is watered frequently. It soon becomes filled with roots, and once this has happened, those that have fulfilled

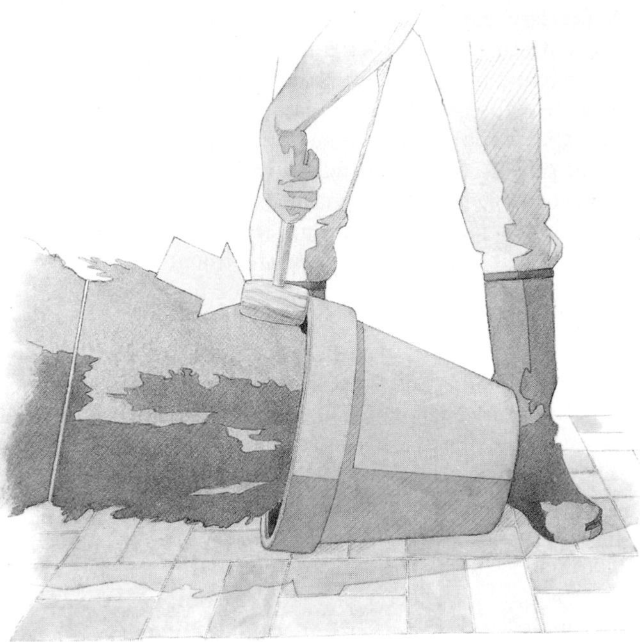

Removing a large plant from a pot
1. Tie the branches together.

2. Lie the plant on its side and turn the pot round, tapping the rim lightly with a mallet to loosen the earth.

their purpose begin to die. This means regular repotting; about once every three or four years. In the meantime, scrape off the surface layer of compost (soil) each spring, and replace it with fresh. Small plants in small containers do not need repotting. Change the compost (potting mix) in large window boxes in sections; replant only some plants as it becomes necessary.

Tie the branches of large plants to make them easier to handle. Lay the plant down on its side and turn the pot round, tapping the rim lightly with a mallet. The pot will come away easily if the soil has been allowed to dry out for two or three days. The process will be even easier if the pot has been lined with an insulating material against the cold, or the container is a wooden one which can be taken apart. Remove about a third of the compost (potting soil) from around the plant's roots. Replant and fill the space with fresh. The best time for repotting is at the very beginning of spring.

PATHS AND STEPS

It needs to be easy to move around the garden, but the paths and steps must be in harmony with the rest of the garden.

The function of the path

Paths can have quite separate, even totally different functions. They may, for example, form an important integral part of the overall design, with the garden actually structured and organized around them as a main feature. Alternatively, they may simply be a way of getting from one part of the garden to another; a purely functional role in which they have to be as discreet as possible, blending in and forming part of the background.

It is important to think about the purpose of a path before building it, and to make it harmonize with the style of the garden. For example, narrow winding paths would look ridiculous in a formal French-style garden; equally, magnificent straight avenues intersecting at right angles would be totally wrong in an informal cottage garden.

The formal garden

When you are planning a neat, formal garden, design the layout of the paths before the rest of the garden. Start with a main path, which should always begin from a man-made opening, such as the front door of the house, or the gate, or as a link between the two. If the garden faces a road, it probably needs a drive big enough for a car, and an area in front of the house for cars to turn round. If the garden is large enough, put another path across the drive at right angles, and about half the width of the drive. If it is larger still, these four rectangles or squares can be further divided into triangles with diagonal paths.

In a really huge garden, divide the whole of it into three large rectangles. Repeat the pattern of paths in each one: main drive, path at right angles to it, then diagonal path.

The purpose of the main path is not to reach a particular place, as it would be in an informal garden, but to justify its presence to the eye. It must, therefore, end with a focal point: a vista, a

Steps should fit in with the local style and the materials from which the house is made. This flight of steps is made of shale and gives a pleasant, structured feeling to the garden.

fountain, a statue, an arbour, or something similar.

The informal garden

The paths in an informal garden should not be designed until the rest of the garden has been planned. Paths here are not so much decorative, as functional, providing a way of wandering round the garden and discovering its beauties. They have the practical role of allowing you to reach all parts of the garden when working on it.

Unless you are an expert gardener, it is unwise to lay them out in the early days of the garden, at least in any permanent form. Lay them out based on your overall plan, but the final design will be refined by everyday use.

As far as possible, avoid straight lines, including zigzags, so that there are surprises round each bend. Do not stress the curves too much unless the garden is very large or on a slope. In a medium-sized, flat garden use slight curves, and put a clump of bushes, a raised flowerbed or some kind of obstacle on the inside of the curve so that there appears to be a reason for the curve. A winding path means the whole garden cannot be seen at a glance, and the feeling of discovering the unknown makes the garden seem bigger. Similarly the width of the path can vary as it goes along, the same way as a river bed. This also adds to the natural feel of the garden.

The only path that needs to be built straight away is the one leading to the garage, if there is one, for obvious reasons of convenience. Make it as curved as possible, so that the garage is not immediately visible from the beginning.

As well as the main path, build a series of small ones leading to all the parts of the garden in regular use. They should blend in with the scenery and not be prominent. The centre of the lawn is usually much trodden on and, if you always follow the same route, it soon shows signs of wear. To avoid this, lay a Japanese-style path of non-slip flagstones.

A hillside flight of steps decorated with flowers. This arrangement creates a link between two separate levels with the minimum of clutter. The steps themselves function as a mini-garden.

Steps

The rules for steps are the same as those for paths. The more natural the appearance of the garden and the farther from the house, the more informal and inconspicuous steps should be.

To stop a lawn wandering onto flowerbeds or paths, make a border out of bricks or railway sleepers (ties).

Use them only when necessary, and use as few as possible. As you get closer to the house or an artificial surface, you can make them more significant, using heavy, well-structured materials.

If you want to place formal steps in a fairly informal area, make them large, wide, and smart-looking. This turns them into separate features, a focal point in the same way as a fountain or a statue. There are some fine examples in overlapping half moon shapes or right-angled flights, which form proper terraces.

Materials

Grass is the commonest material for making paths. The simplest way to create paths in a wild meadow or an orchard is with a lawnmower. To stop the grass wandering on to flowerbeds, place a row of bricks, paving stones, or railway sleepers (ties) along the side. A grass path would be ideal were it not that it retains moisture and is fairly easily damaged. It also requires careful maintenance.

Sand and gravel can produce uneven results. They tend to disappear into the underlying soil unless there is a layer of firmly rolled clinker or crushed pebbles or special felt beneath. Peoples' feet sink into gravel, and sand makes a lot of dust when it is dry. However, these are good drainage materials, and gravel is useful for warning you of approaching visitors, as it is impossible to walk on it without making a noise. There is a sand made of fossil coral which settles down in time to give a hard but porous surface. This is undoubtedly the most suitable material when it can be obtained.

Asphalt is not very elegant, but it is useful for drives leading to garages.

Other materials are solid and so ideal by nature. Bricks, set on edge, can make very attractive designs, but this will get worn as the years go by. Paving stones often look very smart and do not wear out, but they are expensive and hard work to lay. They are in an infinite variety, but note that pure white always looks artificial.

Shingle is attractive, easy to make into a path, and hard wearing, but it is fairly uncomfortable to walk on. It is also difficult to push a wheelbarrow along a shingle path.

Flagstones look good, especially large ones in soft colours. However they are quite expensive to buy.

A grass path with mixed borders on either side. As well as being pleasant to walk on, a grass path brings out the attractions of the plants beside it. Its disadvantage is that it needs a lot of care.

Building a path
Place the paving stones on a bed of sand, with a layer of clinker or crushed pebbles underneath so that the path is perfectly drained.

Shale and slate often look rather drab and become very slippery as soon as it starts to rain. Granite, sandstone, basalt, and many light-coloured limestones, give a better effect.

Concrete gives good results. Effective but inconspicuous, it is particularly suitable for small strip paths leading to garages. There are even paving stones made of honeycombed concrete in which grass can be planted.

It is possible to use concrete and gravel flagstones. These have something of an artificial look to them, but are still an improvement on slates with clear joints, which have been popular in the past. Whichever materials you use, do not use more than two in combination.

Making a path

The top surface of a path should be slightly lower 2–7 in (5–19 cm) than the rest of the garden. The surface should be slightly cambered to allow water to drain off.

Start with a layer of drainage material, such as crushed pebbles or clinker. Place the material itself on top: this may be sand, gravel, or sand into which paving stones or bricks are embedded. Alternatively, cover the drainage material with a thin layer of concrete. Spread well compressed sand on this layer to hold the stones themselves, which are irregularly shaped and different thicknesses, and join them using mortar. Place flagstones and flat stones of even thickness on a bed of fine mortar. After two or three days this will bind them together. The mortar joining the stones is not essential; sand is equally suitable. Another possibility is to leave gaps in the underlying layer of concrete, so that plants can be put in between the flagstones giving the path a more natural look.

Building steps inside a building requires very stringent guidelines, which need to be followed to the letter. In a garden there are fewer restrictions. The steps should be quite long – between 16 and 24 in (40 and 60 cm) – or even $3\frac{1}{2}$ ft (1 m), and 6 to 8 in (15 to 20 cm) high. Ideally, the steps should all be the same size, for reasons of comfort. How wide they are will depend on the situation.

The nosing of the step must be very solid, which can be achieved by firmly fixing either concrete or wooden crosspieces into the earth. The riser of the step is smaller and does not support any great weight, so it can be less firmly built than a path is. If the steps are the only way of getting from one part of the garden to another build a smooth ramp up the side or the middle of the flight of steps so that a wheelbarrow or lawnmower will go up it.

Make sure water can drain away from the path easily and if there are any areas which are not draining properly, correct the problem at once.

In icy weather, a hard path will become slippery whatever material is used. If this happens, sprinkle sand on it; never use salt as this will burn the neighbouring plants irretrievably when the ice melts and will also attack certain types of support.

Weeds are more likely to be a problem on a sand or gravel path. There are a number of special weedkillers which will get rid of these; alternatively, use a hoe.

WALLS AND FENCES

The idea of enclosing a garden predominates in Europe. While walls, fences and other means of enclosure certainly exist throughout the world, they are less consistently part of every household's garden. There are many different ways of enclosing a garden, and while some are very attractive others are less so.

The wall

The wall is the most traditional way of surrounding a garden, though it is becoming less common nowadays because it is expensive. A wall is made of stone and can be either dry or pointed. Walls offer a certain amount of protection against unwanted visitors; they help to keep the noise down, reflect the light if they are pale in colour, and store up heat during the day to release it at night. On top of all this, they are very long lasting. On the other hand, they are very expensive to build, and being impermeable they encourage wind eddies and do not make good wind breaks.

Building a wall will require planning permission, and you should also ensure that it is built within the boundaries of your property, unless the neighbours would like to make it a party wall, in which case it can be built straddling the two properties.

Always use a material which will go well with the house or at least with the local style. Although a reasonably experienced do-it-yourself enthusiast may be able to build a small wall, it is usually wiser to leave the job to an expert. There are no aesthetic guidelines to follow concerning the height, thickness and shape of a wall; the only rule is that it should fit in with its environment.

A wall is an important feature of the garden's overall appearance. It can also be used as a base for plants. Here it brings out the attraction of rhodendron bushes which are more than a hundred years old.

A wooden fence around a country cottage. A fence should always fit in with the style of the garden and the house itself. Here, it is an attractive part of a small, informal garden and a house with a strong regional feel to it.

The fence

The most common form of enclosure for a garden is a fence. It is infinitely variable in appearance, durability and cost.

Fences do not accumulate heat during the day, they last a limited amount of time, whatever precautions are taken, and they are easy to climb over. On the other hand, they are very easy to build and some types make good wind breaks. Moreover, because they are permeable, they do not cause wind eddies.

There are a variety of materials that can be used for fencing. Your choice will depend on whether or not the fence is to be visible; if it is, you may prefer the fence to harmonize with the style of the house and the surrounding landscape, if it is not it could be purely utilitarian.

Wood is a good choice for a visible fence as it will fit in easily almost anywhere and there are a huge variety of forms it can take: chestnut palings, woven sheets, cross pieces, picket fences, smooth timber and so on. An alternative is extruded plastic, which is quite conspicuous but can sometimes go very well with the style of the house. The Japanese use bamboo to make fences which are works of art. Bamboo fences are available in the West, but they are very expensive.

If the fence needs to be as inconspicuous as possible, wire mesh, stretched on wire between stakes placed about 6 ft (2 m) apart will do the job quite satisfactorily. This type of fence is normally best suited to somewhere well away from the house, like a vegetable garden or orchard which is hidden from view by a hedge, for example. Metal, in the form of square rods or wrought iron, should be used with care, as it is not suited to every situation.

Combining a fence and a wall

One compromise between a fence and a wall is to use both in the form of a low, solid wall surmounted by a fence. With this method, the bases of plants will benefit from the heat stored up by the wall, while the durability of the wall will also extend the life of the fence. A further benefit is that the fence being light and relatively permeable will serve as a good wind break.

Gates and openings

Gates and door-shaped openings need to harmonize both with the materials used for the wall and those of the house, but must also be a suitable size for both the house and the garden. Huge ornamental gates are still all too often used as entrances to quite modest gardens and houses. Also, be very careful with gates which are sold ready made, with their supporting posts. The latter are often unattractive and very rarely suit the overall appearance of the house.

Lower gates present less risk of error because of their small size. Do not overload them with wrought iron embellishments which are supposed to be decorative. Gates with spikes can be very dangerous for children. The simplest way to discourage gate climbers is by putting stretched wire mesh inside.

If you do not enclose your garden, you may be liable in case of accidents occurring on your land, even if the people concerned are trespassing. On the other hand on some newly built estates, for example, walls or fences are not allowed as the gardens are designed to be open-plan.

SPECIAL CORNERS

A garden should have at least one, but ideally a selection of special corners, which welcome quiet reflection. They also make walking through the garden a pleasure, and sometimes allow the visitor an opportunity to enjoy an attractive view.

The patio

The patio is perhaps the most popular of these special corners. Neither house nor garden, it is halfway between the two. The material that it is made of should either match that of the house, or be totally inconspicuous. Never make a patio the centrepiece of the garden. Choose somewhere where there is plenty of light for a patio. You can always shade it during the summer, and the sunny position will be appreciated when the weather is cool.

Do not make the patio a separate feature of the garden – it should be part house and part garden. Although its relationship with the house is an inherent one, because they are both made from artificial materials, the relationship between patio and garden can be a difficult one to forge.

On a traditional patio, bring in some plant life using troughs or large pots filled with plants and flowers and arranged in a regular design. For a less formal approach, use containers of widely different shapes and sizes and scatter them around irregularly. Put some ground-covering plants in between the paving stones, for an even more informal and natural style. For a

A paved terrace between a house and its garden. The link between the world of nature outside the house, and the artificial environment inside it, is created using pots of shrubs and flowering plants. The large curtains of greenery around the edges give it an intimate feeling.

modern look, simply place raised plant troughs around the edge of the patio.

Bear in mind that a patio should not be a spectacular display. The main aim is to create a tranquil place which is reasonably sheltered from the gaze of other people. If it is at the front of the house, or on a raised hillside, and there is no privacy, screen it with a line of shrubs along the edge. Plant raised beds of shrubs in alternate rows so that anyone on the patio will get the impression of informality and does not feel completely separated from the rest of the garden.

The pergola

A pergola, as an extension of the house, is a collection of horizontal crosspieces on uprights usually made either of wood or in the same material as the house. If located on the patio, it should not cover more than half its area. This will allow plenty of light but means that shade is also possible when required.

A pergola is also used to cover a path or create a separate area of shade from the house. If necessary, replace it with an arbour, the framework of which gives scope for a greater variety of shapes.

Arbours have another use: they create a destination for anyone walking through the garden to aim for. Whether the sense of distance is real or illusory, it still has the same effect. Arbours also provide a focal point for the end of a path or for the crossing of two paths. Or, they can be decorated with an object, such as a bench, a fountain, a table or a statue.

A quiet, secluded corner at the bottom of a garden. The bench is hidden in a screen of macleaya (plume poppy), sage and wild roses. Asparagus adds its decorative foliage to this delightful jumble of plants.

Benches

A bench can in itself create a special corner and should not be placed in the garden at random. There should always be some kind of justification for a bench's presence: it might be a position close to the house, on the patio, or in a corner of the garden where people most often go. Place a bench at a viewpoint, in the shade of a tree, or alternatively in a hidden corner where it can serve as a retreat.

Banquettes

An amusing alternative to a bank is the less often used garden banquette from the Middle Ages and Renaissance. To make one, place stakes along the line of the banquette, sticking out 16 to 20 in (40 to 50 cm), then weave flexible branches in between them, packed tightly together. Fill it in with earth and then sow it with grass and tiny flowers. The brushwood can be replaced with stone or other forms of wood if required.

Wells

Water is an essential feature of any garden. It is at its best in ponds and wells. The undeniable beauty of some wells means that many people want one, but they are major items in a garden so choose carefully. Some gardeners are fired with enthusiasm and bring in old wells from outside; these are often very attractive, although sometimes do not fit in with their new environment.

Whether it is built from scratch, restored or imported, a well needs to be in harmony with the local style. If it is common in your area to use rough-cast walls using small frost-riven limestone quarry-stones, for example, then do the same for your well.

Part of the charm of this old fountain comes from the fact that it is covered in moss and ferns.

Where the well goes will depend on where there is available water. Wherever it is placed, make it stand out a little by clearing a small space around it. If done carefully, the rim, or the centre if it is a covered well, can be decorated with masses of flowers.

Fountains

Fountains have appeared in gardens for almost as long as wells, and they pose the same aesthetic problems of style and good positioning. A fountain should neither be hidden away so that it never gets properly viewed, nor placed where it competes with another prominent feature of the garden, such as a flower bed. It will gain by being made to stand out against a plain background. This could be the crossing of two paths, a wall, or an arbour of greenery.

If the garden does not have a spring in it, the fountain will need to use water from the public supply. As this can be expensive, it may be better to use a pump which recycles the water. Top up the water which has evaporated regularly. The problem with this type of pump is that it is somewhat susceptible to clogging up with dust and algae. So use an effective filtering system which comes with a supplier's guarantee. Algae can be eliminated using products made specifically for this purpose, but these will also prevent fish and plants living in the fountain.

Swimming pools

This recreational area of the garden rarely fits in with its surroundings. An artificial swimming pool should be as discreet as possible, and tastefully disguised. Place low bushes, hedges or perennials round the edge of it leaving a reasonable gap to allow people to get round the pool. Never plant tall trees, even evergreens, near a pool, as they will not only keep the sun off it but their leaves or needles will also fall into the water. Although it may be tempting to plant grass around the pool, this is not a good idea as wet grass is very slippery – added to which, anyone diving into the pool will take some of the grass with them.

Collapsible swimming pools are a great deal cheaper and the wide variety of sizes they come in means there is one for almost any garden. Place them on a perfectly flat surface, but not on grass as this will discolour in a few days. Set aside an area of bare earth, paving stones or gravel, and surround it with bushes.

GARDENING TECHNIQUES

GROWING CONDITIONS

Creating a garden involves combining, in a harmonious mixture, plants suited to the climate and soil of your garden. Unfortunately, a single garden is rarely ideal in all respects. It is usually possible to improve the soil, but less easy to change the climate. In this instance, the option is to create a micro-climate by putting up windbreaks and protecting plants against frost.

Gardeners are never satisfied with the growing conditions in their gardens; this is hardly surprising, given that they are invariably trying to grow a range of plants whose needs are often very different. However, there is not the slightest reason why you should not grow, say, cabbages, which love alkaline soil, alongside rhododendrons, which will grow only in acid conditions; all you need is a little knowledge. The logical approach is to grow only plants suited to a particular area or even a particular garden, but that is asking a lot of gardeners. Therefore, the following chapter includes all aspects of improving growing conditions in gardens, so that plants can flourish.

THE NATURE OF THE SOIL

Soil is made up of complex organic and inorganic materials in a delicate balance. A 'good soil' is one that is capable of growing a wide range of plants.

The topmost layer of the soil, or topsoil, is the most important in gardening. Its fertility derives from a wealth of living micro-organisms, which need air, food and a favourable environment to grow. The gardener's first job is to keep the topsoil fertile by maintaining its organic matter and plant food content. It quickly deteriorates if neglected.

There are many kinds of soil, depending on local geology. Alluvial soils, often the most fertile, tend to be found in valleys and the flood plains of rivers. Deep, friable and recently deposited alluvial soils are often quite fine, and are found in areas where streams and rivers abound. Older, sedimentary soils appear when the waters covering submerged areas recede. These are normally of sandstone, chalk or limestone. The oldest soils are frequently the poorest: mostly volcanic in origin, they are the remains of primeval rocks. They are found in many upland regions. They are often characterized by a dry and pebbly, with a thin layer of topsoil.

A soil for every garden

Although soil type is not determined by geology alone, it is certainly an important factor. The earth's crust has folded, slipped, collapsed, and moved to mix soils, so the more rivers, mountains or faults an area has, the greater the chance of finding different soils. Centuries of farming have also changed some soils dramatically: constantly tended and improved, their fertility has increased. Other soils have been left idle and wild plants colonized them. The topsoil may have hardened and the microbial population dwindled. Nonetheless, they still promise well for future cultivation if trouble is taken to work and improve them. Organic soils of woods or forests are rich in humus, accumulated from innumerable seasons of decomposing leaves. Such soils are often acid and, although they seem rich, often need fertilizers, as their nutrients are so easily leached out by water.

The naturally occurring vegetation often gives a rough idea of the soil type. Foxgloves, heather, bracken and other heaths like blueberries indicate an acid, often poor soil; poppies, clover and thistles often indicate a generally fertile alkaline soil; convolvulus (bindweed), dandelions, couch grass (quack grass), dog roses and hawthorn point to heavy but rich soil. Lastly, bulrushes, sedges and reeds are often signs of moist, peaty soils. The density of the wild plants also indicates the fertility of the soil; sparsely-covered ground usually means that the soil is poor and that nutrients are quickly washed out or that growing conditions are difficult in some other way.

pH

Like all substances, soil has an overall chemical reaction, which may be acid, alkaline or neutral. This reaction is measured by its pH on a scale from 0 to 14; pH7 is neutral. In practice, soils are termed neutral if they have a pH of 6–7 and the widest choice of plants succeed on them.

Acid soil generally has a pH between 4.5 and 6. The lower the pH the more acid it is and the more difficult it is for plants to grow because the acid reaction slows bacterial activity and makes it difficult for organic matter to decompose. Acid soils are improved by liming with ground chalk or limestone.

Alkaline soils are usually found over chalk or limestone. Chalky soils normally have a pH between 7.6 and 8.5. If the pH rises higher than this, only the most lime-loving plants can survive, but most garden plants tolerate up to pH8.

The pH is measured by chemical reagents which colour soil samples and different-sized kits are available from garden centres. Electronic measuring devices have recently appeared on the market. These measure pH instantly: all you have to do is put the electrodes in the soil.

As a rule, the best soil for a garden is a slightly acid one, especially for growing ornamentals. In the kitchen garden, a slightly alkaline soil is better, except for growing potatoes and asparagus which like acid soil. Do not confuse 'best' with 'essential'; perfectly good results may be gained from the vast majority of soils.

Analyzing the soil

It is worth analyzing the soil before planting a garden. While soil type should not put you off buying a house, as it is always possible to improve soil, you should have a fair idea of its

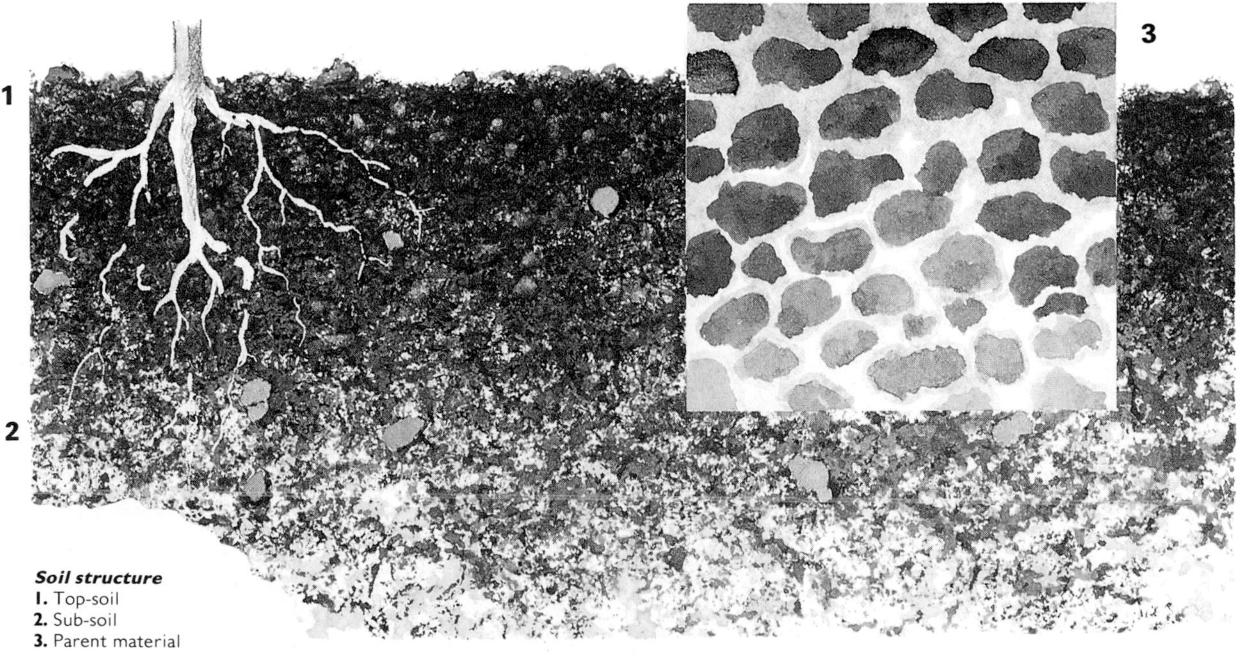

Soil structure
1. Top-soil
2. Sub-soil
3. Parent material

Mountain jasmine grows naturally in sandy soil, which is easy to work but inherently unstable as it does not hold nutrients.

composition before buying plants. A complete in-depth soil analysis by a laboratory is expensive. An adequate and quick analysis can be done with a do-it-yourself soil-test kit. This consists of chemicals which react and colour samples of soil according to their acidity or alkalinity. The results are then compared with a colour chart provided in the kit. As well as kits for testing the acidity/alkalinity of soil, there are others for testing the soil's nutrient content.

Collect a number of cup-sized soil samples from all over the area to be tested; take samples 10–15 ft (3–4.5 m) apart and from a depth of about 9 in (23 cm). Place all the samples in the same bucket, stir and test two samples. The average of the two readings provides a good working basis for the whole plot.

When using a soil-testing kit, leave the soil in a dry place for a few hours to remove its natural moisture; an accurate chemical reading can only be taken from dry soil.

Soil structure

A soil may be heavy, light, friable, soft, compact, sticky, open, moist, cold, hard or pebbly, these descriptions relating to both the texture and the structure.

The texture depends on the size of the individual mineral particles; a clay soil, for example, has a fine texture, while a gravelly soil has a coarse or open texture.

The structure of a soil is the way in which the soil particles are held together. Thus, pure clay and sand have a poor structure, while a well-cultivated loam usually has a good structure. Organic matter is largely responsible for creating a good structure, so it is important to maintain the level of organic matter in a soil. It helps to bind sandy soils together and opens up clay soils. A high proportion of clay particles results in compact heavy soil.

Soil contains a considerable amount of air: the fewer the clay particles, the more air. Aerating the soil improves its fertility and drainage, so it is important to keep an open structure by regular cultivation. Soil also contains tiny capillary channels formed by the empty spaces between the particles. These act as channels for air, water and roots. They have a vital role to play, especially in a drought, as it is through them that water rises.

Heavy soils are apt to cake and crack in dry summer weather but regain their muddy consistency with the first rains.

Clay soil in which lavender grows here holds nutrients well. It is rich but heavy and sticky and often difficult to work.

Rain or artificial watering soaks into the soil through capillary channels. Some of it is absorbed by the roots of plants and some is held by the soil to a greater or lesser extent depending on structure and composition. Any water which is not retained continues downwards, taking the dissolved minerals beyond the reach of the plants. This is why very porous soils are often starved, as the slightest rain leaches out nutrients.

Soil constituents

Soil has four main physical constituents: sand, limestone, clay and humus. The proportions in which they occur determine a soil's texture and structure: sandy, chalky (or alkaline), clay and humus-rich (or peaty).

Sand, being formed of grains of varying sizes, does not bind together well, and gives the soil a light texture. Limestone or chalk is present in the form of fine particles of calcium carbonate. These are quick to join together when wet, but crack when dry or frozen. Limestone – or chalk-based soil has a pale, whitish appearance. Clay often occurs with iron salts, giving the soil a reddish colour. This colloidal element forms a sort of impermeable dough which hardens and then cracks as it dries. Clay tends to make soils airless by clogging up the capillary channels, but it can be improved by adding bulky organic matter or a lime or gypsum dressing. Humus, produced from decaying organic matter, is a dark brown or black, spongy substance which holds water well. Rich in bacteria it is the 'living' constituent and major controlling factor of any soil.

Physical characteristics of soil

The physical characteristics of soil comprise texture, density, stability, durability, ability to warm up, permeability and aeration.

The coarser a soil's texture, the more permeable, aerated and easier it is to cultivate, while very fine constituents tend to amalgamate to form a sticky, moist, impermeable soil. An open texture is equally important for plants in pots, as it prevents the roots from being asphyxiated. The presence of grit in the soil helps ensure aeration. If a soil's individual components collect together into 'crumbs' and 'blocks', the soil is said to 'flocculate'. If it is regularly worked, it becomes less dense and the amount of air it holds increases. In general terms, a fine textured soil is called 'heavy' and a coarse or textured one is referred to as 'light'.

Stability concerns the natural movements to which soil is subject. Sandy soils are the least stable. Their constituents can be carried away by wind or water, and they are quick to erode. Their stability can be greatly improved by adding humus, which adheres well to sand particles, binding them together.

This woodland soil, where ferns prosper, is rich in humus.

The stability of some soils can vary with the seasons. For instance, the alkaline soils crack in hard frost, and plants are lifted. Both alkaline and clay soils shrink in summer, in heat and drought, causing cracks which quickly dry roots out. Soils low in humus are the least stable.

Resistance can be judged by the difficulty involved in digging and otherwise cultivating a soil. The more compact, moist and sticky a soil, the more resistance increases. Organic materials added to a soil lighten it and improve its balance. Clay soils are less prone to cracking in summer if well supplied with humus, which forms a moisture reservoir. If soil sticks to tools, this increases resistance, too.

The temperature of a soil governs how early or late plants develop. Sandy soils and those rich in humus tend to be the warmest. Cold soils are moister, but have the advantage of not drying out in summer. Darker soils absorb heat, so spreading compost over the soil in later winter encourages plants to begin growing.

Soils in windy areas tend to be cold because water evaporates quickly. Very light and open soils, such as sandy soils, are especially susceptible to frost. Heavy soils, on the other hand, particularly clay, can suppress growth in rainy areas, although in hot areas they act as useful moisture reservoirs. The coarser the soil particles, the more permeable the soil. Soil fertility depends partly on its ability to retain water: to be productive, soil needs to retain about 25 per cent of its own volume of water.

Aeration of the soil depends on its texture and structure. The more granular the soil, the better aerated it is and the more easily water can penetrate.

The importance of the subsoil

Subsoil affects the structure and behaviour of the topsoil, especially if the latter is thin: the thicker the topsoil, the less important the subsoil. If a light, unstable topsoil overlies a similar subsoil, the latter accentuates the soil's coldness and its close, airless nature. A sandy topsoil over a heavy subsoil can work well, as the latter acts as a natural reservoir. The same goes for a clay topsoil over a sandy subsoil, which helps correct the clay's poor drainage.

Different types of soil

Each soil has its own characteristics and needs individual treatment.

Silica soils

These soils are rich in sand, containing between 70 and 80 per cent. Light, yellow, friable and supple, silica soils should not be confused with fine, alkaline sands which lack the porosity of silica sand. Loose structure makes sandy soils unstable and vulnerable to wind and rain.

Silica soils are generally acid and easily worked. The fertility is usually good if they contain enough organic matter. They warm up rapidly, and are well aerated, easy to improve and do not become sticky, even when it rains. The natural vegetation on such soils includes chestnut, birch, pine, fern, heather, blueberries, rhododendrons, broom, sorrel, small reeds, foxgloves and gorse. Very porous silica soils, however, cannot hold on to nutrients and so they tend to be starved. They dry up in the sun and are often eroded by heavy rain, particularly in sloping gardens.

The best way to improve them is by adding organic matter, such as well-rotted garden compost or farmyard manure. This acts as a sponge and helps the soil retain moisture and nutrients. Top-dress or dig in at a rate of 10–15 lb per sq yd (5–8 kg per m^2) or apply as a 3–4 in (8–10 cm) thick mulch. Alternatively, apply proprietary composite manures at the recommended rate.

Do not work sandy soils too deeply and dig them over just before planting. Use little base fertilizer, but add quick-acting fertilizers regularly, and organic matter every year.

Trees which like fairly dry sandy soil include acacia, ash, birch, catalpa, cedar, chestnut, cypress, ginkgo, gleditsia (honey locust), Judas tree (redbud), laburnum (golden-chain), larch, magnolia, some maples, pine, ornamental plum, sequoia, larch and walnut. Shrubs include barberries, broom, ceanothus, elaeagnus (Autumn olive), flowering currant, forsythia, gorse, halesia, hamamelis (witch-hazel), hazel, heather, hibiscus, holly, kerria, lilac, laurel, lavender, osmanthus, privet, rosemary, hypericum (St John's wort), santolina (lavender cotton), spiraea, viburnum and yucca. Climbing plants which prefer light soil include aristolochia (Dutchman's pipe), fremontodendron and ivy. Suitable hardy perennials and half hardy annuals include achillea (Yarrow), alyssum, anthemis (golden marguerite), aubretia, chamomile, Cineraria maritima (dusty miller), cistus, helianthemum, iris, lavatera, mallow, marigolds, poppies, some saxifrages, sedum, speedwell, thyme and valerian.

Alkaline soils

These can be recognized by their whitish colour and very fine texture and they contain at least 15 per cent calcium carbonate. Chalky, or limestone, soils are often pebbly. Very sticky in winter, they are quick to dry out in summer and cracks appear on the surface. However, a chalky subsoil acts as a good water reservoir.

Their natural vegetation is made up of 'chalk- or lime-loving' species, such as buttercups, clover, cornflowers, fumitory, wild mustard, poppies and thistles. Woody subjects which favour chalky soils include beech, blackthorn, hazel, juniper and mountain ash. If the lime content is less than 30 per cent, these soils are rich in wild flowers.

Warm chalk or limestone soils are pleasant to work in dry weather, and are quick to recover after drought, with their characteristics resembling those of silica soils. There are also alkaline sands. Unfortunately, alkaline soils quickly become sticky and are somewhat unstable, especially after frost.

The best way of improving alkaline soils is by adding acidic organic matter, particularly sphagnum moss peats. Rotted cow manure is also suitable. Add organic matter regularly, as it quickly decomposes in alkaline soil. Growing green manure crops, such as white clover or mustard, helps build up the soil's moisture-holding ability.

In dry areas, autumn planting is often better than spring so that the plants are well established before the risk of summer droughts.

Many plants like alkaline soil: in the kitchen garden, cabbages do particularly well, as do

Gorse and plants in the heath family are naturally suited to poor, acid, sandy soils.

Poppies are particularly fond of alkaline soils. These are often fertile and covered in an abundance of wild flora.

other plants of the Cruciferae family. Trees which grow well in alkaline soils include alder, amelanchier (shad), ash, catalpa, cherry (prunus), firs, hawthorn, horse chestnut, hazel, holly, Judas tree or redbud (cercis), lime (linden), some maples, pine, plum, poplar, sequoia and willow; and among shrubs, barberries, box, caragana (pea shrub), cistus, colutea (bladder senna), cornelian cherry (cornus mas), cotoneaster, flowering currant, garrya, kerria, lavender, privet, lilac (syringa), Spanish broom, spindle tree (Euonymus), spiraea and sumach (rhus). Climbing plants such as clematis, honeysuckle, ivy, jasmine and virginia creeper (parthenocissus) are suitable as are a large number of hardy perennials, including aconitum (monk's hood), golden alyssum, anchusa, aquilegia (columbine), anemone, arabis (rock cress), aubretia, campanula (Carpathian bellflower), centaurea (cornflower), day lily (hemerocallis), doronicum (leopardsbane), erigeron (sea-holly), gaillardia, geraniums (hardy), gypsophila (baby's breath), helianthemum, hollyhock, iberis (candytuft), iris, platycodon (balloon flower), poppy, scabious, valerian and veronica.

There are also several groups of plants which do not like lime in the soil and consequently develop chlorosis.

Clay soils

These reddish brown earths consist of at least 30 per cent clay in the form of very fine colloidal clay particles. If there is a shortage of organic matter, the particles stick together and form sticky clods. These soils are nearly always rich in plant foods. Their natural vegetation is generally fairly rich, even dense.

The great advantage of clay soils is that they retain nutrients and moisture. They can be deeply worked and offer excellent anchorage for most plants, especially trees and shrubs. They are fairly stable and support demanding species. When saturated with moisture, however, they are slow to warm up, so plants start to grow later in spring. In winter, if the drainage is poor, the roots tend to suffocate, and the soil is virtually impossible to work. In summer, when it dries out, clay is often hard to wet as the water forms streams on the surface and does not penetrate.

These soils benefit from the addition of large quantities of organic matter. Top-dress or dig in well-rotted garden compost at the rate of 10–15 lb per sq yd (5–8 kg per m^2) or apply as a 3-4 in (8–10 cm) thick mulch, ideally added when you turn the soil over in the autumn. Growing green manure plants also helps improve clay soils, as does liming. Lime breaks up the clay and causes the particles to flocculate. Liming is best done in spring, using two handfuls of ground chalk or limestone per square yard (m^2). Repeat every three years to be effective without damaging plants. In soils which are far too heavy, a herringbone pattern of plastic drains must be laid. Plastic pipes or, less commonly nowadays, clay ones are laid in trenches 1½ ft (45 cm) deep on a bed of gravel and then covered with more gravel to stop them getting choked with soil.

Work clay soils deeply to make them as open as possible. Some experts advise adding sand to lighten them, in which case you can use fairly coarse silica (horticultural) sand, together with organic matter, such as well-rotted compost or manure. However, enormous quantities are needed to be effective. Dig clay soils in autumn, so the winter frosts break up the clods to a good depth. There are also effective specialist products for improving clay soils. They are stable and often long-acting, but are not a substitute for bulky organic matter.

Many plants like clay soils because they are so rich. Only fragile-rooted species find it hard to live on such heavy soil. Trees which like clay soils include alder, ash, beech, cytisus (broom), elm, gleditsia (honey locust), hawthorn, hazel, hickory, holly, hornbeam, Judas tree (redbud), lime (linden), locust tree, oak, plane (sycamore in USA), plum (prunus), poplar, willow and many conifers. Shrubs such as amelanchier (shad), aucuba, barberry, buddleja (butterfly bush), box, caragana (pea shrub), colutea (bladder senna), cotoneaster, cytisus (broom), deutzia, elder (sambucus), flowering currant, halesia (silver-bell), kerria, lilac, privet, mock orange, osmanthus, roses, spindle tree (euonymus), spiraea, viburnum, weigela and witch-hazel also do well here. Climbing plants, such as clematis, jasmine, honeysuckle, climbing roses and virginia creeper; hardy perennials such as anemones, astilbe, bee balm, bergenia, campanula, centaurea (cornflower), cimicifuga, erigeron (sea-holly), filipendula (meadowsweet), golden rod, heleniums, hostas, hypericum (St John's wort), *Iris kaemferi*, ligularia, lobelia, michaelmas daisies, mimulus, marigold, primula, rodgersia, peonies, polemonium (Jacob's ladder), saxifrage, tradescantia (spiderwort), trollius (globe flower) also do well in this kind of soil.

Moist soils

These forest, undergrowth and fen soils contain at least 10 per cent humus, and are dark brown, almost black. They have a spongy consistency, and are usually moist and acid.

Their natural vegetation includes buttercups, broom, colchicum, carex, ferns, fungi, marsh marigold, mosses, poplars, rushes, reeds, willows and wood anemones.

The dandelion is a common plant on clay soils.

Light, easy to work, rich in nitrogen and bacteria, these soils are fertile but unstable. They are quick to dry out in summer and difficult to rewet. Being spongy, they tend to retain water in winter which retards plant growth in spring.

The main way of improving an acidic humus-rich soil is by liming in autumn, giving two handfuls of ground chalk or limestone per square yard (m^2). If a humus-rich soil lies over impermeable subsoil, land drains may be needed to restore it to health. Watering with liquid manure helps stimulate microbial activity and adding a clay/lime mixture (marl) also helps the overall balance. Spread an even layer of 6 in (15 cm) and work it into the humus. Dig over humus-rich soils shallowly in spring.

The best plants to grow in humus-rich soil are acid-lovers and those that like shade or semi-shade. Trees include alder, birch, catalpa, laburnum (golden-chain), poplar, liquidambar (sweet gum), magnolia, red oak, rhododendrons, nyssa (tupelo) and willow. Shrubs include pieris (andromeda), arbutus, arctostaphylos (bearberry), azalea, bilberry (blueberry), calycanthus (sweet shrub), cassiope, ceanothus, clethra (summersweet), daphne, dogwoods, fothergilla, enkianthus, gaultheria (wintergreen), gorse, halesia (silver-bell), hydrangea, kalmia (mountain laurel), leucothoe, mock orange (philadelphus), pernettya, spiraea, viburnum and winter sweet (chimonanthus). Conifers which are at home in humus-rich soil include *Abies balsamea* (balsam fir), *Juniperus communis*

Disease-free fertile soil will ensure success with nearly all types of plants and create a well balanced garden.

(common juniper), *Juniperus virginiana* (red cedar), *Pinus rigida* (pitch pine), *Pinus contorta Pinus strobus* (white pine), and *Thuja* (arborvitae). Among suitable climbing plants are ivies, stephanandra and wistaria. Suitable herbaceous plants include a stilbe, astrantia, *Iris pseudacorus*, lysimachia, lythrum (loosestrife), Japanese anemones, aquilegias (columbines), arabis (rock cress), aruncus, bergenias, doronicum (leopardsbane), epimedium, hardy geraniums, hellebores, hostas, lamium, ligularia, lily of the valley, lobelia, marsh marigold, peltiphyllum, *Polygonum affine*, pulmonaria (lungwort), rodgersia, sidalcea, tiarella (foam flower), trollius (globe flower) and waldsteinia (barren strawberry).

Open soils

For gardening, open-textured medium loams which contain 50–70 per cent sand, 20–30 per cent clay, 5–10 per cent lime and 5–10 per cent humus are best. They are balanced, homogeneous, rich and fertile and almost anything grows on them. They are difficult to achieve and need regular fertilizing and cultivation to keep them in good condition. Open soils are not so easy to cultivate as sandy or very humus-rich soils and they are unsuitable for plants, such as heathland plants, which need poor growing conditions.

Open soils must be regularly maintained with well-rotted manure or compost at least every two years at 13–17 lb per sq yd (6–8 kg per m^2) preferably when digging in autumn. Organic manures sold in garden centres are also suitable. It is important to avoid making open soils too acid by adding organic matter (unless this is done deliberately to grow heathers and related plants). It is also worth checking that additives are neutral with pH of 7.

Soil chemistry

The bulky organic matter of a soil is broken down by micro-organisms to produce nutrients, in the form of mineral salts, for plants. The fertility of the soil depends on its reserves of such available nutrients. All the nutrients plants absorb are mineral in origin.

There are 12 essential elements. Those required in the largest amounts are nitrogen (N), phosphorus (P) and potassium (K), together with Calcium (Ca), magnesium (Mg) and sulphur (S). The remaining six are called trace elements and are required in minute quantities: iron, manganese, copper, zinc, boron and molybdenum.

Nitrogen

This element is responsible for leafy growth,

Soil reaction is measured on a graduated scale from 0 to 14. The ideal soil has a pH of 6.5 to 7.5.

Like all leafy vegetables, cabbages need plenty of nitrogen.

and is designated by the chemical symbol N. It is always the first element listed in the various chemical mixtures used in the garden, particularly on packets of fertilizer.

Nitrogen is present in a number of different forms in the soil, but the nitrogen in nitrates is the form which plants find easiest to absorb. Nitrates are produced when ammonia is converted by specialized bacteria known as 'nitrogen fixers'. The nitric acid formed quickly combines with bases in the soil to produce various nitrates: calcium nitrate, potassium nitrate and magnesium nitrate.

Nitrogen stimulates growth, which is why some nitrate-based products are marketed as 'lightning' fertilizers. It promotes the growth of stems and leaves, and is vital for building proteins by means of photosynthesis. It dramatically increases yields of leafy vegetables, such as lettuces and cabbages, and gives leaves a bright green colour. It also promotes the growth of grasses so that lawns become thicker.

However, nitrates are quick to dissolve and easily leached out of the soil. If used to excess, nitrates can scorch plants and promote soft and sappy growth, vulnerable to pests and disease. Plants in soils containing an excess of nitrogen tend to have fewer flowers and fruits.

Plants hungry for nitrogen include lawn grasses, cabbages, lettuce, leeks, pampas and other decorative grasses and ornamental green-leaved plants.

Nitrogen deficiency shows in plants as a characteristic yellowing around the central veins of the leaves. This can usually be remedied by adding a nitrate-based fertilizer.

Some plants, particularly those of the pea family such as clover, peas and beans, are able to absorb atmospheric nitrogen into their roots. They may be grown as green-manure, to dig into and enrich low-nitrogen soils.

Phosphates

Phosphoric acid is the form of phosphorus that plants can use. It is denoted by the chemical symbol P_2O_5 and always follows nitrogen in the contents list of fertilizers. It helps flowers develop and assists fertilization, preventing flowers fading too quickly, and helping fruit set earlier and ripen better.

Equally important is its role in developing strong root systems. It makes the stems more rigid and gives plants a better natural resistance to disease. It is essential for plants' general health. Plants can only absorb phosphates easily in the presence of lime, so phosphorus is often unavailable in very acidic soils. It is slow acting and most soils carry an adequate supply. All flowering plants, especially roses, fruit trees, tomatoes and strawberries are fond of it.

Phosphatic fertilizers should be given regularly to heathland plants such as rhododendrons and azaleas. Finely granulated or powdered products are preferable, as they can be easily worked into the surface of the soil. It is very important to mix the product well into the soil. Bone meal and super-phosphate are the most common phosphatic fertilizers.

Potash encourages high quality and tastier fruit.

Potash

This oxide of potassium, designated by the chemical symbol K_2O on packs of fertilizer, is always the third ingredient to be listed, after phosphoric acid. It plays an extremely complex part in all stages of plant development.

Potash helps form necessary reserves for feeding seeds, and is essential for all bulbous and tuberous-rooted plants, and for fruit. Potash helps plants absorb nitrogen and strengthens their tissues. It makes seeds stronger, roots hardier, fruit sweeter, and improves flavour all round. It also helps plants resist diseases, drought and frosts. Lastly, it helps bulbs and tubers survive the winter.

Potash tends to be held too tightly by the soil. Though present in clay soils, potash can sometimes be 'locked in' and must be added regularly. Liming acid soils helps the assimilation of potash. Potash is also slow-acting and not very dramatic in its effects. All fruiting, tuberous and bulbous plants, such as strawberries, tomatoes, onions, irises and dahlias, need potash.

Calcium

Calcium is mainly present in the form of calcium carbonate, i.e. lime or chalk. Its main function is as a regulator, and it should not be regarded as a nutrient. It affects pH, and in high concentrations makes soils alkaline.

Calcium gives a certain rigidity to plant cells. It also flocculates clay and helps plants to absorb fertilizers, at the same time preventing overfeeding. Finally, it activates the decomposition of organic matter and plays an important part in transporting nutrients within the plant. By lightening the texture of heavy soils calcium helps plants absorb phosphoric acid, and is a physical and chemical corrective to the soil.

Calcium can create a chemical imbalance in the soil, making it too alkaline. Acid-lovers or calcifuges, such as rhododendrons, have difficulty in absorbing certain elements in the presence of too much chalk or limestone.

Most of the Cruciferae family, such as cabbages and turnips, many trees and some of the

Rose 'O sole mio' All rose fertilizers are rich in potash and magnesium. The latter is a trace element present in the chlorophyl molecule.

Leguminosae family, such as peas and beans, love alkaline soil.

Occasionally adding some handfuls of chalk or ground lime to household compost speeds its decomposition.

Magnesium

Used by plants in the form of magnesia, i.e. magnesium oxide (MgO), magnesium is an important element as it controls feeding and helps form sugars, proteins and vitamins. It is useful for all plant tissues and produces regular growth. In very light or acid soils, it is often found in a form which plants cannot use. Excess potash also tends to make it difficult for plants to absorb magnesium. Tomatoes, roses, fruit trees, carrots and lettuces in particular need magnesium.

Some fertilizers, such as nitrate of lime or basic slag, contain magnesium. A shortage of magnesium shows as chlorosis (paling) between the main leaf veins. The older leaves at the base of a shoot or stem are the first to be affected.

Sulphur

Sulphur is present in amino-acids, and plants generally use it in the form of sulphates. Sulphates in the soil come from the breakdown of organic matter or the mineral constituents of the bedrock. Plants are also capable of absorbing sulphur as sulphur dioxide (SO_2) in the atmosphere via their leaves, in exactly the same way as they absorb carbon dioxide.

Sulphur plays an important part in the production of proteins and the forming of bulbs and roots. Abundant in soil, it can also be added as a sulphate fertilizer, such as sulphate of ammonia, potassium sulphate or superphosphate, but it is easily washed away by rain.

Plants of the Cruciferae, Leguminosae and Liliaceae families, especially garlic, leeks, onions and tulips, need adequate supplies of sulphur.

Trace elements

Trace elements are the six remaining elements that plants need in minute quantities.

Iron assists in the production of chlorophyll. Failure to absorb iron results in yellowing, or chlorosis, of the leaves, starting with the youngest. An excess of lime is generally the cause of iron deficiency and can be remedied by adding iron chelates (not to be confused with iron sulphates which are used to destroy moss on lawns).

Boron plays its part in plant respiration and in the cell walls, or cellulose. The symptoms of boron deficiency, which is very rare, are browning of the inside of roots or fruit, diseases of the core of fruits and the formation of woody cells. Beetroot (beets), vines, pear and apple are most sensitive to this deficiency, which can be alleviated by adding borate fertilizers.

Copper acts as an enzyme activator in the production of chlorophyll and many proteins. Rare but spectacular, copper deficiency dramatically slows down growth, and leaves become

Without boron, the heart of a pear becomes cork-like and brown and the flesh gritty.

discoloured. Very sandy, acid soils are likely to be deficient in copper.

Manganese is generally associated with iron in photosynthesis, which is why a deficiency often shows as chlorosis. Treatment is applying basic slag containing 2–4 per cent manganese, together with acid organic matter.

Molybdenum is much appreciated by melons, cucumbers and cauliflowers, and is important for legumes, helping them fix atmospheric nitrogen in the nodules on their roots. Any deficiency is particularly noticeable in acidic soils. Liming is usually enough to enable plants to absorb the tiny amounts of molybdenum they require.

Zinc affects the growth of plants, helping form sugars and hence food reserves. Zinc deficiency is particularly serious in fruit trees; their leaves turn white and no fruit develops. Zinc deficiency is aggravated by excessive liming, heavy or badly-worked soils, and can be corrected by adding manure. Deficiencies are extremely rare.

There are other trace elements in the soil, such as aluminium, chlorine, cobalt, iodine and vanadium, but in such infinitesimally small doses that it is virtually impossible to control their action, and deficiencies are virtually unheard of. In most cases, balanced manuring is enough to eliminate any risk of deficiency.

Organic additives

Improving soils physically usually involves enriching them with organic matter. This, in turn, forms humus, which retains water, balances the pH and joins with clay to produce a lighter soil or with sand to increase its absorptive capacity. Micro-organisms in the soil enable it to metabolize the nutrients in the organic matter, especially nitrogen.

Manure

Manure adds humus and is of great benefit to the soil structure. The traditional material for improving garden soil, manure consists of farm animal droppings mixed with straw, ideally rotted for a number of months before use. During that time enough heat is generated to destroy most harmful organisms. The finished product contains plant nutrients, particularly nitrogen, and many trace elements. Used fresh before decomposition, manure can scorch plants and cause rotting. Increasingly rare in urban areas, farmyard manure has largely been superseded by proprietary products, many of which are simply well-rotted manure mixed with peat and then sealed in bags.

Manure is mainly used in autumn as base dressing which is dug in when the soil is turned over. It can also be used as a mulch for keeping down weeds and conserving moisture.

Proprietary products based on dehydrated manure, in granules, or decomposed, in sacks, are more manageable for small gardens. They are quicker to spread and their quality is assured, but they do not supply the organic matter in the desirable bulky form.

Contrary to popular opinion, horse manure is not necessarily the best. It is very strong and can cause severe scorching. Cow manure is usually better; it is more stable and better suited to the wide range of plants grown in the garden.

Peat

The product of mosses and rushes in moist, low-oxygen environments, peat is a fossil substance in an advanced state of decomposition. It adds

Section through a peat bog. The lighter surface layer consists of lighter coloured peat, the lower layer of well rotted dark peat.

little or no nutrients to the soil, but markedly improves its physical structure, making it lighter. Sphagnum moss peat is a spongy, partially decomposed substance, mainly added to sandy soils or mixed with sand and potting compost for sowing seeds, rooting cuttings and general potting. Light and easy to use, sphagnum moss is inert and acid, and may exacerbate the problems of acid soils.

Moss peat tends not to release all its water for plants to use, and when dry, it is difficult to moisten. It is especially useful for reducing the alkalinity of chalky soils and for adding to homemade seed and potting composts.

Sedge peat (unavailable in the USA) is formed from dead reeds, rushes, sedges, willow and alder scrub. It is more decomposed than moss peat and is darker and finer in texture, though less acid. It is normally formed in warmer areas than is moss peat. Most sedge peats are found in wet areas overlying rock or clay. They contain more organic matter than moss peat, by bulk, are moist, readily release their water to plants and have a long-lasting effect on soil. Mixed with rotted manure, both types of peat are extremely effective soil improvers.

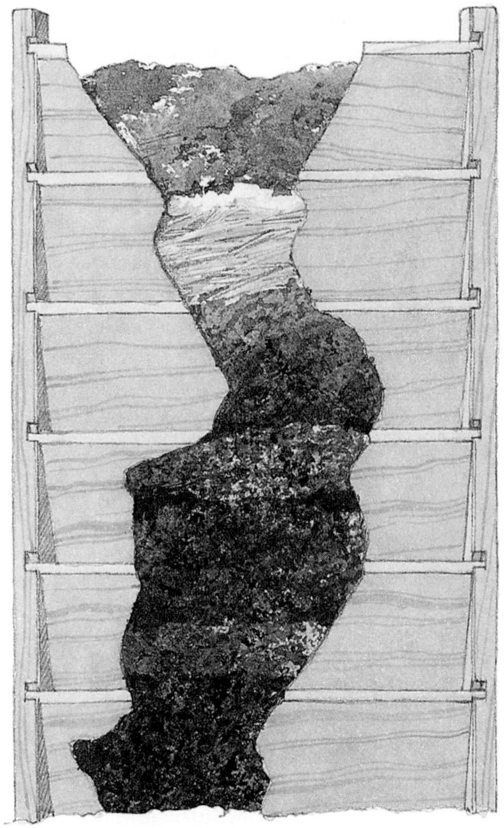

Section through a compost bin. In this case, the layers of waste vegetation are separated by layers of straw. Ventilation is provided by holes drilled in the walls of the bin.

Garden compost

Garden compost is rotted waste vegetation from the garden and home, as opposed to seed and potting composts, which are loam- or peat-based mixtures in which seeds and plants are grown. Garden compost is applied to the soil in one of several ways and is usually full of nitrogen, rich and moist. It is well suited to improving soils with its high content of organic matter. Although some uses require garden compost to be completely decomposed, partial decomposition is normally sufficient when it is being dug in.

Composts can be produced from any or all of the following: lawn mowings, most weeds, soft hedge clippings, spent vegetables, flower stalks, leaves, soft prunings, sawdust and wood ashes, straw and hay, pet droppings and animal manures. To these can be added organic household waste such as cabbage leaves, vegetable peelings, tea leaves and dead flowers. Avoid composting too many evergreen leaves and pine needles. The roots of perennial weeds, such as dock, bindweed and ground elder, should be thoroughly dried to kill them before they are composted, failing which they should be burnt.

Woody materials, such as thick hedge clippings and prunings, take longer to decompose but ultimately provide the most humus, as long as they are chopped into small pieces beforehand. There are several excellent mechanical shredders available for doing this. Once shredded, they are best mixed with softer material before composting.

Carpet sweepings used to be first-rate raw material for compost but nowadays these may contain nylon which never rots. However, sweepings and dust from vacuum cleaners are suitable for incorporating in moderation. Newspaper, again in moderation, should be shredded first. Newspaper contains no plant foods, but adds bulk.

The decomposition of waste plant materials is carried out by micro-organisms which need air and moisture to survive and work. Too much air, however, leads to slower decomposition because the raw material dries out quickly. Too much moisture forces air out of the heap and thus kills many micro-organisms. They also need nitrogen to flourish and, although a certain amount is provided by plant remains, the process is greatly speeded up by the addition of extra nitrogen from proprietary compost activators. These release nitrogen in a suitable form for use on a compost heap. For example, sulphate of ammonia on its own creates excessively acid conditions, but most proprietary activators have an ingredient to prevent this.

Types of compost heap The nature of a heap depends on: how much raw material is available; how much compost is needed; and whether the compost is needed all at once or throughout the year. If there is a small amount of raw material or if the need for compost is limited, a bin is better. If there is enough raw material and large amounts of compost are needed, one or more conventional heaps is more sensible. This is also the better system if compost is needed only once a year, say for autumn digging. If an ongoing supply is needed for various jobs throughout the year, it is better to have a number of small heaps or bins.

Bins have a number of advantages. They are tidier looking than conventional heaps. Bins which incorporate ventilated polythene sheeting or are made of more substantial plastic, wood, or brick, retain moisture better than ordinary heaps and also retain heat to varying degrees. Those made of wire or plastic mesh must have a polythene liner fitted to retain the moisture. A cover or top keeps out the rain and retains the heat within the compost.

A compost heap should be as round or square as possible, for maximum heat generation and fast, even decomposition. The ideal width is 4–5 ft (1.2–1.5 m), with the length depending on the amount of compost being made; 6 ft (1.8 m) is normally long enough for most households.

The ideal site is in the angle of a fence or wall where two sides are already provided. A sunny position, with a high ambient temperature, helps speed up decomposition.

Put a sheet of corrugated iron against the wall or fence to stop it deteriorating. The other two retaining walls can also be corrugated iron with air holes pierced in it. Alternatively, use uprights with horizontal planks nailed at half-inch (13 mm) intervals.

Most gardens produce a good range of raw materials; mix them together as the heap is built up, layer by layer. Try to mix dry and wet materials together and spread them evenly over the surface of the heap. Firm down unshredded twiggy material to retain the heat and moisture, by excluding large air pockets. It is seldom necessary to water a heap, unless a large amount of dry material, such as straw has been added. However, evaporation takes place in summer and an occasional watering may be needed in a dry year, particularly if the heap is not covered or enclosed.

In the past, and before the introduction of efficient activators (still scarce in the USA), a compost heap was built up in the course of one year, turned inside-out and upside-down in the early winter and left for another year to rot down completely. An activator makes this unnecessary. Once a heap or bin is complete, and provided that it has been made properly, cover it and simply leave to rot down.

Proprietary 'garden' composts

These are substances produced by combining various decomposing organic materials: clippings, peelings, manure, algae, sewage sludge, rotted bark, sawdust and leaves. Some are of industrial origin, others are treated household waste; the quality depends on their constituents and treatment. They are usually sold through garden centres and generally make good organic additives provided they have been completely broken down and stabilized. Often rich in organic matter and fairly cheap, they do not smell if well decomposed.

Fertilizers

Fertilizers are materials which provide nutrients for plants; whether organic or mineral, a fertilizer is always a chemical substance. Unlike bulky additives, which act on the soil structure as well as providing nutrients, mineral fertilizers affect only its chemical substance.

Most fertilizers contain the three main nutrients: nitrogen, phosphates and potash. There are simple fertilizers containing a single nutrient, dual fertilizers, with two, and complete fertilizers with three and sometimes more.

Green manures

Green manuring is the practice of growing plants, mainly leguminous, for the purpose of ploughing or digging them in as they approach maturity. Green manures improve the soil in the same way as other bulky organic materials do. Leguminous plants, such as peas, vetches and clovers, also add to the nitrogen content of the

Acid-loving plants, such as rhododendrons and azaleas, grow best in sandy, acid soil.

soil, thus encouraging stronger crops.

In a garden, the most appropriate plants for green manure are mustard, rape or buckwheat (annual rye) for general soil improvement, and clover for adding nitrogen. These are cut down and dug or ploughed in when they are fully grown but before flowering to prevent the plants seeding.

As well as the structure of the topsoil being improved by green manuring the subsoil is also broken up because the roots penetrate deep into the ground.

The drawbacks of growing green manure include losing part of the growing season with the expense and effort entailed. Green manure requires a lot of water, and can also encourage slugs and snails by providing them with a superb supply of protected, underground food.

Green manures are best used to bring fallow soil back into use, and are particularly useful for increasing the retentive power of sandy soils.

Straight fertilizers

These are mainly used to correct a chemical imbalance in the soil or to stimulate plants which need a particular element. Straight fertilizers are widely used by professionals and are often cheap, but must be used properly. Straight fertilizers supply either nitrogen, phosphates or potash; all are available in both organic and inorganic forms.

Straight fertilizers are best used by an experienced gardener with a sound knowledge of plant nutrition and how fertilizers work. They are specially useful for prompt action against nutrient deficiencies.

Dried blood (not available in USA)

Highly valued in organic gardening, dried blood contains 10–13 per cent organic nitrogen, which it releases slowly. At 3½ oz per square yard (100 g per m^2), it acts as a tonic on flowers and certain vegetables; and can be used under cover in spring. Its drawbacks are its unpleasant smell and its tendency to scorch young plants, such as pricked-out seedlings.

Hoof and horn (not available in USA)

This contains 12–15 per cent organic nitrogen. It is slow-acting and useful for feeding trees, shrubs, vines, roses and lawns. Apply in early spring, at 3½ oz per square yard (100 g per m²). It is an excellent base fertilizer to use when planting.

Other 'straight' fertilizers which add organic nitrogen to the soil include oilcake (4–7 per cent), wool scraps (4–9 per cent) and feathers (4–6 per cent).

Sulphate of ammonia

This inorganic fertilizer, in the form of crystalline pellets, contains 21 per cent nitrogen. It is used at 1–2 oz per square yard (25–50 g per m²) on vegetables, especially cabbages, radishes, turnips, potatoes and lettuces. Used as a spring and summer dressing; its stimulating effect lasts for several weeks.

Ammonium nitrate

This inorganic fertilizer contains 20–34 per cent nitrogen. It is an excellent foliage stimulant and has a longer-lasting effect than sulphate of ammonia. Use it in the spring at 1 oz per square yard (25 g per m²), especially on lawns and lettuces.

Other simple nitrogen fertilizers include calcium cyanamide, with 18–22 per cent ammoniac nitrogen; sodium nitrate, with 16 per cent ammoniac nitrogen; and calcium nitrate, with 15 per cent of ammoniac nitrogen and 26–28 per cent lime.

Superphosphate

This phosphate fertilizer is extracted from natural phosphate quarries in North Africa. It contains 18 per cent phosphoric acid, plus lime and sulphur. Use on acid soil at 2 oz per square yard (50 g per m²), preferably once plants are full size. Triple superphosphate contains 48 per cent phosphoric acid.

Potassium sulphate *(sulphate of potash)*

Obtained by chemical treatment of synvinite, potassium sulphate contains 48–50 per cent potash. It is good for fruit and potatoes, and is used as a base fertilizer at 1 oz per square yard (25 g per m²).

Straight fertilizers supply a specific element, as and when needed, to counteract a natural deficiency. They are concentrated and easy to use but some are rich in lime and unsuitable for alkaline soils.

Some sulphate of ammonia can also be used to enrich compost or accelerate the decomposition of organic matter.

Dual fertilizers

These contain two nutrients and have a wider

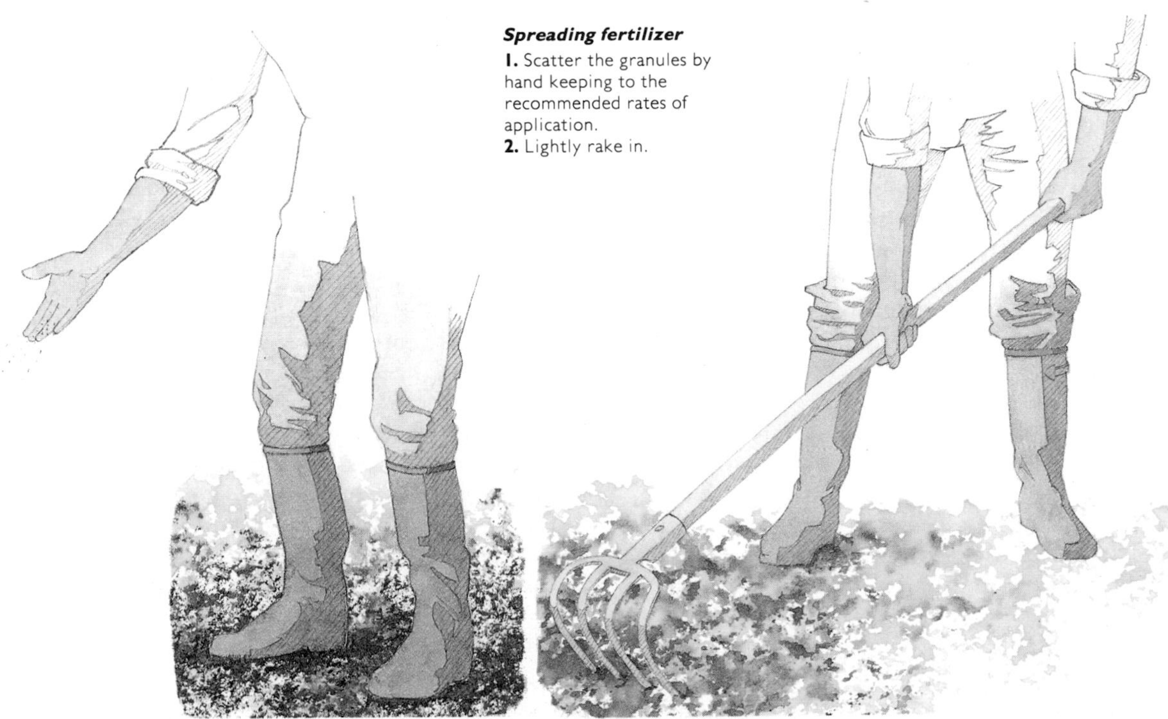

Spreading fertilizer
1. Scatter the granules by hand keeping to the recommended rates of application.
2. Lightly rake in.

range of effects than single fertilizers but are limited in number. They are seldom offered in garden centres and can be expensive, but are easily obtained from agricultural suppliers.

Potassium nitrate

A soluble and easily absorbed inorganic fertilizer, potassium nitrate, is used in spring and often forms part of compound fertilizers. Particularly suitable for fruit trees, bushes and strawberries at 2 oz per square yard (50–60 g per m^2), it needs a little working in. Potassium nitrate also makes a good liquid feed, when dissolved in water, for greenhouse and outdoor tomatoes.

Compound, or general, fertilizers

These combine nitrates, phosphates and potash. Their contents are always expressed as a percentage: a product labelled 10:10:10 contains 10 per cent of each. Complete fertilizers are available in inorganic, organic and mixed form, as liquids, granules or microgranules. Complete compound fertilizers are by far the most convenient and widely used sources of plant foods, especially in gardens. They should always be used, unless there is a particular reason for applying a more specific type containing just one or two elements.

Compound fertilizers are labelled according to their use. 'Universal' fertilizers are suitable for general cultivation and are often applied as base dressings before sowing or planting. Compound fertilizers are sold for specific purposes: roses, other flowers, vegetables, ericaceous plants, citrus fruits, cacti, orchids, indoor plants, lawns, and so on.

In practice, however, vegetable fertilizer can be given to flowers or fruit trees, rose fertilizer can feed other flowers and shrubs, and straight lawn fertilizer can be given to lettuces. Use common sense, check the composition of the fertilizer before use to make sure that its contents match the needs of the plants concerned, and follow the manufacturer's instructions.

Complete organic fertilizers

These products consist solely of organic ingredients and are coming back into fashion. Liquid seaweed is common in the USA, while 'blood, fish and bone' (5–5–6.5) is widely used in Europe. Organic fertilizers are available in liquid, powder or stick form. Guano, with its balanced composition, is particularly valuable for flowers and vegetables, but too low in potassium for fruit.

Organic fertilizers mixed with well-rotted organic matter, such as peat and manure are also available. They fertilize and improve the soil, have a long-lasting effect and do not scorch plants.

FERTILIZER WEEDKILLER

A special type of fertilizer combines fertilizer and weed killer. Lawn fertilizer/weed killer and moss killer mixtures are widely available. These products do two jobs in one application, which is not the least of their advantages. Although fairly expensive, they are very effective, the fertilizer encouraging the grass to grow in the gaps left by the dead weeds and/or moss. To obtain best results, apply in mild weather on damp soil.

Complete artificial fertilizers

These chemical fertilizers, usually highly concentrated in granule or liquid form, are easy to use and store. They have little or no smell, and their composition varies according to intended use. Those rich in magnesium and marketed as slow-release fertilizers are especially useful for woody and perennial plants and lawns.

Slow-acting fertilizers are used annually; excessive use can damage plants and soil in a long term way which is difficult to correct.

Some fertilizers are available with a vermiculite or peat base, for better, more economical dispersion of the product. They are lighter by volume than mineral-based fertilizers with a similar nutrient value.

Granular fertilizers

Most garden fertilizers are in granular or microgranular form; these are easy to scatter by hand or to use with a fertilizer distributor for a more even application. Some granular fertilizers stick together in a moist atmosphere and need to be stored in an air-tight container in a dry place.

Liquid fertilizers

Long reserved for indoor plants, these are now becoming increasingly popular outdoors because they are easy to use. Some experts advise watering plants all year with a liquid fertilizer and get excellent results.

Generally less concentrated than granules, they reduce the risk of scorching if used according to the manufacturer's instructions. Some liquid fertilizers are foliar feeds applied with atomizers or hose end diluters on to foliage.

A number of different formulas of liquid fertilizers are available, for use as a quick tonic to recently moved plants or those suffering from weather damage.

WATER IN THE GARDEN

Biology has long emphasized the importance of water in the appearance of life on earth, and so it is hardly surprising that water is the main constituent of plant tissues (up to 90 per cent of their weight). The presence or absence of water governs plant life, which depends directly on various forms of precipitation from the atmosphere. Rain in spring renews the soil's reserves of water; in winter there is snow. In summer, atmospheric moisture appears as dew, and water vapour condenses on to leaves. In autumn there is fog.

In reverse, evaporation caused by the heat of the sun reduces the soil's water reserves and makes plants wilt, and ordinary plant transpiration (rather like sweating) and bad drainage cause further water losses. The gardener must make up for the deficiencies in the atmosphere at the right moment, to create an equilibrium. Fortunately there are watering techniques and equipment available that save effort and time.

The garden should have plenty of taps for watering. Here, one is incorporated into an ornamental water trough.

Water in the soil

The roots of plants absorb all soil nutrients in soluble form, and water is therefore essential. The soil's water-retentive power depends on the hygroscopic capacity of its constituent particles. The finer the soil particles, the better they are at holding water, since each grain is covered with a thin film of water.

An impermeable soil is less likely to surrender its water to plants than an open soil. Plants may wilt completely in a clay soil with a 15 per cent water content, but the water content in a sandy soil has to fall below 8 per cent to achieve the same effect. On the other hand, the porosity of a soil reduces its water-retentive power; a sandy soil needs to be watered more frequently than a clay soil.

Water collecting in the subsoil of impermeable ground harms most plants, particularly in winter and early spring. It is especially liable to asphyxiate roots but also encourages a number of serious fungus diseases, such as club root in brassicas, mildew, withering in conifers, damping-off of seedlings, root rot, black spot on rose bushes, etc.

Water in the air

It is easy to forget how important atmospheric moisture is to plant life. The moist climate of Great Britain plays a large part in the exceptional beauty of English gardens; hot, dry countries have a different vegetation, capable of withstanding dry atmosphere. A high moisture content encourages the growth of vegetation; a dry atmosphere, however, causes increased plant transpiration and wilting.

During a dry spell, water generously, although this will not halt the cycle of transpiration which means that the more you water, the more the sun evaporates the water, and the more plants try to absorb.

In practice, do not hesitate to soak leaves or spray plants when the weather is very hot. This

A damp climate encourages the growth of herbaceous perennials and wild gardens.

is best done in the evening when the sun is less liable to scorch the wet leaves and when the stomata are more closed. These are the pores which absorb the gases that the plant needs and through which water vapour passes during transpiration.

In the greenhouse, high humidity must be combined with adequate air circulation to prevent the spread of fungal disease.

Watering

Watering is called for whenever the natural water supply is insufficient or when specialized growing techniques are involved. Most gardens depend on mains water supply, but running water in channels is a method often used in very arid parts of the world. Rainwater can be stored by leading the roof gutters and down-pipes to a water barrel or a large buried cistern with an immersion pump. Rainwater is slightly mineralized and relatively pure in less polluted areas.

When to water

In a temperate climate in the spring, the best time to water is in the late morning, once the soil has warmed up slightly. In summer, the best time to water is in the evening, to prevent the leaves scorching and water evaporating too quickly. Avoid watering in the middle of the day in sunny weather, as the droplets will act like lenses, focusing the sun's rays and possibly burning the foliage.

Sprinkler equipment

A wide range of equipment is available; choice depends on the area to be treated, the plants grown and the type of water supply.

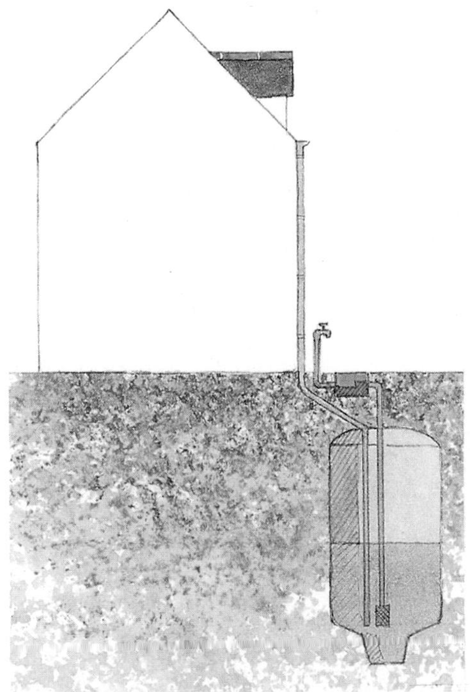

Sophisticated rainwater collection system. The main gutter leads to an underground tank including a settling chamber. An external pump enables the water to be drawn as and when required.

Output

Output is a given period of time. The quantity of water is measured in cu.ft/hr (m^3/hr) or gallons/min. (litres/min.).

Pressure

This is the force with which the water emerges from the taps (or pump). In many areas, the pressure in summer is much less than in winter, and equipment should be selected accordingly. To measure output, simply turn the tap fully open and fill a 2.2 gallon (10 litre) bucket or watering can. Measure the time in seconds required to fill the bucket or watering can. The hourly output in gallons is obtained by dividing the number of seconds taken into 3600 (seconds in an hour) and then multiplying the capacity of the bucket or can by that number.

Hoses

Hoses are an essential part of a sprinkler system, allowing adjustment of the water supply. If only a fixed pressure is available, to increase the output, use a larger diameter hose.

Where the water pressure is consistently high, use a $\frac{3}{4}$ in (19 mm) diameter hose; if it is lower, a $\frac{5}{8}$ in (15 mm) diameter hose is better. The form of the hose is also important. There is a wide range of reinforced hoses available, with a PVC core covered in woven, overlapping or braided polyester fibre. Other hoses are made of PVC and rubber, and are more rigid but also heavier.

A fixed sprinkler operated at very low pressure.

Rotary sprinkler. This system distributes the water in a fine shower and is particularly suitable for flower borders and nursery beds.

Cheap hoses are rarely satisfactory in terms of rigidity. Before buying, check that hoses do not kink easily. Flat hoses are now available in packs: light and easy to carry, they are practical but not designed for intensive garden use. They also have to be unwound completely before being used.

Joints

Automatic joints, usually of plastic, are becoming increasingly widespread. They are cheap and are good enough for ordinary use. These joints can connect two hoses, a sprinkler and a hose, or a hose and a tap; they also enable branches and different sprinkling areas to be covered, if required. It is essential to know exactly what you need if you are to choose the right equipment from among all the different joints.

An on/off fitting at the end of a hose stops water backfiring if you want to disconnect the sprinkler without being showered. It is a useful device if you have a number of sprinkler areas.

Static sprinklers

These are simple mechanisms, fixed on a skid or stuck into the ground. They have few or no moving parts and spread water over a usually circular area; some models are adjustable to cover larger or smaller areas. Static sprinklers are used for delicate plants and rock gardens and spread a fine spray over an area of 269–1076 sq ft (25–100 m^2).

Static sprinklers are cheap and long lasting. They can remain outdoors all year round in a slightly concealed spot. Simply connect them when watering is required.

Rotary sprinklers

Also known as lawn sprinklers, rotary sprinklers operate at normal tap pressures, the area covered depending on their size and height. Rotary sprinklers are unpowered: the pressure of water alone makes them work. The numerous models available, with various arrangements of holes in the arms and end nozzles, spray the water in different, often decorative patterns.

Rotary sprinklers give a light, fine spray of water, and are ideal for delicate plants, especially young seedlings. In larger gardens, tripod-mounted models can cover areas of around 1615–2150 sq ft (150–200 m^2).

Oscillating sprinklers

These consist of an arm with holes or nozzles which move from side to side, controlled by an adjustable hydraulic mechanism. Oscillating sprinklers operate at standard tap pressure and cover square or rectangular areas (most other sprinklers water in circles). They can also be set in several different positions. Oscillating sprinklers can cover 2150–3765 sq ft (200–350 m^2), and the shape of the area they cover makes them particularly suitable for the kitchen garden.

Pulsating sprinklers

These are the most powerful form of sprinkler available to the amateur gardener. They need a high water pressure to work well and cover circular or conical areas. The sprinkler mechanism relies on a plate being moved under the power of a jet crossing the nozzle: this makes the sprinkler head move in jumps. Depending on the model, the jet has a range of up to 50 ft (15 m), and maximum area covered is 7500 sq ft (700 m^2). Because of their powerful jets, they are best suited to watering large lawns and shrub borders.

Using tripod-based models makes the jet reach even further, and reduces the force of the water so that it falls in a fine spray.

Sprinkler terminals or nozzles

This term covers the innumerable wands, sprayers and gadgets, some with adjustable jets, which can be fitted to a hose for localized watering. Some of the more powerful ones can be connected to a detergent tank for washing cars or pavements; others are controlled by pressing a button.

Sprinkler terminals are best used for automatic joints and a hose-end stop, and can often be used instead of traditional sprinklers.

Oscillating sprinkler. This is the only effective sprinkler for watering square or rectangular areas.

The watering can

The symbol of watering in a bygone age, the watering can is simple to use and still essential

Pulsating sprinkler. Intended for large areas, particularly lawns, it requires a minimum 3 bars pressure. The jet can reach up to 50 ft (15 m) covering an area of 700 sq. yds (700 m^2).

Pop-up sprinkler. The pressure makes the sprinkler come out of its housing. It works according to a pre-selected programme and then disappears back into the ground.

for limited, localized watering. Many plastic models with or without a rose are available, and it is still possible to buy zinc or copper versions for those nostaligic for old-time gardening.

A watering can with a capacity of $3\frac{1}{2}$ pints (2 litres) and a long spout is useful for plants in small containers, and a $10\frac{1}{2}$ pint (6-litre) watering can with a rose is useful for watering young plants and for general use. If you have a good sprinkler system, you do not need anything larger than this.

Complete watering systems

The last word in sprinkler systems, these highly developed set-ups combine a complete network of buried pipes with overhead or retractable sprinklers. They give very precise watering control, with a complete network of jets accurately covering pre-seclected areas of the garden, and are controlled by actuators or remote hydraulic controls. Watering can be adjusted to suit the needs of plants and the pressure available.

The dozens of models available can theoretically be assembled by the user. However, it is essential to design the system properly, arranging watering areas so that they overlap by one third. It is better to hire a specialist to install a system of this kind in a complicated layout. If it is just a matter of watering a lawn, a simple system is easy to install yourself.

Drip feed systems

These low pressure systems, which are becoming ever more sophisticated combine an economical use of water with feeding the plants. Each nozzle in the system delivers approximately 1 gallon ($4\frac{1}{2}$ litres) of water an hour to the roots of each plant. The 'drip feed' system reduces evaporation losses and prevents plants drying out but it involves an unsightly criss-cross of pipes on the ground and also has to be changed completely when used on short term plants such as vegetables. Drip feed is certainly the most labour-saving watering system as it also allows you to liquid-feed the plants.

Automatic equipment

Electronic or mechanical programmers are widely available. The most complex models work to the minute on many watering areas and can be programmed several days in advance. Linked to hygrometric probes, they automatically cut off watering once the moisture in the soil reaches an adequate level. Linked to photo-electric cells, they only start watering when the sun goes down. There are also flow control valves which measure the quantity of water emitted and automatically cut off the water when necessary.

Programming your watering, even with a simple timer, can avoid floods and excess water consumption. Programming units are not con-

Watering pistol. Used for spraying plants in hot weather and for all pinpoint watering.

fined to integral water systems, but can be used on very simple systems.

Water-saving techniques

Organic additives, such as well-rotted garden compost, combine with the soil to form a kind of 'natural sponge'. This retains water well, particularly in sandy soils.

Mulching with lawn mowings, well-rotted compost, pine bark or leaf mould all reduce evaporation considerably and help keep the soil moist. Mulching is very beneficial to hardy perennials and low-growing species. Ground cover plants act in the same way as mulching and form a decorative carpet, but they absorb water themselves.

Perforated black polythene may be laid on the ground around roses and shrubs, and then covered with gravel or pulverised bark. This controls weeds as well as conserving moisture.

Removing the hard crust from the soil by hoeing allows atmospheric moisture to reach the surface roots. Hoeing also stops water moving upwards by capillary action, and so reduces evaporation at the surface and retains the sub-soil water reserves.

Water retainers are fairly recent products. They consist of hygroscopic silicates or naturally occurring alginates capable of holding 50 to 100 times their own volume of water to form a non-liquid reserve. They have produced excellent results in very sandy soils but their 'active life' is relatively short.

Combatting excess water

A highly water-retentive subsoil tends to asphyxiate roots, especially in winter. Saturated soil is also slow to warm up in spring and en-

Trickler. This is a water-saving system. It is mainly used for vegetables, hedges and shrubberies.

courages fungus and bacterial diseases. As well as using bulky soil additives, it is often necessary to use other methods of soil drainage improvement.

Drainage is the best method of correcting permanently saturated soil. Clay drains are no longer widely used because of their fragility; instead, rows of PVC pipes are placed in sloping trenches 16 in (40 cm) deep. The pipes are laid on a bed of gravel and covered with gravel so that they cannot move and so the plants' roots cannot enter and block them. These main drains are placed lengthways along the garden, about 33 ft (10 m) apart and run to a collecting tank or to a ditch. Secondary drains 10 ft (3 m) apart and at an angle join the main drains in a V-shaped pattern. If digging deep, such as when planting an orchard, place a light plastic mesh over the drainage lines.

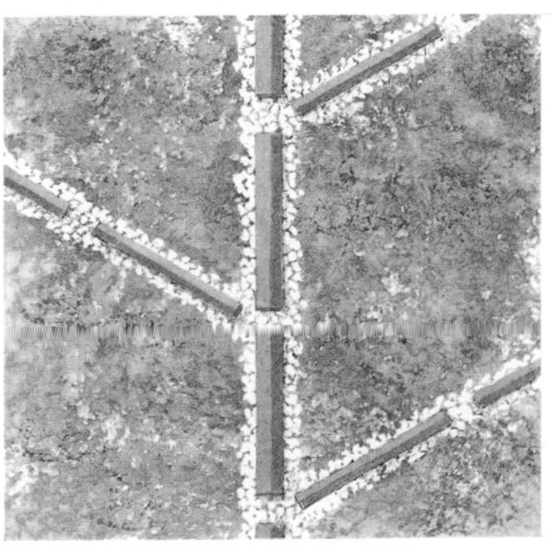

Drainage
1. Drains are laid on a bed of pebbles and covered with soil, each slightly separated from its neighbour.
2. Drain layout. All lead to a central collector.

Raised beds also help prevent waterlogging. Low walls, railway sleepers (railroad ties), and logs will keep the plants 12–20 in (30–50 cm) above the natural ground level; with the slope resting on a bed of cinders or gravel to improve drainage. Gaps in retaining walls and spaces between sleepers or logs also allow excess water to drain off.

CLIMATE

Climate has a much greater effect on growing conditions in the garden than you might think. The climate of an area enormously affects the plants that can be grown there. Some need more heat or moisture; many cannot withstand the rigours of winter. Others, such as bulbs, must have a certain amount of cold weather if they are to develop completely.

Different climates

Each garden has its own micro-climate; a wall exposed to the sun, a hedge or a position in a town centre may be enough to change climatic conditions completely. It is still useful however to understand the main climatic groups.

The oceanic climate dominates most coastal regions, which benefit from the influence of the sea and often have high humidity but are also liable to very high winds and floods. The oceanic climate is comparatively mild and stable: mild winters and often cool summers. In warmer countries, gardeners in coastal areas are able to grow many temperate-climate species which like moisture and hazy sun.

A near-oceanic climate is often found inland where the influence of the sea is still discernible. It has distinct but moderate seasons, often with heavy rainfall. In these areas, plants must be hardier to survive than those nearer the coast.

The continental, or inland, climate occurs in regions well away from any moderating maritime influence. The continental climate has very distinct seasons, often with scorching summers and very cold winters, so only hardy species survive as permanent planting and much use is made of seasonal plants, to take advantage of the good summer weather.

A mountain climate is found in areas of high altitude: the main features are a significant drop in temperature, 1.8°F (1°C) for every 650–1000 ft (200–300 m), and the long winters. Plant life varies considerably, depending on the direction in which the slopes face. In the northern hemisphere, west-facing slopes are normally the wettest, north-facing the coldest, and south-facing slopes, the driest. Gardeners in these areas should allow for these factors and use mainly mountain species. These are often more compact than their lowland counterparts because the snows last so long and flowers only emerge in spring.

A mild maritime climate enables supposedly delicate plants, such as Lavatera olbia *and agapanthus, to acclimatize.*

You must always bear in mind that it is wiser to grow plants to suit the local conditions rather than try to alter the conditions to suit the plants. This should be attempted only when you are fully confident about your own knowledge and experience. New gardeners in particular should always grow plants suited to their particular conditions; a word with an experienced local gardener soon points the newcomer in the right direction. Later, when experience has been gained or, if appropriate, a greenhouse has been bought, the range can be extended.

Sunlight

Sunlight is one of the main factors governing the success of a garden. Of course, there are species which grow best in the shade, but far more that demand strong light.

In the northern hemisphere, the sunniest spots face south. A west-facing position gets sunlight in the afternoon, when the sun is high in the sky and at its hottest. Such sites may also be exposed to relatively strong winds, particularly in coastal areas.

To help plants get more sunshine, make your

Saint-Jean-Cap-Ferrat *On the French Mediterranean coast, the virtually sub-tropical climate allows palm trees and succulents to be grown in the open.*

borders slope towards the west or south. This practice is very beneficial to early seedlings and helps protect against cold in winter.

There are a number of shading techniques to reduce the amount of sunlight plants receive: planting a light-leaved tree, shading grids, mulching young plants lightly, netting or growing plants in a slight hollow, where the difference in levels shades delicate young plants.

Areas of light and shade in a garden allow a wide variety of species. In areas with little sun, make as many open areas as possible by concentrating the tallest plants away from the direction of the sunlight. In the hottest areas, extend the shade by planting trees. In coastal areas, where the sky is often hazy, trees close to the house may increase the humidity and make the rooms even darker.

Wind

Wind is harmful to garden plants. It tends to dry out both the soil and the plants, break branches, flatten flowers and seriously impair pollination.

Use a windbreak to protect plants. A windbreak forces air to pass through a filter, slowing it down considerably. Windbreaks can be barricades of branches, bamboo, wood or fine-mesh fencing, or lines of hedges.

A well-designed windbreak can be effective over a distance of up to 20 times its own height, so that a 10 ft (3 m) high hedge gives some protection to a distance of about 200 ft (60 m) on its lee side, with a maximum effect to 100 ft (30 m).

A windbreak must be permeable to be effective; if it is too solid, it acts like a wall,

Windbreaks

1. Very impervious barriers, such as walls, are inefficient as they only divert the force of the wind and can add to its destructive powers with turbulence.

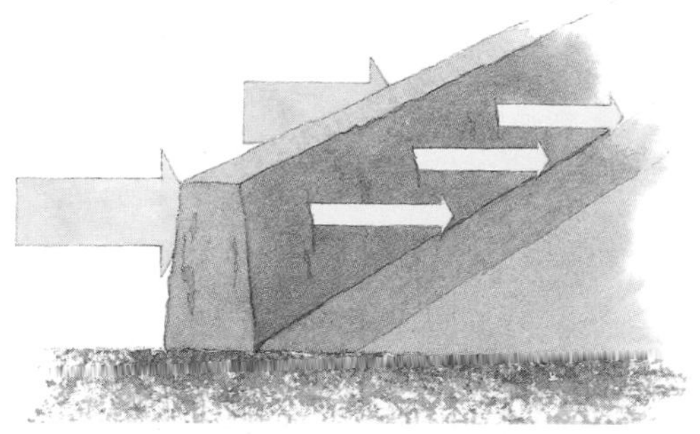

2. A hedge, on the other hand, slows down the wind speed by filtering it through its branches.

A hedge windbreak must contain a mixture of shrubs and tall bushes, with at least 33 per cent evergreens.

setting up major turbulence on the lee side in an area equal to twice its height. The best results are achieved with a permeability of 50 per cent.

In the garden, the ideal windbreak and one which remains attractive all year round, is a free-standing hedge with foliage from top to bottom in a mixture of deciduous and evergreen plants, such as hornbeam, holly, cupressus, hawthorn or privet. In mild localities, species such as olearia, escalonia and tamarix could be used. Spacing depends on species and ultimate size. On a larger scale, you could plant clumps of trees, such as robinia (honey locust), rowan (mountain ash), lime (linden), or holly, keeping in mind that they may shade the garden as well as shelter it.

Once you have chosen your species, plant them in two or three fairly closely-packed rows to allow the foliage to intertwine. Place larger species in the background.

Conifers, apart from *Chamaecyparis* (cypress), do not make good windbreaks as their foliage is too impenetrable. *Thuja* (arbor-vitae), Leyland cypress and yew can only be used in ornamental screens.

Rain

Rain is only slightly mineralized and free of lime, unlike most town water. A fine, conti-

Frost protection systems
1. A pane of glass resting on pegs ensures a more rapid warming of the soil.
2. A new plant protected by cloth or polythene held by pegs.
3. Tie cardoons, gynerium (a tender reed) and kniphofia (red-hot poker) into bundles for protection.

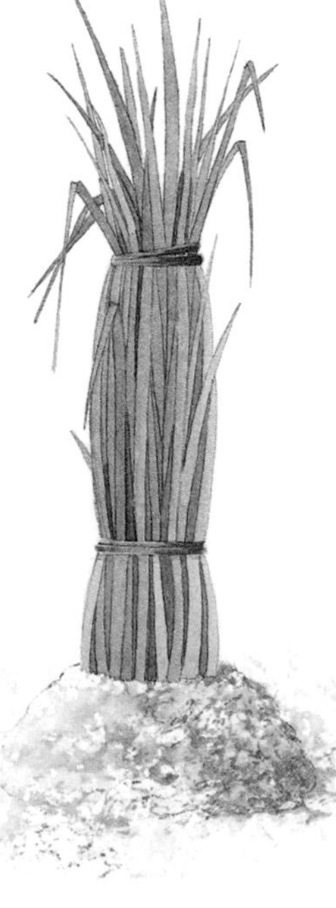

nuous rain, such as a gentle mist, can have beneficial effect, since it penetrates the soil gently and does not run off in torrents.

Violent rain can seriously damage plants, especially seedlings and plants in containers. It can form streams and torrents on sloping ground, eroding the soil. Where the atmosphere is polluted, rain carrying corrosive dust and active chemical agents may be harmful to plants, as is the case with the acid rains downwind of industrial regions.

Rainfall on its own is rarely enough to meet all the needs of garden plants and is usually supplemented by watering.

Putting plants under cover, such as in a greenhouse, on a verandah, in a frame or tunnel protects them from the physical damage caused by heavy downpours. If erosion channels start to form, particularly in sloping gardens, stepped terraces are an excellent solution. Provide channels or ditches to drain off excess water. These are essential precautions in areas subject to repeated storms.

Snow

Snow is usually beneficial, as it gives plants a natural covering in winter, under which the temperature never falls below about 28°F (−2°C). This blanket of snow prevents one side-effect of frosts: scorching followed by desiccation. The weight of snow can be a problem however, as it may distort or even break conifer and broad-leaved evergreen branches, and can smother young spring plants. Shake snow off conifer branches, but do not uncover the kitchen garden or lawn. Sprinkle coarse sand on iced-over paths.

Frost

Frost occurs when water crystallizes, and may be dangerous for plants. When water freezes, it expands, and is liable to burst plant cells. In theory, all plants ought to freeze below 32°F (0°C), the freezing point of water; in practice, their resistance depends on a number of factors.

The hardiness of plants varies according to the permeability of their cells. Impermeable cells usually burst, while permeable cells allow the water, which would otherwise freeze inside their walls, to escape. The more permeable the cells, the hardier the plant.

The sap's content of mineral salts also has a major effect; the more salts it contains, the less likely it is to freeze, rather like anti-freeze. Sap is particularly rich after a hot, sunny summer, which also hardens the external tissues of plants, especially bark.

It is difficult to put plant resistance on a scale, as the type of cold matters as much as the temperature. A single night at +5°F (−15°C) may be much less harmful than a month of +14°F (−10°C): after a month, all available water in the soil will have turned into ice, so plants die of thirst. The presence of wind, which furthers desiccation, compounds the damage done by frost.

The type of soil is another factor. Compact soils freeze *en masse* and can cause rot and neck

4. An upturned flower pot filled with straw protects the root stock of delicate perennials and some bulbs or rockery plants which dislike the damp.
5. Stool layering bush roses.
6. In very cold areas, protect standard roses with straw matting. The head of the shrub is wrapped in a plastic bag filled with straw.

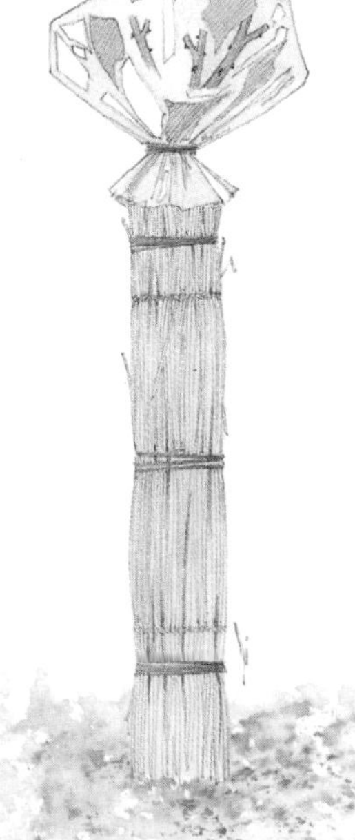

Greenhouses or conservatories are an effective and attractive way of protecting plants from bad weather.

rot once they thaw. Even after the surface soil has thawed, the sub-soil may still be frozen and will stop water draining away causing waterlogging.

Choosing the hardiest species or varieties of a genus helps, as does siting them in sheltered spots in corners, by walls or hedges and in sun. Transfer tender pot plants indoors or to a greenhouse, frame (fixed or moveable), or even a plastic tunnel. Light and inexpensive, plastic tunnels protect plants from wind and rapid temperature changes, and retain moisture, but they are not efficient for retaining heat. A mulch of straw or dry leaves at least 4 in (10 cm) thick, and covered with a sheet of plastic protects dormant perennials and bulbs. Shrubs and trees can be surrounded with a vertical mesh at least 8 in (20 cm) from the trunk(s), forming a 'cage' filled with straw or leaves, at least 20 in (50 cm) high. Most shrubs protected in this way will flower again the following season. Protect the tops of plants with a double thickness of garden netting or plastic mesh covered with a plastic top. Do not allow the netting or mesh to touch the leaves or they might be damaged.

As well as these familiar techniques, cold can also be turned against itself. Snow is very useful, as the temperature beneath 20 in (50 cm) of snow rarely falls below 32°F (0°C). If you act at the start of a freeze, when the temperature is still only 23–28°F (−5–−2°C), you can spray water on shrubs and trees for frost protection. Tie them in bunches first to prevent them deforming under the weight of the film of ice which will form. Use a spray gun filled with lukewarm water. The ice formed acts to some extent in the same way as snow. This method is widely used in orchards to protect the blossom from late spring frosts.

PLANT PESTS AND DISEASES

The number of insects, fungi, bacteria and viruses which attack plants is astounding. Unfortunately, garden pests often develop a resistance to initially effective products and there are still serious diseases, such as fireblight and Dutch elm disease, for which there is no treatment. There are also innumerable viral infections, which can only be eliminated by long, costly genetic selection.

Pests and disease control has made great advances in producing chemicals which are relatively harmless to humans but very effective against pests and diseases. All products now on the market have undergone lengthy, complex and rigorous testing, at enormous cost. This does not mean that these products can be used willy-nilly or without precautions.

Always follow the manufacturer's instructions scrupulously, keep garden chemicals in their original packaging and wear gloves and protective clothing while spraying. Any chemical, however, can be potentially dangerous if misused. Do not make up unprescribed mixtures. Spray or dust downwind to prevent contact with the chemicals, and do not smoke, drink or eat while using them. Store garden chemicals out of the reach of children. Clean sprayers thoroughly after use.

Avoid treating plants during the day in summer as the water droplets may act as lenses and burn the leaves. Never treat plants in full flower, as spraying may make the flowers wilt and drop prematurely. It may also kill pollinating insects.

Rinse equipment after use, and run clean water through the spray wand to clear it of all traces of chemical.

If you suspect that you have been poisoned, contact a doctor or hospital immediately, taking with you the bottle or packet of chemical and any packaging.

Mealy bugs (Cochineals) bite the plant and suck the sap. Their sticky excretions are easily recognised.

Insecticides

These are designed to destroy harmful insects, and may kill those attacking the plants after treatment, as well as those already present.

Insecticides can be classified by the way in which they work and what pests they affect. Insecticides are available in liquid and solid forms.

Soil insecticides are available as microgranules or powder, and are used to destroy cutworms, wireworms, grubs and vegetable root flies.

Systemic insecticides are sold as liquids or granules. Ant-killers, often containing pirimiphos-methyl, are powders used at any time of year in many countries.

A good working knowledge of pest identification helps you select the most suitable insecticide. As a rule, a systemic insecticide, such as dimethoate (cygon), and a stomach poison, such as derris (rotenone) or permethrin (pyrethrum), will solve most problems, together with a granular soil insecticide for killing root-eating pests.

Winter washes

Spraying fruit trees and bushes in winter with tar oil (dormant oil in USA) kills the overwintering stages of many of the worst pests, including greenfly eggs. It is a dirty job, so wear old clothes and rubber gloves, and proceed after pruning to avoid having to handle oily branches.

Tar oil has a scorching effect on foliage, so cover any plants, including lawns, beneath the trees being sprayed with newspaper during spraying.

Avoid winter washing when the temperature is below freezing, and apply the spray so that it gets under the bark, into all the crevices and runs down the branches and trunk.

Contact insecticides

These penetrate insects through their 'skin', the pest merely has to touch the product (or be touched by it) for the insecticide to start destroying them. Contact insecticides are designed as curatives when insects are already on plants, but can also prevent further infestation.

The most common contact insecticides are lindane, also known as gamma HCH or Isotox, and the new synthetic pyrethroids, such as permethrin. The latter is very quick acting and non-persistent; it is soon broken down into harmless materials so that treated fruit and vegetables can usually be safely eaten the day after treatment. These products, in powder or liquid form, are sprayed on plants during the growing season. They are also toxic if ingested and therefore harmful to bees and other beneficial or harmless insects.

Always spray or dust the top and underside of all leaves, shoots and branches to ensure good control. Treat plants at the first sign of trouble; never allow an attack to get out of hand.

Ingested insecticides

These poison insects internally, as they eat the plant tissues.

The Colorado beetle, a beautiful coleopterous insect, ravages potatoes and completely devours the leaf, leaving only the veins. A preventive insecticide can be used to avoid this kind of damage.

Non-systemic ingested poisons have little effect against sucking insects of the greenfly or aphid type. Contact or systemic insecticides have to be used.

Common stomach insecticides include products containing derris (in rotenone), carbaryl (sevin) and malathion; malathion is versatile, and can be used against red spider mites. Preparations combining contact and ingestion insecticides are available, and have wider-ranging effect.

Ingested insecticides must be applied carefully and thoroughly to all parts of the infested plants. Suggested safety intervals between treating and eating vegetables must be adhered to.

Systemic insecticides

These are absorbed by the plant and carried in the sap, acting 'from the inside'. They cannot be washed away by rain, and are longer-lasting than non-systemic products, but take some days to become fully effective. Some are not suitable for use on fruit and vegetable crops, but these are rare.

A common systemic insecticide is dimethoate (cygon). This is available either on its own or in combination with other insecticides, which act in different ways, so that the range of pests controlled is increased.

Malathion is partially systemic; it enters a leaf but is not carried to other parts of the plant. It is effective against sucking insects feeding on the underside of leaves sprayed only on the upper surfaces.

Systemic products are increasingly being used on young plants against greenfly and other sucking insects. Dimethoate (cygon) preparations are sprayed onto leaves; granular soil insecticides raked in on moist soil.

Systemic insecticide is the main type used against greenfly and other sucking insects, such as capsids and red spider mites. Dimethoate (cygon) lasts for about three weeks after application, but is ineffective against caterpillars and most other biting/chewing pests.

Ant-killers

Powders with lindane, carbaryl (sevin) or pirimiphos-methyl (not in USA) are common, together with a range of products based on borax. Many countries market anti-ant tubes, which contain semi-liquid sugared pellets, for spreading across ants' paths.

There are also borax-based bait traps, which quickly destroy ant-nests, as the ants transmit the poison on contact.

Bait traps should always be used when there are young children or pets around.

Special precautions

Insecticides contain inflammable solvents, with low flash points, so they must be kept out of full sun and not exposed to sources of heat. They withstand cold well, but avoid exposure to prolonged periods below freezing.

'Natural' insecticides

The term 'natural' is a loose one, meaning different things to different people. In terms of insecticides, it refers to pyrethrum (derived from an African daisy), rotenone-based (derris) and 'biological' insecticidal preparations of

Bacillus thuringiensis, a bacterium effective against the caterpillars that attack cabbage-family plants. These products are environmentally safe.

Acaricides or miticides

Acaricides (miticides) are often classed as insecticides, but act specifically against mites, principally red spider mites. Most available preparations are based on dimethoate (cygon), which acts against egg, larva and adult mites. It is not particulary toxic to mammals (including humans) but should not be applied less than two weeks before picking.

Cucumbers and other cucurbits in greenhouses are particularly vulnerable to red spider mites, and acaricides (miticides) help protect them.

Caterpillars, or butterfly larvae, attack leaves making holes which can lead to serious damage.

Fungicides

These products are used against fungal diseases. They are mainly preventative, creating a protective layer on the surface of plants, but some can retard, or even halt, the development of fungi which are already present. Fungicides commonly available each control a wide range of fungus diseases, so a host of separate products is not necessary.

Contact fungicides

Copper, sulphur, maneb, zineb and thiram are the most commonly used contact products in the garden. They are mainly used preventatively, whether in powder or liquid form, they must be applied as soon as leaves appear and re-applied regularly, according to the manufacturer's instructions.

Contact fungicides have largely been replaced by systemic fungicides, such as benomyl, which are both preventative and curative. However, a few fungi, such as botrytis or grey mould, are developing resistance to some of the systemics, so a limited return to contact fungicides may be beneficial, particularly where resistance is known to exist.

Tomato mildew. When it attacks the fruit, mildew causes severe decay which can decimate the harvest. Preventive treatment is essential.

Systemic fungicides

Like their insecticide counterparts, these products are absorbed by the plant and carried in the sap. The fact that they cannot be leached out by rain makes them particularly useful in rainy seasons when fungi grow best. They also have a long active life within the plant.

Systemic fungicides are applied with a sprayer between mid-spring and early autumn, as soon as the first attacks appear. Spray mainly on the undersides of leaves if the weather is very humid.

Systemic fungicides are based on chemicals including benomyl, triforine, thiophanate-methyl and carbendazim, and can treat a wide range of susceptible fungus diseases.

Mixing chemicals

Mixing two or more fungicides for use in a single operation is rarely necessary, but it is often convenient to mix a fungicide and an insecticide to make a combined pest- and disease-control spray. This is often used for treating roses. Unless there is a specific recommendation to the contrary, most commonly used insecticides and fungicides can be mixed quite safely provided only one of each is included.

It may also be convenient to add a foliar feed to the spray, but the more chemicals you include, the more liable it is to be an incompatible mixture.

Fungicides for commercial use

These act against certain specific fungi, or in conjunction with certain crops. Anti-mildew preparations are usually a versatile mixture of several fungicides, and can be used against a variety of leaf moulds, such as rust, spots and anthracnose. However, most of these materials are only available to commercial growers.

Total products

These are designed to combine the effects of insecticide, acaricide (miticide) and fungicide. Total products are very useful for amateurs, as it is not necessary to identify the exact pest or disease and then buy a specific preparation to treat it.

Total products are available as dry powder, soluble powder, spray liquid and aerosols. The liquid products are generally best as they are simple to use and have higher concentrations of active ingredients than other forms.

Total products are most effective in spring, but can be used throughout the growing season. There are 'all purpose' sprays for general garden use, but they are mainly used for treating roses and lawns, for which combined weedkiller, fertilizers and mosskiller preparations are also available.

Anti-pest preparations

This category covers all products designed for use against animals other than insects.

Slug killers

Also known as molluscides, these are usually metaldehyde-based. Most are in the form of mini-pellets, and destroy slugs and snails. Put small heaps down near vulnerable plants, especially lettuces and the young hardy perennials, such as delphinium, on humid evenings. Metaldehyde is highly toxic to all forms of animal life. Hiding slug pellets under half-round tiles or inside tunnels and frames, places which slugs adore but are out of reach of pets, wild birds and animals is clearly a sensible precaution.

Hosta is a delicacy for slugs and snails, which can reduce its leaves to tatters in a few days.

Mole killers

This includes a wide range of products, some of dubious efficiency. The commonest is a smoke canister which is lit, then pushed into the main burrow beneath the 'hills'. Some anti-mole products kill the moles; others simply drive them away. Most gardeners are unwilling to kill moles, and prefer simply to drive them into other gardens.

There are hundreds of methods of combatting moles, from the empirical to the barbaric. One effective solution is to destroy earthworms with worm repellents, thus starving the moles.

Rat- and mice-killers

There are specific preparations for use against rats, field mice and voles: these are anticoagulants (such as warfarin), and must be put outside known holes. The best time to use them is in autumn and late winter.

Do not allow rodent killers to come into contact with the hands, because they pick up human scents and the rodents will not take them. Rodent killers can kill other animals as well; place them out of range of household pets. In the USA, these can only be used by licensed professionals.

Herbicides

Designed to kill weeds, herbicides or weedkillers act selectively or indiscriminately, in which case they are referred to as total, or broad spectrum, weedkillers. Chemical weedkillers are one of the fields in which research has made most progress in recent years.

Total, or broad spectrum, weedkillers

These kill plants indiscriminately. Several are based on a single active ingredient, such as glyphosate or paraquat. Others combine several chemicals, making them effective against the widest possible range of plants, and over the longest possible time. The fact that most modern products are applied only once a year shows how effective they are.

Total weedkillers are most effective in early spring on a slightly moist soil, irrespective of the state of vegetation. They are diluted and applied with a watering can or a sprayer fitted with a hood around the nozzle to prevent the material drifting on to wanted plants. Total weedkillers must not be applied close to ornamental plants or crops. Proceed with care near boundaries; the roots of a neighbour's plants may well reach into your garden. Prescribed dosages vary from one product to another, so follow instructions carefully.

Bare soil, or pre-emergent, weedkillers

These products have many uses, depending on the chemicals they contain but they all kill germinating weed seeds without affecting plants already present.

Also known as pre-emergent, preventative, or residual, weedkillers, they have an active life which varies from a few weeks up to a year. They can be used at any time during the growing season but spring is usually best because fewer weed seeds will have germinated.

Most preventative weedkillers are used under ornamental trees, including conifers, shrubs, roses and fruit trees and bushes. They are available as dry (mini-granular) applications and for diluting with water.

If the leaves of cultivated plants come into contact with 'bare soil' weedkiller, watering them is enough to wash it off and prevent damage. Some 'bare soil' weedkillers can be used at no risk to existing plants, but are virtually useless against hardy big-rooted weeds such as couch (quack) grass, thistles and convolvulus (bindweed).

Systemic weedkillers

These substances are the last word in weapons against unwanted weeds. They are carefully designed to destroy only the plants with which they come into contact. Systemic weedkillers are absorbed by leaves and carried by the sap to all parts of the plant, destroying it completely. Those containing glyphosate even eliminate the most invasive species. Selective systemic weedkillers are also available.

Total systemic weedkillers should only be applied to weeds in full growth, and are only fully effective at temperatures over about 59°F (15°C). Large areas of ground can be cleared effectively by applying them, but they can also be applied locally with a brush, a sponge or a special roller, and are ideal for destroying convolvulus (bindweed). To clear the ground for a lawn, for example, a single application of systemic weedkiller suffices. Depending on which one is used, cultivation may start within a matter of days.

Special precautions

Never mix weedkillers. Some products, princi-

WEEDS

Bindweed, a serious garden weed, is easily recognised by its twisting brittle roots. It is almost impossible to get rid of it completely.

A 'weed' is any plant growing wild. Some weeds are even considered attractive, such as dandelions, purslane, poppies, centaury and daisies.

There are two types of weeds: annuals and perennials. The annuals, the seeds of which are usually carried by birds and the wind, are liable to overrun a garden and are very difficult to eliminate. In principle, one has only to stop them flowering and they eliminate themselves. Examples are persicaria, with creeping roots and little pink flowers; hogweed, with large fleshy roots and slightly prickly leaves; stinging nettle; feverfew, with slightly greyish stumpy foliage; red or white dead-nettle, common in shaded areas; chenopodium (fathen), a tall plant with a hard stem and small greenish spiky flowers; euphorbia (spurge), with stems which secrete a poisonous milk; groundsel, with small yellow flowers and annual meadow grass (Poa annua), which invades lawns.

Hardy perennial weeds are much more of a nuisance as they last from one year to the next and spread with every season. Their root system is often deep and their strong growth frequently makes them more resistant to weed killers. The most common types are dandelion; bindweed, which wraps itself round the smallest support and very quickly overruns the garden; prickly leaved thistles; couch-grass (quack or witchgrass), with its creeping roots; buttercups, with long suckers which invade lawns; the perennial nettle, which likes rich soils full of humus; large sagebrush, which can often grow over 5 ft (1.5 m) tall; clover, which attacks lawns; and the deep rooted and extremely vigorous horsetail.

Many weeds have medicinal properties which make them highly sought after in the countryside, but that is no consolation for the gardener.

It should be mentioned that some plants can become undesirable in the long run due to their tendency to overrun the garden. For example, marigolds, eschscholzia (California poppy), annual chrysanthemum, bamboo, euphorbia lathyris (caper spurge or molewort).

Weeds do, however, have a positive side. They often tell you the quality of the soil as some species will only grow in certain types of soil.

pally sodium chlorate, can present a fire risk, so must be used with extreme care and in suitable areas. Follow the manufacturer's instructions carefully, to prevent disasters and to get the best results.

Total weedkillers
These are sold as soluble powders, liquids and microgranules for direct use on weeds, and are gradually becoming available in self-dissolving packs, thus avoiding any need for measuring doses. These products are intended solely for clearing paths and other non-cultivated areas.

Lawn weedkillers
These destroy broad-leaved weeds without harming grass. They should be used from mid-spring to early autumn in dry weather, and can be used safely at the foot of trees growing in the lawn. They should be applied not less than three days before and after mowing. Only apply them on established lawns, unless specifically recommended for newly sown or turfed areas.

Vegetable weedkillers for use on specific crops
These are usually available only to commercial growers. They are highly selective, although carrot weedkillers can also be used on celery, leeks, potatoes and asparagus, and strawberry weedkillers on beetroot, spinach beet and endives. They are applied when the weeds appear.

Shrub weedkillers (not available in USA)
These protect rose bushes which have been in the ground for at least six months, shrubs over a year old and established conifers, and some can also be used on well-established hardy perennials. There are often considerable restrictions about using shrub weedkillers, the instructions must be carefully read and fully followed.

Troublesome weedkillers (not available in USA)
These are systemic products capable of destroying the toughest weeds; some pose no risk whatever to lawns.

Undergrowth killers (not available in USA)
These are extremely powerful, and are mainly designed for use against nettles, docks and brambles, but may also be used against elder and other woody weeds. They are applied after brushwood has been cut down and the new shoots have reached 1 ft (30 cm) in height. After a month, the ground can be cultivated.

The buttercup quickly overruns crops, particularly lawns. It is very hardy and not easily killed, other than by weedkiller.

Spraying equipment

Sprayers
These are essential gardening tools; keep one for insecticides and fungicides, and another for weedkillers. To prevent any confusion, buy different colours for each purpose. If only one sprayer is used for all purposes small amounts of residual weedkiller can seriously damage plants when the sprayer is next used for insecticides.

Hose-end sprayers
These connect to an ordinary garden hose and the water pressure automatically draws pesticide or fertilizer from the attached reservoir, and dilutes it. The dosage is automatic and it also eliminates the need for carrying water, but is only practical in small gardens. Hose-end sprayers are also ideal for treating tall trees, as the water pressure can lift the mixture well up into them.

Pump-action spray guns
These work on the same principles as a bicycle pump. The diluted mixture is contained in a tank or bucket, and pumping creates air pressure to eject it. In some models, the pressure is enough to reach a considerable height. They are large and can be awkward to carry, but reducing their capacity would also reduce their performance. Applying the mixture evenly also takes a certain amount of concentration.

Pumps, although very old-fashioned, are excellent for treating the upper branches of trees and save the gardener having to use a ladder.

Pressure sprayers

The commonest models consist of a $\frac{1}{2}$–$2\frac{1}{2}$ gallon (2–12 litre) tank and a built-in pump which also acts as a grip. The tank is filled with the diluted chemical and the pump is operated to build up the pressure. Pressure sprayers are operated by an on/off tap which allows the liquid to pass along an external tube, up the lance and out of the nozzle.

In most models, the nozzle is adjustable from a strong jet to a fine mist. The more expensive models have telescopic wands, directable nozzles and often extensions. Most have translucent tanks for checking the level of the liquid.

A 1.1 gallon (5 litre) model, carried by hand, is occasionally useful for an amateur gardener although trigger sprayers are more practical in most situations.

Constant pressure spray guns

These sprayers, with plastic or stainless steel tanks, are carried knapsack fashion and are popular with market gardeners. They often have a large capacity, 3.3–3.6 gallons (14–16 litres), and are worked by a pump system operated continuously by hand. The best designed models also have a pressure regulator to make spraying more even. Pressurized sprayers are particularly useful in large gardens or for frequent use.

Trigger sprayers

These are small, cheap, light, spray guns 0.8–3.5 pint (0.5–2 litre) often used for spraying indoor plants. Some have robust, adjustable heads. They are easy to use; the tank is filled with the mixture and the trigger squeezed to operate the pump mechanism.

Cheap models have a rather limited life but they are quite adequate where only limited use is required.

Atomizers

These are fitted with a motor and are carried on the back, and have a powerful jet which can easily reach over 30 ft (9 m). They economize on insecticide or herbicide, which they atomize, finely and evenly spreading the chemical, but they are heavy and bulky. Renting an atomizer is sensible for occasional use.

Tips for successful treatment

It is not enough to have the right product and the proper equipment: you will also need a degree of skill and to take some precautions.

Some insect pests, particularly greenfly, aphids and red spider mite, have started to develop a resistance to certain insecticides, so changing the chemicals you use at regular intervals is a sensible precaution; check that the new one contains different active ingredients.

Read the manufacturer's instructions and follow them scrupulously, even if the doses prescribed seem weak.

Observe minimum times before harvesting edible crops as some substances take longer to wear off than others.

THE SAFE USE OF GARDEN CHEMICALS

The effective use of garden chemicals is just one aspect of pest, disease and weed control; their safe use is just as important.

This includes the safety of the user, other people, pets, wild animals and birds, harmless and beneficial insects and, of course, the safety of the plants being treated.

Instructions concerning safe handling and use of the chemical are found on the label. These normally include the wearing of gloves, washing the face and hands before eating, drinking or smoking after using the chemical and staying out of any drift when spraying.

It is important to show consideration for other people when using garden chemicals. Try to prevent spray chemicals drifting on to other people's property: insecticides and fungicides and especially weedkiller.

'Pets' includes cats, dogs, rabbits, tortoises, fish and caged birds. Cats and dogs seldom ingest any plants that have been treated chemically, simply because they are mainly carnivorous. However, cats spend a lot of time cleaning themselves and, if thoughtlessly applied garden chemicals end up on their coats, it can lead to upset stomachs (though seldom anything worse).

Slug pellets in particular have to be handled and applied with care. The alternative to pellets is to use non-chemical traps, such as upside-down halved grapefruit skins, put out in the evening, and checked for slugs in the morning.

Rabbits, guinea pigs and other grazing pets, including tortoises, are especially susceptible to injury from chemicals. Because they eat greenery and are frequently kept on the lawn in the summer, special care must be taken to prevent them eating plants which have been treated.

Chemicals in fish ponds can be especially dangerous and carelessly applied sprays can quite often drift into caged bird feed containers.

Wild animals should be given the same consideration as domestic animals. The most important precautions are those to be taken when using slug pellets and rat/mouse poison. Rodent poisons must be treated in the same way as slug pellets so that *only* rats and mice are affected.

The creatures most likely to be inadvertently harmed by garden chemicals are, unfortunately, helpful to gardeners. These include bees, which pollinate fruit and vegetable flowers as well as make honey, and ladybirds, lacewings and hoverflies, which prey on insect pests and help to keep their numbers down.

Use insecticides which are specific to given pests, such as pirimicarb against aphids. However, there are very few that are completely safe so other precautions are needed.

Where possible, delay any spraying until the evening when most bees have returned to their hives for the night. This, though, still leaves ladybirds and other predators vulnerable. The general rule is to avoid spraying if there is a worthwhile population of beneficial insects on the target plants: ladybirds, lacewings, hoverflies, centipedes, violet ground beetles, rove beetle (Devil's coach-horse), ichneumon flies and many small or even tiny parasitic wasps.

Finally, there is little point in trying to protect plants from the ravages of pests and diseases if they are then killed by chemicals. Read and understand the instructions on the labels before treatment and carry it out as recommended. Probably the most elementary mistake is to get the dilution rate wrong. An even more basic precaution is to make sure that the chemical you are planning to use is safe for the plants that are to be treated. A chemical that is safe to use at one time of the year may be harmful at another. This is always stated on the label.

The safe disposal of garden chemicals, either as concentrates or as surplus diluted sprays, is important. It is wise to dispose of chemicals when their labels have been lost or are unreadable and when a quantity of diluted spray is left over after treatment. In most cases, concentrates in dry form (powders granules and dusts etc) can be wrapped in newspaper, sealed in a plastic bag and put in the dustbin. For liquid concentrates, check with your local authority for the appropriate disposal method. The best way of getting rid of what is left in the bottom of a sprayer is to offer it to a neighbour for treating his or her own plants.

These methods of disposal are only applicable to garden chemicals in normal domestic amounts. Farmer and grower products and larger quantities are subject to strict regulations.

BIOLOGICAL PEST AND DISEASE CONTROL

Any account of pest and disease control would be incomplete without reference to biological control. This is the practice of making positive use of other living organisms. In nature, this is taking place the whole time, for example, when ladybirds eat greenfly or aphids. In a garden the beneficial insects are unlikely to keep the undesirable ones at an acceptably low level. In a greenhouse, however, the beneficial insects can be nurtured and prevented from escaping. Commercial greenhouse nurseries are making increasing use of biological control, because it is less time-consuming than chemical control and people are less attracted to food that has been treated with chemicals.

This method of pest control is also available to amateurs but currently there are only parasites available for controlling whitefly and red spider mite, and other pests within the greenhouse will be untouched.

PESTS, DISEASES AND PHYSIOLOGICAL DISORDERS

For a given climatic zone, no matter where it may be, the pests and diseases tend to be similar, though small differences in temperature can cause variations. Legislation also influences the pest and disease population of a country. The Colorado beetle, for example, is widespread in

	SYMPTOMS	*DIAGNOSIS*	*CONTROL MEASURES*
On leaves	Pale, discoloured leaves, with large numbers of tiny puncture holes. Drying out.	Red spider mites.	Apply suitable insecticide once every 14 days from late spring to early autumn in hot, dry weather.
	Small moth-like flying insects ⅛ in (3–4 mm) long. Plant becomes sticky and stops growing.	Whitefly.	Apply suitable insecticide as soon as seen and repeat at weekly intervals.
	Small black spots on leaves and stems. Leaves drop off rapidly.	Anthracnose.	Spray preventatively as soon as leaves appear. Repeat weekly until late spring.
	Leaves turn brown and curl up.	Scorch.	Multiple causes: too much fertilizer or sun; pollution; exposure to weedkiller or wind.
	Leaves discoloured and often shrunken at the middle; turn yellow, white then red.	Nutrient/trace element deficiency.	Add all-round (general) fertilizer or spray with a general feed immediately.
	Leaves nibbled, sometimes down to veins. Caterpillars on leaves.	Caterpillars, winter moth, saw-fly.	Preventative or remedial spraying.
	Leaves turn yellow, veins remain green, slow growth.	Chlorosis.	Lower the soil pH by watering with chelated iron.

mainland Europe but in the UK is only found very occasionally, as local outbreaks in imported vegetation. In the UK, this is a notifiable pest and ruthlessly wiped out.

Pesticides also vary enormously from country to country; one in common use in one country can be illegal in another.

The following chart, listing the major pests and diseases of temperate climates, gives the active ingredients, rather than proprietary brands, of chemical control. For example, the systemic insecticide dimethoate is available in a dozen different proprietary products, and listing them all is impractical. All pesticide, insecticide and fungicide products list the active ingredients on the label, so it is simply a matter of checking them .

PRODUCTS	*ADVICE*	*VULNERABLE PLANTS*
Specific Dicofol-based or most systemic insecticides.	Use when first seen. Some winter sprays kill the overwintering eggs.	Fruit trees, vines, conifers (especially blue pines), roses, dahlias, strawberries.
Multi-purpose insecticides (synthetic pyrethroid bases)	Burn worst-affected plants.	Any plants grown under glass. Also brassicas.
Copper or zineb based fungicides.	Pruning trees and shrubs drastically gives additional protection.	Beans, cucumber, grape, willows, poplars, cherries, planes, redcurrants, raspberries, peas, lettuce, melons.
None. Water generously with fresh water and correct or protect against cause.	Do not add fertilizer. Dig down to roots to see if they are alive.	All.
Quick-acting nitrogen fertilizer for nitrogen deficiency. Seaweed-based fertilizers for trace element deficiencies.	Enrich the soil with manure or garden compost.	All.
Contact-type insecticides like lindane, permethrin or a biological spray based on *Bacillus thuringensis*.	If preventative treatment is carried out effectively in spring, specific treatment is rarely needed.	Most plants including fruit trees, roses, shrubs, cabbages, radishes and turnips.
Add moss peat to the soil or chelated iron solution.	Do not apply iron sulphate as spray as this harms the foliage.	Pears, azaleas, rhododendrons, roses, magnolias, hydrangeas, camellias etc.

	SYMPTOMS	*DIAGNOSIS*	*CONTROL MEASURES*
On leaves	Brown through to cream pustules on leaves. Plants become sticky and stop growing.	Cochineal insects.	Spray when attack begins and follow up weekly for a month.
	Black charcoal-like powder on leaves, sticky texture. Plant asphyxiates.	Sooty mould.	Clean affected leaves and spray against aphids, thrips and scale insects.
	Leaves turn white, curl up, soften along stems.	Frost.	Protect plant to limit future damage.
	Large flying insects eating leaves.	Cockchafers or May bugs.	Spray contact insecticides if swarms appear. Attack larvae (white worms).
	Leaves holed and nibbled, with traces of clear slime.	Slugs and snails.	Pick off the pests regularly. Set traps and scatter proprietary pellets in mild, moist weather.
	Brown spots on leaves which shrivel and wither.	Mildew or leaf spot.	Spray fungicide preventatively, repeat every 10–12 days for major attacks or in wet weather.
	White mould all over leaves and stems. Plant reacts by shrivelling up.	Oidium fungus.	Spray preventatively early in season, repeat every 10 days in damp weather.
	Clusters of small green or black insects gathering on young shoots. Leaves curl up and some develop reddish brown blisters.	Aphids.	Apply systemic insecticides every 3 weeks or dig in insecticide granules around non-edible plants. Remove dense colonies by cutting off affected shoots.
	Leaves riddled with little holes and nibbled edges. Sometimes a characteristic smell.	Various beetles and weevils.	Good garden hygiene helps. Preventative multi-purpose remedies. Spray twice with contact insecticide at 10-day intervals.

PRODUCTS	*ADVICE*	*VULNERABLE PLANTS*
Oily or oil-based insecticides or malathion.	Use cotton bud soaked with beer, petrol (gasoline) or vinegar to remove cochineals by hand.	Citrus fruits, palms, hydrangeas, rose laurels, fruit trees, succulents, palm laurels.
Use systemic insecticides.	Act quickly.	Fuchsias, roses, evergreen shrubs, young plants.
None.	Do not underestimate risk of severe frost, even in supposedly mild areas.	Tender and half-hardy species, young plants.
Lindane, carbaryl, malathion, synthetic pyrethroids.	Attacks occur in cycles; treat soil over this period with a soil insecticide. Thorough cultivation and good weed control help.	Oaks, maples, chestnuts, beeches, limes, many ornamental shrubs and even lawns.
Metaldehyde, methiocarb.	Use a product containing a pet repellent.	Lettuce, rockery plants, seedlings, delphiniums, bulbs etc.
Thiram, mancozeb, triadimeton, zineb, thiophanate-methyl, maneb, copper.	Best in damp weather with temperatures over 50°F (10°C).	Vines, potatoes, tomatoes, onions, cabbages etc.
Micronized sulphur, fenarimol, triforine, dinocap (karathane).	Don't use sulphur at temperatures below 50°F (10°C) or over 77°F (25°C) or in full sunlight.	Oaks, roses, fruit trees, redcurrants, begonias, vines, chrysanthemums, mahonias, artichokes, hydrangeas.
Dimethoate, disulfoton, pyrethroids, rotenone (derris) malathion.	Granular formulations are very easy to use; action lasts for 2 months. Become effective after 8–10 days.	Most plants are vulnerable including roses, redcurrants, broad beans, nasturtiums, apples, plums, cherries.
Lindane, carbaryl, malathion.	Overgrown shrubs, woodpiles and neglected areas are favourite hide-outs for beetles and weevils.	Fruiting and ornamental shrubs, cabbages, buddleias, hydrangeas, dahlias.

	SYMPTOMS	*DIAGNOSIS*	*CONTROL MEASURES*
On leaves	Characteristic orange-brown pustules appear on undersides of leaves, which often fall off.	Rust.	Preventative sprays in spring, plus curative fungicide when attack starts.
	Leaves discolour and turn silver. Tiny stinging insects on undersides.	Thrips.	Spray or apply systemic insecticide on ground.
	Retarded growth; leaves slowly discolour, marble and shrivel.	Viruses.	No direct remedy. Destroy infected plants and select plants for resistance.
On stems	Bark splits, lesions appear; tissucs turn brown, rough and swollen.	Canker.	On large branches, gouge out the diseased tissue and treat with fungicidal paint. Cut back branch below affected section to healthy wood.
	Young and older shoots dry out drastically as if charred. Plant quickly dies.	Fireblight or bacterial canker.	No effective counter-measures. Remove and burn infected plants as soon as possible.
	Seedlings turn brown and rot. Soil sometimes covered in fungus.	Damping-off.	Good ventilation, steady temperature reduces risk of infection. Cleanliness and treatment of seedlings with fungicide solution.
	Bark nibbled at ground level; stunted growth.	Rabbits and/or hares.	Protect young plants with plastic collars or netting, or use rabbit-proof fencing.
	Deep wounds in stems at ground level. Plants die.	Cutworms.	Spread soil insecticide granules when planting.

PRODUCTS	***ADVICE***	***VULNERABLE PLANTS***
Thiram, mancozeb, triamedifon, thiophanate-methyl.	Keep reputedly vulnerable plants apart to avoid contamination. Destroy badly infected plants. Burn diseased leaves.	Geraniums, roses, hollyhocks, weeping willows, poplars, euphorbia, marigolds, chrysanthemums, anemones, larches, pines, mint.
Dimethoate, disulfoton, bromophos, lindane.	The control measures for aphids usually work for thrips.	Gladioli, iris, marigolds, dahlias, peas, chrysanthemums.
None but control pests like aphids which spread virus.	Avoid propagating vulnerable plants especially strawberries.	Strawberries, lettuce, cucumbers, melons, marigolds, chrysanthemums, iris, dahlias.
None.	Always use clean tools, and protect major pruning cuts with fungicidal paint.	Apples, plums, hornbeams, sorbus, hawthorn, maple, ash, birch.
None.	Don't plant vulnerable species. Follow crop rotation sequences.	Members of the *Rosaceae* family (roses), cotoneaster, hawthorn, pyracanthas, pears, marigolds, clematis, dahlias, chrysanthemums.
Thiram.	Use as open a compost as possible; if necessary with vermiculite or perlite added.	Any plants sown under cover.
None.	Put down bait with seed or granules near plants to prevent damage.	Fruit trees, lettuce, hostas, lilies, heathers.
Lindane.	Destroy insects after cultivating. Treat regularly at temperatures over 68°F (20°C)	Tomatoes, lettuce, cabbages, various root vegetables.

	SYMPTOMS	*DIAGNOSIS*	*CONTROL MEASURES*
On stems	Plants fail to grow. Holes appear on trunks together with sawdust. Trees quickly die.	Bark beetles.	Cut off and burn damaged shoots and branches. Apply preventative spray weekly in mid-spring.
On roots	Roots and necks of plants nibbled in ground or where stored.	Voles and fieldmice.	Put poison bait, where legal, under loose corn near plants. Otherwise use traps.
	Plants cut off cleanly at neck.	Mole-crickets.	Disguise insecticide granules as bait.
	Plants up-rooted; small earthmounds on lawn or in beds.	Moles.	Use traps. Treat lawns with a wormkiller.
	Plants cut at ground level. Fleshy roots or tubers riddled with holes.	Wireworm.	Spread insecticide granules when planting.
On fruit	Round holes with a saw-toothed edge at base of fruit. Flesh eaten away.	Wasps.	Find nests and destroy. Pick fruit before it is completely ripe.
	Fruit nibbled in a number of places, especially when in storage. Scampering noises in stores at night.	Dormice or field mice.	Use Warfarin as bait where legal (illegal in USA) or use traps.
	Concentric mould spots on maturing fruit.	Monilia.	Preventative fungicide sprays shortly before the fruit is picked.
	Grey fur on fruit. Fruit quickly rots.	Grey mould (Botrytis).	Use fungicidal powder or spray before damage appears, especially in damp weather.
	Apples and pears develop brown spots then crack. Spots on leaves.	Scab.	Preventative fungicidal sprays at all stages of growth.

PRODUCTS	*ADVICE*	*VULNERABLE PLANTS*
Synthetic pyrethroids.	Increase potassium and phosphoric acid content of soil to make trees more resistant.	Fruit trees, conifers, lilacs, laburnams.
Chlorophacinone, Warfarin etc. (illegal in USA).	Always put bait under tiles or PVC drains, since these rodents will only eat under cover.	Apples, beetroot, carrots, turnips, fruit trees.
Lindane, bromophus.	Best used in evenings on moist soil.	Strawberries, vegetables, newly planted flowers.
Alphachloralose.	Also use alphachlorolose with smoke cartridges and bait.	Lawn, kitchen garden.
Lindane.	Hoeing and turning over surface will expose most larvae and leave them open to attack by birds.	Vegetables (mainly root vegetables), strawberries.
None.	Do not treat with insecticides when the fruit is nearly ripe.	Pears, plums, peaches, vines.
Chlorophacinone, coumafene (illegal in USA).	Use bananas as bait to avoid any confusion.	Any fresh fruit.
Folpel, thiram, mancozeb.	Don't leave rotten fruit on trees, pick it and burn.	Pears, apples, plums, apricots.
Iprodione.	Avoid soaking plant foliage when watering.	Tomatoes, vines, raspberries, strawberries.
Bordeaux mixture, captan, maneb, carbendazim.	Burn diseased leaves.	Pears, apples, plums, pyracanthas, willows.

PLANTING

Planting is the most important stage in the life of a plant; poor planting can stunt or kill a plant, even a healthy one. Planting must also be well thought out and should make a major contribution towards improving the appearance of a garden.

For new plants to become established they need decent soil conditions and room to grow. Knowing the ultimate height and spread of a plant helps to position it well. If a tree is too large, for example, it will cast too much shadow and prevent other plants growing around it. There is the risk of invasion with some plants which may threaten buildings, especially if there are large branches weighing down on a roof. It is wise to draw up a plan and then check the needs of the plants you have selected, first making sure that you know where you can buy them.

Taking this approach will ensure that your garden is a success. In the following pages, you will find all the essential techniques for planting and information about the care the plants need afterwards.

BUYING AND COLLECTING PLANTS

Open- or field-grown plants have to be planted at different times of year, but the popularity of plants raised in containers has made planting almost a year-round operation. The enormous commercial use of heated greenhouses means that garden centres can now offer flowering geraniums from early spring, forced vegetable plants from the end of winter and packeted roses from early autumn.

Plants grown in containers for at least one full season beforehand should already have a complete root system and are less liable to be harmed by being transplanted. Generally speaking, the more roots a plant has, the better its chances of becoming established. However, the older and bulkier a plant, the more important good planting is and, as the larger plants are generally

Buying geraniums in a garden centre. Always go for the sturdiest and bushiest plants.

more expensive, small, young plants are a better choice. A 3ft 3 in (1 m) high *Thuya* (arborvitae), for example, has a better chance of establishing rapidly than a 6½ ft (2 m) one, which may often need a complete season to settle in and start growing again. Even so, young plants must also be vigorous, healthy and well formed, and the strongest, best-shaped specimens should always be chosen.

Where to buy and how to start

Ten years or so ago, plants were sold at the nurseries which grew them; only a few had mail-order facilities or catalogues. The development of modern sales techniques means that plants are now available in a variety of outlets, from mail order to discount stores. Unfortunately, cut-throat competition has reduced the range of plants available from many nurseries and garden centres making gardens more uniform.

Nurseries

The main growers, nurseries, are the best sources for unusual plants. Plant-raising nurseries are becoming increasingly rare, and are being replaced by growers who buy young plants from specialists, grow them on for a year or two and then sell them. Many of them issue lavishly illustrated catalogues. Growers may undertake to deliver plants within a certain radius, or send them by carrier. Most nurseries, local or regional, have sales outlets open to the public on a self-service basis, where you can choose the plants you want. In some cases, you can select plants while they are still in the nursery bed.

Nurseries – advantages

The nursery is the ideal place for direct contact with skilled specialists who are ready to give advice. They are the places where most plants are raised. They may then be sold direct to the gardener or, more usually, to garden centres or other retail outlets.

It is worth visiting local nurseries. You may find plants you have not heard of, but which appeal to you, as well as the more ordinary plants.

Drawbacks

Nurseries are usually in suburban or rural areas, so visiting them takes time. Some highly industrialized nurseries have only a very limited range, and if they only supply the trade, are not open to the public. Lastly, horticultural specialists often speak a language which is incomprehensible to many people and may even put customers off. This, though, is rare nowadays.

Tying up conifers in a nursery. Planted out in the open, the trees are well suited to a temperate climate.

Garden Centres

Garden centres are often sales outlets for nurseries to which they are attached. They usually offer a wide variety of garden products, such as stakes, ties, peat, sundries and fertilizers, and often have a wider range than the nursery itself: trees and shrubs, roses, fruit trees, bulbs, flowering plants, vegetables, indoor plants, seeds and so on. Other garden centres buy in all their plants, relying entirely on wholesale growers.

Advantages

Garden centres are designed for the ordinary gardener, in terms of the range of products sold and advice available. Their 'supermarket' style, careful layout and promotions make them equally accessible to the beginner and more experienced gardener.

Drawbacks

Some garden centres have a limited range of plants, with no collectors' items or outstanding specimens. The quality may vary and they are often crowded, which can be a nuisance.

It is often better to buy plants from a garden centre on a weekday rather than at a weekend, when t[illegible] can be extremely crowded, especially during good weather. It is also wise to visit them at the start of the planting season, as the range is at its widest then.

Mail order

Mail order is widely available, especially for the sale of Dutch bulbs, but general mail order companies also produce their own plant catalogues and some nurserymen specialize in mail order. The mail-order system works well in most countries depending on local legislation. Mail order can be an excellent way of buying, provided that you choose wisely and time it well.

Advantages

You can make your selection at home without wasting time, with reference books to hand to check the appearance, size and growing conditions required of particular plants. Catalogues often offer unusual plants at bargain prices and are especially useful in areas where nurseries and garden centres are rare.

Drawbacks

It is impossible to select the quality of the plants or control exactly when they are delivered; ordering large plants may involve expensive delivery charges. Catalogue illustrations also tend to be 'glamourized' and, more seriously, some plants resent being transported in this way. Lastly, there may be no way of contacting the professionals directly, and the only advice available to the customer is that in the catalogue.

The best way of testing a catalogue is to make your initial order small but varied; depending on the results, it may then be worth getting together with a group of fellow gardeners and putting in a bulk order to cover the carriage costs.

Superstores (discount stores in USA)

A superstore is a giant self-service store with a wide range of products. There is a garden section in most large food and DIY superstores. As many of these outlets have no outside storage facilities, they are restricted to selling 'pre-packed' plants, packs of bulbs or roses, seeds, 'boxed' fruit trees, indoor and hedge plants.

Advantages

You can buy a number of different things at the same time, and prices are also often very cheap. Self-service shopping means you can take time to make your choice.

The main things worth buying are special offers. Sundries are also often much cheaper than at other outlets. Try to buy plants that have just been put out for sale, rather than ones that have been on the shelves for some time.

Disadvantages

Their range is limited to the most popular plants, so it is rare to find anything unusual or exceptional. The plants may not always be top quality. Plants are not always stored under ideal conditions and, lastly, it is very rare that sales staff are experts.

Plant fairs

These are becoming increasingly popular, and may involve gardening clubs, specialist nurser-

Every year, producers, nurserymen and collectors show their latest creations at large, international exhibitions.

ies, botanic gardens, arboreta landscape gardeners and collectors selling unusual or fashionable plants.

Advantages
These fairs are a chance to find little-known or rare species and consult professionals and keen amateurs.

Disadvantages
The fairs are not always widely publicized, and often the only way to find out what is being sold is to pay to get in. The plants available may be expensive and available only in limited numbers. Fairs also attract so many visitors that it is difficult to buy in peace.

Remember that, if a plant is rare, it is often because it is difficult to grow. Lastly, attend fairs as soon as they open, to avoid crowds and the risk of the best plants being sold out.

Presentation

How plants are packaged usually depends on the outlets through which they are sold. Specific terms describe this and it is essential to know what they are to avoid mistakes, disappointment or confusion, especially with mail order purchases.

Bare-rooted plants
This usually refers to woody, deciduous plants, such as roses, many shrubs and fruit trees and bushes, and herbaceous perennial plants which are lifted and sold directly from nursery beds. Bare-rooted plants should only be sold when dormant, usually from late autumn to early spring.

Light and easy to carry, bare-rooted plants are often cheaper than those in soil or containers. When buying a bare-rooted plant, check that it has a strong, large and healthy root system and that it has not dried out. If not planted immediately, bare-rooted plants must be stored in the nursery in moist peat or heeled in temporarily at home.

Root-wrapped or balled plants
This type of presentation is disappearing in favour of plants in containers, but is still popular at some superstores in Europe. Balled plants are dug up from the open ground and their root balls wrapped in protective hessian sacks (burlaps) or plastic envelopes, which must be

Many shrubs are now sold in containers. This enables them to build up a strong and extensive root system so that planting them in the garden is easy and successful.

removed before planting. Balled plants are usually planted when dormant, from late autumn to early spring.

Avoid evergreen plants, such as conifers, with wilted or brown foliage. Check that the root ball has been kept moist.

Plants in containers
Most garden plants are available container-grown, which avoids root disturbance associated with planting. Containerized specimens can be planted when flowering, without risk, as the plants have been grown in these containers, and have a compact but full root system.

Containerized plants can be planted at any time of year, provided the ground is not frozen or waterlogged. Young containerized plants become established more easily than older ones.

Small containerized plants
Young flowering plants, tiny trees and shrubs for training as bonsai, and vegetables are often sold in little plastic pots. As they have well-

Blue fir with roots wrapped in sacking (burlap). You can check that the tree has not suffered too much from being dug up by examining the foliage.

established root systems, they last well in shops and usually take well. Plant out or transplant into a larger container quickly, as they have usually reached the limits of their growth in the pot. The potting compost or soil quickly dries out, and once this happens the chances of survival are dramatically reduced.

Pressed-ball plants

These plants (often grown in six-packs) come with a square compressed clump of peat-based compost, which helps the plants become established quickly after transportation. This method is frequently used with young vegetables and seasonal bedding plants, such as pansies, geraniums, French marigolds and impatiens.

Using pressed-ball plants is the cheapest way of stocking a kitchen garden or flower bed in a very short time. Keep them moist and in the shade until planted, as they dry out quickly.

Plants in bags

Roses are often sold in plastic bags, with colour reproductions of the variety on the covers. Plants in bags generally have bare roots packed in damp peat or moss, and the bag has airholes to prevent too much moisture building up.

Check the condition of bagged plants, make sure the branches are alive and healthy and that the peat has not dried out. Buy plants in bags when they are dormant, before shoots appear on the branches.

Pre-packed plants

Packaged for self-service stores in an elegant box which combines colours and advice, boxed plants are usually top-of-the-range roses, deciduous shrubs or fruiting plants. They are similar to bagged plants. Again, check that the plant is in good condition and avoid totally concealed specimens which are impossible to examine.

Buying trees and shrubs

Trees, shrubs and conifers offered in soil or containers are usually sold by height. The price usually increases faster than the size of the plant but, the taller a plant, the older it is. Avoid buying specimens that are too small, less than 16 in (40 cm) or too tall, over 5 ft (1.50 m) as they may be difficult to establish. With slow-growing varieties, such as box or holly, it is best to buy a 24–32 in (60–80 cm) specimen, as smaller plants take years to reach this size.

Standard trees

When choosing a standard, be sure that your garden is big enough to accommodate the full-

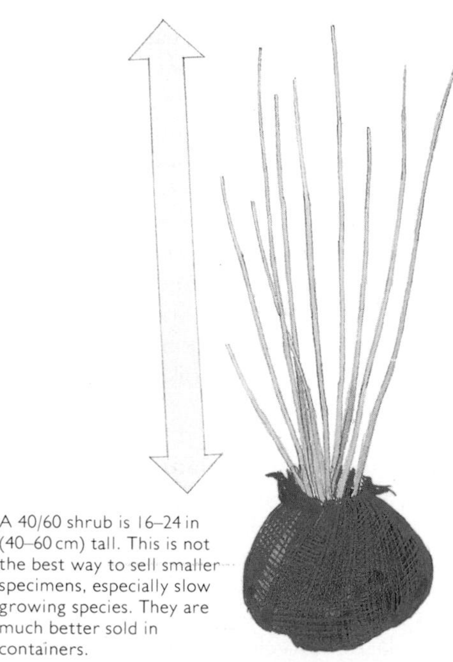

A 40/60 shrub is 16–24 in (40–60 cm) tall. This is not the best way to sell smaller specimens, especially slow growing species. They are much better sold in containers.

grown tree and that you will be able to put a ladder and other fruit-gathering equipment where the tree has been planted. If a standard is to produce a reasonable crop, it will grow so tall that the only way to pick fruit will be with a tall ladder. However, these trees, particularly cherries, are attractive in this form.

Half-standards

The trunk of half-standards is limited to about $4\frac{1}{4}$ ft (1.30 m) in height. The branches are perfectly developed, but the tree is smaller than the standard. Restricting their growth makes the trees more suitable for medium-sized gardens. Dwarf and semi-dwarf trees are also available in the USA.

2–3 years

These young, unformed trees need to be pruned into shape. For experienced gardeners, they offer an excellent price/performance ratio. They are the trees to choose if you want something that you can shape as you wish. 'Weeping' varieties are already shaped and are easier to train.

Maidens or whips

Maidens are one-year-old budded or grafted plants. Fruit trees are often sold at this age. Designed to be pruned into shape, they come as a single stem, often with a few lateral shoots known as 'feathers'. Maidens are a very cheap way of buying a tree, but you need to know how to prune them correctly.

Carrying plants

Plants can be bulky and difficult to carry, especially in large sizes or quantities, so take your own transport when buying from a nursery, garden centre or self service store. Pot plants should be tightly packed to prevent their shifting in transit; take boxes to contain them or plastic sheeting to protect the car. When buying in spring or summer, do not leave plants in the car in the sun as they will dry out quickly.

If you have to transport plants on the roof rack, as is often the case with trees, put the roots, and as much of the tree or trees as you can, in plastic bags. In winter, add a layer of straw or sacking. Always lay plants with the roots forward, to offer less wind resistance, and if the branches extend about 3 ft (1 m) beyond the end of the car, hang a red warning cloth.

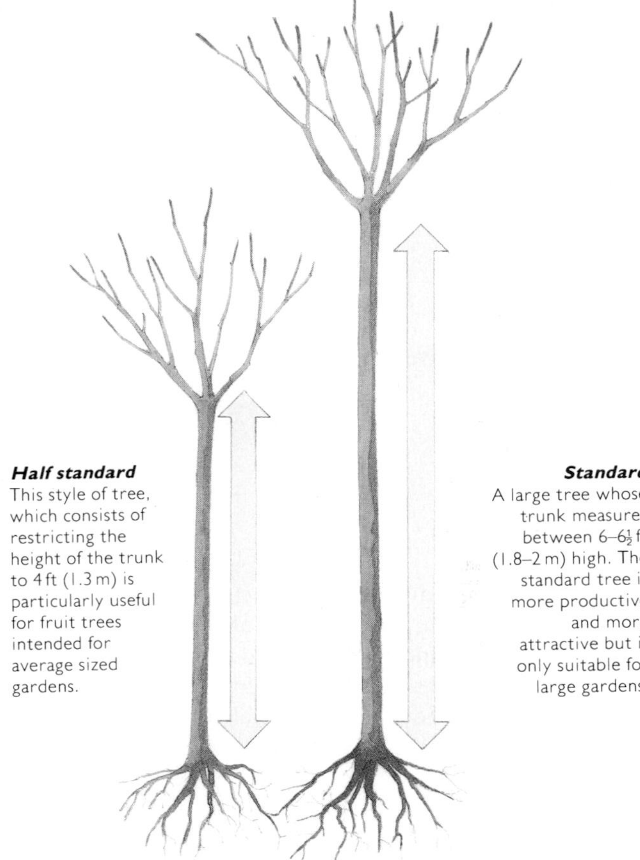

Half standard
This style of tree, which consists of restricting the height of the trunk to 4 ft (1.3 m) is particularly useful for fruit trees intended for average sized gardens.

Standard
A large tree whose trunk measures between 6–$6\frac{1}{2}$ ft (1.8–2 m) high. The standard tree is more productive and more attractive but is only suitable for large gardens.

If you cannot shut the rear door with the plants inside, tie the door down securely to prevent it opening completely. Keep the windows of your vehicle open to let out any exhaust gases that enter the passenger compartment.

When plants arrive

Prepare the site for plants ordered from a nursery well in advance, unless the weather is very cold, in which case the planting holes would freeze. If new arrivals cannot be planted immediately, keep them in a sheltered position; against a south-facing wall, for example. Dig a trench 12–16 in (30–40 cm) deep and lay the plants in this trench at an angle, covering the roots with soil.

Examine plants bought by mail order as soon as they arrive; do not hesitate to return second-rate, damaged or dried-out plants and insist on their being replaced, even if it is difficult to get a refund. Send your parcels by registered post to keep a record of when the parcel was returned.

Plants arriving during frosts always pose a particular problem. Do not unwrap them, but

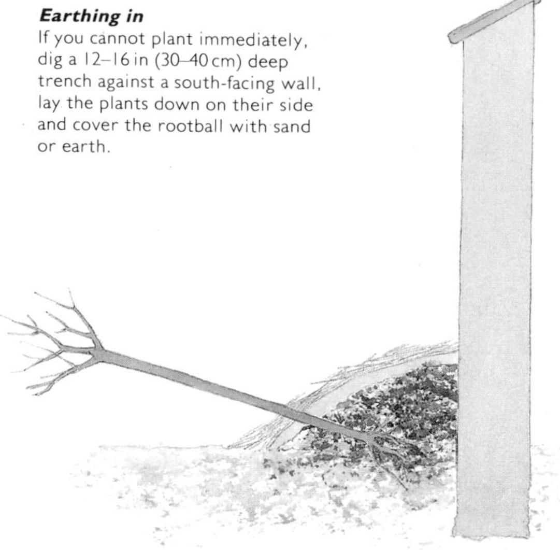

Earthing in
If you cannot plant immediately, dig a 12–16 in (30–40 cm) deep trench against a south-facing wall, lay the plants down on their side and cover the rootball with sand or earth.

put them directly in a trench and give additional protection, such as a tarpaulin or straw. Alternatively, stand them in a frost-free (or nearly so) shed or garage until conditions improve. While conscientious nurseries will not make deliveries in very cold weather, mail order parcels may arrive at any time.

People whose work takes them away from home should make special arrangements when buying plants by mail order, or at least insist on them being sent by recorded delivery, as many non-specialist carriers store plants in cold and draughty warehouses.

Preparing for planting

If plants fail to establish, this is often due to poor planting. Digging a little hole and slipping the plant in is not enough. People with 'green fingers' may seem to succeed effortlessly, but this is usually due to their experience rather than any magical ability. Planting means successfully installing a plant in a new environment and there are a number of essential considerations.

Designing a layout

A planting layout is essential to the success of a beautiful garden. Include as much information as possible on the plants already in the garden. It is not always easy to identify some plants when they are dormant, or to remember all their features. In the case of bulbs and some hardy perennials, it may be impossible. Who can accurately recall the exact shade of a border months after flowering? Noting these details avoids putting plants of the wrong kind or colour together and helps you visualize the effect of differing heights. Unless the garden is planned beforehand irritating mistakes may occur: dwarf asters will be invisible if thoughtlessly planted behind phlox, for example.

Choose the sites of trees and shrubs carefully. Take the shapes, leaves and colours into consideration, but height is the decisive factor. Do not overlook any legal restrictions concerning plant heights and party walls and neighbouring property.

A plan is not always enough; common sense is also required. Plants may only reach their full height a long time after they are planted and, unless you allow for this, your garden may look unbalanced for many years. Consider family needs when planning; take care in siting a play area, for example.

You do not have to design your garden to the last inch; just note the distances between plants and their approximate spread. Consult this plan before introducing new plants in autumn and early spring. It is advisable to include such fixtures as main drains, sprinkler systems and lighting cables on the plan to avoid problems when digging holes for new plants, and to mark the positions of your house and other buildings. Note the direction the garden faces.

Preparing the soil enables you to adjust it to suit the plant concerned. Ideally choose species which tolerate or thrive in the existing soil type.

Prepare the planting position in advance by digging the hole sufficiently wide and deep to accommodate either the spreading root system of a bare-rooted plant or the compact rootball of container-grown plants.

Incorporate peat, pulverized bark or well-rotted garden compost into the bottom of the hole and the dug-out soil. In autumn or winter incorporate bone meal with the dug-out soil; in spring and summer use a general fertilizer.

When planting, break up the soil as much as possible. Double dig heavy or previously uncultivated soil, digging to two spades deep, and keeping the topsoil and subsoil separate.

Preparing plants

Plants must be fresh and their rootballs moist. Avoid the hottest times of day when planting in summer and plant on a relatively cool evening. This is also the best time for watering, so the sun's rays are not magnified by the drops of water and scorch the foliage.

In winter, never plant when the soil is frozen or water-logged.

If newly bought plants are dry at the roots, stand the roots in water and do not plant them until the following day.

Planting in autumn

Autumn is the traditional time for planting, when nurseries offer a full selection of trees, shrubs, conifers, climbing plants and roses. Autumn is also the time to plant bulbs for flowering in spring.

Dormant plants planted in autumn suffer less shock than if they are moved when fully active. Autumn and early spring are best for planting bare-rooted deciduous plants. Less hardy species and those with fleshy roots benefit from spring planting.

Planting bare-rooted plants

This mainly involves fruit trees and trees, such as willow and poplar, which establish easily. Ornamental trees are usually sold root-wrapped or in containers.

Method Make the hole deep and wide enough to take the spread-out roots comfortably. If a stake is needed, put it in place after the hole has been dug but before the tree is planted. Drive the stake in upright slightly off centre, so that the tree can be centred. The stake should be placed in the direction of the prevailing wind, to help support the tree. The top of the stake should come to just below the lowest branch.

Trim back excessively long roots with secateurs (hand pruners) and remove any damaged or crushed roots.

Position the tree in the centre of the hole, roots flat on the bottom of the hole and evenly fanned out. Ideally, one person should cover the roots with soil enriched with organic matter while a second holds the tree upright, shaking it gently so that the soil particles fill the spaces between the roots. If necessary, use a stick to push the soil into the smaller spaces. When the hole is half full compress the soil with your feet, holding the tree to keep it upright. Replace the rest of the soil, firming it down as you go, until the hole is full. Unless the soil is naturally heavy and poorly drained, finish by forming the soil into a shallow dish around the base of the tree. Fill this with water after planting, to settle in the tree. The dip also collects rainfall, taking advantage of natural watering.

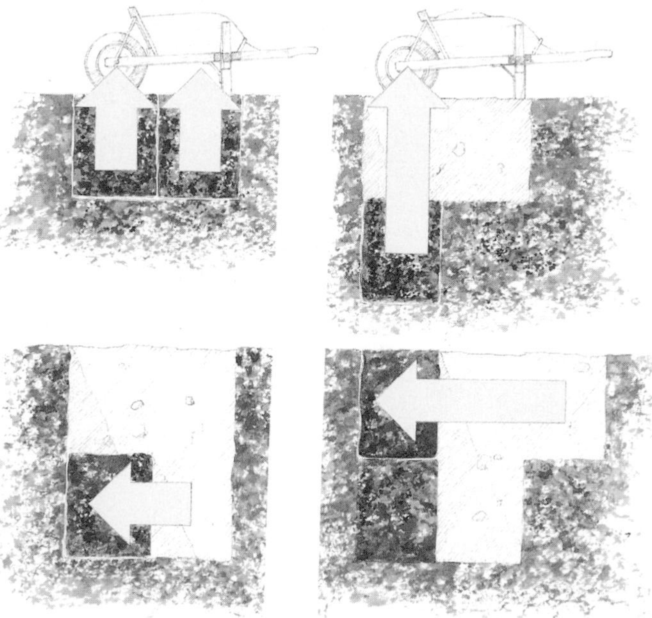

Double digging
Double digging is just an extension of single digging in that the trench formed by throwing the topsoil forward is itself dug to a full fork's depth.

Spread a mulch of well-rotted garden compost or manure around the base of the tree, to further increase the soil's moisture-holding capacity, and protect the roots from sudden drops in temperature. Do not let the manure or compost touch the trunk, or it is liable to rot.

Tie the tree to the stake, preferably using a proprietary tie which will not damage the trunk. Finally, lightly prune the branches reducing their length by about a third and giving the plant a well-proportioned appearance.

Planting containerized or balled trees

The vast majority of trees and shrubs are sold containerized or root balled. They can be planted all year round, provided the weather and soil conditions are suitable.

Method Planting is the same as for bare-rooted trees, except that no root preparation is involved. Try to remove the plant from its container without breaking the rootball. Remove a clay or plastic pot by tapping it gently against the side of a table or other hard surface. If roots show through the drainage holes, you may have to break the pot if tapping fails to dislodge the plant.

Plant trees and shrubs with their rootballs wrapped in protective hessian sacking (burlap). Once it is in the hole, cut the top of the sacking, so that it falls open and exposes the rootball.

Planting bare rooted trees

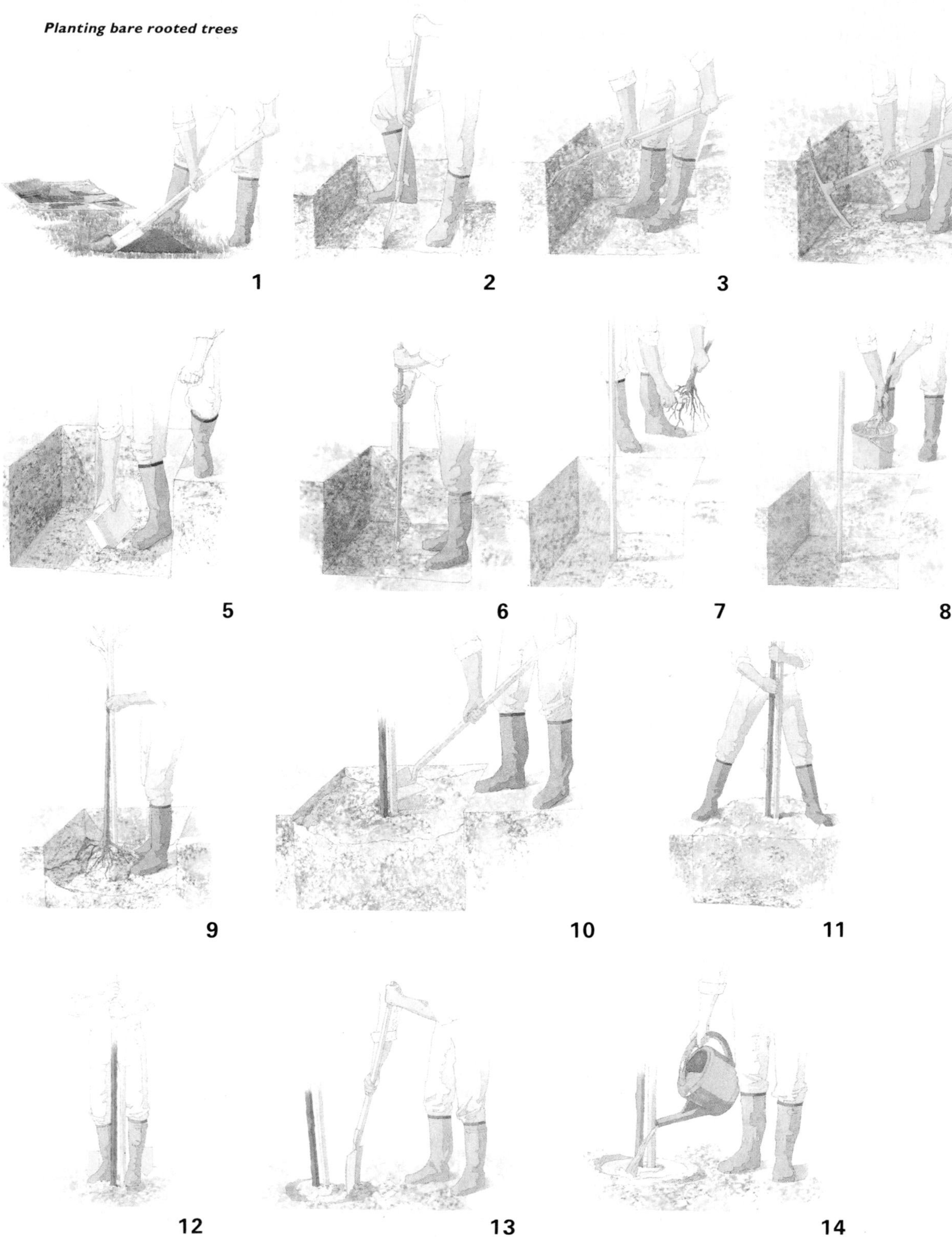

1–2. First dig a hole deep enough to accommodate the spread out root system. **3.** Loosen sides of the hole. **4.** Pickaxe or fork the bottom to break up the soil. **5.** Throw in one or two handfuls of slow acting fertilizer. **6.** Drive in the stake vertically and slightly off centre. **7.** Trim the ends of the roots with secateurs (hand pruners). Remove any damaged pieces. **8.** (Optional.) Dress the roots by dipping them in a semi-liquid compost made of cow-dung and clay. **9.** Place the tree in the centre of the hole with its roots well spread out and flat. **10.** Fill the hole with soil. **11.** Gently shake the tree so that the soil gets into all the small pockets. **12.** Firm the soil with the foot while holding the tree. **13.** Dig a circular moat around the tree. **14.** Water copiously. Finally, tie the tree to its stake.

This avoids disturbing the rootball; the new roots soon grow through the bottom of the sacking, which in time rots away.

If the sacking is plastic, stand the tree or shrub in the bottom of the planting hole and proceed as for hessian sacking (burlap), but try to remove as much of the plastic as possible, by sliding it up from the base.

Black, plastic (polythene) containers also have to be removed completely. Stand the plant in the bottom of the planting hole and slit the container from the rim to the bottom of the hole in about four places, then pull it away from under the roots.

It is essential that the rootball remains intact. Moistening the rootball generously before planting is essential to prevent wilting, and also to make the soil hold together and thus less liable to crumble when the container is removed. If the roots crowd round the edge of the pot and form a spiral in the base, this can prevent a plant becoming established. Try to uncurl coiled roots and spread them out in the planting hole.

Planting shrubs

Whether grown in containers or bare-rooted, ornamental shrubs or small fruit bushes are planted in the same way as trees, except that the holes are smaller and no stakes are required.

Planting roses

Roses are planted in the same way as other shrubs and must have a sunny location, sheltered from the wind, if they are to flower well.

Hybrid tea and floribunda roses should be planted 18–30 in (45–80 cm) apart, according to cultivar; miniatures, 10–12 in (25–30 cm) apart. Standards and weeping standards are often planted singly as focal points, but if more than one is planted, space them 4–6 ft (1.2–1.8 m) apart. Plant species and shrub roses 5–10 ft (1.5–3 m) apart, again depending on the cultivar. Climbers and ramblers vary enormously in size; the label should indicate the space needed.

Method Roses are sold bare-rooted, during the dormant season, and in containers all-year-round.

Most roses are sold pruned back to an average height of 12–16 in (30–40 cm). Shorten the branches by half to an outward-facing bud.

During planting make sure that the point at which the bush was budded is ½ in (1 cm) below ground level. Finish by watering generously.

Pre-packed roses often have dry roots; if so immerse the roots completely in a bucket of water for a half hour before planting. Remove any root suckers before planting.

Planting hedges

Root-balled or container grown specimens are less risky, although bare-rooted plants are cheaper and, correctly planted, can give good results.

Planting distances vary depending on the species used, from 12 in (30 cm) for dwarf box to 24 in (60 cm) for laurel and privet.

Method Prepare the soil well before planting, incorporating organic matter and removing

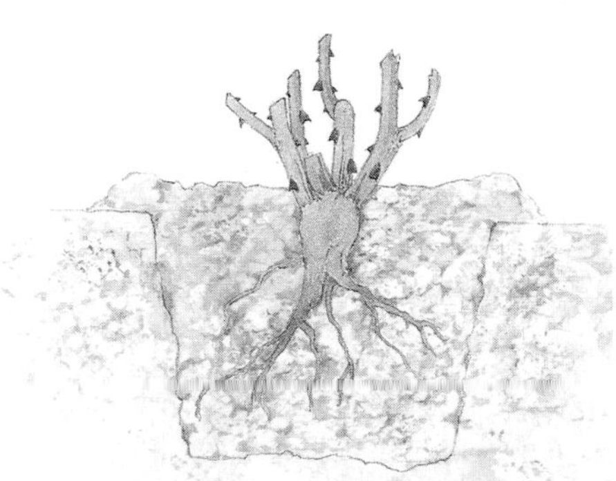

Plant roses in a sunny position, making sure that the graft union is just below the surface. Prune back the branches and give plenty of water.

Planting a hedge
Dig a trench 2 ft (60 cm) deep and 16 in (40 cm) wide. Partly fill with soil enriched with organic matter and arrange the plants at the recommended distance apart. Water copiously.

perennial weeds. Run a taut line where you want the hedge and set the plants the right distance apart. Water generously, even if the soil is moist.

Deciduous hedging plants are planted when dormant; plant conifer hedges, such as *Thuya* (arborvitae) or Leyland cypress in late spring or early summer.

Planting bulbs

Plant spring-flowering bulbs from early autumn to early winter. Generally, the size of a bulb governs the depth at which it is planted. Bulbs are buried to about twice their height, 2–2½ in (5–6 cm) for grape hyacinths, scillas, blanda anemones etc., and 4–5 in (10–12 cm) for tulips, hyacinths and narcissi (daffodils in USA). Bulbs look best planted in groups of at least five large, or ten smaller species. Planting distances vary from ¾–1⅛ in (2–3 cm) for small bulbs, to 4–6 in (10–15 cm) for tulips, narcissi (daffodils in USA) and hyacinths.

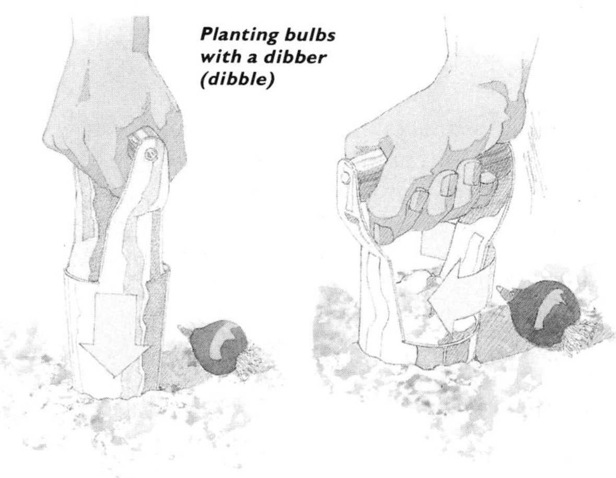

Planting bulbs with a dibber (dibble)

1. Push the dibber straight down into the soil.

2. Twist and pull to remove a plug of soil.

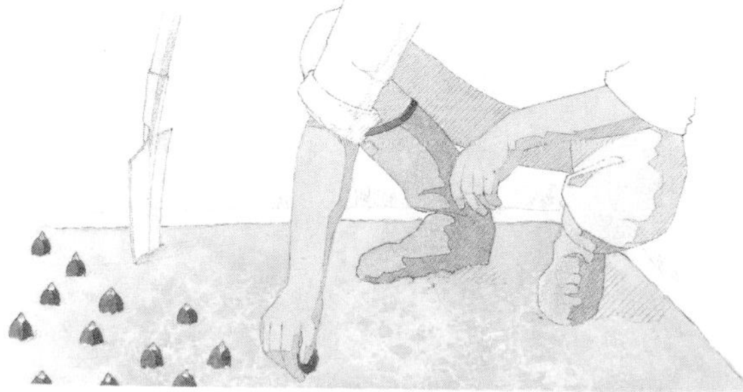

Dutch method of planting bulbs
Scrape off a layer of soil from the surface of the bed. Arrange the bulbs neatly and cover with a thin layer of soil.

Method On slopes where nothing but bulbs are planted, use the Dutch method, which makes it easier to space plants regularly. Remove the soil to the required depth, lay the bulbs in a regular pattern and reapply the soil.

In European gardens, the bulbs are planted with biennials, such as pansies, myosotis (forget-me-nots) or wallflowers. Plant the biennials first and then the bulbs, so you do not accidentally disturb planted bulbs. Using a bulb planter or trowel, make a suitably sized hole, then place the bulb in the hole and fill with soil.

If planting bulbs in heavy soil, place a little grit or coarse sand in the bottom of the planting hole before putting in the bulb, and mix a little peat in the soil to be returned to the hole. This helps drainage and prevents the bulb rotting. The soil must not contain any fresh manure or unrotted organic matter.

In Europe, you can buy perforated plastic baskets which hold a number of bulbs. By planting the bulbs in the basket it is easy to recover them once they have flowered to put other plants in their place.

To give the impression of bulbs growing naturally on a lawn, scatter the bulbs over the ground and dig them in where they fall.

Planting in spring

Spring planting, depending on the weather, can start in early spring and continue until early summer. Spring planting saves plants from the rigours of winter, and is usually the season for planting evergreen and not quite hardy species. Once spring growth has started, do not buy or plant bare-rooted plants, only root-wrapped or containerized ones.

Planting conifers

Conifers can be planted in early autumn but only where winters are mild and the soil light. The best time for planting conifers is from mid- to late spring. Most conifers are sold in containers and in temperate climates can be planted until the end of early summer.

Method Conifers are planted in the same way as other shrubs and trees, but avoid waterlogged soils, as an impermeable soil often encourages the rot *Phytophora cinnamomi*. Poor or sandy soil may retard the growth of some conifers.

Thick conifer foliage, which lasts throughout the winter, always presents a considerable target for wind. Large plants should be anchored to

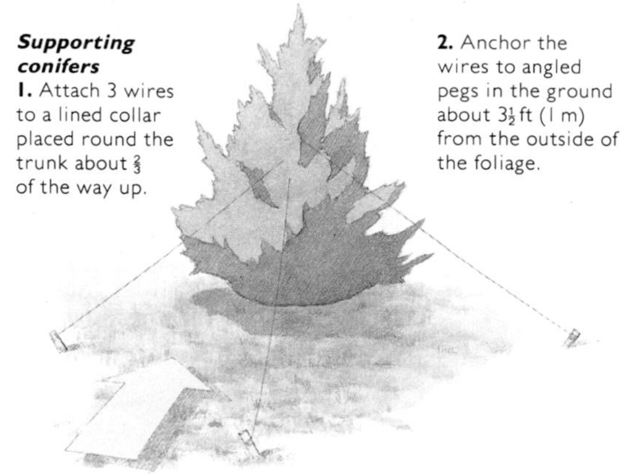

Supporting conifers
1. Attach 3 wires to a lined collar placed round the trunk about ⅔ of the way up.
2. Anchor the wires to angled pegs in the ground about 3½ ft (1 m) from the outside of the foliage.

resist sudden gusts until they become established. Tie three taut wires to a padded collar fixed to the trunk about a third of the way up the tree. Hold the wires in the ground by stakes angled outwards about 3 ft 3 in (1 m) out from the base.

Finish by watering generously, about 4.5 gallons (20 litres) for a plant 5 ft (1.5 m) tall. In hot, sunny weather, spray the foliage of newly planted conifers at the end of the day to prevent drying out.

Planting heathland (ericaceous) plants

Rhododendrons, azaleas, camellias, andromedas and kalmias (mountain laurel) cannot tolerate lime in the soil and must be planted in soil with a pH of less than 6, specially treated, if necessary. If your soil is not suitable, it is best to grow these plants in large tubs containing ericaceous compost. Smaller species and cultivars can be grown in raised peat beds. Apart from magnolias, heathland (ericaceous) plants are relatively easy to transplant.

Method Planting heathland (ericaceous) plants is the same as for other trees and shrubs. Moisten the rootball before removing it from the pot. Water generously, as sandy soil has trouble re-absorbing water when dry.

Most heathland (ericaceous) plants prefer semi-shade and a cool, moist atmosphere. Plant them away from draughts, which tend to prevent flowers forming. Frequent mulching helps maintain a high proportion of organic matter and keep the temperature down.

Planting climbing plants

The best time for planting climbing plants is spring. Apart from ivy and some other evergreens, most climbing species are not decorative in winter. The climbers in the nurseries and garden centres will be prettier in spring. Many will be available in containers.

Supports for climbing plants are essential and should be installed before planting. Even self-clinging plants, such as Virginia creeper, ivy and climbing hydrangeas, need wires or netting to start with.

Method Dig the planting hole at least 12 in (30 cm) from the base of a wall, place the rootball in the hole, burying it to the same depth as it was in the container, so the surrounding soil is level with the top of the root ball. This is important with clematis. Put some large stones or tiles around the base of clematis stems to protect them from the heat. Clematis are particularly fond of having 'their feet in the shade and their heads in the sun'.

Spread out the stems of climbing plants in a fan over the support, or in a spiral if training the plant up in a column. Tie the branches lightly with plastic ties or twine.

Planting plants root-wrapped in acid soil

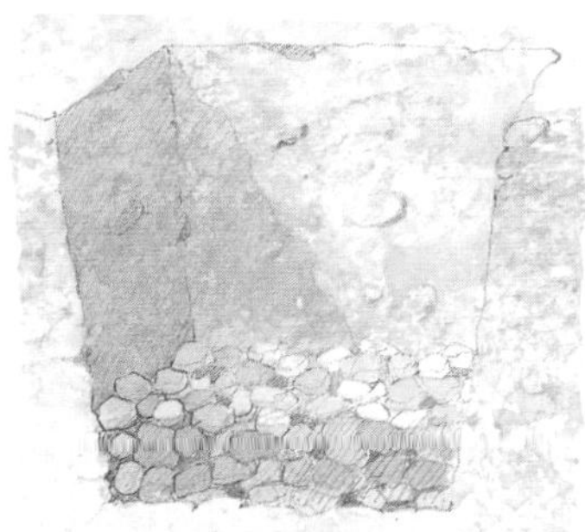

1. Dig a 20 in (50 cm) deep hole and put a layer of broken pots on the bottom.

2. Line the sides with garden felt.

3. Plant the rootball having first soaked it thoroughly.

Planting clematis
1. Dig a hole as close to the support as possible.
2. Lay the rootball on its side in the bottom.
3. Fan out the stems over the support and loosely tie the branches to it with plastic ties.
4. Place a tile or broken clay pot over the base of the stems to protect them from the sun.

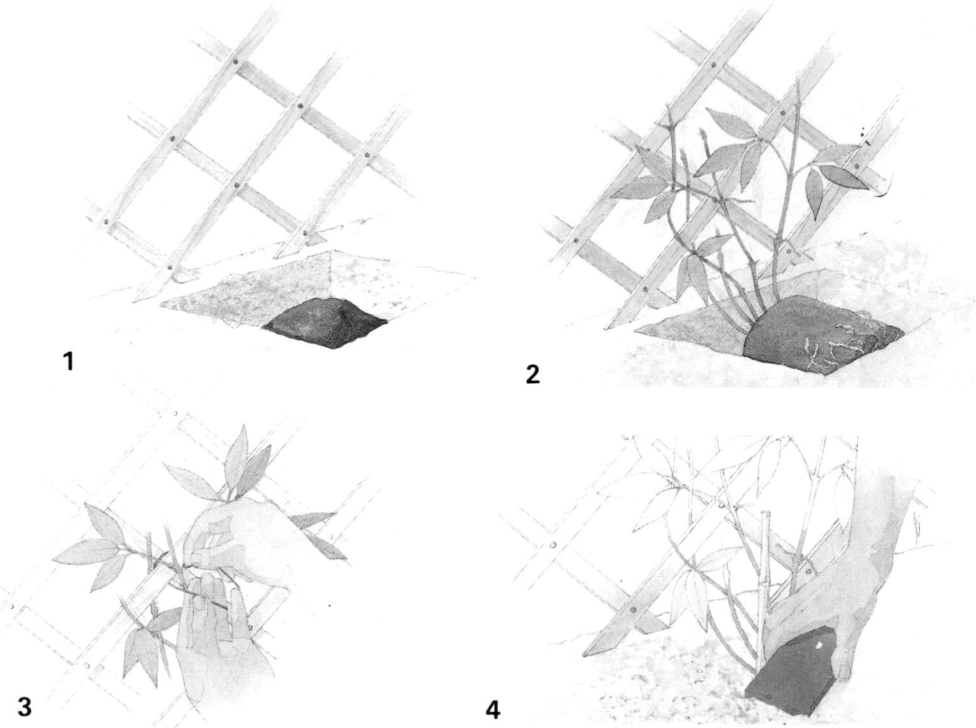

Water generously if the weather is fine and hot.

If buying very young plants with just a single stem, as is often the case with clematis, you can group two or three together to give a larger clump.

Train new stems evenly as they grow.

Planting aquatic plants

Plant aquatic plants in late spring, once the pond has warmed up sufficiently. The depth of water needed varies according to the species. Aquatic plants are usually supplied in a perforated mesh container. If not, repot in perforated plastic baskets or terracotta pots. Use heavy soil, clay if possible, and avoid peat and light fibrous matter which is liable to float to the surface.

Method Cover the surface of the soil or compost in the pot with gravel or pebbles, to prevent soil floating to the surface and fish nibbling around the roots. Lower the plant gently into the water to prevent the pond being muddied.

Positioning plants in the centre of a pond is easiest working in twos, each person holding one end of two cords threaded through either

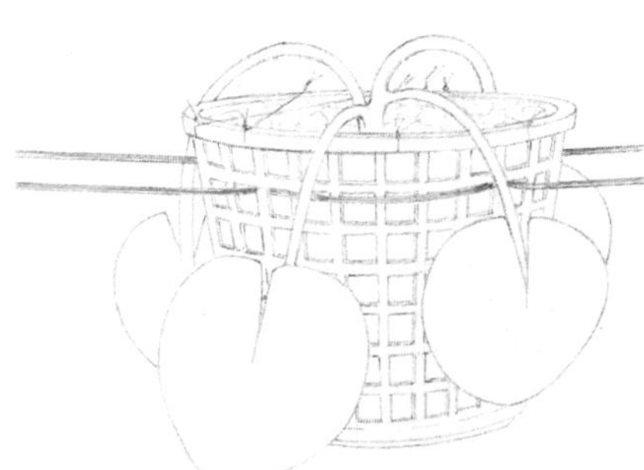

Planting aquati
plants
1. Re-pot the plan
plastic basket or a
perforated clay pc
2. Cover the surfa
the pot with stone
gravel.
3. Loop string thr
both sides of the
planter and positi
the pot in the rec
spot above water.
Then lower it int
water and pull th
string free.

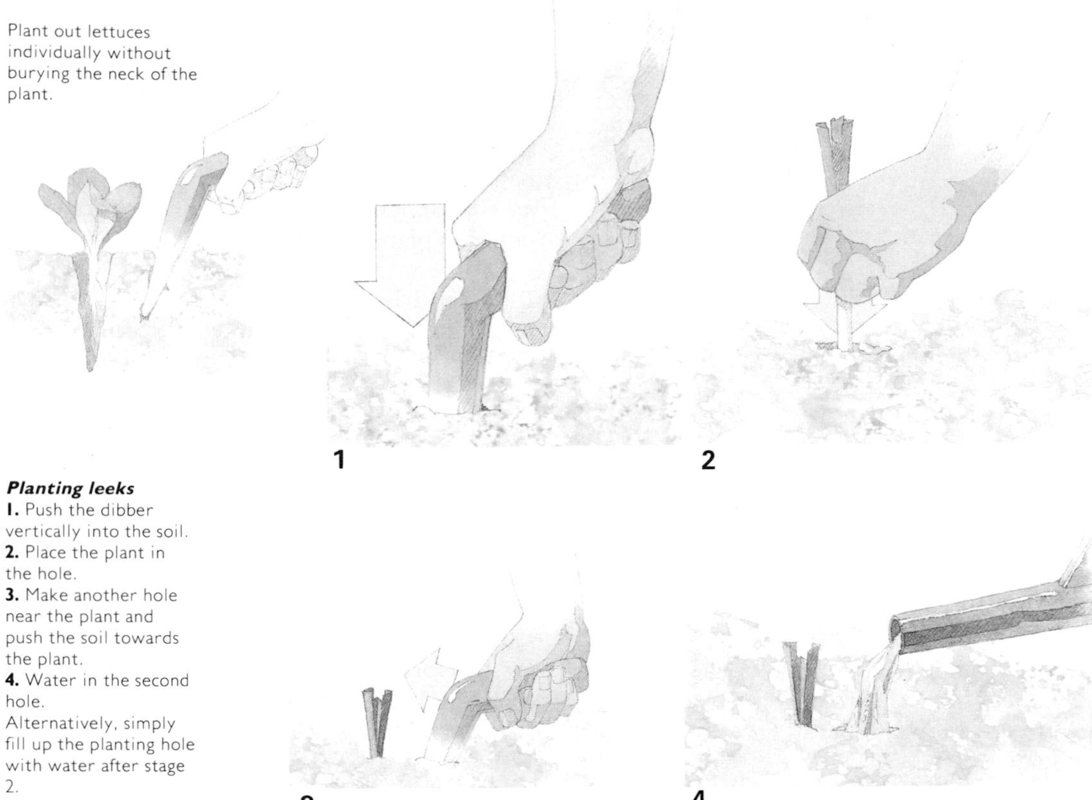

Plant out lettuces individually without burying the neck of the plant.

Planting leeks
1. Push the dibber vertically into the soil.
2. Place the plant in the hole.
3. Make another hole near the plant and push the soil towards the plant.
4. Water in the second hole.
Alternatively, simply fill up the planting hole with water after stage 2.

side of the planting basket. The pot is then moved into position over the water, and gently lowered and the cords removed.

Totally submerged plants, such as myriophilles, are weighted and put in plastic netting cylinders held upright in an underwater tank. They will then root themselves and can grow in peace, protected from fish by the vertical netting.

To prevent plants floating to the surface, criss-cross the top of the pot with plastic-coated galvanized wire.

Planting vegetables and fruit

Some vegetables, such as cabbages, tomatoes and leeks are traditionally germinated in seed trays or nursery beds, and then planted out. You can raise plants from seed or buy seedlings from garden centres or growers.

Method Plant bare-rooted vegetables as soon as possible after buying or digging up. Revive them for ten minutes by immersing in water. Cut back leek and onion leaves before planting to 6 in (15 cm). Lettuce is shallowly planted, so the heart is *not* buried. Push a dibber vertically into the soil and insert the plant in the hole created. Use the dibber again to lever soil back over the roots and against the lower part of the stem. This creates a cavity beside the plant for watering. Use this method for lettuce, leeks, onions and all brassicas. Water the plants freely after planting.

Strawberries may be planted through black plastic sheeting which is perforated with the trowel at regular intervals. The plastic film prevents weeds growing, protects the fruit from rot and keeps the soil moist.

Ideally plant in the evening, to prevent plants wilting in the sun.

Planting annuals and bedding plants

Most annuals and summer bedding plants are sold in trays or peat pots.

Wait until the risk of frost is past before planting in borders that have previously held spring-flowering bulbs and plants.

Method All bedding plants must be thoroughly charged with moisture when planted, so water thoroughly an hour or two before planting. This applies to plants in pots or trays as well as young plants in the open ground.

Plant firmly and water well, even if the root

To plant strawberries through polythene, cut a cross in the sheet with the point of a trowel.

ball is already wet; the plant's immediate environment must be damp to encourage new roots. If dry, adjacent soil will absorb the water from the root ball by capillary action.

If raising your own bedding plants, it is best to grow them in peat pots which the roots can penetrate. When planting peat pots, you will need to use a bulb dibber to give bigger, more even holes.

Planting in summer

This is becoming easier thanks to the increasing use of containers, and allows you to fill gaps in your garden. Planting rules are the same. The best time to plant is in the evening, once the worst heat of the day is over, with watering daily until the plant is established.

Planting irises

Irises are traditionally planted in summer, after flowering, or in the early autumn. You can divide existing plants then to rejuvenate them, or replace them with other varieties. This is quite common, as the best-looking varieties may degenerate after a few years.

Method To renew most rhizomatous species, use a 4 in (10 cm) length of rhizome with a clump of leaves; do not use excessively soft rhizomes or any with signs of injury or disease. Cut back the leaves to leave a fan about 6 in (15 cm) long. Plant so that the upper surface of the rhizome is just showing above the soil, and firm the soil, then water for the next 2–3 weeks, if the soil is dry.

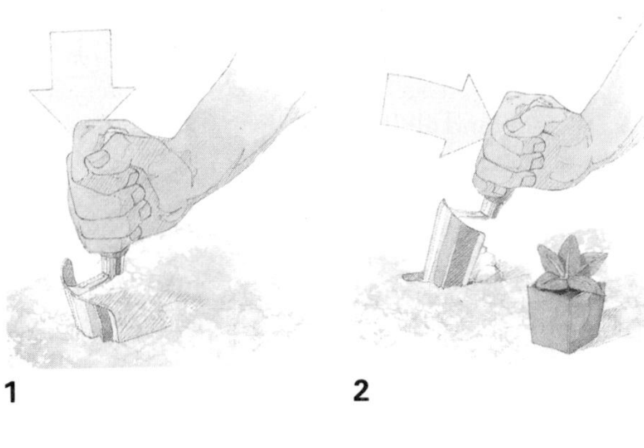

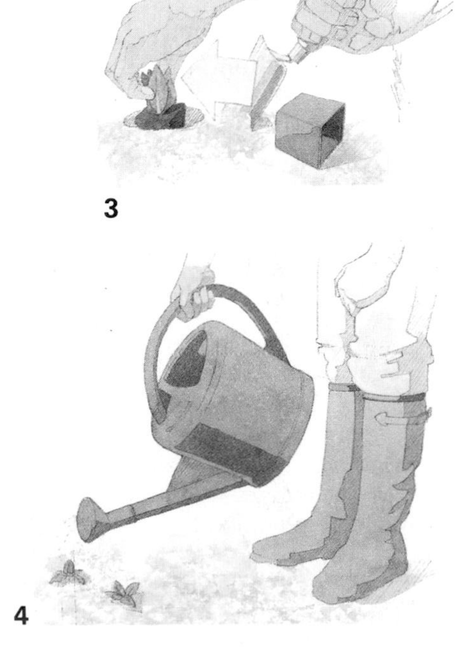

Planting bedding plants
1. Push the trowel vertically into the soil.
2. Pull the trowel towards you to make a hole.
3. Place the young plant in the hole having first moistened the root ball. Push back the soil around it.
4. Water copiously.

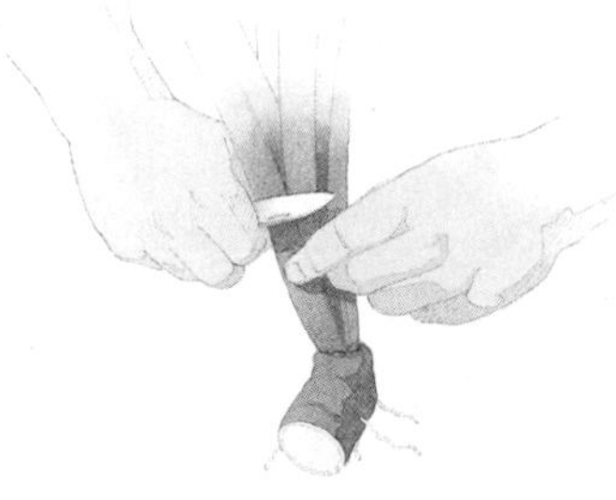

Planting irises
1. Trim the leaves to a third of their length.
2. Make a medium sized hole with a trowel.
3. Put the rhizome in the hole but do not bury it completely and carefully firm the soil.

AFTER-CARE

Protect the roots of plants planted in autumn; a mulch 2–4 in (5–10 cm) thick can stop frosts reaching the roots; but keep the mulch away from the trunk or stems. Use well-rotted leaf mould, garden compost, peat or pine bark, which will slowly decompose and enrich the soil.

With spring planting, water the plant daily for a week after planting, to help the roots establish. Do not give newly planted plants fertilizer, beyond that originally added to the soil, for at least a month; adding it too soon is liable to harm the roots.

Protect against winds in exposed areas, especially by the sea; a temporary windbreak in the direction of the prevailing winds ensures adequate protection.

Treat all new plants, especially roses, against sucking insects such as aphids and greenfly, to prevent new shoots from being weakened and distorted. Apply a systemic insecticide as soon as the first foliage appears.

Yellowing, falling leaves may be a sign that the soil is too heavy or too dry. Dig a trench around the plant and improve the soil by adding well-rotted organic matter. With deciduous plants, drastic pruning is often enough to stimulate new vigorous growth.

With fruit trees, remove the fruit in the first year after planting, so the tree can concentrate its energy on woody growth and give a better yield in following years.

PROPAGATING PLANTS

Propagating garden plants is both pleasant and fascinating; it can also be profitable. Of course things are not always easy, and luck and good intentions are not enough to fill a garden with new varieties. Some propagating techniques are within the scope of a beginner, others require more experience.

PROPAGATION FROM SEED

Germinating seeds under the right conditions is the most natural method of plant propagation and the most widely used for vegetables, annuals and herbaceous perennials and even ornamental trees and shrubs.

Propagation from seed is economical, as most plants produce seeds in large quantities, and the best method if you want plants in large numbers. The seed must be of good quality, most seed merchants offer selected seed which guarantees that the results are largely true to type and that a high rate of germination occurs. Gardeners can collect seeds from stock they find attractive, but the results are more unpredictable, as some plants cross-breed with their neighbours, and the new plants may not have the characteristics you want. This applies particularly to fruit trees, which are always cross-fertilized, since they are unable to fertilize themselves with their own pollen. Sowing the seeds of a Golden Delicious apple, for example, is bound to produce apple trees, but not necessarily of the same variety.

Advantages of propagating from seed

As well as producing many young plants in a limited space and a relatively short time, most propagation from seed is simple and within the capabilities of the beginner. Most non-woody plants, such as annual and perennial flowers, vegetables and grass, germinate without too much trouble. Many trees and shrubs are a bit more challenging.

Generally speaking growing from seed produces plants very quickly. It may take up to two years before hawthorn seedlings appear, but most species germinate within two weeks or a month. Chicory can take just 48 hours, but 5–7 days is average for most other herbaceous plants, hardy vegetables and hardy annual flowers. The development which follows is very fast, and many can be grown in the position where they are to crop or flower. Thinning out seedlings is all that is necessary.

Lastly there is the entertainment value of growing from seed. Growing your own plants is a modest but rewarding business. Just watching how children behave towards plants they have grown shows how much joy watching a developing plant can bring.

Drawbacks

Some plants, such as fruit trees and bushes and many hybrids, especially the F1 types, never reproduce faithfully from seed, and strains eventually degenerate if grown from generations of seed collected from the garden. This problem does not arise with naturally occurring species and varieties, but even then, any given population always produces a few mutations. Seeds from a green-leafed species, for example, may produce one or more purple-leaves mutants or 'sports', more compact or more slender in shape. In some cases, this is used to create a new cultivated variety but mutants are usually of little value and are discarded.

Unless you know exactly what you are doing, it is always best to buy a reliable brand of seeds and to avoid growing your own seeds. A further problem in growing from garden seeds is that you may unwittingly carry over diseases, particularly those caused by viruses.

Species grown from seed often differ in appearance and bearing. In any given population of ornamentals, some grow faster than others; some are squat, others slender. This variation hardly matters in lettuce and most vegetables, but can be annoying if a uniform effect, such as in a summer bedding scheme, is the object. F1 hybrids are uniform, but, as previously stated, do not breed true from seed.

Selecting seed

Seed growers select parent stock and make stringent checks on the trueness to type and yield of their seed according to local legal stipulation.

Germination tests are regularly carried out at seed laboratories. Packets of seed are marked with 'sell by' dates; it is always best to sow all the seed from one packet in the year it is bought. The germination rate of spinach, for instance, drops by about 50 per cent by the second year, once the packet has been opened. There are two main categories of seeds available: F1 hybrids and ordinary open-pollinated seeds.

Most F1 hybrids are new varieties or in great demand and are obtained by crossing two parent stocks with very specific characteristics. This selection calls for highly complex methods, particularly *in vitro* pollination. Under identical growing and development conditions, this produces uniform offspring, useful in uniform bedding schemes or for producing uniform crops of vegetables.

F1 hybrids cost money but guarantee uniformity of colour, earliness, resistance to disease and compactness. The so-called 'classical' varieties are often adequate for ordinary use; they are less expensive, but usually of high quality. Some, such as Marmande or Moneymaker tomato, Big Boy tomato, Roma tomato, Beefsteak tomato or Nantes carrot, have remained popular for 20 years or more, and are still being improved.

Sowing in open ground

This involves sowing seed in specially prepared soil in the garden, either where it is to mature or in a seed bed. It is used for most hardy flowers and vegetables or those sown at a time of year when the weather is good enough for them to germinate.

Requirements for success

To germinate, seeds need a dark, moist environment which is warm enough to ensure that the seedlings can grow without check.

Preparing the soil well is important: the tiny root which emerges from the seed must have light, open soil to find its way between the particles. Heavy, compact, hard, suffocating soil soon stops the seedling developing. Cultivating and breaking down the soil well before sowing, and the removal of all annual and perennial weeds is essential. Mixing the soil with peat or garden compost may also be of great benefit. The soil should be tamped down lightly once the seed has been sown to remove air pockets which would dry out the rootlet when it emerges.

Method Dig over the soil, carefully removing stones and weed roots, especially couch grass and convolvulus. Organic matter, such as manure or compost, is added during digging. Never use fresh manure, which is liable to cause disease and rot, particularly damping-off in seeds. Depending on the size of the plot, digging can be done with a spade, a garden fork for stony or heavy ground, or a rotavator. Rotavating is done in two stages, first with the plough to turn over the soil deeply and roughly, then working it down into a manageable tilth with a rotavator. Ploughing is done once a year, preferably in autumn. This is followed, in the spring, by cultivating and raking to remove the last stones and roughly level the surface of the soil. Use a hand cultivator initially, a tool with three to eight triangular teeth. If you use a rotavator, the need for raking is much reduced.

Finally, level the surface of the seed bed with a rake. Hold it as upright as possible so that it just brushes the surface of the soil. Work in short strokes, moving the rake backwards and forwards.

If you are making a seed bed, make it no more than 4 ft 3 in (1.30 m) wide; the ideal width is 3 ft 3 in (1 m) so that the centre can be easily reached, and plastic tunnels or frames fit neatly on top. Length is less important, but leave a narrow path between beds to make maintenance easier. Sowing in open ground is divided into two types: either sowing on the spot (*in situ*,) or sowing in nursery rows.

Sowing on the spot (*in situ*)

This involves scattering seed on land or sowing it in rows, where plants remain throughout their lives. Lawns are a good example of *in situ* sowing. Many hardy annuals and perennials are also sown *in situ*, as are fast-growing vegetables, such as spinach, lettuce and radish, and plants with edible roots, such as carrots, beetroot and turnip. As handling is kept to a minimum, the chances of success are high.

Do not sow too thickly, as this causes overcrowding and involves thinning the seedlings out later, which can be wasteful. Sowing on the spot is the easiest method but can waste seed, unless you use a mechanical seed drill. (A seed drill is really only justified when you are growing very large numbers of plants in rows.)

Sowing in a nursery bed

Nursery sowing is common practice with bedding plants, such as pansies, wallflower and forget-me-not; as well as hardy perennials such as delphiniums and campanulas; and some vegetables such as early lettuce, leeks, cabbages and tomatoes. It involves preparing an area of the garden solely for raising seedlings. The nursery bed must be sheltered from prevailing or cold winds and preferably out of the harshest rays of the sun. Against a south-east facing wall is ideal, screened or shaded if necessary. Frames can also be used if required.

Alternatively, seeds of plants that are to be transplanted later can be sown in nursery rows between established plants.

Plants with very small seeds and less hardy plants are often sown in nursery rows, as are the relatively slow-growing woody plants. Nursery sowing makes looking after the plants easy, and prevents overcrowding. If they are sown too thickly, the seedlings can be thinned or pricked out. Flower borders and vegetable plots tend to be more regimented, in contrast to the more informal effect of *in situ* sowing. Nursery sowing is also more time consuming, as it involves thinning and transplanting the plants.

Sowing under cover

This method is used for all half-hardy and tender annuals, perennials and woody plants: begonias, petunias, French marigolds, ageratums, peppers, aubergines (eggplants), melons and tomatoes, for example.

It can involve sowing seed under cloches or in frames, but more usually a heated greenhouse or a warm room. The seeds and resulting seedlings are protected from low temperatures and frost.

Sowing indoors

The natural warmth of a house is excellent for germinating many seeds. They are grown in plastic or clay pots, small propagators, seed-trays or peat pots. The growing medium is very important; it must be light, warm and water-retentive to encourage germination. Peat and loam-based seed composts (planting mediums) are available in the shops, and are ideally suited. It is seldom worthwhile making your own seed compost (planting medium), as it involves sterilizing loam and the money saved does not make up for the usually inferior-quality results.

Once they have germinated, seedlings raised indoors should be as close as possible to a well-lit window, but protected from the sun by gauze, or the plants quickly wilt. Turn the trays regularly so the seedlings don't grow lopsidedly towards the source of light. Radiators can be used to accelerate germination, but do not allow the seeds to become too hot or the compost will dry out.

Sowing under cloches

This involves sowing in the open, but under cover. The soil must be light and well drained, so that the high moisture levels under glass or plastic do not lead to rot or damping-off. You can shallow hoe out a trench or drill, about 2 in (5 cm) deep, replacing the original soil with peat-based seed compost (planting medium). Ventilate the frame or cloche as much as possible, protecting it with straw mats if there is a risk of frost. Heating cables can be buried in the ground. These work on a low voltage and encourage the seeds to germinate.

Sowing in drills
Using a seeder to sow the seeds in a drill drawn along a line with a hoe.

Sowing techniques

Sowing methods differ according to the type of seed, its size and how it is sown.

Sowing in rows

Seeds are sown thinly and evenly in drills of varying depth made with the point of a hoe, following a taut line to ensure that the row is straight. This technique is used mainly with vegetables sown *in situ* and annuals, perennials and woody plants sown in nursery beds. Sowing in rows makes maximum use of space and makes pricking out or thinning easier. There is a risk of seedlings being over-crowded, and there are various ways to prevent this; mixing tiny seeds with sand, for example, station sowing, or spacing of seeds large enough to handle, and thinning.

Broadcasting

This consists of scattering seeds as evenly as possible by hand over prepared ground, and is widely used for sowing lawns. Seeds sown in seed trays are often broadcast sown. All seeds sown indoors, in drills, pots or trays are also sown loose, although in this case the process is more like dusting than sowing.

For effective broadcasting over a wide area, such as a lawn, hold the seed tightly in your fist. Raise your forearm level with your shoulder, then throw your hand sharply forwards, opening your fist and stretching your fingers as much as possible.

When sowing small patches of ground, use a to-and-fro movement as if dusting the ground with the seed, working about 6–8 in (15–20 cm) above the ground.

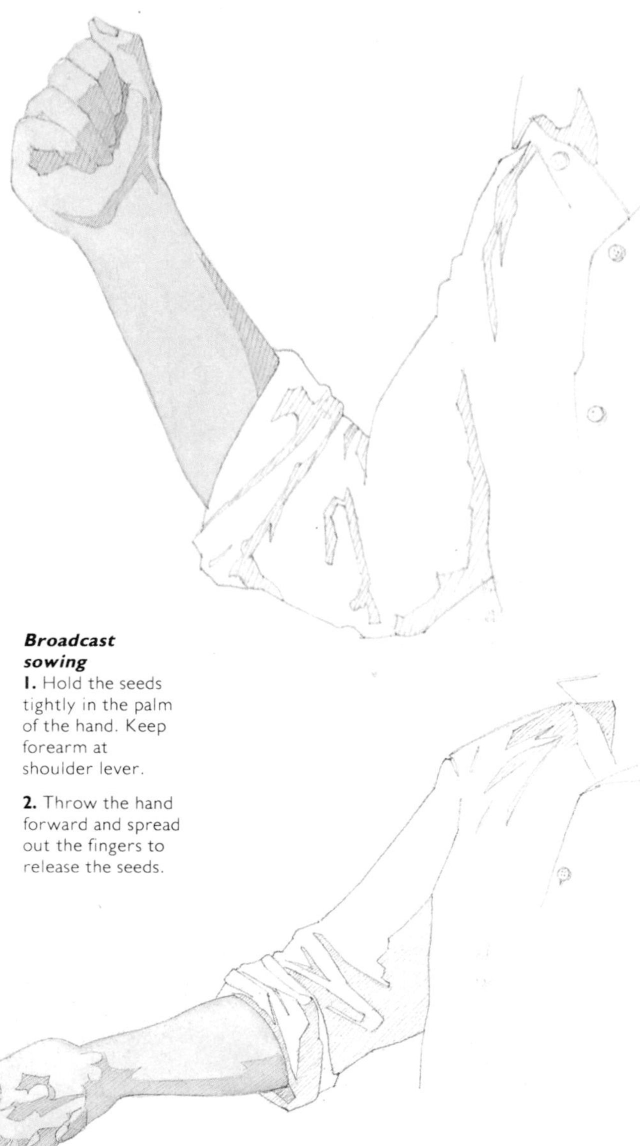

Broadcast sowing
1. Hold the seeds tightly in the palm of the hand. Keep forearm at shoulder lever.

2. Throw the hand forward and spread out the fingers to release the seeds.

Sowing small seeds

Very small seeds are usually left uncovered, and the surface on which they are scattered should be as smooth as possible to ensure even germination. Prepare pots and trays carefully, using sieved seed compost (planting medium) for the top, ¼ in (5 mm) layer, and gently pressing it down with a presser (wood block). Water with an atomizer or sprayer.

There is a special technique for sowing small seeds, such as petunias or begonias. You can mix them by hand or make a home-made seeder. Fold a sheet of paper in half and put the seeds inside, along the fold. Tap the underside of the fold with your finger and the seeds will fall out gently and evenly.

Sowing large seeds

Handling large seeds presents no problems. Dwarf and runner beans, peas, broad beans, sweet peas, melons, marrows, pumpkins and nasturtiums can be sown directly in peat pots or *in situ*. Sowing one or two seeds per peat pot avoids the check that seedlings are liable to receive when the roots are disturbed while being pricked out. Once the seedlings are sufficiently developed, those in pots are moved into large pots or planted outside. The compressed peat which forms the pot decomposes under the action of the moisture in the soil or compost.

Sowing in clumps
Place groups of 3 to 5 seeds in the drill, evenly distanced at the recommended spacing.

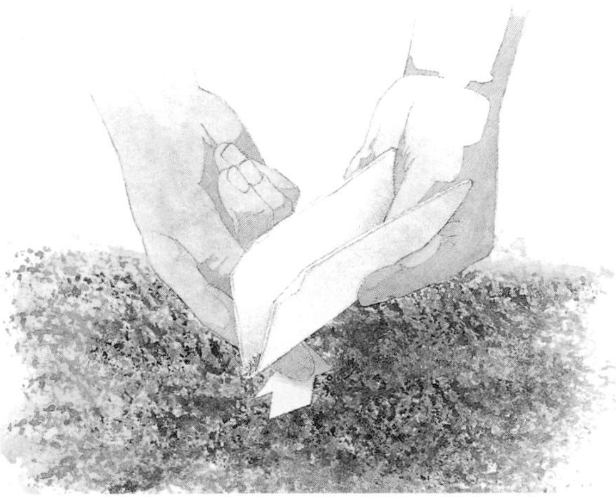

Sowing small seeds
1. Put the seeds in a sheet of paper folded in half.
2. Tap the underneath of the paper with the finger to sprinkle the seeds.

Aftercare

Just sowing seeds and covering them is no guarantee that they will germinate; there are a number of conditions which have to be fulfilled to get good results.

Covering the seed

Seeds must be covered with a light, fine soil; if sowing in containers, use sieved or fine grade soil. Only tiny seeds are left uncovered.

The larger the seed, the deeper it must be buried. As a general rule, a seed should be covered with three to five times its own thickness; cover lawn seed, lettuces, French marigolds with ½ in (1 cm) of soil, for example. Peas and beans need 2–2½ in (5–6 cm); and root vegetables, 1 in (2–3 cm).

Tamping

This involves firming down the seed after sowing and covering, and is carried out with the back of a rake for seeds sown in drills or in the open ground, or with a wooden presser for seeds sown in pots or trays. Firming down ensures that the seed comes into close contact with the soil without air pockets forming. Tamping should be done gently; the soil should be firm but not hard, and it should never be done if the soil or compost is soaking wet. With lawns the soil is often firmed with a roller before sowing rather than after. The natural moisture in the soil would mean that the seed would tend to stick to the roller if it were used after sowing.

Watering

Watering follows sowing, whatever the method used. A moist environment is essential for germinating seeds. If sowing in the open, allow about 1 gallon of water per square yard (4½ litre per m^2), applied with a watering can with a fine spray. If sowing in pots or seed-trays, semi-

Covering the seeds
Pull a layer of soil over the drill with the back of a rake, about 3 to 5 times the thickness of the seeds.

Tamping
After sowing in drills, tamp down the soil with the back of a rake.

Thinning
Thin out and single the seedlings carefully to the recommended spacing.

immerse them in a trough of water until the compost (planting medium) darkens in colour, then allow to drain.

A second watering is rarely required before seeds in cloches or frames germinate; too much water can lead to them damping-off. Condensation visible on the glass or protective cover indicates sufficient moisture and may indicate the need for increased ventilation.

Seeds sown in the open should be watered whenever the soil is dry; as often as once a day in hot weather. Use a fine spray or it will damage the young plants, wash away the soil, or form a crust when it dries.

Thinning

This involves moving excess plants and is carried out once seedlings are large enough to handle with ease. Generally, the weaker specimens are removed, ideally without damaging their neighbours. The thinning-out distance varies and is sometimes expressed in fingers or hands; 'three-finger' thinning means leaving a space three fingers wide between adjacent plants.

After thinning, water the remaining plants if the soil is dry, and press the soil down lightly, by hand, to re-firm them if necessary.

Pricking out

This is done as soon as seedlings have two true leaves, which appear after the two seed leaves, or cotyledons. Pricking out consists of transplanting seedlings evenly spaced apart, into seed-trays or peat pots.

The young plants are fragile and must be handled carefully. Pricking out requires a small, flat tool, such as a wooden ice lolly (popsicle) stick or spoon handle to lever the plant from its pot, and a pencil-like dibber for making the holes into which the roots are put. To avoid touching the delicate leaves, the plant can be lifted and supported by the lever and by a pencil partially split along its length.

Bury the seedlings up to the first pair of leaves, to encourage the seedling to produce vigorous, branching roots. Use a low-nutrient or multi-purpose compost (planting medium) – peat-based composts are fine.

Pricked-out plants are watered lightly, then returned to the greenhouse staging or window sill. Protect from bright sunlight and high temperatures for a few days. Keep the atmosphere moist but not saturated.

Final planting

Once plants are sufficiently well developed and the weather is suitable, they are planted in their final positions. Plants grown under cover should be gradually acclimatized to outdoor conditions, or 'hardened off'. Plants under cloches should be progressively exposed to the air. Put plants grown indoors or in a greenhouse in a cold frame or a sunny, sheltered bit of

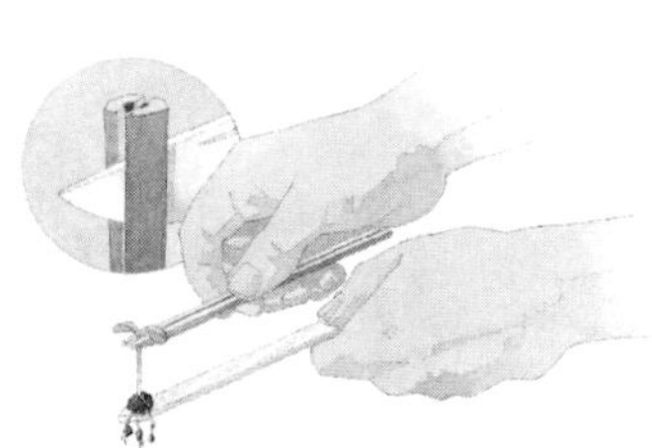

Pricking out
1. Gently lift out the seedling from the seed tray using a lollipop stick, or something similar.

2. Lift the seedling with a paper stick cut to the shape of prongs, without touching the leaves. Alternatively hold the seedling very gently between finger and thumb by a leaf.

3. Make a hole in the potting compost with a pencil or dibber.

4. Plant the seedling up to the first pair of leaves and firm into place with the dibber and/ or fingers.

garden for ten days or so before planting out. Take them in at night or when frost threatens.

Some plants, such as the cabbage family and leeks, are usually buried deeper than they were previously, while lettuces are planted with their growing point well above the soil to prevent them rotting. Smaller, bare-rooted plants are usually planted with a dibber (dibble). The plant is lowered into a hole and the dibber (dibble) is pressed into one side and pushes the soil against the plant, with a sideways movement. This creates a hole beside the plant for watering.

Labelling

Make sure that all batches and rows of seeds are properly labelled on plastic in indelible ink; alternatively fold the empty seed packet and put it in a corner of the plot or at the end of a row, although bad weather is liable to make it illegible.

Spacing between rows

This is important when sowing vegetables *in situ* and is based on the size of fully grown plants, while also allowing access between the rows for maintenance. Rows should be at least 8 in (20 cm) apart: the more widely spaced the plants, the easier they are to maintain. Sowing and planting distances are given on seed packets so there is no need for overcrowding or wasted space.

Handling seed

Try to avoid touching seed with your hands, especially fine seed; some people's pores secrete acids and other substances which could inhibit germination. This might explain why some gardeners never succeed in growing parsley, while others have 100 per cent success rate. It is better to use scissors to open the packet and sow the seeds directly from it. A seed sower is always useful; choose an easily-adjusted model which is simple and reliable.

Coated or pelleted seeds

Fine seeds are coated with a layer of clay which breaks up in contact with soil moisture. The main advantages of using coated seeds are that it makes sowing much easier and reduces the need for thinning-out later. Coated seed is expensive, however.

Peat tablets

These flat discs are soaked in water and expand to form pots; some have plastic mesh for added strength. Nasturtiums, tomatoes, melons and sweet peas benefit from being sown in expanded peat tablets or peat pots, as this avoids the need for pricking out.

Stratifying

This is used to break the dormancy of hard seeds, including many tree seeds. Ripe seeds are bruised, to encourage the flesh to rot, then mixed or layered with moist loam, peat or sand, and placed in a dark cold frame or buried in the open ground for the winter. The vegetable compartment in a refrigerator can also be used. In spring, stratified seeds are sown in trays in the usual way.

Soaking seeds in hot water, 104°F (40°C), for one or two hours helps break the dormancy of sweet peas, as does scratching the seed surface in one place.

On contact with water, peat pellets swell to form a little compost module for sowing large seeds.

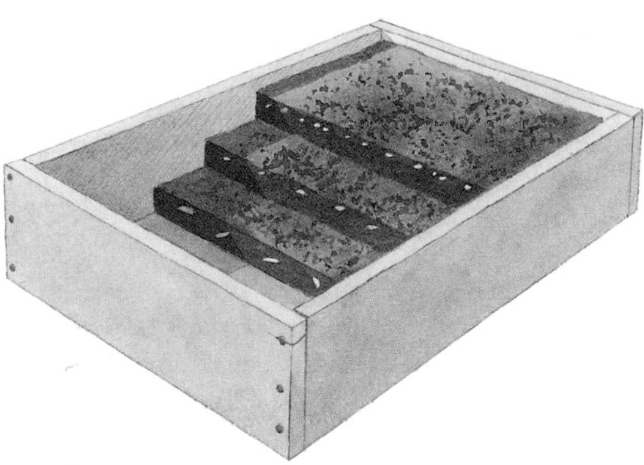

Stratifying seeds
Keep hard seeds between layers of a slightly damp sand outside throughout the winter.

CUTTINGS

This method involves growing a new plant from part of an existing one, such as a shoot, leaf or root. It is widely used for propagating ornamental shrubs, some trees and conifers and numerous hardy perennials.

Taking cuttings is an asexual, or vegetative, method of reproduction, and except in a few isolated cases, the new plant is identical to the parent. Populations of plants, or clones, taken from cuttings are also uniform and have similar growth rates, foliage and yields. Taking cuttings is the standard method of propagating named varieties of perennial trees, shrubs and herbaceous plants. A cutting taken from a healthy specimen will usually be disease-free.

A large number of cuttings can be taken from a single parent without harming it. *Lonerica nitida*, geraniums, fuchsias and privet root with an 80 per cent success rate for amateurs, approaching 100 per cent for professionals.

Requirements for success

A piece of plant must survive long enough without nutrients to produce roots and become self-supporting. Moist, but not saturated, warm surroundings encourage most cuttings to 'take' root. Cuttings must be taken at a precise stage in a plant's development if they are to survive the intervening period before they root. Cuttings can be taken from soft spring shoots, semi-woody shoots in summer or woody shoots at the end of the growing season. Each requires a different technique.

Choosing the rooting compost

The compost (planting medium) is a vital factor in successful rooting. The best rooting medium is light, moist, porous and aerated. The tiny rootlets must find a way between the soil particles and cannot penetrate large lumps. They also need air to breathe and moisture, as the roots take the nutrient mineral salts in soluble form. On the other hand, plants quickly asphyxiate if there is too much water. Cuttings taken in water are an exception; and the structure of the roots which develop is completely different. Cuttings taken in water should be planted in compost as soon as they root, if they are not to rot when their growing environment is changed.

A mixture of equal parts sand and moss peat usually gives excellent results for a seed and cutting planting medium. This medium has no nutrients for the cutting, which lives off its own reserves, but provides it with ideal conditions in which to produce its roots. Rooted cuttings must be potted on into compost (potting medium) that does contain nutrients if they are not to suffer. Use a good, loam-based or 'multi-purpose' medium.

Vermiculite is increasingly used in professional cutting mediums. This inert substance, which looks like sawdust, is superbly aerated and encourages the production of a healthier root system.

Tools

You need a good pair of scissors or secateurs (hand pruners), a sharp knife or razor blade and containers with covers. Mini-propagators available in the shops are not always deep enough for cuttings; some cuttings need at least 8 in (20 cm) between the cover and the surface of the compost (soil). A miniature greenhouse can be made from a tray or pot, with wire or canes to support a transparent tent of plastic film. This is placed over the tray or pot full of cuttings, and keeps the humidity high. Some cuttings, such as those of pelargoniums (geraniums) and cacti, need dry air.

There are deeper and larger propagators available, usually equipped with an electrical heating system. These are a great help in the rooting of cuttings and the germination of difficult seeds.

After the initial watering, mist spray if necessary, to maintain a high moisture level. If heavy condensation appears on the glass or plastic, wipe it off and ventilate the propagator briefly.

Rooting hormones

Available in sachets or tubes from garden centres, rooting hormones come in the form of a white powder and promote the growth of roots. They are especially useful for rooting conifer cuttings, which hardly ever succeed without the aid of hormones. Dip the cut end in the powder, then tap it gently, to remove any excess. Rooting hormones are sold in the shops under several names and some brands also contain protective fungicide.

As cuttings develop

There is not much to see while a cutting is taking root; as long as the stem and leaf keep their original colour, and don't shrivel, all should be well. Shoots rarely appear on a cutting in less than a month after insertion, as all the cutting's energy is concentrated on producing roots, which takes from ten days to several months, depending on the plant, time of year and conditions. Remove any flower buds or flowers that may form while the cutting is rooting. Black spots, withering, collapse or drying out are signs that the cutting is not taking. Examine cuttings regularly and remove any that are dying or already dead, to prevent the others being attacked by a parasitic fungus, the symptoms of which include a blackening of the tissues and leaves dropping.

Once the cuttings take

If the cuttings are still healthy after a month, this means that they have rooted or are in the process of doing so. Lift a sample cutting to see how the roots are developing. Once they are $1\frac{1}{2}$–2 in (3–5 cm) long, pot the young plants.

Rooted cuttings must be lifted carefully to avoid damaging the delicate young roots. Never pull out a rooted cutting; use a small dibber, digging it vertically into the tray and using a back-and-forth movement to lift the cutting out.

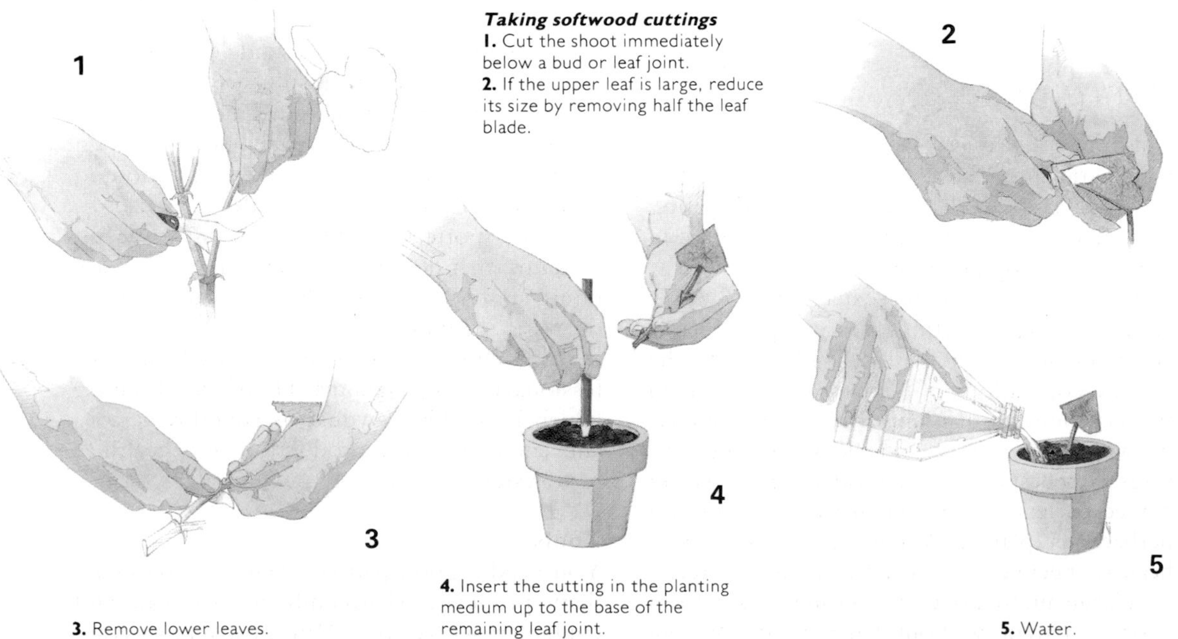

Taking softwood cuttings
1. Cut the shoot immediately below a bud or leaf joint.
2. If the upper leaf is large, reduce its size by removing half the leaf blade.

3. Remove lower leaves.

4. Insert the cutting in the planting medium up to the base of the remaining leaf joint.

5. Water.

Use a small clay or plastic pot, or a peat pot; root systems can become tangled when rooted cuttings are planted out into seed trays.

Do not try to pot up cuttings before the roots have formed and branched. Planting outside should not normally be done until a year after the cutting has rooted.

The first winter is often a difficult time for all young plants; shelter them in a cold frame or plastic tunnel for protection. With species which produce a strong tap root, cut this back by a third at the time of potting up, to promote the growth of the root system and make transplanting easier.

Softwood cuttings

This method involves young shoots, preferably taken in spring, when the sap is rising. Given the right conditions, softwood cuttings quickly produce roots, but it often involves precise heat and moisture control. Dahlias and many begonias can be propagated in this way, as can forsythias, weigelas and fuchsias.

In short, this is the quickest type of cutting to root but, if conditions are not right, it is also the most delicate and the most liable to die.

Many spring cuttings are taken from parent stocks over-wintered under cover, then encouraged to produce new shoots, given extra heat. Chrysanthemums, dahlias, cannas, pelargoniums (geraniums), heliotropes, anthemis (chamomile) and fuchsias are thus propagated.

Method Use shoots 6 in (15 cm) long, with five or six leaves. Cut the shoot below a bud or a leaf, then remove the two leaves at the base of the cutting with a razor blade or sharp knife.

If the cutting has large leaves, such as one of the decorative-leaved begonias, cut back the leaves by half. Using a dibber (dibble) to make the hole, insert the stem vertically into the medium down to the point where the leaves start. Hormone-rooting powder can accelerate the formation of roots, but is not necessary. Cover the cuttings with clear polythene to keep the atmosphere moist until they root.

For tuberous-rooted plants, such as dahlias, cannas and tuberous begonias, remove the cutting with a small part of the 'heel' or hard bases attached, using a sharp knife. The heel should be ½–1 in (1.5–2.5 cm) long and about ¼ in (6 mm) thick.

Use non-flowering shoots, if possible. If there are flowers, remove them when preparing the cutting. Soft cuttings benefit from being grown in a heated propagator which speeds the rooting process and increases the chances of success.

Rooting

New growth normally indicates that roots have formed. Pot up in a potting or multi-purpose soil. Place under cover in a well lit spot, shaded from direct sunlight. Maintain humidity with the exception of succulent, grey-leaved and fleshy leaved cuttings, which are liable to rot in high humidity, and avoid over-watering.

Semi-ripe cuttings

This method is the most commonly used for many shrubs and flat-leaved conifers, such as *Thujas* (arbor-vitae), *Chamaecyparis* (false cypresses), Leyland cypresses and *Cupressus* (true cypresses), but not conifers possessing needles. It is used from late summer to early autumn, when the young shoots are changing from their soft, supple state, to their woody state.

Cuttings are taken from the ends of the healthy non-flowering shoots, preferably well developed side shoots. Semi-ripe cuttings should be 2–6 in (5–15 cm) long, depending on species. The shorter the cutting, the better its chances of rooting. Rosemary cuttings should be 2–3 in (5–7 cm) long, while *Prunus laurocerasus* (cherry laurel) or *Thujas* (arbor-vitae) can be up to 6 in (15 cm).

Method Taking semi-ripe cuttings is similar to the method for softwood cuttings, except that the foliage is removed for about a third of the length of the stem, and the cutting is inserted much deeper into the compost (potting soil); the deeper it is buried, the better its chances. Again, with large-leaved species, the leaves are cut back by half to prevent wilting.

Using hormone-rooting powder is of great benefit, especially for conifers, azaleas, rhododendrons, and camellias. Dip the lowest ½ in (1 cm) of the cutting into the powder and tap off the excess before inserting the cutting.

Semi-ripe heel cuttings

This method is useful for hard-wooded species such as pyracantha, box, *Euonymus* (spindle tree) and nearly all conifers. The method involves pulling off, not cutting, the shoot, together with a piece of the old wood from which it grew. The heel thus obtained is shortened to about ¾ in

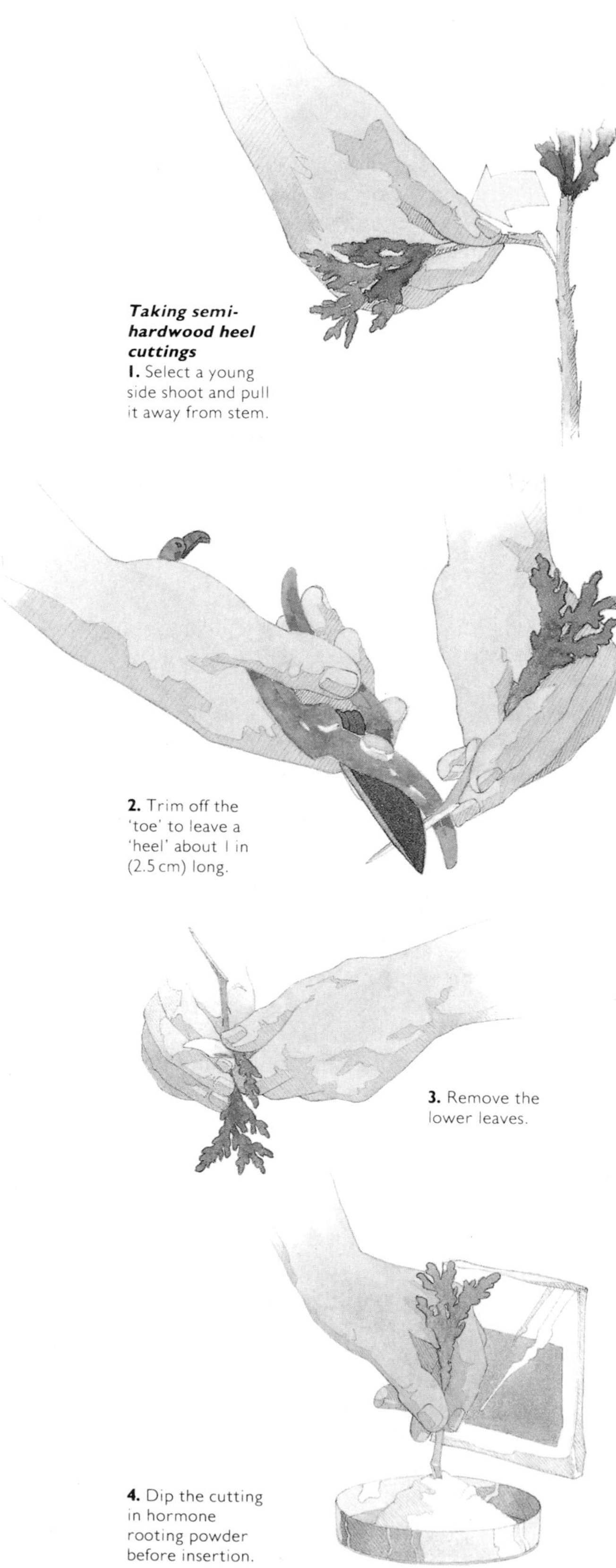

Taking semi-hardwood heel cuttings
1. Select a young side shoot and pull it away from stem.

2. Trim off the 'toe' to leave a 'heel' about 1 in (2.5 cm) long.

3. Remove the lower leaves.

4. Dip the cutting in hormone rooting powder before insertion.

(1.5 cm) and if uneven, its surface should be trimmed with a sharp knife or razor blade.

A cutting with its heel attached can be taken by lightly scoring the parent branch with a pruning knife.

The best time to take semi-ripe cuttings is generally in late summer. Before this, the shoots are often too soft; any later and they have a tendency to harden and are more difficult to root.

Water generously after insertion then cover with cloches or clear polythene to prevent them drying out. Do not water if condensation appears on the sides of the cloche, but check the soil regularly.

Insert cuttings in free-draining soil in a semi-shaded spot.

Rooting

The first signs of rooting appear after about six weeks, in 'easy' plants such as *Lonicera nitida* (honeysuckle), privet, *Euonymus* (spindle), *Eleagnus* (Russian olive) and rosemary. Cuttings can be regarded as successful if they show no signs of withering or blackening after a month. After six weeks or so, uncover the cuttings and leave in the open until late autumn, then put them under frames or a plastic tunnel to protect them against frosts.

The first potting takes place the following spring; the young plants remain in these pots for two or three months, after which they are potted into larger containers and richer soil. At this point, the growing tips are pinched to encourage branching. They are finally planted out in the spring of the second year or, in areas where the climate is mild, in autumn, provided they are at least 8 in (20 cm) high.

HARDWOOD CUTTINGS

This requires the ripe, hard shoots of deciduous trees and shrubs, and is carried out in late autumn or early winter, immediately after the leaves have fallen. Use the terminal shoots which developed in the previous season. Choose shoots that are not too thick and woody as the more mature the wood, the less chance it has of putting out roots.

Hardwood cuttings can be taken from roses, especially the species and old varieties, forsythias, prunus, hydrangeas, currants, lilacs, dogwood (*Cornus*) and deutzias, Hardwood cuttings are 5–8 in (12–20 cm) long.

Another type of heel cutting

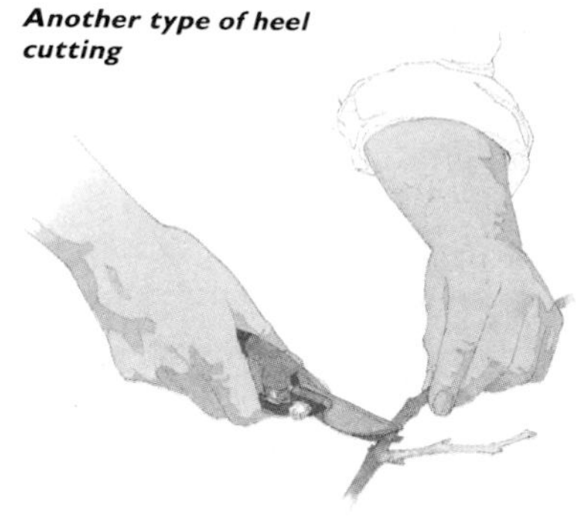

1. Take a cutting with a section of the parent stem attached.

2. Plant the cutting to a depth of one or two buds.

3. Water well.

Method This is the same as for other stem cuttings but preparing them is simpler. Take the cutting to just below a bud.

Hardwood cuttings may be gathered in bunches of about a dozen, tied together with a piece of twine or string and labelled with their name and variety. The cuttings are inserted to a depth of three quarters of their length in a V-shaped trench. A layer of coarse sand, 1 in (3 cm) deep, in the bottom of the trench assists drainage. Insert the cuttings against the vertical wall of the 'V', push back and firm the soil.

Keeping a heel attached is not necessary; simple nodal (cut to a bud) cuttings root better than those with heels.

Eye cuttings

These are used mainly for ornamental vines and Virginia creeper; fruiting vines are usually propagated by grafting, to avoid attacks of phylloxera beetle.

Eye cuttings are short lengths of hardwood shoot usually containing from one to three buds. About $\frac{1}{2}$ in (1 cm) of shoot is left below the bottom bud and this is pushed into the rooting medium so that the lowest bud is at soil level. The roots will be produced from just below the bud in the buried portion.

Cuttings containing more than one bud are laid on their sides, and barely covered with

Taking hardwood cuttings in early winter

1. Cut the shoot on a slant below a bud.

2. Make bundles of a dozen cuttings. Plant them out 3/4 deep in a hole.

3. In the spring, space the cuttings out in open ground leaving only 2 buds above the surface.

rooting medium. This gives a greater chance of success in rooting but it reduces the number of young plants obtained from a given length of shoot or cane.

Sapling cuttings

Willow and poplar cuttings are taken from well-developed, one-year-old branches up to 5 ft (1.5 m) long and as straight as possible. The base of the branch is cut in a 'V' to assist insertion and the giant cutting is pushed into the soil, buried for about a third of its length.

Protect hardwood cuttings with a cloche in colder areas or during heavy frosts. Natural soil moisture levels in winter are enough to make watering unnecessary. In dry areas, mix moss peat into the soil in which the cuttings are inserted, to prevent the soil drying out. After a cold spell, check that the cuttings have not been lifted by the frost; tread them back in if necessary.

Taking sapling cuttings
1. Take the cutting up to about 3 ft (1 m) long.

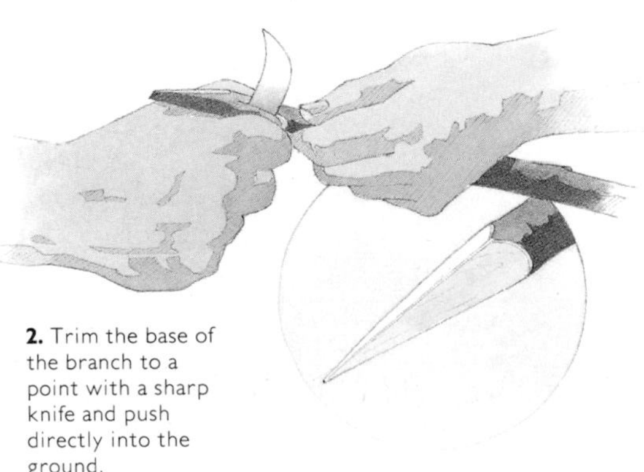

2. Trim the base of the branch to a point with a sharp knife and push directly into the ground.

Rooting

Some species root rapidly after planting, others wait until spring. Remove the cuttings from their trenches in autumn and plant individually where they are to grow.

Pinch the growing tips of new shoots, to promote branching and to give well-rounded, balanced plants.

CUTTINGS IN WATER

This is widely used with indoor plants, less so with garden ones. Willows, impatiens, coleus, ivy and sometimes geraniums can be rooted in water. Except for willows and some house plants, cuttings in water are always taken from soft, new shoots in full leaf, about 6 in (15 cm) long. The leaves are removed from the entire underwater section; and the leaves of large-leaved species are trimmed to avoid wilting. This method can be used from mid-spring to early autumn, but is most likely to succeed between mid-spring and early summer.

Method Fill a transparent glass with water to ½ in (1 cm) from the top. To keep the cuttings in place, stretch a piece of aluminium foil over the rim and make holes in it for three or four cuttings. Remove the lower leaves, then immerse the stem for about half its length. Place in a shady, relatively humid room, such as a kitchen or bathroom.

Good results with indoor plants can be obtained by adding a few drops of liquid fertilizer to the water.

Rooting

This may take two or even three months for woody plants, though willows show the first signs of rooting within a week or two. Soft, herbaceous plants, such as impatiens and coleus, may start rooting in under two weeks.

Roots which develop in water are almost transparent, delicate and often straight and fleshy, and can supply the plant with its normal needs and enable it to develop for a short while. This is the method on which hydroculture (hydroponics)is based. On the other hand, these roots show a definite dislike for soil so pot up rooted cuttings as soon as the first roots appear, in peat-based potting or multi-purpose type potting soil. Once potted, the cuttings should develop normally but must be given abundant water for the first few days to encourage them to produce normal roots.

Rooting cuttings in water
1. Trim large leafed species by removing $\frac{2}{3}$ of the foliage.
2. Add 2 or 3 drops of liquid fertilizer to the water.
3. Push the cutting through a sheet of tin foil stretched over the top of the glass filled with water. Half the cutting must be underwater.

LEAF CUTTINGS

These are used mainly for propagating fleshy leaved house plants, such as *Saintpaulia, Begonia rex, Streptocarpus* and *Sansevieria.*

Warm, close, moist growing conditions are needed, and the method works best during the growing season, from mid-spring to early autumn.

Method There are several methods. With begonias, for example, a whole leaf is placed on the surface of seed compost (medium), with the leaf stalk, cut off to about $1\frac{1}{2}$ in (4 cm), pushed into the compost (medium). To encourage roots to develop, make small cross incisions through the main veins at 2 in (5 cm) intervals with a razor blade. The leaf must come into contact with the compost (planting mix); place a few small pebbles on the areas between the veins to weigh down the leaf. Never cover the slit veins as the roots and new shoots emerge from them.

Another method with *Begonia rex* is to cut the leaf into postage stamp-sized squares and lay these on the surface of the compost (planting medium) with a pebble on each. Each 'stamp' must contain at least one main vein from which the plantlet will grow.

African violet leaves, instead of being laid flat on the surface of the compost (planting medium) are inserted in it. Most of the stalk is left on, and the lower 1 in (2.5 cm) of stalk is buried at a slight angle in the compost, so the leaf stands clear of the compost (medium).

Strap-shaped *Streptocarpus* leaves are cut into 1–2 in (2.5–5 cm) sections, and these are inserted, right-way up and at a slight angle, into the compost, in the same way as *Saintpaulias.*

Rooting

This takes at least a month, during which the leaf must not rot, but must remain turgid and healthy. Succulent leaves hold enough moisture to ensure that they survive, and they can be put vertically into the compost (medium), just slightly buried.

Rooting is indicated by the cutting's healthy appearance and the appearance of plantlets on the leaf surface, in the case of begonias, or at its base, in the case of succulent plants. Remove the plastic cover of the tray or propagator as soon as shoots appear, but maintain a high humidity. Avoid over-watering succulent leaves, or they and, later, the young plants will rot.

Leaf cuttings
1. Cut into the biggest veins on the underside of the leaf. Place the leaf bottom down on the compost.
2. Stick small staples through the leaf to keep it in contact with the planting medium.

LEAF BUD CUTTINGS

This is mainly used for vines and commercially, for camellias; roots appear, not from a leaf, but from an axillary bud in the axil of the leafstalk.

This is done in winter when the plants are dormant. As with leaf cuttings a moist, close atmosphere is necessary, and a propagator or closed frame is ideal.

Method For a vine, select a young shoot with well-developed eyes, and cut it into $1\frac{1}{4}$ in (3 cm) sections, each with a well developed bud. Cut away the sliver of shoot behind the eye lengthways, using a razor blade or sharp knife and place on the compost (medium), cut side down, after brushing the exposed section with hormone-rooting powder.

With camellia, take a leafy shoot of this year's growth. Cut the centre section of the shoot into short lengths, each containing a leaf with its basal bud and 1–2 in (2.5–5 cm) of shoot below the bud.

Insert each cutting into the compost (planting medium), either vertically with the eye at surface level or horizontally with the eye half-buried. A heated propagator provides the ideal environment, with a temperature of 72–74°F (22–23°C). Alternatively, put the tray with the cuttings on top of a radiator. Prop up each camellia leaf, which otherwise tends to overbalance the cutting, with a matchstick.

Rooting

This takes a month or more, and is indicated by the development of small shoots. Young plants are fragile for some time; pot them up when the shoots are 2 in (5 cm) high, into individual peat

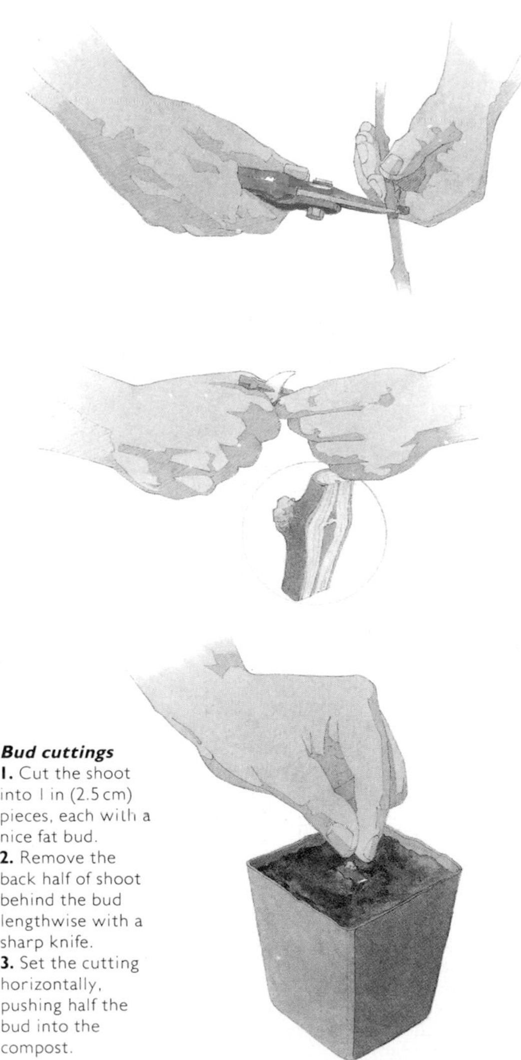

Bud cuttings
1. Cut the shoot into 1 in (2.5 cm) pieces, each with a nice fat bud.
2. Remove the back half of shoot behind the bud lengthwise with a sharp knife.
3. Set the cutting horizontally, pushing half the bud into the compost.

or plastic pots. Plant out in the spring of their second year. The success rate with vines may reach 80 per cent, but rarely exceeds 60 per cent with camellias.

ROOT CUTTINGS

This method is mainly used for hardy perennials, especially phlox, hollyhocks, Oriental poppies and certain primulas. Cuttings are taken in winter or in early spring, and rooted indoors.

Method Cut root sections 1 –2 in (2.5–5 cm) long in winter and insert them flat or vertically, right way up, in peat-based compost (planting medium). Lay thin, flexible roots flat on the compost (medium) and cover with ½ in (1 cm) of fine sand. Insert thicker roots upright, with the top section level with the surface. Place in a well-heated room. New shoots appear in spring.

Prune the base of the root in a 'V' to make it easier to handle and also to indicate which end is which; a short piece of fleshy root is fairly uniform throughout its length. Protect the cuts on large roots from infection with a sealing mastic.

Rooting

Once new growth appears, remove the glass or plastic cover to increase ventilation. Move the young plants away from the sources of heat, after rooting. Once any threat of frosts has passed, put the young plants out in the open. Pot them up towards the end of spring; the final planting out takes place in late summer when the plants are well developed.

SCALE CUTTINGS

This method is used for propagating lilies, and involves making new plants from the scales of the bulb. Scales are removed in mid-autumn, when bulbs are planted, and placed in a tray or pot filled with seed compost (potting soil) .

Method Each scale is treated like a leaf cutting and is capable of producing a little bulb at its base. Use the outermost scales, as they are the largest and most mature, and can be removed without damaging the parent bulb. Do not take more than five scales from a bulb if you want to plant it. A little sideways pressure on the scale is enough to detach it from the bulb. Insert each scale upright and the right way up in the compost, covering its base to about ½ in (1 cm). Enclose the tray with polythene or place a plastic cover on top, and put it under a cold frame or in a bright but cool room indoors. Do not water them until they start to grow; too much water can cause rottting.

Root cuttings
1 and **2.** Cut some pieces of root 2–3 in (5–8 cm) long.
3. Insert large roots upright with the top flush with the soil. Thin roots such as Phlox, are better laid flat in a seedtray and buried ½ in (1 cm).

Rooting

In a few weeks, a bulbil should form at the base of each scale; this bulbil will then produce two delicate leaves. Leave the bulbils in the original tray for at least a year while the plants are developing. The food reserves in the scale ensure that the bulbil survives until roots have formed. The following autumn, prick out the young plants in boxes or individual pots; it takes three to five years for the bulbs to flower; expect 50 per cent of your plants to reach maturity.

DIVISION

Many hardy perennials have a woody, rhizomatous or stoloniferous rootstock which enables them to increase in size. Once clumps have reached a certain age, usually four to five years, it is best to divide them, reducing their size and rejuvenating them. This helps plants produce

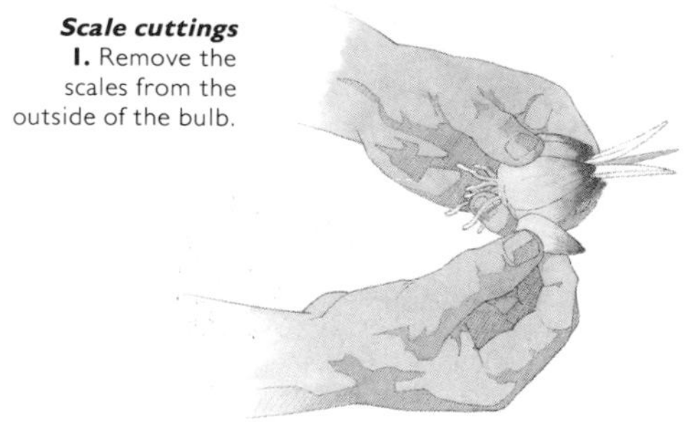

Scale cuttings
1. Remove the scales from the outside of the bulb.

2. Insert the scales upright, about ½ in (1 cm) deep in the planting medium.

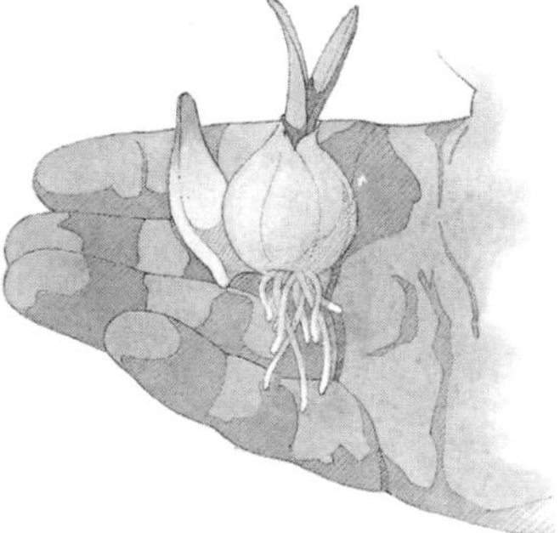

3. Young lily bulbs will have formed on the base of the scale by next season.

more flowers, improve the general tone of the clump and remove dead or unsightly parts. Any small sections not used for immediate replanting can be potted up and/or planted in nursery rows and used to produce new plants identical to the parent.

Division is one of the simplest methods of propagating plants. Unlike cuttings, which require very specific growing conditions and are not self-sufficient, division involves complete sections of plant, with roots, leaves and stems. In most cases, all that is needed is to put the divided sections into fresh soil, and they will quickly develop. Provided that the conditions are good and that certain precautions are taken, this method of propagation is virtually always successful.

Advantages

Division is quick and simple. The only equipment needed is a spade or a couple of digging forks, or for rhizomatous or delicate plants, a sharp knife.

The work is carried out on open ground, and new plants can be planted in their final positions straight away. With rhizomatous species, division gives a relatively large number of new plants.

Drawbacks

There are few snags, but those that do exist should be borne in mind. After several generations of division, degeneration may set in, with a tendency for cultivars to revert to type. In some irises, for example, varieties of a particular shade have a tendency to revert to a pale blue after a few years. Dividing clumps may also spread or carry over pests and diseases, especially viruses.

Requirements for success

Division has to be done at the right time: generally, in spring or autumn, just as new growth is starting, or dormancy is setting in, respectively. Some plants such as German or flag iris, are traditionally lifted and divided after flowering.

Dig up the parent plant with care, keeping as much of the root system intact as possible. Ideally, each newly divided clump should have three shoots and a healthy root system.

A good sharp cut with a clean tool gives plants the best chances of taking without being attacked by parasites. The roots and shoots should also be balanced: too few roots result in the shoots wilting.

The soil should be suitable for the type of plant being divided, and weed free. Once the divided plants have been planted, water generously.

Dividing rhizomatous clumps

German, or flag, irises and montbretias are examples of plants which develop from rhizomes: underground stems, full of sap and capable of putting out roots and shoots. A fragment of rhizome with an eye can, theoretically, grow into a complete new plant.

Dividing an herbaceous clump
1. Uproot the plant with a fork.

2. Separate into 2 in (5 cm) sections with a sharp knife or by pulling apart.

Method This consists of digging the plant up once it has flowered. Use a fork to dig up the rhizome then, with a sharp knife, divide the rhizome into sections, each with a few leaves. The sections need not have roots though it helps if they have. Each section should be at least 2 in (5 cm) long, ideally 4 in (10 cm). Re-plant sections shallowly but firmly, with the upper half of the rhizome exposed. Trim the leaves, reducing them by about half, then water generously.

Use only the outer, young rhizomes; discard the centre, which is the oldest part and hence produces the fewest flowers. A good young rhizome should be firm, thick, well swollen and as even as possible. Discard all soft, damaged or spotted sections.

Rooting

This is usually immediate; even irises thrown on a compost heap or left in a box in the open air often root and continue growing quite normally. Avoid compact, heavy, waterlogged soil, and avoid using too much organic matter, particularly fresh manure. Yellowing leaves at the tip of the clump is nothing to worry about provided that the heart stays green. In many cases, a proper shoot only appears in the spring following division.

Dividing fibrous clumps

This method is used for hardy perennials such as heleniums, phlox, helianthus (sunflower), asters and anaphalis (life-everlasting), with an extensive, dense root system of small, tangled roots. The clump is dug up as a whole, preferably with a fork in heavy soils and a spade in light ones.
Method Shake the earth from the roots, select well-developed young, outer portions and pull them gently apart with your fingers. Each new

Dividing a rhizomatous clump (e.g. iris)
Cut the clump in sections with a sharp spade or border spade.

Dividing fibrous root stock
Carefully tear the mass in half by hand.

clump should have three to five shoots. However, one shoot is enough, even if you want many new plants. If you do have just one shoot plant it in a peat pot, so it can develop well in the nursery.

In the open ground, re-plant the clumps slightly deeper than previously, then water generously with a watering can fitted with a fine hose. For very tangled plants that are difficult to separate intact, use two forks back to back, inserted in the heart of the clump. Pull the two handles together, to divide the clump.

Rooting
Adding peat to heavy soils in the new planting positions helps plants take rapidly. Keep the plants well watered, especially in hot, sunny weather.

Dividing tubers

Tubers of dahlias, cannas, tuberous begonias and even potatoes can be cut into sections before planting. In theory, a bit of a tuber just needs a well-developed eye to form a new plant; but in practice, it is better to use larger pieces. Tubers are divided immediately before being planted in the open, or before the plants start producing leaves in a greenhouse, as in the case of cannas. You need a clean, well-sharpened knife.

Method This varies according to the plant but all tubers need at least one well-developed, viable growth point. Divide clumps of dormant dahlia tubers in spring, immediately before planting. Split up the tuberous root clump into as many small tubers as needed; each new section must contain at least one tuber with some of last year's dead stem attached. This ensures that live buds are present, where the tuber and stem join; from these buds, new plants grow.

Cut begonia tubers, potatoes and Jerusalem artichokes vertically in half. Pot up dahlias, cannas and begonias immediately, in multipurpose compost (potting soil) and place under cover.

It is sensible to treat the cut surface with a thin coating of sulphur or some other fungicidal dust, to reduce the risk of rot and diseases. Let canna tubers grow under glass and produce roots and shoots, before dividing them.

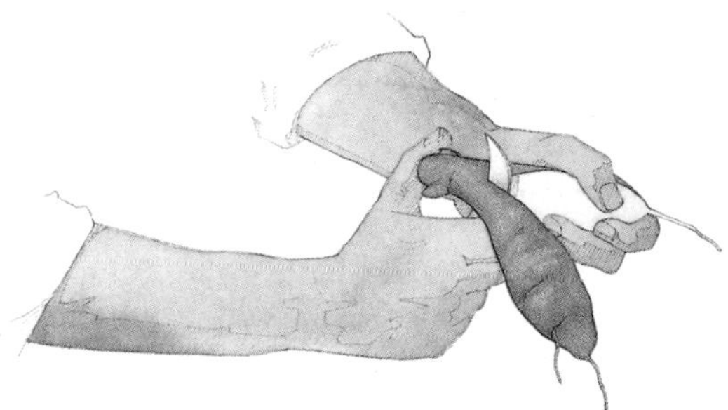

Dividing tubers
Cut the tuber in half, lengthways, with a sharp knife.

Rooting
Newly divided tubers develop faster if they are given slight warmth. Wait until frost has finished before planting out. Plants propagated in this way can flower in their first summer.

Fleshy root division

This method is used for plants such as rhubarb and hosta with solid, fleshy roots that form a compact, hard mass. In autumn, or from midsummer onwards for poppies, dig up the clump, using a spade, preserving as many of the fine, young roots as possible.

Method Cut up the clump like a pie, using a sharp spade or border cutter. Each new section should have at least three old stems. Plant the sections again immediately, at the same depth as previously.

Make the cut as neat and clean as possible.

Rooting
This is fairly predictable, but poppies do not like being disturbed and should only be divided when flowering is reduced.

Separating runners and suckers

Runners are produced by plants such as strawberries and *Chlorophytum* (spider plant), and are small plantlets which develop at the ends of long stems. Very often, the plantlets already have roots themselves.

Side shoots can develop at the base of some plants, such as artichokes, and suckers may also be grown in pots under cover until late spring, this often increases their chances of rooting. In the case of grafted cultivars, such as roses or plums, suckers come from the rootstock and have no horticultural value. These shoots are best discarded, unless used as rootstocks themselves. Suckers from variegated or double varieties may revert to the species with plain green leaves and single flowers.

Success rate
The chances of success are high if the shoots have enough roots, but you have to wait until the next spring to be sure that the plants are

Separating runners
Once roots have formed on the plantlet, cut the runner from the parent plant with secateurs (hand pruners) and plant out.

grow from buds which develop on lateral roots. Unlike other side shoots, the young plants may appear some distance from the parent. Bamboo, raspberry, rhus (sumac) and ailanthus (tree-of-heaven) shoots can be separated from their parent and planted separately.

Method Separate the runner or shoot carefully from its parents to keep it intact. It is easier with above-ground shoots or runners than with some suckers, which may join the parent root deep in the soil,

Preserve as much of the root system as possible. Plant in potting compost, in the case of *Chlorophytum* (spider plant) and *Saxifraga stolonifera*, or in the open. Artichoke side shoots can

Separating side shoots
Dig all round the parent plant to expose the side shoot and remove it with a sharp knife.

developing well. Strawberries, on the other hand, often show signs of growth just a week after being separated from the parent plant. These suckers should be given the same treatment as the parent plant.

Layering
1. Strip the leaves from the section of stem to be used for layering.

2. Dust the area to be buried with hormone rooting powder.

3. Peg down the section to be buried. Raise the end of the branch.

4 and **5.** Securely stake the raised end. Cover the buried section with a sand and compost mixture.

LAYERING

This method involves encouraging a stem to produce roots while still attached to the parent plant. Since the layered stem has an uninterrupted supply of sap, the chances of success are better than with cuttings. Runners are one form of natural layering; blackberries, ivy, honeysuckle, some dogwoods and hydrangeas tend to layer of their own accord as soon as their branches or stems touch the ground.

Layering techniques differ, depending on the characteristics of the plants. Species with flexible branches are bent down and buried in the soil, while more rigid species are earthed up so that sections of stem are in contact with the soil. The layer is separated from the parent plant once roots develop.

Advantages

Layering requires no special equipment and it can be used to propagate plants, such as rhododendrons, magnolia and fig, which are normally difficult to propagate by cuttings. Layered plants are not subject to 'stress' and, if a layer fails to root, this does not affect the parent plant.

Drawbacks

Only a limited number of plants are suitable and layering only produces a few plants. This is why professionals do not use it very much nowadays. Layering is often a lengthy process; rooting can take several months or even as long as two years.

Requirements for success

Choose a flexible young shoot, one or two years old, and as close to the ground as possible. Rooting hormones can speed root growth, especially on slow plants. The soil should be light and friable and the parent plant in good condition and growing well; semi-shade is helpful. Autumn is the best time for layering.

Ground layering

This is the most commonly used method, and consists of bending a low branch and half burying it in the ground. Some flexible shrubs, such as dogwood, or climbing plants, such as clematis, lend themselves to this technique.

Method Bend over a low, flexible shoot so that it forms a 'U' shape. Bury the base of the 'U' 2–3 in (5–7 cm) deep. The above-ground stem beyond the layer should be 6 in (15 cm) long. Hold the buried section in place with small wire hoops, like staples. Turn the end of the branch upwards and tie to a cane. Cover the buried section with a mixture of sand and compost.

Make a few light incisions on the lower part of the buried section, preferably below an eye, to promote the growth of roots.

You can bury the layer in a large pot in the ground, filled with suitable compost (soil) and with a minimum of root disturbance.

Rooting

The appearance of roots is not easy to detect, so wait until shoots appear on the buried stem before separating the plant. Water the layered section regularly, mulching the soil in hot dry weather.

Chinese layering

This is also suitable for plants, such as hazel, forsythia, honeysuckle, willows and ivy, which have long, supple shoots.

Method Bury a long shoot in a shallow trench with the last few inches of stem at the end exposed and bent upwards. The branch is initially buried in 2 in (5 cm) of sand soil, then by means of three successive earthings, the layer is eventually covered with about 8 in (20 cm) of soil, improving the rooting considerably. Earthing up frequently encourages the side shoots growing from the buried stem to produce roots. Keep the soil or compost moist.

Rooting

This coincides with the development of side shoots. Wait until the rooted shoots are dormant before severing them in the autumn. Some plants, such as garrya (silk-tassel bush), do better if the rooted layers are potted up for at least a season before being planted out.

Serpentine layering

This involves burying a long supple shoot in several places along its length, giving a shape reminiscent of a sea serpent. Vigorous climbing plants, such as clematis, honeysuckle, jasmine, passion flower, *Vitis coignetae* (crimson glory vine) and wistaria are suitable.

Etiolation layering
1. Remove the leaves from the section to be buried.

2. Lay the shoot in a shallow ½in (13 mm) deep drill. Only the end should be upright. Provide support as and when necessary.

Method The section of stem nearest the plant is buried for about 6 in (15 cm), then lifted out and rebedded at intervals along its length; the end of the shoot is tied to a cane. Rooting is encouraged by scoring a few light incisions on the bark of the buried sections. Applying rooting hormone powder to the wounds helps and wire hoops can secure the buried sections of the shoot in place.

Twisting the section to be buried so that the bark is broken also promotes the development of roots, but be careful not to snap the shoot. Using pots for serpentine layering makes transplanting easier; place the buried sections in pots instead of in the open ground.

Rooting

Timing depends on species. Spring layers can often be severed in the autumn once the leaves have fallen. Carefully dig up each new plant with a ball of soil attached to the roots. Each buried part of the layer is capable of producing a new plant.

Rooting
The success rate is high. The young shoots often produce side shoots during the growing season. Detach each shoot at its base by hand and replant quickly, before the roots dry out. Lastly, trim the young plants, cutting the above-ground growth back by a third to encourage plants to establish and grow well the following year.

Air-layering

This method is used on indoor plants, such as *Ficus, Dracaena* and *Yucca*, but can also be used on magnolias, hibiscus, viburnums and some conifers. It is done in spring or summer, and consists of encouraging above-ground branches, that are one to two years old, to produce roots.

Method Remove the leaves from the section to be layered, 6–15 in (15–38 cm) above the growing tip, make an oblique, $1\frac{1}{4}$ in (3 cm) long notch in the leafless section. Do not cut through the heart of the branch; one third of the way through is best. Dress the cut with a hormone rooting powder and wedge open by inserting a matchstick. Wrap the leafless section in damp moss, then cover the whole section in a plastic sleeve, tied tightly at the top and bottom.

A method more commonly used with indoor plants can also be applied to hardy species whose

Serpentine layering
1. Twist the shoot to be layered so that the bark is split.
2. Lift and bury the stem several times until you reach the end of the stem, which should be staked.

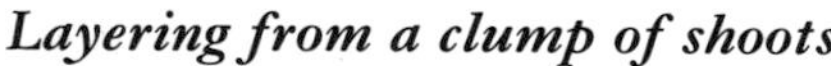

Layering from a clump of shoots

This is known as stooling or mound layering and is carried out on plants whose rigid stems cannot be bent over and buried in the soil. The soil is earthed up around the base of the plant, so that young shoots can root while attached to the parent. This technique is used with *Cydonia* (quinces), *Chaenomeles speciosa* (Japanese quinces), willows and some apple rootstocks. The earthing up is carried out when the shoots are 8–10 in (20–25 cm) tall, and separation takes place in the early winter.

Method To produce as many new shoots as possible, the parent plant is cut back almost to ground level in winter. The young shoots grow from the crown and when these are 8–10 in (20–25 cm) high, they are earthed up to half their height, to encourage roots to grow from the buried portion. If the soil is heavy and lumpy, adding a 50:50 peat sand mix is helpful.

They are successively covered with soil during the growing season. By midsummer, the bottom 6 in (15 cm) of stems should be buried. Keep the soil moist at all times. Separation is carried out in early winter.

Stooling weakens the parent so use it only on strong, well-established plants and allow two seasons normal growth before stooling again.

Layering a stool (stooling)
Cut down the parent shrub during the winter. In mid spring cover it with soil and repeat as the shoots grow.

bark comes away easily. Carefully remove a ring of bark about ½ in (13 mm) broad with a razor blade. The exposed part is then treated with hormone-rooting powder, wrapped in moss and covered with a polythene sleeve, as above.

Keep a high level of moisture around the layer. Opaque plastic is better than transparent plastic, as roots will develop readily in darkness.

Rooting

This is a lengthy, often difficult process; it takes an average of two or three months for the layering to succeed. Failure does not threaten the health of the plant, however, and the cut section often heals of its own accord.

GRAFTING

Grafting is a surgical operation performed on plants, to combine two related individuals in such a way that the lower, rooted section, or stock, supports a decorative or productive aerial part, or scion.

It is complicated and requires patience. Most grafting techniques work well on young specimens, but it is harder to graft a plant aged 20 or more years or to graft one more than 4 in (10 cm) in diameter. A small shoot, up to 6 in (15 cm) long is the usual size of scion, but a single bud may also be used. This is called 'budding', but the same principles apply.

Advantages

Grafting is used to propagate plants, such as fruit trees, large-flowered roses, coloured-leaf conifers, weeping trees and double-flowered lilacs, which cannot easily be obtained by simpler methods.

Grafting can also be used to create unusual shapes, such as one variety of cactus grafted on another. Grafting can also enable a species to adapt to a soil which would normally be unsuitable for it: pear trees, for example, can adapt to alkaline soil if grafted on to *Cydonia oblonga* (quince) rootstocks.

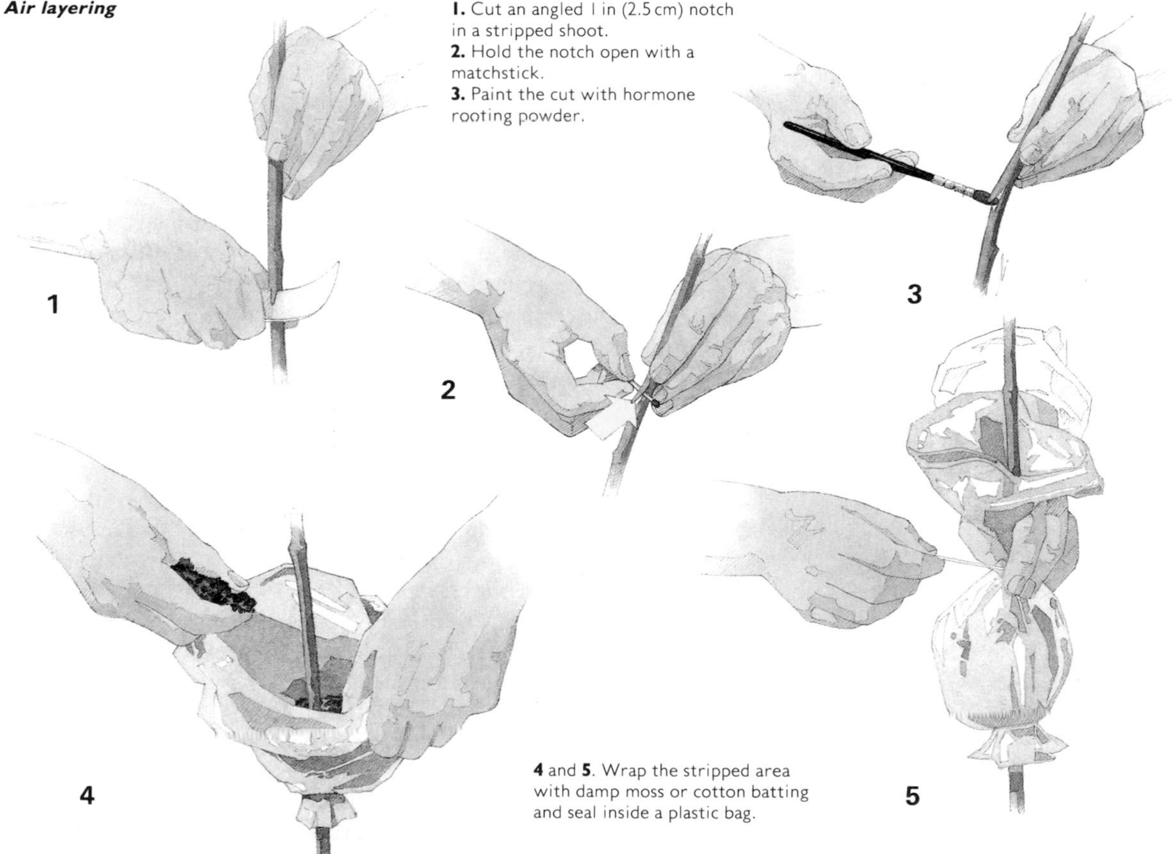

Air layering

1. Cut an angled 1 in (2.5 cm) notch in a stripped shoot.
2. Hold the notch open with a matchstick.
3. Paint the cut with hormone rooting powder.

4 and **5**. Wrap the stripped area with damp moss or cotton batting and seal inside a plastic bag.

Grafting is also used to make plants resistant to some diseases; fruit and grape vines, for example, can be protected from phylloxera by grafting on to stocks of American origin. Grafting also enables a plant's vigour to be controlled by choosing a specific stock: fruit trees, for example, are grafted on to rootstocks that give particularly vigorous or slow-growing trees. Lastly grafting may be the only way of propagating a favourite variety, such as older varieties of pear, apple or rose, which cannot be found in the shops.

Grafting gives enormous control over a plant. By combining a selected stock and a given scion, you can determine the ultimate size of a plant. Grafted plants often gain in vigour, bloom earlier and produce more fruit.

Grafting can also be an opportunity to indulge in botanical fantasies, as a number of varieties can be grown on the same plant. Red and yellow roses can flower on a single bush, or peaches and plums on the same tree. While this is fun, it has no real advantage as one variety will eventually overpower the other.

Drawbacks

Grafting is usually restricted to woody species, though not all woody species can be grafted.

For a graft to succeed, the two specimens must be compatible, belonging to the same family, and the same or a closely related genus. Apples can be grafted on to apples, roses on to roses, pears can be grafted on to quinces, and lilacs on to privet. It is even possible to graft tomatoes on to potatoes. As a rule, though, the options are limited and amateurs do not have access to all modern rootstocks bred by research institutes.

Grafting requires practice and skill, and the initial success rate is liable to be low.

Rootstocks

Also known as the stock, this provides contact with the soil, giving the composite plant strength and hardiness. Intermediate stocks are sometimes used, especially on fruit trees, for straight stems.

Intermediate stock can also be used to overcome incompatibility between stock and scion; William's or Bartlett pear, for example, is incompatible with quince rootstock. If a chip or shoot, of another pear variety, such as Conference or Anjou, is inserted between the rootstock and the William's or Bartlett scion, a perfectly good and strong tree results.

There are a number of ways of obtaining stocks. The oldest method is to select wild plants which offer the best chances of adapting to local soil and weather conditions, such as *Rosa canina* (dog rose) for roses, wild plums for plums, hawthorn for pears and so on. Wild stocks can be hard to find, as the hedgerows in which they thrived are now rare.

Using wild stocks for grafting is haphazard, as there is no guarantee that those selected are healthy or of the vigour required. Also, if you are raising more than one tree or shrub, it is most unlikely that wild rootstocks will give consistent results.

Another method is to sow the seeds of a hardy but unexciting variety to give stock on to which more exotic varieties can be grafted.

Fruit tree pips and stones and rose seeds germinate easily and in large numbers; the best plants can be used as stocks to practise simple grafting techniques, such as shield budding.

Professionals use selected stocks with well-known characteristics, of which dozens exist for fruit trees and roses in particular. Few are offered in nursery catalogues, as it is not in the nurseryman's interest to encourage amateurs to do their own propagating. Selected stocks carry names which mean more to the professional than they do to the amateur, and it is essential to know the characteristics. With vines, for example, only *Vitis riparia* or hybrid rootstocks can guard against phylloxera.

The scion

This is the above-ground section of the plant, and is the variety chosen to be propagated. Scions should always be taken from healthy plants, true to type and in their prime. For spring grafting dormant scions are used. The shoots from which the scions are cut should be straight, healthy, terminal growths. They are gathered during winter pruning in the case of fruit trees, and are heeled in by burying them almost completely in sand at the base of a north-facing wall. Bunches of scions should be labelled with the name of the variety to avoid confusion later on.

For budding in summer, the scion shoots, or bud sticks, are gathered the same day as they are used. They are then wrapped in moist linen and put in a cool, dark place to prevent them wilting (the vegetable compartment in a refrigerator will do perfectly).

Requirements for success

The right tools are essential. You need a suitable grafting knife. There are a number of types available, including those with pointed and spatula blades for shield budding, crown and spliced-side grafts. Those with blades with rounded ends, or 'vine grafting knives', are used for cleft, whip and tongue grafting. You will also need a saw and a good pair of secateurs (hand pruners). Lastly, for cleft grafting you need a mallet and wooden wedges for opening the cleft. For tying in the scions, you need twine or plastic tape and grafting wax, available ready to use from good garden centres.

The success of grafting in general, and budding in particular, is affected by the weathe1. The scion, whether a shoot or a bud, must never dry out, so it is important to tie in the scion correctly and firmly and then, if not using plastic tape, apply a coating of wax to make it completely airtight.

Grafting deciduous trees, shrubs and fruit trees is carried out in early spring; grafting evergreens and conifers, in late spring. These timings give the scions the whole growing season in which to become established. Budding is normally done in summer. All these operations are carried out on plants growing in the open ground.

'Bench grafting' is done under cover in late winter and early spring. This involves grafting short scions on to lifted rootstocks; the completed grafts are plunged into damp sand until they can be safely planted outside.

Although techniques differ, the success of a graft depends on using absolutely clean, well-sharpened tools to give neat, clean cuts. There must be good contact between the scion and the stock; a tiny air gap is often enough for one of the parts to dry out and prevent a quick and strong union taking place. Ties should always be tight and any exposed cut surfaces well covered with wax, especially for cleft grafts.

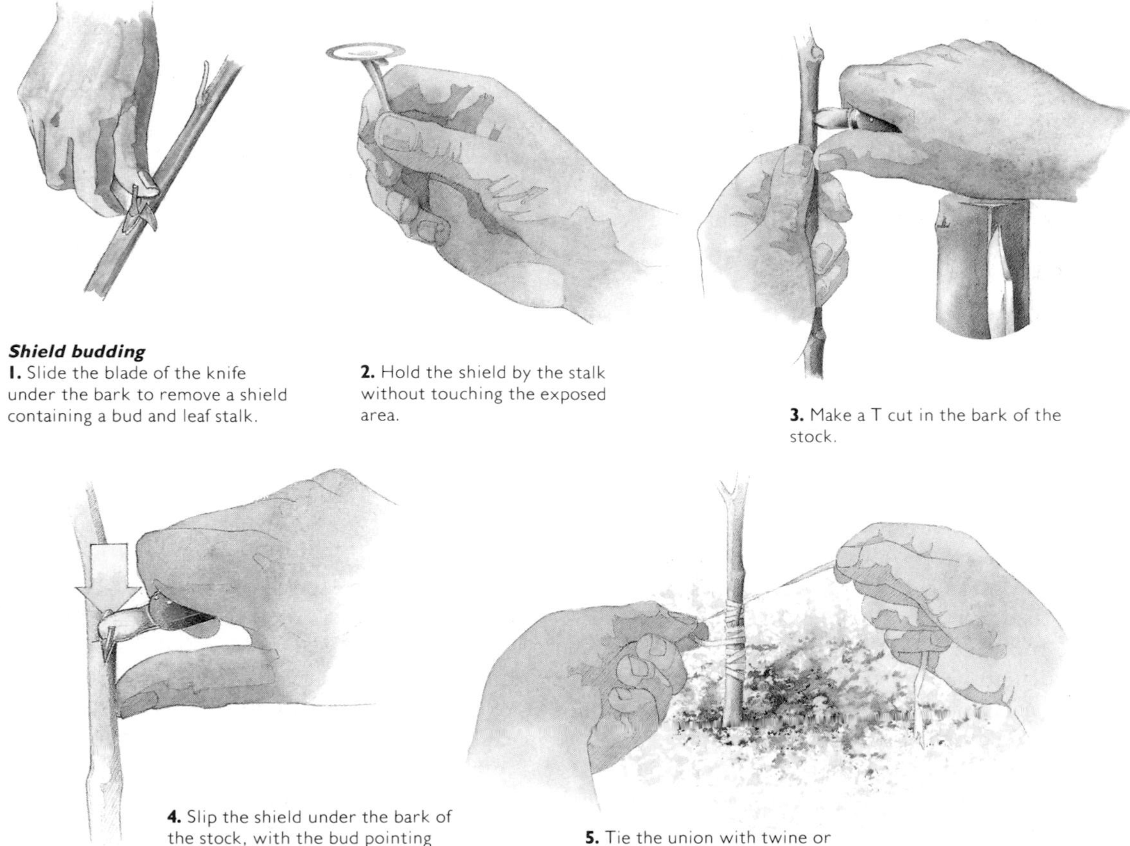

Shield budding
1. Slide the blade of the knife under the bark to remove a shield containing a bud and leaf stalk.

2. Hold the shield by the stalk without touching the exposed area.

3. Make a T cut in the bark of the stock.

4. Slip the shield under the bark of the stock, with the bud pointing up, using the grafting knife spatula.

5. Tie the union with twine or plastic tape.

Shield budding

In theory, this is the simplest method. It involves making a very small wound which heals quickly. Shield budding is normally carried out from about midsummer until early autumn, on rootstocks already planted out in the ground.

It is the usual way of propagating hybrid tea, floribunda and climbing roses and is used for old-fashioned varieties as well. Most fruit trees are also propagated by budding; the required variety being budded on to known clones of vegetatively propagated rootstocks.

With this type of budding, the bud remains dormant until the following spring when it grows out to form the new plant.

Shield budding consists of sliding an eye bud of the variety to be propagated under the bark of the stock. This type of budding is made on the stem, just above the neck of the stock where the stem and the root meet. Stem budding, which is carried out higher up the stem of the rootstock, is mainly used for producing espalier fruit trees, which are to be trained on wires. In this case, buds are often inserted under the bark of the stock at the exact points where the branches of the espalier are wanted, saving a considerable amount of time in forming the tree.

Standard roses are formed by inserting buds even higher up the main stem but this system is also useful with cherries, where it is known that the scion variety is particularly susceptible to some disease, such as bacterial canker.

Method Bud-sticks are gathered just before budding and buds in the centre of the shoots are used. With the point of a budding knife, make a T-shaped cut, about 1 in (2.5 cm) long, in the bark of the stock. Use the spatula of the knife to lift the bark carefully without pulling it off. A shield bud will only unite with a stock carrying a good supply of sap and whose bark does not stick too tightly. Strip the bud-stick of its leaves but retain the leaf stalks. To take the shield bud, put the knife blade about ½ in (1 cm) below the bud; then with a lengthways pulling movement, slide the blade under the bark and lift a shield 1 in (2.5 cm) in length. Hold the bud by the leaf stalk, and avoid touching the shield. Immediately slide the shield under the bark of the stock, making sure it is the right way up, with the bud above the stalk.

Use the spatula of the knife to push the bud into the cut without damaging it; the bud must be in complete contact with the stock. If the shield is too long, cut off the protruding section with the knife. Once assembled, bind the bud to the stock with twine or plastic tape. Leave the eye open to the air, to develop freely. Budding patches, consisting of a small piece of rubber and a staple, are available from specialist suppliers. Simply put the rubber over the graft and hold it in place with the staple to give a firm tie. This has the advantage of speed, and is widely used commercially.

Make sure that the bud does not have any slivers of heartwood attached to it, which can happen if the budding knife was inserted too deeply when the bud was taken. If in doubt, discard, and use a new bud. Shield budding only succeeds with young stocks less than ¾ in (2 cm) in diameter. If the specimens to be grafted are larger than this, other methods are used.

Success rate

The leaf stalk next to the bud eventually indicates whether the bud has taken. If the stalk falls naturally in autumn, when the other leaves on the stock do, the stock has accepted the bud.

Once the bud has developed a shoot about 12 in (30 cm) long in the following summer, prune the stock down to about 4 in (10 cm) above the new shoot, to give a 'peg' for attaching the young shoot to a support, and getting an upright plant by the end of the season. Standard roses, for example, need straight stems and all side shoots which appear from it must be removed, except of course, the ones budded on. Plants which produce branches at the base, such as bush roses, do not need a peg, and the stock is cut just above the new shoot.

Cleft grafting

Its main use is grafting fruit trees of one variety to the stock of another variety. It is carried out in spring, and involves first pruning branches back then grafting the desired variety to the end of the pruned-back branch. Cleft grafting may also be used where buds failed to take the previous summer; the stock is left to develop for a year, to broaden sufficiently. Branch stumps and stocks for cleft grafting should be about 1 in (2.5 cm) in diameter.

Cleft grafting is widely used on high-stemmed fruit trees, which are first sometimes shield budded with an intermediate stock to

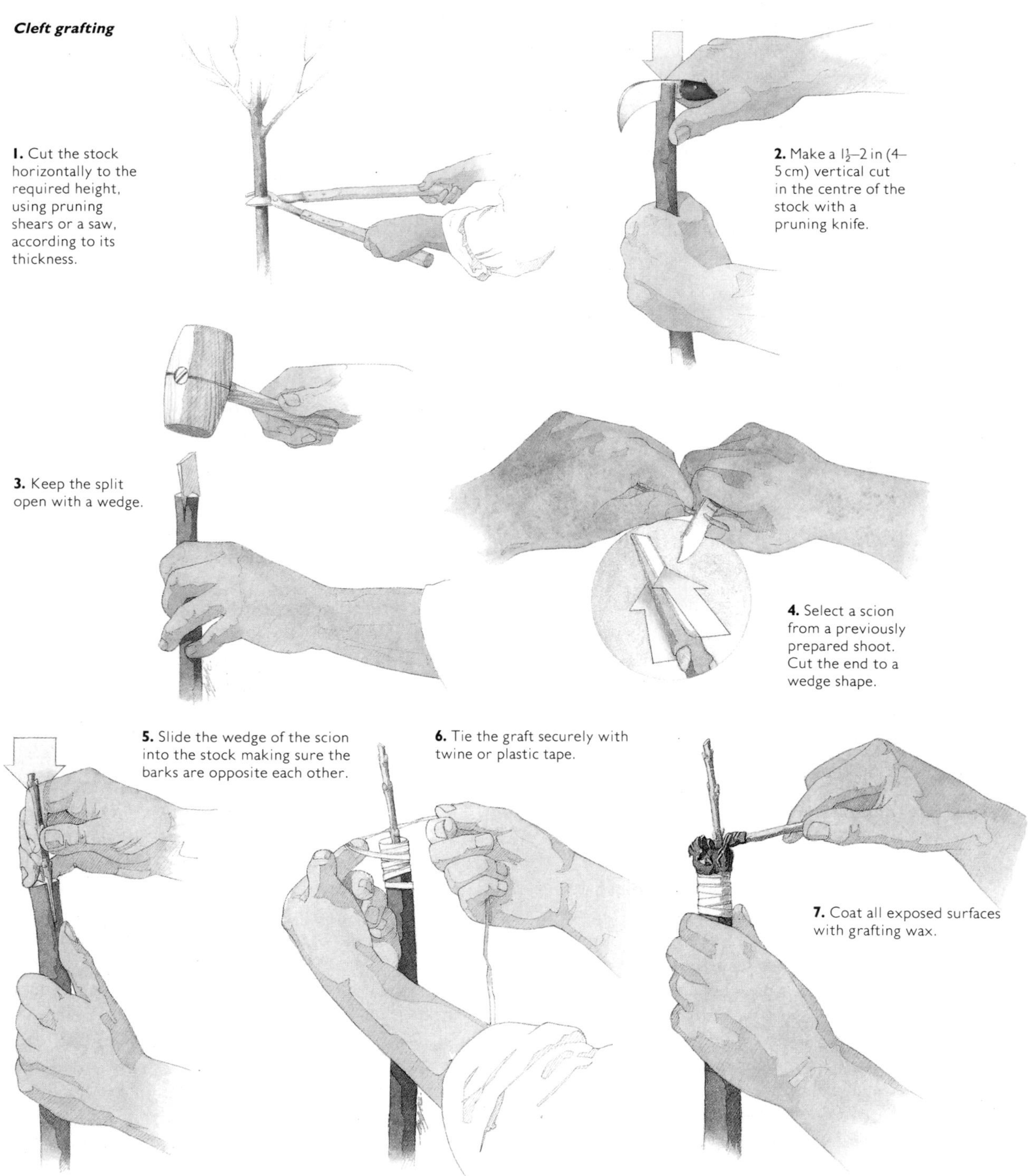

give a straight trunk. Citrus fruits, standard and weeping roses, wisteria and beech are also grafted by this method.

Method Cleft grafting requires some preparation. The scion shoots are taken in late autumn and heeled in until spring. About two weeks before grafting the stock is cut down to the required height. It is often necessary to use a lopper, a kind of two-handed secateurs (pruners), to make the cut as clean and horizontal as possible.

Begin by making a split across the stock about $1\frac{3}{4}$ in (4.5 cm) in length, using a garden knife or special clefting tool and a mallet to help the blade penetrate into tougher wood. Proceed gently, to avoid splitting the wood too deeply. If necessary, insert a small wooden wedge to hold the cleft open. The scion should have healthy, well-developed buds. Cut the lower part of the scion into a V-shape for about $1\frac{1}{4}$ in (3.5 cm) either side of a bud. The 'V' should be fairly acute, to avoid excessively enlarging the cleft.

The average scion should have three viable eyes, including that at its base, and should be 2–3 in (5–7 cm) long. The graft is made by inserting the V-shaped end of the scion into the cleft in the stock, until the eye at the base of the 'V' is well into the cleft. The barks *must* meet. A single scion is used when grafting a new tree but, when grafting another variety on to a mature tree, more than one scion is used.

The maximum width of a branch stump suitable for grafting is about 4 in (10 cm), and up to three scions are normally inserted, to ensure that the end of the stock branch heals. After two or three years and when the scions are growing strongly, all but one is removed, otherwise a weak point would be created by several branches originating from the same stump.

A successful graft brings the scion and stock into as close contact as possible. Once the graft has been made, tie it firmly to close the cleft and exclude all air. Raffia (twine) can be used for single cleft grafts but, for multiple cleft grafts or with more than one scion, use plastic tape. Any exposed parts are then coated with grafting compound, applied along the cleft and to the upper end of the scion.

To make raffia (twine) supple, stronger and easier to tie, soak it in water for half-an-hour or so before using; many professionals keep the skein in a bucket of water while working.

It is often unnecessary to tie large cleft branches, $2\frac{1}{2}$ in (6 cm) or more with raffia; the strength of the wood trying to close up the split is usually quite sufficient to hold the scion firmly in place. However, the union still needs complete waxing to make it airtight. If the cleft is wide, a soil plug can be pushed in to stop hot wax penetrating and causing damage.

Success rate

The scion and stock should fuse within two months of grafting; this shows in the swelling of the buds on the scion, especially that at its base, and is followed by the emergence of new shoots. The union must remain intact; if necessary tie a short cane to the stock and secure the scion to it. If surface cracks appear on the wax, add another layer of wax. Any shoots which form on the stock should be removed.

Inlay grafting

This version of cleft grafting eliminates the space between the stock and scion and involves inserting a scion with three viable buds into a triangular cleft in the stock. It is sometimes used with stone fruits as it prevents grafting compound running over the open wound. Grafting broom hybrids on to laburnum rootstocks is also done in this way. However, it is more difficult than ordinary cleft grafting, as the cuts must meet correctly. Most species which can be cleft grafted can also be inlay grafted. The best time for inlay grafting is spring.

Method Using a single-trunk branchless stock with a maximum diameter of $1\frac{1}{4}$ in (3.5 cm), cut it through horizontally at the intended height of the graft. With a grafting knife, cut a narrow triangle or notch on the side of the stock at the top. The triangle or notch should point downwards and stop short of the centre, or core, of the stock. Next, make a wedge-shaped cut on the base of the scion on either side of a bud. Ideally, the wedge should fit perfectly into the triangle or notch in the stock, but matching the angles is not easy, though the technique can be mastered with practice. If necessary, increase the size of the triangle or notch, to accommodate the scion, rather than try to trim the scion to fit.

With a good inlay graft, the barks meet and the scion is held firmly in place by the stock, but it also needs tying in with plastic tape or twine. There is no need to cover the scion entirely. Finally, apply grafting compound wax to any parts still exposed, especially the cut surfaces of the stock and the tip of the scion.

The scion benefits from being wrapped in a protective, waxed paper sleeve for about ten days after grafting.

Success rate

The scion should join on to the stock in the weeks following grafting. The buds on the scion will swell, then burst, producing young leafy shoots. This is the time to make sure that the union is holding well, as ties may become loose under the effects of the weather. If a tie is too tight, cut it with the tip of the grafting knife on the side of the stock opposite the scion, once the graft is seen to be successful. Inlay grafts of cherries often develop only one shoot but pinching the growing tip once the shoot is 16 in (40 cm) long encourages branching. Start pruning the branches to give the required shape in the year after grafting.

Crown grafting

Crown grafting is the collective name given to any type of grafting involving removing all the large branches of a tree and grafting scions of a new variety on to the stumps to produce, in effect, a new tree. Cleft, oblique cleft, rind, modified rind or veneer grafts are usually employed.

Crown grafting is used mainly on apple and pear trees, to improve the variety. The existing tree must be healthy and no more than 20 years old; older trees are better replaced. Stone fruit trees are unsuitable, as the gum exuded reduces the chance of success and weakens the tree itself.

Method Using a saw, cut back the branches to 4 in (10 cm) in diameter and graft each branch separately. Pare back the cut with a sharp knife to remove any rough tissues. Like the cleft graft, the rind graft is commonly used for crown grafting. A vertical cut about $1\frac{1}{2}$–2 in (4–5 cm) long is made in the bark at the top of the stump with the point of a grafting knife, and bark is peeled back from the wood. The scions are, again, one-year-old shoots, with three viable, well-developed buds, taken in winter and heeled in. Make a long, slanting cut behind the lowest bud, to give as much surface contact with the stock as possible. Slide the scion under the bark of the stock. If the scion is narrow, the bark is only lifted on one side (a modified rind graft). The eye at the base should be below the top of the stock. Between three and seven scions can be grafted on to the branch, depending on the size of the stock. Tightly bind each graft with twine or plastic grafting tape; about four or five turns is enough. Crown grafts should be waxed more generously than others; the cut surface of the stock should be completely covered, as should all other exposed surfaces. Because of its size and vulnerable position at the end of a branch, a

Inlay grafting
1. Cut the stock horizontally and make a V shaped notch to one side.
2. Cut the scion to a triangular wedge on the side opposite a bud.
3. Push the scion into the stock.
4. Tie with twine or plastic tape.
5. Coat exposed areas with grafting wax.

1

2

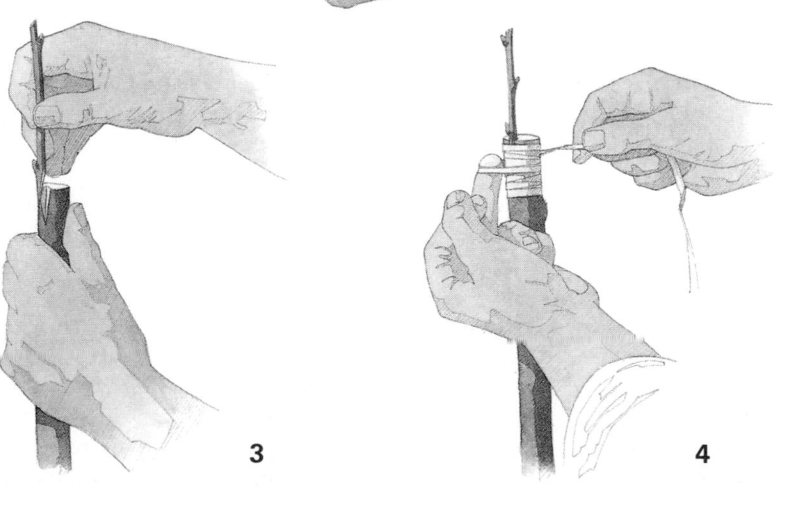

3

4

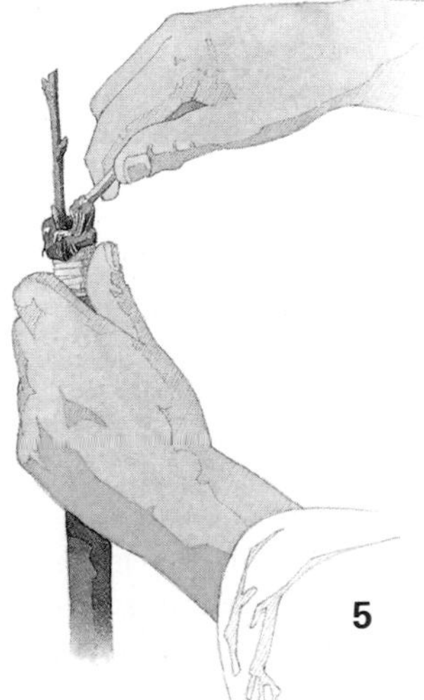

5

Rind or crown grafting

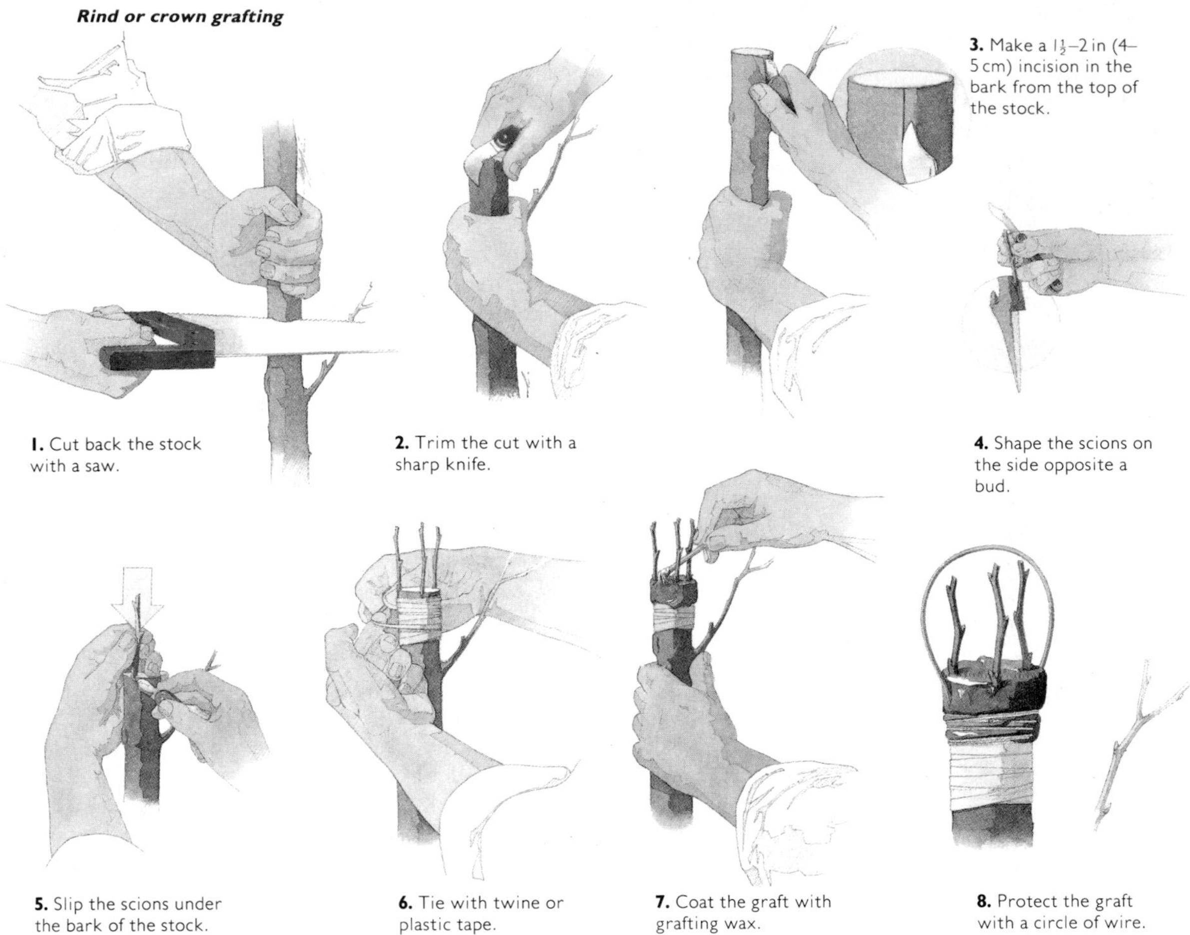

1. Cut back the stock with a saw.

2. Trim the cut with a sharp knife.

3. Make a 1½–2 in (4–5 cm) incision in the bark from the top of the stock.

4. Shape the scions on the side opposite a bud.

5. Slip the scions under the bark of the stock.

6. Tie with twine or plastic tape.

7. Coat the graft with grafting wax.

8. Protect the graft with a circle of wire.

crown graft must be protected from birds perching on the scions. A wire hoop over the tops of the shoots, held in place by string should suffice. As crown grafts are relatively fragile, a second coating of compound applied a month after the first is advisable.

Leaving a small lateral shoot just underneath the graft helps draw the sap towards the grafts. Shaping the top of the sloping cut on the back of the scion helps it stand more vertically.

Success rate

A strong union takes a fairly long time, but if the buds on the scions stay reasonably healthy and show a tendency to swell, all is well. Sap-drawing shoots and branches on the stock should be removed in the winter following grafting. Usually only one scion in each crown is kept; the others are gradually removed in the course of two or three annual winter prunings. With larger crown grafts, the excess scions are removed within two years.

Whip (and whip-and-tongue) grafting

This method, used for vines, fruit trees, ornamental trees, shrubs including clematis and roses is a fairly delicate operation because, unlike other grafts, the stocks used are not rooted. Vines are whip grafted during the winter, preferably under cover and in a heated atmosphere, while ornamental species tend to be grafted in spring, also under cover. For vines, use a stock of *Vitis riparia* or one of its hybrids, to avoid attacks of phylloxera.

Method There are two variations: whip and whip-and-tongue grafting. Simple whip (or splice) grafting consists of pruning the stock and scion diagonally, so the two cut surfaces match perfectly, then tying them together. The diagonals must be parallel, so that the stock and scion 'lock' together in a straight join. The scion has only one bud, so a number of plants can be obtained from a single shoot and therefore a higher yield achieved than with other methods.

Whip-and-tongue whip grafting is based on the same principle. The stock should be 6–8 in (15–20 cm) long to root well. The scion and stock must be roughly the same diameter: each is cut to the same angle and with about 2 in (5 cm) of exposed surface. A small protruding tongue is made by slitting each cut surface for $\frac{1}{8}$ in (3 mm) of its length, so the two sections can be interlocked. This gives a larger contact area and the stock and scion remain in close contact while being tied in. Both types of graft need waxing.

Success rate
Success requires keeping the plant warm for at least a month. Vine bud grafts should be buried in a large tub containing a mixture of moist sand and peat, and given bottom heat. It takes 30 to 40 days for the plant to root well. Fruit trees and other indoor grafts are planted fairly deep in boxes of sand and kept under cover at about 59°F (15°C) and should not be brought out until mid-spring. By this time, the eye of the scion should have produced a young shoot which needs to be supported with a stake. Simple whip-grafted shrubs are kept at 44–50°F (7–10°C) until the risk of frost is past. These scions often develop early, which makes protecting them even more important. Ventilate well and cut the ties during the summer.

Approach grafting

This method is often used when other forms of grafting are unsuccessful and is widely used on citrus fruit, magnolias and camellia. It often happens in nature that two intertwined branches fuse; because the stock and scion are receiving nutrients from their own roots, this is a relatively easy method and can be done at any time during the growing season. It can also be used to reconstitute a broken main branch.
Method This involves wounding both stock and scion and then bringing the two wounded surfaces into close contact, without detaching the scion from its parent until the join has succeeded. You can plant a scion close to the stock or use separate pots. The stock and the scion are prepared by removing their leaves for about 4 in (10 cm) of their length. A sliver of bark, $1\frac{1}{2}$–2 in (4–5 cm) long, is removed from each. The wounds should be shallow, no more than $\frac{1}{4}$ in (6 mm) wide, and the same length. The best system is to cut away the sliver from the stock then mark the size of this on the scion.

Whip and tongue grafting

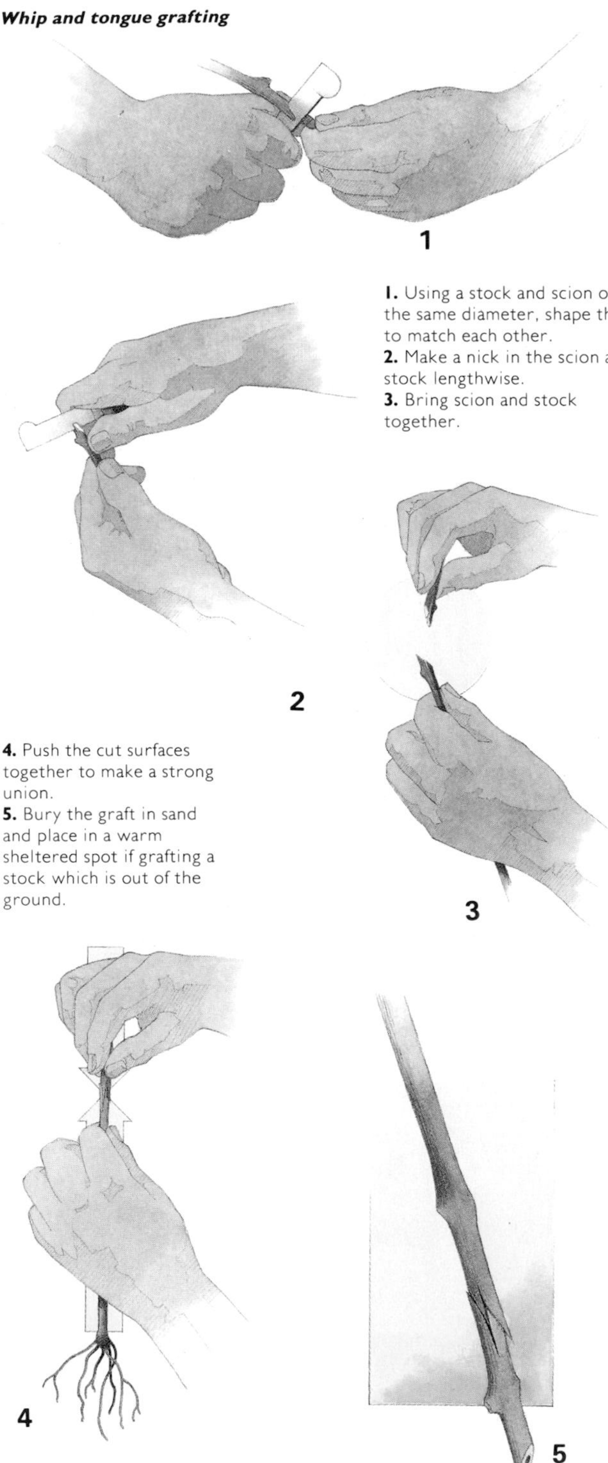

1. Using a stock and scion of the same diameter, shape them to match each other.
2. Make a nick in the scion and stock lengthwise.
3. Bring scion and stock together.

4. Push the cut surfaces together to make a strong union.
5. Bury the graft in sand and place in a warm sheltered spot if grafting a stock which is out of the ground.

The two sections are brought into contact with one another, then tied, preferably with wool for smaller plants and a rubber band or cotton thread for the larger ones. Grafting wax is usually needed. The best branches are those sheltered from strong winds and excessive sun, so the grafted tissues do not dry out. Spray the graft with cold water in hot weather.

Success rate

This is relatively slow; the approach graft must not be severed until the end of the scion has grown considerably and lateral shoots have developed. The scion is usually separated from its natural roots in stages and is cut just below the join.

Side grafting
1. Remove the leaves from the stock and the graft over about 4 in (10 cm).

Spliced side grafting (Veneer side graft)

This method is mostly used for grafting coloured-foliage varieties or conifers. It involves working with very young plants with thin, and hence, delicate shoots. Containerized stocks, grown from seed and not more than two years old, are used. The grafting is done at the base and under cover, preferably in mid-to-late spring or early autumn, although it can be done successfully any time.

Method This involves inserting a scion into an oblique cut made in the stock. Start by stripping the base of the stock of its needles up to about ½ in (1 cm) above the level of the potting compost with a sharp knife. Then, make a small sideways cut at the foot of the stock, about a third of the way into the stock.

Take the scion at the time of grafting from a young tip shoot (preferably lateral) of the variety to be propagated. It should have three or four clumps of needles over about 3–4 in (7–10 cm) of its length. Cut its base into a 1 in (2.5 cm) wedge either side of a group of needles, then insert the wedge into the cut in the stock. All exposed sections must match perfectly. Tie well with twine or plastic tape, but waxing is not necessary.

The graft must be kept moist; use a metal hoop stuck in the pot with a transparent plastic bag over it for about a month.

2. Strip 1–2 in (2.5–5 cm) of bark from the stock and make a slanting cut with the knife. Do the same with the scion.

3. Bring the two exposed areas together.
4. Tie with twine, plastic tape or an elastic band.

Success rate

Uniting usually takes 6–7 weeks and is shown by the shoots developing from the scion. Once the scion is clearly growing, the stock can be gradually cut back three or four times during the course of the season, until it has completely gone. The young plants should be left in their pots until the following year when they are potted on, and then spend a further season in a container before finally being planted out.

PRUNING

Garden design often attempts to imitate nature, but it is natural to want to combine plants from different origins and growing environments. And because cultivated plants have different growth rates and vigour, gardening involves trying to prevent the stronger plants from displacing the weaker. Plants in the wild are engaged in a relentless struggle for territory, and this fierce competition often leads to distorted form and inextricable tangles. Grown as garden plants, they are modelled by the skilful hand of the gardener so that each achieves optimum appearance.

Pruning is one of the gardener's main ways of keeping the garden beautiful. Plants can survive without pruning, but it can improve a plant's balance, grace, flowering and fruiting. Pruning should never be mutilation but a means of balancing a plant, cutting it back to make it grow and perform better in the long run.

Why prune?

It is essential to know basic plant physiology to understand the benefits of pruning and why one branch is pruned rather than another. A branch has a terminal shoot which ensures that its length continues increasing and, at the junction of each leaf and branch, is a small latent axillary bud or 'eye'.

The terminal shoot dominates the others, as it produces growth inhibitors which prevent the axillary buds developing. Removing the terminal shoot makes these buds develop, enabling a plant to form a lateral branch or branches if the end breaks. Without this regenerative ability, there would be no point in pruning. It accelerates the natural process of branching and can be used to prevent a tree or shrub becoming leggy. Wild plants regularly renew themselves by shedding growth, and produce new, strong and healthy shoots and branches. As new growth comes from the terminal bud, trees and shrubs in the wild eventually become drawn out and bare at the base. Pruning counteracts these effects by encouraging the formation of lateral, or 'side', shoots closer to the base and/or main trunk or stems.

Light promotes the production of flower buds and pruning can allow light to reach the shoots and branches, resulting in increased flowering.

Pruning has a complex effect on fruiting, but basically strength is inversely proportional to fertility, and the more a tree grows, the less fruit it yields. Fruit tree and shrub pruning limits the production of the leaf and stem growth and encourages the production of flowers. Some plants tolerate pruning better than others: apples and pears for instance, can take drastic pruning, while cherries and plums resent pruning, which is liable to result in excessive growth and 'bleeding'.

A branch which is cut tends to grow all the more. However, too much pruning, particularly of the wrong sort, causes a plant to lose its strength and slow down. This is because of the way sap circulates in a plant. The terminal shoots on branches receive the most 'raw', or rising sap, but this stimulates the development of leaves and woody tissue. The shorter the distance between the branch and the shoot, the

The principle of pruning
Removing the end bud on the branch allows side buds to develop, which encourages branching.

more sap the shoot receives and the more it grows. Less favourably positioned parts, especially lateral shoots, mainly receive 'processed' or descending sap. Transformed by photosynthesis in the leaves, this processed sap is full of nutrients, and promotes the formation of reproductive organs, resulting in the development of flowers and fruit. This is why most plants bear fruit or flowers on their side shoots.

Advantages of pruning

Pruning improves the shape of plants and gives them a pleasant outline. This 'maintenance' pruning is carried out at intervals according to the speed of growth. Bonsai trees, for instance, are shaped by repeated treatment in this way.

Pruning keeps plants a reasonable size and stops them smothering others.

Pruning can allow plants with very different growth rates to exist alongside one another. Limiting the size of the strongest plants encourages the growth of the less vigorous ones.

Pruning also stimulates flowering by limiting the number of leafy shoots. The production of many branches reduces the vigorous growth of a tree and encourages it to flower; as flowers are inevitably followed by fruit, it gives a higher fruit yield.

Pruning can also improve the strength of a weak specimen, as pruning stimulates more growth. Pruning also rejuvenates plants, by removing old branches to encourage young ones. Lastly pruning can help to prevent disease, such as cankers, which infect shoots and branches.

Drawbacks of pruning

Pruning always involves risk, as removing a branch not only shocks a plant but also wounds it. This wound is open to pests and diseases, which can easily invade the plant's internal tissues. Pruning at the right time, which varies from plant to plant, does much to reduce this risk. A newly pruned plant is liable to check its growth drastically for several weeks and some do not flower the year they are pruned.

The drastic pruning often carried out on trees in towns or by the roadsides lowers their natural defences and renders them more vulnerable to diseases and pests.

In the garden it is possible to imitate nature and respect plants at the same time.

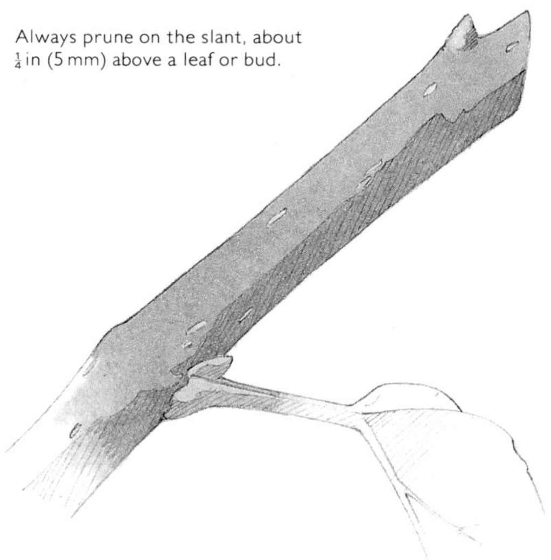

Always prune on the slant, about $\frac{1}{4}$ in (5 mm) above a leaf or bud.

Techniques

Pruning means cutting; pinching, cutting back, rejuvenating, trimming, lopping, disbudding, debranching, pollarding, topping and sawing are just a few of the many pruning terms.

The aim of pruning is usually to encourage the development of one or more shoots to replace the one being pruned, so cuts are made above a bud or shoot. In pruning carried out during the growing season, the cut is made above a leaf, the axillary bud becoming the terminal bud and often growing out. This principle never varies. The distance between the cut and the top of the shoot should be about $\frac{1}{4}$ in (5 mm). The pruning cut should be as close as possible to the replacement bud, but not so close that it damages the new terminal bud.

When lopping an adult tree, the pruning is quite drastic; the branch is cut back to above a better placed branch, or large shoot.

Shaping

This is formative, or maintenance, pruning which creates or retains an attractively shaped woody plant. Secateurs (hand pruners) are usually used, but a saw or chainsaw may be needed for large trees. First, remove any surplus branches and straggling shoots, then clear the centre of the tree and remove overcrowded branches.

Cutting to size

This is one of the commonest reasons for pruning. When undertaking this work, remember that hard pruning encourages a plant to

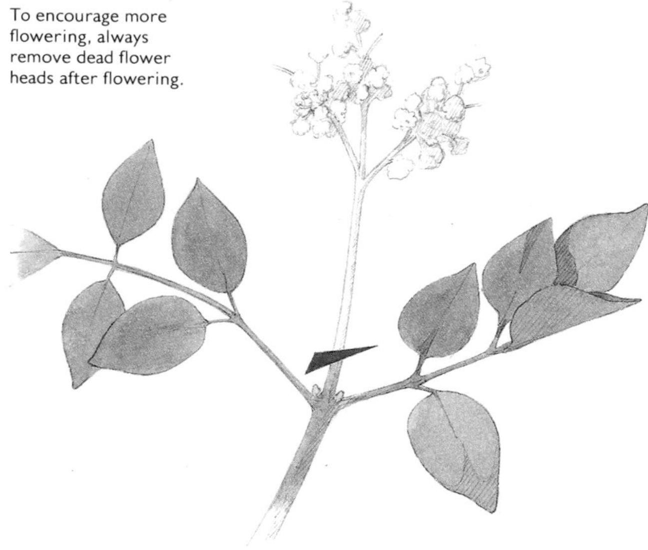

To encourage more flowering, always remove dead flower heads after flowering.

grow all the stronger. It involves reducing the current season's shoots in number and length during the growing period, which tends to reduce vigorous growth. Pruning again in winter enables you to correct the shape. This operation often has to be repeated for a number of years.

Severe pruning low down increases the vigour of certain trees and shrubs, such as buddleja (butterfly bush).

Increasing flowering

This is done by increasing the number of shoots of flowering age, as it is mainly the lateral branches which produce flowers. This often involves pinching or, more exactly, tipping the shoots after the normal flowering period.

Improving fruiting

This is much the same as increasing flowering, as fruit derives directly from flowers. The aim is to restrict the number of leafy shoots and limit their size to encourage the production of blossom and, subsequently, fruit. Too much foliage hides the fruit from the sun and makes it ripen more slowly; it also hampers the production of blossom buds for the following year. Thinning out excess young fruit prevents the tree becoming exhausted, gives the remaining fruit better quality and leads to more consistent yields.

Strengthening plants

Some decorative shrubs benefit from pruning at the end of the growing season, or in the case of flowering shrubs, after flowering has finished. Thin out branches and shoots and remove some of the old shoots to encourage new growth. New growth usually has green bark, while other branches are usually dark brown. Some shrubs, such as buddlejas (butterfly bush), dogwood and willow, can also be cut back completely to just above the ground every 2–3 years to renew their branches completely.

Pruning for health

Many diseases can be limited or controlled by pruning. Cutting off young shoots covered with mildew, for instance, considerably reduces attacks by this disease. Any shoots removed should be burnt immediately. Removing rose leaves infected with black spot, tree fruits with brown rot and strawberries with grey mould slows the disease down, making it easier to control, if necessary, by spraying.

Dead wood and broken shoots and branches should be pruned off, cutting the branches back to healthy wood.

The direction in which a terminal bud faces governs the direction in which the new shoot will grow, and it is generally best to prune back to an outward-facing bud.

Pinching out the terminal shoots usually encourages the lower buds to grow, thus giving a denser structure, and often improving flowering. Pinching out can be done with your fingernails on soft young shoots.

Training

General pruning principles also apply when training young trees or shrubs, especially fruit trees trained into cordon, espalier, fan, or other shapes. Despite the fact that these methods are extremely labour intensive, they are popular today because they produce trees which require less space.

The cordon consists of a single vertical or oblique stem furnished with fruiting spurs. The espalier has a vertical stem from which, at regular intervals and on each side of the stem, horizontal branches are trained out sideways.

Espalier-trained fruit tree.

> **PLANTS WHICH SHOULD NOT BE PRUNED**
>
> *Generally speaking, plants which branch normally, need not always be pruned. Conifers may need to be pruned occasionally but be sure not to cut their leading shoot as this will spoil their shape.*
>
> *Palm trees, bananas, cycads and ferns will never need to be pruned. Camellias, azaleas and rhododendrons will only need to be pruned for shape and then straight after flowering.*

This system is usually kept for apples and pears. As the name indicates, fan trees have a short trunk from which radiate a number of main, lateral and sub-lateral branches and shoots. Although apple and pear trees are grown as fans, this method is really intended for stone fruits (especially peaches and nectarines) because of the way in which they carry their fruit.

All three methods need the support of wires either stretched against a wall or fence, or in the open. Cordons normally have three wires at 2½ ft (75 cm), 4½ ft (1.3 m) and 6½ ft (2 m) above ground. To these, oblique canes are fixed to which the actual trees are tied and trained. For espaliers, the number of wires used depends on the number of tiers required for the tree. The wires should be 15–18 in (38–45 cm) apart. When growing fan-trained trees, the wires will need to be about 6 in (15 cm), or two courses of bricks, apart. As with cordons, canes are tied to

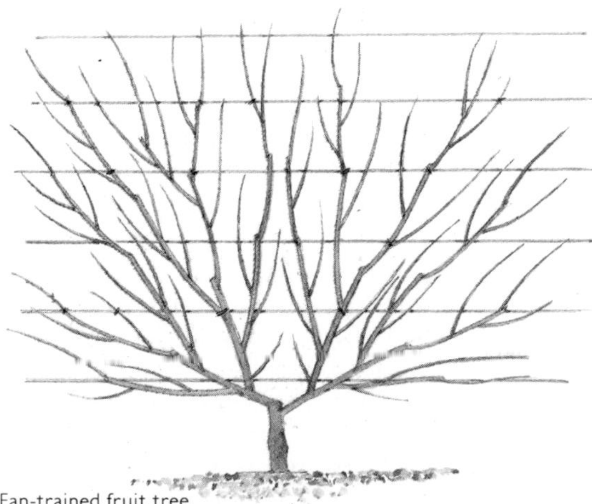

Fan-trained fruit tree.

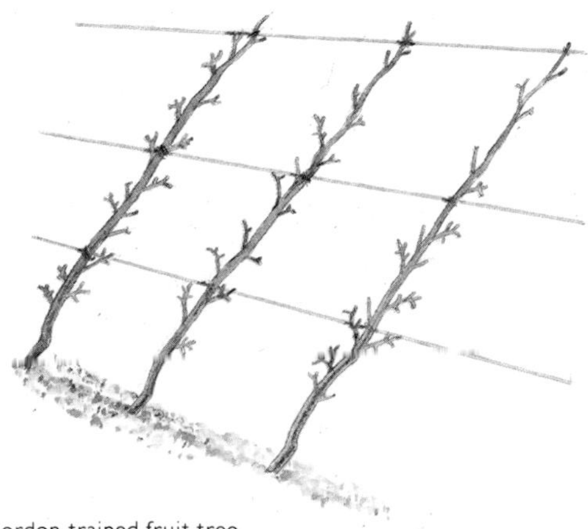

Cordon-trained fruit tree.

the wires to which are trained the main and secondary branches. Smaller ones are tied direct to the wires.

Cordons

To form a cordon tree, the central shoot is allowed to grow unhindered until it reaches the top training wire. When lateral shoots grow directly from the main stem, prune them back to about 3 in (8 cm) long in mid summer to form fruiting 'spurs'. Established cordons are pruned only in the summer, and only once they have reached the top training wire. In mid or late summer, all new side shoots which are hardening at their base (semi-ripe) and which are growing directly from the main stem are nipped back to 3–4 in (8–10 cm) long. Those growing from existing side shoots or spurs are taken back to 1 in (2–3 cm). Any that are not semi-ripe are left and pruned in early autumn. Extension growths that come from the earlier pruning are cut hard back in late autumn once the leaves have fallen.

Espaliers

If you start with a one-year-old (maiden or whip) tree, an espalier is formed by cutting it back to 2–3 in (5–8 cm) above the bottom training wire. The top bud will grow upwards to continue the main stem, the next two produce shoots which will be trained out sideways along the wire to form the first tier of horizontal branches; the initial cut should be made with this in mind. From then on, the system is broadly the same each winter. The top bud being for extension growth, the next two for another tier of branches. Once established and of fruiting age, espaliers are pruned only in the summer and in exactly the same way as cordons. Shoots arising from the horizontal arms of the tree are treated in the same way as those on the upright central stem.

Fan-trained

Maiden (or whip) peach and plum trees for fan-training should be cut back to 2 ft (60 cm) tall in the spring after planting. The aim is to produce two good laterals pointing in opposite directions on either side of the main stem and no more than 1 ft (30 cm) from the ground. If there is already a suitable side shoot 1–2 ft (30–60 cm) up the stem, shorten the main stem back to it.

If there are only buds (no side shoots), wait until two well-placed shoots have started to grow out; the main stem above then can be cut back to the top one in the summer.

Late in the following winter, shorten back the two laterals to 12–18 in (30–45 cm) long and train them out at about 45 degrees. Thereafter, cover the wall or fence by tying in suitable shoots and removing all others.

Once fan-trained plum trees have covered their allotted space, any shoots that are growing directly towards or away from the wall or fence are rubbed out as soon as they are seen in the spring. Those shoots that are required to extend a branch or fill a space are tied in as the summer progresses. Shoots not required for this should have their tops pinched out (stopped) when they reach 6–7 in (15–18 cm) long. These will form the fruiting spurs.

Peaches are treated somewhat differently because they only fruit on the shoots that grew in the previous year. In the spring, all badly placed shoots are rubbed out as for plums. Later, the remainder are tied to the training wires so that they are approximately 6 in (15 cm) apart along the top and bottom of the branch. Once these shoots have fruited in the following summer, they are either cut hard back to produce more shoots or tied in to fill any available space.

Training a free-standing tree

This method is mainly used on fruit trees bought as one-year-old maidens (or whips), but can also be used on ornamental trees grown from seed or bought as saplings. The method is exactly the same for a half standard (trunk 4½ ft (1.4 m) high) and standard (trunk at least 6 ft (1.8 m) high) tree. If starting with a maiden, which has a single stem, and sometimes a few small lateral branches or 'feathers', cut it back by a third or even half its length at the time of planting, above a well-developed bud. By the end of the first full growing season, the main stem will often have grown by nearly 7 ft (2 m) and you can start pruning the main branches to the height you want.

Allow the branches to grow naturally during the following season then, in winter, remove the lowest shoots unless you want a short trunk, and leave only the three top shoots. Cut these back to between a third and half their length, always cutting to an outward facing bud. The main branches should make a fairly open angle with the trunk, to give the tree strength and solidity. Excessively upright main branches are liable to

Training a free-standing tree
Year 1: Cut back the main shoot by a third or even half of its length to above a bud.

Year 2: Remove low branches and cut back upper branches to a third of their length to an outward pointing bud, if appropriate.

Year 3: Shape the branch framework by balancing the laterals.
Year 4: The tree is formed.

develop parallel to the main trunk, and tend to break, especially stone fruit trees, plums in particular.

In the second year the tree fills out and secondary branches appear. To encourage their appearance, especially in the case of cherry trees, tip back the growing points of the main shoots in summer.

In the following winter, cut back all branches by a third to a half, to encourage branching. Trim the shape to an even size to prevent the tree becoming lop-sided. Finally, cut back to three or four buds all the lateral shoots not intended to form part of the branch structure, keeping the best placed outer branches.

In future years, pruning consists of controlling the proportions of the main and secondary branches and removing any inward-growing shoots. As the tree develops, intervals between prunings will lengthen until, eventually, winter pruning alone is enough.

Training a dwarf pyramid

The dwarf pyramid is a form suited to apples on rootstock M9 or M26, and pear trees on quince rootstock.

A maiden planted in autumn or winter is cut back to 20–25 in (50–60 cm) above ground, to a well-developed bud, preferably on the side opposite that to which the tree was budded or grafted. During the growing season, the terminal bud will develop into a strong vertical shoot and the three or four lower buds will send out laterals.

These are left intact until the following winter, then cut the leading (top) shoot by 8–10 in (20–25 cm) pruning to a bud facing away from the angle of the branch to obtain an upright trunk. Cut lateral shoots back by half and check that the branches are balanced. Keep up to four well-spaced branches. If two branches grow from the same place, remove one.

Pyramid training
Year 1: Cut back the top shoot to a bud 20–24 in (50–60 cm) from the ground.

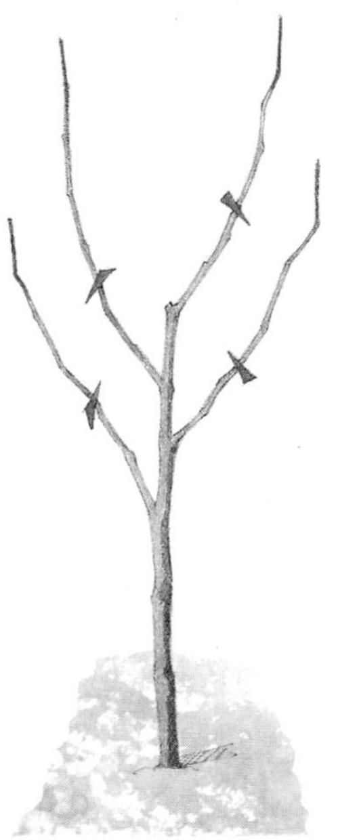

Year 2: Cut back the central leading shoot and the side shoots to half their length.

Year 3: Allow the main branches to lengthen by about 10 in (25 cm) each year.

During the next growing season prune back the new shoots to five leaves from the base in early summer and back to three leaves in late summer to encourage branching, but leave the leading shoots on the central stem and on main branches intact.

In following years, extend the ends of the main branches as before, cutting back to alternating terminal eyes. The branches of a pyramid tree should be nearly horizontal, to slow the rise of the sap and increase productivity. Vigorous and vertical or nearly vertical woody shoots should be removed completely, and the lower branches should be longer than the upper ones. In the first few years, staking is sensible.

Training a palmette

Palmette fruit trees (palm-shaped espaliers) are trained against a wall or a framework. In addition to its beauty, a palmette takes up very little space, making it suitable for small gardens, but the branches need constant maintenance to retain their highly distinctive form. There are a number of versions: vertical, oblique or tiered. The example that follows is the classic four-branched Verrier palmette, which is the easiest and is well suited to apples and pears growing on stocks of average strength. A maiden is cut back to 12 in (30 cm) from the ground in the first winter, above a bud facing away from the wall or frame. Three terminal buds are kept in spring: one at the front and one on each side.

The shoots which form are trained along canes tied to the frame, which consists of three vertical battens 18 in (45 cm) apart and one horizontal batten 12 in (30 cm) from the ground. As the laterals grow they are turned up at the ends and tied to the frame. Gradually re-adjust the canes to lower the lateral shoots little by little until they are horizontal on the wooden batten, a position usually achieved by the end of the season. Train the shoot emerging from the upper eye vertically on the upright batten. Make sure that the ties are not too tight on the branches.

The following winter, cut the lateral branches back to two-thirds of their length to a bud facing away from the frame and just before the branch curves, then tie in the shoot. Prune one upright branch back to the first front-facing bud above the upper horizontal batten, to establish the shape of the palmette and increase the flow of sap to the laterals.

During the growing season, train the terminal shoots on lateral branches along the frame and tie in the upright branch as it grows. Pinch back any lateral offshoots to three buds.

In the winter of the third year, complete the framework. Prune the two lateral branches to a front-facing bud 14–18 in (35–45 cm) above the bend. The central stem is pruned back to a sideways-pointing bud. In spring, fix two vertical battens 12 in (30 cm) apart, and, as they grow, tie the uppermost shoots of the vertical stem to them, removing all other shoots, to form a central U whose branches gradually become parallel with the frame.

Thereafter, prune annually by cutting the central branches hard back, and prune for fruiting by nipping all new side shoots back to three buds in the summer. Check the ties at each stage.

Training a double U

This style, as elegant as the palmette Verrier, gives balanced growth. The palmette tends to produce heavy growth in the central branches, and requires a great deal of maintenance pruning. The double U is an alternative form of training, also suitable for apples and pears.

Cut a maiden down in winter to a sideways pointing bud about 8 in (20 cm) from the ground. As soon as leaves appear, remove all

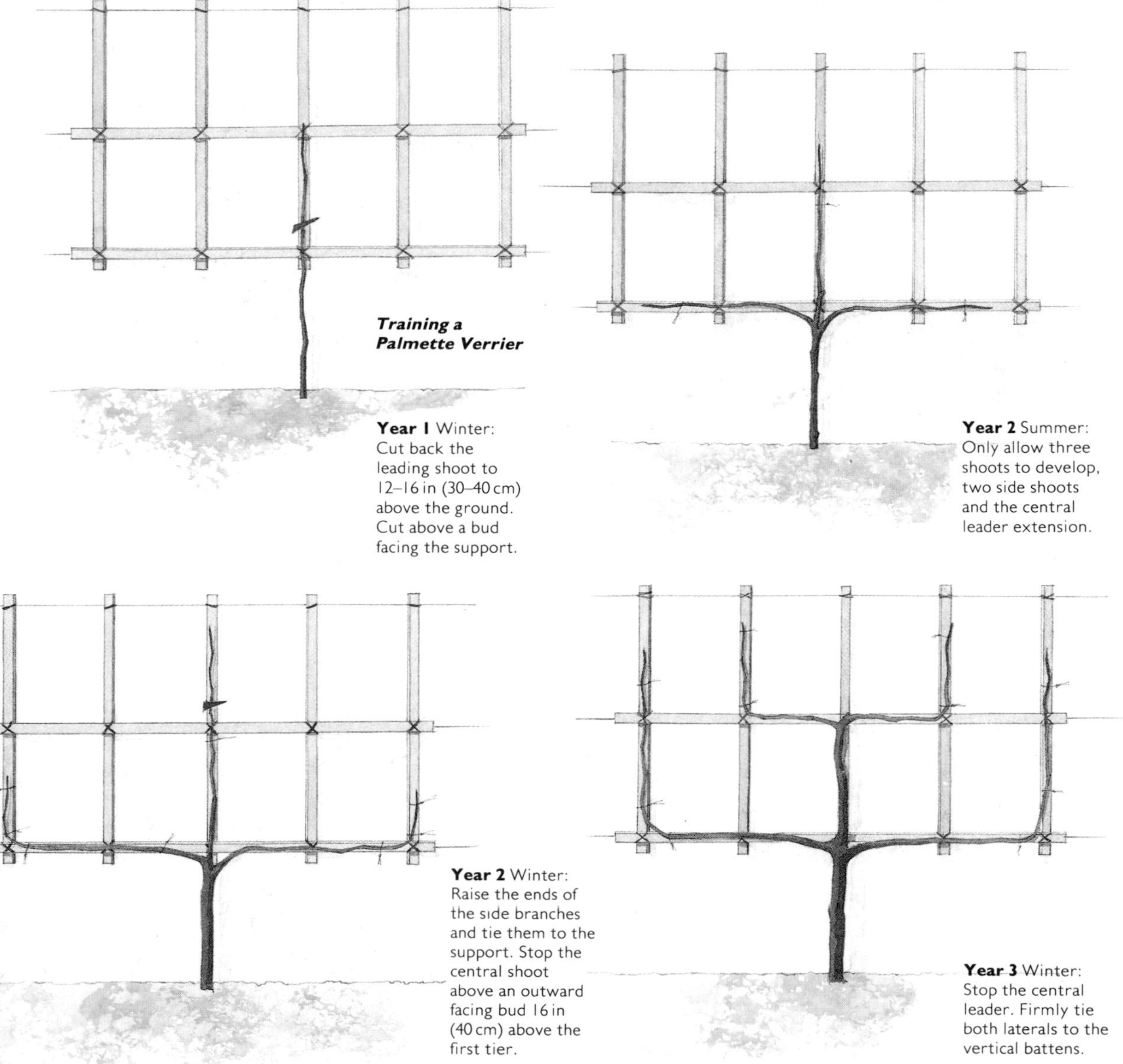

Training a Palmette Verrier

Year 1 Winter: Cut back the leading shoot to 12–16 in (30–40 cm) above the ground. Cut above a bud facing the support.

Year 2 Summer: Only allow three shoots to develop, two side shoots and the central leader extension.

Year 2 Winter: Raise the ends of the side branches and tie them to the support. Stop the central shoot above an outward facing bud 16 in (40 cm) above the first tier.

Year 3 Winter: Stop the central leader. Firmly tie both laterals to the vertical battens.

Training a Double U

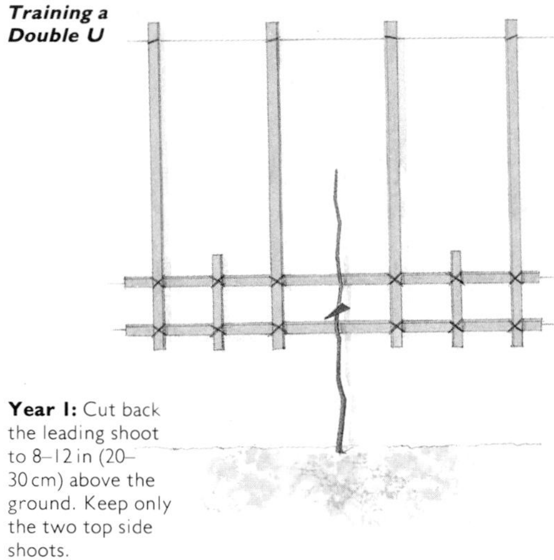

Year 1: Cut back the leading shoot to 8–12 in (20–30 cm) above the ground. Keep only the two top side shoots.

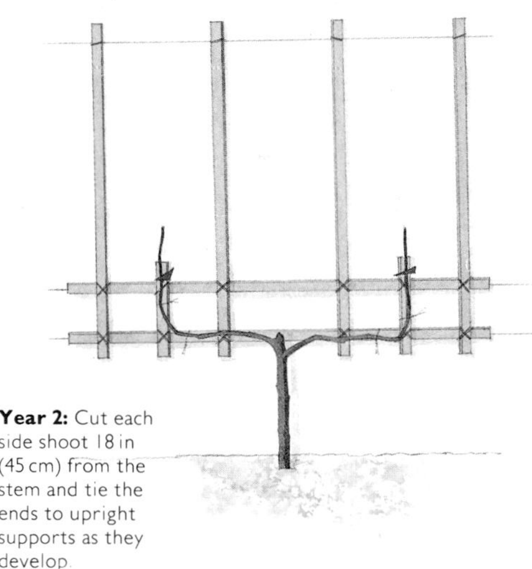

Year 2: Cut each side shoot 18 in (45 cm) from the stem and tie the ends to upright supports as they develop.

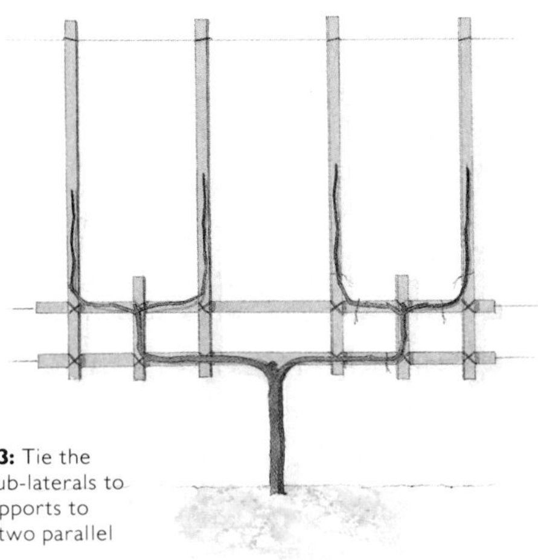

Year 3: Tie the four sub-laterals to the supports to make two parallel U's.

but the top two lateral shoots; train these horizontally by attaching them to vertical canes and gradually lowering them towards the horizontal. Finally, attach them to short vertical battens at 18 in (45 cm) from the main stem.

In the second winter, cut back each lateral shoot to a sideways-pointing bud about 9 in (22 cm) above the bend and remove all secondary shoots.

In the spring, fix four new long vertical battens 12 in (30 cm) and 24 in (60 cm) on each side of the main stem. This creates a frame with two long vertical battens each side, 12 in (30 cm) apart, and 6 in (15 cm) either side of the original short vertical batten.

Train the young terminal shoots up these as they grow, pinching back any secondary shoots to three leaves.

In following years, the double U is strengthened by pruning the leaders in winter to just 10–12 in (25–30 cm). Pinch back side shoots to three buds to encourage fruiting.

The double U contains several right-angle bends, which must be formed gradually. Let them begin to develop before bending them, as bending causes a slowdown in growth, undesirable during training.

Training a horizontal cordon

This is a single horizontal branch or a pair of branches pointing in opposite directions, trained 16 in (40 cm) above the ground, and is normally only used on apple trees growing on M9 or M27 rootstock.

Horizontal apple cordons are decorative but do not fruit heavily, although better yields can be obtained with 'spur' varieties such as Starking or Discovery Spur.

In the winter of planting, tie a maiden tree vertically to a frame which already has a horizontal wire positioned 16 in (40 cm) above the ground. Once leaves appear, push a cane into the soil at an angle and train the young shoot to it. Progressively lower the cane, with the shoot attached, to the horizontal.

At the end of the season, fix the maiden to the horizontal wire. During midsummer, cut back any vertical secondary shoots and pinch back weaker shoots to five leaves. Leave the extension leader intact.

In the winter after planting, shorten the leader by about a third, to a bud pointing downwards. Cut back lateral shoots to three eyes.

A GOOD ANGLED CUT

It is often recommended that pruning cuts be made at an angle above a bud. This means that the cut must start above the bud and travel downwards. In this way, the hand holding the secateurs (hand pruners) is in a logical position, but more importantly, raindrops can more easily fall off behind the bud and the bud is therefore better protected from late spring frosts.

During the growing season, fix the leading shoot to an angled cane when it is 16 in (40 cm) long. Gradually lower it in line with the wire and attach it. Never force the branch into a horizontal position, or the fibres will break, which weakens the tree. Remove side shoots from the upper part of the cordon and pinch back the others to five leaves.

In subsequent years, prune the cordon by about one third of its length each year; the pruning in all cases is to a downward-facing eye in winter.

Maintenance pruning

Each time you cut a branch on a tree, a shrub or any plant, this is pruning. Some pruning is carried out as dictated by immediate need or imagination, without following a special method, while other kinds of pruning call for skill and experience. In neither case should pruning amount to mutilation and some general principles should always be borne in mind. For example always have in mind a replacement for a branch you intend to prune and, when pruning, consider the future development of the branches, the behaviour of buds and the direction in which future branches will grow.

Pruning is to improve the circulation of sap on a continuous basis and give more light to leaves; it helps the plant grow. It is also part of maintaining the garden and keeping it carefully tended. A good gardener should have a pair of secateurs (hand pruners) nearby at all times.

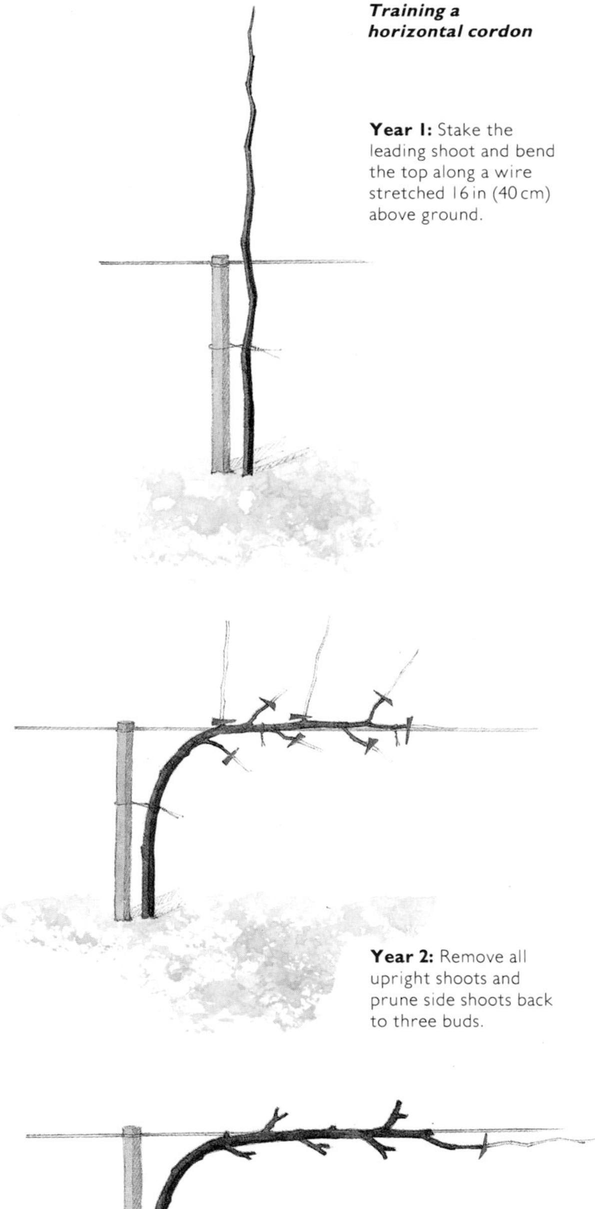

Training a horizontal cordon

Year 1: Stake the leading shoot and bend the top along a wire stretched 16 in (40 cm) above ground.

Year 2: Remove all upright shoots and prune side shoots back to three buds.

In subsequent years, prune all spurs and cut back the leader to one third of its original length.

Pruning hedges

Trimming a hedge is a simple task, usually consisting of keeping the hedge to the desired height and shape. Different methods are used, depending on the hedging plants, and whether the hedge is informal or formal.

Trimming informal hedges

These hedges are usually flowering such as berberis (barberry), roses or escallonia, which retain their natural growth habit. Trimming is done to keep the hedge to sensible proportions and to thin outside branches. Free form hedges are usually trimmed once a year, either in late spring after flowering, or in early spring before flowering, depending on whether the plant flowers on new or one-year-old wood.

Method To keep the hedge looking natural, use secateurs (hand pruners) or a pruner (lopper) to thin out branches, rather than shears or a hedge trimmer. Remove branches growing towards the centre of the hedge, but on no account cut outward-facing branches. These are the highly visible ones, and removing them would leave ugly gaps. Cut back to a young branch or a fork between two branches. To restrict the height of the hedge cut the terminal shoots above a leaf, in an irregular pattern to allow the hedge to retain its natural shape. Do not remove the leader (terminal) in conifers until the hedge has reached its full height.

Do not hesitate to cut out several branches and open up the centre of informal hedges well. Severe pruning encourages the growth of vigorous new shoots, makes the branches denser and so gives a fuller hedge.

Cut away dead wood and every three to five years cut major branches back to a third of their length, to rejuvenate the hedge and encourage branches at the base. Conifers, however, cannot stand drastic trimming.

Thin *Thuja* (arbor-vitae) hedges from the inside using secateurs (hand pruners).

Cut thick branches with pruning loppers above a young shoot or at a fork.

Trimming formal hedges

This should be carried out one or more times during the growing season, depending on the rate of growth. Trim the hedges whenever the shoots reach 8–12 in (20–30 cm) in length and are no thicker than a pencil. Some species, such as euonymus, box and ivy grow slower than others, such as privet, cherry laurel or *Thuja* (arbor-vitae), and need less frequent trimming. Uncontrolled growth leads to the base of the hedge becoming bare.

Method An electric- or petrol-powered hedge trimmer is the best tool for long hedges, as they give a clean, fast cut and are labour- and time-saving. However, they are heavy to handle with outstretched arms. A straight cut can be obtained by stretching a cord along the proposed top of the hedge and cutting everything above it.

Young hedges are trimmed more drastically than adult ones, to increase the density of the hedge. Apart from conifers, which are left to grow naturally to the required height, other hedging plants have their annual growth cut back by half until they reach the desired height. Once a hedge is fully grown, it may need rejuvenating occasionally by much harder cutting to encourage more young shoots to develop.

Angle the sides of formally pruned hedges inwards to make the hedge narrower at the top and fuller at the base; for example, hedges 3 ft (1 m) wide at the top should be about 4 ft (1.3 m) wide at their base. Hedging plants with particularly hard wood and thick stems, such as box or hornbeam, require petrol-driven equipment or large two-handled loppers.

To make a square hedge, use a line stretched horizontally at the right height as a guide.

Pruning shrubs

Shrubs are often left to grow as they will and then become a tangle of branches with few flowers, competing with the plants around them and robbing borders of much of their attraction. Pruning helps keep shrubs to a reasonable size, and can also improve their performance. Young shrubs grown informally rarely require pruning, but may need it as they get older and become sparse at the base. As a rule, though, only shrubs which flower on the current season's growth, such as buddleia (butterfly bush), or on one-year-old wood, such as deutzia, need a systematic annual trimming.

The methods of pruning below relate to various types of growth; in some cases, a combination of two methods may be required.

Tidying

Remove faded flowers by hand, using scissors or a small pair of secateurs (hand pruners), before fruit or seedheads appear to encourage the production of more flowers. Remove dead or damaged branches as soon as seen.

Method When removing dead or diseased branches, cut back to healthy wood. Diseased or broken branches should be dealt with as soon as

TOPIARY

The art of topiary involves sculpting plants into precise shapes and requires perfect mastery of pruning. No other skill is required, except perseverence, regularity and a good eye backed up with some artistic talent. As soon as the required shape is achieved, do not let the plant and the branches grow on for too long. Cones, balls and other geometrical shapes are obviously much more difficult to maintain than free shapes because of their regularity. From the technical point of view, only use hand shears and trim when the shoots are 2 in (5 cm) long.

Example of the art of topiary. Drive lined with yew trees in Vaux-le-Vicomte, France.

Removing faded flowers with secateurs (hand pruners).

possible to prevent any fungal diseases spreading. Cut back to 4 in (10 cm) below the damaged section to be certain of removing any contaminated wood. Trim any wounds over ½ in (1.25 cm) in diameter with a garden knife and coat with a healing compound, if desired.

If a shrub has a lot of weak or dead wood, apply a fast-acting general fertilizer in spring, to encourage new growth.

Water shoots

Fast-growing shrubs or those in particularly favourable settings may produce upright over-vigorous shoots, or water shoots, which look unattractive and upset the balance of the plant. Prune back to ground level or to the base of the water shoot as soon as seen.

Cutting back

Plants which have been neglected for some years and whose lower sections are bare, and evergreen shrubs, such as aucubas and laurels, which do not like regular pruning are cut back hard in late winter or early spring.

Method Use a narrow-bladed handsaw or long-handled secateurs/pruners. Cut to 8–10 in (20–25 cm) above the ground to encourage new growth or, if a plant is crowded at its base, remove many of the branches completely. Hard pruning cannot be used on all long-neglected shrubs as some cannot produce new growth on old wood. Cover the wounds with a layer of healing compound, then scatter 2 or 3 handfuls of general fertilizer per shrub and mulch with well-rotted garden compost, leaf mould or wood chips.

Thinning

Thinning is carried out after flowering or in late winter for decorative leaved plants. Frequency and severity depend on the rate of growth. It is equally suitable for shrubs, such as forsythia,

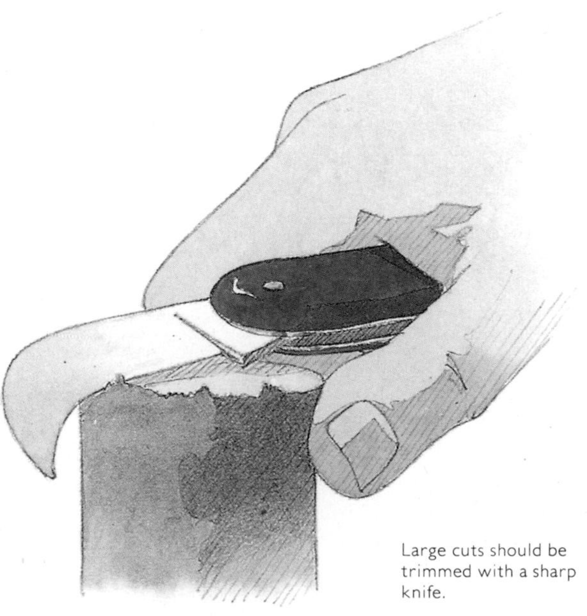
Large cuts should be trimmed with a sharp knife.

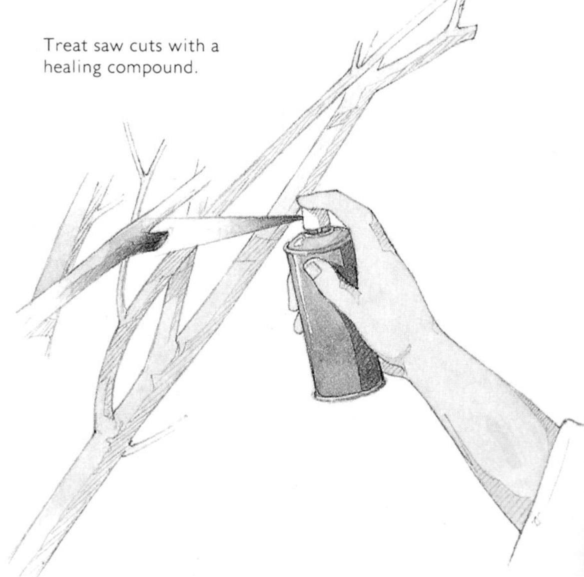
Treat saw cuts with a healing compound.

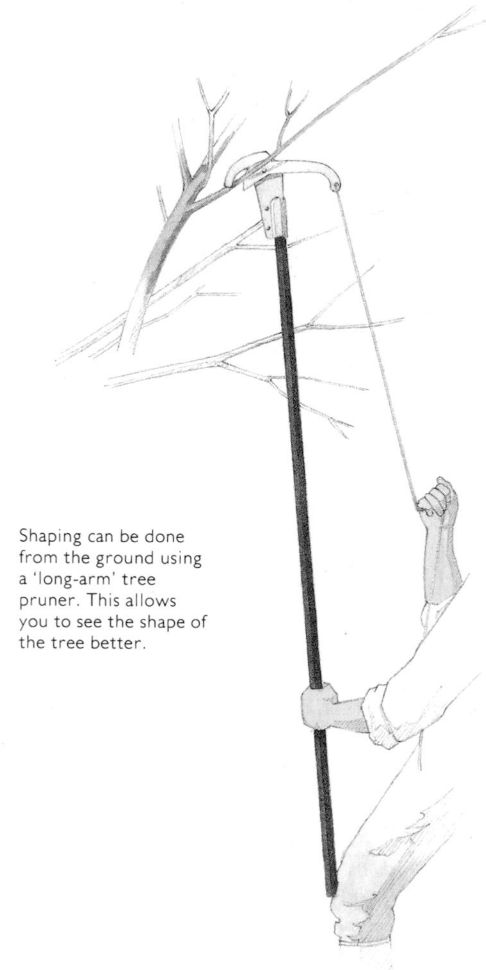

Shaping can be done from the ground using a 'long-arm' tree pruner. This allows you to see the shape of the tree better.

which flower directly on the main branches, as on those such a lilacs and deutzias, which flower on lateral shoots.

Method Using secateurs (hand pruners) or a lopper, cut off the oldest flowering branches as soon as the flowers fade, removing about a quarter of the oldest stems. Balancing the remaining branches evens the plants and encourages the laterals, which are the ones that will bear flowers the following spring.

Branches often flower less after their fourth year, so cut old wood right back to a new strong branch. On the other hand, kerria flowers on one-year-old wood, so remove the stems once they have flowered.

Stooling

This severe system of pruning involves cutting back all top-growth to the central stool, or clump. A few half-hardy flowering subjects such as fuchsias, are treated in this way but its main use is for hardy shrubs which are grown either entirely for the brightly-coloured bark on their one- or two-year-old shoots or for their bark and foliage. Those grown for their bark alone include several dogwoods (*Cornus*) and willows (*Salix*) and also some *Rubus* (bramble) species, such as R. *cockburnianus*. *Cornus sibirica albovariegata* is grown for its very attractive variegated leaves.

Method Remove most, or all, the previous year's shoots, to encourage strong new shoots each spring. It is carried out annually or every two years. You can also allow half the stems to remain for a second year, for a continual visual barrier or internal windbreak.

Stooling also benefits *Prunus triloba*, which flowers very early. Once flowering is over, cut

Cutting back
1. Cut all shoots at the base.
2. When new shoots develop, remove the old ones.

Thinning
Thinning consists of cutting out the oldest flowering branches after they have flowered and then balancing the remainder.

Creating a stool
Cut all the branches back to a stump below the first branching using a small hand saw.

the shoots short to keep the shrub dense and free flowering.

General fertilizer applied each spring will make up for this treatment, which tends to exhaust the shrub.

Rejuvenation

Some shrubs, such as all the *Ribes* (flowering currants), *Symphoricarpos* (snowberry), *Berberis* (barberry), *Cytisus* (broom) and hydrangeas need occasional hard pruning for rejuvenation although it should not be so severe that flowering is dramatically reduced the following year. Specimens over three years old require maintenance pruning each year to maintain an open form and flower well.

Method In early spring, prune branches over three years old back to ground level, to encourage the growth of new shoots. In the case of vigorous shrubs, cut two-year-old branches back by half.

Leave dried hydrangea flowerheads on the bush through winter to protect the following year's flower buds against severe frosts. In spring, cut these back to two plump flower buds.

Rejuvenation consists of removing an old branch above a young vigorous shoot.

Thinning out

Giving branches more space is beneficial to dense-growing plants, such as potentillas, viburnum and euonymus. Thinning is done at the start of the growing season, and speeds the onset of growth.

Method Use secateurs (hand pruners) to cut out branches which are badly positioned or too dense, as with informal hedges. Thinning need not be carried out every year; once every two or three years is enough. Treat any large wounds with healing compound.

Thinning is a matter of instinct. If a shrub which needs this kind of treatment has been well handled in the first few years after planting, it will not need much effort expended on it. The right approach is to follow the natural trend of the plant and not to force it.

Pruning when planting

Deciduous shrubs often need pruning hard immediately after planting to encourage the production of vigorous shoots, and also to remove any dead wood. The branches are shortened back by between about one quarter and one third.

Pruning for growth

Some species, such as *Hamamelis* (witch hazel) and magnolias, are pruned in their first two years after planting to prevent branches over-lapping, to eliminate surplus shoots, and to remove forks on branches with too many sideshoots. The opening up of the shrub not only encourages growth and flowering but also reduces the risk of disease.

Pruning evergreens

Many evergreen shrubs have dense, regular growth which needs no pruning, but flowering evergreen, such as heather, lavender, rosemary and ceanothus, may need pruning in spring or after flowering in the same way as hedges, to improve the general shape and encourage further flowering.

Removing suckers

Some shrubs, such as hazel and lilacs, produce suckers. If these are suckers from the rootstock, remove them at the point where they join the stock, unearthing them to pull them off at the root. A natural tendency to produce suckers usually needs to be suppressed, so it is usually better to pull them off rather than cut them off. If suckers are cut off, even more suckers are encouraged to grow.

Thin out shrubs with secateurs (hand pruners) by cutting any branches which are crossing in the centre.

Lopping

Lopping involves large ornamental trees which need regular, major pruning to keep them a reasonable size and attractive shape. It is a job for a trained tree surgeon because of the dangers involved. Lopping thins out branches and reduces their size, and involves completely removing large branches.

To remove suckers, dig out the soil and find the point where they join the parent root. It is better to pull them off than to cut them as the latter leads to the development of even more.

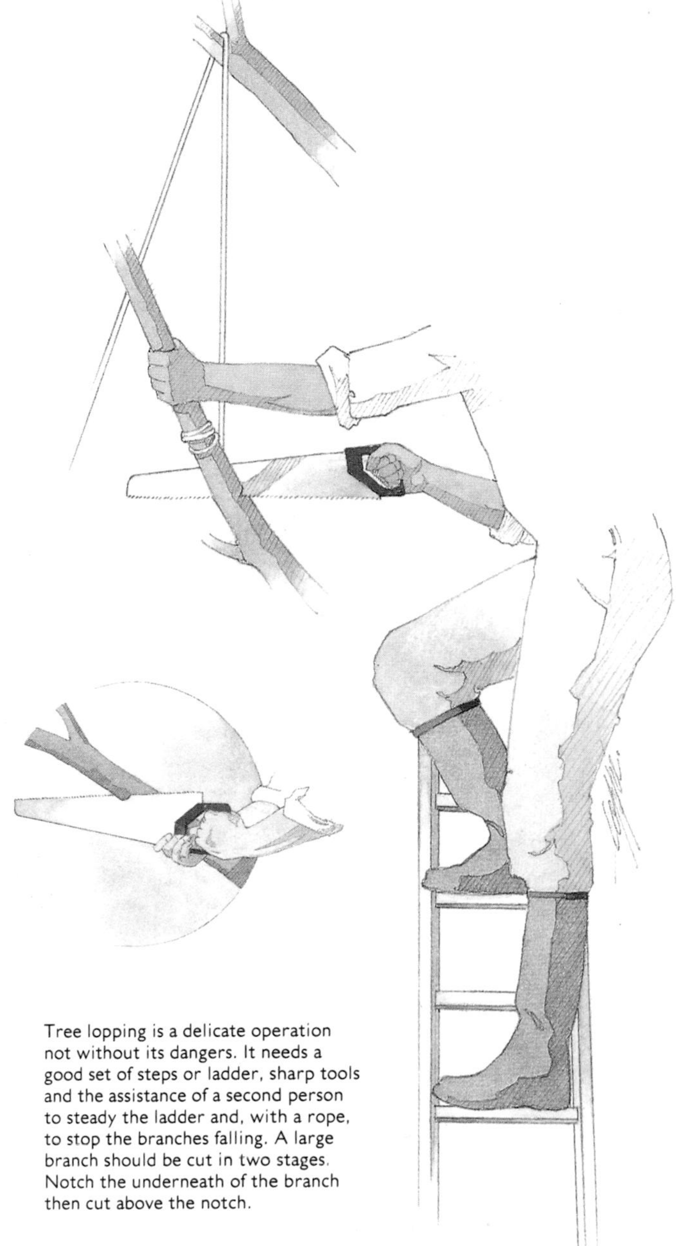

Tree lopping is a delicate operation not without its dangers. It needs a good set of steps or ladder, sharp tools and the assistance of a second person to steady the ladder and, with a rope, to stop the branches falling. A large branch should be cut in two stages. Notch the underneath of the branch then cut above the notch.

Method Lopping takes place when trees are dormant, because wounds heal more easily and the absence of leaves makes it easier to assess the shape of the tree. This is best done by a professional, but if you are going to do it yourself, you will need an assistant on the ground to get a better view, to direct the cutting, to point out the branches to be removed, and to steady the ladder. An assistant can also guide the branches as they are lowered by rope. For safety, it is essential to work out where each branch is likely to fall, and to arrange for a clear space in which they can land. A rope must be tied around each branch before it is cut. If a branch is overhanging a building, it must be held by a double rope and its weight taken to stop it falling as soon as it is cut.

Use a small, light, well-balanced chainsaw, with a sharp chain and find a good sitting position in the tree so that you can saw with precision. Large branches are removed bit by bit; never have such heavy, bulky pieces that it is impossible to control their fall. To prevent splitting, a saw cut about 1 in (2.5 cm) deep is made underneath the branch, then the branch is cut downwards from above so it comes cleanly away from the trunk. All wounds should be trimmed with a garden knife and coated with healing compound, especially on fruit trees which are highly susceptible to diseases such as Silver Leaf.

Chainsaw chains wear out quickly and often need sharpening after three quarters of an hour's continuous use. Having a spare chain is easier than trying to sharpen a chain on site. (Chain maintenance should be entrusted to a specialist.)

Pruning to increase fruiting

Fruit trees and shrubs are capable of producing fruit on their own without any pruning, but suitable pruning increases their yield without the trees or shrubs exhausting themselves, and increases the size of the fruit. Pruning to increase fruiting involves removing the unnecessary parts which use sap to the detriment of the fruit. It also means replacing fruit-bearing branches, such as worn-out vines, when they are no longer productive. More than with any other form of pruning, predicting this is the main art of pruning to increase fruiting but this ceases to be a problem once you understand how plants grow. Think carefully before using the secateurs (pruners). It has to be said, however, that the detailed explanations given in these pages can never replace practical experience gained on the spot.

Pruning apple and pear trees

These grow in a similar fashion, and are pruned in virtually the same way. Pruning to increase fruiting is only carried out on fully-grown trees. Standards and half-standards (dwarfs and semi-dwarfs) need less pruning than formally grown espaliers, dwarf pyramids and cordons.

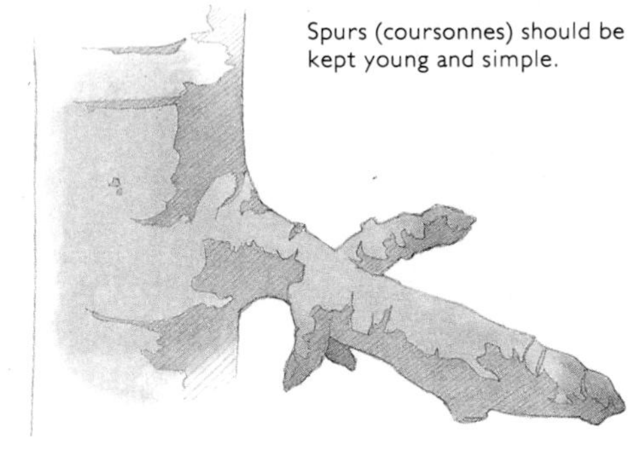

Spurs (coursonnes) should be kept young and simple.

Growth buds develop mostly on leafy shoots.

Fruit spurs (dards) can develop into growth buds or fruit buds according to how the tree is managed.

Tree structure

Understanding the parts of a tree helps make sense of pruning for fruit. The trunk, the lower part of the tree and main channel for the sap, rises directly from the ground and produces branches at varying heights depending on initial training. The main branches issue directly from the trunk and their positioning gives the tree its overall shape. Formally trained cordons, espaliers and fans usually have fewer main branches than free-standing trees. On formally trained fruit trees, the aim is to encourage fruit on the main branches; some varieties are much more willing to do this than others.

Growth buds are small, pointed buds, sometimes consisting of little more than a small scar on the shoot with a minute bud in the base. Growth buds are found in the leaf axils. In a one-year-old shoot, the growth buds get progressively smaller the further away they are from the growing point. They often turn into leafy shoots but may also, with the right treatment, develop into fruit buds in subsequent years.

Dards are intermediate between growth buds and fruit buds. They stand away from the shoot on small, woody spurs. Once formed, dards tend to be unpredictable and may do one of three things in the following year: stay as they are and simply enlarge; grow out into shoots; or turn into fruit buds. Which course they take depends on how much sap reaches the dard. This is governed by the way in which the tree is pruned and managed.

Fruit buds, also known as flower buds and blossom buds, are bigger and plumper than the others. In their simplest form, they are single buds standing out from the shoot and were growth buds during the previous growing season. On older shoots and branches, they grow in fruiting spurs with one or more other fruit buds and growth buds. In spring, they open into a flower which gives rise to fruit, if successfully fertilized.

A fruit spur is a woody, wrinkled, twisted shoot growing on a branch, and carrying a number of plump buds close together. Spurs must always be retained during pruning as they are the main fruiting organs of a fruit tree, though excessively large and complicated spurs should be thinned out.

When a ripe fruit is harvested from a spur, it leaves behind it a fleshy knob, or lump, which normally carries two or more buds. These may be either growth buds, dards, fruit buds or a mixture. What they actually are will depend on the type and variety of fruit and how well the tree has been looked after. These knobs should never be cut off.

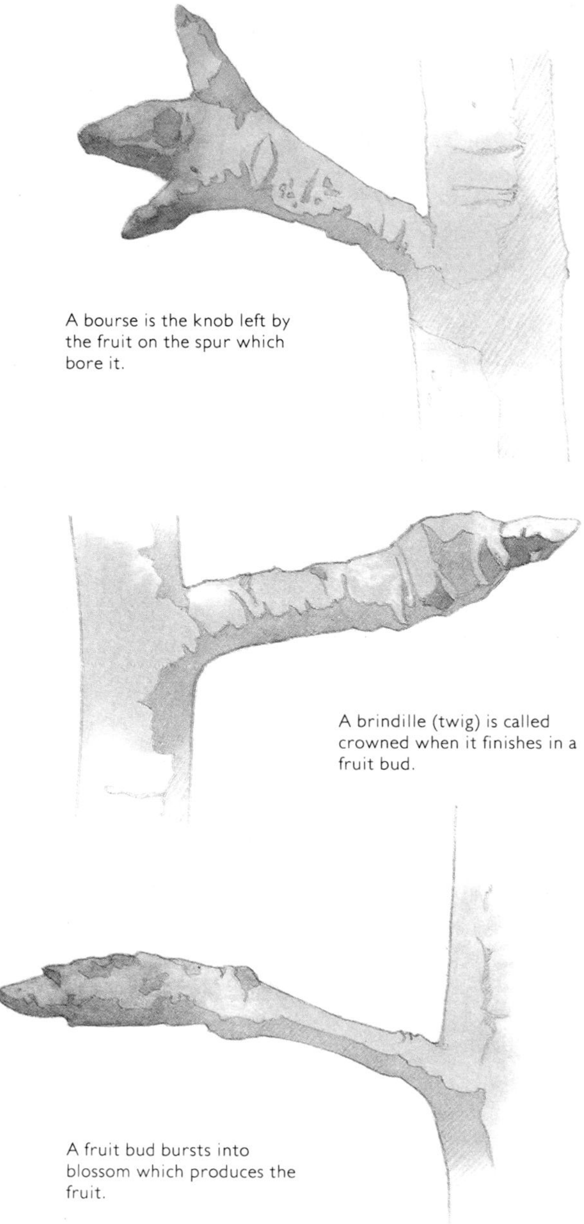

A bourse is the knob left by the fruit on the spur which bore it.

A brindille (twig) is called crowned when it finishes in a fruit bud.

A fruit bud bursts into blossom which produces the fruit.

A brindille is a short, thin shoot, 4–12 in (10–30 cm) long, which starts life as a dard. They are usually fertile and will, within a year or two, develop a fruit bud on the end. They should not be pruned out, unless for some reason they develop into normal shoots.

In this context, a 'sucker' refers to an unusually vigorous woody shoot which often grows from the upper surface of a branch which has recently become bent down, usually through the weight of fruit. The French call these suckers, very appropriately, 'gourmand' (glutton) shoots, because they use a great deal of sap at the expense of fruit size and fruit bud production. Unless they are used for replacement branches, they should be removed as soon as they appear.

How fruiting occurs

A young apple or pear tree, less than 3–4 years old, normally carries only growth buds. Some of these grow out into woody shoots during the next growing season. At the same time, many of the remaining buds which have not developed into woody shoots will develop into blossom buds for flowering in the following spring. One of the aims of pruning for fruit, rather than for growth, is to encourage the formation of these blossom buds.

The more vigorously a fruit tree grows, the less fruit it produces, as most of its energy goes into producing new growth and wood. On the other hand, a sickly tree usually puts all its effort into producing fruits, to perpetuate the species, and very little growth is made. Both extremes are equally undesirable.

It is important to balance these two processes, by pruning and general tree management, such as feeding. There are two main times of the year when fruit trees are pruned; the summer and the winter. The different times of pruning also demand different methods.

Winter pruning deals principally with the shaping of the tree and the distribution of shoots and branches. Summer pruning is to encourage the developing fruitlets and the formation of blossom buds for the next year, and to reduce the tree's vigour.

Winter pruning using the three-bud system

The three-bud pruning system is traditional for apple and pear trees because it restricts the growth of a tree while encouraging the development of blossom buds. Also known as 'spur pruning' and 'tipping and spurring', this involves shortening back nearly all the one-year-old shoots to within three buds of their base. Shoots required to form new branches or to extend the ends of existing branches are cut back by about a third. Any 'gourmand' shoots or suckers unsuitable for new branches should be cut back to their points of origin. If shortened to three buds, they simply produce thick growth.

Unfortunately, not all varieties of apple

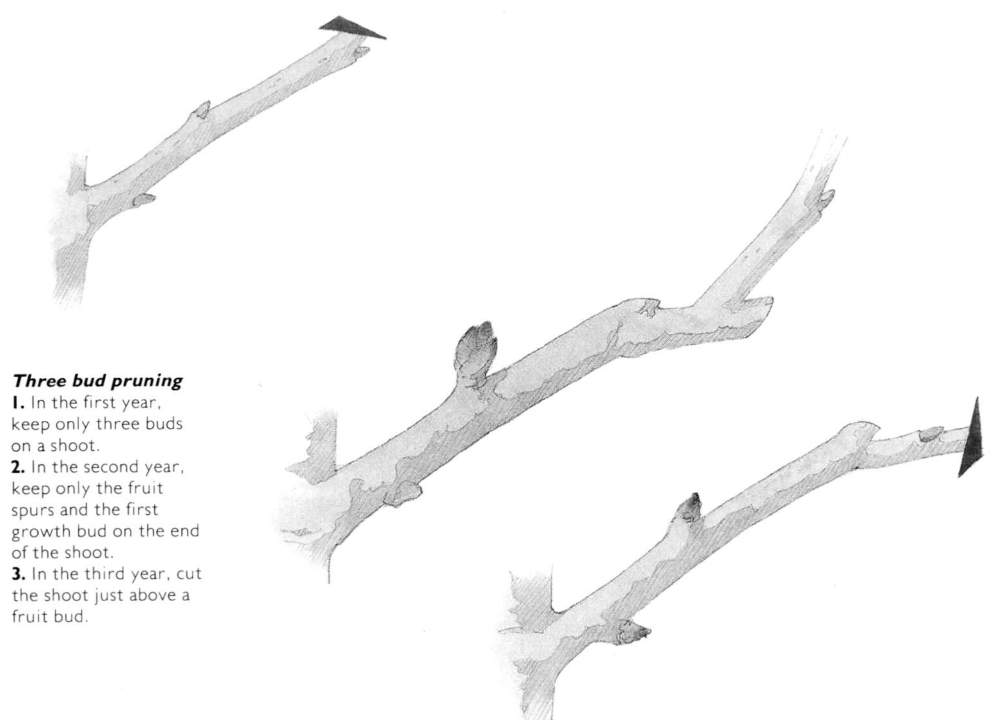

Three bud pruning
1. In the first year, keep only three buds on a shoot.
2. In the second year, keep only the fruit spurs and the first growth bud on the end of the shoot.
3. In the third year, cut the shoot just above a fruit bud.

respond to the three-bud system, although most pears do. Tip bearers, such as Worcester Pearmain, and those with excessive vigour, such as Bramley's Seedling, which is also a tip bearer, should be pruned less severely.

Prune pears first, then apples, because pears start into growth earlier. This pruning encourages the formation of fruiting spurs and keeps the size of the trees well within bounds. It does not always lead to the heaviest crops as much potential cropping wood is removed.

Method A one-year-old shoot on a branch is leafless when pruned, so the buds along its length should be easy to see. In most varieties, these will all be growth buds.

Ignore the cluster of buds at the base of the shoot. Count the lowest three clusters spaced further apart and cut the shoot above the third, giving a spur some 3 in (7.5 cm) long. In spring, the topmost one or two buds grow out into shoots, and the lowest one often just forms a rosette of leaves.

If only one bud produces a shoot, the other two may well develop into fruit buds.

When pruning the following winter, do not cut back to the first of these newly formed fruit buds, or one, and possibly more, will produce a weak cluster of flowers and a strong shoot in the spring. In the winter after the initial pruning, cut back any new shoots to three buds. Subsequently leave at least two growth buds so that the blossom buds will all develop strong flower clusters.

Once a spur system is three years old, you can then start pruning back to a fruit bud. Once a spur carries fruit a knob forms, which is more likely to produce further fruit buds than a pruned shoot.

Do not automatically cut thin, sometimes fertile, shoots or brindilles back to three buds. Many carry a fruit bud on the end and should be retained.

Less severe pruning systems are used commercially, and many are quite easily adapted for use in gardens. They involve less work and time and the trees will start fruiting younger.

Summer pruning

Increasing a tree's yield can involve pruning during the growing season to restrict growth and to encourage the development of blossom buds. Summer pruning can save a whole year by encouraging the development of fruit buds without passing through the intermediate stage of dards. Nipping and pinching out are done at varying times during the growing season, depending on variety and the effect desired.

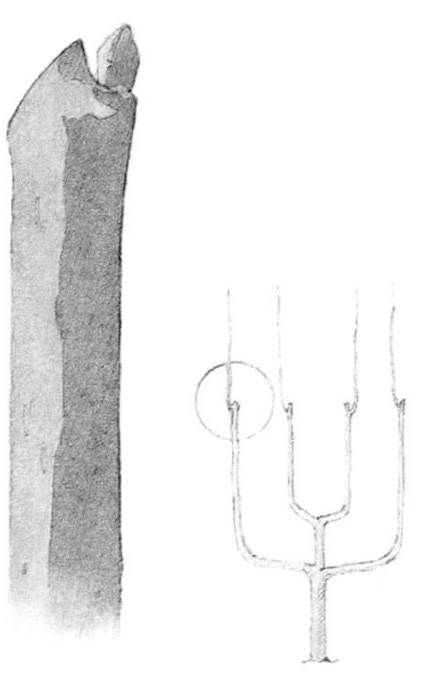

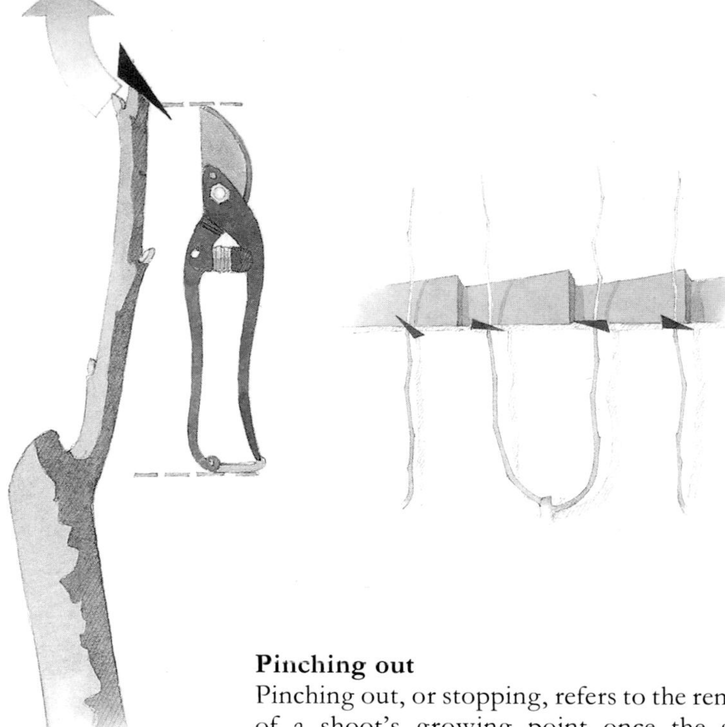

Pruning extension growth
To extend main branches, prune above a growth bud facing away from the shoot it is on. The extension should not exceed 8–10 in (20 25 cm).
When the top of the tree reaches the desired height, cut back the extensions to the height of the wall, fence or other support.

Nipping

This involves removing poorly placed and unwanted new shoots and forms part of the summer pruning of apples and pears. It diverts much of the tree's energy from the formation of shoots into the existing fruit buds. Nipping out young shoots gives fruitlets a greater supply of sap and allows more sun to reach them.

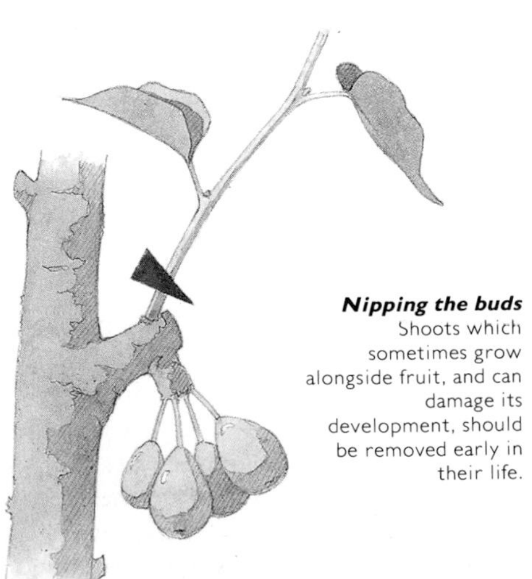

Nipping the buds
Shoots which sometimes grow alongside fruit, and can damage its development, should be removed early in their life.

Pinching out

Pinching out, or stopping, refers to the removal of a shoot's growing point once the shoot reaches a certain length, and is another part of summer pruning of apples and pears.

Normally it can be done with the fingernails but, if left too long, secateurs (hand pruners) may be needed. Stopping encourages the formation of side shoots on the stopped shoot and the formation of fruit buds towards its base. The first pinch is made on shoots 8–12 in (20–30 cm) long; stop the shoot above the fourth or fifth leaf. Once side shoots reach 4–6 in (10–15 cm) in length, about six weeks after the first pinching, pinch them back to two leaves.

The more vigorous the tree, the sooner and shorter it should be pinched, while fertile trees are pinched less and later in the season. Never pinch out extension growth on main branches, which should be pruned in winter.

Summer pruning allows work to be carried out in advance of winter by removing, for example, much of the new growth beyond a fruit bud or fruit shoot. You can also simplify some branches slightly by removing clearly out-of-place young shoots.

Apple cordons often produce large numbers of vertical wooden shoots; bend these shoots over towards the foot of a tree to limit their growth. Hooped branches are tied to the main branch of the cordon and cut off in winter above the fertile buds.

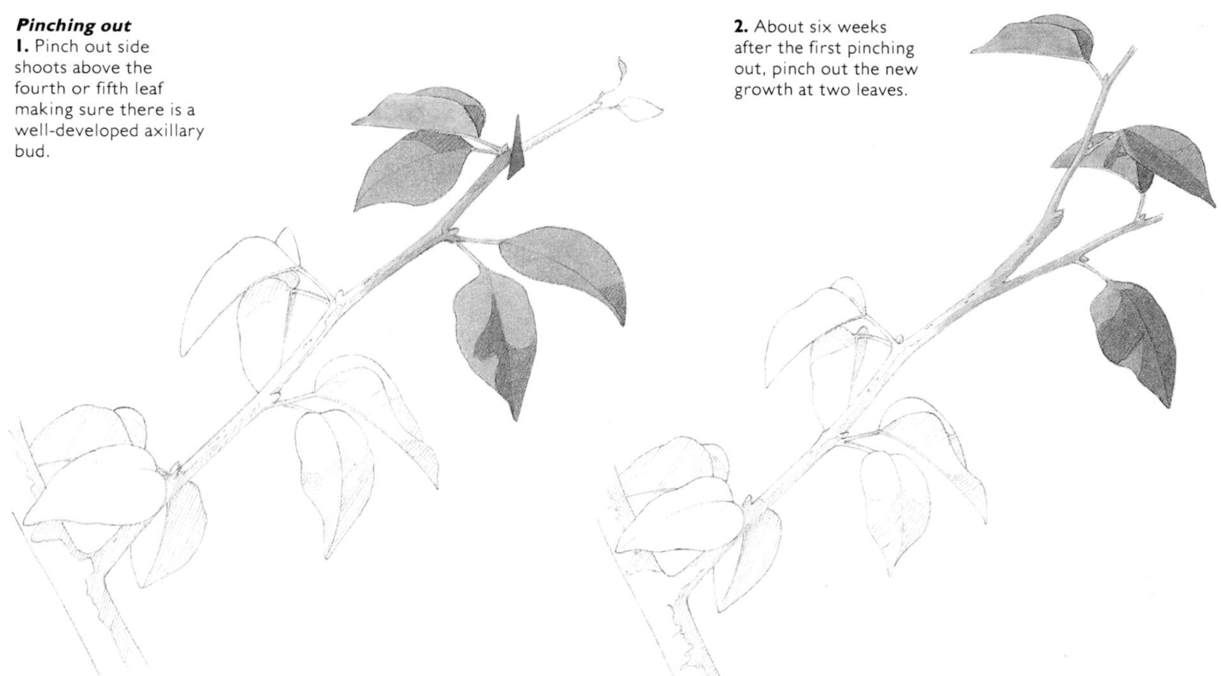

Pinching out
1. Pinch out side shoots above the fourth or fifth leaf making sure there is a well-developed axillary bud.

2. About six weeks after the first pinching out, pinch out the new growth at two leaves.

Pruning stone fruit trees

Cherries, plums, apricots and peaches are stone fruits and are pruned differently from apples and pears. Unless a young tree is in the process of being built up or formally trained, stone fruit trees should be pruned as little as possible. Where Silver Leaf fungus is a problem try to avoid pruning during winter, when the spores of the fungus are being released. The disease nearly always enters a tree through an open wound so winter pruning is asking for trouble. In areas where this disease is not prevalent, late winter pruning is appropriate.

In the growing season, remove dead, dying or broken branches and keep the tree open and airy. Some cherry trees' upward growth can be restricted by cutting back the young terminal shoots to half their length in winter. However, in general terms, pruning should be kept to a minimum. Use healing compound on wounds.

Pruning peach trees

Peach trees are pruned from late winter to early spring, as soon as the flower buds are clearly visible. Flowers only appear on the one-year-old wood; when a branch has once carried fruit, it never does again and often dies. Lastly, any flower bud which fails to open in the year after its formation usually reverts to a growth bud.

The different parts

There are two very distinct types of bud, growth buds and blossom buds, that will frequently be growing together. As with apples and pears, peach growth buds are small and pointed, and blossom buds are plump and round. The bud clusters on a healthy one-year-old shoot frequently consist of a growth bud flanked by two blossom buds, but may be only one of each or even just single buds. Each bud should be identified before you cut back a shoot.

A wood shoot is an ordinary one-year-old shoot with buds along its length. On many peach trees, wood shoots appear in groups. 'Gourmand' shoots (suckers)are very vigorous wood shoots, which can be over 5 ft (1.5 m) long and may drain a tree's strength. On vigorous peach trees, they are often found on the upper surface of an arching branch. A mixed shoot usually has two or three growth buds at its base, four or five fruit buds in the middle and more growth buds at its end. A cluster consists of growth and blossom buds grouped closely together on a spur. It may produce fruit, shoots or both.

Method Most pruning is done back to one or two growth buds at the base of a shoot, to provide its replacements. A normal shoot is pruned back to two or even three eyes, if the shoot is really healthy, after fruiting. 'Gour-

Prune a peach shoot above the third or fourth flower bud, leaving a growth bud at the end to grow out.

When a shoot has fruited, cut it back to the new shoot(s) at its base. These can be either tied in as they are or shortened to 3–4 flower buds, according to space.

mand' shoots (suckers) are cut less severely, back to 8 to 10 eyes, and may be bent over and tied down to restrain them.

Shoots containing blossom and growth buds may be pruned above the third or fourth bunch of flowers, with a wood shoot or growth bud accompanying the last flower bud left at the end to draw the sap. If there are less than two viable growth buds at the base of the shoot, nip out the flower buds until beyond the second growth bud, as these provide future replacement shoots. Remove any growth buds between two flower buds to prevent shoots drawing off the sap to the detriment of the flowers.

Leave shoots intact or, if there is a growth bud at the base, cut the shoot back to that bud, to encourage a stronger one to develop.

Finally, a shoot which has borne fruit and also carries other shoots can be cut back to a young one. If there are two good shoots, leave the one further from the main branch intact, and cut the other back to two growth buds from the base.

After fruiting remove all old wood, particularly if it has borne fruit. Cut back extension shoots on the end of branches by 12–20 in (30–50 cm) to an outward pointing bud.

Summer pruning

Peaches tend to produce a considerable number of leafy shoots, so pruning in early summer is essential. Remove badly placed or unwanted new shoots as soon as they appear. Do not touch the two replacement shoots at the base of a branch, but remove all but sap drawers and extension shoots.

Pinching out

This should be carried out continuously during the growing season, to restrict the development of shoots. Pinch back the leading extension shoot to three or four leaves. Prune back new shoots which are not wanted for fruiting or extension to four or five leaves as soon as they are over 8 in (20 cm) long. Pinch back to two leaves any secondary growths and pinch back vigorous replacements to 12 in (30 cm).

If a branch is weighed down with fruit, the crop has to be thinned once or possibly twice. When the fruitlets are about the size of a hazel nut, reduce pairs of fruit to singles, and remove imperfect and badly placed fruit.

Natural fruit drop follows in early summer; once it is over, thin fruits to about 8 in (20 cm) apart.

Cut back the fruited shoots of early varieties as soon as picking is finished, to two or three growth buds at their base. This helps the wood ripen.

Leaves directly shading the fruit can be removed to allow the fruit to ripen.

Pruning dessert-grape vines

Grapes only appear on the current season's canes, and the extent of pruning can vary with the variety. There is the classical two-bud pruning system and the three- or four-bud system, used on muscat grapes. If you are not sure which method is more appropriate, ask your nurseryman.

Winter pruning

Winter pruning is carried out in early winter, to encourage the development of replacement canes. Most vines have a structure of permanent branches which carry one or more fruiting canes; winter pruning removes the canes which have fruited and makes space for the new fruiting canes in the following year. Whether the vine is grown in a greenhouse or outdoors, the principle is exactly the same.

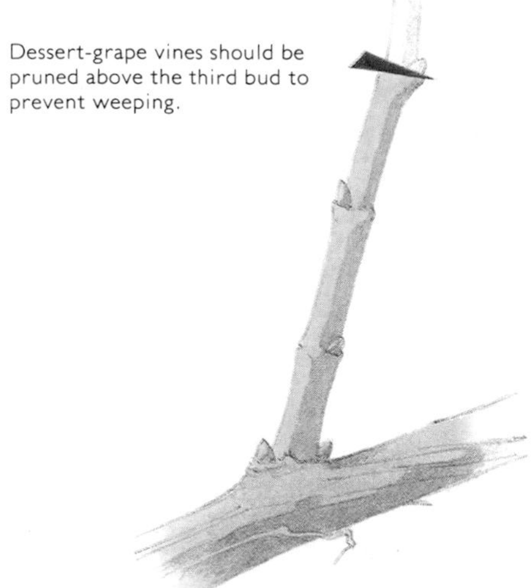

Dessert-grape vines should be pruned above the third bud to prevent weeping.

The first stage in winter pruning is to remove any shoots which have fruited. Replacement shoots are pruned to two buds.

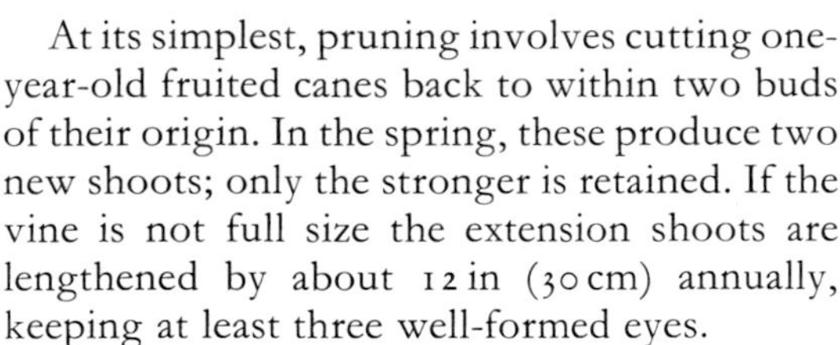

At its simplest, pruning involves cutting one-year-old fruited canes back to within two buds of their origin. In the spring, these produce two new shoots; only the stronger is retained. If the vine is not full size the extension shoots are lengthened by about 12 in (30 cm) annually, keeping at least three well-formed eyes.

Guyot training

The Guyot system is a popular system of training, especially for wine vines. Following winter planting, cut down the vine to three buds from the ground.

In the first growing season, allow one shoot to develop; rub out all others as soon as they appear. In winter cut back this shoot to about four buds. During the second growing season, keep only the two top buds.

Cut one shoot back to two buds and shorten the other to six buds, which produce fruiting laterals next year. Bend the longer shoot down and tie it to a supporting wire.

During the following, third, growing season, shoots will develop from most of the buds on the longer cane. These laterals produce flower trusses and are stopped at two leaves beyond the second or third truss. Pinch back all other shoots to one leaf.

The cane reduced to two buds the previous winter should send out a shoot from each. These two are left intact.

In winter, cut out the fruited laterals completely, together with their parent cane. From then

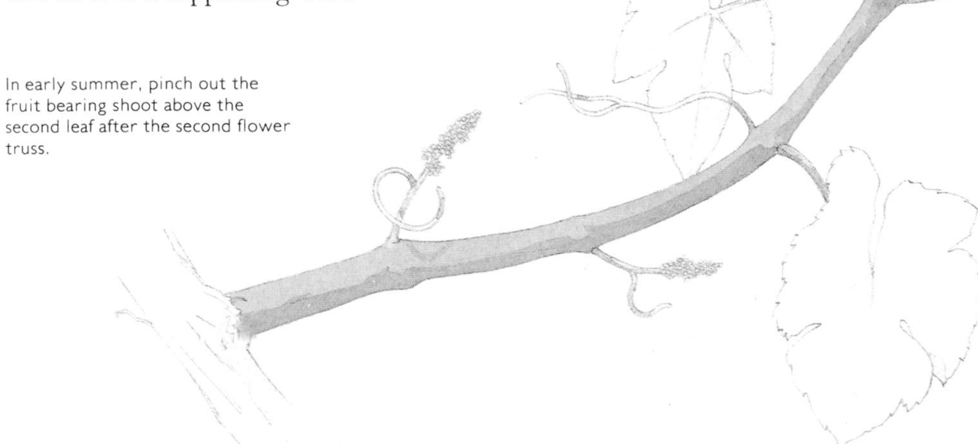

In early summer, pinch out the fruit bearing shoot above the second leaf after the second flower truss.

on, simply follow the same routine each year; cut out the fruited laterals and parent cane and shorten back one of the replacement shoots to two buds and the other to six.

Summer pruning
Summer pruning depends on the training system used, but the purpose in all cases is to remove unwanted shoots and restrict the sometimes excessive vigour of others. Nip back shoots which appear from small axillary buds. Nip back to one bud or leaf when three leaves appear.

Pinching out
Pinch out the tip of a fruiting cane above the second leaf after the second cluster of flowers.

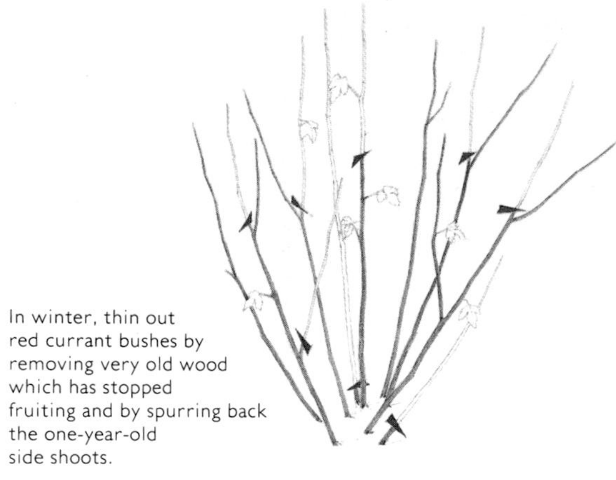
In winter, thin out red currant bushes by removing very old wood which has stopped fruiting and by spurring back the one-year-old side shoots.

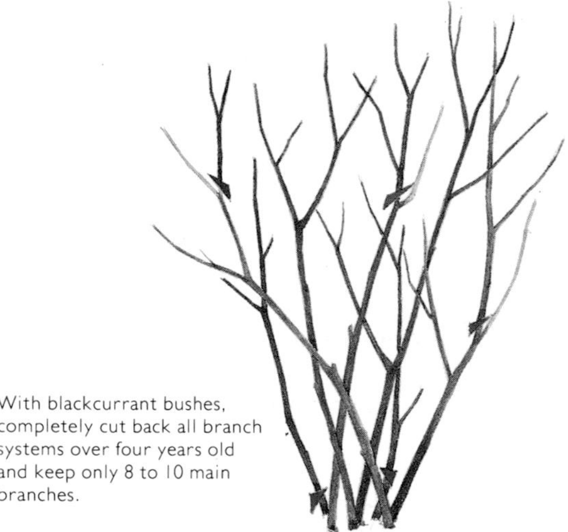
With blackcurrant bushes, completely cut back all branch systems over four years old and keep only 8 to 10 main branches.

Pruning soft fruits

The term 'soft fruit' covers red, black and white currants, gooseberries and raspberries.

Winter pruning of red and white currants and gooseberries is similar because all fruit on short fruiting laterals that form on the main branches. After planting a young, dormant bush retain four or five strong shoots and cut them back by half; remove the rest. These pruned shoots will produce two more shoots each, which, in the following winter, are cut back by half. Cut back any other new shoots to two buds. Thereafter, cut back all branch leaders by about a third and all other new shoots to two buds. This builds up a branch system well furnished with fruiting spurs.

These fruits may also be grown as single and double cordons; once the permanent framework is established all side shoots are cut back to about two buds in the autumn. In midsummer, shorten back the new shoots to 5–6 in (13–15 cm) so that more sun can reach the ripening fruit.

Blackcurrants
Blackcurrants fruit best on young shoots, up to five years old. Cut out the oldest branches when the leaves start to fall in the autumn. Work out the age of the branches by counting back the years of growth; the wood gets darker as it ages.

Pruning raspberries
This depends on whether the variety is summer or autumn fruiting. Summer-fruiting varieties fruit on canes that grew in the previous year and fruited canes are pruned back to ground level straight after harvesting.

Thin new canes if necessary allowing 4 in (10 cm) between each, and support them on wires.

Autumn varieties fruit on the current season's canes; the fruited canes remain until the following spring, when they are cut to ground level as soon as there are signs of growth.

Pruning flowering shrubs

Shrubs, such as forsythia, which flowers in spring, usually do so on the shoots that grew in the previous growing season. Prune straight after flowering to allow the maximum time for next year's flowering shoots to grow. Shrubs, such as most bush roses, which flower after the start of summer, do so on the current season's growth and are best pruned in spring.

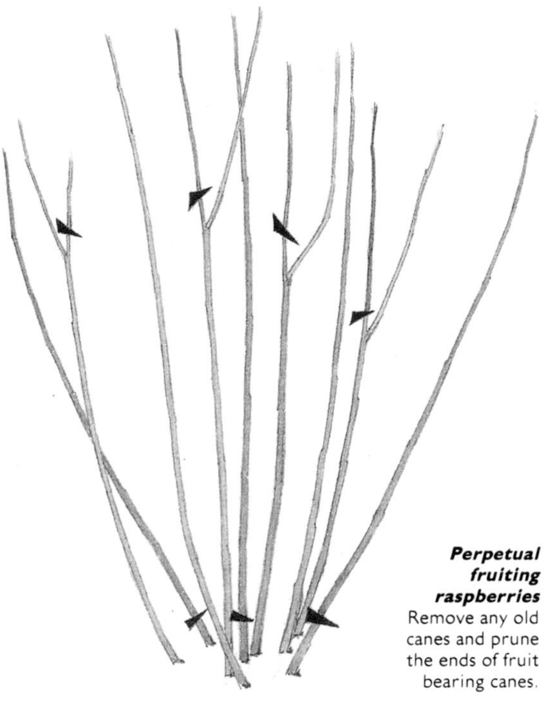

Perpetual fruiting raspberries
Remove any old canes and prune the ends of fruit bearing canes.

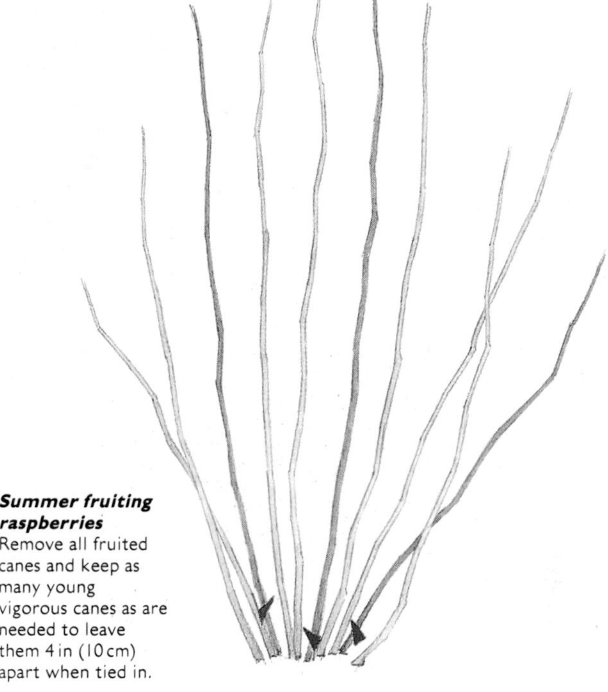

Summer fruiting raspberries
Remove all fruited canes and keep as many young vigorous canes as are needed to leave them 4 in (10 cm) apart when tied in.

Pruning rosebushes

The most popular bush roses are hybrid tea roses, with their large, spectacular flowers; and floribunda roses, with clusters of smaller flowers. Both flower throughout the summer and autumn. The flowers appear on the current season's wood and the plants are pruned annually to promote young growth and prevent the plants growing bare at their bases.

Method Dead-head and tidy bush roses up in the late autumn but leave the main pruning until spring. After a mild winter, growth starts early but new shoots are usually too soft to withstand sharp frosts. Once the worst of the weather is over all new growth that normally follows pruning is likely to survive.

Floribundas are usually more vigorous than hybrid teas, and are more lightly pruned. Cut out any badly placed or overcrowded shoots. Remove weak, feeble or broken shoots, or prune back to a strong bud near the base. Cut back strong, hybrid teas to about 12 in (30 cm) high; floribundas to about 18 in (45 cm), pruning weaker shoots harder to induce them to grow strongly.

Hard pruning encourages strong, new growth. Prune a neglected rose bush moderately in the first year, removing some of the old wood and keeping most new shoots. The following spring, harder pruning can be carried out. Always remove suckers from the rootstock, which are usually straight and vigorous, with completely different foliage and flowers from the named variety.

Hybrid tea rose bushes need hard pruning. Keep only 5 or so main branches usually pruned to 3 buds.

Shrub roses are pruned like ornamental shrubs simply by thinning. This is a rugosa shrub rose.

Pruning climbing roses

Climbing roses have long flexible shoots and branches which hook on to support with their thorns. Many flower continuously throughout the summer; others flower in short bursts.

Method First, build up a framework to fill out the allotted area of fence or wall. Simply cut back flower-bearing shoots to two or three eyes and remove badly placed branches. Once the framework is complete, treat it as permanent, removing and replacing them only when old, and flowering starts to diminish.

Cut weak side shoots hard back to about two buds, and just tip and tie in the strong ones. Tipping induces them to produce two or more new shoots rather than just one extension.

Pruning rambler roses

These roses usually only have one flowering period, and are always pruned after flowering, from late summer to early autumn.

Method Untie the rose and spread its branches out on the ground. Prune out the old, dark brown ones that have already flowered; the young green ones will carry next year's flowers. If there are not enough new shoots to fill the space, keep some older stems, but prune the laterals back to two buds from the base. Re-tie the branches as before.

Burn all prunings because diseases such as black spot and mildew are carried over to the following year on the shoots and wood.

Pruning standard roses

Standard roses are bush varieties grafted on to tall stocks. Prune the branches back in late winter to three to five buds, retaining only five to eight main shoots. After flowering has finished, cut back flowered shoots by about half

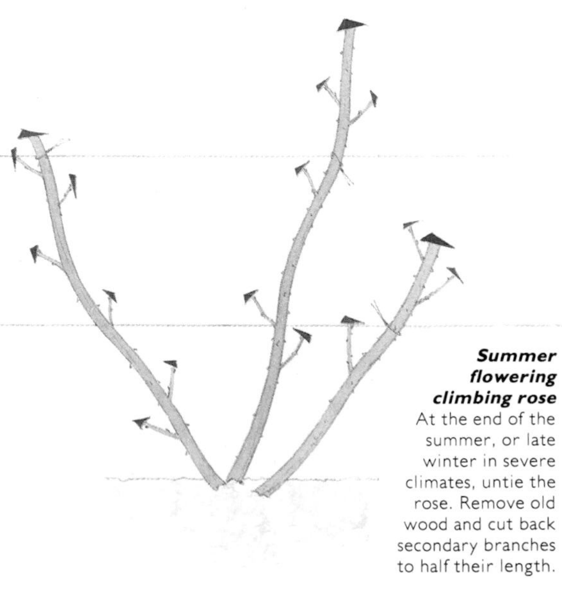

Summer flowering climbing rose
At the end of the summer, or late winter in severe climates, untie the rose. Remove old wood and cut back secondary branches to half their length.

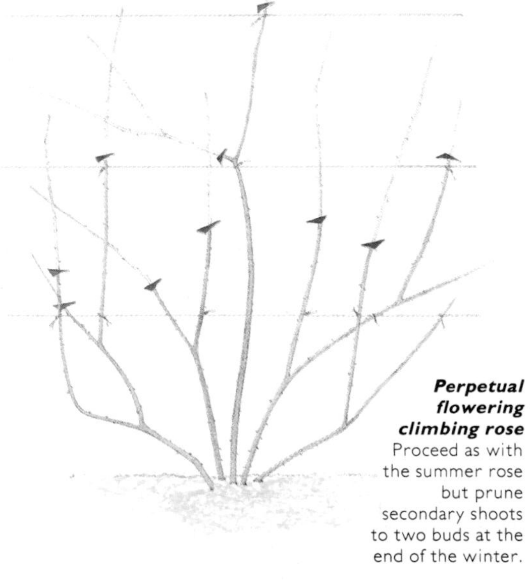

Perpetual flowering climbing rose
Proceed as with the summer rose but prune secondary shoots to two buds at the end of the winter.

Standard rose
In late winter early spring, cut back the young shoots to 3 or 5 buds. Keep only 5 to 8 shoots.

Weeping rose
Pruning weepers consists of removing any shoots which are too upright. Prune the hanging branches similarly to climbing roses.

to a strong bud. Always prune to outward-facing eyes and cut out branches growing towards the centre. Autumn pruning limits the volume of branches and reduces its exposure to the wind, which helps prevent the plant being rocked or broken.

Pruning weeping roses

Weeping roses are often rambler varieties grafted on to tall stocks.

Method In mid to late summer, prune off all flowered shoots, leaving the new shoots to flower next year. If there are few young shoots, keep some old ones but cut back the flowered side shoots to two buds. Try to balance the shape of weeping roses with the main shoots roughly equal in length, otherwise uneven growth results. Train the branches to an umbrella-shaped frame, cut hard back branches growing formally.

Pruning shrub and old roses

Species roses and some old shrub varieties require little pruning.

Method After flowering in autumn, cut away overcrowding or weak, thin growth. In late winter, prune spindly, poor flowering side shoots back to the main stem.

Pruning climbing plants

Ivy and Virginia creeper need no special pruning, but other climbing plants like wistaria benefit from systematic pruning to encourage direction and shape.

Pruning clematis

The pruning of clematis is surrounded by an air of mystery, to an even greater extent than roses.

Shrub and old fashioned roses
After flowering, reduce the number of branches to open out the shrub and cut back the longest ones to a quarter of their length.

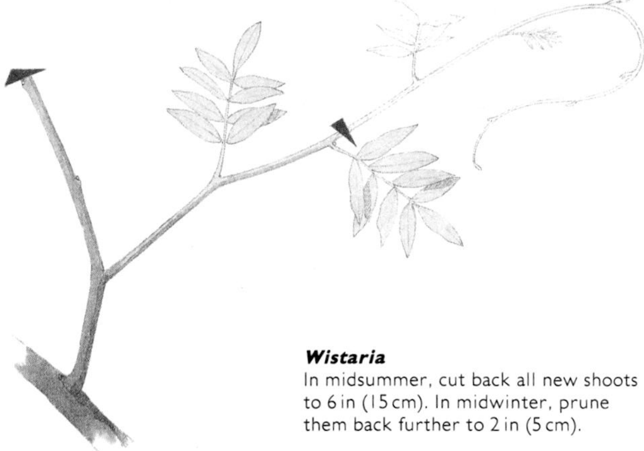

Wistaria
In midsummer, cut back all new shoots to 6 in (15 cm). In midwinter, prune them back further to 2 in (5 cm).

The main reason for this is probably that, like roses, not all species and varieties are pruned in the same way. There is no mystery whatever about the actual pruning, which is perfectly straightforward. The only problem lies in identifying to which group your clematis belongs. Broadly speaking, there are three groups: Group 1 is pruned hard back to within 1–2 ft (30–60 cm) of the ground before early spring when the buds are coming to life again; Group 2 is, if necessary, pruned towards the end of the winter; Group 3, which flower twice a year, are best left unpruned, but if pruning is preferred it should occur before early spring.

Group 1 consists of those species and varieties which flower after about midsummer on the current season's new shoots. Many of the popular large flowered hybrids are in this group. Because they have to produce the shoots before they flower, they should be pruned hard (to within 2 ft (60 cm)) in the early spring. The *Jackmanii* and *Viticella* species and hybrids make up the greater part of this group:

Ascotiensis
Barbara Jackman
Comtesse de Bouchaud
Ernest Markham
Etoile Violette
Gipsy Queen
Hagley Hybrid
Huldine
Jackmanii and varieties
Lady Betty Balfour
Madame Baron Veillard
Madame Edouard Andre
Madame Julia Correvon
Margot Koster
Margaret Hunt
Niobe
Perle d'Azur
Pink Fantasy
Rouge Cardinal
Serenata
Star of India
Venosa Violacea
Victoria
Ville de Lyon
Voluceau
Viticella

The pruning of species and varieties in Group 2 rather depends on the size and condition of the individual plant. The group is made up of species and varieties which flower in the early summer on the shoots that grew in the previous year. For example, *Clematis montana* and *C. macropetala*. This is the largest group and needs no regular pruning but should be cut back with a severity that is dictated by the condition of the plant. During their early life, plants will need little pruning beyond encouraging them to grow in the right direction. However, if, in later life, they outgrow their position, an occasional hard pruning in the late winter will sort them out and bring them back into good shape. This is by far the largest group and really typifies clematis pruning. By and large, any species which does not fall into Groups 1 or 3 is in Group 2. All varieties and species in this group flower before about midsummer on the previous year's growth. The clematis is pruned as and when required during the winter. In most cases, none will be needed and very seldom every year.

Group 3 varieties and species tend to have an early flush on last year's shoots and then a longer but less spectacular show later in the summer, and into early autumn. This later display is on the current season's new shoots. For best results, these should be left unpruned but, if just the later flowers are wanted or if there is not enough room to let them go wild, prune them as for Group 2 before early spring. Group 3 includes:

Belle Nantaise
Blue Diamond
C.W. Dowman
Duchess of Edinburgh
Elsa Spath (Xerxes)
Fair Rosamund
Henry I
John Warren
Lady Caroline Nevill
Lawsoniana
Marie Boisellot (Madame le Coultré)
Romana (*Hybrida seiboldii*)
Sealand Gem
Silver Moon
W.E. Gladstone
Will Goodwin
William Kennett

If in doubt, leave a clematis unpruned until you have established its group.

A-Z OF GARDEN PLANTS

Note to the reader

- Plants have been allocated a zone on the basis that they can withstand the minimum winter temperature of that zone and also conditions in zones of higher numbers. To establish the zone rating of a particular area, see pages 583–5.
- The species zone applies to all sub-species, cultivars and varieties within that species.
- Use of common names and availability of cultivars varies not only from country to country, but also within one country.

Abelia

Caprifoliaceae

There are approximately 30 species belonging to this genus, native to Asia and Mexico. About ten are in cultivation.

A. floribunda (zone 9) is an attractive semi-evergreen shrub which can reach 10ft (3m) in height and almost as much across. Covered in early summer with delicately scented, tubular pink flowers, the shrub is sensitive to frost and needs the warmth and shelter of a south-facing wall.

A × grandiflora (zone 8) is a slightly hardier garden hybrid with equally widespread semi-evergreen foliage and pink and white flowers, carried from mid summer to early autumn.

Cultivation. Abelias thrive in all types of well-drained soil, including calcareous soil, in sunshine or partial shade. They need protection from cold wind. Plant in autumn or spring.

Pruning need not be carried out every year, and involves cutting out dead wood at the end of winter and thinning after flowering. Propagation from semi-hardwood cuttings taken in summer.

Abies

Silver fir, *Pinaceae*

A genus of about 40 species of evergreen conifers native to the Northern Hemisphere which have a distinctive conical shape and form vast plantations in mountain regions. The leaves are needle-shaped, shorter than those of the pine and grow from the branches singly, rather than in twos or threes. Both male and female flowers appear as catkins on the same tree, with the female flowers occupying the top branches. The fruit is an upright cone with thin scales.

A. alba (*A. pectinata*) – zone 5 – European silver fir, can attain 170 ft (50 m) in height. Forming the basis of mountain forests in Germany, France and Switzerland, it differs from the *Picea* by its upright cones whose scales are shed at maturity. The leaves are arranged in two rows and have two white lines underneath. The tree is not suited to a hot, dry climate or low-lying areas subject to prolonged frost.

A. cephalonica (zone 5), Greek fir, grows to a height of 120 ft (37 m) and has sharp-needled, leathery leaves 1 in (2.5 cm) long and white underneath. They are carried around the entire circumference of the branch. The upright cylindrical cone measures more than 4 in (10 cm) in height. A species at home in alkaline soil and resistant to disease, it produces new growth early in spring, so is unsuitable in frost pockets.

A. concolor (zone 5), Colorado white fir, is a native of the western U.S. and Mexico, and achieves 100 ft (30 m) in height. Its grey bark is grooved and furrowed when mature, and the thick, round blue-grey leaves are 2 in (5 cm) long. The slightly downward pointing branches bear cones 4 in (10 cm) long. A fast-growing tree which needs little attention.

A. koreana (zone 5), Korean fir, grows very slowly to 16 ft (5 m) in height. The leaves are short, and white on the undersides. This species is characterized by the attractive violet cones which are produced even on very young trees.

A. pinsapo (zone 5), Spanish fir, measures about 100 ft (30 m) in height and as in *A. cephalonica* has very short needles arranged right round the circumference of the branches. It tolerates chalk soils and hot, dry climates.

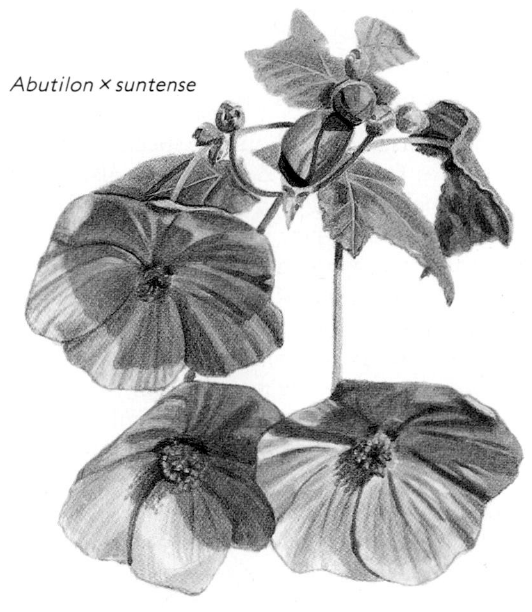

Abutilon × suntense

Firs are used as specimen planting or as part of a wind break, slow-growing species are suitable for a small garden.

Cultivation. Plant in early or mid spring when new growth first appears. Firs are very hardy by nature but they can suffer from being alternatively exposed to frosts and thaws. Cool, deep, moist but well drained soil is crucial. Most dislike air pollution and withstand moderate shade.

Prune only to reduce a forked leader to one shoot. Propagate by seed in spring, keeping seeds cold or stratifying them, or by grafting blue or pendulous species and cultivars.

Silver firs are prone to attacks of sap-sucking adelgids, which are related to aphids.

Abutilon

Malvaceae

This genus is represented by about 100 species from tropical or subtropical regions. Flowering all summer long, these woody or herbaceous plants can reach 15 ft (4.5 m) or more in height. The leaves are heart-shaped or palmate and the flowers hang from the leaf-axils.

A. theophrasti (*A. avicennae*) – zone 9 – Indian mallow, with small yellow flowers, measures 3 ft 6 in–6 ft 6 in (1–2 m) in height.

A. megapotamicum (zone 9) is an evergreen shrub growing to 6 ft 6 in (2 m) in height, with little yellow, red and purplish flowers. It has a graceful habit of growth and pointed, coarsely toothed leaves.

A. vitifolium, with blue-lavender flowers and downy-grey foliage, can reach 26 ft (8 m) in height. The cultivar 'Album' has white flowers; 'Veronica Tennant' has mauve flowers.

There are a number of hybrids, with flowers in shades of pink, orange, lemon and white, and with yellow-mottled leaves, such as *A. pictum* 'Thompsonii'. *A.* × *suntense*, a hybrid of *A. vitifolium* and *A. ochsenii* has slightly smaller flowers than *A. vitifolium* and with the darker coloured flowers of the second parent.

Abutilons are used in mixed borders and as specimen plants on the lawn.

Cultivation. Abutilon is easy to grow out-of-doors in frost-free latitudes but prefers the protection of a wall and some must be brought into a cool greenhouse in other climates. It grows in any well-drained soil which is not calcareous. Protect with straw in winter and cut back greenhouse specimens by half in spring. Remove dead and frost damaged shoots of hardy species at the same time in spring. Propagate by seed in spring or early autumn, or by semi-ripe cuttings planted out in the open air in summer.

Acacia

Wattle, mimosa, *Leguminosae*

A genus represented by about 1,200 species of usually fast-growing trees and shrubs, of which half are from Australia and the others are from subtropical Africa and the Pacific Islands. The street tree commonly cultivated and sometimes erroneously called 'acacia' is in fact false acacia (honey locust), or *Robinia*.

A. baileyana (zone 10), Cootamundra wattle, is a graceful species up to 30 ft (9 m) high, with bluish foliage and pure yellow flowers from late winter to early spring.

A. dealbata (zone 9), silver wattle or florists' mimosa, has attractive, fern-like leaves and pure yellow, fragrant flowers. It can reach 25 ft (7.5 m) or more in height. Cultivars include 'Bon Accueil', 20–23 ft (6–7 m) in height, with yellow flowers in late winter to early spring; 'Le Gaulois' 25–26 ft (7–8 m) which unfolds enormous gold coloured flowers in late winter, or early spring; 'Mirandolle' which measures 13–17 ft (4–5 m) high and is covered in yellow flowers in early winter; 'Pendula' (weeping

mimosa) 6 ft 6 in (2 m) whose flowers appear in early spring; 'Reve d'Or' which is 12–16 ft (4–5 m) high and flowers in late winter to early spring; and 'Virginia' which is 6 ft 6 in–10 ft (2–3 m) tall and has orange flowers which blossom from late winter to early spring.
A. howitti (zone 10), sticky wattle, 12–15 ft (4–5 m) high which has yellow flowers in mid to late spring, is rather sensitive to the cold.
A. karroo (zone 10), karroo thorn, 10–13 ft (3–4 m) is very prickly and can create a very effective defensive hedge.
A. longifolia (zone 9), Sydney golden wattle, attains a height of 26 ft (8 m) and tolerates alkaline soil. It produces attractive lance-shaped leaves and pale yellow flowers in early to mid spring. It is one of the hardiest species.
A. podalyriifolia (zone 10), Queensland silver wattle, native to Tasmania and Australia, reaches 15 ft (5 m) in height, and has silvery foliage and trunk. Flowers, which are bright yellow, appear in early to mid spring.
A. pravissima (zone 9), ovens wattle, reaches 10 ft (3 m) in height, and has unusual, triangular silvery foliage and pure yellow flowers from early to mid spring. It is relatively hardy and generally trouble-free.
A. rhetinodes (zone 9–10), four seasons wattle, reaches 20 ft (6 m) in height. It has willow-like leaves and yellow blossoms, less spectacular than other species but appearing all year in Australia, and from spring through to autumn in northern temperate climates. It is suitable for all types of soil.

Species of *Acacia* are generally used as cut flowers, especially in the south of France. Their rapid growth is greatly valued and in gardens the light foliage and magnificent winter or spring flowers of pale yellow or orange can look very decorative.

Cultivation. Acacias are easy to grow in areas where the orange tree is grown. Plant in neutral or peaty well drained soil in a sunny, sheltered position. Otherwise, cultivate in pots or open beds in a cool greenhouse.

Use a dressing of organic fertilizer and water freely. Propagate by seed or by grafting between early and late summer, or by cuttings of semi-hardwood twigs with a heel.

Root mealy bugs may attack the roots, causing foliage wilt, and some species are sensitive to calcareous soils. If this is a problem graft the subject on to *A. rhetinodes* which is quite able to tolerate such soils.

Acaena

New Zealand burr, *Rosaceae*

A genus consisting of about 100 species, coming principally from New Zealand, but also from South America and Polynesia. The plants form a huge evergreen carpet. The flowers are insignificant and not very interesting but the spiky fruits which follow them have a decorative effect.
A. buchananii (zone 7), originating in New Zealand, measures 1–2 in (2.5–5 cm) in height with a spread of 24 in (60 cm). This plant, with prostrate stems, has pinnate leaves $\frac{1}{2}$–$\frac{3}{4}$ in (1.5–2 cm) long, composed of round, grey-green leaflets, with a blue sheen on both sides. Prickly, globular, green or yellow burrs appear in mid summer.
A. microphylla (zone 7) from New Zealand, measures 1–2 in (2.5–5 cm) in height, with a spread of 24 in (60 cm). The stems are prostrate and branching, with pinnate leaves, 1–2 in (2.5–5 cm) long. Its rounded leaflets are notched and dentate. The crimson, spiky globular burrs are $\frac{1}{2}$–$\frac{3}{4}$ in (1–2 cm) long and appear in mid summer. It is an attractive species with green-bronze foliage, sometimes turning yellow or rusty.
A. novae-zelandiae (zone 7), from New Zealand, measures 2–3 in (5–7.5 cm) in height and has a spread of 3 sq ft (1 m^2) or more. It produces trailing, bronze foliage and crimson burrs. These are easy plants to grow and are hardy. They are used as ground cover but can be highly invasive, smothering weaker plants nearby. They are suitable for growing in the spaces between paving stones, or as a ground cover for spring-flowering bulbs.

Cultivation. Plant in quite light, even poor, and well-drained soil, in sun or partial shade, any time from autumn to spring.

Propagate by seed or by division and replant any time from autumn to spring.

Acantholimon

Prickly heath, prickly thrift, *Plumbaginaceae*

A genus comprising 120 species, some of which are very attractive and ideal rockery plants. They come from the Mediterranean area and require a prolonged drought in summer and, above all, dryness in winter. Naturally disliking all humidity except when the snow thaws, these plants have adapted to harsh growing conditions and seem to thrive on them.

A. glumaceum (zone 8), from Asia Minor, is 4 in (10 cm) high with a spread of 20–30 in (50–80 cm). This hardy species is easy to cultivate and forms thick cushions of dark evergreen foliage out of which burst little mauve-pink flowers on slender spikes about 6 in (15 cm) long, in mid summer.

A. venustum (zone 8), from Asia Minor is 4 in (10 cm) high, with a spread of 9–12 in (20–30 cm). It has spiky rosettes of blue-grey leaves; the flower spikes, 8–10 in (20–25 cm) high, carry pink flowers. It is a more beautiful species than the preceding one, but more difficult to grow.

Cultivation. Place the plants in extremely gritty soil mixed with a little peat. In open ground they must be protected from winter rain with a small pane of glass placed directly above the clumps or wire supports, so the air can circulate beneath.

Propagate by layering, or from 2 in (5 cm) cuttings taken in late summer, and rooted in sand under a cold frame, where they remain throughout the winter.

Acanthus

Bear's breeches, *Acanthaceae*

This genus is represented by some 30 species mostly originating in the Mediterranean region. Striking plants for borders.

A. mollis (zone 6–7) growing high, with a spread of 2–2½ ft (60–75 cm), is a hardy herbaceous plant. The decorative, deeply toothed bright green leaves die back in the winter. The white flowers are carried on long spikes, and have mauvy pink bracts which remain after the flowers fade. The flowers open in mid to late summer. Acanthus plants are hardy; they look magnificent planted in isolated clumps and integrate well in perennial borders. They can be grown successfully in large tubs or urns.

Cultivation. *A. mollis* likes light, deep and well drained soils, and sun or partial shade. Plant in mid autumn or the end of spring, space 2 ft (60 cm) apart. In poor soil it will require some fertilizer in spring. Cut back the stems to ground level after flowering. Acanthus resent root disturbance, but can be propagated by division in spring, and also by root cuttings in spring or by seed sown in gentle heat. All species are generally trouble-free

Acer platanoides

Acer

Maple, *Aceraceae*

A genus of over 100 deciduous trees and shrubs from the Northern Hemisphere, some of which have given rise to numerous cultivars. They are valued for their ornamental qualities, the beauty of their trunks and their autumn colours. Clusters of little green, red or yellow flowers appears in spring at the ends of the branches. The fruits are distinctive, double-winged keys.

A. campestre (zone 6), field or hedge maple, rarely grows taller than 33 ft (10 m). The leaves, 2–4 in (5–10 cm) long, have 5 lobes and turn bright yellow in the autumn. The tree is characterized by a light, gnarled trunk and ridged branches. It grows throughout Europe, except in mountainous areas and the Mediterranean region and prefers a limy soil. It is sometimes used for hedging.

A. davidii (zone 6) from China measures less than 33 ft (10 m) in height. The dark-green leaves are ovate with red petioles, and turn a lovely golden colour in autumn. The fruits are red and the highly decorative bark is striated white, especially when grown in shade.

A. griseum (zone 6), paperback maple from China, measures less than 16 ft (5 m). Its trifoliate leaves turn scarlet in the autumn and its old tobacco-coloured bark peels off in large flakes, to reveal the bright orange, young bark beneath.

A. japonicum (zone 7), Japanese maple, is a slow-growing multi-stemmed shrub or small tree, up to 16 ft (5 m) in height. The rounded leaves with numerous shallow, pointed lobes are soft green, and turn a vivid red or yellow in the autumn. The drooping clusters of red flowers come out before the leaves. Grow in cool soil in a semi-shaded place. This species from Japan has produced many horticultural variants, such as 'Aconitifolium', with deeply divided leaves which turn bright crimson in the autumn; 'Aureum', which is slow-growing with yellow leaves; 'Vitifolium' which has leaves with 10 to 12 lobes and brilliant autumn colour.

A. monspessulanum (zone 7), Montpellier maple, is a native of Mediterranean shores and the Near East. A slow-growing shrub or small tree, it can reach 20 ft (6 m) high. It has small, three-lobed leathery dark green leaves which are dull blue-green underneath. The wings of the fruit are parallel. In its natural environment it grows in rocky soil in full sun and turns a beautiful colour in autumn. It makes an excellent specimen in a small garden.

A. negundo (zone 5), box elder, is a fast-growing tree from North America and measures 50–66 ft (15–20 m) high. Unlike other species of *Acer*, it has pinnate leaves, with three to five leaflets, and its branches are covered with a silvery bloom and drooping racemes of fruit on female trees. Found along waterways, it can tolerate all types of soil and is used as a wind break. Most commonly seen are the cultivars 'Variegatum', with white variegations, 'Elegans' with yellow variegation and 'Auratum', with striking golden leaves.

A. opalus (*A. opulifolium*) – zone 6 – Italian maple, has leaves like the snowball tree, (*Viburnum opulus*), and originates from South and Central Europe. It rarely grows more than 25 ft (7.5 m) high. The crown is spreading and leaves usually have five shallow lobes. Clusters of yellow flowers come out in early and mid spring before the leaves and, for this reason, it is one of the more ornamental of the many spring-flowering trees.

A. palmatum (zone 7), Japanese maple, measures between 17–23 ft (5–6 m) in height. Originally from Japan, China and Korea, and well known to Bonsai lovers, this elegant tree generally presents a dense, rounded and spreading crown. The leaves are deeply lobed, and normally light green, but bright red, bronze or purple in spring and autumn. It likes moist, well drained soil and a sheltered and shaded position away from the wind. There are numerous cultivars with various habits of growth, leaf colours and shapes. The following are recommended: 'Atropurpureum', with bronze-crimson leaves; 'Aureum', with yellow leaves; 'Dissectum Atropurpureum', with deeply divided purple leaves; 'Dissectum Flavescens', which is similar, but with yellow-green leaves; 'Linearilobum', with leaves which have very long narrow lobes; 'Osakazuki', with brilliant scarlet autumn colour; and 'Senkaki', the coral-bark maple, characterized by yellow autumn colour and coral-red bark.

A. platanoides (zone 4), Norway maple, grows up to 50 ft (15 m) high. It is similar to sycamore, but distinguished by its non-scaly trunk. The large, five-lobed leaves are green on both sides, and it is often cultivated for its rapid growth and striking stature. There are numerous cultivars, including 'Columnare', with an erect habit; and 'Goldsworth Purple' and 'Schwedleri', which have striking purple foliage. The latter are less vigorous and better adapted to smaller gardens.

A. pseudoplatanus (zone 5), sycamore (in UK), originally from Europe and Western Asia, can reach more than 66 ft (20 m) in height. The grey bark peels off the trunk in vertical flakes. The leaves have five deep lobes, dark green on the top and glaucous on the underside, and can be up to 8 in (20 cm) long. It thrives in northern temperate climates, in deep, cool soil. There are numerous forms and cultivars, including forma *purpureum*, which has leaves with purple undersides; 'Brilliantissimum', with pink new growth which ages to yellowish and finally to green; 'Erectum' (syn. 'Fastigiatum'), which has an erect habit; 'Simon-Louis Frères' which is slow-growing and has leaves variegated with purple and cream; and 'Worleei' with leaves which are golden-yellow for most of the year. At the end of the summer the leaves of these varieties are often marked with tar spot, the black spots of the *Rhytisma* fungus.

A. saccharinum, (*A. dasycarpum*) – zone 4 – silver maple, must not be confused with the sugar maple (*A. saccharum*) which is the emblem of Canada. Originally from eastern regions of North America, this species reaches a height of 33 ft (10 m). Primarily planted for decoration, it has toothed leaves and each leaf has five deep lobes characteristically silver underneath. This species has given rise to fastigiate cultivars, such as 'Pyramidale', and cultivars with golden leaves, such as 'Lutescens'.

A. sempervirens (A. creticum) – zone 7 – Cretan maple, is native to the Eastern Mediterranean. It is a slow-growing shrub or small tree, and its leaves remain green until Christmas in more northerly regions.
Cultivation. These trees like full sun or partial shade, especially golden-leaved forms, which can scorch in full sun. A rich neutral, or limy, well drained soil is best. Plant in autumn or spring; bare-rooted specimens can be planted in winter or spring. Protect Asiatic species from late frosts followed by morning sun, and from cold winters.

Propagate from seed, which can be successful if stratified just after the harvest, or by cuttings in late winter or early spring; named cultivars must be grafted in summer or winter, on to rootstocks of the species.

No regular pruning is needed, but remove dead or damaged wood or reverted branches from variegated forms in autumn. Diseases such as mildew, tar spot, anthracnose and canker along with pests such as tunnelling insects and caterpillars of certain moths can attack this species.

Achillea

Yarrow, milfoil, *Compositae*

This genus comprises some 85 species of hardy herbaceous perennials from Europe, the Middle East and Northern Asia.
A. filipendulina, can reach 32 in–4 ft (80–120 cm) in height, with a similar spread. It has finely divided, grey-green ferny foliage, and is covered from mid summer to early autumn with large, flat, lemon-yellow compact flower-heads, which are as attractive dried as they are fresh. Cultivars include 'Coronation Gold' and 'Gold Plate' both with deep-yellow flowers.

Other popular species and cultivars include *A. millefolium* 'Cerise Queen' with deep pink flowers in early to mid summer and *A. ptarmica*, 'The Pearl', with little white double flowers. Tall-growing achilleas are a traditional feature of herbaceous or mixed borders, low growing species are planted in rock gardens. Some forms are quick spreading and without careful attention can be invasive.
Cultivation. Plant in autumn or spring in well drained soil and in full sun. Cut the dead stems back to ground level at the end of autumn, when the flowers have finished.

Propagation is by dividing clumps in the spring.

Acinos

Calamint, *Labiatae*

This genus comprises 10 perennial species.
Acinos alpinus (*Calamintha alpina*) (zone 6) grows 4–10 in (10–25 cm) tall with a spread of 1 ft (30 cm). It is a perennial plant or sub-shrub and has long stems covered with black hairs. The oval leaves with short petioles are toothed at the ends and are opposite, arranged in fours around the stem. Purplish-blue flowers in loose whorls have white patches on their lower lips; occasionally they may be pink or white. They bloom from early to late summer.

Grow in a rockery with *Aquilegia vulgaris, Stachys lanata* or ornamental grasses for an especially stunning effect.
Cultivation. Plant in damp soil between limestone rocks in full sun, or grow in a trough. Propagate by seed, cuttings or division in the spring.

Aconitum wilsonii

Aconitum

Aconite, Monk's hood, *Ranunculaceae*

A genus comprising some 100 species poisonous in all parts, from Europe and Asia.

A. napellus (zone 6) is a perennial herbaceous plant from 3 ft 6 in–4 ft (1–1.2 m) high, with a 16–24 in (40–60 cm) spread. The dark green leaves are glossy and deeply divided. The intense blue flowers appear in mid-to-late summer on long spikes, and have hood-shaped petals. They are excellent flowers for use in fresh or dried flower arrangements and can be grown in a herbaceous or mixed border.

A. Wilsonii from China flowering in early autumn is somewhat similar.

Cultivation. The aconite prefers cool, deep, moisture-retentive soil, enriched with peat or well rotted manure. It should be planted in full sun or in partial shade in mid autumn or the start of spring, 16 in (40 cm) apart.

It is important to water it during a dry spell, give it ample fertilizer each spring, and cut off stems after flowering. It is hardy in all regions, however, protect the crowns in winter with straw or dead leaves.

Propagate by division of clumps in spring or by sowing seed in a cold frame in early spring, for planting out in autumn.

Acorus

Sweet flag, sweet sedge, myrtle grass, *Araceae*

A. calamus (sweet flag) – zone 5 – and *A. gramineus* (zone 6–7), are the only two species in this genus.

Coming from marshes and edges of waterways in the Far East, *A. calamus* has made itself at home in the temperate zones of Europe and America. It is grown for its foliage, not its modest green flowers. Its leaves are about 20 in (50 cm) long, clear green and spear-shaped. *A. gramineus* is smaller, with narrower leaves, and is native to Japan. The white-variegated forms are the most commonly used as ornamentals in water gardens, with plants of the same shape, such as irises, or of contrasting shape, such as marsh marigold (*Caltha palustris*).

Cultivation. The rhizomes have to remain permanently in moisture, any soil type is acceptable. Sweet flags can easily be divided in spring and autumn.

Actaea

Baneberry, *Ranunculaceae*

A genus comprising eight species of herbaceous perennials which come from northern temperate forests. They have attractive fern-like leaves, and their white flowers on terminal racemes are followed by ornamental red, black or white fruits. The plants are poisonous.

A. rubra (zone 4–5), native to North America, measures 2 ft (60 cm) in height and spread. This pretty forest plant is characterized above all by its bright-red ovoid berries, carried well above the leaves.

A. spicata (zone 4–5), herb Christopher, is native to Europe and Asia and measures 16–20 in (40–50 cm) in height and spread. It carries round, black berries from early to mid summer.

These hardy plants are ideal for shady borders and wild or woodland gardens.

Cultivation. Plant in rich, moist and well drained soil, in shelter or partial shade. *A. spicata* likes chalky soil.

Propagate by division in early autumn.

Actaea rubra

Adenophora

Ladybells, *Campanulaceae*

About 40 hardy herbaceous species comprise this genus, with fleshy, thick rhizomes.

A. tashiroi (zone 7), from Japan and South Korea, is 12–16 in (30–40 cm) high, and should be planted 8 in (20 cm) apart. The stems have fairly dense basal, alternate, ovate leaves $\frac{3}{4}$–1 in (2–3 cm) long. The bell-like, violet-blue flowers are 1 in (2.5 cm) long and carried singly or in erect, rather sparse clusters in mid summer.

A close relative of *Campanula*, adenophora is planted in herbaceous borders, wild gardens and rockeries.

Cultivation. Plant in sun or partial shade, in ordinary or chalky well drained soil. The plant resents root disturbance.

Propagate by seed as soon as the berries are ripe.

Adenostyles

Compositae

A genus with three, hardy, herbaceous perennial species which are hairless or covered with white down, originating from the mountains of Europe or Asia.

A. alpina (zone 5–6), native of the Alps and Corsica, grows 12–16 in (30–40 cm) high and 16 in–2 ft (40–60 cm) in spread. It has a compact habit and heart-shaped, toothed leaves with grey-green undersides. Mauve, light-pink or white flowers open in mid to late summer.

These suit wild gardens or big rockeries and take their place next to rhododendrons with *Actaea spicata, Petasites paradoxus*, etc.

Cultivation. Plant in shade or partial shade in a moist soil during the summer.

Propagate from seed or division in spring time.

Adonis

Ranunculaceae

A genus consisting of 20 species of generally hardy annuals or perennials. The two hardy perennial species given below are outstanding.

A. amurensis (zone 5), from Manchuria and Japan, grows 10–16 in (25–40 cm) high. The bright-yellow bowl-shaped flowers are 2 in (5 cm) across, and appear in late winter or early spring. The fern-like leaves are pale green. 'Flore Pleno', the double-flowered form, is often grown.

A. vernalis (zone 5) comes from Europe and Siberia, and grows 8–12 in (20–30 cm) high. The flowers are pale yellow and open out flat in full sunshine during mid spring.

Adonis vernalis

They are suitable for a rockery, planted with spring-flowering bulbs, for growing in pans or in an alpine house.

Cultivation. Grow in light, moist soil, and full sun or light shade. Plant 1 ft (30 cm) apart from early to late summer, when the plants are dormant; new growth appears at the end of the autumn. Fertilize every three years with bonemeal. After flowering, propagate by division replanting immediately or by sowing seed in a pot in a cold frame in summer. Germination can take up to a year.

Aechmea

Bromeliaceae

A large genus of over 150 species from tropical America. Among the epiphytic forest plants, these bromeliads are one of the most dangerous for the tree in which they grow. Rain water can fill their enormous rosettes, making them too heavy for the trees to support. This causes a number of branches to break suddenly, ridding the tree of its undesirable guests! From the centre of the large prickly rosettes, depending on the species, grows an enormous flower-spike which displays the most vivid colours. *A. fasciata* (zone 10) possesses grey foliage, flecked with green, which contrasts with the delicate pink and cherry red of the flower spike.

Less commonly cultivated is *A. chantinii*, with bright orange flowers; and *A. fulgens* var.

discolor, which has red berries following the attractive purple flowers.

Cultivation. Aechmeas grow in a well drained position and need a short dry period between each watering. After flowering, the plant produces seeds which take five years to reach flowering size. The mother plant then dies, but produces a number of side-shoots which can be detached and potted up separately.

In the home, aechmeas need full sun to flower. Water very frequently during summer but much less in winter.

Aeschynanthus

Basket plant, *Gesneriaceae*

This genus contains around 100 species from tropical areas of the Far East. Most are evergreen climbing, trailing or creeping herbaceous plants. The leaves are opposite and often somewhat fleshy. The clustered tubular flowers are showy and sometimes have a small hood formed from the upper petals. They may be grown in hanging baskets or as climbers but need protection except in very warm climates.

A. marmoratus (*A. zebrinus*) (zone 10+), from Burma is a trailing plant with stems reaching to 2 ft (60 cm) long. The waxy, dark green leaves are oval, 3–4 in (7.5–10 cm) long, veined, yellowish-green above, but purplish below. Green flowers, blotched dark brown, appear in summer and autumn.

A. speciosus (*A. slendens*) (zone 10+) comes from Malaysia. It is a trailing plant with stems reaching 2 ft (60 cm) in length. The waxy narrow leaves are usually borne in whorls and the erect, bright orange flowers are carried in large clusters in summer and autumn.

A. × *splendidus* (*A. parasiticus* × *A. speciosus*) (zone 10+), a hybrid, is a vigorous trailing plant with stems to over 3 ft (90 cm) long with thick, narrow-oval leaves up to 5 in (13 cm) long. The erect, bright orange-red flowers are blotched with brown-red, and formed in summer and autumn.

Cultivation. Frost-tender plants needing a minimum temperature of 65°F (7°C), a fairly humid atmosphere and a bright position out of direct sun. Mist frequently and water regularly during the growing season but sparingly in winter. Repot every two to three years in spring. Propagate by stem cuttings in spring and summer, using bottom heat.

Aesculus

Horse chestnut, *Hippocastanaceae*

A genus of 13 deciduous trees or shrubs from the Northern Hemisphere, some of which can reach 80 ft (25 m) in height, with umbrella-like crowns. The bark, first grey then brown, often becomes scaly with age. The leaves are large and digitate. The flowers, in erect showy racemes, appear mostly in spring. The fruit is a spherical capsule which is prickly in some species and resembles a chestnut, with one large seed inside.

A. hippocastanum (zone 6), common horse chestnut, originally from the Balkans, can reach 80 ft (24 m) in height. It is among the most spectacular of flowering trees. The leaves are robust and unfold very early in spring, and the numerous flowers appear in great white candles, emerging from brown, sticky buds. The leaves, mid to dark green, have five to seven leaflets. It is difficult to grow plants in the shade of horse chestnut, but winter-flowering species, such as winter aconite, *Eranthis hyemalis*, take advantage of the tree's dormancy to flower. The cultivar 'Baumannii' ('Flore Pleno') has sterile, double white flowers; because it doesn't set seed, it is often planted in built-up areas.

A. pavia, red buckeye, grows 8 ft 6 in (2.5 m) high. This species, from the southern United States, has embossed leaves, red flowers and smooth fruits. It is small enough to be grown in an average garden.

A. × *carnea* (*A. rubicunda*), red horse chestnut, is a hybrid of species, resembling *A. hippocastanum* but with red flowers and slightly prickly fruits. The deep-pink flowered form 'Briotii' is also grown.

The horse chestnut is particularly suitable for large gardens and in urban areas as a street tree.

Cultivation. Choose one with a good rootball and plant in the autumn or spring. Horse chestnuts are very hardy and resistant to pollution, and tolerate most soils, but prefer cool, open soils. Avoid a position in very strong sunshine which, together with a dry soil causes the foliage to turn brown in summer. In summer, water newly planted trees.

Propagate from seeds planted as soon as they fall and cover with their own depth of soil. Varieties are normally grafted. The tree is prone to anthracnose, and leaf spot fungal disease.

Aethionema

Stonecress, *Cruciferae*

Around 40 perennial or shrubby species round the Mediterranean basin comprise this genus. *A. grandiflorum*, (zone 7) from Lebanon, is the largest, growing 12 to 16 in (30–40 cm) high and 2 ft to 2 ft 6 in (60–80 cm) across. It carries attractive mounds of sea-green foliage. Its domed heads of pink flowers last from late spring to early autumn.

The cultivar 'Warley Rose', 9 in (25 cm) high and 16 in (40 cm) across, is one of the most popular rock garden plants, for its blue-grey foliage and bright-pink flowers, larger than those of the species. A very decorative plant, its flowers last from late spring to early autumn. These attractive dwarf bushes with evergreen leaves are invaluable for a rock garden.

Cultivation. Plant in well drained, gritty, poor or chalky soil, in full sun. Cut back ruthlessly after flowering, to induce compact growth. Frost can cause die-back at the top of the branches, and in a harsh winter the mature branches freeze, but the plant makes up for lost growth. Dampness is more dangerous than frost.

Work well rotted compost into the soil every third spring. Propagate the species from seed or by taking 2 in (5 cm) cuttings from lateral branches from early to mid summer and then put them under a cold frame. 'Warley Rose' is always propagated from cuttings.

Agapanthus

African blue lily, *Amaryllidaceae (Alliaceae)*

This genus is comprised of ten species of perennial plants from South Africa.

A. africanus (*A. umbellatus*) (zone 10) is a perennial with tuberous roots, growing 2 ft–2 ft 6 in (60–80 cm) high and 16–20 in (40–50 cm) across. Its ribbon-shaped, evergreen leaves are mid-green, and 20 to 40 flowers form dense, blue-mauve umbels, which blossom on leafless stems from mid summer to early autumn. It is excellent for container growing, or grouping in mixed borders.

It is semi-hardy, and best suited to Mediterranean and Atlantic climates. Hardier hybrids, such as 'Blue Giant' and Headbourne Hybrids are more suitable for cooler areas.

Agapanthus

Cultivation. Agapanthus likes fertile, well drained soil and sheltered, sunny sites. In mid spring, plant the fleshy roots 4 in (10 cm) deep and 6 in (15 cm) apart; in colder areas plant deeper. In summer, it needs frequent watering. After flowering, cut back the flowering stems to the base. In cold climates, protect with a mulch of dry leaves in winter, or bring indoors over winter in a cool but frost-free place.

Propagate by division of clumps in the spring.

Agastache

Giant hyssop, *Labiatae*

A small genus comprising sun-loving, moderately hardy, perennial plants whose scented leaves are similar to that of the bergamot.

A. foeniculum (*A. anethiodora*) – zone 8 – from N. America, grows 3 ft 6 in–4 ft (1–1.2 m) high. It is shrub-like, with scented leaves resembling those of the mint, and indigo-violet flowers carried in large spikes at the top of each branch, in mid summer.

A. mexicana (zone 9) comes from Mexico and grows 2 ft (60 cm) high and 1 ft (30 cm) across. The splendid spikes of sage-like flowers vary

from dark pink to crimson. This species is short-lived and confined to regions with a mild, dry climate. Giant hyssop is useful to liven up the back of large herbaceous borders, but in the colder areas needs protection in winter.
Cultivation. Plant in any well drained soil in sun. Incorporate well-rotted manure in the soil before planting.

To propagate, sow in early spring in a box placed in a cold frame, or lift and divide in spring.

Agave
Agavaceae (Amaryllidaceae)

This is an important genus from South and Central America comprising about 300 tropical and subtropical species, of which two or three are hardy in northern climates.
A. americana, century plant, grows 3 ft 6 in (1 m) high and twice as much across. It forms a stemless rosette of sharply pointed, fleshy, strap-shaped leaves. It flowers when 10 or more years old, after which it dies, usually leaving offsets. The variegated forms, such as 'Marginata', with thin white leaf margins, and 'Medio-picta' with a central yellow stripe, are often grown as house plants.
A. macroantha, from Mexico, grows only 6–10 in (15–25 cm) high, and its rosettes of grey-green leaves, bordered with brown thorns, form slow-spreading clumps.
A. virginica correctly named *Manfreda virginica,* a native of southern USA measures 12–18 in (30–40 cm) across. The soft leaves are deciduous and dark green in colour and the flower stem can reach the height of a man. Greenish fragrant flowers bloom in summer. A species which is interesting rather than attractive.
Cultivation. Agaves need a very sunny position and well-drained, gritty, soil as a protection against winter dampness. Grow young plants sheltered from frost for two to three years.

Propagate by offset or seed. Young plants are very sensitive to frost but hardiness develops.

Ageratum
Floss flower, *Compositae*

This genus is composed of about 40 annual and biennial herbaceous plants, and they are among the more popular tender summer bedding plants.
A. houstonianum (*A. mexicanum*) – zone 6 – grows 6 in–2 ft (15–60 cm) high, depending on the variety. Sky-blue pompon flowers appear on this bushy annual, from mid summer to early autumn; flowering can be interrupted by a very dry spell. The cultivars 'Blue Blazer' and 'Blue Cap', 6 in (15 cm) high, have deep-blue flowers; 'Blue Mink', 10 in (25 cm) high, is admired for its lavender blue flowers; and 'North Sea', 6 in (15 cm) high, has reddish mauve flowers.
Cultivation. Plant in moisture-retentive soil in a sunny or lightly shaded, sheltered position after the last frost. Sow seed in a warm greenhouse from late winter to mid spring. Prick out into pots or boxes and pinch out the young plants to make them bushy and to encourage them to flower over a longer period. Progressively harden off before planting in the final position. Water when the weather is dry. Red spider mite can infest the foliage, causing it to discolour and dry out.

Agrostis
Gramineae

This genus contains 120 annual or perennial species, many of which are used in lawn seed mixtures. A few are grown for the graceful flower-spikes, which are very soft, and fawn, red or white. These are invaluable for fresh and dried flower arrangements.
A. stolonifera (*A. alba*) – zone 4 – creeping bent, is 12–18 in (30–45 cm) high, often wide spreading. Velvet bent (*A. canina*) – zone 4 – comes from mountain meadows or the Mediterranean coast. Cloud grass, *A. nebulosa* (zone 9) is grown for its delicate, white flower panicles, giving the impression of a white haze, seen from a distance. It grows up to 18 in (45 cm) high. For best effect place near the more erect grasses.
Cultivation. Propagate in spring by sowing seeds collected from the previous autumn.

Ailanthus
Tree of heaven, *Simaroubaceae*

A genus of five deciduous trees from Asia and Australia.
A. altissima, (A. glandulosa) – zone 7 – has a straight trunk and quite dense, pinnate foliage

carried on thick, spreading branches. It comes originally from northern China and can grow 65 ft (20 m) high. The leaves resemble those of ash, and can be up to 3 ft 6 in (1 m) long on young plants. The small, yellow male or female flower clusters appear in early summer on the same or on different trees, but have no beauty. The fruits are key-shaped and conspicuous, like those of the ash tree. It often colonizes wasteland and derelict sites in towns. The new leaves unfold late in the spring. The smell of the foliage when crushed and of the male flowers is quite unpleasant. The tree of heaven is used as a street or specimen tree, or to stabilize slopes. Prune annually because it draws a lot of nutrition from the top soil.

Cultivation. Plant in autumn or spring. The tree of heaven is fast growing and resists pollution, and is therefore often used as a street tree in warmer areas. It grows best in a rich, deep soil, in any aspect, even beside the sea. It can also tolerate pruning and can be maintained as a shrub.

Propagation is by seeds, separation of suckers, root cuttings or grafting. Because of the odour of the male flowers, female trees are more commonly grown, and these are propagated vegetatively.

Ajuga

Bugle, *Labiatae*

A genus comprising 50 species of hardy annuals and herbaceous perennials.

A. pyramidalis (zone 6), from Europe, grows 10–14 in (25–35 cm) high, with a spread of 8–10 in (20–25 cm). The toothed leaves are light green. The flowers, in spikes, are blue with purple bracts and appear in late spring.

A. reptans (zone 6), also from Europe, grows 4–8 in (10–20 cm) high, with a spread of 16–20 in (40–50 cm). This plant produces long leafy runners, which can be invasive. The species has large, dark-green leaves in rosettes, and dark-blue flowers in late spring or early summer. The cultivars are more popular, and include 'Atropurpurea' ('Purpurea'), with dark-purple foliage, and 'Burgundy Glow', with purple, cream and bronze foliage. All can be used as ground cover, in a rock garden, herbaceous border, or wild garden, as long as there is ample moisture. They are excellent under trees and shrubs.

Cultivation. Plant in rich, well drained soil in shade, partial shade or in sun. Colouring is often better in sun, but growth can be stunted by hot, dry conditions.

Propagation is from seed or by division of clumps in spring or autumn.

Akebia

Lardizabalaceae

A genus of two species of twining climbers with semi-evergreen foliage from Asia. The most commonly grown is *A. quinata* (zone 8) which is very hardy and vigorous, growing more than 40 ft (12 m) in height. Its palmate leaves are leathery and dark green, with five leaflets; they are shed during harsh winters. Bunches of fragrant but modest-looking brown-purple hanging flowers appear in mid to late spring and are followed by edible, sausage-shaped purplish fruits which are produced only in sheltered spots. Plant in sun or shade in good soil and near support, such as a tree or pergola, which it will soon cover. It grows well on a trellis against a wall facing the sun.

Propagate in autumn by taking semi-ripe cuttings, layering or from seed in early spring. Prune untidy branches after flowering.

Akebia quinata

Albizia

Leguminosae

This genus is represented by several species of deciduous tree or shrub, rarely growing more than 13 ft (4 m) in northern latitudes. The habit is spreading and the double pinnate leaves resemble those of mimosa (*Acacia dealbata*) but are bigger and lighter green. The leaflets fold up at night. The charming, fluffy flowers are composed of numerous stamens united into a tuft. The fruits are hanging pods.

A. julibrissin (zone 9), silk tree, from Iran to China, is the only species hardy enough to withstand severe frost. The unusual, petal-less flowers look like little pink brushes and appear towards the end of the summer.

The cultivar, 'Rosea', has deeper pink flowers. Albizia is grown for its light foliage and beautiful flowers. It is best against a south-facing wall, in northern temperate climates and is suited to the seaside. It lacks the scent of the mimosa, but the albizia has the advantage of being slightly hardier. It flowers when young, and plants can be raised annually to use in bedding-out schemes.

Cultivation. Plant in the spring after the danger of frost has gone. For the first few years, stake the stem. Albizias prefer a warm, open, well drained soil. To get a little trunk to form, cut off lower branches. In the areas with severe, prolonged frost, albizias are best planted in a pot and overwintered in a cool greenhouse, then placed outdoors during the summer, where the wood can ripen and produce flowers. It can suffer from mimosa wilt, or can produce spots on the branches which are black at first, becoming red then pink.

Propagation is from seed after soaking. Young plants grow very rapidly.

Alisma

Alismataceae

A. plantago-aquatica (zone 6), water plantain, is an aquatic plant, belonging to a family which is found on all continents except the Antarctic. This hardy species is found in calm waters in temperate zones all over the world, and varies in size between 8 in–3 ft (20–90 cm). It has oval, pointed leaves and in summer carries large panicles of small pink flowers, like those of gypsophila. They open, for pollination, in the afternoons. The life-cycle is unusually short, the seeds reaching maturity 8 to 12 weeks after the start of growth. The water plantain is very prolific and its runners can be invasive. Due to its strong, tuberous root system it is very useful

Albizia julibrissin 'Rosea'

for stabilizing steep river banks and the shallow waters of pond margins.

Propagate by seed or by division in spring or autumn.

Allium

Amaryllidaceae, (Alliaceae)

A genus of about 700 species of often bulbous, perennial plants, many with a strong smell when bruised. Many are cultivated as ornamentals or for food.

Garlic (zone 7)
A. sativum is a hardy perennial, cultivated as an annual or biennial. Bulbs are 1½–2½ in (4–7 cm) in diameter and produce stalks 20 in (50 cm) high, terminating in an umbel of whitish-green or pink flowers, together with numerous bulbils. Cultivars can be distinguished by their colour. Pink garlic is planted later and lasts longer than white garlic.
Cultivation. Garlic favours a rich, well drained, sandy soil which has not been manured for three years. The same ground can be used year after year if the preceding year's growth is good. Otherwise, the bulbs must be planted on a new site or the soil must be changed or improved. Garlic is not affected by bad frosts but it likes plenty of sunshine.

Garlic can be planted from late autumn onwards in a light soil, but mid winter planting is better in areas with a heavy or damp soil. Healthy, large cloves are detached from a bulb and planted, pointed-end upwards, 6 in (15 cm) apart within the row, 1 ft (30 cm) apart between the rows. Barely cover the top with soil. Good cultivation will help keep pests and diseases away. Harvest when the tops turn yellow at the end of the summer, 4 to 5 months after planting. Take care when lifting, using a small fork or spade, to avoid damaging the bulbs. Remove any remaining soil, then put out to dry in the sun. To store the bulbs, tie the yellowed dead leaves together, and hang in a cool, dry, frost-free place, or place them on a shelf.

Welsh onion or **Japanese bunching onion** (zone 4)
A. fistulosum, Welsh onion or bunching onion, originated in cultivation and grows about 1 ft (30 cm) high. It is perennial, forming a compact clump of green stems which are quite thick and slightly bulbous, and similar in appearance to spring onions. It produces bulbils at the base.
Cultivation. This onion prefers a cool, dry position, and does well in any aspect. Lift and divide the clumps in early spring or mid autumn, every three years, and replant at 4 in (10 cm) intervals, in rows 8 in (20 cm) apart. You can also sow seeds in early or mid spring in rows 8 in (20 cm) apart. Firm the ground well and thin to 2–4 in (5–10 cm) apart. Harvest throughout the year, as required.
Uses. Welsh onion is used for seasoning sauces, and the leaves are popular eaten raw in salads.

Chive (zone 4)
A. schoenoprasum, chive, comes originally from the Mediterranean basin and does not exceed 12 in (30 cm) in height. This perennial plant is like a spring onion, but with much finer stems.
Cultivation. Instructions for chives are the same as for Welsh onions, but reduce the distance between the rows to 6 in (15 cm). To prolong the harvest, protect in winter with straw or peat, or pot up and place on a cool, sunny windowsill. Plants can remain in place for three or four years, after which the clumps should be lifted and divided.
Uses. The leaves of the chive are used finely chopped to enhance omelettes, salads, sauces, soups and cottage cheese.

Shallot (zone 5)
The shallot was for a long time considered to be a separate species, *A. ascalonicum*, but is now regarded as a variety of the onion. The bulb measures ¾–1 in (2–2.5 cm) in diameter when mature. This hardy plant, cultivated as an annual or biennial, has been grown since the Dark Ages. Among the best cultivars are 'Hâtive de Niort', 'Giant Yellow', 'Dutch Red' and 'Long Keeping Yellow'.
Cultivation. After selecting healthy bulbs from the previous harvest, plant them in light, well drained soil which has not been recently manured, preferably in a sunny position, from mid winter to early spring. They should be planted 6 in (15 cm) apart and at least 1 in (2 cm) deep. Hoe them regularly and water only in dry weather. In early summer, gently pull the soil away from the bases of the clumps to encourage ripening. The shallot can be attacked by pests such as onion fly and eelworm, or by various fungal diseases including white rot, saddleback,

neck rot and downy mildew. Gather the bulbs when the leaves turn yellow and leave them to dry, ideally in the sun, for a few days. Keep only healthy bulbs and store them in a box or hung up in a net in a cool dry place.

Uses. Used as a flavouring and also as a pickling onion.

Onion (zone 4)

The bulb of *Allium cepa* measures 2–4 in (5–10 cm) in diameter and the plant grows 20 in (50 cm) high. Onions recommended for sowing in spring and harvesting in autumn are 'Ailsa Craig', 'Hygro', 'North Holland Blood Red' and 'Rijnsburger'. Cultivars for autumn sowing include 'Autumn Queen' and 'Reliance'. The Japanese cultivars bridge the gap between spring and autumn onions and can be sown in the summer; good cultivars are 'Buffalo', 'Express Yellow', 'Extra Early Kaizuka' and 'Senshyu'. American cultivars for cool temperate areas include 'Sweet Spanish' and 'Yellow Globe Hybrid'. For the south and west of the U.S., 'Walla Walla Sweet' and 'Granex Yellow Hybrid' are suitable.

Cultivation. Sow spring types any time from the end of winter to early spring, in light, well drained soil in a very sunny position in rows 1 ft (30 cm) apart. Thin subsequently at 5 in (12 cm) apart within the row. New spring onions are sown in early to mid spring placed in rows spread 8 in (20 cm) apart. They should be thinned to $2\frac{1}{4}$ in (6 cm) within the row. Autumn types are sown as seeds from late summer to early autumn. The young plants are the size of a pencil and are sown every 5 in (12 cm) in rows 10 in (25 cm) apart. In USA, grow long-day types in Northern areas (Yellow Globe Hybrid) or short day types in Southern areas (Graney Yellow Hybrid). Where available onion sets may be bought to save time. These are planted out in late spring.

Weed by hand. Watering is unnecessary except during a prolonged dry spell. The onion cannot tolerate fresh manure and excessive humidity. Grow them as a root vegetable but without fertilizer. Japanese cultivars should be sown in mid summer and harvested a year later; they do not store well. The onion fly, thrips and stem and bulb eelworm all feed on it. There are numerous diseases to which they are susceptible including blackrust, bulb or neck rot and finally rust. Too early sowing into cold, loose soil can cause bolting.

The harvest will yield 3–5 lb (1.5–2.25 kg) per yard (metre) for white onions and 3–10 lb (1.5–4.5 kg) per yard (metre) coloured onions. Gather new onions in early to mid summer to eat fresh, and onions sown in spring, in early autumn. Those sown in autumn will be gathered in mid spring to early summer.

Leave onions gathered in early summer to early autumn to dry in the sun before putting them in boxes in a dry, well-ventilated place.

Uses. New onions should be eaten fresh; onions sown in spring or autumn can be stored.

Allium christophii

Leek (zone 5)

Allium ampeloprasum var. *porrum*, leek is a native of France and Southern Europe. Its stem measures $2\frac{3}{4}$–8 in (7–20 cm) depending on the cultivar. This hardy plant is a biennial cultivated as an annual. Early leeks are lifted in the autumn and early winter and include the cultivars 'Early Market' and 'Grennervilliers-Splendid'. Mid-season forms are harvested from mid winter to early spring and the following are recommended: 'King Richard', 'Argenta', 'Snowstar' and 'Musselburgh'. Late cultivars are lifted in early to late spring and include 'Winter Crop', 'Giant Winter-Catalina' and 'Giant Winter-Royal Favourite'.

Cultivation. Propagate by seed. In spring sow seeds in a warm, shaded spot in rows 6 in (15 cm) apart for early leeks. Sow other cultivars in open ground in rows 6 in (15 cm) apart. Transplant when the plants are 8 in (20 cm) high into deep, friable soil free from fresh manure. Make holes with a dibber (dibble), 9 in (23 cm) apart and 6 in (15 cm) deep. Drop the seedling into the hole then water thoroughly. Hoe regularly between the rows and water copiously in summer. In autumn, gradually earth up the soil around the stems, to blanch them. Wait four or five years before replanting in the same place.

Spanish garlic (zone 6)
Allium scorodoprasum, Spanish garlic or Spanish shallot, native of the Caucasus and Middle East measures 16–32 in (40–80 cm) in height. This hardy plant differs from the garlic *A. sativum* by its flat leaves and its umbels of flowers which have numerous reddish bulbils.
Uses and cultivation. See **Garlic**.

Ornamental Allium
Among the 700 species of allium, a number are quite decorative. The sometimes fragrant flowers can be yellow, pink, blue, purple or white according to the species. The leaves of many species smell of onions if handled or crushed. The size of the plants varies from 4 in–4 ft (10 cm–1.5 m).
A. aflatunense (zone 7), from China, has strong stems 30–48 in (75–120 cm) high, which carry spherical umbels of pinkish-purple flowers in late spring or early summer.
A. christophii (*A. albopilosum*) – zone 9 – is 18–36 in (45–90 cm) high and comes from Central Asia. The umbels are usually 8 in (20 cm) across, but can reach 1 ft (30 cm) in diameter, with up to 80 very fine, silvery purple flowers borne on long peduncles in early summer. They are excellent in dried flower arrangements.
A. giganteum (zone 7), from the Himalayas grows up to 5 ft (1.5 m) tall, with huge, tightly packed globes of star-shaped rosy pink flowers.
A. karataviense (zone 7), coming from Central Asia, grows 8 in–1 ft (20–30 cm) high. The leaves are broad, spreading and long-lasting. The spherical umbels of dull purplish pink flowers appear in early summer.
A. moly (zone 6), is a native of southern Europe and grows 1 ft (30 cm) high. The bright-yellow flowers are large and open in early summer. It is an excellent plant for rock gardens and borders, but can be invasive.
A. neapolitanum (zone 7), originates from the shores of the Mediterranean, and has white flowers with a pleasant scent, carried on 12–20 in (30–50 cm) stalks in late spring to early summer. 'Grandiflorum' is a form often grown.

Larger ornamental species are grown in clumps in beds or borders, expecially between shrubs. Annuals can be used to hide the foliage which starts to wither and become unsightly in early summer. Smaller species are excellent in rock gardens and as edging.
Cultivation. Plant in the autumn in good, well drained soil in full sun. Larger varieties may need staking. Leave undisturbed for several years, until huge, dense clumps form. The clumps can be lifted and divided at the end of the summer.

Alnus
Alder, *Betulaceae*

A genus of 35 fast growing, hardy deciduous trees, most from the Northern Hemisphere. The flowers are borne on separate male and female catkins in late winter to early spring. The fruits are small, round or ovoid cones, strikingly beautiful on the leafless winter branches.
A. cordata (zone 6), Italian alder, has glossy, heart-shaped leaves and an elegant pyramidal silhouette up to 50 ft (15 m) high and 20 ft (6 m) across. It is more tolerant of chalk and dry soil than other species.
A. glutinosa (zone 5), common alder grows up to 90 ft (27 m) high. This tree, a native of Europe, western Asia and North Africa, grows rapidly when young and has small oval leaves. It is tolerant of waterlogged soil. There are several cultivars, including 'Aurea', with light-yellow leaves; 'Imperialis', with finely dissected leaves; and 'Laciniata', with a more erect habit than the species and leaves which are coarsely divided. Alders are used as hedges or specimen trees, especially near water, and they need plenty of light.
Cultivation. Plant bare-rooted specimens in autumn or winter and container-grown plants at any time of year. The alder is as happy on lowland as in the mountains and will grow in all kinds of moist soil, though shallow chalk is unsuitable. Pruning is of limited use but is well tolerated by the tree. Vigorous offshoots will grow from the stump.

Propagation is from seeds in winter or by leafless cuttings in the open ground. The leaves may be attacked by certain fungi but without serious effects.

Aloe

Liliaceae

This genus is represented by about 360 species, mostly from South Africa and often wrongly confused with agaves, which belong to the *Agavaceae* family. Aloes are stemless or woody plants, with leaves arranged in fleshy or leathery rosettes. Erect clusters of flowers vary from cream, yellow, coral and vermilion to dark red.

A. arborescens (zone 9–10), stag's antler, or candelabra Aloe, with stems up to 15 ft (4.5 m) high, has 31 in (80 cm) racemes of red-coral flowers which appear from early winter to early spring. There are numerous hybrids.

A. ciliaris (zone 9–10), climbing aloe, often reaches 17 ft (5 m) in height and has green leaves with white toothed edges and bright red flowers. Flowering is almost continuous in winter and creates a cascade of colour in a rockery or on trellis against a wall.

A. striatula (zone 9–10), reaches approximately 6 ft 6 in (2 m) has mid-green leaves striped with pale green. Tightly bunched, light yellow flowers appear from mid winter to early summer.

Cultivation. Plant in sunny, well drained soil in Mediterranean areas and as greenhouse pot plants in cooler areas. As they create a tropical atmosphere, aloes are superb in rock gardens and stone walls. Put fast-growing varieties on their own.

In temperate climates, overwinter in a cool greenhouse, water occasionally and frequently in summer.

Propagate by division of clumps from offsets, or by hormone treated cuttings, well dried before being placed in a sandy soil. Propagation be seed is not recommended owing to the strong tendency to hybridisation.

Alonsoa

Mask flower, *Scrophulariaceae*

The genus consists of six species, all originating in tropical America. They are bushy, half-hardy perennials, usually treated as annuals, with clusters of lipped or pouched flowers. They can either be grown outdoors, or indoors as summer-flowering or winter-flowering pot plants.

A. acutifolia (zone 9), from Peru, is 2–3 ft 6 in (60 cm–1 m) high, with large scarlet flowers; var. *candida* (*A. albiflora*) has white flowers. *A. warscewiczii* is erect and clump-forming measuring 3 ft 6 in (1 m) in height, and bearing scarlet and orange flowers for the whole summer.

Cultivation. In frost-free areas; plant in moist well-drained soil in a sunny position. In colder regions, put into a pot and in winter bring into the greenhouse.

Propagation is from seeds. Sow in late winter or early spring for outdoor summer flowering. Prick out and then harden off (if raised under glass), before planting out in late spring. For indoor summer-flowering pot plants sow in late winter, and for winter flowers in late summer.

Alstroemeria

Peruvian lily, *Amaryllidaceae*

Alstroemeria aurea 'Lutea'

This genus includes about 50 tuberous-rooted hardy herbaceous plants from South America. They are grown for their delicate flowers, which bloom from early summer to early autumn.

A. aurantiaca (zone 8), from Chile, grows 3 ft (90 cm) high and is the hardiest species. Its tall, straight, cylindrical stem carries orange flowers stained with pink or purple. The leaves are lanceolate and slightly glaucous. 'Lutea' has yellow flowers streaked with red. 'Ligtu Hybrids' *Alstroemeria* are commonly grown in warmer or more sheltered areas. They vary in height and produce flowers which may be yellow, orange or pink.

Alstroemerias are planted in groups in borders and make attractive cut flowers. Leave clumps undisturbed for several years.
Cultivation. Grow in fertile, well drained soil in a sheltered, partially shaded position in hot climates, and in full sun in cooler climates. Stake if necessary. In winter, protect with a thick mulch of leaves or peat.

Propagate by lifting and dividing the tubers in autumn or in early to mid spring. Seeds are stratified in pots or in a cold frame in mid to late autumn, for lifting in early spring. Plant out in mid to late spring, taking care not to damage the fragile roots.

Althaea

Hollyhock, *Malvaceae*

A genus composed of a dozen species of biennial or perennial plants from Europe and N. Asia.
A. rosea (zone 6), the hollyhock, is a very hardy biennial or perennial often grown as a half-hardy annual. It can grow to over 6 ft 6 in (2 m) in height and carries attractive, funnel-shaped flowers all along the stems. The flowers can be single, semi-double or double, and range in colours from white, pink and yellow to very dark red. Some are laced or ruffed.

'Chater's Double' has double flowers and the colours are sold either separately or in mixtures. Hollyhocks can be grown in borders.
Cultivation. To grow as biennials, sow in open ground from early summer to early autumn in a sheltered sunny spot. Plant out in autumn or spring 16 in (40 cm) apart. Water well in hot weather. Stake taller varieties and those growing in exposed positions.

Double-flowered hollyhock

To keep plants a second year, cut off the flower stems at the end of the flowering season. After that, the plants become less vigorous and should be replaced with those grown from seed. To grow as annuals, sow seed in late winter. Keep at a temperature of 55°F (13°C). Prick out into pots and harden off (if raised under glass) for planting out in late spring. Red spider mite or caterpillars can affect the leaves, and rust can create brown or orange pustules.

Alyssum

Cruciferae

This genus is comprised of more than 100 species of hardy annuals or herbaceous perennials and evergreen sub-shrubs, found wild from southern Europe to Siberia.
A. argenteum (zone 4), comes from Europe and grows 12–20 in (30–50 cm) and 10–14 in (22–55 cm) across. This dense, bushy plant has silver grey foliage and large clusters of bright-yellow flowers from early to late summer. Growing it next to *A. saxatile* assures continuous flowering for two to three months as the two species flower sequentially.
A. montanum (zone 4), mountain gold, grows up to 6 in (15 cm) high, and 12–20 in (30–50 cm) across. It is a prostrate, very hardy evergreen with grey-green foliage and fragrant, bright-yellow flowers from late spring to early summer.
A. saxatile (zone 6), rock madwort, gold dust, measures 10–12 in (25–45 cm) in height and 20–28 in (50–70 cm) across. This evergreen sub-shrub is covered in golden flowers from mid-spring to early summer. 'Citrinum' is one of the most beautiful cultivars, with lemon-yellow flowers. 'Compactum' is smaller than the species, and 'Flore Pleno' has golden-yellow double flowers.

The species described are suitable for rock gardens, low walls, pavements, borders, etc.
Cultivation. *Alyssum* species thrive in full sunlight in all well drained soils, including calcareous soils. Cut back perennial species ruthlessly after flowering, to keep them compact, which helps them tolerate winter dampness. Dead head annual alyssums by clipping them lightly with shears.

Propagate by taking cuttings of 2–2¾ in (5–7 cm) after flowering. Place in a cold frame, in a mixture of equal parts of peat and coarse sand. Alternatively, sow under glass in early spring with gentle heat, planting out in late spring, or sow outdoors in late spring.

Amaranthus

Amaranthaceae

A genus of about 50 half-hardy annuals, some of which are grown for their attractive flower heads, others for their foliage.
A. caudatus (zone 6), love-lies-bleeding, from the tropics, grows 3 ft 6 in (1 m) high, but there are many dwarf forms available. Long, red, hanging flower spikes appear from mid summer to mid autumn. The cultivar 'Viridis' has green flowers.
A. hypochondriacus (zone 6), Prince's feather, grows 4–5 ft (1.2–1.5 m) high. It is similar to *A. caudatus*, but has upright not hanging, spikes.
A. tricolor (zone 5), is also a tropical plant and grows 1 ft 8 in–3 ft 6 in (50 cm–1 m) high. Its green foliage is flecked with yellow, bronze and brilliant red and the flowers are dark red and often striped. There are many good cultivars, including 'Joseph's Coat', 'Flaming Fountains', and 'Illumination'.
A. salicifolius (zone 6), has thin, drooping bronze green leaves marked with orange.

Amaranthus caudatus

Having decorative foliage and flowers they are attractive in flower beds and used for both fresh or dried floral decoration, grown as half-hardy annuals.
Cultivation. Sow under some form of shelter, in colder regions under glass with some heat, in mid spring transplant, harden off progressively then plant outdoors in late spring to early summer. Space them at a distance of 16 in (40 cm) in deep moist soil. Greenfly can be a problem on the leaves.
Cultivation. Amaranthus is suited to all types or soil, preferably in a sunny position. In mid spring sow in open ground in spaced rows of 10 in (25 cm). Thin out at 6 in (15 cm) and water when dry. Gather the leaves and then the small black seeds when required.
Uses. The leaves can be eaten raw in salads or cooked like spinach. They have great nutritional value. The seeds can be made into a flour which is added to the wheat flour for making crêpes or porridge.

Amaryllis

Belladonna lily, *Amaryllidaceae*

This genus comprises a single bulbous species originating from South Africa.
A. belladonna (zone 8–9), belladonna lily, is moderately hardy, and produces 6–12 fragrant funnel-shaped, pink flowers on a 20–42 in (50 cm–1 m) stem in autumn. There are white and deep pink cultivars. Long strap-shaped leaves appear after flowering in late winter or early spring.
Cultivation. Plant in light, well drained soil in full sun, in a sheltered position in late spring or early summer. In a Northern European climate, plant the bulb 6–8 in (15–20 cm) deep, against a sunny wall, or the wall of a greenhouse.

Propagate by dividing clumps of lilies in summer.

Amelanchier

Snowy mespilus, June berry, *Rosaceae*

A genus of 35 shrubs or small trees from Europe, Asia and North America, which rarely reach more than 30 ft (9 m) in height, and are usually half that. The small, ovate leaves are deciduous, and black edible berries follow the white flowers carried in spring.

A. lamarckii (zone 5), shadbush, from North America is the most common and often grown incorrectly as *A. canadensis* or *A. laevis*. It prefers a lime-free rich soil and can grow near the sea. A prolific flowerer, this species is also valued for its foliage which turns red, yellow and orange in autumn.

A. rotundifolia (*A. ovalis, A. vulgaris*) – zone 6 – with oval leaves is an attractive species from Southern Europe, often growing in poor soil. It forms a shrub up to 10 ft (3 m) high and large, white flowers with long thin petals appear in early summer. It can be used as hedging or as a specimen shrub.

Cultivation. Plant in autumn or spring. They are all very hardy, and enjoy a sunny position and rich loamy soil.

Propagate from seed, when fresh, or by layers or division. They can be attacked by fireblight and caterpillars.

Amsonia

Apocynaceae

A genus comprising about 20 hardy herbaceous perennials from North America and Japan which are all poisonous. They can reach 3 ft 6 in (1 m) in height with alternate, willow-like leaves and clear, light-blue funnel-shaped flowers from early to mid summer.

A. tabernaemontana (zone 6), has arching stems 3 ft (90 cm) high and clusters of starry, blue-grey flowers.

Cultivation. *Amsonia* species are simple to grow and long lived in heavy damp soil in sun or partial shade.

Propagation is by dividing clumps in early spring or by cuttings in summer.

Anacyclus

Mount Atlas daisy, *Compositae*

This genus of nine species includes attractive rock garden plants.

A. depressus (zone 7–8), from Morocco, measures 4 in (10 cm) high and 8 in (20 cm) across. It forms a neat mat of deeply dissected leaves with white, daisy-like flowers, purplish underneath and carried on short stems, from late spring to early summer.

Cultivation. Not easy, this plant needs a stony calcareous soil in full sun. Protect from winter rains with a pane of glass placed horizontally above the plant, held on wire supports.

Propagate from seed in early autumn.

Ananas

Pineapple, *Bromeliaceae*

This genus of eight herbaceous perennials from tropical America includes *A. comosus* (zone 10), the well known fruit intensively cultivated in tropical areas. At the centre of its rosette of green spiny leaves, more than 3 ft 6 in (1 m) in length, grows a cone-like inflorescence of purple flowers followed by an edible fruit. It is a fast-growing terrestrial plant, but difficult to grow indoors or in the greenhouse as a fruiting crop. In full sunlight the leaves turn pink. *A. comosus* 'Variegatus' has creamy-yellow margined leaves and is a valuable and attractive ornamental plant.

Cultivation. Most bromeliads need a dry environment with warm, still air. In temperate climates grow indoors. Plant in late spring or early summer in a mixture of loam, peat and sand. Water frequently, but leave compost to dry out between waterings. Pot on every year.

Propagate by suckers, if produced. Cut them from the mother rosette, allow to dry for a day or two, then place on sand with strong bottom heat. The rosette of leaves at the top of a pineapple can be rooted. Slice the top off a fresh, ripe fruit, then dry the rosette for several days before planting in a rich, well-drained potting compost, which should be watered from time to time.

Androsace

Rock jessamine, *Primulaceae*

A genus comprising about 100 dwarf species, those from Asia generally being easier to grow than those from Europe.

A. carnea (zone 4), from Europe is a small perennial which puts out rosettes of tiny serrated, awl-shaped evergreen leaves to a height of 2 in (5 cm). Pink flowers are grouped clusters in late spring to early summer.

A. sarmentosa (zone 4), is from the Himalayas. This plant with runners has rosettes of grey hairy leaves measuring $2\frac{3}{4}$–4 in (7–10 cm) in diameter. Pink flowers appear in late spring to early autumn on 4 in (10 cm) long stems.

Cultivation. These plants thrive best in moraine conditions with exposure to winter snow. Plant in a mixture made up of equal parts leaf mould, gravel, neutral soil and coarse bulk of sand on a scree slope. The soil must be moist in spring but never waterlogged in winter.

Propagate by seed in mid to late summer. Seeds need exposure to freezing conditions and can take a year or more to germinate. You can also remove rosettes in early summer and root them in a cold frame.

Anemone

Windflower, *Ranunculaceae*

A genus represented by about 150 species of hardy herbaceous perennials mostly from Europe, Asia and North America.

A. × *hybrida* (zone 6), Japanese Anemone, grows 2–3½ ft (60 cm–1 m) high, with a spread of 1 ft–20 in (30–50 cm). It has large lobed, dark-green leaves and saucer-shaped flowers 2–3¼ in (5–8 cm) in diameter in shades of pink, red and white with a central mass of yellow stamens. They flower from late summer to mid autumn; there are single, semi-double and double forms.

Cultivation. Plant between mid autumn and early spring, 12–16 in (30–40 cm) apart, in full sun or partial shade and in moist, well drained or even dry soil. The fleshy roots are delicate and take several years to become established. After flowering, cut the stems down to the base.

Propagate by division of established clumps in autumn or spring, from root cuttings in winter, or from seed.

Anemone × hybrida

A. apennina (zone 7), from Italy grows 6 in (15 cm) high. It has light blue flowers 1–2 in (3–5 cm) across, which appear in mid to late spring. This rhizomatous plant can be grown in borders or rock garden, and is best in partial shade.

A. biflora (zone 6), from Central Asia, grows 4–6 in (10–15 cm) high. Its bright red flowers, 1 in (3 cm) across, open in early to late spring. This tuberous species requires full sunshine and may be grown in a pot which can be kept completely dry in summer.

A. blanda (zone 6), from Greece, grows 4–6 in (10–15 cm) high. The star-shaped flowers are blue, white, pink or lavender, 1–1½ in (3–5 cm) across, and open in late winter or early spring. Grow in partial shade, in a warm spot and well drained soil.

A. coronaria (zone 7), florist's anemone, comes from the shores of the Eastern Mediterranean and grows 4–16 in (10–40 cm) high. The flowers, 2–3¼ in (5–8 cm) in diameter, are red, blue, violet, crimson or yellow with black stamens. Flowering takes place in spring when planted in autumn, or in summer if planted in spring. St Brigid and de Caen are popular.

A. nemorosa (zone 6), wood anemone, is found throughout Europe and grows to a height of 6–8 in (15–20 cm). The flowers, 1 in (2.5 cm) across, are white, light pink or lavender and appear in early spring. 'Robinsoniana' is a large flowered cultivar. Prefers rich soil in light open woodland and is excellent for naturalizing.

Cultivation. Plant rhizomatous species in damp soil and tuberous species in well-drained soil. Plant the tubers with the buds upwards. Propagate by division.

Anethum

Dill, *Umbelliferae*

Of the two species of this genus, dill is an annual plant, coming originally from southern Europe.

A. graveolens (zone 7) reaches 2–2½ ft (60–80 cm) in height. Small yellow flowers open in large umbels between mid spring and mid summer followed by oval seeds.

Cultivation. Dill prefers light soil in a warm position and needs to be sown in mid spring in rows 8 in (20 cm) apart. Then thin out in the row to 8 in (20 cm).

Gather leaves for culinary purposes in summer as required. Harvest mature seeds in late summer to early autumn and keep them in a jar.

Angelica
Umbelliferae

Few of this genus of 50 herbaceous species are of garden value except *A. archangelica* (zone 7), angelica, a biennial from Europe and Asia. It grows 3½–5 ft (1–1.5 m) high and produces grooved stems and deeply dissected yellowish-green sheathed leaves. Large, white, flat flower heads crown the stems in mid summer.
Cultivation. Angelica prefers fresh, rich, deep soil, in sun or light shade, and can tolerate a fairly exposed position. Sow seeds as soon as ripe in late summer to early autumn in rows 3 ft 6 in (1 m) apart, or purchased seeds in spring. Thin to 2 ft (60 cm). Alternatively, sow seeds where they are to grow, spaced 3 ft 6 in (1 m) apart, in groups of three seeds. When the seedlings appear, thin out to leave the strongest seedling at each station. Water copiously during a dry spell. Gather stems, leaves and roots from late spring to early summer a year after sowing. If you cut back the stems before they flower, the plant behaves like a perennial and grows for another year or two.
Uses. Stems and petioles are used in confectionery, baking and for flavouring raw salad, soups and sauces. In an infusion, the fresh leaves and dried roots are a tonic.

Antennaria
Compositae

This genus consists of about 45 species of hardy perennials with evergreen foliage.
A. dioica (zone 5–4) cat's ear, comes from Europe and North America. It is extremely hardy and grows 4 in–1 ft (10–30 cm) high, 16–20 in (40–50 cm) across. From rosettes of white cottony leaves, clusters of decorative white or pink, fluffy flowers opening in late spring to early summer. Suited to a rockery, it can also be used for overplanting spring-flowering bulbs and in cracks between paving stones.
Cultivation. Can be easily grown in light but very well drained soil in full sun.

The mat-forming stems root as they cover the ground, and these can be detached and grown on separately. Alternatively, propagate by splitting clumps in spring or after flowering in late summer, or sow seeds in spring and place in a cold frame.

Anthemis
Compositae

This genus consists of about 100 annual, biennial and perennial species native to Europe; few are cultivated.
A. tinctoria (zone 5), ox-eye chamomile, is a hardy herbaceous perennial, 8–30 in (20–75 cm) high, with mid-green deeply dissected leaves, woolly white underneath. In summer it is covered with a profusion of yellow daisy-like flowers. It is useful for rock gardens, flower beds or as cut flowers. Several cultivars are grown, including 'Kelway Yellow', with yellow flowers; 'Grallah Gold', with golden-yellow flowers; and 'Wargrave', with pale cream-yellow blooms.
Cultivation. The ox-eye chamomile requires a sunny position and well drained soil.

Plant in autumn or spring 12–16 in (30–40 cm) apart, and stake larger-growing varieties. Cut off faded flowers to stimulate new growth, and cut back to base of stems at the end of autumn.

To propagate, divide clumps in autumn or spring, or take cuttings in mid to late spring.

Anthriscus
Umbelliferae

Of 12 species in this genus, only one is usually cultivated.
A. cerefolium (zone 7), chervil, is a hardy biennial usually grown as an annual, from the Mediterranean and Middle East. It grows 12–20 in (20–50 cm) high and has deeply dissected parsley-like foliage. The smooth-leaved variety has a very strong scent, but curly chervil has a more delicate, aniseed flavour.
Cultivation. Chervil does well in any soil. Sow successfully in a sunny aspect at random or in rows 8 in (20 cm) apart from early spring to early autumn. From late spring to late summer sow in partial shade to prevent the plants going to seed. Cover seeds with ¼ in (6 mm) of compost. Thin out to 12 in (30 cm) apart. For winter gathering, sow in mid autumn under a heated frame. Water in dry weather; as soon as the flower stems appear, pinch them out.

Start to gather the leaves 6 to 8 weeks after sowing, cutting loose to the root. It is liable to attacks of mildew or rust.

Uses. Chervil enhances salads and soups but its aroma is lost in cooking. It can also be used as an infusion (tea).

Anthyllis

Leguminosae

Twenty species of herbaceous perennials or small shrubs spread throughout Europe, North Africa and Asia make up this genus.

A. montana (zone 6), from Europe and Algeria, is a prostrate deciduous sub-shrub, 6–12 in (15–30 cm) high, with a spread of 12 in (30 cm). The white, hairy, dissected leaves are made up of 8 to 15 pairs of long leaflets. Deep-pink, globe-shaped flower heads with pea-shaped flowers appear from early summer to early autumn.

A. vulneraria (zone 5), ladies fingers, from Europe and North Africa, is a herbaceous plant, 6–9 in (15–23 cm) high, and 16 in (40 cm) across. It has red, pink or white flowers with an inflated calyx.

These species are best in sunny rockeries or walls, but larger shrubby species can be grown in a mixed border.

Cultivation. Anthyllis grows in the wild in dry grassy areas. They require a poor, gravelly soil in full sun.

Propagate by sowing fresh seeds in a tray in early to mid autumn. Germination takes place the following spring. Herbaceous species can be lifted and divided in autumn or spring, and shrubby types can be propagated from cuttings.

Antirrhinum

Scrophulariaceae

The genus including about 40 annual or perennial species and some sub-shrubs from Europe and North America.

A. majus (zone 5–6), common snapdragon, is perennial, ranging from dwarf cultivars 4 in (10 cm) high, to plants 5 ft (1.5 m) or more high. Usually grown as a half-hardy annual, this species has spikes of yellow, white, pink or red pouch-shaped flowers from mid summer until the first frosts, whose sweet scent attracts bees. Cultivars include 'Rocket', 2–3½ ft (60 cm–1 m) high, in single colours; 'Madame Butterfly', up to 3 ft 6 in (1 m) high, with double flowers. Floral Carpet is a dwarf strain, in mixed colours. The snapdragon is grown in borders or in pots. Larger cultivars make good cut flowers and dwarf cultivars go well in rockeries and are excellent for bedding.

Cultivation. Sow in a greenhouse, in mid to late winter, prick out in early spring, and pinch out the young plants to encourage branching. Plant in rich, moist but well drained soil in a sunny open position in early summer, 1 ft (30 cm) apart; stake larger varieties. Water well and cut faded flowers to prolong flowering period. Damping off can kill the young plant; downy and powdery mildew and rust can disfigure the leaves.

Apios

Leguminosae

A genus of 10 species occasionally cultivated.

A. americana (A. tuberosa) (zone 9–10) groundnut or potato bean, is a perennial native to North America. It has mealy, sweet tubers, 6 in (15 cm) in diameter, and twining stems that reach an annual height of 6½ in–13 ft (2–4 m). These carry unusual, brown-purple fragrant flowers. Grow against a warm sunny wall or up a trellis.

Cultivation. Plant tubers 6 in (15 cm) deep and 12–16 in (30–40 cm) apart in well-prepared ground. Keep the soil cool in dry weather and mulch with straw if required. After two years gather the tubers in autumn and let them dry out before storing in a well ventilated place. Propagate by dividing tubers.

Uses. The tuber can be eaten cooked like a potato and the seeds, fresh and dried, can be prepared like beans.

Apium

Umbelliferae

Among the 20 temperate-climate species of this genus is *A. graveolens* (zone 6–7), celery, a native to Mediterranean coastal regions. This biennial measures 12–20 in (30–50 cm) high. Grown as an annual, it forms leaves with pulpy, long ribbed edible petioles. There are white, pink or red cultivars, the white being the earliest to mature and least hardy, the red maturing last and being the hardiest, and the pink, mid-way between the two.

The hardier trench cultivars include 'Giant Pink', 'Giant Red' and 'Fordhook'; frost-tender, self-blanching cultivars include 'Golden Self Blanchers', 'American Green' and 'Ivory Tower'.

Cultivation. Celery can follow on from root vegetables. It is considered by some beneficial to plant next to cauliflower, onions, leeks and tomatoes. Plant in a rich, deep and moisture-retentive soil in an open position in full sun, in early to mid summer 10 in (25 cm) apart in each direction. In the winter before planting, enrich the soil with plenty of manure or compost. For the white, pink or red cultivars dig a trench 15 in (38 cm) deep 15 in (38 cm) wide. Half refill the trench with a mixture of soil and compost. The remainder of the soil is used for earthing up later on. The self-blanching type are not planted in trenches, but in blocks 9 in (23 cm) apart in all directions. Water regularly in dry hot weather, avoiding soaking the leaves. Earth up (i.e. mound the soil) lightly when the plants are 14 in (35 cm) high. Earth up again twice at 2–3 week intervals. The final earthing up should be level with the base of the leaves, 3 weeks before picking. When earthing up remove suckers and dead leaves and gently tie in the leaves when you start.

Propagate from seed in a nursery bed, sown in mid spring to early summer. If sowing outdoors in cool climates, warm the soil first with cloches. Seeds can also be sown in a greenhouse with heat in early spring. Prick out into boxes. Place these in a cool frame to harden off then plant out in the open 10 in (25 cm) apart. Celery leaf spot and heart rot are the two main diseases. The main pests are celery beetle, celery fly and celery leaf miners. Slugs and snails also enjoy this vegetable.

Aponogeton

Water hawthorn, *Aponogetonaceae*

An exclusively aquatic sub-tropical or tropical genus including more than 40 species from Africa, Australia and India.

A. distachyus (zone 9), Cape pondweed or water hawthorn, is a rhizomatous plant which lives submerged in 6–20 in (15–50 cm) of water. The leaves are ovate, sometimes with brown markings, and float on the water like water lily leaves. At the top of the fleshy stem is a two-forked inflorescence which opens above water level. The waxy flowers are fragrant and their pure-white colour contrasts strikingly with the black

Aponogeton distachyus

stamens. Flowering begins in early summer and ends with the first frost.

Cultivation. The pondweed does not like limy soil or water. Plant in a rich, peaty mixture in spring. Although flowering is more prolific in full sunlight, it prefers semi-shade. Seeds are plentiful and germinate spontaneously on the surface. The young plants should be protected from frost for the first winter and planted in place the following spring. Alternatively, divide and replant the tuberous root.

Aquilegia

Columbine, *Ranunculaceae*

This genus contains about 70 species of herbaceous perennials from North America, Asia and Europe.

A. vulgaris (zone 4–5), columbine or granny's bonnet, is very hardy and grows $1\frac{1}{2}$–$2\frac{1}{2}$ ft (45–75 cm) high, with a 12–20 in (30–50 cm) spread. It has fern-like, graceful foliage, deeply dissected and glaucous green. The petals are characterized by their long spurs, often a different colour to the sepals. There are a number of large-flowered hybrids in cream, yellow, pink, red or blue. Columbines are excellent for cutting; flowering is in late spring and the plant is generally used in mixed planting. Smaller species are useful in rock gardens.

Cultivation. This plant favours moist but well drained soil, enriched with compost or leaf mould, and full sun or light shade. Plant at 12 in (30 cm) intervals in autumn. Cut back flower stems to their base in autumn, and dead head alpine species.

Aquilegia vulgaris

Propagate by division of clumps between mid autumn and early spring or by sowing seeds thinly in a shady place or in pans in a cold frame. Self-seeding often occurs, and the best plants can be retained. The plants can be attacked by aphids and leaf miners.

Arabis

Rock cress, *Cruciferae*

This genus consists of around 100 hardy annuals and evergreen perennial plants, originating in the mountains of the Northern Hemisphere. Only a few are cultivated.

A. caucasica (A. albida) (zone 4–5), common white cress, comes from south-east Europe and Caucasus. It grows 6–12 in (15–30 cm) high and 16–24 in (40–60 cm) in spread. One of the most widely found of rock cresses, it is often confused with *A. alpina*. In early to mid spring delicately scented white flowers appear over its mounds of decorative grey foliage. Cut back ruthlessly after flowering.

A. ferdinandi-coburgi 'Variegata' (zone 4–5) grows 4 in (10 cm) high, with a spread of 12–20 in (30–40 cm). Its flowers are white and appear in early to mid-spring, and its dark-green foliage has a distinctive white edge.

Cultivars include 'Flore-Pleno', with white double flowers which come later and last longer than those of the species, continuing for two months; and 'Rosea', which has pale-pink flowers.

All these perennials are at home in a rock garden, on a wall, or in the front of a herbaceous border. *A. caucasica* can be invasive, but its cultivars are more restrained. Common white cress is often grown with alyssum and aubrieta, for a spectacular spring show.

Cultivation. Plant in autumn or spring in light, well drained soil in partial shade.

Propagate by stem cuttings taken in spring after flowering and put in a cold frame, or by division of clumps in early autumn.

Aralia

Araliaceae

This genus is represented by about 35 trees, shrubs and herbaceous perennials from North America, Malaysia and Australia. The shrubs, which are often unjustly overlooked, have attractive compound, dissected leaves and white flowers in panicles. Some species are spiny.

A. elata (zone 7), Japanese angelica tree, usually forms a large, suckering, spiny-stemmed shrub, up to 10 ft (3 m) or more. Its large, deciduous leaves, to 4 ft (1.2 m) long, are fringed with white in the cultivar 'Variegata' ('Albomarginata'), and with yellow in 'Aureo-variegata'.

A. spinosa 'Hercules Club' (zone 8) from southeastern USA, has large leaves on a spiny stem and large, cream clusters of flowers in late summer. It is similar to *A. elata* but less hardy.

Cultivation. Plant in partial shade in ordinary, well drained soil. *A. elata* likes dry rocky soil and a fairly sheltered position for preference. Propagate from seed, suckers or root cuttings in spring.

Araucaria

Araucariaceae

This genus comprises 18 large evergreen conifers from the Southern Hemisphere, with branches arranged in tiered whorls on a straight trunk. The shape of the leaves varies from broad to needle-like, according to species. Fruiting is not common in cultivation but male and female cones are generally borne on different trees.

A. araucana (A. imbricata) (zone 6), monkey puzzle or Chile pine, from S. America, measures 80 ft (24 m) or more in height. The dark-green leaves are rigid, leathery and spine tipped. Globular cones 4–6 in (10–15 cm) in diameter are shed on maturity. Hardy in Northern Temperate climates, the monkey puzzle tolerates exposure to wind and makes an excellent specimen tree on a lawn. It grows best in a moist climate rather than hot, dry conditions.
A. bidwillii (zone 9–10), bungy bungy pine has broad leathery leaves. On the same branch there may be long or short needles. This species from Queensland is not very hardy.
A. heterophylla (A. excelsa) (zone 9–10), Norfolk Island pine, is distinguished by its very fine bright green, awl-shaped leaves on the horizontally tiered branches. The juvenile form is grown as an indoor plant while small.
Cultivation. Plant outdoor monkey puzzles in spring using small plants under 12 in (30 cm) high. Grow greenhouse species in pots of potting compost. In winter keep at a temperature of 41°F (5°C) – the compost (soil) should be just moist. In spring and summer water well. Pot on annually. Propagate by seed or cuttings placed in shade.

Arbutus
Ericaceae

This genus consists of 20 evergreen trees and large shrubs from Europe and N. America.
A. unedo (zone 9), strawberry tree, is a large shrub or small tree 12–26 ft (4–8 m) high, with a 10 ft (3 m) spread. Its glossy, toothed dark-green evergreen foliage; pink or white, bell-shaped flowers in summer and red-orange fruits are equally decorative. The fruits are edible but insipid. It is moderately hardy and prefers a warm, sunny, sheltered spot, especially when young. It makes a good specimen plant, and is especially good in maritime conditions in which it generally thrives.
Cultivation. *Arbutus* species like well drained, lime-free soil, although *A. unedo* tolerates lime. Use pot-grown plants, since arbutus transplants badly if open grown. Plant in autumn or spring in a sunny, sheltered spot. Protect its roots in winter in the cooler regions, with straw. Pruning is not usually necessary.

To propagate, take semi-hardwood cuttings with a heel in mid to late summer.

Arctostaphylos
Ericaceae

A genus represented by 50 species of small trees and shrubs with deciduous or evergreen foliage. The clusters of small, white or pink flowers are followed by decorative berries.
A. alpina (zone 2), black bearberry, comes from polar regions and flowers in late spring and early summer. The fruits are dark purple.
A. uva-ursi (zone 1–2), bearberry, also comes from polar regions. It has a creeping habit and grows 8–12 in (20–30 cm). Pink flowers appear from mid-spring to mid summer, followed by bright-red berries. Its stems are self-rooting.
Cultivation. The smaller species are excellent rock garden plants. All prefer conditions similar to those for rhododendrons: cool, acid, and moist but well drained soil. However, they prefer full sun to shade.

Propagate by layering in early spring or seed in early to mid autumn.

Arctotis
African daisy, *Compositae*

Arctotis × hybrida

A genus consisting of around 60 half-hardy annual and herbaceous perennial plants from Africa.

A. × *hybrida* (zone 6) is a half-hardy perennial, grown as an annual. It has solitary flower heads carried on stems 1–2 ft (30–60 cm) high. The flowers range from white, cream, pink, apricot, orange and yellow to red; many have zonal markings and central discs. In bad weather and in the afternoon the flowers close up.

This plant is ideal in borders and for flower arrangements. It can also be grown in pots.

Cultivation. Grow in an open soil in a sunny site. When the plants are 5 in (10 cm) tall, pinch out growing tip to encourage bushy growth. Support tall plants and dead-head. To propagate, sow seed in early spring at a temperature of 64°F (18°C). Prick out, and if necessary harden off, before planting out in mid to late spring. Alternatively, take cuttings at any time, and insert in a very sandy compost. Damping off can be a problem but sandy compost and good aeration helps prevent this disease.

Ardisia

Myrsinaceae

Around 42 species make up this genus from tropical or subtropical regions. Shrubs or trees with evergreen foliage, they have white, red or dark mauve flowers in panicles, according to the species, followed by red or purplish fruits.

A. crispa, coral berry, (zone 10+), from the East Indies, grows 3½–4 ft (1–1.2 m) high. The foliage is dark, shiny green and the flowers are red or pink and red. Fruits remain on the tree for some time.

A. macrocarpa (zone 10+) from Nepal reaches 5–6½ ft (1.5–2 m) in height. It has pink waxy flowers and bright red fruits.

Cultivation. Plant in peat-based compost and grow in a heated greenhouse, or as a house plant. Shade from direct sunlight.

Propagate from seed in a mixture of equal part loam and peat with a little sand added to it, use bottom heat and keep moist.

Arenaria

Sandwort, *Caryophyllaceae*

A genus consisting of 150 species of hardy and half-hardy annuals, herbaceous perennials and evergreen sub-shrubs distributed throughout the temperate world. Many are attractive rock garden plants, forming cushions of evergreen foliage, enlivened by small star-shaped flowers which are usually white.

A. balearica (zone 5), from the Balearic Islands and Corsica, grows ½ in (2 cm) high and 24 in (60 cm) across. It forms a thick mat of minute, glossy, ovate leaves in bright green; small flowers appear over the leaves in mid to late spring. It is hardy, adapts to shady places, covers the ground whatever the contour and favours cold, humid places.

A. tetraquetra (zone 4), from the Pyrenées and Spain grows 4 in (10 cm) high and 1 ft (30 cm) across. Its overlapping leaves are arranged in four lines down the stem, and it forms a grey-green carpet-like lawn. White single flowers appear in early summer.

Cultivation. Plant in light, well drained, sandy or gravelly soil in full sun for most species, though *A. balearica* prefers shade. Dead-head after flowering.

Propagate by division or by taking ½–1 in (2–3 cm) cuttings in mid spring and place in cold frame.

Argemone

Prickly poppy, *Papaveraceae*

A genus composed of 10 species of hardy and half-hardy plants.

A. mexicana (zone 5–6), Mexican poppy, from Central America, grows 2 ft (60 cm) high. This annual has spiny glaucous leaves with white marking; when cut, the stem exudes a vivid, yellow sap. The large single, scented flowers resemble orange or yellow poppies. They are followed by prickly seed capsules.

Cultivation. Treat as a hardy annual. Sow under glass in early spring or in situ in late spring, in a light, sandy dry soil. Choose a warm, sunny spot and plant 1 ft (30 cm) apart. Dead-head to encourage further flowering.

Arisaema

Araceae

A genus composed of 150 species of tuberous-rooted plants, mainly from the Himalayas, China and Japan, although one species is North American. They are hardy or half hardy and the foliage is dissected or lobed. The coloured spathe forms a hood enclosing the spadix, which bears the insignificant true flowers.

A. candidissimum (zone 7–8), grows up to 14 in (35 cm) when in flower. The white or green and pink-striped spathe surrounds the green spadix in summer, and the leaves have three leaflets.

A. griffithii (zone 7–8), from China, grows 16–24 in (40–60 cm) high. The large spathe is ribbed and mottled brown, purple and green, and the impressive foliage is made up of three leaflets.

A. sikokianum (zone 7–8), from Japan grows 18 in (45 cm) high. The spathe is white inside, and dark brown and green outside, and the ivory, club-shaped spadix forms in spring. Leaves with three to five leaflets appear later.

A. speciosum (zone 9), from the Himalayas is almost hardy and measures 20–32 in (40–70 cm) in height with a spathe striped with purple and white and a cream and purple spadix and leaves with three leaflets measuring 16 in (40 cm) in spread. This is a truly spectacular plant.

A. triphyllum (zone 4–5), Jack in the pulpit, comes from eastern North America, is very hardy and grows 1 ft (30 cm) high. The white-veined brown flowers are ribbed green and the leaves have three leaflets.

Arisaema candidissimum

Cultivation. The plants prefer a partly shaded position in rich, well-drained soil, with peat and well rotted leaf mould or compost-added. They should remain cool through the summer. Plant the tuber in autumn, 6 in (15 cm) deep in a pocket of river sand.

Where hard frosts occur, lift the tubers and overwinter buried in dry soil in a cool but frost-free spot. Replant in spring.

Propagate by removing offsets as growth is about to start, in spring. Place the rootless offsets in peat-based cutting compost, with some heat. Alternatively sow in a mixture of equal parts peat, compost and sand. Cover with a layer three times the diameter of the seed and leave for two to three years before lifting.

Arisarum

Araceae

A genus of three species of herbaceous perennials related to *Arisaema*.

A. proboscideum, (zone 7–8), mouse plant, originates in the Apennine mountains. It grows 2–3¼ in (5–8 cm) high, and 8 in (20 cm) across and is the most common species grown. The dark green leaves are arrow-shaped, and small, erect grey-white spathes with blades extended into a long tail surround a spadix which is grey at the top. Flowering occurs in late spring to early summer.

A. vulgare (zone 8), from southern Europe, grows 4–8 in (10–20 cm) high, and 1 ft (30 cm) across. Striped or spotted stems have arrow-shaped leaves. The purple spathe with a white spadix forms in late spring.

Cultivation. These plants require shade and a cool, moist soil. Protect the rhizomes in winter with a layer of leaf mould. Propagate by seed or by division in the spring.

Armeria

Thrift, *Plumbaginaceae*

The genus consists of 80 species of tufted, hardy, perennial plants, mainly from Europe.

A. maritima (zone 5–6), sea pink, grows 6–12 in (15–30 cm) high, and 12 in (30 cm) across. It forms evergreen cushions of grassy, green foliage. Rounded heads of pink, red or white flowers cover the plants in early to mid summer. It is useful for borders, beds and rock gardens.

Cultivation. Plant between early autumn and mid spring 8–12 in (20–30 cm) apart. It favours sun and well-drained, even sandy soil, and thrives in coastal conditions. Cut off faded flowers to show the foliage to best advantage.

Propagate by division of clumps in late winter or early spring; place the newly divided sections in a cutting compost and cover with a pane of glass. Alternatively, sow seed in sandy, loam-based compost and place in a cold frame.

Armoracia
Cruciferae

This genus of five species includes *A. rusticana* (*Cochlearia armoracia*) – zone 6 – horseradish, a hardy perennial native to Western Europe. It grows 3 ft 6 in (1 m) high and is cultivated for its large white-to-yellow root which has a strong, peppery flavour. Its rough-looking leaves are long and ovate, and grow in rosettes. Its small, white flowers open in summer, but it has no decorative value.

Cultivation. Horseradish thrives in fresh, rich and deeply dug soil. Sow seed in sun or partial shade in early to mid spring. Thin to 16 in (40 cm) apart. In mid to late autumn of the second year lift the roots, which keep several months in the cellar in boxes of sand. Alternatively, plant roots in late winter, setting them 12 in (30 cm) apart, with the top of the root just 2 in (5 cm) below the ground. Lift during the summer. To propagate, cut the roots into 3 in (7.5 cm) sections, place in a hole 15 in (38 cm) deep, and fill with new loam.

Uses. Grated horseradish can be used instead of mustard in raw salads, mayonnaise, and various other dishes. In England horseradish sauce is the traditional accompaniment to roast beef. The roots can also be used in infusions (teas) and poultices to ease various ailments.

Arnebia
Boraginaceae

Twenty-five species of annual or perennial plants comprise this genus.

A. pulchra (*A. echioides*) – zone 5 – prophet flower, originates from the Caucasus and grows 8–12 in (20–30 cm) high, with a 12–16 in (30–40 cm) spread. The leaves are rough and lanceolate. The flowering stems bear clusters of golden yellow flowers with one small purple blotch on each petal. These eventually fade and disappear completely. It blooms in early to mid spring, and often produces a second, smaller crop of flowers later. Arnebia is a useful perennial for the rock garden or for the border, but it may be short lived.

Cultivation. Plant in autumn or spring in moist, but well drained, neutral or acid soil. Choose a sunny position, such as a rock garden.

Propagate by lifting and dividing well established plants in spring; by taking root cuttings in autumn; or by sowing fresh seeds from autumn onwards.

Arnica
Compositae

About 30 species of herbaceous perennials from the Northern Hemisphere make up this genus and all of them have yellow, daisy-like flowers. The leaves usually form a basal rosette.

A. montana (zone 4–5), arnica, mountain tobacco, comes from the European alps and grows 8–20 in (20–50 cm) high, with a spread of 4–8 in (10–20 cm). Its erect stem bears large, vivid, golden-yellow flowers opening in late spring to early summer.

Cultivation. Plant in spring in full sun in a peaty, moist soil. Mountain tobacco is extremely hardy.

Propagate by seed in late summer to early autumn from fresh seed sown in a frame. Germination is lengthy and can sometimes take two years. Alternatively, divide the plant in spring.

Artemisia
Compositae

This very large polymorphic genus includes many shrubs and perennials with attractive aromatic foliage, and which are very hardy and useful garden plants. Most have insignificant yellow flowers which are pinched out in bud, to promote dense foliage and a compact growth habit. The plants are suitable for borders, rock gardens and alpine houses.

A. abrotanum (zone 6) old man, southernwood, lad's love, from Southern Europe, grows 4 ft (1.2 m) high and as much across. The soft-stemmed shrub is grown for its decorative silvery grey-green foliage which is feathery and aromatic.

A. lactiflora (zone 6), white mugwort from China and India, grows to 6 ft (1.8 m) high. It is a herbaceous perennial with jagged green leaves, but its main attraction is its huge plumes of creamy white, fragrant flowers, carried at the end of the summer.

A. ludoviciana (zone 6), white sage, grows 2–4 ft (60–120 cm) high, bears grey-white, narrow woolly leaves and small white flowers. Easily confused with *A. gnaphalodes.*

These species can be used in mixed beds or at the back of herbaceous borders.

Cultivation. Grow in light, well drained soil in full sun or light shade; plant in autumn or spring, 16–24 in (40–60 cm) apart, more for southernwood.

In spring, mulch with peat; cut back the stems of herbaceous perennials to the base in autumn.

Propagate by division in autumn or spring; or taking cuttings of woody species, with a heel, and rooting in sand and a frame.

Tarragon

A hardy perennial plant native to Central Asia, *A. dracunculus*, tarragon, grows 2–3 ft (60–90 cm) high. It forms a bushy plant with stems covered with small lanceolate leaves and, in summer, dull, greenish-white flowers. It has little decorative value, but the leaves have a delicious flavour.

Cultivation. Tarragon likes light, rich, fresh, well drained soil without excessive humidity, especially in winter. Place the small plants 15 in (37 cm) apart in a sheltered, sunny position in spring. Pinch out flowering stems to promote bushiness and an ongoing supply of fresh leaves. The plant has a sprawling habit of growth and the rhizomes can spread some distance. Flavour and vigour deteriorate after two to three years, so lift and replant young rhizomes or take stem cuttings in spring or summer, place in a cold frame, then plant out the following spring. Alternatively, treat as an annual, sown under glass and planted out, 12 in (30 cm) apart, in spring.

Gather the largest stems as required. At the end of the summer dry the stems out in the shade and keep the dried leaves in a jar or freeze if required.

Uses. The leaves are excellent in salads, egg, fish and chicken dishes and are used to flavour gherkins, vinegars or mustard.

Arum

Araceae

Around 20 species of tuberous-rooted plants make up this genus which are perennial and hardy.

A. italicum (zone 6), from southern Europe, measures 1 ft 6 in (45 cm) high and 1 ft (30 cm) across. The arrow-shaped leaves appear in autumn and the greenish-white spathe stained with red covers the yellow spadix at the beginning of the year. The decorative but poisonous orange-red berries follow in autumn. 'Pictum' is a cultivar with attractive leaves veined and marbled with white.

A. maculatum (zone 4–5), cuckoo pint, or lords and ladies, comes from Europe. It grows 8 in–1 ft (20–30 cm) high. The arrow-shaped, bright-green leaves usually with dark spots appear early in the year. Flowers similar to those of the species above in late spring are followed by poisonous coral red berries at the end of summer. These plants make good ground cover between shrubs and in shaded borders.

Cultivation. Plant in a cool moist soil. They survive summer drought if grown in full or partial shade. They often produce seedlings, otherwise propagate from seed at the end of autumn or by division just as new growth begins; place rootless pieces in heat to encourage root growth.

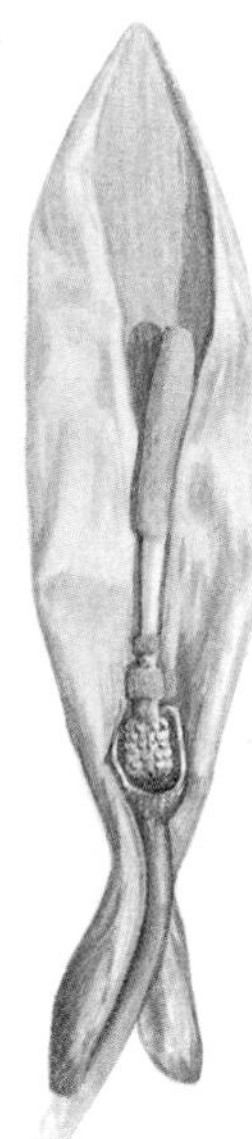

Arum italicum

Aruncus

Goat's beard, *Rosaceae*

This genus is represented by one species native to the Northern Hemisphere.

A. dioicus, (*A. sylvester*) – zone 6 – is a herbaceous perennial growing 4–6½ ft (1–2 m) high and 2–3½ ft (60 cm–1 m) across. The decorative, clear, green foliage and the long, upright plumes of small, creamy white flowers open in early to mid summer. These are followed by ornamental, but poisonous, seed heads on female plants. Grow by the sides of a pond or ornamental pool, at the back of a flower bed or in an isolated clump.

Cultivation. It likes partial shade in a moist, preferably peaty soil. Plant deeply, between autumn and early spring, 2 ft (60 cm) apart. Water well in dry weather, and cut back the stems to the base in mid autumn. Propagate by division of clumps in mid autumn, or by seed. Leaf miner larvae can seriously damage the leaves.

Arundinaria

Bamboo, *Gramineae*

With 150 species, *Arundinaria* constitutes one of the most important genera of bamboo. Originally from the temperate zones of the world, they range from moderately hardy to very hardy. Some species are re-classified as belonging to other genera, including *Sasa, Sinarundinaria, Pleioblastus* and *Pseudosasa*. From 2–30 ft (60 cm–9 m) in height, tall-growing clumps make good focal points and screens, and shorter-growing types make good ground cover, though they can be invasive. Some are also excellent for container growing.

A. gigantea (zone 8–9), southern cane, is one of the tallest bamboos and also one of two native to the United States. The pioneers used it as an indication of fertile land. Its rapid growth makes it more suitable for parks and excludes it from small gardens.

A. humilis (zone 4–5), is correctly known as *Pleioblastus humilis* and comes from Japan. It does not exceed 5 ft (1.5 m) in height but is highly invasive.

Cultivation. All species like rich moist soil, and sun or light shade. Protect from cold winds and water in dry weather.

Propagate in late spring by division of clumps or from cuttings of stolons. Use a little heat if possible.

Arundo

Gramineae

A genus of three reed grasses, ranging in origin from the Mediterranean to Japan.

A. donax (zone 9), from the Mediterranean, is the largest of the European grasses, and forms huge clumps of leafy, grey-green canes. The variegated form, *A. donax* 'Variegata', has green leaves, striped white and creamy yellow. It is shorter but less hardy than the species. The dry stems of Provence cane are used as wind breaks and are called '*canisses*' in France.

Cultivation. The Provence cane, in spite of its name, is hardy in areas where frosts are not severe, as long as the stems are cut back and covered with straw for winter protection. Plant in moist, even wet soil in early spring. It is ideal for seaside hedges or sandy spots.

Propagate by seed, division of clumps in spring, or placing cuttings of flowering stems, taken in early summer, in water, to induce the growth of shoots at the nodes; when the roots appear, pot up.

Asarum

Aristolochiaceae

Around 70 species of low-growing perennials originating in Europe, Asia and North America comprise this genus. The leaves are often heart-shaped and green, like those of cyclamen.

A. canadense (zone 3), wild ginger, is a deciduous plant with downy leaves 2–7 in (5–18 cm) across. Brownish-purple flowers in spring.

A. europaeum (zone 3–4), asarabaca, or wild ginger, is found in Europe to western Siberia. It grows 4–10 in (10–25 cm) high and 3 ft 3 in (1 m) across. This hardy plant has dark-green, evergreen kidney-shaped leaves. The little, bell-shaped, brown flowers on short stems open in mid spring and early summer.

All species grow best in woodland conditions and are propagated from suckers. They make excellent, carpeting ground cover.

Cultivation. Plant deeply in a cool soil rich in leaf mould, in full or partial shade.

Propagate from suckers, lifting and dividing in spring, or from seed.

Asclepias

Milkweed, *Asclepiadaceae*

A genus comprising 120 species of herbaceous perennials, shrubs and sub-shrubs, some of which are hardy. The stems contain a milky sap, hence the common name.

A. syriaca (A. cornuti) (zone 5), parrot flower or milkweed, from North America, grows 4–6 ft

(1.2–1.8 m) high. It is a hardy plant with creeping roots, a single robust stem and ovate opposite leaves which are downy underneath. The umbels of pendant purple to white, fragrant flowers appearing mid to late summer are followed by large bent bird-like fruits.

A. tuberosa (zone 9), butterfly weed, from North America, grows 16–24 in (40–60 cm) high, and 12–20 in (30–50 cm) across. The lanceolate leaves are alternate. Large umbels of bright-orange flowers appear at the end of downy erect stems in mid to late summer. It is not reliably hardy, and can be difficult to establish, but its flowers are extremely attractive to butterflies. These two species suit borders protected from cold winds.

Cultivation. In spring, plant in sun or partial shade in a peaty, light, rich soil which remains cool in summer, 20 in (50 cm) apart. Increase by division or by seed in spring and plant out as soon as possible.

Asparagus
Liliaceae

This genus consists of 300 species of shrubs, hardy or tender and climbing perennials with tuberous or fibrous roots, some of which are grown as house plants for their ornamental foliage.

A. officinalis (zone 3–4), edible asparagus, is a native of the Mediterranean area and has been grown since the 15th century. It forms clumps 5–6½ ft (1.5–2 m) high and is hardy.

Cultivation. Choose light, sandy loam, with a well drained subsoil, in a sunny position and sheltered from the wind. As seeds take several years to crop, obtain young crowns from garden centres or by mail-order. Most seedsmen offering vegetable seeds also stock 1–2 year old asparagus crowns. Dig in plenty of manure in the winter prior to planting. In late winter, apply chalk (lime) 2 oz/sq yd (50 g/1 m) and subsequently 3 oz (75 g) of a general fertilizer yearly. Plant the crowns in trenches 14 in (35 cm) wide and 10 in (25 cm) deep, spaced 4½ ft (1.4 m) apart in early spring in a Mediterranean climate and in mid spring in a temperate one. At the bottom of the trench make a longitudinal mound 4 in (10 cm) in height, and every 20 in (50 cm) place the crowns, spreading the roots out well. Cover them with 2–3¼ in (5–8 cm of light soil, after applying a light covering of fertilizer 1 oz/yd (25 g/1 m) of trench, completely filling the trench by hoeing in the course of the season.

Water well after planting and regularly during summer. Hoe the top soil so as not to damage the roots and crowns and cut the fern-like foliage down in autumn, once it turns yellow. Cut down any female stems as soon as berries start to form, to prevent inferior seedlings. Always keep the asparagus bed totally free of weeds.

Start harvesting in the third year when yields of 14 oz–1 lb 8 oz (400–700 gm) per plant can be expected. With a knife cut the spears when these appear 3¼–4½ in (8–10 cm) above the ground, making the cut 4 in (10 cm) below the ground. Spread the harvest over six weeks. Asparagus can be frozen. Stop cutting at the end of spring or beginning of summer. Apply fertilizer at the rate of 9 oz/sq yd (225 g/1 m^2). After the harvest in autumn cut the foliage to ground level and mulch with manure, compost or seaweed 2–3 in (5–7.5 cm) thick. At the end of winter rake 4 oz/yd^2 (120 g/m^2) of soot (wood ash) on the rows. Asparagus beetle and asparagus fly can attack the plant. Violet root rot, spear blackspot due to frost and rust are common problems. Re-plant the bed every 15–20 years.

Uses. Asparagus is appreciated for its tasty and edible young stems known as spears.

Asperula
Rubiaceae

A genus comprising 90 species of hardy herbaceous and alpine plants, many from Europe and Asia, with leaves and stipules forming whorls on stem.

A. nitida (zone 7–8), a perennial from Greece and Asia Minor, grows 2¾–4 in (7–10 cm) high. With a spread of 9 in (23 cm). It forms small green tufted cushions. The pink tubular flowers are clustered at the top of the stem and open in late spring to mid summer.

A. odorata (zone 6), a woodruff, is a perennial found in Siberia and Europe, and grows 6–8 in (15–20 cm) high, and 12–16 in (30–40 cm) across. The mid-green, bristle-tipped leaves are in whorls of eight. The white, cross-shaped flowers open late spring and early summer. It grows best in woodlands or partial shade and the whole plant is fragrant when dried. It spreads by stolons, and can be invasive.

A. suberosa (zone 7–8), a native to Greece, grows 1½–2 in (4–5 cm) high and 6 in (15 cm) across. This is a tufted, semi-trailing plant with leaves with silvery white hairs. Pale-pink, tubular flowers cover the plant in late spring and early summer. This alpine species is suitable for rockeries and borders, but needs protection from winter damp.

Cultivation. Provide a dry, well drained soil for alpines, herbaceous species prefer moist soil. Protect alpine species from winter damp, with a sheet of glass.

Propagate herbaceous species by division in spring; take soft, basal cuttings of alpine species in spring, and root in a cold frame.

Asphodeline

Liliaceae

Genus represented by approximately 15 European, tuberous-rooted perennial plants.

A. lutea (zone 7–8), asphodel, is also called king's spear and Jacob's rod. Originally from the Mediterranean, it grows 28 in–4 ft (70 cm–1.2 m) high and 1 ft (30cm) across. The grassy leaves are glaucous. In late spring, it produces spikes of yellow, star-like fragrant flowers. The seed heads are equally attractive.

Cultivation. Plant singly or in groups in borders or woodland gardens. It tolerates heavy frost, but prefers Mediterranean climates.

Asphodeline lutea

Plant in spring or autumn, 10 in (25 cm) apart, in a sheltered, sunny spot in well drained, dry soil. Asphodel is especially suited to the seaside. Cut back stems in late autumn.

Propagate by division of clumps either in spring or autumn.

Asphodelus

Liliaceae

A genus comprising some dozen species of annuals or rhizomatous herbaceous perennials originating from an area between Western Europe and the Near East.

A. albus (zone 7–8), asphodel, is native to Southern Europe, and its flower spikes grow 20 in–3½ ft (50 cm–1 m) high. Its linear-lanceolate leaves are 2 ft (60 cm) high, and its spikes of white flowers, overlaid with brown veins, open in spring and summer.

A. ramosus (zone 7–8), indigenous to the Mediterranean, grows 28 in–5 ft (70 cm–1.5 m) high. The grey-green, linear leaves are triangular in cross section, and the white flowers growing up in large branching racemes right from the base open in early to late summer.

Interplant asphodels with late-flowering subjects, such as nerines or agapanthus, for maximum garden colour.

Cultivation. Asphodels tolerate ordinary, even calcareous, soil provided it is well drained. They do need heat and direct sunlight to flourish. Plant 10–16 in (25–40 cm) apart.

Propagate by division of tuberous roots in spring.

Asplenium

Aspleniaceae (Polypodiaceae)

A genus represented by more than 650 species of fern found throughout the world.

A. trichomanes (zone 7–8), maidenhair spleenwort, grows 8 in (20 cm) high and across. It is hardy, but vulnerable to prolonged, heavy frosts. Its narrow pinnate fronds have blackish brown stems and pale-green, rounded pinnae. The central, fertile fronds are deciduous, and the sterile fronds form evergreen rosettes.

The maidenhair spleenwort is particularly suited to rockeries, walls, patios and shaded beds, and can be grown as a pot plant in a cool greenhouse.

Cultivation. Maidenhair spleenwort is one of the rare ferns that thrive in calcareous soils in partial or full shade. Plant between spring and autumn, preferably in cool, damp weather. Upkeep only involves watering in dry weather.

Propagation is generally from spores, which germinate freely in summer or by division of its crowns in spring.

Aster
Compositae

There are numerous species of these hardy herbaceous perennial plants: flowering in spring (*A. farreri*); summer (*A. amellus*); or in autumn (*A. novae-angliae, A. novi-belgii*); and a huge range of heights.

A. novi-belgii (zone 6), michaelmas daisy, grows 11 in–4 ft (30 cm–1.2 m) high, has produced a vast group of hybrids, including 'Blondie' (semi-double white), 'Lassie' (pink, double), 'Marie Ballard' (light blue, double), 'Freda Ballard' (red, semi-double) and 'Winston S. Churchill' (red). All have small, narrow, green-pointed leaves, and are grown for their dazzling, yellow-centered, display of flowers. The small, daisy-shaped flowers grow in clusters in colours ranging from white through to crimson.

Michaelmas daisies and other taller species give a large splash of colour to herbaceous or mixed borders. Many forms are strong growing, even invasive, and should be kept well away from more delicate plants. Smaller species, such as *A. alpinus*, are good in rock gardens.

Cultivation. Grow in well drained soil, spaced 12–16 in (30–40 cm) apart, in full sunlight. In spring, dress with fertilizer, and water regularly in dry weather. Larger varieties may need staking. Removal of faded flowers prolongs the flowering period. Cut back stems at the end of autumn. Division of clumps in spring is the best method of propagation, selecting the outer positions for replanting. Many species degenerate unless lifted and divided every two or three years. The two main diseases of michaelmas daisy are wilt and mildew.

Asteriscus
Compositae

The genus includes three Mediterranean species.

A. maritimus, (Odontospermum maritimum) – zone 9 – from the Mediterranean, grows 6–8 in (15–20 cm) high and 8–12 in (20–30 cm) across. This half-hardy herbaceous perennial produces a profusion of golden, daisy-like flowers on short stems in late spring, above a tuft of silky haired grey leaves. It is suitable for seaside planting, rockeries, low walls and scree.

Cultivation. Plant in a dry sunny, spot in maritime or frost-free gardens. In cold temperate climates, grow it in an alpine greenhouse.

Astilbe
Saxifragaceae

A genus comprising 25 species of herbaceous perennials, most coming from China and Japan. *A.* × *arendsii* (zone 5–6) is a hybrid growing 2–3 ft (60 cm–1 m) high, and 1–2 ft (30–60 cm) across.

The deep-green foliage is deeply divided, elegant and decorative. Upright, fluffy plumes

Astilbe × arendsii

of tiny flowers, in shades of white, red, mauve or pink are produced in summer. Popular cultivars include the pale pink 'Bressingham Charm'; the bright red 'Federsee'; crimson 'Fanal'; and white 'White Gloria'. Dwarf cultivars, such as those of *A.* × *crispa*, for rock gardens are also available. Astilbes can be grown in beds, borders and pool-side planting schemes. They make excellent ground cover and tolerate boggy soil.

Cultivation. Plant in sun or light shade between mid autumn and late winter, 1 ft–16 in (30–40 cm) apart, in deep fertile soil. Mulch with peat, compost, leaf-mould or well rotted manure every spring.

Water generously in dry weather. Cut back stems to the base in mid autumn. Every 3–4 years divide the clumps, to rejuvenate the plants.

Astragalus

Leguminosae

This genus is very important, comprising nearly 2000 species, spread mainly throughout the Northern Hemisphere, but little-known in cultivation. They are herbaceous perennials or subshrubs, bearing white, yellow, blue or purple pea-like flowers. Some are totally unable to survive damp winters.

A. monspessulanus (Montpelier astralagus) – zone 9–10 – is native to southern Europe and North Africa. It grows 4–6 in (10–15 cm) high, and 16–20 in (40–50 cm) across. It is a small stemless perennial, with pinnate leaves and purple or violet flowers in short clusters.

A. galegiformis (zone 7), from the Middle East grows to 5 ft (1.5 m) with a spread of about 3 ft (90 cm). The leaves are pinnate and spikes of creamy yellow flowers appear in summer.

Cultivation. Plant in a warm, dry sunny location. It tolerates limy soils, but protect it from winter rain, with a pane of glass. The plant grows very long roots which push their way through the rocky soil to find the water and minerals it needs. Taller herbaceous species are suitable for a sunny border in well-drained soil.

Propagate in early spring by sowing seeds in an earthenware pot in a cold frame.

Astrantia major

Astrantia

Masterwort, *Umbelliferae*

A genus comprising around ten species of hardy herbaceous perennials, native to Europe.

A. major (zone 9), is a clump-forming plant which grows 24–28 in (60–70 cm) high, with a spread of 12–20 in (30–50 cm). Its mid-green leaves are divided into three leaflets. The star-shaped, pinkish white flowers open in early to mid summer and are good for cutting and the attractive bracts dry well.

A. minor (zone 5), grows 8–12 in (20–30 cm) high, and 16 in (40 cm) across. Similar to, but with much smaller greeny white flowers than the species above, it flowers in mid to late summer and thrives on calcareous soils.

Both are suitable for a herbaceous border, informal ground cover or wild gardens.

Cultivation. Plant in any well drained soil, in light shade or sun, between mid autumn and late spring; water regularly during dry spells.

Propagate by sowing fresh seeds in a cold frame in mid autumn; germination takes place the following spring. Alternatively, increase by division of roots in autumn or spring. Generally free from pests and diseases.

Athyrium

Aspleniaceae

There are almost 200 species of this genus from all over the world; a few can be planted in open ground in temperate zones.

A. filix-femina (zone 4–5), lady fern, is hardy and forms part of the European forest flora. Quite large, it reaches 2–3 ft (60–90 cm) in height, and 2 ft (60 cm) across. Its deeply dissected fronds are bright green and invaluable in making dried or fresh flower arrangements. Plant in a group either in a shady, damp herbaceous border, or in isolated beds, or in wild or woodland gardens. They are attractive in a water-side setting.

Cultivars. Cultivars in the Plumosum group have finely divided, green fronds; 'Victoriae' has lattice-like crisp fronds.

Cultivation. Plant in spring or early autumn in a fairly shady position in moist, deep soil which is neutral yet rich in humus. In early spring, mulch with peat or leaf mould.

Propagate from spores or division of clumps in spring.

Atriplex

Chenopodiaceae

Some 100 species of annuals, herbaceous perennials and shrubs comprise this genus, some cultivated for ornaments and others as food.

A. halimus (zone 8–9), tree purslane, sea orach, is a shrub 3½–6½ ft (1–2 m) high with 3½ ft (1 m) spread. It has decorative, silvery-grey stems and foliage but its green flowers are insignificant. It is excellent near the sea for its resistance to salty spray. Its foliage is evergreen in Mediterranean areas, and deciduous in colder regions. Not very hardy, the tree purslane is confined to regions with a mild climate. In warmer areas, tree purslane is often used for hedging, or ground cover for slopes.

Cultivation. Plant in autumn or spring, in any type of well drained soil, whether sandy or salty, in full sun or light shade. Avoid heavy, rich soils.

Pruning is rarely necessary. Propagate by division of clumps in autumn or spring or by taking cuttings from flowering shoots.

Garden Orach

A. hortensis (zone 5–6), orach or mountain spinach, comes from Northern Europe and grows 3 ft 6 in–6 ft 6 in (1–2 m) high. This annual which is sometimes used instead of spinach has erect and bushy stems. Purple-leaved forms may also be used as ornamentals in summer bedding schemes.

Cultivation. Sow the seeds successionally, in rich or ordinary soil, from late winter to late summer, in rows 20 in (50 cm) apart. Cover with ½ in (13 mm) of soil and thin later to 16 in (40 cm) apart. In summer water copiously and mulch. Pinch off the ends of the stems to encourage the growth of large leaves. Orach is vulnerable to various pests such as slugs and snails. Cut the leaves 30 to 40 days after sowing.

Uses. The leaves are eaten cooked like spinach, in soup, or raw, in salads.

Aubrieta

Cruciferae

A genus consisting of a dozen species of hardy, evergreen perennials which originate in the mountain regions of the Mediterranean, from Italy to Iran. Several are grown as popular rock garden plants.

A. deltoidea (zone 4–5), aubrieta, is a prostrate mat-forming and trailing plant, 6 in (15 cm) high, and 1–2 ft (30–60 cm) across. The clumps of small, wedge-shaped leaves are covered in flowers in spring.

From the species, numerous cultivars have been developed with red, pink or violet, single or double flowers, some with golden- or silvery-variegated leaves.

Cultivars include 'Bressingham Pink', with large, double pink flowers; 'Dr Mules', with prolific dark, violet-blue flowers; 'Argenteo Variegata', with white variegated foliage and delicate blue flowers; and 'Carnival', with large purple flowers.

Cultivation. A good rock garden plant, Aubrieta thrives in well drained limy soil with a gravel surface dressing and a sunny position. It can also be planted on banks, in walls, and as edging to herbaceous borders. Mulch sparingly with well-decayed organic matter every three years as this plant does not tolerate fertilizers. Propagate by taking soft wood cuttings in spring or by division of clumps after flowering, or by removing rooted layers.

Aucuba

Cornaceae

This Asian genus includes three species of evergreen shrub with male and female flowers on separate plants.

A. japonica (zone 6) is popular for its hardiness and ability to do well in difficult conditions, such as salty spray, atmospheric pollution and dense shade. This bushy shrub can grow 6½–10 ft (2–3 m) high with a 3½–6½ ft (1–2 m) spread. Its fairly uninspiring purplish spring flowers are followed in the autumn by bright red ovoid long-lasting berries on the female plant as long as there is a male plant nearby for pollination.

There are a number of cultivars, some with variegated leaves, of which the male clone 'Maculata' with yellow-spotted leaves is the most common. Aucuba can be used as hedging, in a border, or planted on its own.

Cultivation. Plant in autumn or spring in any soil, dry or damp, in sunshine or shade. Prune only to curb excessive growth.

Propagate from semi-ripe cuttings at the end of summer, or by removing rooted layers.

Azara

Flacourtiaceae

This genus of tender evergreen shrubs from South America has green foliage and clusters of scented, petal-less flowers from pale cream to yellow, which open in spring to summer.

A. integrifolia (zone 9), from Chile grows 20–40 ft (6–12 m) high. The compact clusters of yellow flowers open in early spring. The cultivar 'Variegata' has dark-green leaves edged with pale pink in spring which changes to cream or white in summer.

A. microphylla (zone 9–8), also from Chile, is the hardiest species. It forms a superb dark-green bush 6½–10 ft (2–3 m) high, and carries deep-yellow, vanilla-scented flowers in late winter. The leaves of the slow-growing cultivar 'Variegata' have a pale yellow margin.

Cultivation. Azara is normally hardy in latitudes where the olive tree grows and tolerates a certain amount of frost. Plant against a warm, sheltered spot in cool areas. Propagate either from root cuttings or from hardwood cuttings with a heel placed in gentle heat.

Azolla

Fairy moss, *Azollaceae*

A genus of tropical, free-floating aquatic plants, with delicate, fern-like foliage, from temperate and sub-tropical regions.

A. caroliniana (zone 9–10), from temperate America, has fan-like branches of closely packed tiny, fleshy blue-green leaves which form a dense carpet ½–¾ in (13–20 mm) thick in still water. The fronds turn red in autumn.

This plant creates a very attractive floating carpet on the surface of the water but it often becomes invasive.

Cultivation. Azolla requires warm calm waters with a pH close to 7 (neutral).

Propagate by division of clumps. In a very cold area, overwinter by placing in a basin in a cool room. Can be invasive in ponds.

Azorella

Umbelliferae

A genus consisting of around 70 mostly perennial species from South America, with evergreen foliage and a habit similar to the mossy saxifrages but uninteresting flowers.

A. trifurcata (Bolax glebaria) – zone 5 – from Chile and the Magellan Straits, grows 1–2 in (2.5–5 cm) high, with a 1 yd² (1 m²) spread. Its dense, dark-green cushions of foliage are an attractive feature; the small, dull-yellow flowers appear in summer. It is useful in a rock garden, and between paving cracks, but treat with care, as it is very brittle.

Cultivation. Plant in spring in a moist but well drained, gritty soil, neither too dry nor too damp, in sun or partial shade. From time to time a large section of the clump will die off. They are resistant to cold, if the soil is not too damp, but in cold regions, grow in an alpine house.

Propagate from cuttings from rosettes between the start of autumn and place in a layer of sand in a cold frame.

Ballota
Labiatae

A genus containing around 30 species of perennials and sub-shrubs with deciduous or semi-evergreen foliage, native to the Mediterranean, Europe and Western Asia. Most of the species are classed as weeds.

A. pseudodictamnus (zone 7), native to the Mediterranean, grows 1–2 ft (30–60 cm) high, and 2 ft (60 cm) across. It is a slow-growing, branching sub-shrub, with white, woolly stems and grey, woolly heart-shaped leaves in opposite pairs. Its white tubular flowers, spotted with purple, appear in mid summer and are not striking.

The plant is grown for its foliage and is ideal for silver and grey gardens, rock gardens and herbaceous borders, especially with ornamental grasses.

Cultivation. Grow in ordinary, well-drained garden soil in full sun. The plant is hardy but does not tolerate wet winters.

Propagate by taking cuttings 3 in (7.5 cm) long in mid to late summer, of non-flowering side shoots, and place in cold frames in a sandy soil.

Baptisia
False indigo, *Leguminosae*

A genus containing 35 species of hardy, herbaceous perennials native to North America, with an erect habit and flowers resembling those of the lupin.

B. australis (zone 4–5), a hardy native of North America, grows 2–4 ft (60 cm–1.2 m) high, and 20–30 in (50–60 cm) across. This is a very popular plant with trifoliate blue green leaves, and spikes of indigo-blue, pea-like flowers, which appear in early summer. The dark-grey, inflated seed pods are good for drying.

Because of its height it is used towards the back of herbaceous borders.

Cultivation. Plant in cool, deep lime-free soil in a sunny or semi-shaded position in autumn or spring. The plant will not flourish if it lacks sun. Support with stakes or twiggy sticks, if growing in an exposed position, and prune back to the ground in late autumn. The plants are deeply rooted, and dislike disturbance.

Propagate by sowing seeds in spring in trays in cold frames or by dividing roots which are woody between mid autumn and early spring.

Barbarea
Land cress, *Cruciferae*

Around 12 species of biennial or perennial herbaceous plants make up this genus. These upright branching plants originate from the temperate regions of the Northern Hemisphere. Several species are grown as salad vegetables, but others are weeds.

B. vulgaris (zone 6) grows 1–2 ft (30–60 cm) high and 8–16 in (20–40 cm) across. Its yellow flowers only appear with sufficient sun in late spring to early summer. Cultivated varieties include 'Flore Pleno' which has a double flower and 'Variegata', with yellow-spotted foliage.

This species is used in ornamental gardens in rock gardens or to edge flower beds.

Cultivation. Plant in an ordinary rich garden soil in a sunny position.

Propagate by dividing clumps every year in autumn or by seeds or cuttings.

Cress
B. praecox (zone 6), garden or land cress, is a European plant which prefers a cool position. This perennial grown as an annual produces rosettes of deeply divided leaves. It is a very strong flavour and is usually cut when about 6 in (15 cm) high.

Cultivation. Rotate in the same way as common cress, *Lepidum sativum*. Garden cress grows better next to potatoes.

Sow the seeds monthly from spring to end of summer quite thinly in a rich, moist soil in the shade, in rows 10 in (25 cm) apart and thin to 8 in

(20 cm) apart. Water generously in summer. Remove the flowering shoots which appear in the second year to prolong the crop. Only the outer leaves are picked. Garden cress is susceptible to flea beetle.

Basella
Basellaceae

A small genus of tuberous rooted plants from tropical areas. *B. alba* (zone 9–10), Malabar spinach is grown as an ornamental and cultivated as a spinach-like vegetable. It is a half-hardy climbing plant growing rapidly to produce stems to 17 ft (5 m) in one season. Clusters of small white fragrant flowers appear during the autumn.

The species is perfect for adorning a trellis with its abundant stems and is edible.

Cultivation. Plant deeply in a rich sandy soil with plenty of organic matter in mid to late spring. The position is not too important, but the warmer the better. Plant several tubers in the same spot while still small (less than 2 in (5 cm) long) and if these are not lifted for the winter they should be protected with a thick mulch of straw. Propagate from the brittle stem tubers.

Bauhinia
Leguminosae

The genus is composed of about 250 species of often climbing shrubs, native to the tropics. Most have distinctive evergreen foliage, divided into two kidney-shaped lobes or leaflets, and the orchid-like flowers form in clusters. Most species are tender and may only be grown outdoors in frost-free climates.

B. corymbosa (zone 10+), native to Southern China, is a superb climbing plant. The shoots are downy and the flowers are pink with red stamens appearing in summer.

B. natalensis (zone 10+), native to Natal, produces white flowers in early autumn.

B. variegata (zone 10+), the orchid tree or ebony wood, is indigenous to India, and grows 17–20 ft (5–6 m) high. Its red flowers, flecked with white and yellow, bloom in early summer.

Cultivation. Plant in trays of sandy loam and peat in a heated greenhouse. Propagate by seeds, root cuttings or semi-hardwood cuttings in sand under glass with bottom heat.

Begonia – tuberous hybrid

Begonia
Begoniaceae

Begonias form a large family of up to 900 species, most from the tropics, many of which are popular house or bedding plants grown, for flower or foliage. They vary considerably in habit; erect, climbing or trailing and with tuberous, fibrous or rhizomatous roots. None are truly frost hardy.

Tuberous-rooted begonias

B. evansiana (B. grandis) – zone 9–10 – from China is half hardy, 1–2 ft (30–60 cm) high, with white or pink flowers appearing on drooping stalks in autumn. The heart-shaped leaves are glossy green and red below.

B. sutherlandii (zone 9), from South Africa, has slender pendant stems 1–2 ft (30–60 cm) long, and orange flowers appearing in summer. Its leaves are light green veined with red. As this species is half hardy, it should be sheltered and kept dry in winter. It is useful for hanging baskets.

Cultivation. The hardier tuberous-rooted begonias are grown in sheltered borders and beds in very mild gardens. They need a deep mulch in autumn, to protect them from frost. Most, however, permanently need greenhouse conditions, or are lifted and dried off in autumn, then replanted in spring.

Plant in spring in light, well drained soil, rich in humus, in sun or partial shade. These species and their hybrids are particularly susceptible to mildew.

Propagate by stem cuttings, division of tubers or bulbils which may appear in the leaf axils of some species.

Begonia × *tuberhybrida* (zone 10), hybrid tuberous-rooted begonias. This enormously popular bedding and pot plant grows 12–24 in (30–60 cm) high and across. Its flowers may be single, semi-double, double or fringed; many look like huge double roses. There are single and bi-coloured forms, with contrasting edges or flushes. They flower abundantly in summer until the approach of cold weather.

These begonias are particularly suitable for sunny or lightly shaded bedding schemes and window boxes. Those with pendulous habit are excellent for hanging baskets.

Cultivation. Plant in spring when the danger of frost is past, in rich, free-draining soil 2–3 in (5–7.5 cm) deep and shelter. Lift before the first frost, gradually allow the tubers to dry off before removing any soil or compost clinging to them and store in a cool, dry place at 50°F (10°C).

Belamcanda

Iridaceae

A genus composed of one or two species, rhizomatous plants, similar to iris in the shape of its leaves, and native to Western Asia.

B. chinensis (zone 8–9), leopard flower or blackberry lily from China, Japan and India, measures 3 ft (90 cm) high. Its rigid leaves form spikes. Its flower shoots are forked and produce cup-shaped, orange flowers smudged with reddish brown, 2 in (5 cm) in diameter, in mid to late summer.

The intergeneric hybrids × *Pardancanda norrisii*, obtained from crossing *Belamcanda chinensis* and *Pardanthopsis dichotoma* (*Iris dichotoma*), are much hardier, and produce stunning, iris-like flowers in shades of red, orange, yellow, blue and purple.

Cultivation. Plant in a well drained, rich sandy loam in a sunny position, 1 ft (30 cm) apart, provide with a thick mulch for winter protection. This plant is relatively short-lived.

Propagate by division in spring, or by seeds in mid autumn sown in cold frames. Germination takes place in the following spring.

Bellis

Daisy, *Compositae*

A genus of about 15 species of hardy herbaceous perennials from the Mediterranean and other parts of Europe. Cultivated plants of *B. perennis* (zone 4–5) are often grown as biennials but the quality of the flowering falls considerably after the second year. Cultivars (zone 4–5) have double flowers, in colours from white to pink and crimson. They make pretty edging to spring and early summer borders, and ground cover for bulbs. They are excellent subjects for window boxes and flower pots. Taller-stemmed cultivars make beautiful cut flowers.

Cultivars include the large-flowered types such as 'Monstrosa' or 'Giant Double'; and dwarf double varieties, such as 'Pomponnette', 6 in (15 cm) with small double flowers. 'Alba Plena', with double white flowers, and 'Dresden China', with double pink flowers. Seed may be in mixed or individual colours.

Cultivation. Sow in early to mid summer in shady seed beds. Transplant in early to mid autumn or early spring, 4 in (10 cm) apart; protect seedlings in harsh winters. Daisies like a cool aspect and light soil, but avoid excessive water. They transplant very easily. Sterile cultivars, such as 'Dresden China' are propagated by division.

Bellis perennis 'Pomponnette'

Berberis

Barberry, *Berberidaceae*

This genus includes a large number of species and cultivars of deciduous or evergreen shrubs with a spreading habit. Reaching 3–9 ft (1–3 m) high and of similar or greater width, they are often grown for their foliage, flowers and decorative fruit. Most are spiny, and many of the deciduous types have good autumn colour.

They can be grown as specimens, in mixed planting, as hedging or as ground cover.

Species and cultivars

Among the deciduous barberries are *B. aggregata* (zone 6), from China, with a height and spread of 5 ft (1.5 m). Its foliage turns red-orange in autumn, and its pale-yellow flowers are followed by scarlet berries.

B. darwinii (zone 6–7), a moderately hardy native of Chile, has shiny evergreen foliage, and orange-yellow flowers, followed by bluish-black berries. It is excellent for hedging and can grow 10 ft (3 m) high and wide.

B. × *stenophylla* (zone 6), is a hybrid with very small, dark-green evergreen leaves, yellow flowers and dark, purple-black berries. It has an arching habit of growth, and is good for informal hedging, as specimen plants, and as ground cover for banks. It has a height and spread of 10 ft (3 m), but there are many dwarf cultivars.

Berberis × rubrostilla

B. thunbergii (zone 6), Japanese barberry, has deciduous, light-green foliage, turning orange-red in autumn, pale yellow flowers and scarlet berries. It is tolerant of shade and poor soils, and grows 5 ft (1.5 m) high and wide. There are variegated purple- and yellow-leaved cultivars, and numerous dwarf forms.

Cultivation. Plant in autumn or early spring, in a sunny position for deciduous types, and sun or light shade for evergreens. Any ordinary well drained soil, even chalk, is fine. Plant 16–24 in (40–60 cm) apart for a hedge.

Only hedging plants require regular pruning. Prune deciduous plants in autumn and evergreen types after flowering.

Propagate from cuttings towards the end of the summer. Some plants are affected by rust.

Bergenia

Elephant ear, *Saxifragaceae*

This genus includes six species from the Himalayas and Siberia, most grown as ornamentals.

B. cordifolia (zone 4–5), Siberian saxifrage, is a hardy, herbaceous perennial, 1 ft (30 cm) high and 12–20 in (30–50 cm) across. The large, evergreen leaves are leathery, rounded and heart-shaped at the base. They are a glossy, bright green, turning red in autumn. At the beginning of spring, spikes of mauve-pink flowers appear. There are cultivars and hybrids with white, crimson and lilac flowers.

Bergenia is suitable for herbaceous borders, ground cover, and grows well in containers.

Cultivation. Plant in mid autumn or early spring 16 in (40 cm) apart. It grows in any soil, even calcareous soils, if these are well drained, and in semi-shade. After flowering, cut off the stems. *B. cordifolia* may be affected by leaf spot, recognized by brown spotting on the leaves. Lift and divide plants after several years, when they become too dense.

Beta

Beet, *Chenopodiaceae*

A small genus of herbaceous plants, some of which have been developed as edible crops.

B. vulgaris (zone 5), is a biennial plant of uncertain origin. The wild species has produced

Ruby chard

many horticultural sub-species, including the beetroot with its swollen roots and high sugar content.

Beetroot (beets) is cultivated as an annual. It grows 12–18 in (60–80 cm) high and its swollen red roots can reach a diameter of 4 in (10 cm). Among the long-rooted, maincrop cultivars are 'Forono' and 'Cylindra'; among the round-rooted cultivars 'Boltardy', 'Detroit Globe' and 'Monopoly'.

Cultivation. Choose an open sunny site, preferably with a light sandy soil, that has been manured for the previous crop, following on from brassicas, such as cabbage or broccoli, for example.

Incorporate some peat in the soil the previous autumn and two weeks before sowing apply a base fertilizer and rake this soil level. When thinning out apply a general fertilizer. Sow monthly from spring to early summer in drills 1 in (2.5 cm) deep, 4–6 in (10–15 cm) between plants and 12–15 in (30–38 cm) between the rows according to cultivars.

During the summer, water regularly. When hoeing never touch the roots, weed by hand if necessary so as not to damage them. Harvest before the first frost and store in peat, in boxes kept in a cool spot. The leaves are twisted off but not cut. The yield is about 1 lb (5 kg) for every foot (30 cm). The time from sowing to picking is 10 to 15 weeks.

Beetroot (beets) can be affected by rust and by violet root in areas where this is a problem. Leafminers and heart rot can also be a problem and the plants bolt with irregular watering.

Uses. Beetroot can be eaten raw in salads, cooked or pickled or put in the deep freeze.

Sea-kale beet, Swiss chard, leaf beet

B. vulgaris subsp. *Cicla*, sea-kale beet, is grown only for its leaves. These are 20–28 in (50–70 cm) long and 4–6 in (10–15 cm) wide. Among the cultivars grown are 'Silver Beet' and 'Sea-kale Beet' with white midribs and leaf veins and 'Rhubarb Chard' and 'Ruby Chard' with long crimson leaf stalks and midribs.

Cultivation. Sow the large seed capsules individually in rich, cool soil, in early spring to mid summer, in rows 16 in (40 cm) apart. Cover the seeds with $\frac{3}{4}$–1 in (2–2.5 cm) of soil and thin the seedlings to one per station.

Water every 10 days with a fertilizer rich in nitrogen during the summer. Hoe to keep weeds down, and mulch to retain soil moisture. The sea-kale beet exhausts the soil and should only be replanted in the same place once every three or four years. Remove any flower heads that start to form.

Harvesting is from mid summer to late autumn and averages 3 lb per square foot (5 kg/m^2). Pests and diseases are the same as for beetroots.

Uses. The green leaves may be eaten like spinach, and the succulent midribs of chards may be cooked like asparagus, in breadcrumbs or in sauce.

Betula

Birch, *Betulaceae*

About 60 species of shallow-rooted, relatively short-lived deciduous trees and shrubs from the Northern Hemisphere comprise this genus, the tallest reaching 90 ft (27.5 m).

The birch has a slender and very elegant habit. Many species are grown for the thin, white, peeling bark and golden autumnal colours, a few have coloured barks.

The small, often triangular leaves are toothed. Flowering takes the form of hanging male catkins, first formed in autumn, and female flowers, shaped like cylindrical cones, opening in late spring. The birch seed is very small and winged.

B. papyrifera (zone 3–4), paper birch, originating from North America, is 60–70 ft (18–21 m)

high. Closely related to European birches, this species is distinguished by its very white bark.
B. pubescens (zone 4), downy birch, is a European species most often found in wet, marshy ground. The smoothy, downy branches are more erect and reddish, distinguishing the tree from *B. pendula*, silver birch.
B. pendula (B. verrucosa) – zone 4–5 – silver birch, grows between 50–60 ft (15–18 m) high. The silver birch is characterized by its columnar habit and its fine, spreading, pendulous branches. It is very common in Europe, but in the south it is restricted to mountain areas. It adapts to dry, shallow soil, but grows faster in cooler soil. The weeping cultivar, 'Youngii', is usually grafted to make a mushroom-shaped tree.

Many are tough, pioneer trees, tolerant of extremely dry or wet soil and sun or shade. There are numerous cultivars suitable for smaller gardens.

Cultivation. Plant container grown specimens or those with root-ball in autumn or spring. All are very hardy, but have varying soil requirements according to different species.

Propagate by seed, sown outdoors, pressed onto the surface of the soil and protect by a covering of brushwood until germination. Named varieties are propagated by grafting or by hardwood cuttings. Birches can be attacked by gall-producing insects. Bracket fungus can denote that the tree is nearing the end of its life.

Biscutella

Cruciferae

Forty-five species of hardy annual or herbaceous perennial plants, originating from central and southern Europe, make up this genus.
B. laevigata (zone 4), buckler mustard, is a perennial 8–24 in (20–60 cm) high and across, with erect often-branching shoots. The downy, smooth or dentate leaves form rosettes. Its yellow flowers, in loose, branching clusters, appear in late spring or early summer and are followed by flattened fruits, which resemble pairs of spectacles.

This is the only species cultivated by alpine garden enthusiasts, in rock gardens or tubs, with *Aster alpinus* and various mountain pinks.

Cultivation. Sow in a poor, calcareous soil in a sunny position; they do not tolerate transplanting, but self seed readily.

Blechnum

Blechnaceae

A very large genus of ferns found throughout the world.
B. spicant (zone 3–4), hard fern or deer fern, is 12–18 in (30–45 cm) high and across. It is a hardy evergreen perennial producing a clump of shining fronds. The tough sterile fronds form cushions; the taller, more slender fertile fronds bear rows of spore-cases on the pinnae, and appear in summer in the centre of the clump. Hard ferns can provide a pretty carpet under trees or shrubs, in shady rock gardens, banks and beds.

Cultivation. Plant in spring in a cool, semi-shaded or shady position, in deep, lime-free soil, enriched with peat or leaf mould. Propagate by sowing spores or by division in spring of its rhizomatous roots.

Bletilla

Orchidaceae

This is a small genus of terrestrial orchids from Eastern Asia.
B. striata (zone 9–10), is a moderately hardy herbaceous plant, with long, sword-shaped,

Bletilla striata

pleated leaves, and a 1 ft (30 cm) stem carrying sprays of deep mauve flowers in early summer. This species provides a beautiful display in sheltered or semi-shaded beds or a cool greenhouse. There is a white form available.

Cultivation. Plant the swollen, tuber-like pseudobulb 2 in (5 cm) deep, in spring. Choose a semi-shaded spot with well drained gritty soil, enriched with peat and compost. In colder regions, protect the plant with a layer of peat or leaf mould in winter; in the damp and frosty regions, grow in pans and overwinter in a greenhouse.

Propagate by dividing the pseudobulbs.

Borago

Boraginaceae

Three species of hardy herbaceous plants from the Mediterranean area comprise this genus.

B. officinalis (zones 6–7), borage, is a hardy annual, growing 20 in–3½ ft (50 cm–1 m) tall. The plant has hollow stems bearing ovate leaves covered with rough silvery hairs. Pendant flowers in the form of five petalled luminous blue stars are borne from mid spring to early autumn.

Borage has been used for several centuries as a medicinal plant, and is used to add colour to salads and summer drinks. It is an attractive plant for the kitchen garden, rock garden, wild garden or herbaceous border.

Cultivation. Borage can be grown in virtually any soil, but prefers a sunny aspect in a well-drained soil.

It self-seeds readily and any surplus seedlings should be removed. In the kitchen garden, sow seeds successfully from mid spring, in shallow drills, and thin out to one plant every 12 in (30 cm).

Boronia

Rutaceae

This genus is represented by about 90 species of tender to semi-hardy shrubs or sub-shrubs originating in Australia, often grown for cut flowers. They have fine foliage and clusters of fleshy flowers mostly ranging from carmine to maroon.

B. heterophylla (zone 10), has an erect but straggly habit, and grows 4–6 ft (1.5–2 m) high. Drooping clusters of scarlet, fragrant flowers appear in mid spring.

B. megastigma (zone 10), scented or sweet boronia, is 20–24 in (50–60 cm) high. The nodding, vanilla-scented flowers are maroon on the outside and yellow on the inside. It is used in the manufacture of perfume.

B. serrulata (zone 10), is a small species with abundant, deep pink, fragrant summer flowers.

Cultivation. Plant in peaty, lime-free soil, in a shaded or semi-shaded position. Prune hard after flowering. In areas with damp, frosty winters keep in a greenhouse. Boronias tend to be short lived.

Propagate by seeds in covered pans, or by semi-ripe cuttings inserted into a mixture of sand and peat, and placed in a propagator in a cool greenhouse.

Bougainvillea

Nyctaginaceae

The genus comprises over 15 species of tender climbing plants from tropical America. While the flowers are insignificant, much colour is derived from their long-lasting bracts.

B. glabra (zone 10), the paper flower from Brazil, grows up to 15 ft (4.5 m). Insignificant white flowers appear from early summer to mid autumn, surrounded by spectacular purple bracts, fading to pink. It, and the cultivar, 'Sanderiana', which is 26 ft (8 m) tall and has mauve-pink bracts, adapts well to pot culture. The flowering period is from late spring to early autumn.

Cultivars include 'Killie Campbell', with orange bracts; 'Snow White', with white bracts; 'Golden Glow', with yellow orange bracts; 'Mrs Butt', with crimson bracts; and 'Variegata', with white-variegated leaves. Some of these are of the hybrid *B.* × *buttiana*, which has *B. glabra* as one parent.

Cultivation. Plant bougainvillea in a rich, well-drained soil in a sunny, sheltered position in frost-free climates; or for the cold areas, in a greenhouse. Cut back the main shoots of mature plants by a third of their length, and shorten all side shoots almost back to the main shoots. Propagate by semi-ripe cuttings from mid-spring to late summer placing these in sand, under glass keeping an ambient temperature of 70°F (21°C). These plants are susceptible to scale insects, red spider mite or mealy bugs.

Boykinia
Saxifragaceae

This genus consists of about eight plants resembling the herbaceous saxifrages, differing in slight botanical features. They are natives of North America and East Asia.

B. aconitifolia (zone 6–7), from eastern North America, has large clumps of rounded, dissected leaves and branching heads of small, creamy white flowers. It grows to about 3 ft (90 cm).

B. rotundifolia (zone 7), from California, is similar.

Cultivation. The plant thrives in shade, and cool, lime-free soil. It is suitable for the wild garden and the smaller species do well in the rock garden or alpine house. Cut back frosted foliage.

Propagate by seed or by division.

Brassica
Cruciferae

This large genus of about 30 herbaceous plants includes many cultivated as economic crops for hundreds of years. In addition to specific cultivation notes, see general cultivation notes for brassicas at the end of this entry.

Cabbage
B. oleracea, cabbage, is a species growing spontaneously on European shores, including the Mediterranean. It measures 3¼–6 in (8–15 cm) in height. It has produced numerous horticultural groups with distinct characteristics.

Kale (Borecole)
B. oleracea Acephala Group grows up to 3½–5 ft (1–1.5 cm). A biennial variety of the wild cabbage, it produces long stalks bearing very curly leaves 20–28 in (50–70 cm) long. There are two basic types: plain and curly leaved.

'Thousand head' has plain leaves and 'Dwarf Green Curled' and 'Tall Green Curled' are curly-leaved cultivars. They tolerate a wide range of soils and stand up well to the cold, so are well suited to cold winter regions.

Cultivation. Grow in full sun, in a poor, firm soil, which is undug but weeded and manured from the previous crop. In spring, sow in the open in drills, thin to 9 in (23 cm) and transplant into permanent position 2 ft (60 cm) apart in both directions, when the young plants are 6 in (15 cm) high.

Hoe regularly. At the end of summer rake soil up to the base of the first leaves. Pick from early winter through to early spring, cutting the centre of each plant first, to encourage succulent side shoots. Kale is also used for cattle feed, but for the table only pick tender leaves. Thirty weeks is the approximate time between sowing and harvesting, the yield is about 1½ lb (.7 kg) per plant.

Cauliflower and broccoli
B. oleracea Botrytis Group, cauliflower and broccoli, are annual or biennial plants producing hearts of congested, aborted flowers, 14 in (35 cm) in diameter. Sprouting broccoli has a loose cluster of flower heads which may be green or purple.

Cultivars. These are distinguished according to their period of yield. Summer yields are the following: 'Alpha', 'All Year Round', 'Andes' and 'Snowball'; autumn yields cover: 'Flora Blanco', 'All Year Round', 'Autumn Giant', 'Nevada'. In milder climates the following broccoli are grown for a late winter yield: 'Angers Early', 'Snow White'; and for the spring yield, these two are grown: 'Pinnacle' and 'St George'.

Cultivation. Choose an open site where the ground has been well prepared the previous autumn and where planty of manure has been incorporated. Rake in a general fertilizer before planting. Sow in a seed bed in the open, in early spring, in drills 9 in (23 cm) apart, and plant out into permanent positions 2 ft (60 cm) apart, when each plant has about half a dozen leaves. Water in well and water in dry periods throughout the growing season, giving an occasional feed with an artificial fertilizer. Protect cauliflower heads from sun or snow by breaking leaves over the curd and earth up in the autumn. Start picking cauliflower as soon as possible even when the heads are still small. Cauliflowers can be stored for a few weeks after picking, provided they are dug up with a root ball and hung upside down in a cool shed. Cut broccoli when the spears are well formed but before the buds have opened. Cut the central spear first, then the side ones when 4 in (10 cm) long, as they develop, but never allow the heads to flower or production will stop. The expected yield is 1 to 4 lb (0.5–1.8 kg) per plant depending on variety and maturity.

Brussels sprout
The Brussels sprout, *B. oleracea* Gemnifera Group, grows up to 3½ ft (1 m) high. It is another descendant of the wild cabbage; it is a biennial with a weak terminal bud and small, firm round buds along the stem.
Cultivars. Early cultivars include: 'Pegasus', 'Peer Gynt' and 'Jade Cross'; semi-late cultivars are: 'Widgeon', 'Citadel'; and finally, late cultivars: 'Huizer's Late' and 'Fortress'.
Cultivation. Grow where it gets sun for a few hours a day. Dig out the soil the previous autumn, adding plenty of organic matter. It prefers a firm, limy soil with not too much nitrogen. Sow in the open in a sheltered nursery, in spring in drills 9 in (23 cm) apart and plant out 1 to 5 weeks later when 6 in (15 cm) high, into permanent position 2½ ft (75 cm) all round. Hoe frequently and keep well watered throughout the growing season, using an occasional foliar feed. Mulch, and stake the taller plants especially those exposed to the wind. In the autumn earth up to the lower leaves. Pick from mid autumn through to early spring depending on cultivars. Pick the lower sprouts first and work up the stem ending at the top with the leafy greens. The average yield is about 2 lb (1 kg) per plant, with 28 weeks elapsing between sowing and picking.

Round cabbage, white cabbage, red cabbage, Savoy cabbage
The round cabbage, *B. oleracea* Capitata Group, is another variety of wild cabbage. It includes red cabbages and white cabbages, which have smooth leaves and the Savoy cabbage, which has crinkled leaves. The heart is 8–24 in (20–60 cm) in diameter.
Cultivars. The following are ready to be picked in autumn: 'Minicole', 'Winnigstadt', 'Rearguard'; in winter: 'Polinius', 'Holland Late Winter', all of which are white cabbages. Summer cutting cultivars include 'Hispi' and 'Primo'. Summer and autumn red cabbage cultivars include 'Ruby Ball' and 'Red Dutch'. Summer cultivars of Savoy cabbage include: 'Best of All'; autumn cultivars are 'Silva', 'Savoy King'; and late winter cultivars: 'Winter King', 'Omskirk', 'Aquarius'.
Cultivation. Cabbages thrive in a sunny position, in a cool, deep and compact soil, rich in humus. Leave a few months between digging and planting having previously incorporated plenty of organic matter and lime if necessary. Sow seeds in the open in drills 9 in (23 cm) apart, from mid winter through to early autumn. Lift the plants at the 5–6 leaved stage, on a moist day, and plant firmly in position 2 ft (60 cm) apart all round, having previously raked in a general fertilizer. Hoe regularly until the plants suppress weed growth, keep well watered and use a foliar feed. In winter, firm any plants loosened by the frost. Thirty five weeks is the approximate time between sowing and harvesting, the expected yield being 1 to 3 lb (0.5–1.4 kg) per plant.

Kohlrabi
B. oleracea Gongylodes group, kohlrabi, is a biennial descendant of wild cabbage grown as an annual. The rounded, swollen stems are edible, grow up to 10 in (25 cm) in diameter; the leaves are not eaten.
Cultivars. 'White Vienna' and 'Purple Vienna' are popular types.
Cultivation. Grow in full sun in a cool, well manured soil, which has been well dug during the winter. Sow seeds in shallow drills 1 ft (30 cm) apart, from early spring through to early summer, thin out the seedlings to 8 in (20 cm) apart in the row. Plant the young plants 6 weeks later when large enough to handle, leaving 12 in (30 cm) between them. Water well during a dry spell and mulch as they must grow quickly especially in the early stages to give tender stems. When these are the size of tennis balls pull out usually two months after planting.

Turnip
B. rapa Rapifera Group grows up to 1 ft (30 cm) high. A biennial plant with round leaves, it produces a white fleshy root, 2–4 in (5–10 cm) in diameter.
Cultivars. Cultivars are distinguished by shape, since there are round, flattened and long-rooted types, and by seasons. Early cultivars include 'Purple Top Milan' and 'Snowball' and later ones 'Golden Ball' and 'Manchester Market'.
Cultivation. The cultivation for turnip and swede is very similar. They require a rich well manured soil, with lime if necessary. Allow the soil to settle after digging, and like many brassicas firm the soil before planting out. For early turnips sow seed under a cloche at the beginning of the year. Otherwise sow both vegetables from early spring to early autumn, first in drills 15 in (38 cm) apart, thinning in stages to 6 in (15 cm) apart and then planting out in their permanent positions 1 ft (30 cm) apart.

Keep the crop well watered as uneven water supply encourages splitting. Harvest turnips when they are the size of golf balls. Later, lift the remainder of the crop, remove the leaves and store in boxes between layers of peat and sand and placed in a dry shed. Swedes can be left in the ground and dug up when required. Pick about 10 weeks after sowing up to the end of winter.

Swede
B. napus Napobrassica Group is a form of the wild swede, measuring 3½ ft (1 m) tall. It is a biennial, grown as an annual, with long stems and yellow, fleshy, edible roots 8–12 in (20–30 cm) long.
Cultivars. Rounded root cultivars 'Marian', yellow with a purple top and 'Best of All'.
Cultivation. See cultivation for turnip.

Chinese cabbage, Pe-tsai
B. chinensis, Chinese cabbage or pak-choi, forms a heart 6 in (15 cm) in diameter and from 10–12 in (25–30 cm) in height, and looks a little like the 'Large Roman' lettuce.
Cultivars. F1 hybrids 'Kido' and 'Tip-Top'.
Cultivation. Grow in cool, light soil. May be planted in the same spot after two years.

Sow seeds from early to late summer, in rows 12 in (30 cm) apart, and thin out to 10 in (25 cm). Keep the soil moist and mulch when necessary. Pick three months after planting, from early to late autumn.

Ornamental cabbage
Ornamental, coloured-leaved cabbages, derived from *B. oleracea*, are lovely with herbaceous perennials or as decorative edging in vegetable gardens. They are grown as biennials. Their leaves are wavy and fringed, with red or white colouring on a green background; the colouring becomes more pronounced as the temperature drops, especially welcome when the garden is still quite bare at the end of winter.
Cultivation. Sow in the open ground from late spring to early summer. Prick out twice to obtain hardy plants. Plant deeply as the head can become quite heavy and unstable. They can be stored through the winter under a veranda or in a cold frame, if intended for indoor decoration.

Cabbage family: general cultivation notes
Most brassicas prefer a firm, limy soil. Always rotate crops and never follow one brassica crop with another. Follow on from peas or beans which provide the necessary nitrogen. Brassica pests include pigeons, slugs, snails, cabbage caterpillars, flea beetles, cutworm, mealy aphid and cabbage white fly. The diseases that affect the brassicas include mildew, clubroot, white rust, black rot and leaf spot. Magnesium and manganese deficiences can cause particular leaf discoloration and a boron deficiency can lead to brown curd in cauliflowers.

Brodiaea
California hyacinth, *Liliaceae*

This genus includes 15 moderately hardy species found in western North America. They grow from corms and flower in late spring or summer, producing small umbels of 4 to 9 star-shaped, lavender or violet flowers.
B. californica (zone 9), from northern California, grows up to 2 ft 6 in (75 cm) high. Grow at the foot of a sunny wall or in a conservatory in exposed areas.
Cultivation. Plant in autumn, in a rich sandy soil in full sun. Protect from the cold, and lift and divide established clumps every few years.

Propagate from seeds or by division.

Brunnera
Siberian bugloss, *Boraginaceae*

A small genus of European plants represented in cultivation by *B. macrophylla* (zone 6), a hardy plant 18 in (45 cm) tall, with a spread of 16–24 in (40–60 cm). The leaves are large and heart-shaped and continue to increase in size through the summer. It carries clusters of vivid blue flowers, like forget-me-not, from mid spring to early summer, and sometimes flowers again in the autumn. The cultivar 'Variegata' has leaves marked with creamy white.
B. macrophylla, makes excellent ground cover especially in woodland gardens or mixed borders.
Cultivation. Plant in mid autumn or early to mid spring, 12–18 in (30–45 cm) apart; it prefers a cool, moist soil, enriched with manure or well rotted leaf mould, and semi-shade. Water during dry spells, remove dead flowers and mulch with manure in the spring.

Propagate by seed or by division in autumn or spring.

Buddleja
Loganiaceae

Around 100 deciduous or evergreen trees and shrubs from E. Asia, South America and South Africa make up this genus. They range from hardy to half hardy, and are grown for their flowers, which are extremely attractive to butterflies.

B. davidii (zone 6–5), butterfly bush, is native to China and the most popular species cultivated. It is extremely hardy, and grows as high as 13 ft (4 m), and as much across. Its long, arching stems bear lanceolate, mid-green deciduous leaves and long dense panicles of fragrant flowers are carried on new wood throughout the summer. Cultivars include 'White Profusion', white; 'Pink Pearl', pink; 'Ile de France', violet; 'Royal Red', rich red.

B. globosa (zone 7–8), from S. America bears balls of bright yellow flowers in early summer.

The taller-growing *B. alternifolia* (zone 6) has lightly fragrant lavender flowers in rounded clusters all along the pendulous stems in early summer. It can be grown as a multi-stemmed shrub, or trained as a weeping standard.

Cultivation. Plant in autumn or spring in a sunny aspect. It adapts to most soils, including dry, poor and even calcareous types.

Prune buddlejas that flower on new wood annually, in early spring. Hand pruning, to within 6 in (15 cm) of the ground, limits growth and stimulates flowering. Buddlejas, such as *B. alternifolia* that flower on the previous year's growth, should be pruned back lightly, immediately after flowering. Propagate by hardwood cuttings in winter. Young shoots may be attacked by greenfly.

Buddleja globosa

Bupleurum
Umbelliferae

This genus includes 150 species of herbaceous plants and sub-shrubs, native to Europe, Asia, Africa and North America. The leaves are undivided with parallel veins and yellow, euphorbia-like flowers are arranged in umbels.

B. rotundifolium, (zone 4–5), hare's ear, is a hardy annual, 6–12 in (15–30 cm) tall. It has broad, lanceolate blue green leaves, and branched stalks of greenish yellow flowers from early to mid summer. Plant with other lime-loving rock garden plants, such as *Aster alpinus*, edelweiss, *Linum*, saxifrage, etc.

Cultivation. Plant in sun or light shade 12 in (30 cm) apart in a humus-rich, stony calcareous soil where it will create little cushions over the flat stones.

Propagate from seeds in spring.

Buxus
Box, *Buxaceae*

The genus includes around 30 species of evergreen shrubs and small trees from Southern Europe, Western Asia and America. Box is long lived and some can eventually reach a height of 30 ft (9 m).

B. sempervirens (zone 4), common box, grows slowly to a height of 15 ft (4.5 m), eventually making an attractive, graceful tree if left to grow naturally. Its bark is fine and grey; the leaves are small, oval, glossy green and leathery. Small greenish aromatic flowers appear in spring, followed by horned seed capsules. There are many cultivars, including dwarf, variegated, and weeping forms.

Box is a popular hedging plant.

Cultivation. Plant in autumn or spring. When planting as a hedge, space the species 18 in (45 cm) apart; space dwarf edging varieties 6 in (15 cm) apart. Box is extremely hardy and will tolerate all kinds of soil, especially calcareous ones, and any aspect. It is also extremely tolerant of pruning, and is often used in topiary.

Propagate from cuttings in late summer or autumn. Rust can attack the leaves.

Caesalpinia

Leguminosae

This genus contains about 100 deciduous trees, shrubs or climbers, tropical or subtropical in origin and usually bearing clusters of yellow flowers with long, spectacular stamens. Some are hardier than others but most need frost-free climates.

C. gilliesii, bird of paradise shrub – zone 9–10 – from Argentina is a deciduous shrub or small tree and can reach 30 ft (9 m) high, grown against a wall. It has light, green bi-pinnate leaves and its yellow flowers with coral-red stamens appear in mid to late summer.

C. japonica (zone 9) is a fiercely thorny, lax or rambling shrub, 10 ft (3 m) or more high and wide. Its brilliant yellow flowers with scarlet stamens are borne in large hanging panicles on the previous year's wood in mid to late summer. It is slightly hardier than *C. gilliesii*.

Cultivation. Plant in full sun and shelter, or against a sunny wall. Avoid limy or heavy clay soils. Protect with netting, bracken or sacking against winter frost.

Propagate from seed after soaking overnight in warm water. Place in a mixture of equal parts of garden soil, leaf mould and sand.

Calanthe

Orchidaceae

This genus of orchids contains about 120 species which are usually terrestrial, from Asia and Australia. Some species are evergreen, others deciduous. Many are grown as greenhouse plants but some species from temperate Japan are quite hardy. They have bulbous roots and rosettes or broad, erect leaves. The flowers are carried on stems 1–2 ft (30–60 cm) high, in early summer.

C. discolor (zone 9–10) carries mauve or chocolate-coloured flowers, with white edges. They are sweetly fragrant. Its variety *flava* (*C. striata, C. sieboldii*), has bright yellow flowers with white lips.

C. tricarinata, has yellow flowers with red lips.

C. vestita carries white flowers, sometimes with a pale pink lip, from mid autumn to late winter. It is a deciduous species with flower stems 3 ft (1 m) long each of which carry between 20 and 30 blooms.

Cultivation. They prefer a mild climate, shelter and damp, peaty, humus-laden soil but will tolerate a limy one. Plant in semi-shade, in a cool spot. Barely cover the roots when planting. Water generously in hot weather.

To propagate, divide the clumps carefully in early spring. As for all orchids, growing from seed is very difficult.

Calceolaria

Scrophulariaceae

This genus comprises more than 300 herbaceous and woody species, native to South and Central America, grown for their pouch-shaped flowers. Some of the perennials from mountainous regions of the Andes will thrive in a temperate climate, and their small size means that they are perfectly suited to the rock garden.

C. biflora (zone 6), a perennial native of Chile and Argentina, is 10 in (25 cm) tall with basal rosettes of dark-green, oval leaves. Its abundant pale-yellow, pouched flowers, often in pairs, bloom in early summer. Grow in semi-shade in cool, well drained soil.

C. darwinii (zone 5), from Patagonia, grows 6 in (15 cm) tall, and is a fine species for the rockery. Its leaves are similar to those of *C. biflora*. Its yellow flowers, speckled with brown and with a prominent white bar, have inflated lower lips, and bloom in late spring to early summer.

C. integrifolia (zone 7–8), bush calceolaria, grows 2 ft (60 cm) high, or up to twice that given greenhouse conditions. Although it has a woody base, it may be cultivated as an annual, as it will not survive the winter out-of-doors in colder areas. It produces small, yellow flowers in tight inflorescences, and will continue to bloom until the frosts arrive.

Cultivation. Plant rock garden species on a cold facing slope in a crevasse filled with a mixture comprising 70 per cent peaty compost (an ericaceous mix) and 30 per cent coarse sand.

Protect rock garden species with a pane of glass from winter rains; otherwise grow in an alpine house. Calceolarias are very sensitive to chemical fertilizers.

Propagate by sowing seed in mid spring. Before planting, treat the soil with a fungicide, as the roots are very susceptible to fungal attack.

Calendula

Compositae

This genus consists of about 20 species of small shrubs and annuals, mostly from Mediterranean regions.

C. officinalis (zone 6), pot marigold, is a hardy, free-flowering annual. It is fond of a gentle and humid climate but is easily pleased. Its almost procumbent stems bear bright green pungent leaves and single or double, yellow or orange flowers. Pot marigold is suited to the cottage garden and makes an excellent cut flower.

Cultivars. 'Fiesta Gitana' grows 1 ft (30 cm) tall, and has mixed, coloured flowers. Cultivars with single colours include 'Lemon Queen', 'Orange King' and 'Indian Song', with golden-yellow, dark-centred flowers.

Cultivation. Sow the seed in autumn in situ if the soil is dry and light. Otherwise, sow from early spring to early summer in the nursery or directly into the open ground. Pinch out the young plants to encourage branching. Dead-head, to encourage further flowers, and prevent self-sown seedlings, which can be a nuisance.

Pot marigold may be attacked by cucumber mosiac virus (which shows as irregular yellowing and distortion of the leaves), mildew or rust appearing as orange pustules on the leaves.

Calliandra

Powder-puffs, *Leguminosae*

There are about 200 species representing this genus, from tropical America, Madagascar and India. The evergreen trees and shrubs, 6.5–10 ft (2–3 m) tall, sport globular clusters of flowers, with spectacular tufts of stamens, varying from white to red. The light green foliage is finely divided. They are hardy only in frost-free areas.

C. brevipes (zone 10+), an elegant native of Brazil, grows 5–6½ ft (1.5–2 m) tall. The flowers are bright pink and bloom in late summer and early autumn.

C. portoricensis (zone 10+) produces white flowers in mid to late summer and is native to Central America.

C. tweedii (zone 10+), flame bush, a native of Brazil, grows 10 ft (3 m) tall, and is the most spectacular of the genus. The yellow flowers with very long, bright red stamens bloom from early spring to mid autumn.

They are usually grown as specimen shrubs.

Cultivation. Most species are frost sensitive and prefer to be planted in a warm and sunny position, inside a heated greenhouse. Pot these into an open compost of loam and peat.

Propagate from cuttings of ripe wood in gentle heat or from seed.

Callicarpa

Beauty berry, *Verbenaceae*

There are nearly 150 species of shrubs in this genus from tropical and subtropical areas, some of which can be grown in cooler climates.

C. bodinieri (zone 8) from China is a small, fairly hardy, erect shrub which can reach a height of 8 ft (2.5 m). Its clusters of pink or mauve flowers appear in summer but its main attraction lies in the purple berries that follow, and the deciduous leaves which turn a spectacular rose purple in autumn.

Cultivation. Plant in spring, in a well drained fertile soil, in a sunny, sheltered spot, preferably against a warm wall. In colder areas, protect the base of the plant in winter by a mulch of branches or straw. Prune the previous year's wood back at the end of winter. Berries are more freely produced if several plants are grown together.

Propagate from softwood cuttings in early summer, or by seed.

Callirhoe

Poppy mallow, *Malvaceae*

The genus has its origins in North America and comprises eight, mostly perennial, species. Its rhizomes are turnip-shaped, its leaves are arranged alternately and are deeply lobed, and the flowers showy.

C. involucrata (zone 7) grows to 8 in (20 cm) with a spread of 16–24 in (40–60 cm). This is a perennial, trailing plant with hairy, hand-shaped leaves. Funnel-shaped flowers range from pink to bright scarlet with white bases and bloom non-stop from early summer to mid autumn.
Cultivation. Plant in dry soil in full sun. It is suitable for a dry rockery, bank, border, balcony or kitchen-garden.

Propagate from seed sown in situ in spring and thinned to the required distance. If sown early enough, it may produce flowers the same year. It can also be increased by the cutting of young shoots placed in a sandy soil in a frame.

Callistemon

Bottlebrush, *Myrtaceae*

Around 20 species make up this genus of elegant shrubs which originate in Australia. Measuring 6½–10 ft (2–3 m) they have evergreen, light foliage, but are grown for their bottle-brush like spikes of flowers, with their tufts of red, bright pink or yellow stamens, crowned by a tuft of leaves. They are hardy only in frost-free areas.
C. citrinus (*C. lanceolatus*) – zone 9 – is 6½–10 ft (2–3 m) tall, and its leaves are lemon-scented when crushed. In mid summer, it produces ruby-red flowers. 'Splendens' has bright crimson flowers with longer stamens.
C. pallidus (zone 9), 10–13 ft (3–4 m) high, has pale-yellow flowers, from early to late summer.
C. viminalis (zone 10), weeping bottle brush, 20–30 ft (6–9 m) tall, has a weeping habit and is rather more tender than the above-named species. Red flowers are produced from late spring to late summer.
Cultivation. Grown in full sun, in moist but well drained, lime-free soil. Plant in a 10–12 in (25–30 cm) pot with a loam-based compost and keep in a cool greenhouse in winter months. Their supple branches can be attached to a support, pallisade fashion. Water freely during the growing season.

Propagate from cuttings.

Callistephus

China aster, *Compositae*

This is a genus of one species, *C. chinensis* (zone 6), which is an annual excellent for late summer borders, for cutting and container growing. It includes a wide range of single and double-flowered cultivars in white, pink, red, purple or blue, sold in single or mixed colours.
Cultivars. 'American Beauty', 28–32 in (70–80 cm) tall carries large double flowers. 'Ostrich Plume' 12–20 in (30–50 cm) tall, has early flowers with feathery, reflexed petals. 'Princess', 24–28 in (60–70 cm) tall, has large, double flowers with a quilled, cushion-like centre; 'Super Chinensis' carries semi-double flowers; 'Giant Single Andrella' 24 in (60 cm) tall, produces large, single flowers with yellow centres.
Cultivation. Callistephus can be grown as half-hardy or hardy annuals. Sow under glass in mid spring and plant out in late spring, or sow direct in late spring for a late summer display. Space out at 8 in (20 cm) apart for small varieties, 16 in (40 cm) for medium-sized ones and 24 in (60 cm) for the larger kind.

Because the plants are vulnerable to wilt, avoid planting in the same spot two years running. Pinch the young plants to encourage branching, and stake the larger varieties. Remove faded flowers to extend the flowering period.

The plant may be attacked by cucumber mosaic virus (evident from yellow patches on leaves and deformed flowers), black neck (blackening at the base of the stems) and fusarium wilt. Foliage is susceptible to attack by various aphids and caterpillars.

Calluna

Ling, heather, *Ericaceae*

Calluna vulgaris (zone 5), the only species in the genus, is hardy in all regions and found wild in Europe and Asia Minor. Ling has produced many cultivars whose height and spread vary from 4–28 in (10–70 cm). Their evergreen, scale-like leaves in green, grey ('Silver Queen') and even orange-red ('Multicolor') hues are particularly attractive. Generally they flower from early summer to autumn, having terminal spikes of small, bell-like flowers in colours ranging from white, pink, red or purple.

Ling is useful planted in groups, in beds with other acid-loving plants, in the rockery or simply as a ground cover.
Cultivation. Provided that it has a damp, light, enriched peaty soil, Calluna is easy to grow. Plant in autumn or spring, 8–20 in (20–50 cm)

apart, according to variety, in sun or semi-shade. Add a peat mulch in spring, and water in dry weather.

Remove dried and dead flowers in spring; to avoid the plant becoming straggly it is also worthwhile cutting them back after a few years, by trimming down to old wood.

The easiest method of propagation is to take cuttings of lateral shoots at the end of summer.

Caltha

Marsh marigold, kingcup, *Ranunculaceae*

Around 10 perennial herbaceous species make up this genus. Of north-temperate origin, the plants are aquatic relatives of the buttercup with large golden-yellow flowers and wide, round toothed brilliant green leaves.

C. palustris (zone 6), found wild in N. America and Europe, is typical of the genus. The cultivar 'Alba' has white flowers and yellow stamens, while 'Floreplena' has bright yellow double flowers.

Easy to grow, they do best on river banks or around pools and are indispensable for any damp spot in the garden. Plant with rushes, water-loving irises or sedges with grey leaves for the contrast of their upright foliage.

Cultivation. Quite hardy even in the harshest of climates, marsh marigolds will grow in just about any soil and flower abundantly in the spring, in sun or semi-shade.

They grow prolifically in damp soil so propagation is easily achieved by dividing the clumps at the beginning of spring or in autumn. Alternatively, sow ripe seeds during summer or the following spring.

Calycanthus

Sweet shrub, allspice, *Calycanthaceae*

This genus, native to North America, has sea-green, oval, downy leaves. Aromatic flowers are either yellowish- or red-brown.

C. floridus (zone 7–8), Carolina allspice, comes from southeast USA and grows up to 10 ft (3 m). The mahogany coloured, aromatic flowers come out in early to mid summer.

C. occidentalis (*C. macrophyllus*) – zone 8 – Californian allspice, bears large $2\frac{3}{4}$ in (7 cm) long flowers which are also mahogany, but paler, in early to mid summer. It will produce less

Caltha palustris

flowers than *C. floridus* and is more tender.

They can be grown as specimens, as hedges or in groups.

Cultivation. Preferably plant in a good, moist, open lime-free soil although it is adaptable to most soils.

Propagate from seed or by layering.

Camassia

Quamash, *Liliaceae*

This genus of bulbs comprises five species which originate in North and South America. The pear-shaped or spherical bulb will produce a rosette of linear, green or sea-green leaves in spring, and in early summer the flower-stem bears a raceme of 10 to 20 star-shaped flowers, similar to those of the asphodel, ranging in colour from white to pale violet or blue.

C. cusickii (zone 7) grows 20–32 in (50–80 cm) tall with pale blue flowers and blue-green leaves.

C. quamash (*C. esculenta*) – zone 7 – quamash, is similar, but is smaller and with flowers which may be white, pale blue or deep violet-blue.

C. leichtlinii (zone 7), generally 3 ft (90 cm) tall, can grow to 4 ft (1.3 m). Its flowers range from white to deep violet or blue.

Camassias are hardy plants that naturally grow in damp prairies and look best when planted in groups for naturalizing in grass, in a wild garden, or in the mixed border.

Cultivation. Plant in early to mid autumn in a heavy soil which will not dry out.

Propagate from ripe seed sown outdoors; it flowers after four years. The clumps of bulbs can be split up in early autumn.

Camellia japonica cultivar

Camellia
Theaceae

Some 80 species of evergreen trees and shrubs from Asia make up this genus and include the species from which tea is obtained.

These splendid shrubs are well known for their evergreen glossy foliage and spectacular blooms in winter or spring. The single or double flowers come in tints ranging from pure white to bright red and the plants can grow 5–13 ft (1.5–4 m) tall and almost as wide. Camellias will generally survive quite hard frosts and can be planted in colder climates, but because they flower in winter and early spring they need to be protected from snow which will spoil their blooms.

Cultivars. The better known are derived from *C. japonica* (zone 6–7), with leathery brilliant, deep-green leaves, and flowers in late winter. 'Adolphe Audusson' bears semi-double scarlet flowers with yellow stamens; 'Alba Simplex' has single white flowers; 'Gloire de Nantes' carries semi-double pink flowers. The hybrid group *C. × williamsii* (zone 7), often needs to be sheltered by a wall and will flower from late autumn to early spring, like the famous 'Donation' which has semi-double, pearly pink flowers. *C. sasanqua* (zone 7–8), with white and pale pink flowers, also blooms from autumn to spring and like the hybrids requires wall protection in cold areas.

Camellias must have a lime-free, light and moist soil (if possible enriched with peat) and combine well with azaleas and rhododendrons.

Cultivation. Plant camellias in early autumn or spring in a semi-shaded spot where they will be sheltered from cold winds and the morning sun to allow any frosted blooms to thaw out gradually.

A mulch of leaf-mould will benefit them in spring. It is advisable to remove the dead flowers on *C. japonica* varieties.

Propagate in late summer by semi-hardwood cuttings or by leaf cuttings inserted in pots containing sandy peat, plunged in a cool frame.

Camellia sasanqua

Campanula
Bellflower, *Campanulaceae*

This large genus comprises about 300 species of biennial and perennial herbaceous plants found in most regions, and characterized by their usually bell-shaped flowers in shades ranging from white to violet-blue. Leaves are usually round or oval, more or less toothed, mid green.

Among the most commonly grown in zones 5–6 are *C. carpatica*, 8–12 in (20–30 cm) tall, with saucer-shaped flowers of white or blue; *C. cochlearifolia*, 4–6 in (10–15 cm) with abundant white or blue flowers; *C. latifolia*, 2.5–4 ft (0.8–1.2 m), has long clusters of tubular white or violet blue flowers; *C. medium*, Canterbury bell, up to 3 ft (90 cm) tall is biennial and has white, pink or blue flowers; the cup and saucer variety, 'Calycanthema' is a pretty cottage-garden plant; *C. persicifolia*, 24 32 in (60–80 cm), which has evergreen basal leaves and clusters of saucer-shaped white or blue flowers; *C. portenschlagiana*, 4–8 in (10–20 cm), with long-lasting purple-blue flowers. All flower from early summer through to early autumn.

Depending on their size, campanulas can be grown in the rock garden, wall crevices, or in herbaceous and mixed borders.

Campanula latifolia cultivar

Cultivation. Plant in sun or semi-shade in autumn or spring, in a fertile, well-drained soil, if possible enriched with manure or compost. Each year add compost in spring and cut back dead growth.

Campanulas can be propagated from seed, from cuttings, or by dividing clumps in the spring. Slugs and snails may attack the young shoots and some species are prone to attacks of rust, which produces orange patches on the leaves.

Campsis

Trumpet creeper, trumpet vine, *Bignoniaceae*

This genus comprises two species of vigorous, deciduous climbing shrubs.

C. grandiflora (zone 9), from China, grows to 30 ft (9 m) and is not as hardy as the next species but equally attractive.

C. radicans (zone 8–9), from North America, 40–50 ft (12–15 m) tall, is a hardy deciduous species. It bears pinnate leaves 2–4 in (5–10 cm) long and has clinging stems. Its orange-red flowers, somewhat similar in shape to foxglove's trumpets appear in mid to late summer.

C. × *tagliabuana* (zone 8–9) is a garden hybrid between the two species and has inherited the more hardy attributes of its North American parent.

They are all best treated as semi-hardy and grown against a wall or up a tree-trunk in a warm, sunny and sheltered position.

Cultivation. Plant in any ordinary, even a chalky soil, in full sun.

Propagate from root or woody cuttings in spring, under glass, at a temperature of 70–75°F (21–24°C) or by layering the suckers in the summer.

Canna

Indian shot, Canna lily *Cannaceae*

The genus includes about 25 rhizomatous species from tropical and warm temperate America. At flowering time the lanceolate to heart-shaped leaves with sheathing bases are borne on a stem about $3\frac{1}{2}$–6 ft (1–1.8 m) long with a cluster of showy flowers at the top.

C. indica (zone 9–10), Indian shot, is some $3\frac{1}{2}$–5 ft (1–1.5 m) tall. This tender plant carries narrow, bright red or orange flowers with yellow spotted lower lips. It blooms throughout summer.

Many named hybrids are commercially available, with an interesting variety of leaf colour. 'Le Roi Humbert', 'Red King Humbert', for example, has bronze leaves and deep red blooms and large flowers in brilliant hues.

Cannas are used to provide variety in summer bedding schemes and mixed borders.

Cultivation. Plant in spring after the frosts, in a rich, well-irrigated soil in a very sunny position.

When autumn frosts arrive cut back the stems and pull up the rhizomes, which should then be stored in a cool, dry place, in either sand or peat.

Propagate by dividing the rhizomes, but leave at least three to five eyes per division. It is easy to grow from seed sown in early spring in a warm house and plants will flower in a year. The seed cases should be soaked and to facilitate germination, the testa (seed coat) filed through before sowing.

Cantua

Polemoniaceae

This genus is represented by six species originating in the Andes of South America. Branched and bushy, these shrubs bear delicate, long-lasting leaves and long tubular flowers arranged in compact clusters. Cantuas need a frost-free climate, or they can be grown in a cool greenhouse.

C. buxifolia (zone 9–10), magic flower of the Incas, from Peru, Bolivia and Chile, is 6½ ft (2 m) tall. Its tubular flowers in tints of cameo pink, scarlet and fuchsia bloom in late spring to early summer.

C. bicolor (zone 10), from Bolivia, will grow to 6½ ft (2 m) tall and has yellow and red flowers.

In suitable climates they can be used to decorate rocky banks.

Cultivation. The bushes will not tolerate a highly alkaline soil.

Propagate from cuttings, which should be placed under glass with slight bottom heat, or from seed.

Capparis

Caper-bush, *Capparidaceae*

The genus is represented by about 250 species of erect or climbing shrubs, which originate in warm temperate regions. Their stems are often spiny and the flowers range from white to purplish violet, depending on the species.

C. spinosa (zone 10), common caper, is a superb shrub sadly under-used, some 5 ft (1.5 m) tall. Pinkish white flowers with long carmine-pink stamens bloom in early to mid summer. The flower-buds, known as capers, should be picked just before they open if they are to be used for pickling.

In frost-free climates it can be used as a specimen shrub, as a hedge or at the back of a mixed border, otherwise grow in a warm greenhouse.

Cultivation. Plant in light, well-drained, sandy loam. It is a straggly shrub and should be cut back regularly to encourage bushiness.

Propagate by layering or by cuttings placed in sand, under glass with bottom heat.

Capsicum

Pepper, pimento, *Solanaceae*

These annual or perennial plants are natives of tropical South America.

C. annuum (zone 10), sweet pepper, grows up to 1–3 ft (30–90 cm) high and bears hollow fruits from 1–6 in (3–15 cm) long in various shapes; the fruit has a thick skin which is green at first, then ripens through yellow to red or black, or may remain orange or yellow, according to cultivar.

C. frutescens (zone 10), chilli pepper, is a perennial which has smaller fruit than the sweet pepper. The fruit may be green or red and is strong-flavoured. The dried fruits are powdered to produce cayenne pepper.

Cultivars. *C. frutescens* includes such cultivars as 'Cayenne Chilli' and 'Chilli Serrano'. *C. annuum* has many fine cultivars e.g. 'Big Bertha', 'Canape', 'Early Prolific', 'Gold Star', 'Gypsy', 'New Ace', and 'Worldbeater'. Other cultivars of both species are grown as pot plants for the decorative quality of their fruits.

Cultivation. In regions with frost these plants cannot ripen thoroughly, therefore greenhouse conditions are needed at least to start them off. Then plant them out in a warm, sheltered place in the garden. Sow seed in early spring in heat in pots or pans. As soon as the seedlings can be handled they should be put into small pots and kept heated until the roots have developed. Plant into larger pots and gradually harden off before planting in the open at distances of 2 ft (60 cm) apart in late spring, against a warm wall or sunny sheltered corner. Alternatively the large pots can stay under glass provided the compost is rich and they are well fed.

Weed by hand and water regularly. Remove some flowers to obtain larger fruit. As soon as the latter appear, water with a liquid fertilizer, once every ten days. Spray with warm water when pollination takes place.

Output should be 3 lb sq yd (1.5 kg m²) and you can harvest from open ground until late summer or until mid autumn in the greenhouse. They can be stored for several months, provided that the fruit has been picked with some of its stalk, and then hung up with a length of string in a dry place.

Pests to watch out for include red spider mites and aphids as well as grey mould, a fungal disease which may affect the fruit.

Cardamine

Cruciferae

The genus consists of about 130 herbaceous, annual or perennial species which originate in temperate zones. The perennial species have creeping, sometimes tuberous rhizomes. The annuals are common weeds of uncultivated ground.

C. pratensis (zone 5), lady's smock or cuckoo flower, is found in Europe, Asia and North America. It grows 12–20 in (30–50 cm) tall with a spread of 8 in (20 cm), it has a creeping rhizome, and is often considered undesirable. Leaves are divided into 3–11 leaflets. The lilac-pink flowers come out in spring. The double-flowered form 'Flore Pleno', which is better for garden purposes looks quite charming with *Caltha palustris* 'Florepleno' as a partner.

Cultivation. Plant from mid autumn to early spring, in a heavy, moist soil, in sun or semi-shade.

The double-flowered form does not set seed, but can be divided in spring after it has flowered or, alternatively, from leaf cuttings inserted in moist soil.

Cardiocrinum

Giant Himalayan lily, *Liliaceae*

The genus comprises three perennial bulbous species which are found in a wide region from the Himalayas to China and Japan. The bulb produces a stem which can grow over 6½ ft (2 m) tall at flowering time, after which it dies. Such plants are called monocarpic. However, it leaves small offset bulbs which grow on and flower some years later. The flower spike is made up of 4–25 trumpet-shaped flowers, which are white with a dark purple centre and achieve an impressive size. Heart-shaped leaves are arranged in a basal rosette and also alternately up the stem.

C. cordatum (zone 7) is 4–6 ft (1.2–1.8 m) tall. White flowers with yellow or purple spots inside appear in late summer.

C. giganteum (zone 7), giant Himalayan lily, can grow 6–13 ft (1.8–4 m) in height and bear as many as 25 large, white scented flowers with purple stripes inside, in mid summer.

These plants are best in the semi-shade cast by shrubs or in a woodland clearing. A group of three or five is more impressive than just a single specimen.

Cultivation. In autumn or the beginning of spring, plant deeply in a damp humus-rich soil, which is light and well drained. The Eastern Atlantic climate is particularly suitable for them. A bulb planted too near the surface could well suffer in colder climates in winter.

Propagate from the bulblets or from seed; the latter should be vernalized (subjected to a cold temperature) and will usually only germinate after a year.

Carduncellus

Compositae

About 30 species of biennial or perennial plants constitute this genus. Natives of the Mediterranean region, the plants are spiny, often without stalks, with a basal rosette of leaves.

C. rhaponticoides (zone 6), a native of North Africa, is 4 in (10 cm) tall with a spread of 6–12 in (15–30 cm). Its large rosette lies flat on the ground and consists of deep green spatula-shaped leaves edged with whitish hairs, and with petioles and central veins of red. Bluish-violet flower-heads, 2 in (5 cm) wide, resembling those of the knapweed (*Centaurea*), appear singly at the centre of the rosette in late spring or early summer.

The species is happy in a rock garden or trough, with other low-growing species, such as *Anacyclus depressus, Erinus alpinus*, or *Sedum dasyphyllum*.

Cultivation. Plant in spring in full sun, between stones. The sub-soil should be well-drained for, although the plant is hardy, it will not tolerate winter wet. Propagate from root cuttings of lateral shoots at the beginning of spring. Alternatively, increase by division.

Carex

Sedge, *Cyperaceae*

Sedges are quite common in damp places, where they will form compact, but hardly attractive clumps. They are remarkably hardy, however, and valuable for their ability to stabilize banks. Among the 1000 known species, less than 10 have any real ornamental value.

C. acutiformis (zone 6), which is 2 ft (60 cm) tall, has a sea-green sheen. It is notable for its unusual black flowers, which it bears in spring. Its growth should be checked by surrounding it with taller, robust plants such as the grass *Miscanthus sinensis* or the club-rush *Scirpus lacustris*. It can be planted on river banks or any slightly flooded spot.

C. pendula (zone 6), is a tall species which likes shade and a damp, humus-rich soil. It produces large clumps of light green leaves and has decorative hanging spikes.

C. morrowii (zone 9), a native of Japan, is a dwarf compact species. The cultivar with white-variegated leaves, 'Variegata', makes a pretty ground cover for a damp spot.

Cultivation. The plants are easy to cultivate and may be propagated in spring by division.

Carica

Pawpaw, papaya *Caricaceae*

A genus of about 20 evergreen trees native to tropical America, one of which is an important economic plant.

Carica papaya (zone 10+) is a semi-woody plant from South America, usually growing 10–13 ft (3–4 m) tall, and sometimes as much as 26 ft (8 m).

The jagged leaves form a tuft at the top of the trunk. Creamy white flowers are grouped in the leaf-axils. Outdoors it needs a very warm climate; indoors it needs stove conditions to survive for long.

Cultivation. Plant in a rich, well-drained but damp loamy soil in full sun. The pawpaw or papaya needs frequent watering and fertilizing.

Propagate from fresh seed in a sandy soil with gentle heat. Treat the seedlings with care as they are subject to damping off. Alternatively, take cuttings from mature shoots together with an entire leaf and place in sand, under glass with some bottom heat.

Carissa

Apocynaceae

This genus is represented by 37 evergreen trees native to tropical or subtropical regions.

C. grandiflora (zone 10), Natal plum, is a large spiny shrub, growing 10–20 ft (3–6 m) tall. It comes from Natal in South Africa and grows best in frost-free areas.

This species has fragrant white flowers from mid summer to mid autumn, and its edible red fruits have a mild flavour.

Cultivation. It can be grown in almost any soil, though a mixture of peat and loams suits it best, and it will tolerate light frosts.

Propagate from cuttings placed in a mixture of equal parts of soil, leaf-mould and sand, with bottom heat.

Carlina

Compositae

The genus comprises 28 herbaceous biennial and perennial species found in the mountains of Europe and Asia. Thistle-like, they are spiny plants with flower-heads wider than they are tall.

C. acaulis (zone 5), stemless carlina thistle, from Europe is 8 in (20 cm) tall, has jagged, evergreen leaves and stemless, brilliant silver-white flower-heads which appear in mid summer. Var. *caulescens* is characterized by its flower-heads being borne on prominent stalks, 4–10 in (10–25 cm) tall.

It makes a lovely plant for a rock garden with limy or chalky soil, or at the front of a well-drained sunny border. It dries well.

Cultivation. The plant prefers a poor, gravelly, well-drained soil, and it benefits every five or six years from a little fresh cow dung, which it is used to in its alpine meadow habitat.

To propagate, seeds collected in the autumn are sown the following spring, in well-drained soil.

Carpenteria

Tree anemone *Hydrangeaceae* (*Philadelphaceae*)

The genus is represented by a single species – a splendid shrub from California.

C. californica (zone 8–9), bushy in appearance, is $6\frac{1}{2}$–10 ft (2–3 m) tall. Its brilliant green foliage is evergreen and its large, fragrant white flowers, $2\frac{3}{4}$–$3\frac{1}{4}$ in (7–8 cm) wide are reminiscent of a wild white rose with bunches of golden stamens.

Cultivation. Plant in a light, well-drained loamy soil, in a sunny position. Protect in areas affected by frost. Its supple branches allow it to be trained on a wall, where it looks particularly attractive.

Propagate by layering or from suckers, or by taking cuttings and placing under glass, in summer, in a mixture of equal parts soil, leaf-mould and sand.

Carpinus

Hornbeam, *Betulaceae*

A genus of over 30 deciduous trees from temperate regions in the Northern Hemisphere.

C. betulus (zone 6), common hornbeam, is found mainly in lowland areas, easily recognized by its grooved trunk. It can reach a height of 66 ft (20 m); its crown is ovoid and the branches are slender. The dark grey bark is smooth and the oblong, toothed leaves are 2 to $3\frac{3}{4}$ in (5–8 cm) long. Flowers grow in hanging catkins, male or female. The fruits, called achenes, are surrounded by a wing, deeply divided into three lobes. It makes good hedging material, its dead leaves keeping their brown coloration throughout the winter.

Hornbeam has produced several horticultural forms, somewhat shorter than the species itself. 'Fastigiata', for example, has a useful narrow upright shape. Other North American and Chinese species are also worth cultivating.

Cultivation. Plant in autumn or in spring. For hedges, planting distance should be 5 ft (1.5 cm) and clipped every summer. The hornbeam is quite hardy and will grow in a deep clay or lime soil, cool and damp.

Propagate from seed, sown in the spring, after they have been vernalized (subjected to a cold temperature); cultivars must be grafted.

Carum

Umbelliferae

This genus of annual, biennial or perennial herbaceous plants has only one species of importance.

C. carvi (zone 7), caraway, is a biennial native of Europe and Asia as far east as northern India. It has slender stems topped with umbels of white flowers, 1–2 ft (30–60 cm) tall, in early to mid summer in the year following their sowing. The lacy ornamental leaves are aromatic, as are the seeds, which are commonly used for culinary purposes.

Cultivation. In late summer to early autumn, sow in rows 12–16 in (30–40 cm) apart and thin out to 14 in (35 cm). Caraway grows best in well-drained soil, in full sun.

Pick the young leaves as they are required. Cut the umbels after flowering, before the seeds start to ripen, and hang them in a warm, well-aired place where they can continue to ripen, placing a canvas or cloth underneath to catch falling seeds.

Uses. Commonly used in cake-making, the seeds can also be used to flavour many dishes such as soup, sauerkraut, game, vegetables and cheese.

Caryopteris

Bluebeard, *Verbenaceae*

About six shrubs or herbaceous plants make up this genus, all native to East Asia.

C. × *clandonensis* (zone 6–7), a hybrid between two of the species, is a small shrub which will grow only to $2\frac{1}{2}$–$3\frac{1}{2}$ ft (80 cm–1 m) tall and wide. It has slender, grey-green, faintly aromatic deciduous leaves and is best loved for its autumn blooms, which last from late summer to the first frosts. It bears clusters of small, bright blue, tubular flowers.

It is hardy just about anywhere, except in extremely cold climates and is particularly suitable for a mixed border or in the herb-garden with other aromatic plants.

Cultivation. Plant in autumn or spring in any well-drained soil, preferably one which is light and limy. It prefers full sun, but will tolerate some shade.

In colder regions, protect in winter with a mulch of dry leaves and in spring cut to within 6 in (15 cm) of the ground. In mild climates, at the beginning of spring cut out any dead wood and trim back shoots from the preceding year's growth by an inch or so.

Propagate from semi-hardwood cuttings in late summer to early autumn and place in a cold frame.

Cassia

Senna, shower tree, *Leguminosae*

The genus is represented by some 530 species of plants originating in tropical and sub-tropical regions. They can range from perennial bushy plants to trees 33–50 ft (10–15 m) tall. The airy foliage is bright green and its flowers are usually borne in clusters, rarely singly, and in most species are golden-yellow. The pods are used in pharmacies and the herbalist's shop.

C. marilandica – zone 10 – (correctly *Senna marilandica*), wild senna, Maryland senna, from south-eastern United States, is 3½–5 ft (1–1.5 m) tall. It is an erect semi-woody plant with few branches and brilliant green foliage. Clusters of yellow flowers appear in late summer to early autumn.

C. corymbosa – zone 9–10 – (*C. floribunda* and properly *S.* × *floribunda*), is a native of Mexico, which grows up to 6½–10 ft (2–3 m) tall. A lovely erect shrub, it bears bright green foliage with large, brilliant yellow flowers in corymbs, which appear in late summer to early autumn, but it is susceptible to severe frost.

C. fistula (zone 10), golden shower, which comes from India and Sri Lanka, will grow 6½–10 ft (2–3 m) tall. Yellow flowers are carried in large clusters, 12 in (30 cm) long; its long pods are used by herbalists. This shrub must be grown in frost-free areas.

Cultivation. Plant in a dry, well-drained soil in a sunny position or in a glasshouse.

Propagate from semi-hardwood cuttings or seed.

Cassiope

Ericaceae

Consisting of some 12 species, this genus of hardy dwarf somewhat heath-like evergreen shrubs, which originate in the Northern Hemisphere, bear small, very compact leaves and white or pink flowers. They are sometimes mistakenly classified as belonging to the genus *Andromeda*.

C. fastigiata (zone 6), a native of the Himalayas is an erect shrub 8–12 in (20–30 cm) tall. It has deep green leaves bordered with white. Its white flowers appear in late spring.

C. hypnoides (zone 4), which comes from the Arctic regions of Europe and North America is a moss-like, mat-forming shrub. It will grow up to 2-4 in (5–10 cm) and its white flowers appear in early summer.

Cultivation. Plant in moist well-drained acid (non-limy) soil, in a shady or semi-shady position (a cold-facing aspect is ideal). They will suffer from drought.

Propagate from seeds, by layering, or semi-hardwood cuttings of non-flowering shoots, which should be placed under glass.

Castanea

Chestnut, *Fagaceae*

The genus comprises a dozen or so deciduous trees and shrubs from northern temperate regions. The genus includes *C. dentata*, the US chestnut and *C. Mollisima*, the Chinese chestnut. Like the walnut, the sweet or Spanish chestnut, *C. sativa* (zone 6), has been cultivated for a long time and many, improved, chestnut-producing cultivars have been developed.

A deciduous tree, it can grow as high as 66 ft (20 m) and has a substantial trunk with obliquely ribbed bark. The oblong leaves are toothed and the flowers, carried in catkins, appear in early to mid summer. The nuts are produced in mid autumn, either singly or in groups of two or three, in a spiky fruit case which splits open on ripening.

The sweet chestnut is an imposing tree, usually planted as a specimen; it is wise to bear in mind that it needs plenty of room.

Cultivation. It likes a deep, acid or neutral soil, so alluvial soil in a non-alkaline area will suit it best. It can be affected by various diseases such as canker, chestnut blight or ink disease and will tend to produce many suckers and die back.

Propagate from seed, or in the case of cultivars, by spring grafting. Stock for grafting should be taken from disease-free specimens.

Catalpa

Indian bean, *Bignoniaceae*

The catalpas are hardy, deciduous trees native to America and east Asia which grow rapidly to a height of 33 ft (10 m). They prefer shade and spread out as they mature. Large heart-shaped leaves are carried on stout branches and bell-shaped flowers appear in summer in long panicles at the ends of branches.

C. bignonioides (zone 7), from the eastern USA, is 25–50 ft (8–15 m) tall. Its light-coloured bark tends to crack with age, and the leaves develop quite late in the spring. Wide-open white flowers have small yellow and purple spots in their throats. The decorative bean-shaped fruits persist throughout the winter. There is a dwarf variety, 'Nana', whose very compact head is in the shape of a ball 6½–10 ft (2–3 m) in diameter.

This is a tree for a park setting, but can be used in the garden, provided it is kept small by pruning well each winter. This will check its flowering, but will increase the size of its leaves to provide a beautiful foliage effect. Even better for this purpose is the rich yellow-leaved cultivar, 'Aurea'.

Cultivation. Plant in autumn or spring in a moist loamy soil. This catalpa is quite hardy but is intolerant of positions that are too exposed to the wind or where the soil becomes too dry.

Propagate from seed in spring or cuttings of short side shoots, which in late summer will root easily under glass with some bottom heat.

Catananche

Compositae

The genus includes five species of hardy, herbaceous perennials or annuals from Mediterranean areas.

C. caerulea (zone 7), Cupid's dart, is a perennial 16–28 in (40–70 cm) tall with a spread of 12–16 in (30–40 cm). Its silvery grey leaves are narrowly lanceolate. From mid summer to early autumn there is a non-stop display of slender stems carrying flower-heads of violet-blue with brownish, papery bracts.

This hardy plant suits a large sunny rock garden or flower border. The flowers are good both for cutting and drying.

Cultivation. Cupid's dart is a floriferous plant, but short lived, rarely more than two or three years. It is best to plant it in a dry, light, well-drained soil in full sun.

To propagate, sow seed in mid to late spring in a seed tray in a cold frame.

Catananche caerulea

Ceanothus

Californian lilac, *Rhamnaceae*

This genus of over 50 evergreen and deciduous shrubs, mostly from California but some from eastern North America, are greatly appreciated for their stunning blue, sometimes pink or white, flowers. *C. Americanus* is hardy to zone 4 and popular in the USA. Deciduous hybrids, such as 'Gloire de Versailles' (zone 8), with bright blue flowers, or 'Marie Simon' (zone 8), with pink, are hardy in most regions, whereas evergreen species like *C. impressus* (zone 9) or *C. thyrsiflorus* (zone 7–8) are safer in a Mediterranean-type or mild oceanic climate.

These vigorous shrubs grow, depending on the species or cultivar, 3½–10 ft (1–3 m) tall with the same spread and may be grown against a sheltered wall or in a mixed border. They flower prolifically and bear clusters of small star-shaped flowers. Some are spring flowering and others bloom in summer and into autumn.

Cultivation. Plant in autumn or spring, avoiding really cold weather, in a deep, fertile, well-drained soil, preferably non-alkaline, in full sun or in the shelter of a wall. Some species suffer

Ceanothus 'Marie Simon'

from chlorosis (yellowing of the leaves) when planted in soils that are too calcareous.

Evergreen ceanothus should be pruned by cutting back the previous year's growth by a half in mid spring. The deciduous species can be cut back even more at the same time.

The easiest method of propagation is to take semi-hardwood cuttings in late summer to early autumn.

Cedrus

Cedar, *Pinaceae*

These are tall conifers growing to around 100 ft (30 m). When young they are slender and supple, becoming broader with age. Wide spreading branches are supported by a massive trunk. Evergreen, needle-shaped leaves are grouped in rosettes on short branchlets. The cones are large and barrel-shaped.

C. atlantica (zone 6), Atlas cedar, from North Africa, is about 100 ft (30 m) tall and its 1 in (2 cm) long leaves are green or sea-green. Its cones can grow to 3¼ in (8 cm) with the central cone lasting longer than that of the cedar of Lebanon. The following cultivars are widely available: 'Glauca', blue Atlas cedar, is one of the most spectacular of the conifers, with fine blue-green needles; 'Pendula', the weeping cedar, is characterized by a short stocky appearance with branches which hang down to the ground; it has blue-green or green leaves and its spread can be quite considerable.

C. deodara (zone 6), Himalayan cedar, from the high forests of Afghanistan and the west Himalaya, sometimes grows to more than 100 ft (30 m). The needles are longer than those of the previous species and may turn red and die during harsh winters, to be replaced in the spring. Its slow-growing cultivar, 'Aurea', reaches about 17 ft (5 m), its new shoots flushed with gold.

C. libani (zone 6), the cedar of Lebanon, originates in Turkey, Syria and the Lebanon and grows up to 100 ft (30 m). This species grows quite slowly with a narrow conical habit in its young stage but with horizontal branches when mature.

Cedars are most commonly found as specimens in parks and because of their root activity and eventual size should not be planted near buildings. As young trees they are beautiful and can be planted in smaller gardens provided they are replaced after about 20 years.

Cultivation. Plant with a root ball in the spring in a sunny position. Cedars, with the exception of *C. deodara*, are very hardy. This species does not usually like cold and damp winters. They are not particular about soil, but prefer a rich loam and an open subsoil so that they can spread their roots.

Propagate from seed in the spring by collecting cones and sowing seeds immediately, and plant out in the open nursery the following spring. In the case of cultivars, graft in late winter or early spring using the parent species as stock.

Celmisia

Compositae

The genus comprises some 60 species originating in New Zealand and Australia, most of which are herbaceous or sub-shrubs, perennial and more or less hardy. Felted leaves are

arranged in rosettes or along branches. Pure white daisy-like flowers, occasionally mauve or light yellow, have yellow or purple centres.
C. bellidioides (zone 6) is 3¼–4 in (8–10 cm) tall with a spread of 8 in (20 cm). This is the easiest species to grow, being very hardy. It has flat clumps of dark green leaves and flowers on short stems, from late spring to mid summer.
C. spectabilis (zone 7) is 14–16 in (35–40 cm) tall with a spread of 20 in (50 cm) and is the largest of its genus. The long, broad, pointed leaves are grey, and white flowers 1–2 in (3–5 cm) in diameter appear in summer.

Celmisias can be grown in well-drained rock gardens where winters are not too severe, or in an alpine house.

Cultivation. Plant in well-drained, moist, peaty soil in the sun or semi-shade. While they are fond of atmospheric humidity they do not like too much water on their leaves in the winter. Propagate by division in spring.

Celosia

Cockscomb, woolflower, *Amaranthaceae*

The genus includes some 60 annual species from tropical and subtropical regions.
C. cristata (zone 10), cockscomb, is 2 ft (60 cm) tall. Plumed flowers vary from yellow to red.
Cultivars. The dwarf 'Lilliput' or 'Jewel Box' 9 in–1 ft (21–30 cm) tall, have flowers of many colours; 'Plumosa', 10 in (25 cm) tall, is dwarf with red plumes; 'Exhibition Triumph', 28 in (70 cm) tall, has yellow, red, pink or violet plumes on a background of bronze-green leaves; 'Apricot Brandy' has orange plumes on compact plants.

Cockscomb is grown in summer flower beds and makes an excellent cut flower.

Cultivation. Sow in heat in early spring. Plant out and gradually harden off the young plants until their final planting in late spring or early summer. It likes a well-drained, but rich, deep, peaty soil. Water generously in dry weather.

The neck and roots can be attacked by rot, which will cause wilting and eventual death.

Celtis

Nettle tree, hackberry *Ulmaceae*

These are deciduous trees and shrubs, some of which make good shade trees for sunny countries. *C. occidentalis* is the native US hackberry and hardy to zone 2. A few species come from the Mediterranean region, but others are tropical and rarely cultivated.
C. australis (zone 9), originating in southern Europe can grow up to 66 ft (20 m) tall. Its round, bushy crown somewhat resembles the cherry-tree. It has a massive, grooved trunk with grey bark, smooth in young trees, but growing rough with age. Lanceolate, pointed and toothed leaves are pubescent on the underside. The flowers are insignificant and are followed by violet or reddish fruits, which look rather like cherries.

This tree grows well in frost-free areas and its wood is used to make handles for tools and pitch-forks, in other areas it tends to be cut back by frost with the result that it seldom forms a trunk of any size.

Cultivation. Plant at the end of winter or in spring. The nettle tree prefers rich, cool soil, but will also do well in drier conditions. Young trees grow well in shade.

Propagate from seed or by cuttings or from suckers, which are often plentiful.

Centaurea

Knapweed, *Compositae*

The genus comprises about 450 species, many native to the Mediterranean region. The plants are herbaceous and most are hardy.
C. montana, a perennial that grows up to 12–20 in (30–50 cm). It forms loose clumps with narrow, lanceolate, mid-green leaves. It is grown for its solitary flower-heads which are cornflower blue; white and pink cultivars are also available. Flowers are borne from early to late summer.

Other hardy decorative perennial species include *C. dealbata*, which is much the same size and has lilac-pink or sometimes purple flowers and *C. macrocephala*, which produces large, yellow flower-heads on robust stems about 4 ft (1.2 m) tall in early to mid summer. These species can all be used in borders.
C. cyanus, the cornflower, is an annual about 2–3 ft (60–90 cm) tall with bright blue flowers, and there are other colours available – white, pink, red and purple. Also an annual, *C. moschata*, sweet sultan, is a little shorter and its lovely fringed flowers and its colour range includes yellow, but not blue. Both these annuals are good cottage-garden plants flowering during

Centaurea cyanus

the summer and into autumn, and are excellent for cutting.

Cultivation. Easy to please, these plants just need a well-drained sunny or only lightly shaded spot. Plant 12–16 in (30–40 cm) apart. The larger plants may need staking.

Remove dead flowers and cut the stems back in the autumn. Propagation of the perennials is by dividing the clumps in spring every three years. Seeds of the annual species should be sown where they are to flower in early autumn or early spring.

Centranthus

Valerian, *Valerianaceae*

The genus comprises some nine herbaceous annual and perennial hardy species found wild in Europe.

C. ruber (zone 6), red valerian, grows 20–30 in (50–80 cm) tall. It has oval bluish-green leaves and red or bright pink flowers, borne in erect panicles, from early spring to early autumn. 'Albus' has white flowers.

Very ornamental, red valerian can be used in herbaceous borders and to cover dry walls, but it can seed itself around rather too much.

Cultivation. The plant thrives in a poor, well-drained chalky soil, in full sun. It is not unusual to see it growing in walls or on chalk cliffs. But it can also adapt to cool soil, provided that it is well-drained.

To propagate, sow seed directly into the soil in late spring to early summer and thin the young plants out 12–16 in (30–40 cm) apart.

Cephalaria

Dipsacaceae

This genus comprises 65 species of annual, biennial or perennial herbaceous plants, occasionally shrubs with heads of flowers like those of the scabious to which it is related. The four-petalled flowers are blue, lilac, yellow or white.

C. gigantea (zone 6), giant scabious, a native of the Caucasus, grows 8½ ft (2.5 m) tall with a spread of 3½ ft (1 m). This perennial, hardy plant has leaves divided into four to six pairs of leaflets and the flower stems are grooved, with a few branches. The bright yellow flower-heads are up to 2¼ in (6 cm) in diameter, from mid to late summer.

It should be planted alone or in groups, in a mixed border, or with other large plants, such as *Cirsium japonicum* or *Echinops ritro*.

Cultivation. Plant in a humus-rich soil, which is not too damp, in sun or semi-shade, in mid autumn or early spring.

Propagate by division in spring.

Cerastium

Caryophyllaceae

The genus comprises 60 hardy annuals and herbaceous perennials some of which are ornamental but others are rather weedy.

C. alpinum (zone 5), a native of Europe, is 2–3¼ (5–8 cm) tall with a spread of 10–16 in (25–40 cm). This grey, velvety plant has oval, lanceolate leaves with solitary white flowers which appear in late spring to early summer and are 1 in (2 cm) in diameter. It is well suited to the rock garden and looks lovely planted in wall crevices.

C. tomentosum (zone 5), snow-in-summer, is also from Europe and is 4–8 in (10–20 cm) tall with a spread of 4 ft (1.2 m) or more. It is mat-forming, compact and invasive. The leaves are downy, silvery grey and narrowly lanceolate. Small white flowers are carried on slender branched stems in late spring to early summer.

Most species are too invasive for the rock garden where they will swamp other plants, but they can be used to stabilize a sunny bank, where their evergreen leaves will provide year-round decoration.

Cultivation. Plant in a gritty, well-drained soil in the sun, in early spring, but *C. tomentosum* will accept a cool soil, as long as it is well drained. Propagate by dividing the plants in spring.

Ceratophyllum

Hornwort, *Ceratophyllaceae*

The genus comprises two species of entirely submerged, aquatic plants.
C. demersum (zone 6) found wild in Europe and North America is submerged to a depth of 3½–6½ ft (1–2 m). This is a hardy, herbaceous plant with much-branched stems and roots. The deeply divided leaves are arranged in whorls; its flowers are insignificant. Fertilization takes place under water.

The plant can be grown out-of-doors in a pond and in warm conditions it will grow rapidly.
Cultivation. Plant in a pond filled with clean water. During winter the stems lie along the bottom and will rise to the surface in spring.

To propagate, cut pieces of the stem and submerge them, weighing them down with a stone. They will produce roots quickly and the stems will grow until they reach the surface.

Ceratostigma

Hardy plumbago, *Plumbaginaceae*

The genus comprises about eight species of half-hardy, herbaceous perennial or sub-shrubs, the garden species coming from the Himalayas and China.
C. plumbaginoides (zone 7–8), the most hardy, is 8–16 in (20–40 cm) tall with a spread of 20–24 in (50–60 cm). It is a more or less herbaceous plant with mid-green leaves which often turn scarlet in the autumn. From mid summer to late autumn blue flowers, 1 in (2 cm) in diameter appear in terminal clusters.

This species can be used as ground cover because of its spreading habit and is especially attractive in the autumn when its blue flowers are displayed against its red foliage.
C. willmottianum (zone 8), Chinese plumbago, is taller at 4 ft (1.2 m), with similar flowers, but likely to be cut back by frost and although woody can be treated as a herbaceous perennial. It looks especially fine with the white-flowered autumn bulb *Zephyranthes candida*.
Cultivation. Easy to grow with no special conditions. Plant in mid spring in a well-drained soil, in full sun with shelter from the cold winds in winter.

Damaged shoots should be cut back to the ground in early spring. Add fertilizer every three years.

Propagate by dividing clumps and replanting at once, in mid spring or for more woody species from 3¼ in (8 cm) cuttings with a heel, inserted in a rooting compost and kept at a temperature of 60–64°F (16–18°C) during the summer.

Cercis

Leguminosae

A genus of about seven slow-growing deciduous trees from North America, southern Europe and Asia with unusual flowers appearing before the leaves in late spring. Commonly grown in the USA is *C. Canadensis*.
C. siliquastrum (zone 7), Judas tree, is native to the Mediterranean region and commonly cultivated. Growing up to 17 ft (5 m) or more it is a spreading, moderately hardy, tree with a short sinuous trunk and gnarled, dark-coloured bark. It has round bluish-green leaves and its clusters of bright pink pea-like flowers, which appear in spring, sprout at the ends of new shoots, on the old wood and even on the trunk itself. Seeds are contained in flattened pods that last until the following spring.

It is a useful specimen tree for small gardens.
Cultivation. Ideally it enjoys a deep sandy loam in a sunny position where it can tolerate dry conditions. It is best to plant young trees directly in the ground in their permanent positions: they resent root disturbance later on, their roots dying back. The tree can be pruned and trained.

It can be attacked by coral spot in areas where this is a problem. Cut back to healthy wood straight away. Propagate only from seeds.

Ceterach

Rusty-back fern, *Aspleniaceae*

This genus includes about 10 species from Europe and Asia.
C. officinarum (zone 6), is a small fern, commonly found on old walls. A very hardy, European herbaceous perennial reaching 2–8 in (5–20 cm) in height. Its fronds are deep matt green on the upper surface but underneath are covered in

rust-coloured scales. Fronds are divided into rounded pinnae which may be slightly toothed. They may wilt during a period of drought, but will spring up again after watering.

The fern grows well in rock gardens and slightly shaded dry, stone walls.

Cultivation. Plant in spring in barely moist, preferably limy soil, in a slightly shaded position. It is usually propagated from its spores.

Chaenomeles

Japonica, Japanese quince, *Rosaceae*

This genus consists of three species, which are very hardy, deciduous shrubs growing up to 6½ ft (2 m) tall with a similar spread. The leaves are toothed, darkish green, and the plant is at its most decorative in early spring, when the flowers appear before the leaves.

Cultivars. Most commonly grown are cultivars of *C. speciosa* or *C.* × *superba* (zone 6), like 'Crimson and Gold', which is wide-spreading with crimson flowers and golden yellow stamens; 'Knap Hill Scarlet' which has orange scarlet flowers; 'Nivalis', with large pure white flowers and 'Moerlosii' with large white flowers overlaid with pink.

Japanese quinces can be grown against a wall or fence or used in a mixed border. The fruits may be used in jellies or conserves but are astringent if eaten raw.

Cultivation. These are extremely easy plants to grow and should be planted between the autumn and spring in either the sun or shade in any soil even limy soil. They require very little upkeep. Pruning is not absolutely necessary, but they can be thinned out after flowering. Where plants are trained against a wall, the previous year's growth should be cut back drastically at the beginning of summer.

Propagate from heeled semi-hardwood cuttings in late summer or by layering the long, supple shoots at the end of summer.

Chaenomeles speciosa

Chaerophyllum

Umbelliferae

A genus of about three species from northern temperate regions, one of which is cultivated. *C. bulbosum* (zone 6–7), tuberous or turnip-rooted chervil, is a biennial plant native to central Europe. The size of a carrot, its grey-white, fleshy cylindrical root produces a flowering stem nearly 6½ ft (2 m) tall, with umbels of white flowers in the late spring or early summer following its planting.

Cultivation. In early to mid autumn, sow seed as soon as ripe in rows 8 in (20 cm) apart and thin out seedlings in each row to 4 in (10 cm). The seeds germinate in late winter. Tuberous chervil prefers a cool, rich soil that has not been freshly manured.

As soon as the leaves turn yellow, towards the middle of summer, lift the roots and allow them to dry out on the ground before storing them like potatoes in a shed until the following spring.

Uses. Unlike the ordinary chervil, *Anthriscus cerefolium*, its stem and hairy, divided leaves, are toxic. Only the roots are edible, and their flavour improves with storage. They are cooked like potatoes.

Chamaecyparis

False cypress, *Cupressaceae*

This genus of seven species of evergreen conifers comes from Asia and North America and is reminiscent of *Cupressus*. Because of their conical shape they also look like *Thuja*, but differ in their fruits and branches. Their leaves consist of scales, and barely visible flowers appear in a flattened, fan shape at the tips of the branches. The fruit is a small, globular cone about ½ in (1 cm) in diameter.

C. lawsoniana (zone 7), Lawson's cypress, is a native of north west North America and can grow up to a height of 66 ft (20 m) and even 190 ft (60 m) in its wild state. This large, conical tree has gracefully arched branches. Too large for the smaller garden, it makes an excellent windbreak. Hedges should be pruned regularly to keep them thick and compact. There are many horticultural forms, which may be slow-growing or dwarf or with various leaf colours and habits.
C. obtusa (zone 7), from Japan, is slow-growing but can reach over 70 ft (21 m) in height. Numerous cultivars with a range of habit and leaf colour are available.

The use of these trees varies considerably, given the wide number of cultivars. The larger forms make excellent specimen trees while the dwarf and slow-growing cultivars can be grown as features in rock gardens or among heathers.
Cultivation. Plant in spring. Older trees may be transplanted quite readily.

This genus is hardy, but prefers a maritime climate. It needs a cool, well-drained soil, but will take to a poor, limy one, although its growth will be slower. Any position will suit it, and it will do quite well in the shade.

Propagate the species from seeds sown in spring. Named varieties must be propagated from cuttings, with a heel, inserted during autumn in sandy soil in a cold frame.

Chamaemelum

Chamomile, *Compositae*

Coming from western Europe and the Mediterranean region, this genus consists of three species of herbaceous perennials.
Chamaemelum nobile (*Anthemis nobile*) (zone 6), common chamomile, grows 6–8 in (15–20 cm) high. A hardy species, it makes a thick carpet of deeply dissected, scented green foliage. Small single daisy-like white flowers, double in 'Flore Pleno', open during the summer. The cultivar 'Treneague' does not flower and is the best form for making a small fragrant lawn.

It is a suitable plant for sunny border fronts, or rock and herb gardens.
Cultivation. Common chamomile prefers a clay soil which is not too damp. Propagate in spring by seed, division or cuttings. Sow the seed *in situ* in mid spring and thin out to 1 ft (30 cm) apart. For a lawn thoroughly prepare the plot by digging, adding manure and letting the area settle for a few weeks; keep the planting distance to 4 in (10 cm). Hand weed and keep watered for the first season. The first cut should be done with shears.
Uses. The dried flowers can be used in infusions (tea), as a tonic, in shampoos to lighten hair, in eye baths and liqueurs. Gather the flower buds in dry weather, before they are fully open, and allow them to dry in shade before storing in a jar.

Chamaerops

Fan palm, *Palmae*

C. humilis (zone 9) is the only palm tree in this genus and grows wild in southern Europe and northern Africa. It is a dwarf suckering shrubby palm, with fan-shaped leaves to 3 ft (90 cm) across. In cultivation the trunk may reach 5 feet (1.5 m) or more.

It goes well with other exotic-looking plants such as the yucca, New Zealand flax or bamboo.
Cultivation. It is hardy in milder regions, but where there are prolonged frosts cover the base and trunk with a thick mulch for protection. This will also encourage new growth. Its growth is slow and it will need several years to establish itself. A well-drained soil suits it best and plenty of water in the summer.

Propagate from seeds or by division, but both methods are very slow.

Cheiranthus

Wallflower, *Cruciferae*

A genus of about 10 species of annuals, biennials and perennials from temperate regions.
C. cheiri (zone 6), wallflower, from southern Europe has given birth to countless cultivars. Grown as biennials, they are hardy and produce aromatic flowers in spring. They are in fact woody and can survive from year to year in less exposed areas. Their yellow, orange or brown, single or double flowers appear from mid spring to early summer. Cultivars include: 'Primrose Monarch' which reaches 18 in (45 cm) tall with golden yellow flowers and 'Orange Bedder', 12 in (30 cm) which has attractive rich orange flowers.
Cultivation. Sow in pots or peat pots from late summer to late autumn, for planting in late

winter or early spring. They can also be sown in open ground in late spring to early summer for planting out in the autumn. They prefer a well-drained, even stony ground. Bury the neck of each plant well and pinch out the ends of shoots to encourage it to branch out. Young plants may be destroyed by birds or slugs, and powder and downy mildew may affect the leaves, giving them a white appearance.

Chelone

Scrophulariaceae

Around six species native to the mountains of North America make up this genus which is related to *Penstemon*. These hardy perennials stand tall and erect and have leaves interspersed with clusters of flowers at the sides or ends of the stalks.

C. obliqua (zone 5), turtle-head, which is native to southeastern US, is around 3 ft (90 cm) tall with a spread of 12–16 in (30–40 cm). Its stems are branched and its leaves are broad and lanceolate with large veins. Brilliant, deep pink or purple flowers appear from late summer to early autumn. The form 'Alba' has white flowers; 'Praecox Nana' is only 12 in (30 cm) tall and flowers earlier.

This is a good plant for a wild garden or herbaceous border.

Cultivation. Plant in a damp soil, which is not too rich, in either sun or semi-shade, in autumn or spring.

Propagate by division in autumn and from seeds, in spring, or by cuttings of young shoots inserted in a sandy soil in a cold frame.

Chenopodium

Chenopodiaceae

This genus includes about 150 annual and perennial herbaceous plants, few of horticultural interest.

C. bonus-henricus (zone 6), Good King Henry, is a hardy herbaceous perennial found wild in Europe, with branched, upright stems growing to a height of 18 in (45 cm). The large, triangular leaves are arrow-shaped; greenish flowers are arranged in spikes and appear during mid summer.

Cultivation. Grown as a substitute for spinach, it needs a deep, rich, dry soil. As the plant is hardy, it can be propagated by division in mid spring. Replant each division every 16 in (40 cm), in rows spaced out to 20 in (50 cm). Harvest from mid to late spring but don't cut too much as this will reduce the future yield. After picking, manure and water well.

Uses. Leaves may be eaten cooked or raw.

Chimonanthus

Calycanthaceae

A genus of about six species of deciduous shrubs from China.

C. praecox (*C. fragrans*) –zone 7–8 – wintersweet, is a shrub with brilliant green leaves, which can grow up to 6½–10 ft (2–3 m) tall. It is quite hardy but often needs several years before reaching its full flowering potential. It is grown for its winter flowers of light yellow and their heady, spicy fragrance.

Chimonanthus may be planted on its own, in a mixed border or in the colder areas against a sun-facing wall.

Cultivation. Plant in early autumn or spring, when the sun is warm, either in full sun or semi-shade, in an ordinary, well-drained, even limy soil.

Water in dry weather; prune when flowering is over for the wall-trained plants, shortening strong shoots, and cutting back the weak ones.

It may be propagated from seeds in autumn or by layering the long shoots at the end of the summer, or in early spring.

Chimonobambusa

Bamboo, *Gramineae*

This is a genus of bamboo of about 12 species from China, Japan and the Himalayas.

C. marmorea (zone 5), the hardiest, is a native of Japan and will tolerate temperatures as low as 14°F (−10°C) or less, though its foliage may suffer. It is a graceful plant with slender leaves. As a mature plant, it will not grow taller than 6½ ft (2 m); its new shoots are a purple-tinged green. Somewhat invasive, it looks very decorative when confined to a tub. There is a cultivar with variegated foliage.

C. falcata (zone 6), comes from the northwest Himalayas. Even more elegant than the preceding species, it has one of the finest displays of leaves. Shoots grow up to 10 ft (3 m), with dark red sheaves when young. This kind of bamboo may flower and its seeds germinate easily. It will suffer in a heavy frost, or temperatures lower than 14°F (−10°C).

Chionanthus

Oleaceae

This genus comprises 120 species of shrubs or small trees from China, Japan, east North America and parts of tropical and subtropical Africa and Asia. The flowers have very narrow petals.

C. retusus (zone 6), from China, is a rounded shrub or small tree with widespread branches growing up to 40 ft (12 m) high. The oval or round leaves, 1½–4 in (4–10 cm) long are shiny green above. Snow-white flowers in panicles 2–3¼ in (5–8 cm) long, bloom at the end of terminal shoots from late spring to early summer and are followed by oval-shaped dark blue fruits in early or mid autumn.

C. virginicus (zone 6), fringe tree, is a shrub or small tree from eastern North America, 10–17 ft (3–5 m) tall, with strong, straight branches. Oval leaves, 3¼–8 in (8–20 cm) long are deep green above. Pure white, slightly aromatic flowers appear on loose panicles 4–8 in (10–20 cm) long in late spring to early summer.

These species look best when planted on their own.

Cultivation. Plant in a deep fertile, moist loam, which can be slightly peaty, in a sunny position. Propagate from cuttings 2¾–4 in (7–10 cm) long from lateral branches and place in a cold frame. Alternatively, both species can be layered.

Chionodoxa

Glory-of-the-snow, *Liliaceae*

This genus is very much like the squill and includes some six species from the eastern Mediterranean. The small, hardy, ovoid bulb produces two longish leaves in spring, followed by a short flower stem with 2 to 15 very early, white, blue or pink star-shaped flowers.

C. luciliae (zone 5), from west Turkey, is 8 in (20 cm) tall, and produces one or two lavender-blue flowers with white centres.

C. sardensis (zone 5), also from west Turkey, is 4–8 in (10–20 cm) tall and has up to 12 bright blue flowers, sometimes with a white centre.

These are excellent plants for the rock garden, containers and border fronts.

Cultivation. Plant in a good soil, in semi-shade or full sun.

Propagate by division of offsets or from seeds, leaving the young plants undisturbed for two or three years before transplanting.

Chlidanthus

Perfumed fairy lily, *Amaryllidaceae* (*Liliaceae*)

The genus comprises only one bulbous species, *C. fragans* (zone 8), which is a native of the mountains of Peru.

In spring the bulb puts forth blue-green, linear leaves, which are followed in summer by a flower stem about 12 in (30 cm) long bearing two to four large lemon-yellow, trumpet-shaped, fragrant flowers.

Cultivation. Plant the bulb in spring, 6–8 in (15–20 cm) deep, in a rich, well-drained soil, at the base of a wall in full sun.

It can also be grown in a pot, keeping bulbs cool and dry during the winter, but in the open air during the rest of the year. Propagation is by removing offsets when repotting.

Chlorophytum

Liliaceae

A genus of well over 200 species of evergreen, herbaceous perennials which grow in tropical regions especially Africa and India. The plants have short rhizomes bearing tufts of lance-shaped leaves. The flowers, usually white or greenish are star shaped with six petals, formed on thin, often branched stems. Only one species is commonly cultivated, grown for its attractive foliage as a pot plant or in summer bedding schemes.

C. comosum (zone 10+), spider plant, from South Africa, is a tufted plant with very narrow green leaves up to 18 in (45 cm) long spreading from rosettes. The numerous flowers are white, to ¾ in (20 mm) across, produced on long slender, branched or unbranched stems to over 2 ft (60 cm) high sporadically throughout the year. Small rosettes of leaves may appear on the flower stems forming plantlets.

Several different cultivars are grown with leaves variegated with longitudinal stripes of white, cream or yellow.

Chlorophytum comosum variegated cultivar

Cultivation. These frost-tender plants, usually used for indoor decoration, survive a minimum temperature of 45–50°F (7.5–10°C). They are grown in a rich sandy compost and will tolerate most light conditions but avoid direct sunlight or dark corners. Water freely in the growing season but sparingly during the winter. Remove flowering shoots, any dead leaves and any offsetts which can be used for propagation. Repot in the spring.

Propagate by seed or division in spring; some of the plantlets produced may be detached and potted-on using any potting medium. These plants are comparatively pest and disease free but should insects attack them use a systemic insecticide.

Choisya

Rutaceae

A genus of seven species from Mexico and south west USA of which one is widely grown.

C. ternata (zone 8), Mexican orange, is a lovely evergreen shrub growing up to 6½ ft (2 m) or more tall with a similar spread. It is decorative with bright green foliage and white, sweet-scented flowers in spring and often a repeat performance in the autumn. It suffers in severe frosts and should be grown against a sunny wall in colder climates.

The Mexican orange, when grown against a wall provides a lovely backcloth for herbaceous flowers or with other shrubs.

Cultivation. Plant in mid to late spring in any light, well drained, even limy soil, in sun or light shade.

Water in dry weather. Pruning is not absolutely necessary, but it can be thinned out after flowering in spring, and any frosted branches should be cut out in early spring.

The easiest method of propagation is from semi-hardwood cuttings at the end of summer, placed in gentle heat or from older wood placed in a cold frame.

Chrysanthemum

Chrysanthemum, *Compositae*

Although this large genus of more than 200 species has been split into several genera by some authors, the plants described have been retained under the better known name *Chrysan-*

themum for simplicity. Several are annuals but those described below are all herbaceous perennials.

The florist's chrysanthemums are of complex parentage derived from several Asiatic species. They are best treated as half-hardy perennials and are available in a large range of forms and colours, including double flowers with incurved petals and anemone-centred, with single outer florets.

Other species have flowers similar to the common daisy, but can come in a range of colours and habits. Blooms appear from early summer and will last till the autumn. Flowering is prolific and the plants make a lovely basis for herbaceous and mixed borders. The alpine species are perfect for the rock garden.

C. alpinum (zone 4), a native of the European Alps, forms clumps of about 6 in (15 cm) across studded in late summer with little white daisies with yellow hearts.

C. maximum (zone 4), Shasta daisy from the Pyrénées, up to 3 ft (90 cm) tall, is grown for its large white flowers with yellow centres, which appear from early to late summer. There are several cultivars with larger flowers, some double or fringed, like 'Aglaia', 'Bishopstone', and 'Wirral Supreme'.

C. rubellum (zone 6), autumn daisy, is another species of hardy chrysanthemum or possibly a hybrid of unknown origin, which flowers from late summer to early autumn. There are various cultivars in shades of pink and yellow, like 'Clara Curtiss' (clear pink) and 'Duchess of Edinburgh' (reddish-brown).

Anemone-centred florist's chrysanthemum

C. uliginosum (zone 5), from eastern Europe, is an autumn flowering daisy growing to 6 ft (1.8 m) in a fertile, damp soil. It has single, white flowers with bright yellow centres.

C. weyrichii (zone 6), comes from the mountains of Japan. This mat-forming plant has a woody rootstock and numerous, pale green leaves. Pink flowers with golden yellow centres appear at the end of summer.

Cultivation. Plant in a fertile, cool, but not damp soil (except *C. uliginosum*).

They can be divided at the beginning of spring. Cuttings can be taken at the same time or in the autumn placing these under a cold frame. Botanical species can be increased from seed.

They can suffer from mildew and aphids. Treat with an appropriate fungicide and insecticide, respectively.

Chrysogonum

Compositae

This genus is native to North America and consists of only one species, *C. virginianum* (zone 5–6), a hardy herbaceous plant that grows up to 8 in (20 cm) with a spread of 12–20 in (30–50 cm).

It has fresh, light-green leaves which are oval and stalked. Yellow daisy-like flowers, 1–2 in (3–5 cm) in diameter appear in late spring and continue through to early autumn.

This is a hardy, easy-to-grow plant, popular for its long flowering period. It is suitable for a rock garden or the front of a border, but its spread may need checking occasionally.

Cultivation. Plant in a dry, well-drained peaty soil, in sun or semi-shade. Propagate from runners or by division in spring.

Cicer

Chick pea, *Leguminosae*

A large genus of about 40 herbaceous plants which includes one of the world's most important pulses.

C. arietinum (zone 9–10), the chick pea is an annual plant from southern Europe growing up to 20–24 in (50–60 cm). The short husks, like the stalks and leaves, are covered in down and contain one or two seeds.

Cultivars. These include the 'White-seed chick pea' and the 'Round-seed chick pea'.

Cultivation. It grows well in a dry soil, and enjoys the warmth of a dry, frost-free climate.

Propagate from seeds in mid to late winter, in rows 8–12 in (20–30 cm) apart, then thin out to 8–10 in (20–25 cm) between the plants within the row.

Keep young plants clean and weed free. It is attacked by the same pests as the pea.

Cicerbita

Compositae

The genus comprises 18 species of tall, hardy, latex-producing plants, which are native to the mountains of temperate zones. Stems bear lobed leaves and the flowers are usually blue.

C. alpina (zone 5), blue sow thistle, from the European Alps and Scandinavia, grows up to 3 ft (90 cm) with a spread of 3½ ft (1 m).

This species has branched stems with reddish down. The leaves are blue-green, and it has violet-blue flowers 1 in (2.5 cm) in diameter, which appear on spikes from early summer to early autumn.

The plant is ideal for a wild garden and large borders associated with such genera as *Adenostyles, Aconitum* and *Actaea.*

Cultivation. Plant in a damp humus-rich peaty soil in semi-shade, either in autumn or spring.

Propagate from seeds or by division in spring.

Cichorium

Compositae

A genus of eight, mainly European species, including two important salad plants.

C. endivia (zone 7–8), curly chicory is an annual or biennial from Asia, naturalized in the Mediterranean region, from which the endive has been produced. Numerous leaves arranged in a rosette 12–16 in (30–40 cm) in diameter are curled, jagged and more or less toothed. They are sometimes blanched before use.

Cultivars. Cultivars for early sowing include 'Moss Curled' and late sowing 'Batavian Green', and 'Green Curled'.

Cultivation. Plant in a deep, rich, well-drained soil in a sunny position. It should be planted in soil in which cabbage, radish and turnip were cultivated the previous year. The soil needs well-rotted manure dug in during the winter. Sow in spring, in a nursery bed for autumn use or in the open ground in summer for winter and early spring crops. Plant out 14 in (35 cm) apart from spring to early autumn.

Water regularly, preferably with a watering can directed so as not to wet the leaves, and hoe frequently. Look out for aphids and for snails and slugs on the roots.

Other cultivars of chicory are suitable for forcing to produce tight conical blanched heads for salads or cooking. These are sometimes referred to as Brussels chicory.

Cultivars. 'Normato' and 'Witloof'.

Cultivation. Plant in the sun in a light, fertile, even limy soil, manured for the previous crop of cabbages, radishes and turnips. Sow from mid spring to early summer, in rows 10 in (25 cm) apart, then thin plants out to 6 in (15 cm) apart after two weeks. Only water in times of drought, and mulch with straw in summer. For forcing and blanching, the plants are lifted in the autumn until just before the first frost when they are replanted in special forcing beds which are frost free but not too warm. The leaves are cut, the crowns are covered with peat or sand so as to blanch the new young leaves before harvesting. Field mice and cats can be a problem, as are snails and slugs. Aphids can attack the roots and the leaves can be affected by rust.

Uses. These plants are very popular in winter salads. The cultivar 'Witloof' can also be grown for its roots which when chopped, roasted and ground can be used as a substitute for coffee.

C. intybus (zone 7–8), wild chicory, has been developed as a salad crop from a perennial herbaceous plant found wild in Europe. Its salad cultivars are similar in habit to lettuce. The sky-blue daisy-like flowers held on stems up to 5 ft (1.5 m) make an attractive wild form.

Cultivars. 'Sugar Loaf', 'Treviso' with red leaves veined white and 'Palla Rossa' with dark red-green leaves.

Cultivation. The cultivation is the same as for Brussels chicory, but when sowing, the distances are 12 in (30 cm) apart for the rows and 10 in (25 cm) apart for the plants in the row.

Cimicifuga

Bugbane, *Ranunculaceae*

The genus is represented by 15 species of hardy

herbaceous, perennial plants from Japan, Siberia, North America and Europe.
C. racemosa (zone 5), native to North America will grow to 4–5 ft (1.2–1.5 m) tall with a spread of 16–24 in (40–60 cm). The bright green leaves are fern-like. The plant flowers in mid to late summer with bottle-brush like spikes of small, slightly fragrant, star-shaped, pure white flowers. *C. racemosa* is an excellent cut flower, or for the back of a hardy border or among low shrubs. It is happy almost anywhere.
Cultivation. Plant in a shady situation in autumn or spring in a deep, moist soil, enriched with manure, compost or leaf-mould.

In windy, exposed positions, it needs the support of a stake. Cut stems down during the autumn, and in the spring enrich the soil with compost or manure.

Propagate by seed sown in a cold frame as soon as it is ripe or multiply by division in the spring.

Cineraria

Cineraria, *Compositae*

Botanically speaking, the garden or florists' cineraria has been re-classified as *Pericallis hybrida*. In the past it has been included in the genus *Senecio* as *S. cruentus*. The plant described here, however, is better known under the name of cineraria and is listed here for the sake of simplicity. It originates from the Canary Isles.

Cineraria is a 20 in (50 cm) tall perennial with a spread of 12–16 in (30–40 cm). It is hardy in warm, frost-free climates but is generally grown as a biennial house or pot plant. It flowers from early winter to early summer depending on the time of sowing. Many cultivars have been bred and provide a wide range of colourful displays in homes and greenhouses throughout the winter.
Cultivation. To propagate, sow seeds in boxes filled with a light, sandy compost in spring, at a temperature of 57–60°F (14–16°C), then prick out the young plants into progressively larger pots. Finally, plant cineraria in 6 in (15 cm) pots filled with compost. Keep the temperature quite cool after the first buds have appeared; add fertilizer every fortnight; keep the soil damp, but not too moist. Regular and careful watering are now needed, with plenty of ventilation, but without draughts, and plenty of space around each plant.

In order to maintain a buoyant but moist atmosphere in autumn a little heat in the greenhouse might be needed. The plants are liable to attacks from greenfly, leaf miners, white fly and mildew.

Cinnamomum

Lauraceae

These trees, native of eastern Asia, can grow up to 66 ft (20 m) high.
C. camphora (zone 9), camphor tree, is hardy in frost-free regions. It has large, evergreen, leathery, aromatic deep green leaves. Greenish-white flowers appear in large multiple blossoms in spring. If any part of the plant is distilled, it will produce camphor. The wood used to be utilized in cabinet-making to make 'moth-proof' cabinets for storing silk or wool.
C. aromaticum (*C. cassia*) (zones 9–10) from China and *C. zeylanicum* (zone 10) from Sri Lanka can, with care, be grown in some mild regions and are a source of cinnamon. The spice produced from the bark of the latter species, is the main one used in commerce.
Cultivation. Plant in a peaty soil, in a moist climate. In countries having frost these trees are grown in hot houses. Propagate from seeds or cuttings or by layering, to produce a quick show of bushy, spectacular young plants.

Cirsium

Thistle, *Compositae*

The genus covers around 200 species of annual, biennial and perennial herbaceous plants from the northern hemisphere most of which are pernicious weeds.
C. rivulare (zones 4–5), however, is an ornamental thistle, 4–5 ft (1.2–1.5 m) tall with a spread of 2–3 ft (60–90 cm). Its jagged, spiny leaves are deep green, and clusters of purplish-pink flowers appear in early to mid summer.

Whether on their own or in groups, its erect growth makes a distinctive feature for the back of a flower border.
Cultivation. Plant out in spring or early autumn. It enjoys a well-drained, fairly deep, humus-rich soil and likes to be in full sun.

Remove dead flowers and cut down the dead stems in the autumn. Propagate by division in early autumn or spring.

Cissus

Grape ivy, *Vitaceae*

A genus of about 350 species, usually evergreen shrubs, which climb by means of tendrils. They are native to tropical and subtropical regions throughout the world. Several are cultivated for their ornamental foliage as house or greenhouse plants but few could be grown outdoors, except in very warm conditions. Most have small greenish flowers in clusters.
C. antarctica (zone 10+), kangaroo vine, is native to Australia and is easy to grow as a house plant even in poor light. The ovate leaves are leathery, glossy dark green and toothed and may reach 6 in (15 cm) in length.
C. discolor (zone 10+), begonia or rex-begonia vine is found in Java and Cambodia. The leaves are somewhat similar in shape and size to the previous species but a velvety green in colour with silvery white bands above and reddish below. The tendrils, leaf stalks and stems tend to be red.
C. rhombifolia (zone 10+), grape ivy, is from parts of Central and South America. There is confusion in cultivation over the name of this plant and it may be sold incorrectly as *Rhoicissus rhomboidea*. The leaves of this species have three coarsely toothed leaflets which are rhomboidal in shape and dark glossy green in colour. The tendrils are forked at the tips.
C. striata (zone 9–10), miniature grape ivy, comes from Chile and parts of Brazil. It has three to five shiny green toothed leaflets and is a vigorous plant, which may climb to 30 ft (9 m) in height and is almost hardy in some areas.
Cultivation. These plants are tolerant of varying conditions of light, temperature and moisture. They enjoy semi-shade, away from direct sunlight. Most like it cool, a minimum of 45°F (7.5°C), except for *C. discolor* which needs a minimum of 60°F (16°C), and occasional misting when necessary. Repot in spring, ensuring good drainage. Water well during the growing season but sparingly during the winter. Pinch out tips of plant to encourage bushiness. Propagate by stem cuttings in spring or summer.

Cissus antarctica

Cistus

Rock rose, sun rose, *Cistaceae*

About 20 shrubs make up this genus most of which are cultivated. Evergreen Mediterranean shrubs, they can grow up to 6½ ft (2 m) tall with an equal spread, depending on the species. Their attraction lies in their large, but short-lived, white, pink or purple, saucer-shaped flowers which are profusely carried from late spring to mid summer. They are not hardy in colder climates. *C.* × *corbariensis* and *C. laurifolius* (zone 8), both with white flowers, are among the most hardy. *C. incanus* (*C. villosus*) – zone 9 – with rose-pink to purple flowers is a somewhat tender species.

The greatest effect can be achieved by growing these plants in groups on sunny banks and below sunny walls.

Cultivation. They are fairly easy to grow and are happiest in an open, sunny position, but sheltered from the cold winds. In the colder regions, it is best to wait until the end of spring before planting them against a wall, well exposed to the sun, in a light well-drained, even dry soil. Most cistuses will manage just as well in a sandy or limy soil, and will tolerate salt spray.

Prune at the beginning of spring to remove dead wood and retain a good shape. Frost-damaged shoots should be cut at the end of spring. Propagate from semi-hardwood cuttings with a heel at the end of summer.

Citrullus
Cucurbitaceae

A genus of three annual and perennial herbaceous plants climbing by tendrils.
C. lanatus (*C. vulgaris*) (zone 10), water melon, is an annual from central and southern Africa. It has much the same characteristics as the melon, but bears fruit four to five times larger with red or pink flesh and green skin, weighing 10 to 50 lb (4.5 to 22.5 kg) or even 100 lb (45 kg).
Cultivars. 'Sugar Baby'.

Citrus
Citrus fruits, *Rutaceae*

The genus of about 16 evergreen, usually spiny, trees and shrubs from southeast Asia includes those producing edible citrus fruits. Many have been hybridized to produce the fruits known today.

Bergamot tree (zone 9–10)
C. aurantium subsp. *bergamia* is a shrub of uncertain origin, measuring 13–17 ft (4–5 m) tall. It has bright green evergreen leaves with winged leaf-stalks and highly aromatic white flowers followed by pear-shaped, thin-skinned yellow fruits 3–4 in (7.5–10 cm) across. Its leaves and bark are also aromatic. The essence, which is taken from the fruit zest makes up the base of Eau de Cologne.

This is a lovely tree which can be planted alone as a feature.

Citron tree (zone 9–10)
C. medica, a native of southwest Asia was introduced into the Mediterranean region some time towards 300 BC. It is an elegant bush with bright green, tough and brilliant foliage. The white flowers tinged with pink are highly perfumed. It bears large yellow fruits, each weighing up to 8 lb (4 kg) with either acid or mild pulp. The mild form of citron-tree has white clusters of flowers, while the acid form has purple flowers.
Cultivars. 'Corsican' has soft fleshy fruit; 'Diamanthus' has acid flesh; 'Buddha's Hand' with fat, finger-like fruit.

The citron tree is largely grown for its extremely thick fruit rind which is used in jam-making and for candied peel.

Citrus limon

Grapefruit (zone 10)
C. paradisi is possibly a hybrid and is often confused with the pomelo tree, *C. grandis*. It is vigorous and at maturity reaches over 40 ft (12 m). It bears large, brilliant green leaves and very aromatic clusters of white flowers. Large, flattened, globular fruits form clusters (the origin of the name grapefruit). Their thick skin is greenish, or yellow, sometimes tinted with pink or red depending on the cultivar. The pulp is juicy and aromatic, slightly acidic, more or less sugary, with a hint of bitterness according to cultivars. It is thought to be of Polynesian origin.
Cultivars. 'Marsh' has a yellow peel and pale yellow pulp; 'Thompson' a pinkish-gold peel and pinkish-purple pulp; 'Ruby', a pinkish-orange peel and deep red pulp.

Lemon tree (zone 9–10)
C. limon is a hardy tree of 20 ft (6 m), characterized by its elegant habit and lightly thorny stems. The tough leaves are brilliant green with narrow-winged leaf stalks. It bears clusters of flowers which are purple on the outside and white on the inside which give off a sweet perfume. Brilliant yellow, thick-skinned, oval

fruits have an acidic pulp except for some cultivars like the 'mild' lemon which is grown commercially. The lemon tree now grown in the Mediterranean region will tolerate a temperature of 25°F (−4°C).
Cultivars. 'Four Seasons' produces flowers and fruit nearly all-year round; 'Eureka' has the same characteristics; 'Sicilian Monachello' is particularly resistant to pests and diseases; 'Bloody Variegated' has a distinctive pink flesh and its leaves and bark are variegated; 'Meyer' is resistant to cold.

Mandarin; tangerine; satsuma (zone 10)
C. reticulata is a beautiful shrub from Vietnam and China, 13–17 ft (4–5 m) tall, with shiny green foliage and a naturally rounded shape. The mandarin tree has white, star-shaped flowers with a delightful scent, grouped in small clusters at branch ends, and flattened fruits. The colour, aroma and appearance of the peel and the taste of the pulp differs widely, depending on the cultivars.
Cultivars. 'True Mandarina', 'Ponkan', 'Kinokuni', 'Cleopatra'. The satsuma is the least sensitive to cold of the citrus fruits and among the cultivars are 'Wase', a very early cultivar which bears fruit from the beginning to mid autumn, and 'Owari', which bears its fruit in late autumn.

Pomelo, shaddock tree (zone 10)
C. grandis is a beautiful tree with a pleasant natural shape enhanced by deep green brilliant leaves with a very broad-winged leaf stalk. Highly aromatic flowers appear in terminal clusters. Large green fruits, 10–12 in (25–30 cm) in diameter, turn yellow on maturity. The peel is thick and spongy and the slightly bitter pulp is sugary and juicy, although a bit tasteless. As it is so attractive, the pomelo is usually best displayed on its own.

Seville or sour orange tree (zone 9–10)
C. aurantium, from southeast Asia, differs from the sweet orange in several botanical characteristics. It has bright green, wavy edged leaves with broad-winged stalks and deliciously aromatic white flowers, from which neroli essence is taken. Thick-skinned, orange-coloured fruits are too bitter to be eaten, but are used in preserves or marmalade and in liqueurs such as Cointreau. There are some ornamental cultivars such as: 'Gratino' which has serrated leaves; 'Nice Flower-girl' with double flowers; 'Large Bouquet' with very large fruits; 'Chinese Boxtree' or 'Myrtle-leaved', a splendid shrub with tiny fruits; 'Chinese Crispifolia', an erect plant with highly aromatic fruit.

Citrus sinensis

Sour Lime (zone 10)
These are hybrids of the lemon tree with foliage akin to that of the citron tree. The flowers, which are purple on the outside, are aromatic, and the round, flat, pure yellow fruits have either an acidic or sickly sweet taste, depending on the cultivar.
Cultivar. The most common is 'Marrakech Sour Lime', which bears prolific fruit and flowers.

Sweet lime (zone 10)
C. aurantifolia is a small tree, widely grown for the juice of its fruit. It has little in common with the lemon tree, although the fruit can replace the lemon, but with quite a different flavour. It is a small, erect, thorny tree, 13–17 ft (4–5 m) tall and has brilliant green leaves and purple shoots. Its white flowers have a light perfume and it bears average-sized bright green fruit with juicy, green flesh which has a pleasant taste.
Cultivars. Small fruited – 'Mexican Lime', 'Bedi Lime', 'Yung Lime', which has no thorns; large fruited – 'Tahiti Lime'.

Sweet orange tree (zone 9–10)
C. sinensis is an elegant tree from China and Vietnam, 17–20 ft (5–6 m) tall, and is popular

for its fine, brilliant green evergreen foliage. The flowers, which are borne in terminal clusters, have a heavenly aroma in spring. The globe-shaped, dark and sweet fruits mature between late autumn and mid spring, depending on the cultivar. Hybridizing between various citrus species has given rise to many cultivars.
Cultivation. Broadly speaking, all citrus trees and shrubs are cultivated in a similar way. For their fruit they must have a completely frost-free climate, although they can be grown as ornamental plants in colder areas provided they are given glasshouse protection in the winter, the fruits remaining small in size and number.

Apart from the sun and light, these trees enjoy a good loam, with some sand to help drainage. Incorporate plenty of decayed manure annually in the ground, and during the growing season apply liquid feed.

When kept in tubs in cold areas, the compost should be a good loam containing organic matter, and the drainage should be efficient. An annual top dressing of manure and soil is beneficial. During the growing season water well and syringe (mist) the foliage morning and afternoon, but avoid overwatering. The plants should always be taken in for the winter when the minimum temperature is 45°F (7.5°C) and the temperature under glass must never fall below this figure. Scale, mealy bug, and red spider mite can affect these plants.

Citruses can be grown from seed, but it is more usual to graft or bud in order to retain the particular characteristics of each cultivar.

Clarkia
Onagraceae

This genus is composed of some 30 species of annuals from both North and South America.
C. unguiculata (*C. elegans*) – zone 5 – clarkia is up to 3 ft (90 cm) tall. It has large single or double flowers about 2 in (5 cm), in white, pink, red or lavender, which bloom from mid summer to mid autumn.
C. pulchella (zone 5), is about 20 in (50 cm) tall. A more branched species, it bears smaller flowers than the previous species in much the same range of colours.

They are all well suited to annual and mixed borders; they also make excellent cut flowers.
Cultivation. They are easily raised by sowing the seed where the plants are needed, in early autumn or in spring in any good garden soil in the sun – they do tolerate semi-shade. Thin out gradually until a spacing of 8–12 in (20–30 cm) is attained. Pinch out young plants to encourage branching and keep the soil moist. The plants can be destroyed by neck and stem rot.

Clematis
Clematis, *Ranunculaceae*

This is a large genus of about 230 woody climbing or sometimes herbaceous plants from many areas of the world. The petiole acts as a tendril, so that the plant can cling to all kinds of supports to great heights. Some species and cultivars flower over a long season.

Small-flowered clematis
C. alpina (zone 5), a native of northern Europe and northern Asia, 6½–10 ft (2–3 m) tall is very hardy. Blue, star-shaped flowers with white staminodes in the centre appear in mid to late spring.
Cultivars. 'Frances Rivis', brighter blue than species; 'Ruby', rose-red flowers with white centre.

Clematis 'Ville de Lyon'

C. armandii (zone 7–8), from China, is over 33 ft (10 m) tall, fairly hardy with shiny evergreen leaves and creamy-white flowers in dense clusters in mid spring.
Cultivars. 'Apple Blossom' has bronze leaves and pink tinged flowers.
C. chrysocoma var. *sericea* (zone 6–7), China 20 ft (6 m) tall, is hardy and has pure white flowers in late spring.
C. cirrhosa, (zone 8), southern Europe, 10 ft (3 m) tall, fairly hardy, evergreen, bears bell-shaped light yellow flowers tinged with purple in winter.
C. × *durandii* (zone 7), is a hybrid, 10 ft (3 m) tall, very hardy with indigo-blue flowers which appear in summer.
C. × *eriostemon* (zone 7), a hybrid 5–8½ ft (1.5–2.5 m) tall, very hardy, with nodding fragrant bluish-purple flowers borne at the end of summer. It is usually represented in gardens by the cultivar 'Hendersonii'.
C. × *jouiniana* (zone 7), is another hardy deciduous hybrid 10 ft (3 m) tall, whose small yellowish-white flowers, tinted with lilac, open at the end of summer and in autumn.
Cultivars. 'Mrs Robert Brydon', blue; 'Praecox', lavender-blue flowering in mid summer.
C. macropetala (zone 5), China and Siberia, is 8½ ft (2.5 m) tall, very hardy, double lavender-blue flowers in late spring to early summer.
Cultivars. 'Markham's Pink', a light pink.
C. montana (zone 6), Himalayas, 33 ft (10 m) tall, is deciduous and abundant white flowers appear in late spring.
Cultivars. 'Elizabeth', pale pink, slightly fragrant flowers; 'Grandiflora', larger white flowers; 'Rubens', rose pink flowers with bronze-green leaves; 'Tetrarose', with deep pink, large flowers.
C. tibetana subsp *vernayi* (*C. orientalis*) (zones 5–6), orange-peel clematis, from northern Asia, is 20 ft (6 m) tall and is a deciduous species with bell-shaped nodding yellow, aromatic flowers which come out from late summer to mid autumn, followed by decorative downy silvery grey seed-heads.
C. paniculata (zone 6–7) from Japan. Vigorous climber to 30 ft (9 m) or more. White flowers scented like hawthorn and 1 in (2 cm) across in early to mid autumn.
C. rehderiana (zone 6), China, over 23 ft (7 m) tall is deciduous and produces small, pale yellow, fragrant flowers in the autumn.
C. tangutica (zone 6–7), from China, is 17–20 ft (5–6 m) tall, and produces light yellow flowers in mid summer, similar to but less solid than those of *C. orientalis.*
C. vitalba (zone 5), traveller's joy, old man's beard, of hedgerows from Europe, grows over 13 ft (4 m) and is a very vigorous species with creamy white, fragrant flowers from mid summer to early autumn followed by fluffy white to grey seed-heads.
C. viticella (zone 6), from southern Europe, is over 13 ft (4 m) tall, very hardy and produces blue nodding flowers from mid summer to early autumn.
Cultivars. 'Kermesina', deep red flowers; 'Abundance' light purple flowers with darker veins; 'Minuet', cream with purple bordered flowers; 'Royal Velour', purple velvety flowers; 'Alba Luxurians', white with dark anthers.

Large-flowered clematis
All these cultivars are derived from hybridizing several species. Their height varies from 5–10 ft (1.5–3 m) and flowers are white, pink, mauve, red, blue or violet, single or double, and can be up to 10 in (25 cm) wide.

All clematis mentioned, small as well as large-flowered, are suitable for decorating pergolas, arbours, trellises and tree trunks and for growing over shrubs.
Cultivation. Choose a rich, loamy well drained moisture-retentive soil. Many grow naturally in

Cleome spinosa

chalky or limestone soils. A good mulch at the base will help keep the roots cool, as will a few stones. In summer water well.

Clematis are good climbers and need sturdy supports whether natural or artificial. Pruning is aimed at keeping these plants under control, determined by the space available and to encourage flowering. Those that flower on the previous year's wood such as *C. montana* are pruned after flowering, those that flower on the current year's wood, *C. viticella*, are pruned in early spring.

Propagate the species by seed. Layering is another method: make an incision in the stem, surround it with a peaty compost and separate from parent plant the following year when the layer has taken root. Or take cuttings in early summer, placed in sand in a heated frame.

Their most damaging disease is clematis wilt: cut back to healthy wood, drench with fungicide and it is more than likely that new growth will appear from below ground.

Cleome
Capparidaceae

The genus is made up of about 150 species of annual and perennial herbaceous and shrubby plants from tropical and subtropical areas.

C. hasslerana (*C. spinosa*) – zone 6 – spider flower, may, when conditions are good, grow to over 4 ft (1.2 m) tall. This is a lovely branched, aromatic spiny plant grown as a half-hardy annual with fine clusters of pink or white flowers with long stamens.

Cultivation. Sow under glass in early to mid spring. Pinch out in mid spring and harden off gradually. Plant out in late spring, 20 in (50 cm) between plants, in a light, rich soil in a warm situation. If allowed to go to seed, it will re-seed in subsequent years.

Clerodendrum
Verbenaceae

This is a genus of over 400 climbing and shrubby species from tropical and warmer areas of which a few are cultivated and one or two are hardy.

C. trichotomum (zone 7), is a hardy bushy tree or large shrub which produces decorative fruits, growing up to 13 ft (4 m), with large deciduous

Clerodendrum trichotomum var. *fargesii*

leaves. The flowers blooming in mid summer are star-shaped, white and fragrant and bloom in mid summer; each is surrounded by an inflated red calyx. The flowers are followed by brilliant blue berries. In var. *fargesii* the leaves and stems are less hairy and its fruits are produced more freely.

This species is excellent for shrub borders.

Cultivation. Plant in early or mid autumn in a well-drained soil in a sunny, sheltered position. Propagate by division. The planted fragments will take immediately.

Clethra
Clethraceae

The genus covers some 60 species of shrubs or small trees from America and eastern Asia with lanceolate or oval leaves. Flowers, which are borne in panicles are fragrant, white or pink.

C. alnifolia (zone 5), sweet pepper bush, from eastern North America grows up to 6½ ft (2 m). It has oval leaves and white, aromatic flowers on spikes which bloom from mid summer to early autumn.

Cultivars. 'Paniculata' is similar to the species but with more attractive flowers and of vigorous growth. 'Rosea' has pale pink flowers.

C. arborea (zone 9), lily-of-the-valley tree, is about 20 ft (6 m) tall and comes from Madeira. Its white flowers bloom from late summer to mid autumn, but it can only be grown in mild frost-free areas.

Cultivation. Clethras prefer a moist, acid soil. Propagate from seed, summer cuttings placed in sand in a heated frame, or by layers in the spring.

Clianthus

Leguminosae

This genus of two species which are semi-climbing tender shrubs with evergreen pinnate leaves bear large flowers in white, red or scarlet clusters. Native to Australia, New Zealand.

C. formosus (*C. dampieri*) (zone 10), desert pea, a native of Australia is 3½–4 ft (1–1.2 m) tall. It has green-grey velvety leaves and bright scarlet flowers with a dark, raised blotch, 4–5 in (10–13 cm) long which appear in groups of five or six from mid summer to early autumn.

C. puniceus (zone 9–10), glory pea, a native of New Zealand, is 3½–4 ft (1–1.2 m) tall. It has leathery, bright green leaves and large pendulous scarlet flowers about 4 in (10 cm) long from early to mid summer.

Clianthus should be staked or allowed to fall over a wall, slope, or to decorate a pillar.

Cultivation. It will grow well in warm frost-free areas in sheltered situations but, where winters are frosty it must be grown in a glasshouse. Propagate from seeds or from cuttings, in sand with bottom heat.

Clianthus puniceus

Codiaeum

Variegated laurel, *Euphorbiaceae*

This genus of about six species, found mainly in the islands of the Pacific ocean and Malaysia, consists of mostly evergreen shrubs. Only one is cultivated for its ornamental, brightly coloured foliage, usually as decoration in the house or greenhouse although in tropical areas it has been used for hedging.

C. variegatum (zone 10), croton, Joseph's coat, is assumed to be native to Polynesia for although it has been cultivated and interesting forms have been selected by native peoples for many years it has not, for certain, been found in the wild. It forms a small shrub to 3 ft (90 cm) or more in height with glossy, leathery leaves in a range of shapes, from narrow lance shaped to ovate, entire or lobed. Some are twisted or curled and the basic green colour may be blotched, spotted or tinged with many colours including shades of red, yellow, orange or pink. The small flowers when formed are less significant.

Many named cultivars are available, among them: 'Bravo' with a wavy leaf marked with yellow; 'Reidii' with an ovate, red, yellow and green leaf; 'Craigii' with a green and yellow leaf, three pointed at the apex.

Cultivation. These plants enjoy some direct light in the morning or evening, a steady temperature of at least 60°F (16°C) and a moist atmosphere with no draughts. Repot in spring in a peaty compost and propagate by stem cuttings.

Codonopsis

Bonnet bellflowers, *Campanulaceae*

The genus covers some 30 species of hardy perennials from Asia. They are climbing or rambling plants with tubers and single, bell-shaped flowers.

C. clematidea (zone 6), from central Asia, is 24 in (60 cm) tall with a similar spread. The branched stalks are erect and supple, carrying opposite, oval, pointed grey-green leaves. The large bell-like flowers have turned-up edges and are pale porcelain blue with browny yellow bases and tinged with black. This is a decorative species which flowers from mid to late summer.

C. meleagris (zone 6), from China, is 4–12 in (10–

Codonopsis clematidea

30 cm) tall with a spread of 12–16 in (30–60 cm). It is an erect plant with wide elliptical and dark green rosette-like leaves crowded at its base. Terminal, bell-shaped, single flowers are creamy coloured with a chocolate-brown marbled base. It blooms from early to mid summer.

Erect species are grown in a rock garden or on a wall; the climbing species, which are often invasive, should be kept clear of fragile plants. **Cultivation.** Plant in a humus-rich soil, in either shade or semi-shade. Propagate from seeds or by dividing older clumps in the spring.

Coix

Gramineae

A small genus of three or four annual grasses represented in cultivation by *C. lacryma-jobi* (zone 10), Job's tears, which will grow to over 3 ft (90 cm). This is an unusual grass with branched stems bearing short, wide leaves and produces small glossy, white or grey seeds that look like pearls.

Cultivation. Sow under glass in heat, in late winter or early spring and plant out in late spring. They can also be sown in the open in spring, in an open warm sunny position, spaced out at 8 in (20 cm).

Colchicum

Autumn crocus, *Liliaceae*

The genus covers some 50 species with corms from Europe, north Africa, and Asia. Those described here are hardy. In most species long and fairly wide pleated leaves emerge in the spring, with a seed capsule at ground level which lasts until early summer. Mauve, pink or white flowers appear in autumn before the leaves. They are not true crocuses.

C. autumnale (zone 4), a common European plant has soft rosy lilac flowers and is the easiest species to grow. It blooms from early to late autumn.

C. agrippinum (zone 8), a possible hybrid, bears speckled violet-purple flowers with pointed, tapering segments, and is easy to grow in any sunny position.

C. byzantinum (zone 5), another possible hybrid, blooms a little earlier with wide open, pale lilac-purple flowers.

C. cilicicum (zone 5), a native of Turkey, Syria and Lebanon, bears lilac to rose-purple coloured flowers that appear in mid-autumn. Leaves grow quite quickly after the plant has flowered.

C. luteum (zone 7), a native of the Himalayas, has yellow flowers in spring to early summer and is best grown in an alpine house.

C. speciosum (zone 5), is one of the finest of the autumn crocuses, with very large rosy-purple flowers having a green tinged perianth tube.

Colchicum byzantimum

The cultivar 'Album' has white flowers. There are many hybrids including 'Waterlily', which has double pink, long-lasting flowers.

Autumn crocuses create fine splashes of colour in the lawn or rock garden from late summer to mid autumn. They need a warm and sunny position in a well-drained soil and thrive in very dry summers.

Cultivation. Plant bulbs in good well-drained but moisture retentive soil at about 4 in (10 cm) deep, from mid to late summer so that they develop a good root system before flowering.

They do not need a cold period in order to bloom. The flowers will appear at the right time of year even without soil and water. Leave the plant undisturbed unless you wish to increase them, in which case lift in summer, divide, and replant. Plants of this genus are extremely poisonous.

Coleus

Labiatae

This genus includes about 150 species, most of which are herbaceous perennials from tropical regions in the Old World.

C. blumei (zone 10+), flame nettle of Java is a tender plant which does well indoors and is often treated as a half-hardy annual for summer bedding. It has small blue flowers, but it is the multicoloured foliage in shades of yellow, purple or red developed by hybridizing that is by far the most important.

Cultivars. The 'Rainbow' series, 10 in (25 cm) tall, has leaves in a wide range of colour markings, while the 'Milky Way' series is dwarf with deeply cut leaves in an equally exciting range of colours. Var. *verschaffeltii*, 12 in (30 cm) tall, has deep purplish-red leaves.

Tropical-looking effects can be created with the flame nettle. Plants grown from cuttings of one plant will give a more uniform result than if grown from the seed mixtures.

Cultivation. Sow those which can be obtained from seeds from mid winter to early spring, in the hot house. Prick out the seedlings in mid spring into pots and harden off gradually before planting out in late spring. For the named cultivars take cuttings in early autumn and from the resulting plants take further cuttings in late winter. After hardening off, plant out at distances of 12 in (30 cm) after the last frosts are well over.

Columnea

Columnea, *Gesneriaceae*

The genus comprises over 150 species, often epiphytic, evergreen herbaceous perennials or sub-shrubs from tropical America.

C. gloriosa (zone 10+), goldfish plant, comes from Costa Rica. The pendulous stems of this sub-shrub are 2–4 ft (60 cm–1.2 m) long and covered with green hairy leaves. Scarlet hooded flowers, 2–2¼ in (5–6 cm) long, have a small yellow patch in the throat and are borne profusely through mid autumn to mid spring.

The plant is grown in hanging baskets for its showy hooded flowers which are produced close together in the leaf axils.

Cultivation. Propagate between early and late spring by cuttings 3¼ in (8 cm) long from non-flowering shoots; put in pots containing a peat-based compost (potting soil) and keep at a temperature of 64–71°F (18–22°C). When plants are well developed transfer them, at a spacing of 8–10 in (20–25 cm), to hanging baskets with a mixture of peat and soil. Throughout the flowering season keep the temperature at 57–60°F (14–16°C) and keep moist to ensure a continuous display of flowers.

Colutea

Bladder senna, *Leguminosae*

The genus covers over 20 deciduous shrubs from Europe and Asia.

C. arborescens (zone 6), from the Mediterranean region, is a spreading shrub which can grow over 12 ft (3.7 m) tall and with the same spread. It is hardy in many areas. Light green pinnate leaves give it an airy grace and its pea-shaped yellow flowers, which appear throughout the summer, are followed by strange, decorative inflated fruits which turn brown, fading to almost white

Bladder senna can be used as a specimen shrub or take its place in a bed of shrubs.

Cultivation. Easy to grow, it will adapt to just about any soil, prefering well-drained, even poor soil, limy or sandy. It can be planted between the end of autumn and spring, in full sun or semi-shade.

It does not need any special attention but, as it flowers on the current year's wood, it should be pruned in the spring. Remove dead or weak wood and cut back to within a few buds of the old wood. It can be propagated from seeds sown in the ground at the beginning of spring, or from semi-hardwood cuttings (with a heel) at the end of summer.

Comptonia

Myricaceae

This genus contains just one species which is a native of North America.

C. peregrina (zone 6), sweet fern, from the eastern USA, grows up to 2–4 ft (60–120 cm) tall. This is a lovely aromatic shrub which has downy brown branches with narrow, fern-like deciduous green leaves. The male flowers are in the form of cylindrical catkins, the female flowers are globular catkins; they appear in early to mid spring.

Cultivation. Plant in a moist heathland (acid) soil in a well-shaded position. Propagate from layers or by removing suckers.

Convallaria

Lily of the valley, *Liliaceae*

The genus covers one variable species found in Europe, Asia and North America.

C. majalis (zone 4) is a hardy herbaceous perennial, 6–8 in (15–20 cm) tall with a spread of at least 20–24 in (50–60 cm). It has elliptical mid-green leaves arranged in pairs, and blooms from mid to late spring. The clusters of bell-shaped, white, waxy-looking flowers have a lovely strong scent. Variants are available with pink or double white flowers.

The plant is too invasive for flower beds, but is useful as groundcover or in a shrub border in semi-shade. It will grow in most regions.

Cultivation. The plant prefers a cool, humus-rich, well-drained soil.

Plant crowns in autumn, at 4–4¾ in (10–12 cm) apart in a sunny or semi-shaded position.

Maintenance is quite easy: mulch with compost or leaf mould every spring. Propagation is done by dividing the crowns in the autumn or at the beginning of spring.

Convolvulus tricolor

Convolvulus

Bindweed, *Convolvulaceae*

The genus comprises around 250 annuals and herbaceous perennials, shrubs and sub-shrubs, often twining, from all parts of the world. Several species are pernicious weeds, but the following selection is blameless in this respect and worth growing.

C. cantabrica (zone 8–9), is a pink-flowered convolvulus from the Mediterranean region and south east Europe. It is 10–14 in (25–35 cm) tall with a spread of 20–24 in (50–60 cm). This is a perennial with downy, branched climbing stems, which produces its large flowers from early summer to early autumn.

C. cneorum (zone 9), shrubby convolvulus, from southern Europe grows up to 2–5 ft (60 cm–1.5 m) tall with the same spread. This small bushy shrub has a silky, silvery down covering its leaves and bears clusters of pink-tinged white flowers at the end of its stalks in early summer.

C. mauritanicus (zone 9–10), from north Africa is 4–6 in (10–15 cm) tall with a spread of 3½ ft (1 m). It is a prostrate, twining perennial plant with mid green leaves and blue flowers which are 1 in (2.5 cm) across and appear throughout summer. It is useful in hanging baskets or containers.

Cultivation. Plant in mid spring in any dry, well-drained soil, in full sun.

The plants cannot tolerate cold and winter damp thus becoming more difficult to grow the further north you garden.

Propagate from cuttings, 2–4 in (5–10 cm) long, taken from lateral shoots; place these in sand under a cold frame in early or mid summer.

C. tricolor, (*C. minor*) (zone 5), an annual from southern Europe, is 16 in (40 cm) tall with tricoloured flowers – orange-yellow throat surrounded by a white area and blue edges – which bloom in early and mid summer. The flowers open by day and close at night. Seeds are available for plants with specific coloured flowers, but are usually sold in mixed colours.
Cultivation. Sow early or mid spring under shelter in pots of seed compost (potting soil) or, better, as these plants resent root disturbance, in peat pots. Plant out in late spring, 1 ft (30 cm) apart, being careful not to break up the soil. To avoid root disturbance, you can sow directly *in situ* in late spring in groups of two or three seeds. Pinch out young plants and remove dead flowers to extend the flowering season.

Coreopsis

Tickseed, *Compositae*

This genus is represented by about 120 species of hardy annuals and herbaceous perennials native to America and tropical Africa.
C. grandiflora (zone 6), from southern USA, is a perennial growing to over 20 in (50 cm) tall with a spread of 16–20 in (40–50 cm). Narrow leaves are mid green and the plant flowers profusely from early summer to early autumn. The golden-yellow flowers are daisy-like and make lovely cut flowers. The plant is suitable for herbaceous and mixed borders. 'New Gold' and 'Sunray' are double cultivars.
C. verticillata (zone 6) from USA grows 18–24 in (45–60 cm) with yellow flowers borne midsummer to early autumn. Cultivars include 'Zagreb' and 'Moonbeam'.
Cultivation. Plant in autumn or at the beginning of spring 16 in (40 cm) apart. This species prefers light, well-drained soil and full sunlight. Stake in windy positions. Water during dry periods and dead-head regularly to encourage further flowers. Propagate by division in mid autumn or early spring, or from seeds sown in spring. The plant is short-lived but self-seeds.

Coriandrum

Umbelliferae

A genus of two annual species from western Mediterranean regions, one of which has been used as a herb for many centuries.
C. sativum (zone 7–8), coriander, is 20–30 in (50–80 cm) tall and produces much-divided leaves like parsley, but larger. White flowers appear in mid summer, followed by seeds which initially give off an unpleasant rubbery smell, but once ripe their scent is quite pleasant.
Cultivation. Coriander does best in a limy permeable soil and requires a warm position. Sow in place from mid spring to early summer in rows 12 in (30 cm) apart. Thin out to 10 in (25 cm). Hoe and water when necessary.

Remove leaves as and when required. Wait for seeds to ripen before removing umbels. Hang the stems in a dry, well-aired place, out of the sun. Allow these to dry before shaking them on a cloth to recover the seeds.
Uses. Coriander leaves are good for decorating and flavouring a variety of dishes. The seeds are also useful for flavouring various meat dishes.

Coriaria

Coriariaceae

The genus covers about five species from the Himalayas, Japan, New Zealand, South America and the Mediterranean region. They are shrubs or sub-shrubs with small flowers, but their fleshy, coloured fruits are poisonous.
C. japonica (zone 9), from Japan, grows up to $3\frac{1}{2}$ ft (1 m). It is a delightful shrub, popular for its decorative red fruits.
C. myrtifolia (zone 9), redoul, from southern Europe, is a shrub 6–$6\frac{1}{2}$ ft (1.8–2 m) tall. It produces a lovely foliage, and in late spring and summer small greenish flowers appear in erect clusters, followed by glossy purple-black fruits.
C. napalensis (zone 9), from the Himalayas, is 10 ft (3 m) tall, the tallest of all the species. Greenish-brown flowers appear in late spring to early summer followed by purple-black fruits.
Cultivation. These are not hardy where the winters have prolonged periods of frost and should be protected in all but the mildest of relatively frost-free climates. Plant in the open, in any soil. Propagate by removing suckers and runners in the autumn or by seed or cuttings.

Cornus

Cornel, dogwood, *Cornaceae*

This genus of 45 species, mostly from northern

temperate zones, includes mostly deciduous shrubs and shrubby trees ranging from 3½–23 ft (1–7 m) tall and their leaves are usually entire, lanceolate and opposite. Small, but decorative flowers are in some species surrounded by petal-like bracts.

C. alba (zone 4–5), from Siberia and Korea, is a bushy shrub and can grow up to 10 ft (3 m). The young stems are bright red in the winter and should be cut back to encourage a greater display. The most common variegated-foliage cultivars are 'Elegantissima' with white margined leaves, and 'Spaethii' with yellow variegated leaves.

C. controversa (zone 7), from Japan and Formosa, grows slowly and erectly, and is most noticeable for its horizontal tiers of branches.

C. florida (zone 5), flowering dogwood, from the eastern USA, can grow up to 17 ft (5 m). Clusters of flowers in late spring are encircled by four white bracts, which are pink in f. *rubra*. The leaves of both forms turn bright red in autumn, and look good as isolated specimens.

C. kousa (zone 5), from Japan and Korea, grows up to 10–13 ft (3–4 m) tall with the same spread. In late spring four large, white bracts encircle the flowers like butterfly wings and the subsequent fleshy red fruits look like strawberries. Autumn foliage is richly coloured. Plant at the back of a bed or in a clearing, in a rich, cool, non-alkaline soil. The more vigorous var. *chinensis* is more commonly grown.

C. mas (zone 6), cornelian cherry, is a slow-growing tree and reaches 25 ft (7.5 m) with a rounded top. In late winter and early spring it is covered with clusters of small, pale yellow flowers. Red, edible fruits appear in early to mid autumn. It grows extremely well in a dry, alkaline soil. It can be planted under large trees or used as a backing for a flower border.

C. sanguinea (zone 6), common dogwood or bloodtwig, will grow up to 13 ft (4 m) tall and is very branched. The branches are sometimes red on the exposed side and leaves turn a brilliant red in autumn. White flowers appear in late spring and are followed by black fruits. Plant randomly for a natural hedgerow look. This shrub does well in a poor, dry soil. It is very vigorous, produces suckers and may be pruned in the spring.

All these ornamental dogwoods are suitable for small gardens.

Cultivation. In general, the dogwoods will grow in just about any kind of soil and will thrive in shade as well as sun. Plant in autumn or spring. At the end of winter prune those species that are grown for the colour of their young stems.

Cornus kousa var. *'chinensis'*

Propagate suckering species by removing rooted suckers in late autumn; others by cuttings in late autumn and early winter.

Cortaderia

Pampas grass, *Gramineae*

The genus comprises about 15 species of hardy grasses from South America, including *C. selloana* (zone 8–9), which is the well-known pampas grass. This grows up to 5–10 ft (1.5–3 m) tall, when in flower, with a spread of 3½–6½ ft (1–2 m). It is more or less evergreen and the numerous blue-green leaves to 6 ft (1.8 m) long are arched, making a dense, tufted clump. The inflorescences are long silvery white plumes on stalks to 3 ft (90 cm) or more; they appear at the beginning of autumn.

Cultivars. 'Pumila' is only 4 ft (1.2 m) tall; 'Gold Band' has leaves striped gold; 'Rendatleri' has purplish plumes.

As a specimen, pampas grass will decorate a lawn or it can be associated with shrubs for the contrast of its habit. It is hardy in many regions except those that suffer particularly harsh winters.

Cultivation. Plant in mid spring in a sunny position sheltered from the wind and in a deep, well-drained soil. Remove the dead leaves either by cutting or burning in early spring. In very cold regions protect the stump in winter with straw or dry leaves. Propagate by dividing clumps in the spring.

Corydalis

Papaveraceae (Fumariaceae)

Out of about 300 species of herbaceous plants spread across the temperate zones of the north and parts of Africa, some species are useful for their profuse small tubular flowers and decorative fern-like leaves.

C. cashmeriana (zone 6), from the Himalayas, is a lovely species with a cluster of tubers and delicate, blue-green leaves. Its flowers, carried on stems 8 in (20 cm) tall, are an unusual bright blue and bloom in late spring to mid summer.

C. lutea (zone 6), a native of Europe, grows up to 1 ft (30 cm) tall with a similar spread. This is an ideal plant for walls and rocky places in a shady position; its yellow flowers start appearing in mid spring and continue to late autumn.

C. solida (zone 6), which grows naturally in chalk in woody regions, has blue-green leaves and bears purple or creamy white flowers in early to mid spring and is an easy plant for a semi-shaded position.

Cultivation. These are hardy plants and mostly not too demanding as far as soil is concerned; they will grow in limy soil provided that it is well drained, especially in winter. *C. cashmeriana*, however, is more particular: it needs a siliceous, moist peaty (non-limy) soil, in a semi-shaded position; the soil must be well drained, but never allowed to dry out, and it prefers humid conditions.

The plants seed themselves readily. Remove young plants from the garden with plenty of soil around the roots and replant where desired.

Corydalis cashmeriana

Corylopsis

Winter hazel, *Hamamelidaceae*

About seven species of deciduous shrubs or small trees make up this genus from northeast Asia.

C. glabrescens (zone 6), from Japan, grows up to 10 ft (3 m) and not quite as wide. Green leaves are bristle-toothed and pale yellow flowers bloom early to mid spring.

C. pauciflora (zone 6), from Japan, is a lovely shrub with spreading habit which grows up to 5–6½ ft (1.5–2 m) tall and is often wider than it is high. Its brilliant green, rounded leaves appear after it has produced its pale yellow, aromatic flowers, two to three in each cluster, borne on the naked branches in early to mid spring.

C. spicata (zone 6), also from Japan, is a closely related species with longer flower spikes and purple-bronze tinted leaves in autumn.

The shrubs prefer a mild climate without cold winters and spring frosts which damage the flowers. They need the shelter of a south- or west-facing wall in colder regions, or better still, the protection of other trees or shrubs.

Cultivation. Corylopsis like a moist, humus-rich, preferably peat-enriched soil. They should be planted between autumn and spring in the sun or slight shade. They do not require a great deal of care once planted, except an occasional thinning out of frost-damaged twigs after flowering. The simplest method of propagation is to layer the supple stems in the autumn, or by cuttings.

Corylus

Betulaceae

This genus of 10 deciduous trees and shrubs from the Northern Hemisphere includes the hazels and filberts.

C. avellana 'Contorta' (zone 5–6), corkscrew hazel, is an ornamental tree which can grow as tall as 10–13 ft (3–4 m), with almost the same width. It has unusual twisted spiral branches and is particularly decorative in winter. The leaves are mid green and in late winter it produces yellow pendent catkins. It also bears nuts. It is hardy in most regions as is another decorative species, *C. maxima* 'Purpurea' (zone 5–6), which has large purple leaves.

Both species may be planted as specimen shrubs, in a mixed border or shrub bed.

Cultivation. Plant between autumn and spring in a well-drained, preferably loamy, even chalky soil, although they will also do well in clay soils. They enjoy a position in full sun or slight shade.

In order to obtain a good shape it is best to prune them for a few years after planting, cutting back by half the old wood to stimulate a bushy growth. Propagation is by layering the supple stems in autumn.

Cosmos

Compositae

The genus includes 20 or so species of annuals and perennials from tropical and subtropical America.

C. bipinnatus (zone 5–6), cosmos, from Mexico is an annual up to 3½ ft (1 m) tall. Slightly stiff, but branched with feathery leaves it bears large white, pink or scarlet flowers with a yellow centre. 'Sensation' is 2½–5 ft (80 cm–1.5 m) tall with large, variously coloured flowers.

This cosmos can be grown in semi-wild parts of the garden as well as in mixed borders. They are useful for cut flowers.

Cultivation. Sow in early to mid spring under glass or in a nursery bed in late spring. Pinch the tips of young plants to encourage branching. Plant out at the end of spring in a dry, poor soil in full sun and towards early summer, thin to 16 in (40 cm) apart. Remove dead flowers to extend flowering period. Young shoots may be attacked by aphids.

Cotinus

Smoke bush, *Anacardiaceae*

A small genus of about four species of deciduous shrubs from the Northern Hemisphere.

C. coggygria (syn. *Rhus cotinus*) (zone 6–7), Venetian sumach or smoke bush, from Europe is a lovely deciduous shrub with a decorative foliage producing brilliant autumn colours. The name 'smoke bush' comes from the feathery heads of purplish-pink flowers that it bears in the summer. It can grow up to 6½–10 ft (2–3 m) tall with the same spread. It is hardy in most regions, but needs shelter from cold winds.

Cultivars. There are various highly decorative forms like f. *purpureus* with green leaves and purplish-pink flowers or 'Royal Purple' with deep purple foliage.

They can be grown on their own or as backgrounds for smaller shrubs and perennials.

Cultivation. The smoke bush grows well in a light, well-drained, even sandy soil in full sun. Plant between autumn and spring when the weather is mild. A mulch of peat or well-decomposed compost in spring is beneficial. Water during dry spells. Propagate by layering the flexible stems in early to mid autumn, or by removing and transplanting rooted young suckers.

Cotoneaster

Rosaceae

The genus covers about 50 species of deciduous and evergreen shrubs from Europe and Asia with decorative foliage, flowers and coloured autumn berries. They are all extremely hardy and easy to grow.

C. franchetii (zone 5), from western China, is over 6½ ft (2 m) tall and has the same spread, with arched stems and evergreen grey-green leaves, pink and white flowers and numerous orange fruits.

C. horizontalis (zone 5), from China, is a low-growing shrub with a herringbone arrangement of branches and small deciduous leaves. In spring it is covered with white flowers, tinged pink, followed by red berries and its leaves colouring orange-red.

C. lacteus (zone 5), 10–13 ft (3–4 m) tall, is evergreen with white flowers and clusters of red berries.

C. microphyllus (zone 5), is low-growing to prostrate, with small evergreen leaves, white flowers and scarlet berries.

Coming in so many shapes and sizes the numerous species have many uses in the garden: as a ground cover, to decorate walls, as specimens, as hedges, in mixed borders, and some are small enough for window boxes, troughs and rock gardens.

Cultivation. Plant in autumn or winter in any kind of soil, even a dry and rocky site in sun or shade, is suitable. They may need occasional tidying: in the spring for evergreens and at the end of winter for deciduous species.

Propagate by semi-hardwood cuttings at the end of summer or from seed. The destructive bacterial disease of fireblight can affect this genus, and the only sure way to bring some measure of control is to cut out affected parts – if necessary the whole bush – and burn immediately.

Crambe

Cruciferae

The genus covers some 25 species of herbaceous annuals and perennials from Europe, western Asia and tropical Africa. They often take the form of large plants with thick stalks, glaucous leaves and white flowers arranged on spikes or in clusters.

C. cordifolia (zone 4), from the Caucasus and Afghanistan, is 5–6½ ft (1.5–2 m) tall with a spread of 2–3 ft (60–90 cm). Its leaves are extremely large, rounded and with irregular indentations; initially violet, they turn green as they mature. Numerous white, aromatic flowers on tall leafless stems in great panicles appear in early summer.

C. maritima (zone 5), sea kale, from Europe, is 3½–5 ft (1–1.5 m) tall with a spread of 3½ ft (1 m). The oval blue-green leaves are similar to those of the cabbage and large heads of white flowers are produced in early summer. In addition to its decorative value it is also grown as a winter vegetable. The white leaf stalks can be eaten as soon as they appear or after forcing, in the manner of chicory. White, etiolated shoots taste a little like cauliflower. *C. maritima* does very well near the sea, suffering salt-spray, with no ill effect.

Both species make fine additions to large herbaceous borders where their scale gives a dramatic architectural quality among more traditional plants, or in the kitchen garden to add a flowery note.

Cultivation. Plant in a deep, rich, preferably limy soil in a sunny position.

Propagate from seeds planted in the position in which they are to grow in the spring, or from root cuttings 4–6 in (10–15 cm) long, taken in the autumn.

Crassula

Crassulaceae

Mostly South African, this genus covers 300 species of succulent herbaceous perennials and shrubs, but only one is hardy.

C. sedifolia (*C. milfordae*) (zone 8–9), a native of the Drakensberg, is 2 in (5 cm) tall with a spread of 8–12 in (20–30 cm). Its tiny, fleshy bronze-coloured leaves are displayed in rosettes making thick cushions. Small white flowers are borne on 1–2 in (3–5 cm) stems from mid to late summer.

This species is best grown in a rock garden.

Cultivation. Plant in full sun in rock crevices, in a well-drained soil. Propagate by removing some rosettes in early summer and rooting them in sand under a cold frame, before placing them in their final positions in the summer.

The tender species which follow make attractive pot plants for the house or greenhouse and may survive outdoors in frost-free areas without excessive humidity.

C. arborescens (*C. cotyledon*) (zone 10) is a vigorous shrub to about 3 ft (90 cm) or more in height. The wide, grey-green leaves have a red edge and the white to pale pink flowers may be formed on plants growing in the ground but rarely on pot-grown plants.

C. portulacea (*C. argentea*) (zone 10), jade plant, is not dissimilar to the previous species, but the red-edged leaves are glossy dark green and spathulate in shape. The clusters of starry pinkish white flowers open in spring.

Cultivation. The tender succulents are easy to grow in a freely draining compost (potting soil). In the growing season they like plenty of sun, air and water, and during their resting period they enjoy cool dry conditions. Propagate from seed, from offsets, or from stem or leaf cuttings which should be allowed to dry before inserting in a cutting compost (potting soil).

Crataegus

Rosaceae

This is a genus of nearly 300 small thorny, deciduous trees and shrubs, which can grow up to 26 ft (8 m) tall, from north temperate regions. They have small, often lobed leaves and usually white, aromatic flowers which appear in mid spring, followed by red fruits with a flavourless pulp.

C. crusgalli (zone 6) from North-East America is a thorny-branched tree with a wide spread. The glossy green leaves turn bright red in autumn. white flowers bloom in clusters in early summer.
C. monogyna (zone 6), common or singleseed hawthorn from Europe and western Asia, is a familiar tree which, if used in isolation has a fine, rounded shape. Its leaves are deeply lobed and the red fruits bear just one seed. It is commonly grown in Europe but will not tolerate an acid soil. There are cultivars with erect or weeping habit.
C. oxycantha (zone 5), hawthorn or May, is often confused with the preceding species, but can be distinguished by its less lobate leaves and by its fruits which are two or three seeded. It does well in a cool location, in the shade. There is a red, double-flowered cultivar 'Paul's Scarlet'.
Cultivation. Plant in autumn or spring, in a good loamy soil leaving at least 5 ft (1.5 m) between each tree for taller varieties and less for the shorter ones. Propagate from seeds that have been stratified for 18 months. Hawthorns are quite hardy and will stand up well to pollution. They can be attacked by fireblight, powdery mildew and leafblotch; caterpillars can damage the leaves.

Crinum
Amaryllidaceae

This genus is mostly a tropical one of 120 bulbous species. The large, pyriform or oval bulbs produce long strap-shaped leaves and a flower stem topped by umbels of star- or tubular-shaped flowers in the summer.
C. amoenum (zone 10), from Burma, is 2 ft (60 cm) tall when in bloom, and bears about 10 star-shaped, fragrant white flowers tinted pinkish-red on their undersides. The species is best suited to a frost-free climate or grown in a heated greenhouse elsewhere.
C. asiaticum (zone 10), from tropical southeast Asia, is a strong plant. Its attraction lies in the large leaves which are over 3 ft (90 cm) long. Star-shaped, white, aromatic flowers, numbering about 20, are produced. Like the preceding species it is not hardy, so must be grown in a frost-free climate.
C. moorei (zone 9–10), from South Africa, has flower stems 30 in–3½ ft (80 cm–1 m) tall, each bearing 10 funnel-shaped white to pink flowers. This is best suited to a mild climate.

Crinum × powellii

C. × *powellii* (zone 9–10), a hybrid of *C. moorei* and *C. bulbispermum*, is a hardier perennial creating large clumps, with pink flowers much like the preceding species.
Cultivation. In areas of frost-free winters crinums will do well if planted in a rich soil in a sunny position. *C.* × *powellii* can be grown outside in mild areas provided it is placed in a well-sheltered warm position. When pot-grown in a greenhouse they need a sunny position and compost consisting of a turf loam, fibrous peat and charcoal. Propagated from seeds the plant will take some time before flowering, but sooner if started from offsets. In common with all Amaryllidaceae, it is best not to disturb the root system once planted, but when necessary, repotting is best done in the spring.

Crocosmia
Montbretia, *Iridaceae*

The genus comprises about seven species with corms from southern Africa. The plants look rather like small gladioli. In spring the corm produces long, smooth or folded leaves and clusters of tubular yellow or orange flowers appear on spikes from the summer onwards.
C. × *crocosmiiflora* (zone 7–8), 20–30 in (50–80 cm) high, is a hybrid with flowers ranging from yellow to orange-red. Several good cultivars are now available, such as 'Citronella' with

lemon-yellow flowers and 'Solfatare' with apricot-yellow flowers and bronzy foliage.
C. masonorum (zone 7–8), grows up to 3½ ft (1 m). Its lanceolate leaves are pleated and in mid to late summer, orange-red flowers are held erect along curved flower stems.
Cultivation. Plant in spring at 6–8 in (15–20 cm) apart in a light well-drained soil, which should be watered in dry summers. In northern regions plant in full sun in front of a wall.

Cover with a layer of dead leaves before frosts arrive. Cut back stems when the flowering season is over. If necessary you can lift the corms and store them over the winter. This will provide many new corms to increase your stock. Otherwise, collect mature seeds in the autumn and sow at once in a sandy mixture under a cold frame.

Crocus

Crocus, *Iridaceae*

A genus of generally hardy plants with corms with some 80 species found from Europe to Central Asia. They can always be relied on to bloom, whether they be autumn- or spring-flowering species. In some species, the leaves appear after they have flowered.

Crocus sativus

Autumn-flowering species
C. laevigatus (zone 6), from Greece, has flowers ranging from white to mauve which appear in late autumn or winter. 'Fontenayi' has deep lilac-striped flowers and is easy to grow.
C. ochroleucus (zone 6), Syria and the Lebanon, produces leaves and creamy white flowers with yellow throats in late autumn.
C. sativus (zone 6), saffron, has grey-green leaves in mid autumn appearing before its wide-open flowers which are lilac-purple with darker veins. It is distinguished by its large branched, orange-red stigmas. It used to be widely cultivated for its stigmas, which contain the valuable spice, saffron. But it is not easy to grow in northern regions. It is best to lift and divide the corms every two years replanting them in good fresh soil. Unknown in the wild, this species is sterile and multiplies vegetatively.
C. speciosus (zone 5), from Asia Minor, produces pointed, violet-blue flowers in early autumn and multiplies quickly. It has itself given rise to a number of forms.

Winter- and spring-flowering species
C. ancyrensis (zone 5), from Turkey, produces very precocious orange yellow flowers.
C. chrysanthus (zone 5), from the mountains of Yugoslavia and Greece, is the ancestor of many hybrid forms under cultivation, with colours which vary from pale yellow to mauve. It is easy to grow, very precocious and produces abundant flowers in late winter and early spring.
C. angustifolius (*C. susianus*) (zone 5), from southwest Russia bears yellow flowers marked with wide purple-brown lines on the outside in early spring.
C. tomasinianus (zone 5), which is close to *C. vernus*, has very narrow leaves and pale lilac flowers, which can appear as early as late winter. It is easy to grow in a lawn or rock garden and will self-seed.
C. vernus (zone 5), from Europe, has given rise to giant-flowered cultivars, the so-called Dutch crocuses, which offer a rich choice of colours between early and mid-spring.

Many crocuses can be forced, except for yellow varieties, which are difficult to control. Do this in the same way as recommended for hyacinths; keep in the dark during the winter months. The flowers will wither very quickly if they get too warm. Crocuses should be planted in the rock garden, window boxes, a lawn, the edge of a flower border, or around specimen trees.

Cultivation. Plant in a well-drained soil, in a sunny position, in the autumn, 4 in (10 cm) deep and as much apart and cover corms with 2 in (5 cm) of soil. Avoid the use of fertilizers as these will damage them, particularly on lawns.

Field mice and slugs eat the corms, and birds can damage the flowers. The latter can be prevented by stringing black thread between pegs.

Cucumis

Cucurbitaceae

A genus of about 30 species of annuals or herbaceous perennials, many climbing or trailing with tendrils, from tropical regions.

C. sativus (zone 7+), cucumber, is an annual probably from the eastern Himalayas with stems of 4 ft (1.2 m) tall which can climb to 8½ ft (2.5 m) in the greenhouse, and bears fruits 6–16 in (15–40 cm) long.

Cultivation. Cucumbers enjoy a rich, well-drained soil in a warm, sunny position. However, in areas where the winters are long, with lengthy periods of frost cucumbers can be grown in a greenhouse by selecting the appropriate cultivar and provided it is not grown with other plants, as they have a growing regime particular to them. The greenhouse soil should consist of two parts loam, one part compost together with the addition of sterilized bonemeal. Alternatively, grow in large pots using a proprietary compost (soil mix) or in growing bags.

Sow seed in early spring in small pots and when these have developed into the four-leaf stage, plant out, watering them in well. The stems are trained up canes or wires and stopped when they reach the top of the greenhouse; the lateral shoots are trained horizontally. Retain the female flower with a miniature cucumber behind it and pinch out the tip at two leaves beyond it. All the male flowers should be removed, to avoid bitter fruit. The soil must be kept moist but never waterlogged and you must ensure a moist, well-ventilated, buoyant atmosphere at all times. As soon as the fruits begin to appear start feeding once every two weeks. Pick the cucumbers when they are oblong and before they turn yellow, otherwise new fruits will cease to appear. Harvest throughout the summer. Indoor cucumbers are liable to attacks of whitefly and this must be controlled at once, likewise with red spider mites.

Many cultivars have been bred for growing outdoors. For these, choose a site that is warm and sheltered from the wind and with a humus-rich, well drained soil. Dig holes 12 in (30 cm) wide, 12 in (30 cm) deep and 18 in (45 cm) apart and fill with a mixture of soil and compost and sprinkle a fertilizer on the surface. Sow three seeds 1 in (2.5 cm) deep, a few inches apart in each pocket in late spring. After germination, thin out, retaining the strongest plant. Alternatively sow in pots under glass and harden off before planting, with a minimum of root disturbance.

Keep the soil moist and water around the base of each plant. When the fruits start to appear, water with a liquid feed.

Pinch out the leading tip at the seven-leaf stage to encourage a bushy plant with many laterals. It is important with the outdoor cultivars not to remove the male flowers as these are needed for fertilization.

Harvesting starts in mid summer and continues until the first frosts.

Snails and slugs can be a nuisance and should be controlled. Mildew, leaf blotch and various virus diseases can affect cucumbers.

Gherkins are the young fruits of a different species *C. anguria*, an annual from tropical America. The fruits are used boiled or pickled. Sometimes immature cucumbers are also used as substitutes.

Cultivation. Sow in the greenhouse or in open ground as recommended for cucumbers. Pick the greenhouse varieties from early summer onwards and outdoor ones from early autumn. Pick frequently so the fruits are prevented from growing large.

Cucurbita

Squash, pumpkin, *Cucurbitaceae*

This genus, somewhat similar to *Cucumis*, contains about 27 species from tropical and subtropical America. Several species have been cultivated and developed for hundreds of years by the indigenous peoples of South and Central America. The range of size, shape and colour of the fruits is large. Confusion is caused by the use of the common names, squash and pumpkin, for several different species.

Winter squash (zone 8–9)

C. maxima is an annual which produces fruits with a wide range of shapes and sizes depending on the cultivar.

Cultivation. Plant in a well-manured soil in a sunny sheltered position. Water liberally, especially when the weather is warm and dry. Mulch each plant and feed every two weeks with a liquid fertilizer as soon as the first fruits appear.

Propagate from seeds under glass or *in situ* in early to mid spring; sow in pots with three or four seeds under glass and harden off before planting out. Retain the best seedling and plant out in late spring. In the open sow three seeds in each seed-hole which should be spaced 1½–2 ft (45–60 cm) apart. Retain the strongest plant and cut the others down to ground level. The retained plant can be allowed to run over the ground or up a trellis. Harvest as soon as the leaves start to yellow.

Marrow, squash, courgette, zucchini (zone 6–8)

C. pepo, vegetable marrow or squash, is an annual plant, with trailing stems which can grow up to 10–13 ft (3–4 m) long. The fruits are large, and variable in size, shape and colour. Those usually grown as vegetable marrows have dark green cylindrical fruits striped and marbled with white, and they are cut when about 2 ft (60 cm) long. Courgettes (zucchini) are derived from cultivars which produce many fruits suitable for cutting when only a few inches long.

Cultivation. Propagate from seeds sown in mid to late spring in peat-filled seed holes in the open ground in a cool, richly manured soil. Place four to five seeds in each hole, which should be spaced apart and eventually retain just one or two plants per seed-hole.

In order to extend the fruit-bearing period pick the courgettes (zucchini) at regular intervals as soon as they have reached a length of 3¼ in (8 cm). For larger marrows, let them grow and cut them when they are mature at the end of autumn. Mature fruits can be preserved for several months at a temperature of 50°F (10°C). Cut fruits as they appear from mid summer through to early autumn.

Pumpkin (zone 9–10)

This almost globular, large fruit with orange skin and cream to pale orange flesh is used for sweet or savoury dishes. It is also probably from the species *C. pepo*.

Cultivation. Sow in mid or late spring under glass and plant out in late spring or sow directly at the same time of year in a sunny position, at 20 in (50 cm) apart. Allow the plants to grow along the ground. The pumpkin is a heavy drain on the soil's fertility and should only be grown in the same position every five years.

Weed regularly and keep the soil moist. The pumpkins should be picked in mid autumn until frosts appear. They can be stored throughout the winter in a warm place. Watch out for red spider mite or aphids on the leaves and cucumber mosaic virus on the whole plant. Subject to mildew and grey rot.

× Cupressocyparis

Cupressaceae

× *C. leylandii* (zone 5), Leyland cypress, is a bigeneric hybrid between *Cupressus macrocarpa* and *Chamaecyparis nootkatensis*. The seeds were first sown in 1888 and raised by a Mr Leyland. One of the most commonly used evergreen conifers, once established it will grow more than 3½ ft (1 m) a year.

It is generally quite a hardy tree and is best seen when planted alone: its shape is erect and regular with a deep green, shiny foliage. Fifty years after planting, under good conditions, it can grow to the very respectable height of 83 ft (25 m). The cultivar 'Robinson's Gold' is slightly slower growing with bronze-yellow foliage in spring, later turning to gold-yellow and then lemon-green.

It is ideal for creating a quick evergreen screen. Prune if you wish to grow as a hedge.

Cultivation. It is suited to all types of soil but will need an organic ferilizer if it is to grow quickly. When planting, leave plenty of space for its future growth. Hedges should be pruned every year in early autumn.

Propagate from cuttings with a heel under a cold frame in the autumn.

Cupressus

Cypress, *Cupressaceae*

This is a genus of 13 evergreen conifers from the Northern Hemisphere, generally conical or very

narrow in shape. They are distinguished by the foliage consisting of scales and cylindrical or angular branches, which are not as flat as those of *Chamaecyparis*. The flowers are very small catkins and fruits are globular cones covered with scales which spread open when they ripen.
C. arizonica (zone 6), Arizona cypress, from southwest USA and Mexico will grow to over 66 ft (20 m) and is conically shaped with a wide base. It has a fine red bark and the bluish leaves give off an unpleasant smell. It can be used in avenues or can be planted alone, but don't prune. It is a hardy tree and can tolerate temperatures of − 2°F (− 20°C).
C. glabra (zone 6), smooth cypress, comes from further west and is sometimes thought to be the same species. It has smooth bark and is the one more commonly grown.
C. macrocarpa (zone 8–9), Monterey cypress, from California, will not grow taller than about 80 ft (24 m) in its natural state. The mature tree is recognised by the flat top and horizontal branches. Its green foliage is pleasantly scented. It needs a mild coastal climate and makes a good windbreak. For this purpose keep the planting distance at least 6½ ft (2 m).
C. sempervirens (zone 8–9), Italian cypress, has been cultivated for many years around the Mediterranean and can reach a height of 100 ft (30 m). Its dark grey-green leaves are distinctly aromatic. The most popular shape is narrow and conical but another form has wide-spreading branches. It does not tolerate extreme cold which weakens it and makes it sensitive to attack by parasites and diseases. It has great charm when planted in isolation, and it can be used as a windbreak.
Cultivation. Plant in spring. Although generally hardy, some cypresses, such as *C. sempervirens*, require a Mediterranean climate. They grow quickly even in poor soils. Pruning is usually only necessary for those grown as a hedge. Some pruning at planting time will help a tree to bush out. Water liberally in the first year.

Insect attack or frost damage will leave a tree open to fungal diseases causing decay.

Propagate from seeds in the spring.

Cyclamen
Primulaceae

This genus covers around 15 tuberous species spread across the Mediterranean region as far as

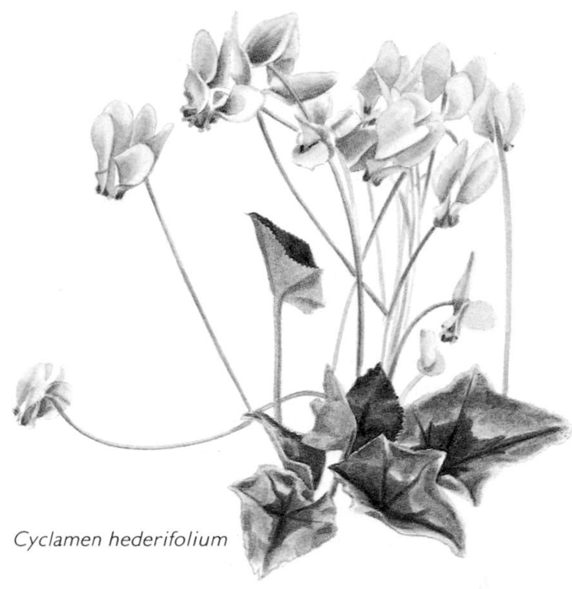

Cyclamen hederifolium

Iran. They are small plants, measuring 6–8 in (15–20 cm) across, which in spring or autumn produce heart- or kidney-shaped, or rounded leaves which may be marbled with silver, and sometimes have scalloped edges. Flowers range in colour from white to deep pink and have characteristic reflexed petals. They appear in either spring or autumn and most of the species are hardy.

Summer- to autumn-flowering species
C. cilicium (zone 6), from southern Turkey, has pale pink flowers blotched with darker pink at mouth. A white form is occasionally found. Leaves are either heart- or orb-shaped.
C. hederifolium (zone 6), from the Mediterranean region, produces pink flowers. Its leaves vaguely resemble those of the ivy and are heart-shaped, scalloped and spotted with silver. This is a common species and is easy to grow.
C. purpurascens (zone 5), from Europe, produces pale to deep pink flowers and small round leaves. This hardy species is becoming rare in the wild and is therefore protected. It flowers in late summer in its alpine habitat.

Spring-flowering species
C. coum (zone 6), from Asia Minor, is a hardy species having flowers which range from white to red; its leaves are round or kidney-shaped.
C. libanoticum (zone 8), from the Lebanon, has pale pink flowers and heart-shaped leaves.
C. persicum (zone 9–10), from the Near East, has pale violet flowers and heart-shaped, marbled

leaves. Many cultivars have been bred from this tender species for growing in greenhouses and homes. These have much larger flowers than the wild species.
C. pseudibericum (zone 6), from Turkey, produces magenta-coloured scented flowers, and heart-shaped leaves. It should be protected from the cold.

Cyclamen can be grown in rock gardens, under shrubs or in north-facing borders.
Cultivation. Cyclamen require a light, well-drained rich soil. Plant the tubers near the surface; they may need to be protected from hard frosts and wind, and they enjoy some shelter from the sun in summer. Avoid moving mature tubers.

Propagate from fresh seeds, which should be soaked for 24 hours in lukewarm water before sowing in a sandy compost in a shallow pan placed in a cool, damp atmosphere. They will flower after two or three years. Cover the pan with wire against rodents. The adult plants may be attacked by the grey mould fungus.

Cydonia
Quince, Rosaceae

This small deciduous tree is the only member of its genus and is in the same family as cherries, peaches, plums and many other fruit trees.
C. oblonga (zone 7), probably comes from Central Asia and was introduced many centuries ago to the Mediterranean region. It produces pink or white flowers in late spring followed by edible, aromatic, yellow pear-shaped fruits.
Cultivation. The quince needs a sunny position and well-drained soil. Several cultivars have been raised to suit various soils and climates.

The species itself can be propagated from seeds or from cuttings, while horticultural cultivars should be grafted on to the species rootstock.

Cynara
Compositae

A genus of 10 perennial species from Mediterranean area, large and thistle-like.
C. scolymus (zone 8), globe artichoke, is not too hardy but will last three to five years or more in a favourable climate. Reaching a height of 6 ft (1.8 m) with a spread of about 3½ ft (1 m) in diameter, it has been grown for its edible flower heads since the 15th century.
Cultivation. Some varieties are quite hardy, but in colder zones their crowns should be protected with straw and peat during winter.

The artichoke will thrive in a light but rich, soil in a sunny position. Dig deeply the previous autumn, incorporating plenty of manure. Plant suckers (sections of shoots with some roots) in mid spring at 4 ft (1.2 m) intervals after trimming, which should be done partly by removing damaged sections and partly by cutting off the ends of the leaves. At the end of winter and before planting, add some well-decomposed compost, reinforced with artificial fertilizers (sulphate of potash and super phosphate) at the rate of 2 oz/sq yd (56 g/m^2) each. Water liberally when the weather is dry. Feed in spring with sodium nitrate or sulphate of ammonia in heavier soils, using ½ oz/sq yd (15 g/m^2). In summer use undiluted liquid fertilizer frequently. Cut heads when fully developed but before the scales begin to open. Remove the lateral flower buds before they are 1 in (2.5 cm) in diameter to encourage the main heads to grow much larger.

The artichoke can be attacked by slugs, earwigs and aphids. It can also suffer from white mould, withered petals and root rot.

Cardoon
C. cardunculus (zone 8), cardoon, grown as an annual, is 6 ft (1.8 m) or more tall. It is much like the globe artichoke, but its leaves and flower heads are more spiny. While it is chiefly grown as a vegetable for the value of its blanched leaf stalks, its silvery leaves and large thistle-like flower heads make it an imposing plant for flower borders.
Cultivation. Plant in a sunny position in deep, rich and non-limy soil. Sow in late spring in seed-holes using three seeds per hole, and burying them to a depth of 1 in (2.5 cm) and thinning to one as soon as possible. The trenches in which these are sown should be 1½ ft (45 cm) wide, 1 ft (30 cm) deep, and 5 ft (1.5 m) apart from centre to centre if there is more than one trench. Well-rotted manure to a depth of 3 in (7.5 cm) should be well mixed with the soil in the bottom of the trench the previous autumn. Water liberally and add a nitrogenous fertilizer while the plants are growing. Mulch in summer.

Cynara scolymus

Blanch in early autumn when soil and foliage are dry: draw the leaves together and tie firmly with raffia (twine), winding a strip of brown paper from the bottom up and then earth up to a height of 1 ft (30 cm). Cover them with straw or old sacking to a thickness of 3 in (7.5 cm), kept secured by raffia (twine) to protect from frost. Pick them three to five weeks later. If you wish to keep plants for the following year, lift the remaining plants before the frosts arrive and store until needed in a cool, dry place, with the straw or sacking (burlap) still in place. You should obtain a yield of 6½ lb/sq yd (3 kg/m²). Protect the seeds from mice.

Cynoglossum

Hound's tongue, *Boraginaceae*

The genus comprises some 50 to 60 species of herbaceous perennials and biennials, growing in temperate or subtropical areas of the world.

C. nervosum (zone 7), a native of the Himalayas, will grow up to a height of 1–2 ft (30–60 cm) with a spread of 2 ft (60 cm). It has a bushy shape and hairy stems. The lanceolate, pale green leaves are covered in short bristly hairs with well-defined veins. Luminous, deep blue flowers are arranged on cymes and bloom from early to late summer. This is one of the few perennials in its genus, but it is rather short lived.

Cultivation. It will thrive in any good soil, either in sun or semi-shade.

Propagate from seeds in the spring. Sow where they are to flower.

Cyperus

Cyperaceae

The genus covers over 500 species of herbaceous plants which are found world-wide in tropics, subtropics and temperate zones. Their leaves are narrow and grass-like.

C. esculentus var. *sativus* (zone 9), chufa or tigernut, a native of the Mediterranean region, rarely flowers but produces pleasant-tasting edible tubers, which have been used as a vegetable since ancient times. It is grown in much the same way as the potato.

C. involucratus (*C. alternifolius*) (zone 9), umbrella plant, from the warmer parts of Africa, is well known, and often grown as an indoor plant. Hardy in the mildest climates, the leaves should be trimmed back and the stump covered to protect from cold.

C. longus (zone 6), sweet galingale, from Europe, Asia and North Africa can grow to a height of 4 ft (1.2 m). Umbels bear reddish-brown flower spikes with leafy bracts. This is the hardiest species and can grow under 16 in (40 cm) of water. It produces attractive clumps in the water garden.

C. eragrostis (*C. vegetus*) (zone 7), galingale, is from warm-temperate America and was naturalized several decades ago in southern Europe. It forms clumps of narrow, light green leaves, with umbels of flower spikes, initially green and then turning fawn. It can be useful for disguising the base of taller plants along the margins of a water garden.

Cyphomandra

Solanceae

This genus comprises 30 species of shrubs and trees from South America.

C. betacea (syn. *Solanum betaceum*), (zone 10+), tomato tree, is from Peru and is 13–17 ft (4–5 m) tall. Clusters of small greenish-pink to white flowers appear from mid spring to early autumn and are followed by orange fruits the size and shape of large plums; the skins of the fruit are bitter, but the pulp is tasty, both raw or stewed.

Cultivation. The tomato tree is grown in a warm house except in Mediterranean climates where it will grow quickly in the open. It bears fruits in its second year. Plant in a very sunny position in a compost made up of equal parts of ordinary soil and leaf-mould.

Propagation is easy from seeds; cuttings may be taken and placed under glass in late summer. Under glass the main pest is red spider mite.

Cypripedium

Lady's slipper, *Orchidaceae*

This is one of the most fascinating of all the orchid genera. It contains 35 species native to the more temperate regions of the northern hemisphere. Like its close relative, *Paphiopedilum*, it produces one sac-like inflated pouch often of a different colour to the other four petals. The leaves are usually pleated. Some species are tender but the most attractive are often the easiest to grow.

C. reginae (zone 5), showy lady-slipper, which comes from the peat bogs of eastern North America, survives cold winters well. In the spring it produces extremely beautiful, delicate white flowers with a pink pouch. In a sunny position and in constantly moist, non-alkaline soil it can be quite spectacular. Plants available in the trade are generally collected from the wild and will be short-lived in the garden. It is better to enjoy them in the wild than to deplete native populations.

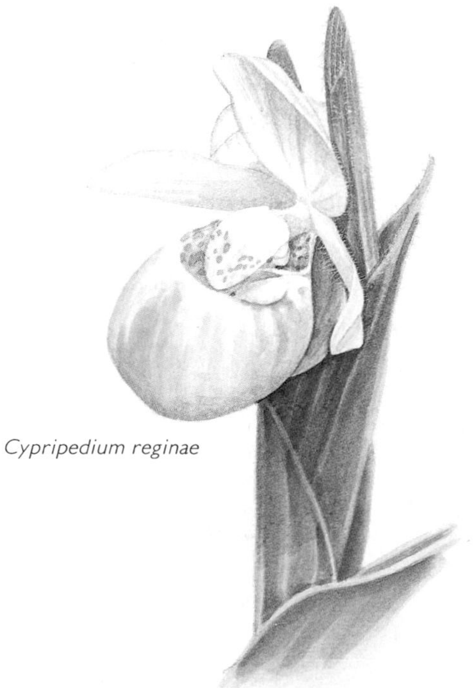

Cypripedium reginae

C. calceolus (zone 5), which has a golden-yellow pouch and four reddish-brown, twisted petals in spring, is a widely distributed plant but in Europe it is, sadly, under threat of dying out because it has been dug up to supply the market.

C. japonicum (zone 5), is one of the eastern Asiatic species which bears a greenish flower with pink pouch in the centre of two fan-shaped leaves.

Cultivation. They do well in partial shade in a cool, open, well-drained soil rich in humus.

When planting in autumn, place the central crown just below the surface and firm well, checking that it remains this way during the winter frosts, when it can be lifted above ground. Propagate in spring by dividing mature clumps.

Cytisus

Broom, *Leguminosae*

This genus includes about 30 species of shrubs from Europe, Asia and North Africa, many of which are well known for their abundant late-spring flowers. Hardy in most regions are cultivars derived from *C.* × *praecox* (zone 6), a hybrid $3\frac{1}{2}$–$6\frac{1}{2}$ ft (1–2 m) tall with the same spread, having arched stems, greyish-green deciduous leaves and cream to yellow flowers. 'Albus', has ivory-white flowers; 'Allgold', golden-yellow flowers. Other species to be noted include, *C. scoparius* (zone 6–7), broom, which can grow over $6\frac{1}{2}$ ft (2 m) tall with the same spread; it has upright green branches, deciduous leaves and yellow flowers. Hybrids of mixed parentage include: 'Burkwoodii' with cerise flowers bordered with gold; 'Lena', flowers light yellow and red; 'Windlesham Ruby', flowers deep red; 'Hollandia' with cream and cerise flowers.

Brooms can be used in shrub borders and mixed borders, the smaller forms are suitable for rock gardens or to clothe sunny slopes.

Cultivation. Plant in autumn or spring, preferably in full sun in an ordinary, well-drained, even dry and sandy soil. They need little care and will do well in dry weather. Trim back each year after they have flowered, to maintain a dense bush. Mites can attack leaves, producing gallnuts. Propagate from semi-hardwood cuttings at the end of summer.

Daboecia

St Daboec's heath, *Ericaceae*

A genus comprising two species of small evergreen shrubs from Europe.

D. cantabrica (zone 6), native to Ireland, France and Spain, measures up to 2 ft (60 cm) in height and spread. The leaves are stiff and pointed, dark green with a silvery underside. The flowers are pinkish-purple and appear from late spring to the beginning of winter. There are cultivars with pink, purple, white or crimson flowers.

This fine shrub is suitable for rock or heather gardens and makes excellent ground-cover.

Cultivation. Like all heaths and heathers, plant in a humus-rich peaty soil or a light sandy lime-free loam, in a sunny or partly shaded position. A light pruning of the dead flowers in the spring will encourage it to be more dense and more floriferous.

Propagate from mid summer to mid autumn, by removing shoots $\frac{3}{4}$–2 in (2–5 cm) long from lateral branches, with or without heels. Then plant in a very well-drained compost in a semi-shaded position under a cold frame.

Dahlia

Compositae

A genus containing 20 or more tuberous plants native to Central America and Columbia, dahlias were introduced to Europe at the end of the 16th century. The many horticultural forms found in gardens today have originated from repeated hybridization. Dahlias flower from mid summer until the first frost. They are prized for their numerous flowers which come in all shades of the spectrum except blue. They are classified for shows according to the type of flower they produce and its diameter.

Single-flowered dahlias (zone 9) have a central disc surrounded by a single row of florets; one example is the yellow 'Yellow Hammer'.

Anemone-flowered dahlias (zone 9) have one or more rows of flat ray-florets surrounding tubular central florets sometimes of a contrasting colour. 'Lucy', for example, has purple petals outside and yellow inside.

Collerette dahlias (zone 9) have a single row of flat ray-florets outside a ruff of smaller florets, sometimes of a different colour, and a central disc. One example is 'Chimborazo' with maroon outer petals and a yellow ruff.

Paeony-flowered dahlias (zone 9) consist of at least two rows of flat-ray florets and a central disc. The pink-purple 'Fascination' is an example.

Decorative dahlias (zone 9) have flowers which are wholly double, with no central disc, and flat, slightly twisted florets radiating outwards. Cultivars belonging to this group are also categorized by their height: 'Alva's Supreme', a *giant* with yellow flowers; 'Purple Joy', a *medium* with purple flowers; and 'Biddenham Sally', which is *small* and pink-flowered.

Ball dahlias (zone 9) are fully double and their petals incurved for more than half their length;

Pompon dahlia

they are arranged in spirals to form a spherical flowerhead which, to fall into this category, must be more than 2 in (5 cm) in diameter. One of the many cultivars in this group is the reddish-pink 'Nijinsky'.
Pompon dahlias (zone 9) are popular for their small spherical heads (up to 2 in/5 cm) consisting of radiating florets rolled inwards for more than half their length. The white 'Little Willow' is an example.
Cactus and *semi-cactus dahlias* (zone 9) have double flowers with radiating, pointed florets rolled outwards or tubular in shape. Some cultivars in this group are 'Pink Symbol', pinkish-purple; 'At Last', red and yellow; 'Highgate Lustre', bright orange; 'Kathy', lilac; 'Lady Linda', primrose yellow.

Different and improved cultivars in all categories appear quite frequently, often ousting existing ones because of their superiority or because of a change in fashion. A specialist society refines the classification to ensure the highest standards in exhibiting.

The dahlia is a striking plant for decorating a garden, either in beds on their own or in mixed borders. They are also ideal as cut flowers for all kinds of floral arrangements.
Cultivation. Plant dahlias from mid spring to early summer when the danger of frost has passed. Prepare the soil by double digging and incorporating plenty of manure the previous autumn. These plants enjoy a sunny situation. Plant robust growers $3\frac{1}{2}$ ft (1 m) apart and smaller ones 16–24 in (40–60 cm) apart, inserting a strong stake first. Remove the lateral buds to obtain larger flowers. At the end of the season, after the first frost, cut the stems down to 6 in (15 cm) above ground level, then lift the tubers carefully with a fork. Keep them in a cool dry, frost-free place at a temperature of 43–50°F (6–10°C). Propagate by division, before planting, or by cuttings in late winter when the tubers have been forced in gentle heat.

Dahlias may suffer from various virus diseases such as mosaic, and fungal diseases such as powdery mildew or wilt. It is quite normal for the tubers to be slightly shrivelled at planting time and they should be dusted with copper lime or sulphur to discourage fungal attack. Slugs and snails are fond of new shoots as are earwigs and blackfly. The tarnished plant bug can cause the malformation of flowers and the distortion of leaves by sucking young shoots and flower buds.

Danae

Alexandrian laurel, *Liliaceae*

A genus of a single evergreen species whose 'leaves' are really flattened stems which function as leaves.
D. racemosa (syn. *Ruscus racemosus*) (zone 5), Alexandrian laurel from Asia Minor, is a small shrub $3\frac{1}{2}$–5 ft (1–$1\frac{1}{2}$ m) in height, with an elegant appearance with arching branches and small, narrow, shiny evergreen 'leaves'. Its small greenish-yellow spring flowers will produce small reddish-orange berries in autumn if the summer has been hot.

It can be used among shrubs or in a mixed border. Its branches are good for cutting as winter decoration.
Cultivation. Alexandrian laurel should be planted in autumn or spring, in a moist, humus-rich soil, in shade. Once planted, it will not need much care apart from watering during dry spells in summer. It is possible to propagate it by taking hardwood cuttings in winter, but this is a slow and unreliable process; increasing by seed or division is better.

Daphne

Thymelaeaceae

This genus consists of 50 species of evergreen and deciduous shrubs from Europe and Asia, many with fragrant flowers. The plants are poisonous.
D. mezereum (zone 3–4), mezereon, from Europe, is an attractive bushy deciduous shrub $3\frac{1}{2}$–5 ft (1–1.5 m) high and 20–42 in (0.5–1 m) in spread. Its main decorative value lies in its flowers, which appear from late winter to mid spring, in closely packed clusters of dark pink, highly scented flowers, appearing before the greyish-green oblong leaves develop. The blooms are followed by decorative red berries. There is also a white-flowered form. Like other species of daphne, notably the small trailing *D. cneorum*, with dark evergreen leaves and dark pink flowers in late spring to early summer, it is completely hardy.
Cultivation. Plant in autumn or at the beginning of spring, in ordinary cool well-drained, lime-free soil, preferably in a slightly shaded position sheltered from cold winds.

There is little else that needs to be done apart

from watering in dry weather, as it does best in dampish conditions. Normally there is no point in pruning except for thinning out slightly, or shaping it.

Propagation is by semi-hardwood cuttings with a heel taken in late summer, or from seed. The leaves and young shoots are sometimes attacked by greenfly.

Datura

Solanaceae

This genus contains some 15 species of herbaceous plants or shrubs, native to North America. It is divided into two genera by some specialists: *Datura*, which contains the herbaceous plants with large erect trumpet-shaped flowers, and *Brugmansia*, which are shrubs with large pendent trumpet-shaped fragrant flowers. All are highly poisonous.

Datura

D. metel (zone 10), an annual from tropical regions which reaches 3–5 ft (90 cm–1.5 m) in height, with dark green leaves and, in summer, large white flowers to 10 in (25 cm) long which are beautifully scented after dusk. Round prickly fruits follow on.

D. metel var. *chlorantha* (zone 10), of unknown origin, reaches 2–3½ ft (60 cm–1 m) in height and is highly decorative. It has scented greenish-yellow double flowers in mid summer to mid autumn.

D. stramonium (zone 6), the thorn-apple, is an annual which comes from North America but is widely naturalized in Europe. It has white flowers and thorny fruits with an unpleasant smell. It is used as an ingredient in some pharmaceutical products.

Treated as half-hardy annuals they can be grown in mixed borders.

Brugmansia

B. arborea (zone 10), a native of Peru and Chile, is a shrub to 10 ft (3 m) with large leaves, 12–16 in (30–40 cm) in length, and white, highly scented pendent flowers, 8–10 in (20–25 cm) long, produced throughout summer.

B. × *candida* (zone 10), Angel's trumpet, reaches over 15 ft (4.5 m) in height. It has pink or creamy-white pendent flowers, 1 ft (30 cm) long. The cultivar 'Plena' ('Knightii') has semi-double flowers.

Brugmansia × candida

B. sanguinea (zone 10), a native of Peru, Chile and Colombia, has orange-red flowers with a yellow tube throughout summer.

B. suaveolens (zone 10), native to Brazil, is a shrub to 12 ft (3.7 m) with large leaves and fragrant large white flowers 8 in (20 cm) long in summer.

These shrubby species can be grown in a cool greenhouse and may be taken outside in containers for the summer.

Cultivation. Daturas are easy to grow in a warm sheltered place or conservatory in colder regions. They enjoy light sandy soils and need plenty of growing space. Propagate by seeds sown in a hotbed.

Brugmansias can be increased from 6 in (15 cm) long cuttings, placed in sandy soil with bottom heat. Young shoots with a heel will also root easily.

They are subject to attack by scale insects.

Daucus

Umbelliferae

A genus of about 20 herbaceous plants from Europe, Asia, Australia and Africa of which the best known is *D. carota* (zone 5), carrot, a biennial grown as an annual for its swollen edible roots which can be up to 10 in (25 cm) long.

Cultivation. Carrots like a sunny position and deep, light, sandy soil, which has been well manured for the previous crop. Sow from early spring, once a month for succession. Two weeks before sowing, rake in 4 oz/sq yd (113 g/m^2) of a general fertilizer. Sow in drills, ½ in (13 mm) deep, 10 in (25 cm) apart. Then spread a general

Davidia involucrata

compost on the furrows and water in well. Thin out to between 4 in (10 cm) and 8 in (20 cm) apart, depending on the final size of the carrots. When hoeing between the rows slightly earth up the plants so as to avoid the tops of the roots becoming green.

Carrots can be eaten when ready or stored in a clamp for early winter use. When harvesting, water the night before to make them easier to pull up.

The main pest is carrot fly and everything should be done to avoid an attack, from thinning out and picking in the evening when the flies are not about, to filling the holes by watering, and the use of chemical control. Also, it is a good idea to grow this crop with chives, onions or leeks, whose scent will reduce the risk of carrot fly infestation. Avoid irregular watering during dry conditions.

Davallia

Davalliaceae (Polypodiaceae)

This genus consists of about 40 species of ferns from tropical and warm temperate regions.

D. fejeensis (zone 10), rabbit's-foot fern from Fiji has finely dissected triangular-shaped fronds 1–2½ ft (30–76 cm) long. Scaly rhizomes are ½ in (13 mm) thick. The cultivar 'Plumosa' is even more feathery. They make good basket plants.

D. mariesii (zone 10), squirrel's-foot fern, from east Asia is a small, elegant fern, but not very common. It is only hardy in warm climates, but can be grown in a cool greenhouse, where it may keep its leaves in winter. It reaches 6–12 in (15–30 cm) in height with large, pale green, finely divided fronds which are triangular in shape.

Its creeping, scaly rhizomes are a decorative reddish-brown. It likes partial shade and in the greenhouse can be used in a hanging basket.

Cultivation. Plant this fern in spring, burying the roots but leaving the rhizomes to grow on the surface of the soil. It needs a slightly shaded, humus-rich, damp but not waterlogged soil. Propagation is by spores or by division of the rhizomes in spring. In colder areas, grow in the greenhouse in pots containing a well-drained mixture of leaf mould and silver sand.

Davidia

Dove tree, handkerchief tree, *Nyssaceae*

This genus contains only one species of deciduous tree from China.

D. involucrata (zone 6–7), has always been a source of great curiosity. It was Abbé David, in 1869, who was the first European to note, in the mountains of western China, an extraordinary tree with huge white flowers hanging on the branches like handkerchiefs. These flowers, produced abundantly in late spring, are actually bracts and the true flowers are very small. The species shares this unusual feature with the dogwood, to which it is related. It resembles a lime or linden tree in its leaves and outline.

Cultivation. It is completely hardy and will grow in any soil that is moist and does not dry out in summer. Propagation by seeds may be a bit tricky but cuttings of side shoots taken when the wood is hard but not yet ripe are easy.

Decaisnea

Lardizabalaceae

This genus consists of two species of small shrubs with magnificent deciduous leaves. The clusters of flowers are not especially attractive,

but they are followed by beautiful blue or yellow fruits which are edible, though not particularly distinctive in flavour. These plants are native to China and the Himalayas.
D. fargesii (zone 8) is $6\frac{1}{2}$–10 ft (2–3 m) or more in height. It has very large leaves up to 3 ft (90 cm) long composed of up to 25 brilliant green leaflets, and clusters of greenish-yellow flowers in late spring and early summer. These are followed by blue cylindrical fruits reaching 4 in (10 cm) in length.
D. insignis (zone 8) has the same features, but its fruit is yellow.
Cultivation. These plants thrive best in a moist loam and like a warm climate with a south-facing aspect, out of the wind and sheltered from the late frosts. Propagation is by seeds, or cuttings, struck in a frame.

Delosperma
Aizoaceae

A genus of about 140 species of succulent plants from South Africa and Madagascar.
D. cooperii (zone 9), from South Africa, one of the few succulents that are almost hardy in a northern climate, grows to a height of 4 in (10 cm) with a spread of 4 ft (1.2 m), making it a very good ground-cover plant. The fleshy leaves are almost cylindrical. The long stems take root as they grow, and the star-shaped flowers, appearing in summer, are purple to ruby red with white centres.

This plant can be grown with other succulents such as sedums and sempervivums, but as it spreads very quickly, do not plant it near slow-growing plants.
Cultivation. Plant in very well-drained soil in a sunny position. In areas with damp winters, protect from the rain with a pane of glass. In these conditions, the plant will survive a temperature of 17–14°F (−8– −10°C).

Propagate by taking cuttings in mid to late spring; these will take root very quickly under a frame in a sunny position.

Delphinium
Ranunculaceae

There are around 250 species of herbaceous perennials from Europe, Asia and America in this genus.
D. elatum (zone 6), a species found wild in Europe and Asia, reaches 6 ft (1.8 m) in height. The elegant green leaves are palmate and deeply divided and the blue flowers borne on spikes from early to mid summer. It is the main parent of most of the garden hybrids which have long, thick spikes of spurred flowers in shades of blue, violet, white or pink, with a darker or lighter central eye. Reds are now being developed.
Cultivars. The hybrids can be divided into dwarf cultivars, 32–48 in (0.8–1.2 m) high, such as 'Blue Dawn', blue tinged with pink; and giants, which reach 5–6 ft (1.5–1.8 m) in height, which include: 'Black Knight', dark blue; 'Blue Bird', light blue; 'Galahad', white. There are other groups of delphinium with branched but less tightly packed inflorescences, such as the 'Belladonna' delphiniums with shorter spikes formed throughout the summer.

Delphiniums look at their best with other flowers in a herbaceous or mixed border, planted in groups at the back. They make excellent cut flowers for dramatic arrangements.
Cultivation. Delphiniums need deep, fertile soil with plenty of humus, and a sunny, sheltered position. Plant them either in autumn or spring. They are fairly delicate plants, and need a certain amount of care and attention if they are to flower well: manuring in spring, watering in dry weather, staking if they are large, removing dead spikes and stems at the end of autumn. Delphiniums are fairly susceptible to powdery mildew, black root rot and viruses. Plants that are severely affected should be lifted and destroyed. It is best if they are renewed every three to four years by division or taking cuttings in spring.

Dentaria
Toothwort, *Cruciferae*

This genus numbers some 20 species of herbaceous perennial plants from northern temperate regions that are closely related to the genus *Cardamine*. Often with creeping rhizomes, they have flowers in terminal clusters at the beginning of the year and are ideal for the wild garden or under shrubs.
D. bulbifera (*Cardamine bulbifera*) (zone 5), coralwort, from Europe and Caucasia is found in beech forests and measures 12–28 in (30–70 cm) in height with a spread of 12 in (30 cm). The upper leaves are simple with bulbils in their axils

and the lower ones pinnate. Its pale lilac flowers grow in short, thick clusters in mid to late spring.

D. enneaphyllos (*Cardamine enneaphyllos*) (zone 4), from S. Europe, grows to 8–12 in (20–30 cm) with a spread of 12–16 in (30–40 cm). The leaves have three leaflets or more in whorls of two to four. The pale yellow flowers are drooping and bloom in early to mid spring. Its time of blooming makes it a good partner for *Daphne mezereum* and *Hepatica nobilis*.

Cultivation. Plant in damp, humus-rich soil in a shaded woody position.

Propagation is from seed or division, in spring or autumn.

Desfontainia

Loganiaceae (*Potaliaceae*)

A genus of one or more species of evergreen shrub from South America.

D. spinosa (zone 8–9), not a common shrub, is compact in habit and reaches 10 ft (3 m) in height and spread. Its small, shiny evergreen dark green leaves resemble those of holly. This decorative foliage becomes even more attractive in early summer with the arrival of fine, tubular, pendent scarlet flowers edged with yellow. It is only hardy in areas with fairly mild winters.

It can be planted on its own, in a mixed border, or shrub border, preferably where climate is not too dry.

Cultivation. Desfontainia likes moist, humus-rich soil, and a semi-shaded position, sheltered by a wall in colder climates. Plant between autumn and spring, when the weather is mild. In spring, it likes a peaty mulch, after which its only other need is watering in dry weather. There is nothing to be gained by pruning it.

Desfontainia spinosa

Propagate by seed or by taking 3 in (7.5 cm) long semi-hardwood with a heel in late summer or tip cuttings.

Deutzia

Hydrangeaceae (*Saxifragaceae*)

This genus contains about 40 species of deciduous shrubs, mostly from Asia. Many of those cultivated in gardens are hybrids between species. They are hardy, sturdy, tolerate air pollution and produce large numbers of flowers in late spring or early summer. They form spreading bushes, often wider than they are high.

The cultivar 'Elegantissima' (zone 6–7) has slightly perfumed pale pink flowers; 'Mont Rose' (zone 6–7) is a vigorous shrub with purplish-pink floral buds which open out into paler pink flowers. The species *D. gracilis* (zone 6–7) has shoots covered in profuse, pure white flowers.

These pretty shrubs are well suited to small gardens and can be grown either on their own as specimens, in mixed borders or shrub borders.

Cultivation. Plant in ordinary soil between autumn and spring, in a sunny or slightly shaded position.

They will need virtually no more attention apart from watering in dry weather, but they appreciate a mulch of manure or compost in spring. Prune them after they have flowered, removing old, overcrowded growth.

Propagation is by semi-hardwood cuttings taken in late summer.

Dianthus

Carnation, pink, *Caryophyllaceae*

This genus includes about 300 species of annual, biennial or perennial plants, mostly found in Europe and Asia.

D. alpinus (zone 4), alpine pink, native to the mountains of eastern Europe, grows to a height of 4–6 in (10–15 cm) with a spread of 8–16 in (20–40 cm). It forms clumps of linear, green leaves with many pink flowers in early to mid summer. It is the source of several cultivars ranging from pale pink to bright red in colour. The plant should be grown in a light, well-drained limy soil.

D. deltoides (zone 5), maiden pink, widespread in

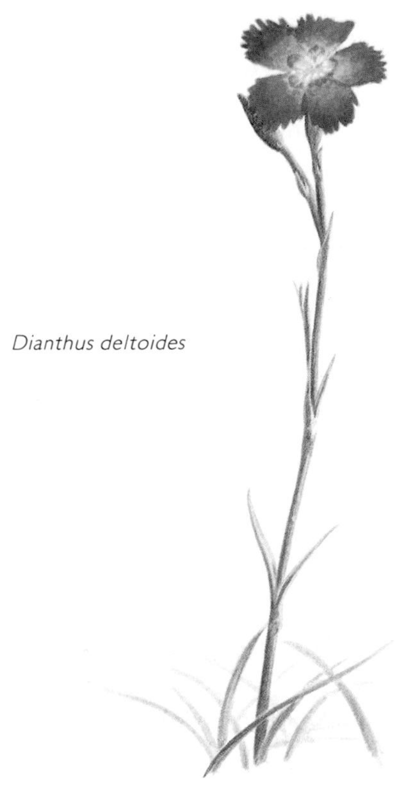
Dianthus deltoides

Europe and Asia, measures up to 9 in (23 cm) in height, with a spread of 16–20 in (40–50 cm). This species has green or blue-green foliage which, in dry soil, is sometimes tinged with bronze. It carries a succession of deep pink flowers throughout the summer.

D. neglectus (zone 4), is native to the European Alps and measures 1½–4 in (3–10 cm) in height, with a spread of 6–8 in (15–20 cm). This is a dwarf which makes a dense cushion of highly decorative stiff leaves. The large flowers are a beautiful luminous pink and appear in early to mid summer. This species is best grown in rock crevices containing rich, stony soil with plenty of humus.

D. plumarius (zone 4), the common pink, is native to Europe. It reaches 10–12 in (25–30 cm) or more in height, with a spread of 12–16 in (30–40 cm). The wild form is not so common in cultivation, but it has given rise to the numerous types of garden pink. These form low-growing carpets of glaucous leaves and the flowers, often scented, are single or double, ranging from pure white to crimson, including every shade of pink. They flower from late spring to mid summer.

D. barbatus (zone 6), sweet William, comes from southeast Europe and grows to a height of 1–2 ft (30–60 cm). Strictly a short-lived perennial it is best grown as a biennial. The single reddish flowers in flattened heads appear in early to mid summer. A wide range of colour forms are available from white to purple.

D. caryophyllus (zone 8), bears fragrant red, pink or white flowers in summer. It is 10–20 in (25–50 cm) tall and is the parent of the carnation, which is grown in large numbers commercially as a cut flower in a wide range of colours.

The smaller species are best suited to rock gardens and larger ones to the front of herbaceous borders. Although they are not as highly scented as the florists' varieties, they are strikingly colourful and form clumpy growth with numerous flowers.

Cultivation. Plant the species in a gritty well-drained soil in a sunny position.

Sweet Williams (*D. barbatus*) are treated as biennials. Sow seed in late spring in a cold frame; plant out into a nursery bed; plant into their final position in a rich well-drained loam. Cuttings of semi-ripe material can be taken in summer, or plants can be divided in early autumn.

The hardy cultivars of pinks (*D. plumarius*) should be planted out in a rich gritty well-drained soil in early autumn, the less hardy ones can be overwintered in a cold frame. After flowering take cuttings (pipings) and place in a sandy compost under glass. When rooted gradually let in air and harden off.

Carnations (*D. caryophyllus*) need plenty of light in a greenhouse, good ventilation and a temperature of at least 45°F (7°C).

Propagation by seed is possible in spring but, of course, it does not guarantee purity of cultivar. In early summer, take cuttings 3–4 in (7.5–10 cm) long from the lateral branches and plant them in a mixture of peat and sand under a cold frame.

Put the young plants in pots in late winter or early spring, in light, nourishing compost, then repot a month later into larger pots containing soil with a high leaf-mould content. Pinch out the plants to encourage lateral shoots to grow; this should be done twice more before mid summer if the plant is to flower in winter.

Diseases usually associated with these plants are spot, ring spot, leaf rot, wilt or stem rot, smut, and split calyx, and some viruses.

The more common pests which affect these plants are red spider mite, carnation fly, and the caterpillars of one or two moths such as the tortrix moth.

Diascia rigescens

Diascia
Diascia, *Scrophulariaceae*

This genus includes about 50 species of annual and perennial herbaceous plants native to South Africa. They are erect or prostrate with opposite leaves and terminal or axillary clusters of flowers, each with two spurs, that bloom throughout the summer months.
D. barbarae (zone 9), measures about 1 ft (30 cm) in height. The toothed leaves are opposite and oval. The clusters of terminal flowers have pink petals spotted with green, to ¾ in (20 mm) in diameter in summer. Grow as a half-hardy annual in cooler regions. It can be used in a sunny position in a rock garden, but not where the soil dries out – it may then survive the winter.

Dicentra spectabilis

D. rigescens (zone 9), is a robust species with stems up to 22 in (55 cm) which may be erect or decumbent. Its rose-pink flowers are closely packed and the plant is perennial in mild regions.
'Ruby Field' is a selected form.
Cultivation. Plant in any type of well-drained soil in a sunny position. These plants will not survive severe frosts but cuttings can be over-wintered in a sheltered place.
Propagate by division and seeds in spring.

Dicentra
Fumariaceae

This genus contains around 20 species of hardy herbaceous perennials, native to North America and Asia.
D. spectabilis (zone 7), bleeding heart or Dutchman's breeches, comes from China and Japan and measures 1–2 ft (30–60 cm) in height, with a spread of 16–24 in (40–60 cm). The blue-green leaves are finely divided. Its beautiful flowers, which appear in late spring to early summer, are heart shaped and form long clusters on arching stems. The outer petals are red or pink with white inner petals protruding from them. There is an all-white form that is quieter but equally appealing.

It is a good plant for mixed borders, and especially between shrubs or in woodland clearings where its young foliage will be protected from late frosts.
Cultivation. Plant either in early autumn or mid spring, 16–20 in (40–50 cm) apart. It thrives best in a deep, moist, well-drained soil, enriched with peat or leaf mould. It prefers a semi-shaded position protected from cold winds. Manuring is advisable in spring.

Propagate in spring, either from seeds or by dividing the clumps being careful not to damage its fragile fleshy roots.

Dictamnus
Rutaceae

This genus contains a single species of hardy herbaceous perennial.
D. albus (*D. fraxinella*) – zone 7 – false dittany, burning bush, native to Europe and Asia, measures 2–3 ft (60–90 cm) in height, with a spread of 16–20 in (40–50 cm). The shiny, dark

green aromatic leaves are deeply divided and the white or purplish pink flowers are formed in a loose cluster on erect flower stems 8–12 in (20–30 cm) in length. They are highly scented, with stamens longer than their sepals, and appear in early to mid summer. Occasionally on a hot summer's night, the highly flammable essential oils contained in the seed pods and other parts of the plant ignite spontaneously (or you can use a match – the plant will not be damaged). Some people may develop an allergy to this plant. It is a hardy species which may form part of a sunny herbaceous flower border with the pale blue flowers of *Iris pallida*.
Cultivation. Grow in any ordinary soil, on the dry side and leave in place. Propagate by sowing freshly harvested seeds directly into the soil in late summer or early autumn.

Dieffenbachia 'Exotica'

Dieffenbachia

Dumb cane, leopard lily, *Araceae*

A genus of about 25 species of evergreen perennials native to tropical America. They may be woody based and they have erect stems with tufts of attractive large oval to lance-shaped leaves. The insignificant flowers are clustered on a spadix surrounded by a narrow leaf-like spathe. The sap is poisonous to humans and pets; it can seriously affect the eyes, and causes swelling in the mouth and temporary loss of speech – hence one of its common names. Always wash your hands after handling these plants.
D. seguine (zone 10), is a tufted plant growing to about 3 ft (90 cm) tall, but sometimes much larger, with a similar spread. The glossy dark green leaves are broad lance-shaped to about 18 in (45 cm) long. There are many cultivars with a wide range of leaf variegation.
Cultivars. 'Amoena' (*D. amoena*) is a more robust cultivar to nearly 6 ft (1.8 m) high. It has dark green leaves with creamy white bars along the lateral veins; 'Exotica' has a white midrib and extensive creamy white blotches on its green leaves; 'Rudolph Roehrs' ('Roehrsii') has leaves which are yellowish-white but have a green midrib and are edged with green.
Cultivation. These plants are frost tender, needing temperatures of at least 60°F (16°C) and partial shade in summer, but brighter light in winter. They are usually grown in glasshouses or for decoration in the house but must be kept well away from children. Water well in summer allowing the top of the compost (soil) to dry out between watering. Keep in a moist atmosphere. Propagate by cuttings or pieces of leafless stem placed horizontally in the compost (soil). Scale insect or red spider mite are common pests.

Dierama

Iridaceae

About 20 herbaceous plants from South and East Africa with corms and evergreen grass-like leaves make up this genus. Its graciously arching stems bear pendent bell-shaped flowers.
D. pendulum (zone 8), from South and tropical East Africa, grows to 3½ ft (1 m) in height. Linear, erect leaves and pink flowers appear in early to mid summer.
D. pumilum (zone 8), is similar but smaller, about 2 ft (60 cm) tall.
D. pulcherrimum (zone 8), wand flower or angel's fishing rod, from South Africa is 5–6 ft (1.5–1.8 m) tall. This species is also similar but taller and it flowers in late summer.

These species are best suited to a rock garden, beside water in which they will be reflected, or in a herbaceous border in association with plants having broad leaves for contrast.
Cultivation. Plant the corms in spring at a depth of 6 in (15 cm) in humus-rich, well-

Dierama pendula

drained soil, in a sunny or partly shaded position 12–20 in (30–50 cm) apart.

Cover with a mulch of dead leaves in areas with very cold winters.

Propagate from offsets of the corm at planting time in spring.

Diervilla

Bush honeysuckle, *Caprifoliaceae*

This genus comprises two or three deciduous shrubs native to North America.

D. sessilifolia (zone 5), of southeastern USA, reaches 5 ft (1.5 m) high and has oval leaves some 6 in (15 cm) in length. Tubular flowers of sulphur-yellow appear in clusters at the tops of the shoots from early to mid summer.

Cultivation. Plant in a deep, rich, moist loam in a sheltered sunny or partly shaded position in autumn or spring. It will need watering in dry weather and likes a spring mulch of manure or compost. It is not essential to keep it pruned, but as it flowers on the current year's wood it can be pruned in the spring before new growth appears and this will encourage it to produce a mass of flowering shoots.

Propagate in mid to late summer by taking semi-hardwood cuttings with a heel from non-flowering shoots.

Digitalis

Foxglove, *Scrophulariaceae*

A genus comprising about 20 species of biennial and perennial herbaceous plants native to Europe, central Asia and northwest Africa.

D. purpurea (zone 5) is generally a biennial $3\frac{1}{2}$–5 ft (1–1.5 m) high with a spread of 16–20 in (40–50 cm). It is highly poisonous. Most of its leaves form a basal rosette above which is held the one-sided flower spike. The flowers, which bloom in summer are tubular, usually purplish-pink in colour spotted with darker purple. Some plants may have white or pale pink flowers. In the cultivar 'Excelsior' the flowers are carried in horizontal fashion and all around the stem.

Foxgloves should be grown in bold groups in herbaceous or mixed borders, and woodland clearings in a wild garden.

Cultivation. Plant 20 in (50 cm) apart in mid autumn or late spring in a moist, well-drained soil enriched with leaf mould. Choose a sunny or partly shaded position. Remove any dead flowers to encourage the growth of lateral shoots and in autumn cut the stems right back in case any of the plants prove to be perennial.

Propagation is by seed under a cold frame in spring, or outdoors in early summer.

Diospyros

Ebenaceae

This is primarily a tropical genus of nearly 500 species including some which provide ebony for cabinet makers.

D. kaki (zone 9), kaki or Chinese persimmon, a native of China, is the main species seen in gardens. It is hardy in warmer areas. A medium sized tree, reaching 20 ft (6 m) high, it is covered with bright yellow-orange fruits the size of a tomato, with a persistent calyx formed only on female trees. They ripen at the beginning of winter when the tree has already lost its leaves, so the effect is spectacular. Kakis are edible and cultivars have been bred with fruits of a particularly good flavour; they are sold as persimmons.

D. virginiana (zone 7), native to North America, is another species which is hardy in temperate climates, though less commonly grown in Europe than the previous species. The flowers are yellowish-white and the fruits, although

edible, are not always produced in cultivation. The tree, sometimes imposing, at 50 ft (15 m) or more, is grown for its autumn leaf colours and for the decorative qualities of grey bark with deep rectangular cracks.
Cultivation. Both species described here will grow in almost any soil provided it is properly drained. Growth is slow, but fertilizer and a sun-facing wall will help. The trees in the case of *D. kaki* are propagated by seed except for the cultivars of *D. kaki* which should be grafted on seedlings.

Dipelta
Caprifoliaceae

This genus contains four species of deciduous shrubs from China.
D. floribunda (zone 5–6), is a large bushy shrub reaching up to 15 ft (4.5 m) in height and 6½–10 ft (2–3 m) across. Its leaves are dark green, but its chief decorative value lies in its peeling bark and its clusters of pale pink flowers with spots of yellow on the throat that bloom in late spring to early summer.
D. yunnanensis (zone 5–6), is slightly smaller, with glossy leaves and creamy white flowers tinged with pink.

Both are hardy everywhere except in the coldest climates and look handsome whether grown in isolation or as a background plant on a bank.
Cultivation. The dipeltas are easy to grow: plant in autumn or spring, in a good loam in a sunny or partly shaded position, and protected from cold winds. The only pruning needed is to thin out after flowering, if necessary. The easiest method of propagation is to take semi-hardwood cuttings in mid to late summer.

Disanthus
Hamamelidaceae

A genus of a single species from Japan.
D. cercidifolius (zone 6) is a fairly uncommon shrub that grows to a height of 10 ft (3 m). In habit it resembles the witch hazel, to which it is related, but its mid-green, rounded leaves are similar to those of the Judas or redbud tree. It is at its most attractive in autumn, with its small, dark purple flowers and brilliant crimson-purple, orange and scarlet leaves. It is quite hardy and can be grown as a specimen or as a background for a border.
Cultivation. This shrub should be planted in autumn or spring, preferably in a partly shaded position, in a lime-free soil, enriched with peat, that is well drained but always moist. The only care it needs is watering in dry weather. It can be readily propagated from cuttings.

Distylium
Hamamelidaceae

This genus contains about six evergreen trees and shrubs from China and Japan.
D. racemosum (zone 7), Isu tree, southern Japan, grows to between 3½–5 ft (1–1.5 m) in height. The small, star-shaped red flowers appear in early to mid spring. The cultivar 'Variegatum' has narrow leaves edged and blotched with yellow.
Cultivation. Distylium enjoys a sandy soil in a partly shaded position. It does best in a Mediterranean-type climate. Propagate by taking cuttings in spring.

Dodecatheon meadia

Dodecatheon

Shooting star, *Primulaceae*

This genus contains about 15 very similar herbaceous species, most native to North America. The flowers with reflexed petals are like small cyclamen. They like cool, shaded sites and, being perennials with a short growth cycle, they emerge from the ground in early spring and disappear in late summer.

D. meadia (zone 6) grows to about 2 ft (60 cm) tall. It has broad oblong leaves of a soft attractive green and, during late spring and early summer, umbels of 10 to 20 purplish-red flowers with yellow anthers.

D. pulchellum (zone 6) grows to a height of 8–12 in (20–30 cm). A smaller species than the previous one but much like it.

Cultivation. Grow in a cool, damp peaty soil, in the shade. Every two or three years, place a layer of sphagnum peat on the surface of their growing site. Propagate by dividing the root clump when the plant is dormant, in late summer, and replant immediately, or alternatively grow from seed.

Doronicum

Leopard's bane, *Compositae*

A genus containing 35 hardy herbaceous perennials native to Europe and Asia.

D. austriacum (zone 6) grows to about 18 in (45 cm) in height, with a spread of 12–20 in (30–50 cm). The leaves are dense and heart-shaped with a toothed margin and mid-green in colour. The flowers, which appear in late spring, are daisy-like, bright yellow and up to 2 in (5 cm) in diameter.

This plant is suitable for herbaceous or mixed borders, or in the partial shade of trees or shrubs, where its yellow can replace that lost by the demise of the daffodils.

Cultivation. Plant in autumn or spring, 12–16 in (30–40 cm) apart, in a sunny or part-shaded position and a deep, moist soil containing plenty of humus. The plant will need staking if it is in a windy position. Dead flowers should be removed to encourage further flowering. Cut the stems right back in autumn. The leopard's bane may suffer from mildew, a disease whose symptoms appear as whitish spots on the leaves of plants.

Propagation is by division of the root clumps in autumn or spring, preferably once every three or four years.

Doxantha

Bignoniaceae

This genus consists of a single species, *D. capreolata* (zone 10) should correctly be named *Bignonia capreolata*. It is a creeper growing up to 33–40 ft (10–12 m) in length, from the southern USA. It has leaves made up of two leaflets and a terminal tendril, and clusters of two to five curved, tubular orange-red flowers which appear in late spring to early summer. The cultivar 'Atrosanguinea', has longer, narrower leaves and purple or violet flowers.

Cultivation. The doxantha is only hardy in completely frost-free areas; elsewhere, it should be grown in a greenhouse where it likes a rich porous soil and needs frequent watering. Use it to cover large trees or the trellises and walls of a conservatory. Propagate by seed or cuttings taken in spring inserted in sand under glass with bottom heat.

Draba

Cruciferae

There are about 300 species in this genus, but only a few are cultivated in gardens. Most are dwarf tufted plants native to mountainous areas in the Northern Hemisphere, and many are difficult to grow without an alpine house.

D. aizoides (zone 4), whitlow grass, is an evergreen perennial 4 in (10 cm) high and native to Europe. It forms small, densely packed cushions producing small yellow flowers in spring.

D. sibirica (zone 3), is a perennial from Siberia and Greenland. It has prostrate rooting stems with evergreen leaves and heads of 10 to 20 yellow flowers in spring.

D. aizoides is ideal for planting in rock crevices, while *D. sibirica*, makes good groundcover for small rock gardens interplanted with dwarf bulbs.

Cultivation. These two species are fairly easy to grow, and tolerate a limy soil. Plant in a sunny position, in poor, sandy or gravelly, but well-drained soil. For *D. sibirica*, remove dead flowers. Do not feed as, in winter, the snow will bring these plants enough nutrient. Propagate by dividing the root clumps after flowering. Alternatively raise new plants from seed.

Dracaena

Agavaceae

This genus includes about 40 species of trees and shrubs from tropical and subtropical areas of Africa and Asia. Several are cultivated in the house or greenhouse for their attractive foliage, but could not be grown outdoors except in very warm climates. Many may become very large, even in pots, so are useful as imposing specimen plants. Many have a palm-like habit; their flowers are rather insignificant.

D. deremensis (zone 10+) is found in tropical East Africa. It is rather slow growing but may reach 10 ft (3 m), even in a pot, with cane-like stems covered with long, narrow glossy green leaves. Several cultivars are available, such as 'Warneckii' which has leaves with longitudinal stripes of creamy white.

D. draco (zone 10), dragon tree, from the Canary Islands, is the hardiest species which may survive outside in Mediterranean-type climates. The thick trunk bears rosettes of thick blue-green, sword-shaped leaves and when injured exudes a reddish resin, or, dragon's blood.

D. marginata (zone 10+), Madagascar dragon tree, is native to Reunion Island. It is an erect, sometimes branched plant reaching 6 ft (1.8 m) and the very long, narrow green leaves with a narrow red margin clasp the stem. 'Tricolor' has leaves striped with cream and edged red.

D. sanderana (zone 10+), ribbon plant, from Central Africa, may reach 6 ft (1.8 m) in height and bears long, narrow, pale grey-green leaves margined with cream.

D. surculosa (*D. godseffiana*) (zone 10+), gold dust dracaena, comes from Central Africa. It is a bushy plant with rather broad leaves which are dark green and covered with yellow to white spots and small blotches.

Cultivation. These plants enjoy warm moist conditions with a temperature not less than 55°F (13°C) in a semi-shaded position. Keep the compost (soil) moist at all times, watering less in the winter. Repot into larger pots every two or three years. Propagate by removing the crown, making a clean cut and inserting it into cutting compost (potting soil) with bottom heat. Alternatively, air layer, or lay 3 in (7.5 cm)-long pieces of stem on top of the compost (potting soil). Avoid dry air and cold draughts, both of which will cause browning of the leaf tips and their margins.

Dracaena marginata 'Tricolor'

Dracocephalum

Dragon's heads, *Labiatae*

Forty-five species of annual and perennial herbaceous plants from central Europe and Asia go to make up this genus, together with one species from North America.

D. ruyschiana (zone 6), is a perennial, native to Europe, and measures 16–24 in (40–60 cm) in height, with a spread of 16 in (40 cm). The plant has erect stems with short hairs, bearing lanceolate leaves with recurved edges. Whorls of two to six tubular flowers are violet, sometimes pink or white, and form a dense terminal spike from mid to late summer. This is for a rock garden or the front of a herbaceous border.

Cultivation. Plant in spring in a dry, sandy soil in a spot which catches the sun at midday but is in semi-shade the rest of the time. Propagation is by division in spring or by cuttings.

Dracunculus

Araceae

A genus of three species from the Mediterranean region and the Canary Islands similar to Arum.

D. vulgaris (zone 6), dragon arum or dragon plant, comes from the Mediterranean region from Corsica to Turkey, but has become naturalized in some cooler areas. Its tuber is large, rounded or flat, and produces large, deeply divided leaves on a purple-mottled leaf stalk 20–42 in (50 cm–1 m) in height. A tall, narrow, dark reddish-purple spathe with a blackish-red spadix develops at the end of spring or early summer.

This is a striking plant but should be grown some distance from the house as it gives off a strongly unpleasant smell of rotting flesh which attracts flies.

Cultivation. Plant in a sunny but sheltered place in a rich, sandy soil. Plant the tubers 6 in (15 cm) deep. In summer allow the plant a period of rest by not watering it.

Propagate by dividing the tuber.

Drimys

Winteraceae (Magnoliaceae)

This genus contains nine species of striking trees or shrubs native to South America, Australia, New Zealand and Borneo. They are distinguished by their shiny evergreen foliage and clusters of small flowers which are often delicately perfumed.

D. lanceolata (D. aromatica) (zone 8), mountain pepper, from Tasmania and New South Wales, has oblong leathery leaves and cream-coloured flowers in corymbs, in late spring.

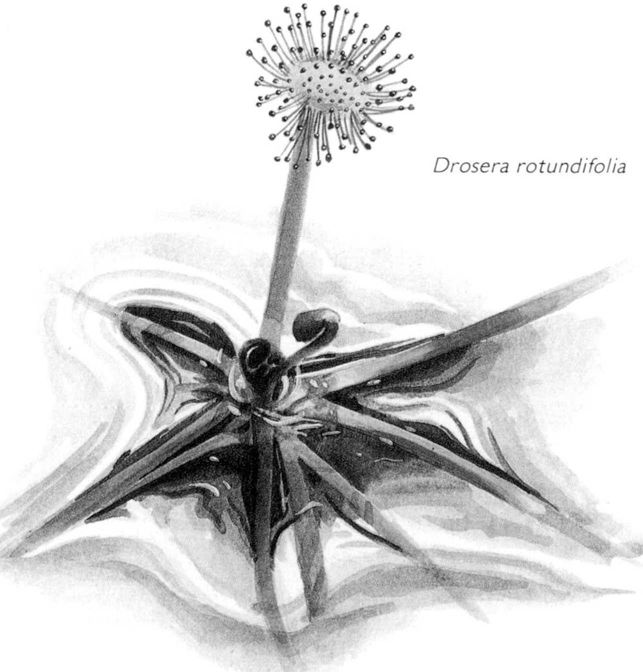

Drosera rotundifolia

D. winteri (zone 8), winter's bark, from South America has cream flowers which give off a delicate perfume in spring and aromatic grey bark.

Cultivation. Both like a warm sandy soil in a semi-shaded, sheltered position in a mild climate and will be cut back in regions where the winters are hard.

Propagation by cuttings of half-ripe shoots.

Drosera

Sundew, Droseraceae

This genus consists of nearly 100 species of insect-eating plants which form small rosettes. Species exist in every continent and many are found in acidic peat bogs. The leaves are covered in red glandular hairs, which secrete a sticky glistening fluid. Insects attracted by this get stuck and die of exhaustion, when they are digested by enzymes secreted by the leaf. Only the carapace of the insect, which is made of chitin, cannot be absorbed by the plant. The carnivorous habit enables these plants to thrive in the poor conditions in which they live.

D. rotundifolia (zone 5), round-leaved sundew, is the commonest species, found throughout temperate regions and also one of the few which are easy to grow.

Cultivation. It is a delicate plant to grow as it needs an artificially created peat bog. Grow in a mixture of peat and sphagnum moss with good drainage in a pot standing in a saucer of water, preferably in a greenhouse. Do not use limy water. A pot of pure peat sometimes gives satisfactory results. It enjoys full light.

Propagate from seed.

Dryas

Rosaceae

This genus is composed of two species from arctic and alpine regions of the Northern Hemisphere.

D. octopetala (zone 3), mountain avens, is a creeping mat-forming shrub from Europe and North America measuring only 4 in (10 cm) in height but with a wide spread of 20–42 in (50 cm–1 m). This hardy sub-shrub has small, evergreen leaves, indented like those of an oak, dull green above, white beneath and bears white flowers with eight petals in late spring to early

summer. The cultivar 'Minor' (zone 3–4) is similar, but more compact.
D. drummondii (zone 4), native to North America is similar, but its flowers are creamier and somewhat nodding; they are borne mid to late summer.

They are suitable for covering the ground in rock gardens and on screes.
Cultivation. Dryas like a gravelly, limy soil in a sunny position. Add a small amount of leaf mould every two to three years. Propagate by seed, in early spring, or heel cuttings placed in sand in early autumn.

Dryopteris

Shield fern, buckler fern, *Aspleniaceae*

A genus represented by 150 ferns from all parts of the world.
D. filix-mas (zone 4–5), the male fern, is a large forest-dwelling fern, from Europe and North America, which may reach between 2–4 ft (60 cm–1.2 m) in height and spread. This is a completely hardy perennial with deciduous leaves. Its young yellowish-green, finely divided fronds turn a much darker green during the summer.

This beautiful fern sometimes turns up in gardens, uninvited, because of its wind-blown spores. There are several cultivars with crisped, crested or forked fronds that make a delightful change from the species itself.

It is best suited to a separate bed, as ground-cover, or in a shady mixed border. Its foliage is useful for summer and autumn flower arrangements.
Other species. *D. cristata* (zone 4–5), from northern Europe, Siberia and North America, has yellowish-green fronds and narrow, delicately cut leaflets; *D. affinis* (*D. pseudomas*) (zone 5), from Europe to Himalayas, has golden-green evergreen foliage and stems covered with brown scales. *D. dilatata* (zone 4–5), broad buckler fern, is variable in size but can be as much as 5 ft (1.5 m) tall, and its fronds are broader than the other species.
Cultivation. These ferns are easy to grow. Plant in spring, in neutral or peaty (acid) soil, not necessarily very damp, and in a shaded or partly shaded position. It is best to cut the stems right back in autumn.

They are easy to propagate by sowing spores or by dividing the root clump in spring.

Dryopteris dilatata

Drypis

Caryophyllaceae

A genus with but a single species, native to an area extending from Italy to Greece.
D. spinosa (zone 9–8), measures 4–6 in (10–15 cm) in height with a spread of 8–12 in (20–30 cm). It is a sub-shrub with tiny awl-shaped evergreen leaves, and stiff much branched, square stems. It forms a rounded prickly bush with small pale pink or white flowers in early to mid summer. For rock gardens only.
Cultivation. Plant in spring in a sandy, gravelly soil in a sunny position. This plant resists the cold well, provided the soil is dry in winter, so it should be quite satisfactory for it to be protected by a pane of glass, where the winters are wet, or grown in an alpine house. Propagation is by seed sown in a sandy compost in spring or by cuttings.

Eccremocarpus

Glory flower, *Bignoniaceae*

This genus includes five species of hardy and tender climbing plants with divided leaves and abundant clusters of tubular flowers native to South America.

E. scaber (zone 8), from Chile, reaches 13–17 ft (4–5 m) in height. It may die down to soil level in a cold winter but new shoots should reappear in spring. The leaves are compound, pinnate and with tendrils. The orange-red tubular flowers are ¾–1¼ in (2–3 cm) long and appear in clusters from early summer to mid autumn.

Cultivation. Grow in a rich, light soil. Sow in late winter in gentle heat, pot on in early to mid spring before planting out in a sheltered position in late spring, with 32 in (80 cm) between each plant. Tie against a wall facing the sun; young plants will need staking. The following winter protect the roots with straw and peat, and in mid spring, cut out completely any branches killed by frost.

As it flowers in its first year it can be treated as an annual in regions with very cold winters.

Eccremocarpus scaber

Echinacea

Cone flower, *Compositae*

This genus contains nine species of hardy herbaceous perennials from North America similar to *Rudbeckia*, but differing in the colour of their flowers.

E. purpurea (zone 5), purple cone flower, native to eastern North America, grows to a height of 32–48 in (80 cm–1.2 m) and a spread of 16–20 in (40–50 cm). The leaves are lanceolate, rough and slightly toothed. The flowers, 3–4 in (7–10 cm) in diameter with purple rays and an orange centre, appear individually at the ends of branching stems. There are several cultivars with colours ranging from cream to carmine red. They flower from mid summer to early autumn. All are good subjects for herbaceous and mixed borders.

Cultivation. Plant in a deep rich, well-drained soil, in a sunny position. Propagate by dividing the root clumps in autumn or spring.

Echinops

Globe thistle, *Compositae*

A genus containing over 100 hardy herbaceous plants native to Europe, Asia and Africa.

E. ritro (zone 5), from Europe and Asia, is 3½–4 ft (1–1.2 m) in height with a spread of 16–24 in (40–60 cm). The leaves are very decorative: bluish-green on their upper surface, and silvery on the lower, highly indented like those of thistles, but not as prickly. The metallic-blue globular inflorescences, appearing in mid to late summer, are very popular for flower arrangements, either fresh or dried. The globe thistle is best suited to herbaceous and mixed borders.

Cultivation. Plant in deep, well-drained soil, even dry, in a sunny position, in autumn or spring, 20–24 in (50–60 cm) apart. Cut the stems down to soil level in autumn. Propagate by dividing the root clumps at the planting times.

Echinops ritro

Echium

Boraginaceae

A genus of 40 species of tender and hardy herbaceous plants from Europe, Asia and Africa.

E. russicum (*E. rubrum*) (zone 6), from east and southeast Europe, grows to a height of 3½ ft (1 m). It is a hardy biennial with narrow, pointed leaves and tubular red to violet flowers with yellow projecting stamens, flowering from late spring to mid summer.

E. vulgare (zone 6), viper's bugloss or blueweed, is also from Europe, and measures 20–28 in (50–70 cm) in height and 12–16 in (30–40 cm) across. It is biennial, but grown as an annual in cold climates, with a compact, bushy appearance. The plant bears dark green, pointed leaves with purple flowers turning to violet, growing in dense spikes throughout the summer.

These plants make excellent decoration for herbaceous borders in climates which do not have excessively cold winters.

Cultivation. Both species like dry, light soil and a sunny position. They will accept a moist soil but will produce fewer flowers. Propagate in early autumn by sowing outdoors in areas with mild winters, or in early spring elsewhere. Thin out the young seedlings so that the plants will have a reasonable distance between them when they are fully grown.

Edraianthus

Grassy-bells, *Campanulaceae*

A genus of about 24 species of herbaceous perennials, native to southern Europe and western Asia. The genus is closely related to *Campanula*, with linear leaves and erect bell-shaped flowers.

E. graminifolius (zone 6), a native of Albania, Italy and Greece, measures 4–6 in (10–15 cm) in height with a spread of 8–12 in (20–30 cm). Its leaves are grass-like. The creeping stems bear five to eight bell-shaped violet-blue flowers in a cluster during early to mid summer.

E. pumilio (zone 7), from Yugoslavia, is 1½–2 in (4–5 cm) high and 8 in (20 cm) across. This greyish-green plant forms a cushion of needle-shaped leaves about ½ in (13 mm) long. The solitary bluish-violet bell-shaped flowers are 1¼ in (3 cm) long, and appear in large quantities in early to mid summer.

Both species grow well in a rock garden or a dry stone wall.

Cultivation. Plant in limestone scree mixed with leaf mould, in a dry, sunny position.

Propagation is by seed in late winter, under a cold frame.

Ehretia

Boraginaceae

This genus contains 50 species of tender trees and shrubs native to tropical regions. They have bright green evergreen or deciduous leaves and pyramid-shaped inflorescences of small white, scented flowers.

E. thyrsiflora (*E. acuminata*) – zone 10+ –, from tropical Asia and Australia, grows 20–30 ft (6–9 m) in height. The large oval leaves are toothed and the numerous white flowers give off a honey-like scent.

E. macrophylla (zone 10+), from western China, is a deciduous tree which grows to a height of 20 ft (6 m) or so. It resembles *Paulownia* and has large leaves 4–7 in (10–18 cm) long and large inflorescences of small white, pleasantly scented flowers followed by fleshy fruit.

Cultivation. The ehretia grows best in areas where the winters are mild. It will grow from the base if cut down by frost. Plant in ordinary soil.

Propagation by seed or cuttings.

Eichhornia

Pontederiaceae

Formerly known as *Pontederia*, this genus contains seven species of aquatic plants with blue flowers native to tropical and subtropical America.

E. crassipes (zone 10), water hyacinth, widespread in stagnant water in warm areas throughout the world, is undoubtedly the best known. The plant forms a rosette of floating leaves with swollen leaf stalks. A cluster of lilac-blue flowers with a bright yellow centre grows from the centre of the rosette. The flowers measure about 1½–2 in (5–7 cm) across. The water hyacinth is killed by frost, but grows very fast. In northern climates, it should be placed on the water as soon as there is no risk of further cold weather. It will then flower in late summer and die in autumn. It makes a fine partner for the delicate pink blooms of the flowering rush, *Butomus umbellatus*.

Cultivation. These plants are increased by dividing the clumps in spring. Where there are hard frosts the plants can be overwintered in pots or moist soil (not in water), placed in the dark and kept frost free.

Eichhornia crassipes

Elaeagnus

Oleaster, *Elaeagnaceae*

A genus of some 40 species of hardy and tender shrubs with evergreen or deciduous leaves. They are highly decorative and come from Asia, North America, and southern Europe.

E. angustifolia (zone 6) from Europe and West Asia, grows up to 15 ft (4.5 m). Deciduous tree with wide spread, spiny branches and grey-green slender leaves. Silvery flowers borne early summer.

E. pungens (zone 6), from China and Japan, is 5–13 ft (1.5–4 m) high, but not as wide, and the hybrid *E.* × *ebbingei* is 5–10 ft (1.5–3 m) high and with a similar spread. The former has leathery, shiny green leaves, and the latter's are silvery grey below. Their inconspicuous flowers are sometimes followed by red berries.

Cultivars. *E. pungens* 'Maculata' (zone 6), has green leaves with a golden yellow, central blotch. *E.* × *ebbingei* 'Gilt Edge' has its leaves edged with golden yellow.

These shrubs make good hedges, particularly near the sea, and are interesting features in mixed or shrub borders. They are also useful for providing foliage for floral arrangements.

Cultivation. Plant in early autumn or spring, in an ordinary well-drained soil, and in a sunny or partly shaded position. When used as a hedge the planting distance should be 15–20 in (38–50 cm). Water in dry weather until they become established. Trim in summer.

Propagation is by semi-hardwood cuttings taken in late summer or early autumn.

Elodea

Hydrocharitaceae

This genus includes about 12 species of submerged aquatic plants from the Americas.

E. canadenis (zone 5), Canadian pondweed, is a submerged, filiform plant native to North America (as its name indicates). Unknown in Europe until the middle of the 19th century, the plant rapidly took over this new territory and now inhabits many streams and rivers. It bears male and female flowers on separate plants. Only one female plant was imported into Europe, so circumstances forced it to multiply vegetatively. In an ornamental pond, it oxygenates the water and limits the growth of algae.

Cultivation. Elodea can rapidly take over large stretches of rivers; in a garden pool do not allow it to cover more than half the surface.

Elsholtzia
Labiatae

A genus of about 35 tender and hardy shrubs with lanceolate, aromatic leaves from Europe and Asia.
E. polystachya (*E. fruticosa*) – zone 5 – from the Himalayas, is the most vigorous species. Sometimes reaching 6½ ft (2 m) in height, it bears numerous spikes of small white flowers in early to mid autumn.
E. stauntonii (zone 7), from China, reaches a maximum height of 5 ft (1.5 m) and its leaves, when rubbed, are mint scented. The purplish-pink flowers in autumn make it an excellent shrub for associating with other late-flowering shrubs having similar requirements, such as *Caryopteris* × *clandonensis*.
Cultivation. As these shrubs are only hardy in truly temperate climates, it is best to cut them hard back in autumn (which needs to be done if they are to produce plenty of shoots in the following year) and place a mulch over their roots. The soil must be well drained and its planting site must be in full sun.

They can be propagated by green cuttings in summer, or by sowing seed under glass in spring. In either case, the new plants should be protected from the cold in their first winter.

Elymus
Lyme grass, *Gramineae*

A genus of about 100 species of often invasive grasses from the northern temperate zones. Only a few species are suitable for growing in gardens, and should only be planted where there is plenty of space or where other plants will not be adversely affected by them.
E. arenarius (zone 4–5), blue lyme grass, native to Europe and Asia, grows to 3½–4 ft (1–1.2 m) in height and is variable in spread. In good conditions, it will cover several square feet/metres. This is a hardy suckering perennial with ribbon-shaped bluish-grey leaves.
Cultivation. Plant in sandy, well-drained soil in a sunny position. Propagate by removing suckers during the growing period.

Embothrium coccineum

Embothrium
Proteaceae

This genus is made up of about eight evergreen trees and shrubs mostly from the Andes of South America.
E. coccineum (zone 8), Chilean firebush, from Argentina and Chile, is a large, but rather uncommon upright shrub or small tree growing to 13–20 ft (4–6 m) in height and 6½–10 ft (2–3 m) wide. It has very eye-catching clusters of scarlet-orange flowers in late spring and early summer. It has shiny, green lanceolate leathery leaves which are evergreen in mild climates. Only hardy in areas with mild winters, it is a fine species to plant in isolation or in light undergrowth.
Cultivation. Plant in a sunny position in spring, or in the shelter of a wall exposed to full sun. It succeeds best in deep, moist, but well-drained peaty (acid) soil or an open sandy lime-free loam. It is advisable to protect the roots in winter using straw or dead leaves. The easiest way to propagate is to use the suckers which grow from the base of the tree, or from seed.

Enkianthus
Ericaceae

A genus of 10 or so species of hardy deciduous shrubs, native to the Himalayas, China and Japan.

Enkianthus campanulatus

E. campanulatus (zone 6), redvein enkianthus, from Japan, grows to a height of 6½–10 ft (2–3 m) with a spread of 3½–6½ ft (1–2 m). The elegant dark green foliage grouped at the ends of the branches turns to dazzling shades of scarlet and bronze-red in autumn. It flowers in spring, producing dense decorative clusters of small bell-shaped flowers ranging from creamy yellow to orangey yellow. These are followed by small pendent fruits.

It is a good plant for growing alongside other acid-loving shrubs such as azaleas, rhododendrons, camellias, and heather.

Cultivation. Plant in a sunny position sheltered from cold winds. It enjoys a soil enriched with peat or heath-mould, but dislikes lime.

Propagate by seed or by taking semi-hardwood cuttings with a heel in late summer or early autumn.

Ephedra
Ephedraceae

This genus contains 40 species of shrubs, sometimes climbing, from temperate and subtropical areas. The stems are green and the leaves, reduced to scales, are soon shed. The flowers appear in the form of catkins.

E. distachya (zone 7), from southern Europe and western Asia, grows to 3½–5 ft (1–1.5 m) in height. It is characterized by its erect and rigid habit of growth which makes it look like the horsetail (*Equisetum*). The whitish catkins are followed by bright red berries in autumn.

Cultivation. Ephedra can only be grown in good sandy soil in a frost-free climate. It does not require a great deal of water. It grows well in rock gardens and on banks. Propagation is by seed, layers or by division in spring.

Epilobium
Willowherb, *Onagraceae*

A genus of more than 200 species of herbaceous perennials, annuals, biennials and sub-shrubs.

E. angustifolium (zone 4), rosebay willowherb or fireweed, from Europe, Asia and North America, is up to 5 ft (1.5 m) tall and spreads by means of rhizomes and a considerable amount of seeding. Its spikes of purplish flowers make it attractive, although it is best confined to the wild garden. There is a fine white cultivar, 'Alba' and there are sterile clones of both forms.

E. dodonaei (zone 4), a native of Europe (often confused with *E. fleischeri*, which is a smaller plant), grows to 2 ft (60 cm) in height and spread. It is a compact perennial plant with grey-green narrow willow-shaped leaves. It is slightly stoloniferous but not invasive. The tubular flowers, with four, dark pink petals, appear throughout the summer.

E. pedunculare (zone 6), from New Zealand, is a perennial prostrate plant with creeping stems

Epilobium angustifolium

and rounded leaves ¼ in (6 mm) in diameter, often bronze-coloured. The small flowers are pale pink to white and appear in summer. This species may become invasive in damp, semi-shaded soil and also seeds itself readily and can become a weed. This is best suited to a rock garden or the front of a herbaceous border.
Cultivation. Plant in spring in a well-drained soil, in a sunny position.

Propagation is by seed in late winter, in a seed tray under a cold frame.

Epimedium

Barrenwort, *Berberidaceae*

This genus includes about 20 species of hardy perennials with unusual spurred flowers and evergreen or semi-evergreen leaves from Europe and Asia.
E. grandiflorum (zone 6), from East Asia, measures 12 in (30 cm) in height with a spread of 16–20 in (40–50 cm). The leaves are divided, with oval leaflets. The large flowers are light red or pink, and white and appear in spring.
E. × *rubrum* (zone 6), a cross between *E. alpinum* and *E. grandiflorum*, grows to a height of 9 in (23 cm) with the same spread. It has soft green leaves tinged with red when young, and very bright autumn colours. Its crimson flowers appear in spring.
E. × *versicolor* (zone 6), a hybrid of *E. grandiflorum* and *E. pinnatum* var. *colchicum* measures 12–16 in (30–40 cm) in height and spread. The foliage is similar to that of the previous species. The flowers are yellow, tinged with red, and appear in spring. 'Sulphureum' has pale yellow flowers.

These plants look striking in a shaded part of the garden in front of shrubs, such as rhododendrons, grown with foliage plants like *Hosta, Rodgersia* or ferns.
Cultivation. Plant in autumn or spring, in a moist humus-rich soil, in shade or semi-shade. Do not let the soil dry out in summer.

Propagate by dividing the root clumps in summer.

Equisetum

Horsetail, *Equisetaceae*

Horsetails have no flowers and, with tree ferns, represent vestiges of the ancient carboniferous forests. Some species, such as the meadow horsetail, *Equisetum arvense*, are weeds and very difficult to eradicate. Others are slower growing and attractive.
E. hyemale (zone 4), common scouring brush, from Eurasia and northwest North America, forms erect rush-like stems about 3 ft (90 cm) long, without leaves, lasting all winter. It often occupies banks to a depth of 4 in (10 cm) or so of water.
E. hyemale var. *robustum* (zone 4), is a giant version of the previous plant, reaching up to 10 ft (3 m) in height.
E. scirpoides (zone 2–3), is a dwarf species from the north polar regions and in cool soil it forms a prostrate or erect plant of evergreen filaments.

Because of their precise, geometric appearance, horsetails play an important role in Japanese-style gardens.
Cultivation. All these species will grow in any soil. They are propagated by dividing the root clumps while they are growing.

Eranthis

Winter aconite, *Ranunculaceae*

A genus of about six small tuberous hardy perennial plants native to Europe and Asia. This plant is poisonous.
E. hyemalis (zone 6), grows to a height of 4 in (10 cm) and is found in undergrowth in southern Europe. The plant flowers even earlier than

Eranthis hyemalis

the snowdrop. The flowers are a shiny golden yellow and have a collar of deeply incised leaves.
Cultivation. Leave the small rhizomes to soak for 24 hours before planting in early to mid autumn. The winter aconite will grow well beneath deciduous trees, and although it likes winter sunshine, in semi-shade, the flowers last longer.

Propagate by dividing the rhizomes and replanting them immediately, or by sowing seeds in trays, keeping them in a cold frame for two years before planting out.

Eremurus

Foxtail lilies, *Liliaceae*

This genus contains 35 hardy herbaceous species with fleshy roots. In spring a basal rosette of linear, green or greenish-grey leaves, triangular in section, appears. The dense floral spikes develop at the end of spring.
E. himalaicus (zone 7), from the Himalayas, 5–6½ ft (1.5–2 m) tall has pure white flowers in early summer.
E. robustus (zone 7), from central Asia, is 3½–5 ft (1–1.5 m) tall, with bright yellow flowers in summer.
Cultivation. At the end of summer plant the tubers in groups of three or five, burying them 6 in (15 cm) deep on a mound of sand and in well-drained soil, enriched to quite a depth with well-rotted peat. Choose a sunny position at the foot of a wall, sheltered from cold winds.

The plants need to be kept dry in summer to induce flowering. In winter, in the absence of snow to protect the dormant buds from cold winds, protect the crowns by placing an inverted pot over them.

Propagation can be a slow process. Sowing seeds will give a large number of plants which will flower after four to six years. However, older tubers may divide naturally and form several crowns more quickly. Take care not to damage or break the long roots when lifting them.

Erica

Heath, heather, *Ericaceae*

This numerous genus includes about 650 species of evergreen shrubs and small trees from Europe, the Mediterranean region and South Africa. Those from the latter region are grown as house plants. The hardy types are grown for their dense clusters of small bell-shaped flowers in colours ranging from white to red and some are also grown for the decorative value of their coloured foliage; cultivars with yellow, grey, gold and reddish leaves are available. These plants should be grown in groups in borders and rock gardens. The most commonly grown species and cultivars from Europe are hardy anywhere.

Erica ciliaris

E. herbacea (*E. carnea*) – zone 5 – winter heath, 4–12 in (10–30 cm) high, flowers in winter and is tolerant of alkaline soils; *E. cinerea* (zone 5), bell heather, 6–16 in (15–40 cm) high, is summer-flowering; *E. ciliaris* (zone 5), Dorset heath, 1 ft (30 cm) high, has pale green leaves and rose-red flowers from mid summer to autumn. *E.* × *darleyensis* (zone 5) is a hybrid 1–2 ft (30–60 cm) high, which flowers from late autumn to mid spring, also fairly tolerant of alkaline soils; *E. vagans* (zone 6), Cornish heath, 10–16 in (25–40 cm) high, flowers in summer. Finally, *E. arborea* (zone 8), the tree heath, is better in a slightly milder climate, when it may reach 6½–10 ft (2–3 m) in height and spread, with white flowers in spring. Its variety *alpina* (zone 7) grows to 8 ft (2.5 m) and is hardy.
Cultivation. Heathers are easy to grow even in conditions which are not ideal. They have a preference for a peaty humus-rich, light soil (such as heath-mould), and some will tolerate slightly limy soil.

Plant them either in autumn or spring, in a sunny or partly shaded position 8–20 in (20–50 cm) apart, depending on the variety. In spring, the plants like a peat mulch. After that, the only attention required is watering in dry weather, especially during the first year after planting. It is also advisable to remove dead flowers in spring, whatever the type of heather by clipping them over. Winter-flowering heathers will not need any further pruning, but those that flower in the summer should be pruned after a few years to encourage further flowering. Simply cut back the old woody stems in spring. Heaths can be grown from seed sown in a sandy peat in spring. Also propagate by taking cuttings of semi-ripened twigs, 1 in (2.5 cm) long, placing them in pots containing a sandy peat, topped with silver sand and left undisturbed until the following spring.

Erigeron

Fleabane, *Compositae*

A genus represented by more than 200 species of herbaceous annuals, biennials or perennials, natives either of Europe or North America.
E. speciosus (zone 5), is a hardy perennial from western North America growing to 16–24 in (40–60 cm) high and 12–20 in (30–50 cm) across. The stems bear lanceolate leaves and clusters of daisy-like lilac-coloured flowers in summer. Many cultivars and hybrids with other species are available in a wide range of pinks, mauves, blues and violets with single or semi-double flowers.
Cultivation. Plant 12 in (30 cm) apart in autumn or spring. The fleabane likes well-drained soil, enriched with manure or garden compost, and a sunny position. It is advisable to add manure in spring and to stake the plants if the site is windy. Remove the dead flowers to encourage further flowering and cut down the stems in autumn.

Propagate by seed sown in early summer outdoors or by division in autumn.

Erinus

Scrophulariaceae

A genus consisting of two hardy perennial species with evergreen leaves, native to the mountains of Europe and North Africa.
E. alpinus (zone 4), fairy foxglove, from the Pyrenees and European Alps, is $3\frac{1}{4}$–4 in (8–10 cm) high with a spread of 4–6 in (10–15 cm). This is a small ground-covering plant with many leafy stems and dark green spatulate leaves. It has profuse tiny pink flowers in spring. The cultivar 'Albus' has white flowers; 'Dr. Hannelle', carmine red; 'Roseus', soft pink. They all grow best in rock gardens.
Cultivation. Plant in spring in well-drained soil, even alkaline, in a sunny or partly shaded position.

Propagation is by seed sown in seed trays, in early spring, under a cold frame or by sowing *in situ* in crevices. It is a short-lived plant but once established will spread its seeds abundantly in the garden. Remove any plants which grow where they are unwanted. They can also be divided.

Erodium

Storksbill, *Geraniaceae*

This genus is very closely related to the geraniums. It contains some 60 species growing in temperate and subtropical climates of Europe, Asia, Australia and America.
E. petraeum subsp. *crispum* (*E. cheilanthifolium*) (zone 8), Spain and Morocco, grows to 4 in (10 cm) in height. It has attractive deeply divided, evergreen downy grey foliage. The flowers are grouped in twos or fours on each stem, and are white to pale pink, with darker pink veining. The plant flowers from early summer to early autumn.
E. reichardii (*E. chamaedryoides*) (zone 8–9), from the Balearic Islands, measures 1–3 in (2.5–7.5 cm) in height, but spreads to between 8–16 in (20–40 cm). It is a dwarf perennial which makes good ground cover without being invasive. The plant bears white flowers, veined with pink, from late spring to late summer. The cultivar 'Roseum' has pink flowers veined with purple, $\frac{3}{4}$ in (2 cm) in diameter, and is highly decorative. Grow in well-drained soil and a partly shaded position. Protect in winter in cold climates with a carpet of dry leaves.

The plants in this genus are not always easy to grow, but they are attractive in a rock garden.
Cultivation. Plant in dry, gravelly soil in a sunny position. A 2 in (5 cm) gravel mulch on the surface of the soil will be of benefit in areas with damp winters.

Propagate by seeds which germinate easily or by taking cuttings from the base of the main stems, in late spring or early summer, and keep under a cold frame, before planting out.

Eryngium × oliverianum

Eryngium

Sea holly, *Umbelliferae*

A genus containing 230 species of perennials, some frost resistant and others not, native to Europe, America, Australia and Asia.

E. bourgatii (zone 4–5), from the Pyrénées, is a hardy herbaceous perennial 16–24 in (40–60 cm) high with a spread of 12–20 in (30–50 cm). It is a decorative plant, with silvery, deeply cut slightly prickly leaves and flowers in dense silvery-blue heads surrounded by bracts forming a silver collar in mid to late summer. This plant looks good in rock gardens or at the front of herbaceous or mixed borders; it is also suitable for dried flower arrangements.

E. × oliverianum is a hardy hybrid of uncertain parentage, up to 5 ft (1.2 m) tall with blue-green basal leaves and mauvish bracts around its bluish flower heads.

Cultivation. Plant in autumn or spring 12 in (30 cm) apart. Any well-drained soil is suitable, provided it is in a sunny position. Cut the stems right back after flowering and, if drying the flowers, cut them before they have fully opened.

Propagation is by seed, or by root cuttings taken in late winter, and placed under a cold frame before planting out in autumn.

Erysimum

Wallflower & blister cress in USA, *Cruciferae*

This genus contains around 80 species of annuals, biennials and sub-shrubs from Europe and Asia. Most of them are hardy, and resemble wallflowers, to which they are closely related.

E. linifolium (zone 5–6), native to Spain, is 8 in (20 cm) or more tall with a spread of 16 in (40 cm). It is an evergreen perennial growing in erect clumps with entire linear leaves. The flowers are lilac or mauve, growing in terminal racemes from mid spring to early summer.

E. pulchellum (zone 7), native to Greece and Asia Minor, is a perennial, 6–12 in (15–30 cm) high with a spread of 16–20 in (40–50 cm). It is a ground-covering plant with ascending stems and long, toothed spathulate leaves and bright yellow flowers in mid to late spring.

E. pumilum (zone 5), Europe, is a perennial 2–4 in (5–10 cm) high with a spread of 8 in (20 cm), forming cushions of ground cover. The scented lemon-yellow flowers appear throughout summer.

These species are best suited to a sunny position in a rock garden.

Cultivation. Plant in spring in a sunny position, in ordinary soil, not too rich but well drained. Short-lived plants, they will live longer in poor soils.

Propagate by seed, division or by taking cuttings 2–3 in (5–7.5 cm) long from the lateral branches in mid to late summer, and plant in sand in a cold frame.

Erythrina

Coral tree, *Leguminosae*

This genus comprises about 100 species, native to the tropical regions of the world. Most are trees, though some are spiny herbaceous plants. Only the latter kind can be grown outside the tropics, in mild, frost-free areas. A warm greenhouse is necessary for the trees.

E. crista-galli (zone 9–10), cockspur coral tree, from South America, grows to $6\frac{1}{2}$–$8\frac{1}{2}$ ft (2–2.5 m) or more. It is a bushy plant with a strong, woody rootstock. The branches are spiny and the leaves composed of three leathery, shiny green leaflets. The large vermilion red flowers grow in spikes from mid summer to mid autumn. Branches which have flowered die after

doing so. The cultivar 'Compacta' is a more compact plant with blood-red flowers and is said to be more free flowering.
E. herbacea (zone 10), native to southeast USA is a sub-shrubby deciduous plant 4–5 ft (1.2–1.5 m) high. It has large clusters some 20–24 in (50–60 cm) long of scarlet-garnet flowers.
E. vespertilio (zone 10), native to Australia, is a very decorative specimen shrub.

These plants look superb either on their own or in groups of three to five.
Cultivation. Plant in open soil in a very sunny position. *Erythrina crista-galli* needs frequent, copious watering in summer. Keep it protected with a covering of leaves where the winters are particularly cold or grow in a warm house.

Propagate by seed after soaking these for 24 hours, and germinate using bottom heat. Cuttings of young shoots with a heel, planted in a sandy soil in spring, again with some bottom heat is another method of propagating.

Erythronium

Dog's-tooth violet, adder's tongue, *Liliaceae*

A genus of 20 bulbous species, widespread in the Northern Hemisphere, with long, pear-shaped corms. The floral spike bears one or more star-shaped flowers, usually with recurved white, yellow or bright pink petals. The flowers, resembling small lilies, appear in mid to late spring.
E. Americanum (zone 6), yellow dogtooth violet, grows to 1 ft (30 cm). Leaves 6 in (15 cm) long, mottled brown and white. Flowers are solitary, yellow often spotted red at the base inside, and bloom mid-spring.
E. dens-canis (zone 5), dog's-tooth violet, is native to Europe, growing to 4–6 in (10–15 cm) high and producing solitary white or bright pink flowers on each stem. The oblong leaves are marbled and blotched with brown. Its corms resemble the canine tooth of a dog.
E. hendersonii (zone 6), native to northwest USA, grows to 8–10 in (20–25 cm) in height and has solitary lavender flowers in spring to summer. Keep it dry in summer. The leaves are mottled and have a wavy margin.
E. 'Pagoda' (zone 6), is a hybrid, 8–12 in (20–30 cm) high, with three to four lemon yellow flowers and mottled leaves.
Cultivation. The soil needs to be humus-rich and well drained. The bulbs are best planted in small groups at a depth of 4 in (10 cm), in autumn, in light undergrowth.

Propagate by seed, but the plants will take five years to flower. They can also be propagated by offsets.

Escallonia

Grossulariaceae (*Saxifragaceae*)

A genus of about 40 species of evergreen trees and shrubs, native to South America. The majority of those grown are cultivars, ranging between 5–10 ft (1.5–3 m) in height and with a spread of 3½–6½ ft (1–2 m). *E. rubra* var. *macrantha* from Chile is but one of their several parents. It has bright red flowers during summer and is useful as a hedge, especially in seaside locations.
Cultivars. 'Donard Radiance' has dark green evergreen leaves and elegant pink flowers which appear in early to mid summer; 'Pride of Donard' has bright red flowers appearing in early to mid summer; 'Apple Blossom' has shiny evergreen leaves and large numbers of pale pink flowers from early summer to autumn.

The cultivars are hardy (zone 7) and are particularly suitable for coastal gardens since they can put up with salty spray. They can be used in hedges, on their own, or as part of a mixed border.
Cultivation. Plant in spring in an ordinary well-drained soil, in full sun in cold regions, or use the protection of a wall. As a hedge they should be planted 12–15 in (30–38 cm) apart.

Propagate by semi-woody cuttings taken in late summer or early autumn, put into pots in a sandy soil, placed in gentle heat.

Escallonia rubra var. *macrantha*

Eschscholzia

California poppy, *Papaveraceae*

A genus consisting of some 10 annual and perennial species native to western North America.

E. californica (zone 6), reaches a height of 12–20 in (30–50 cm). This easy-to-grow annual has strikingly coloured, yellow or orange flowers from early summer to mid autumn.

Cultivars. Seed is in mixed colours including white, pink, red and yellow as well as cultivars of distinct colours. 'Ballerina', 8 in (20 cm) tall, has large semi-double flowers with fluted petals.

Cultivation. Sow where the plant is to grow in early autumn in a mild climate, or in early spring where winters are cold. Lightly cover the seeds with a sprinkling of seed compost. Thin out to a distance of 6 in (15 cm). The California poppy tolerates poor dry soils. Remove faded flowers to encourage further flowering and to prolong the season, sowing may be staggered from early spring to early summer.

Eucalyptus

Gum tree, *Myrtaceae*

This vast genus consists of about 450 species and hybrids of aromatic fast-growing evergreen trees, mostly native to Australia and Tasmania. Most are tropical or sub-tropical, but those that grow at a high altitude are hardy in temperate climates. However, this hardiness is relative, as they scarcely tolerate temperatures lower than 14°F (−10°C), and stand cold winds even less well than low temperatures.

In these conditions, the parts above ground die, but the roots survive, and send up shoots the following year. Their rapid growth quickly makes one forget the effects of a hard winter. Their juvenile leaves are distinct from the adult foliage.

E. camphora (zone 7), is a small tree from New South Wales perfectly adapted to waterside growth or very wet places.

E. dalrympleana (zone 7), from Tasmania, grows very quickly. The trunk is covered with a patchwork of bark that is as decorative as its grey-green foliage.

E. gunnii (zone 7), cidergum, also from Tasmania, is a handsome tree with silvery leaves. It is very amenable to pruning and is often cut back annually for the sake of its round, juvenile foliage.

E. parvifolia (zone 7), small-leaved gum, from New South Wales, is a shrub with glaucous foliage. It is one of the hardiest species best adapted to northern temperate climates.

Eucalyptus comes into its own in gardens planned with blue, grey and white as the theme. Their particular habit and foliage will add an exotic touch and their white flowers are quite striking. When cut back every year, most species associate well with white variegated grasses, such as *Phalaris arundinacea 'Picta'* or *Miscanthus sinensis*.

Cultivation. All types of soil suit eucalyptus, but they enjoy a rich soil, with some decayed manure and charcoal to keep it open. *E. parvifolia* tolerates chalk, but most species prefer a moist soil, rather than a dry one. The only means of propagation is by seed, sown in pots of light sandy soil with gentle heat. Transplanting should never be done with the roots exposed to the air but always with a rootball which should be covered.

Eucomis

Pineapple lily, *Liliaceae*

This genus of about 10 species originates in tropical and southern Africa. The foliage forms a rosette, from which the flowering spike rises to a height of 32 in (80 cm). This carries a dense cylindrical raceme of small star-shaped flowers, which last several weeks, surmounted by a crown of short, leafy pineapple-like bracts.

E. bicolor (zone 10), has large green leaves with wavy edges. The star-shaped flowers are green, edged with purple.'Alba' has greenish-white flowers without coloured margins.

E. comosa (*E. punctata*) (zone 10), pineapple flower, has large smooth-edged leaves measuring up to 20 in (50 cm) long. The upper side of the leaves and the flower stem are spotted in purplish-brown. The flowers are a greenish or brownish-white, and bloom from mid summer to early autumn.

Cultivation. Plant in rich soil in a sunny position sheltered from cold winds. The wrinkled, conical bulbs should be planted in spring at a depth of 8 in (20 cm). Protect with a layer of dead leaves in winter. In very cold climates grow in pots in a greenhouse.

Propagate by means of seeds or by offsets.

Eucomis bicolor

branches during its first winters.

Propagate by means of semi-hardwood cuttings, taken in late summer or early autumn.

Eucryphia

Eucryphiaceae

A genus consisting of five species of evergreen trees and shrubs from Australia and Chile.

E. glutinosa (*E. pinnatifolia*) (zone 8), from Chile, is pyramidal in habit, and measures 10–13 ft (3–4 m) or more in height, with a spread of 6½ ft (2 m). In many gardens it is likely to be partly deciduous. In summer, the plant is covered with large pure white flowers, with yellow-gold stamens grouped in a central cluster.

In regions with mild climates, this species can be grown as a solitary specimen or as background to a border.

E. × *nymansensis* (zone 8), is a hybrid between *E. glutinosa* and another Chilean species, *E. cordifolia*, which can reach 50 ft (15 m), and will tolerate limy soils.

Cultivation. Plant at the beginning of autumn or spring in moist, well-drained, lime-free soil (especially in the case of *E. glutinosa*). This should be deep, and in a sheltered position in full sun or half-shade. Protect with straw or

Euonymus

Spindle tree, *Celastraceae*

This genus consists of about 180 species of trees and shrubs with deciduous or evergreen leaves, and tall, dwarf, spreading, or climbing in habit. They are prized for their varied and decorative foliage as well as for their characteristic pink and orange fruit. They are native to many parts of the Northern Hemisphere.

E. fortunei (zone 6), from Asia, is notable for its hardiness and its tolerance of atmospheric pollution. It has given rise to several cultivars with decorative evergreen foliage, such as 'Colorata', with spreading habit and green leaves that become tinted with red in winter, or 'Emerald 'n' Gold', a dwarf shrub with golden variegated foliage.

E. europaeus (zone 5), spindle tree, found wild in Europe, is deciduous and notable for the abundance of its pink and orange fruit in autumn, which are especially prolific in the cultivar 'Red Cascade'.

E. japonicus (zone 7), is a slightly less hardy evergreen species from Japan of which there are several variegated cultivars.

These plants are easy to grow, and can be used for hedging, the smaller evergreen species as ground cover, or in island shrub borders or mixed borders.

E. kiautschovicus (zone 5–6), Manhattan, from East Central China. It is an evergreen or semi-deciduous shrub up to 10 ft (3 m) tall with oval leaves 2–3 in (5–7.5 cm) long. Flowers are greenish-white, fruit is pink and almost ½ in (13 mm) across with beautiful orange-red seedcoats.

Cultivation. They do well in all ordinary soil, even limy ones, and enjoy sun and half-shade. The variegated forms benefit from the protection of a wall or other shrubs. Plant in autumn or spring; 16–24 in (40–60 cm) apart if they are to form a hedge. Young plants need to be watered in dry weather. Hedges should be pruned in summer.

Propagate deciduous species by seed, layers or cuttings. With the help of some bottom heat, propagate the evergreen species any time of the year. Aphids, caterpillars and scale insects may attack the young shoots and prevent fruiting. Spray immediately with a contact insecticide when any of these appear.

Eupatorium

Boneset, *Compositae*

A genus comprising more than 1000 species of herbaceous plants and shrubs, hardy and tender, native to America, Asia and Europe.

E. maculatum (zone 6), is a native of North America, and measures up to $6\frac{1}{2}$ ft (2 m) in height, with a spread of $3\frac{1}{2}$ ft (1 m). The glaucous red-streaked stems carry lanceolate to oval leaves in whorls of three to six. Its flowers in the form of flat purple corymbs appear from mid summer to early autumn.

E. purpureum (zone 6), Joe-pye weed, also from North America, is similar to the above species, with flowers ranging from pale pink to purple. 'Atropurpureum' has dark brownish-red flowers and purple stems.

Both species are hardy perennials suitable for large beds and wild gardens where they combine well with species of *Lythrum, Ligularia, Tradescantia, Hemerocallis*, and *Trollius*.

Cultivation. Plant in heavy, marshy, clay-rich soil, in a sunny or half-shaded situation, either in autumn or spring.

Propagate by division of root stock in spring.

Euphorbia

Spurge, *Euphorbiaceae*

A genus comprising more than 1000 species which come from most temperate and subtropical regions. It includes annuals, biennials, perennials, shrubs, and spiny succulent cactus-like species. All have a milky latex which may be poisonous. Their flowers, generally insignificant, are surrounded by long-lasting coloured leaves, known as bracts.

The following three species are only hardy in a Mediterranean-type climate, where the first two are suitable for cactus gardens along with other succulents. Elsewhere they should be grown under glass.

E. fulgens (zone 10+), scarlet plume, from Mexico, is notable for its slender, flexible stems, which carry fleshy leaves and insignificant flowers surrounded by vermilion bracts during winter.

E. milii (*E. splendens*) (zone 10+), crown of thorns, is native to Malagassy and reaches a height of $2\frac{3}{4}$–$3\frac{1}{2}$ ft (80 cm–1 m). It is a thickly branching shrub covered with sharp spines, and has umbels of flame-red bracts during winter.

E. pulcherrima (zone 10+), poinsettia, from Brazil, is grown as a pot plant for home or greenhouse decoration during the winter, although in its native habitat it is a shrub over 12 ft (3.7 m) tall. It has narrowly ovate leaves and insignificant greenish flowers, but the latter are surrounded by leafy bracts of a showy bright red. Cultivars are also available with bracts in shades of pink or white.

Cultivation. When grown under glass these tender species need plenty of light, although some shade from hot summer sun is necessary. The temperature should not be much below 60°F (16°C). *E. fulgens* and *E. millii* need moderate watering during spring and summer, less in winter. *E. pulcherrima* needs more water in the summer and if its leaves begin to wilt (but do not over water). In general, the compost should be allowed to become slightly dry before watering. A humid atmosphere is desirable for *E. fulgens* and particularly for *E. pulcherrima* while it is flowering – achieve this by misting. Several euphorbias from temperate regions are hardy and good garden plants suitable for herbaceous and mixed borders; smaller species

Euphorbia characias

are best grown in a rock garden. Among the best are:
E. characias (zone 7), from southern Europe, is a statuesque, evergreen semi-shrub up to 3 ft (90 cm) tall, with whorls of grey-green leaves and large flower heads with yellowish bracts in early spring. While it is not hardy in severe winters, its self-sown seedlings often survive.
E. griffithii (zone 6), from the Himalayas, is a somewhat spreading herbaceous perennial 2½ ft (76 cm) high with, in its cultivar 'Fireglow', brick-red bracts during late spring and early summer.
E. myrsinites (zone 6), from southern Europe and parts of Asia Minor, is a prostrate evergreen perennial about 6 in (15 cm) tall and 2 ft (60 cm wide). Whorls of somewhat succulent, blue-grey leaves carry a good display of yellow bracts in early and mid spring.
E. epithymoides (*E. polychroma*) (zone 6), from central and southeast Europe, is a herbaceous perennial with bright yellow bracts from mid spring to early summer and makes hummocky growth up to 18 in (45 cm) tall and wide.
Cultivation. Plant in autumn or spring in any reasonable, well-drained soil in sunny sites. Propagate by seeds in early spring, or by cuttings of basal shoots in a cold frame during mid and late spring. Division of some species is possible in autumn and spring.

Exacum
Gentianaceae

A small genus of about 25 species of herbaceous plants which are found in tropical areas of Asia and India. One species is frequently grown as a flowering pot plant and usually treated as an annual or biennial.
E. affine (zone 10+) Persian violet, is native to the island of Socotra in the Indian Ocean. It forms a small bushy plant under 1 ft (30 cm) high with small, glossy, bright green, ovate leaves. The fragrant, star shaped flowers about ¾ in (20 mm) across have five purplish-blue petals with a conspicuous cluster of stamens with yellow anthers in the centre. The flowering season lasts from summer through to late autumn after which the plants are normally discarded.

Exacum affine

Cultivation. Keep in good light but away from hot sun. As it enjoys damp conditions, keep the compost (soil) moist and mist frequently. Propagate by sowing seed in late summer.

Exochorda
Pearl bush, *Rosaceae*

A genus consisting of four hardy deciduous shrubs, native to central China and Korea. Often neglected, they are elegant in habit and have magnificent white flowers in spring.
E. korolkowii (zone 6), from Turkestan, measures 13 ft (4 m) in height. It is notable for its elegant form and its white flowers that bloom in mid and late spring.

The cultivar 'The Bride' has larger flowers, measuring 1½–2 in (4–5 cm) wide.
E. racemosa (*E. grandiflora*) (zone 6), originates in northern China. It reaches 13 ft (4 m) in height, with an upright habit. The flowers bloom in racemes of about ten. This species is unsuitable for chalky soils.
Cultivation. Plant in a rich loam in a sunny position although in the warmer regions some will benefit from the light shade of larger trees. Prune lightly after flowering is over.

Propagate by seeds, layering or, in the case of *E. racemosa*, by suckers.

Fabiana

Solanaceae

A genus of about 25 tender species of shrub from South America.

F. imbricata (zone 9), comes from the Andes, and is of medium size, measuring 5 ft (1.5 m) or more in height, and resembles heather in habit. The slightly viscous, evergreen scaly leaves grow all along the branches. In summer, the tube-shaped white flowers are abundant. The cultivar 'Prostrata' (zone 8–9) is a dwarf form with mauve flowers, slightly hardier than the type species. It is half-hardy, and should be kept in a cold greenhouse in winter, except in milder regions.

Fagus sylvatica

Cultivation. It prefers neutral or acid soil, a sunny position, and a mild rainy climate. It blooms in a sunny position, and can also be grown in a cold greenhouse.

Propagate by means of cuttings taken in summer and placed in well-drained soil, or in a greenhouse in spring.

Fagus

Beech, *Fagaceae*

This genus consists of some 10 species of deciduous tree from the Northern Hemisphere with male and female catkins produced on the same tree.

F. grandifolia (zone 4), American beech, is from Eastern North America. Large suckering deciduous tree up to 80 ft (24 m) tall. Leaves up to 5 in (13 cm) long and heavily veined. Its fruit husks are covered with recurved prickles.

F. sylvatica (zone 5), common beech in UK and European beech in USA, from Europe, has a rounded crown that may reach a height of 130 ft (40 m). The straight trunk is covered with smooth ash-grey bark. Its buds taper to a point and its alternate, wavy edged leaves turn gold in autumn. The fruits, known as beech-nuts, are enclosed in a prickly casing with a silky lining.

The tree makes up a large part of northern European forests, and when in full leaf its canopy produces deep shade in which little else will grow.

Cultivars. 'Albomarginata' has leaves edged with creamy white; 'Riversii' is a good form of the copper beech; f. *laciniata* has deeply cut leaves, and is among the most beautiful of deciduous trees; while f. *pendula* has pendent branches.

The beech is ideal for large gardens, and as their dead leaves are retained for a long time it makes good hedges.

Cultivation. Beech enjoy a light or medium soil, and do best on chalk. Seeds gathered at the end of summer should be kept in slightly damp sand, and sown in spring.

Most cultivars need to be grafted, and cannot be propagated by means of cuttings. Beech is one of the finest deciduous hedging materials, plant from mid-autumn to early spring, 1–2 ft (30–60 cm) apart. Trim in late summer or early autumn. Beeches should never be transplanted with bare roots, but should be lifted with a rootball. Woolly beech aphid can be a nuisance.

Fatsia japonica
'Variegata'

Fatsia
Araliaceae

A genus of one species of evergreen shrub or occasionally a small tree from Japan. It is usually grown for its glossy foliage as a house or greenhouse plant in cooler climates, although it will survive outdoors in many areas with a little frost and is worth trying in sheltered places.
F. japonica (zone 9–10) is usually grown as a bushy shrub which, even in a pot, may reach 6 ft (1.8 m) in height. The palmate leaves up to 15 in (38 cm) across are divided to nearly halfway into about nine toothed lobes. The rounded heads of small creamy white flowers are formed in autumn and followed by shiny black berries. 'Variegata' has leaves variegated with white.
Cultivation. This quick-growing indoor plant enjoys a well-lit, well-ventilated warm situation. Water frequently during the growing season, sparingly in the winter. To encourage a bushy habit cut back the tips in the spring. Repot annually at the same time. Propagate by sowing seed in the spring or take stem cuttings in the summer.

Felicia
Compositae

A genus consisting of over 60 species of not particularly hardy herbaceous annuals, perennials, or sub-shrubs from South Africa with daisy-like flowers.
F. amelloides (Agathaea coelestis) (zone 9), blue daisy, measures 16–20 in (40–50 cm) in height, with a spread of 20 in (50 cm). This bushy perennial can tolerate a winter outside in milder climates, but is otherwise grown as an annual. The sky-blue flowers literally cover the foliage from early to late summer, making a most decorative plant for the fronts of borders, or in rock gardens and containers.
Cultivation. Plant in spring, in ordinary well-drained soil, in a sunny position. Protect with a cloche during winter. In climates where the winters are cold, grow in a greenhouse.

Propagate by means of cuttings 2–2¾ in (5–7 cm) long from mid to late summer, and place in a cold frame in sandy soil.

Festuca
Fescue grass, *Gramineae*

A genus represented by 80 species of perennial grasses, many of which are used in lawns, native to Europe.
F. glauca (zone 6), from Europe, is hardy in all temperate regions, and has ornamental bluish-green foliage. Its leaves are narrow, and each plant forms dense clumps of about 8 in (20 cm) in height. In early and mid summer it has small bluish spikes of flowers.
F. amethystina (zone 6), from central Europe, is an evergreen perennial, with bluish foliage and violet flower spikes which grow up to 18 in (45 cm) tall.

These small grasses are useful as foliage foils for the front of a mixed border, for sunny slopes or for contrast in a rock garden.
Cultivation. Plant the clumps 6–8 in (15–20 cm) apart between autumn and spring in a sunny position. The soil should be light and well-drained. It is worth removing the flowers which tend to distract from the beauty of the foliage.

Renew the clumps by division in autumn or spring, every four or five years.

Ficus
Fig tree, *Moraceae*

A genus of about 800 tropical trees, shrubs and climbers, several of economic importance.

Ficus benjamina

F. carica (zone 7–8), is the only species that is moderately hardy in northern temperate climates. The fig tree is a typical feature of the Mediterranean region, and does not grow to be tree-sized except in warmer regions. In harsher climates the aerial parts are regularly killed off in winter, but grow again from the roots to form a small bush. When trained against a south-facing wall, it can produce a reasonable crop of fruit in colder regions. For this purpose, the best choices are such cultivars as 'Brown Turkey', 'Brunswick' or 'White Marseilles'.

The fig tree is prized as much for its fruits as for its large and decorative lobed leaves. For ornament it may be associated with other large-leaved trees such as *Magnolia grandiflora*.

Cultivation. The fig does well in fertile soil that is well-drained without being dry, and can tolerate lime. It needs watering during the growing season.

It can be propagated by means of cuttings placed in heated, humid conditions at the beginning of summer, or by layers or suckers.

Several of the tender subtropical and tropical species which follow are grown as foliage plants indoors in zones where they are unsuitable for cultivating outdoors.

F. benjamina (zone 10+), weeping fig, grows in tropical Asia where it reaches 70 ft (21 m) or more but in a container forms a small tree with an attractive pendulous habit. The glossy green ovate leaves have a long tapering tip and several variegated-leaved forms are available.

F. deltoidea (*F. diversifolia*) (zone 10+), mistletoe fig, from Malaysia, forms a slow-growing shrub reaching about 2 ft (60 cm) high when pot grown. It has leathery, dark green, obovate leaves and globose yellow fruits even when the plant is small.

F. elastica (zone 10+), rubber plant, native to India and Malaysia, is cultivated in tropical areas for the latex from which rubber is produced. As an indoor plant it will eventually form an impressive specimen with large shining leaves up to 12 in (30 cm) long. 'Decora', one of the more commonly grown cultivars, has broader leaves, pinkish tinged as they unfold.

F. lyrata (*F. pandurata*) (zone 10+), fiddle-leaved fig, grows in tropical West Africa as a climber attached to other trees. The lustrous green leaves have wavy edges and are an unusual shape.

F. pumila (*F. repens*) (zone 10+), creeping fig, from eastern Asia and northern Australia, is a climbing or trailing plant, with small oval or heart-shaped leaves when grown in a container.

Ficus lyrata

Ficus pumila

F. radicans (zone 10+), from southeast Asia, eventually makes a trailing plant with leathery, narrow oval leaves which in 'Variegata' have an irregular creamy white margin.
Cultivation. These plants enjoy heat and the temperature should not drop below 55°F (13°C) in winter. The tree types need good light and the compost (soil) should be allowed to dry out between watering. The trailing species need shade, frequent watering and misting. Repot every two or three years. Propagate by stem cuttings in summer.

Filipendula

Meadowsweet, *Rosaceae*

A genus represented by about 10 herbaceous hardy perennials from Europe and Asia.
F. vulgaris (*F. hexapetala*) (zone 6), dropwort, is a hardy herbaceous perennial that reaches 20–36 in (50–90 cm), with a spread of 16–24 in (40–60 cm). The foliage is bright green and finely cut, recalling that of ferns. It blooms in early and mid summer with small creamy-white flowers tinted with pink, grouped in feathery panicles.
F. rubra (zone 6), queen of the prairie, native to the eastern USA is up to 7 ft (2.1 m) tall and 2 ft (60 cm) wide with large flower heads, up to 1 ft (30 cm) across, in summer carried over deeply divided foliage.
Cultivation. Plant in autumn or spring. *F. vulgaris* requires a dry soil in a sunny position, while *F. rubra* must have damp soil in either a sunny or half-shaded position. Top-dress with a compound (general) fertilizer in spring, and cut back to ground level in autumn.

Propagate by means of division of the crown in autumn or spring.

Foeniculum

Fennel, *Umbelliferae*

A genus of one species of biennial or perennial herbaceous plant, now widespread in Europe but probably a native of southern and south western Europe.
F. vulgare (zone 6–7)has flowering stalks which reach more than $6\frac{1}{2}$ ft (2 m) in height during summer. The finely incised foliage, topped by umbels of small yellow flowers, gives off a strong smell of aniseed when it is rubbed. Its variety *purpureum* had purple-bronze foliage which contrasts with its flowers making it a good plant for a sunny mixed border.
F. vulgare var. *dulce* is grown for flavouring and essential oils, while *F. vulgare* var. *azoricum* produces swollen leaf bases and, when blanched, is eaten as a vegetable and known as Florence fennel or finnochio.
Cultivation. Florence fennel can follow root vegetables in crop rotation. It does well in light, rich, moisture retentive soil in a warm position.

It can be sown in two ways: in warmer regions, from mid to late summer, to produce a crop from early winter to early spring; or alternatively, in colder regions, from mid spring to mid summer to give a crop from late summer to early winter. In both cases sow seeds in drills 16 in (40 cm) apart, and cover the seeds to a depth of $\frac{3}{4}$ in (2 cm). Thin out to a distance of 6 in (15 cm).

Water liberally in warm weather. Mulch as necessary. Keep the leaf bases covered with earth until they are well developed, so that they become blanched. Continue the earthing-up process until the covering is 8 in (20 cm) deep. Cut the 'bulbs' at their base when they are fully blanched.
F. vulgare (var. *dulce*) also requires a well-drained soil in a sunny position. In mid and late spring sow three or four seeds per pocket 20 in (50 cm)

apart, and retain the best plantlet. Crowns can be divided in mid autumn.

Gather the leaves as and when needed, and the umbels at the end of summer. If you want to encourage leaf growth, cut out the flowering shoots.

Uses. The leaves add flavour to raw vegetables, grills and sauces for fish.

Forsythia

Oleaceae

A genus consisting of seven species of deciduous shrub, originating in eastern Asia and southeast Europe.

It is one of the most colourful plants, compact in habit, signalling the approach of spring with yellow, bell-shaped flowers which appear on the wood before the leaves, entirely covering the branches.

F. × *intermedia* (zone 6), is a robust hybrid between *F. suspensa* and *F. viridissima*. The flowers are a luminous yellow-gold, in hanging clusters of two to three and bloom in early and mid spring. The dark green, sometimes trifid leaves appear after flowering is over in mid spring. 'Arnold Giant' has numerous large leaves but is less free flowering; 'Beatrix Farrand' has flowers nearly 2 in (5 cm) long; 'Lynwood' has a very compact habit and flowers freely; 'Spring Glory' is free flowering with bright yellow flowers.

F. ovata (zone 6), from Korea, has somewhat drooping branches and rarely exceeds a height of 5 ft (1.5 m). In early spring, yellow flowers sprout from the branches, along with oval leaves. This species flowers less abundantly than *F.* × *intermedia*, but earlier in the year.

F. suspensa (zone 6), originates in China,. and measures from 6½–10 ft (2–3 m) or more in height. The long, supple, arching branches are pendulous but can be trained along a wall. The butter-yellow flowers bloom early in the year. 'Atrocaulis' has young stems that are dark purple, with lemon-yellow flowers; var. *fortunei* is larger and more erect; var. *sieboldii* is small and finely branching.

F. viridissima (zone 6), from China, measures 6–8 ft (1.8–2.4 m) in height. The narrow leaves turn purplish in autumn.

F. × *intermedia*, can be used in isolation, or in hedges along with cotoneasters, cherry trees and whitebeams. For training on a wall, *F. suspensa* is the best choice, as long as it is firmly fixed. Its variety, *sieboldii*, provides excellent ground cover for north-facing slopes.

Cultivation. Plant in mid to late autumn 3½ ft (1 m) apart in ordinary garden soil with good drainage. In the case of *F. suspensa* prune to within a few inches/centimetres of the old wood when flowering is over.

To propagate, use layering in the case of *F. suspensa*, which naturally roots as its branches touch the ground. Generally speaking, propagate by means of cuttings from new growth, in mid autumn, putting 8–12 in (20–30 cm) cuttings in the open garden in well-drained soil, and planting into their final positions the following year.

Fothergilla

Hamamelidaceae

A genus consisting of two species of deciduous shrub that originates in southeast USA. The shrubs are notable for their petal-less flowers with prominent creamy white stamens looking like a bottle brush, and their flamboyant autumn leaf colours. The flowers usually appear before the leaves.

F. gardenii (zone 7), reaches 3½ ft (1 m) in height, with a spread of 4–5 ft (1.2–1.5 m). Oval leaves.

F. major (zone 7), measures 6–10 ft (1.8–3 m) in height, and varies in spread between 4–6 ft (1.2–1.8 m). The flowers are strongly scented, and are followed by wrinkled leaves, blue-green on the underside, which turn green, yellow, and red before falling.

Cultivation. Fothergillas do well in moist lime-free soil, rich in organic matter. They are at home by a riverbank or pond, and prefer dappled light.

Propagate by collecting and sowing the seeds in an earthenware pan, filled with a mixture of peat and leaf mould in humid conditions. Those who are patient enough to wait two years may get good results. Alternatively, layer or, in summer, take cuttings with a heel from firm wood and place in gentle heat.

Fragaria

Strawberry, *Rosaceae*

A genus of about 12 species, most from Europe.

F. vesca (zone 6), wild strawberry, grows wild in

many countries and has given rise to many cultivars of alpine strawberry. The plant takes the form of compact clumps 8–12 in (20–30 cm) in diameter and 6–8 in (15–20 cm) in height. The commercial strawberry is of more complex parentage.

Cultivars. The perpetual-fruiting varieties, 'Aromel', 'Gento', 'Trellisa' and 'Sans Rivale' produce a first crop from early to mid summer, and a second from late summer to mid autumn, sometimes as late as the first frosts. Summer-fruiting varieties, like 'Belrusi', 'Cambridge', 'Cambridge Vigour', 'Grandee', 'Gorella', 'Tamella' and 'Royal Sovereign' produce a single, but large crop in early summer.

Cultivation. The strawberry needs a sunny situation and soil that is moist but not too damp, fairly light and well manured. It takes a lot of nourishment from the soil, so there should be a gap of 7 to 10 years before replanting it in the same place, and before doing so add fertilizer to the soil.

Plant 16–20 in (40–50 cm) apart, level with the soil surface, taking care not to cover the tops of the plants. Planting can be done by inserting the plants in a stretch of plastic perforated with holes at regular intervals in order to keep the soil moist and weed free. Otherwise use a layer of straw around the plants before flowering takes place. Leave 15 in (38 cm) between the plants and 30 in (76 cm) between the rows. Fertilize between the time of flowering and gathering the crop. This should be applied every ten days, as a liquid feed. In autumn, spread seaweed compost or manure, and dig it into the soil the following spring.

Each plant can produce 2 lb (1 kg) of fruit. To hasten ripening by two or three weeks, cover part of the crop with a polythene (plastic) tunnel in spring. Pick the fruits as and when they ripen, retaining the stalk. Burn any spoilt fruit in order to avoid diseases.

The strawberry plant propagates itself by means of runners or stolons. However, strawberry beds should be renewed every three years. In spring, keep a healthy and vigorous row for propagation; remove all the flowers, and allow to grow without fruiting. Separate the newly formed plants in early autumn and plant immediately.

They may be attacked by birds, slugs and snails, aphids, red spider mites, and eelworms, and they may also suffer from viruses, grey mould, and mildew.

Fraxinus

Ash, *Oleaceae*

A genus containing over 60 species of deciduous trees, from north-temperate regions which reach a height of up to 100 ft (30 m). They have an upright habit, with a rounded or spreading crown. They have brown or black velvety buds and pinnate leaves. The flowering ash has showy flowers but in other species they are rather inconspicuous and appear before the leaves. Male, female, and hermaphrodite plants are found. The fruits are winged, and grouped in clusters.

F. americana (zone 6), white ash, from East USA is a good specimen tree and grows up to 35 ft (10.6 m).

F. excelsior (zone 6), common ash in UK but European ash in USA, from Europe is easily recognized, and much grown for its foliage and the quality of its wood.

F. ornus (zone 7), flowering or manna ash, from southern Europe and Asia reaches a maximum of 23–26 ft (7–8 m) in height. It has been much planted for its white inflorescences that appear on the ends of the twigs in early summer. Outside the flowering season it is difficult to distinguish it from the common ash, except by the slightly fewer leaflets and its brighter buds.

The common (European in USA) ash can be grown as a specimen tree or in avenues. It is only suitable for large gardens.

Cultivation. Plant in a deep, fertile loam; they are adaptable to various soils. Plant in autumn or spring. When young, the ash is tolerant of shade.

Propagate by means of seeds in spring, after these have been stratified.

Susceptible to mildew and the ash bark beetle.

Freesia

Iridaceae

These plants with corms are natives of southern Africa, and are naturalized in parts of the Mediterranean. There are about 20 species, and numerous garden hybrids of mixed parentage. The corm produces a single flowering stem, which carries from 2–10 tubular, highly scented flowers, arranged horizontally, variable in colour. The hybrids have large, brilliantly coloured flowers.

Freesia cultivar

Cultivation. Corms should be planted in a sheltered situation in rich, well-drained soil. Plant in spring after allowing the corms to pass the winter in a cool, dry place, at around 50°F (10°C). Otherwise, they are better grown in pots or in a greenhouse. It does well in mild climates.

Freesias are propagated from seeds and flower within a year. Sow as soon as ripe in pots containing a light sandy compost, in a cold frame facing the sun. Otherwise multiply by separating the corms.

Fritillaria

Fritillary, *Liliaceae*

There are about 100 species of fritillary, which are found in various parts of the Northern Hemisphere. The bulb is egg-shaped or round, from $\frac{3}{8}$–$3\frac{1}{2}$ in (1–9 cm) in diameter. In spring this produces straight or spear-shaped leaves, alternate, opposite, or whorled. The flowering stem carries bell-shaped flowers, which vary in number and colour.

F. acmopetala (zone 6), from Asia Minor, reaches 16–20 in (40–50 cm) in height. It carries solitary flowers with green petals, marked reddish-brown. The narrow leaves are blue-green. Hardy in well-drained soil, it benefits from dryness in summer. It does well in rock gardens.

F. imperialis (zone 5), crown imperial, also from Asia Minor, is up to 3–4 ft (90 cm–1.2 m) tall. It has three to five pendent orange or red flowers with brown or yellow centres, carried in a whorl and surmounted by a tuft of leaves, in mid spring. 'Lutea', a yellow form is just as beautiful. This species is hardy, and prefers rather dry soil in summer.

F. involucrata (zone 5), originates in southern France, and reaches 1 ft (30 cm) in height. This hardy fritillary produces solitary green flowers marked with purplish-brown, and alternate glaucous linear leaves.

F. meleagris (zone 5), snake's head fritillary, originates in Europe and grows in moist meadows. It measures 1 ft (30 cm) in height, and produces solitary purple or pinkish flowers chequered with white. A white form 'Alba' also exists. It is very hardy, requires damp soil and will self-seed when happy.

F. pontica (zone 5), from Turkey, reaches 8–14 in (20–35 cm) in height, and has solitary light green flowers, often marbled with brown, and glaucous leaves. Plant in well-drained soil that is dry in summer.

F. pyrenaica (zone 5), from the Pyrenees, measures 1 ft (30 cm) in height, and produces solitary, brown to purplish flowers, chequered with a lighter colour, yellower inside. It is hardy in well-drained soil.

Cultivation. This varies according to the species, but generally speaking, fritillaries do well in a well-drained, fertile soil in a sunny position. More delicate species can be grown in a cold frame or in an alpine house. Carefully plant the

Fritillaria imperialis

bulbs at a depth of 4–6 in (10–15 cm) from early to late autumn. Do not disturb them unless the bulbs become congested. Remove dead stems in summer.

Propagate by means of fresh seed, sown as soon as ripe, in a frame in mid to late summer, and then over winter at a temperature of 41°F (5°C). When the plantlets come up in spring, prick out and pot on. Finally transplant into their permanent sites in the garden at least one year later. Alternatively, a quicker method of increase is to separate the bulb offsets when the bulbs are being lifted every two or three years to ease congestion. Mulching is advised.

Fuchsia cultivar

Fuchsia

Onagraceae

Most of the 100 species or so originate in Central and South America, but a few come from New Zealand. Few are entirely hardy in a northern temperate climate.

F. magellanica (zone 8), from southern Chile and Argentina, forms small bushes $3\frac{1}{2}$–5 ft (1–1.5 m) tall covered in small, somewhat bell-shaped flowers of various shades of red and purple from midsummer till the first frosts. The plants generally die down in winter, to send out new shoots the following spring. Var. *molinae* has pale pink flowers.

F. procumbens (zone 9), is a New Zealand species, hardy in mild climates. It is a creeping plant with summer flowers that are unusual rather than attractive; its calyx tube is yellowish, its sepals are purple and green, but it is without petals. Small, pinkish oval fruits follow in autumn. It will be killed if the temperature drops below 23°F (−5°C).

From among the multitude of hybrids bred from crossing many species since the 19th century, the following are worth mentioning: 'Lady Thumb' semi double with small simple carmine red and white flowers; 'Riccartonii' is almost hardy with shorter and broader flowers than *F. magellanica*; 'Alice Hoffman' is dwarf with pink and cream flowers; 'Isabel Ryan', red veined with white, or the dwarf 'Bashful' with double corolla, white flushed with red.

Cultivation. Whether grown in containers or in the garden, these plants tolerate all types of soil, even limy as long as it is sufficiently rich and moist. They flower in shady places, but do so more abundantly in a sunny position. In colder climates, the tender species can be grown in a greenhouse and planted outdoors in summer.

They are easily propagated at the beginning of summer by means of cuttings inserted in equal parts of peat and sand. Rooting takes ten days.

Especially in the case of the hybrids, it is advisable to treat regularly against white fly, red spider mites, mealy bugs, and mildew. Regular spraying with insecticides and fungicide will help to control these. A sudden change of temperature can cause the leaves to turn yellow and fall but a return to a steady regime will prevent this from happening again.

Gaillardia

Blanket flower, *Compositae*

This genus is represented by some 30 species of hardy perennial and annual herbaceous plants from northern temperate zones and S. America. *G. aristata* (zone 6), native to western USA, is a herbaceous perennial 20–28 in (50–70 cm) high, with a spread of 16–20 in (40–50 cm). The spear-shaped greyish-green foliage is covered with large flowers from mid summer to mid autumn. These are daisy-like and brightly coloured, with a yellow corolla and reddish brown centre.

Hybrids with an annual species are even more colourful, although short-lived. They include 'Burgundy', which is wine-red; 'Goblin', yellow and red, and only 10 in (25 cm) high; and 'Mandarin', orange-flame and red.

They are suitable for borders.

Cultivation. Gaillardia does well in a light and well-drained soil. It benefits from a sunny position, and tolerates shade. Plant in spring, 16–20 in (40–50 cm) apart.

Stake if necessary; remove faded flowers to stimulate further flowering. In autumn cut back the stems to ground level.

Propagate by means of seeds in spring, placed under a cold frame, or *in situ*. Alternatively propagate by cuttings taken in late summer and wintered under glass.

Galanthus

Snowdrop, *Amaryllidaceae*

Small bulbous plants from Europe and the Middle East, some 12 species in all, distinguished from their relatives, the snowflakes (*Leucojum* species) by the internal floral segments, which are shorter, single, and marked with a green streak.

G. elwesii (zone 5), giant snowdrop, from Asia Minor is similar to but larger than the next species.

G. nivalis (zone 5), common snowdrop, from Europe, has snow-white flowers, with three green crescent-shaped streaks, and blooms in mid and late winter. It has given rise to several garden varieties, some with double flowers; all are hardy.

G. reginae-olgae (*G. nivalis* subsp. *reginae-olgae*) (zone 6), flowers in autumn to spring before its leaves appear.

Snowdrops can be grown with other early-flowering bulbous plants.

Cultivation. Plant the bulbs in good garden soil in a sunny or half-shaded position, to a depth of 4 in (10 cm), in early autumn. *G. elwesii*, however, enjoys a warm sunny position.

Propagate by dividing the clumps as soon as the foliage has died down and replant immediately.

Alternatively, sow seed as soon as it is ripe, either in the open or in a cold frame; it should germinate in the spring.

Galega

Leguminosae

A genus consisting of six species of hardy perennials, mostly from Europe and Asia, with very rapid growth. They have dense racemes of flowers in summer.

G. officinalis (zone 6), goat's rue, from Europe and the Middle East, is $3\frac{1}{2}$–5 ft (1–1.5 m) tall. This species has light green, pinnate leaves, and 2 in (5 cm) long spikes of flowers in early and mid summer. Cultivars include 'Alba', white; 'Bicolour', white and blue; 'Lady Wilson', mauve and cream.

G. orientalis (zone 7), from the Caucasus, reaches a height of 32 in (80 cm). Its leaves are oblong, and the stems hairy. The flowers are a bluish-mauve. It may become invasive.

Cultivation. Plant in well-drained, even stony soil, in full sun, 32 in (80 cm) apart.

If necessary, the plants may be supported by pea sticks. Fertilize well. Cut back faded flowers to ground level in summer to stimulate a second flowering.

Propagate by means of division of roots in mid autumn, replanting the pieces where they are to flower, or by seed sown in a nursery bed in mid spring, planting out in summer to flower the following year.

Galtonia

Liliaceae

This genus consists of three bulbous species that originate in the mountains of southern Africa. In spring, the pear-shaped bulb produces long, straight leaves. The flowering spike carries 10–20 white or green bell-shaped flowers.

G. candicans (*Hyacinthus candicans*) (zone 7–8), summer hyacinth, cape hyacinth, measures 28 in–4 ft (70 cm–1.2 m) in height. White, pendent, bell-shaped flowers appear between early summer and mid autumn, depending on climate and date of planting. The leaves are grey green.

This bulb mixes well with the blue flowers of agapanthus in a mixed border.

Cultivation. Plant the bulbs in spring to a depth equal to three times their height, in a well-drained soil and a sunny position.

Propagate by means of seeds or division of bulbs. Slugs may prey on the foliage.

Gardenia

Rubiaceae

This is a large genus of about 200 species of evergreen trees and shrubs native to the tropical and subtropical regions of Africa and Asia. Most have scented flowers with thick, white or cream petals, and they must be grown as pot plants in all but warm climates.

G. jasminoides (*G. florida*) (zone 10+), Cape jasmine, common gardenia, comes from southern China. As a pot plant it forms a small bushy shrub with attractive, glossy, dark green leaves often in whorls of three. The white flowers produced from summer to winter, are about 3 in (7.5 cm) across and in cultivation, the form with double flowers is the one most usually grown, although in the wild the flowers are single with five petals. Its fragrant flowers are used for buttonholes and for scenting tea.

Cultivation. Avoiding the direct midday sun, these plants like plenty of light and a warm humid atmosphere. Keep the compost (soil) moist with soft (lime-free) water during the growing season in an ambient temperature of not less than 60°F (16°C). Repot every two or three years with a moisture-retaining compost (potting soil). Propagate by taking stem cuttings in spring or summer, using bottom heat.

Garrya

Silk-tassel bush, *Garryaceae*

A genus consisting of some 13 species of hardy and tender evergreen shrubs originating in North America and the West Indies.

G. elliptica (zone 7), from western North America is fairly hardy. It reaches 8½–10 ft (2.5–3 m) in height and is of very compact habit. The grey-green oval leaves are leathery and have a wavy edge. Long grey catkins 6–8 in (15–20 cm) are produced in late winter and early spring. The female plants, once fertilized, produce groups of small black fruit. It is better to choose male plants, which are thicker and flower more densely. This shrub may be used as a hedge, or as a specimen in mild localities.

Cultivation. Plant in spring, in well-drained soil, and in a sunny position that is protected against cold winds. *G. elliptica* is tolerant of shade, sea-mist, and pollution. Protect young shrubs from the cold during their first year.

Propagate either by seeds or cuttings. In the latter case, semi-hardwood cuttings 4 in (10 cm)

Garrya elliptica

long are taken in the summer and should be placed in a sandy loam under a frame. Re-pot the following spring, and plant out in its growing site the following year.

Gaultheria

Ericaceae

A genus consisting of about 150 species of evergreen shrubs originating in Australia, New Zealand, North and South America, and Asia. The flowers are small but abundant, and like small Chinese lanterns. They are followed by fruits in fleshy capsules.

G. procumbens (zone 5), checkerberry, partridge berry or creeping wintergreen, originates in North America, and reaches a height of about 6 in (15 cm) with a spread of 3 ft (90 cm). Its shiny, dark green alternate leaves turn reddish in winter. The summer flowers are cream or pink in small racemes, and the autumn fruits are small red berries.

G. shallon (zone 6), originates in western North America, and may reach 6 ft (1.8 m). This thick and bushy shrub spreads by underground stems to form dense clumps. It has evergreen leaves and pinkish-white flowers in early summer followed by dark purple fruits.

G. trichophylla (zone 4), is a native of the Himalayas, 6 in (15 cm) in height, with a spread of 1 ft (30 cm). It produces solitary pink flowers followed by blue fruits. This species is suitable for town gardens, and provides excellent groundcover.

Cultivation. Plant in a damp and in a lightly shaded place. Normally, no pruning is necessary; however, *G. shallon* can be cut back in mid or late spring if it becomes too straggly.

Propagate by seed or by division of rooted offsets in autumn, planting immediately in a good peaty soil, or by taking cuttings from side shoots in late summer, placed in a mixture of peat and sand.

Gaura

Onagraceae

A little-known genus of 21 North American plants of which only one species is frequently cultivated.

G. lindheimeri (zone 7), measures 4 ft (1.2 m) in height, with a spread of 3 ft (90 cm). This short-lived perennial is unusual in the abundance of its pinkish-white flowers in spikes from late spring to mid autumn.

Cultivation. Plant in spring, in any kind of well-drained soil, in a sunny position.

To propagate, sow seed in pots outdoors in early spring, and transplant into a sunny border as soon as the plants can be handled.

Gazania

Treasure flowers, *Compositae*

This genus is represented by 40 species of herbaceous perennials from tropical and southern Africa.

G. ringens (zone 9) reaches 8 in (20 cm) in height, with a spread of 1 ft (30 cm). The spatulate leaves are dark green on the upper face and silky grey on the lower face. It flowers from mid summer to early autumn in the form of orange daisy-like blooms marked with black and white at their base, which only open in sunshine. *G.ringens* is grown as a half-hardy annual in colder regions, either at the edge of a mixed border or for bedding. It is only hardy in places with mild Mediterranean-type climates.

The majority of gazanias available are hybrids between this species and several others. Their flowers are in shades of orange, red and yellow and some have all-grey foliage.

Cultivation. Plant in spring, 1 ft (30 cm) apart, in a sunny position in well-drained soil. Remove faded flowers.

Propagate by means of seeds kept in heated sheltered conditions and planted out in early summer. Alternatively, take cuttings of basal side shoots in mid to late summer and winter in sandy soil in a closed-frame.

The stems and leaves are vulnerable to botrytis, or grey mould.

Genista

Broom, *Leguminosae*

A genus containing nearly 90 species of deciduous hardy and tender shrubs, which come from Europe. The leaves are simple or trifoliate and the stems, often green are sometimes spiny. They produce, usually yellow, pea-like flowers in profusion.

G. aetnensis (zone 7), Mount Etna broom, from Sicily and Sardinia, 10–13 ft (3–4 m) or more in

Gentiana sino-ornata

height, is almost a small tree. It has pendulous branches, and grows naturally on the Sicilian volcano which gives it its common name. Its leaves are sparse but in mid and late summer, it bears golden yellow flowers along the shoots. It is fairly hardy, and does well in dry soil.

G. cinerea (zone 7), from southwest Europe, 10 ft (3 m) in height, is an elegant shrub with slender branches, with clusters of bright yellow flowers in summer.

G. hispanica (zone 8), Spanish gorse, from southwest Europe, reaches up to 2–3 ft (60–90 cm) in height. It is a branching, spreading, and spiny shrub, not hardy in colder regions. The yellow-gold flowers are carried in clusters 1 in (2.5 cm) across in late spring.

G. lydia (zone 6), from eastern Europe, reaches 24–32 in (60–80 cm) in height. This small species with a pendulous habit produces an abundance of vivid yellow flowers in clusters along the branches in late spring.

G. pilosa (zone 7), 1½ ft (45 cm) high, less bushy in habit, produces yellow flowers in late spring and early summer.

G. sagittalis (zone 6), from southern Europe, measures 4–8 in (10–20 cm) in height. This is a prostrate species with winged stems; its subspecies *delphinenis* is smaller and does well in rock gardens.

G. tinctoria (zone 5), dyer's greenweed, from most of Europe, reaches 8–32 in (20–80 cm) in height in cultivation, with a spread of 6 ft (1.8 m). Its yellow flowers are held in erect racemes. There are several varieties and cultivars: var. *alpestris* is very low-growing; 'Plena', also low, has double yellow flowers; 'Royal Gold', a small shrub to 2 ft (60 cm) high that flowers all summer.

The larger species are suitable for mixed borders, many make excellent ground cover, and are suitable for furnishing sunny slopes.

Cultivation. As brooms do not tolerate root disturbance, plant pot-grown plants in well-drained soil, in mid spring. They do not benefit from fertilizer. Choose a sunny position. Pruning is usually unnecessary, but old branches can be thinned out after flowering and pinching out the tips of young plants will encourage a more bushy habit.

Propagate by taking cuttings in early autumn. Place these in a mixture of $\frac{1}{3}$ leafmould and $\frac{2}{3}$ sand; pot on in spring, and plant out in mid autumn or late winter; Good results may also be had from seeds.

Gentiana

Gentian, *Gentianaceae*

Gentiana asclepiadea

This genus has 300 species mostly from mountainous areas in temperate regions. It does not consist only of blue-flowered low-growing alpines, but also includes taller species, like the yellow gentian (*G. lutea*), which can reach a height of 3½ ft (1 m).

G. asclepiadea (zone 5), willow-leaved gentian, from central and southern Europe and western Asia, is 3 ft (90 cm) tall. Arching stems carry paired leaves and deep blue trumpet-shaped flowers that bloom from late summer to early autumn. The white-flowered form 'Alba' is equally beautiful. It is completely hardy and does well in mixed borders or in semi-shade in open woodland situations.

G. septemfida (zone 5), from west Asia and the Caucasus, is one of the easiest alpine species. Spreading, finally erect stems carry several bell-shaped blue flowers in mid and late summer. There are several good hybrids with related species.

G. sino-ornata (zone 5), from southwest China, grows in rosette form with prostrate, narrow-leaved stems up to 8 in (20 cm) long, each of which bears a large funnel-shaped royal blue flower in early and mid autumn.

Cultivation. The willow-leaved gentian prefers moist, peaty soil preferably enriched with well-rotted manure or compost, in a lightly shaded position. It needs no attention other than mulching with leafmould each spring, and watering during dry spells. Cut the stems back to ground level in late autumn. *G. sino-ornata* must have a moist, lime-free soil; in dry areas it will be better in part shade. *G. septemfida* will accept most reasonable soils and prefers full sun.

Geranium sanguineum 'Striatum'

In general, propagate from seeds sown as soon as they are ripe in a light porous mixture of loam, sharp sand and peat in equal parts. Alternatively, take cuttings in spring, or divide fibrous-rooted kinds in spring when growth is about to start.

Geranium

Cranesbill, *Geraniaceae*

Perennial geraniums should not be confused with florists' geraniums, belonging to the genus *Pelargonium*, which are not hardy.

The genus *Geranium* comprises up to 300 species of herbaceous perennials and some annuals and biennials from many parts of the world. Most are hardy in northern temperate climates. Usually they flower abundantly, having flattened cup-shaped flowers ranging in colour from white and pink to blue and purple. Depending on size and habit, geraniums can be used in herbaceous or mixed borders, as groundcover, or in rock gardens.

G. cinereum (zone 5), from the Pyrenees, is 6–8 in (15–20 cm) high with lilac-pink flowers, having darker veins, held above greyish leaves.

G. endressii (zone 5), also from the Pyrenees, is 12–16 in (30–40 cm) tall. It carpets the ground and has pale pink flowers tinged with lilac. It flowers from early summer to autumn.

G. 'Johnson's Blue' (zone 6), probably a hybrid between *G. himalayense* and *G. pratense*, is 16–20 in (40–50 cm) high, somewhat creeping, with palmate leaves and large violet-blue flowers from early summer onwards.

G. pratense (zone 6), meadow cranesbill, from Europe and Asia, has large violet-blue flowers veined with purple, 2 in (5 cm) wide, which appear in early and mid summer.

G. sanguineum (zone 6), bloody cranesbill, from Europe, forms a carpet of foliage, 8–10 in (20–25 cm) high with deep pinkish-magenta flowers in late spring to late summer. 'Album' has white flowers, and its form 'Striatum' (var. *lancastriense*) has rose-pink flowers with darker veins.

Cultivation. These plants are easy to grow. The soil should be well-drained, and the position sunny or half-shaded. Plant in autumn or spring. They need little care other than cutting back the flowering stems once the blooms are spent, and tidying up in the autumn.

Propagate by division or by seeds sown in a cold frame in spring.

Gerbera

Compositae

A genus of 35 perennial herbaceous species from South Africa, tropical regions and the Andes. *G. jamesonii* (zone 9–10), Transvaal or Barberton daisy, is from the Transvaal and is perennial when kept under glass, but treated as half-hardy in cold regions where planted out. The flower heads that spring from the rosette of leaves resemble large daisies, yellow or orange-red in colour. They generally grow to 20–24 in (50–60 cm) in height. Gerberas make excellent cut flowers owing to their lasting properties.
Cultivar. 'Happipot' is a series of dwarf hybrid plants measuring 8–12 in (20–30 cm). It flowers early, and is usually sold in a mixture of colours with semi-double or double flowers.
Cultivation. Sow in late winter or early spring, in a greenhouse. Do not store the seeds, as these quickly lose their power to germinate. Prick out and pot on in mid spring. In warm areas plant out in late spring. Choose a warm and sheltered position. They will come into flower in the second year. In the colder areas keep in a greenhouse. Gerbera do not tolerate cold or excessive humidity. Remove faded blooms to prolong flowering. Leaf spot can be a problem.

Geum

Avens, *Rosaceae*

A genus represented by about 65 species of herbaceous plants which originate in Europe, Asia, North America and Chile.
G. chiloense (zone 6), from Chile, is a herbaceous perennial, 16–20 in (40–50 cm) in height, with a spread of 12–16 in (30–40 cm). The pinnate foliage is mid green and its flowers are scarlet. From early summer to early autumn various cultivars produce single or double flowers with large bowl-shaped corollas. 'Lady Stratheden' is double yellow and 'Mrs Bradshaw' is double scarlet.

It is a good cut flower, and is best grown in mixed or herbaceous borders.
Cultivation. Plant in early autumn or early spring, 12–16 in (30–40 cm) apart, in ordinary well-drained soil. This should preferably be enriched with peat or leaf mould. The position should be sunny or half-shaded. In windy places the plant should be supported by twiggy sticks. Cut back the stems to their base when flowering is over.

Propagate every three or four years, as the plants are not very long-lived. This can be done either by seeds or division of the clump in spring.

Gillenia

Rosaceae

A small genus that includes two species of herbaceous perennial from North America.
G. trifoliata (zone 7), Indian physic, measures 2–3½ ft (60 cm–1 m) in height, with a spread of 20–28 in (50–70 cm). This hardy perennial is bushy in habit, with stiff stems and alternate, trifoliate toothed spear-shaped leaves. The loose panicles of white flowers with red contrasting calyces bloom from early to mid summer. This species associates well with shade-loving plants, such as *Kirengeshoma palmata*, hostas, *Aruncus sylvester* etc.
Cultivation. This beautiful plant should be placed in a lightly shaded position under trees. The soil should be moist and heavy, and not limy.

Propagate by means of seeds sown in a tray in mid autumn, and keep in a cold frame all winter; germination will take place the following spring. Alternatively increase by division in the spring.

Ginkgo

Maidenhair tree, *Ginkgoaceae*

Ginkgo biloba

This genus has only one species, *G. biloba* (zone 4), a hardy deciduous tree from southern China that may reach more than 100 ft (30 m) in height. It is a 'living fossil', a type of plant that first appeared in the age of the dinosaurs. It is often included with conifers, but its method of fertilization is similar to that of ferns and it produces ovoid fruits, fleshy outside and hard inside. In China, ginkgos may live for 1000 years. The trunk and larger branches may have outgrowths known as bosses. The straight stems have several upright main branches. The fan-shaped, notched leaves resemble the leaflets of the maidenhair fern, and grow from short woody spurs. In autumn they take on magnificent golden tints.

The male tree bears small hanging catkins but the 'fruits' do not appear on the female trees until they are over about 40 years old. They resemble small plums and, once fallen, give off an unpleasant smell. Male trees are more popular for this reason and come into leaf and shed their leaves earlier than the females. Cultivars are available with fastigiate, strictly conical or weeping habits and variegated foliage.

Ginkgos make fine specimen trees for large gardens.

Cultivation. The ginkgo is an undemanding tree as far as soil is concerned. It grows very quickly in rich deep soils. Avoid damp soil.

Propagate by means of cuttings in early and mid spring, or by seed which has been stratified, sown in a cold frame in spring.

Gladiolus

Sword lily, *Iridaceae*

A genus consisting of about 180 species, mostly from southern Africa, but a few from southern Europe and the Mediterranean region. The corm produces rigid, spear-shaped leaves in spring or autumn. They bear several tubular wide-mouthed flowers of various colours. Numerous large-flowered hybrids have been produced.

G. callianthus (zone 9), from East Africa, is 2–3½ ft (60 cm–1 m) in height, and produces from 2–10 large scented flowers, white with a dark purplish red centre. These start to bloom in late summer. This species is often sold in garden centres and catalogues under the name of *Acidanthera murielae*.

G. cardinalis (zone 9), from southern Africa, grows 3½ ft (1 m) high, and produces 2–8 scarlet flowers with a white mark on the lower segments. It blooms in summer and needs a cool greenhouse except in the mildest areas.

G. communis (zone 6), from the Mediterranean region, reaches a height of 20 in–3½ ft (50 cm–1 m), and has bright pink flowers. The darker purple-red flowers of its sub-species *byzantinus* appear in early summer. This is a hardy species but must be kept dry in summer.

G. imbricatus (zone 5), reaches 12–32 in (30–80 cm) in height, which originates in the damp plains of central Europe and further east, is hardy; it produces reddish purple flowers in early summer.

G. orchidiflorus (zone 9), from the Cape, reaches 1½ ft (45 cm) in height. Its fragrant late-spring flowers are spectacular: greenish-white with a purple spot.

G. papilio (zone 6), from southern Africa, reaches 20 in–3½ ft (50 cm–1 m) and is stoloniferous. The flowers are yellow or pinkish-white, blotched with purplish red on lower lobes. It needs a sheltered position in exposed areas.

The hybrids, of which there are hundreds of cultivars in a wide range of colours, are principally grown for cut-flower arrangements. The wild species are less common but prized by gardeners for their unsophisticated charm.

Cultivation. All forms need a well-drained soil in a sunny position. Plant corms 4 in (40 cm) deep in a ground that has been double dug and enriched with well-rotted leaf mould and com-

Gladiolus callianthus

Gladiolus communis subsp. *byzantinus*

post, the previous autumn. Over-winter the corms in a cool dry frost-free place at a temperature of 50°F (10°C). Deep planting prevents the plants from leaning over too much as a result of wind or the weight of their flowers. It is a good idea to provide stakes for the tall large-flowered hybrids.

Propagate by means of division of new corms. Gladioli may suffer from attacks of dry rot, leafspot and neck rot.

Glaucidium

Paeoniaceae

A Far Eastern genus of a single species that is not common.

G. palmatum (zone 7), from Japan, is 2 ft (60 cm) tall, with a spread of 28 in (70 cm). This plant has a short tuberous rhizome and unbranched stems that carry two or three vine-like leaves to 1 ft (30 cm) across on long stalks. The upward-facing poppy-like flowers are 2¼–2¾ in (6–7 cm) across, have four lavender petals and numerous stamens. They flower in mid and late spring. There is also a white-flowered form which is rather rare.

Cultivation. It needs shelter from cold winds, a partially shaded position, and humus-rich, lime-free soil.

To propagate, sow seeds in early autumn and keep the tray in a sheltered spot. Germination will take place the following spring.

Glaucium

Horned poppy, *Papaveraceae*

A genus of about 25 species of annuals, biennials and herbaceous perennials from Europe and Asia.

G. flavum (zone 6), sea poppy, from Europe, is generally biennial, has glaucous foliage, and spectacular bright yellow flowers from early summer to early autumn, which are followed by very long fruits in cylindrical husks. It is 20 in (50 cm) tall, and suitable for sunny herbaceous borders.

Cultivation. Sow in late spring or early summer in a cold frame, and plant out in any reasonable soil in mid autumn, leaving 16 in (40 cm) between plants. Seeds can be sown *in situ* in early to mid spring, and thinned out as necessary. It does not transplant well.

Glechoma

Labiatae

A genus consisting of 10 to 12 species of low-growing perennials, native to temperate Eurasia, usually with blue-violet flowers.

G. hederacea (zone 5), ground ivy, is 4–8 in (10–20 cm) tall, and spreads over several square feet/metres. The creeping, suckering stems do not carry flowers, they are on the erect stems in whorls from early spring to early summer. The evergreen leaves are rounded with crenate edges. 'Rosea' has violet-pink flowers; 'Variegata' (zone 9) has white markings on its leaves but is less hardy and useful in a cool greenhouse.

This attractive creeping perennial is used as groundcover among shrubs, on dry stone walls, or anywhere where it cannot invade the space of prized plants. It may be used with species of *Ajuga*, *Corydalis*, or *Lamium maculatum* and *Viola odorata* all of which are vigorous enough to fend for themselves.

Cultivation. Plant in well-drained soil that keeps its moisture and is rich in humus, either in sunshine or shade, in autumn or spring.

Given the right conditions, this plant will colonize a large area very quickly but care must be taken because of its invasive character.

Propagate by transplanting rooted suckers.

Gleditsia

Honey locust, *Leguminosae*

A genus of 14 species of trees from the Northern Hemisphere and South America, some of which are cultivated as ornamentals.

G. triacanthos (zone 7), is a tall deciduous tree, from eastern USA, with a spreading crown consisting of numerous branches with strong branched spines up to 12 in (30 cm) long. The leaves are compound, their pinnate form giving a fern-like effect and light shade. They become golden in autumn. The insignificant greenish flowers grow in small clusters but the fruits, which need a sunny climate for their development, are of an impressive size more than 1 ft (30 cm) long and are curved bright-mahogany pods which last a long time on the tree.

Non-spiny varieties exist and there are cultivars of a pyramidal habit or with golden young leaves; 'Sunburst' is a good form of the latter. It is planted in parks and used to form low hedges.

Cultivation. Gleditsia is hardy and fast-growing in almost all types of soil, especially if this is rather dry. When young, it is tolerant of shade. Plant in autumn or spring. Propagate from seed.

Globularia

Globe daisy, *Globulariaceae*

This genus consists of 22 species of sub-shrubs or herbaceous plants, many native to the Mediterranean region, which form tight clumps from which small blue flowers emerge.

G. cordifolia (zone 5), is a prostrate evergreen shrub from central Europe and the Pyrenees. The small leaves are fleshy and leathery, and the flowers, in globular heads with long peduncles, are mauve-blue. Subsp. *alba* has white flowers. It blooms from late spring to mid summer.

G. nudicaulis (zone 5), from the mountains of Europe, is a herbaceous plant 4–12 in (10–30 cm) in height, upright in habit, with large blue-mauve flowers from early to late summer.

Cultivation. Globularias are well suited to sunny rock gardens in regions with a mild winter climate, where the soil is stony, warm and limy. An exception to this is *G. nudicaulis*, which prefers deep, moist soil.

Propagate by means of seeds, or by division.

Gloriosa

Liliaceae

A genus consisting of one tender, scrambling species, native to the tropical regions of Africa and India.

G. superba (G. rothschildiana) (zone 10+), has finger-shaped tubers each of which produces a stem 5–6½ ft (1.5–2 m) long. This is held upright by the tendrils at the ends of the leaves. Solitary pendulous flowers 4 in (10 cm) in diameter, variously coloured in red and yellow, are carried on long stems from the leaf-axils, the petals are often wavy and reflexed like those of a Turk's-cap lily.

It can be allowed to climb the rafters in a greenhouse.

Cultivation. Plant the rhizomes in late spring, either in a pot containing a peat-loam compost or where the plant is to grow outdoors in rich

Gloriosa superba

and well-watered soil. Flowering takes place after three months. The tuber is planted horizontally. It is important that one of its extremities should be budding.

When the leaves dry out in autumn, keep the plant in a cool and dry place 50°F (10°C), taking care not to break the tubers if they are lifted.

Propagate by means of seeds sown in pots containing a light sandy compost and plunged in bottom heat. It will be three years before the first flowers appear. Otherwise, by careful division of offsets from the tuber.

Glyceria

Manna grass, *Gramineae*

A genus of 16 grasses from all parts of the world. *G. maxima* (zone 6), reed grass, grows in all the temperate damp regions of the Northern Hemisphere. It is about 3–6 ft (90 cm–1.8 m) high and a rapid spreader. *G. maxima* 'Variegata', has leaves prettily striped with creamy yellow and is most decorative for a water garden. The type species has little ornamental value but is useful at the edges of a pond as cover for wildlife or shelter for fish. Birds feed on the seeds.

Cultivation. Propagate by removing rooted stolons, and replant immediately.

Godetia

Satin flower, *Onagraceae*

Godetias belong, strictly, to the genus *Clarkia* and are just as easily grown. Brilliantly coloured annuals, the single or double flowers of *G. grandiflora* – zone 6 – (correctly *Clarkia amoena whitneyi*) bloom from early summer to early autumn. The 'Azalea-Flower' types are about 12 in (30 cm) tall with large double flowers, and wavy edged petals. The seeds are generally sold in mixed colours.

Cultivation. Sow *in situ* in early autumn, or in early to mid spring. Thin out progressively to a distance of 8–12 in (20–30 cm) between each plant. Pinch out the growing tips of young plants to encourage branching. Godetias do well in peaty soils but not too rich as this reduces flowering. They tolerate a little shade, and should be well-watered.

The stem and base of the plant may be attacked by rot.

Godetia amoena

Gomphrena

Amaranthaceae

A genus consisting of about a hundred species of annuals, biennials and herbaceous perennials from tropical Asia, Australia and America. *G. globosa* (zone 9–10), globe amaranth, is 1 ft (30 cm) or more high. This bushy annual has tiny white, pink, or purplish-red flowers in globe-shaped heads from mid summer to early autumn.

This plant is suitable for annual or herbaceous borders and is prized for its long flowering period and use as a dried flower.

Cultivation. Sow the seed in a sheltered place in early or mid spring. Plant out in late spring in a well-drained soil, in a sunny position.

To obtain dried flowers, cut just before they reach maturity and hang in bunches in a dark, airy place.

Grevillea

Spider flower, *Proteaceae*

This genus of over 200 species is composed mainly of evergreen trees and shrubs native to Australia. Some are important sources of timber and several are grown for ornamental purposes, though few are hardy enough to be grown in areas with climates colder than those of the Mediterranean type. The flowers are formed in showy racemes, but in some species the foliage is, because of its decorative value, of equal importance.

Grevillea robusta

G. robusta (zone 10+), silky oak, comes from eastern Australia. It has finely divided, fern-like leaves when it is young and it is for this characteristic that it is usually grown as a pot plant. In the open in suitable climates it will reach nearly 100 ft (30 m) in height and the golden-yellow flowers are only formed once the tree is mature.

G. rosmarinifolia (zone 9–10), from New South Wales, is one of the hardier species of the genus. It forms a small shrub with narrow dark green leaves and short terminal clusters of red, sometimes pink or white, flowers in early summer.

G. sulphurea (*G. juniperina*) (zone 9), also from New South Wales is the hardiest grevillea and somewhat similar to the previous species, but its flowers are pale yellow.

Cultivation. *G. sulphurea* and *G. rosmarinifolia* are frost-sensitive plants, needing the protection of a sun-facing wall in areas where frost is prolonged. When planting, add peat to the soil and keep away from lime. In colder regions they make good conservatory plants. Propagate by semi-hardwood cuttings taken in summer, placed in a frame with bottom heat. *G. robusta* is even more tender but can be grown as an indoor plant. Choose a cool well-lit position where temperatures do not drop below 45°F (7°C). Water and feed well from spring to autumn, sparingly in winter. Repot every spring until too large, then discard. Easily grown from seed sown in spring or summer.

Gunnera
Gunneraceae

A genus consisting of some 40 species of herbaceous perennials, which are natives of Malaysia, Hawaii, South Africa, and South America. Few are hardy in northern temperate climates with the exception of the two species described below. Even so, these must be protected from the cold in winter.

G. magellanica (zone 8), from Argentina and Chile, is only 4 in (10 cm) tall, with a spread of 16–24 in (40–60 cm). This mat-forming plant with kidney-shaped leaves has spikes of green flowers 3¼ in (8 cm) high. These appear in mid and late summer.

G. manicata (zone 8), from Colombia and Brazil, measures 5–8 ft (1.5–2.4 m) in height; it is the largest species in the genus. Its lobed, toothed, and wrinkled rhubarb-like leaves may reach 6 ft (1.8 m) across and are carried by enormous spiny petioles. The upright greenish flowers form conical panicles 2 ft (60 cm) or more high.

Gynura aurantiaca

The flowers appear as early as mid spring but develop only slowly, sometimes not until late summer in cooler regions. The seeds rarely mature because of lack of heat. *G. manicata* is a good lakeside plant.

Cultivation. Plant in deep, moist, rich soil in a sunny or half-shaded position in spring.

During their period of vegetative growth, these plants require a great deal of water. Every two years, lightly hoe in well-rotted manure round the root stock. In winter cover the crowns with their own dead leaves or with bracken.

Propagate by means of seeds in early or mid spring. Ripe seeds should be placed in a tray that is kept constantly wet, at a temperature of 68–71°F (20–22°C). Keep the young plants under a cold frame during their first winter. Or multiply by division.

Gynura

Compositae

This genus includes about 50 species of climbers, shrubs or perennials, from tropical areas of Africa and Asia. Most bear yellow to orange dandelion-like flowers but those in cultivation are usually grown for their decorative foliage.

G. aurantiaca (zone 10+), velvet plant, is native to Java but is naturalized in many areas of the world where the climate is similar. It is a scrambling or climbing plant reaching about 10 ft (3 m) or so in height. The dark green, ovate, coarsely toothed leaves are over 6 in (15 cm) long, and the stems are velvety, covered with purple hairs. The orange-yellow flower heads are born in loose clusters in winter but the scent is unpleasant. 'Purple Passion' is a common cultivar with smaller, slightly narrower leaves, reddish-purple below.

Cultivation. A brightly lit position with some direct sun and a minimum winter temperature of not less than 50°F (10°C) is suitable for this species. Water well during the growing season. When necessary repot in spring. Propagate by taking stem cuttings.

Gypsophila

Caryophyllaceae

A genus containing some 125 species, annual or perennial, native to Europe, Asia, Australia and New Zealand.

G. elegans (zone 6), from the Caucasus and east Turkey, is an elegant annual about 12 in (30 cm) tall, with white or pink flowers on branching stems.

G. paniculata (zone 6), baby's breath, from Europe and Asia is a hardy herbaceous perennial 20 in–3½ ft (50 cm–1 m) in height, with a spread of 2–3 ft (60–90 cm). It has linear foliage and a great number of small, starry white flowers, arranged in light panicles on thin, much-branching stems during the summer. In 'Bristol Fairy' the flowers are double.

It provides good flowers for cutting and drying, and is an excellent addition to mixed and herbaceous borders. It looks well in the company of fleabanes (*Erigeron*) and phlox.

Cultivation. Plant in fertile soil, preferably limy and well-drained and in a sunny position. It should be planted in clumps in mid autumn or early spring 24–32 in (60–80 cm) apart.

Propagate by means of seeds sown in early spring and placed in a cold frame, or in the case of *G. paniculata* by taking cuttings from the base of the shoots in spring, to be planted in autumn.

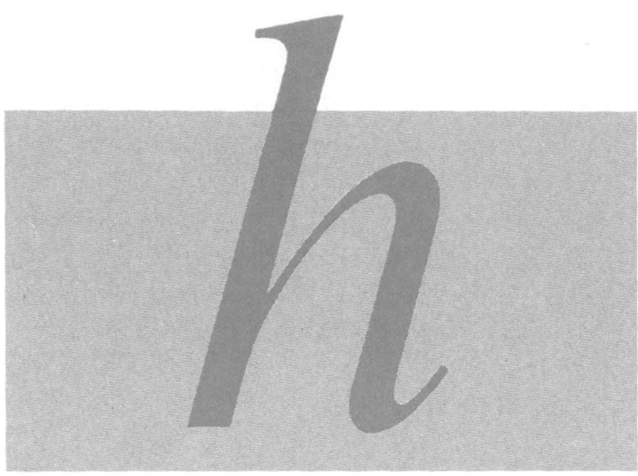

Haberlea
Gesneriaceae

A genus of one species from the Balkans, *H. rhodopensis* (zone 6) measures 8 in (20 cm) in height and spread. It is a hardy perennial with wrinkled and spear-shaped evergreen leaves. The wide-mouthed, bell-shaped flowers are lilac-blue with a yellow centre. These bloom from late spring to early summer. 'Virginalis' has white flowers.
H. rhodopensis enhances shady rock gardens. With the years, the plant forms colonies of thick, decorative cushions.
Cultivation. Plant outside in a rock garden, sheltered from the wind, in humus-rich soil, or on a dry stone wall.

Propagate by seeds in a seed-tray in spring. Divide older clumps after flowering is over, and plant out the pieces immediately.

Hacquetia
Umbelliferae

H. epipactis (zone 5), the only species of the genus, originates in alpine regions of central Europe with alkaline soil, and measures 4–10 in (10–25 cm). This is a hardy perennial with a tuberous rhizome and round palmately lobed leaves. The flowers, appearing before the leaves in spring, are grouped in yellow heads, surrounded by a yellow-green leaf-shaped involucrum.

This attractive plant does well in shady places in rock gardens or between shrubs.
Cultivation. Plant in moist, humus-rich even limy soil, in shade or half-shade. In order to thrive, this plant must remain in the same place for some years without being disturbed.

Propagate by division of older plants in spring, before growth starts, or by mature seeds.

Halesia
Snowdrop tree, *Styracaceae*

A genus consisting of five species of hardy elegant deciduous trees and shrubs, originating in North America and China. The leaves are light green, translucent and numerous. The bell-shaped flowers appear in late spring followed by winged fruits.
H. carolina (H. tetraptera) – zone 7 – from southeast USA, reaches 30 ft (9 m) in height. Its flowers are in hanging bunches, springing from the shoots of the previous year.
H. monticola (zone 7), reaches nearly 100 ft (30 m) in the wild and produces larger flowers and fruit in great profusion. Its form *rosea* produces pink flowers.
Cultivation. Plant in a deep, damp, lime-free sandy soil, near trees offering partial shade.

Propagate by seeds in a cold frame. Layering is simpler, if one is prepared to wait two years for the results.

Halimodendron
Leguminosae

This genus has a single species of deciduous shrub, a native of southeast European Russia to central Asia, which is remarkable for its tolerance of calcareous, salty soil.
H. halodendron (H. argenteum) (zone 6), salt tree, is spreading in habit, and reaches 6½ ft (2 m) in height. The beautiful pinnate leaves end in a spine. Purplish-pink flowers appear in clusters in early summer, followed by inflated pods. The cultivar 'Purpureum' has flowers of a deeper colour.
Cultivation. Propagate by means of seeds, or by grafting on to laburnum.

Hamamelis
Witch hazel, *Hamamelidaceae*

A genus consisting of five or six species of hardy deciduous shrubs, native to America, China and Japan. They have an elegant habit and leaves that turn yellow and red before falling in autumn. The witch hazels are prized for their winter flowering. The spider-shaped, usually yellow flowers are often scented, and appear on the branches in late winter before the leaves, surviving frost.

H. × *intermedia* (zone 6), a hybrid of *H. japonica* and *H. mollis* reaches 6½ ft (2 m) in height. The yellow or orange flowers have long curling petals. The oval leaves turn yellow in autumn. There are numerous cultivars: 'Carmine Red', with copper-coloured petals; 'Jelena', with orange flowers and fine autumn colours; 'Ruby Glow', with coppery red flowers and fine autumn tints.

H. japonica (zone 6), from Japan, reaches 8 ft (2.4 m) in height. The brilliant green leaves turn red in autumn. Its variety *arborea* has a much larger, more tree-like habit.

H. mollis (zone 6), from China, reaches 8 ft (2.4 m) in height. With upright branches, this shrub has downy leaves that turn yellow in autumn. The scented flowers are golden yellow, tinged with red at their base.

Cultivation. Plant in moist soil in a sunny, sheltered place, either in mid autumn or spring. Propagate by means of seeds but bear in mind germination takes two to three years; plant out one year after first repotting. Alternatively graft on seedlings of *H. virginiana* in spring, under glass.

Hebe

Shrubby veronica, *Scrophulariaceae*

A genus consisting of about 75 species, native mainly to New Zealand. These small evergreen shrubs used to be classed as *Veronica* but differ from that genus by being shrubby and also in minor botanical features. They are generally hardy but need protection from the cold in some regions.

H. × *andersonii* (zone 8), measures 32 in (80 cm) in height. The leaves are thick, fleshy, and pointed and the racemes of bluish-purple flowers bloom in summer. 'Andersonii Variegata' has leaves with a creamy-white edge. Neither are particularly hardy.

H. cupressoides (zone 7), has scale-like blue-green leaves similar in shape to those of *H. ochracea*. The pale blue flowers form in summer.

H. macrantha (zone 8), has bright green leaves, and large white flowers.

Hebe × andersonii

H. ochracea (zone 7), measures 32 in (80 cm) in height. The overlapping yellow-green leaves are similar to those of the cypress. The white flowers with four petals are grouped in racemes, and appear in summer.

H. pinguifolia (zone 6), has small oval blue green leaves and white flowers in profusion.

H. salicifolia (zone 7), has pale green pointed leaves and white or lilac flowers.

There are numerous garden hybrids, many of which are moderately hardy and suitable for seaside gardens.

Cultivation. Hebes do well in all soils, and are resistant to pollution. They can be cut back by severe frost, but growth starts again from the base.

Propagate by means of cuttings during summer inserted in a mixture of sand and leaf mould.

Hedera

Ivy, *Araliaceae*

There are some four to five species of ivy, hardy evergreen climbing shrubs, mainly from Europe and Asia.

H. canariensis (zone 7), from North Africa and the Canaries, climbs to 15–20 ft (4.5–6 m). It is a decorative species with large leaves but vulnerable to frost 14°F (−10°C). Its cultivar 'Gloire de Marengo' has leaves edged with creamy yellow and is often grown as a house plant. Useful for trellises in either a sunny or half-shaded position.

H. colchica (zone 7), from the Caucasus and Asia Minor, reaches 50 ft (15 m) in height. Fairly hardy and fast-growing, this species has large leaves, up to 10 in (25 cm) long.
H. helix (zone 4), the common European ivy, is a vigorous hardy climber with small leaves. There are numerous cultivars many with leaves variegated with cream, yellow or greyish-green.

Ivy can be grown on walls, trellises, old trees, or pillars, or as ground cover.
Cultivation. Plant out in autumn or spring in ordinary soil. Any pruning should be done in spring before growth starts.

Propagate by taking cuttings 4–6 in (10–15 cm) long. Plant out at the foot of a cold-facing wall in ordinary soil in autumn, or place in a cold frame in mid autumn in pots of peat and leaf mould, before planting out in the open, in sun or shade.

Hedychium

Ginger lily, *Zingiberaceae*

A genus consisting of 50 rhizomatous herbaceous perennials originating for the most part in the eastern Himalayas. These half-hardy plants may reach 10 ft (3 m) tall. They have handsome leaves and their fragrant flowers are tubular, variable in colour, with long protruding stamens.
H. coccineum (zone 10+), reaches a height of 6½ ft (2 m) or more and has orange-red flowers in summer to autumn and leaves 12–20 in (30–50 cm) long.
H. coronarium (zone 10+), from tropical Asia, reaches 6½ ft (2 m) or more in height, and has white flowers in spring. The leaves are 24 in (60 cm) long. A similar species is *H. flavescens*, which has yellow flowers.
H. gardnerianum (zone 9–10), reaches 3½–6½ ft (1–2 m), and has white and yellow flowers with bright red stamens in summer to autumn and leaves of 10–16 in (25–40 cm) long.
H. gardnerianum and *H. coronarium* are decorative species that flower spectacularly. They can be used to provide a tropical look to summer bedding.
Cultivation. Hedychium should be treated in the same way as cannas: it needs sunshine, frequent watering and rich soil, and a conservatory in the areas affected by long periods of frost. In the latter case, plant in good loam, well-decayed manure and sand to provide good drainage. Propagate by seed, or by division of the rhizomes.

Helenium

Sneezeweed, *Compositae*

A genus containing some 40 species of hardy herbaceous annuals and perennials originating in North America.
H. autumnale (zone 6), sneezeweed, is a hardy herbaceous perennial, reaching 32 in–5 ft (80 cm–1.5 m) in height, with a spread of 12–20 in (30–50 cm). The mid green foliage is spear-shaped, and produces daisy-like yellow flowers with a yellow domed central disc from late summer to mid autumn.
Cultivars. 'Moerheim Beauty' is bronze-red; 'Mahogany' is gold and brownish-red; 'Pumilum Magnificum' is butter-yellow and 24 in (60 cm) tall.
H. autumnale is suitable for herbaceous or mixed borders.
Cultivation. Plant in well-drained soil, in a sunny or half-shaded position, in autumn or spring. Leave a distance of 16 in (40 cm) between each plant.

Stake in windy situations and water during dry spells. Remove faded flowers to encourage further flowering.

Propagate by means of division of root stock in autumn or spring, or the species from seed.

Helianthemum

Rock rose, *Cistaceae*

A genus consisting of about 100 species of hardy or half-hardy herbaceous plants or sub-shrubs distributed in Europe, North Africa to central Asia, and North and South America. Most of those grown in gardens are hybrids and cultivars with brilliantly coloured flowers and evergreen foliage. The flowers are short-lived but numerous.
Cultivars (zone 5). These flower in late spring and early summer. 'Bengal Rose' is a robust plant with a good spread, slightly glaucous green foliage, and single bright-pink flowers; 'The Bride' has silvery foliage and large creamy white flowers; 'Ben More' is mat-forming, with glossy green foliage and brilliant pure orange flowers; 'Tigrinum Plenum' has green foliage and large double orange flowers; 'Rhodanthe

Carneum' has flesh-pink flowers and silver leaves; 'Mrs C.W. Earle' has a vigorous growth of foliage, and double red flowers.

Helianthemums grow well in rock gardens and on sunny banks.

Cultivation. Plant in a limy, gravelly soil in a sunny position. Dress with leaf mould every two or three years. A surface layer of gravel is advisable in damp climates.

The hybrids sometimes reproduce themselves by seed, but the plants that arise from this seeding rarely come true to type. Take soft-stem cuttings 2–3¼ in (5–8 cm) long, after flowering is over. These should come from side shoots, and be placed in gentle heat.

Helianthus

Sunflower, *Compositae*

A genus represented by over 50 species of hardy annuals and perennials, originating in North America.

H. annuus (zone 6), is the well-known annual which can reach 10 ft (3 m) with flowers up to 14 in (35 cm) across, one to each plant. 'Flore Pleno' has double flowers.

H. decapetalus (zone 5), is a perennial herbaceous plant reaching 3–5 ft (1–1.5 m) in height, with a spread of 20–32 in (50–80 cm). The stems have large oval leaves, which are mid green and toothed, and large brilliant yellow flowers resembling daisies appear from mid summer to early autumn. 'Loddon Gold' is a double-flowered cultivar.

Helianthus species

Sunflowers are decorative when cut, and suitable as background subjects in herbaceous and mixed borders.

Cultivation. Plant the perennial in autumn or spring, leaving 20 in (50 cm) between plants. The soil should be well drained and the position sunny. Stout stakes should be used; faded flowers can be removed, and the stems cut back to their base in autumn.

Propagate by means of seeds sown in a seedbed in spring, the plants to be put in their final positions in autumn. Alternatively increase by division in mid-autumn. Seeds of the annual should be shown *in situ* in early to mid spring.

This species is sensitive to grey rot during damp weather.

Helichrysum

Everlasting daisies, *Compositae*

A large genus consisting of more than 400 species of shrubs, annuals and herbaceous perennials. These originate in Europe, Africa and Australia, usually in hot and dry places.

H. bracteatum, strawflower, from Australia, is treated as a half hardy annual. Some 3 ft (90 cm) tall it has double straw-like flowers in shades of red, pink, orange and white. The blooms are long lasting if cut before fully open.

H. italicum (H. serotinum, H. angustifolium) (zone 7–8), curry plant, from southern Europe reaches 8–12 in (20–30 cm) in height, with a spread of 12–20 in (30–50 cm). This dense dwarf shrub has narrow, straight, silvery, evergreen leaves which when rubbed, give off a strong curry-like smell. In early and mid summer, numerous heads of pale yellow flowers appear.

H. milfordiae (H. marginatum), measures 1⅛–2 in (3–5 cm) in height and 6–12 in (15–30 cm) in spread. This attractive cushion-like perennial has small rosettes of elliptical evergreen leaves, covered with silvery hairs. It produces large, solitary, daisy-shaped flowers, carmine-red in bud, and opening white. They flower from early to mid summer.

The dwarf species do well in a sunny, dry rock garden, the taller ones in borders.

Helichrysum bracteatum

Helichrysum milfordiae

Cultivation. Plant in a sunny position in poor, dry, and well-drained soil, in spring. During the winter, the perennial species tolerate cold but not humidity. Protect by placing a sheet of glass over the clumps.

Propagate perennial and shrubby species by means of cuttings 2–3¼ in (5–8 cm) long, taken in spring and placed in sand in a cold frame. *H. bracteatum* is propagated by seed sown under glass in late winter or early spring, hardening off and finally setting out in mid to late spring.

Heliopsis
Compositae

A genus containing about a dozen annual or perennial herbaceous species from America.
H. helianthoides var. *scabra* (zone 5), native to North America, is 28 in–4 ft (70 cm–1.2 m) tall, with a spread of 16–24 in (40–60 cm). It is a bushy plant with spear-shaped leaves and yellow daisy-like flowers that appear from mid and late summer to autumn. Cultivars exist with semi- or fully-double flowers in all shades of yellow.

This hardy perennial is suitable for herbaceous and mixed borders.
Cultivation. Heliopsis will tolerate most kinds of garden soil but is best in rich, well-drained soil, and in a sunny position.

Propagate by dividing the crowns from mid autumn to mid spring, when it is not frosty.

Heliotropium
Boraginaceae

A genus consisting of about 250 species of annuals and shrubs from tropical and temperate areas of the world.
H. arborescens (H. peruvianum) – zone 10 – cherry pie or heliotrope, from Peru, measures 6 ft (1.8 m) in height. It is a perennial in greenhouse conditions, but may be planted out as an annual throughout summer. Its violet, vanilla-scented flowers appear in early summer.
Cultivar. 'Marine', 15 in (38 cm) tall has midnight blue-purple flowers.
Cultivation. Sow seed in early spring in a heated greenhouse. Prick out and pinch to encourage branching. Preferably pot on and place in progressively cooler conditions. Plant out in late spring in a sunny situation, spaced out at 12 in (30 cm) intervals.

Plants kept in a greenhouse can be propagated by taking 3¼ in (8 cm) cuttings in early autumn or late winter. Place these in a light mixture, pinch, pot on and plant out in late spring; water well in dry weather.

Helipterum Everlasting flower, *Compositae*

A genus consisting of about 60 species of annual and herbaceous perennials and shrubs from South Africa and Australia.
H. manglesii (zone 7), is a hardy annual that reaches 1–2 ft (30–60 cm) in height. It has oblong glaucous leaves and pink or white papery flower heads with yellow centres from mid summer to early autumn.
H. roseum (Acroclinium roseum) – zone 7 – from Western Australia, reaches 1–2 ft (30–60 cm) in height. The leaves are glaucous and very narrow. Its flowers are larger in overall span but with smaller centres than those of the previous species.

Both do well in annual beds and are prized as cut flowers.
Cultivation. For growing in a greenhouse, stagger the sowing from late winter to late spring. Outside sow in mid spring *in situ*, choosing a sunny, even dry, place with light soil. Thin out to a distance of 6 in (15 cm).

If the 'everlasting' flowers are to be kept, cut them before they are fully open, and hang in bunches in a dark, airy place.

Helleborus

Ranunculaceae

A genus consisting of about 20 species of herbaceous perennials, originating in Europe and Asia.

H. niger (zone 6), Christmas rose, from the mountains of Europe, reaches 8–16 in (20–40 cm) in height, with a spread of 16–20 in (40–50 cm). The foliage is dark green, leathery, and deeply lobed. From early winter to early spring, large white flowers with yellow anthers appear.

H. orientalis (zone 7), Lenten rose, from Greece and Asia Minor is about 2 ft (60 cm) tall by 1½ ft (45 cm) wide. Its leaves are evergreen and its cream flowers, fading to brown, often spotted crimson, appear in late winter to early spring. There are many cultivars with flowers in shades of crimson, purple and pink. They are ideal plants for siting under deciduous trees or shrubs or beneath shady walls. Their flowers are long lasting when cut.

Cultivation. Plant in deep humus-rich soil that is moist but well-drained, in mid autumn. The position should be partially shaded, and a distance of 16 in (40 cm) left between each plant. In cold regions, the flowers of *H. niger* should be protected by a cloche. Cut back the stems when they have stopped flowering. Avoid disturbing them once planted.

Propagate by division of the roots in spring or by seeds sown in a cold frame in summer.

Hellebores may suffer from round black spots on the leaves.

Helleborus orientalis

Helxine

Urticaceae

A single half-hardy perennial species, originating in the western Mediterranean region.

H. soleirolii (soleirolia soleirolii) – zone 9 – mind-your-own-business, mother of thousands, measures 1⅛–4 in (3–10 cm), with a spread of 20–36 in (50–90 cm). This mat-forming plant has very fine stems that take root as they grow. The evergreen leaves are small and round, and form a fresh green compact carpet. The cultivar 'Argentea' has leaves streaked with white; 'Aurea' has golden foliage.

Helxine grows well in the company of bulbs or the hardy cyclamen; in mild localities it can be invasive.

Cultivation. Plant in moist, humus-rich, and well-drained soil in a shaded or part-shaded place, in spring.

During a hard winter, the plant may lose its leaves. It will survive, however, and the clump will soon recover.

Propagate by removing sections of a clump and replanting immediately, or by cuttings.

Hemerocallis

Day lily, *Liliaceae*

A genus consisting of some 15 species of rhizomatous herbaceous perennials from central Europe to China and Japan.

H. fulva (zone 5), reaches 2–3½ ft (60 cm–1 m) in height and forms clumps of arching ribbon-like mid green leaves. The large trumpet-shaped flowers of a rusty orange-red resemble those of lilies, and bloom from early to late summer. The colour range of these very numerous cultivars now includes pink and purple, passing through red and yellow to bronze and some are scented.

Day lilies are excellent for herbaceous or mixed borders and look particularly fine when planted near water.

'Kwanso Flore Plena' is an old variety with semi-double orange-buff flowers.

Cultivation. They should be planted 16–20 in (40–50 cm) apart, in autumn or spring. The soil should be deep and humus-rich, and the position sunny or half-shaded.

They benefit from an annual dressing of well-rotted manure, in spring, and the stems should be cut back to the crown after they have

Hemerocallis cultivar

flowered. Propagate by division of the roots in autumn or spring.

Hepatica
Ranunculaceae

A genus consisting of 10 species of hardy perennials, with semi-evergreen foliage. These originate in the forests of the northern temperate zone.

H. americana (zone 6) is a native of eastern North America and measures 6 in (15 cm) high. Blue flowers carried during early spring.

H. nobilis (H. triloba) (zone 6), is a native of Europe, Asia and measures 4 in (10 cm) in height with a spread of 12–20 in (30–50 cm). This attractive plant gradually spreads and has medium-green trilobed leaves. The anemone-like flowers, $\frac{3}{8}$–$\frac{3}{4}$ in (1–2 cm) across, are blue, but there are white, pink or purple forms. They bloom from late winter to mid spring.

Cultivation. Plant in moist, slightly limy, humus-rich soil. This should be done in autumn, and the position can be sunny or partially shaded.

Propagate by means of division at the end of summer, replanting the sections immediately, or raise from seed sown in a moist soil in shade, in a nursery bed and plant out in autumn or spring.

Hepatica nobilis

Heracleum
Umbelliferae

A genus consisting of 60 species of hardy, herbaceous, biennial and perennial plants, of which a large number are too weedy for garden use.

H. mantegazzianum (zone 7), giant hogweed, from the Caucasus, measures 6½–13 ft (2–4 m) in height, with a spread of 2½–5 ft (80 cm–1.5 m). It is a spectacular species with deeply incised leaves that reach 3½ ft (1 m) in length. The strong stems are ridged and spotted with purple, emerging from the clump of leaves in mid and late summer, carrying white flowers in huge cartwheel-like heads, which may be more than 3½ ft (1 m) in diameter.

This dramatic biennial is only suitable for large wild gardens or along the edges of ponds. Its sap can cause a skin rash, especially in sunlight.

Cultivation. Plant in rich, deep and moist soil, in a sunny or half-shaded position, from mid autumn to early spring.

Cut back the stems after they have flowered and before they start seeding, for this plant is capable of invading an entire garden by this means.

Propagate by sowing fresh seeds in autumn, in the place where the plant is to grow. Germination takes place the following spring. Remove unwanted plants when they are young, as the plant has a long tap-root, which is very difficult to extract, especially with older specimens.

Hesperis

Rocket, *Cruciferae*

A genus consisting of about 30 herbaceous biennials and perennials from Europe and Asia. *H. matronalis* (zone 5), sweet rocket or dame's violet, from Europe, is about 32 in (80 cm) tall. It is a short-lived perennial but can be grown as an annual. This species has branching stems of pink, mauve or white flowers that bloom in early summer and are fragrant in the evenings. Seed is usually available in a mixture of white, mauve, and purple-red, but may also be obtained in separate colours.

Cultivation. Sow seed in open ground in mid spring. Plant out to a distance of 1 ft (30 cm) between plants in late spring early summer.

Propagate the double form by division or cuttings.

Heuchera

Alumroot, *Saxifragaceae*

A genus represented by about 50 herbaceous perennials native to Mexico and North America. *H. sanguinea* (zone 6), coral bells, measures 18 in (45 cm) in height and has a spread of 1 ft (30 cm). Hardy in most regions, its evergreen leaves are heart-shaped and decorative, often marbled with light green. Flowering lasts from early summer to early autumn. Its small, red, bell-shaped blooms, grouped in long panicles, can be used for fresh or dried arrangements.

Cultivars. *Heuchera* 'Palace Purple' has purple leaves and sprays of small white flowers; *H. cylindrica* 'Greenfinch' has spikes up to 2½ ft (75 cm) tall of olive-green flowers which are good for flower arrangers.

Heucheras and the many cultivars and hybrids can be grown in the front of herbaceous or mixed borders, along a path as an edging, or as ground cover.

Cultivation. Plant in light, well-drained soil in a sunny or partially shaded position in autumn or spring, leaving 1 ft (30 cm) between plants.

It is advisable to top-dress with well-rotted manure in spring. Cut the flower stems to their base after flowering, and every three or four years in the spring lift the plants that are becoming woody and divide before replanting.

The species can be propagated by means of seeds sown in a cold frame in spring, to be planted out in autumn. Otherwise divide in autumn.

Hibiscus

Rose mallow, *Malvaceae*

A large genus comprising 200 decorative shrubs of elegant habit, both deciduous and evergreen. The flowers have five large and brilliantly coloured petals often with a coloured spot at the base and the stamens merge to form a column. The flowers are short-lived, but many are produced continuously for some months. Many species originate in tropical countries, and are grown as indoor or greenhouse plants but the one described may be grown outside.

H. syriacus is good for small gardens, for hedges, or in containers.

H. syriacus (zone 7), originates in eastern Asia, and may reach 10 ft (3 m) in height. This species is an attractive long-flowering shrub – from mid summer to the first frosts. It has oval deciduous leaves, toothed and generally trilobed. Many cultivars were bred in France during the first half of the 19th century.

Cultivars. Today there is a wide choice of colours. Single flowers: 'Hamabo', with large bluish white flowers with crimson eye; 'Blue Bird', large blue flowers with a dark heart. Semi-double flowers: 'Jeanne d'Arc', white; 'Elegantissimus', violet-pink. Fully double flowers: 'Duc de Brabant', dark red.

Cultivation. Hibiscus requires a sunny position, and rich, sandy, moist soil. It should be planted in autumn or spring.

As the flowers are borne on the current season's wood prune in early spring. Young plants should be protected from frost.

Propagate from cuttings taken in autumn from the mature wood of the current season's growth.

Hieracium

Hawkweed, *Compositae*

A genus consisting of more than 150 perennial species, mostly originating from temperate regions. They are not often grown in gardens, as they are usually invasive. Their flowers are similar in construction to those of a dandelion. *H. aurantiacum* (zone 6), fox and cubs or orange hawkweed, from Europe, measures 8–12 in (20–

30 cm) in height, with a spread of more than 3½ ft (1 m). This creeping plant has underground and aerial stolons, bearing rosettes of leaves covered with greyish hairs. The decorative red-orange flowers bloom early to late summer.

It can be invasive, so it is advisable to set aside a place for it in the middle of flagstones or on a dry stone wall, at a distance from less robust species. It is suitable for growing with grasses in a meadow garden.

H. villosum (zone 5), from central Europe, is 6–12 in (15–30 cm) tall with a spread of 1 ft (30 cm). Evergreen rosettes of whitish-grey leaves with long soft hairs are topped by yellow flowers from mid summer to early autumn. It requires well-drained soil. One feature of this plant is that it is very tolerant of being trampled.

Cultivation. *H. aurantiacum* requires a neutral or peaty soil that is moist and rich, either in a sunny or partially shady place. *H. villosum* prefers well-drained limy soil, and a sunny position.

Propagate by division, or by seed in spring.

Hippeastrum cultivar

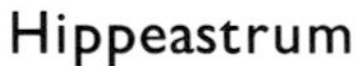

Hippeastrum

Amaryllidaceae

This genus includes about 75 bulbous plants which are native to tropical Central and South America. People frequently use the common name 'amaryllis' for these bulbs, but this causes considerable confusion with a distinct hardier genus, *Amaryllis*, from South Africa. Most of the plants grown are hybrids of complex parentage derived from several different species; as well as the named cultivars, many unnamed seedlings are sold by colour. These are popular house plants grown for their large showy flowers formed in winter and spring.

H. × *ackermannii* (zone 10+), is the scientific name given to the hybrids which are usually seen in cultivation. These have a large bulb with several dark green strap-shaped leaves, each nearly 2 ft (60 cm) long, often appearing after the flowers. A stout flowering stem, taller than the leaves, bears two to four or more very large trumpet-shaped flowers which are in a range of shades of white, red, pink or orange and sometimes striped.

Cultivation. Unless forced, hippeastrums will normally flower in the spring. They enjoy a well-lit position with some direct sun and with temperatures of 65°F (18.5°C) and above. Commence watering and feeding in the spring when growth starts, and allow the plants to rest when the foliage begins to die down in early autumn. Plant each bulb into a compost (potting soil), half-burying it in a pot that is only slightly larger than the bulb. Repot every three to five years and propagate by separating and replanting the offsets.

Hippophae

Elaeagnaceae

A genus of three species of deciduous trees and shrubs from Europe and Asia.

H. rhamnoides (zone 5–6), sea buckthorn, is a shrubby deciduous tree that does not exceed 10 ft (3 m) in height, of spreading habit and thorny branches. The narrow silvery leaves resemble those of the white willow (*Salix alba*). The clustered flowers are insignificant, but the profuse edible yellow-orange berries, which cover the branches of female plants, persist all winter, attracting birds. A nearby male plant is needed for the production of berries. It is found among the scree by mountain streams, and along the European Atlantic coasts.

It can be used to make hedges, to stabilise earth on slopes and in seaside gardens.

Cultivation. This shrub is hardy and undemanding of soil type. It is advisable to plant specimens of both sexes to encourage the formation of fruit. It does well in a sunny or partially shaded position, and tolerates sea-mists and salty ground. Plant in autumn or spring. For hedging purposes, leave a distance of 5–6½ ft (1.5–2 m) between plants.

It may benefit from summer pruning. Propagate by means of seeds, or separation of suckers.

Holboellia

Lardizabalaceae

This genus consists of five species of climbing shrubs, which originate in the Himalayas and China, with leathery evergreen leaves, and flowers that differ according to the sex of the plant. The female plants produce cylindrical edible red or purple fruits.

H. coriacea (zone 8), from western China, grows to 26 ft (8 m) in height, and is a superb climber whose bunches of female flowers are greenish-white while those of the male are purplish. They bloom in mid and late spring.

H. latifolia (zone 8), from the Himalayas has greenish-white scented male flowers and purple female flowers, followed by purple edible fruit.

Cultivation. These fast-growing climbers do well in light non-limy fertile soil in a sheltered position. They are hardy in frost-free climates.

Propagation is by seed, layers or soft-wood cuttings.

Hosta

Plantain lily, *Liliaceae*

A genus represented by about 40 species of herbaceous perennials, originating in China, Japan and Korea.

H. fortunei (zone 5), measures 24–32 in (60–80 cm) in height with a spread of 16–20 in (40–50 cm). This species has decorative green leaves, grey green below with deeply indented veins and a heart-shaped base. The lilac, trumpet-shaped flowers appear in early and mid summer on tall spikes.

H. sieboldiana (zone 5), has broad leaves, sometimes up to 1 ft (30 cm) wide, with a distinct point and blue-green in colour. Its flowers, held on rather short stems are white, delicately flushed lilac.

Hosta sieboldiana

Hostas form clumps of beautiful foliage, usually broad in outline, a perfect contrast for sword-like foliage or the fronds of ferns.

A large number of cultivars, many with variegated leaves are available as well as several other species which are equally good garden plants.

Cultivation. Plant in spring or autumn 16 in (40 cm) apart. The amount of sunshine and shelter does not matter greatly, as long as the soil is moist, well-drained, and enriched with leaf-mould or garden compost.

Keep watered during dry weather; remove faded flowering spikes and add well-rotted manure in spring.

Propagate by means of division of clumps, in winter or spring. The foliage may be eaten by slugs.

Hottonia

Water violet, *Primulaceae*

This genus contains two aquatic species native to Eurasia and North America that are useful as oxygenators for shallow pools and aquaria.

H. palustris (zone 7), featherfoil, from Eurasia, has much divided leaves from which stems rise up to 1 ft (30 cm) above the surface of the water, carrying in spring and early summer, whorls of scented lilac flowers. In autumn, winter buds are formed which sink to the bottom mud – the

remainder of the plant disappears. These start into growth when the water warms to continue the annual growth and flowering cycle.
Cultivation. Hottonias like shallow water in sun or partial shade and will tolerate brief periods of drought, during which the leaves form a rosette attached to the mud.

Propagate from seeds sown in the spring or by dividing the rooting stems at the same time.

Houttuynia
Saururaceae

A genus of one species from Japan and China, which grows in moist places near water, both shaded and sunny.
H. cordata (zone 6), is 12–20 in (30–50 cm) tall, with heart-shaped, dark green leaves that smell of oranges when rubbed. The small white flowers resemble those of the dogwood, and have a peppery smell. In the right conditions it is a good spreader.

The overall effect of this plant is attractive; its heart-shaped leaves contrast well with the linear foliage of *Iris eusata* which likes the same conditions.
Cultivars. A form with double cone-like flowers, called 'Flore Pleno', makes more impact; and 'Chamaeleon' with leaves variegated with cream and red makes a superb foliage effect.
Cultivation. This plant grows well in a moist loam, even shallow water. To propagate the species sow seed; otherwise divide or remove suckers from the parent plant in mid spring or late spring, and insert in damp soil.

Hoya
Asclepiadaceae

A genus of nearly 100 species of evergreen twining or sprawling shrubs which are native to the islands of the Pacific and southeast Asia. The plants have opposite fleshy leaves and hanging clusters of unusual flowers with five waxy petals. Most species are suitable for house or greenhouse decoration, in all but tropical climates, as climbers with support or in hanging baskets.
H. bella (zone 10+), miniature wax plant, is found in India where it grows as an epiphyte on larger woody plants. The pendulous stems bear oval leaves and the clusters of flowers appear in summer. Each flower is nearly ½ in (13 mm) across with white petals and a red centre.
H. carnosa (zone 10+), wax plant, is found in many parts of the Pacific from southern China to northern Australia. It is a vigorous climber reaching over 20 ft (6 m) with leaves to 3 in (7.5 cm) long. The fragrant flowers, each over ½ in (13 mm) across, have white petals with a pink centre, turning to pink as they age. They are borne in large clusters from spring to summer. This species will tolerate slightly less tropical conditions, but it does need a minimum temperature of about 55°F (13°C). 'Variegata' is similar but the leaves have a creamy white margin.
H. coronaria (zone 10+), from Java, is similar but has larger leaves and larger yellowish-white flowers with red spots in the centre.
Cultivation. These plants need a position that is well lit with some direct sun and an ambient temperature of 55°F (13°C) or above in winter. The trailing *H. bella* prefers higher temperatures and less light. During the growing season feed regularly and water well, allowing the surface of the compost to dry out between waterings. Hoyas prefer not to be disturbed when in bud or in flower, also avoid any sudden changes in

Hoya carnosa 'Variegata'

temperature while they are in flower, allowing the dead flowers to fall. Repot in spring only if necessary.

Propagate in the spring using stem cuttings from mature shoots.

Humulus

Hop, *Cannabidaceae*

A genus consisting of two species of perennial herbaceous climbers from north temperate regions.

H. japonicus (zone 7), Japanese hop, can grow to more than 23 ft (7 m). This species is usually grown as an annual and forms a thick curtain of large, deeply incised leaves.

H. lupulus (zone 7), common hop, is the species whose fruit is used for brewing. Its vine-like leaves have fewer lobes than the previous species. Its golden-leaved form 'Aureus' is more ornamental than the normal form.

Both hops will quickly decorate a trellis, a pergola or a dead tree.

Cultivation. These climbers should be grown in fertile soil in a sunny position. Growth is very rapid, and can be made even more so if the soil is enriched with leaf mould or well-rotted manure.

Propagate by seeds, sown *in situ* either in early autumn in a mild climate, or elsewhere in early or mid spring; alternatively by division.

Hutchinsia

Cruciferae

This genus has only one species, a perennial which originates in the higher reaches of the Alps and Pyrenees of Europe.

H. alpina (zone 4), Chamois cress, is 2–4 in (5–10 cm) in height, with a spread of 12–20 in (30–50 cm). It is an evergreen cushion-forming plant with tufts of glossy deeply cut leaves. The flowering stems carry white blooms $\frac{3}{16}$–$\frac{5}{16}$ in (5–8 mm) in diameter, which appear from late spring to early summer.

It is a good rock garden plant and associates well with alpine androsaces, drabas and primulas. It can also be grown in troughs.

Cultivation. Grow in a shady limestone scree, in order to protect it from the strongest rays of the sun.

Propagate by seeds in a tray in late winter, in a cold frame, or by division at the same time.

Hyacinthus

Hyacinth, *Liliaceae*

A genus of three or four bulbous plants from the Mediterranean region.

H. orientalis (zone 4), native to the eastern Mediterranean, is prized for its fragrant spikes of flowers, 4–8 in (10–20 cm) tall. The flowering period, early to mid spring, can be extended by means of forcing techniques. The wild form has been considerably improved by Dutch breeders, and the range of colours is now very wide.

Cultivars. 'Pink Pearl', dark pink; 'Anna Marie', light pink, late flowering; 'Delft Blue', strong blue, late flowering; 'Jan Bos', red, early flowering; 'Ostara', deep blue-violet; 'L'Innocence', white; 'City of Haarlem', yellow.

For an early display of colour there is no better plant for a formal bedding scheme with the additional attraction of its fragrance.

The bluebell belongs to the genus *Hyacinthoides*.

Cultivation. When flowering is over, it is usual to discard the bulbs that have been planted in the open, in pots, or window boxes. They do not flower so well the following year – the bulbs have a tendency to weaken, the flowering spikes become smaller, and the flowers more thinly spread. However, there is no reason why they should not be replanted in the less formal parts of the garden.

Hyacinths said to be 'forced' can be grown in a glass containing water. For this to be successful, specially prepared bulbs should be purchased, like 'Anne Marie', 'Jan Bos', and 'Delft Blue'. The containers should then be placed in a cool, dark place, between 48–55°F (9–13°C) for eight weeks, and then for three weeks in a dark, warm place 64–68°F (18–20°C). During the latter period, the shoot grows longer, and as soon as the flower buds appear among the leaves, the hyacinths should be brought in to the light.

The species can be propagated by seeds in a cold frame. Prick out the young plants and place in a nursery bed or tray the second year. Flowering takes place three to six years after sowing. Propagation by division of bulbs is not easy, and best left to professionals.

Bulbs can sometimes be affected by certain rotting fungi, one of which causes the disease known as yellows. Bulbs so affected should be destroyed.

Hydrangea

Hydrangeaceae

This genus includes 23 species of shrubs and climbing plants, both deciduous and evergreen, natives of China and Japan, Himalayas and America. There is a large number of cultivars and hybrids. Most species produce flowers in corymbs, those at the centre being fertile, while those round the edge are large and sterile. Many cultivars have all-sterile flowers.

H. arborescens (zone 7), from eastern USA, reaches over 6½ ft (2 m) in height. The oval leaves are bright green. The large creamy white flattened corymbs, 6 in (15 cm) in diameter, appear in mid and late summer.

H. aspera (zone 7), from China, has wide hairy leaves, and purplish pink flowers in early and mid summer.

H. serratifolia (H. integerrima) (zone 8), from Chile, is a climbing species with evergreen leaves, with creamy white flowers in late summer.

H. involucrata (zone 9), from Japan, has slightly thorny branches, and wide rough leaves that are paler on the underside. Blue or pink fertile flowers surrounded by white sterile flowers appear in late summer to early autumn.

H. macrophylla (zone 7), from Japan, reaches a height of 5 ft (1.5 m). The rounded leaves are bright green, and the flowers pink or blue. Since the last century, many cultivars have been bred from this species. The flower colour is governed by aluminium in the soil.

Cultivars. The Hortensias or mop-headed hydrangeas have globular heads of all-sterile flowers: 'Altona' red, sometimes turning blue; 'Ami Pasquier', dark red to purple; 'Deutschland', which has attractive foliage in autumn, and deep pink flowers; 'Générale Vicomtesse de Vibraye' bright pink or blue; 'Goliath', with large dark pink flowers; 'La France', with large pink to blue heads; 'Madame E. Mouillère', with white flowers and large separate petals.

Lacecaps have a flattened inflorescence with fertile and sterile flowers: 'Blue Wave', very vigorous and profusely flowering, with blue flowers; 'Mariesii', with pink or blue flowers; 'White Wave', with white flowers.

H. paniculata (zone 7), from Japan and China, has elongated panicles resembling those of the white lilac in late summer, which turn pinkish in autumn.

H. petiolaris (zone 7), is a climbing species from Japan, with small dark green leaves. A large number of white flowers appear in early and mid summer. When planted at the foot of a north-facing wall, it will grip and climb up.

H. quercifolia (zone 7), from southeast USA, has smooth five- to seven-lobed leaves and yellowish-white flowers in midsummer.

H. sargentiana (zone 7), from China, has hairy branches, and dense corymbs of lilac-pink flowers in mid and late summer.

Cultivation. Plant in humus-rich soil, sheltered from cold winds. Hydrangeas do well in a damp oceanic climate. In a limy soil it suffers from chlorosis, the leaves turning yellow.

The flower colour of *H. macrophylla* is affected by altering the pH of the soil. Acidifying the soil by adding aluminium sulphate to water, will obtain bluish flowers can be obtained; for pink, add powdered chalk. Pinch young shoots to cause branching. Cut *H. macrophylla* down to within 2 in (5 cm) of the ground every three of four years.

These plants may be attacked by eelworms, scale insects, red spider mites, powdery mildew, and viruses.

Propagate by taking cuttings of half-ripened leafy twigs 4–6 in (10–15 cm) long, placed in a mixture of sand and peat with a little bottom heat; *H. quercifolia* and *H. sargentiana* are best layered.

Hypericum

St John's wort, *Guttiferae*

A genus of over 350 species of shrub, both deciduous and evergreen, and herbaceous perennials.

H. calycinum (zone 6), rose of Sharon, Aaron's beard is 12–18 in (30–45 cm) tall and wide spreading. Its leaves, soft green in spring and copper-coloured in winter, are sometimes destroyed by frost, but new shoots appear the following season. Large yellow flowers with many stamens appear in summer. Excellent ground cover but may become invasive.

H. × inodorum (H. elatum) (zone 6), reaches a height of 5 ft (1.5 m). Its foliage is aromatic and the small, yellow flowers are followed by attractive red fruit. It is fairly hardy.

H. × moseranum (zone 7), 20 in (50 cm) in height has flowers 2 in (5 cm) across, with very beautiful yellow anthers that appear in summer and

autumn. 'Tricolor' has leaves edged with pink and white and prefers shaded positions.
H. patulum (zone 6), from southwest China, reaches a height of about 3½ ft (1 m). The branches are reddish and supple, and the leaves partially evergreen. The golden yellow flowers are formed throughout the summer.
Cultivars. *H.* 'Hidcote' (zone 6), is an evergreen shrub, up to 5 ft (1.5 m) tall with profuse golden-yellow flowers in midsummer to autumn.
H. 'Rowallane' (zone 8), reaches 6½ ft (2 m) in height, has fine yellow-gold flowers from spring to autumn, but is only moderately hardy. It needs a partially shaded position.
H. polyphyllum (zone 6), from Turkey, is a small sub-shrub with bluish-green leaves and golden flowers, 2 in (5 cm) across, from midsummer to autumn. It is suitable for rock gardens.
Cultivation. Plant in well-drained soil, in a sunny position. *H. calycinum* does equally well in shade, and can be pruned to within 2 in (5 cm) of the ground to form compact clumps.

Propagation is easy for all species; by seed for the species, or by cuttings taken in midsummer and placed in a mixture of sand and peat, by rooted runners or, in the case of *H. calycinum*, by simple division of the clumps using a spade.

Hypoestes
Acanthaceae

This genus of about 40 species from tropical Africa and Asia includes evergreen shrubs and herbaceous perennials. Several are cultivated for their ornamental foliage for house or greenhouse decoration. The tubular flowers are two-lipped and often formed in terminal spikes.
H. aristata (zone 10+), from South Africa, is a bushy herbaceous plant or sub-shrub over 3 ft (90 cm) tall. The green leaves are ovate, and up to 3 in (7.5 cm) long. It has showy, deep pink to purple flowers each up to 1 in (2.5 cm), formed on long spikes, and flowers from late winter to spring.
H. phyllostachya (often incorrectly known as *H. sanguinolenta*) (zone 10+), freckle face or polka dot plant, comes from Madagascar. It is a bushy herbaceous plant or sub-shrub, 2 ft (60 cm) or more tall. The unusual showy leaves are ovate, to 2 in (5 cm) or more long, and dark green, covered with irregular pink spots. Insignificant lavender-coloured flowers.

Hypericum calycinum

Cultivation. Frost-tender plants, they require a minimum temperature of 50°F (10°C) and bright light. Water frequently in the growing season but less in winter. Cut back straggly plants and propagate by cuttings in spring and summer. *H. phyllostachya* can be treated as an annual, being propagated from seed.

Hyssopus
Labiatae

A genus of five hardy shrubby species, native to Europe and Asia.
H. officinalis, hyssop, from southern Europe, reaches 16–24 in (40–60 cm) in height, with a spread of 16 in (40 cm). The aromatic leaves are linear and spear-shaped. The tubular flowers in terminal racemes, are usually blue, but sometimes white or pink. They bloom from mid summer to early autumn.

This plant has almost evergreen foliage, and makes a decorative edging. Young leaves can be eaten raw in salads, used for soups and stuffings, or for infusions when dried.
Cultivation. Plant in garden soil, in a sunny or partially shaded position, in autumn or spring.

Propagate by means of seeds in early spring, in a tray in a cold frame, or outside in mid spring. Basal cuttings can be taken in spring.

Ilex

Holly, *Aquifoliaceae*

A genus consisting of about 400 species of shrubs and trees, many from the Northern Hemisphere, with deciduous or evergreen foliage. Their fleshy fruit is red, orange or black. There are many hybrids and cultivars but as many are dioecious, berries are only formed on female plants if there is a male plant nearby.
I. × *altaclerensis* (zone 6), a hybrid of *I. aquifolium* and *I. perado*, 25 ft (7.5 m) tall and 10 ft (3 m) wide, has given rise to numerous cultivars: 'Hodginsii' is a male form with large leaves, which resists pollution; 'Balearica' a thornless female form, profusely fruiting; 'Camelliifolia', pyramidal in habit, with usually spineless leaves, is female; 'Golden King' is actually a female with green, almost spineless leaves, edged with gold; 'Lawsoniana' has leaves with a central gold splash.
I. aquifolium (zone 6), common holly, 25 ft (7.5 m) high and 15 ft (4.5 m) wide, produces a large quantity of fruit on the female plant if there is a male nearby. It can be used to form hedges that are both decorative and impenetrable. It has given rise to numerous cultivars, many slower growing and smaller. With green foliage: 'Angustifolia' with small narrow leaves, 'Ferox', hedgehog holly, with spines on leaf surface. Cultivars with variegated foliage: 'Argentea Marginata', 'Argentea Pendula', 'Ferox Argentea', 'Golden Queen', 'J.C. Van Tol', 'Silver Queen'.
I. cornuta (zone 6), horned holly, from China, is a slow-growing shrub, up to 8 ft (2.5 m) tall and broad, with curiously rectangular leaves.
I. crenata (zone 6), from Japan, is less than 10 ft (3 m) tall, very bushy, and has given rise to several cultivars: 'Convexa' has small leaves, convex above and 'Mariesii' is very dwarf and of stiff habit with tiny round leaves, barely ½ in (13 mm) long.
I. opaca (zone 6), American holly, grows slowly in a pyramid shape up to 50 ft (15 m). An evergreen, it shows white flowers in spring and berries range in colour from yellow through to red.
Cultivation. Holly grows in any kind of soil, both in sun and shade. However, when planting, it is important to obtain specimens with a good rootball, or better still, container-grown. For fruiting to occur plant a male holly in the middle of a group of female ones. For hedging, plant 15–30 in (40–75 cm) apart, in early autumn or late spring, watering well in dry conditions; trim in mid-summer.

Seeds should first be stratified before sowing in the open, preferably in a vermin-proof nursery bed. They should remain there for two years before being lined (planted) out for another two years before planting out in their final positions. Otherwise, take cuttings of mature wood of the current season's growth in summer. Insert in a mixture of sand and peat, covered with a frame; re-pot two years later.

Illicium

Anise tree, *Illiciaceae*

This genus consists of about 40 species of evergreen trees and shrubs that are native to the southern USA and Asia. They have aromatic star-shaped fruits and some are used for pharmaceutical purposes.
I. anisatum (zone 8), Chinese or Japanese anise, is native to China and Japan. It reaches 10–13 ft (3–4 m) in cultivation, and has glossy deep green leaves. It has greenish yellow flowers in spring.
I. floridanum (zone 8), purple anise, is a native of southern USA that reaches 5–6½ ft (1.5–2 m) in height, and is noted for its glossy, bottle-green foliage, and its pendent flowers. These are maroon-purple, and bloom in late spring and early summer.
I. henryi (zone 8), from western China, measures 5–6½ ft (1.5–2 m) in height, and has brilliant pink fragrant flowers.
Cultivation. Illiciums do well in a mild frost-free climate. Plant in a peaty soil in a sunny position. Propagate by layering or by cuttings.

Impatiens walleriana cultivar

Impatiens

Balsam, *Balsaminaceae*

A genus that contains about 850 species of annuals or herbaceous perennials, hardy or tender, from many parts of the world. All are vigorous and profusely flowering and have seed capsules which burst open when ripe, thus scattering the seeds.

I. balfourii (zone 10), from the Himalayas, reaches 24 in (60 cm) and forms fine clumps, with bright pink and yellow flowers marked with white. Strictly a perennial, it is usually treated as a half-hardy annual.

I. balsamina (zone 10), touch-me-not or rose balsam, from India and China, measures 2 ft (60 cm) in height with an upright habit and few branches. It is a tender annual and produces flowers that are white, pink, or red in colour from early summer to mid autumn. Double-flowered cultivars, usually shorter, are available.

I. glandulifera (zone 7), from India, may reach more than 6½ ft (2 m) in height growing in rich moist soil. The pinkish-purple flowers appear in racemes from late summer to mid autumn. It is an annual that self-seeds and best kept to the wilder parts of the garden.

I. walleriana (zone 10), busy lizzie, from east Africa, may reach 2 ft (60 cm) in height. It often has dark foliage, and forms compact rounded clumps. It is a tender perennial used for summer bedding in semi-shade, or for home and greenhouse decoration.

Cultivation. Sow in late winter and early spring in clean leaf mould, widely spaced, in a heated greenhouse. Prick out in mid spring, and reduce heat progressively. Plant out in late spring and in early summer, 12 in (30 cm) apart. They can also be sown outside in spring.

I. walleriana can be propagated by cuttings taken in spring from plants kept inside over the winter. All balsams prefer damp humus-rich, non-limy soil. They do not like dry conditions.

Incarvillea

Bignoniaceae

A genus of around 12 species of perennial plants with fleshy roots resembling dahlia tubers; from the Himalayas and eastern Asia.

I. delavayi (zone 8), from west China, is sold as a bulbous plant. Its large pinnate leaves form a clump with the flowering stem reaching 16–28 in (40–70 cm) in height. Bright rose-red, trumpet-shaped flowers, marked with orange and brown in the throat, appear in early summer.

These plants may be grown at the front of sunny herbaceous borders.

Cultivation. Plant the roots in spring in rich soil, 20 in (50 cm) apart in a sunny position. The soil should be well-drained, and the plant protected during winter with a layer of dry leaves.

Propagate by seeds sown in a cold frame in mid spring; plants will take two or three years to reach flowering size. Division is possible in the autumn.

Indigofera

Indigo, *Leguminosae*

A large genus of about 700 species of herbaceous plants and deciduous and evergreen shrubs, that originate in tropical and subtropical areas. Indigo is extracted from the stems and flowers of *Indigofera tinctoria.* Some species survive in colder climates and have attractive pea-like flowers during the summer.

I. heterantha (I. gerardiana) (zone 8), from the northwest Himalayas, reaches 5 ft (1.5 m) in height and may reach 10 ft (3 m) when grown against a wall. The elegant, deciduous pinnate foliage is similar to that of a vetch. The flowers are pink-purple.

I. potaninii (zone 8), from China, reaches 6½–10 ft (2–3 m) in height. Its foliage is darker than that of *I. heterantha*, and the flowers significantly more profuse.

Cultivation. Plant in light, dry, well-drained soil. Pruning is only necessary to tidy up damage caused by a hard winter.

These shrubs are propagated by means of semi-hardwood cuttings placed in a slightly heated frame, or by seeds; prick out the young plants in pots as soon as possible, and leave to overwinter under glass until the spring.

Inula

Compositae

A genus of nearly 100 species, mostly perennials that originate from Europe, Asia and Africa.

I. magnifica (zone 5–6), from the Caucasus, may reach 6½ ft (2 m) in height and spread. The stems are lightly covered with hairs and mottled with purple. The leaves are rough stalked and elliptical, dark green in colour, and may reach 3½ ft (1 m) in length. The flowers in wide-spreading corymbs measure 4¾ in (12 cm). The centre of the flower is orange, and the ray florets are yellow-gold. It flowers from mid to late summer.

This tall plant is for the back of large herbaceous borders, but smaller species are more suitable for a rock garden or for gaps left in crazy paving (flagstones).

Cultivation. *Inula magnifica* tolerates dryness and needs a sunny position. All types of garden soil suit it, but the best results are to be had from moist, rich soil. Topdress with well-rotted manure every two or three years.

Propagate by means of seeds in spring, or by division after it has flowered.

Ipomoea

Morning glory, *Convolvulaceae*

There are some 500 species in this genus of herbs and shrubs, which come from tropical and warm temperate regions. They are generally climbers with large, funnel-shaped flowers and stems that gain a hold by twining.

I. purpurea (zone 10+), morning glory, from tropical America is an annual climber growing very rapidly to more than 10 ft (3 m) in height. The funnel-shaped blue-purple flowers formed in the leaf axils, appear from midsummer to early autumn.

Ipomoea tricolor

I. tricolor (zone 6), from tropical America, is a perennial climber which, in gardens, is treated as a half-hardy annual. It climbs to about 8 ft (2.5 m) and has large purplish-blue flowers with a whitish throat. There are several beautiful cultivars, for example: 'Flying Saucers' has blue flowers, striped white; 'Wedding Bells' has rosy lavender flowers. This species also blooms from mid summer to early autumn.

Cultivation. Soak the seeds for 24 hours before sowing, to facilitate sprouting. Sow in early or mid spring in pots of peat under glass. Plant out in late spring 12 in (30 cm) apart, or sow in early summer where the plants are to grow, in a warm and sunny site. If necessary, guide the young shoots towards their support.

Remove flowers as and when they fade, in order to prolong the flowering season. In colder areas they are best grown in a greenhouse.

Iresine

Bloodleaf, *Amaranthaceae*

This genus includes about 80 species of mainly herbaceous perennial plants from tropical and temperate regions, especially from South America and Australia. The flowers are small and insignificant but the cultivated species have

brightly coloured, opposite leaves. They are useful for greenhouse or indoor decoration, in pots and hanging baskets. They are also suitable for summer-bedding schemes.
I. herbstii (zone 10+), beefsteak plant, from South America is a perennial up to about 2 ft (60 cm) high but often less if grown as an annual. The stems are red and the rounded, purplish-red leaves with paler or yellowish veins, are notched at the apex. 'Aureoreticulata' is similar but has bright green leaves with yellow or red veins.
I. lindenii (zone 10+), bloodleaf, is native to Ecuador and forms a bushy perennial about 2 ft (60 cm) high with spread of about 1½ ft (45 cm). The dark red leaves are narrowly lance-shaped, 2–4 in (5–10 cm) long.
Cultivation. These frost-tender plants need a minimum temperature 50–60°F (10–16°C). They should be grown in a good loam, and bright light is necessary to retain the leaf colour. Propagate by cuttings and pinch out tips to obtain bushy plants.

Iris
Iridaceae

There are about 300 bulbous and rhizomatous species in this genus which come from the Northern Hemisphere, roughly from the Arctic Circle to North Africa. Most have beautiful flowers and many are easy to grow. Generally, their foliage is narrow and sword-like. The flowers consist of six petals, the outer three are known as falls, while the inner three are called standards. In some species, the falls have a series of coloured hairs – the beards – in the middle of their inner parts. Between the standards, and arching over the falls are three style-branches. Other species are beardless. With flowers of every conceivable colour, other than a true red, a joint flowering season of eight or nine months, and between them suitable for most positions in the garden, what better genus could there be?

The two basic groups have been divided into several sections and subsections, the chief of which are given below, with a few representatives and their varying cultural requirements.

Bulbous irises are divided into three sections:

1. **Xiphiums.** Known as Spanish iris in the USA, these are characterized by their channelled, narrow leaves and unbranched stems carrying one to three flowers.
I. latifolia (zone 5), from the Pyrénées, is 2 ft (60 cm) tall, with violet-blue flowers with golden marks on the falls. Its leaves appear in late winter and it blooms in mid summer.
I. xiphium (zone 5), Spanish iris, from the western Mediterranean region, is 20–28 in (50–70 cm) tall, with purple flowers marked yellow on the falls. They bloom in early and midsummer, and its leaves persist through the winter. From this species and others, many hybrids, known as Dutch and English irises, have been produced in a wide and varied range of colours.
Cultivation. Plant in autumn, the English iris in rich damp soil, Spanish and Dutch irises in well-drained soil in a sunny site – some protection may be necessary in cold areas for the latter two. Propagate from bulbils after the foliage has died down.

2. **Reticulatas.** These have small bulbs with netted tunics and, in late winter, a single flower to each stem. Their leaves are tubular and usually appear with the flowers.
I. danfordiae (zone 4–5), from Turkey, is 4 in (10 cm) tall and has bright yellow flowers spotted with green.
I. histrioides (zone 4–5), from Turkey, is 5 in (12 cm) tall with gentian-blue flowers, the falls spotted with yellow and white.
I. reticulata (zone 4–5), from Turkey, the Caucasus and Iran, is 6 in (15 cm) tall, with light blue to purple flowers, the falls marked in bright orange.
Cultivation. Plant in autumn in a well-drained soil – they like limy soils – in a sunny rock garden. When flowering is over feed with a general fertilizer to help the bulbs build up for the next season's flowers. If the bulbs become overcrowded they can be lifted when the foliage has turned yellow, divided and replanted.

3. **Junos.** These are distinguished by the bulbs having fleshy roots and often grey-green leaves whose bases are folded around the stem. The flowers, which arise from the leaf axils, have considerably reduced standards.
I. bucharica (zone 6), from central Asia, is 12–16 in (30–40 cm) tall with cream to yellow flowers marked with gold. It blooms in mid and late spring and is the easiest to grow of this section.

Bearded iris

Cultivation. Coming from arid regions they need well-drained sunny pockets in the rock garden, or they can be grown in deep pots in an alpine house. Propagate by division when the foliage had died down, ensuring that the fleshy roots do not dry out.

Rhizomatous irises can also be divided into categories:

1. Bearded. These have a fan of broad leaves and large surface-creeping rhizomes (underground stems).
I. germanica (zone 4–5), flag iris, probably originated in the Mediterranean region. Between 2–3 ft (60–90 cm) tall, it has a fan of more or less evergreen leaves and, in early summer, large purple flowers with a yellow beard on the falls. It has been largely superseded by numerous hybrids of mixed ancestry with a great range of colours and heights: tall, 28 in (70 cm) and over; intermediate, 10–28 in (25–70 cm); dwarf, 3–10 in (7.5–25 cm). The latter are best planted in rock gardens or border fronts in places without too much competition from other plants.
I. pallida (zone 6), from Italy and Yugoslavia is similar, but 3 ft (90 cm) tall. It has lavender-blue flowers with a yellow beard and good grey-green leaves, which remain attractive for a long time. Even better for foliage effect are its variegated forms: 'Argentea' with white-striped leaves and 'Aurea' with gold-striped leaves.
Cultivation. Plant the rhizomes in early or mid summer in any reasonable garden soil, but not too acid, previously prepared with some good garden compost, in sunny positions. The rhizome should just be showing and not allowed to dry out. Wind-rock can be lessened by cutting the leaves down by several inches/centimetres. Propagate by dividing the rhizomes after flowering is over, replanting only the newer growth.

2. Beardless. In addition to having beardless flowers, the rhizomes are more slender, fibrous and below the surface of the soil. There are several series, but only four will be considered here.

(a) Sibiricae. These have grassy foliage and groups of flowers on tall stems.
I. sibirica (zone 4), from central Europe and Russia, is the best known in this subsection. About 3 ft (90 cm) tall, it has blue flowers, which appear in early summer, but cultivars have been developed which extend the range of colours.
Cultivation. Plant in late autumn in good moist soil in sunny positions. Propagate by dividing the rhizomes after flowering has finished or when growth starts in mid spring, using the outer, newer growths.

(b) Spuriae grass. These are clump forming, with reed-like foliage.
I. graminea (zone 5–6), from central and southern Europe and the Caucasus, is 10 in (25 cm) tall with fragrant purple flowers, the falls veined blue on white. They appear in early summer.
I. orientalis (zone 5), from Asia Minor, is 3 ft (1.2 m) tall with cream flowers, falls marked in gold. It blooms in mid to late summer.
Cultivation. Plant in mid or late autumn in any reasonable soil in a sunny position. When the foliage has died down the rhizomes can be divided but they will take a year or two to settle before they flower again.

(c) Laevigatae. These must have moist conditions.
I. ensata (I. kaempferi) (zone 5), Japanese iris, from China and Japan, is 2 ft (60 cm) tall, with 4–8 in (10–20 cm) wide flowers, the falls streaked with yellow. Many cultivars have been produced in a broad range of colours, from blue through red-purples to pink and white. The flowers may be single or double and they appear in mid and late summer.

I. laevigata (zone 5), from China and Japan, is about 2 ft (60 cm) tall, with three 6 in (15 cm) wide, deep blue-purple flowers and deciduous grassy leaves. There are several cultivars with flowers of blue or white; they bloom in early summer to autumn.

Cultivation. Plant in spring, or mid summer to early autumn in boggy soil alongside water. The soil for *I. ensata* must be lime free; *I. laevigata* should be planted in about 4 in (10 cm) of water. Propagate by dividing the rhizomes after flowering has finished; the divisions must be replanted immediately.

(d) Californicae. The irises in this group have evergreen leaves and dainty flowers on branched wiry stems.

I. douglasiana (zone 5), from southern California to Oregon, is about 20 in (50 cm) tall with flowers of lilac-purple, lavender or whitish in summer.

I. innominata (zone 5), from California and southwest Oregon, is 8 in (20 cm) tall and in summer has yellow to lilac or bluish flowers, variously veined with lavender or deep purple.

The Pacific Coast Hybrids has been produced from crossing these species and others. Between 10–16 in (25–40 cm) tall, they have flowers in shades of blue-purple, reddish, yellow or white, variously veined.

Cultivation. Plant in late autumn in sun or part shade in lime-free soil (*I. douglasiana* will accept a little lime). Rather short-lived, these irises can be propagated from seed sown in autumn or mid spring in seed compost at a temperature of 45–50°F (7–10°C). Plant out as soon as the seedlings can be handled. They can also be propagated by dividing the rhizomes in early autumn.

3. Lophiris. Also known as Evansias, these have thin rhizomes and a conspicuous crest or cockscomb along the centre of the falls.

I. cristata (zone 5), dwarf crested iris, from eastern North America, is 6 in (15 cm) tall, with deciduous leaves. Its lilac to white or blue flowers, falls whitish with white and yellow crests, appear in mid and late spring.

I. japonica (zone 6), from China and Japan, up to 2 ft (60 cm) tall, has pale lavender flowers, spotted purple and an orange crest on the falls. The flowers bloom in mid spring.

Cultivation. Plant these species in spring or early summer in semi-shade. They do not like a limy soil. Propagate by dividing the rhizomes in early summer, after the plants have flowered.

Diseases. Bulbs can be affected by rot, and mould when they are stored. The rhizomes of bearded irises can be attacked by rhizome rot, but this can be discouraged by planting the rhizomes at the correct depth, with their upper part above the ground.

Ixia

African corn lily, *Iridaceae*

This genus, which originates in southern Africa, is represented by 45 species with corms and is not hardy. The corm is spherical and the leaves are sword-shaped. It produces spikes of 6 to 12 flowers that are variable in colour, often having a dark centre.

I. viridiflora (zone 10), is about 1 ft (30 cm) tall and has flowers of a brilliant green with a purplish-black centre which appear in late spring and summer.

The flowers grown in gardens are hybrids of this species and others, and are usually sold in mixed colours. Occasionally, named cultivars are available, like 'Panorama' whose flowers are purple outside and fuchsia-pink inside.

Cultivation. The requirements of these flowers are almost identical to those of freesias, but they prefer full sunshine. They are hardy in Mediterranean-type climates where they flower in spring. In colder climates they can be grown in pots in a greenhouse.

Ixiolirion

Lily of the Altai, *Amaryllidaceae*

This genus includes three hardy bulbous species that range from the Near East to central Asia. They have a rosette of narrow leaves and the flowers are carried in an umbel in spring to summer. The leaves usually die down at the time of flowering.

I. tataricum (zone 7), from southwest and central Asia, produces 6 to 12 blue or light violet star-shaped flowers. It is a variable species and some forms have been recognized as distinct and called *I. ledebourii* and *I. montanum*.

Ixiolirions are suitable for warm rock gardens, otherwise they are best grown in an alpine house.

Cultivation. Plant in autumn in a sunny position. Propagate by seeds, or by division of clumps.

Jacaranda
Bignoniaceae

A genus represented by about 30 species of small trees or shrubs from tropical America, with large bipinnate leaves. They reach 26–32 ft (7–8 m) in height with light, semi-evergreen foliage and a superb display of blue-violet flowers.
J. ovalifolia (J. mimosifolia) (zone 10), is native to northwest Argentina and produces blue-violet flowers in mid summer. They are carried in large terminal panicles.

In those regions where it is hardy it makes a fine specimen tree.
Cultivation. This species enjoys a peaty soil in a mild Mediterranean-type climate. Tip the crown to encourage the plant to bush out.

Propagate by means of half-ripe cuttings in summer and place in a mixture of peat and sand, under a cloche, where it is kept shaded until rooted. In colder areas this plant must be grown in a heated greenhouse.

Jasione
Campanulaceae

The genus includes 20 species of herbaceous perennial and biennial plants, native to Europe, the Mediterranean region and southwest Asia.
J. perennis (zone 4), from western Europe, reaches a height and spread of 8–16 in (20–40 cm). This hardy perennial plant forms a clump consisting of rosettes of small downy, obovate leaves. The lilac-blue flowers take the form of rounded capitula, $1\frac{1}{8}$ in (3 cm) in diameter, and appear in summer.
J. humilis (zone 4), is a carpeting perennial, from the Pyrenees, whose root produces numerous rosettes of hairy leaves. The flowerheads are profuse, blue, and $\frac{3}{4}$ in (2 cm) in diameter. It forms fine flowering clumps from mid summer to early autumn.
Cultivation. Plant in a sandy soil. Propagate these species by seeds in late autumn in a seed tray under a cold frame. These perennials can also be increased by division.

Jasminum
Jasmine, *Oleaceae*

A large genus consisting of some 450 species of deciduous and evergreen shrubs and climbers from tropical and temperate regions.
J. azoricum (zone 10), from Madeira, measures 23 ft (7 m) in height, and can be grown in a warm, completely frost-free climate. This twining climber has evergreen foliage and very fragrant white flowers that bloom from early summer to autumn.
J. beesianum (zone 7), from China, is $6\frac{1}{2}$ ft (2 m) tall, and quite hardy. This species may form an erect shrub and only climbs well in a half-shaded situation. The dark-green, simple deciduous leaves are $1\frac{1}{8}$–2 in (3–5 cm) long. The light red fragrant flowers appear in late spring, and are followed by black fruits.
J. humile (zone 7–8), from western China and the Himalayas, reaches a height of $3\frac{1}{2}$–13 ft (1–4 m), and is fairly hardy. The yellow flowers appear in mid and late summer in cooler temperate regions, and between early spring and late spring in warmer regions. The leaves are trifoliate and semi-evergreen. This species should be protected against hard northern winters.
J. mesnyi (J. primulinum) – zone 9–10 – primrose jasmine, from western China, climbs to a height of about 13 ft (4 m), but is far from hardy. Vulnerable to frost, it should be grown either in regions with very mild winters or in a greenhouse. This evergreen climber produces bright yellow often semi-double flowers from late winter to early spring in warmer regions, and a month later in colder ones.
J. nudiflorum (zone 6–7), winter jasmine, from China, climbs up to 10 ft (3 m) or more, and should be trained as it grows. It is notable for its yellow flowers that spring from dark green stems from early to late winter. In regions with a

harsh climate, plant it at the foot of a north-facing wall, but sheltered from cold winds.

J. officinale (zone 7), common or white jasmine, from Iran, India and China, grows to 33 ft (10 m), and is hardy. This is the well-known species with fragrant white flowers all summer. The plain green deciduous leaves are made up of five to seven leaflets. The cultivar 'Aureovariegatum' ('Aureum') has leaves blotched with yellow. The form *affine* has larger and more numerous flowers, whose buds are tinged with pink.

J. polyanthum (zone 10), pink or Chinese jasmine, from western China reaches 6½–13 ft (2–4 m), and grows well in warm climates. It is an evergreen or semi-evergreen climber that is vulnerable to frost and does best in a cold greenhouse. Fragrant white flowers, pink in bud, bloom in mid and late spring or earlier if the plant is grown in a greenhouse.

J. × stephanense (zone 8), 10–17 ft (3–5 m) high, is fairly hardy. Its semi-evergreen leaves, which are sometimes variegated, are single or pinnate with three to five leaflets. The fragrant pale pink flowers bloom in early and mid summer. In colder climates, it needs protection during hard winters.

All jasmines can be used to clothe pergolas, trellis or pillars.

Generally, they should be planted in a sunny, sheltered place, with the exception of *J. beesianum* and winter jasmine, both of which require some shade.

Cultivation. Ordinary well-manured soil is adequate. In the case of pot-grown plants, prune the shoots that have flowered. In the open they can be allowed to grow freely, thinning out if they become overgrown.

Propagate from semi-ripe cuttings in late summer or by layering in early autumn. It is possible to sow seed of the hardy species under a cold frame in autumn. Good results may also be obtained from layering.

Jeffersonia
Berberidaceae

This genus contains only two species, which are hardy perennials. The leaves grow from ground level on long stems and the flowers are solitary, in the form of pendent cups on wiry stems.

J. diphylla (zone 6), twin leaf, originates from northwest North America, and is 3–6 in (7.5–15 cm) tall and wide. The shield-shaped leaves are divided into two oval lobes and the white flowers appear in late spring.

J. dubia (zone 6), is a native of Manchuria, and is 6–12 in (15–30 cm) in height and spread. The foliage is glaucous, becoming dark brown in autumn. The solitary, cup-shaped, lavender-blue flowers bloom in mid and late spring.

These species can be used in a shaded rock garden along with anemones and epimediums, for example.

Cultivation. Plant in moist, humus-rich soil, but make sure it is one which does not retain water in winter.

Propagate by division in late summer, replanting the root fragments immediately; alternatively sow seeds as soon as they are ripe.

Juglans
Walnut, *Juglandaceae*

This genus of 21 species consists of deciduous, mostly tall, trees, with straight and slender trunks. The compound pinnate leaves have a varying number of leaflets. The flowers appear in spring, male and female on the same tree, the former as pendent catkins, the latter, upright. The fruit is a hard shelled nut enclosed in a thin fleshy coat.

J. nigra (zone 6), black walnut, from North America, grows to 100 ft (30 m), and is easily distinguished from the common walnut by its leaves. These are toothed, 1–2 ft (30–60 cm) long, with 11–23 leaflets. Its bark is deeply furrowed.

J. regia (zone 6), common walnut, (English walnut in USA), has long been cultivated in Europe for its fruit and there are numerous cultivars. The leaves are compound, with five to nine untoothed leaflets. Its bark remains smooth for a long time.

Walnuts make fine specimen trees for large gardens.

Cultivation. The walnut is hardy, and grows rapidly. Its buds tolerate late frosts. Although best grown in moist, deep soils, it accepts poorer ones.

These trees demand a lot of growing space and are intolerant of shade. Plant in autumn or spring, with a good rootball.

If pruning is necessary, do this when the trees are in full leaf or when totally dormant to avoid excessive bleeding.

Juncus

Rush, *Juncaceae*

A genus consisting of over 200 species of herbaceous perennials having a world-wide distribution, but few in the tropics. They have narrow leaves, insignificant flowers and grow in marshy ground or at the edge of ponds.
J. effusus (zone 5), common throughout the temperate regions, has produced two cultivars grown for their unusual appearance: 'Spiralis', with strange spirally twisted leaves, forming a dishevelled clump, and 'Vittatus', with longitudinally yellow-striped leaves.
Cultivation. Plant in wet soil or even in water, in spring. Propagate by division of clumps.

Juniperus

Juniper, *Cupressaceae*

A large genus of about 50 species of evergreen conifers, including upright and low-growing shrubs, and trees. The needle-like juvenile leaves may become scale-like with age. The female flowers become a berry-like fruit.
J. chinensis (zone 5), from Japan and China, is a medium-sized shrub or erect tree. It has scales and needles on adult plants and round black fruits with white bloom. It is one of the most frequently cultivated conifers and has given rise to a large number of garden cultivars, both upright and spreading in habit, with foliage of various colours. The cultivar 'Pfitzerana' with arching branches is a popular form, generally considered to be a hybrid of *J. chinensis* and *J. sabina.*
J. communis (zone 4–5), common juniper, from temperate zones of the Northern Hemisphere, is a small tree that can reach 33 ft (10 m) in height or it may take the form of a spreading shrub. It grows slowly and is tolerant of all types of soil, including poor and limy ones. The needles are grouped in threes and the fruit has the appearance of a bluish berry. Various cultivars exist that are upright, compact, spreading, or dwarf in habit, with leaves of various colours.
J. communis subsp. *nana (J. nana)* (zone 4–5), the dwarf juniper, has a prostrate habit, and shorter needles.
J. horizontalis (zone 5), creeping juniper, native to North America, is spreading or even creeping in habit. It grows slowly but can eventually cover a large area. The glaucous leaves turn bronze in winter. Several cultivars with good glaucous leaves are available. It does well in damp soil.
J. oxycedrus (zone 9), prickly juniper, from southern Europe, is a conical shrub or small tree, to 30 ft (9 m) in height. The branches are supple, with sharp glaucous needles; fruits are reddish and its pale wood is strongly scented. In Europe, it prefers more southerly climates.
J. sabina (zone 3–4), originates in the mountainous regions of southern Europe and into Asia. It is often creeping in habit but may reach 15 ft (4.5 m) in height. The leaves of mature specimens consist of scales with a disagreeable smell. There are several cultivars.
J. virginiana (zone 4), red cedar, originates in east and central North America; it can reach 100 ft (30 m) in height and has a conical habit. The branches carry scale-leaves, with needles dotted among them; its small fruits are bright blue. Several cultivars exist.

Spreading junipers can be used as groundcover; shapely dwarves are good for rock gardens; larger forms associate well with heather or as isolated specimens.

Cultivation. The species described are all completely hardy, and undemanding where the nature of the soil is concerned. More often than not, they tolerate a chalky soil. However, they need sunny, open positions. Plant in spring, when the new foliage is beginning to grow. Choose a plant with a good rootball, or container-grown plants.

Junipers do not object to pruning.

Propagate by sowing seeds in spring, after stratification, by taking cuttings in summer, or by layering in the case of the prostrate varieties.

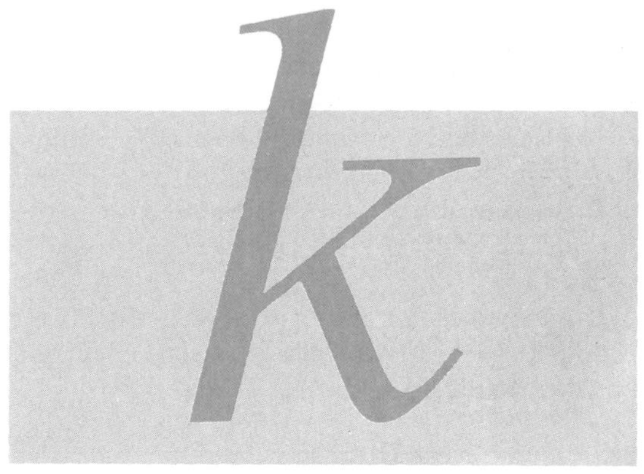

Kalanchoe

Crassulaceae

This is a genus of about 125 species of succulent plants many of which are native to Africa. They have tubular flowers with four petals and simple opposite fleshy leaves. They are usually grown as house or greenhouse plants for flower or foliage, but can be grown outdoors in warm and rather dry conditions.

K. blossfeldiana (zone 10+), flaming Katy, is from Madagascar as are all the other species described here. It is often grown as a winter-flowering pot plant, forming a small perennial with clusters of numerous bright red flowers and glossy green leaves. Cultivars are available with flowers in many colours from red to yellow or orange.

Kalanchoe blossfeldiana

K. daigremontiana (Bryophyllum daigremontianum) (zone 10+), good luck plant, devil's backbone, is an unusual plant with leaves to over 6 in (15 cm) long bearing numerous tiny plantlets around the margins. These may be detached and potted-on to produce new plants. *K. tubiflora* (*Bryophyllum tubiflorum*) also has plantlets but the leaves are cylindrical and blotched with brown.

K. tomentosa (zone 10+), panda plant, is a small, slow-growing shrub with thick, felted leaves covered in silvery hairs and marked at the edges and tips with dark brown.

K. uniflora (zone 10+), is a trailing species, useful for a hanging basket, with small rounded leaves and inflated bright pinkish-purple pendulous flowers.

Cultivation. Kalanchoes, along with other succulents, need plenty of light and temperatures of not below 50°F (10°C) during the winter. Keep well watered during the growing season. Allow the compost to dry out after flowering for five or so weeks, during their resting period. Repot with a free-draining compost (potting soil). Propagate in spring or summer by taking leaf or stem cuttings, allowing these to dry out for a day or two before inserting them into a mixture of sand and peat; where possible take offsets or in the case of *K. daigremontiana* and *K. tubiflora* remove plantlets.

Kalmia

American laurel, *Ericaceae*

A genus represented by about seven species of small but elegant shrubs, native to North America, with brilliant evergreen but poisonous foliage. The flowers are bell-shaped and grouped in terminal corymbs.

K. angustifolia (zone 4), sheep laurel, reaches at most 6½ ft (3 m) in height. The attractive deep pink flowers appear at the ends of the branches in late spring and early summer. 'Rubra' has darker red flowers.

K. latifolia (zone 4), calico bush or mountain laurel, 10 ft (3 m) in height, is a bushy shrub with leaves that are dark green above, and yellow-green on the underside. The pink corollas are deeply pleated; the flower buds, too, are decorative.

Rhododendrons, azaleas and Pieris are suitable associates.

Cultivation. Kalmias should be grown in a peaty, humus-rich soil in some shade, or in a

Kalmia latifolia

trench filled with heath mould to a depth of 16 in (40 cm).

Propagate by seed, cuttings, layers and offshoots.

Kalopanax
Araliaceae

A genus represented by a single species of deciduous tree that is hardy in temperate regions, originating in the Far East.
K. pictus (K. septemlobum, K. ricinifolius) – zone 6–7 – reaches 80–90 ft (24–27.5 m) in the wild. It has a thick trunk, and its branches bear short, stout spines. The leaves are palmate, 10–14 in (25–35 cm) in diameter, with seven triangular or oval lobes. Small white flowers in compound umbels, 16–24 in (40–60 cm) in diameter, appear in early and mid summer. In autumn they turn to beautiful shades of yellow. The leaf-lobes of the variety *maximowiczii* are more deeply divided.
Cultivation. Plant in deep soil, in a position sheltered from cold winds. Propagate by seeds.

Kerria
Rosaceae

A genus containing one small, commonly grown shrub, originating in China and Japan, with light green incised deciduous leaves. The yellow flowers appear in mid to late spring on branches grown the previous year.
K. japonica (zone 7) reaches 5–6½ ft (1.5–2 m) in height. The stems are green, and supple. 'Plenifolia' with double flowers is most frequently grown; 'Variegata' ('Picta') has white-edged leaves, but is not quite as hardy.

Kerria is hardy, but should be planted against sun-facing walls in exposed areas.
Cultivation. Plant in all types of garden soil. Prune when flowering is over to keep it under control.

Propagation is very easy, as the plant produces suckers naturally. Cuttings may also be taken from side-shoots.

Kirengeshoma
Hydrangeaceae (Saxifragaceae)

This genus contains one species of great beauty, yet rarely grown.
K. palmata (zone 7) is a native of Japan and Korea and measures 3 ft (90 cm) in height with a spread of 2 ft (60 cm). It is a hardy perennial with opposite angular palmate leaves, bright green in colour. In early autumn the yellow flowers bloom, giving a cloud-like effect in their profusion. Each one is 1⅛–1½ in (3–4 cm) long and resembles a hanging bell. Place in a prominent position in a bed, along with *Tovara virginiana* 'Painter's Palette' and *Lysimachia clethroides.*
Cultivation. Plant in a sunny position in deep, damp, non-limy soil with plenty of leaf mould. Regions with a high level of humidity in the air are most suitable for it. Where the winter temperatures are low, protect it with a layer of dead leaves.

Propagate by sowing seeds during late autumn in a tray with bottom heat. Keep them at this temperature for a month, and then place the tray in a cold frame. Germination takes place the following spring when the temperature rises.

Kniphofia
Torch lily, red-hot poker, *Liliaceae*

A genus containing some 70 species of herbaceous plants, many from southern Africa. Many hybrids (zone 7) have been raised, ranging in height from 3–4 ft (90 cm–1.2 m) or more. The leaves are ribbon-like, of a medium green, and the stems bear long spikes of yellow, orange or red tubular flowers from mid summer to mid autumn. 'Goldelse' is soft yellow and early; 'Royal Standard' is red and yellow and flowers later.

Kniphofias are suitable for both herbaceous and mixed borders.

Cultivation. Plant in spring, 20 in (50 cm) apart, in deep well-drained soil in a sunny position. Where the winters are severe cover them with leaf litter.

Cut down the stems to their base to encourage a second flowering. It is advisable to topdress with manure in spring, and do not allow young plants to dry out.

Propagate by division of roots in spring, or by seeds.

Kochia

Chenopodiaceae

This genus is sometimes included in *Bassia*. The species come from Europe and Asia and include perennial and annual herbaceous plants, and shrubs.

K. scoparia (zone 10), burning bush or summer cypress, from southern Europe to Japan, is grown for its decorative foliage. This annual plant, around 3 ft (90 cm) tall, has an egg-shaped habit, with straight, bright green leaves which turn deep red or purple in the autumn; its flowers are insignificant.

Kochia is useful for summer bedding displays with colourful annuals.

Cultivation. Plant in rich, light, well-drained soil, in a sunny position. Sow under glass in early to mid spring. Harden off the plants before planting out in the open in late spring. Alternatively, sow them *in situ* in late spring.

Koeleria

Gramineae

This genus was named after Louis Koeler, author of a work on this important family, and includes about 25 species of grass, many native to Europe.

K. Macrantha (K. gracilis) – zone 2–3 – is the only species of interest from the ornamental point of view. It is a low-growing 12 in (30 cm) plant with glaucous foliage, covered during summer with very compact silvery, green or purplish flowers which can be dried.

Cultivation. This grass does well in dry ground, and looks particularly good in the company of other grasses.

Propagation is not difficult: either by division of clumps, or by sowing seeds collected in autumn, sown in the following spring.

Koelreuteria

Golden-rain tree, *Sapindaceae*

This is a genus of three deciduous trees, which may reach 33 ft (10 m) in height. They are notable for their elegant habit, large domed crown, and the large compound pinnate leaves. The seeds are produced in inflated bladder-like capsules.

K. paniculata (zone 7), Pride of India, from China and Korea, has compound leaves with between five and nine toothed leaflets. The small yellow flowers appear in summer in long panicles, even on young trees. The fruit is decorative, and is a three angled capsule which resembles a lantern.

The golden-rain tree grows rapidly when young, more slowly as it ages. It is well suited to small gardens.

Cultivation. Plant in autumn or spring. It is quite hardy, and can be grown in all types of soil. A sunny sheltered position suits it best.

Propagate by means of seeds in spring, or by root cuttings.

Kolkwitzia

Beauty bush, *Caprifoliaceae*

A genus of a single species similar to *Abelia*.

K. amabilis (zone 7), from China, is a deciduous twiggy shrub with brown peeling bark, 10 ft (3 m) tall and 8 ft (2.5 m) wide. The oval, light-green leaves take on pleasing autumn tints. In late spring and early summer, very fine yellow-throated pink bell-shaped flowers appear in groups of four or five.

Cultivation. Plant in a warm place in any type of soil, well protected from wind in front of a wall, for instance.

Propagate by means of cuttings placed in a mixture of peat and sand. Plant out the following year.

Laburnum

Leguminosae

A genus consisting of two, hardy, deciduous trees and shrubs from southeast and central Europe, with trifoliate leaves, and racemes of numerous yellow pea-like flowers.

L. alpinum (zone 6), Scotch laburnum, from southern Europe, grows to about 20 ft (6 m). Long racemes of scented yellow flowers appear in late spring. The leaves are dark green above and blue-green on the reverse side. There are several cultivars: 'Pendulum' grows slowly and has weeping branches; 'Pyramidalis' has erect branches.

L. anagyroides (zone 6), from central and southern Europe, reaches 6½–17 ft (2–5 m) or more in height. It flowers in early summer, with shorter racemes than those of *L. alpinum*.

L. × *watereri* (zone 6), golden-chain-tree a hybrid of the two previous species, has flowers in racemes 8–12 in (20–30 cm) long. 'Vossii' is the best cultivar, having racemes 2 ft (60 cm) long.

The branches can be trained up a pergola, alternating with wistaria. Do not plant laburnums in a garden frequented by young children, as all parts of the tree, and above all the seeds, are highly poisonous.

Cultivation. Plant laburnum either from a container or bare rooted, in winter; it takes root easily.

Provide a stake for young trees during the first year. Branches may be removed if the tree becomes too large.

Propagate by mature seeds in autumn; prick out the following spring. Cultivars may be grafted on to the type species.

Lactuca

Compositae

A genus of about 100 annual, biennial and perennial herbaceous plants found in many parts of the world.

L. sativa (zone 5), garden lettuce, is an annual or biennial plant that probably originated in southern Europe. Lettuce plants measure from 6–16 in (15–40 cm).

Cultivars. Lettuces may be divided into three groups.

Butterhead or cabbage lettuce form a round or flattened close-knit heart of leaves. Crisp hearts, with wavy, crisper leaves are also part of this group; for summer harvesting, sow in succession from spring to summer. Cabbage lettuce: 'Sigmahead', 'Sigmaball', 'Suzan', 'Fortune'. Crispheart lettuce: 'Webbs Wonderful', 'Windermere', 'Lake Nyah'. Autumn cabbage lettuce are sown in summer to mature in autumn: 'Avondefiance'. Winter cabbage lettuce are sown in autumn to mature in spring: 'Valdor', 'Arctic King'; types for growing in a frame or greenhouse: 'Dandie', 'Kwiek', and the crisphearts 'Novita' and 'Marmer'.

Cos lettuce are elongated in shape. Among the suitable cultivars are: 'Little Gem', 'Density', 'Lobjoits Green Cos'. They can be gathered in spring and autumn.

Loose-leaf lettuce do not form a heart of any kind, but have foliage that grows again after it has been gathered. They can be grown all year: 'Salad Bowl' and 'Red Salad Bowl'.

Cultivation. Lettuce does not readily exhaust the soil, and can be grown in the same spot up to three years in succession. Choose a sunny position, and plant in a moist, well-manured soil, one that was well prepared the previous season.

Propagate by means of seeds sown at intervals from late winter to early autumn. From late winter to mid spring, sow in a nursery bed, or under a frame or plastic tunnel. Plant out 8–10 in (20–25 cm) apart in the row. From mid spring, sow where it is to grow spaced out to 10–12 in (25–30 cm); cover the seeds with less than half an inch (a few millimetres) of soil and tamp down. Water, and thin out the seedlings. It is important to hoe often and water copiously. The soil should not be allowed to dry out in summer; if necessary provide a mulch or cover the base of each plant with a plastic film to retain moisture. Unless growth is steady, the lettuce will tend to bolt (run to seed). Expect a yield of 30 heads per 30 ft (9 m) row. Gather when the heads begin to form and when the leaves are well formed. In the case of loose-leaf lettuce, gather the leaves as and when they are needed.

Birds can be a nuisance; slugs and snails can do a lot of damage. Among the other pests are leaf and root aphids, the larva of crane fly and cutworms. Lettuce can also suffer from mildew, botrytis and lettuce mosaic.

Lagerstroemia
Lythraceae

A genus consisting of about 50 species of deciduous often tender trees and shrubs, originating in tropical Asia and Australia.
L. indica (zone 9), crape myrtle, from China and Korea, flowers in summer in warmer regions, and in early autumn in cooler places. The flowers are profuse, and may be pink, purple, or even white. They have many wrinkled narrow petals, and grow in terminal panicles. The grey bark is smooth and decorative.

It can be pruned to form a bushy shrub reaching 10–13 ft (3–4 m) in height, or as a small tree, pruned to form a rounded shape.
Cultivation. Lagerstroemia is a warmth-loving plant, and does not do well in damp climates; a hot summer is necessary for good flowering. Consequently, it should be planted in front of a sunny wall in the cooler regions. Ordinary well-drained soil is adequate.

Propagate by means of half-ripe cuttings in spring, inserted either where the plant is to grow, or in trays, when the rooted cuttings are planted out the following year.

Lagurus
Gramineae

A genus of one species of annual grass that originates in the Mediterranean region.
L. ovatus (zone 7), hare's-tail grass, is a softly hairy plant with short flat leaves, and reaches some 16 in (40 cm) in height. It is grown for its white, downy flowers, $\frac{3}{4}$–$1\frac{1}{2}$ in (2–4 cm) long, which are used in dried flower arrangements.
Cultivation. It does well in well-drained, sunny positions, especially in sandy soil by the sea. The seeds should be sown in early autumn, and the young plants should spend the winter in a cold frame. In regions with a harsh climate, it should not be planted out until mid spring.

Lamium
Labiatae

A genus consisting of about 40 species of hardy herbaceous perennials and annuals, originating in Europe, northern Africa and western Asia.
L. maculatum (zone 5), dead nettle, is a hardy plant measuring 8–12 in (20–30 cm) in height with a spread of 20–24 in (50–60 cm). The leaves are decorative, being evergreen, with a silvery central stripe. The spikes of small, tubular, purple pink flowers appear from mid spring to early autumn. Cultivars with silvery leaves and white or pink flowers are available.

It is used in herbaceous and mixed borders and in rock gardens; it also makes excellent ground cover but can become invasive.
Cultivation. Plant in autumn or spring, 16–24 in (40–60 cm) apart. It does well both in sunny and shaded places, and is tolerant of all types of soil, even poor and dry ones. When used for ground cover, cut down the flowering stems when flowering is over, in order to keep the foliage dense.

Propagate by division of clumps in autumn or spring.

Lantana
Shrub verbena, *Verbenaceae*

A genus represented by about 150 species of tender shrubs originating in tropical America and Africa. Some species are thorny. The foliage is a soft green in colour and the brightly coloured, often bicoloured, flowers are in terminal clusters.
L. camara (zone 10), from tropical America, reaches 5–$6\frac{1}{2}$ ft (1.5–2 m) in height. It has flowers that open chrome-yellow and mature to orange and red appearing from late spring to mid autumn. Cultivars are available with a wide range of colours.
L. montevidensis (L. sellowiana) (zone 10), is pendulous in habit, and has mauve or lilac-pink flowers that bloom from mid spring to late autumn. It can be placed in a mixed border, in a rock garden, or on slopes, which it will cover by cascading down them.

Cultivation. Lantanas can only be grown in a warm frost-free climate. Otherwise they can be bedded out for the summer or grown in a greenhouse. They require frequent watering, and plenty of organic fertilizer.

Propagate by means of soft cuttings in spring. Seeds give unpredictable results because of hybridization.

Lapageria

Chilean bellflower, *Smilacaceae (Liliaceae)*

A genus of a single species of tender or semi-hardy climbing plant.

L. rosea (zone 9), from Chile, growing to 17 ft (5 m) is the national flower of Chile. It has large 2–4 in (5–10 cm) oval, evergreen leaves. During summer to autumn it produces impressive purplish-pink, pendent, bell-shaped flowers. These are followed by large, edible, yellowish-green berries.

Lapageria should be trained up a trellis in a well-sheltered spot (such as a west-facing wall). It needs warmth and partial shade, or it can be grown in a cool greenhouse.

Cultivation. Plant in light, well-drained soil. Water well in periods of drought and protect during winter.

Propagate by layering vigorous shoots in a mixture of sand and peat in spring or autumn, or sow seed in a sheltered place in spring, at a temperature of 53°–60°F (12°–16°C). It is only necessary to prune dead growth or weak shoots in early spring.

Larix

Larch, *Pinaceae*

A genus of nine hardy conifers with deciduous foliage. They are pyramidal in habit with a conical crown, and spreading branches that take on magnificent tints in autumn. The short branchlets carry fine needle-like leaves, joined in rosettes like those of the cedar of Lebanon. The flowers are globe-shaped catkins, and both sexes grow on the same plant. The cones are small, 1½ in (4 cm), with thin scales.

L. decidua (L. europaea) – zone 5 – from Europe, reaches 100 ft (30 m) in height. The needles of this conifer are extremely narrow and the cones are a reddish-violet colour when their scales are new.

L. kaempferi (L. leptolepis) – zone 5 – Japanese larch, has larger needles than the preceding species, and ovoid cones whose scales have a curved edge. This species is more frequently planted as it is more resistant to disease.

L. laricina (zone 5), American larch, grows to 80 ft (24 m) with spreading branches, fine branchlets and small cones. Young shoots are grey, male flowers grow in small clusters and female flowers are small with pale green, red-margined bracts.

Larches grow quickly, and are only suitable for large gardens.

Cultivation. Larches require a great deal of light and do best in moist soil; plant in spring. They cast a light shade, so that plants or grass which accept semi-shade can be grown beneath them. The European larch can be killed by a fungus under unfavourable conditions, for example an excessively humid climate.

Propagate by seeds, after they have been stratified.

Lathyrus

Ornamental pea, *Leguminosae*

A genus of about 150 species of hardy and tender herbaceous plants from north temperate

Lathyrus cultivar

regions, tropical East Africa and temperate South America.

L. latifolius (zone 6), everlasting pea, is a vigorous scrambling perennial up to 8 ft (2.4 m) long. It has winged stems and large rose-purple flowers during the summer months; 'White Pearl' is a beautiful white form.

L. odoratus (zone 6), sweet pea, is an annual, originally from Italy. The cultivated forms vary in height from 18 in (45 cm) to 10 ft (3 m). There are cultivars with flowers in virtually all colours except a true yellow and orange, and most are fragrant. They appear during summer and early autumn.

L. tuberosus (zone 5), tuberous or earth-nut pea, from Europe and western Asia, is a perennial with bright pink flowers in mid summer. It scrambles up to 5 ft (1.5 cm), its many shoots coming from an edible tuberous root.

The two perennial peas can be allowed to scramble through shrubs, over a bank or, with the aid of supports, up a wall. Sweet peas, supported by twiggy sticks, are generally grown for cut flowers, but they can also be used in borders, supported by tripods or pillars, or trelliswork to form a screen.

Cultivation. Any good well-drained garden soil, not too acid, is suitable for the perennial species, which should be planted in mid autumn or early spring. Sweet peas need added organic matter and copious watering when conditions are dry. Cutting their flowers for indoor use and dead heading to prevent seed formation helps to prolong their flowering season.

Propagate the perennial species by seed sown in early spring under a cold frame; pot up seedlings and plant out in autumn. Division of the roots in spring is sometimes possible. Sweet peas can be sown under glass in late winter, potted on, and planted out in a sunny position in mid spring. Soaking the seeds in water for 24 hours, or nicking the hard seed coats assists germination.

Sweet peas are subject to various rots, which lead to wilting and mildew.

Laurus
Sweet bay, *Lauraceae*

A genus of two evergreen trees or shrubs from the Mediterranean region.

Laurus nobilis (zone 7), bay laurel or sweet bay, is hardy, though its aromatic foliage can be damaged by frost. Growing up to 40 ft (12 m) tall, it prefers mild and sunny climates.

In colder regions, it can be grown against a wall, and in suitable climates can be used as hedging. It can also be grown in tubs in unheated conservatories; the tubs should be as small as practicable. It is quite amenable to pruning and can be clipped into formal shapes such as globes or cones.

Cultivation. The laurel can be planted with a good rootball or as a container-grown plant. When grown in a tub it needs regular feeding. Frost-damaged branches can be trimmed without ill-effects. To grow as a standard, allow one stem to develop by removing the side branches except those at the top. These will bush out, and the whole can be shaped.

Propagate by seeds, or by cuttings taken in summer.

Lavandula
Lavender, *Labiatae*

A genus consisting of some 20 species of mostly hardy evergreen shrubs. These have aromatic foliage, and many species originate in southern Europe.

L. angustifolia (zone 7), common or English lavender, is a sub-shrub to about 2 ft (60 cm) in height. The narrow leaves are grey-green and particularly aromatic. Small lavender-purple flowers form dense heads in summer.

Numerous cultivars are grown: 'Hidcote' has darker flowers and is more compact; 'Munstead' has bluish flowers.

L. stoechas (zone 9), French lavender, is notable for its large leaf-like purple bracts above the flower spike.

Cultivation. Lavender grows in ordinary, well-drained soil. Plant in spring. In order to form hedges, plant 10–12 in (25–39 cm) apart, and cut back each spring, nearly down to the previous year's growth, to keep the hedge bushy.

Propagate by seed or by means of half-ripe cuttings with a heel, taken in summer, placing these in a mixture of sand and peat in which the root will take easily. Plant out the following spring.

The most serious disease is shab which causes wilting of stems and shoots. They can also be affected by the cuckoo-spit insect (froghoppers in UK and leafhoppers in USA).

Lavatera trimestris

Lavatera

Tree mallow, *Malvaceae*

A genus consisting of 25 species of shrubs, annual, biennial, or perennial herbaceous plants from Europe, Asia, Australia and western North America.

L. olbia (zone 7), a native of central and southeast Europe, may reach 6½ ft (2 m) in height and spread. This is a soft-stemmed shrub, woody and many-branched at its base, and with soft, greyish, five-lobed leaves. The large 2¾–3¼ in (7–8 cm) flowers are purplish pink and open trumpet-shaped, resembling those of hibiscus. The cultivar 'Rosea' has pinker flowers than those of the type species. It flowers from early summer to mid autumn.

L. trimestris (zone 6), from the Mediterranean region, is an annual up to 4 ft (1.2 m tall). It has profuse rose-pink flowers in mid to late summer. Two good cultivars are 'Mont Blanc' with white flowers and 'Silver Cup' with silvery pink flowers.

Cultivation. *L. olbia* does not tolerate extreme cold. In cooler regions plant in a sunny position in any well-drained soil. Take particular care that it is sheltered from cold winds.

Propagate by division of root stock in spring, or in autumn in regions with a mild climate.

The annual is propagated by seeds sown in autumn in mild climates, or in spring in cooler climates.

Ledum

Ericaceae

A genus of three or four small hardy shrubs that originate in cold and humid Arctic regions.

L. groenlandicum (zone 4), Labrador tea, from North America and Greenland, is about 3½ ft (1 m) tall, with an upright habit and twisted branches. It has shiny evergreen leaves that are rust felted on the underside. Profuse white flowers in terminal umbels appear from mid spring to early summer.

L. palustre (zone 4), marsh ledum (wild rosemary in the USA), from all parts of the Arctic has smaller leaves with recurved edges, reddish underneath and white flowers.

Cultivation. These plants must have lime-free peaty soils, doing best in silica-rich soil. They should be sheltered from direct sunlight, in the shade of trees, for example.

Propagate by means of seed, cuttings, layers or division.

Lens

Lentil, *Leguminosae*

A genus of six herbaceous plants from Mediterranean and west Asia.

L. culinaris (zone 9), the lentil, is an annual that has been grown since the Stone Age. Its fragile stems are 14–16 in (35–40 cm) tall. After flowering the plants are covered with small round pods that generally contain one seed.

Cultivation. Grow lentils in a light sandy soil and a warm position. Sow the seeds in open ground in early-mid` spring, in rows 18 in (45 cm) apart and cover with a thin layer of fine soil. Hoe after the seeds have sprouted, and earth up lightly.

Gather the plants when they turn yellow, before they are completely ripe. The cut plants will finally mature in storage. Only dehusk as and when needed.

Uses. The cooked seeds are used in soups or purées, or eaten cold with dressing.

Leonotis

Labiatae

This genus includes about 15 species of herbaceous plants and sub-shrubs, mostly native to

Africa, which are not very hardy in colder climates.

L. leonurus (zone 9), lion's ear or lion's tail from South Africa, is a shrub that can be grown in milder temperate regions. Up to 6 ft (1.8 m) tall, its characteristics are lance-shaped toothed foliage, and unusual hairy, bright, red-orange flowers in whorls 2 in (5 cm) long, towards the ends of the stems. These bloom in late summer and autumn.

Cultivation. Plant in rich loamy soil, in a well-drained and sunny position or a greenhouse in the colder areas. Prune after flowering. Young plants should be cut back from time to time to encourage branching.

Propagate in spring by means of cuttings placed under a frame in a sandy soil. The young plants, pricked out in pots, should not be planted out until the following spring.

Leontopodium

Edelweiss, *Compositae*

This genus contains about 30 species of herbaceous alpine plants, one of which has become symbolic of alpine flora, and protected in the wild. However, it is widely available from nurseries.

L. alpinum (zone 4), originates in the mountains of Europe. Some 6 in (15 cm) or more in height and spread, it is a densely woolly plant with whitish foliage and white flowers. These are small, occur in groups of seven or nine per capitulum and are surrounded by woolly bracts in a star shape. They bloom in early and mid summer.

Leontopodium alpinum

Edelweiss is suitable for rock gardens.

Cultivation. Plant in very poor, gravelly, limy soil in a sunny position so that the plant remains dwarf and maintains its woolly covering. Avoid damp conditions in winter.

Propagate from seeds in late winter, sown in a sandy compost and placed in a well-aired cold frame, alternatively by division.

Lepidium

Pepper grass, *Cruciferae*

This genus includes about 150 herbaceous plants from all parts of the world.

L. sativum (zone 6), garden cress, is an annual originating in the Middle East, which has been cultivated for a very long time. The stems are 8–24 in (20–60 cm) tall, and carry indented leaves that are spicy to the taste. The roots, leaves, and seeds can all be eaten.

Cultivation. When grown in the open, the soil should be light, fairly moist and moderately manured. Sow the seed from spring to mid autumn in rows 10 in (25 cm) apart, and use as soon as ready. As cress grows quickly from seed, sowing can be staggered on a regular basis, throughout the season. Alternatively, sow 3 in (7.5 cm) deep in boxes with good drainage, containing a compost of soil and peat. Keep the compost moist, especially in dry weather.

It is liable to be attacked by flea beetles.

Leptospermum

Myrtaceae

This genus is represented by 30 species of small trees or shrubs, originating in Australia, Tasmania and New Zealand. They have evergreen foliage, and white, pink, or red flowers that bloom from late spring to late summer.

L. lanigerum (zone 9), measures 20–33 ft (6–10 m) in height. This is a vigorous tree, noted for its light foliage and white flowers that bloom in early and mid summer.

L. scoparium (zone 9), Manuka or New Zealand tea tree, reaches 5–6½ ft (1.5–2 m) in height, with aromatic leaves and it is covered with white flowers in summer. It is a vigorous species.

Cultivars. 'Album Flore Pleno', compact and bushy, with white double flowers; 'Boscawenii' has large flowers which are rose pink in bud, and white with a pink centre when they open; 'Decumbens', with a low-growing habit and long-lasting pale pink flowers; 'Keatleyi' with flowers of a fresh pink, and grey-green leaves and shoots that are tinged carmine red; 'Red Damask', later flowering with dark red, fully double blooms.

Cultivation. Plant in a light sandy soil in a sunny position, or in a partially shaded place if the climate is warm and frost free. Otherwise in very cold areas grow in a greenhouse.

Propagate by seeds in spring, in a greenhouse, or in mid summer by semi-ripe stem cuttings, under glass, with gentle heat.

Lespedeza

Bush clover, *Leguminosae*

This genus of about 40 species includes perennials, sub-shrubs and shrubs, from temperate North America, tropical east Asia and Australia.

L. thunbergii (zone 7), nakai, from China and Japan, is a semi-woody perennial that may reach a height of about 6½ ft (2 m) and more in spread. Its leaves are deciduous and, like many plants in the family, trifoliate; it comes into growth late in the season. When its arching stems are carrying many racemes of rose-purple pea-like flowers in late summer and autumn, it is an attractive sight. It is hardy, except in the coldest climates and although its stems may be cut back by frost, new growth will arise from the woody rootstock the following season.

Cultivation. Plant in spring. It will grow in ordinary well-drained soil with humus added; it needs a sunny position protected from the wind. Cut away all dead stems in spring.

Propagate from seed, or by dividing the rootstock in the spring.

Leucojum

Snowflake, *Amaryllidaceae*

A genus of bulbous plants containing 10 species, which originate in Europe, North Africa and the Middle East. The rarer species from warmer countries are grown in pots, and kept cool and dry during winter. The two species described below are quite hardy. The flowers are generally white with a green mark at the end of the six equal segments.

L. aestivum (zone 5), summer snowflake, is native to Europe, and rapidly forms dense clumps 16 in (40 cm) high. The flowering stems are the same height, and carry several flowers in late spring to early summer. It grows easily in a sunny position, either in a border, or naturalized in the wilder parts of a garden.

L. vernum (zone 5), spring snowflake, is native to Europe, and is often confused with the snowdrop, but its flowers are larger with segments of all the same length, which end in a green spot. The flowers appear in late winter and early spring. This species grows naturally under trees or on a lawn with crocuses and scillas.

Cultivation. Plant the bulbs in autumn 4 in (10 cm) apart and at an equal depth. Both species are easily grown, and do well in somewhat rich, moist clay soil. Both sun and shade suit them.

Propagate by division of clumps.

Leucothoe

Ericaceae

Most of the 40 small shrubs of this genus from America and Asia are evergreen, but some are deciduous. They are very similar to *Pieris* having bell-shaped white flowers grouped in racemes, reminiscent of those of lily-of-the-valley. They flower for a very long time.

L. fontanesiana (L. catesbaei) – zone 6 – dog-hobble, from southeast USA, 2–6 ft (60 cm–1.8 m) in height, has arching branches and makes excellent ground cover. The foliage takes on a coppery tint in winter. It flowers in late spring.

L. grayana (zone 6), from Japan, has semi-evergreen foliage that turns red in autumn and the shoots are red in winter. The white flowers appear during the summer.

Leucothoes can be planted along with other plants that prefer acid, heathy soil, such as rhododendrons, kalmias, and pieris.

Cultivation. These shrubs need acid soil, without lime, so should be planted with a mixture of peat or heath mould.

Propagate either by means of seeds, though these are very fine, or by division of clumps in autumn, or by layering. Propagation by means of cuttings in a heated greenhouse or frame.

Levisticum

Umbelliferae

L. officinale (zone 7), lovage, the only member of the genus, is a perennial, widespread in southern, central and eastern Europe. It has sturdy stems, many-branched at the top, and reaches $3\frac{1}{2}$–$6\frac{1}{2}$ ft (1–2 m) in height. The ribbed stems, like the leaves, are smooth. The latter are dark green and deeply pinnate. The yellowish flowers, carried in umbels, bloom in mid and late summer, and are followed by small oval fruits.
Cultivation. Sow where the plant is to grow, in mid or late spring in moist, well-drained soil. Only keep a single plant, which is quite sufficient for the needs of one family. Gather the seeds in autumn, when they have ripened.

Propagation by division is possible in early spring. Leave a space of 24 in (60 cm) between each plant. Plants more than four or five years old should be discarded.
Uses. The leaves add a pleasant flavour to soups and all cooked dishes.

Lewisia

Portulacaceae

A genus consisting of about 20 species from western North America. Many are quite beautiful, but may be difficult to grow, and do best in an alpine house.
L. cotyledon (zone 7), is a perennial measuring 8 in (20 cm) in height with a similar spread. The evergreen foliage is in a basal rosette. The flowers, held in panicles, are white veined with pink, and bloom from early to late summer. This species has given rise to numerous cultivars and hybrids: 'Sunset Strain' has variable but vivid flower colours; var. *heckneri* has pink flowers; 'George Henley' has red flowers.

This species is one of the most decorative rock garden plants.
Cultivation. Lewisias are difficult to grow when exposed to persistent humidity in winter and a cold greenhouse or frame might be more suitable. In a rock garden, plant in a well-drained soil in vertical fissures of rocks, facing the sun. The fleshy roots can tolerate prolonged periods of drought.

Propagate by means of seeds in late spring and early summer, in a cold frame, or by division.

Lewisia cotyledon

Leycesteria

Caprifoliaceae

A genus represented by six species of small bushy shrubs. These are much-branching and deciduous, and originate in China and the Himalayas. The small flowers in hanging racemes are white, yellow, or pink, surrounded by showy bracts. These are followed by small, fleshy berries.
L. formosa (zone 7–8), Himalayan honeysuckle, from the Himalayas and China, reaches $6\frac{1}{2}$ ft (2 m) in height and has an upright habit. The white flowers with garnet-red bracts bloom profusely from early summer to early autumn. They are followed by reddish-purple berries.
Cultivation. Plant in ordinary, moist, light, woodland soil, in a half-shaded situation. *L. formosa* can be grown in regions with a mild winter. Mulch in winter, and cut back in spring.

Propagate by seeds in spring, by half-ripe cuttings in late summer, or soft-stem cuttings in mid spring.

Liatris

Blazing star, *Compositae*

A genus represented by about 40 species of herbaceous tuberous plants, originating in North America.
L. spicata (zone 6), gayfeather, is a hardy perennial 16–32 in (40–80 cm) tall with a spread of 12–20 in (30–50 cm). It has mid-green grass-

like leaves and purple-pink flowers grouped in long bottle-brush-like heads that bloom from the top in early autumn.

It is an interesting plant for herbaceous or mixed borders, and does well as a cut flower.
Cultivation. Plant in a moist soil containing plenty of humus, and preferably enriched with peat or leaf-mould. Choose a sunny or partially shaded position. Plant in spring or autumn, 16 in (40 cm) apart. Water during dry spells and remove dead flowers to encourage further flowering. Slugs tend to eat the young shoots.

Propagate by division in spring to rejuvenate the plants, or sow seeds in early autumn.

Ligularia
Compositae

A genus represented by 180 herbaceous perennial species, originating in the temperate regions of Europe and Asia.
L. dentata (L. clivorum) (zone 6), from China is a hardy species that is 3½–5 ft (1–1.50 m) tall, with a spread of 32 in–3½ ft (80 cm–1 m). The leaves are decorative, being large and heart-shaped. Panicles of large yellow-orange flowers with a yellow central disc appear in early and mid summer.

Ligularia przewalskii

L. przewalskii (zone 6), from northern China, is even taller but has deeply divided leaves and its smaller flowers are carried on near-black stems in a dramatic spike. It blooms in summer and early autumn.

Ligularias look best as a single specimen on the edge of a stretch of water with other bold plants in the background, such as skunk cabbage (*Lysichiton americanum*) and purple loostrife (*Lythrum salicaria*).
Cultivation. Plant in autumn or spring, 3½ ft (1 m) apart, in deep, damp, fertile soil, in semi-shade. Large amounts of water are necessary in dry weather. Stake large specimens in windy places, topdress with manure in spring, and cut the stems down to the base in autumn. It is advisable to divide the clumps in spring every three or four years.

Ligustrum
Privet, *Oleaceae*

A genus consisting of about 50 species of hardy deciduous or evergreen flowering shrubs, native to Europe, Africa, Asia and Australia. Several are a familiar sight in gardens, and are grown mainly to form hedges because of their rapid growth and their ability to tolerate ruthless pruning.
L. japonicum (zone 6), from China, Japan and Korea, is fairly compact in habit, and has evergreen foliage similar to that of the camellia. The panicles of tubular white flowers appear in mid summer to early autumn, but the elongated fruit only ripen in warmer climates.
L. lucidum (zone 6), from China, has oval evergreen leaves, and produces panicles of white flowers in late summer and autumn. There are several cultivars, among them: 'Aureovariegatum' with yellow-variegated leaves, and 'Tricolor' with white-edged leaves, pinkish when young.
L. ovalifolium (zone 6), from Japan, is deciduous or semi-evergreen. It produces creamy white flowers in mid summer.

Privets can be allowed to grow naturally as single specimens or in tubs when they can be clipped to a formal shape.
Cultivation. Privets do well in all soils, even calcareous ones. They tolerate pollution, and are long-lived in tubs. They grow quickly, and for hedging purposes small ones should be planted in autumn to spring in well-prepared garden

soil, 12 in (30 cm) apart. Hedges can be trimmed at any time.

Propagate by hardwood cuttings, placed in a cold frame in a mixture of peat and sand.

Lilium

Lily, *Liliaceae*

A genus of about 100 species of bulbous plants originating in the Northern Hemisphere that are for the most part hardy. The sumptuous flowers, in the shape of turbans, cups or trumpets carried on rigid stems, are often scented. Taken as a whole, their flowering period covers late spring to early autumn. Depending on the species, their leaves are in whorls (verticils), scattered or spirally arranged on the stems. Their bulbs consist of a basal plate topped by tightly packed scales. In some species further bulbs are produced at the ends of shoots arising from the parent bulb, while in others the stem meanders underground before reaching the surface, rooting as it goes. Further bulbs are produced on the wandering stems – the species in which this happens are called stem rooting. Unlike some bulbs, the daffodil, for example, those of lilies do not have a dry enveloping tunic.

L. auratum (zone 7), golden-rayed lily, originates in Japan and in ideal conditions will reach a height of 8 ft (2.4 m). This has one of the largest flowers of all lilies, 10 in (25 cm) or more across, and they are scented. Cup-shaped, they have a golden stripe running down the centre of each white, brown-flecked segment. Bulbs should be planted in moist, but well-drained acid soil. There are several good cultivars and hybrids have been produced by crossing with other species.

L. candidum (zone 5), Madonna lily, which comes from southern Europe and the Near East, has fragrant, white funnel-shaped flowers which bloom in early summer on stems up to 5 ft (1.5 m) tall. This species does not tolerate the close proximity of other lilies. Plant in a limy soil in early and mid autumn. A rosette of wavy edged leaves will appear and persist throughout winter.

L. henryi (zone 6), a native to the mountains of central China, is some 6½ ft (2 m) tall. It is a vigorous species with, during late summer, orange Turk's-cap flowers spotted with black. It does well in deep alkaline soil.

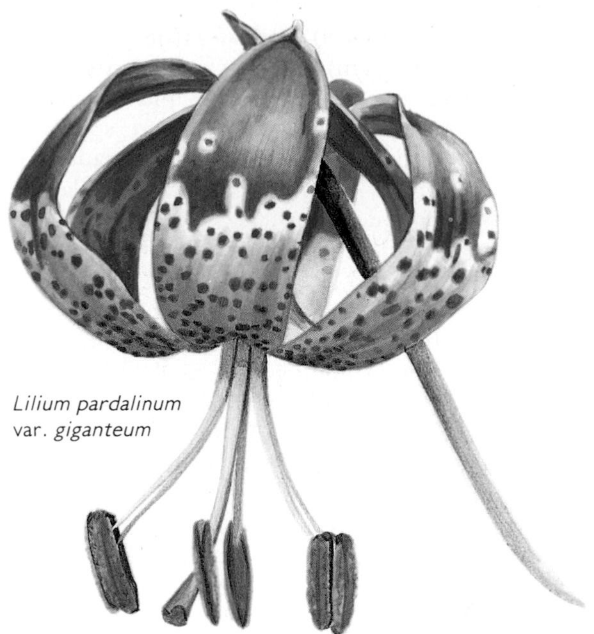

Lilium pardalinum var. *giganteum*

L. martagon (zone 4), Turk's-cap lily, originating in Europe and Asia, is a variable species whose flowers are usually rose-purple and 1½ in (4 cm) long. It blooms in midsummer on stems about 4 ft (1.2 m) high and does well in all soils, in both sun and shade. Its white form is vigorous and easy to grow. In Europe it is protected and must not be picked or dug up.

L. pardalinum (zone 8), panther or leopard lily, from Oregon and California, is 5–7 ft (1.5–2 m) tall with nodding, strongly reflexed orange-red flowers, spotted in crimson or brown. Blooming in early and mid summer its bulbs spread by means of rhizomes. The var. *giganteum* has larger, bright red flowers with yellow centres, spotted purple-brown.

L. pyrenaicum (zone 6), from the Pyrénées, is 3½ ft (1 m) tall and has orange, red or yellow Turk's-cap flowers, spotted with purple or red, similar in size to those of *L. martagon*. Also, it produces 2 to 10 flowers compared with the 5 to 50 of *L. martagon*. The large bulb should be deeply planted in moist, humus-rich soil in sunny or partially shaded positions.

L. regale (zone 5), regal lily, from China, is 4–5 ft (1.2–1.5 m) tall, pleasantly scented and, while not robust, it is an undemanding species. Sometimes confused with the Madonna lily, it flowers later, in mid summer, and its white trumpet-shaped blooms are longer and pinkish-purple on the outside. Several hybrids have been developed with pink or yellow flowers.

L. speciosum (zone 8), orginates from Japan, and is up to 5 ft (1.5 m) tall. This is the 'florists' lily, with fragrant, white or pale pink, pendent Turk's-cap flowers, with crimson spots. It blooms during mid summer to early autumn, requires moist peaty soil and can be planted among rhododendrons.

Hybrids. Lilies are a popular genus on which much work has been done by hybridists to produce a wider range of colours and plants that are less fussy in their requirements. For convenience in exhibiting and cataloguing they have been grouped in several divisions which reflect their origin and affinities.

There is only space here to mention two of the divisions:

Asiatic Hybrids are derived from several Asiatic species and their hybrids. Among the best are those known as Mid-Century Hybrids, whose flowers may be outward facing, pendent or upright. A good example of the latter is 'Enchantment' with nasturtium-red blooms.

American Hybrids have been produced from some American species, including *L. pardalinum*. This division incorporates a group known as Bellingham Hybrids, among which is 'Shuksan', with Turk's-cap flowers of orange, flushed red with maroon-black spots.

Cultivation. In general, plant immediately after the plant has died down, 5 in (18 cm) deep for those that root from the base of the bulb (*L. candidum* should have its nose just below the soil's surface), and 10 in (26 cm) for stem-rooting species and hybrids (*L. auratum* is one of these). A good garden soil enriched with plenty of leaf mould is suitable. As lilies enjoy a cool root-run with sun on their foliage and flowers they can be planted among shrubs. Ensure that the drainage is good, and water only at the base.

Propagate from seed, bulbils from leaf axils, scales, or offsets, depending on the species. Handle each stage with care to avoid damage and drying out.

They can be affected by virus, lily beetles, and lily thrips.

Limnanthes

Limnanthaceae

A genus of about seven annuals from western North America.

L. douglasii (zone 5), poached-egg flower, is a hardy, fast-growing annual, which in late spring and early summer is covered with white flowers with a large yellow centre. It grows to a height of scarcely more than 6 in (15 cm), and can be used at border fronts, for bedding and rock gardens. It seeds itself naturally in the right conditions.

Cultivation. Sow *in situ* in late autumn in a mild climate, or in early spring in colder regions. Lightly cover the seeds. Thin out if necessary to a distance of 4 in (10 cm) between plants.

Limoniastrum

Plumbaginaceae

A genus consisting of ten stocky, bushy shrubs, originating from the western Mediterranean. They have glaucous green leaves, evergreen and fleshy, and spikes of purple-pink flowers that appear from early to late summer.

L. monopetalum (zone 8–9), measures $3\frac{1}{2}$ ft (1 m) in height, and has pinkish blue flowers that bloom from mid summer to early autumn.

Limoniastrum grows well on the tops of walls, and makes a good dried flower.

Cultivation. Plant in dry sandy soil in a sunny position, by the sea on dunes or slopes. It needs a warm climate, and is very tolerant of salt.

Propagate by means of seeds or by division in spring.

Limonium

Sea lavender, *Plumbaginaceae*

A genus represented by about 150 species of herbaceous annuals and perennials and subshrubs found in dry or maritime areas of eastern Europe and the Mediterranean region.

L. latifolium (zone 5), sea lavender or statice, from eastern Europe, is a hardy plant, 24–28 in (60–70 cm) in height, with a spread of 16–24 in (40–60 cm). It has evergreen leathery leaves in a basal rosette. From mid summer to early autumn it produces numerous loose racemes of small lavender-blue flowers.

Limonium is suitable for cut flower arrangement, both dried and fresh, and is best planted in mixed borders. Flowers for drying should be gathered before they are in full bloom.

Cultivation. Plant in autumn or spring in a sunny position, 16 in (40 cm) apart. Ordinary well-drained soil is sufficient, even if poor and dry.

Propagate in late winter or early spring by sowing seeds in a cold frame. Prick out the seedlings, harden off and transfer to a nursery bed, leaving them to grow until planting in their flowering site the following autumn. Alternatively, take root cuttings in early spring; keep in a cold frame until a few leaves appear and then transfer to a nursery bed and grow on, again planting out in the following autumn.

Linaria

Toadflax, *Scrophulariaceae*

This genus consists of about 100 species of hardy and half-hardy annual and perennial herbaceous plants, and sub-shrubs.
L. alpina (zone 4), is native to the European Alps, with a height and spread of 6–10 in (15–25 cm). This hardy perennial forms a compact mat of grey-blue leaves. From early to late summer, racemes of violet flowers with orange throats appear.
L. purpurea (zone 5), from Italy, but naturalized in many parts of Europe, reaches 20–36 in (50–90 cm) in height. It is a hardy perennial with mid-to grey-green linear leaves. The flowers are bluish-purple streaked with white, grouped in flexible spikes, and appear from mid summer to early autumn. The cultivar 'Canon Went' is very decorative, with greyish-blue foliage and soft pink flowers.

The alpine species is for rock gardens or gaps left in paved areas. *L. purpurea* is for mixed borders or the wilder parts of a garden.
Cultivation. These plants do well in all types of well-drained soils in sunny places. Add gravel to heavy soil.

Most species seed themselves in the garden. Sow in a tray in late winter and place in a cold frame, before planting out when the weather is warmer.

Linnaea

Caprifoliaceae

A single species of hardy creeping evergreen shrub, named after the father of botanical classification, Carl von Linné.
L. borealis (zone 3), twinflower, originates in mountainous and Arctic regions of the Northern Hemisphere, and is 4–8 in (10–20 cm) high with a spread of 24 in (60 cm). It has small, oval, dark-green leaves that grow in pairs. The slender stems carry flowers in groups of two. These, shaped like nodding trumpets, are a soft pink or white appearing from late spring to mid summer.
Cultivation. This plant needs constant moisture and humidity. Plant in a shaded rock garden in peaty soil mixed with leaf mould.

Linnaea produces suckers; remove these when they have become established in spring and replant immediately, or alternatively propagate by divisions or cuttings.

Linum

Flax, *Linaceae*

This genus is represented by more than 200 species of annuals, biennials, herbaceous perennials and shrubs, which originate in Europe, Algeria and southeast Asia.
L. narbonense (zone 5), is a herbaceous perennial from the Mediterranean region. Some 16–24 in (40–60 cm) tall and with a spread of 1 ft (30 cm) it is generally hardy. It has straight, grey-green foliage. From early summer to early autumn, numerous panicles of deep, clear blue cup-shaped flowers appear.

Linum perenne

L. perenne (zone 6), is a short-lived hardy perennial from central and eastern Europe. Up to 2 ft (60 cm) tall, its leaves are slightly narrower than the preceding species and its flowers, which appear in summer, are a little smaller but of an appealing shade of blue.

Both these species are suitable for herbaceous and mixed borders.

Cultivation. Plant in autumn or spring, 1 ft (30 cm) apart in well drained soil, preferably enriched with manure or leaf mould. They need a sunny position in order to flower abundantly. In severe winters *L. narbonense* needs some protection and it should be watered during dry spells. Cut down in autumn.

Propagate by seeds sown in pots placed in a cold frame at the beginning of spring.

Lippia
Verbenaceae

A genus of about 200 species of mostly tender shrubs from Africa and America.

L. citriodora (L. triphylla) (zone 8–9), lemon-scented verbena, is a shrub that originates in Chile. It has long stems with deciduous lance-shaped pale-green leaves, with a sweet lemony smell. In summer it is covered with loose spikes of small pale purple flowers.

Cultivation. This is a tender plant, but can withstand a temperature as low as 5°F (−15°C) in well-drained soil, and when cut back to ground level. In colder regions, it is better grown in a container and over-wintered in a sheltered place. Otherwise, plant out in light, well-drained soil in mid spring, in a sunny position. Leave 24–28 in (60–70 cm) between plants.

Take half-ripe cuttings in late summer or early autumn. It may be some time before they show signs of having rooted.

Uses. The fresh leaves add flavour to raw vegetables or can be used as an infusion.

Liquidambar
Hamamelidaceae

A genus of four large deciduous trees from North America and Asia that may reach more than 100 ft (30 m) in height.

L. styraciflua (zone 6), sweet gum, originates in the eastern USA, and reaches 60 ft (18 m) or so in cultivation. Young specimens are conical in habit, a characteristic that disappears with age as the crown widens out. The maple-like leaves are alternate, dark green in colour, and take on splendid autumn colours – dark purple, scarlet and yellow. The flowers appear in spring but are inconspicuous and the fruits are roundish hanging clusters.

It is a handsome tree, suitable for parks and large gardens.

Cultivation. Plant in autumn or spring. It is quite hardy, and grows quickly, preferring moist or even damp soil, with little or no lime.

Propagate by means of seeds in spring. Germination is irregular.

Liriodendron
Tulip tree, *Magnoliaceae*

A genus of two deciduous trees from China and North America.

L. tulipifera (zone 6), originates in North America. This large deciduous tree, with an imposing columnar habit, may reach 130 ft (40 m) or more in height in its native habitat. The leaves are unusual in being more or less lobed according to the age of the tree. They have truncate ends and take on beautiful golden tints in autumn. In winter, it is easily recognizable by its large flattened buds. In early and mid summer it produces large yellowish-green tulip-shaped flowers with an orange mark at the base of each petal. This tree is principally grown in parks or large gardens. 'Fastigiata' is recommended for small gardens, as it only reaches a modest height and is columnar in habit.

Cultivation. The tulip tree does well in a variety of climates, and prefers moist, deep, well-drained soil, even heavy soil. Plant in spring. Bought trees should be young with a rootball or be container-grown.

Propagate by means of seeds in autumn or spring, in a moist sandy loam, in the shade.

Liriope
Lilyturf, *Liliaceae*

A genus consisting of five somewhat tender evergreen herbaceous perennial species from Asia.

L. muscari (zone 9), originates in China, and is 12–20 in (30–50 cm) tall and wide. The compact clump bears dark-green, glossy, linear leaves. The spikes of bluish-lilac bead-like flowers bloom from early to late autumn.

L. spicata (zone 10), from Japan, China and Korea, has flowers of a lilac or white colour in dense spikes 2–3¼ in (5–8 cm) long. These appear from late summer to mid autumn.

They are excellent ground-cover plants or for border edges.

Cultivation. Plant in spring in well-drained, even light sandy soil in a sunny or partially shaded position.

To propagate, lift the stoloniferous rhizomes in spring, divide and replant immediately.

Lithospermum
Boraginaceae

A genus consisting of about 60 species that are native to Europe, Asia and North America. They include hardy and half-hardy herbaceous perennials and sub-shrubs. The genus *Lithospermum* has lost species to *Lithodora*, but the plants are still often sold under their earlier name.

L. diffusum (Lithodora diffusa) – zone 6 – from France and Spain is 8 in (20 cm) tall with a spread of 2 ft (60 cm). This is a hardy sub-shrub with dark, leathery, oval, evergreen leaves. It has flowers ⅜ in (1 cm) in diameter with five open lobes of a gentian blue from late spring to early summer. 'Grace Ward' has larger flowers and 'Heavenly Blue' has clear, paler blue flowers.

L. oleifolium (Lithodora oleifolia) – zone 7 – from the Pyrenees is 6 in (15 cm) high with a spread of 12–16 in (30–40 cm). This low-growing sub-shrub had grey-green leaves, and produces sky-blue flowers from late spring to early summer and is suitable for the rock garden or alpine house.

L. purpurocaeruleum or more correctly *Buglossoides purpurocaerulea* (zone 6), is 12 in (30 cm) tall, with a spread of 3½–6½ ft (1–2 m). This is a low-growing, creeping perennial, with self-rooting stems. Its linear leaves are wrinkled, and its flowers are red in bud and become blue on opening in early summer. This species provides useful ground cover in large gardens, along with *Geranium sanguineum* and *Anemone sylvestris*.

Cultivation. Plant in mid and late spring in a sunny position. The soil should be a well-drained, moisture-retentive sandy peat. While *L. diffusum* must have an acid soil, *L. oleifolium* and *L. purpurocaeruleum* thrive on a limy one.

Propagate by means of seeds, or by cuttings taken from side shoots in mid summer placed in a cold frame, or by division.

Lobelia
Campanulaceae

A genus consisting of more than 350 species of hardy or half-hardy annuals, herbaceous perennials, and sub-shrubs, many from tropical America.

L. cardinalis (zone 7), cardinal flower, native to Eastern and Central North America, may reach 36 in (90 cm) tall. This short-lived herbaceous perennial has upright branching stems, with lance-shaped, mid green toothed leaves. The racemes of five-lobed scarlet flowers bloom from mid to late summer. It needs winter protection in the cold regions.

L. erinus (zone 6), originates in South Africa, and is 4–8 in (10–20 cm) tall. This dwarf, carpet-forming plant, used in bedding, is a perennial but is always grown as an annual. The oval leaves are bright green tending to turn reddish. The flowers are pale blue, and appear in profusion from late spring until the first frosts. There are numerous cultivars, some with a

Lobelia cardinalis

trailing habit, of which the most commonly marketed are: 'Crystal Palace', with dark blue flowers, and 'Rosamund', crimson with a white eye, and the trailing 'Blue Basket' with violet-blue, white-eyed flowers.
L. fulgens (zone 8–9), is native to Mexico, and measures 16–36 in (40–90 cm) in height. This perennial plant has a rosette of linear, dentate, reddish leaves. The spikes of scarlet flowers bloom from late summer to late autumn. The hybrid 'Queen Victoria' has flowers of a particularly brilliant red.
L. syphilitica (zone 7), blue cardinal flower, is a hardy perennial, native to the USA, and up to 3 ft (90 cm) tall. Its leaves are light green and long spikes of light blue flowers appear from mid summer to early autumn.

The annual species is used in bedding schemes, border edgings and hanging baskets. The perennials described here are suitable for herbaceous beds.
Cultivation. The perennial species should be planted in mid spring in rich moist soil, in a sheltered, partially shaded situation, leaving 4–6 in (10–15 cm) between the plants.

Perennial species need protection in winter, especially when they are in exposed situations. Cover the roots with dead leaves or fern fronds, when the foliage has been cut to ground level.

To propagate *L. erinus*, sow in a tray in late winter, keep at a temperature of 60–64°F (16–18°C), prick out and progressively harden off until they are finally planted out in late spring, when the danger of frost has passed.

Divide the perennial species in spring, re-planting the divisions immediately.

Lomatia

Proteaceae

A genus represented by 12 species of trees and shrubs originating in Australia and Chile. They are elegant evergreens that reach 3½–13 ft (1–4 m) in height.
L. ferruginea (zone 9), is native to Chile and Patagonia, and reaches 30 ft (9 m) in height. Its pinnate leaves are deep green; short racemes of cream and scarlet flowers appear in mid summer.
L. myricoides (zone 8), originates in Australia, and is 5–6½ ft (1.5–2 m) high. It has an upright habit with dark bottle-green leaves, and creamy white flowers from early to mid summer.
L. tinctoria (zone 8), originates in Tasmania. It is a small shrub some 24–32 in (60–80 cm) high and has long racemes of yellow, scented flowers.
Cultivation. Plant in light, humus-rich, lime-free soil in mild climates, or in a cool greenhouse. Propagate by cuttings from well-ripened shoots, placed under a cloche with some bottom heat.

Lonicera

Honeysuckle, *Caprifoliaceae*

This genus contains nearly 200 species of deciduous and evergreen climbers, or erect shrubs, many with fragrant flowers.
L. × *americana* (zone 5–6), is a hybrid of *L. caprifolium* and *L. etrusca* and may climb to a height of more than 33 ft (10 m). This hardy species is characterized by young shoots of a violet colour, and green leaves that are glaucous on their undersides. The large, white, fragrant flowers bloom in early and mid summer, and fade to yellow tinged with purple red.
L. × *brownii* (zone 5–6), is a hybrid of *L. sempervirens* and *L. hirsuta*. It climbs to 10–17 ft (3–5 m), and is equally hardy. Its deciduous or semi-evergreen oval leaves are glaucous on their undersides, and scarlet flowers are produced throughout summer.
L. etrusca (zone 7), originates in the Mediterranean region, and grows up to 33 ft (10 m). It has glaucous leaves, deciduous or semi-evergreen, and its young stems are purple. In early and mid summer scented flowers appear – creamy yellow, tinged reddish-purple on the outside.
L. × *heckrottii* (zone 6), is probably a hybrid of *L.* × *americana* and *L. sempervirens*. It reaches 13 ft (4 m) but is not a vigorous climber; its leaves, too, are glaucous on their undersides. The scented flowers are yellow-orange inside and bright pink outside; they bloom from early to late summer.
L. henryi (zone 6), originates in China, and climbs to 30 ft (9 m). This hardy species is evergreen or semi-evergreen and has downy stems. The reddish-yellow flowers appear in early and mid summer.
L. japonica (zone 6), originates in China, Japan and Korea, and reaches 30 ft (9 m) in height, and is notable for its evergreen foliage and the scent of its white flowers which change to yellow. The flowers are grouped in twos in the angle of the

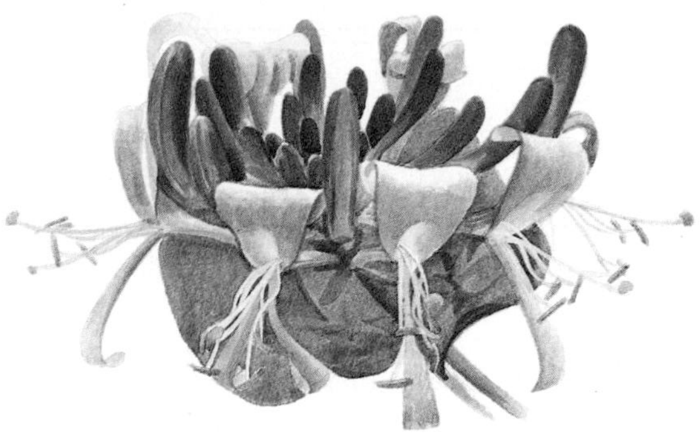

Lonicera periclymenum

leaves and the stem and bloom in early and mid summer. There is a cultivar, 'Aureo-reticulata', having leaves veined in yellow. It is not as hardy, losing its leaves in hard winters.

L. periclymenum (zone 6), wild honeysuckle, from Europe, reaches 10–20 ft (3–6 m) in height, and is hardy. Its dark green leaves are glaucous on the underside, and the scented flowers are yellowish-white tinged with purple outside. 'Belgica', the early Dutch honeysuckle is more compact and begins to flower in late spring; 'Serotina', the late Dutch honeysuckle begins to bloom in summer.

L. tragophylla (zone 6), from western China, climbs 6½–10 ft (2–3 m) and is quite hardy. It is notable for the profusion and size of its flowers, which are bright yellow, and bloom in early and mid summer. Its leaves are also large, and blue-green in colour.

All these species are suitable for decorating trellises, pergolas, pillars, or old trees.

Cultivation. Plant honeysuckle in ordinary, well-drained moist soil in a sunny or partially shaded situation, one preferably free from late frosts. Keep roots cool.

All species can be propagated by means of half-ripe cuttings taken in mid and late summer, giving them some bottom heat; layering is also possible from late summer to late autumn.

Poorly cultivated plants are liable to be attacked by aphids.

Loropetalum

Hamamelidaceae

A genus of one or two evergreen shrubs from the Himalayas, China and Japan.

L. chinense (zone 9), is a shrub that can reach 6 ft (1.8 m) or so. Its flowers closely resemble those of witch hazel, but are white, with long ribbon-like petals and appear in late winter and early spring. The leaves are oval and dark green.

Cultivation. Loropetalum needs a peaty loam and a climate that is mild without being too hot, or a cool greenhouse. It will tolerate oceanic or Mediterranean-type winters, where it can be planted in humid conditions in the shade.

Propagate by means of seeds, cuttings, or layering.

Lotus

Leguminosae

The genus consist of 100 species that originate in America, Europe, Asia, the Canary Islands and certain parts of North Africa. They are herbaceous perennials or rarely annuals. The leaves are pinnate, with flowering stems branching from the leaf stalks, producing blooms that are yellow or pink, more rarely white.

L. corniculatus (zone 5), bird's-foot trefoil, is found throughout the Northern Hemisphere and measures 4 in (10 cm) in height with a spread of more than 3½ ft (1 m). This hardy perennial has creeping stems with compound leaves of five leaflets. Flowering from late spring to early autumn, its umbels of five to six flowers are yellow, tinged red in mountainous regions but yellow at lower altitudes. 'Pleniflorus' ('Plenus') has double flowers and is less vigorous.

Plant in a rock garden along with species of *Alyssum, Armeria, Thymus* and *Veronica.*

Cultivation. Any reasonable well-drained soil and a sunny position are all that is needed. As these plants, even the double-flowered variety, generally seed themselves in the garden, they can be propagated by lifting the young plants with plenty of soil around their roots and planting in the chosen spot.

Ludwigia

False loosestrife, *Onagraceae*

This genus contains about 75 species, mostly aquatic, from warm regions of the world.

L. uruguayensis (Jussiaea grandiflora) – zone 10 – from southeast North to South America is the best-known of the creeping or floating species. The leaves are mid-green, glossy and oblong. The yellow flowers measure more than 2 in (5 cm) in diameter and appear in summer.

Ludwigia uruguayensis (Jussiaea grandiflora)

This species can be associated with other summer-flowering plants that grow well on river banks such as yellow loosestrife and zantedeschias.

Cultivation. The plant is not deep-rooted, but forms a thick carpet over the water as it grows. At the onset of winter the topgrowth disappears, leaving the roots and resting buds submerged. In this state the plants can survive light frosts and with the rising temperatures of late spring, growth is renewed.

Lunaria

Money flower/plant, *Cruciferae*

This genus contains three biennial or herbaceous perennial plants from Europe. They produce mauve flowers in spring, and in summer form large flattened fruits of silvery transparent appearance that are used in dried arrangements. The ornamental part is the internal wall of each 'pod', without the external husk and the seeds.

L. annua (L. biennis) – zone 6 – honesty, is an annual or biennial which reaches 3½ ft (1 m), with mauve flowers that appear from mid spring to early summer. During the night they give off a scent similar to that of violets. 'Alba' has white flowers, while 'Variegata' has mottled cream leaves.

L. rediviva (zone 6), is a perennial up to 2 ft (60 cm) tall, with pale mauve to white scented flowers in spring. Its pods are more elliptical than those of the previous species.

Cultivation. Money flowers prefer light soils that are rich in humus, and prefer some light shade. Sow in a prepared seed-bed in mid and late spring; thin out and plant where they are to grow in early autumn.

Lupinus

Lupin, *Leguminosae*

A genus containing 200 species of hardy and half-hardy annuals, herbaceous perennials and sub-shrubs from North and South America and the Mediterranean region.

L. polyphyllus (zone 6), from west North America is a herbaceous perennial that is hardy in most climates, measuring 3½–5 ft (1–1.5 m) in height, with a spread of 20–24 in (50–60 cm). Its leaves are digitate, consisting of several spear-shaped green leaflets. It flowers from late spring to early summer, with long, thick, upright spikes of blue pea-like flowers.

Many cultivars in a wide range of colours, both self-coloured and bicoloured have been raised from these species, some of which are only 2 ft (60 cm) tall. Some seed strains come more or less true, and desirable forms can be increased from cuttings.

L. subcarnosus (zone 6), Texas blue-bonnet, is an annual, about 1 ft (30 cm) tall with rich blue flowers often marked with white or yellow on the standards.

Suitable for herbaceous or mixed borders.

Cultivation. Plant the perennial in a sunny or lightly shaded position, in any good non-limy soil, not too rich in organic matter. This should be done in autumn or spring, leaving 20 in (50 cm) between each plant.

Remove spikes with faded blooms to encourage further flowering; support with a stake in windy situations and cut the stems down to ground level in autumn.

Sow the seeds of the annual species *in situ* in spring. For the perennial species sow the seeds in a sheltered position and transplant quickly into their permanent site, (they do not like being moved) or propagate by division in spring, or by cuttings taken from basal shoots at the same time; plant out in autumn.

Lupins are vulnerable to virus diseases, whose symptoms are marbling, striping, and browning of the leaves. Plants suffering from this should be destroyed.

Luzula

Woodrush, *Juncaceae*

This genus contains about 80 herbaceous perennials with grass-like leaves, often having long white cottony hairs along their margins. They come from cold and temperate regions. Their flowers are similar to those of reeds, but the plants generally grow in drier places.

Grow them with shrubs in the foreground of a partially shaded herbaceous border, or in wooded clearings.

L. nivea (zone 5), snowy woodrush, is found from Spain to Poland, and reaches 12–16 in (30–40 cm) in height. It has loose clumps of evergreen leaves. The white flowers, which appear from early to late summer, can be used in cut flower arrangements.

Cultivation. Luzulas enjoy partial shade, and a dryish soil, rich in humus. Plant 12–16 in (30–40 cm) apart.

Propagate by division in spring.

Lychnis

Campion, *Caryophyllaceae*

A genus represented by about 35 hardy and half-hardy annuals and herbaceous perennials originating in north temperate regions.

L. coronaria (zone 5), dusty miller, rose campion, from southern Europe is a hardy herbaceous plant reaching 3 ft (90 cm) in height, with a spread of 12 in (30 cm), which adapts to most climates.

The leaves are silver-grey, spear-shaped and, like the stems, have a woolly appearance. From mid summer to early autumn red or white flowers appear in succession on branching stems.

Suitable for mixed or herbaceous borders, this campion is good as a cut flower.

Cultivation. Plant in a sunny or lightly shaded position, in ordinary well-drained soil. A short-lived perennial, it is usually grown as a biennial. Provide stakes for support in windy situations, remove faded flowers to prevent self-seeding, and cut down to its base in autumn.

Propagate by seeds in a cold frame at the beginning of spring, and plant out in early summer.

Lycium

Box thorn, *Solanaceae*

A genus represented by about 10 species of shrubs and shrubby trees that originate in temperate and sub-tropical regions. Low-growing or climbing in habit their tubular flowers vary from white to violet-purple, and bloom from late spring to early autumn.

L. barbarum (L. halimifolium) (zone 7), Duke of Argyll's tea tree, originates in China. It is 10–13 ft (3–4 m) tall and variable in habit; it may be spiny or not, a climber or a shrub with pendulous branches. The leaves are green or grey-green and from early summer to early autumn, it carries small profuse purple flowers, which are followed by scarlet berries.

It is especially suitable for conditions in seaside gardens.

Cultivation. Plant in a good light soil. This shrub grows rapidly and is useful for covering slopes or arbours. It does well in a mild climate.

Propagate by seed or by layering, removing suckers, or by hardwood cuttings, in spring or autumn.

Lycopersicon

Tomato, *Solanaceae*

A genus of seven species from west South America one of which, the tomato (*L. esculentum*), is a perennial grown as an annual for its fruit.

Cultivation. Tomatoes may be grown outdoors in a warm sheltered position or under glass, when the yield will be more than double. Whichever, plant fairly deeply in fertile soil, in a sunny position. Two weeks before planting apply a general fertilizer. Plant 20 in (50 cm) apart in rows 32 in (80 cm) apart, and provide stakes, strings or wires for support.

Tomatoes need copious watering, preferably at the base of the plant. From the time when the fruits set until they are picked feed the plants with a proprietary tomato fertilizer. Check daily and pinch any side-shoots to form one single main stem and stop the plant when the top of the support is reached. The side-shoots spring from the angle between the leaves and the main stem. Remove the lowest leaves to encourage circulation of air around the base of the plant.

The so-called bush varieties do not grow more than 2½ ft (75 cm) tall. Bush-like in habit, supports are unnecessary and there is no need to pinch out the side-shoots. However, as many of the fruits are at ground level, straw or plastic sheeting must be placed around the plants to prevent the tomatoes from becoming soiled.

Spray regularly in the morning to encourage pollination and the setting of fruit.

In late winter or early spring propagate by seeds sown in a tray placed in a heated glasshouse. Provide plenty of light, and a minimum temperature of 50°F (10°C). Prick out when the first true leaves appear into 2¾ in (7 cm) pots. Plant in their final positions when they reach a height of 6 in (15 cm).

Tomatoes are subject to the following problems: stem rot, root rot, leaf mould, wilt and viruses, also to whitefly and red spider mite.

Lysichiton (Lysichitum)

Araceae

This genus consists of two species of hardy herbaceous perennials. The flowers resemble those of the *Arum*, but are more spectaclar.

L. *americanus* (zone 5), skunk cabbage or bog arum, originates in western North America, and is 28 in–4 ft (70–120 cm) tall and wide. It is long-lived and in time forms considerable clumps of soft green leaves, 32 in–3½ ft (80–100 cm) long. The flower is a large yellow-gold spathe measuring 12–16 in (30–40 cm), enclosing a thick greenish spadix. It blooms in spring, early or late according to the climate.

L. *camtschatcensis* (zone 6), originates in Kamchatka, and has a height and spread of 2–3½ ft (60–100 cm). It is similar to the above species, but smaller. The magnificent spathes are pure white but do not often produce seed.

They are dramatic subjects for waterside planting.

Cultivation. These plants need deep, humus-rich soil that stays damp throughout the period of growth.

Propagate by seeds in a tray kept constantly wet at a temperature of 71°F (22°C). The secret of success lies in the freshness of the seeds, as their power to germinate only lasts some weeks. Alternatively divide the rhizomes, or remove young offset plants.

Lysimachia

Loosestrife, *Primulaceae*

A genus containing about 150 herbaceous perennials or shrubs from Europe and Asia.

L. *clethroides*, from China and Japan, reaches a height up to 3 ft (90 cm). Mid-green leaves turn orange or red in autumn. White star-shaped flowers bloom mid summer to early autumn.

L. *nummularia* (zone 5), Creeping jenny, from Europe is a creeping prostrate perennial with golden flowers in summer. It is useful for covering the ground in dampish semi-shady places. The form with yellow foliage, 'Aurea', is better looking.

L. *punctata* (zone 5), yellow loosestrife, from southeast Europe is a hardy perennial, between 24 in–3½ ft (60 cm–1 m) high with a spread of 24–32 in (60–80 cm). It has spear-shaped dark green leaves, and long spikes of cup-shaped bright yellow flowers. They bloom from early to late summer.

This species does well in herbaceous or mixed borders.

Cultivation. Plant in autumn or spring, 24 in (60 cm) apart. L. *punctata* grows well in ordinary, rather damp peaty soils. The position should be sunny or partially shaded.

This species is somewhat invasive, and its growth may have to be checked. Water in dry weather, and stake if necessary. Propagate by division of clumps in autumn or spring.

Lythrum

Lythraceae

A genus represented by more than 30 species of herbaceous perennials which originate in the temperate zone of the Northern Hemisphere and many other parts of the world.

L. *salicaria* (zone 5–6), purple loosestrife, from the north temperate zone of Eurasia is a hardy perennial, 32 in–4 ft (80 cm–1.2 m) high, with a spread of 16–24 in (40–60 cm). The foliage is dense, mid green, and spear-shaped. From early summer to early autumn, dense spikes of small, star-shaped flowers appear, ranging from pink to purple.

It provides excellent material for cut-flower arrangement, as well as complementing mixed and herbaceous borders, especially near water.

Cultivation. Plant in autumn or spring, 20 in (50 cm) apart, in a sunny or half-shaded position. The soil should preferably be damp or even marshy, and enriched with well-rotted manure or garden compost. It should be well watered after planting. Cut stems down in autumn. Only sterile cultivars, such as 'Morden's Pink', should be grown as the species is very invasive and is taking over marshy meadows in North America.

Propagate this plant by division.

Maackia
Leguminosae

This genus is represented by six to eight species of elegant shrubby trees which come from eastern Asia. The deciduous leaves are composed of many blue-green leaflets. The white to greenish-white flowers appear from early to late summer in terminal racemes.

M. amurensis (Cladrastis amurensis) – zone 5 – from Manchuria, reaches 40 ft (12 m) in the wild but much less in cultivation. It has fine foliage, and produces small greenish-white flowers in long, dense, erect racemes in early and mid summer.

Cultivation. Plant in deep, fertile soil, in a sunny or partially shaded position. Propagate by seeds as soon as these have been gathered, or by layering.

Macleaya
Plume poppy, *Papaveraceae*

A genus consisting of two species of hardy herbaceous perennials, native to China and Japan, sometimes sold under the generic name *Bocconia*.

M. cordata (zone 7) reaches a height of 4–8½ ft (1.2–2.5 m). The leaves up to 20 in (50 cm) across, are deeply lobed, grey-green above, and grey-white below. Plumes of numerous tiny white flowers, to 3½ ft (1 m) high, appear in mid to late summer. It is invasive.

M. microcarpa (zone 7) is similar, but has buff-coloured flowers. It is even more invasive making it less suitable for smaller gardens.

With attractive foliage and flowers, these plants are decorative in isolated groups, or at the back of large borders.

Cultivation. In spring plant deeply in humus-rich soil in a sunny position. Cut dead stems down to ground level in autumn as part of the pre-winter maintenance programme.

Propagate in mid spring by division or from root cuttings with an eye and replant immediately

Magnolia
Magnoliaceae

This genus consists of about 100 species of mostly hardy trees and shrubs, native to China, Japan and the USA. They are elegant in habit, with decorative leaves and spectacular flowers.

M. campbelli (zone 7), from the Himalayas, forms a deciduous tree to 33–50 ft (10–15 m) in height in cultivation. It should be planted in mild areas where flowers are less damaged by frost. The large cup-shaped fragrant blooms, up to 10 in (25 cm) across, may be white, pink or purple and occur towards the top of the tree. The tree does not flower until it is about 20 years old, but up to the age of 40 years it blooms profusely in early spring.

M. delavayi (zone 8–9), undoubtedly has some of the largest leaves of any tree growing in temperate regions. They are evergreen, and blue-green below. In late summer and early autumn it produces creamy white fragrant flowers, up to 8 in (20 cm) in diameter. Except in the mildest areas, it is best grown against a wall.

Magnolia grandiflora

M. denudata (zone 7), lily tree, from China, is rounded in form reaching 30 ft (9 m) in height. The flowers are large, up to 8 in (20 cm) across, pure white, fragrant, and appear before the oval downy leaves.

M. grandiflora (zone 8), southern magnolia, native to southern USA, forms a dense pyramidal tree to 66 ft (20 m). It has dark evergreen leaves, shiny above, with rust-coloured down beneath. During late summer and autumn it produces large creamy, fragrant flowers. Several forms are available such as 'Exmouth', which has a more erect habit and 'Goliath' with larger flowers.

M. kobus (zone 6), introduced from Japan, is a deciduous tree over 33 ft (10 m) tall with rather small white flowers in spring. It is quite hardy and lime tolerant but does not flower freely when young.

M. liliiflora (zone 7), native to China, is a deciduous spreading shrub useful for the small garden except on chalk soils or exposed areas. The white flowers are purple on the underside, and appear in late spring and early summer.

M. × loebneri (zone 7) is a hybrid, forming a small tree or shrub flowering freely when young. Several forms are available, including 'Leonard Messel' with lilac pink flowers in spring.

M. × soulangiana (zone 7–8), saucer magnolia, which is a hybrid between *M. denudata* and *M. liliiflora*, is usually a wide-spreading deciduous tree to 6½–13 ft (2–4 m). The flowers are tulip-shaped, white inside and purplish outside, and appear in mid to late spring before the leaves. 'Lennei' is an attractive large-flowered form that sometimes flowers again in autumn.

M. stellata (zone 7), star magnolia, from Japan, is a compact deciduous shrub with fragrant, star-like white flowers produced before leaves in spring. It is highly suitable for small gardens.

Cultivation. Magnolias are not difficult to grow, provided that the soil is deep, rich, and well-drained. A few tolerate alkaline soil. They should be planted with a rootball or as container-grown plants. Take care not to break their branches, which are very fragile. Plant in spring, even if in flower.

Most magnolias are hardy, but do best in mild or protected areas when buds and flowers are less likely to be damaged by frost. The leaves of all types may be damaged by frost and should be protected from cold winds.

M. grandiflora can be pruned to shape; other magnolias only require any dead wood to be removed as necessary. The trees can be killed by root rot, therefore it is best to plant in late spring when growth is underway.

Propagate species from seeds sown in trays containing a mixture of soil and leaf mould, or from cuttings of young growth placed in a cold frame.

Mahonia

Berberidaceae

This genus of about 70 species native to North America and Asia consists of mostly hardy, slow-growing, usually evergreen shrubs. They are grown for their yellow flowers, usually blue-black berries and attractive foliage.

The Asiatic species are more ornamental than the American ones, but less hardy. They are less branched and have very long leaves with up to 25 or more spiny leaflets. The long racemes of yellow flowers may persist all winter.

M. aquifolium (zone 5), Oregon grape, native to northwest North America, is a hardy compact shrub 5–6½ ft (1.50–2 m) in height, with pinnate, spiny leaflets. The clusters of yellow flowers appear from mid winter to mid spring, and are followed by abundant blue-black fruits. It is the parent of many hybrids.

M. bealei (zone 7), a native of China, is taller and more robust with denser, more upright racemes than *M. japonica*.

M. japonica (zone 7), from China, reaches 6½ ft (2 m) in height, bears long pendulous racemes of fragrant lemon yellow flowers and leaves to 1½ ft (45 cm) with up to 19 leaflets. 'Charity', with up to 20 racemes of flowers is one of the hybrids

Mahonia aquifolium

produced from this and another Asian species. *M. repens* (zone 6), native to western North America, is a low-growing, suckering shrub rarely exceeding 20 in (50 cm) in height. The pinnate leaves have three to seven spiny leaflets and clusters of deep yellow flowers which open in spring.
Cultivation. Mahonias will grow in most soils in shade or semi-shade, including under trees. Sow the seeds immediately after collection in a proprietary seed compost. However, it is more usual to take semi-hardwood cuttings in summer.

Malcolmia
Cruciferae

A genus of about 30 annual and perennial species native to Mediterranean area.
M. maritima (zone 5), Virginia stock, is an annual that reaches 6–12 in (15–30 cm) in height with grey-green foliage, and four-petalled flowers of white, pink, mauve or red. They can flower as soon as a month after sowing.
Cultivation. This little annual grows well in most soils in sunny positions. Sowing should be staggered from early spring to early summer for a succession of flowers, and should be done *in situ*. Thin young plants to 8 in (20 cm) apart. Further sowings may be made in early autumn in order to obtain an early display the following spring.

Malope
Malvaceae

A genus of three to four species of annuals, native to the Mediterranean region, grown for their showy flowers which last well as cut flowers in water.
M. trifida (zone 6) reaches 16 in (80 cm) or more in height. The leaves are three lobed and the large, solitary pink to purple flowers to 4 in (8 cm) across, are veined with a darker purple. They bloom from early summer to early autumn. 'Alba' has white flowers, and 'Rosea' has flowers flushed pink.
Cultivation. Sow in early and mid spring *in situ*, preferably in a light soil and an open position. Thin out progressively to a final spacing of 1 ft (30 cm) between plants. It seeds itself readily from one year to another.

Malus
Flowering crab apple, *Rosaceae*

A genus of about 25 hardy deciduous trees from north temperate regions, many of which are grown for their ornamental flowers and fruit.

Apples are one of the most important of the hardy fruits and several species, such as *M. pumila* and *M. praecox*, are probably involved in their parentage. As many as 2000 cultivars have been named of which about 200 are commonly grown: the cooker 'Bramley's Seedling', and 'Cox's Orange Pippin' a dessert apple are examples.
M. floribunda (zone 6), from Japan, flowers profusely in mid spring. It reaches 23–26 ft (7–8 m) in height with a rounded crown; oval, narrowly toothed leaves and pale pink flowers. The fruits are round, small and yellow.
M. tschonoskii (zone 6), originates in Japan and is pryamidal in habit, though erect when young. It is noted for its white flowers, flushed with pink which appear in late spring followed by large, mid green, oval leaves. These take on brilliant scarlet tints in autumn and the fruits are greenish-yellow tinged purple.
Cultivars. Many hybrids have been raised for their decorative value. 'Profusion' with purplish-red flowers in late spring; 'Golden Hornet', which has white flowers at the same time and a wonderful display of bright yellow fruits that persist long after the leaves have fallen; 'John Downie' has white flowers and a good crop of yellow fruits flushed with crimson which are useful for preserves.

Ornamental crab apples are particularly suitable for small gardens.
Cultivation. All apple trees should be planted between mid autumn and early spring. They prefer good loamy, well-drained soils and flower best in full sun. As with cherry trees (*Prunus*), the flowers only persist in fairly cool climates, particularly at higher altitudes; elsewhere, the petals soon fall.

Propagate species from seed; varieties and hybrids need to be grafted on a rootstock.

Malva
Mallow, *Malvaceae*

A genus represented by about 30 hardy annuals and short-lived herbaceous perennials, native to

Europe and the Mediterranean region, suitable for the herbaceous or annual border.

M. alcea (zone 6), mallow, is a herbaceous perennial, reaching $2\frac{1}{2}$–$3\frac{1}{2}$ ft (75 cm–1 m) or more, with a spread of $1\frac{1}{2}$–2 ft (40–60 cm). The leaves are light green, deeply lobed with toothed margins. From mid summer to mid autumn, clear pink flowers $1\frac{1}{2}$–2 in (4–5 cm) across are freely formed on branching stems.

M. moschata (zone 6), musk mallow, is similar, but grows to about 2 ft (60 cm). The white form, 'Alba', is particularly desirable. It flowers in summer.

M. sylvestris (zone 6), common mallow, is biennial or perennial and grows to 3 ft (90 cm). Unlike the other two species its leaves are entire. Its flowers are rose-purple with darker veins; they appear from early summer to early autumn. Because of its leafy nature, this species is best confined to the wilder parts of a garden.

Cultivation. All species thrive in a well-drained soil, even if poor or dry, and succeed in a sunny or partially shaded position. Plant in autumn or spring, 16–20 in (40–50 cm) apart.

Remove faded flowers to encourage a second flowering, and cut down to the base in autumn. The leaves may be affected by rust (brownish orange pustules). In spring take cuttings from new shoots and root these in sandy soil in a frame. Alternatively sow seeds in trays of seed compost in spring and place in a cold frame, to be planted out in autumn. They are both likely to self-seed.

Malva sylvestris

Mandevilla
Apocynaceae

A genus of a large number of species of tender shrubs and climbers (sometimes placed in the genus *Dipladenia*), originating in Argentina, Mexico and India, of which the following is half-hardy and may be grown outdoors in a Mediterranean-type climate or a conservatory elsewhere.

M. laxa (M. suaveolens) – zone 9 – Chilean jasmine, originates in Argentina, Bolivia and Peru, and reaches 20 ft (6 m) and more in height. It has fresh green deciduous or semi-evergreen foliage, and pure white, fragrant, trumpet-shaped flowers formed in clusters of five to fifteen in late spring and summer.

Where this species is hardy it can be trained up trees and walls or over pergolas. Alternatively, grow in a conservatory.

Cultivation. Plant in a good well-drained soil, in a sunny or partially shaded position.

Propagate from seed in spring, or by semi-hardwood cuttings of short lateral shoots in summer. Insert these in pots of sand and place in a cold frame.

Maranta
Marantaceae

A genus of about 20 species of low-growing perennial plants, native to tropical America. Many are cultivated in the house or greenhouse for their distinctly patterned and coloured foliage.

M. bicolor (zone 10+), from Brazil and Guyana, is a low-growing, tufted herbaceous plant with oblong, blue-green leaves which are reddish-purple underneath. The centre of each leaf has an irregular paler zone and a row of darker blotches on each side. The flowers are whitish in short spikes.

M. leuconeura (zone 10), prayer plant, from Brazil, is a herbaceous plant with a short stem from which arise oblong leaves about 6 in (15 cm) long, often purplish below, especially under any blotches on the upper surface. The

leaves tend to stand upright at night but lie flat during the day giving the common name. The small white to mauve flowers are formed in a slender upright spike. The cultivar 'Erythroneura' ('Erythrophylla'), herringbone plant, has the leaf veins marked red with a paler yellowish-green midrib and darker green areas between the veins. *M. leuconeura* var. *kerchoviana*, rabbit foot or rabbit tracks, has light green leaves with dark brown blotches between the lateral veins, which become greener on aging, while var. *massangeana* has a wide irregular pale green or silvery zone along the midrib, and white lateral veins on a dark velvety green leaf.
Cultivation. Frost-tender plants requiring a minimum temperature of 50–60°F (10–16°C). They need constant high humidity in a shaded position away from draughts and should be grown in a rich open compost (potting soil). They are not suitable for growing outdoors except in tropical climates. Propagation is by division of the crowns or by cuttings. Too wet a compost (soil) and too low a temperature will cause the leaves to go limp and the rotting of stems, expecially in winter, while dry air will cause leaf fall, and direct sunlight leads to leaf scorch.

Marrubium

Horehound, *Labiatae*

This genus consists of 30 species of mostly herbaceous perennials. They may be hardy or half-hardy, and originate mainly from the shores of the Mediterranean sea.
M. supinum (zone 6), from Spain, measures 8–16 in (20–40 cm) in height, with a similar spread. It forms cushions, and has round, downy, grey-white leaves. The small lilac-pink flowers bloom in early and mid summer.

This species and some of its relatives are grown mostly for their beautiful foliage, as the flowers are insignificant. They are ideal for rock gardens in hot, dry places.
Cultivation. Plant in a mixture of gravel and good soil, and cover the surface with a layer of gravel. Long periods of humidity do not suit them, but it is worth making the effort to ensure conditions are right for the sake of their beautiful foliage.

Raise from seed sown in the open in early spring or propagate from cuttings taken in spring, placed in a cold frame.

Matteuccia

Aspleniaceae

The genus contains three species of hardy deciduous ferns from north temperate regions, characterized by somewhat invasive underground stems.
M. struthiopteris (Onoclea germanica, Struthiopteris germanica) – zone 5 – Ostrich fern, is 3½ ft (1 m) or more in height and spread. It forms a shuttlecock-like rosette of upright, sterile, bright green fronds, which are deeply divided and bipinnate. The fertile fronds, which are brown and shorter, often last through the winter. It is seen to best advantage when planted in isolated clumps at the edge of water or in a bog garden.
Cultivation. Plant between autumn and spring in a lime-free soil containing loam and plenty of leaf mould, in a slightly shaded position. The soil must be damp throughout the year. It needs no attention other than an occasional topdressing of organic matter, such as well-rotted compost, if the soil is poor.

It can be propagated by division of the rhizomatous roots in autumn or winter.

Matthiola

Stock, *Cruciferae*

This genus is represented by some 50 species of annuals, biennials, perennials or subshrubs native to Europe and western Asia.
M. incana (zone 6), is a perennial which may reach 2½ ft (76 cm) in height with long, grey-felted leaves. The fragrant flowers are formed in upright racemes, from early summer to early autumn. Cultivated forms are variable in colour from white, pink, red, lilac, purple, violet to yellow. 'Excelsior', which reaches 3 ft (90 cm), has double flowers and makes an excellent cut flower. Other cultivars have a more compact habit. All of these cultivars are grown as annuals or biennials.
Cultivation. Stocks can be grown outdoors or as pot plants for the conservatory. Sow seed in early summer; when large enough to handle prick out seedlings into their final pots where they will flower the following year. The compost should be well-drained and never over-wet as young plants are prone to damping off, and adult plants to mildew.

Mazus
Scrophulariaceae

The genus consists of 20 to 25 species of herbaceous plants from Asia to Australia.
M. pumilio (zone 7) originates in Australia and New Zealand, and is 2–4 in (5–10 cm) high and 1–2 ft (30–60 cm) across. It spreads by creeping underground stems. The backward-curving oval leaves are dark green and each slender stem carries one to six, white or bluish-white, 2 in (5 cm) flowers with a yellow throat, in late spring and early summer.
M. reptans (zone 6), from the Himalayas, is a hardy perennial and measures 2 in (5 cm) in height, with a spread of 1–2 ft (30–60 cm) with prostrate rooting stems bearing short, erect leafy shoots. This carpet-forming plant has purplish-blue flowers streaked with white and yellow from mid spring to mid summer.

Their habit makes them suitable for rock gardens or spaces between paving stones.
Cultivation. Plant in moist, peaty, lime-free soil in a sheltered sunny position. In winter, cover with a layer of pine needles.

In autumn propagate by dividing the clumps after flowering or alternatively raise from seed.

Meconopsis grandis

Meconopsis
Papaveraceae

A genus of about 40 species of hardy herbaceous perennials, native to Asia and Europe.
M. cambrica (zone 5–6), the Welsh poppy, is native to Europe. It has a height and spread of over 1 ft (30 cm). The leaves are mid green, deeply incised and slightly downy. From late spring to summer the poppy-like yellow or orange flowers bloom in profusion. It may die after it has flowered, but seeds itself readily.
M. cambrica can be used in semi-wild parts of the garden, herbaceous borders and rock gardens.
M. grandis (zone 6), from the Himalayas, reaches well over 3½ ft (1 m) and bears large, blue, pendent flowers in early summer. The hairy basal leaves are oblong and somewhat toothed. This, like the other Asiatic species should have a cool, partly shaded position, as in a woodland clearing, in a lime-free soil, kept moist with plenty of humus.
Cultivation. In spring, plant 1 ft (30 cm) apart in light, fertile soil. *M. cambrica* does well in sunny and shady positions. Remove dead flowers to prolong the flowering season and cut down the stems in autumn. Sow seeds as soon as they ripen in a sheltered place, and plant out in autumn. Downy streaks, the sign of mildew, may cover the leaves, stems, and flowers.

Medicago
Medick, *Leguminosae*

A genus of about 50 species of herbaceous perennials and shrubs from southern Europe and Africa.
M. arborea (zone 9), moon trefoil, from southern Europe, is a tender evergreen shrub growing to 6½ ft (2 m) with trifoliate leaves. The bright yellow pea-like flowers are formed in short racemes from late spring to early autumn.

It is best grown in a sheltered position against a sunny wall, or in colder areas, in a cool greenhouse.
Cultivation. This species tolerates most soils. Propagate from cuttings. Bottom heat will encourage rooting.

Melia
Meliaceae

A genus of about twelve species of trees native to the tropics and sub-tropics.

M. azedarach (zone 10), bead tree or Persian lilac, 40–50 ft (12–15 m) tall, has beautiful deciduous mid green bipinnate leaves and large panicles of small lilac-coloured, scented flowers, in summer. These are followed by long-lasting yellow bead-like fruits.
Cultivation. Hardy in Mediterranean-type climates and in protected positions, such as against a sunny wall. It tolerates dry conditions and needs a good well-drained soil. Raise from seed.

Melissa

Balm, *Labiatae*

A genus of four to five species of herbaceous perennials native to Europe and Asia.
M. officinalis (zone 6), lemon balm, from the Mediterranean region, has branching stems of 1½–2 ft (45–60 cm). These carry toothed oval leaves, lemon-scented when crushed and three to six flowered whorls of white or pinkish flowers in summer. 'Aurea', whose leaves are splashed with gold, is a good-looking form.
Cultivation. Lemon balm thrives in all soils, but prefers moisture and a shady position. Every four years, divide the old clumps in mid autumn, and replant the sections at intervals of 16 in (40 cm). Plants seed themselves more than readily. Protect in winter during frosty weather.
Uses. Gather the leaves when the plant is in fresh growth to add flavour to raw vegetables and cooked dishes. Infusions of the leaves have antispasmodic and digestive properties.

Mentha

Mint, *Labiatae*

A genus of about 25 species of hardy herbaceous perennials from temperate regions of the Old World. Having aromatic foliage, many are used for culinary purposes.
M. × *piperata* (zone 5–6), peppermint, is a vigorous and invasive European perennial. It has upright reddish stems that reach 1½–2 ft (45–60 cm). The spear-shaped leaves are toothed, and spikes of purplish flowers appear in summer.

Other species include *M. spicata*, common or spearmint; *M.* × *rotundifolia*, round-leaved mint, widely used in the kitchen; *M. pulegium*, pennyroyal, and *M. requienii*, Corsican mint, which is prostrate and suitable for carpeting paved areas.

Cultivation. Although mints prefer to be planted in a rich, moist, well-manured soil, they grow well in most places regardless of exposure to sun. Divide clumps in autumn or early to mid spring.

Gather the leaves as and when they are needed, and dry them in a shady place for later use.
Uses. The fresh leaves add flavour to salads, omelettes, and couscous. Infusions (teas) have digestive and stimulant properties and when inhaled ease throat and bronchial infections. Mint essence is said to be a good antiseptic.

Menyanthes

Marsh trefoil, buck-bean, bog-bean, *Gentianaceae*

M. trifoliata (zone 6), the only member of the genus, is a herbaceous perennial, native to the cooler temperate regions of the Northern Hemisphere.

It has large green leaves divided into three leaflets, each up to 3in (7.5 cm) long. White or tinged pink the fringed star-like flowers, measuring about 1 in (2 cm) across, appear in spring, in clusters on erect stems.

This attractive plant never reaches more than 1 ft (30 cm) and makes excellent ground cover in a moist situation.
Cultivation. Grow in a damp place, or in water 4–6 in (10–15 cm) deep. It develops quickly, and associates well with plants with variegated foliage, such as *Acorus calamus* 'Variegatus' or the zebra rush, *Scirpus lacustris* subsp. *tabernaemontani* 'Zebrinus'.

Propagate by dividing the clumps during the growing period, from late spring to early autumn, or by cutting 1 ft (30 cm) lengths of root with a terminal bud and pushing them into soft mud.
Uses. Even today the bitter leaves of this plant are taken for various complaints of the digestive tract or used in the brewing of a bitter type of beer.

Menziesia

Mock azalea, *Ericaceae*

A genus of seven hardy deciduous shrubs from North America and Japan, useful for the woodland garden.

M. ciliicalyx (zone 6), native to Japan, is a branching shrub to $3\frac{1}{2}$ ft (1 m) high. In late spring or early summer it bears nodding pink urn-shaped flowers, each about 1 in (2.5 cm) long.
Cultivation. Grows well in light shade on the edges of woodland. Plant in moist, well-drained, lime-free loam or a peaty soil.

Propagate by sowing seeds in late winter in well-drained sand and peat. Keep at a temperature of 55°F (13°C) and prick out seedlings when large enough to handle, keeping them in a frame during the winter. Plant outside in a nursery bed the following autumn and in their final positions a year later. Otherwise, take heeled cuttings in summer.

Mertensia
Boraginaceae

The genus contains about 40 species of hardy herbaceous perennials from western Europe, Asia and North America. Most are fairly small plants with attractive tubular funnel or bell-shaped blue flowers suitable for the rock garden or ground cover. Taller species such as *M. virginica* enjoy woodland conditions.
M. maritima (zone 5), oyster plant, native to northern Europe, reaches about 1 ft (30 cm) in height with stems spreading to 3 ft (90 cm). The leaves are blue-green and the bell-shaped light blue flowers are borne in summer. It prefers a well-drained sunny position.
M. virginica (zone 5), Virginia cowslip, from eastern USA, is between 1–2 ft (30–60 cm) tall with smooth greyish leaves and drooping sprays of tubular purple-blue flowers in spring. In midsummer it dies down completely to reappear in early spring.
Cultivation. Plant in early spring in sun or partial shade. The soil should be rich in humus, moist, but well-drained in winter.

Propagate by division after flowering is over. The pieces of root should be replanted immediately. Sow seeds as soon as they are ripe.

Mespilus
Medlar, *Rosaceae*

A genus of one species from southeast Europe and Asia Minor.
M. germanica (zone 7) is hardy, and closely related to the hawthorns. It forms a small, wide-spreading, deciduous tree, 10–13 ft (3–4 m) in height, and as an ornamental, is best planted as a specimen. The oblong leaves are slightly hairy, and become tinged reddish-brown in autumn. The white or pink-tinged flowers formed in late spring are followed by brownish fruits which are edible, and should be gathered when over-ripe after the first frosts. Grafted cultivars have larger fruit than the species.
Cultivation. Medlars are easily grown in all well-drained soils and prefer an open sunny position.

Propagate by means of stratified seeds that have been collected and cleaned in autumn. It can be cleft-grafted in mid spring on to hawthorn or on to a seedling medlar in order to obtain a standard tree.

Mimulus
Monkey flower, *Scrophulariaceae*

This genus comprises about 150 species of annual and perennial herbaceous plants, most of which have showy flowers. They are distributed in South Africa, Asia and America.
M. cardinalis (zone 8), scarlet monkey flower, originates from a region extending from Oregon to Mexico. It is an erect perennial reaching 3 ft (90 cm), with narrow, clammy leaves toothed at the margins. The flowers are red or red with yellow throats, and appear from early summer to early autumn.

Mimulus cardinalis

M. guttatus (*M. luteus* of gardens) – zone 5 – monkey musk, comes from a territory that extends from Alaska to New Mexico, and has numerous sub-species. It is a summer-blooming perennial 2 ft (60 cm) in height with yellow flowers to $\frac{3}{4}$–2 in (2–5 cm) long, streaked with reddish-brown.

Both are short-lived perennials, and are suitable for beds, rock gardens, bog gardens and the edges of ponds.

Cultivation. Plant out 8–12 in (20–30 cm) apart in spring when the frosts are over. They need a moisture-retentive soil and a sunny or partially shaded position to succeed.

Cut down dead stems in late autumn, and where winters are cold protect with a cloche or a plastic tunnel.

Sow seeds in late winter under glass in gentle heat 60–64°F (16–18°C). Prick out and harden off before planting out in the open ground.

Minuartia

Caryophyllaceae

This genus contains about 120 hardy species of mostly herbaceous plants originating in Europe, Asia and America, from Alaska to Chile.

M. laricifolia (zone 4), native to the mountains of southern and central Europe, is 6 in (15 cm) in height, with a spread of 12–20 in (30–50 cm). The grass-like foliage is dark green and the white flowers on thin stems appear in early summer. This hardy creeping plant forms a loose mat, and is useful for rock gardens.

Cultivation. Plant in a sunny corner of a rock garden in moist, light, gritty soil containing some organic matter.

Propagate either by division or by taking cuttings from the base of the stems in early and mid summer and placing them in a cold frame in a sandy mixture.

Mirabilis

Nyctaginaceae

A genus of 45 species of annual and perennial herbaceous plants natives of warmer areas of America, with showy flowers.

M. jalapa (zone 10), marvel of Peru or four o'clock plant, from tropical America, is a large perennial, reaching more than 32 in (80 cm), and may have red, pink, white or yellow funnel-shaped flowers from mid summer to early autumn which open late in the afternoon, and close the following morning.

Mirabilis jalapa

It is usually grown as a half-hardy annual except in warm climates.

Cultivation. Sow seeds in a greenhouse or warm frame in early spring. Prick out and, after hardening off, plant outside in late spring in the open ground.

Plant, 16 in (40 cm) apart, in a deep and well-prepared friable loam, in a sunny position, where it will tolerate dryness but not excessive heat. By the end of the season the roots become tuberous, and can be kept like those of dahlias during winter. They can then be divided in the spring, before planting out.

Miscanthus

Silver grass, *Gramineae*

This genus is represented by about 20 hardy perennial species of grass from various parts of Asia.

M. sacchariflorus (zone 6), silver banner grass is the tallest species, measuring from $6\frac{1}{2}$–10 ft (2–3 m) in height. The mid-green alternate leaves are spear-shaped, and a variegated form has a white central vein. It flowers in the form of an elegant silvery plume but only in warm climates.

M. sinensis (zone 6), Chinese silver grass, measures from $3\frac{1}{2}$–$6\frac{1}{2}$ ft (1–2 m) in height. It has given rise to several cultivars with variegated foliage, such as 'Zebrinus' with leaves banded with yellow, 'Variegatus' with leaves with longitudinal white stripes and 'Gracillimus' with finely textured foliage.

The larger species can be used as hedges or wind-breaks during the summer, but they are best in large herbaceous or mixed borders, where their foliage contrasts with broader foliage and acts as a background for brightly coloured flowers, or as isolated specimens. The white-variegated cultivars may be used in the planning of white gardens. Their flowerheads are suitable for dried arrangements.

Cultivation. These plants are extremely hardy and easy to grow. Unlike bamboos, they renew their stems every year, and die back totally during winter. They require a moist soil, or frequent watering during summer.

Propagate by division of clumps in autumn or early spring.

Mitella

Miterwort, *Saxifragaceae*

A genus of about eight small hardy herbaceous perennial plants, native mainly to North America.

M. diphylla (zone 6), mitrewort, is 8–10 in (20–25 cm) high when in flower, with a spread of 28 in (70 cm). The green leaves are broad and heart-shaped, with three or five lobes. The racemes of small whitish flowers appear in mid and late spring.

This plant quickly covers the ground with its suckers. It should be grown in shade or partial shade in woodland or rock gardens. Shade-loving bulbous plants that will penetrate its foliage are good partners for it.

Cultivation. Plant in moist, peaty soil and protect from cold winds during winter.

Propagate by seed, by division or by removing suckers in early summer, and replanting them immediately.

Molinia

Gramineae

A genus represented by about three species of grass from Europe and Asia.

M. caerulea (zone 4–5), purple moorgrass, native to Europe, reaches 20 in–3½ ft (50 cm–1 m) in height, forming clumps of glaucous leaves, from which purplish flower spikes grow at the end of summer. The form 'Variegata' is neater, not as tall and conspicuously striped with cream.

This species can be used with other grasses in a bed devoted to them, or as a foil for flowers in herbaceous or mixed borders.

Cultivation. Molinia grows naturally in marshy places and peaty soils and adapts well to all damp conditons. It is propagated by division.

Moltkia

Boraginaceae

This genus consists of six species native to southern Europe and Asia. They are herbaceous perennials or sub-shrubs, mostly hardy.

M. petraea (zone 7) is native to Greece and reaches 12–18 in (30–45 cm) in height, much taller in warm conditions. The whole plant is covered with a silky down. It has grey-green linear leaves and tubular pinkish-blue flowers which turn deep blue-violet, and appear from late spring to late summer.

It can be used in a rock garden, in troughs, on dry stone walls, or stony slopes.

Cultivation. Plant in a sunny position in well-drained calcareous soil, consisting of gravel and leaf mould in equal parts, covering the soil with a final layer of gravel up to 4 in (10 cm) deep.

To propagate, sow fresh seeds in a tray in mid autumn, and keep them in an unheated frame

Moluccella laevis

over winter until germination takes place the following spring. It can also be propagated from cuttings or by layers.

Moluccella

Shell flower, *Labiatae*

This genus contains about four annuals and perennials from the Mediterranean region to northwest India. They are appreciated for their unusual green flowers.

M. laevis (zone 8), bells of Ireland, reaches 12–20 in (30–50 cm) in height. It is a half-hardy annual from Syria with light green, roundish leaves with long stalks, and upright spikes of white flowers in whorls of 5 to 10, each enclosed in a large bell-shaped green calyx.

They are decorative in borders and are suitable for both dried or fresh flower arrangements.

Cultivation. Plant in light, humus-rich soil in a sunny dry position.

Propagate by means of seeds in spring, under glass. Prick out in trays or in a nursery bed, and then finally plant *in situ* in late spring.

Monarda

Wild bergamot, *Labiatae*

This genus is represented by about a dozen hardy herbaceous annual and perennial plants native to North America and Mexico.

M. didyma (zone 6), Oswego tea or bee balm, is a herbaceous perennial that is hardy in most climates. It is 2–3½ ft (60 cm–1 m) tall, with a spread of 16–24 in (40–60 cm). The aromatic leaves are mid green, and oval in shape. Scarlet tubular flowers are densely grouped at the ends of the stems, and appear from early summer to early autumn. Cultivars in a range of colours are available, among them: 'Snow Maiden', white; 'Croftway Pink' pink; 'Prairie Night', purple-violet.

Monarda is suitable for moist parts of herbaceous or mixed borders and near ponds.

Cultivation. *M. didyma* is sun loving and thrives in a soil that is not too dry but humus rich and moisture retentive. It is best planted 16 in (40 cm) apart, forming a spreading clump. Cut the stems down to their base in autumn.

Every three or four years, propagate by dividing the clumps in spring.

Monarda didyma

Montanoa

Tree daisy, *Compositae*

A genus of 22 tender shrubs from Central and South America, grown primarily for their attractive foliage. They bear small daisy-like flowers in autumn and winter.

M. bipinnatifida (zone 10) reaches a height of 6½–10 ft (2–3 m) and has large, deeply bipinnate leaves and, in winter, flowers similar to those of *M. mollissima*.

M. mollissima (zone 10) is 6 ft (1.8 m) tall with yellow-centred white flowers in autumn.

Cultivation. These cool-greenhouse plants grow well in a good loam and sand; only in a Mediterranean-type of climate can they be grown outside.

Propagate from seed or from root cuttings, or, better still, stem cuttings from the shoots of the previous year's growth when it will grow to maturity within the year.

It associates well with other tropical plants such as cannas, banana plants and the cultivars of *Ricinus communis*.

Morina

Morinaceae

A genus consisting of about 17 species of herbaceous perennials originating in the Himalayas and southwestern China.

Morina longifolia

M. longifolia (zone 8–9), whorlflower, from Nepal, is 24–32 in (60–80 cm) tall. Its thick fleshy roots are reminiscent of those of asparagus. The basal rosette of thistle-like leaves, gives off a smell of balsam when rubbed. The whorls of flowers are tubular, white on opening, becoming pink and then crimson towards the end of the flowering period. They appear one after the other from mid summer to mid autumn.

This plant can be used in a rock garden or herbaceous border.

Cultivation. Plant in spring, leaving 12–16 in (30–50 cm) between plants, in rich, well-drained soil in a sunny or partially shaded position.

In late autumn, cut down the stems and protect with a layer of dead leaves.

Propagate in spring by sowing seeds in a tray in a cold frame, and plant out the seedlings in their permanent positions with some shading, as soon as danger of frost has passed. Alternatively, divide and plant immediately after flowering in order to enable the plant to establish itself before the winter sets in.

Morus

Mulberry, *Moraceae*

This genus consists of seven species of deciduous trees and shrubs from subtropical Asia that do not usually exceed 33 ft (10 m) in height, notable for their longevity. They have a rounded crown and fairly large, alternate, entire and often lobed leaves. The flowers in small pendulous catkins, are insignificant but are followed by juicy fruits in blackberry-like clusters.

M. alba (zone 7–8), white mulberry, originates in China, and was once grown to feed silkworms. The leaves are broad, often three lobed; the fruits are white or pink, sweet but insipid. Several cultivars are known with very large or deeply lobed leaves, and others with a weeping habit.

M. nigra (zone 8), black mulberry, native to western Asia, also has a rounded crown. The rough leaves are wide, oval, and toothed, and the dark red fruits are sweet and edible. This is a slow growing tree thriving best in milder, drier areas. The black mulberry has been cultivated for hundreds of years for its edible fruits which are delicious raw or in cooking.

Cultivation. Mulberries do well in most soils, even if poor and dry, but they do best in a warm well-drained loam. Although they are drought resistant, growth is better in warm moist conditions. Plant with a good rootball and water well in autumn or spring. They will tolerate some pruning.

Propagate by means of seeds in spring, after these have been stratified; by 1 ft (30 cm) long summer cuttings, or by cuttings taken after the leaves have fallen, planted deeply, 10 in (25 cm), in a sandy soil in a shady border.

Muehlenbeckia

Polygonaceae

A genus of about 15 species from the temperate zone of the Southern Hemisphere. These are woody perennials, either upright, prostrate or climbing, and have decorative foliage.

M. axillaris (zone 7), creeping wire-vine, native to New Zealand, Tasmania and Australia, is 8 in (20 cm) tall with a spread of 4 ft (1.2 m) or more. This hardy creeping plant forms compact mats, its blackish stems resembling thin strands of wire. The small leaves are round, alternate, shiny greenish-brown. The insignificant greenish flowers produce fruits with black glossy seeds.

This species is useful for providing ground cover in a rock garden or a border.

Cultivation. It does well in a sunny or partially shaded position and in a soil that is not too dry. In a severe winter it may loose its foliage but the plant is frost-resistant, and new leaves will appear in spring.

Propagate by cuttings taken in late summer rooting them in a sandy medium in a cold frame.

Musa

Banana plant, *Musaceae*

This genus includes nearly 40 species of tender perennial plants, with large shiny evergreen leaves. The curious flowers are held in a spectacular pendent raceme.

M. basjoo (zone 9), Japanese banana, up to 10 ft (3 m) tall, has bright green leaves about 4 ft (1.2 m) long.

M. ensete (zone 10), from Ethiopia, reaches 30 ft (9 m) in open ground and has wide leaves of a shiny green up to 5 ft (1.5 m) long.

A banana tree gives the smallest garden an exotic atmosphere; in a conservatory or greenhouse it needs a large container.

Cultivation. Grow in moist, rich soil in a sunny position. They need frequent watering and generous amounts of organic fertilizer. Banana trees are only hardy in warm mild and totally frost-free climates, elsewhere they need a large spacious heated glasshouse or conservatory in order to flourish.

Propagate by means of seeds that have been soaked for 24 hours in tepid water, and placed in a tray with bottom heat. Alternatively, remove strong suckers and place them in pots on a hotbed.

Muscari

Grape hyacinth, *Liliaceae*

A genus of about 60 species of hardy bulbous plants native to Europe and the Near East. They are usually low-growing with flowers, often blue, grouped in small spikes from early to late spring. Some species have a musky scent.

M. armeniacum (zone 7) originates in southern Europe and Turkey, and reaches 6–8 in (15–20 cm) in height. The bell-shaped flowers are fragrant, cobalt-blue edged with white, and appear in mid spring. In the monstrous garden form 'Blue Spike' each flower produces a tiny inflorescence.

M. botryoides (zone 6), from southern Europe, is 6–8 in (15–20 cm) tall with sky-blue flowers which bloom slightly later. 'Album' is an attractive white form.

M. comosum (zone 8), tassel hyacinth, from western Europe, is 8–16 in (20–40 cm) tall. This species is distinguished by a tuft of sterile violet flowers above a loose inflorescence of fertile olive-green flowers. In the form 'Plumosum' all the flowers are sterile and violet-blue with feathery violet filaments.

With other species, such as *M. latifolium* and *M. aucheri* (*M. tubergenianum*), it is possible to have a succession of flowers in different shades of blue throughout the spring. Muscari are particularly suitable for rock gardens, border fronts and pots or for naturalizing in sunny areas in short grass.

Cultivation. Plant in autumn, as early as possible, in a sunny position in a rich and well-drained soil 2–4 in (5–10 cm) apart, and as deep. In the spring before they flower, cover the area in which the bulbs were planted with a top dressing of new soil.

By lifting the bulbs periodically it is possible to obtain small offsets which can be planted elsewhere. As a rule, there are plenty of self-sown seedlings.

Mutisia

Climbing gazania, *Compositae*

A genus of 59 species of evergreen erect or climbing shrubs from South America.

M. ilicifolia (zone 9–10) is a tender climbing plant native to Chile whose striking flowers are reminiscent of those of *Gazania*. It climbs vigorously to 13 ft (4 m) by using tendrils at the ends of the leathery holly-like leaves, which are woolly below. The flowers are profuse, daisy-like, 2–3 in (5–7.5 cm) across ranging in colour from pink to mauve with yellow centres. These colourful blooms appear from summer to early autumn.

Cultivation. Mutisia is only hardy in warm, mild climates. Usually it needs a sun-facing wall or better still a greenhouse. It needs a rich and well-drained soil.

It can be propagated by seed in very warm areas, or by means of cuttings placed in warm humid conditions in sand under glass, in late summer, or by semi-hardwood cuttings in spring.

Myoporum
Myoporaceae

This genus comprises about 30 species of tender, evergreen trees and shrubs that originate in Australia, New Zealand, China and Japan with small, white or pink flowers sometimes dotted with purple. Some species are hardy enough for milder, more or less frost-free climates of the Mediterranean type, otherwise they need the protection of a cool greenhouse.
M. laetum (zone 9), Ngaio, from New Zealand, reaches 20 ft (6 m) in height, a small tree or shrub, with beautiful narrow bottle-green leaves. The white flowers in clusters are spotted with violet, and appear in mid and late summer followed by reddish juicy fruits.
Cultivation. In a cool greenhouse it should be planted in a compost of loam, peat and some sand.

Propagate by means of half-ripened shoots under glass.

Myosotis
Forget-me-not, *Boraginaceae*

These annual, biennial or herbaceous perennial plants in this genus of 50 species from temperate regions are generally grown as biennials and, because they are so straightforward to cultivate, are very popular.
M. alpestris (zone 4–5), about 8 in (20 cm) tall, forms pretty blue carpets in spring to accompany bulbs and other perennial plants. It begins to flower in late spring and may continue into summer. Among the many cultivars are: 'Bouquet' with indigo blue flowers, and 'Carmine King' with carmine-pink flowers.
Cultivation. Use a clean and well-prepared site that is moist, well drained and in a sunny or partially shaded position.

Raise from seed sown in spring in a warm moist nursery bed. Prick out when large enough to handle in the bed in which they were sown, and then plant out into their permanent positions in the autumn. Perennial species can be divided, or raised from cuttings under shaded glass in summer.

Mildew can cause a greyish dust to appear on the plant, causing premature desiccation and this must be controlled immediately it appears if you are to save the plant.

Myriophyllum
Water milfoil, *Haloragidaceae*

The name *Myriophyllum* comes from the Greek 'myrios', many, and 'phyllon', leaf. The genus contains about 40 bog or totally aquatic species, from all parts of the world. The flowers are insignificant, but the foliage decorative.
M. aquaticum (*M. proserpinacoides*) – zone 10 – water feather or parrot's feather, is the most ornamental species. The stems usually float in the water but upright leafy stems rise 4–8 in (10–20 cm) above the water. The leaves, in whorls of about five, are finely divided. This plant comes from Brazil, Chile and Argentina so it is half hardy in temperate climates but can be used in aquaria or greenhouse pools.

In frost-free climates myriophyllum looks well in association with water irises, *Eichhornia crassipes*, and small rushes.
Cultivation. It can be propagated from cuttings taken during the growing season.

Myrrhis
Myrrh, sweet cicely, *Umbelliferae*

M. odorata (zone 6), the only member of the genus, is a herbaceous perennial found wild in much of Europe. The hollow stem rises to a height of 2 ft (60 cm) or more when the umbels of white flowers are at their fullest development in early summer. The green leaves are triangular in outline, and deeply incised in many leaflets. They smell like aniseed.
Cultivation. This fragrant herb does well in most situations with a moist soil, as may be found in a partially shaded woodland clearing. Sow in early or mid spring, or divide the clumps in mid autumn, leaving a distance of 2½ ft (75 cm) between plants.
Uses. The fresh leaves are gathered when needed. They give flavour to cooked and raw vegetables and reduce acidity in rhubarb, but are mainly used in salads. The seeds can be used while still green in the same way as aniseed.

Myrsine
Myrsinaceae

This genus includes five species, mostly from tropical or subtropical areas.

M. africana (zone 9), Cape myrtle, from eastern and southern Africa, the Himalayas and China, is a hardy small evergreen shrub measuring about $3\frac{1}{2}$ ft (1 m) in height, and has leaves reminiscent of those of the myrtle. It has small brownish-red flowers in late spring and when male plants are present, the female plants produce attractive pale blue berries about $\frac{1}{4}$ in (6 mm) across.
Cultivation. It does well in ordinary soil, as long as this is not too calcareous (alkaline).

Propagate by means of cuttings.

Myrtus

Myrtle, *Myrtaceae*

This genus contains six species of shrubs and small trees, with aromatic evergreen mid green foliage. Clusters of small white scented flowers appear in spring and summer followed by black berries.
M. chequen, (*Luma chequen*) – zone 7–8 – Chilean myrtle, 10 ft (3 m), a native of Chile, is a thick-set and very elegant shrub with plain evergreen foliage and white scented flowers that bloom from early summer to mid autumn. This species requires moist soil.
M. communis (zone 8–9), common myrtle, 10–17 ft (3–5 m) tall, grows wild in southern Europe and western Asia. The leaves are dark glossy green and it is appreciated for its superb white scented flowers that bloom from late spring to mid summer. These are followed by purple-black berries. The cultivar 'Flore Pleno' has double flowers, but these have no scent. *M. communis* var. *tarentina* is more compact, with smaller leaves and whitish berries.

Myrtles are frost sensitive but can be planted to form hedges in mild climates or as solitary specimens, against a sheltered wall in cooler areas.
Cultivation. Plant *M. communis* in well-drained soil – it does not object to dry chalky soils. It is a good seaside plant, enjoying the generally milder climate of the coast.

Propagate by means of seeds, or by semi-hardwood cuttings taken in early and mid summer and placed under a cloche.

Narcissus

Daffodil, *Amaryllidaceae*

There are about 27 species in this genus of bulbous plants, mostly originating in western Europe and the Mediterranean region. The majority are more or less hardy. Several species are included in the parentage of the large number of cultivars grown in gardens (see below). Those with large coronas (trumpets) are very popular but double and smaller flowered types are also widely grown.
N. bulbocodium (zone 8), hoop petticoat, originates in an area ranging from southwest France to Morocco, and reaches 4–6 in (10–15 cm) in height. It has yellow flowers, and a well-developed corona, whose shape is indicated by its common name. It flowers in late winter to

Narcissus 'February Gold'

early spring. It is easy to grow, and does well in a lawn.

N. cyclamineus (zone 8) originates in the Iberian peninsula. It is 4–8 in (10–20 cm) tall, and has small bright yellow flowers with the perianth entirely reflexed. It blooms in late winter to early spring. This species is easily grown in rock gardens and in naturalized light shade under trees.

N. jonquilla (zone 8), wild jonquil, is native to the Iberian Peninsula. Its fragrant, yellow flowers are in umbels of two to five, with small coronas. It has narrow dark green rush-like leaves.

N. poeticus (zone 6), poet's narcissus or pheasant's eye, originates in Europe, and reaches 12–20 in (30–50 cm) in height. It is notable for its scent and late flowering (mid spring to summer). The white perianth surrounds a small corona, which is orange-red or sometimes yellow with a red edge. This species can be grown in damp meadows, and moist clay soils.

N. pseudonarcissus (zone 5), wild daffodil or lent lily, originates in Europe, and is 8–12 in (20–30 cm) high. This is a well-known species with a long yellow trumpet, and has one of the largest flowers of the genus, appearing in early and mid spring. It naturalizes easily in damp meadows.

N. tazetta (zone 7) has a wide distribution, spread from southern Europe to Japan, by way of North Africa, the Middle East and China. It reaches over 18 in (45 cm) in height and bears umbels of 3 to 15 scented white flowers with small yellow coronas in late winter and early spring.

Cultivars. More than 1000 cultivars and hybrids are available for garden use. Mostly large flowered, they are superb for spring displays in borders or, the more vigorous kinds, naturalized in grass and woodland clearings. Patio containers and window boxes can be a riot of colour and several forms can be forced for indoor use. For exhibition purposes and ease of cataloguing, garden daffodils and narcissi are classified into twelve divisions, one of which includes the wild species and their immediate hybrids. There is a miscellaneous division and the others are concerned with the size and shape of the corona or with their relationship to the wild species that has contributed to their make up. For example, crosses made between *N. cyclamineus* and trumpet daffodils have produced several desirable hybrids, one of which is 'February Gold'. About 12 in (30 cm) tall, it has inherited the reflexed petals of the one and the larger trumpet of the other. It is classed as a Cyclamineus Narcissus.

Cultivation. The garden varieties are easy to grow. The bulbs should be planted in autumn in moist clay soil in an area with a little shade. They should be buried quite deeply 4–6 in (10–15 cm), and placed a similar distance apart. The bulbs should remain in the ground for several years, and should not be disturbed too often. It is also important not to remove the foliage until this has completely faded.

Propagate by division of clumps every three or four years, once the leaves have turned yellow. Replant the bulbs at once.

Daffodils are vulnerable to various fungal diseases which affect the leaves (white mould), the roots (white root rot), or the bulbs (grey bulb rot). Their main pests are slugs, bulb and stem eelworms, bulb flies and narcissus fly.

Nasturtium

Watercress, *Cruciferae*

This genus consists of six species of perennials from Europe to central Asia.

N. officinale (zone 6), an aquatic, grows naturally near springs and in clear running water. It has stems 2–4 in (5–10 cm) long with compound leaves, which have an agreeably sharp flavour and are used for salads.

Cultivation. While watercress is best grown in running water, it does well in permanently moist soil in a partially shaded position. It may also be grown in a container, as long as the water is clean and frequently renewed.

Propagate by means of seeds sown at the rate of $\frac{1}{8}$ oz per sq yd (4 g per m^2), or by cuttings dibbled in very damp soil in late spring and early summer. It is also possible to sow seeds in a pot resting on a saucer constantly refilled with water. Whether cuttings are placed in a seed bed or a basin of water, replant the leafless branches at intervals of 2 in (5 cm) and keep them in the shade until they take root. In a seed bed, water generously, preferably with an automatic system. When it is grown in a basin, ensure that the water does not become stagnant.

The plants may be attacked by shrimps, slugs, caddis-fly larvae, chironomids, cress-flies and aphids.

Gather by using scissors, never by hand, avoiding cutting too far down.

Neillia

Rosaceae

This is a small genus of deciduous Asian shrubs related to *Spiraea*.

N. thibetica (N. longiracemosa) – zone 6 – native to China, has erect, downy stems 5 ft (1.5 m) high. The toothed, oval leaves are sometimes three-lobed. The dense racemes of tubular pink flowers appear in late spring and early summer.

N. thyrsifolia (zone 6) is smaller, with a spreading, rounded habit and arching stems. Its white, scented flowers are borne on the tips of the shoots, or in the axils of the uppermost leaves.

Cultivation. Neillia does well in all soils, except very dry ones. It is hardy, but if damaged by frost, cut the shrub down to ground level, and new growth will shoot from the base.

Propagate by seeds or semi-hardwood cuttings.

Nelumbo

Lotus, *Nelumbonaceae*

A flower sacred to Oriental civilizations from India to Japan, the lotus has inspired many works of art. In the gardens of the Alhambra in Spain, there are basins derived from the shape of the closed and open Nelumbo blossom.

N. lutea (zone 9), American lotus, has yellow flowers, blue-green, shield-shaped leaves and originates in North America. It can take several years to become established.

N. nucifera (zone 9–10), sacred lotus, is of Asiatic origin and has red to pink flowers and greyer, paddle-shaped leaves.

The leaves of both species sometimes rise more than 5 ft (1.5 m) from the surface of the water on long petioles; floating leaves are only a transitional stage.

Though hardy in some cooler temperate regions, the lotus needs to be brought in for the winter where the frosts are hard.

Cultivation. Grow in 4–12 in (10–30 cm) deep water in a pond or tank or tub which can be brought in during the winter. Bury the rhizomes in early spring 3 in (7.5 cm) deep in a rich organic mixture of loam and cow manure. It disappears completely during winter to emerge once more in spring, and flowers throughout summer. Seeds the size of a small almond ripen in the fruit and these can be sown in spring. In mid spring, the rhizomes can be divided, and the sections replanted immediately.

Nelumbo nucifera

Nemesia

Scrophulariaceae

A genus of about 50 annual or herbaceous perennials, many from South Africa, with brightly coloured flowers.

N. strumosa (zone 7–8) is a compact dwarf half-hardy annual, about 10 in (25 cm) tall, which flowers from late spring to early autumn. It is suitable both for borders and window boxes. The flowers are funnel shaped, and can be white, yellow, orange, red, purple or blue, in pastel or bright shades, and with or without a contrasting eye.

Cultivars include 'Blue Gem', 8 in (20 cm) high; and 'Carnival Mixture', 7 in (18 cm) high, known for its very large flowers in various shades.

Nemesia can be used in formal bedding schemes or informally, in mixed borders. They are excellent cut flowers and can be grown as pot plants for a cool greenhouse.

Cultivation. Sow under glass in early spring, then prick off the seedlings into boxes, harden off and plant out, or sow outside, *in situ*, in late spring. Leave 4 in (10 cm) between plants when planting out. Nemesia prefers a sunny spot and a light peaty soil, rich in organic matter. Water in dry weather, and cut back after the first flowering, to obtain a second flush in autumn. *N. strumosa* is the least affected by adverse weather conditions.

Nepeta

Labiatae

This genus is represented by about 250 species of annuals or herbaceous perennials, which originate in Europe and Asia.

N. × *faassenii* (zone 6), catmint, is a hardy herbaceous perennial, 12–16 in (30–40 cm) in height, with a similar spread. Its narrow leaves are silver-grey and aromatic, and its small, tubular, pale-lavender flowers are produced throughout summer, as long as it is regularly dead-headed.

Nepeta is used in herbaceous beds, as edging for paths or flower beds, or in rock gardens.

Cultivation. Plant in a sunny position in spring, 12 in (30 cm) apart, in ordinary, well drained soil, especially sandy or limy soil. It dislikes cold, wet winters.

Topdress with manure and cut the stems down to their base in the spring.

Propagate by division in spring or by taking 3 in (7.5 cm) long cuttings from early shoots in late spring or early summer and placing them in a cold frame.

Nerine

Amaryllidaceae

This genus includes about 30 species of half-hardy bulbous plants, which originate in southern Africa. The strap-shaped leaves usually appear in spring and the umbels of trumpet-shaped flowers, borne on slender, elegant stems, at the end of summer.

N. bowdenii (zone 9) grows 28 in (70 cm) high, and produces 6 to 12 pink flowers with sinuous petals and prominent stamens in autumn. This species has given rise to several cultivars such as the more robust 'Fenwick Variety', and the silvery-pink flowered 'Pink Triumph'.

Cultivation. Plant 4–6 in (10–15 cm) deep in spring, in well-drained soil and in full sunshine, at the foot of a sunny wall, or in a pot. Nerines need a resting period between the time when the leaves die down and the flower buds reappear, and will tolerate long periods of drought in summer. Protect from hard frosts with a thick mulch, or move the pot to a cool but frost-free spot indoors. Lift and divide or repot only when the plants become crowded and flowering is affected – usually after four to five years. If potted use a compost of fibrous loam with some sand to ensure good drainage. Propagate by means of offsets.

Nerium

Apocynaceae

This genus consists of three species of tender, evergreen shrubs, erect and stocky in habit, with attractive lanceolate mid green leaves. All parts of the plants are highly poisonous.

N. oleander (zone 10), the oleander or rose bay, grows wild in the Mediterranean region and reaches 15 ft (4.5 m) or more in height, forming an upright, suckering shrub. The bright pink flowers are very spectacular, and appear from early summer to early autumn. This species has given rise to cultivars with single or double, white, pale yellow, apricot, pink or carmine flowers, some of which are fragrant.

Nerium can be used in spot planting or hedges.

Cultivation. This shrub tolerates all types of soil, but needs full sunshine, dry conditions and a mild, frost-free climate. It is moderately hardy in areas with hot summers. It can also be grown in tubs, and overwintered in a cool greenhouse. Cut back after flowering to encourage new growth; they are sometimes trained as standard trees, on a single, leafless trunk.

Propagate by taking cuttings from the mature shoots in spring. Place in wet soil, or in a jar of water, and pot when the root system is well developed, into a compost of loam and manure in equal proportion.

Neriums are prone to attacks of red spider mite and mealy bug.

Nicandra

Solanaceae

This genus is represented by one annual with decorative calyces, excellent for using in dried flower arrangements.

N. physaloides (zone 7), shoo-fly plant, was introduced from Peru. It grows 20 in–3½ ft (50 cm–1 m) high and has pale blue, bell-shaped flowers with white centres, in summer. They are followed by small, apple-shaped inedible fruit covered in an inflated, membranous green calyx.

Cultivation. Grow as a hardy or half hardy annual, starting out under glass, in early spring or sowing outdoors in ordinary soil in mid spring. If started under glass, prick out in mid spring and gradually harden off. Plant out in late spring, 12 in (30 cm) between plants.

To preserve as dried flowers, cut the branches before the first frosts, remove the leaves, and hang in a dry and well-ventilated place.

Nicotiana

Tobacco plant, *Solanaceae*

A genus consisting of about 65 species of annuals or herbaceous perennials, mostly native to tropical America. Some species are grown as annuals in cooler temperate climates, for their decorative, scented flowers.

N. alata (N. affinis) – zone 6 – grows 32 in (80 cm) high, but there are also compact, dwarf forms. The flowers are white, pink, or red, and resemble those of the petunia but are more upright, and resist bad weather better. There are various cultivars, including 'Lime Green', 32 in (80 cm) high, with pale yellow-green flowers, and 'Sensation Mixed', which has a range of colours.

Cultivation. Sow in early spring in a heated greenhouse. Do not cover up the seeds. Prick young plants into boxes. Harden off and plant out in late spring, in a deep rich moist soil, leaving 12 in (30 cm) between plants. Support tall-growing types with stakes. The flowers of many tobacco plants open at the end of the day, and partial shade encourages the flowers to open earlier. Some cultivars have been bred to open and remain open all day. Remove faded blooms to encourage further flowering.

Nigella

Love-in-a-mist, fennel flower, *Ranunculaceae*

A genus represented by about 15 species of hardy annuals from Europe and Asia with fine green foliage. These are extremely easy to grow.

N. damascena (zone 5), love-in-a-mist, grows 20 in (50 cm) high, and flowers from early summer to early autumn. The sky-blue, saucer-shaped flowers are surrounded by feathery foliage and followed by striking inflated seed pods, green with maroon stripes. Some cultivars have double flowers, and strains of mixed colours are sold, including white, blue, pink, purple, mauve and rosy-red.

This plant will grow in any well drained soil, and sun or light shade. The flowers are excellent for cutting, and the seed pods can be used in dried flower arrangements.

Cultivation. Sow where it is to grow, in spring, or, where winters are mild, in autumn, for an earlier crop of flowers. Nigella does not transplant well. Thin to 6 in (15 cm) apart. The plant self seeds freely.

Nolina

Agavaceae

This genus contains about 25 species of remarkable plants from southern USA and Mexico which cannot be grown out of doors except in very mild and warm climates. Nolina resembles the yucca in habit, but the leaves are more supple. The small whitish flowers appear in racemes on mature plants. The base of the trunk is often swollen and topped by a rosette of strap-shaped leaves.

N. longifolia (zone 10), 5–10 ft (1.5–3 m) high, has thin, rough-edged green leaves that curve elegantly downwards, and can be 10 ft (3 m) long. The flowers are greenish-white. It makes a superb specimen plant, giving a tropical look to a garden or greenhouse.

Cultivation. Plant in a rich fibrous loam, preferably rich in silica to provide ample drainage. Water well when growing but sparingly when resting. Propagate by means of cuttings, root fragments, or seeds.

Nuphar

Yellow water lily, *Nymphaeaceae*

A genus represented by about 20 aquatic plants. It belongs to the same family as *Nymphaea* but is less ornamental, although most species are hardier.

N. lutea (zone 6), yellow water-lily, is the most widespread European species, and is found also in Asia and N. America. It grows best at the edge of slow-moving water where the very large rhizomes are buried in the mud to a depth ranging from 16 in–6½ ft (40 cm–2 m). From these spring orbicular, dark, shiny-green leaves. Summer flowering takes the form of numerous yellow-gold flowers which look like enormous buttercups resting on the water surrounded by large dark leaves.

Cultivation. Plant the rhizomes in spring in fertile mud, by strapping them between two turves, turned grass-side inwards, or in perforated aquatic baskets, filled with heavy loam, lowered into the water. Propagate by division of rhizomes in spring.

Nymphaea

Water-lily, *Nymphaeaceae*

A genus represented by about 50 species of hardy and tender aquatic plants. These have been immortalized by Monet, and are synonymous with romantic stretches of water. An enormous number of hybrids has been created since the last century, in all colours except blue, a colour only found in the tropical *N. caerulea* which is the blue sacred lotus of Ancient Egypt.

The cultivars are categorized according to size: miniature, medium, and large, and choice is determined by the depth and surface area of the water in which it is to be grown.

Most species are suitable for depths ranging from 12–20 in (30–50 cm). The deeper growing forms are recommended for large ponds.

Cultivation. Plant the rhizomes in spring in fertile, muddy soil. If necessary, use a mixture of moist clay and leaf mould, wetted to a cement-like consistency, and placed in a perforated, aquatic planting basket. Propagate from seed sown in shallow pans of loam and charcoal and only just covered with water at a temperature of 70°F (21°C).

Once planted, Nymphaea flowers every year, from spring to autumn. The flowers open in mid-morning and close in the late afternoon, but do not open on sunless days. Each flower lasts three to five days, but as many as 20 at a time may be produced by a single plant.

They are prone to leaf spot and stem rot, water lily aphids and water lily beetle. If these are chemically controlled, any livestock in the water, such as fish or frogs, should be considered.

Ocimum

Basil, *Labiatae*

A genus of plants from warm climates. The two species below are commonly used as culinary herbs.

O. basilicum (zone 9), sweet basil, is a half-hardy annual from Asia, tropical Africa and the Pacific islands. It has oval, glossy leaves and grows more than 18 in (45 cm) high. Its insignificant white flowers appear in racemes, and are best pinched out in bud. The best ornamental cultivar is 'Dark Opal', with metallic purple leaves.

O. minimum (zone 9), bush basil, originates in Chile and is more compact, with smaller leaves. It is often grown in a pot on a windowsill and reaches 6–12 in (15–30 cm) in height in the right conditions.

Cultivation. Grow basil in the warmest and most sheltered spot in the garden or on a sunny windowsill. Sow in a tray in mid spring, and place in a cold frame. After pricking out, harden off and plant out in the garden in late spring or early summer, depending on climate, 8 in (20 cm) apart in light, rich soil. Water well until established.

For salads, gather the leaves as needed. To harvest for drying, cut down to a few inches from the soil in mid to late summer and tie up into a bunch. Dry upside down in an airy, shady place. When the leaves are papery and bone dry, store in a jar for the winter.

Pot up some plants at end of summer and place in a greenhouse for winter. These plants can also be propagated by cuttings of young shoots which should be placed in sand in a closed frame.

Oenothera

Evening primrose, *Onagraceae*

This genus is represented by about 80 species of herbaceous annuals, biennials, perennials and sub-shrubs. These originate in North and South America. Many are cultivated for their showy flowers; there are species and cultivars for growing in borders, in the wild garden and on dry slopes. Dwarf forms are suitable for rock gardens.

O. biennis (zone 6) is a hardy biennial, 3 ft (90 cm) high, with lance-shaped leaves and pale yellow flowers which open in the evening. It can be grown as an annual and will flower the first year from seed. Self-sown seedlings can be a nuisance.

O. tetragona (zone 5), evening primrose, is a hardy herbaceous perennial, from east North America, 2 ft (60 cm) high, with a spread of 12–16 in (30–40 cm). The oval, mid-green leaves are semi-evergreen in mild areas, it blooms abundantly from early summer to early autumn and the short-lived flowers are bright yellow, funnel-shaped, with a silky appearance. They open in daytime.

Cultivation. Plant perennial species in autumn or spring, 12 in (30 cm) apart, in an open sunny position, in a well-drained sandy loam. Water in dry weather. Cut the stems down to their base in autumn.

Propagate biennials and perennials by seed sown in mid summer for the following year. Named forms should be propagated by division of clumps in spring or autumn or by cuttings, before flowering starts, inserted in a sandy compost in a cool frame.

Olea

Olive tree, *Oleaceae*

A genus of about 20 evergreen trees and shrubs of which the olive tree, *O. europea* (zone 10), is the best known. In the Mediterranean basin, it is often the main feature of the landscape and has been cultivated since ancient times, for its great economic importance. There are several selected cultivars. The tree grows to 30 ft (9 m) high, and has a rugged, much branched habit of growth, and attractive grey green foliage.

Cultivation. Olive growing is limited to regions where the temperature never falls below 10°F (−12°C), and where the summers are hot and dry. It resists drought, and grows in any well-drained soil.

It can be grown in slightly less favourable areas, but is unlikely to bear fruit.

Plant olive trees with a good rootball, never bare rooted. Water during the first two summers and protect from the cold during the first two winters. Growth is slow, and it usually takes at least ten years for the first crop.

Propagate by cuttings in spring, taken the previous winter from branches three or four years old, and stratified horizontally in sand.

Olearia

Daisy bush, tree daisy, *Compositae*

This genus contains over 100 species of sun-loving shrubs or tree that originate in Australia and New Zealand. These are noted for their attractive evergreen foliage, and their profusion of usually white, daisy-like flowers in summer. Not all are hardy, but most are wind resistant and easy to grow. Some are excellent for maritime planting.

O. arborescens (zone 9) may quickly reach 12 ft (3.7 m) in height, but it is not very hardy and suited only to mild climates. The dark-green, glossy leaves are silvery on the underside. The clusters of white flowers appear in late spring and early summer, and smell like violets.

O. × *haastii* (zone 8) is the hardiest species, and is resistant to pollution, so can be grown in towns. It makes a rounded shrub, up to 8 ft (2.5 m) high and across. Its small green leaves are white felted on the underside, and the white flowers are very profuse in summer. This shrub makes excellent hedges.

O. ilicifolia (zone 8–9) is a medium-sized shrub up to 10 ft (3 m) high and wide, with green spiny holly-like leaves. The very numerous, small, strongly scented flowers are formed in early summer.

O. semidentata (zone 9) is a very attractive but tender shrub with large pale lilac pendent flowers, purple in the centre, in early summer.

Olearias may be used as specimen plants or as hedges, and most are useful in maritime districts, because they are resistant to salt and sea winds.

Cultivation. All these species thrive in ordinary, even chalky, garden soil, as long as it is well-drained. *O.* × *haastii* is hardy, but the other three species need protection from cold and frost, and are best against a sunny wall or in a cool greenhouse. For hedges, plant 20 in (50 cm) apart.

If the shrub is attacked by frost, or has grown straggly at the base, cut it back hard in spring.

Propagate by cuttings taken in autumn, and placed in sandy leaf compost and give gentle bottom heat. *O. semidentata* should be propagated from semi-ripe cuttings of lateral shoots, taken in mid summer.

Omphalodes

Navelwort, *Boraginaceae*

This genus is represented by about 30 species of annuals and herbaceous perennials, originating in Asia Minor, southern Europe and Mexico.
O. verna (zone 6), blue-eyed Mary, creeping forget-me-not is a stoloniferous, hardy herbaceous perennial from southern Europe, 4–8 in (10–20 cm) high, with a spread of 12 in (30 cm). The mid-green leaves are oval or heart-shaped. From early to late spring, the plant bears small, bright-blue flowers with a white throat, similar to those of the forget-me-not.

O. verna provides good carpeting ground cover, and is used in the front of herbaceous borders, or as a rock garden plant, and for naturalizing in a light woodland.
Cultivation. Plant in mid or late spring, leaving 12 in (30 cm) between plants, in moist, peaty soil and light shade. Water freely in dry weather.

Propagate by division in spring, or after flowering is over or by seed.

These plants are susceptible to slugs.

Onoclea

Sensitive fern, *Aspleniaceae*

O. sensibilis (zone 5), sensitive fern, is the only representative of its genus, and is a perennial fern from northern Asia and North America, hardy in most climates. Its deciduous foliage grows 1–2 ft (30–60 cm) high, and forms clumps up to 3 ft (90 cm) across. In spring, crook-shaped shoots develop into large, sterile light-green, deeply incised fronds, which turn red with the first frosts hence its common name. The fertile fronds do not appear until summer, and change from green to brown. The spores are released the following spring.

This plant spreads rapidly by rhizomes, and is useful ground cover in damp, shaded positions.
Cultivation. Plant the rhizomes shallowly, in spring, in shade or partial shade, and peaty, permanently damp soil. The roots must remain damp all year round.

Propagate by means of spores, or by division of rhizomes in spring.

Onopordum

Giant thistles, *Compositae*

This genus consists of about 30 species of annuals, biennials and herbaceous perennials with a wide range of habit, but all with thistle-like flowers.
O. nervosum (O. arabicum) – zone 7 – a biennial, tall, branching plant, originates in southwest Europe, and reaches 10 ft (3 m) in height, with a spread of 30 in (75 cm). The strong woolly stems carry large silvery oval leaves, prickly and prominently veined on the undersides. The reddish-purple flowers are 2 in (5 cm) in diameter and appear in mid summer. They are dramatic in wild gardens and at the back of a border.
Cultivation. Plant in fertile, well-drained soil, in a sunny position. Dead head to prevent self-sown seedlings, which can be a nuisance.

Propagate in late spring by seeds sown *in situ*, and thin out to a distance of 30 in (75 cm).

Onosma

Golden drop, *Boraginaceae*

A large genus of over 70 species of hardy or tender annuals, biennials, perennials and sub-shrubs from Mediterranean regions and Asia. The foliage is often hairy and flowers, arranged in one-sided inflorescences, may be yellow, white, pink or sometimes bicoloured.
O. alborosea (zone 7) is a perennial from southeast Europe, growing 6 in (15 cm) high, with a spread of 16 in (40 cm). This bushy species is woody at the base and has oval spear-shaped leaves covered with stiff hairs. The stems carry several flowers which open white, becoming pink and then violet-red. Flowering takes place in late spring and early summer.

Onosmas are suitable for rock gardens, hot banks, walls, troughs or planted between paving stones.

Onosma alborosea

Cultivation. This plant likes a deep sandy or gritty, well drained soil in a sunny situation.

Propagate annuals from seeds sown in the open ground in mid spring. Perennials can be increased from cuttings taken in summer and placed in a cold frame.

Opuntia

Prickly pear, *Cactaceae*

This is the only genus in a large family to include some species that are hardy in mild temperate climates. All originate in the American continent, and need a lot of space in cultivation. They have jointed stems, many flattened into sections which are easily rooted.

O. ficus-indica (zone 10), prickly pear or barbary fig, is a large, tree-like plant with flattened stem sections and bright-yellow flowers. It is widely cultivated in warmer parts of the world and the red juicy fruits are edible.

O. rafinesquei (zone 10) is widely naturalized in the Americas and has oblong joints and bright-yellow flowers in summer.

O. humifusa (zone 10) is a dwarf, prostrate species, 4 in (10 cm) high, but spreading to 3½ ft (1 m) wide. The stem sections are spineless and cover the ground. The flowers are similar to those of *O. rafinesquei*.

O. imbricata (zone 10), chain-link cactus, is the tallest of the hardier species. It measures about 5–10 ft (1.5–3 m) in height, with cylindrical stem sections. The purple flowers appear in the summer months.

Cultivation. Outdoors, this plant should be grown in a sunny position, with at least four hours of direct sunlight a day, in a very well drained, calcareous soil. Under glass grow in pots of rich soil and water frequently during the summer. Repot annually in spring.

Growth is speeded if it is generously watered in summer during periods of drought; high-potash feed promotes flowering.

Each joint may be separated from the original plant, and easily takes root.

Orchis

Terrestrial orchids, *Orchidaceae*

These are orchids from Europe, Asia and North Africa, with small tuberous roots. This genus has given its name to the family as a whole, Terrestrial orchids are found in sunny meadows and along the edges of forests; the following moderately hardy species are cultivated, and available from specialist nurseries. All have lance-shaped leaves and spikes or racemes or typical orchid flowers in summer.

O. purpurea (zone 5), lady orchid, grows 18 in (45 cm) high, and has fragrant, purple and pink flowers, with densely spotted lips.

O. militaris (zone 5), military or soldier orchid, so-called from its upright carriage, has spidery,

A protected species of European orchid

magenta purple flowers and handsome, broad, green foliage. It grows 18 in (45 cm) high.
Cultivation. Plant in sun or semi-shade, in moist, humus-rich soil; avoid sand, clay or chalk soils. Propagate by division of tubers.

Never remove orchids from their natural surroundings; it is illegal in many countries, disturbs the ecological balance and transplanting is unlikely to be successful.

Origanum
Labiatae

A genus of sub-shrubs or perennial herbaceous plants of which three or four with especially aromatic foliage are commonly used for culinary purposes.
O. *majorana (Majorana hortensis)*, sweet or knotted marjoram, is a tender sub-shrub, native of North Africa, and usually grown as a half-hardy annual in cooler climates. The reddish stems form a bush about 1½ ft (45 cm) high, with small, entire, oval leaves. The plant bears clusters of small, white, pink or mauve flowers in grey, knot-like bracts at the ends of the stems in early summer.
O. *vulgare* (zone 5–6), oregano, is a perennial of European origin, and like marjoram, has reddish branches reaching 1–1½ ft (30–40 cm) in height. The aromatic leaves are oval, and the flowers are purplish to white. There is a yellow-leaved form in cultivation.
Cultivation. Sow O. *majorana* under glass in late winter, harden off, then plant in a warm, sunny spot in late spring, in light, well drained soil.

Alternatively, sow outdoors in mid and late spring in rows 12–16 in (30–40 cm) apart, and thin to a distance of 1 ft (30 cm). Gather the leaves and young shoots just before the plants flower in late summer and early autumn. Dry them in a dark airy place. Easily raised from seed, by division or from cuttings of young shoots.

Grow oregano in light, well-drained soil in a sunny, sheltered position. Divide established clumps in early spring and replant 1 ft (30 cm) apart. Alternatively sow *in situ* in mid spring in rows 12–16 in (30–40 cm) apart, and thin out to leave around 1 ft (30 cm) between plants.

Gather leaves and young shoots when flowering starts in mid summer and dry in a shady, well ventilated place.

Ornithogalum
Liliaceae

These hardy and tender bulbous plants are very widespread in Europe, Asia and Africa. Over 100 species exist, all with linear leaves, sheathed at the base. The white, star-shaped flowers often have a greenish tinge.
O. *arabicum* (zone 9–10), star of Bethlehem, is a moderately hardy species with blue-green linear leaves 12–16 in (30–40 cm) long. The 2 ft (60 cm) stems bear rounded flower-heads of up to 12 large, brilliant, white fragrant flowers with projecting blackish green ovaries, opening in late spring and early summer. Plant in spring in cool climates, and lift in autumn; in milder climates the bulbs are best planted in autumn. They are also grown in pots under glass.
O. *pyrenaicum* (zone 6–7), French asparagus, is a European woodland plant, with racemes of 30–50 small greenish yellow flowers in early summer on 2 ft (60 cm) stems. It will tolerate shade.
O. *nutans* (zone 6–7), drooping star of Bethlehem, is originally from the Caucasus, but grows wild in western Europe in damp meadows. The drooping flowers are white, striped with green, and open in spring. It thrives in light shade and is naturalized easily.
O. *umbellatum* (zone 6–7), star of Bethlehem, comes from Asia, North Africa and southern Europe. Its leaves have a silvery white midrib, and grow 8 in (20 cm) long. The green-striped white flowers are grouped in flat umbels, and bloom in spring, but only during the brightest hours of the day. When planted in numbers, this hardy plant forms a remarkable white carpet.

Ornithogalum can be grown in pots, rock gardens, short grass or borders, and many are excellent for naturalizing.
Cultivation. Plant hardy species in autumn in a well drained soil and grow the tender species in pots, in a cool, dry place, such as a conservatory. The foliage soon dies down after flowering. Hardy species can be left undisturbed for many years.

Osmanthus
Devilweed, *Oleaceae*

A genus represented by about 15 species of evergreen, slow-growing shrubs or small trees,

originating in North America and Asia. Many are hardy and some may be confused with *Ilex* (holly), but *Osmanthus* can be distinguished by its opposite, spiny leaves. The purple-black, olive-like fruits are only produced in warm areas, but the plants are largely grown for their fragrant flowers.
O. delavayi (zone 7), from China, may reach 20 ft (6 m) in height. The small, fragrant, tubular white flowers appear in clusters in mid-spring. The ovate leaves are dark glossy green and the fruits blue-black.
O. heterophyllus (zone 7), Chinese holly, from Japan, has a dense, bushy habit. The leaves are variable usually, with large triangular teeth. The white flowers are very fragrant, and appear in autumn. This plant forms excellent hedges, and there are several variegated forms.
O. yunnanensis (zone 7–8), from China, is a shrub or small tree to 20 ft (6 m) or more. Its oblong, dark green leaves can be more than 8 in (20 cm) long. The creamy white or pale yellow, very fragrant flowers appear at the end of winter.
Cultivation. Osmanthus can be grown in all soils, including limy ones, and in sun or partial shade. Avoid planting in exposed positions.

Propagate by cuttings taken in mid summer and given a little bottom heat; or raise from fresh seeds.

Osmunda
Osmundaceae

This genus contains about 10 species of ferns, some of which are hardy.
O. regalis (zone 8), royal fern, reaches 3–6½ ft (1–2 m) in height and spread. It is a hardy deciduous perennial with large, sterile, bright green and deeply incised fronds on the outside of the clump. The fertile, spore-bearing fronds form in the centre. Its attractive young crook-shaped fronds are reddish, and turn green as they unfold, eventually becoming yellow brown in autumn.

This is a particularly striking and decorative fern, and gradually spreads by means of rhizomes and almost black roots. It is an excellent plant for water edges and moist soils.
Cultivation. Plant the rhizomes shallowly in early spring in sun or shade. The soil should be peaty, rich in humus, and permanently wet as the roots need a constant supply of water. Mulch with leaf mould in spring.

Sowing spores is a delicate operation; division of clumps in spring is an easier and more satisfactory method of propagation for most gardeners.

Osteospermum
African daisy, *Compositae*

A genus of 70 species of herbaceous and sub-shrubby perennials from South Africa to the Middle East, which are not fully hardy. The species described here look wonderful when in full bloom at the front of sunny borders or below sunny walls, or they can be grown in a cool greenhouse or conservatory. They were once placed in the genus *Dimorphotheca*, under which name they are sometimes sold in garden centres.
O. ecklonis (Dimorphotheca ecklonis) (zone 9), native to South Africa, grows to a height of 16–24 in (40–60 cm) with a spread of 16 in (40 cm). It is a bushy perennial with upright branches bearing bright green lanceolate leaves and white flowers 2¼–3¼ in (6–8 cm) in diameter, with a deep purple-blue central disc, and blue-purple underneath petals. It blooms in mid to late summer, but it does not like frost.
O. jucundum (Dimorphotheca barberae) (zone 9), is an almost sub-shrubby perennial with large daisy-like flowers, whose petals are purplish both above and below. It is 18 in (45 cm) tall, but there is a dwarf form, 'Compactum', which is rather hardier. They flower from late spring to autumn.
Cultivation. Plant out in mid to late spring in light, well-drained soil, in a warm, sunny place. In areas with mild winters, protect the roots with a cloche; elsewhere, where the winters are hard grow the plant in a cool greenhouse, or treat as an annual or half-hardy perennial.

Propagate in mid to late spring by seeds sown where they are to be grown. Thin out as soon as the young seedlings appear. The plants should flower eight weeks after sowing.

Othonna (Othonnopsis)
Compositae

This genus consists of eight species of tender perennials and sub-shrubs native to Africa and Asia, but only one can be considered as half-hardy.

O. cheirifolia (zone 9), from North Africa, grows 8–16 in (20–40 cm) high, with a spread to 20 in (50 cm). This evergreen perennial has thick, spatulate bluish-grey leaves and single, yellow flowers, about 1½ in (4 cm) across, in early and mid summer.

This plant is suitable for a rock garden but needs protection in winter in all but mildest areas.

Cultivation. Plant in light, well drained soil in mid spring, in a warm, sunny, sheltered spot. The fleshy leaves are intolerant of humidity in winter, and of temperatures lower than 17°F (−8°C).

Take 6 in (15 cm) cuttings from side shoots when flowering is over and place these in a cold frame. Alternatively, propagate by division.

Ourisia

Scrophulariaceae

This genus consists of about 24 species, native to South America, Tasmania and New Zealand. They are moderately to very hardy, low-growing perennials, with tubular or funnel-shaped red, pink or white flowers.

O. coccinea (O. elegans) – zone 5–6 – from the Andes, grows 8–9 in (20–25 cm) high, with a spread of 1–2 ft (30–60 cm). This carpet-forming plant has oval leaves and small clusters of drooping, scarlet flowers, 1 in (2.5 cm) long, appearing from late spring to early autumn.

O. macrocarpa (zone 6) grows 16–20 in (40–50 cm) in height when in flower, with a spread of 3–6½ ft (1–2 m). This is a vigorous species with thick, creeping rhizomes, and has close-set, smooth, dark green leaves. The mimulus-like flowers, appearing in late spring and early summer, are white with yellow throats. They are arranged in regularly spaced whorls on upright stems.

Ourisias, depending on species, can be planted in tubs, peat beds or rock gardens where they form a close carpet of leaves.

Cultivation. Plant in cool, moist, lime-free soil with a high peat content. Choose a partially shaded position, and, ideally, a mild climate and protect the plant from damp and humidity in winter.

Propagate by seeds or by division in spring.

Oxalis

Wood sorrel, *Oxalidaceae*

This genus is made up of some 500 sub-shrubby or herbaceous plants, some with bulbils. Most are tropical, but some are hardy and may be grown outside in temperate regions, for their flowers and compound, palmate foliage.

O. acetosella (zone 5), wood sorrel, is a hardy woodland plant found all over the Northern Hemisphere. It grows 2 in (5 cm) high and 12 in (30 cm) across. It has pale-green, shamrock-like leaves and tuberous roots, by which it spreads rapidly, and it also self seeds. The flowers are white or pink and appear in spring.

O. adenophylla (zone 6) comes from Chile, and grows 4 in (10 cm) high and 8 in (20 cm) across. It is hardy and forms rosettes of silvery-green, crinkled leaves. Large, pink bell-shaped flowers appear from late spring to mid summer.

O. depressa (O. inops) – zone 7 – is a South African species. It spreads rapidly enough to be invasive, and forms a carpet of bright-green, trifoliate leaves. Its bell-shaped flowers, to ¾ in (2 cm) across, are bright-pink, white or violet, and are carried throughout summer.

O. laciniata (zone 5) is a small, very hardy rhizomatous plant to 4 in (10 cm) high, from Patagonia. The silver-grey leaves are made up of 9–12 leaflets. It flowers in shades of blue and lavender, with darker veining, in summer.

Many species are suitable for the rock garden or alpine house, and shade lovers can be planted in the woodland garden, but some can become pernicious weeds.

Cultivation. The species listed should be planted in rich, well drained peaty or gritty soil in spring or autumn. They prefer a warm site, but need to be watered during dry spells. Semi-hardy species should be grown under glass or given winter protection.

Propagate by division of rhizomes or separation of bulbils in early spring.

Pachysandra

Spurge, *Buxaceae*

This genus contains four species of hardy dwarf evergreen shrubs or sub-shrubs, useful as ground cover in shaded areas.

P. terminalis (zone 7), Japanese pachysandra or spurge, native to Japan, is the most commonly grown species. It measures 1 ft (30 cm) in height, with a spread of 20 in–3 ft (50 cm–1 m), and has dark-green, toothed, diamond-shaped leaves, 3–4 in (8–10 cm) long. The insignificant flowers have no petals, but four greenish white sepals. They are carried in terminal spikes, 1–2 in (2–5 cm) long, in early spring. There is a white variegated form which is also popular.

Cultivation. Plant in rich, moist soil in shade, even under trees, in autumn or spring.

To propagate, lift and divide in early spring, replanting the sections immediately. Alternatively, take cuttings in summer.

Paeonia

Peony, *Ranunculaceae*

A genus represented by about 30 species of herbaceous perennials or shrubs, mostly hardy and originating in Asia, North America and Europe, and grown for their showy flowers.

P. lactiflora (zone 6) is a hardy herbaceous perennial from northeast Asia, 2–3 ft (60–90 cm) high, with a spread of 2 ft (60 cm). The foliage is dark green, and the white flowers are large and scented, with a central mass of yellow stamens. They bloom in late spring or early summer. The true species is rarely grown in gardens, but there are numerous cultivars, with single, semi-double or double and sometimes scented flowers in white, pink, carmine, crimson and rose.

P. mlokosewitschii (zone 6), from the Caucasus, has grey-green leaves and single lemon-yellow flowers in spring. It is herbaceous and 2 ft (60 cm) in height. The seed pods are striking.

P. officinalis (zone 6) is a herbaceous perennial bearing single crimson flowers in late spring to early summer. It is 2 ft (60 cm) high with a spread of 3 ft (90 cm), and has deeply cut green leaves.

P. suffruticosa (zone 7), tree peony, reaches 5–6 ft (1.5–1.8 m) high and across. A shrub, it has single white to pink flowers in late spring. Many cultivars have been developed from it offering the gardener a choice of flower colour.

Herbaceous peonies can be used in isolated clumps and in herbaceous or mixed borders.

Paeonia mlokosewitschii

Cultivation. Plant in deep, moist, well drained soil, alkaline rather than acid, with plenty of well rotted manure or garden compost incorporated. Plant in sun or partial shade in autumn or spring, leaving 2½–3 ft (75 cm–1 m) between herbaceous plants, more for tree peonies.

All need top dressing with well rotted manure in autumn and a good mulch in summer. Avoid disturbing or moving the plants, as they are slow to establish themselves. Water during dry spells, and support with stakes in windy positions. In autumn, cut flowers and leaf stems down to their base.

Propagate by division in autumn or sow seed, as soon as it is ripe, in a cold frame.

Peonies may be attacked by various fungus diseases, the most serious of which is peony wilt. This causes young leafy shoots to wilt and turn brown in spring, followed by grey fungal growth at the base of the stem. The remedy is to cut these out below ground level and burn immediately. Use a fungicide at the base of the plant to prevent recurrences.

Pancratium

Sea lily, *Amaryllidaceae*

This genus contains 15 bulbous plants; the species listed below are from the Mediterranean region and suitable only for mild, sheltered gardens. The smooth, strap-shaped glaucous leaves have often faded by the time the plant produces its large, white, scented, daffodil-like flowers. These are grouped in umbels of five to twelve blooms.

P. maritimum (zone 9), sea lily or sea daffodil, is a semi-evergreen found growing by the sea. The stems are about 1 ft (30 cm) high, and flowers appear in late summer. It is one of the most beautiful species of the *Amaryllidaceae* native to Europe, but only hardy in mildest districts.

P. illyricum (zone 8–9), from Corsica, is similar but deciduous, taller and hardier. It flowers in late spring and early summer, quickly forming large clumps in favoured areas. It is the best species to plant outdoors in cool climates.

Pancratium is best suited to rock gardens.

Cultivation. Bury the bulb 8 in (20 cm) deep in a bed of coarse sand in a very sheltered, warm, sunny position, and avoid disturbing for several years. Protect in winter with a thick mulch. *P. maritimum* is nearly hardy in mild areas, otherwise grow under glass in open compost and place in a cold frame in summer. *P. illyricum* is hardy in most areas given the protection of a wall.

Propagate from seed or from bulbils, planted in a light sandy soil, when they will flower after two or three years.

Papaver

Poppy, *Papaveraceae*

This genus is represented by about 50 herbaceous annuals, biennials and perennials. Most are hardy, originating in Europe, North Africa and Asia, and are grown for their bright-coloured flowers.

P. alpinum (zone 5), alpine poppy, is a perennial though it is usually raised from seed like an annual. The grey-green dissected leaves form low mounds and the flowers may be red, orange, yellow or white. Its height and spread is 4–10 in (10–25 cm).

P. nudicaule (zone 5), Iceland poppy, from sub-Arctic regions in the north, is grown as an annual or a biennial. The white or yellow flowers are fragrant and come out in summer. The leaves are green and the plants reach 1½–2½ ft (45–75 cm) high and 1–1½ ft (30–45 cm) across.

P. orientale (zone 6) from Armenia, is a hardy herbaceous perennial, growing to over 3½ ft (1 m). The dark-green, deeply divided leaves are thick, wrinkled, and hairy, and the large, bright

Papaver 'Oriental poppy'

scarlet flowers, blotched with maroon at their centres, open in early summer. This species has given rise to the Oriental poppies, in a range of pink, red, white, salmon and scarlet, some double or with frilled petals.

P. rhoeas (zone 6), field poppy, grows wild in Britain. Its red flowers with a black centre appear in summer. Height is 2 ft (60 cm) and spread is 1 ft (30 cm).

Cultivation. Plant in ordinary, well drained, sandy soil, preferably not too rich, in autumn or spring. Choose a sunny spot and space plants 2 ft (60 cm) apart.

Stake the plants, and remove faded flowers to encourage a second flowering, after which cut stems down to the base.

Mildew may form yellow streaks on the leaves and cover their undersides with a greyish fuzz, but this is not serious.

Propagate by division of roots in spring, or from root cuttings in winter placed in a cold frame. Oriental poppies are short lived where winters are warm.

Parthenocissus

Vitaceae

This genus contains about 10 species of climbing, mainly deciduous, plants. They climb by twining tendrils or grip with adhesive suckers on to almost any surface. The foliage of most species is spectacular in autumn, but the flowers that appear at the end of spring are insignificant, and are followed by black berries, in hot summers.

P. quinquefolia, Virginia creeper, from southern and eastern United States, is a vigorous and very hardy creeper, to 70 ft (20 m) high, and can become invasive. It clings by adhesive pads to many types of surface. The green leaves usually have five leaflets, each 4 in (10 cm) long, and turn brilliant scarlet in autumn.

P. tricuspidata, Boston ivy, is native to China, Japan and Korea. It is a hardy, vigorous plant gripping with its adhesive tendril tips. The leaves are very variable: trifoliate or ovate on the young plants, and deeply three lobed on the older ones. They turn deep crimson in autumn.

The form 'Lowii' has smaller, three-to-seven-lobed leaves. 'Purpurea' has reddish-purple leaves throughout summer.

These species are ideal for covering walls, pergolas, arbours or old trees.

Cultivation. Grow in any moist, loamy soil, preferably not acid. Young plants should be supported with sticks until they become self-clinging. If the plant is to climb up a pillar, pergola or tree stump, shorten young shoots in summer and cut back in winter each year to limit growth.

Scale insects, weevils, aphids and glasshouse red spider mites can be a problem, and mildew and honey fungus may occur.

The simplest means of propagation is by layering, which frequently happens naturally, or take cuttings.

Passiflora

Passion flower, *Passifloraceae*

A very large genus of woody and herbaceous climbing plants, most of which are tender. The parts of the unusual flower are so arranged that they were said by missionaries to symbolize the passion of Christ: the three stigmas represented three nails, the five anthers represented the five wounds, the corona represented the crown of thorns, and so on.

P. × *allardii* (zone 9) may be grown outside in very mild districts. The white petals are tinged pink and the corona white and deep bluish-purple.

P. caerulea (zone 8), passion flower, is from Brazil and Peru and hardy on a sheltered, sunny wall in milder areas. It is vigorous, climbing by tendrils, and can send out stems 17 ft (5 m) long during the course of a summer. The semi-evergreen leaves are palmate, and divided into 5 to 7 spear-shaped lobes. The solitary flowers appear from early summer to early autumn, and are 4 in (10 cm) across, pale blue to bluish white, with a central blue-purple corona. In severe winters, it may be killed back to ground level, but often sends out new growth in spring.

P. edulis (zone 10), passion fruit, purple granadilla, from tropical South America, can reach a height of 23 ft (7 m) or more but is not hardy. The evergreen leaves are trilobed, and the flowers, 2–2¾ in (5–7 cm) across, are white with a purple corona, appearing in mid and late summer. It is cultivated in warm climates for its edible orange to purple fruits.

P. quadrangularis (zone 10), granadilla, from tropical South America, can reach 26 ft (8 m) or more, and is not hardy. The oval leaves are semi-evergreen. The scented flowers, 3¼–4 in (8–

10 cm) across, have white, pink or purple petals and a purple striped corona, and bloom in summer. They are followed by yellow-to-purple, edible, egg-shaped fruits over 8 in (20 cm) long.

Hardy passion flowers can be trained up a trellis on a sheltered wall in a mild climate, but others must be grown in heated greenhouses.

Cultivation. Plant in well drained soil either in a greenhouse, when it can be trained along wires, or against a sunny wall. Alternatively, grow in pots of potting compost. Water sparingly in winter, but copiously in summer. Shade the greenhouse in winter. Prune in late winter in a greenhouse, and in mid spring outdoors.

Passion flowers are susceptible to cucumber mosaic virus.

In spring, propagate by 6 in (15 cm) long cuttings with a heel inserted into a sandy compost under glass, or sow seed. Maintain a temperature of 64–68°F (18–20°C) in both cases.

Paulownia

Scrophulariaceae

A genus of about six species of deciduous trees from east Asia. The large, foxglove-like flowers appear in spring before the heart-shaped leaves, in erect terminal panicles, and the flower buds form at the end of summer. The fruits are egg-shaped capsules, 1½ in (4 cm) long, opening on two valves to release the winged seeds.

Paulownia tomentosa

P. tomentosa (P. imperialis) – zone 7 – Princess Tree, from China, is majestic in habit growing to 50 ft (15 m), with a rounded crown. Its mauve flowers bloom in late spring and are similar in shape to the white flowers of *Catalpa*. Paulownia leaves are large, downy and opposite.

It is grown in parks and large gardens, but with regular pruning, may be suitable for small gardens. Heavy pruning results in the leaves growing enormously large. They are sometimes stooled and grown in bedding-out schemes for the tropical appearance of their leaves. Stooled plants carry no flowers. Paulownias do not always flower freely when young or after severe winters.

Cultivation. Paulownia becomes hardier with age, but its buds may be damaged in very hard winters with intermittent mild spells. Grow in rich, well drained loam in a sunny situation, sheltered from icy winds. Plant in autumn or spring.

Propagate by seeds or cuttings.

Pelargonium

Geraniaceae

A genus consisting of 250 species of mostly tender sub-shrubs, herbaceous and succulent plants, with deciduous or evergreen foliage. These are often sold under the name of geranium, but should not be confused with the true *Geranium*, which is perfectly hardy.

P. × *domesticum* (zone 9–10), regal, fancy or show geraniums; Martha or Lady Washington geraniums in USA, are a hybrid group of compact plants growing to 2 ft (60 cm) or more. They have lobed, toothed leaves and large, showy flowers in white, salmon pink, red and purple. The flowers are often blotched or veined with darker shades. They are best grown in pots indoors, on a windowsill perhaps, or in the greenhouse.

P. endlicherianum (zone 7), from Asia Minor, is the only species that is hardy in cooler temperate climates. It is herbaceous and grows 8–10 in (20–45 cm) high and across. It has small, roundish silvery and slightly hairy leaves, 1–2 in (2.5–5 cm) in diameter. The pink flowers, streaked with carmine, appear in early and mid summer. Grow in very well drained stony soil, in a sunny rockery.

P. peltatum (zone 9–10), ivy-leaved geranium, from South Africa, is a straggling, sub-shrubby species with branches more than 3½ ft (1 m) long. The plain green fleshy leaves resemble those of ivy and the pink flowers bloom from late spring to mid autumn. It is the main parent of many ivy-leaved pelargoniums with a wide range of flower colour; some forms have attractively variegated foliage. Ivy-leaved geraniums are especially suitable for hanging baskets, pots and window boxes.

P. zonale (zone 9–10), zonal geranium or horseshoe geranium, from South Africa, has produced a race of hybrids know as *P. × hortorum*, which may reach 6½ ft (2 m) in height. These branching shrubs are characterized by round green leaves, with a bronze or chestnut horseshoe-shaped zone in the centre. The flowers appear in round umbels from late spring to mid autumn, in white, pink, red, purple or bicoloured; single or double; and early or late-flowering. These are often used in bedding schemes, where uniformity is important. They are also popular house plants.

There is also a wide range of species grown as house plants for their flowers and sometimes scented foliage.

Cultivation. Plant pelargoniums in well drained but only moderately rich compost; they flower best when pot bound. In late spring, when the danger of frost has passed, plant out in containers or open ground in a well drained soil in a sunny position. In very mild areas, pelargoniums can remain outdoors all year round, and they often grow quite large, with thick stems.

Apply a liquid feed every ten days to plants in pots from late spring to mid autumn. In winter, keep plants in a frost-free garage or basement with some light. Water sparingly once a month, cut down the thin stems that grow during this period, and repot or plant out in late spring. Whitefly can be a problem; treat regularly with a systemic insecticide.

Propagate from seeds sown in mid winter, or from cuttings taken from non-flowering shoots in mid summer. Place in pots of sand in a cold frame, with a high level of atmospheric humidity. Replant the rooted shoots individually into potting compost. Pinch out the tips when the plants are 6–8 in (15–20 cm) high, to encourage bushiness. Cuttings are susceptible to fungal attack causing black-leg. Discard and burn affected parts of the plant and take fresh cuttings.

Pelargonium peltatum

Pennisetum

Gramineae

A genus of more than 70 species of annual or perennial grasses, many from tropical regions.

P. alopecuroides (zone 9), Chinese fountain grass, comes from Asia and is an attractive long-lived perennial with fine green leaves, which are almost as decorative as the dense, cylindrical, bottle-brush-like, purplish plumes. These appear in late summer and are useful in dried-flower arrangements. The parchment-coloured leaves are also an attractive feature in winter. The plant grows to 2–2½ ft (50–75 cm). It is moderately hardy, but needs protecting for the first few winters after planting, with a mulch of leaves or bracken. Fountain grass can be used in mixed borders or in single clumps, as specimens.

Cultivation. Plant in spring in well drained soil, in a sheltered, sunny or partly shaded position. In cold climates, with severe winter weather, the plants are best lifted in autumn, potted up in loam-based compost, and overwintered in a cool greenhouse. Plant out in spring.

They require little attention other than the removal of the plumes at the end of winter.

Propagate by dividing the clumps in spring.

Penstemon

Beard-tongue, *Scrophulariaceae*

A genus of some 250 species of herbaceous plants or sub-shrubs, mostly native to North America and Mexico, with showy flowers.

P. hartwegii (zone 8–9) is a moderately hardy herbaceous perennial, 1½–2 ft (45–60 cm) high, with a spread of 1–2 ft (30–60 cm). It has semi-evergreen, narrow leaves and scarlet, tubular flowers appearing throughout the summer.

It is one of the parents of the hybrids, *P.* × *gloxinioides*, grown for bedding. These come in a wide range of colours including red, purple, white and pink.

Penstemons are suited to herbaceous or mixed borders and summer bedding schemes. Most should be treated as half-hardy perennials and propagated annually, unless the winters are very mild. Smaller species are useful in the rock garden.

Cultivation. Provide a well drained soil, enriched with organic matter, such as garden compost or well rotted manure. It dislikes damp winters and drying spring winds, and prefers a sheltered sunny position. Plant in early to mid spring, 1–1½ ft (30–45 cm) apart. Remove dead flowers to prolong the flowering season. In mild climates cut the plants right back in autumn and protect the roots.

Propagate from cuttings in autumn, overwintered in a cold frame for planting out in spring; or from seed sown under glass in late winter or early spring.

Peperomia

Radiator plant, *Piperaceae*

This is a very large genus of about 1000 species of herbaceous plants most of which are native to tropical and subtropical areas of South America. The cultivated species are grown for their decorative leaves which have a range of shapes and sizes, often coloured or variegated. The tiny white or cream flowers on long narrow spikes are less significant. These plants will not survive outdoors except in climates with a constant warm temperature.

P. argyreia (P. sandersii) – zone 10+ – watermelon begonia, is from many areas of tropical South America. It is a compact bushy plant with fleshy, dark green oval leaves up to 4 in (10 cm) long, striped with broad bands of silver, on long red leaf-stalks joining the undersurface of the leaves.

P. caperata (zone 10+), is probably native to Brazil but its exact origin is uncertain. It forms a tufted plant up to 6 in (15 cm) high with many leaves on pinkish-red leaf stalks. The oval dark green leaves have sunken veins giving them a puckered appearance. Tiny white flowers are borne on narrow spikes well exceeding the foliage in height.

P. magnoliifolia (zone 10+), desert privet, from the West Indies and Central America, is an erect branching bushy plant to 10 in (25 cm) in height. The thick, fleshy, glossy green leaves are almost rounded, and 4 in (10 cm) or more across.

P. rotundifolia (P. nummulariifolia) – zone 10+ – from tropical America, is a creeping, low growing, carpet-forming plant. The stems are slender with tiny, bright green, fleshy, rounded leaves about ⅓ in (8 mm) wide. It can be used in hanging baskets.

Cultivation. These frost-tender plants require a minimum temperature of 50°F (10°C) or more and a bright or partially shaded place. A peat-based soil is ideal but the plants are sensitive to overwatering. Propagate by division, seed, or leaf and stem cuttings.

Perilla

Labiatae

This genus is represented by about five species of Asian annuals used for bedding, for gaps in borders or in the greenhouse for their ornamental foliage.

P. frutescens 'Crispa' (*P. frutescens* var. *nankinensis*) – zone 10 – Nanking perilla, is a vigorous plant which forms dense clumps, with bronze-purple, deeply toothed leaves with wrinkled edges, and inconspicuous white flowers. The cultivar 'Atropurpurea' has dark purple, cut leaves. It grows 2 ft (60 cm) or more high, and is attractive with silver-leaved plants.

Cultivation. Grow as half-hardy annuals. Sow in a greenhouse in early to mid spring. Prick out and harden off gradually. Plant out in late spring in moist soil and full sun, spacing the seedlings 1 ft (30 cm) apart. Pinch out the tips to encourage a bushy habit and prune back if necessary. Alternatively, grow in pots of potting compost under glass. It often self-sows.

Pernettya

Ericaceae

A genus comprising about 20 species of shrubs, native to the Southern Hemisphere, with evergreen leaves and attractive fruit.

P. mucronata (zone 5–6), from Chile, is the most commonly available species, and grows about 4 ft (1.2 m) high, spreading by suckers and forming dense thickets. The leaves are pointed, spine tipped and dark, shiny green. The plant is functionally dioecious, with plants being either male or female, and the small, white, bell-shaped flowers appear in the leaf axils in late spring. The small berries are shiny, spherical and pink, purple, white or red, about ½ in (1 cm) across. The berries persist until spring. There are many named cultivars with larger berries of a selected colour.

Plant in groups with at least one male plant to 5–10 females to ensure the females are pollinated and produce fruit.

Cultivation. This species is reasonably hardy and prefers cool, well drained, lime-free soil. It tolerates shade, but is more compact and free fruiting in sun. It can be grown in a peat bed in association with azaleas or rhododendrons. It also makes excellent ground cover.

The plant may lose its leaves as it gets older; if this happens, cut back to the old wood and new shoots will sprout.

The species is self-seeding, but to retain the colour of the parent, take cuttings 2 in (5 cm) long in early autumn and place them in a mixture of sand and peat in a greenhouse; or remove suckers in autumn and grow them on in the same mixture.

Persea

Lauraceae

A genus of over 100 tropical evergreen trees.

P. americana (P. gratissima) – zone 10 – avocado pear, may grow 30 ft (9 m) or more high. It has attractive dark green leaves, glaucous below, and greenish flowers grouped in clusters. Its large, shiny green, pear-shaped edible fruits are very popular alone or in salad dishes. It can be grown as a foliage plant in the house until it gets too big.

Cultivation. This plant only grows outdoors in a very warm frost-free climate, where it requires a rich soil and a sunny position. Elsewhere it can be grown successfully as a house plant.

Propagate by sowing the stone of an avocado pear in a moisture-retaining compost and pot on into a larger pot in a rich soil-based potting compost.

Petroselinum

Parsley, *Umbelliferae*

This genus of annual or biennial herbaceous plants contains an important culinary herb.

P. crispum (P. sativum, P. hortense) – zone 6 – parsley, is a biennial plant native to southern Europe, western Asia and North Africa. The stems grow 8–16 in (20–40 cm) long; common parsley bears deeply divided leaves, and curly-leaved cultivars have crisped leaves. Either type makes an attractive edging to a herb garden.

Cultivars.'Moss Curled', 'Consort' and 'Curlina' are curly leaved types. 'Plain-leaved' is a common parsley with a stronger flavour.

Cultivation. Parsley prefers cool, rich soil. Choose a sunny spot in spring but partly shaded in summer, as it soon runs to seed in full sun. Though biennial, parsley is often grown as an annual and if its flowering stem is ripped out, it behaves as a perennial. Older plants tend to produce tough foliage, and are best replaced. Sow successionally in a border from late winter to early autumn, in rows 10–12 in (25–30 cm) apart. To improve germination, soak the seeds in water for 24 hours before sowing. Just cover the seeds and firm the earth well. Thin the seedlings to 3 in (8 cm), and water in dry weather to prevent bolting.

Start picking the leaves 10–12 weeks after sowing. For late autumn and winter supplies, sow seed in late summer or early autumn and protect with cloches.

Parsley can occasionally be attacked by a fungus which causes the leaves to go brown and then white. Destroy all infected plants and start again on fresh ground.

Uses. Eat the leaves fresh in salads, cooked dishes and seasonings. Parsley sauce is a traditional accompaniment to boiled ham. A refreshing infusion (tea) can be made by pouring boiling water over the leaves.

Petunia

Solanaceae

A genus of some 35 annual or perennial herbaceous plants. The popular plants grown for bedding, tubs etc, are included under *P.* × *hybrida* (zone 9). These are tender perennials grown as half-hardy annuals, forming bushy plants 8–18 in (20–45 cm) high and bearing large showy white, pink, yellow, purple, blue, red or bicoloured funnel-shaped single or double flowers throughout summer.

Grandiflora hybrids have large flowers, which can be marked by rain. The Cascade series has trailing stems and single flowers. It is ideal for hanging baskets, window boxes and ground cover. Multiflora hybrids, such as the Resisto series, have many smaller but more rain resistant flowers and more flowers. There are also compact types, 6 in (15 cm) high, ideal for edging beds.

Cultivation. Sow in a warm greenhouse in early to mid spring. Prick out as soon as large enough to handle. Pinch out the tips to encourage bushier plants. Plant out in late spring 1 ft (30 cm) apart, in a well drained soil and sunny position. Remove the faded flowers so that flowering lasts as long as possible.

Petunias are vulnerable to various types of rot, and a number of viruses, which may cause blotching and deformation of the leaves, stems and flowers.

Phalaris
Gramineae

A genus of about 15 species of annual and perennial grasses, mostly from Mediterranean areas.

P. arundinacea (zone 4) is usually represented in gardens by the cultivar 'Picta', known as ribbon grass or gardener's garters. It is a vigorous perennial which can become invasive, growing 4 ft (1.2 m) and with leaves striped longitudinally with white. The compact, straw-coloured inflorescences have little visual merit but make a good contrast to purple-leaved subjects.

Cultivation. Plant at any time of year, in a dry, damp or even waterlogged position, up to 4 in (10 cm) underwater, in sun or light shade.

The plant reproduces vegetatively at an extraordinary rate, and the smallest piece of root will rapidly establish itself.

Phaseolus
Leguminosae

This genus includes twining annual or perennial plants, some grown for their edible seeds or complete seed pod. The dwarf or French beans or snap beans are derived from *P. vulgaris*, (zone 6) a twining annual or bushy plant native to South America. The stems grow 1–10 ft (30 cm–3 m) long. Some, such as 'Blue Lake' are climbing French beans, and are grown on support. Dwarf French or snap beans such as 'Masterpiece' are upright plants, needing little support. Others may have yellow or purple pods. Runner beans or pole beans in America have been developed from *P. coccineus* (zone 6) and are vigorous plants requiring support except for one or two recently developed plants, such as 'Pickwick'. Beans grown for drying include 'Chevrier Vert' and 'Flaveol'.

Cultivation. Grow beans as the first plant in a crop rotation. Sow in a sunny position, in light, cool, well manured soil. Give the soil time to warm up and sow in late spring when there is no risk of frost. Before sowing apply fertiliser, and rake to produce a fine tilth. Beans are sown outdoors from mid spring to mid summer, or in late spring to early summer for shelling varieties. For succession, sow seeds ever two or three weeks, in pockets of two, eliminating the weaker plant after germination. Seeds are sown 2 in (5 cm) deep, 9 in (23 cm) in the row and 24 in (60 cm) between the rows.

After sowing, protect plants from mice or slugs. For the taller growing plants insert sturdy stakes.

Hoe shortly after the seedlings appear, then again three weeks later, and earth up the young plants. In summer, water generously but do not wet the leaves unless the weather is very hot, in which case spray foliage with water to encourage the flowers to set. When the flowers have appeared apply liquid feed every ten days. Pick as soon as ripe to ensure a succession.

To produce dried beans, leave them to ripen completely and then dry them out so that they will keep.

When picking is over pull out plants and burn or cut down the plants to ground level in order to dig in the nitrogen-rich nodules.

Black bean aphid is the main pest. Discourage by pinching out young shoots, and control with sytemic insecticide spray. Anthracnose is the main disease.

Philadelphus
Mock orange, *Hydrangeaceae (Saxifragaceae)*

A genus of approximately 65 species of medium-sized, hardy deciduous shrubs, most of which have masses of pure-white, fragrant flowers with golden stamens in summer. They are often incorrectly known as syringa; the common name 'mock orange' comes from their orange-blossom like fragrance.

P. coronarius (zone 6) grows 12 ft (3.5 m) high, with a stiff, slightly arching habit and oval leaves. The creamy white, highly scented flowers appear in late spring and early summer. The cultivar 'Aureus' has bright yellow young leaves.

P. microphyllus (zone 8) from southwest USA is rarely over 4 ft (1.2 m) high and has small, oval leaves and large, white fragrant flowers, either solitary or in groups of two or three in early summer.

Many hybrids have been bred, especially in France, including 'Avalanche', with solitary flowers and arching habit; 'Belle Etoile', with pure white flowers with maroon blotch at base of petals; 'Minnesota Snowflake', ultra-hardy, with double flowers, bred in USA; 'Virginal', vigorous growth, with scented semi-double flowers, and 'Etoile Rose', with solitary flowers whose bases are spotted with carmine-pink.

Philadelphus can be grown as a flowering hedge but is more often seen in shrub or mixed beds.

Cultivation. Plant in ordinary soil, in early to mid spring. Philadelphus are tolerant of chalky soils and drought, but do not tolerate water-logged soils. They will grow in the shade, but will flower better in a sunny position. Every two years, after the plant has flowered, prune the previous year's flowering wood. Old, leggy plants can be pruned hard; new growth will spring from the base.

Propagate from 1 ft (30 cm) long hardwood cuttings and plant them outdoors in a protected position, away from full sun. The plant may be affected by black aphids.

Phlomis

Jerusalem sage, *Labiatae*

A genus of approximately 100 species of small, hairy shrubs, sub-shrubs and herbaceous plants native to the Mediterranean and Asia.

P. fruticosa (zone 8), Jerusalem sage, is hardy in all but the coldest areas, and grows 32–42 in (80 cm–1 m) high and 2 ft (60 cm) across. Its evergreen, oval leaves are thickly covered with grey hairs, and have a woolly, almost felted, appearance. The erect stems carry inflorescences of tightly packed whorls of tubular, bright-yellow flowers in the axils of the upper leaves.

Cultivation. Plant in a sunny, sheltered position in autumn or spring, away from cold winds and in light, well drained, even dry, soil. Remove unwanted and frost-damaged branches in autumn or spring.

Propagate the plant by semi-ripe cuttings in the summer placing them in a cold frame, for planting out the following year.

Phlox

Phlox, *Polemoniaceae*

A genus of some 60 species of herbaceous perennials, hardy and half-hardy sub-shrubs and annuals, most of which are native to North America and Mexico, and grown for their showy flowers.

P. drummondii, from Texas, is a half-hardy annual reaching 15 in (38 cm) high and 9 in (23 cm) across. Its white, red, pink and purple flowers open in mid summer to early autumn. A number of garden cultivars are available.

P. paniculata (zone 6), summer phlox, is a herbaceous perennial, growing 2–3½ ft (60 cm–1 m) high and 16–24 in (40–60 cm) across. The stems bear mid-green leaves and almost spherical terminal corymbs of small, violet-purple flowers. It is one parent of the many hybrids more commonly grown in gardens, with flowers in shades of white, pink, red, violet-blue

Phlox cultivar

and purple, some with a contrasting centre.

P. subulata (zone 6), moss phlox, an alpine sub-shrubby species from the eastern United States, forms a mat of green leaves and has purple to pink flowers in mid to late spring. Pink, blue and mauve cultivars have been developed from it. It reaches 2–4 in (5–10 cm) high and up to 1½ ft (45 cm) across.

Perennial phlox are usually planted in flower beds where it adds bright colour in mid and late summer. The small or creeping species are widely grown in rock gardens and dry stone walls or raised beds. The annual species are also suitable for mixed borders, but smaller forms can be used for bedding and for growing under glass, to flower in spring.

Cultivation. Plant herbaceous perennial phlox in fertile, well drained soil in sun or light shade in autumn or spring, spaced at 16–20 in (40–50 cm) apart. If the soil is poor, add a complete fertilizer; avoid chalk or clay soils. Water if the soil is dry, and manure in spring. Stake if in an exposed position, and cut back to ground level in autumn.

Propagate by dividing the clumps in autumn or spring, using the plants on the outside of the clump. They must be lifted and divided every 3–4 years, or they degenerate.

Stem eelworms may make the shoots wither and the leaves turn yellow, in which case propagate by root cuttings taken in late winter or early spring, and grow in a cold frame.

Wilt may affect these plants, in which case destroy the whole plant.

Phoenix

Palm tree, Phoenix, *Palmae*

P. canariensis (zone 10), Canary Island date palm, is endemic to the Canary Islands and is now widely grown in areas with a very mild climate, planted in rows or used for shade.

The tree has a smooth, stout, grey trunk, and may grow to a height of more than 66 ft (20 m). The crown of leaves at the top of the tree is spectacular, containing more than 200 finely divided, pinnate fronds each up to 15 ft (4 m) long, and arching outwards and downwards.

P. dactylifera (zone 10+), date palm, is similar and cultivated in suitable climates for its fruit. It is suckering when young, and its trunk is more slender, and its crown sparser, than the Canary date palm.

Cultivation. Phoenix grows in well drained soil, where the winter temperature does not fall below 21°F (−6°C). The seeds germinate easily, but it may be more than ten years before the tree starts developing a trunk. The date palm is propagated from suckers or offsets from young trees.

Phragmites

Reed, *Gramineae*

Reeds are a very common sight in marshy areas the world over. There are three species, but *P. communis* (zone 5), common reed, is the most common and tallest European reed, growing up to 17 ft (5 m) high. It is used for thatching.

It is only suitable as a garden plant for the margins of lakes or large ponds where it has space to spread. In smaller areas it quickly becomes invasive.

Cultivation. Propagate by dividing the rhizomes and replanting them immediately in 2–12 in (5–30 cm) of water.

Phyllitis

Aspleniaceae

A genus of four species from many parts of the world, unusual among ferns because of their entire, rather than divided, fronds.

P. scolopendrium (Asplenium scolopendrium) – zone 6 – hart's tongue fern, is a hardy evergreen perennial, from the Northern Hemisphere, growing 12–20 in (30–50 cm) high, and 8–16 in (20–40 cm) across. It has long, fresh-green fronds, and there are a number of highly decorative cultivars such as 'Crispum'.

This is an easy fern to grow, even on chalk, and can be grown in a pot. It likes a shaded, damp spot beneath trees, in a rock garden or a cool, shady border. It cannot tolerate drought.

Cultivation. Plant in cool, humus-rich soil in spring.

Propagate from spores, or by dividing established clumps in spring.

Phyllodoce

Mountain heath, *Ericaceae*

This is a genus of approximately six species of dwarf, heath-like shrubs, no more than 20 in

(50 cm) high. They are native to Europe, Asia and Africa, and have a dainty, compact habit of growth and narrow, evergreen leaves. Flowering is from mid spring to mid summer; the bell-shaped flowers are carried in clusters on short racemes.

P. breweri (zone 6) 6–12 in (15–30 cm) high and across, is native to California. It forms tufts of shiny green foliage and purplish-pink flowers in late spring and early summer.

P. nipponica (zone 6), 6–10 in (15–25 cm) high and across, comes from Japan. It bears umbels of pinkish-white flowers in late spring.

Cultivation. The shrubs are especially suited to rock gardens and alpine gardens in cool, moist, semi-shaded position in lime-free soil. They thrive in areas of high rainfalls, and especially dislike dry air and soil. In other respects, cultivation is the same as for heather.

Propagate from cuttings or layering.

Physalis franchetii

Physalis

Chinese lantern, Cape gooseberry, *Solanaceae*

A genus of roughly 100 species of annuals or herbaceous perennials, with berries enclosed in an inflated calyx.

P. alkekengi (zone 7), bladder or winter cherry, is a half hardy herbaceous perennial, originally from Asia. It grows to a height and spread of 18 in (45 cm) and has coarse, mid-green, oval leaves. The small white flowers are inconspicuous and appear in mid to late summer. In autumn, the flowers are followed by berries enclosed in bright orange-red, inflated calyces, resembling Chinese lanterns when fully grown. Popular for dried-flower arrangements.

P. franchetii, often included as a subspecies of the above, is taller with longer, more pointed, lanterns.

Grow physalis in a herbaceous border, although it spreads rapidly and can be invasive.

Cultivation. Plant in spring, 16–20 in (40–50 cm) apart, 3 in (7.5 cm) deep, in ordinary, well drained soil in sun or light shade.

For drying, cut the stems when the fruits start to colour. Hang right-way up, in a cool, dry, airy place; if hung upside-down, the lanterns stick out at odd angles, once dry. Cut right back in autumn.

Propagate by division. It can also be grown as a half-hardy annual, from seed sown in a cold frame in spring.

Physoplexis

Horned rampions, *Campanulaceae*

A genus of one hardy herbaceous perennial, similar to *Phyteuma* and cultivated in rock gardens.

P. comosa (Phyteuma comosum) – zone 5 – is native to the Dolomites and grows 2–4¾ in (5–12 cm) high. In its native land, the plant grows between limestone rocks. It forms clumps of indented, oval pointed leaves. Unusual, claw-like purple flowers appear in short-stemmed clusters, at the centre of the clump, in mid summer. Each flower has a protruding style.

Cultivation. *P. comosa* needs a fertile, very well drained soil in limestone scree or rock gardens, and a sunny position. Protect this species from slugs, as they are very partial to it. It can also be grown in an alpine house. To propagate, sow seeds in autumn.

Physostegia

Labiatae

A genus of some seven species native to North America.

P. virginiana (zone 6), obedient plant, or lion's heart, is a hardy herbaceous perennial reaching 20–32 in (50–80 cm) high, and 16–24 in (40–

60 cm) across. It has irregular, long, indented leaves. Long spikes of small, close-set, snapdragon-like pink flowers appear on the stem from late summer to early autumn. There are white and dark-rose cultivars. The common name comes from the fact that the flowers have hinged stalks and pushed to one side, they stay there. The obedient plant is good for cutting. Grow in herbaceous or mixed borders.

Cultivation. Plant in autumn or spring, 20 in (50 cm) apart, in moist soil, enriched with organic matter, in sun or light shade.

Mulch in spring, water in dry weather and stake in an exposed position. Cut the stems back in autumn.

Propagate by division in autumn or spring, or take cuttings of young shoots in spring.

Phyteuma

Horned rampions, *Campanulaceae*

A genus of approximately 40 species of hardy herbaceous perennial plants native to Europe.

P. hemisphaericum (zone 5), a native of the Alps, grows 2–4¾ in (5–12 cm) high. It has numerous stems, with grass-like leaves and groups of 10 or 12 blue or milky-white flowers in globular heads in early summer.

This species is ideal for rock gardens, but other larger species can be grown in the front of borders.

Cultivation. *P. hemisphaericum* needs light, fertile, slightly acid, well drained soil and sun or light shade. Water freely in dry weather. Top dress annually with a mixture of leaf-mould, or peat.

To propagate, sow seeds in late winter and germinate in a cold frame, or alternatively divide in spring.

Phytolacca

Phytolaccaceae

A genus of 25 species of tender and hardy trees, shrubs or herbaceous perennials.

P. americana (P. decandra) – zone 6 – poke weed or red ink plant, is a hardy perennial, native of the United States. Its oval, green leaves are tinged with red in autumn and the erect stems are wine coloured. It grows 3–10 ft (1–3 m) high. The spikes of white flowers appear from summer to early autumn, and are followed by purplish-black berries with red juice. Poke weed is a coarse, unpleasant smelling and invasive plant, and it is also poisonous, but it has a striking habit of growth, and is particularly attractive in autumn.

This and *P. clavigera*, smaller, less coarse and with pink flowers, are suitable for a wild garden or mixed border.

Cultivation. Plant in cool, well drained but moisture-retentive soil in sun or light shade. Avoid windy locations. Cut the stems right back in late autumn. Propagate by division, sow in seed trays in spring, then prick out the seedlings into pots, to be planted out the following spring. The plants self seed freely.

Picea

Spruce, *Pinaceae*

A genus of about 30 species of hardy evergreen conifers, normally very tall, sometimes reaching more than 170 ft (50 m) in height. They have a slender, conical habit, even when mature. The trunk is straight, with spreading branches, but the lower branches only last in isolated specimens. Many species have pendulous branches. The needle-like leaves are spirally arranged around the branches and leave small, peg-like stumps when shed. The male and female flowers appear as catkins, both on the same tree. The fruits are pendent cones which ripen in their first year and fall to the ground after releasing the seeds.

P. abies (P. excelsa) – zone 4 – common or Norway spruce, is fast growing, sometimes reaching more than 130 ft (40 m) in height and is noted for its longevity. It is commonly found in Alpine regions at heights of 2,600–6,500 ft (800–2,000 m), along with pine. It is grown for timber and as Christmas trees. There are a very large number of cultivars, varying in size, habit and colour, and many are smaller and more suitable for the average size garden than this species.

P. glauca (zone 5), white spruce, occupies much of Canada and northern United States. It is similar to the Norway spruce, but is smaller and has grey-green foliage and small brown cones. A very well known cultivar is var. *albertina* 'Conica', a slow-growing dwarf shrub with a dense, perfectly conical shape.

P. orientalis (zone 5), oriental or Caucasian spruce, is native to Asia Minor. It is similar to *P.*

abies but slow growing for the first 15 years. The small, dark, glossy green needles are pressed against the branch. The purple cones are 3 in (7 cm) long, becoming brown when mature; they are not produced on young trees. This is an easier tree to grow than *P. abies*, as it is more resistant to drought. The form 'Aurea' has yellow new growth, eventually turning green in summer.

P. pungens (zone 5), Colorado or blue spruce, comes from the Rocky Mountains. It is generally slow growing, with attractively tiered horizontal branches. The dense, long needles are green in type species but var. *glauca* has bluer needles. The cone is 3–4 in (7.5–10 cm) long, cylindrical and light brown. It likes very cool or even damp soils. As a garden tree, it is best replaced after 25 years, before it loses its lower branches. It should not be confused with *Abies concolor* (Colorado white fir). There are several cultivars with very blue foliage, some of which are slow growing or dwarf in habit making them suitable for small gardens.

P. sitchensis (zone 6), Sitka spruce, comes from western North America, where it sometimes grows to a very great height. It has fine needles and pale brown cones to 4 in (10 cm) long. This tree likes a damp climate and damp soil. It has the unfortunate habit of retaining dead inner branches and twigs, which the outer, living foliage isn't dense enough to hide; this can look unsightly.

Spruces are very versatile; in parks and large gardens they can be grown in isolation or as shelter belts or wind breaks but dwarf cultivars are also suitable for small gardens and rock gardens.

Cultivation. Plant spruces in spring in moist, fertile and preferably acid soil; shallow, dry, chalky soil is unsuitable. If the leading shoot is forked, prune one away to retain only one leading shoot. The species described above are very hardy, adapting easily to most environments and types of soil, and are fast growing. However, they can be affected by drought in summer when planted in flat, open country – especially if there is only a thin layer of topsoil. So avoid soils that are too dry, shallow and chalky.

Propagate by seed in spring, after leaving the seeds in damp sand to make them swell. Varieties, especially dwarf forms, are propagated from cuttings or by grafting in summer months.

Pieris

Andromeda, *Ericaceae*

A genus of about 10 species of mostly hardy, evergreen shrubs native to China, the United States, Japan and the Himalayas. They are grown for their lily-of-the-valley like flowers and attractive foliage, which is often brightly coloured when young.

P. floribunda (zone 6), from southeastern USA, is rounded, bushy and slow growing, gradually reaching a height and spread of 6 ft (1.8 m). It carries numerous, erect flower panicles in late spring.

P. formosa (zone 6), from the Himalayas, grows 6½–13 ft (2–4 m) or more high. The young shoots are red, but gradually turn dark glossy green. The flowers appear in pendent clusters in mid to late spring. The young shoots of *P. formosa* var. *forrestii* remain a shiny red colour for about a month; there are cultivars available with even redder young foliage.

P. japonica (zone 6), 6½ ft (2 m) high, has coppery young foliage and drooping flower panicles in spring.

P. 'Forest Flame' is an extraordinary hybrid; the young shoots turn from red to pink, taking the whole summer to do so.

Pieris can be grown in mixed or shrub borders or woodland gardens. The larger forms

Pieris formosa

make good specimen shrubs. They associate especially well with other ericaceous plants, such as heathers, rhododendrons and azaleas, for instance.

Cultivation. Grow in peaty, lime-free soil, rich in humus. Plant in early spring. Pieris is shallow rooted, so water in dry weather and mulch annually in spring with leaf mould. They are vulnerable to spring frost damage, and prefer shelter and light shade.

Propagate from seed or by layers or offsets if these are present. Alternatively take cuttings of short side shoots with a heel in late summer.

Pimpinella

Umbelliferae

A genus of about 70 annuals or perennials, few of which are cultivated. A hardy annual, native to Greece, *P. anisum* (zone 5), anise or aniseed, has erect stems up to 20 in (50 cm) in height. It has fine, indented, celery-like leaves. The yellowish-white flower umbels appear in summer and autumn. The leaves and oblong, aromatic greenish-grey fruits are used as flavouring.

Cultivation. Sow outdoors in spring, in light soil and in sun. Pick the leaves as required. Pick the umbels when they are completely ripe, dry in a shaded position and remove the seeds by hand.

Uses. The leaves are pleasantly scented and can be used to season cooked vegetables or salads. The seeds are used to make liqueurs and aniseed balls. Aniseed can also be made into infusions (tea).

Pinguicula

Butterwort, *Lentibulariaceae*

The butterworts are insectivorous herbaceous perennials, some of which are hardy. They come from boggy areas in many parts of the world and are characterized by their pale-green rosette of sticky leaves. This stickiness traps small insects, which are then digested by a fluid secreted by specialised cells on the leaf blade. They have attractive, violet-shaped flowers, often with a long spur, in mauve, white, pink or yellow. *P. grandiflora* (zone 4) originates from the Pyrenées and is the species commonly cultivated in bog gardens or damp, mossy pockets by the side of pools. Its purple flowers are carried on shoot stalks in early summer.

Pinguicula grandiflora

Cultivation. In mountainous areas, pinguiculas live in waterlogged places which are constantly cool, and they need these conditions to thrive. Grow in acid soil with plenty of sphagnum moss incorporated. Tender species are suitable for the greenhouse and alpine house; grow these in well drained pots filled with peat sphagnum moss.

Propagate by seeds, by leaf cuttings placed in a mixture of peat and sand, or by division.

Pinus

Pine, *Pinacaeae*

A genus of about 70 species from the Northern Hemisphere forming evergreen, usually very tall, conifers often conical in outline when young. In some the leading stem disappears when the tree reaches maturity. The needles are normally long and grouped in twos, threes of fives. The flowers are unisexual catkins, male and female appearing on the same tree followed by cones.

P. mugo (*P. montana, P. mughus*) – zone 4 – mountain or mugo pine, is a bushy tree or shrub native to the mountains of central Europe and grows slowly to a height of only 6½ ft (2 m). It varies in appearance, but is usually gnarled or picturesque looking, and sometimes of creeping habit. The needles are in pairs and it has very small cones. It is a hardy plant and grows even in poor dry or alkaline soils. It is ideal for rock gardens and container growing.

P. nigra (zone 5), Austrian pine, is native to central and southeast Europe and grows to 66 ft (20 m) or more. The long, fine dark green needles are grouped in pairs. The cones are ovoid or conical, to 3 in (7.5 cm) long. This very hardy pine is fast growing, tolerant of exposure and thrives in dry alkaline soil.

P. nigra var. *maritima*, Corsican pine from southern Europe, reaches well over 100 ft (30 m). It bears pairs of greenish-grey needles. The tree prefers hot, dry summers and acid soil, though it tolerates alkaline soils and also pollution.

P. pinaster (*P. maritima*) – zone 7 – maritime pine, is native to the western Mediterranean, and reaches over 80 ft (24 m) in cultivation. It bears pairs of deep, glossy green needles 4–8 in (10–20 cm) long, and brown cones 4–6 in (10–15 cm) long which may last for several years on the branches and even the trunk. It is hardy in a reasonably mild climate and will grow in poor sandy soils, but is vulnerable to scale insects.

P. pinea (zone 9), stone pine or umbrella pine, comes from the Mediterranean and grows 25 ft (8 m) high and wide. It has a distinctive habit with a flat-topped crown, similar to an umbrella, and only bears branches towards the top of the tree, even when young. The pairs of leaves are 3¼–6 in (8–15 cm) long. When mature, the tree bears large oval cones containing edible seeds. It is hardy and tolerant of drought but prefers a maritime climate.

P. strobus (zone 5), Weymouth or white pine, is native to eastern North America. It is a fast growing pine, similar to Bhutan pine, but with smaller leaves in groups of five and slightly shorter cones. It is very hardy and will grow in most types of soil, but is not especially attractive when mature, and is vulnerable to blister rust. The form 'Nana' 24 in (60 cm) high and wide, forms a dense hummock of bright-green needles, and is popular for rock gardens.

P. sylvestris (zone 4), Scots pine, has various habits, depending on its geographical origins and on local conditions. It is rarely more than 100 ft (30 m) high, and is recognizable by the reddish brown bark, often heavy branches, and pairs of fairly short grey-green needles, and small, dull, grey-green cones. This is a very hardy, widely cultivated species. There are numerous dwarf or slow growing cultivars for small gardens.

P. wallichiana (*P. excelsa*) – zone 6 – Himalayan or Bhutan pine, is native to the Himalayas and grows to 100 ft (30 m) or more. It has blue-green needles in groups of five, up to 7 in (17.5 cm) long, often drooping elegantly. The cones are cylindrical, curved, 8 in (20 cm) long and very resinous. It is very hardy but needs shelter from severe wind, and makes a good specimen tree for large gardens. Its shape when young is conical, but it forms a broader, irregular crown when mature.

Pines are suitable for large gardens, and dwarf or slow-growing cultivars may be suitable for small gardens, or rock gardens. Some are useful as windbreaks and for maritime planting or even for containers. Commercially, they are the predominant timber tree in the Northern Hemisphere.

Cultivation. Plant pines with bare roots or balled in spring, when growth starts. Some species, such as Corsican pine, only transplant well when under 1 ft (30 cm) high. Pines are very hardy and tolerate most climates, whether inland or by the sea; dry or moist air, even with salt; most soils and most locations. Many are vulnerable to heavy pollution in industrial areas. After spring growth has started, prune double leads to one leader as soon as possible, and cut off the dead lower branches flush with the main stem where bark is a feature.

Propagate by seed in spring after stratifying the seeds, or alternatively by grafting on to their own type in late winter, with some protection from sun and cold winds.

In some countries, rust is an important disease. Among the pests are the pine shoot moth and pine weevil whose flight-holes allow drops of resin to exude.

Pisum

Pea, *Leguminosae*

This genus of hardy climbing annuals includes several species, of which *P. sativum* is the most well known.

P. sativum (zone 6), pea, is a hardy climbing annual grown as a vegetable, with stems 1–6½ ft (30 cm–2 m) high. It produces pods 2¾–6 in (7–15 cm) long; the whole pod of mange-tout or sugar peas, is eaten, but only the seeds of garden peas are eaten.

Cultivation. Unlike most other plants, the pea and other legumes add nitrogen to the soil. Plan a three-year rotation and plant peas after a root vegetable. Peas like fairly cool soils which are well drained and aerated, and dislike drought, excessive heat and fresh manure. Round seeds are hardier and have a lower sugar content than wrinkled seeds. Sow the seeds in rows as wide apart as they grow tall, 2–3 in (5–7.5 cm) deep, 1 in (2.5 cm) apart. In areas with a mild winter, sow round-seeded peas from mid autumn to mid winter. Round-seeded peas and mange-tout can also be planted in any area from late winter to mid spring. Sow wrinkle-seeded peas successionally from mid spring to early summer, and early round or wrinkled seeded peas in mid summer for an autumn crop.

Hoe in two stages; first, after the shoots have appeared and then when they are 8–10 in (20–25 cm) high, when the plant can be earthed up and the taller varieties supported with nets, pea fences or twiggy pea sticks. Water in dry weather and mulch in spring with leaf mould or lawn mowings to conserve moisture. Expected yield from a 30 ft (9 m) row is 30 lb (13.5 kg). Approximate time between autumn sowing and picking is six months and three months for spring sowing. Pick the pods in dry weather, about three weeks after they have flowered.

Peas are vulnerable to pea weevil, pea aphid, pea moth, pea thrips, seed beetle, slugs and snails, pea downy mildew, and powdery mildew, root rot, foot and halo blight. Coating seeds with a fungicide is a good preventative measure. Good quality seed and good cultivation helps prevent most of the above.

Platanus

Plane (sycamore in USA), *Platanaceae*

A genus of large deciduous trees with wide-spreading branches, some growing to 130 ft (40 m) in height. The tree has a distinctive bark: normally smooth, it flakes during the summer, winter and spring revealing the cream or brown young wood. The large, maple-like leaves are palmately lobed, and turn golden in autumn. The flowers are small, growing in clusters, and are followed by seeds in distinct pendulous balls. There are two main species: *P. orientalis* (zone 7), Oriental plane from southeast Europe (sycamore in USA) and *P. occidentalis* (zone 7), buttonwood from North America. *P.* × *acerifolia* (*P.* × *hispanica*) (zone 7), London plane, is believed to be a hybrid of these two species. It grows to over 100 ft (30 m) high, with a straight trunk and rounded crown. The leaves are three to five lobed and the flowers appear in clusters in mid to late spring.

Plane trees are tolerant of pollution and hard pruning, and much planted in cities, large gardens, parks and streets.

Cultivation. The plane likes deep, cool, well drained soil but dislikes chalky soil. Plant in autumn or spring.

The tree is prone to chlorosis, plane tree anthracnose (especially in towns) leading to canker on stems in severe cases.

Propagate by seed in spring, or from cuttings 8–12 in (20–30 cm) long with a heel, taken in autumn and placed in a cold frame. Planes can also be layered.

Platycodon

Balloon flower, *Campanulaceae*

A genus consisting of a single species, native to the Far East.

P. grandiflorum (zone 6) is a long-lived, hardy herbaceous perennial. It grows 16–24 in (40–60 cm) or more high, and 12–16 in (30–40 cm) across. It is clump forming and bears oval, bluish-green leaves and spherical buds which open into large blue or white, cup-shaped flowers, from summer to autumn. Several forms with pink or mauve flowers are available, some with semi-double flowers.

It is suitable for the front of herbaceous or

Platycodon grandiflorum

mixed borders, and is especially attractive with fuchsias.

Cultivation. Plant in autumn or spring, 16 in (40 cm) apart, in ordinary, well drained soil and an open, sunny or partly shaded position. Avoid moving the plants and cut the stems right down to ground level in autumn to ensure a flourishing plant for the following year.

Propagate at the beginning of spring, either by seed under a cold frame, or by division of old plants.

Pleione

Orchidaceae

These unusual, Asian orchids have showy flowers and in milder areas some can be grown outdoors if protected from frost. They are half-hardy and deciduous; their small pseudo-bulbs, 1–1½ in (2.5–3 cm) wide, lodge in mossy hollows in rocks in the temperate regions of the Far East. The flowers appear in winter and spring and each flower may be more than 4 in (10 cm) across, making it the largest of the hardier orchids.

P. bulbocodioides (*P. formosana*) – zone 9 – 4 in (10 cm) high, is one of the best known, most robust and most attractive. It bears bright pink and white flowers, often marked or shaded with cream and yellow; these appear in spring before the leaves.

P. yunnanensis (zone 9–10) is similar, but with smaller flowers.

P. × *confusa* (*P. forrestii*) – zone 10 – is a delicate plant, but is the only cultivated species with yellow flowers.

Cultivation. Many species survive the colder winters if given ideal soil conditions and protected with open-ended cloches from mid autumn to mid spring. Choose a sheltered, partly shaded position and very well drained gritty soil, enriched with leaf mould or peat. They are ideal species for growing in alpine houses.

Pleiones propagate naturally by forming new pseudo-bulbs every year.

Poa

Meadow-grass, *Gramineae*

This is a widespread genus of about 250 species of annual or perennial grasses, with flattened spikes of up to 10 florets. Some species are used as lawn grasses and a few as ornamentals.

Pleione bulbocodioides

P. glauca (zone 4) grows in most of the colder regions of the Northern Hemisphere. It forms a tufted plant to 15 in (37 cm) with stiff, blue-green leaves.

P. chaixii (zone 4) from Europe and southwest Asia grows 3½ ft (1 m) high and 20 in (50 cm) across. The sharply pointed leaves are bright green and ⅜ in (1 cm) across. The flower spikes appear in early summer growing to a length of up to 10 in (25 cm).

Cultivation. Sow or plant in autumn or spring, in any soil and in sun or light shade. Propagate from seed or by dividing the clumps in spring.

Polemonium

Jacob's ladder, *Polemoniaceae*

A genus of 30 species of hardy herbaceous perennials, grown for their clusters of mainly blue flowers, with golden stamens.

P. caeruleum (zone 6), Jacob's ladder, is native to the Northern Hemisphere. It grows 2 ft (60 cm) high and 1 ft (30 cm) across, forming clumps of arching leaves of numerous, ladder-like pointed leaflets, hence its common name. Racemes of blue, cup-shaped flowers appear in early summer. There are dark-blue and white flowered forms available. It self seeds.

P. carneum (zone 6), a native of western North America grows to 16–20 in (40–50 cm) in height and spread. It is moderately hardy and produces

spreading, branched stems with mid-green, pinnate leaves, narrow leaflets and flesh-pink flowers, $\frac{3}{4}$–$1\frac{1}{4}$ in (2–3 cm) in diameter, growing continuously from late spring to mid summer. There are deep-pink forms available.
P. foliosissimum (zone 6) from western North America, grows $2\frac{1}{2}$ ft (75 cm) high and 20 in (50 cm) across. Its mauve-blue flowers with their orange stamens appear in summer.

Larger species are particularly suitable for mixed borders and smaller ones for rock gardens.
Cultivation. Plant in ordinary soil, in sun or part shade. They prefer a rich soil, and soon tend to exhaust it.

To propagate, sow seeds in spring in a seed tray kept at 68°F (20°C). Reduce the temperature to 50–55°F (10–13°C) when the seeds start to germinate. Alternatively divide in the spring or autumn. Established clumps need regular division, otherwise they degenerate.

Polygala
Milwort, *Polygalaceae*

A large genus comprising approximately 450 species of sub-shrubs, annuals and herbaceous perennials, some tender and from the tropics, but others hardy.
P. calcarea (zone 5), a native of Europe, grows 2–4 in (5–10 cm) high and 1 ft (30 cm) across. This perennial forms a dark-green carpet of spreading stems, covered in oval leaves. The racemes of large, winged bright-blue flowers appear in summer.
P. chamaebuxus (zone 6), ground box, a native of Europe, grows 6 in (15 cm) high and 12 in (30 cm) across. It is a dwarf sub-shrub with evergreen, leathery oval leaves and procumbent stems. The pea-like flowers are yellow and cream or yellow and purple, and appear from mid spring to early summer, six per 1–2 in (3–5 cm) long raceme.

The small hardy species of this genus are suitable for rock gardens.
Cultivation. The two species above prefer well drained, limy soil, but *P. chamaebuxus* likes a cool, moist position, humus and light shade, while *P. calcarea* prefers full sun.

Propagate from cuttings, 2–3 in (5–7.5 cm) long, of lateral shoots, taken in early to mid summer. Plant in a cold frame in equal parts sand and peat, and keep the cuttings shaded.

Polygonatum
Solomon's seal, *Liliaceae*

This genus contains about 50 species of hardy herbaceous perennials, grown for their attractive foliage, graceful, arching growth and small, bell-like flowers.
P. biflorum (*P. commutatum*) – zone 5 – originally from North America, grows 2–$6\frac{1}{2}$ ft (60 cm–2 m) high, and has pairs of oval to lanceolate, green leaves, and white or greenish-yellow bell-shaped flowers in summer. This plant is particularly suited to large, shaded gardens.
P. odoratum (*P. officinale*) – zone 5 – a European native, grows 16–24 in (40–60 cm) high, and 12–16 in (30–40 cm) across. It has alternate, pale-green leaves on the upper part of the angular stems. The pendent, green-tipped, white fragrant flowers appear singly or in clusters of two to four in late spring to early summer, and are followed by bluish berries.

These plants are lovely in woodland gardens, associate well with ferns and hostas, and are useful in flower arrangements.
Cultivation. Plant in cool, peaty, humus-rich soil in shade or part shade, avoiding hot, dry situations. Cut the stems down to soil level in late autumn. Mulch with leaf mould once a year.

Propagate by dividing the root clumps in mid autumn or early spring, and replant these immediately since the plants resent disturbance.

Sawfly caterpillars can be troublesome in late spring.

Polygonum
Knotweed, *Polygonaceae*

A genus of about 150 species of annuals and herbaceous perennials or sub-shrubs, native to many parts of the world, and many of which are grown for their flowers. The common name comes from the swollen stem joints, or 'knots'.
P. affine (zone 6), from Nepal, a herbaceous perennial sometimes grown in rock gardens, has had at least two cultivars developed from it – 'Darjeeling Red' and 'Donald Lowndes' – and it is usually these which are grown in the garden. 'Darjeeling Red' is a low spreading plant with dark green leaves and spikes of deep pink flowers, appearing in mid summer to early autumn. 'Donald Lowndes', which is more compact, has rose-red flower spikes in early

summer. The foliage is bright green when young, but darkens with age. Both cultivars are 6–9 in (15–23 cm) high and reach 18 in (45 cm) across.

P. amplexicaule (zone 6), mountain fleece, from the Himalayas, is a hardy, clump-forming herbaceous perennial which grows 32–48 in (80 cm–1.2 m) high and 24–32 in (60–80 cm) across. It has large, pointed, heart-shaped leaves and masses of erect, dense spikes of small, crimson flowers from early summer to autumn. Forms with white, scarlet and pendulous flowers are available.

This species can be used in herbaceous or mixed borders, and associates well with asters, but other species can be invasive, and suitable only for wild gardens.

P. baldschuanicum (zone 7), Russian vine, is well known for the speed with which it will grow along a wall or trellis. This makes it an invaluable screening climber. Eventually it will reach 40 ft (12 m) high. The leaves are bright green and it has clusters of white or pale pink flowers in mid summer to early autumn.

Cultivation. Plant herbaceous perennials in autumn or spring, 2 ft (60 cm) apart, in rich, cool, moist soil and in sun or part shade. Cut the stems back in autumn, after the flowers have died. *P. baldschuanicum* should be planted in spring in any type of soil or aspects, against some sort of support. Propagate by division in autumn or early spring. Take cuttings of *P. baldschuanicum*.

Polygonum amplexicaule

Polypodium

Polypody, *Polypodiaceae*

This very large genus contains ferns found in many areas of the northern temperate regions, often grown for their attractive foliage.

P. vulgare (zone 6), common polypody, is a hardy, shade-loving perennial, growing 1 ft (30 cm) or more high and across. It has arching, mid-green fronds divided into entire leaflets. They retain their fresh green colour from sum mer, when the new leaves appear, to late winter. There are several very decorative cultivars, including 'Cornubiense', with lacy fronds, and 'Cristatum' with crested bright green leaflets.

This plant is excellent as ground cover in shaded areas.

Cultivation. This easy-going plant resents disturbance and requires only humus-rich soil and light shade to thrive. Plant in spring, burying the roots just below the surface, but placing and fixing the rhizomes at ground level. Rust sometimes develops on the fronds in the form of small orange-brown pimples. Remove plain leaves which appear in crested or lacy cultivars.

Propagate in spring by division.

Polystichum

Shield fern, *Aspidiaceae*

This genus is represented by some 200 species of evergreen fern found throughout the world.

P. acrostichioides (zone 5), Christmas fern, from North America. Grows to a height of 3 ft (90 cm) and the dark green fronds retain their colour through winter. Used for Christmas decoration in USA.

P. setiferum (zone 6), soft shield fern, is a vigorous, evergreen hardy perennial, with a height and spread of 2–4 ft (60 cm–1.2 m). The bipinnate fronds are covered in brown, cottony scales, turning light green as they unfold.

There are many cultivars. The 'Acutilobum' ('Proliferum') group has finely divided foliage and small plantlets on the midribs which can be used for propagation. Plants in the 'Divisilobum' group also have finely divided fronds. These are large, impressive but not invasive

ferns which can be grown as specimens or in shaded mixed borders, in woodland gardens or spaces between paving stones.
Cultivation. Plant in early spring in a shaded or partly shaded position, preferably in a limy soil containing plenty of organic matter. The soft shield fern is tolerant of drought.

Propagation is by spores sown as soon as ripe, by division of the crowns in spring, or by potting up the plantlets which grow on some varieties.

Populus

Poplar, *Salicaceae*

These are large, fast-growing, hardy deciduous trees widespread over the Northern Hemisphere, normally of tall, columnar habit with a straight trunk. The flowers take the form of male and female catkins in spring, usually on separate trees. The fruits are capsules of numerous seeds with long white cottony hairs which ensure distribution by wind.
P. alba (zone 6), white poplar, grows to 40 ft (12 m) high and can be recognized by its smooth bark, and the white underside of the lobed leaves, which are especially noticeable in the wind. The leaves turn golden yellow in autumn. The tree is tolerant of alkaline soil, drought and sea spray, and often forms a mass of suckers round the trunk.
P. × *canescens (alba* × *tremula)* – zone 6 – grey poplar, is now considered to be a natural hybrid of the white poplar and the aspen. It is similar to *P. alba* but distinguished by the grey undersurface to the leaves. It also likes alkaline soil.
P. nigra (zone 6), black poplar, has a rough bark and very distinctive, glabrous, triangular or diamond-shaped leaves which are green on both sides. It may eventually grow 100 ft (30 m) high. One of the most common cultivars is *P. nigra* 'Italica', the Italian or lombardy poplar, tall and columnar, with ascending branches. It is nearly always male, stands up well to windy conditions and is often used to form windbreaks.
P. tremoloides, quaking aspen, a tree growing up to 200 ft (60 m) in wild. Slender trunk, bright green (above) leaves, which are finely toothed and roundish.
P. tremula (zone 6), aspen, is a smaller tree and rarely reaches a height of 66 ft (20 m). It has small, round leaves with long petioles, which tremble at the slightest breath of wind.

Poplars should only be grown where there is plenty of room available. They make fine windbreaks and screens and grow well in damp soil. Their roots, however, are wide spreading, invasive, and can damage drainpipes and building foundations.
Cultivation. Plant in late autumn or early spring in fairly rich, cool or damp soil.

Propagate from seed, suckers or from strong leafless cuttings taken in spring and inserted in the ground.

Poplars, expecially young trees, are vulnerable to leaf blight and other diseases but the species above are fairly resistant to disease.

Portulaca

Portulacaceae

A genus of annual or perennial succulents which grow wild in many areas, especially warmer regions.
P. grandiflora (zone 9–10), sun plant or moss rose, is a semi-prostrate tender perennial, grown as a half-hardy annual. It has bright green foliage and red, succulent stems. Its large, saucer-shaped flowers come in brilliant reds, yellows, purples or white, and close at night and on dull days. There are single-colour seeds strains, double and dwarf varieties, and those which remain open all day. They are excellent as edging for borders and in rock gardens.
Cultivation. Choose a hot, sunny spot and well drained, even poor, soil. Sow under glass in early spring, prick out, harden off and plant after the last frost. Water only when it shows signs of wilting. Alternatively sow *in situ* in mid to late spring and thin as necessary.
P. oleracea (zone 7), purslane, is a creeping plant with small fleshy, edible leaves and yellow flowers in summer.
Cultivation. This species exhausts the soil after a time, and should not be replanted in the same place until two or three years later. It needs light, well drained soil and a warm, sunny position.

Sow thinly from mid winter to early spring on a hot bed or under a cold frame, and prick out in mid spring. Alternatively, sow thinly outdoors from late spring to late summer, in rows 10 in (25 cm) apart, then thin out leaving one seedling every 8 in (20 cm). Sow the seeds at intervals to prolong the productivity of the plant.

Keep the soil well weeded and hoed, and water the plant in dry weather. Pick from mid summer until the first frosts.
Uses. The leaves can be eaten raw in salads, cooked like spinach, or used in soups.

Potentilla

Cinquefoil, *Rosaceae*

This genus consists of about 300 species of annuals, herbaceous perennials, shrubs or sub-shrubs from the Northern Hemisphere. The perennials and shrubs are grown for their colourful flowers which appear over a long season, usually from late spring to late summer, and for this reason are particularly prized.
P. atrosanguinea (zone 6), from the Himalayas, is a hardy herbaceous perennial with grey, strawberry-like leaves and deep-red flowers in summer. It is the parent of many garden hybrids with single, semi-double or double flowers in orange, yellow, scarlet, coral, mahogany and crimson.
P. fruticosa (zone 7), shrubby cinquefoil, is a small deciduous shrub about 3 ft (1 m) high found wild in Europe, North America and Asia. It has delicate, pinnate foliage and bears small, bright-yellow, rose-like flowers throughout the summer. The species is rarely grown but many hybrids and cultivars have been developed with similar habits but with white, pale yellow, orange, apricot or reddish flowers.
P. nitida (zone 7), a dwarf herbaceous species, reaches only 2–3 in (5–7 cm) high and is grown in rock gardens or used as a ground cover plant. The pale pink flowers with dark centres open in summer.

P. atrosanguinea can be used in herbaceous or mixed borders, shrubby potentillas can be used for hedging, and low-grass forms make excellent ground cover. Dwarf ground-hugging forms are ideal for rock gardens.
Cultivation. Plant in early spring, 18–24 in (45–60 cm) apart, more for shrubby species, in ordinary, well drained soil and a sunny, open position. Water well in dry weather, mulch in spring and cut herbaceous potentillas back in autumn. Cut weak shoots of shrubby potentillas out at ground level and after flowering remove spent shoots. Water well in dry weather, mulch in spring and cut back in autumn. Propagate by division in autumn or spring, from seed, cuttings or offsets.

Primula

Primulaceae

This genus includes over 500 species of hardy and half-hardy herbaceous plants, most of which are native to North America, Europe or Asia. The leaves form rosettes and the showy, five-petalled flowers appear in spring or summer, singly or in clusters. The smaller species are especially useful for the rock garden or peat bed and the taller species can be used in borders, woodland areas or beside ponds. Some are suitable for the alpine house and others for spring bedding.

The smaller species flowering in early spring include *P. vulgaris* (*P. acaulis*) – zone 6 – primrose, to 4 in (10 cm), with rosettes of wrinkled leaves and solitary yellow flowers; *P. auricula* (zone 5), bears ear, dusty miller, 4–6 in (10–15 cm) high, with rosettes of greyish-green, fleshy, farinose leaves and yellow fragrant flowers; and *P. juliae* (zone 6), which forms a small cushion with rounded leaves and bright-purple flowers with yellow throats.

Larger plants include *P. denticulata* (zone 5), drumstick primula, from the Himalayas, which grows to 1 ft (30 cm) and has tightly packed, globose heads of small, mainly purple, flowers in spring; *P. florindae* (zone 5), giant cowslip, from Tibet growing 16–20 in (40–50 cm) high, with lemon-yellow flowers in summer grouped in loose terminal umbels, and *P. pulverulenta* (zone 6) native to China, 24–32 in (60–80 cm)

Primula vulgaris

high, with large narrow oval leaves and stems bearing whorls of deep-red flowers.

Many hybrids have been raised, among the most popular of which are polyanthus, hybrids of *P. vulgaris*. These are used as pot plants and for spring bedding and come in a virtual rainbow of colours, some bicoloured, others semi-double or double.

Cultivation. Primulas like deep, cool, humus-rich soil which is well drained, and sun or light shade.

Mulch annually in spring, water in dry wether, and dead head if time permits.

Propagate by division after flowering, but some primulas can be propagated from cuttings and others produce seed freely and the seedlings can be used to maintain the stock. Alternatively, sow in the autumn and place in a cold frame when germination will take place the following spring. Polyanthus and drumstick primulas are often grown as half-hardy annuals or hardy biennials.

Primulas are subject to fungal attack, crown and root rot and downy mildew, all of which should be controlled as soon as infection appears.

Prunella

Labiatae

A genus of about seven easily grown species of small, hardy, herbaceous perennials.

P. grandiflora (zone 5) is a native of Europe and grows 6 in (15 cm) high and 20–32 in (50–60 cm) across with green or purplish oval leaves. The tubular flowers are violet or purple, and arranged in dense spikes 2–4 in (5–8 cm) long from late spring through the summer.

P. × *webbiana*, probably a hybrid, grows 8–12 in (20–30 cm) high and 20–32 in (50–80 cm) wide. The leaves are shorter than those of *P. grandiflora* and the flowers bright purple. There are several cultivars including 'Loveliness' with pale violet flowers and 'Pink Loveliness' with light pink flowers.

Prunellas are grown in rock gardens, though they can be invasive, but make good ground cover on moist soil.

Cultivation. Plant in spring, in ordinary, fairly cool soil and in sun or light shade. These plants self seed readily, so dead head flowers as soon as the flowers fade.

Propagate by seed in early spring, by division in early autumn, or by removing the rooted side-shoots and planting them out.

Prunus 'Kanzan'

Prunus

Rosaceae

The 200 species of this genus, mostly native to the Northern Hemisphere, include a large number of trees and shrubs with attractive flowers. Many are widely grown in gardens for their ornamental value, and others are grown for their edible fruits.

P. avium (zone 6), wild cherry, is native to Europe and Asia, and grows 50–66 ft (15–20 m) high. It has a narrow habit when young, but as the tree grows older, the branches begin to slope and the tree acquires a more rounded outline. The white flowers appear in mid to late spring, followed by small, sweet, blackish-red cherries containing a large stone. It is one of the parents of the cultivated fruiting cherries.

P. cerasifera (zone 6), cherry plum, grows 17 ft (5 m) high and carries profuse clusters of white flowers followed by edible red fruit. There are several purple leaved forms, including 'Pissardii'. These normally produce large numbers of flowers, but bear few fruit. They are good hedging plants and should be clipped after flowering.

P. laurocerasus (zone 8), common laurel or cherry laurel, comes from Asia Minor and is useful as a fast-growing evergreen up to 17 ft (5 m) in height. It has elongated, leathery, shiny leaves and clusters of white flowers, followed by black, shiny inedible fruit. It can be grown in shade, as an isolated specimen or hedge, but is not hardy in extremely cold areas. 'Otto Luyken' has narrower leaves, compact habit and is very free flowering; it, and the similar 'Zabeliana' are excellent ground cover.

P. lusitanica (zone 7), Portugal laurel, is a bushy shrub growing 10–17 ft (3–5 m) high. It has evergreen, lanceolate, shiny dark-green leaves, and in early summer, long racemes of white, scented flowers. It is more tolerant of shade and alkaline soils, and considerably hardier than *P. laurocerasus*.

P. padus (zone 6), bird cherry, grows 50 ft (15 m) high. It looks like wild cherry, but has drooping clusters of fragrant white flowers, and acrid-smelling bark. There are several cultivars with double or pink flowers and coloured foliage.

P. serrula (zone 6), a native of China, grows 33 ft (10 m) or more high. It has slender, willow-like leaves but is remarkable for its shiny, peeling, mahogany-coloured bark. Its flowers are white and rather small.

P. serrulata (zone 5–6), is a widely-spreading, flat-topped, double-flowered cherry, and has given rise, probably with other species, to the large number of cultivars known as Japanese flowering cherries. 'Kanzan', with upright habit and pompons of purple-pink flowers, is one of the best-known and frequently planted. 'Shirotae' ('Mount Fuji') has wide-spreading horizontal or drooping branches. The flowers are semi-double, white and scented, and appear at the same time as the first leaves.

P. subhirtella (zone 6), higan, or spring cherry, is native to Japan and has slender branches. It has soft pink small flowers very early in spring. Several forms are grown, including 'Autumnalis', with semi-double almost white flowers opening in mild spells in late autumn and often throughout winter.

Apricot tree (zone 8–9)
P. armeniaca is an attractive round-headed tree, growing 30 ft (9 m) high. It has fairly smooth oval leaves and pinkish or white flowers in spring.

Almond tree (zone 8)
P. dulcis (*P. amygdalus*), may grow to 33 ft (10 m) in height. The large, ornamental pink or white flowers are formed early.

Cherry tree (zone 6–7)
P. cerasus grows to a maximum of 20 ft (6 m). In mid spring it bears clusters of pure white flowers, which are very decorative but the fruit is red and acid. Some of the edible cherries have been derived from this species.

Peach tree (zone 7)
P. persica is a bushy tree growing to a height of about 20 ft (6 m). It is similar to the almond but less robust. It has equally decorative rose pink flowers in spring.

Plum tree (zone 6)
P. domestica grows to a maximum height of 20 ft (6 m), with a fairly slender shape. The rather small but numerous white flowers are formed in spring. This species has given rise to the many forms of plum such as greengage, damsons.

Cultivation. Plant in autumn or spring. Most Prunus enjoy warm sunny situations and the lower altitudes, avoiding shade and frost pockets. This applies particularly to the fruiting trees which need a full day's sun. Cherries and plums are hardier but apricots, peaches and nectarines need to be grown against a warm sunny wall in cooler areas.

All these trees thrive in a deep (2 ft/60 cm), well drained rich loamy calcareous soil, especially for the stone fruits which rely on good drainage, lime and a plentiful supply of water during the growing season.

Any pruning is aimed at letting the light into the tree and this is done during the early summer to allow the wounds to callas over quickly and prevent the entry of certain diseases.

Propagation of the ornamental species consists of taking cuttings of young wood becoming firm and with a heel. The fruit trees are grafted in the spring on to the appropriate stock or, budded in the summer.

The main diseases are peach leaf curl, silver leaf and powdery mildew as well as pocket plum, blossom wilt and whither lip.

The main pests are birds and wasps, the maggots of various moths (red plum maggot) and certain mites (plum gall mite).

Pseudotsuga

Pinaceae

This genus consists of about six species of large conifers, related to the spruces and firs, and native to western North America and Japan. The needles are fine and green or glaucous. The flowers take the form of male and female catkins, growing on the same tree in spring. The fruits are pendent cones, $2\frac{1}{4}$ in (6 cm) long, which have conspicuous bracts protruding between the scales.

P. menziesii (P. taxifolia, P. douglasii) – zone 5 – Douglas fir, from western North America, is a very tall, fast-growing, slender conifer reaching about 300 ft (90 m) in the wild. As it matures, it develops a broad, flat-topped crown. The foliage is aromatic and green to blue green. It is too big for ordinary gardens but is sometimes grown as a tall hedge.

P. menziesii var. *glauca* (zone 5), Colorado Douglas fir, is hardier, smaller and slower growing, usually well under 100 ft (30 m). It often has very blue foliage.

Cultivation. All are very hardy, thriving in deep, moisture-retentive but free-draining soil. They dislike poor, calcareous or waterlogged soil but are tolerant of dry weather in summer. They grow best in areas of high rainfall, but the Colorado Douglas fir is tolerant of dry conditions, and also shallow soil. Plant in spring.

Propagate by seed in spring after stratification of the seeds. Grey mould fungus can attack seedlings but the most serious problem is canker and die back caused by a fungus.

Pulmonaria

Lungwort, *Boraginaceae*

A genus of approximately 10 species of European herbaceous perennials, which are hardy and more or less evergreen.

P. saccharata (zone 6) grows 8–12 in (20–30 cm) high, 2 ft (60 cm) across. It has large, rough, very decorative oval leaves, spotted with silvery grey. The tubular, pink flower heads appear in spring and turn to blue as they age.

The plant makes very good ground cover in the border or wild garden.

Cultivation. Plant in a shaded position in ordinary soil, in autumn or spring and 12 in (30 cm) apart. Keep well watered in dry weather and cut the stems back after flowering.

Propagate by division in autumn or early spring, or transplant the self sown seedlings.

Pulsatilla

Pasque flower, *Ranunculaceae*

This genus consists of approximately 30 species of herbaceous perennials with showy early flowers, mostly native to Europe or Asia.

P. vulgaris (zone 5), pasque flower, is hardy, reaching a height and spread of 8–12 in (20–30 cm). The mid-green leaves are very finely divided and violet, cup-shaped, anemone-like flowers, 2–3¼ in (5–8 cm) in diameter, are produced in mid to late spring. The pasque flower has decorative woolly seed heads. There are forms available with pink, white, blue and red flowers. Plant in herbaceous borders or rockeries.

Cultivation. Plant in early autumn, 12 in (30 cm) apart. *P. vulgaris* likes well drained soil, preferably containing plenty of organic matter, and an open, sunny position. It is an easy plant to grow, but dislikes damp winters. Do not move it once it has been planted, as it is deep rooted.

Propagate by seed under a cold frame either from mid summer onwards or during winter.

Punica

Pomegranate, *Punicaceae*

Of this genus of two species, only one is grown: a small, deciduous tree or shrub.

P. granatum (zone 10), pomegranate, grows to 20 ft (6 m) high. It has a bushy, erect habit, and is often thorny. Its small, bright-green, deciduous leaves turn brilliant yellow in autumn, and, in late spring, it carries scarlet flowers. Forms with white, pink and double flowers are available. The fruit, which is only produced in warm climates, is large, globular and golden yellow, turning to carmine as it ripens. It has a leathery skin and the seeds are surrounded by a juicy edible, acidic pulp.

Pomegranates make attractive hedges in mild climates.

Cultivation. Plant in any well drained soil, however poor or dry, and in a sunny position. In late spring, prune the older and weaker wood, as the flowers appear on the current year's wood; in winter, it is not easy to distinguish live wood from dead. Water frequently and provide a good mulch. Propagate by seed, by cuttings or by grafting, using seedling stock of the type.

Pyracantha

Firethorn, *Rosaceae*

A genus of approximately ten species of mostly hardy, thorny evergreen shrubs with attractive

corymbs of white flowers, and clusters of small, inedible fruits, much loved by birds.
P. angustifolia (zone 6), from China, grows 12 ft (3.7 m) high, and has narrow, mid-green leaves, grey and hairy below. The white flowers appear in early summer, followed by clusters of orange-yellow fruits retained for much of the winter.
P. atalantioides (zone 6) is a larger, often nearly spineless, shrub with shiny, dark-green leaves. The white flowers in late spring and early summer are followed by clusters of red, long lasting fruits. 'Aurea' has yellow fruits.
P. coccinea (zone 6), from S. Europe, has oval or obovate, glossy green leaves, white flowers in early summer and bright-red fruits.
P. crenato-serrata (zone 6) grows 15 ft (4.5 m) high. It has obovate leaves, white flowers and numerous small, red fruits which last all winter.
P. crenulata (zone 7–8), from the Himalayas, is less frequently grown and less hardy. It has orange-yellow fruits.

There are numerous cultivars and hybrids.

The firethorn can be grown as a specimen tree, against a wall, or as a small hedge.

Cultivation. Pyracanthas are easy to grow even in poor or chalky soils, provided they are well drained. Plant as specimen in open ground where pruning is hardly necessary, or 20 in (50 cm) apart to form hedges. Wall-trained firethorn must be carefully tied in and, as with hedges, cut back after flowering.

Propagate by removing the pulp from the seeds and stratifying them, or by taking heel cuttings and planting under a frame.

Pyracanthas are liable to attack by scab, causing the foliage to wither and fall, and are susceptible to fireblight when it is best to cut back affected parts and burn immediately.

Pyrethrum
Compositae

Although correctly in the genus *Tanacetum*, the following plant is included here, where it is better known.
T. coccineum (Pyrethrum roseum) (zone 6), pyrethrum daisy, from the Middle East, is a hardy herbaceous perennial. It grows 2–3½ ft (60 cm–1 m) high and 20 in (50 cm) across. It has fine, feathery, bright-green foliage and large, single, red, daisy-like flowers in early to mid summer. Many single and double forms in white, pink, red and crimson are available. This is an excellent cut flower, and grows best in a herbaceous or mixed border.

Cultivation. Plant in fertile, neutral or alkaline soil in an open situation in autumn or spring, 20–24 in (50–60 cm) apart. Use pea sticks to stake the plant if necessary, water in dry weather, and remove the stems once the flowers have died to encourage second flowering.

Propagate in autumn or spring by division, or from cuttings in early spring.

The main pests are aphids, eelworms and leaf miners. The powdered flower heads of *T. coccineum* yield a strong non-poisonous insecticide.

Pyrus
Pear, *Rosaceae*

A genus of about 20 deciduous trees including a few of ornamental value.
P. communis, pear, is a deciduous tree about 50 ft (15 m) high, fairly twisted in appearance if allowed to grow unchecked. The leaves are similar to those of the apple but glossier and colour well in autumn. Numerous clusters of white flowers are carried in spring. This is the species from which culinary pears have been developed.

Cultivation. Pears like well drained, deep soil which has neither too much clay nor too much sand, but will not tolerate chalk. Water well during first year to help pear become established. Then dress annually with fertilizer in late winter. Mulch in spring. They need shelter and protection from spring frosts. Pyrus produce new growth readily therefore prune well to encourage the younger branches.

Pick the pears from the tree when they are just ripe and still firm, from mid summer to late autumn. Propagate by sowing seed or grafting on the same species or on quince trees obtained from cuttings. The main disease encountered with this species is fireblight and this should be checked after flowering.

Quercus
Oak, *Fagaceae*

There are around 250 species of oak, native to temperate regions of the Northern Hemisphere. They are deciduous or evergreen trees, occasionally shrubs, with simple, often lobed leaves. The male and female flowers appear on the same tree in the form of catkins. The fruit is an acorn enclosed in a scaly cup.

Q. alba, white oak, is a deciduous tree which grows up to 150 ft (45 m) and is common in the USA. It has never succeeded for long in the UK.

Q. ilex (zone 8), evergreen or holm oak, is native to Mediterranean areas and is a fine, round-headed, evergreen tree, growing to 90 ft (27.5 m) high. The bark is dark, only slightly cracked, and not corky. It has leathery, more or less toothed glossy dark green leaves, often grey hairy below. It is highly resistant both to drought and heat, but comparatively sensitive to cold. However, it grows well in any warm, well drained soil, and is excellent for sea-side planting.

Q. palustris, pin oak, a deciduous tree, it is densely leafy and grows up to 100 ft (30 m). Shiny green leaves are wide and obovate to oval.

Q. robur (*Q. pedunculata*) – zone 6 – the pedunculate, common or English oak, may grow to 100 ft (30 m) or more, upright if grown in woods but spreading in open positions. It is a deciduous, long-lived tree which only begins producing fruit when it is many years old. The common oak is a magnificent tree, but does not thrive on poor, acid soils. The cultivar 'Fastigiata' is columnar.

Q. rubra (zone 6), red oak, is native to eastern North America. It may reach 70 ft (21 m) or more in height and is usually grown for the large leaves, which turn red or yellowish-brown in autumn. It is fast growing and tolerant of most conditions.

Q. suber (zone 9), cork oak, is a wide-spreading evergreen tree from the Mediterranean region, with remarkably thick corky bark which is harvested commercially. It thrives best in mild, damp areas.

Oaks are normally grown in large gardens and parks or in the countryside and are not suitable for small gardens. Evergreen oaks, however, can be used for hedging.

Cultivation. Most species are very hardy. The Mediterranean species are more sensitive to the cold. Plant in autumn or spring and propagate by seed or by grafting varieties on to the rootstock of the parent.

The main disease of oaks is oak mildew and the main pest is the oak leaf-roller moth which can cause a certain amount of defoliation.

Ramonda

Gesneriaceae

Three species of hardy evergreen perennials, similar in appearance to the African violet, make up this genus. They are native to the mountains of Europe and are examples of what botanists call 'relic plants' as they are considered to be proof that several million years ago Europe had a tropical climate and when this changed, only a few species were able to adapt themselves to the cooler climatic conditions.

R. myconi (zone 4), has flat rosettes of hairy evergreen leaves which grow larger as the plant matures. Stems 6–8 in (15–20cm) grow from

Ramonda myconi

this rosette, bearing violet-purple, saucer-shaped flowers 1½ in (3 cm) in diameter, with a conspicuous cone of yellow stamens. There are also equally attractive forms with white or pink flowers. The plant flowers in late spring and early summer.
Cultivation. Plant in early spring in a gravelly, humus-rich soil in the shaded gaps between the rocks in a rock garden or dry wall, away from the sun. These plants will live for many years once established.

Propagate by seed in early autumn, or by division.

Ranunculus

Buttercup, *Ranunculaceae*

This genus comprises about 250 species of annual or herbaceous perennial plants, some with tuberous roots, and mostly native to temperate regions of the world.
R. *asiaticus* (zone 6), garden ranunculus, is native to the Middle East. It grows 12–16 in (30–40 cm) high. The leaves are mid-green and deeply divided. The large flower heads, 3 in (8 cm) across, include garnet red, white and various shades of yellow; there are many cultivars with single, double or semi-double flowers. They make excellent cut flowers, and bloom in late spring and early summer.
R. *calandrinioides* (zone 7), a native of Morocco, grows to a height of 4–6 in (10–15 cm) and spreads 16–20 in (40–50 cm). This is a beautiful, delicate, species with smooth, greyish-green oval-to-lanceolate leaves with long petioles and wavy margins. The flowers are white, tinged with pale pink, and 2 in (5 cm) across, appearing in early to mid spring.

Many species are suitable for gardens; most are easy to grow and are well suited to rock gardens, flowerbeds, alpine houses or window boxes. Others may be invasive and considered weeds.
Cultivation. Plant between early autumn and mid spring when weather conditions are favourable. Most species can be grown in ordinary soil in a sunny position.

R. *asiaticus* is hardy in most areas although it will need a mulch of dead leaves in areas where the winters are hard. Alternatively, lift when the leaves turn yellow, dry the tubers then store in a cool, frost-free place and replant in spring. Choose a moist, sunny situation in a loamy soil in a border or rock garden. Plant the claw-like tubers, pressing them firmly into place, with the points down, 2 in (5 cm) deep, 6 in (15 cm) apart, in spring.

R. *calandrinioides* is hardy but it will need a sheltered position where the winters are severe, or it can be grown in an alpine house.

Raoulia

Compositae

This genus consists of 20 species of small, hardy or semi-hardy evergreen plants from New Zealand.
R. *australis (*R. *hookeri)* – zone 5–6 – is native to New Zealand, and grows 1 in (2.5 cm) high with a spread of 12–20 in (30–50 cm). The plant forms a carpet of small, silvery-grey spatulate leaves, with heads of tiny yellow flowers in early to mid summer.

This species is suitable for rock gardens, troughs or between paving stones, and can also be grown in an alpine house. It will withstand temperatures down to 5°F (−15°C).
Cultivation. Plant in well drained, gritty soil, in a sunny position. Protect from damp in winter by placing a sheet of glass over it. Propagate by splitting the root clump in mid summer, or by seed.

Raphanus

Radish, *Cruciferae*

A genus of eight species of herbaceous plants from Europe and Asia.
R. *sativus* (zone 5), radish, has been growing in China and Egypt since ancient times. It is a hardy biennial grown as an annual, 2¼–6 in (7–15 cm) high when it matures in spring and summer, but is usually harvested for the swollen round, long or ovoid root long before it flowers and matures.
Cultivation.
Summer varieties. These are usually sown in succession from early spring to late summer, although they can be sown earlier under glass. Quick growth results in succulent, tender crops.

Choose a site with a friable soil, which has been manured for a previous crop. Before sowing, apply a general fertilizer and work to a fine tilth. Sow thinly in drills ½ in (1 cm) deep, in rows 6 in (15 cm) apart. Cover with sifted soil, and firm the surface well. Hoe between rows, thin if necessary, and weed regularly and provide a steady supply of water. Pick radish immediately they are ready. Expected yield is approximately 12 lb (5.5 kg) in a 30 ft (9 m) row. Because of the short time between sowing and picking radishes can be sown as catch crops between other crops before these mature fully. The most usual diseases are downy mildew and scab. A common pest is the flea beetle and also birds.

Winter varieties. These are much less common and are sown in mid summer in rows 12 in (30 cm) apart and thinned to 8 in (20 cm) apart within the row. Otherwise treat as above, except that where the winters are hard cover with a litter of bracken until picked. These strong-flavoured radishes are large and can weigh up to 1 lb (0.5 kg). They are sliced raw and eaten in salads.

Rehmannia

Scrophulariaceae (Gesneriaceae)

A genus of 10 species of semi-hardy herbaceous perennials, from Asia.

R. *elata (R. angulata)* – zone 10 – Chinese foxglove, is native to China and grows 20–32 in (50–80 cm) high and 1 ft (30 cm) across. It has a basal rosette of leaves, and the foxglove-like flowers are purplish-pink, yellow inside and with scarlet spots. These appear throughout the summer. It is normally grown as a biennial. The plant is used in herbaceous borders or in conservatories or cool greenhouses.

Rehmannia elata

Cultivation. In areas with a mild winter these plants can be grown outdoors in a sheltered, sunny location, in ordinary garden soil. In colder climates, overwinter the plants in a cold greenhouse to protect them from the frost.

Propagate in early spring by sowing seed in a seed tray and keeping it at a temperature of 55–60°F (13–16°C). Prick out into pots, then harden off before planting outside.

Reseda

Resedaceae

A genus of approximately 60 species of herbaceous plants from Mediterranean regions and Asia. These plants are a source of yellow dye, scented, and always grown as annuals in cooler climates.

R. *odorata* (zone 7), mignonette, is a bushy, North African plant growing 1 ft (30 cm) high, and bearing close-set clusters of highly scented creamy white but insignificant-looking flowers. It blooms from early summer to mid autumn, if sown in succession. 'Machet' has dense spikes tinged with red which are highly scented.

These flowers are highly attractive to bees, and can be grown in a bedding scheme or border. They are good for cutting and can also be grown as a later winter-flowering pot plant.

Cultivation. Sow under glass in spring. Prick out, harden off and plant out in late spring. Alternatively, sow outdoors in late spring, 6 in (15 cm) apart. Mignonette likes a light, well drained, peaty soil, preferably alkaline, in a sunny position.

Rheum

Rhubarb, *Polygonaceae*

A genus of approximately 50 species of herbaceous perennials from Europe and Asia, some of which are grown for ornamental purposes and some for cropping.

R. *palmatum* (zone 5), ornamental rhubarb, from China, is hardy everywhere. It grows 5–6½ ft (1.5–2 m) high, and 3½–5 ft (1–1.5 m) across, and

is a decorative, clump-forming plant, with large, deeply cut leaves, reddish when young. The cultivars 'Atrosanguineum' and 'Bowles Variety' ('Bowles Crimson') are more striking, with their richer red leaves, remaining red on the undersides all season long. Small, pink or red flowers grow in large plumes on the stem in early summer. This species can be grown as a specimen on the lawn or beside a pond or lake.
R. *rhubarbum*, garden rhubarb, from Manturia. Large perennial, cultivated for edible leaf stalks (leaves are poisonous). Easy to grow in a sunny site with an annual dressing of well-rotted garden compost in late winter. It does not like a climate with hot summers and warm winters.
Cultivation. Plant in winter, in a moist, fertile, humus-rich soil, in a sunny or partly shaded position, 3½ ft (1 m) apart.

Water in dry weather. Cut the stems back in autumn.

Propagate by seed or by division in early spring.

Rhododendron

Rhododendron, *Ericaceae*

This genus consists of some 800 species of deciduous or evergreen trees and shrubs. They are native to the Northern Hemisphere especially America, the Himalayas, Burma and China. They are popular because of the extraordinary variety, richness and diversity of colours their flowers possess. This genus, the most important for lime-free (acid) soil and semi-shade, also includes the deciduous azaleas and many hundreds of hybrids.
R. *arboreum* (zone 6–8), from the Himalayas, grows 20–26 ft (6–8 m), far taller in the wild. It has large, shiny leaves, 8 in (20 cm) long, with a silvery down on their undersides. The flowers, from white to red, are bell-shaped, 2 in (5 cm) across and deep, and grow in dense heads from late winter to mid spring. It is semi- to moderately hardy.
R. *augustinii* (zone 7), grows 6½–10 ft (2–3 m) high, with small, pointed leaves with scaly undersides. The shrub is completely covered in large numbers of lavender or pale-blue, funnel-shaped flowers in late spring. This quick-growing Chinese species is ideal for woodland planting.
R. *auriculatum* (zone 6), from China, grows 10–17 ft (3–5 m) high and has large, oval leaves. It is

Rhododendron augustinii

unusual in that the large, white, scented flowers are carried in mid to late summer.
R. *barbatum* (zone 7), from the Himalayas, grows 17–26 ft (5–8 m) high. It has pinkish-brown, peeling bark and lanceolate leaves 6–8 in (15–20 cm) long. The scarlet flowers are bell-shaped and grow in large, dense globular heads in early spring.
R. *callimorphum* (zone 5–6), from Yunnan and Burma, 5 ft (1.5 m) high, has round leaves which are green on top and greenish-blue underneath. The flowers are bell-shaped, dark pink in bud, paler with a crimson blotch at the base, from mid to late spring.
R. *calophytum* (zone 6), from western China, grows 40 ft (12 m) high, with leaves about 1 ft (30 cm) long. The bell-shaped flowers grow in loose trusses of about 30 and are white with a large crimson blotch. This is one of the hardier of the large-leaved species, but should be sheltered from wind.
R. *campanulatum* (zone 5–6), from the Himalayas, grows 10 ft (3 m) high. It has peeling bark and oval leaves covered in a fine rust-coloured down underneath. The flowers, which appear in mid spring, are open, bell-shaped and vary from pink to lavender.
R. *campylocarpum* (zone 7), from the Himalayas, grows 5–10 ft (1.5–3 m) high, with glossy, dark-green, oval leaves. The bell-shaped flowers are bright or pale yellow, and appear in late spring. It does not flower when young, but is one of the best yellows for general planting.
R. *campylogynum* (zone 6), from the eastern Himalayas, is dwarf, to 2 ft (60 cm) in height. It has dark-green, lustrous leaves and nodding waxy, bell-shaped purplish to pink flowers in late spring or early summer.

R. *catawbiense* (zone 6), rosebay rhododendron, from southeastern USA, is a dense, hardy shrub, 6½–10 ft (2–3 m) high, and thicket-forming when mature. Its glossy leathery leaves are 6 in (15 cm) long. The flowers in large trusses are bell-shaped and vary from pink to lilac or white. It is the parent of many garden hybrids.

R. *ciliatum* (zone 8), from the Himalayas, a dome-shaped shrub, grows 5 ft (1.5 m) high. Its leaves, fringed with hairs, are 3¼–3½ in (8–9 cm) long. The scented flowers are pale pink to almost white and bell-shaped, appearing in early to mid spring. It flowers at a young age.

R. *cinnabarinum* (zone 5–6), from the Himalayas, is 5 ft (1.5 m) or more high, with oval leaves and waxy, pendant, narrow funnel-shaped red flowers appearing in late spring.

R. *crassum* (zone 8–9), from Yunnan and Burma, grows 20 ft (6 m) high, with pointed, oval leathery leaves, rust-coloured below. The highly scented flowers are white and funnel-shaped, appearing in early to mid summer. It is only moderately hardy and is sometimes grown as a conservatory plant.

R. *discolor* (zone 5–6), from central China, grows 20 ft (6 m) high. It has narrow, oblong leaves, and white to pink-tinged fragrant trumpet-shaped flowers in early to mid summer. It is the parent of many hybrids.

R. *falconeri* (zone 7), from the Himalayas, grows up to 33 ft (10 m) high. It has very large leaves, 1 ft (30 cm) long, with rust-coloured undersides. The bell-shaped, creamy yellow flowers with a dark purple blotch appear in large clusters in mid to late spring. It needs shelter to thrive.

Rhododendron 'Winsome'

R. *ferrugineum* (zone 5–6), is a dwarf species, 4 ft (1.2 m) high, native to the Alps, with dark-green, oval leaves. The bright-pink flower clusters appear in early summer.

R. *fictolacteum* (zone 5), from Yunnan, is about 30 ft (9 m) high, and is one of the hardiest of the large-leaved species. It has leathery leaves 8–12 in (20–30 cm) long. The creamy white flowers with a crimson blotch are 2½ in (6 cm) wide and open in mid to late spring.

R. *forrestii* (zone 5–6), from China, is a slow-growing, prostrate shrub, growing to a maximum of 1 ft (30 cm) high. It has round leaves, and scarlet, bell-shaped flowers to 1½ in (3.5 cm) in diameter, appearing in mid to late spring. It needs moist soil and partial shade if it is to thrive.

R. *fulvum* (zone 5–6), from western China, is 17 ft (5 m) high, with especially attractive dark-green leaves, felted with red-brown below, and white-to-pink flowers in spring.

R. *haematodes* (zone 5–6), from Yunnan, is slow-growing and compact, to 3 ft (1 m) high. It has oval or oblong leaves and scarlet red bell-shaped flowers in late spring.

R. *hippophaeoides* (zone 5), from Yunnan, is an erect shrub reaching 5 ft (1.5 m) in height, with narrow, grey-green leaves. The flowers are lilac to pink and funnel-shaped, appearing in early to mid spring. This species tolerates boggy soil.

R. *hirsutum* (zone 5), from the Alps of Europe, grows 4 ft (1.2 m) high. It is a twiggy shrub, with oval leaves edged with bristles, and rose-pink flowers opening early in summer.

R. *impeditum* (zone 5–6), is a dwarf species suitable for a rock garden, 6 in (15 cm) high, with tangled mounds of branches, oval leaves and small, bluish-mauve flowers in large numbers.

R. *insigne* (zone 5–6), from China, is slow-growing, eventually reaching 6 ft (1.8 m) or so in height. The undersides of the leaves have a silvery tinge and the bell-shaped flowers are light pink, spotted with deep red, and appear in late spring and early summer. It is extremely hardy.

R. *leucaspis* (zone 7), from the eastern Himalayas, is 1–2 ft (30–60 cm) high. It has oval, bristly, bluish green leaves. White flowers with brown anthers appear in late winter and early spring. It needs a very sheltered site.

R. *lutescens* (zone 7), from western China, grows to about 10 ft (3 m) high, with lanceolate leaves.

Rhododendron 'Hotei'

The flowers, which appear in late winter to mid spring, are pale yellow and the young shoots maroon to red. It is lovely in light woodland.

R. *mucronulatum* (zone 5–6), from northern China, grows 10–13 ft (3–4 m) high. It has deciduous, pale-green, lanceolate leaves and the spectacular, rosy-purple flowers appear at the ends of the branches in mid winter to early spring, before the leaves.

R. *oreotrephes* (zone 5–6), from the Himalayas, grows 6–6½ ft (1.8–2 m) high. The evergreen leaves are oval, greyish green on top and bluish underneath. The freely produced flowers are funnel-shaped in shades of lilac pink, with or without a number of spots.

R. *ponticum* (zone 5–6), grows to 13–20 ft (4–6 m) high. This species is naturalized in England, Ireland and Brittany but is native to western Asia. It has lanceolate leaves and lilac pink flowers in late spring. It is a tough shrub, useful for large hedges and shelter belts, and can be grown in the dense shade of other trees.

R. *racemosum* (zone 5–6), from western China, is 6 ft (1.8 m) high. It bears elliptical leaves which are bluish-green underneath. The small funnel-shaped flowers are pink, appearing along the stems in spring. It is especially attractive planted with heather.

R. *radicans* (zone 5), from Tibet, is prostrate, only a few inches/centimetres high, and makes excellent ground cover for a rock garden. It has small, dark leaves, and solitary, rose and purple, almost flat, open flowers which appear in late spring and early summer.

R. *rubiginosum* (zone 5–6), from western China, is a large, free-flowering species, and may reach 15 ft (4.5 m) or more. It has lilac-pink, funnel-shaped flowers, spotted with dark red, which appear in mid to late spring.

R. *russatum* (zone 5–6), from western China, is a compact shrub 3½ ft (1 m) high, with small leaves under 2 in (5 cm) long. It has deep purplish-blue flowers, with a white throat, which appear in mid to late spring.

R. *sargentianum* (zone 5–6), from western China, is a dwarf, twiggy, dense shrub, 2 ft (60 cm) high. The leaves are oval and aromatic, and the young shoots are scaly. The small, tubular flowers are pale yellow. It needs cool conditions and can be difficult to grow.

R. *thomsonii* (zone 8), from the Himalayas, grows to more than 14 ft (4.2 m) in milder areas. It has oval or oblong leaves, dark green on top and bluish white underneath. The trunk and main branches are cinnamon colour. The branches bear dark red flowers, with a large, cup-shaped calyx, continuously from early to mid spring. These are followed by attractive fruiting clusters, with glaucous capsules set in bright-green calyxes.

R. *wardii* (zone 6), from western China, is up to 20 ft (6 m) high in the wild. It has rounded, dark-green leaves and yellow flowers, sometimes with a bright red blotch at the base. It is the parent of several hybrids.

R. *williamsianum* (zone 8), from western China, is 5 ft (1 m) high, with round, greyish-green leaves tinged with bronze when young. The flowers are bell-shaped, red in bud and turning pale pink when they open in mid spring.

R. *yakushimanum* (zone 5–6), from Japan, is a compact and dome-shaped shrub up to 4 ft (1.2 m) high, with young shoots covered in silvery down. It has shiny, leathery, rounded lanceolate leaves. The flower buds are pink, opening to almost white and appearing in late spring and early summer.

R. *yunnanense* (zone 5–6), from western China, has lanceolate leaves which sometimes fall in cold winters. It grows up to 13 ft (4 m) high and bears enormous crops of pink flowers dotted with brown or crimson in mid spring.

Rhododendrons have been the subject of frequent hybridization by nurseries and keen amateurs. The hybrids come in a multitude of colours and shapes with attractive foliage and flowers.

Cultivation. Most rhododendrons originally come from mountainous areas, where they live in a cool, humid, climate. To reproduce these conditions, plant in a damp but not waterlogged situation, slightly shaded from the sun's rays; underneath a pine or oak tree, in slight shade, is ideal. However, rhododendron adapts fairly easily and even grows in a city atmosphere.

It has a shallow root run, and can be planted in shallow topsoil, but because of its shallow root system, it must not be allowed to go dry and needs to be kept moist at all times.

Rhododendrons need acid soil with pH of approximately 5 or 6. In almost all cases, they need to be planted in a fairly large hole 20 in (50 cm) deep, with plenty of leaf mould, peat or well rotted manure worked into the soil. They are often grown in association with other acid-loving shrubs, such as *Kalmia, Camellia, Pieris*, or heather.

In a limy soil, there is the risk of chlorosis, or yellowing of the leaves. When planting in limy soil, separate the planting pit from the rest of the soil using a sheet of polythene in the bottom of the hole. Wherever possible, water the plant with rainwater.

Give an annual mulch of dead and decayed leaves, to retain moisture and provide the rhododendron with necessary minerals. Prune rhododendrons to remove dead wood and maintain a good shape. Remove dead flowers to encourage vegetative growth.

Species are propagated by seed; pick the seeds when ripe and sow in pots of damp peat. Prick out and re-pot. Propagate hybrids from cuttings kept in a very humid greenhouse in glass-covered seed trays at a temperature of 68°F (20°C), or alternatively by grafting on to the wild species R. *ponticum*, though this technique is not easy. Layering is undoubtedly the easiest method; bury a low branch 2 in (5 cm) in the ground with a U-shaped piece of wire, after making a small, lengthwise slit in the portion of stem to be buried. The layer can be separated two years later from the parent plant.

Rhododendron on the whole are free from serious diseases and pests, the most serious being honey fungus, bud blast, azalea leaf miner and rhododendron bug.

Rhus

Sumach, *Anacardiaceae*

This genus consists of about 200 species, mostly shrubs and small trees, with highly decorative, compound, alternate deciduous leaves and inflorescences with numerous small flowers.

R. *glabra* (zone 5), smooth sumach, grows to a maximum height of 10 ft (3 m). It has smooth leaves with odd numbers of leaflets which turn bright red or orange in autumn. The conical panicles bear numerous flowers, followed by clusters of hairy red fruits, which remain on the female plant for many months. The cultivar 'Laciniata' has deeply cut, ferny leaves.

R. *typhina* (zone 5), stag's horn sumach, is a wide-spreading small tree or shrub and grows up to 20 ft (6 m) high. The young branches are covered in silky down, and the large, pinnate leaves are very attractive, with magnificent autumn colours. The dense, conical and long-lasting fruiting heads are also striking in autumn. It has a suckering habit of growth.

Both can be grown in mixed borders, as specimens in a lawn or on the edge of a woodland garden.

Cultivation. Grow in ordinary or poor, dry soils and a sunny position. Water young plants regularly until established. Both species can be cut down to the ground in spring to obtain a lush, tropical foliage effect. Parts of the plant can be a strong irritant if touched by susceptible people.

Propagate by taking cuttings or layering, or from suckers.

These plants are subject to attacks of coral spot fungus.

Ribes

Saxifragaceae

This genus consists of about 150 species of small, usually spiny, deciduous shrubs with alternate leaves, native to the Northern Hemisphere and South America.

Flowering Currants

R. *alpinum* (zone 5), mountain currant, from Europe, grows $6\frac{1}{2}$ ft (2 m) or more high. It is very hardy, with a twiggy, spreading habit and leaves with three-to-five lobes. It has green, not particularly decorative flowers and red berries which appear at the end of summer if both male and female plants are grown. It does not mind poor soil or shade and can be used as hedging.

R. *odoratum (R. aureum)* – zone 5 – buffalo currant, grows up to 8 ft (2.4 m) high. The erect, arching branches are spineless, and the three-lobed leaves are smooth and pale green. The plant has drooping clusters of tubular, clove-

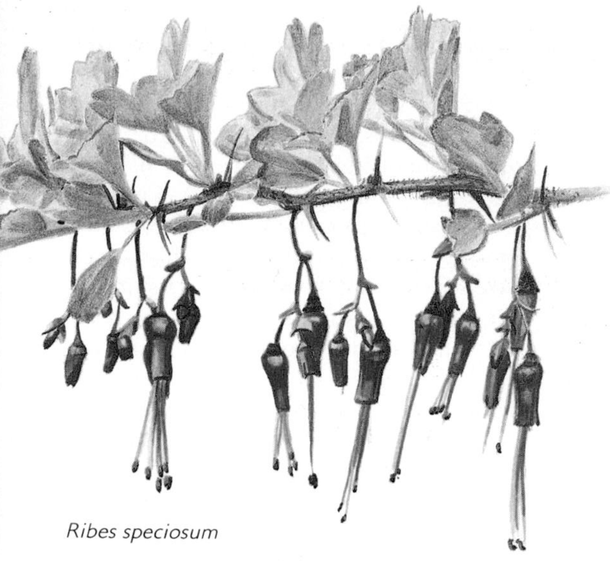

Ribes speciosum

scented, yellow flowers which appear in mid to late spring. It bears edible, purplish-black berries during the summer, and its foliage is colourful in autumn.

R. *sanguineum* (zone 6), flowering currant, reaches a height of 5–6½ ft (1.5–2 m). It has a very spreading habit and rounded, light-green leaves which are highly scented. It bears numerous, pendent clusters of open, pinkish-red flowers before and during the leaf-growing period, followed by black berries in autumn. Some people find its scent disagreeable. There are numerous cultivars with white, crimson or deep red flowers and golden leaves.

R. *speciosum* (zone 7) is a very spiny deciduous shrub from California with striking pendulous red flowers in mid spring.

Cultivation. Plant in mid to late autumn or late winter to early spring in ordinary, well drained soil, in sun or light shade. Cut back weak shoots and prune the branches to half their length in spring after the plant has flowered. If the plant is suffering from disease, cut back to ground level.

Fruiting Currants

R. *nigrum* (zone 6), blackcurrant, is a deciduous shrub with strongly scented leaves. It has pendent clusters of fairly small dull white flowers and edible black fruits. The blackcurrant grows wild in Europe, but it is cultivated both for its berries and its buds, which are used to make cosmetics.

Cultivation. Plant shrubs 6½ ft (2 m) apart, in clean, weed-free soil. Immediately after planting, cut blackcurrants back to 3 in (7.5 cm) above the ground to establish a good root system. Mulch with plenty of well rotted manure, to help retain moisture.

Prune in autumn or after harvesting, to allow light and air to ripen the young wood, by cutting out the three-year-old wood, especially in the centre of the bush. (Old shoots tend to be dark, even black, while young shoots are brown.)

Propagate from cuttings 8 in (20 cm) long, planted out in the open, 6 ft (1.8 m) apart, fairly deep so that only two buds appear above ground. The most common problems are reversion, mildew and the blackcurrant gall mite which causes big bud.

Ricinus

Castor oil plant, *Euphorbiaceae*

The castor oil plant is a perennial in the tropics, but treated as a hardy or half-hardy annual elsewhere. There is only one species native to Africa and the Middle East. Its seeds are deadly poisonous.

R. *communis* (zone 9), castor bean, is fast growing, reaching 5 ft (1.5 m) or more in a single season. It has a stem with few branches, large, palmate leaves and clusters of insignificant green flowers in summer, followed by bristly seed heads. There are several cultivars with purple, metallic-red or green and white leaves. Packets of mixed seeds are available, and there are compact, dwarf forms.

The castor oil plant is very effective on a lawn or in a formal bedding scheme. It can also be grown as a conservatory pot plant.

Cultivation. Sow in a greenhouse in late winter to early spring, having first soaked the seeds in water for a few hours, and plant one seed per pot. Harden the young plants gradually, then plant out 24–42 in (60 cm–1 m) apart in late spring, in soil rich in organic matter.

Robinia

Black or honey locust, *Leguminosae*

This genus consists of several North American species of deciduous trees and shrubs with pinnate leaves and racemes of pea-like flowers.

R. *pseudoacacia* (zone 6), false acacia or black locust, grows rapidly when young, to about 66 ft (20 m) in height. It is sometimes confused with acacia or mimosa. The adult tree has an irregularly shaped crown, with twisted, very thorny branches. The bark is deeply furrowed. The compound, pinnate leaves are light green and the flowers are white and scented, appearing in late spring and early summer grouped in pendulous racemes.

The flowers produce large quantities of nectar, attractive to bees. The fruit is a pod containing a small number of seeds, and is poisonous. It should not be planted in exposed sites, as the branches are easily broken, but may be used to stabilize embankments, or in avenues or as an ornamental tree in a larger garden. There are golden-leaved, upright-growing and repeat-flowering forms.

Cultivation. This is a very hardy tree, tolerant of drought and pollution, and well suited to locations near the sea. It grows in any situation and soil. Plant either in autumn or spring, and stake until established.

Propagate from seed, suckers or cuttings.

Rodgersia

Saxifragaceae

This genus contains six hardy herbaceous perennials native to China, Japan and Nepal.

R. *pinnata* (zone 6), from China, is hardy, and grows 3 ft (1 m) high and 2 ft (60 cm) across. The plant is popular for its eye-catching, decorative, dark-green compound leaves, tinged with bronze. The small, star-shaped pink flowers grow in dense panicles in mid summer. There are cultivars available with white flowers and purple-bronze leaves.

Rodgeresia is best planted on its own near a pond or in a herbaceous border. It makes excellent ground cover.

Cultivation. Plant in shelter and sun or light shade, in a moist soil enriched with manure or garden compost. Water in dry weather, and remove faded flower stems.

Propagate by seed or by dividing the scaly rhizomes in early to mid spring, planting 2 in (5 cm) below the surface of the soil.

Romneya

California poppy, *Papaveraceae*

This genus is variously described as containing either one or two species, native to California and Mexico. They are imposing herbaceous plants or sub-shrubs, with a creeping, woody rhizome.

R. *coulteri* (zone 8), is a magnificent plant with greyish-green stems, 7 ft (2.1 m) high, with alternate, glaucous-green, deeply divided leaves. The poppy-like flowers are 4–6 in (10–15 cm) across, and a shiny, silvery white, with a central boss of yellow stamens. The short-lived flowers are scented and grow from late summer to early autumn. It is semi- to moderately hardy but once established, it can become highly invasive.

Cultivation. Plant in a deep, dry, gravelly soil, at the foot of a sunny wall. The plant does not mind drought, but needs its crown protected in cold winters. Plant in early to mid spring, it resents root disturbance, and is most easily established from a well rooted containerized plant. Once established, it may live for many years and cover several square yards (metres). Cut back in spring.

Propagate from seed in late winter or early spring, germinated at 55°F (13°C). Alternatively, take root cuttings in early autumn and plant in pots placed in a frost-free area, or carefully remove suckers in mid or late spring, and replant separately.

Rosa

Rose, *Rosaceae*

The rose is a shrub with thorny, erect, climbing or creeping stems and compound leaves, varying according to species and climate. It bears flowers growing either singly or in teminal

Rosa foetida 'Bicolor'

corymbs, with five petals and five sepals, very occasionally four. There are around 100 species of roses, spread throughout temperate and tropical areas of the Northern Hemisphere, but many hundreds of hybrids have been raised from them. Modern roses have very complex derivation and their parentage involves many of the species described below.

Species roses
These are grown in the same way as modern roses, except that they are only lightly pruned, to keep them under control and to remove diseased and dead wood.

Roses grown in gardens of Europe from the Middle Ages to the end of the 17th century.
R. *arvensis* (zone 6), field rose, is a trailing or climbing species found wild in the hedgerows of Europe. It has small, single creamy-white flowers which appear in small clusters in mid summer.
R. *canina* (zone 5–6), common brier or dog rose, is a shrub of 12 ft (3.5 m) high and wide, with scented white or pink flowers in early summer. It is often used as the rootstock for modern roses.
R. *centifolia* (zone 6), Provence or cabbage rose, has large, double, open, fragrant flowers in rose pink. It is of hybrid origin. The form 'Cristata' (Chapeau de Napoléon) has moss-like, scented glands on the sepals, which make them appear winged or crested.
R. *damascena* (zone 6), damask rose, is probably of garden origin and was introduced from Asia Minor. It has been in cultivation since the early 16th century or before. It has fragrant semi-double flowers from pale to deep pink in colour. A cultivar of this is the main source of attar of roses in Bulgaria.
R. *foetida* (zone 6), Austrian yellow rose, is a fragrant, single-yellow flowered rose, probably native to southwest Asia but known in European gardens since the 16th century. 'Bicolor', Austrian copper brier, has copper-red flowers with a yellow reverse. All modern yellow roses originate from this species.
R. *gallica (R. rubra)* (zone 6), French rose, grows to 4 ft (1.2 m) high and across. It is a suckering, erect and densely prickly shrub. Its single, carmine-red, highly scented flowers up to 3 in (7.5 cm) across, appear in early summer and are not recurrent. 'Officinalis', apothecary's rose or rose of Provins, has been known since the early 14th century and is considered the red rose of Lancaster. It has fragrant, semi-double flowers.
R. *moschata* (zone 7), musk rose is a lax shrub growing to about 12 ft (3.5 m). The white flowers have a strong musky scent and appear from late summer to autumn. The true musk rose is rare in cultivation and often confused with R. *brunonii.*
R. *pendulina (R. alpina)* – zone 5 – Alpine rose, is a suckering shrub with few thorns and bright-pink flowers, followed by red, flask-shaped hips. It is found wild in central and southern Europe.
R. *sempervirens* (zone 9) is a scrambling shrub with stems to 20 ft (6 m) long. It has single, white, slightly scented flowers and attractive fruit but is slightly tender and not common in gardens.

Roses introduced and raised from the early 18th century.
The number of exotic roses brought back by travellers from India, China, Korea, Japan and America, resulted in a huge increase in the number of cultivars available. The quest for roses producing as many flowers as possible, repeat flowering, large flowers, many petals and attractive colours and scents, was a major concern of the first nursery gardeners.
R. *bracteata* (zone 8–9), Macartney rose, was introduced to Europe at the end of the 18th century from China. It is a rambler with white, lemon-scented flowers. It is not hardy in exposed areas, but flowers over a long period.
R. *chinensis* (zone 7), China rose, includes a race of roses introduced from China with single or semi-double flowers varying from white to crimson in colour. It is of variable habit and size and is the most important parent of the modern roses. 'Semperflorens' ('Slater's Crimson China') has a dwarf habit and semi-double crimson flowers over a long season.
R. *multiflora* (zone 6–7), a species wild in Japan and Korea, is a vigorous rambler with large clusters of white scented flowers in early summer. It is a parent of many rambling roses and of the Polyantha or Pompon roses.
R. × *odorata* (zone 8–9), tea rose, introduced from China, has been hybridized with European roses to give numerous tea roses, which were completely different from existing flower forms, with their extraordinary colours and scents. They had two drawbacks: they were sensitive to the cold, and their slender flower stalks made the

flower heads droop. Most modern hybrid tea roses are derived from early forms of this rose.

R. 'Portlandica' (zone 7), Portland or Scarlet Four Seasons rose, has a low-growing habit and was probably raised around the 18th century. It flowers in summer and early autumn with semi-double, cherry-red, scented flowers and a central cluster of golden stamens. It is named after the Duchess of Portland. This species is a parent of the Portland roses involved in the parentage of the hybrid perpetuals.

R. *rugosa* (zone 6), ramanas rose, is a strong-growing rose from northeast Asia with densely prickly stems and large, fragrant, single, bright-pink flowers.

R. *wichuraiana* (zone 6–7) was introduced from Japan at the end of the 19th century. It has trailing stems and clusters of single white flowers in late summer. It is also an ancestor of many rambler roses of today.

Perpetual-flowering hybrid roses.

Repeated crosses between many of these roses created a series of repeat-flowering hybrids. These roses are completely hardy and flower twice or throughout summer and autumn in a wide range of colour. Most are scented.

Bourbon roses are hybrids developed from a rose found on the French island of Bourbon in the early 19th century. They have a vigorous habit and rounded, double, scented flowers produced intermittently from late spring to early autumn. 'Mme Isaac Pereire' is one of the most fragrant.

Rose 'Madame Isaac Pereire'

Modern Roses

The distinction between old-fashioned and modern roses is subjective. Some authors regard modern roses as being those obtained since the beginning of the 20th century, but according to others, modern roses are those with double flowers, repeat flowering and with typical elongated buds, while old-fashioned roses can be single or double and have more globular buds. It was the development of the hybrid teas with large, complex flowers, which marked the birth of modern roses after the First World War. These are less susceptible to disease and also flower for longer periods during the summer.

Hybrid tea or large-flowered bush roses

These are the result of crosses between tea roses and hybrid perpetuals. They therefore combine the elegance of the tea rose with an abundance of flowers. The first hybrid tea is generally regarded as having been 'La France', a rose obtained by Guillot in 1867 and at the time considered to be a repeating flowering hybrid. Hybrid tea roses make excellent cut flowers, and are particularly suited to growing in beds of roses alone. They like a sunny or lightly shaded position, but some colours, particularly the yellow ones, fade quickly in hot, dry conditions. Hybrid teas often flower from early summer to the first frosts, and grow to a height of 2–4 ft (0.6–1.2 m). They should be planted 20–24 in (50–60 cm) apart. Most are completely hardy. Their characteristic long-stemmed flowers are double, but not always scented.

Floribundas or cluster-flowered roses

These are traditional roses used in rose gardens. They are descendants of polyantha roses, sometimes called poly-poms, characterized by their clusters of small flowers, which were the result of crosses of R. *multiflora* and other roses of the 1870s. These were then crossed with hybrid teas to give floribunda roses which continuously produce large clusters of larger flowers throughout the summer. They are hardy and easy to look after. The distinction between polyanthas and floribundas is a fairly blurred one, but the flowers of floribundas are usually larger with a shape approaching that of hybrid tea although not quite as large. Some cultivars of floribunda roses have flowers almost as large as hybrid teas but in clusters. The term "Grandiflora" has been used in USA, but is not generally accepted in Great Britain.

These are also ideal roses for rose gardens,

but they can also be grown in association with perennial plants in a mixed border.

Modern shrub roses
The distinction between old and modern shrub roses is also a fairly blurred one, based solely on the date they were raised. Although, botanically speaking, all roses are shrubs, the term 'shrub rose' is used as opposed to hybrid tea or floribunda rose. Shrub roses are usually more erect and taller, at 4–10 ft (1.2–3 m).

These are robust, very hardy plants which can be used in isolation or to form hedges, either on their own or together with other shrubs.

Climbing roses
Climbing roses have many different origins. Most ramblers are descended from botanical species, especially R. *multiflora* and R. *wichuraiana*, which are naturally climbing in habit, or at least have long, flexible stems which can be staked up against a support. The others are of various origins, but are sometimes 'sports' or mutations of floribunda or hybrid tea roses, producing a climbing habit. The latter are repeat flowering and often have flowers which are even more attractive than the cultivar from which they originate. They tend to be less vigorous than the cultivars derived from naturally climbing species, which can be exceedingly fast growing. The climbing 'sports' often bear the name of the cultivar they originated from, preceded by the description 'Climbing', such as 'Climbing Shot Silk', or 'Climbing Super Star'. The stems of the more vigorous climbing roses need to be staked up into a fan, or even horizontally, so that they flower all along their length. Most recent cultivars are at least partly repeat flowering, and need a sunny position.

Miniature roses
Miniature roses are small bushes often no more than 20 in (50 cm) high, with the exception of the climbing cultivars. They have become increasingly popular over the past twenty years or so because of their many uses in gardens, whether in borders or rock gardens. They can also be grown in pots or window boxes, and even indoors when they are flowering. Miniature roses are sometimes stem grafted and form small, ball-shaped trees 16–24 in (40–60 cm) in height. The first miniature roses were known over 100 years ago, but their history and parentage is not always clear. They are said to be derived from a minature form of R. *chinensis*.

Ground cover roses
These are roses with long, spreading stems which may form a thick carpet. They are attractive plants for covering an embankment, old tree stump or raised flower bed.

Cultivation. Roses like an open position and, except for some yellow-flowered roses, as much sun as possible. Provide shelter from cold winds, and well drained, deep, fertile soil which is neither too acidic nor too alkaline. The ideal soil is slightly acidic with a pH of about 6.5. Some botanical species grow perfectly well in poor soil. As a general rule, varieties available on sale are hardy everywhere.

Plant any time between autumn and spring, in soil which has been well prepared and dug over beforehand, and with well rotted manure or compost. They also benefit from slow-acting fertilizer, such as bonemeal, dug in the planting hole. Roses sold in containers can be planted even when in full flower, but they need regular watering, until fully established. Bare-root roses should be planted in mid to late autumn.

Different types of roses are planted at varying distances apart: 8 in (20 cm) for miniature roses, about 20 in (50 cm) for large Hybrid Tea and Floribundas and at least 5 ft (1.4 m) for shrub roses.

Flowering is encouraged by the application of rose fertilizer in spring, once a year or every two years. A spring mulch of damp peat, leaf mould, well rotted manure or compost helps keep weeds down and conserves soil moisture.

Dead head regularly except for the roses grown for their decorative fruits, and water regularly in dry weather.

Roses can be pruned at the end of autumn in areas with a mild climate. In colder climates, it is better to shorten the longest branches in autumn and wait until late winter or early spring to prune them properly. The method used for pruning varies depending on the type of rose, but it always involves removing dead, diseased or damaged wood, as well as tangled stems, and clearing out the centre of the shrub to allow air and light to reach the branches. Always cut the stems at an angle, a few millimetres above an outward facing bud.

Hybrid Teas
These should usually be cut back hard in the first and following years, leaving only two or three buds on each stem. The vigorous varieties can be left slightly longer, leaving four buds.

Rose 'Baronne E. de Rothschild'

Floribundas
Cut these short during the first year, then down to medium length, leaving about four buds as these roses produce large numbers of flowers. If overcrowded, remove the older branches.

Climbing roses
Repeat-flowering climbing roses should be pruned in the same way as the other types, i.e. at the beginning of spring, but non-repeat flowering roses should be pruned after they have flowered, at the end of summer. Once the rose has become established on its support it will produce an occasional long and strong shoot and many weaker ones. Retain, and only cut the tip of the strong growth but cut the smaller growth to two or three buds from the base. Repeat-flowering roses should also be pruned after the first flowering, this time removing the branch that has flowered by cutting down to the first true leaf – the one with a bud. This encourages the plant to produce a second large crop of flowers.

Botanical roses, shrub roses and old varieties
Prune lightly, removing dead or weak wood and any surplus or very old wood. If the rose is in an exposed position, cut back any long stems by about a third of their length in autumn, before the winter sets in.

Miniature roses
Remove any dead or weak wood, and prune back the rest with caution to leave four or five buds above the base on each branch.

Roses can be propagated by seed, cuttings or budding, occasionally by grafting as well as from layers or suckers for certain cultivars growing on their own roots. Seed is best for the species, and should be sown in an earthenware pot in a cold frame in mid autumn, when the fruits are ripe and pricked out as soon as ready. Cuttings are the best way of propagating species, single hybrids, shrub roses, old climber and miniature roses. Take cuttings in late summer or early autumn from lateral stems which have not flowered and insert in the ground in a sheltered, shady position. The traditional method used, particularly by professional gardeners, is budding carried out in summer. This involves grafting a bud of the desired variety on to a stock, normally of a wild species such as R. *canina* or R. *multiflora*.

The diseases which most often affect roses are fungal diseases such as mildew, rust and black spot. Mildew forms a whitish felt which covers the leaves and young shoots. Climbing roses are particularly sensitive to this, but there are varieties which are fairly resistant. The symptoms of rust are yellowish spots on the upper surfaces of the leaves during the summer, and orange-brown pimples on the undersides. The disease causing black spots on the leaves may cause them to fall off prematurely.

The most frequent pests are aphids, which mass on the flower buds and multiply very quickly. They require repeated use of systemic or contact insecticide to get rid of them. Various species of caterpillar may eat the leaves and young shoots, sometimes making the leaves curl. Finally, red spider mites often attack the foliage during hot, dry weather.

Rosmarinus

Rosemary, *Labiatae*

This genus consists of two or three evergreen shrubs, native to the Mediterranean area.
R. *officinalis* (zone 7), rosemary, is a dense shrub, up to 3½–6½ ft (1–2 m) high if grown in a sheltered place. Its very fine and elongated leaves are highly aromatic and its small, lipped blue flowers appear in spring, earlier or later, depending on the region. There are many cultivars available, including ones with white, pink and brilliant-blue flowers, and fastigiate and prostrate mat-forming ones.
Cultivation. Rosemary prefers dry, warm soil, but grows in any well drained soil, and in full sun. Trim lightly after flowering and cut out

dead wood in spring. It is normally grown in a herb garden but can also be included in a mixed border, used as hedging or for container growing. Propagate in summer from cuttings 4–6 in (10–15 cm) long. Remove the lower leaves and bury them well in very light sandy soil, preferably in a shaded position in a cold frame. Plant out in the following spring, 32–42 in (80 cm–1 m) apart. Cuttings taken from mature shoots, 6 in (15 cm) long, can be planted *in situ* in early autumn or early spring. Alternatively, sow seeds from mid spring to early summer in a sheltered seed bed, or from early summer to early autumn in open ground. Prick out to a distance of 4 in (10 cm) before finally planting out.

Cut the branches from mid spring to mid autumn and dry them in a dry, shaded and airy place. Shake off the leaves once they have dried and keep these in sealed containers.

Uses. Rosemary is used particularly to flavour cooked dishes such as grills, ratatouille and sauces. The leaves can be made into an infusion (tea), or used to flavour vinegars.

Rubus

Bramble, *Rosaceae*

This large genus consists of about 250 hardy deciduous or evergreen shrubs, native to most regions of the world.

R. *henryi* (zone 5), from China, grows over 17 ft (5 m) high. It is a very hardy scrambling plant, notable for its evergreen, trilobed leaves with a thick white down on the undersides. The pink flowers are unremarkable, and are followed by shiny black fruit.

R. *idaeus* (zone 6), red raspberry, native to Europe, grows up to 8 ft (2.4 m) tall. It is a hardy, deciduous plant which bears fruit in summer or autumn depending on variety. The fruits are excellent for eating fresh, or for freezing and preserving.

R. *laciniatus* (zone 6), blackberry, deciduous shrub grows to 8 ft (2.4 m). Pinkish flowers followed by black fruit $\frac{1}{2}$–$\frac{3}{4}$ in (13–20 mm) long.

R. *occidentalis* (zone 5), black raspberry, from North America grows to 10 ft (3 m). White flowers in June followed by purple-black fruits.

R. *odoratus* (zone 6), from North America, is a suckering shrub with simple deciduous leaves. The large, fragrant, pink flowers open throughout the summer.

R. *phoenicolasius* (zone 7), wine berry, from China, Japan and Korea, grows to 10 ft (3 m) high. It has deciduous leaves made up of three leaflets with white felted undersides. This is a vigorous plant, with attractive stems covered in stiff red hairs, and small pink flowers in early to mid spring, followed by delicious sweet red fruit similar to blackberries.

R. *ulmifolius* (zone 5), native to Europe and the Mediterranean, grows to 3$\frac{1}{2}$–5 ft (1–1.5 m) or more high and is very hardy. Although not a very ornamental species, the cultivar 'Bellidiflorus', with showy, double-pink flowers, is very attractive. The leaves are dark green and semi-evergreen, with glaucous undersides.

All the climbing ornamental species should be grown on a trellis or similar support and the suckering species require a great deal of space. Some are ideal for wild gardens and dainty species can be grown in rock gardens. Some species make excellent ground cover, left to trail and root as they grow.

Cultivation. Plant in ordinary, well manured soil, in sun or light shade; many species will thrive in poor cool soil and deep shade. Cut back old or untidy stems after the plant has fruited. Those grown for their flowers or coloured stems should also be cut back after flowering or fruiting.

Propagate by sowing seeds when ripe or by layering in early autumn, or by division in winter.

Rudbeckia

Cone flower, *Compositae*

This genus contains about 15 species of annual or perennial herbaceous plants from North America. They are easy to grow and produce a profusion of daisy-like flowers.

R. *bicolor* (zone 6), is a half-hardy annual, 1–2 ft (30–60 cm) tall, with many branches, mid-green oblong leaves, and large numbers of flowers from mid summer to mid autumn. The flowers are up to 2 in (5 cm) in diameter, with two or three rows of drooping, golden yellow rays, sometimes brownish at base, and a dark purple central cone.

R. *fulgida* (zone 6), is a hardy perennial species growing 2–3 ft (60–90 cm) high and 1 ft (30 cm) across. The bright-yellow flowers which bloom in late summer have a striking dark purple central cone.

Rudbeckias grow well in a border or annual beds. They also make excellent cut flowers, and the central cones are attractive in dried-flower arrangements.

Cultivation. Plant in any well drained, fertile soil, in a sunny position. Sow annual species in early to mid spring under glass or in a cold frame, and plant out in late spring 20 in (50 cm) apart.

Propagate perennial species from seed sown in a seed bed in late spring and early summer. Plant out in early autumn, 16–20 in (40–50 cm) apart. The plant can also be propagated by division in spring.

Rumex

Sorrel, *Polygonaceae*

This genus consists of about 200 species of herbaceous perennials from temperate regions, most of which are weeds, but one is grown for its edible leaves.

A hardy perennial, native to Arctic and temperate regions of the Northern Hemisphere, R. *acetosa* (zone 5), sorrel, has broad, acid-tasting leaves which begin growing at soil level. In early summer, a flower spike, 32 in (80 cm) high, carries typical, tiny dock-like reddy-green flowers. French sorrel, R. *scutatus*, is smaller but otherwise similar.

Cultivation. Provide light, moist, well-aerated and lime-free soil. Grow it no more than two years running in the same place. Sow outdoors in spring in a border or in rows 1 ft (30 cm) apart. Thin out to 8 in (20 cm) between the plants. Alternatively, divide the root clumps in early to mid spring before planting out. To have a continuous supply of new leaves, pinch out the flower bud as soon as it appears. Start picking the leaves ten weeks after sowing.

This plant's enemies include sorrel fly, sorrel aphid, slugs and snails.

Ruscus

Butcher's broom, *Liliaceae*

This genus consists of six species of evergreen plants from Europe and Asia with leaf-like cladodes (flattened stems) and true leaves reduced to tiny papery scales.

R. *aculeatus* (zone 6) is a hardy, clump-forming sub-shrub, up to 4 ft (1.2 m) high. It is native to Europe and grows wild in woodlands. Its spine-tipped, oval, flattened modifed stems, or cladodes, replace the leaves and carry out their functions. The plant produces inconspicuous but unusual flowers on the cladodes in spring. If male plants fertilize them, the female plants produce globular red berries which remain attractive from autumn until the end of winter. The foliage is used in dried flower arrangements.

Cultivation. Plant female plants together with a male in spring, in any type of soil, even poor and dry, and in any position. They are tolerant of dense shade, and will grow even under hollies.

To propagate, divide the creeping rootstock in spring and replant immediately, or pick the berries and sow. They take at least a month to germinate.

Ruta

Rue, *Rutaceae*

This genus consists of about seven aromatic small shrubs, native to Mediterranean regions.

R. *graveolens* (zone 7), rue, may reach 20–32 in (50–80 cm) high. The evergreen leaves are an attractive glaucous, blue-green, but give off an unpleasant odour when rubbed. Tiny, mustard-yellow flowers appear at the tops of the stems in summer. 'Jackman's Blue' is a cultivar with very blue foliage.

Rue can be grown in a herb garden, mixed border or container. It is sometimes used for low hedging. Some people develop a rash from touching the foliage and seedpods.

Cultivation. Rue prefers dry, light soil and a warm sunny position. Pinch off the flower stems as soon as possible, to keep the plants compact. Trim annually in mid spring to promote bushy growth.

To propagate, take cuttings 4–6 in (10–15 cm) long in early autumn, or sow outdoors in mid spring, then prick out, leaving 2 ft (60 cm) between plants in each direction.

Sagittaria
Alismataceae

This genus includes about 20 herbaceous plants, many aquatic, and most from America.
S. sagittifolia (zone 5), arrowhead, a native of Europe and Asia, belongs to the same family as the water plantain, and is a hardy aquatic plant with stems to 3 ft (1 m) long. It has distinctive arrow-shaped leaves above water, and ribbon-shaped, underwater leaves. In summer, panicles of pure white, three-petalled flowers often with a purplish pink blotch around the brown stamens, appear. It can be invasive.
S. montevidensis (zone 10+), a South American plant, can be grown in a mild climate. This is similar to the common arrowhead, but larger and without stolons.

Arrowheads can be planted on the edge of a riverbank or natural pond, or in containers for the shelf or bottom of an artificial pool.
Cultivation. This marginal plant needs a heavy loam and a water depth of 6–24 in (15–60 cm). In autumn, the arrowhead runners produce egg-shaped tubers which become dormant in winter and form leaves the following spring.

In autumn, separate the tubercles and replant.

Salix
Willow, *Salicaceae*

A large genus of about 300 trees, shrubs and sub-shrubs native to the Northern Hemisphere, with simple, deciduous leaves. There are about 70 species native to Europe. Each plant bears either male or female flowers in catkins which usually appear before the leaves.
S. alba (zone 5), white willow, from Europe, may reach 90 ft (27 m) in height, forming a conical tree with slender branches, pendulous at the tips. These branches are used in basketry. The leaves are lanceolate, and silky grey on both sides, but the catkins are not particularly decorative. This fast-growing species is often grown beside water, and it makes a good windbreak. There are several cultivars with colourful young shoots.
S. caprea (zone 5), goat willow or great sallow, from Europe, is an irregularly shaped bushy shrub to 20 ft (6 m) high. It has large, oval leaves, grey and hairy beneath. The male catkins are the traditional pussy willows, very attractive and appearing before the leaves. This tree tolerates relatively dry soil and it can be stooled. The cultivar 'Kilmarnock' ('Pendula') is a smaller male tree with a weeping habit and is grown as a specimen standard.
S. × *sepulcralis* (zone 6), weeping willow, is one of the most commonly seen willows. It is a hybrid to 40 ft (12 m), with pendulous branches and long, narrow, persistent leaves. The male catkins appear in early to mid spring. The plant is very much at home beside the water but is not suitable for regions with very hot summers, and needs plenty of space.
S. 'Chrysocoma' (zone 6), is similar in appearance, but has golden-yellow branches. It is sometimes sold as *S. alba* 'Tristis' or *S. alba* 'Vitellina Pendula'. It is an excellent specimen tree for a lawn.
S. lanata (zone 4), woolly willow, is native to northern Europe and Asia, and is a slow-growing, alpine shrub, 3½ ft (1 m) high. It is rounded, with distinctly silvery small, oval leaves, branches and catkins. It makes a good rock garden shrub.
S. matsudana (zone 6), Peking willow, from China, is a conical tree, up to 40 ft (12 m) high, with yellow stems and narrow leaves; it is relatively tolerant of drought. 'Tortuosa' is an unusual cultivar, sometimes called the cork-screw, curly or twisted willow, with contoured and twisted branches, much used in flower arranging. The tree should be cut back frequently.
S. purpurea (zone 5), purple willow or osier, from Europe and Asia, is a large, open, graceful shrub, 12 ft (3.5 m) high. It often has highly decorative, purple bark, especially striking when leafless in winter, and narrow leaves. The supple branches are used to make wicker.

Alpine species include the mat-forming *S. reticulata* (zone 4), with wrinkled, rounded leaves with white undersides; and *S. retusa* (zone 4) with tiny smooth, oval leaves, green on both sides. Both these species are dwarf and prostrate, and are suitable for rock gardens.

Willows have varying uses, depending on the species. They may be planted on their own as specimens, used in rock gardens or in hedging. Some forms make good ground cover and others are useful for soil stabilization. The female willow is often more vigorous but the male catkins are usually showier.

Cultivation. Willows are very hardy, fast growing, but short lived trees. They need a deep, moist or damp soil in an open situation where there is no competition from other trees. Plant either in autumn or spring. Prune to remove dead wood or, for trees grown for catkins or coloured bark, prune every 1–2 years.

The willow is easy to propagate from leafless cuttings, from early winter to early spring, planted *in situ*; but half-ripe wood taken in summer also roots rapidly.

Willows are subject to willow anthracnose, willow scab, also to attacks by the gall mite.

Salpiglossis

Salpiglossis, Painted tongue, *Solanaceae*

A genus of about two species of herbaceous plants from the Andes.

S. sinuata (zone 6), is an annual, 32–42 in (80 cm–1 m) high. From early summer to early autumn it bears large, velvety, trumpet-shaped flowers in blue, red, purple, pink and yellow, generally streaked with gold and dark veined. It is sticky all over.

The F_1 hybrid 'Splash' (zone 6) is 1½ ft (45 cm) high, with large yellow, orange, red, blue or mauve flowers. It is ideal for growing in containers and is more tolerant of poor conditions outdoors than the species.

These very decorative, unusual plants are grown as half-hardy annuals, and may be used for bedding or flower arrangements.

Cultivation. Sow in late winter to early spring, under glass. Prick out and plant out in late spring, ¾ in (2 cm) apart, in a sheltered spot. Alternatively, sow the seeds where they are to grow, in late spring. Choose a sunny place. Dry soil is acceptable. Stake if necessary. Dead head to ensure a long flowering period.

Salvia

Labiatae

This large genus consists of about 900 species of hardy and tender shrubs and herbaceous plants from Africa, Asia, America and Europe. Some are grown for the ornamental value of their flowers or leaves, and a few species are grown particularly for their culinary or medicinal properties.

S. officinalis (zone 7), sage, is a sub-shrub native to the Mediterranean, with a branching, very bushy habit, growing 28 in (70 cm) or more high. The highly aromatic, more-or-less evergreen, leaves are greenish-grey on their upper surfaces and whitish underneath. Small violet spikes of flowers appear in summer. There are forms with purple, yellow and attractively variegated leaves. Sage can be grown in a herb garden, mixed border or container, and it can also be used for hedging.

Cultivation. Sage is an easy plant to grow, preferring light, well drained, even limy, soil and sun. Sow outdoors in mid spring, either in a border or in rows 32 in (80 cm) apart, and thin out to 20 in (50 cm) between the plants. Cuttings can also be taken in late summer or early autumn, or the plant may layer spontaneously. In this case, remove the rooted parts in mid autumn or mid spring. Pinch out the flower tips to keep the plants bushy, and prune in mid spring.

Pick the leaves as they are required and for drying purposes before the plant flowers. Replace every three or four years, when the plants become leggy.

Uses. The slightly bitter leaves can be used fresh or dried to accompany rich meats such as goose, duck or pork, or used sparingly in salad. Sage can also be used as an infusion for its properties as a tonic.

Ornamental Species

S. involucrata (zone 9) from Central America is a tender subshrub growing to 4 ft (1.2 m) tall. Bright, pink flowers appear in summer, enclosed in large bracts.

S. nemorosa 'Superba' (zone 6), is a herbaceous perennial 24–32 in (60–80 cm) high and 16–24 in (40–60 cm) across. It is a hybrid with mid green, oblong leaves and carries long spikes of small, violet, tubular flowers with crimson bracts from early summer to early autumn.

Cultivation. Plant in groups 20 in (50 cm) apart, in mid autumn or early spring in ordinary, well drained soil and a sunny position. Stake if grown in an exposed position. Dead head to prolong the flowering period. Cut it down to its base in autumn.

Propagate by division in autumn or spring; dividing every three to four years helps prevent the plant degenerating. Alternatively, sow seed under a cold frame in spring.

Sambucus

Elder, *Caprifoliaceae*

A genus of about 20 species of small, hardy trees and shrubs, native to temperate and subtropical regions, with deciduous, pinnate, opposite leaves. The small, creamy white flowers grow in flat heads, and are followed by profuse red, black or blue berries, much loved by birds. The plant has hollow, pithy stems.

S. canadensis (zone 4), elderberry, from North America, is a suckering shrub, 6½–13 ft (2–4 m) in height. Its flowers grow in broad umbels 6 in (15 cm) across, and are followed by black fruits. Cultivars include 'Aurea', with yellow leaves and red fruits, and 'Maxima', with larger leaves and flower heads 12–16 in (30–40 cm) across. There are fruiting varieties available, for wine-making, pies, jams and cordials.

S. nigra (zone 4), common elder, from Europe, North Africa and Asia, grows 20 ft (6 m) high. It has corky bark and dark-green leaves, usually composed of five leaflets, pungent when bruised. Heavily scented white flowers appear in summer, followed by edible blue-black berries. 'Marginata' has leaves with irregular white margins, 'Aurea' has golden yellow leaves and *f. laciniata* has deeply cut, fern-like leaves.

S. racemosa (zone 5), red elder, from Europe and Asia, grows 6½–10 ft (2–3 m) high. The flowers form a conical head, 4–6 in (10–15 cm) across, and are yellowish-white. Red berries follow in mid to late summer. 'Plumosa Aurea' has golden, deeply cut leaves.

Ordinary elders are best in wild gardens and hedgerows but ornamental-leaved forms are especially suitable for mixed borders and as screening.

Cultivation. Plant in a moist soil; a limy soil is acceptable and choose a sunny or partly shaded position. The golden-leaved cultivars grow more slowly and the yellow colour lasts longer in shade. Prune hard or coppice in winter or early spring for lush foliage effects.

Propagate from seed, ripe cuttings placed in open ground in early winter, or semi-ripe cuttings taken with a heel and placed in a frame.

Sanguinaria

Bloodroot, *Papaveraceae*

This genus is made up of a single species, native to eastern North America. The name of this hardy herbaceous perennial is derived from the blood-red sap which comes from the roots when they are cut.

S. canadensis (zone 4), grows 8–12 in (20–30 cm) high, and 12–15 in (30–37 cm) across. The anemone-like flowers which appear in mid spring, with the leaves, are waxy, pure white, with 8–12 petals around a central boss of yellow stamens, and last only two days. 'Flore Pleno' has sterile, double flowers, lasting longer than the species. The leaves which follow are palmate and glaucous, blue-green. These die down in late summer.

This is a very fine plant, albeit with a short-lived flowering period, for a shaded rock garden or beneath trees.

Cultivation. Grow in well drained soil with plenty of humus, and preferably a shaded position. It is slow growing, but once it has settled in properly it will last many years.

Propagate by dividing the rhizomes after flowering, in late spring or early summer. Take

Sanguinaria canadensis 'Flore Pleno'

care not to damage the roots, and do not lift and divide until the plant is reasonably large, which may take several years.

Sanguisorba

Burnet, bloodwort, *Rosaceae*

A genus of about 18 species of hardy herbaceous perennials, including those formerly regarded as part of the genus *Poterium*.
S. canadensis (P. canadense) – zone 5 – is native to eastern North America. It grows 5 ft (1.5 m) high, and 24 in (60 cm) across. It has elegant, mid-green, pinnate leaves and copious spikes of creamy white, bottle-brush flowers, 6 in (15 cm) long, between late summer and mid-autumn. The flowers are good for cutting.
S. obtusa (S. hakusanensis) – zone 6 – is native to Japan, 3½–4 ft (1–1.2 m) high, and 16–24 in (40–60 cm) across. Its foliage is tinged with grey. The bottle-brush spikes of rose-pink flowers appear throughout summer.

These vigorous plants are suitable for herbaceous borders, in association with asters and polygonums, and provide interest in late summer and autumn.

Cultivation. Plant from mid-autumn to early spring, in ordinary, preferably damp soil, and in sun or light shade. They often need staking.

Cut back in early autumn, after flowering.

Propagate by seed or by dividing and replanting the wide-spreading clumps in early to mid spring.

Santolina

Compositae

A genus of 18 species of hardy of half-hardy subshrubs with finely divided, evergreen, highly aromatic leaves and dainty, button-like flowers, native to Mediterranean regions.
S. chamaecyparissus (zone 7), lavender cotton, is native to southern France, and grows to 16–24 in (40–60 cm) in height and spread. This species forms a dense mound with silvery, woolly, thread-like leaves borne on white downy stems. The golden-yellow flowers appear in mid summer.
S. neapolitana is similar, but the leaves are longer and more feathery.
S. rosmarinifolius (S. virens) – zone 8 – from southern Europe, grows to 32 in (80 cm) in height and spread, with deep-green, thread-like leaves and yellow flowers.

These plants are suited to herb gardens, mixed borders, rock gardens or path edging.

Cultivation. Plant in mid autumn or early spring, in ordinary, well drained soil and a sunny position.

Older plants tend to become leggy; to retain a bushy appearance prune after flowering, to encourage new shoots to develop from the base.

Propagate from mid summer to early autumn by taking cuttings 2–3¼ in (5–8 cm) long and planting them in sand, in a cold frame.

Sanvitalia

Compositae

A genus of about seven species of herbaceous plants from Central America.
S. procumbens (zone 6), creeping zinnia, from Mexico, has trailing stems, no more than 6 in (15 cm) high, and pointed, mid-green leaves. It carries numerous, small, daisy-like yellow flowers with dark centres from mid summer to mid autumn. The cultivar 'Flore Pleno' has double flowers. It is a hardy annual, and is ideal as low edging, or in rock gardens or dry-stone walls. It is also used in window boxes.

Cultivation. Sow in early spring, either in a seed bed or where the plant is to grow. (In mild areas, it can also be sown in autumn.) Prick out or thin out in mid spring, 4 in (10 cm) apart. The plant likes sun and rich, well drained, peaty soil.

Saponaria

Soapwort, *Caryophyllaceae*

This genus consists of 30 species of hardy and half-hardy annuals, biennials and perennials from Europe, Asia and North Africa.
S. caespitosa (zone 7), from the Pyrenées, is a perennial growing 2¾ in (7 cm) high and 8–16 in (20–40 cm) across. It forms dense tufts with oval, evergreen leaves ⅜–¾ in (1–2 cm) long. The flowers are bright pink, and grow in clusters in mid to late summer. It needs a sunny, sheltered site and well drained soil.
S. ocymoides (zone 5), a European perennial, grows 4 in (10 cm) high and 3½ ft (1 m) across. The creeping stems bear oval green leaves and the pink flowers grow in clusters from mid to late summer.

Low-growing soapworts can be used in mixed borders, rock gardens, for edging paths or to cascade over an overhang such as a wall. Dwarf forms can also be grown in an alpine house.

S. officinalis, bouncing Bet, is a perennial 2½ ft (75 cm) high and across. It is naturalized in England, where its leaves were used as a soap for cleaning delicate items. Its campion-like flowers can be single or double and white, crimson or pink. It can be invasive. Taller species of perennial soapwort are good for large mixed borders or the wild garden.

S. vaccaria is an annual with light green leaves. The deep pink star-like flowers are carried in sprays in summer. Height is 2½ ft (75 cm) and spread is 9 in (23 cm). A white form 'Alba' is also grown.

Cultivation. These plants need a light well drained soil and a sunny position. They tolerate limy soils. Prune perennial species after flowering.

Propagate by seed in late winter, sown in a tray and placed in a cold frame, or from cuttings for the perennials.

Sarracenia

Pitcher plant, *Sarraceniaceae*

This genus consists of ten species of hardy and half hardy insectivorous plants, native to North America. The greenish brown, yellow, red or purple leaves are cylindrical or pitcher-shaped and may be several feet high. The edges of the pitchers secrete nectar and this, combined with the very bright colours of the flowers and leaves, attracts insects. These are trapped once in the pitcher, and their bodies are eventually broken down by micro-organisms and enzymes in the pitcher, and absorbed by the plant. In this way, the plant compensates for lack of nitrogenous elements in its environment.

The plant flowers at the end of spring, and is very striking. The nodding flowers are up to 4 in (10 cm) across, with distinctive brightly coloured petals.

S. flava (zone 9), has yellowish-green pitchers up to 2 ft (60 cm) tall and strongly scented yellow flowers.

S. purpurea (zone 8), grows 9 in (23 cm) high. Its pitchers are greenish purple, and its flowers deep purple. It can survive mild winters out of doors.

S. minor (zone 8), has green to purplish pitchers and yellow flowers.

Cultivation. Sarracenia is one of the easiest insect-eating plants to grow outdoors or in a greenhouse in colder areas. Keep continuously damp by growing in a mixture of sphagnum moss and peat. Do not use limy water when you water it.

It can be propagated from seed sown in a cold frame, but this is a slow process. Established clumps can be divided in spring.

Sasa

Bamboo, *Gramineae*

This is a genus of about 25 small bamboos from Japan and Korea, rarely growing to more than 10 ft (3 m) high. Unusual among bamboos, the leaves are large in comparison to the rest of the plant, and are borne on slender stems.

S. palmata (zone 5), is about 6½ ft (2 m) or more high with glaucous canes. Its leaves are 15 × 4 in (37 × 10 cm), with a yellowish midrib. The plant is hardy down to 0°F (−18°C).

S. veitchii (zone 5), is similar to *S. palmata*, but smaller and the leaves have white margins.

These plants are very useful for dense ground cover, but both may be highly invasive.

Cultivation. Grow in moist, fertile soil and in sun or light shade.

Satureja

Labiatae

A genus of about 30 species of annuals or perennials from Europe and North America, several of which are used as herbs.

S. hortensis (zone 5), summer or common savory, is a bushy plant native to the eastern Mediterranean. It is an annual, 10 in (25 cm) high, with stems bearing small, elongated oval highly aromatic leaves and pink tubular flowers in summer.

S. montana, winter savory, is a perennial of a similar size, but with woody, branching stems and tiny, rose-pink tubular flowers, carried in the upper leaf axils in summer. Many people find its flavour coarser than that of summer savory.

Cultivation. Plant in light, well drained soil and a sunny position. Sow in mid to late spring, in a border or in rows 14 in (35 cm) apart and then thin the plants in the row to 1 ft (30 cm).

Alternatively, sow under a frame in early spring and prick out in late spring.

Pick the leaves as needed, usually two and a half months after sowing. Dry them out in a dark place if required. Replace winter savory every two to three years, once its base becomes woody. It is easily propagated by division or from cuttings of lateral shoots taken in spring and rooted in a mixture of sand and peat in a cold frame.

Uses. The strongly flavoured leaves can be used fresh or dry as a flavouring for salads, stuffings, grills, peas and beans. They can be made into an infusion (tea), as a drink, as an aid to digestion, or for gargling.

Saxifraga

Saxifrage, *Saxifragaceae*

A genus of about 300 species of hardy, usually herbaceous perennials, from the mountains of Europe, North America and Asia.

S. fortunei (zone 6), from China and Japan, is a moderately hardy herbaceous perennial 12–18 in (30–40 cm) high, and 8–12 in (20–30 cm) across. Its decorative, deep-green, fleshy, rounded leaves are toothed and lobed, with reddish undersides. Clusters of small, star-shaped, white flowers with irregular petals appear in mid to late autumn.

This species is suitable for herbaceous borders and in woodland gardens, in lime-free soil.

Cultivation. Plant in mid to late spring, 1 ft (30 cm) apart, in a moist but well drained soil containing plenty of humus and enriched with peat or leaf mould. Choose a sunny or slightly shaded position. Remove the flowering stems when the flowers have died.

Propagate by division in early to mid spring.

S. longifolia (zone 4), from the Pyrenees, where it grows on cliffs, is a large and spectacular species when in flower. It has rosettes of silver-grey leaves encrusted with lime on their edges, 6 in (15 cm) or more in diameter, and in early summer an inflorescence, 18 in (45 cm) or more tall, of numerous white flowers. The rosette, which takes four to six years to reach flowering size, dies after flowering – plants that behave like this are called monocarpic. Usually there is plenty of seed for propagation. Hybrids between this species and *S. paniculata*, another encrusted species, are similar, but are perennial in that offset rosettes are produced. The best hybrid is called 'Tumbling Waters'.

Cultivation. This species and its relatives are best planted in gritty soil that contains lime, in sunny (except in very hot districts, where some shade is desirable) rock crevices in a rock garden. Propagate *S. longifolia* from seed; its relatives can be divided after flowering.

S. moschata (zone 4), from the mountainous areas of Europe, is one of several mossy saxifrages that form low evergreen mounds of small, bright green divided leaves. In spring it is covered with creamy white flowers. In this group there are a large number of hybrids having flowers in reds, pinks, white and yellow.

Cultivation. Mossy saxifrages are best in semi-shade, at the foot of rock gardens or as border edging in a soil that does not dry out and preferably limy. Propagate in late summer.

S. oppositifolia (zone 4), purple saxifrage, is a mat-forming plant that grows in upland areas in northern and central Asia, Europe and North America, where it is found in sheltered places on rocks or scree. In late spring or early summer it is covered with bright purplish-red flowers.

Cultivation. Plant in part shade in good soil, adding grit for drainage, but ensure that it does not dry out during the summer months. Propagate by dividing when flowering has finished.

S. × urbium (zone 5), London pride, is a hybrid between two species, often sold under the name *S. umbrosa*, which is one of its parents. It makes slowly spreading evergreen rosettes of somewhat fleshy, spoon-shaped leaves with scalloped edges. In late spring, starry white, red-spotted flowers are carried on stems about 12 in (30 cm) tall. There is a form with yellow-variegated leaves. Easily grown, this saxifrage is a useful ground-cover plant.

Cultivation. Plant in any reasonable soil that does not dry out, in shade or semi-shade. It is easily divided after flowering.

S. stolonifera (S. sarmentosa) – zone 9–10 – mother-of-thousands, from China and Japan, is an evergreen perennial which forms a rosette with runners bearing plantlets at their ends. It has rounded, toothed leaves and clusters of starry white flowers in summer. This plant is less hardy and often grown as a house plant for its pretty foliage. 'Tricolor' has leaves marked with red and silvery-white.

Cultivation. When grown as a houseplant, it enjoys plenty of light, but away from direct sunlight, and temperatures of not less than 40°F

(4.5°C) in the winter. Water well during the growing season allowing the surface of the compost (soil) to dry out between waterings, and sparingly in winter. Repot annually in the spring. Propagate by pegging down plantlets into a cutting compost (medium) and when rooted remove from mother plant.

Scabiosa

Scabious, *Dipsacaceae*

A genus of about 80 annuals and herbaceous perennials from Europe, Africa and Asia.
S. atropurpurea (zone 6), sweet scabious, is a hardy annual with dark crimson flowers which grows 3 ft (1 m) high and 9 in (25 cm) across.
S. caucasica (zone 5), pin cushion flower, from the Caucasus, is hardy almost everywhere. It grows 20–24 in (50–60 cm) high, and 16–20 in (40–50 cm) across. The leaves are lanceolate and mid-green. The plant flowers from early summer to mid autumn, with large, compact heads of lavender-blue flowers. There are numerous cultivars, with white, richer blue or violet flowers.

Scabious is a herbaceous border plant, popular in fresh and dried flower arrangements.
Cultivation. Plant in well drained, preferably limy, soil, enriched with garden compost or manure. Choose a sunny position and plant 16 in (40 cm) apart in early to mid spring. *S. caucasica* is short lived in acid soils.

Scabiosa caucasica 'Moerheim Blue'

Dead head regularly to ensure the plant flowers for as long as possible, and cut the stems back in autumn.

To propagate, divide the root clumps in early to mid spring every three or four years.

Schinus

Anacardiaceae

This genus contains about 27 species of evergreen trees and shrubs from tropical and subtropical America. The clusters of very small flowers are followed by berries.
S. molle (zone 10), pepper tree, comes from tropical South America, and may grow to a height of 33 ft (10 m) or more in the wild. It has an elegant drooping habit and fine, light-green pinnate leaves which give off a peppery smell when rubbed. The clusters of creamy white flowers appear in early summer, followed on female trees by small, shiny, rose-pink berries. It can be planted on its own, as a specimen, as a group or in avenues. It is a common street tree in southern Europe.
Cultivation. Grow in rich well drained soil. It is tolerant of dry weather and adapts remarkably well to areas where citrus fruit grows. Elsewhere, it can be grown in conservatories.

Propagate from seed or cuttings taken in summer and placed under a cloche.

Schizostylis

Iridaceae

A genus of one species of rhizomatous herbaceous perennial from South Africa.
S. coccinea (zone 8), Kaffir lily, is moderately hardy. It grows to 20–32 in (50–80 cm) high, and 12 in (30 cm) across. It has sword-like leaves and long spikes of bright crimson star-shaped flowers in mid to late autumn. If happy, it quickly forms a dense clump. There are several cultivars, including the pink flowered 'Sunrise' and 'November Cheer'. These are excellent flowers for cutting, and can be grown in herbaceous borders or alongside a pond or stream.
Cultivation. Plant in a moist, fertile soil enriched with manure or garden compost, in shelter and sun. Plant 1 ft (30 cm) apart in early to mid spring. Bury the rhizomes $\frac{3}{4}$–2 in (2–5 cm) deep.

Manure the plant in spring. Water generously in dry weather. Cut the stems back in autumn. In colder areas, protect in winter with a mulch of dry leaves or ferns.

Propagate every three to four years in spring by division, to encourage flowering.

Scilla

Squill, *Liliaceae*

This genus consists of about 40, European, Asian and African species of flowering bulbs. Unless otherwise mentioned, the following are hardy and the bell- or star-shaped flowers are usually blue.

S. bifolia (zone 6), from Europe, grows 4–6 in (10–15 cm) high, forming a carpet of narrow leaves in wooded places. It bears one to ten blue, star-shaped flowers on slender stems. The flower stem bends down to ground level to release the seeds when ripe. There are white- and pink-flowered forms available.

S. peruviana (zone 8), Cuban lily, actually comes from the Mediterranean regions, and grows 1–2 ft (30–60 cm) high. It is a magnificent species, but hardy only in mild climates. The plant develops broad leaves in winter, and in spring produces a huge inflorescence in a conical raceme of up to 100, small, star-shaped blue or white flowers. It has a very short dormant season.

S. siberica (zone 5), Siberian bluebell, is native to Russia and grows 6 in (15 cm) high. The cultivar 'Spring Beauty' has dark blue flowers, groups of two to eight, appearing very early in the year. There are also white and bicoloured varieties.

Grow scillas in pots, rock gardens, borders, wild gardens or woods. They are good for providing colour under deciduous trees and shrubs.

Cultivation. Plant in groups in autumn, in moist but well drained soil, 2–4 in (5–10 cm) deep, depending on size. They readily reproduce from offshoots or self-sown seed.

Scirpus

True bulrush, *Cyperaceae*

This genus consists of some 200 species of hardy herbaceous, perennial plants from temperate regions of the world. They resemble species of *Juncus* with their erect, cylindrical leaves. The flowers are uninteresting and appear in small terminal tufts. Only a few species can be used in the garden, as the others are too invasive.

S. lacustris subsp. *S. tabernaemontani* (zone 5), native to Europe and Asia, grows 5 ft (1.5 m) high and 3½ ft (1 m) across. It is an aquatic plant, with mid-green leaves growing from a very hard creeping rhizome. The form usually grown is 'Zebrinus' which grows 3½ ft (1 m) high, and has foliage attractively banded in white. 'Albescens' has creamy white, longitudinally striped stems.

Cultivation. Plant in rich soil, beside the water or in up to 6 in (15 cm) of water.

To propagate, lift and divide regularly in mid spring.

Scutellaria

Skull-cap, *Labiatae*

A genus comprising some 300 species of herbaceous plants or sub-shrubs, with evergreen leaves, found in many areas of the world.

S. alpina (zone 4), alpine skull-cap, comes from Europe and Central Asia, and grows 8 in (20 cm) high and 16 in (40 cm) across. It forms prostrate cushions of creeping stems, with short, erect tips. The leaves are oval and greyish-green. The erect, tubular flowers are violet-blue, often with yellow markings, and appear in late summer. The form 'Alba' has white flowers.

S. indica (zone 6), from China and Japan, grows 6 in (15 cm) or more high and 8–12 in (20–30 cm) across, and also carpets the ground. It has mid-green, rounded leaves covered in white down; racemes of violet-blue flowers 1¼ in (3 cm) long appear from early summer to early autumn.

These are hardy species, best suited to rock gardens or walls.

Cultivation. Plant in ordinary, well drained soil in autumn or spring, in sun or light shade.

Propagate by division in early spring or by taking cuttings 2¾ in (7 cm) long from lateral, non-flowering shoots, in early to mid spring. Plant in sand, with bottom heat, in a frame.

Sedum

Stonecrop, *Crassulaceae*

A genus consisting of over 300 species of mostly herbaceous perennials or sub-shrubs from northern temperate regions.

S. spectabile (zone 5), ice plant, from China and Korea, is a perennial succulent, hardy almost everywhere, 12–20 in (30–50 cm) high and 12–16 in (30–40 cm) across. It has glaucous, fleshy oval leaves. Beautiful mauve-pink flowers appear in large flat heads from late summer to autumn. There are several named cultivars with deeper-coloured flowers. The hybrid 'Autumn Joy' is particularly beautiful, with pale, grey-green leaves and pink flowers eventually turning copper-red in late autumn.

Taller growing species make excellent cut flowers, fresh or dried. They can be planted in herbaceous borders and make good ground cover. Low-growing species are ideal for rock gardens, walls and along paths.

Cultivation. Plant *S. spectabile* in a sunny position, 1 ft (30 cm) apart, in autumn or spring, in ordinary, well drained, even poor or dry soil.

Leave the dried flower heads on the plant until spring, then cut back the old stems down to the cluster of young basal leaves. Propagate by division in autumn or spring.

Sempervivum

Houseleek, *Crassulaceae*

A genus of 40 species of hardy succulents, with mat- or hummock-forming rosettes of evergreen leaves, from Europe, North Africa and Asia. These plants hybridize readily and some species have given rise to many hybrids and cultivars. The rosettes die after flowering but leave offsets.

S. arachnoideum (zone 4), cobweb or spider houseleek, comes from the Alps and Pyrénées. It grows 1½–4 in (4–10 cm) high, and spreads slowly to form groups of rosettes tinged with red, and covered in tangled threads which give it its cobweb appearance. The flower stems are 6 in (15 cm) long and bear bright pink flowers, ¾ in (2 cm) across in early to mid summer. The subsp. 'tomentosum' is more densely webbed.

S. tectorum (zone 5), common or roof houseleek, hens-and-chickens, often found growing on roofs, comes from the Alps and Pyrénées and other parts of Europe. It grows 4 in (10 cm) high with clumps of rosettes spreading to 20–32 in (50–80 cm) across. The leaves are bright green, usually tipped with brownish-red. The flowers are reddish-pink and are borne on spikes growing 20 in (50 cm) or more high, and appearing in mid summer.

Sempervivum arachnoideum

All are suitable for rock gardens, screes, troughs and dry walls. They can also be grown in an alpine house.

Cultivation. Plant in well drained, gritty soil, in a sunny position. These plants tolerate dry conditions. Damp winter weather may harm them, especially in heavy soil. Birds are also fond of the succulent leaves and can cause damage.

Propagate by detaching rooted offsets, and planting immediately.

Senecio

Ragwort, *Compositae*

This genus consists of around 1,500 species of annual, biennial, perennial and woody species from all over the world except the Antarctic. Their common denominator is their daisy-like flowers, which are generally yellow and grow in clusters.

The following two hardy plants are commonly grown:

S. bicolor subsp. cineraria *(S. maritima)* – zone 9 – dusty miller, is native to the coastal areas of southern Europe. Though perennial, it is often used as an annual in cooler climates for its highly decorative, silvery foliage. When it flowers, the stem may grow to a height of 3½ ft (1 m) and bear small yellow heads. These are usually pinched out, because they are not particularly attractive and often interfere with colour schemes. Nipping out the flower heads also helps keep the plants compact. The cultivar 'Silver Dust' has very silvery white, deeply divided leaves. Dusty miller is particularly popular for bedding and as a pot plant.

Cultivation. Sow in late winter to early spring, under glass. Prick out in early to mid spring and plant out 8 in (20 cm) apart in late spring. Pinch out the growing tips to ensure compact growth. To obtain strong plants quickly, take cuttings in early autumn and overwinter in a cold greenhouse. Dusty miller likes plenty of sunshine, and tolerates poor, dry soil.

S. 'Sunshine' (zone 8), is a hybrid between a group of species from New Zealand, often sold under the names *S. greyi* or *S. laxifolius*. It is evergreen, usually about 3 ft (90 cm) high and spreads up to 8 ft (2.4 m) wide. It has oval leaves, dark greenish above but covered with white felt underneath. During the summer it is covered with bright yellow daisy-like flowers. Its greyish appearance provides year-round beauty, and it is especially useful for seaside gardens.

Cultivation. Any reasonable well-drained soil is suitable; it requires full sun and can be planted in spring or autumn. Pruning consists of cutting away the flowering stems when the blooms have faded, and any branches that spoil the shrub's shape. Propagate by cuttings taken in late summer, keeping them under glass.

Some of the tender species are popularly used as decorative plants for greenhouses and conservatories.

S. articulatus (Kleinia articulata) – zone 10+ – candle plant or hot-dog cactus, is a succulent plant from South Africa which has erect cylindrical grey-green jointed stems. The three- to five-lobed leaves are short lived and form at the ends of the young stems in winter. Pale yellow flowers are sometimes produced.

S. confusus (zone 10+), flame vine, from Mexico and other countries of Central America, is a vigorous evergreen climber grown for its clusters of large, brilliant orange daisy-like flowers in summer.

S. macroglossus (zone 10+), Natal ivy or wax vine, is native to South Africa. It is an evergreen, twining, woody climber with fleshy triangular shaped, three- to five-lobed leaves which are dark green and shiny. In winter, white daisy-like flowers about 2 in (5 cm) or more across, with yellow centres are borne in loose clusters. It is usually grown as an attractive foliage plant. 'Variegatus' is similar but the leaves have an irregular creamy white variegated margin.

S. mikanioides (zone 10+), German ivy, is similar to *S. macroglossus* in habit and also native to South Africa. It may be distinguished by the leaves with five to seven more sharply pointed but less fleshy leaves and the flowers, which are smaller, yellow and formed earlier in autumn and early winter.

S. rowleyanus (zone 10+), string-of-beads, from South Africa is one of the succulent species in the genus. The thin trailing stems bear globular, bright green leaves each around $\frac{1}{4}$ in (20 mm) across, and sometimes produce small white flowers. This species makes an unusual plant for a hanging basket.

Cultivation. These plants flourish in bright light, especially *S. articulatus* and *S. rowleyanus*, while the climbing species *S. macroglossus* and *S. mikanioides* will only tolerate full sun in winter. Keep temperatures above 50°F (10°C). Water in summer, scarcely in winter and repot only when necessary. In the case of the climbing species, pinch out the tops to encourage a bushy habit. Propagate by stem cuttings or alternatively by rooted offsets.

Sequoia

Californian redwood, *Taxodiaceae*

A genus of one, very large, evergreen conifer. Its crown is fairly irregular, but thick, and its branches are spreading and drooping. The bark is red, spongy and very thick. The needle-like leaves are dark green and arranged in two rows. It bears cones $\frac{3}{4}$ in (2 cm) long, similar to that of the cypress, at the ends of the branches.

S. sempervirens (zone 6), from California, is regarded as the tallest tree in the world. Some grow to 360 ft (110 m) in height. It is also one of the longest-lived; some are more than 2,000 years old. This species is only suitable for large open spaces and parks, but there are 'dwarf' cultivars, including 'Adpressa', with creamy white shoots in spring; 'Pendula', with a weeping growth habit, and the low-growing 'Prostrata'.

Cultivation. This is a moderately hardy tree, requiring ideally an oceanic climate and a deep, rich moist soil with not too much lime. Plant in spring, in a sheltered position. Stake young plants until their roots are established and mulch annually with well rotted leaf mould. Propagation is mainly from seed, but only a few will germinate. The seedlings are frost sensitive.

Sidalcea
Malvaceae

A genus of 20 species of moderately hardy herbaceous perennials from North America.
S. malviflora (zone 6), chequer mallow, comes from California, and grows 32–48 in (80 cm–1.2 m) high and 20 in (50 cm) across. The slightly lobed leaves are round to kidney shaped, and form a basal clump. The cup-shaped, silky pink flowers are similar to those of the mallow, 2 in (5 cm) in diameter, and grow in stately spikes 10–16 in (25–40 cm) high. The plant flowers continuously from early summer to early autumn.

The species has now been replaced in cultivation by numerous cultivars, often a brighter, or clearer pink.

Plant in herbaceous borders where the basal clumps make excellent ground cover.

Cultivation. Plant in any ordinary, well drained soil in a sunny position. Stake the taller varieties and cut back the stems after flowering to 12 in (30 cm) above the ground, to encourage new flowering lateral shoots to develop. In climates with a cold winter, the plants may be killed by damp.

To propagate, lift in early spring, remove the most vigorous sections from the perimeter of the rootball and replant immediately. The species may be propagated by seed.

Silene
Campion, catchfly, *Caryophyllaceae*

A genus of 500 species of annuals, herbaceous perennials and a few sub-shrubs, native to the Northern Hemisphere.
S. acaulis (zone 4), moss campion or cushion pink, is native to Europe. It is a spreading moss-like plant 2 in (5 cm) high, with tiny, bright-green leaves. In early to mid summer, it is covered with bright pink flowers. It needs poor, gritty soil to flower well.
S. maritima (zone 6), sea campion, from Europe and North Africa, is 8 in (20 cm) high and 16–32 in (40–80 cm) across. It is a hardy perennial with a woody rootstock from which grow many prostrate stems covered in silvery green, lanceolate leaves. The small, white flowers appear from mid summer to early autumn. In gardens, it is largely replaced by varieties such as the double 'Plena' and the pink-flowered 'Rosea'.
S. schafta (zone 6), is native to the Caucasus, and grows to 4–6 in (10–15 cm) high, and 12–16 in (30–40 cm) across. It is a perennial, with spreading clumps of bright green, lanceolate leaves. The flowers are magenta pink and open from mid summer to mid autumn.
S. virginica (zone 6), fire pink, is a perennial growing 1–2 ft (30–60 cm) high. Deep crimson flowers throughout the summer.

Many species are regarded as weeds, but others are suitable for rock gardens, and the annuals are good for bedding schemes.

Cultivation. Plant in ordinary, well drained soil, in sun or light shade.

Avoid disturbing perennials as their roots are fragile. Propagate by seed, in seed trays in a cold frame, with bottom heat in early spring, or sow outdoors in late spring.

Sinapis
Mustard, *Cruciferae*

A genus of ten European species, some grown as fodder or salad.
S. alba (zone 6), white mustard, is an annual, native to the Mediterranean area. It grows quickly, reaching a height of 10–24 in (25–60 cm). It has green, downy leaves. The flowers are yellow, and appear in summer. It is harvested at seedling stage, and used as salad; it is often grown with cress (*Lepidium sativum*).

Cultivation. White mustard prefers a moist, relatively heavy soil and a sunny position. Seed can be broadcast outdoors at intervals, from early to mid spring onward. Cover with a light sprinkling of soil. Alternatively grow under glass in shallow boxes on damp pads of cotton wool, flannel or even kitchen paper. This is more convenient, since there is no soil adhering to the roots. Cover with paper until the seeds germinate, then remove the cover and keep the compost or moisture-retentive medium continuously moist. Temperatures of 55°F (10°C) are necessary. If growing with cress, sow the cress 3–4 days before the mustard so they are ready for cutting at the same time.

Uses. Cut the leaves as required at the seedling stage and use in salads. Steady, quick growth gives by far the best-flavoured leaves.

Sisyrinchium

Blue-eyed grass, *Iridaceae*

These plants are close relations of the iris; the genus comprises about 100 species mainly native to North and South America.
S. californicum (zone 6), golden-eyed grass, is native to California, and grows 2 ft (60 cm) high. Its leaves are slightly glaucous. The large flowers are golden yellow, veined with black, and appear from early summer to mid autumn.
S. graminoides (S. bermudiana) (zone 5), is native to eastern North America and grows over 1 ft (30 cm) high. It has robust stems bearing flattened, lanceolate leaves. The flowers are pale-to-dark blue with yellow centres, and appear at the ends of the stems from late spring to early summer.
S. idahoense (zone 5), originally from North America, grows 8 in (20 cm) high. The plant has very fine, grass-like foliage, similar to *S. graminoides* but with larger, dark-blue flowers with yellow centres, produced from early summer to early autumn.
S. striatum, 2 ft (60 cm) high, has sword-like, evergreen leaves, and spikes of small, yellow, primrose-like flowers striped with purplish brown in early summer.

These plants grow from rhizomes and form tufts of lanceolate leaves which are highly suitable for a rock garden. Larger species are good in mixed borders.

Cultivation. Sisyrinchiums like well drained soil, neither too damp nor too dry, and sun or light shade.

Top dress with leaf mould or peat mixed with well rotted manure every two or three years. Some species are only moderately hardy and need to be protected during cold winters. Remove dead flowering stems in autumn.

As the clumps grow fast, lift and divide from the third year onwards, in early spring, planting them out immediately. Sisyrinchiums often self seed.

Skimmia

Skimmia, *Rutaceae*

A genus of five or six species of slow-growing, aromatic, hardy evergreen shrubs from East Asia, with simple, leathery, green leaves. The male and female flowers are white and star-shaped, appearing on separate plants in some species. The berries are red and long lasting.
S. × foremanii (S. japonica 'Foremanii') – zone 6 – a vigorous female plant, grows about 3½ ft (1 m) high. It has white, highly scented flowers and large numbers of red berries if pollinated by a nearby male plant.
S. japonica (zone 6), from Japan, makes a compact, domed shrub about 3½ ft (1 m) high. It has bright green, leathery leaves. The white flowers are especially fragrant on male plants and the red fruits last all winter. Both male and female plants are needed to produce fruit.
S. reevesiana (zone 6), from China, is a dwarf shrub, growing 2 ft (60 cm) high. It has a compact habit and narrow leaves, often with pale margins. The bisexual flowers appear in late spring on terminal panicles and the red fruits often last until the following season. It cannot tolerate chalky soil.

Skimmias are shade tolerant, and grow well in seaside and urban gardens.

Cultivation. Plant in any well drained, open loam, or a soil containing leaf mould or peat, in sun or shade. Plant male and female plants together to ensure that fruits are produced. Skimmias are subject to chlorosis, but regular applications of organic fertiliser correct the problem.

Propagate by seed from the berries, in mid autumn; alternatively, take cuttings in early autumn and place these in a seed bed in a cold frame, repotting the following year.

Smilacina

False solomon's-seal, solomon's-plumes, *Liliaceae*

A genus of about 30 species of hardy herbaceous perennials growing from rhizomes and native to East Asian and North American woodlands.
S. racemosa (zone 6), false spikenard, is North American and grows 28–32 in (70–80 cm) high and 20–24 in (50–60 cm) across. The elegantly arching stems bear fresh-green, lanceolate leaves, similar to those of Solomon's seal, to which it is related. The terminal spikes, 2–4 in (5–10 cm) long, are made up of cream-coloured scented flowers set closely together, appearing in mid to late spring. These are sometimes followed by red berries. This plant is suitable for shaded flowerbeds, in the company of ferns, Solomon's seal and astilbes.

Cultivation. Plant the rhizomatous roots in moist, well drained humus-rich soil in shade, from mid autumn to early spring. Chalky soils are unsuitable. These are slow-growing plants, and resent disturbance. Remove the dead stems in late autumn.

To propagate, lift and divide the rhizomes of the old root clumps in early to mid-autumn and replant immediately.

Solanum

Solanaceae

A genus of over 1,000 species of trees, shrubs, herbaceous plants and climbers found wild in most parts of the world.

S. tuberosum (zone 5), potato, is a half-hardy perennial 2 ft (60 cm) high with tubers of all shapes and colours, $2\frac{1}{4}$–4 in (6–10 cm) in diameter. It is of uncertain origin, but has been grown for a very long time in South America, and there are numerous cultivars, developed to suit particular soil types and climates.

Cultivation. Potatoes can be grown in almost any soil, but avoid a chalky soil. It is the best crop to begin transforming grassland or wasteland into a vegetable plot. Choose an open sunny position. Dig the soil in the autumn, adding manure. Leave the ground rough over winter.

As soon as the tubers or 'seed' potatoes arrive in late winter, place eye ends uppermost in trays or egg boxes containing a layer of peat, and keep the trays in indirect light, in a frost-free room until shoots grow $\frac{1}{2}$–1 in (1–2.5 cm) long.

Before spring planting, break the soil surface down to a fine tilth and draw drills 5 in (12.5 cm) deep in rows 24 in (60 cm) wide for early varieties, 30 in (75 cm) wide for maincrop varieties. Sprinkle a layer of peat in the bottom of the trench. Place potatoes in trenches 12 in (30 cm) apart for earlies, 15 in (37 cm) for maincrops. Add a further layer of peat and cover the drills to form a slight mound. After planting rake in a general fertiliser. Should there be a danger of frost when young growth appears, slightly cover with soil. When growth has reached 9 in (23 cm) high, break up the soil between the rows, and remove weeds before earthing up to 6 in (15 cm) high.

Harvest earlies as soon as large enough, the maincrop when the haulms have died down. New potatoes do not store well. For storing, harvest on a warm, dry day and leave the tubers on the ground before picking and storing in earth clamps or a frost-free shed. The expected yield is between 45–65 lb (20.5–30 kg) per 30 ft (9 m) row.

Solanum rantonnetii 'Grandiflora'

During the growing season, water well in dry weather.

Potatoes are vulnerable to slugs, wireworms, eelworms, and in some countries, Colorado beetle.

The most prevalent diseases are blight, potato scab, wart diseases and viruses. Never add lime, but when planting on a chalky soil, choose a suitable variety for such soils.

Several of the less hardy species make useful flowering pot plants.

S. capsicastrum (zone 10+), winter cherry, grows in Brazil as a small evergreen shrub but is often treated as an annual when grown as a pot plant. It bears small white flowers and these are followed in winter by scarlet pointed berries up to $\frac{3}{4}$ in (20 mm) long, but these are best kept away from children as they may be poisonous.

S. crispum (zone 8–9), Chilean potato vine, from Chile, is a climbing evergreen shrub grown for its flowers. It is grown outside in suitable climates, but in the greenhouse elsewhere. Large clusters of bluish-purple flowers cover the plant in summer and autumn.

S. jasminoides (zone 9–10), jasmine nightshade, is an evergreen climber capable of reaching 10–

15 ft (3–4.5 m) high. It has star-shaped pale blue flowers in mid summer to mid autumn. 'Album' has white flowers.

S. pseudocapsicum (zone 10+), Jerusalem cherry, is found in many tropical and subtropical areas. It is similar to and often confused with *S. capsicastrum*, but differs in the globose red fruits which are slightly smaller (also poisonous). It also makes a somewhat larger plant which may reach 3 ft (90 cm) or so in height.

S. rantonnetii (zone 10), blue potato bush, from Argentina and Paraguay, is a shrub up to 6 ft (1.8 m) tall in its native habitat. It has oval, generally pointed leaves, and clusters of violet-blue flowers each of which, in the cultivar 'Grandiflora', are almost 1 in (2.5 cm) across. Its fruit is reddish, heart-shaped and drooping.

S. wendlandii (zone 10+), is a giant potato vine from Central America grown for its ornamental flowers. It is a scrambling species with large lilac blue flowers up to 2½ in (6.5 cm) across.

Cultivation. All these plants need bright light with winter temperatures of not less than 50°F (10°C). Keep the compost moist at all times and feed regularly. In the case of *S. capsicastrum* and *S. pseudocapsium*, after flowering (in late winter), prune back and keep dry for a month, then place outdoors before bringing them back inside in late summer. *S. crispum* is best planted permanently in a conservatory.

In all cases propagate by stem cuttings. Overwatering causes the leaves to fall; insufficient light and warm dry air will cause the berries to drop.

Soldanella

Primulaceae

This genus consists of ten alpine plants, native to the mountains of Europe.

S. alpina (zone 4), a herbaceous perennial, is 2–4 in (5–10 cm) high. The erect flower stems rise up above thick, round basal leaves, bearing 2–5 lavender-coloured, fringed, bell shaped flowers in early spring.

This is a plant for an alpine house or a sink garden.

Cultivation. Plant in well drained soil in a sunny position, either at the end of spring or in early autumn.

Place fine gravel around the base of the plant to help keep the leaves dry and retain soil moisture. Where winters are damp protect flower buds with a sheet of glass; slugs can be a problem.

Propagate by dividing the roots in early summer and replanting either directly into the open ground or in a pot. Alternatively propagate by seed.

Solidago

Golden rod, *Compositae*

This genus consists of about 100 species of hardy herbaceous perennials, most native to North America.

S. virgaurea (zone 5), common golden-rod, is a herbaceous perennial, very hardy. It grows 1–3½ ft (30 cm–1 m) high and 1–2 ft (30–60 cm) across. The plant has dense, narrow, mid-green foliage, with long plumes of small yellow flowers from early summer to early autumn. Numerous garden hybrids are available varying in size and shade of yellow flowers.

Golden rod is normally grown in herbaceous borders or wild gardens; smaller hybrids can be grown in rock gardens. They associate well with asters. They make a good cut flower. Taller species can be invasive, both by means of their spreading roots and by self seeding.

Cultivation. Plant in ordinary, well drained, fairly fertile soil. Choose a sunny or slightly shaded position, and plant in autumn or spring, 1–2 ft (30–60 cm) apart, depending on the cultivar.

Manure in spring, stake the taller varieties and cut the plant down to its base in autumn.

Propagate by dividing the root clumps every three or four years in autumn or spring, otherwise the plants deteriorate.

Mildew may affect the leaves.

Sophora

Leguminosae

This genus consists of about 50 deciduous and evergreen, hardy and tender trees and shrubs found wild on most continents.

S. japonica (zone 7), pagoda tree, from China, is a deciduous tree rarely exceeding 66 ft (20 m) in height. It has a broad, rounded crown and a corrugated bark. The leaves are pinnate, and are easily confused with the false acacia, but the 9–15 leaflets are smaller. When mature, the tree bears pea-like, creamy-white flowers in large terminal panicles in late summer, but needs hot, dry summers to flower profusely. The fruit is a pod, not always produced in cultivation. This tree can be grown on its own or alternatively in avenues.

Cultivation. This is a very hardy, fast-growing tree. It is easy to grow in any well drained, fertile soil. Plant it either in autumn or spring, in full sun and shelter. In cold areas, grow in a greenhouse.

Propagate from seed in spring.

Sorbaria

False spiraea, *Rosaceae*

This genus consists of about seven species of hardy, fast-growing shrubs from Asia, with elegant, alternate, deciduous leaves divided into numerous leaflets. The plant bears large panicles of small, white flowers, and has a slightly drooping habit.

S. aitchisonii (zone 6), from West Asia is up to 10 ft (3 m) high. The young stems are red and the green foliage appears very early in season. The large panicles, 20 in (50 cm) long, of white flowers are reminiscent of meadow-sweet, and flower in mid summer.

S. sorbifolia (zone 6), from most parts of Asia, is smaller, with a more erect, suckering habit. Its leaves are similar to those of mountain ash, and it has erect panicles of white flowers in mid summer.

The plants can be grown in mixed borders or near water.

Cultivation. Plant in ordinary, slightly damp soil in a sunny position, in mid to late autumn, or in early spring.

To retain compact growth, prune back the shoots that have flowered to the old wood.

Propagate by suckers in winter or by seed.

Sorbus

Rosaceae

This genus comprises nearly 100 species of mostly hardy European and Asian trees and shrubs, with deciduous leaves, entire in the case of the section Aria and pinnate in the Aucuparia section. Large numbers of decorative white flowers grow in corymbs from late spring to early summer. The fruits are small but usually brightly coloured and fleshy, and very attractive to birds. It is for these, and the foliage, which often colours beautifully in autumn, that Sorbus species and cultivars are grown.

S. aria (Aria section) whitebeam (zone 6), is a European native. It is a slow-growing, round-headed tree, ultimately reaching 60 ft (18 m) or more. Its large leaves with silvery undersides are particularly attractive in bud, and turn gold in autumn, when the scarlet fruits are at their best. It tolerates shallow, chalky soil, industrial pollution and maritime conditions.

S. aucuparia (Aucuparia section) – zone 5 – rowan or mountain ash, is a European tree, smaller than the whitebeam. It has attractive pinnate leaves, richly coloured in autumn, and large numbers of red fruit, much sought after by birds. It is fast growing, and highly pollution-resistant but will not succeed on chalky soils. There are several cultivars, such as 'Fastigiata' and 'Sheerwater Seedling' which have an erect habit.

S. domestica (Aucuparia section) – zone 5 – service tree, from southern Europe, grows to 33 ft (10 cm) or more high. It has open, spreading branches and leaflets are toothed in the upper part only. The tree is sometimes grown for its round or pear-shaped fruits which turn brown as they ripen and are edible when exposed to frost, or bletted.

Sorbus species are used as street or garden trees and can also be made into hedges.

Cultivation. These are very hardy trees, and will live in most well drained, fertile soils. The species in the Aucuparia section prefer a peaty soil, and are generally short-lived on limy or very dry soil. Plant in autumn or spring, in sun or light shade.

Propagate from seed in spring; cultivars are budded or grafted on to the parent or on seedling stock of common rowan.

Spartium

Spanish broom, *Leguminosae*

This genus consists of a single hardy deciduous shrub, native to southern Europe, closely related to *Cytisus* and *Genista*. Its green, erect, gaunt branches give the shrub an evergreen appearance.

S. junceum (zone 7), grows 6½–10 ft (2–3 m) high, somewhat less across. It has very thin, rush-like branches with sparse, tiny leaves, and bears terminal racemes of yellow, pea-like, highly scented flowers for much of the summer and early autumn.

It is very resistant to sea spray and is excellent for maritime positions and for hedging.

Cultivation. Plant pot-grown plants in a sunny position in dry or well drained soil; it thrives in both sandy and alkaline soils. Take care to retain the rootball when transplanting, as a Spanish broom resents root disturbance. To form hedges especially on dry banks, plant 20 in (50 cm) apart, in autumn or spring. Cut back lightly after flowering down to the base of the flowering shoots, but never into old wood.

Propagate from seed germinated in seed trays in autumn, and pricked out into pots the following spring.

Spinacia

Spinach, *Chenopodiaceae*

This genus consists of three annuals. Spinach, *S. oleracea* (zone 6), was probably introduced to Europe during the Crusades from the Middle East. It is cultivated for its edible, succulent leaves which are at least 8 in (20 cm) long. Round-seeded varieties tend to be used for summer planting; prickly-seeded varieties are hardier, and used for winter crops.

Cultivation. Spinach likes a deep, rich, moist soil. Incorporate plenty of well rotted organic manure when preparing the ground. Summer crops benefit from shade. You can sow spinach as a catch crop between peas, cabbage, leeks and beans as they quickly run to seed in full sun. The winter varieties need a warm, sheltered spot. Sow summer varieties every few weeks from spring to mid summer, in rows 12 in (30 cm) apart; thin plants to 9 in (22 cm). Sow winter varieties, which are less rigorous, from mid to late summer and thin to 4 in (10 cm) apart. Before sowing, apply a general fertiliser, then sow seed thinly in 1 in (2.5 cm) deep drills, rake over soil, firm well and water.

During dry spells water copiously; protect winter crops with cloches or straw in cold weather, when harvesting, pick continually, the outer leaves first, to encourage new growth. Avoid picking more than half the leaves on any one plant at any one time. Proper soil preparation, plenty of watering and frequent hoeing help prevent bolting. Other problems are downy mildew, causing yellow blotches on the upper leaf surface, and grey mould on the lower surface; proper thinning and good drainage discourage this disease. Slugs and aphids may also be troublesome. In regions with very hot, dry summers, grow New Zealand spinach (*Tetragonia expansa*) or perpetual spinach (*Beta vulgaris*).

Spiraea

Rosaceae

This genus consists of about 70 species of deciduous shrubs, with a graceful habit and large, showy inflorescences of small flowers. They are native to North America, Asia and Europe. Those listed here are hardy, and grown for their profuse flowers and pleasing foliage.

S. 'Arguta' (zone 5), bridal wreath, or foam of May, is a hybrid of uncertain origin, growing about 8 ft (2.4 m) high and wide. It has narrow leaves, and large numbers of white flowers, all along the branches, in mid to late spring.

S. 'Bumalda' (zone 6), may reach a height of 3 ft (90 cm). It has narrow toothed leaves, reddish when young, and often variegated pink and cream. The bright-pink flowers in flattened corymbs appear continuously from midsummer to early autumn. The cultivar 'Anthony Waterer' is an excellent dwarf shrub with crimson flowers.

S. cantoniensis (zone 6), from China, has a slender habit, and grows to 6½ ft (2 m) in height with wide-spreading, arching, branches. The leaves, sometimes semi-evergreen, are light green underneath, and rhomboidal. White flowers appear in early summer.

S. japonica (zone 6), Japanese spiraea, from Japan, is an erect shrub growing about 5 ft (1.5 m) high. It has lanceolate or oval leaves. The pink flowers appear in large flat terminal corymbs in mid summer. There are numerous garden cultivars, including dwarf forms, forms with crimson flowers and especially good autumn leaf colour.

S. nipponica (zone 6), from Japan, has oval leaves and may reach 8 ft (2.4 m). The white flowers appear at the ends of the arching shoots in early summer. This is one of the showiest plants flowering at this time of year.

S. salicifolia (zone 5), from Europe and Asia grows 7 ft (2 m) high, and has oval or oblong bright-green leaves. The light-pink flowers grow in erect cylindrical panicles from early to mid summer. It is a suckering shrub and may spread quickly, forming dense thickets and becoming invasive in small gardens. It is good for stabilising poor soil.

S. thunbergii (zone 6), from China, is a dense, twiggy shrub 3–5 ft (90–150 cm) high, with small clusters of white flowers growing along the branches before the leaves appear, in early to mid spring. This is the earliest to flower and also has an attractive autumn colour.

Grow species in mixed or shrub borders, or as informal hedging. Dwarf forms can be grown in rock gardens, and large species make handsome specimen shrubs.

Cultivation. This plant likes sunshine, and ordinary, well drained soil with an occasional top dressing of manure. Prune the early-flowering shrubs after flowering, removing weak and old shoots. Cut back the late flowering cultivars, even to the old wood, during the winter.

Propagate the suckering species by division, alternatively by late summer cuttings, or by seeds.

Sprekelia

Jacobean lily, *Amaryllidaceae*

This genus consists of a single species of slightly hardy bulb, native to Mexico and Guatemala, and related to *Hippeastrum*.

Sprekelia formosissima

S. formosissima (zone 10), Jacobean or Aztec lily, is about 1 ft (30 cm) high, with striking, dark-red flowers in the shape of a cross or heraldic lily, on a reddish stem which bears one or two flowers. The leaves appear after flowering is over.

Cultivation. Grow in a pot or in a sheltered place in a rock garden. Plant in spring, with the neck of the bulb only slightly buried. The plant flowers in summer, but sometimes the bulb flowers a month after the initial planting. Over-winter pot-grown bulbs in a dry, cool place with a minimum temperature of 45°F (7°C). Plants growing outside in mild climates do not need watering during summer, once the leaves start to die down. Propagate these plants by separating offsets and planting in an open, well drained compost.

Stachys

Betony, *Labiatae*

This genus consists of about 300 species of hardy and tender herbaceous plants and shrubs, many of which are from Europe, Asia and Australia.

S. Olympica (S. lanata) – zone 7 – lamb's tongue or ear, is a perennial grown for its leaves which have a woolly appearance because of their dense covering of hairs. In mid summer spikes 12–18 in (30–45 cm) high of purple flowers appear on the plants. It is very useful for ground cover.

S. sieboldii (S. affinis) – zone 9 – Chinese or Japanese artichoke, is native to Japan, Korea and northern China. It is a perennial vegetable with edible, knobbly, yellow tubers 4–6 in (10–15 cm) long, composed of several segments. They are crisp, with a nutty flavour. These produce square stems about 16 in (40 cm) high with rough oval, dull green leaves.

Cultivation. This perennial vegetable is easy to grow. It can be left in the same place for several years, or replanted every three years. Plant in mid spring, in light, well drained soil, placing groups of three or four rhizomes 4 in (10 cm) deep and 16 in (40 cm) apart.

Water only in dry weather. Hoe the surface carefully to avoid damaging the rhizomes. Mulch with straw when the cold weather starts. Dig up throughout the winter as required. Propagate by dividing the rhizomes in early to mid winter, and stratify them in damp sand, then plant out in mid spring.

Stephanotis
Asclepiadaceae

A genus of about five species of climbing woody plants from tropical parts of Asia. One species is widely cultivated for its white waxy flowers which are extremely fragrant. It is not grown outdoors except in areas with a constantly warm and fairly humid climate.
S. floribunda (zone 10+), Madagascar jasmine, native to Madagascar, is a woody plant climbing to 15 ft (4.5 m) or more by twining around a support. The dark glossy green leaves are ovate and opposite. The tubular flowers, about 1½ in (4 cm) long, with five flaring lobes, are formed in clusters along the branches from late spring to autumn.
Cultivation. Provide this plant with bright conditions but not direct sunlight, and when in flower, avoid moving and keep the surrounding temperature constant. In winter this should not drop below 55°F (13°C). Keep the compost moist at all times and feed in the growing season. Repot and prune in spring every two or three years. Propagate by stem cuttings in summer, with bottom heat. It is prone to attack by scale insect; treat with systemic insecticides if necessary.

Sternbergia
Amaryllidaceae

This genus consists of about seven hardy bulbous plants with bulbs from the Mediterranean region and southwest Asia.
S. lutea (zone 8), grows 8 in (20 cm) high. It has long, narrow, strap-shaped leaves, lasting from

Sternbergia lutea

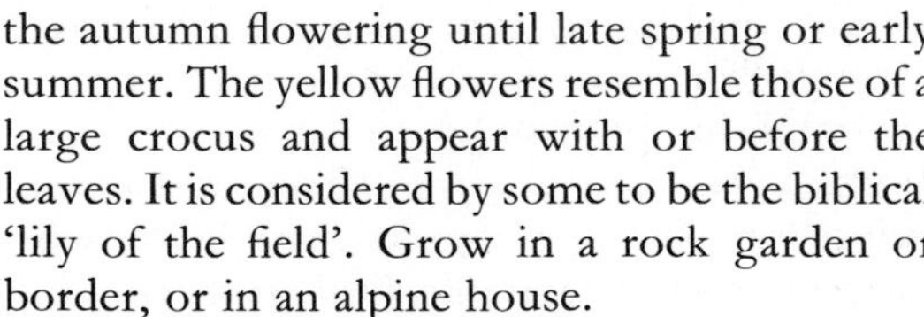

the autumn flowering until late spring or early summer. The yellow flowers resemble those of a large crocus and appear with or before the leaves. It is considered by some to be the biblical 'lily of the field'. Grow in a rock garden or border, or in an alpine house.
Cultivation. Plant in mid to late summer, 4–6 in (10–15 cm) deep. Provide a sunny position and well drained soil. Do not disturb the plants until they become overcrowded and flowering suffers. When this happens, lift, divide and replant immediately.

Propagate by division.

Stipa
Gramineae

This genus consists of about 150 species of tropical or temperate grasses. The name 'stipa' comes from the Greek word *stupe* or 'tow', referring to the use of *S. tenacissima* alfa, or esparto, for making ropes, paper and mats, especially in North Africa. There are several species used in gardens for their highly decorative stems and straw-coloured inflorescences, also useful in dried-flower arrangements.
S. pennata (zone 7), feather grass, from Europe and Asia, grows 20 in (50 cm) high, whereas *S. gigantea* (zone 9), from Spain, may grow 6½ ft (2 m) or more high and resembles a giant oat grass, with purplish inflorescences, eventually turning yellow. It doesn't need staking, and makes weed-proof ground cover.
Cultivation. Plant in dry soil and a warm and sunny position. Sow in spring, to flower one or two years later, or propagate by division. Feather grass is a short-lived perennial, but easily renewed from division or seed.

Stokesia
Compositae

This genus consists of a single species of herbaceous perennial, native to the United States.
S. laevis (zone 6), cornflower aster, grows 12–16 in (30–40 cm) high and 1 ft (30 cm) across. It has glossy lanceolate leaves and blue, cornflower-like flowers, 4 in (10 cm) in diameter, with notched florets. These appear in late summer and autumn. Cultivars are available with white, pink or purple flowers. Plant in the

front of the border, in association with asters or *Achillea* 'Moonshine'.
Cultivation. Plant in light, well drained soil, in sun or light shade in spring. Cut the stems back in late autumn.

Propagate by seed or by dividing the clumps every two or three years, in the spring, and planting out the sections immediately.

Stranvaesia (Photinia)
Rosaceae

This genus consists of about five species of cotoneaster-like shrubs and small flowering trees, all hardy and native to eastern Asia. The evergreen leaves are leathery, oblong and lanceolate, and the white flowers are followed by red fruits, which are not attractive to birds.
S. davidiana (zone 6), is the only species frequently cultivated. It grows about 30 ft (9 m) high and across with erect branches bearing clusters of white flowers in early summer. The pendent clusters of red fruits are carried all along the branches. Use as tall screens, hedging, or in shrub borders. There are prostrate and yellow-berried cultivars.
Cultivation. Grow in good, well drained loam or peaty soil in a sunny position. They tolerate atmospheric pollution.

Collect the ripe seeds in autumn, and sow in seed trays in a frame or in a cold greenhouse. Alternatively, take cuttings from semi-ripe shoots in summer, and root in a mixture of equal parts sand and peat.

Symphoricarpos
Caprifoliaceae

This genus comprises about 17 species of hardy deciduous shrubs bearing ornamental berries. They are native to North America and China, and often used for hedges. They are suckering and thicket forming, and their flowers are not particularly striking, but the fleshy fruits are attractive and useful for flower arranging. In the garden they are largely untouched by birds.
S. albus (zone 5), snowberry, grows to about 4 ft (1.2 m) high. It has oval, opposite leaves and the pale-pink, bell-shaped flowers grow continuously throughout the summer. They produce white berries which last until late winter.
S. orbiculatus (zone 5), coralberry or Indian currant, is usually erect and much branched, less than 6½ ft (2 m) in height. Its oval or round leaves are greenish blue on the undersides. The flowers are whitish and appear throughout the summer, followed by clusters of small purplish-pink fruits which last through the winter. The hybrid 'Hancock' is prostrate, and makes excellent ground cover. Grow in a shrub or mixed border, or as hedging.
Cultivation. The snowberry grows in any soil and in sun or semi-shade. If it is used for hedging, plant 16 in (40 cm) apart, from the end of autumn to spring, trimming it in winter if berries are required. When planting, in early spring, prune to 12–16 in (30–40 cm) above ground. Then prune again, using shears, two or three times a year to keep it even.

Propagate by seed, division or suckers.

Symphytum
Comfrey, *Boraginaceae*

This genus consists of about 35 species of herbaceous plants found wild in Europe and western Asia.
S. officinale (zone 5), is a perennial, native to western, central and southern France. It has winged, branching stems 16–42 in (40 cm–1 m) high. The hairy, coarse leaves are broadly oval to lanceolate. The roots are fleshy and mucilaginous and the young shoots are sometimes eaten. Tubular white, pink and violet flowers appear in early summer.

They are quick spreading plants, making dense ground cover in wild gardens.
Cultivation. Grow in heavy, cool, well drained soil, preferably with a high content of organic matter. Divide the roots in autumn or spring, and plant 2 ft (60 cm) apart. Alternatively, sow seeds outdoors in early to mid spring, in rows 24–28 in (60–70 cm) apart, and thin out to 2 ft (60 cm). This plant can be invasive.
Uses. The young leaves can be eaten raw in salad, or cooked in soup. It is also grown as a green manure.

Syringa
Lilac, *Oleaceae*

This genus includes some 25 species of deciduous shrubs and small trees, native to Europe and

Asia. They are generally vigorous and suckering, with oval, rather uninteresting leaves. The flowers are scented, appearing in terminal panicles on the previous year's wood in spring, and give this popular plant its attraction.

S. × *chinensis* (zone 6), Rouen or Chinese lilac, a hybrid, grows up to 10 ft (3 m) high. It has a dense, graceful habit and attractive, arching panicles of lilac-coloured flowers in late spring.

S. × *josiflexa* 'Bellicent' (zone 6), is one of the finest hybrids, 10 ft (3 m) high, with enormous panicles of clear-pink, scented flowers.

S. laciniata (zone 6), cut-leaved lilac, is a graceful, open shrub 8 ft (2.4 m) high, with deeply cut, leaves and small panicles of lilac-pink flowers. It is rare in cultivation.

S. microphylla (zone 6), is a smaller, spreading plant, 5 ft (1.5 m) high, with round leaves and panicles of red buds, opening to pink highly scented flowers in late spring. It may flower again in autumn. The form 'Superba' is especially free-flowering.

S. × *prestoniae* (zone 5), sometimes referred to as the Canadian hybrids, includes a large number of very hardy, late-flowering hybrids, generally 10 ft (3 m) high, raised in Canada, with flowers ranging from pink to purple. The flowers are borne on the current year's shoots.

S. reflexa (zone 6), 12 ft (3.5 m) high, has drooping panicles of flowers, bright pink outside and whitish inside, and attractive, dark-green leaves. It is very free-flowering, and one of the best species to grow.

S. velutina (zone 6), Korean lilac, grows 6 ft (2 m) high. It has a dense, compact habit; dark-green leaves, paler below; and pale, lilac-pink flowers. It is suitable for a small garden.

Numerous hybrids and cultivars of the garden lilac (*S. vulgaris*) are also available with single or double scented flowers in white, blue pink or purple shades.

Cultivation. Lilacs grow in any soil, especially limy and clay soils. They take one or two years to settle in, and flower best in full sun.

Remove old flowering wood after flowering, to encourage the growth of new vigorous shoots. Extra vigorous shoots can be pinched out in summer.

Propagate from cuttings of semi-ripe wood placed in a warm greenhouse in a mixture of sand and peat; or from layering. All the species can be sown outdoors in early to mid spring. Cultivars can be grafted on to the rootstock of *S. vulgaris*.

Tagetes

African marigold, French marigold, *Compositae*

This genus consists of about 50 annuals and herbaceous perennials from America and Africa. They produce long-lasting flowers from early summer until the first frosts, and have aromatic foliage.

T. erecta (zone 5), African marigold, grows up to 3 ft (1 m) high and has very large flowers. There are dwarf cultivars available. African marigolds have erect growth habits, but pinching out results in more branched plants. The species has single flowers, but garden varieties are double, usually shaped like carnations or chrysanthemums.

Tagetes patula cultivar

T. patula (zone 5), French marigold, reaches about 1 ft (30 cm) and has smaller flowers, and a more branching habit of growth. There are cultivars with single, semi-double and double flowers.

Seeds are available of both species in a wide range of colours from near white to yellow, orange or mahogany brown. French marigolds are often bicoloured. Both African and French marigolds are commonly used for formal or informal bedding, window boxes and tubs; smaller forms make good edging..

Cultivation. Sow from late winter to mid-spring in a warm greenhouse. Cover the seeds lightly. Prick out a month later, and gradually harden off the young plants before planting out in late spring, 1 ft (30 cm) apart, and 20 in (50 cm) apart for the very large African marigolds. This plant lives in any well drained soil, but needs a sunny position. Dead head to ensure a long display.

These plants can be affected by foot rot, stem rot and by grey mould on the leaves.

Tamarix

Tamarisk, *Tamaricaceae*

This genus includes about 50 species of deciduous shrubs and small trees native to Europe, Africa and Asia. The slender branches are finely arching and slightly drooping, and are covered in a multitude of small flowers, sometimes before the tiny leaves have fully developed. They are grown for their plumes of pink flowers, graceful habit of growth and juniper-like foliage.

T. chinensis (T. juniperina) – zone 6 – from China is 6½–10 ft (2–3 m) high. It has very thin, arching branches covered with dense green leaves. The flowers are pink when mature, appearing in late spring on the previous year's branches.

T. ramosissima (T. pentandra) – zone 6 – from the Middle East, is 10–17 ft (3–5 m) high. It has slightly reddish branches with very attractive bluish-green leaves. The flowers appear in long panicles on slender shoots in late summer and early autumn, with the foliage. 'Rubra' is a beautiful, dark pink-flowered cultivar.

T. tetrandra (zone 6), from eastern Europe and the Middle East, has bright green leaves on dark stems and pale pink flowers which grow on the previous year's shoots in late spring and early summer.

Cultivation. Tamarisks like most types of soil, except very limy ones. They also like a sunny position. They are lenient of wind and very resistant to spray if grown near the sea, where they are sometimes used as hedging. To prevent leggy growth, prune species that flower on the current year's wood in late winter; prune those that flower on the previous year's wood immediately after flowering.

Propagate from hardwood or semi-ripe cuttings 18 in (45 cm) long by placing them in sandy soil under a frame or in a seed bed either in early to mid spring or in late autumn.

Taxodium

Cypress, *Taxodiaceae*

This genus consists of two deciduous conifers from North America. They eventually become very tall but are slow growing.

T. distichum (zone 4), bald or swamp cypress, is a deciduous conifer growing to a maximum of 150 ft (45 m), less when cultivated. When young, it has a conical habit which becomes more rounded with age. The bark is thin, pale reddish and fibrous. The needles are short, thin and pectinate, borne on short branchlets which are also deciduous. The leaves are bright green, turning rich brown before falling in autumn. The cone grows on the ends of the branches, and is ovoid, purple when young and 1¼ in (3 cm) long. It resembles that of the cypress, but breaks up when it ripens.

This tree is used in parks and large gardens or as a specimen tree, especially beside water. It is the most suitable conifer for wet soil, where mature trees eventually develop knee-like growths on their roots, projecting above the water or ground.

Cultivation. Plant in spring, in any soil but a chalky one. The bald cypress is very hardy, but it needs hot summers and grows faster in permanently wet soil.

Propagate by seed in spring, having first allowed the seeds to swell by soaking them in water, alternatively take cuttings.

Taxus

Yew, *Taxaceae*

Yews are evergreen conifers native to Europe, Asia and North America. There are about nine similar species of slow growing, long-lived trees.

T. baccata (zone 5), common or English yew, grows 50 ft (15 m) high, and eventually makes a wide-spreading tree. The surface of the trunk is corrugated, with reddish-brown bark. The dark-green needles are similar to those of the fir. The male and female flowers are tiny catkins, appearing in autumn on separate trees. Female trees do not bear cones, but have visible hard seeds surrounded by a red fleshy covering, or aril. Both seeds and leaves are poisonous.

Yew can be grown as a specimen tree, as hedging or screening, or, because it is so tolerant of pruning, as topiary. There are many cultivars, including the upright Irish yew 'Fastigiata', the golden yew 'Aurea', and the dwarf prostrate 'Repandens'.

Cultivation. The yew is very hardy. It prefers a well drained rich, deep soil but enjoys chalk and rocky soils, in sun or shade. Once established, yews tolerate wind and drought.

Propagate from seeds or from cuttings placed under glass at the end of summer. Varieties are often grafted.

Teucrium

Germander, *Labiatae*

This genus consists of about 100 species of herbaceous, hardy or half-hardy perennials and shrubs from many parts of the world.

T. chamaedrys (zone 7), wall germander, from Europe and Asia, is a creeping sub-shrub 6–12 in (15–30 cm) high, and 12–16 in (30–40 cm) across. It is hardy, with dark-green, oval leaves, grey on the undersides and aromatic when bruised. The two-lipped flowers are pale pink, spotted red and white, and borne in spikes on one side of the stems from early summer to early autumn.

T. fruticans (zone 8), shrubby germander, is a loose, lax shrub, to 5 ft (1.5 m) high. It has bright-green leaves, white-felted underneath, and white-felted shoots. Lipped lavender-blue flowers appear in the leaf axils in the summer months.

T. pyrenaicum (zone 4), is native to the Pyrénées, 4–6 in (10–15 cm) high and 12–16 in (30–40 cm) across. This is a hardy perennial with silvery green, scalloped-edged leaves. The small, purple-and-cream flowers are grouped in whorls, appearing throughout the summer.

These species are used for rock gardens, walls and borders.

Cultivation. Plant in spring in any fertile but well drained soil in a sunny position; they tolerate poor soils.

Propagate from lateral cuttings 3 in (8 cm) long, inserted in sand in a cold frame, in late spring or summer. Pot up in light growing medium once rooted.

Thalictrum

Meadow rue, *Ranunculaceae*

This genus consists of about 80 mostly hardy herbaceous perennials, many from northern temperate regions.

T. aquilegifolium (zone 5), is native to Europe and northern Asia, and is both stately and dainty. It grows 28–43 in (70 cm–1.1 m) high, and 12–20 in (30–50 cm) across. The leaves are similar to those of maidenhair fern and the plant bears fluffy, tiny, pale-lilac or white flowers, grouped in large, branching panicles 6–8 in (15–20 cm) long, between late spring and mid summer. There are shorter cultivars, and ones with deep-violet flowers. All of them have attractive seed heads.

T. delavayi (zone 6), is native to China, and grows 4–5 ft (1.2–1.5 m) high and 20–24 in (40–60 cm) across. This is one of the most elegant species of the genus, with finely divided, bright-green foliage with a bluish tinge. The mauve flowers are small but conspicuous, with yellow anthers and grouped in large airy panicles. It flowers throughout the summer. There are both double-flowered and white-flowered forms.

T. kiusianum (zone 7), from Japan, grows 4–8 in (10–20 cm) high and wide. It forms a small clump of smooth leaves divided into lobed leaflets. Purple flowers grow in corymbs in mid to late spring.

The larger species are useful for lightening the appearance of a border, grown with large-leaved plants. The smaller ones are suitable for a shaded rock garden. All species are good for cutting.

Cultivation. Plant in a rich, moist, well drained soil with plenty of humus, in a semi-shaded position, in early spring. Larger species need staking.

To propagate, sow in a seed tray in early spring, and place in a cold frame. Prick out into pots and plant out the following spring.

Thermopsis

Thermopsis, *Leguminosae*

This genus consists of about 30 hardy herbaceous perennials from Asia and North America, similar to lupins.

T. montana (T. fabacea) – zone 7 – from western North America, is 3½ ft (1 m) high and wide. This plant produces underground creeping shoots which in turn produce stems, bearing spikes 6–8 in (15–20 cm) long, covered in lemon-yellow flowers in early summer. The leaves are trifoliate and bluish-green. This species can be invasive.

Grow in a herbaceous border, with *Delphinium, Lupinus, Gillena* and similar plants.

Cultivation. Plant in rich, well drained soil in sun between autumn and spring. In common with lupins, these plants do not like lime. Cut the stems back after flowering; a second crop of flowers may appear in autumn.

Propagate from seed, or by dividing and replanting the sections straight away, in early to mid spring.

Thuja

Arbor-vitae, *Cupressaceae*

This genus consists of about six, mostly slow-growing, small conifers from Asia and North America with flattened sprays of evergreen, aromatic, scale-like leaves. The flowers, in tiny catkins, appear at the ends of the branches. The fruit is a very small, upright cone made up of oblong, overlapping scales, joined to the base.

T. orientalis (Biota orientalis) – zone 6–7 – Oriental thuja, is native to China, and forms a compact, hardy, columnar or conical shrub or small tree to about 30 ft (9 m) high. It has striking vertical branches and branchlets, and small cones with fleshy scales, each with a recurved tip. It is less aromatic than other thujas, and may turn brown in winter, as it is sensitive to the cold. It needs well drained soil. There are several dwarf forms.

T. plicata (T. gigantea, T. lobbii) (zone 4), western red cedar, or giant arbor-vitae, is native to western North America, and can grow up to 170 ft (59 m) or more, though it is smaller when cultivated. The hardy tree retains its conical habit as it grows older. It is fast growing, with dense, very decorative, dark-green foliage and resists cold well, though it may be affected by drought. It is tolerant of chalk soils and some shade. Many cultivars are available.

These species can be made into hedges and large windbreaks and are also used on their own. Dwarf forms can be planted in rock gardens.

Cultivation. Plant in spring in a rich, cool soil and a sunny, sheltered location.

For hedging, plant thujas 2 ft (60 cm) apart, and prune them frequently during the first few years in late summer, early autumn or spring. If necessary, for the larger cultivars remove alternate trees after a few years. Water frequently during the first few summers.

Propagate species by sowing seeds in spring in nursery beds outdoors or in pots indoors. Alternatively take semi-ripe cuttings and place these in a frame in late summer, inserting them in a sandy compost.

Thymus

Thyme, *Labiatae*

This genus comprises around 400 species of hardy sub-shrubs or herbaceous perennial plants. Thyme is well known for its aromatic qualities as a seasoning but the numerous cultivars, with their variation in flowers and very fine leaves, make it an excellent ornamental plant. The flowers appear in early summer, and are attractive to bees.

T. × citriodorus (zone 6), lemon thyme, is 10–12 in (25–30 cm) high and 12–16 in (30–40 cm) across. It has small but broad, lemon-scented leaves and pale lilac flowers in clusters. There are gold- and silver-variegated forms.

T. pannonicus (T. lanuginosus) – zone 7 – has woolly, silvery foliage and pink flowers.

T. serpyllum (zone 6), wild thyme, grows 2¼ in (6 cm) high. It is a creeping species with a spreading habit, forming sheets of colour when in flower. 'Albus' has white flowers, 'Coccineus' has red flowers.

T. vulgaris (zone 7), common thyme, grows wild in Mediterranean climates, and is 8–12 in (20–30 cm) high. It has much branched, woody, often twisted stems and grey, hairy, narrow and recurved leaves. The plant usually has pink flowers. 'Aureus' is a golden leaved form.

Cultivation. This is an excellent rock garden plant, which likes a warm, dry, well drained soil in full sun. Thymes can also be grown in herb or sink gardens, in cracks between paving, or as low edging. In the kitchen, thyme is part of the traditional bouquet garni, and is used to flavour fish, meat and stews. Trim lightly in late summer, after flowering, to keep it compact and to discourage self seeding.

Propagate by dividing the root clumps in spring or late summer for the carpeting type, or taking 2 in (5 cm) heel cuttings in late spring, placing these in a very sandy mixture and repotting the following year. Alternatively sow seed in spring. Common thyme needs replacing every 3–4 years, once it starts to get leggy.

Tigridia

Iridaceae

This genus consists of nearly 30 tender bulbous plants, native to Mexico, Guatemala and South America, where they are found in mountainous areas.

T. pavonia (zone 9–10), peacock flower, tiger flower from Mexico, is 12–16 in (30–40 cm) high. The flowers, up to 6 in (15 cm) across, are an elegant, triangular cup shape, and the erect leaves are similar to *Gladiolus*. The hybrids available for sale are of a wide variety of colours, including white, yellows, reds, pinks, purples and oranges. The centre of the flower is usually spotted or striped. The flowers are short lived, but open continuously from early summer to early autumn.

Cultivation. Grow in a light sandy soil in a warm, sunny spot. Plant 3 in (7.5 cm) deep in groups when the danger of frost is gone, in bedding schemes or borders. Water regularly in dry weather. When the leaves die down, lift, dry and store the bulbs in peat in a frost-free place before replanting in spring. In frost-free gardens, peacock flowers can be left *in situ* for two to three years before being lifted and divided.

The plant propagates readily from offsets or from seed.

Tigridia pavonia

Tilia

Lime, linden, *Tiliaceae*

This genus consists of about 45 large, fast-growing, deciduous trees from the Northern Hemisphere. They have a rounded habit of growth when young. The leaves are usually cordate, often with silvery undersides, and the scented flowers are yellowish, growing in a pendent cyme accompanied by a leafy bract. The flowers are attractive to bees. The fruits are rounded capsules containing one or two seeds.

T. americana (zone 5), American lime, grows up to 130 ft (40 m). Leaves are dark matt green above and light bright green beneath. Popular in USA but little grown in UK.

T. cordata (T. parviflora) – zone 5 – small-leaved lime, is a European native, 80 ft (25 m) high, with a rounded habit and pale bark. The leaves are heart-shaped, with white undersides. It flowers later in the year than the common and broad-leaved limes.

T. × *europea (T.* × *vulgaris)* – zone 6 – common lime, probably a hybrid of *T. cordata* and *T. platyphyllos*, is a fine, robust, long-lived tree with zigzag stems and a dense, suckering habit. It eventually grows to 130 ft (40 m). The leaves are heart-shaped, toothed and glabrous above, with tufts of down on their undersides, on the axil of the veins. Its leaves drop early in autumn and it is prone to aphid attack.

T. platyphyllos (zone 5), broad-leaved lime, has a large crown and dense branches. It is native to Europe, growing wild in mountains with high precipitation, and grows up to 83 ft (25 m) or more in height. The leaves are larger than those of *T. cordata* and are green on both sides. Smaller-growing cultivars include cut-leafed red-twigged and yellow-twigged forms.

Limes are very stately shade trees, and are used as street trees, in parks and in very large gardens. They are resistant to air pollution, and are often planted in broad avenues. They are also tolerant of pruning and pollarding, and the best trees for pleaching, planted 8 ft (2.4 m) apart, topped at the desired height, and the side branches trained to intertwine. Lime flowers are useful in flower arranging.

Cultivation. Limes are very hardy trees, and grow well in deep, loamy soil which stays moist in summer. Plant from autumn to spring in sun or shade. Prune in winter.

Propagate either by seed after stratifying, or by layering; named varieties are grafted. This tree can be infested with aphids which secrete honeydew which in turn becomes covered by sooty moulds.

Tithonia

Tithonia, *Compositae*

A genus of about ten herbaceous and shrubby species from Central America, including an easy-to-grow, half-hardy annual.

T. rotundifolia (T. speciosa) – zone 6 – Mexican sunflower, grows 3 ft (1 m) or more high. It is drought resistant, with vigorous, branching stems bearing large, fairly coarse leaves and red, daisy-like flowers with orange centres from mid summer to mid autumn. The cultivar 'Torch' has larger more vivid flowers, $2\frac{3}{4}$ in (7 cm) in diameter. 'Yellow Torch' has yellow flowers, and 'Goldfinger' is a dwarf form suitable for the front of a border. The flowers last well when cut, provided the cut ends are seared.

Cultivation. Sow in a seed tray in early or midspring, or in late winter or early spring in a greenhouse. Prick out, harden off and plant out in late spring, 2 ft (60 cm) apart, in light soil and full sun. Stake if necessary.

Trachycarpus

Palmae

A genus of about six palms from subtropical Asia.

T. fortunei (zone 8–9), Chusan palm, windmill palm, is possibly native to China, and is the only palm which is almost hardy in a mild, temperate climate. Its habit is very different from the spreading tropical species. The fan-shaped fronds are $3\frac{1}{2}$–5 ft (1–1.5 m) wide, and grow at the top of a tall, single trunk covered in fibres which are the remains of the leaf bases. The palm grows 13 ft (4 m) high after about ten years of cultivation.

Cultivation. This species has the advantage of not being demanding as to the type of soil or the amount of sun or shade it receives. An occasional dressing of manure is beneficial. Avoid exposed places, as wind can shatter the leaves.

Propagate from seed, although the young seedlings take some time to grow.

Tradescantia

Commelinaceae

This genus consists of 65 species of hardy and tender perennials, including some well-known houseplants from North and South America.

T. × *andersoniana* (zone 7), spiderwort or trinity flower, are complex hybrids of *T. virginina*, from eastern North America. They grow 20–24 in (50–60 cm) high and across, with prolific ribbon-like lanceolate, pointed leaves. The numerous, short-lived flowers are $\frac{3}{4}$–1 in (2–3 cm) in diameter, ranging from purple, claret and blue to white, some bicoloured, and appear from early summer to mid autumn.

This easily grown hardy plant forms dense clumps, suited to herbaceous borders and wild gardens. It is invasive.

Cultivation. Plant between autumn and early spring in sun or light shade in any well drained moist soil. Stake if grown in exposed positions.

Propagate by division every three or four years in early to mid spring, otherwise the plant deteriorates. For the tender species, grown indoors, propagate by cuttings inserted in a light compost with some heat.

The following are a few of the tender species useful for homes and conservatories.

T. fluminensis (including *T. albiflora*), (zone 10+), wandering Jew, from South America is a trailing plant with rooting stems up to 2 ft (60 cm) long. The oval leaves are glossy green above, about $1\frac{1}{2}$ in (4 cm) long, sometimes tinged purple below. The white flowers are about $\frac{1}{2}$ in (13 mm) across. 'Variegata' has leaves with irregular stripes of creamy-white.

T. pallida (Setcreasia purpurea) (zone 10+), from Mexico, has creeping stems and slightly fleshy, narrow boat-shaped leaves about 6 in (15 cm) long, bluish-green to purple in colour. Pink flowers are borne in summer. 'Purple Heart' has dark purple stems and leaves, and darker flowers.

T. spathacea (Rhoeo discolor, R. spathacea) (zone 10+), boat lily, Moses-in-the-cradle, from

Central America, has a short stem bearing a rosette of lance-shaped fleshy leaves, to 12 in (30 cm) long, glossy green above and purple below. The white flowers are enclosed in boat-shaped, leaf-like bracts throughout the year. 'Vittata' has leaves striped longitudinally with pale yellow.

Tradescantia zebrina (Zebrina pendula) (zone 10+), silver inch plant, is from Mexico. It is a trailing evergreen plant with stems to 2 ft (60 cm) long. The leaves are bluish-green, purple tinged, with two broad silver bands above and purplish below. Pink flowers are produced intermittently throughout the year.

Cultivation. These plants prefer a bright situation with a minimum temperature of 45°F (7°C). Water and feed during the growing season, repotting when necessary. Stem cuttings, 2–3 in (5–7.5 cm) long, may be taken at almost any time.

T. spathacea is slightly different in that it needs a higher winter temperature, 55°F (13°C) or over, and a position in semi-shade. Keep compost moist, feed and spray regularly. Repot every spring and divide when necessary.

Trapa

Water chestnut, *Trapaceae*

This genus consists of about 15 aquatic plants from many parts of the world, sometimes all considered forms of one species.

T. natans (zone 9), water chestnut, is a very cosmopolitan species, living in lakes throughout the world. It is a floating plant which is weakly rooted in the mud. The submerged leaves are finely divided and the floating leaves are rhomboidal, arranged in a rosette around the central bud. In autumn, the leaves turn bright colours. The spiny fruit are edible.

Cultivation. This plant usually needs a warm house in colder climates. Sow the seeds outside in autumn and plant in a rich loamy soil. The trapa is an annual plant which sows itself readily every year provided the seed is not allowed to dry out.

Trifolium

Trefoil, clover, *Leguminosae*

This genus contains approximately 230 species of perennial or annual plants with varying degrees of hardiness. Few of these species are used in ornamental gardens.

T. repens (zone 5), white trefoil, is an important fodder plant, native to Europe. It grows 2–4 in (5–10 cm) high and 3½ ft (1 m) across. The ornamental cultivar 'Purpurascens', has three to six green-edged purple leaflets, looking rather like a purple-leaved, four-leaf clover. The globe-shaped flowers are identical to those of the white trefoil and appear from early summer to early autumn. The plant spreads rapidly by means of stolons, and is useful as ground cover in association with grasses, but potentially invasive.

Cultivation. Plant in well drained soil in sun or light shade. Increase by seed or by division: dig up the rooted stolons and replant in their final positions.

Trollius

Globe flower, *Ranunculaceae*

This genus includes some 30 species of hardy herbaceous perennials from northern temperate regions.

T. europaeus (zone 5), common globe flower, grows 20–32 in (50–80 cm) high and 12–20 in (30–50 cm) across. The leaves are palmate, strongly indented and toothed and form a basal clump. The large globular orange-yellow, flowers appear in early to mid summer. The form 'Superbus' has lemon-yellow flowers.

The globe flower makes an excellent cut flower and can be grown in a herbaceous border or near a pond. All parts are poisonous.

Cultivation. Plant in a deep, humus-rich moist or even marshy soil, in sun or light shade, in early autumn, 12 in (30 cm) apart. Water copiously in dry weather. Cut off the stems once the flowers have died to encourage further flowering. Cut down in autumn. In spring, mulch with peat or well rotted manure.

Propagate in autumn or spring by dividing the fibrous roots or by sowing seed, in a cold frame; it might not germinate until the second year after sowing.

Tropaeolum

Tropaeolaceae

This genus contains 80 species of annual or short-lived herbaceous perennial, often climbing, plants from Central and South America. Many are easy to grow as hardy annuals.

T. majus (zone 5), garden nasturtium, can grow to a length of more than 8½ ft (2.5 m) but there are dwarf and semi-dwarf forms 6–18 in (15–45 cm) high. There are single, semi-double and double flowered forms, in mixed and single colours. There is also a variegated-leaved form. The climbing or creeping stems bear distinctive round bluish-green leaves which have a peppery taste, and can be used in salads. The spurred, funnel-shaped flowers are yellow, orange or red, and appear from early summer to early autumn.

T. peregrinum (T. canariense) (zone 5), canary creeper, probably from South America, can reach more than 10 ft (3 m) in height. A short-lived perennial, it is usually grown as an annual. The stems are fast-growing and bear five-lobed leaves. The flowers have yellow, fringed petals and cover the plant from early summer to mid autumn.

Nasturtiums can be used for edging, bedding, in hanging baskets or window boxes, or to provide a covering for walls or dry banks. Dwarf forms are good in rock gardens. They can also be used to cover trellises, even in a partly shaded position. Nasturtiums are long-lasting when cut.

Cultivation. Sow from early spring onwards under a frame or in pots of peat, two seeds per pot. Repot, harden the young plants and plant out in late spring. Alternatively in late spring, sow the seeds *in situ*. Plant climbing cultivars 20 in (50 cm) apart and dwarf varieties 12 in (30 cm) apart. Provide twiggy support for climbers. For garden nasturtiums, avoid soils which are too fertile, or the leaves will develop to the detriment of flowers. The canary creeper needs soil of average fertility. The plant can be attacked by aphids, blackfly, cabbage white butterfly and by spotted wilt.

Tulipa

Tulip, *Liliaceae*

This genus comprises approximately 100 species of hardy bulbs, native to Europe, North Africa and Asia.

Garden cultivars are usually listed in catalogues according to when they flower, ranging from early to late spring; the shapes of their flowers; and their parenthood; and these classications are often changed. Tulip 'petals' are

Garden tulip

more correctly perianth segments. Many of the species are equally interesting.

T. clusiana (zone 7), lady tulip, grows 12 in (30 cm) and has pointed white petals, banded with deep pink on the outside, and with a dark violet, basal blotch inside. This is one of the oldest cultivated species, needing well drained soil and hot summers. Unusually for tulips, this species spreads by means of underground stolons.

T. acuminata, T. didieri, T. marjolettii and *T. mauritaniana* (all zone 7), are classified as neo-tulips and may all be derived from *T. gesneriana* from which garden tulips are also derived.

T. acuminata, horned tulip, grows 16–20 in (40–50 cm) high. It has very narrow, twisted, pointed red or yellow petals tinged with red or green, flowering in late spring.

T. didieri grows 20 in (50 cm) high and bears crimson flowers with a purple-black base in late spring.

T. marjolettii has creamy white petals edged with pink, appearing in late spring.

T. mauritaniana is scarlet with a yellow base.

T. greigii (zone 7), from Central Asia, grows 8 in (20 cm) or more high. The leaves are sometimes wavy and are spotted or veined with brown, and the scarlet or yellow flowers, with a black basal blotch, appear from mid spring onwards. This is the origin of the Greigi tulips, and a parent of the Fosteriana and Kaufmanniana hybrids.

T. kaufmanniana (zone 7), water-lily tulip from Turkestan, grows 6 in (15 cm) high. In the wild, this tulip varies in colour, from white to creamy yellow, flushed green or pink on the outside, with a dark yellow centre. There are numerous cultivars which flower in early spring.

T. linifolia (zone 7), from the Middle East and south Russia, grows 6–12 in (15–30 cm) high. It has broad, pointed, scarlet petals with a black basal blotch, which open in mid to late spring. The narrow, red-edged leaves are arranged in a rosette.

T. saxatilis (zone 8), from Crete and Turkey, grows 12–16 in (30–40 cm) high. It has pale-mauve flowers with a yellow centre. It needs a warm, very sheltered place, and is unsuitable for most northerly climates. The leaves appear in late autumn, and a leaf mulch is useful during winter. The plant multiplies rapidly.

T. sylvestris (zone 6), probably comes from Europe and grows 16 in (40 cm) high. It produces yellow, scented flowers in mid spring, with spreading petals. This is a common species, good in light shade, and spreads rapidly in the right conditions.

T. tarda (zone 7), a native of Turkestan, is 6–8 in (15–20 cm) high, and is easy to grow, providing the soil is extremely free draining. It bears star-shaped yellow and white flowers in mid to late spring, often several flowers per stem.

Tulips can be planted in formal or informal bedding or mixed borders. Smaller species and cultivars can be grown in rock gardens, pots or window boxes.

Cultivation. Plant from early autumn to late autumn; later plantings keep the garden in flower until summer. Garden tulips are best planted in a fresh site each year, to avoid disease. Species tulips can be left *in situ* in light soils for several years, before being lifted and replanted. Bury the bulbs about 4 in (10 cm) deep and 5–6 in (12–15 cm) apart; less for garden species, in light, well drained neutral or slightly limy soil, with peat or sand added if necessary.

Dead-head after flowering. Dig up the bulbs of garden tulips once the leaves die down, clean off the earth and dry in the shade before storing in a well ventilated place. Some cultivars will go on flowering year after year. Others will not.

Propagate by separating offsets; seeds take several years to flower. When in store, bulbs can be attacked by green moulds or rodents and in the field by tulip fire. An application of fungicide before storing helps protect the bulbs.

Typha

Reedmace, bulrush, cat's tail, *Typhaceae*

This genus consists of approximately 10 herbaceous perennials growing in wet places in many parts of the world.

T. latifolia (zone 4), great reedmace, is native to most of the Northern Hemisphere and grows 5–5½ ft (1.5–1.8 m) high. It forms large clumps of lanceolate, bluish-green leaves. The strong, brown cylindrical flower spikes appear in mid to late summer with the solid, brown heads of female flowers situated below the loose spikes of male flowers. The flower heads are popular in dried-flower displays. The creeping rhizomes multiply rapidly and can become invasive.

T. minima (zone 4), dwarf reedmace, grows 1–2½ ft (30–75 cm) high. It needs its rhizomatous roots submerged in 2–4 in (5–10 cm) of water to survive in cold winters.

These are waterside plants, the larger species suitable only for large ponds or for lakes, and the smaller, dwarf species for garden ponds.

Cultivation. Plant in spring, in rich soil or mud, submerged in 8 in–4 ft (20 cm–1.2 m) of water for great reedmace, less for dwarf reedmace.

To propagate, separate the rhizomes into sections 2–4 in (5–10 cm) long and replant immediately.

Ulex

Furze, gorse, *Leguminosae*

This genus contains over 20 medium-sized shrubs from Europe and West Africa, with dark green, spiny branches bearing short lived, scale-like leaves and large numbers of golden-yellow pea-like, fragrant flowers in spring and summer. It continues flowering intermittently through winter.

U. europaeus (zone 6), from Europe, grows about 5 ft (1.5 m) high. The cultivar 'Flore Pleno' has double flowers and a more compact habit than the species.

Cultivation. Grow in full sun and in a dry, poor soil to encourage blossoming. Use pot-grown plants, as open-grown plants are difficult to establish. Avoid damaging the rootball. Cut back leggy plants hard in early spring, new growth will spring from the base. The shrubs are highly flammable, and should not be planted near a house in areas that suffer from drought.

Propagate by late summer cuttings placed in a cold frame in earthenware pots containing a mixture of half sand, half peat.

Ulmus

Elm, *Ulmaceae*

A genus of about 18 species of elegant, deciduous trees from northern temperate zones, many susceptible to Dutch elm disease. The flower clusters are formed in spring before the leaves. The leaves are toothed and often asymmetrical at their base and appear at almost the same time as the key or circular-winged seeds, in late spring.

U. glabra (U. montana) (zone 6), Wych elm, is native to Europe and western Asia. It is a more resistant tree, with large, rough, coarsely toothed alternate leaves. The dense clusters of flowers have purplish stamens and seed is produced. The cultivar 'Camperdownii' has weeping branches and a dome-shaped silhouette.

U. parvifolia, Chinese elm, grows up to 40 ft (12 m) with elegant, slender trunk and branches. Leaves are oval to obovate, blunt-toothed and shiny green above, pale green beneath.

U. procera (zone 6), English elm, is a European elm with an erect habit to over 100 ft (30 m) high and thin branches bearing small alternate leaves which turn deep-yellow in autumn. It is particularly vulnerable to Dutch elm disease.

U. pumila, Siberian elm, is a small tree growing up to 40 ft (12 m). Dark green, long oval, coarse-toothed leaves.

Elms were used in large gardens and parks, and as street trees, specimens, hedges, or avenues. They are tolerant of exposure; wych elm tolerates maritime conditions.

Cultivation. Elms are very hardy and will thrive in any type of soil and situation. Plant between mid autumn and early spring.

Propagate by fresh, ripe seeds or by suckers, or layer according to species or cultivar.

European elms are prone to Dutch elm disease, which is carried by the elm bark beetle. Zelkova is often used as a substitute.

Ursinia

Compositae

A genus of about 40 species of annual and perennial herbaceous plants and shrubs, native mainly to South Africa.

U. anethoides (zone 6), is a bushy perennial, 18 in (45 cm) high, treated as a half-hardy annual in gardens. The plant produces finely divided leaves and daisy-shaped orange flowers, opening in the morning and closing in the evening or in dull weather, in mid to late summer. The cultivar 'Sun Star' has a striking claret-red central zone.

Grow as bedding, in mixed borders or pots. They are good for cutting, though they still close at night.

Cultivation. Sow in a frame in early spring. Prick out in mid spring and harden off the young plants before planting in late spring in a warm, sunny position in a light soil. Stake taller varieties. Alternatively take cuttings of the perennial species and place in sand under glass.

Uvularia

Bellwort, merry bells, *Liliaceae*

This genus contains five species of hardy herbaceous perennials native to eastern North America. They are erect plants, related to Solomon's seals, with a thick, creeping rhizome. The arching, leafy stems bear nodding, yellow bell-shaped flowers at their tips. The flowers have narrow, occasionally twisted, petals.
U. grandiflora (zone 6), merry bells, grows 1–2 ft (30–60 cm) high and wide. It is a dainty plant, with downy, slightly pointed, perfoliate leaves. The flowers are pendent, 1½ in (4 cm) long and bright yellow, and appear in late spring. The form 'Pallida' has pale-yellow flowers.
Cultivation. Grow in a well drained, peaty soil in light shade. Propagate by removing single rhizomes in mid spring, before the plant flowers, and replant immediately in a light sandy soil.

Uvularia grandiflora

Vaccinium

Bilberry, blueberry, *Ericaceae*

This genus contains approximately 400 hardy or tender species of deciduous or evergreen shrubs or trees from all parts of the world. Some are grown for their ornamental value, others for their edible fruits. They thrive in conditions similar to those for heathers but need more shade and moisture.
V. corymbosum (zone 5), swamp or high-bush blueberry, is a dense, thicket-forming shrub, 6 ft (1.8 m) high, with deciduous leaves which turn bright red in autumn. The pale pink or white flowers in late spring are followed by edible blue berries. There are many fruiting cultivars; especially in America.
V. myrtillus (zone 4), bilberry, is native to Europe and northern Asia. It has deciduous, finely toothed leaves on dense, branching, bright-green stems 2–4 ft (60 cm–1.2 m) high. Greenish pink, globe-shaped flowers in late spring are followed by edible blue-black fruits.
Cultivation. Plant in moisture-retentive, very peaty soil, in light shade. Plant at least two plants of different cultivars to ensure proper pollination. Water copiously in summer and place straw or decayed leaves around the base of the plant to help retain soil moisture. In winter, prune the old branches which have produced berries, to maintain bushiness and encourage future crops.

A single adult plant of *V. corymbosum* may produce more than 9 lb (4 kg) of fruit. Start picking when the berries are firm and blue. Picking should last four to six weeks. Bilberries are propagated by cuttings but this operation should be left to a professional.

Valerianella

Valerianaceae

This genus consists of about 50 annuals from Europe, Africa, Asia and North America.

V. locusta (V. olitoria) (zone 5), corn salad or lamb's lettuce, is a biennial which grows wild in Europe, forming a rosette of round green leaves 1–4 in (2.5–10 cm) in diameter and 2–2¾ in (5–7 cm) high, with tiny, pale-lilac flowers in spring. It is grown for its smooth tender leaves, for use in salads and soups.

Cultivation. Grow in ground that was prepared for root vegetables which have been harvested. The soil should be deeply dug and moisture-retentive. Keep it weed-free. The crop dislikes heat, but is hardy, and late-summer and autumn sowings provide winter crops.

Propagate by seed sown *in situ*, broadcast, or in drills 6–8 in (15–20 cm) apart, and thinning the plants to 6 in. Cover the seeds with ⅛ in (2 mm) of soil and firm well. Sow successionally in spring and then in late summer and early autumn. Keep the soil moist and shaded while the seedlings are growing and hoe occasionally. In hard winters, protect from frost with straw or bracken.

Harvesting should give from 14–28 oz (400–800 g) of leaves per 1.2 square yards (1 square metre), depending on the variety.

Lamb's lettuce can be affected by rust and mildew.

Verbascum

Mullein, *Scrophulariaceae*

This genus consists of over 300 species of herbaceous perennials or biennials or small shrubs native to Europe, Turkey and Asia.

V. bombyciferum, 4–6 ft (1.2–1.8 m) high, is a biennial species, with very hairy leaves and pale yellow flowers. 'Silver Lining' is an especially attractive form.

V. dumulosum is an alpine sub-shrubby species 6–12 in (15–30 cm) high. It has tufts of grey-green leaves and spikes of yellow flowers in summer.

V. phoeniceum (zone 5), purple mullein, is a herbaceous perennial from southern Europe and Asia, hardy in most climates. It grows 2–5 ft (60 cm–1.5 m) high and 16–24 in (40–60 cm) across. The green or grey foliage is dense and often pubescent. The plant flowers throughout the summer, with white, pink or purple, saucer-shaped flowers on spikes 1–2 ft (30–60 cm) long. This species is suited to an informal garden as a background plant for a herbaceous border, but can also be planted on its own. It is short lived, but self seeds freely.

It is the parent of many hybrids, with yellow, white, pink, purple or orange flowers.

Cultivation. Plant in spring, in sun, and 12–16 in (30–40 cm) apart in ordinary or poor, well drained soil.

The larger varieties might need staking in an exposed position. Dead head after flowering, to encourage secondary spikes to flower. Cut the stems down in autumn and protect the roots in winter in cold climates.

Propagate perennial species in winter or early spring by root cuttings or seed sown under a cold frame. Sow biennials in late summer.

Verbena

Vervain, *Verbenaceae*

This genus is represented by about 250 species from North and South America. Many are showy, tender herbaceous perennials, often grown as half-hardy annuals for summer bedding. They are creeping or erect plants, drought resistant but often short lived. They have toothed leaves and dense, round or flat inflorescences of pink, mauve, red or blue flowers throughout the summer, and until the first frost. Dwarf forms are good for edging, window boxes, hanging baskets and ground cover; taller forms are fine border plants.

V. × hybrida (zone 6), garden verbena, makes an excellent ground cover, and will not grow more than 12 in (30 cm) high without support. There are numerous cultivars with brilliant colours, sold as mixtures or named cultivars; many have contrasting white eye.

V. peruviana (zone 9), from South America, is a procumbent species, 4 in (10 cm) high, covered in small, bright-red flowers. It gives the best results in a warm, sunny position in a rock garden. It is one of the parents of hybrid garden verbenas.

V. rigida (V. venosa) (zone 9), from Brazil and Argentina, may grow 2 ft (60 cm) high. The stems are stiff, erect and branched, bearing small clusters of blue or dark-violet flowers throughout the summer. The plant has tuberous roots. It can be treated as a hardy perennial in warm areas.

Cultivation. Sow in a greenhouse in late winter or early spring. Germination can be unpredictable; prick out, harden off, then plant after the last frost. The hardy perennial cultivars can be propagated by division of the root stock, or from culling. Dead head regularly.

Veronica

Speedwell, *Scrophulariaceae*

This genus contains about 250 species of annual and herbaceous perennial plants, some hardy and some not, mostly from temperate regions. Those described below are all hardy perennials, with slender spikes or racemes of small, saucer-shaped flowers in summer.

V. filiformis (zone 5), from Asia Minor, grows ¾ in (2 cm) high. It is a creeping plant with oval leaves ¼ in (7 mm) long. The plant produces enormous numbers of blue flowers in mid to late spring, but is very invasive, spreading 4 ft (1.2 m) or more. It can be used as ground cover in sun or shade, and in any soil.

V. prostrata, from Europe and Asia, is a mat-forming species, which has deep blue flowers from late spring to mid summer. 'Rosea' is a deep pink cultivar.

V. teucrium (zone 6), is native to Europe and Asia, and grows about 18 in (45 cm) high, and 12–16 in (30–40 cm) across. It has dark-green, evergreen foliage and erect stems, forming dense clumps. The flowers are a remarkable deep-blue and appear throughout summer. Popular cultivars include 'Crater Lake Blue', 'Royal Blue' and 'Blue Fountain'.

V. virginica (zone 6), from eastern North America, grows 4–6 ft (1.2–1.8 m) high, and 20–24 in (50–60 cm) across. It has dark-green lanceolate leaves in whorls, set at intervals up the stem. The flowers are pale-blue and appear in terminal racemes 8–10 in (20–25 cm) long, from mid summer to early autumn. There are white and lilac-pink forms.

The smaller species of speedwell are best suited to rock gardens, and the larger ones to herbaceous borders.

Cultivation. Plant from early autumn to early spring in well drained but moisture retentive soil and in the sun. The species with woolly foliage need fairly dry soil. Dead head after flowering. Tall species may need support. Cut tall-growing species down to ground level in autumn.

To propagate, lift and divide every three years in early or mid spring, replanting immediately. Alternatively take cuttings 2 in (5 cm) long from the lateral shoots in mid to late summer and plant them in a mixture of peat and sand in a cold frame.

Viburnum

Viburnum, *Caprifoliaceae*

This genus consists of some 150 species of mostly deciduous hardy shrubs and small trees with opposite leaves and flowers in corymbs or panicles, some of which may be sterile and are often scented. Most are native to Asia or North America and are grown for the beauty of their flowers, fruits, habit of growth or autumn leaf colours. Their fruits are attractive to birds.

V. betulifolium (zone 6), from China, grows 12 ft (3.5 m). The birch-like, diamond-shaped leaves are deciduous, bright green and toothed. White flowers appear in large corymbs in early to mid summer. In autumn, mature plants produce a large number of translucent red berries which last all winter.

V. × *bodnantense* (zone 6), 'Dawn' is an erect-growing hybrid, 10 ft (3 m) high. It has stiff shoots bearing lanceolate, deciduous leaves. The frost resistant, pink -flushed white flowers appear on the bare branches in mid to late autumn and through winter.

V. carlesii (zone 6), from Korea, is a popular, dome-shaped shrub growing 5–6½ ft (1.5–2 m)

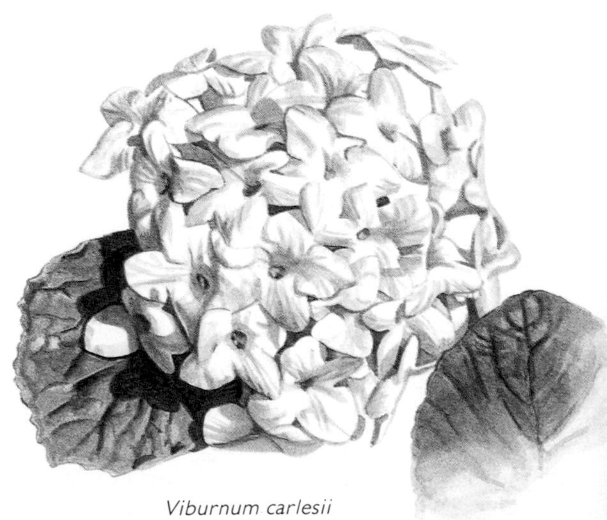

Viburnum carlesii

high. Its irregularly toothed, deciduous matt green leaves, sometimes turn purple-red in autumn. Corymbs of beautifully scented white flowers, tinged with pink, appear in mid to late spring, and are followed by black fruits.
V. dentatum (zone 5), from North America, grows 10 ft (3 m) high. This erect shrub has large, oval, toothed deciduous leaves that colour attractively in autumn. The white flowers grow in large cymes in late spring and early summer, and are followed by blue-black berries.
V. farreri (V. fragrans) (zone 6), from China, grows 6½–13 ft (2–4 m) high and has an erect habit, becoming more rounded as it grows older. It has oval deciduous leaves, bronze when young. The white flowers are finely scented, opening from pink buds. These appear on bare branches in late autumn and continue through winter; in cold winters, flowering occurs in early spring.
V. opulus (zone 6), guelder rose, cranberry bush, grows 6½ ft (2 m) high and has maple-like, lobed, deciduous leaves which turn rich-red in autumn. The inflorescences are flattened and bear small white, fertile flowers surrounded by large showy sterile ones. The translucent red berries are glossy, pungent and long lasting. This species is very widely grown in gardens and grows wild in Europe. It is tolerant of damp soils. The variety 'Sterile' is the popular snowball bush, grown for its huge, globe-shaped heads of sterile flowers.
V. tinus (zone 6), laurustinus, a native of Europe, grows 10 ft (3 m) high. It is a dense, bushy, round shrub with dark, evergreen oval leaves. The flower buds are pink, turning to white when they open, and last all winter. The berries are a metallic blue colour, but need hot summers to develop. Laurustinus is excellent for hedges and screens.
Cultivation. Grow in deep, moist, rich soil; viburnums tolerate limy soil and like sun, but will also grow in light shade. Plant several bushes to ensure cross pollination and proper fruiting. Regular pruning isn't necessary. Trim evergreen viburnums in spring; cut out old or dead wood of deciduous types after flowering.

Propagate by taking 4 in (10 cm) cuttings in late summer inserted into a mixture of sand and peat, with gentle bottom heat. Lax types can be layered; seeds are slow to germinate and may not come true.

This species is often affected by aphids which must be controlled.

Vicia
Leguminosae

This genus consists of nearly 150 herbaceous plants mostly from the Northern Hemisphere.
V. faba (zone 6), broad bean, or fava, is an annual which has been cultivated since prehistoric times. It has square stems 2–3 ft (60–90 cm) high, but there are dwarf cultivars available. The black and white flowers produce green pods of edible beans.
Cultivation. The broad bean can be grown as the first plant in a crop rotation, followed by cabbage. It grows in any soil, but prefers it to be moist and humus-rich and is best in a sunny position. Hoe and water it frequently.

Early crops can be sown in autumn, in shelter and light free-draining soil. In early spring, sow seeds *in situ*, in medium to heavy soil. Sow in drills 2 in (5 cm) deep, with 1 ft (30 cm) between the plants, and 3 ft (90 cm) between the rows. Beans can also be sown under glass, and planted out in early spring. Pinch out the tips when the first pods set, to discourage blackfly. Growing summer savory as a companion plant is also said to deter blackfly, and is an excellent herb for flavouring broad beans. Harvest in late summer when the seeds are about ¾ in (2 cm) across. Cut the tops down but leave the roots in the soil to add nitrogen. Chocolate spot and blackfly can be troublesome.

Vinca
Periwinkle, *Apocynaceae*

This genus consists of seven species of shrubs, sub-shrubs and herbaceous perennials native to Europe, Asia and North Africa. The following make excellent ground cover in semi-shade. Their five-petalled, funnel-shaped flowers appear from spring to mid summer, but flowers are occasionally produced all year round.
V. minor (zone 5), lesser periwinkle, is a hardy, creeping, more or less woody plant, 2–4 in (5–10 cm) high, forming a dense, spreading mat. It has very attractive, dark-green evergreen leaves, and small, bright-blue flowers. There are cultivars with blue, purple, white, pink and wine-red flowers, and double-flowered forms. 'Aurea Variegata' has yellow-variegated leaves.
V. major (zone 6), greater periwinkle, has violet-blue flowers and although the vegetative shoots

are trailing, the flowering stems are upright to 2 ft (60 cm) tall.

Use periwinkle as ground cover, in shrub borders, wild gardens or along the edge of a path. Both can be invasive, though, so keep them away from less vigorous plants.

Cultivation. Plant in any well drained soil, including limy, acid or poor soils, in light shade, in autumn or spring. Remove any unwanted or spindly shoots in spring.

Propagate by division in autumn or spring. The stems are self rooting from the nodes.

Viola

Viola, violetta, violet, pansy, *Violaceae*

This is a huge genus, containing around 500 species of herbaceous, perennial or annual plants. The flowers are distinctively shaped and have five rounded or elongated petals, according to the species. The flowers are usually produced in spring and early summer, and are often repeat flowering. They can be used to edge borders or paths, in rock gardens, as ground cover under trees and shrubs and as spring bedding.

V. cornuta (zone 4), horned violet, found wild in the Pyrénées, is a hardy perennial, growing in clumps 4–12 in (10–30 cm) high. In early to mid summer, it bears large numbers of small blue or violet flowers with long spurs. The evergreen leaves are bright green and toothed. Several cultivars with white, pink or lilac flowers are available. It is excellent, dense ground cover. If cut over after flowering, a second crop of flowers is produced, provided the plant is given adequate water.

V. odorata (zone 6), sweet violet, grows 4–5 in (10–15 cm) high, and 12 in (30 cm) or more across. The leaves are heart-shaped and the plant bears scented, white, pink or purple flowers $\frac{1}{4}$–$\frac{3}{4}$ in (1–2 cm) across from late winter to mid spring. It spreads by underground stolons. There are numerous hybrids.

V. tricolor, heart's ease or Johnny-jump-up, is grown as an annual or biennial. It grows 3–6 in (7.5–15 cm) high, and carries purple, blue, cream or red flowers in mid summer.

V. × *wittrockiana* (zone 5), hybrids include the popular garden pansies in many flower colours flowering at different times of the year. They are grown as hardy or half-hardy biennials or as hardy or half-hardy annuals.

Cultivation. Plant in autumn to flower in early to mid spring. Choose a moist, fertile soil and sun or semi-shade; avoid hot, dry positions. For the hybrids, including pansies, sow in late spring or early summer, outdoors in a cold frame or in a seed bed, to bloom the following spring; or sow in early spring under glass with gentle heat to flower the same year. Dead head regularly to ensure continuous flowering.

Vitis

Ornamental vine, *Vitaceae*

This genus contains some 70 species of climbing deciduous or evergreen shrubs from the Northern Hemisphere, most of which support themselves by twining tendrils. Garden forms are grown for their colourful leaves and attractive, sometimes edible, fruits, produced after hot summers. The flowers are insignificant.

V. amurensis (zone 5), amur grape, from China, Korea and Russia is deciduous, growing to 50 ft (15 m) high. It produces small black fruit and has finely coloured foliage in autumn.

V. coignetiae (zone 6), crimson glory vine, a Japanese species, is one of the largest leaved of the genus. It grows to 80 ft (25 m) and acquires attractive shades of crimson, orange and purple in autumn. It sometimes produces sour, black fruits.

V. davidii (zone 6), from China, has shoots covered with hooked spines, heart-shaped leaves, bright-red in autumn, and black sweet fruits. It is a luxuriant, vigorous vine, up to 50 ft (15 m) high.

V. vinifera (zone 8), common grape vine, can be grown as an ornamental plant, as well as for fruit. Decorative forms include the cut-leaved 'Apiifolia'; 'Incana', with downy white leaves; and the hybrid "Brant", with deeply lobed leaves, brilliant autumn colour and sweet fruits.

All species can be trained on a trellis, a tree trunk or an arbour. Larger species can cover walls or fences.

Cultivation. Grow in deep, rich soil; it tolerates a wide variety of conditions even pebbly ground. Plant with a rootball in early to mid spring, and use a stake to train the plant towards the surface which is to support it. To control size, thin out old growths and shorten new growth in late summer. To propagate, take 4 in (10 cm), semi-ripe or hardwood heel cuttings and place in pots of sand.

Weigela

Weigela, *Caprifoliaceae*

A genus of approximately ten species of deciduous, spreading shrubs with arching, often drooping branches, native to eastern Asia. The early summer flowers are funnel shaped and grow in clusters. Many cultivars and hybrids have been raised. Weigelas are sometimes referred to as *Diervilla*, a former classification.
W. florida (zone 7), is a vigorous spreading shrub growing 8–9 ft (2.4–3 m) high. The flowers are dark pink outside, and lighter inside, and appear in late spring and early summer. A smaller crop of flowers is sometimes produced in late summer and autumn. There are hybrids with purple and variegated leaves, and bright-pink flowers.
W. middendorffiana (zone 7), grows 6 ft (1.8 m) high. The flowers appear in mid to late spring and are bell-shaped and sulphur yellow, with orange spots on the lower lobes. It requires shelter and light shade, the flowers are vulnerable to spring frosts.
W. praecox (zone 7), grows 8–9 ft (2.4–3 m) high. The leaves are hairy on their lower surfaces and the large, deep-pink flowers with yellow marks on the throat appear in late spring, and are honey-scented.

Weigelas can be used in borders and on banks and are tolerant of urban conditions and pollution. Many cultivars are also available.
Cultivation. Grow in deep, fertile soil in sun or light shade. Prune as soon as the flowers are over, by removing the old, flowered shoots, leaving the young shoots untouched. For the plants that flower on the current year's wood, prune in spring before growth starts.

Propagate by taking semi-ripe cuttings in late summer, or by autumn cuttings placed in a seed bed, or by dividing the clumps.

Wistaria

Wistaria, *Leguminosae*

This genus contains about six hardy, tall-growing climbing shrubs from eastern Asia and North America, with pinnate leaves and drooping racemes of showy, pea-like flowers.
W. floribunda (zone 6), Japanese wistaria, from Japan, grows up to 33 ft (10 m) high. It is very hardy, and distinguished by its pendulous racemes, up to 20 in (50 cm) long, of violet,

Wistaria sinensis

scented flowers appearing in late spring and early summer, and its dark green leaves. The form 'Macrobotrys' has flower racemes up to 3 ft (1 m) long.
W. × *formosa* (zone 6), a hybrid of American origin, grows to a similar height and is very hardy. It has silvery, downy leaves and pendulous racemes of pale, violet-pink flowers, which open all at once, in late spring and early summer.
W. sinensis (zone 5), Chinese wistaria, from China, is a very hardy species, growing up to 30 ft (9 m) or more with adequate support. It bears racemes of mauve, scented flowers in late spring, before the leaves; the flowers open simultaneously and sometimes recur in autumn. There are white, dark purple and double-flowered forms.
W. venusta (zone 5), from Japan, grows to a height of 33 ft (10 m) and is also very hardy. Its racemes of white flowers, the largest in the genus, are slightly scented, 4–6 in (10–15 cm) long and appear at the beginning of summer.

Wistarias are ideal plants for pergolas or arbours, or for training against house walls or up a tree.

Cultivation. Wistaria grows in any well drained soil, and needs full sun to flower well. Prune hard in late winter, to keep growth within bounds; shorten the long leafy shoots in late summer, to within 5–6 buds of the base.

Propagate by layering in spring or by cuttings in late summer, kept at 64–68°F (18–20°C). Grafting named varieties on to *W. sinensis* roots is also done.

Wulfenia

Scrophulariaceae

This genus comprises two species of tufted, rhizomatous herbaceous perennials from southern Europe useful for rock gardens.
W. carinthiaca (zone 7), grows 8 in (20 cm) high and 12–16 in (30–40 cm) across. It has rosettes of dark-green, shiny, oval leaves with scalloped red edges. The lipped flowers are blue, purple, pink or white, forming dense, erect spikes, and appear in early to late summer.

Cultivation. Grow in well drained but moisture-retentive soil containing peat and leaf mould. Plant in early spring in a sunny or partly shaded position. Protect from winter wet with a pane of glass placed over the plant. Suitable for rock gardens and alpine houses.

Propagate by seed in early spring, in a seed tray placed in a cold frame, or alternatively lift and divide.

Yucca

Agavaceae (Liliaceae)

This genus is made up of about 40 fairly hardy, tree-like or stemless plants, native to North and Central America, with rosettes of attractive, long evergreen leaves. The white flowers are carried in erect racemes or panicles.
Y. filamentosa (zone 9–10), Adam's needle, from southeast USA grows 24–48 in (60–120 cm) high. It is stemless producing clumps of elongated sharply pointed, blue-green leaves with curly white fibres along the edges. The white flowers appear in 6 ft (1.8 m) high panicles in autumn or late summer. The form 'Variegata' has white-striped leaf edges.
Y. flaccida (zone 9–10), is also stemless, with narrower leaves, and less curly white fibres. The flowers are white and grow in panicles in late-summer or autumn. The variety 'Golden Sword' has creamy yellow variegations.
Y. gloriosa, (zone 9–10), Spanish dagger, is tree-like, slowly reaching 5–6½ ft (1.5–2 m) in height. The leaves have very sharp points and the white flowers are sometimes tinged with red. It flowers in late summer to early autumn, but only on plants five-years old and older.
Y. recurvifolia (zone 9–10), grows up to 6 ft (1.8 m) high. The outer leaves droop, and those at the centre of the plant remain upright. The leaves are blue green and, later, green with age. The creamy white flowers grow in large panicles sometimes more than 3½ ft (1 m) high in late summer. Young plants do not flower. It is a good species for town gardens.

Yuccas make good specimen plants, especially for giving a tropical touch to temperate climate gardens.

Cultivation. Yucca likes a well drained, sandy or rocky, limy soil in full sun. It is resistant to air pollution. It sometimes takes several years before flowering, and flowers best in hot summers. Cut the floral spikes back after flowering.

Propagate by dividing the rhizomes of the parent plant into pieces 2–3 in (5–7.5 cm) long and place in a sandy soil in gentle heat. Stemless species often form basal offsets, which can be removed and planted up separately.

Zantedeschia

Arum lily, calla lily, *Araceae*

This genus consists of eight or nine species of tender to semi-hardy, rhizomatous perennials from South Africa, related to *Arum*.

Z. aethiopica (zone 8–10), grows 20–32 in (50–80 cm) high and 20 in (50 cm) across. It has shiny dark-green, arrow-shaped leaves. The showy, funnel-shaped white spathes, 6–10 in (15–25 cm) long, surround a bright-yellow spadix bearing inconspicuous flowers, and appear from early spring to mid summer, depending on the region.

This species is hardy in areas with a reasonably mild winter if protected during the cold weather, and can be grown in shallow water, lake or pond, or in a herbaceous border. They are excellent for container growing outdoors, then overwintering in a cool greenhouse. The cultivar 'Crowborough' is hardier and more tolerant of any soil.

Z. rehmannii (zone 9), from Transval, grows to 2 ft (60 cm) high and produces white to pink or purple spathes in spring and summer. The mid-green leaves bear white spots under certain conditions.

Cultivation. Plant in a pot, in a mixture of peat, leaf mould, and well rotted manure and submerge in 30 in (75 cm) of water, in full sun. Alternatively, plant in a border in rich, moisture-retentive soil, and protect in cold weather with a mulch of dead leaves. Those grown in water will survive the winter provided the roots are below the frost line.

Propagate by dividing the rhizomes in early autumn ensuring that replanting takes place immediately.

Zauschneria

California fuchsia, *Onagraceae*

This genus comprises four species of hardy perennial sub-shrubs from western North America.

Z. californica (zone 8), from California, is a clump-forming, bushy plant growing 12–20 in (30–50 cm) high and 20–24 in (50–60 cm) across. It has slender, arching stems; pointed, grey-green, lanceolate leaves; and spikes of tubular, vermilion-red flowers from late summer to mid autumn. The leaves are evergreen in mild areas, deciduous in colder ones. The cultivar 'Dublin' is slightly hardier than the species. Grow in a sunny rock garden, or at the foot of a sunny wall.

Cultivation. This plant requires a light, well drained soil, containing sand and gravel, and enjoys a sunny position. Protect the roots in winter with a deep mulch.

Propagate in spring by removing rooted stolons, replanting immediately, or, where winters are cold, take cuttings of side shoots in autumn and put these into pots, in a sandy soil, keeping them in a cool greenhouse until planted out in spring.

Zea

Sweetcorn, *Gramineae*

A genus of four species from Central America, one of which has been grown extensively as a food crop.

Z. mays (zone 9), maize, is an annual plant with stems 5–8½ ft (1.5–2.5 m) high, and ears of yellow, white or bi-colour kernels 6–8 in (15–20 cm) long. There are many cultivars, including early-cropping F_1 hybrids, and hybrids tolerant of cool, wet weather.

Cultivation. Choose a sunny sheltered site, and a well cultivated soil which has been manured for the previous crop. Adding peat helps retain soil moisture. Sow or plant in rectangular blocks, NOT rows, to ensure cross pollination. Either sow seeds in small peat pots under glass in mid spring and plant out when the danger of frost has gone, or sow directly in the ground in mid to late spring, protecting the seedlings with cloches. Sweet corn is sensitive to low temperatures, and needs a minimum of 50°F (10°C) for sowing. Sow 2–3 seeds at a time, 1 in

(2.5 cm) deep, 18 in (45 cm) apart in the row, 24 in (60 cm) between the rows; when the seedlings appear retain the strongest. Keep the plants well watered, keep the weeds down but avoid damaging the surface roots; when these appear at the base, mulch with well rotted compost. Each plant will produce one or more cobs. When the tassels wither, test for ripeness by puncturing the seed: if it exudes a white milky juice it is ready to be picked. Eat immediately for best flavour. Time between sowing and picking is 15 weeks, with an approximate yield of just over 30 cobs for a 30 ft (9 m) row. Treating the seed with fungicidal seed dressing before sowing helps prevent soil-borne diseases. Some varieties need to be grown isolated from other varieties, to prevent inferior crops. Some popular varieties are 'Bantam', 'Silver Queen' and 'Butter-and-Sugar'.

Zephyranthes

Zephyr lilies, *Amaryllidaceae*

This genus comprises about 70 species of mainly summer- and autumn-flowering bulbs from Central and South America, with grassy leaves and crocus-like flowers, which open in a star shape.

Z. candida (zone 9–10), grows 6–10 in (15–25 cm) high. It is moderately hardy, with long, narrow leaves. The white flowers are tinged with red at the base of the petals, and appear from late summer to mid autumn. This plant is suitable for rock gardens and window boxes or a sunny, heated frame in places where they are subject to rain and dampness in winter or summer.

Cultivation. Plant 4 in (10 cm) deep, in spring, in a moist well drained soil and in sun or light shade. Mulch in winter. Leave undisturbed for several years, even slightly pot-bound to encourage flowering. When the clumps become very large, dig up the bulbs in late autumn and remove the offsets, replanting them immediately.

Zinnia

Zinnia, *Compositae*

This genus comprises some 20 species of annuals or perennials, many from Mexico. They are sturdy plants with attractive, daisy-like flowers, in warm colours. There are single, semi-double or double cultivated forms, in an enormous colour range.

Z. angustifolia (zone 6), is an annual which grows 18 in (45 cm). The orange or yellow flowers are single and semi-double, with a maroon centre. They appear from mid summer until the first frosts.

Z. elegans (zone 6), common zinnia, grows 2–3 ft (60–90 cm) high, but there are dwarf forms available. There are cactus-flowered, dahlia-flowered, ruffled and bicoloured forms.

Zinnias are good for borders, summer bedding, container growing, and as cut flowers. Dwarf forms make good edging.

Cultivation. Sow in early or mid spring, under glass. Put in a dark place or cover with a newspaper until germination takes place. Prick out and then plant out carefully in late spring, 12 in (30 cm) apart for dwarf varieties and 20 in (50 cm) apart for taller ones. Zinnias resent root disturbance, and in warm areas, are better sown outdoors *in situ*. Choose a warm sunny place and a rich loamy, well-drained soil. Avoid high humidity and over-watering.

Mildew may attack the leaves and stems, and the flowers may be affected by grey mould in wet weather. Fungi and viruses such as spotted wilt may also cause blotching or distortion of the stems or leaves.

Ziziphus

Rhamnaceae

This genus comprises about 85 species of small, elegant trees which are hardy in areas with a Mediterranean climate.

Z. jujuba (zone 10), jujube tree, or Chinese date, from Europe and Asia, is a spiny deciduous tree to 23 ft (7 m) high. It has light, shiny, bright-green foliage, and bears tiny yellow flowers in the leaf axils in early and mid summer. The edible acid-tasting fruit is oval, dark red, about the size of a large olive, and ripens in mid autumn. It is eaten fresh or dried.

Jujube trees can be grown on their own or in borders; wall protection is essential in colder areas.

Cultivation. Plant in light, porous, dry soil in a sunny position. It does best in areas with hot summers.

Propagate by seed under a frame or by taking root cuttings.

GUIDELINES FOR PLANT HARDINESS

In the matter of plant hardiness, no one can be absolutely sure where a zone border should come, as winters can be unpredictable in their severity. A winter with severe frosts can prove to be less damaging than a slightly warmer one in which there is excessive near-freezing rain; while a persistent freezing wind can lower the ambient air temperature by several degrees through wind chill. There again, a reasonable fall of snow can serve to protect some small plants in their entirety, and the lower parts of larger ones, from the direct adverse effects of frost and wind.

Probably the worst type of winter is one in which there is excessive dampness. This is particularly harmful to evergreens which have to maintain transpiration at all times. So a region which appears, by its average winter temperature, to suit a shrub, might in fact be completely unsuitable on the grounds of its average winter precipitation.

Many rock plants, for instance, come from the high mountain regions of the world. There they have the winter protection of snow. In lowland gardens of Northern Europe and climatically similar areas of North America, the winters can be comparatively mild and wet at the time when alpine plants should be experiencing a cold, dry period of rest. While it is not possible to provide snow, the required dryness can be provided to some degree by planting on the raised areas of the rock garden, and by incorporating grit into the compost and on the surface around the plants.

Wall protection is often advocated for garden plants which originate in climates warmer than those in which they are to be planted, as this gives them some protection against damage from cold winds and frosts.

The climatic conditions of the district in which the garden is situated must be a prime consideration when deciding what to plant, but even within the garden itself there will be microclimates. Some areas may be exposed to the directions from which the coldest winds will come, others will be protected by shrubs, hedges or walls.

By management, you can actually alter these microclimates through the plantings themselves and by use of mulches and other practices, such as those for water control. Through careful selection of the site you can modify air drainage, local wind currents, sun and shade, humidity, the water both on and within the soil, and soil temperature.

ZONES

The Plant Hardiness Zone System used in this book is based on the system devised by *The United States Department of Agriculture* for use in southern Canada and the United States (excluding Alaska and the Hawaiian Islands).

An attempt has been made here to increase the scope of the system to include Australia, New Zealand, South Africa and Western Europe, including the United Kingdom and Eire.

As will be seen from the zone map of the USA, the USDA system divides North America into 10 climatic zones separated by average **minimum** winter temperatures, in stages of 10°F, from −50°F and below at Zone 1, up to +40°F at Zone 10.

For the purpose of this book, a rough translation to Celsius has been made and both the Fahrenheit and the Celsius figures are shown in the key to the maps.

Every plant included in the A–Z of Garden Plants has been given a zone number indicating that it should withstand the **average *minimum* winter temperature of that zone** and **also those zones with higher numbers** and therefore higher minimum temperatures. It must, however, be realised that other factors, such as precipitation patterns and high maximum summer temperatures, may well make life insupportable for plants with low zone numbers.

The zone hardiness ratings are helpful, but they do not conclusively determine whether a plant will thrive in a particular location. For example, many plants that will grow well in zone 9 in the South East USA will not tolerate the dry conditions in zone 9 in the South West USA.

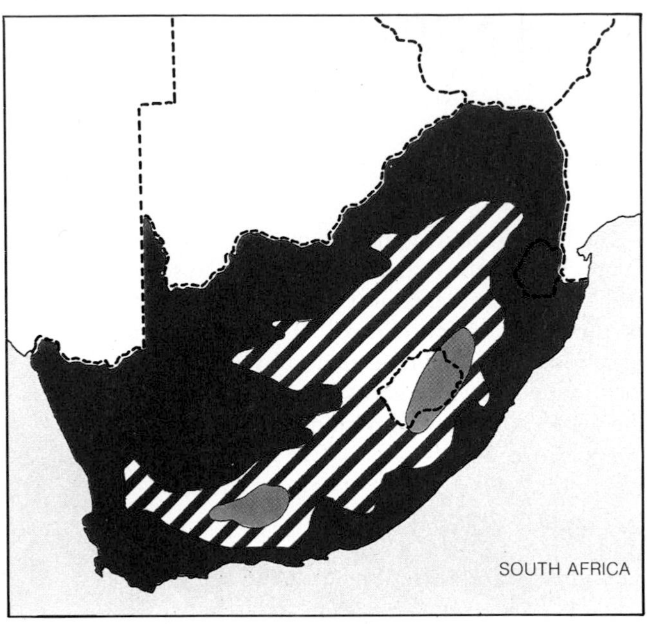

No climatic zone system can be 100 per cent accurate, simply because the variations in annual temperatures and precipitation can be so considerable from one year to another. Working from a basis of averages means that there will be few if any seasons in any area that correspond precisely to the specifications given in a climatic zone system.

Within each zone there are bound to be local variations in climate due to a variety of circumstances. Low-lying areas can be frost pockets, while only a few yards higher up a hillside the growing season may be a good two weeks longer than in a garden near the top. In temperate areas of low summer rainfall, while the climate may be suitable in every other way, supplemental water will be essential for plant survival.

By observing what grows in other people's gardens, or in municipal parks nearby, it is possible to make a reasonable assessment of the planting possibilities for your own garden.

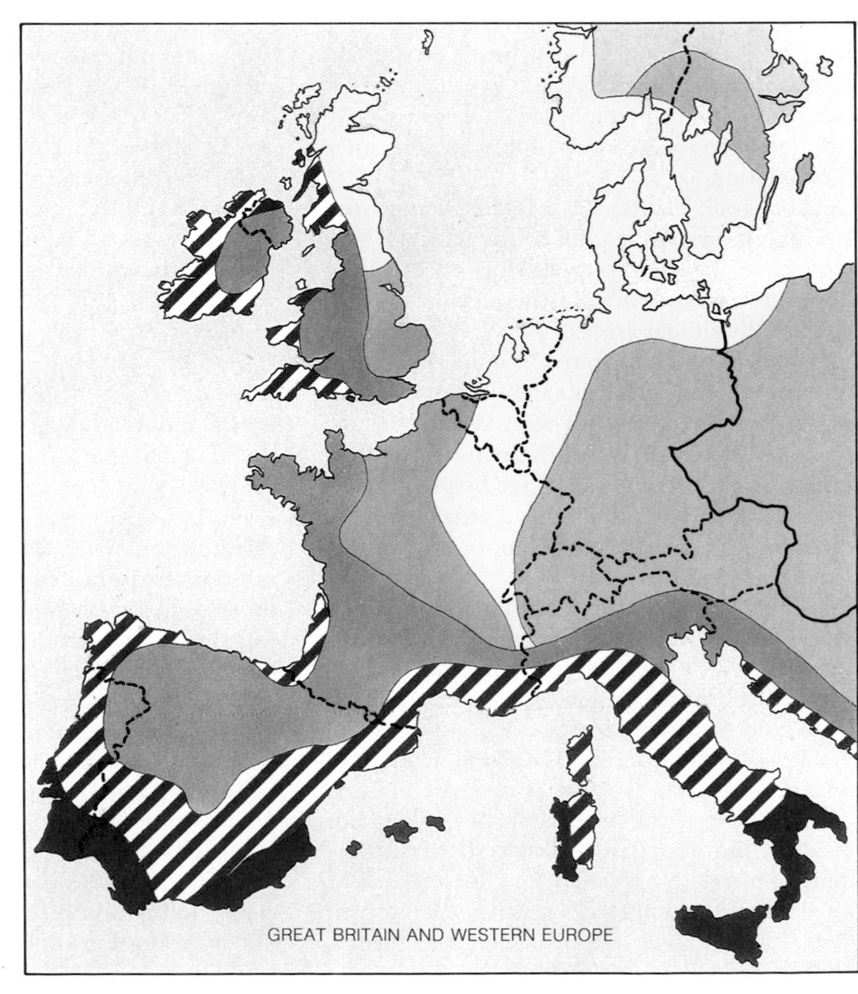

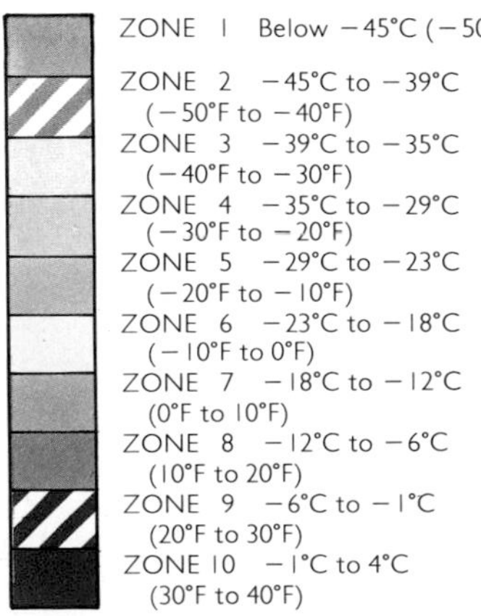

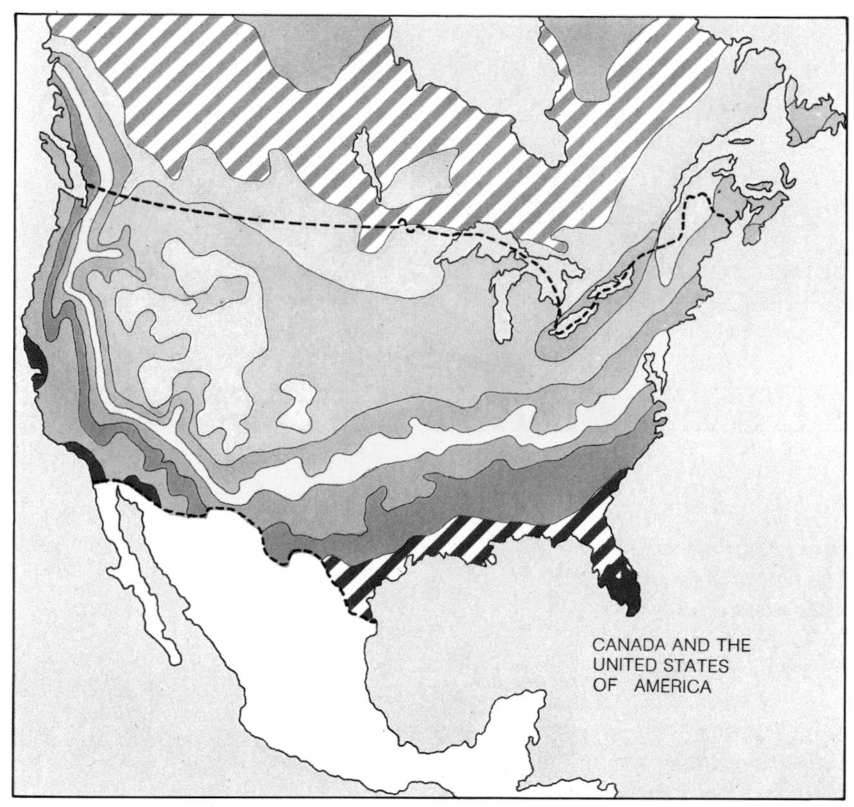
CANADA AND THE
UNITED STATES
OF AMERICA

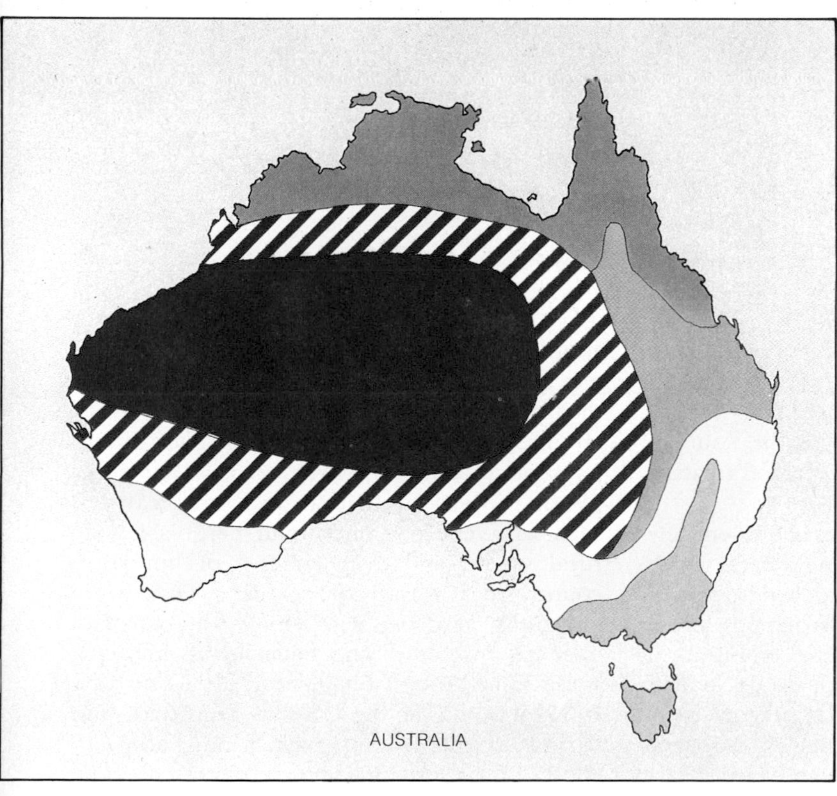
AUSTRALIA

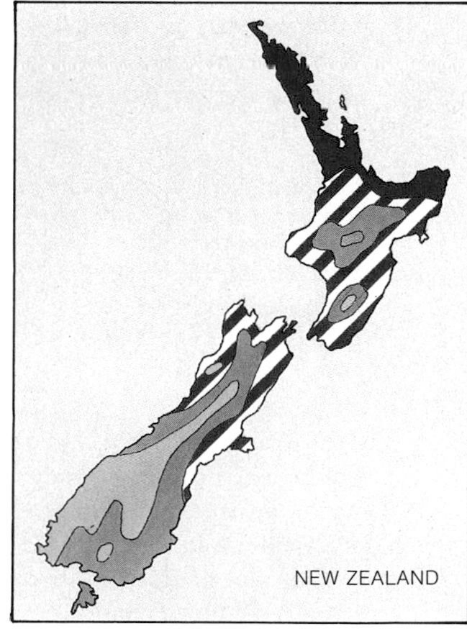
NEW ZEALAND

A PASSION FOR PLANTS

THE CREATORS

Whether painters, architects or gardeners, the following men and women have been guided by a personal vision and design sense; and by a love of their basic materials – plants, the ground form and water. Though imaginative, their work has often been eminently practical. The greatest of them – notably Le Nôtre and Capability Brown – deserve to be thought of as artists, since they have changed the way that we see our environment.

The gardens of the Villa Gamberaia near Florence. The art of topiary was invented when Roman gardeners, in imitation of sculptors, pruned trees into artificial shapes.

PLINY THE YOUNGER

(61–112)

The Roman nephew and adopted son of Pliny the Elder, the encyclopedist, Pliny the Younger was famous for his skill as a lawyer, and amassed a considerable fortune.

Our knowledge of him comes almost entirely from his copious and fascinating letters, which tell of his varied activities and wide circle of acquaintances. Among his most famous letters is the long description of the eruption of Vesuvius in A.D 79 – in which his uncle died while observing and investigating the event.

In his letters, no less than three of his several country properties, their villas and gardens are described. One was on the shore of Lake Como; another in Tuscany, and the third, the Laurentian villa, was near the sea, probably not far from the port of Ostia – though their exact locations are uncertain. The gardens of the Tuscan and Laurentian properties were extensive and complex in their layout, with many formal features, such as avenues, topiary and pergolas; wide rural views; and even an area of 'imitation countryside' within the garden. They were luxurious gardens, with small fountains, an open-air marble dining table incorporating a water-filled trough for floating dishes of food from one end of the table to the other, and various 'garden rooms' with folding doors to allow views out in several directions, and painted scenes of birds and landscapes on the inner walls.

These descriptions were an important source of inspiration both for the gardens of the Italian Renaissance, and for Lord Burlington's villa and garden at Chiswick, near London.

LE NÔTRE, *André*
(1613–1700)

Grandson of Pierre Le Nôtre, gardener at the Tuileries in 1592, and son of Jean Le Nôtre, chief gardener to Louis XIII, André Le Nôtre could hardly escape these influences around him. Yet he first trained as a painter in the studio of Simon Vouet, where Le Brun was a fellow student. By 1637, he was head gardener at the Tuileries, and director of the Jardin du Luxembourg in 1646. He became a royal draughtsman in 1645, and by 1656 was appointed Controller General of the King's Buildings. He worked both for the king, and for lesser patrons. Together with the architect Le Vau and the painter Le Brun, he shared in the creation of the château and gardens of Vaux-le-Vicomte, where he composed a majestic perspective aligned with the house, and placed a fine canal across the long, main axis of the gardens. Commissions flowed from all quarters, at Dampierre for the Duc de Chevreuse, at Anet for the Duc de Vendôme, at Chantilly, at Saint-Germain-en-Laye, at Saint-Cloud, at Meudon . . .

Le Nôtre's most famous work was at Versailles. From the early 1670s until his death in 1700, he was at work designing both the vast prospect as a whole, extending for $1\frac{1}{2}$ miles (2.4 km) from the west front of the château, and the galaxy of features, large and small, which made up the detail of the gardens. His royal master Louis XIV was a passionate garden enthusiast, extravagant, demanding, impatient, and frequently requiring drastic changes or new and extensive developments. The complexity of the schemes involved a bewildering number of different artists and craftsmen – sculptors, architects, hydraulic engineers as well as fountain experts – let alone the arrangements for the supply of new and sizeable trees (for the *bosquets*, or groves, surrounding the sculptured fountains), and of thousands and thousands of flowering plants for the gardens at Trianon. Working *for* Louis, and *with* these many colleagues or assistants (and subject also to the continued restraints of different ministers of finance), Le Nôtre seems to have succeeded triumphantly, both in his art, and friendships.

The parterre of the Orangerie at Versailles, typical of Le Nôtre's style.

From the few drawings that remain, it is clear that he had a perfect sense of balance, scale and proportion. He was a master of optical illusion, able to create a sense of spacious order and balance even when the actual contours of his site were irregular.

Though Louis allowed him to design gardens for many of his nobles in France, Le Nôtre's work abroad was extremely limited. In England, for example, there is no *proof* of his work apart from a single plan for a feature in the royal park at Greenwich – and even that was not executed. His *influence*, on the other hand, was felt from one end of Europe to the other, and the gardens designed by Frenchmen or foreigners who had met him, and studied his achievement at Versailles, could be seen in Russia, Spain, Sweden, Italy and England.

In his last months, when his failing strength left him unable to walk the full round of the gardens, Louis allowed him a *roulotte*, a wheeled chair, in which he was pushed alongside the king, who was seated in another such vehicle. Le Nôtre exclaimed 'Oh, if only my old father were alive to see me now – to see his son, a poor gardener, going round in a chaise beside the greatest king in the world – then my happiness would be complete!'

KENT, William *(1685–1748)*

'He leaped the fence, and saw that all nature was a garden'. Horace Walpole's phrase about Kent's achievement sums him up excellently, for Kent was, more than any other, the English garden designer responsible for initiating the great enthusiasm for 'landscaping' the garden in the eighteenth century.

Kent trained as a painter, spending some seven years in Italy studying and copying the old masters, and imbibing the 'atmosphere' of Italian sculpture, buildings and landscape. For part of the time, he was supported by Lord Burlington, and on his return to England Kent was employed by Burlington to design and execute the interior of his new Palladian villa at Chiswick. In the late 1720s, Kent was commissioned to design parts of the surrounding gardens, which had been begun in somewhat formal style by Charles Bridgeman. Kent's part in the Chiswick gardens was crucial, for he gave to one large area a 'natural' feeling which was virtually unknown in British gardens before this time. The 'lake' or 'canal' which he created at Chiswick has an irregular outline, as if it were not man-made, but an original part of the landscape. At one end of this lake, Kent set a rock-work structure, with arches and a cascade, which was deliberately designed as a ruin – indicating, in the same way, that it was not a new garden building, but one which had been there for centuries, and therefore part of a long-established and 'historic' order of things. Kent quickly acquired the reputation of an innovator, designing 'without level or line' in a freehand manner which was not hampered by formal and geometrical rules.

In the gardens at Rousham, in Oxfordshire, which are his best surviving work, a vital element of the scheme is the repeated use which Kent makes of the landscape outside the gardens – the rural prospects of fields and hedges, with the meandering course of the River Cherwell in the foreground. These views of 'nature' are framed again and again by foreground scenes of an Arcadian kind, with architectural and sculptural features which recall the classical landscapes of Italy, or the paintings of these landscapes by Gaspard Poussin and Claude Lorrain, which Kent had seen and studied during his years in and around Rome. In the area of the 'Elysian Fields', in the gardens of Stowe, in Buckinghamshire, Kent's valley and stream

An eighteenth-century temple in the gardens of Wrest House, Bedfordshire, which were designed by William Kent and Capability Brown.

with temples may be seen as a three-dimensional creation of a 'Claudian landscape'.

BROWN, Lancelot 'Capability'
(1716–83)

Like André Le Nôtre, equally eminent as a garden designer, Capability Brown never wrote a book. Also like Le Nôtre, whose work is virtually all in France, Brown's creations are almost without exception in his native England and Wales. In addition, they seem both to have been charming and approachable characters, liked by their patrons, employees, their colleagues and helpers.

At this point the similarities stop. Brown's training was more modest, as a gardener in the north of England. By 1740 we find him employed by Lord Cobham at Stowe, probably in charge of the kitchen gardens. There, he would have worked under William Kent, who had general control until his death in 1748. Brown was married in 1744 in the little church of St Mary, close to Kent's 'Elysian Fields', and in 1751 he left Stowe to set up in practice as an independent garden designer.

He had already undertaken commissions away from Stowe (with much success, as at Warwick Castle, from 1749 onwards) and was quickly established as the country's leading landscape gardener. Unlike his predecessor Kent, Brown did not give his landscapes a continuous backing of classical reference, but was usually content with a sparse scattering of 'monuments'. Instead, his landscapes present purified, ideal forms of English scenery, perfecting the shape of a valley, a wooded ridge, a sweep of lawn extending to the hills. Almost always, the focus of his landscapes is water, usually in the form of a lake, sometimes a natural river. The lakes are, in most instances, enlarged, either from earlier, existing ponds, or from the accumulated waters of a dammed stream. In this way, Brown created the great artificial lake at Blenheim, by damming the tiny River Glyme. Similarly, the lakes at Petworth in Sussex, at Bowood in Wiltshire, and at Syon Park and Wimbledon Park near London were formed. At Nuneham Courtenay in Oxfordshire and at Warwick Castle, the Thames and the Avon provide the broad expanse of water, while at Audley End, in Essex, the little River Cam is dammed several times to provide the appearance of a noble waterway. Not many miles to the north at Audley End, the Cam has become a more sizeable river as it passes through Cambridge, and here in 1779 Brown proposed to widen the river even further, creating a 'lake' around three-quarters of a mile in length along the 'Backs', the area of ground between the river and several of the colleges. But the colleges could not agree to their several separate gardens being absorbed into a single 'landscape', and his scheme remained no more than an idea.

When asked whether he would consider landscaping someone's property, he often replied (if he was willing) that the land had 'capabilities' which he would develop; hence his nickname.

REPTON, Humphry
(1752–1818)

The Englishman Repton did not turn to garden designing until 1788, when he was 36 years old. He had pursued several careers, and was by then a thoroughly accomplished draughtsman and water-colourist.

When, at last, he tried his hand at 'landscaping', it was at a singularly propitious moment. Capability Brown had died five years before, in 1783, and no obvious successor had appeared among the several garden designers who were practising. Through his skill as an artist, Repton was able to present his clients with pictures of what he proposed which succeeded, again and again, in winning him commissions. His method may now seem a simple one, yet it had not been applied before: he prepared pictures of a composite kind, showing first the scene *as it was*, and then (by lifting up folding flaps of paper) showing the scene *as it would be* if Repton's proposals were carried out. This 'before' and 'after' presentation (often involving several of these 'double' views) was accompanied by careful notes explaining the proposals, and the complete set of papers was usually bound up in elegant covers of red morocco leather, and presented as a 'book' to the client. These handsome Red Books served as a record of how the property had been before Repton's work 'improved' it, and – on display in the client's library – as an admirable advertisement for Repton's practice.

Some two hundred of these Red Books still survive, evidence both of Repton's fine artistic talent, and of his success as a garden and landscape designer. By 1814, in her novel

Mansfield Park, Jane Austen could portray her characters discussing the 'improvement' of a country property, and saying 'Your best friend on such an occasion would be Mr Repton I imagine . . . His terms are five guineas a day . . .'

Repton did indeed seem to become the successor to Brown. His early landscapes, in the 1790s, might often be mistaken for Brown's – as at Shardeloes, in Buckinghamshire, where his landscaping of the fields and woodland fringes on both sides of the Misbourne valley is exactly in the style of an idealized natural scene. Yet in the early 1800s his own and his clients' taste moved away from the purely natural, returning gradually to a pattern of more formal elements close to the house. Where Brown might have proposed, and laid out, a vast sweep of lawn right up to the doors of the house, Repton reintroduced a formal forecourt, or a terrace, with a balustrade, and flower beds. At Endsleigh in Devon, where the house looks out over the grand, wooded valley of the River Tamar, Repton laid out formal terraces beside the house with geometrical flower beds, and with a *fountain* – a feature of an artificial kind which had been all but banished from landscape gardens since the early 1700s. Other fine landscapes which Repton transformed are Attingham, in Shropshire; Woburn Abbey, in Bedfordshire; and Sheringham in Norfolk.

Before designing a garden, Repton prepared pictures showing the scene 'before' and 'after'. This 'after' picture is of his own garden in Romford, Essex.

OLMSTED, Frederick Law *(1822–1903)*

Like Humphry Repton in England, the American Olmsted had several occupations before turning to the designing of landscapes at the age of 36. The impulse came during a visit to England, when, in 1850, he was profoundly impressed both by the design and by the philanthropic purpose of Birkenhead Park, laid out at public expense by Joseph Paxton a few years before. Olmsted was deeply moved that this fine park, created within the city, should be 'for ever the people's own', and he enthusiastically transferred these impressions into his design and proposals for the new Central Park in New York. His design won the competition for this development in 1858, and he and his partner Calvert Vaux (they worked together until 1872, and then separately) subsequently designed many parks in urban regions of the United States. They were the first to style themselves 'landscape architects'.

Central Park, Olmsted's most famous creation, had been proposed as early as 1844, and the ground – that between 5th and 8th Avenues and 59th and 106th Streets – was acquired in 1853. By 1863 the site was extended northwards to 110th Street. The competition for the design, held in 1857, was won the year after by Olmsted the Vaux, and by the autumn of 1859 much of the essential landscaping, including the main ornamental lake, had been achieved.

From the start Olmsted has insisted that the design was conceived as 'a single work of art', with one overriding purpose, 'to supply to the hundreds of thousands of tired workers, who have no opportunity to spend their summers in the country, a specimen of God's handiwork'. This aim to create a city park with a rural character has involved continuing resistance to encroachments, and to the erection of inappropriate buildings; the four existing city streets which had, of necessity, to cross the park from east to west were set in deep walled cuttings, so that they were removed visually from the overall scene, and passed beneath the north-south roads belonging to the park. The roads and paths of the park are with one exception (the Mall) curved and meandering, passing round the irregularly-shaped lakes and natural outcrops of rock.

Today, Central Park is still within the boundaries settled in 1863 – a long, rectangular city

Frederick Law Olmsted.

site now enclosed by tall buildings and towering skyscrapers. It includes areas for games, athletics and sports, for sitting or strolling and enjoying the flowers, trees and open spaces. There is a small zoo, and boating on the main lake – and skating in winter.

Olmsted's other achievements include Prospect Park, Brooklyn; Belle Isle Park, Detroit; the grounds of the Capitol in Washington D.C., and a complex of parks in Boston, notably Back Bay Park, Riverway, Franklin Park, and an area renamed in his honour, Olmsted Park.

ROBINSON, William
(1838–1935)

The Irishman William Robinson was a passionate gardener, who began as a student at the botanic gardens in Dublin. Employed in the winter of 1860–61 on a private estate, he quarrelled with the head gardener and left suddenly, leaving the greenhouse stoves untended, so that many of their plants died.

He came to London at the age of 22, and worked at the Royal Botanic Gardens in Regent's Park. He soon had charge of the herbaceous plants, and began to acquire a reputation for himself as a journalist, writing for the *Gardeners' Chronicle.* He went to France as horticultural correspondent for the London *Times* to the International Exhibition in Paris in 1867.

The visit to France was of decisive importance for him, since he could observe both the wealth of exotic plants which had recently become available, the rigidity of the old French formal gardens, and the modern municipal gardens of Paris. His views, in *The Parks, Promenades and Gardens of Paris* (1869), are vitriolic. Of Versailles, he wrote

> This being one of the most celebrated gardens in the world, it behoves us to examine it somewhat in detail – were we, however, to treat of it in proportion to its real merits as a garden a very small amount of space would suffice.

Soon he produced books of a more 'positive' kind, elaborating what it was that he believed important. In 1870 *Alpine Flowers for English Gardens* and *The Wild Garden* were published, and in 1871 he founded his own journal, *The Garden*, which he edited until 1899. *The English Flower Garden*, the most successful of his many books, appeared in 1883.

His passion was for plants, whether exotic or native, to be seen growing in the way which best suited them, and for gardens which respected the qualities of the plants. 'Wild' gardens, or 'natural' gardens, are his watchwords. In his view a garden plan could not be established until after the plants and trees had been set in place. The plants and trees came first – *their* qualities were what mattered, and should dictate the general form of the garden.

The success of his writings enabled him in 1884 to acquire a property in Sussex, Gravetye Manor. Here, in 200 acres (81 hectares) round an Elizabethan house, he was able to put his theories into practice. He did not in fact advise on many gardens – Shrubland Park in Suffolk is one notable example of his work – but was immensely influential through his writing. His original ideas on gardens were taken up and skilfully adapted by his friend and disciple, Gertrude Jekyll.

JEKYLL, Gertrude
(1843–1932)

An extraordinarily gifted and prolific Englishwoman, Gertrude Jekyll devoted the first half of her life to painting. As a result of problems with her sight, however, she had to abandon both water colours and embroidery in 1891. Since childhood she had a marked inclination for botany and gardening, and she now turned in this direction, encouraged by her friends, the gardener William Robinson (whom she first met in 1875) and the great English architect Edwin Lutyens, with whom she collaborated for many years.

Her sense of pictorial composition and her original ideas on associations of plants quickly made her influence felt on the development of gardening in Great Britain. Her great idea, though it might sound commonplace nowadays, was to juxtapose colours, planting together assemblages that would flower at the same time, to give the harmonious palette which we now associate with the herbaceous border. Her house in Surrey at Munstead Wood, designed by Lutyens, was surrounded by a garden in which over the years she applied her theories on associations of colour.

Between 1880 and 1932, the year of her death, Gertrude Jekyll worked on the designs of more than 300 gardens and her creations inspired some of the finest work that has been done in this century. Most of her designs (though not all of the gardens) still survive, and her many books on gardens have been frequently reprinted. Beginning with *Wood and Garden* (1899) she followed with a flood of titles, now well-known, including *House and Garden* (1900), *Old West Surrey* (1904) and *Colour in the Flower Garden* (1908). Of her gardens, apart from her own at Munstead Wood, notable examples are at Hestercombe (Somerset), Folly Farm and the Deanery (both in Berkshire), Lindisfarne (Northumberland), and The Salutation (Kent). The reputation enjoyed by English gardens at the present time is due in no small part to her efforts.

DUCHÊNE, Achille
(1866–1947)

This important French landscape gardener worked both on his own, and in collaboration with his father, Henri Duchêne (1841–1902), a specialist in the restoration of classical parks and gardens. He played a significant part in the restoration of French formal gardens such as those of Vaux-le-Vicomte, Le Marais, Champs-sur-Marne and Courances, as well as creating those of Voisins and Condé-sur-Iton, inspired by the garden style of the early eighteenth century. The success of Achille Duchêne led to his engagement by the Duke of Marlborough to redesign a part of the gardens at Blenheim near Oxford. The water parterre is derived from Le Nôtre's early water parterre at Versailles.

FARRAND, Beatrix
(1872–1959)

This American landscape architect is most famous for laying out Dumbarton Oaks in Washington D.C., and the Abbey Aldrich Rockefeller Garden, in Seal Harbour, Maine.

In Dumbarton Oaks (1921–1947), she worked with the owner, Mildred Barnes Bliss, to create a series of outdoor 'rooms', those closer to the house, formal in style, then becoming more informal as distance from the house increased. In 1980, *The Plant Book for Dumbarton Oaks* was published; Farrand wrote it in 1942, setting out in detail the origins for the garden, its development and her proposals for management.

The Rockefeller garden (1926–50) was built around oriental sculptures and tomb figures. She also laid out both Princeton University campus and Yale University campus and contributed to the landscape design of several others: Occidental College, Vasser, Oberlin, Hamilton and University of Chicago among them. In England, she contributed to the design of Dartington Hall, and was a great admirer of the English landscape style, especially the work of Gertrude Jekyll, Thomas Mawson and William Robinson.

STEELE, Fletcher
(b.1885)

An American landscape architect trained at Harvard, Steele was influenced by le Corbusier, the Modern Movement, and the landscape designs of the French landscape architects Vera and Legrain.

He travelled extensively in Europe and incorporated various aspects of contemporary European landscape design, including the use of mirrors, manipulation of perspectives and levels, and broken axes, into his own work.

The most notable example is his re-design for the neo-classical garden at Naumkeag, Stockbridge, Massachusetts. His writings include *New Pioneering in Garden Design* (1930), *Landscape Design of the Future* (1932) and *Modern Garden Design* (1936).

CHURCH, Thomas
(1902–78)

One of the most innovative American garden designers of this century, Church's approach

A private garden in Carmel, California designed by Thomas Church.

concerned private American gardens which were essentially small, and often on demanding and irregular sites. His most famous book, *Gardens are for People* (1955), stresses the need to understand the dual requirements of the garden-owner, and of the site itself – and in California, where most of his enormous output was to be found, this frequently implied a restricted and hilly or even mountainous site, to be developed for owners with houses (or requiring new houses) of moderate size.

Given the equable climate, it was possible for Church to develop the theme of the 'interpenetration' of house and garden. Areas of paving were both part of the house and part of the garden; walls of glass allowed the garden to appear as an extension of the building; and skilful touches of asymmetry in paths or levels linked the man-made house and garden with the natural landscape beyond.

Many examples of his work survive, for example the garden of the Sunset Magazine Headquarters, near San Francisco, and the world-famous Dewey Donnell garden, 'El Novillero' at Sonoma, created in 1947–48.

PAGE, Russell
(1906–85)

After training as a painter at the Slade School in London, Page turned to garden design in 1928, and until 1939 collaborated with Geoffrey Jellicoe. After the Second World War, the Englishman settled in France (until 1962), and established a brilliant international reputation as a garden designer, with work executed in France, Britain, Italy and most other countries of Europe, and in the United States.

In Britain, he made notable contributions to the existing gardens at Longleat (Wiltshire), Leeds Castle and Port Lympne (both in Kent), and one of his finest creations in the United States is at Kiluna, on Long Island. He is noted in France for his landscaping of the race course at Longchamps.

In 1962 he published his autobiography, *The Education of a Gardener*, a book of deep and continuing importance for its understanding of the broader and multi-cultural aspects of garden design.

BURLE MARX, Roberto
(b.1909)

The diversity of this Brazilian's interests and activities places him in the orbit of the great artists of the Renaissance, yet his works, whether tiny or immense, are in their conception firmly of the present century. Training as a painter and architect, he was also passionately interested in botany, and his numerous garden and architectural works in Brazil combine the geometrical simplicity of modern architecture with the abundant and varied shapes, textures and colours of Brazilian species. He has made notable 'sculptural' use of the Heliconia genus – relatives of the banana family – some of which are species discovered by Burle Marx himself. In his treatment of ground cover, the palette is strong and vibrant – deep pink, ochre, red or silver, set against vivid greens are typical of his work. The best-known example of his work is the Monteiro Garden, near Rio de Janeiro (1948).

THE BOTANISTS

The first botanists were content to observe plants and their properties in order to improve human health and nourishment, and to accumulate details as a part of the cataloguing of the physical universe. This was, more or less, the concern of Theophrastus, Pliny the Elder and Dioscorides. Gradually, however, the idea developed that the plant kingdom could be classified in terms of natural relationships. In the eighteenth century, a long debate took place between botanists and 'classifiers' of differing opinions. The great Swedish botanist Linnaeus was to prevail, with the view that plants could best be classified according to sexual and reproductive characteristics. Scientists like Lamarck went on to consider the evolution of plants and the different species, and eventually, this led to the foundation of modern genetics. The techniques developed in the nineteenth century were to give rise to many new disciplines while plant anatomy made spectacular progress through this period.

Linnaeus (Carl von Linné)

THEOPHRASTUS
(370–286 BC)

This Greek philosopher and scholar, a disciple first of Plato and then of Aristotle, was the director of the Lyceum, a place in which the garden and its walks played an important role. He was a man of universal interests, and his most important surviving work, *The Characteristics*, is the genial ancestor of all European botanical writing. He also wrote the *Enquiry into Plants*, which has earned him the title of 'the father of botany'. The *Enquiry* contains the first systematic classification in Western writing of the plants of the known world, indicating their nature, characteristics and uses. Some of the plants are (for the fourth and third centuries BC) remarkably 'exotic', and were presumably described to Theophrastus by followers of Alexander the Great, who had seen them in the course of his epic travels of conquest. They include the cotton plant and the banyan.

Theophrastus' garden in Athens was the first to contain collections of rare plants, and was therefore the earliest known botanic garden.

PLINY THE ELDER
(AD 23/24–79)

A man of many parts, Pliny the Elder was in charge of the Roman fleet stationed in the Bay of Naples at the moment of the great eruption of Vesuvius in AD 79. He met his death investigating this 'phenomenon' – a wholly understandable part of his all-consuming interest in the nature and composition of the universe, from its largest and most abstract to its minutest features.

He compiled the *Natural History*, the first 'encyclopedia' written in the western world to survive, and a considerable part of this massive work concerns the plants – whether ornamental, agricultural or wild – known to him, or to his predecessors. Much of his information comes from Theophrastus, but much is added, either from his own, or from other's investigations.

The *Natural History* is divided into 37 'books', and within this scheme, books 12 to 16 cover trees, 17 deals with vines, 18 with plants in agriculture, 20 with medicinal plants, 21 with flowers, 22 with herbs, 23 with fruits and their uses. References to gardens and gardening are few and scattered, though Pliny is the first writer to refer to topiary, the art of clipping trees and bushes into artificial and ornamental shapes, which he says was first practised by a Roman, Gaius Matius, near the end of the first century BC.

DIOSCORIDES
(1st century AD)

Author of *De Materia medica*, Dioscorides is thought to have been an army doctor. His great work, describing an enormous variety of plants, their characteristics and their medicinal uses, exists only in a sixth-century version, illustrated with nearly 400 drawings. This has served as the inspiration for numerous later herbals, first for the second-century Roman writer Galen, and for many subsequent writers. Dioscorides' text was translated into English in 1655 by John Goodyer, and eventually published in 1934 by Robert T. Gunther.

If Theophrastus is the 'father of botany', Dioscorides is the 'father of medical botany'. His analyses of the medicinal properties of plants are thorough, detailed and perceptive. For the opium poppy, for example, he points out that 'ye docoction is drank against want of sleep', but 'being drank too much, it hurts, making men lethargicall and it kills'.

PITTON DE TOURNEFORT, Joseph
(1656–1708)

Pitton de Tournefort was given a broad education under the Jesuits, through whom he studied the classics, physics, anatomy, medicine and philosophy. He later studied botany at Montpellier under Pierre Magnol, after whom Magnolia was named. After journeys in several European countries, he was appointed Professor of Botany in the Jardin Royal des Plantes with additional responsibility for teaching students of medicine. In 1694 he published his first work, *Eléments de botanique ou méthode pour connaître les plantes.*

Soon after, Louis XIV suggested that he undertake a voyage to the Levant to carry out further studies. He left Paris in 1700, accompanied by the artist Claude Aubriet, and a young German doctor, Gundelsheimer. They visited Crete, the Greek islands, Constantinople, the Black Sea coast, Turkish and Persian Armenia, Georgia, Mount Ararat and the borders of Persia and Asia Minor. When Tournefort returned on 3 June 1702, he brought back 1356 new plants, among them the nettle-tree (*Celtis australis*) the acanthus known from Greek art, orchids, poisonous aconites, colchicum, wormwood, the jujube-tree and ephedra, a cure-all

Joseph Pitton de Tournefort

traded by the caravans from China. Tournefort was the first to describe the common rhododendron, R. *ponticum*.

LINNAEUS (Carl von Linné) *(1707–78)*

Linnaeus was born at Råshult, Småland, in the south of Sweden. His father, Nils Ingemarson, had taken the name Linnaeus at the time of his entry to the University of Uppsala in memory of a lime-tree, *linn* in Swedish, which stood on a former family property, *Linnegård*.

As a medical student at the University of Uppsala, Linnaeus began to work on a simplified system for the classification of minerals, animals and plants. After graduation, he went to Holland and worked as doctor to a rich merchant in Haarlem, George Clifford, who possessed a fine garden and glass-houses full of exotic plants. Linnaeus' chief preoccupation remained the classification of living organisms. He perfected a system based on the number of stamens and stigmas in which every plant was designated by two names, one for the genus and one for the species. Linnaeus published his *Species plantarum* in 1753, now considered the point from which all modern plant classification proceeds. A significant acceptance of the Linnaean system came in 1768, when the eighth edition of Miller's *Gardeners' Dictionary* adopted the binomial nomenclature. Though modified and redivided in the nineteenth century, this binary system is still the basis of all plant classification.

During his lifetime, Linnaeus made three important Scandinavian voyages: to Lapland, to the Baltic islands of Öland and Gotland, and, around his fortieth year, to Våstergotland and Skane. He brought back many samples which he kept in the form of herbaria and also published a number of botanical notebooks. An inspiring teacher, he attracted students from several countries. Many were themselves to become distinguished professors of natural history or medicine. They included Pehr Kalm (1715–1779) to whom Linnaeus dedicated the plant kalmia; Peter Forskål (1736–68), who went with the Dane Carsten Niebuhr to Egypt and Arabia – and died there; Fredrik Hasselquist (1722–52), who also travelled in the Levant; Daniel Carl Solander (1736–1782) who accompanied Captain Cook and Joseph Banks on his first circumnavigation of the globe in 1768–71, and Carl Peter Thunberg (1743–1828) who travelled in southern Africa, Java and Japan.

Linnaeus was a tireless correspondent, and achieved immense progress in the efficient classification of the world's plants, more through his encouragement of friends and disciples than from personal travel. From his botanic garden in the university of Uppsala, and from his home at Hammarby nearby, he directed the botanic enquiries of the western world for some 30 years.

Though his health deteriorated after 1763, he lived on to the age of 70. In 1784 his wife sold his collections and library to Sir James Edward Smith, who was to found the Linnaean Society in London in 1788.

BUFFON, G.-L. LECLERC, Comte de *(1707–88)*

Buffon was one of the most respected intellectual figures of the eighteenth century. Voltaire described him as having the soul of a *philosophe* in the body of an athlete. After studies in law, medicine, mathematics and physics, he travelled in Italy and then England. Original work in physics and chemistry gained him admission to the Academy of Sciences in 1733.

Buffon's passion in life, however, was nature in all its forms. In 1739, he was invited to take charge of the administration of the Jardin du Roi. From this appointment, he proceeded to his greatest work, the *Histoire naturelle*, a monumental edifice of classification, research and observation. When the first three volumes appeared in 1749, their impact was felt all over

Georges-Louis Leclerc, Comte de Buffon

Rousseau compiled many volumes of pressed flowers and grasses.

the continent. Publication continued steadily until the whole series was complete in 35 volumes. When he died, he had earned a place in the history of science with his idea that the universe was the product of a slow transformation, and that plant and animal species were born of this evolution. His labours led the way to Darwin, and to the *Origin of Species*.

ROUSSEAU, Jean-Jacques (1712–78)

On Rousseau's tomb, on the 'Island of poplars' in the landscape garden at Ermenonville, there is inscribed one line: 'Here lies the man of nature and of truth'. Rousseau had spent the last few weeks of his life at Ermenonville, as the guest of the Marquis de Girardin, and in this short period had contented himself with the gentle study of nature – 'herborising', as he called it. His other literary, aesthetic and political interests (which had made him a central figure in the eighteenth century) had given way to botany – 'for I know no other study which appeals to me more than the study of plants'.

In a famous section of his novel, the *Nouvelle Héloïse* (1761), he had already described the 'Elysée' created by Julie, the heroine. This was a 'natural' garden, in which the artificiality of human design, and the intrusion of human beings, was avoided as much as possible. In the 1760s, following public hostility to his political ideas, he withdrew from society, and preferred more and more to indulge in solitary meditation, inspired by natural and unspoiled surroundings. His thoughts, or *rêveries*, while studying the flora of the Ile-St-Pierre in the Lake of Bienne, are described in his *Confessions*, then in his *Rêveries*. He compiled many volumes of pressed flowers and grasses, and in 1771–73 wrote the *Lettres sur la botanique*, first published in 1781, and reissued in 1805 with 64 plates by Redouté.

GOETHE, Johann Wolfgang von (1749–1832)

This universal writer – poet, dramatist, novelist, historian, biographer and scientist – was also concerned with gardens and with plants. In his own garden in the park at Weimar, designed and planted by himself, there is one of the most original of all garden monuments, the 'Altar of Good Fortune' (1777); in his novel *Die Wahlverwandschaften*, or 'Elective Affinities' (1809), the 'natural' and 'formal' garden interests of the hero and heroine are carefully described, foreshadowing their divergent attitudes to mar-

Goethe's garden at Weimar.

riage, and in his long essay, *Die Metamorphose der Pflanzen*, written in 1789–90, he makes a serious and influential contribution to the long effort to achieve an adequate classification of plants. Looking back to Linnaeus, he wrote in 1816 'Apart from Shakespeare and Spinoza I know no other master from the past who has so impressed me', and he pursued the attempt to classify plants according to a single yet comprehensive system by elaborating his theory of the *Urpflanze* or 'original plant', from which all subsequent plant growth will have developed. Goethe's thought is therefore leading towards Darwin's theories of evolution, summed up in the *Origin of Species* in 1859.

GRAY, Asa
(1810–88)

Asa Gray was an instructor at Harvard, an eminent botanist, and curator of the Botanic Garden of Harvard University (later Arnold Arboretum) from 1842–72. He promoted the transformation, in 1872, of rolling farmland (left to Harvard for use as a school of horticulture and agriculture) into an arboretum. (The costs were met by a bequest from Hames Arnold, of New Bedford.) Gray chose Charles Sprague Sargent, a former botany pupil of his, as the Director of the Arnold Arboretum.

SARGENT, Charles Sprague
(1841–1927)

This eminent American botanist was the Director of the 245-acre Arnold Arboretum, Massachusetts; the compiler of the enormous *Silva of North America*; and the founder and editor of *Garden and Forest*. He is also the author of *Manual of the Trees of America*.

Upon his appointment, in 1873, to the Arboretum, Sargent persuaded Frederick Law Olmsted to lay out the grounds, and to make the Arnold Arboretum part of a huge system linking various parks around Boston into an 'emerald necklace' of greenery.

He was also able to tempt the great English plant collector, Henry Wilson, to work for the Arboretum, and established exchanges of plant material with European botanical gardens. Joseph Rock, another eminent plant collector, was persuaded by Sargent to provide newly discovered Chinese and Tibetan plants for the Arboretum.

BOTANIC GARDENS

The urge to collect and the activity of collecting are among the most engrossing of human experiences. Curiously shaped seeds or nuts, pine cones, or books of dried flowers and grasses have inspired collectors through the ages, as have collections of plants, grown as part of a garden, or given a whole garden to themselves. In the twentieth century these botanic collections range from small specialist gardens with herbs, bulbs, or heathers to the universal collections of Kew and the spacious areas of selected trees, such as the Arnold Arboretum in Massachusetts, or the Strybing Arboretum in California, real encyclopedias of trees.

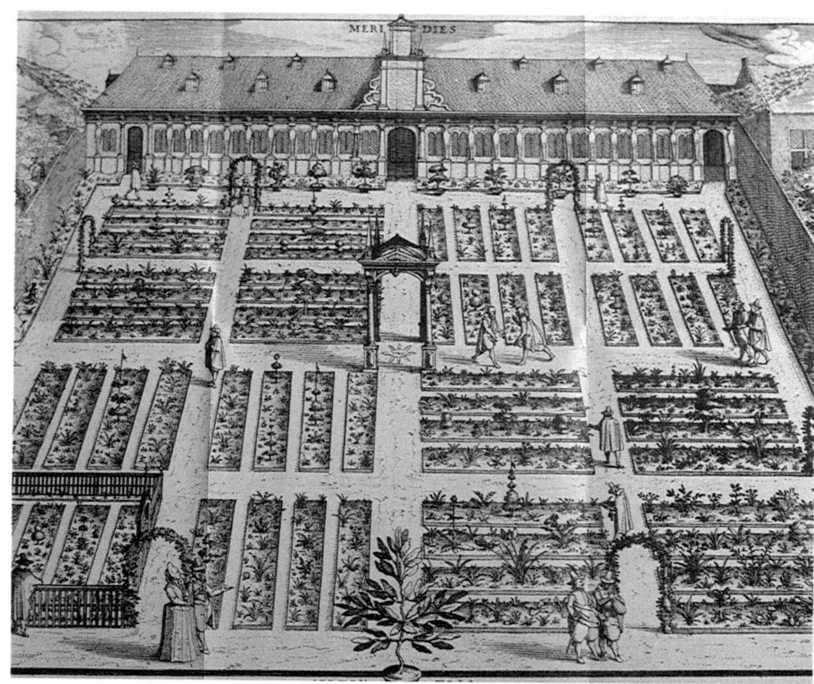

A plan of Leiden Botanic Garden, Holland, showing rows of teaching beds.

THE FIRST BOTANIC GARDEN

The Greek writer Theophrastus was the first serious botanist in the western world. His *Enquiry into Plants*, the description of all the then-known plants, was apparently backed up by a garden, kept by Theophrastus, and many of the plants which he described were probably grown there, so that their properties could be studied. This garden in Athens was therefore – *in all reasonable probability* – the first botanic garden. In his will, Theophrastus left his garden to his students, one of whom was placed in charge as the keeper, the 'tyrant of the garden'.

Today, a botanic garden usually has provision for growing native and exotic plants and hardy and tender ones, with specialized areas and buildings – pools, rockeries, greenhouses – to allow the widest possible variety of plants to be grown. Other buildings may contain related materials: a library, collections of dried plants, exhibitions of different woods. The Royal Botanic Gardens at Kew and the Brooklyn Botanical Garden in New York offer this kind of variety, for inspection, admiration and, possibly, study.

EARLY BOTANIC GARDENS

The early botanic gardens, however, were not directed at the collection and presentation of plants in so universal a way. Until the sixteenth and seventeenth centuries, botanic gardens were entirely or primarily to do with the collection and study of plants for their *medicinal* properties. They were, more precisely, 'physic gardens', and the people who used them, contributed to them and studied the plants were usually doctors, surgeons or apothecaries (chemists or pharmacists), seeking materials valuable for drugs or for healing.

This was the case with 'plant collections' established in Roman times, and with those which the Arab conquerors established in Spain and southern Italy. Such gardens were founded in Moorish Spain by the eleventh century, and, with Arabic influence, at Montpellier in southern France by 1250, then in Salerno in southern

Italy. By around 1333 there was a physic garden in Venice, and not long after, another at Prague.

Then, in 1492, Columbus discovered America, and a continent and countries not mentioned in the Bible were added to human experience. The Renaissance was both a rediscovery of the classical past, and a discovery of the physical world beyond the already-known confines of Europe and the Middle East. So, in garden and botanical terms, the classical writings of Theophrastus, Pliny, Dioscorides and Hero of Alexandria were recovered and circulated again; and botanic glories of the New World were added to those of the Old.

RENAISSANCE BOTANIC GARDENS

When, in 1543 and 1545, the first botanic gardens of the Renaissance were founded in Italy, at Pisa and Padua, they were consciously designed to 'house' the plants from *all parts* of the world. Whereas medieval maps of the world showed three continents, Europe, Asia and Africa, with Jerusalem at the centre, the plan of the new botanic garden at Padua (and of others, such as that at Oxford in 1621) was divided into four equal parts, ostensibly to receive the plants grown in the 'four quarters of the globe', the *four* continents of Europe, Asia, Africa and America.

This was not a practical division, and it was not maintained for long. But the excitement of discovery remained, and in the sixteenth and seventeenth centuries, botanic gardens were founded all over Europe to collect, study and disseminate plants and the knowledge of plants. After Pisa and Padua, there were others in Italy; then Leiden in Holland (1587), guided by the great Clusius (Charles de l'Ecluse); Montpellier in France in 1593, building on the Arabic foundation of the thirteenth century; Oxford in 1621; Paris – the Jardin du Roi, proposed in 1597, founded in 1626, and now the Jardin des Plantes; and in 1665 the botanic garden at the University of Uppsala, in Sweden, was founded – almost as if to prepare the ground for the great Linnaeus, 'father of modern botany', a century later.

Each of these botanic gardens had their great men, their discoveries, their special plants. At Padua, we may still see the palm tree planted in

The botanic garden at Padua, Italy.

1585, and immortalized, in prose, by Goethe, and we may read the contemporary account of *Les Plantes d'Egypte* by Prosper Alpin (pub. 1581–84), which is the first detailed (and beautifully illustrated) account of the Egyptian flora. It is in the form of a dialogue – question and answer– between Melchior Wieland and Alpin himself, the former and later directors of this great botanic centre. Montpellier is associated with Pierre Magnol after whom the magnolia is named, and at the Chelsea Physic Garden, in London, founded in 1673, is associated with Philip Miller.

CHELSEA PHYSIC GARDEN

As its name indicates, the Chelsea Physic Garden was founded in the original tradition of such places, as a garden devoted to plants of interest for their medicinal value. Unlike the renaissance gardens of Padua, Leiden and Oxford, the Chelsea Physic Garden has never been part of a university, but was founded by the *Worshipful Company of Apothecaries*, as a means of furthering medical science. Throughout its history, this has always been its principal function, though its broader recognition as a great botanic garden was firmly established in the eighteenth century under Philip Miller (1691–1771).

Miller was appointed curator of the garden in 1722, remaining in this post almost until his death. In this time, the garden became known throughout Europe, and Miller joined Bernard de Jussieu, Buffon, Ehret, Collinson and Linnaeus as a leading figure in botanic enquiry. His great work is the *Gardeners' Dictionary*, first published in 1731 (a smaller version had appeared in 1724), and reaching eight editions, each one enlarged, in his lifetime. The eighth (1768) is of particular importance in the history of botany, since Miller here adopted (at last, and somewhat grudgingly!) the binomial system of plant classification which Linnaeus had put forward in 1753.

PLACES FOR STUDY

All these gardens, from Theophrastus' time to the present day, have been places of study and instruction – gardens where teachers and students *examine plants*. Though we do not know the plan of the Athenian garden where Theophrastus taught, the layout of the botanic gardens of the Renaissance clearly acknowledged the need for students and teachers to be able to gather round the plants they were discussing. The plans – whether at Padua, Leiden, Oxford or Paris – show the main areas divided into a host of little beds, usually rectangular – and occasional engravings of these gardens show teachers and students gathered round these *pulvilli*, as they were called, in animated discussion. The Latin word *pulvillus* means a 'little cushion', since the small, rectangular beds were often slightly raised, like a pillow or cushion, both for drainage and for ease of inspection.

Botanic gardens ever since have kept some part of their layout as 'teaching beds', some more formal than others. We may see them in the Chelsea Physic Garden, used to display different 'families' of plants, and again at Uppsala in Sweden, in the small and charming botanic garden cared for by Linnaeus. At Cambridge University, the Botanic Garden (a mid-nineteenth century foundation, and much developed since 1951), the areas for plant families are larger, and given gentler outlines, but a narrow strip of rectangular *pulvilli*, around 100 yd (90 m) in length, has been laid out to show the procession of plants introduced to the British Isles from other countries – a *chronological* series extending from the Middle Ages to the present day.

Many forms of plant life do not, however, 'fit' into small teaching beds! The design of modern botanic gardens usually takes this into account, especially when dealing with oddly-shaped and exotic species. One of the most recent foundations is the botanic garden at the University of Düsseldorf, designed by Franz Joseph Greub and laid out in the 1970s. While one area has been given a group of formal teaching beds, other parts are excitingly designed to reproduce the different natural habitats - whether rocky or fertile, shaded or exposed, moist or dry - in which the plants would originally have grown.

Other modern botanic gardens adopt a more informal plan - and with striking success. In the heart of Los Angeles is the 8-acre (3-hectare) botanic garden of the University of California at Los Angeles, where winding paths lead between thickets of acacia and eucalyptus, and beneath the fronded, feathery tops of palms. Not many miles away, the Santa Barbara Botanic Garden has a superlative collection of cacti and desert flowers - acres of them, planted informally, and an astonishing botanic spectacle.

Aswan botanic garden is situated on an island in the Nile.

Major American botanic gardens also include the Arnold Arboretum, part of Harvard University, Massachusetts; the Brooklyn Botanic Garden, New York City; Longwood Gardens, near Kennet Square, Pennsylvania; The New York Botanical Garden; Strybing Arboretum, part of Golden Gate Park, San Francisco; the Fairchild Tropical Garden on the outskirts of Miami; and in Canada, the Montreal Garden.

Two typical American botanical gardens are the Missouri Botanical Garden and the Brooklyn Garden. The former was funded privately; the latter began life as a public institution. Missouri Botanical Garden, in St Louis, is locally known as Shaw's Garden, after its benefactor. The garden was established in 1859, and run by Shaw with the help of his friend and physician, the botanist George Engelman. Today, it houses a botanical library, herbarium, museum and educational facilities, as well as an amazing wealth of plants. The Linnaean House (1882) contains camellias, the huge, domed Climatron holds tropical plants, and there is also a Desert House, a Mediterranean House, and a Floral Display House. The rose garden has over 4,000 plants, and an authentic Japanese Garden has been added recently.

The Brooklyn Garden, of only 50 acres, has an immense diversity of plants as well as an educational program in horticulture, botany and conservation. Founded in 1910, it consists largely of an arboretum of trees and shrubs, with a number of small specialist gardens, including three Japanese gardens, children's gardens, a fragrant garden for the blind with plant labels in braille as well as written, a boulder garden, and several model gardens for teaching. It has one of the finest collections of Bonsai trees in the world.

BOTANIC GARDENS OF THE WORLD

The world's botanic gardens – there are several hundred in existence today – have a dazzling variety of interest: their age, their brilliant collections, their layout, their greenhouses and conservatories, their associations with particular collectors or botanists. In the far south of Egypt there is a botanic garden which may reasonably claim to have the most beautiful site of all: the Aswan Botanic Garden, set on a 17-acre (17-hectare) island in the Nile. On the eastern side of the river is the ancient yet modern city of Aswan, on the other side, to the west – the desert. Seven acres (three hectares) were laid out by Lord Kitchener at the turn of the century – it was then called 'Lord Kitchener's Island' – and the collection of tropical and subtropical plants was extended over the whole island in the 1920s. Today it is notable for the immense variety of palm trees – not merely from Africa and Asia, but also from the Pacific islands and from Australia.

PLANT HUNTERS

Botanists (or some of them!) have been among the most intrepid explorers, running great risks to discover and study new species. They have also been benefactors, since their curiosity and powers of observation have been combined with a wish to improve human health and nourishment. From the sixteenth century onwards, they were involved in the voyages of discovery that opened up the world. Though their contribution to modern culture has been great, they were not at first entirely concerned with botany or gardens, but often had other, more important occupations as well: missionaries, traders, diplomats, doctors or sailors.

A hardy geranium and a helichrysum introduced by plant hunters.

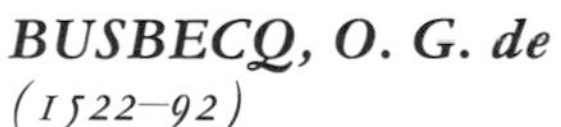

BUSBECQ, O. G. de (1522–92)

Ogier Ghiselin de Busbecq was a diplomat. In 1554 he was sent by the Emperor Ferdinand I to Turkey, as Ambassador to Suleiman the Magnificent, and there, between Adrianople (Edirne) and Constantinople, he saw the *tulip*. It was in the countryside, with 'quantities of flowers everywhere – narcissis, hyacinths, and *tulipans*, as the Turks call them . . . The tulip is admired for its beauty and the variety of its colours'. Wilfrid Blunt suggests that Busbecq 'misunderstood his interpreter', who had compared the shape of the tulip flower with a turban (tulipand); hence the name.

Busbecq brought back to Europe tulip seeds and bulbs, which (he wrote) 'cost me a good deal'. Conrad von Gesner saw them growing at Augsburg in 1559, and his description – with a woodcut illustration – was printed in 1561. Tulips had reached the Netherlands by 1562, England by about 1578, and France by 1608. John Tradescant found in 1618 that they had already reached Russia, and by the 1630s, the craze for rare tulips, in the Netherlands, had become *tulipomania*.

CLUSIUS (Charles de l'ECLUSE) (1526–1609)

Born at Arras, Carolus Clusius, or Charles de l'Ecluse, was educated in classics and the law but swiftly turned away from legal studies to botany. He remained for three years in Montpellier as a student at the university and as guest and secretary of Professor Guillaume Rondelet. In 1552, he travelled in Provence and Brittany, stayed in Paris and went on to Switzerland, Piedmont, Spain and Portugal. He returned with drawings of 200 new species, material for a book on the plants of Spain, dedicated to the Emperor Maximilian II. Summoned to Vienna, he was attached to the Imperial household and collected plants from Austria and Hungary, introducing many new species into the Emperor's gardens. In 1593 he was offered the chair of botany at the University of Leiden, a post he occupied until his death in 1609. He was responsible for the planting of the Hortus Academicus at the University, which quickly became prominent among the botanic gardens of Europe.

Clusius is considered one of the founding fathers of botany, which he treated as a separate discipline, not merely as an annexe of medicine. Clusius is also credited with the start of Holland's bulb industry. Though he did not introduce the first tulip there, he brought several varieties from Vienna which had themselves been brought from Turkey, the home of the tulip. It was said that when he brought these tulips from Vienna, 'no-one could procure them, not even for money. Plans were made by which most of his best plants were stolen by night . . . and by this means the seventeen provinces were well stocked'. He gave his name to *Tulipa clusiana*.

TRADESCANT, John, the Elder
(c.1570–1638)

John Tradescant (the Elder) was responsible for the introduction of several important plants to England, and he and his son John Tradescant (the Younger) are thought to have been the first Englishmen to travel abroad specifically to bring new plants back to their country.

John Tradescant the Elder travelled widely between 1609 and 1627, his journeys allowing and indeed encouraging him to seek out rare plants. He made two journeys to the Low Countries, three to France, one to Russia, and one to a small area of North Africa close to Algiers. His various patrons and employers included Robert Cecil, the 1st Earl of Salisbury; the Duke of Buckingham, and King Charles I and his queen Henrietta Maria, and he was involved both in seeking out plant rarities for them, and in designing their several gardens. He was responsible for garden work for the Earl of Salisbury at Hatfield (Hertfordshire), Theobalds (London) and Cranborne (Dorset), between 1610 and 1614. In 1630, he was appointed royal gardener at Oatlands, in Surrey. From around 1626 onwards, he had also his own garden in Lambeth, which was quickly celebrated for its remarkable collection. In 1637, he was offered the post of keeper of the Oxford Physic Garden, but declined.

Among the many plants he introduced to England were the Siberian larch, purple crane's-bill, spiderwort (*Tradescantia virginiana*) and Virginia creeper.

Apart from gathering plants, Tradescant also collected a great many other rare and curious objects on his travels – a collection known as 'Tradescant's Ark', and kept at his house in Lambeth, on the south bank of the Thames.

TRADESCANT, John, the Younger
(1608–62)

John Tradescant (the Younger) took over from his father as royal gardener at Oatlands, in Surrey. He is noted particularly for his three voyages to Virginia, in 1637, 1642 and 1654, from which he is thought – though without absolute proof – to have brought back several new species, including the red maple, the swamp cypress, the occidental plane and the tulip tree.

On his death, his and his father's collections were taken over by Elias Ashmole, and became the nucleus of the Ashmolean Museum at Oxford, which was founded in 1683. Three generations of Tradescants – the Elder, Younger, and John Tradescant the third – are buried in the churchyard of St Mary's-at-Lambeth. The church is now the Museum of Garden History, and home of the Tradescant Trust.

PLUMIER, Charles
(1646–1706)

Charles Plumier was educated in the Order of Minims. Returning to Marseilles after a period of study in Rome, he collected plants in Provence, Languedoc and Dauphiné, drawing up a herbal with fine illustrations. He was sent on three voyages to the West Indies by Louis XIV in 1689, 1693 and 1695, to study and collect medicinal plants. In 1703 he published his *Nova Plantarum Americanarum Genera*. The first fuchsia is described in this volume.

It is to Plumier that we owe the begonia, the magnolia, named after Magnol, the director of the botanical garden at Montpellier, fuchsia, after Leonard Fuchs, the seventeenth-century German botanist, and lobelia in memory of Mathias de l'Obel . . . He was the first to think of naming plants after botanists, travellers and famous men and women.

KAEMPFER, Engelbert
(1651–1715)

Geographer, doctor and botanist, Kaempfer was appointed surgeon to the Dutch governor of the tiny island of Deshima, the one European trading and diplomatic foothold in the isolated country of Japan. Kaempfer had travelled out to Japan via Persia (his journey took him seven years), and his interests extended far beyond the study of plants. In 1690 and 1691, he was able to join the annual official party of the Dutch ambassador, travelling to the Imperial court, this being his only opportunity to examine the flora of the Japanese mainland (as was the case with his successors in the eighteenth and nineteenth centuries, Thunberg and von Siebold).

In 1712 his *Amoenitates exoticae* (or 'Exotic delights') was published, describing aspects of Japan which he had observed. The fifth section of this work refers to his plant discoveries, which include many species then unknown, but now familiar such as aucuba, hydrangea, ginkgo, skimmia, and several new forms of magnolia, prunus, azalea and tree-paeony, and many camellias.

Nasturtiums, depicted here in a painting by Pierre-Joseph Redouté, were among the many garden plants sent back to France from the Amazon basin by Joseph de Jussieu.

The DE JUSSIEU family

The de Jussieu family left their mark on botany and plant collecting from the early 1700s until the mid-nineteenth century. Of the five who are celebrated for their contributions, three brothers – Antoine, 1686–1758; Bernard, 1699–1777 and Joseph de Jussieu, 1709–79 deserve special mention.

Antoine de Jussieu studied medicine at Montpellier, became fascinated by botany, and made the acquaintance of Pitton de Tournefort, whom he succeeded as professor of botany at the Jardin du Roi in Paris. Studying the growth and cultivation of the coffee plant (introduced from Arabia), he was able in 1719 to provide coffee plants to be taken to the French possessions in the Caribbean, thus beginning the coffee plantations which have prospered in the West Indies ever since.

In 1722 Bernard de Jussieu was invited by his elder brother Antoine to take up the post of demonstrator at the Jardin du Roi. In 1725 he was elected to the Academy of Sciences, and worked on plant classification with such distinction that he became known throughout Europe for his profound knowledge of plants. When Jussieu was visited in Paris by the great Linnaeus, students offered Linnaeus a 'trick' flower, made up from a mixture of plants, and asked him to identify it. Linnaeus tactfully declined to give an answer, saying that 'only Jussieu or God could do so'. Bernard de Jussieu twice travelled to England to obtain plants for the Jardin du Roi, and is supposed to have received a seedling of a cedar of Lebanon – the gift of James Sherard – which he brought back to Paris in his hat. The tree still grows in the garden.

Joseph de Jussieu was more versatile than his brothers, being both botanist, mathematician, physician and engineer. He joined La Condamine's expedition to Ecuador, leaving France in 1735, and explored for plants at Martinique, then San Domingo, and then sailed to Cartagena on the coast of what is now Colombia. From this point he travelled far and long in South America, seeking the mysterious *chinchona* tree whose bark produced the 'powder of the

Jesuits', a cure for fever. At last finding quinine in the Andes of Peru and Ecuador, he had the plant successfully introduced to the Jardin du Roi in Paris.

Then, in the Amazon basin, he discovered the tree called 'cahuchu' by the Indians, and from which they obtained a sort of paste. This was the *hevea* from whose sap rubber is produced. He also discovered, and sent back to France the shrub called 'coca' by the Indians, who chewed its leaves to deaden pain; the medicinal plant ipecacuanha, and two important garden plants, the heliotrope and the nasturtium.

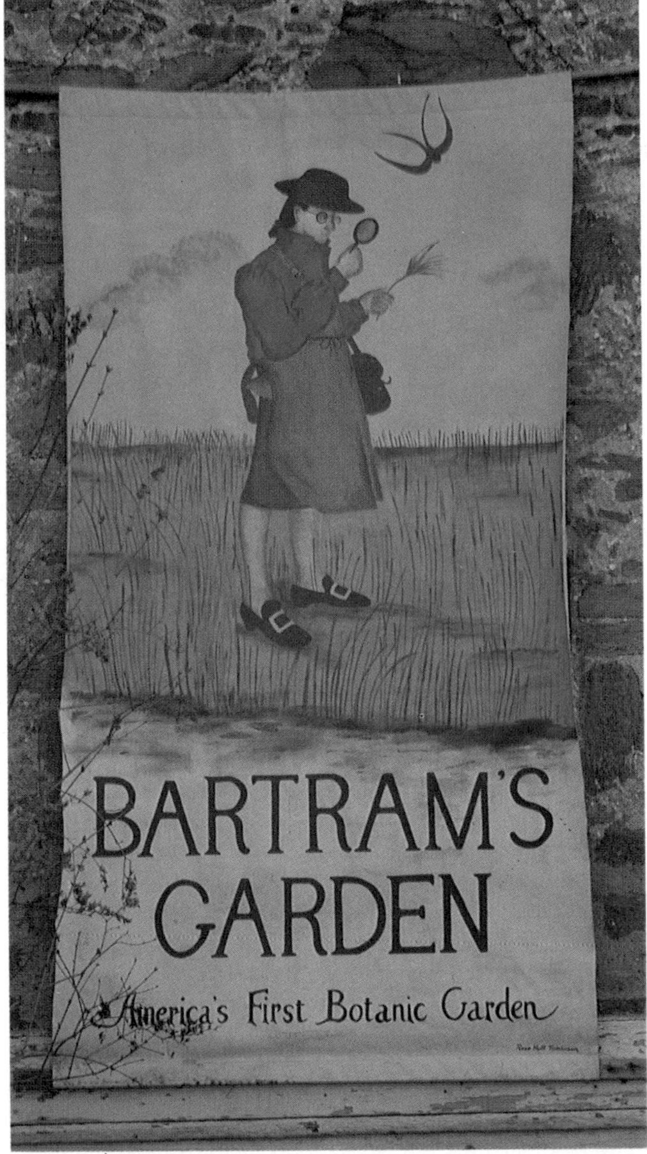

The botanist John Bartram established his own botanic garden.

He did not return to France until 1771, by which time his travels had destroyed both his health and his sanity.

BARTRAM, John

(1699–1777)

A farmer, settled in Pennsylvania on the banks of the Schuykill River, the Quaker John Bartram was a self-taught botanist and an ardent explorer, travelling north as far as Lake Ontario, and south as far as Florida in search of new species. He established his own botanic garden, and from the mid-1730s until 1768 he maintained a lengthy and fruitful correspondence with a fellow Quaker in London, Peter Collinson (1694–1768). He was appointed King's Botanist (to King George III) in 1765.

Collinson, equally enthusiastic in matters of plant-discovery, had his own garden in London, and was instrumental in sending Bartram seeds and materials in exchange for the treasures which came from Pennsylvania. Through Collinson, Bartram supplied plants and seeds to several amateur and professional gardeners in England, notably the Duke of Richmond (at Goodwood, in Sussex), Lord Petre (at Thorndon Hall, in Essex), Philip Miller (at the Chelsea Physic Garden) and Charles Hamilton (at Painshill, in Surrey).

It is thought that Bartram sent some 200 new species from America to England, including many trees now familiar in European settings – American maples, oaks, and pines, *Magnolia acuminata*, and varieties of ash and elm.

POIVRE, Pierre

(1719–86)

Trained as a missionary, Poivre was sent to China in 1741, beginning a career of travel, misfortune and adventure. He became fascinated by botany, and in his last two years in China and Indo-China (until 1745) he travelled widely, studying aspects of agriculture and the varieties of plants which were cultivated.

While returning to Europe, he was stranded in Sumatra (and lost his right hand), and turned to the study of East Indian spices. The spice trade was then controlled by the Dutch, and (after further travels and adventures) Poivre eventually managed to smuggle 3000 nutmeg and other tropical seeds to Mauritius, and thence to the French plantations in the West

Indies. The true black pepper was named *Poivrea* after him.

SOLANDER, Dr Daniel Carl *(1725–82)*

One of Linnaeus' favourite disciples, or 'apostles', Solander travelled from Sweden to England in 1760, where he settled, and where, in the mid-1760s, he was appointed keeper of the Department of Natural History in the British Museum. He is principally noted for his work with Joseph Banks, during Captain Cook's first voyage round the world in 1768–71. During this voyage, he and Banks made notable botanic discoveries on Tierra del Fuego, on the Pacific island of Tahiti, and on the shore of Botany Bay in Australia – Botany Bay being named by Banks for the richness of its hitherto unknown flora.

Solander later accompanied Banks on his expedition to Iceland.

COMMERSON, Joseph-Philibert *(1727–73)*

Commerson's enthusiasm for botany began while he was studying medicine at the University of Montpellier. He rapidly built up a noted collection of plants, and became acquainted (by correspondence) with other botanists of his day, such as Linnaeus and Bernard de Jussieu. In 1766 Bougainville took Commerson with him as botanist on his voyage of exploration. In Uruguay, Commerson discovered the colourful climbing plant which he named *Bougainvillea*, after the expedition's leader, and in 1768 the expedition reached the island of Tahiti, discovered only shortly before by Wallis, and due to be visited soon after by Captain Cook with *his* botanists, Banks and Solander.

During their brief stay on Tahiti, it was discovered that Commerson's young servant was a woman! Her name was Jeanne Baré, and she has the honour of being the first woman to circumnavigate the globe. Commerson however did not return to France. In poor health, he stayed behind on the island of Mauritius, working for a while with Pierre Poivre. After a visit to Madagascar in 1771, Commerson returned again to Mauritius, where he died in 1773. His vast collection of dried plants, drawings and documents reached Jussieu in France a year after his death.

BANKS, Sir Joseph *(1743–1820)*

Banks' wide-ranging botanic and scientific interests were serious and life-long. In 1768 he was the principal figure among the several scientists who went on the *Endeavour*, on Captain Cook's first voyage round the world (1768–71). His assistant botanist was Dr D. C. Solander, and his botanical artist was Sydney Parkinson, who died during the expedition. Parkinson's numerous illustrations, made in Australia and in the Pacific, were engraved, but not printed. The series of over 700 plates has only recently been published, as the magnificent *Flora Banksiana* (1986).

Banks had intended to go round the world again on Cook's second voyage, but Cook would not allow his ship to be modified to accommodate the more luxurious quarters Banks required. Cook set off therefore with new botanists – the Forsters, father and son – and a new artist, William Hodges, while Banks arranged a new expedition for himself, to Iceland, where his studies included the examination of the volcano Mount Hecla. Banks brought back some 40 tons of volcanic lava, which form the nucleus of the rockery in the Chelsea Physic Garden, in London. Returning from Iceland, Banks extended his trip by taking the opportunity to stop off to explore the island of Staffa, in the Hebrides, and named the cavern there 'Fingal's Cave'.

From the 1770s he was the virtual director of the botanic gardens at Kew, and was elected President of the Royal Society in 1778. In 1804, he was one of the founders of the Horticultural Society of London (later to become the Royal Horticultural Society). From Kew, Banks was responsible for training and despatching plant hunters to many parts of the globe – notably Francis Masson to South Africa, William Kerr to China, and Archibald Menzies to South America.

Banks kept up an extensive correspondence with botanists and other scientists throughout Europe. His collections of dried plants and his library came eventually to the British Museum. Banksia, a somewhat delicate shrub with bright tubular flowers, was named after him, and is commonly known in many parts of the world as Australian honeysuckle. The Banksian rose, *Rosa banksiae* (originating in China) is named after his wife, Lady Banks.

Protea. Charles Thunberg introduced many African species into Europe.

THUNBERG, Carl
(1743–1828)

After studying medicine at Uppsala and attending the courses of Linnaeus, Thunberg travelled to Holland, and found a post as ship's surgeon, leaving Europe in 1771 on board a vessel of the Dutch East India Company. His subsidiary task was to find and gather new plants for the collections of Dutch gardens, and his aim was to reach Japan.

However, Thunberg first spent the period 1772–75 in South Africa, exploring untravelled areas and sending back to his patrons specimens of the rich and unique flora. He was to enrich the gardens of Europe with new heathers and gladiolus, and discovered the curious *Protea grandiflora*.

Thunberg later published his *Première Flore du Cap*, which remained the authoritative text on the flowers of South Africa for many years.

Heading again for Japan, he stopped briefly in Batavia (Jakarta), which he visited again in 1776, after his long-awaited stay in Japan – a country where no botanist had been able to collect since Kaempfer at the end of the seventeenth century. He managed to have himself appointed physician to the Dutch governor on the little island of Deshima off Nagasaki, the only place where the Dutch were allowed to reside and carry on commerce.

Using the annual ambassadorial visit to the Emperor as a pretext, he was able to travel through the Japanese archipelago for a few months in 1776.

An acute observer, he was able to describe a wealth of species that have since become garden classics, for example, japonica, kerria, loquat, weigela, deutzia, aucuba, Japanese maple, andromeda, and forsythia. Many of these plants did not reach Europe until much later – forsythia, for example arrived in the 1840s: *F. viridissima*, from China, in 1844, and *F. suspensa*, from Japan, a few years later.

Yet thanks to Thunberg's efforts, new plants from the East Indies and from the Cape found their way into botanic gardens and private collections. When he returned to his native Sweden in 1779, he was appointed to the chair of botany previously held by his teacher, the great Linnaeus. For 50 years he devoted himself to education, to the publication of botanical works such as his *Flora japonica* of 1784, and to accounts of his travels. His name is commemmorated in the pretty *Thunbergia alata*, commonly known as 'Black-eyed Susan'.

MICHAUX, François-André
(1770–1855)

The son of André Michaux (1746–1802), also a botanist, F.-A. Michaux followed his father to the United States in the company of the gardener Paul Saulnier, who was to run the garden that the Michaux's had established in New Jersey, some 6 miles (10 km) from New York. The garden served as a nursery for plants waiting to be sent back to Europe. A similar establishment was created further south, under more clement skies, near Charleston. Michaux searched for plants from Florida to Hudson Bay and the Mississippi. The Charleston garden became a reception centre for plants arriving *in* the United States from other countries. For example, the first ginkgo to be planted in America passed through there, and many azaleas and rhododendrons.

Notable books on American plants by André and F.-A. Michaux include the *Histoire des chênes de l'Amérique septentrionale*, *Flora boreali americana* and *The North American Sylva*.

BONPLAND, Aimé
(1773–1858)

After becoming a ship's doctor, Bonpland met the brilliant Prussian scientist Alexander von Humboldt in 1798, and a lifelong friendship began. Under Humboldt's influence, Bonpland developed a consuming passion for the study of exotic flora. He dreamed of discoveries in South America, a mysterious continent where Humboldt hoped to find confirmation of his ideas on the interdependence of the sciences. They left together on an expedition financed by Humboldt from his large personal fortune.

In July 1799, the two scientists reached Venezuela and quickly came to grips with the green and mosquito-infested regions of the Orinoco jungle. For four years, they wandered in the midst of incredible dangers, Bonpland collecting 6000 new plant species, almost a tenth of the number then known for the whole world! Their successes were largely chronicled and published by Humboldt. After a while in Mexico, they returned to France in 1804, receiving a tumultuous welcome. Bonpland had offered some of his seeds to Joséphine de Beauharnais and she now proposed that he should take charge of her gardens at Malmaison and Navarre, where rare orchids and exotic plants grew in profusion. The post was accepted and Bonpland meanwhile continued a voluminous correspondence with the great botanists of Europe.

His yearning for South America, however, remained and in 1817 he settled in the province of Corrientes in the north of Argentina, in a region disputed by the neighbouring state of Paraguay. Bonpland established a model farm and introduced fruits and vegetables from Europe. Unfortunately, Bonpland fell foul of Francia, the dictator of Paraguay, who had him arrested on suspicion of espionage. His plantation was destroyed and for nine years he was placed under surveillance, living in poverty in a small village where he prepared syrups and decoctions to treat the illnesses of the peasants and Indians, and trying to improve the cultivation of local crops.

Aimé Bonpland

In 1830 or 1831 he returned to France but was once more in Argentina in 1853, and stayed there until his death five years later.

BALDWIN, William
(1779–1819)

A Quaker from Chester County, Pennsylvania, Baldwin studied medicine but loved botany, and corresponded with eminent American botanists. After completing his studies, he became a ship's surgeon, through which he travelled to China, Buenos Aires and, closer to home, up the Missouri River, cataloguing and collecting plants.

RAFINESQUE, Constantine Samuel
(1783–1840)

Born to a French father and German mother, Rafinesque grew up in Sicily, but emigrated and settled in the United States in 1815. He became a professor of botany and natural history in Lexington, Kentucky, and from there, made frequent plant-collecting expeditions to the mid-west. He wrote numerous treatises on plants, and after a century of relative obscurity is now recognized as a brilliant, if eccentric, genius.

SIEBOLD, Philipp Franz von
(1791–1866)

Born into a long line of doctors, Dr von Siebold became a physician in the service of the East Indian Company. Like Kaempfer and Thunberg before him, he managed to have himself sent as physician to the Dutch governor of the island of Deshima, the West's only window on Japan.

He remained in the country from 1826 to 1830 and enjoyed an advantage that neither of his predecessors had possessed. Von Siebold knew how to operate on cataracts of the eye, a problem that the Japanese were then unable to treat. Much in demand, he could travel in relative freedom and was able to collect unknown plants to send to botanic gardens in Europe. It was he who introduced Japanese wistaria as well as many species of bamboo, azalea, camellia, lily and clematis. He was expelled in 1830, for obtaining forbidden maps of the country.

Upon his return to Europe, von Siebold was to open a nursery in Leiden, and in 1835–42 he produced the two volumes of the *Flora of Japan*, in collaboration with J. G. Zuccarini.

He returned to Japan in 1859, living in a house on the outskirts of Nagasaki. There, in the words of Robert Fortune, he established 'small nurseries for the reception and propagation of new plants, and for preparing them for transportation to Europe'. He remained for three years, introducing still more new plants, such as *Spiraea thunbergii*, *Prunus sieboldii* and *Hydrangea paniculata*.

FORTUNE, Robert
(1813–80)

A Scot, Robert Fortune was working at the Edinburgh botanic garden in 1942 when the Treaty of Nankin ended the Opium War and opened the ports of China to the British. The following year, he was sent to China by the Royal Horticultural Society, arriving in Hong Kong. He was to spend the next three years in an extraordinarily fruitful hunt for plants.

Fortune was the first plant hunter to make extensive use of 'Wardian cases' for the transport of his plants. These little portable greenhouses had been invented a few years before by Dr Nathaniel Bagshaw Ward.

In this way, he was able to introduce a considerable number of new plants to Europe, the more common of them including Japanese anemone, *Prunus triloba*, winter jasmine, white wistaria, forsythia, weigela and *Mahonia bealei*.

He was in China again from 1848–58, and later, on his third and final voyage to the Far East, he brought back from Japan the male form of *Aucuba japonica*, without which the female plants, already cultivated in England, would not produce their clusters of decorative red fruit.

HALL, George R
(1820–99)

A graduate of Harvard Medical School, Hall practiced medicine in Shanghai, China. From there, he sent a wealth of plants, long cultivated in China but unknown to the West. These included *Taxus cuspidata*, an oriental yew; the honeysuckle named after him, *Lonicera japonica* 'Halliana'; the water-lily magnolia *Magnolia stellata*; and the Japanese wistaria, *Wistaria floribunda*. He eventually returned to live in Rhode Island, where he grew an impressive collection of Asiatic evergreens.

PARRY, Charles Christopher
(1823–96)

An Englishman by birth, Parry settled in America, where he practiced medicine. From 1846–90, he made many plant-hunting expeditions into Mexico, the mid-west, the Rocky Mountains, and the Pacific coast. His most famous discovery is the blue spruce, *Picea pungens*, which he first saw on Pikes Peak in 1862. Plants named after him include the lovely *Lilium parryi*, *Phacelia parryi* and *Fraseri parryi*.

DAVID, Jean-Pierre Armand
(1826–1900)

Trained as a priest, David entered the order of Lazarists and was appointed to a teaching post at the Collège de Savone, where he established a little museum of natural history. In 1862, he was sent to Peking in China, where the French government was hoping to establish schools. Having collected rare plant specimens, which he sent back to France, he so impressed his correspondents in the Museum of Natural History that they promptly obtained permission from the superior of the Lazarists for him to devote his energies entirely to his botanic and other discoveries.

The work that Armand David accomplished in China was important not only for botany but also for geology, entomology, ornithology, and other sciences. His studies embraced the giant panda, and Père David's deer. After a systematic study of the Peking plain, he left for Jehol in the north of the country and for travels through Inner Mongolia, Central China and Eastern Tibet. He made three expeditions in all, in 1866, 1868–69, and 1872–74. He returned to France in 1874.

Botanists owe to him the discovery of some 250 garden species, such as *Cotoneaster horizontalis*, *Juniperus chinensis* Pfitzeriana, *Acer davidii*, *Prunus davidii* (the original rootstock of which was sent to the Paris Museum where the tree still

Dividia involucrata, the handkerchief tree, discovered in China by Father Armand David.

stands), *Buddleja davidii*, and finally *Davidia involucrata*, the handkerchief tree, discovered near Moupin in Eastern Tibet.

So numerous were David's discoveries that botanists exhausted the terms 'Davidii' and 'Davidiana' and had to use his Christian name, Armand – as in *Clematis armandii*.

DELAVAY, Jean-Marie *(1838–95)*

Jean-Marie Delavay left France as a missionary for China in 1867 and travelled through the Kwangdong and Kwangchi regions.

His first materials were sent to England, but in 1881, on leave in Paris, he met Armand David. David introduced him to A. R. Franchet, the director of the Natural History Museum, and from this point all his discoveries were sent to the French national herbarium. The result of his efforts was one of the finest collections of plants in the world, with over 50,000 specimens and 4000 species, 1800 of them new.

Delavay later concentrated on mountain flora, discovering a great range of plants from primulas, gentians and clematis to conifers and magnolias. In the mountains of Yunan province, he found northerly plants, such as cassiopea or rhododendron, and orchids of the rain forest.

Among the plants which he found were several wild paeonies, including *Paeonia lutea*, with large yellow flowers, and *Paeonia delavayi* whose petals are dark red. There are many plants that bear the name Delavay, the first botanist who among other things came to the conclusion that 'the flora of the European alps, despite its variety, is not more than an offshoot of the alps of Eastern Asia'.

HOOKER, Sir Joseph Dalton *(1817–1911)*

Hooker began his career as a botanist with the *Erebus* expedition to the Antarctic region in 1839, led by Sir James Clark Ross. He visited New Zealand, Australia, Tierra del Fuego and the Falkland Islands, returning with a rich harvest of specimens and observations of flora. In 1847, he left for India where three years of travel would be concentrated mostly in the Himalayas, Nepal and Sikkim.

On his return, he published the description of some 7000 plants and introduced a whole range of rhododendrons which adapted well to European gardens. It was also Hooker who introduced the species *Primula sikkimensis* and *P. capitata* as well as the superb blue orchid *Vanda caerulea*. He worked on a collection of dried plants, gathered from the Galapagos Islands and sent to him by Charles Darwin, his life-long friend.

In 1855 he became Assistant Director of the Royal Botanic Gardens at Kew, and achieved promotion succeeding his father (Sir William Jackson Hooker) as Director in 1865. His later travels took him in 1871 to Morocco for the flora of the Atlas.

Lilium regale, *introduced by Ernest Wilson.*

WILSON, Ernest Henry
(1876–1930)

Wilson was only 22 when he was asked to go to collect seed and new plants from Central China, on behalf of the famous Veitch nursery. He made two journeys for this firm, in 1899–1902 and 1903–05, followed by others to China, then to Japan. He became a member of the staff of the Arnold Arboretum (near Boston, Massachusetts) in 1909, and eventually succeeded, C. S. Sargent as its director.

In the course of his travels in the Far East, Wilson discovered more than 3000 plant species, a good thousand of which could be grown in Europe. His most famous discovery was the royal lily, *Lilium regale*. Other notable plants included *Lonicera nitida*, *Hydrangea sargentiana* and more than sixty rhododendrons, Japanese azaleas and flowering cherries. *Acer griseum*, the paper bark maple, was introduced by him in 1907.

His first published work appeared in 1913, *A Naturalist in Western China*, an account of his travels and botanical discoveries. *China, Mother of Gardens*, followed in 1923. His *Lilies of Eastern Asia* was published in 1925.

KINGDON-WARD, Frank
(1885–1958)

A geographer and plant collector, Frank Kingdon-Ward led more than 25 expeditions in China, particularly to the border regions close to Burma and India. He brought back many new species: rhododendrons, primulas, lilies, gentians and poppies.

Meconopsis*, the Himalayan blue poppy, recently introduced to Europe by Frank Kingdon-Ward.*

An especially valued introduction of his was the blue Himalayan poppy, *Meconopsis betonicifolia*, which he found in south-eastern Tibet. It had first been discovered by Delavay, but its introduction was effected by Kingdon-Ward. Because of his vast experience of the jungle, he was selected during the Second World War to create and run a survival school for men engaged in the South East Asian theatre of operations. Among other things, he taught them how to recognize plants and to learn their uses.

The Romance of Plant Hunting was published in 1924, the best-known of a score of books which he wrote.

ARTISTS AND ILLUSTRATORS

Some of the earliest gardens, those in Egypt, are known to us principally from the illustrations preserved in tombs close to the Nile; as are some of the earliest pictures of botanic interest, like the scene of incense trees with wrapped 'root balls' being carried carefully on board ship, during Queen Hatshepsut's expedition to the land of Punt (c. 1470 BC). But the artists are unknown, as are most of the artists who drew plants in medieval herbals, and those who gave glimpses of gardens in illuminated manuscripts. Not until the Renaissance do the names of the artists survive, and even then the depictions of gardens and plants are mostly incidental, details in broader religious or secular compositions. The genre of plant illustrations was given special encouragement in the sixteenth century when botanic compilations recorded the flood of plants discovered and catalogued, and the art of flower painting was directly affected. We list four notable flower painters from later periods, each famous and each distinctive in their own way.

A gentian, Gentiana acaulis, *depicted in a painting by Pierre-Joseph Redouté.*

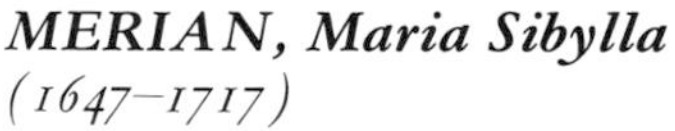

MERIAN, Maria Sibylla
(1647–1717)

The daughter of the topographical artist Matthaeus Merian the Elder, Maria Sibylla Merian is a painter as noted for her delineations of insects as for her pictures of the plants and flowers they flutter round, or feed upon.

In her early thirties, she produced one fine book of botanical illustrations, the *Neues Blumenbuch* of 1680, and the first of her several great works illustrating insects, depicted on or close to the plants they feed on – *Der Raupen wunderbare Verwandlung*, 1679–83. This work, 'The wondrous transformation of caterpillars', went through several editions culminating in *De Europische Insecten* of 1730.

Then in June 1699, when she was 52, she sailed to Surinam, the Dutch colony in South America, and stayed for two years to study and depict the country's insects and flowers. Her book *Dissertatio . . . Surinamensium*, 'Dissertation

A botanical illustration of tulips and fritillaries by Maria Sybilla Merian.

on the generation and metamorphoses of the insects of Surinam', appeared in 1705, with a second, enlarged edition in 1719, two years after her death in 1717 – the publication supervized by her elder daughter Johanna, who went to Surinam to complete her mother's work. Both mother and daughter must count among the most truly 'intrepid' of women artists and plant-lovers, comparable with Marianne North in the nineteenth century.

EHRET, Georg Dionysius
(1708–70)

Born in Heidelberg, Ehret first worked as a gardener, but quickly turned to the depiction of plants and flowers. In his first 30 years he travelled widely, both within Germany, and in other countries of Europe, meeting botanists and plant-lovers, and undertaking many commissions as a botanical illustrator. In France, he met Bernard de Jussieu, who arranged for him to spend the winter of 1734–35 in the Jardin Royal des Plantes, and in 1735 he met Linnaeus when the latter was in Holland. Ehret and the great Swedish botanist developed a firm friendship, and Linnaeus later 'papered' the walls of two rooms in his country house at Hammarby with Ehret's engravings of plants. After one short, earlier visit to England, Ehret returned to England in 1736, staying there for the rest of his life.

He met Philip Miller, curator of the Chelsea Physic Garden, and married Miller's sister-in-law, Susanna Kennet. Though he was to become somewhat cold towards Miller, Ehret provided 16 (of the total of 200) illustrations for Miller's *Figures of the Most Beautiful Plants . . . Described in the Gardener's Dictionary* (1760). His own most famous work was the *Plantae et papiliones rariores* (1748–62), but he was also the artist of the 120 plates in C. J. Trew's *Plantae selectae* (1750–92).

COLDEN, Jane
(1724–66)

This distinguished American botanist was the daughter of Cadwallader Colden, the governor of New York. He was a friend of Linnaeus, a keen naturalist, and encouraged his daughter to learn Latin and draw plants. By 1758, she had compiled a manuscript describing over 400 local New York plants and their uses. This was never published, but was highly esteemed by her father's European correspondents and visiting botanists. After her death, the manuscript was sent to Sir Joseph Banks, and eventually to the British Museum.

REDOUTÉ, Pierre-Joseph
(1759–1841)

Redouté's artistic talents appeared at an early age and he first trained as a lithographer. He joined forces with a botanist, L'Héritier de Brutelle, whose works he illustrated, and then began to specialize in the illustration of botanical specimens, coming under the influence of Gerard van Spaëndonck, the official painter at the Jardin des Plantes. Redouté then became painter successively to Marie-Antoinette, and teacher of Joséphine, Marie-Louise, the Duchesse de Berry, Queen Marie-Amélie and Madame Adélaïde.

Joséphine employed him to illustrate her finest plants, and several splendid folios were

A botanical painting by Marianne North shows the tulip tree, false acacia, mountain laurel and varieties of rhododendron.

produced with his pictures. Of the many works that he illustrated, the best-known is *Les Roses* (1817–44), but he was also renowned for reproductions of lilies and succulent plants. Among other books that were illustrated by Redouté, are Desfontaines' *Flora atlantica*, Bonpland's *La Flore de Navarre* and *Les Plantes rares du jardin de Cels*, and Rousseau's *Lettres sur la botanique*.

He bequeathed to the Museum of Natural History a fabulous collection of 6000 watercolours, called 'Les Vélins' since they were painted on vellum.

NORTH, Marianne
(1830–90)

Already experienced as a botanical painter, and with extensive European travels behind her, Marianne North set out in 1871 for Canada, the United States and Jamaica, with the express purpose of recording in pictorial form the plants of foreign countries.

Between 1871 and 1885, she travelled to all six continents, to countries as far apart as Japan, Egypt, Chile, India, Australia, Borneo and South Africa, her many hundreds of pictures often including a landscape, garden or architectural background to the one or more species which were the main subject. In 1882, a special gallery – the Marianne North Gallery – was opened in the Royal Botanic Gardens at Kew – displaying 832 of her pictures, closely ranged together and covering the entire wall-space of two rooms, according to her own plan.

From 1886 until her death, she was occupied in creating the 2-acre (0.8-hectare) garden of The Mount House, Alderley, in Gloucestershire. Her autobiography, *Recollections of a Happy Life*, was published in 1893, and reissued, in shorter form with many illustrations of her work, as *A Vision of Eden* (1980).

EATON, Mary
(b.1893)

Though she had no special botanical training, Mary Eaton was always intrigued by flowers. In 1909, she visited Jamaica to stay with relatives; there, she painted the local flora and fauna. These paintings were the basis of her appointment to the post of artist to the New York Botanical Garden, where she remained until 1932. The Botanical Garden retains most of the originals, but in Washington D.C., there are approximately 500 of her drawings.

WRITERS

'God Almightie first Planted a Garden', wrote Bacon in 1625. He might have added that garden writing is almost as old, going back to the book of Genesis. Some writers on garden themes are shadowy figures, known only for their books – such as Thomas Hill, or Hyll, whose* Most Briefe and Pleasaunt Treatyse *of 1563 is the earliest printed book by an English garden writer. Was he a gardener himself, and if so, where? Did he garden for others? We do not know. Again, as with the artists who have depicted gardens and their plants as just one part of their work, garden writers often wrote on other subjects as well, or wrote of gardens as a small but enthralling part of a wider concern.

Vita Sackville-West.

THE GARDEN WRITERS

Some of these writers are also known for their gardening skills or general literary skills.

Sir Francis Bacon (1561–1626), statesman and universal writer, whose gardens at Gorhambury in Hertfordshire are a shadowy memory, yet whose marvellous essay *On Gardens* (1625) is in fact but one of the flashes of wisdom on men, manners and the world contained in his *Essays*;

William Shenstone (1714–63), who created the 150-acre (61-hectare) *ferme ornée* of the Leasowes, who was a minor poet, who wrote *Unconnected Thoughts on Gardening* (pub. 1764), and who corresponded copiously with his contemporaries about gardens, literature and life;

Horace Walpole (4th Earl of Orford) *(1717–97)*, moved into two small adjacent buildings close to the River Thames, at Twickenham near London in 1747. The property was called Strawberry Hill. From then until his death he was active in building a 'Gothic' structure, part castle and part mansion, round the original buildings, and in gardening the surrounding grounds, which he was able to extend until they reached the river's edge.

Apart from his thousands of letters, in which gardens are one of the recurrent topics, he kept a private journal describing his 'visits to country seats' over many years, and in 1771 published his perceptive and highly influential essay *On Modern Gardening*, in which his disapproval of formal gardens is as strongly expressed as his admiration of the new style of landscape gardening, given its principal impetus by William Kent, who 'leaped the fence, and saw that all nature was a garden'.

Marquis René-Louis de Girardin *(1735–1808)*, was a soldier, traveller, writer and gardener. In 1766, Girardin inherited his father's estate at Ermenonville, north of Paris and by 1777 his 'landscape' at Ermenonville was virtually complete. Girardin set out his ideas on gardens, landscapes, and their associated *usefulness* in his *De la Composition des paysages* (1777), in which, apart from the main discussion of landscape gardens, he set out the Rousseauan ideas that the beauty of 'natural surroundings' could lead those living in them to a happy and virtuous existence.

Thomas Jefferson *(1743–1826)*, even more than his fellow statesmen, Benjamin Franklin and George Washington, was fascinated by garden matters, both within his own property at Monticello in Virginia, and in gardens great and small in America and in Europe, seen on his visits to France and England in the 1780s.

His *Garden Book*, a journal and notes related to his garden at Monticello, was kept in intriguing detail from 1766 to 1824. He designed both his own garden at Monticello, and the garden-campus of the University of Virginia at Charlottesville. Monticello, built on high ground with views out towards Charlottesville, was begun before his European travels, but is still partly and strongly indebted to the influence of the English landscape garden.

Prince H. L. H. Pückler-Muskau (1785–1871), known as the 'Parkomane' or 'park maniac', who gardened on the grandest and most lavish scale on his estates at Muskau, and at Branitz, in East Germany. He wrote on gardens in *Andeutungen über Landschaftsgärtnerei* ('Observations on Landscape Gardening'), 1834, and superb travel literature in his *Briefe Eines Verstorbenen* ('Letters of the Late x x x') of 1836;

Sir George Sitwell (1860–1943), who first created the gardens of Renishaw, in Derbyshire, and, from 1925 onwards, recreated those at Montegufoni, near Florence in Italy, while producing several historical works, and one of the best studies of the nature of gardens ever to be written – *On the Making of Gardens* (1909);

Vita Sackville-West (1892–1962), who created the great modern garden of Sissinghurst in Kent, with her husband Harold Nicolson, and who wrote novels, garden poetry – *The Garden* (1946) – and many essays on garden matters, contained, for example, in her *Garden Book* (1968).

E.A. Bowles (1865–1954) was a British plantsman whose great passion was his garden at Myddleton House, Enfield, London. Its planting, including a river bank of iris opposite a bank of tulips, became world famous. While his rock garden, flowering in perfect sequence from early spring to midsummer, was a masterpiece. He was the author of a three volume collection which chronicled the development and delights of his garden: *My Garden in Spring My Garden in Summer* and *My Garden in Winter*.

Christopher Lloyd (b.1921) gardens Great Dixter, in East Sussex, England. The gardens of this fifteenth-century manor house were re-designed in 1910 by Gertrude Jekyll, and contain a topiary garden, sunken garden, lily pool, and enormous herbaceous border among other features. Christopher Lloyd inherited the garden from his father, himself an eminent plantsman, and is as knowledgable about his subject as he is an amusing and perceptive writer. His works include the classic *The Well Tempered Garden*, *Clematis*, *Foliage Plants*, *Hardy Perennials*, and *The Year at Great Dixter*.

A.J. Downing (1815–1852), the American precursor of Olmsted, was an enormously prolific writer. His first book, in 1841, was his most impressive: *A Treatise on the Theory and Practice of Landscape Gardening*. It was especially adapted to North America, and intended to improve the gardens of country residences. Other publications include *Cottage Residences*, and *The Fruits and Fruit Trees of America*. He founded the magazine *The Horticulturalist*, and edited it until his death.

Garret Eckbo (b.1910) is an American city planner and landscape architect, who grew up and now practices in California. He is a great innovator, relating garden design to the concepts of modern art, and also to the needs of people who use the gardens. He is professor Emeritus at the University of California at Berkeley; his major publication is *The Landscape We See* (1949).

Lanning Roper (1912–83) was an American by birth, educated at Harvard University, who later settled in England where he practiced landscape gardening. For many years gardening correspondent of *The Sunday Times*, and consultant for the National Trust, he designed various private commissions, and the central garden at the Royal Horticultural Society, Wisley. His books include *Town Gardening* (1957) and *Royal Gardens* (1953).

INDEX

Common names appear in roman type and are cross-referred to genus.
Bold numerals refer to main entries, *italic* numerals to illustrations.

Abelia, **290**
Abies, 170, 171, *214*, **290–1**
Abutilon, **291**, *291*
Acacia, 169, **291–2**
Acacia, false, *see Robinia*
Acaena, **292–3**
Acantholimon, **292–3**
Acanthus, **293**, 596
Acer, 46, 54, 134, *134*, 169, 170, **293–5**, *293*, 606, 608, 610, 612
Achillea, *77*, 169, **295**
Acinos, **295**
Aconite, *see Aconitum*
Aconite, winter, *see Eranthis*
Aconitum, 21, 79, 140, 170, *295*, **296**, 596
Acorus, **296**
Actaea, **296**, *296*
Actinidia, 72, 122–3
Adam's needle, *see Yucca*
Adder's tongue, *see Erythronium*
Adenophora, **296–7**
Adenostyles, **297**
Adonis, **297**, *297*
Aechmea, **297–8**
Aeschynanthus, **298**
Aesculus, 170, **298**
Aethionema, **299**
Agapanthus, 22, 78, *188*, **299**, *299*
Agastache, **299–300**
Agave, **300**
Ageratum, 228, **300**
Agrostis, **300**
Ailanthus, 41, 245, **300–1**
Ajuga, **301**
Akebia, 98, **301**, *301*
Albizia, **302**, *302*
Alder, *see Alnus*
Alhambra, gardens of the, 11, *12*
Alisma, **302–3**
Allium, *99*, 115, *116*, 118, *118*, 123, 173, 174, 175, 223, *223*, 228, **303–5**, *304*
Allspice, *see Calycanthus*
Almond, *see Prunus*
Alnus, 170, 171, **305**
Aloe, **306**
Alonsoa, **306**
Alpine gardens and houses, 88, 95, *95*
Alstroemeria, 78, **306–7**, *306*
Althaea, 41, 55, 170, 241, **307**, *307*
Alton Towers, 40, *40*
Alyssum, 91, 169, 170, **307–8**
Amaranthus, 41, 58, **308**, *308*
Amaryllis, **308**, 442
Amelanchier, 170, 171, **308–9**
Ampelopsis, 72, 79, 98, 150
Amsonia, **309**
Anacyclus, **309**
Ananas, **309**
Anaphalis, 243
Anchusa, *77*, 170
Ancolia, *77*
Andromeda, *see Pieris*
Androsace, **309–10**
Anemone, 21, 41, 52, 170, 171, 172, 220, **310**, *310*, 610
Anemone, tree, *see Carpenteria*
Anethum, 310
Angelica, **311**
Angel's fishing rod, *see Dierama*
Angel's trumpet, *see Brugmansia*
Anise (aniseed), *see Pimpinella*
Anise tree, *see Illicium*
Antennaria, **311**
Anthemis, 169, 235, **311**
Anthriscus, 123, **311–12**
Antirrhinum, **312**
Apios, **312**
Apium, 115, 116, 118, **312–13**
Aponogeton, **313**, *313*
Apple, *see Malus*
Apricot, *see Prunus*
Aquatic plants, 108–9, 222–3, *222*
Aquilegia, 21, 170, 172, **313–14**, *314*
Arabis, 170, 172, **314**
Aralia, **314**
Araucaria, 41, **314–15**
Arbor-vitae, *see Thuja*
Arbutus, 171, **315**
Arctostaphylos, 171, **315**
Arctotis, **315–16**, *315*
Ardisia, **316**
Arenaria, 92, **316**
Argemone, **316**
Arisaema, **316–17**, *317*
Arisarum, **317**
Aristolochia, 169
Armeria, **317–18**
Armoracia, **318**
Arnebia, **318**
Arnica, **318**
Arrowhead, *see Sagittaria*
Artemisia, 123, **318–19**
Artichoke, 245
  Chinese or Japanese, *see Stachys*; globe, *see Cynara*; Jerusalem, 244
Arum, **319**, *319*
Aruncus, 172, **319–20**
Arundinaria, **320**
Arundo, **320**
Asarabaca, *see Asarum*
Asarum, **320**
Asclepias, **320**
Ash, *see Fraxinus*
Ash, mountain, *see Sorbus*
Asparagus, 115, 118, 119, *119*, *162*, **321**
Asparagus, French, *see Ornithogalum*
Aspen, *see Populus*
Asperula, **321–2**
Asphodel, *see Asphodeline*; *Asphodelus*
Asphodeline, **322**, *322*
Asphodelus, **322**
Asplenium, **322–3**
Aster, 58, 171, 243, **323**
Aster
  China, *see Callistephus*; cornflower, *see Stokesia*; tree, *see Olearia*
Asteriscus, **323**
Astilbe, 171, 172, **323–4**, *323*
Astragalus, **324**
Astrantia, 172, **324**, *324*
Athyrium, **324–5**
Atriplex, 134, **325**
Aubergine, 115, 117, 228
Aubretia, 91, 169, 170, **325**
Aucuba, 171, 272, **325–6**, 605, 608, 610
Avens, *see Geum*
Avocado pear, *see Persea*
Azalea, *see Rhododendron*
Azalea, mock, *see Menziesia*
Azara, **326**
Azolla, **326**
Azorella, **326**

Baby's breath, *see Gypsophila*
Bacon, Sir Francis, 616
Balcony gardens, **147–54**
Baldwin, William, **609**
Balloon flower, see *Platycodon*
Ballota, **327**
Balm, *see Melissa*
Balsam, *see Impatiens*
Bamboo, 151, 198, 245, 610
  see also Arundinaria; *Chimonobambusa*; *Sasa*
Banana, *see Musa*
Baneberry, *see Actaea*
Banks, Sir Joseph, 43, **607**
Banksia, 607
Baptisia, **327**
Barbarea, **327–8**
Barbary fig, *see Opuntia*
Barberry, *see Berberis*
Barren strawberry, *see Waldsteinia*
Barrenwort, *see Epimedium*
Bartram, John, **606**, *606*
Basella, **328**
Basil, *see Ocimum*
Basket plant, *see Aeschynanthus*
Bauhinia, **328**
Bay
  laurel, *see Laurus*; rose, *see Nerium*; sweet, *see Laurus*
Bead tree, *see Melia*
Beafsteak plant, *see Iresine*
Bearberry, *see Arctostaphylos*
Bear's breeches, *see Acanthus*
Bear's ear, *see Primula*
Beauty berry, *see Callicarpa*
Beauty bush, *see Kolkwitzia*
Bedding plants, 87, *87*, 223–4, *224*
Bee balm, *see Monarda*
Beech, *see Fagus*
Beet, *see Beta*
Beetroot, *see Beta*
Begonia, 86, 150, 228, 229, 235, 239, 244, **328–9**, *328*, 604
Begonia vine, *see Cissus*
Belamcanda, **329**
Bellflower, *see Campanula*; bonnet, *see Codonopsis*; Chilean, *see Lapageria*
Bellis, 86, **329**, *329*
Bells of Ireland, *see Moluccella*
Bellwort, *see Uvularia*
Beloeil, 28
Berberis, 52, 169, 170, 171, 270, 274, **330**, *330*
Bergamot, *see Citrus*
Bergamot, wild, *see Monarda*
Bergenia, 171, 172, **330**
Beta, 115, 175, 227, **330–1**
Betula, 169, 171, **331–2**
Bignonia, 97, 98
Bilberry, *see Vaccinium*
Bindweed, *see Convolvulus*
Birch, *see Betula*
Bird of paradise shrub, *see Caesalpinia*
Bird's-foot trefoil, *see Lotus*
Biscutella, **332**
Blackberry, *see Rubus*
Blackcurrant, *see Ribes*
Black-eyed Susan, *see Thunbergia*
Black locust, *see Robinia*
Bladder senna, *see Colutea*
Blanket flower, *see Gaillardia*
Blazing star, *see Liatris*
Blechnum, **332**
Bleeding heart, *see Dicentra*
Blenheim Palace, 62, 589, 592
Bletilla, **332–3**, *332*
Bloodleaf, *see Iresine*
Bloodroot, *see Sanguinaria*
Bloodwort, *see Sanguisorba*
Bluebeard, *see Caryopteris*
Bluebell, *see Hyacinthoides*
Bluebell, Siberian, *see Scilla*
Blueberry, *see Vaccinium*
Blue-eyed Mary, *see Omphalodes*
Blue potato bush, *see Solanum*
Blueweed, *see Echium*
Bocconia, *see Macleaya*
Bog-bean, *see Menyanthes*
Boneset, *see Eupatorium*
Bonpland, Aimé, 43, **608–9**, *609*
Bonsai, **46**, *46*, 213, 261, 602
Borage, *see Borago*
Borago, **333**
Boronia, **333**
Botanic gardens, 21, *59*, 60, **599–602**
Bottlebrush, *see Callistemon*
Bougainville, Louis Antoine de, 43, 607
Bougainvillea, 54, **333**, 607
Bouncing Bet, *see Saponaria*
Bowles, E.A., 617
Box, *see Buxus*
Box elder, *see Acer*
Box thorn, *see Lycium*
Boyceau de la Barauderie, Jacques, 21, *21*
Boykinia, **334**
Bramble, *see Rubus*
Brassica, 115, 116, 118, 169, 173, *173*, 174, 176, 182, 223, 227, 228, **334–6**
Bridal wreath, *see Spiraea*
Bridgeman, Charles, 24, 33, 588
Broad bean, *see Vicia*
Broccoli, *see Brassica*
Brockenhurst Park, *14*
Brodiaea, **336**
Broom, 169, 254; *see also Cytisus*; *Genista*, Spanish, *see Spartium*
Brosse, Guy de la, 21
Brown, Lancelot "Capability", 33, 34, 59, 60, **589**
Brugmansia, **387**, *387*
Brunnera, **336**
Brussels sprout, *see Brassica*
Buck-bean, *see Menyanthes*
Buckthorn, sea, *see Hippophae*
Budding, *104*, 105
  propagation by, 249–52, *251*
Buddleja, 52, 171, *262*, **337**, *337*, 611
Buffalo currant, *see Ribes*
Buffon, G.-L. Leclerc, Comte de, **596–7**, *596*
Bugbane, *see Cimicifuga*
Bugle, *see Ajuga*
Bugloss, Siberian, *see Brunnera*
Bulb scales, propagation by, 241, *242*
Bulrush, *see Typha*
Bulrush, true, *see Scirpus*
Bupleurum, **337**
Burle Marx, Roberto, 65, **593**
Burnet, *see Sanguisorba*
Burning bush, *see Dictamnus*; *Kochia*
Busbecq, O.G. de, **603**
Busy Lizzie, *see Impatiens*
Butcher's broom, *see Ruscus*
Buttercup, *see Ranunculus*
Butterfly bush, *see Buddleja*
Butterfly weed, *see Asclepias*
Butterwort, *see Pinguicula*
Buttonwood, *see Platanus*
Buxus, 14, 20–1, 22, 62, 79, 81, 82, *100*, 170, 171, 214, 235, 270, **337**

Cabbage, *see Brassica*
  Chinese, *see Brassica*; skunk, *see Lysichiton*
Cactus, 143, 234, 249
Cactus
  chain-link, *see Opuntia*; hot-dog, *see Senecio*
Caesalpinia, **338**
Calamint, *see Acinos*
Calanthe, **338**
Calceolaria, **338–9**
Calendula, 55, **339**
Calico bush, *see Kalmia*
Californian redwood, *see Sequoia*
Calliandra, **339**
Callicarpa, **339**
Callirhoe, **339–40**

Callistemon, **340**
Callistephus, **340**
Calluna, **340–1**
Caltha, 172, **341**, *341*
Calycanthus, 171, **341**
Camassia, 140, **341**
Camellia, 171, 220, 235, 240–1, 257, 263, **342**, *342*, 605, 610
Campanula, 73, 170, 171, 228, **342–3**, *343*
Camphor tree, *see Cinnamomum*
Campion
moss, *see Silene*; rose, *see Lychnis*; sea, *see Silene*
Campsis, 97, **343**
Canadian pondweed, *see Elodea*
Canary creeper, *see Tropaeolum*
Candle plant, *see Senecio*
Candytuft, *see Iberis*
Canna, 21, 86, 235, 244, **343–4**
Canterbury bell, *see Campanula*
Cantua, **344**
Cape gooseberry, *see Physalis*
Cape pondweed, *see Aponogeton*
Caper-bush, *see Capparis*
Capparis, **344**
Capsicum, 115, 228, **344–5**
Caragana, 170, 171
Caraway, *see Carum*
Cardamine, **345**
Cardinal flower, *see Lobelia*
Cardiocrinum, **345**
Cardoon, *see Cynara*
Carduncellus, **345**
Carex, **346**
Carica, **346**
Carissa, **346**
Carlina, **346**
Carnation, *see Dianthus*
Carpenteria, *96*, **346–7**
Carpet bedding, 87, *87*
Carpinus, 41, 72, 99, 132, *133*, *134*, 171, 190, **347**
Carrot, *see Daucus*
Carum, **347**
Caryopteris, **347**
Caserta, 27–8, *27*
Cassia, **348**
Cassiope, 171, **348**
Castanea, 130, 169, **348**
Castor oil plant, *see Ricinus*
Catalpa, 169, 170, 171, **348–9**
Catananche, **349**, *349*
Catchfly, *see Silene*
Catmint, *see Nepeta*
Cat's ear, *see Antennaria*
Cat's tail, *see Typha*
Cauliflower, *see Brassica*
Ceanothus, *77*, 169, 171, 275, **349–50**, *350*
Cedar, *see Cedrus*
red, *see Juniperus*; western red, *see Thuja*
Cedrus, 169, **350**
Celeriac, *see Apium*
Celery, *see Apium*
Celmisia, **350–1**
Celosia, **351**
Celtis, **351**, 596
Centaurea, 104, *170*, 170, 171, **351–2**, *352*
Central Park (New York), 57–8, *57*, 63–4, 590
Centranthus, 169, 170, **352**
Century plant, *see Agave*
Cephalaria, **352**
Cerastium, **352–3**
Ceratophyllum, **353**
Ceratostigma, **353**
Cercis, 169, 170, 171, **353**
Ceterach, **353–4**
Chaenomeles, 102, 133, 248, **354**, *354*, 608
Chaerophyllum, **354**
Chamaecyparis, 235, **354–5**
Chamaemelum, 141, 169, **355**
Chamaerops, **355**
Chambers, Sir William, 33, *33*, 39–40, 59, 60
Chamomile, *see Chamaemelum*
Chamomile, ox-eye, *see Anthemis*
Champs-sur-Marne, 592
Chantilly, 22, 25, 26, 32
Chard, see *Beta*
Checkerberry, *see Gaultheria*
Cheiranthus, **355–6**
Chelone, **356**
Chelsea Physic Garden, **601**, 607
Chenopodium, **356**
Chequer mallow, *see Sidalcea*
Cherry
bird, *see Prunus*; bladder, *see Physalis*; cherry tree, *See Prunus*; cornelian, *see Cornus*; Jerusalem, *see Solanum*; laurel, *see Prunus*; cherry pie, *see Heliotropium*; cherry plum, *see Prunus*; wild, *see Prunus*; winter, *see Physalis*; *Solanum*
Chervil, *see Anthriscus*
turnip-rooted, *see Chaerophyllum*
Chestnut
horse, *see Aesculus*; sweet, *see Castanea*; water, *see Trapa*
Chick pea, *see Cicer*
Chicory, *see Cichorium*
Chilean firebush, *see Embothrium*
Chimonanthus, 171, **356**
Chimonobambusa, **356–7**
Chinese date, *see Ziziphus*
Chinese fountain grass, *see Pennisetum*
Chinese holly, *see Osmanthus*
Chinese lantern, *see Physalis*
Chinoiserie, 33, *33*, 39–40, *40*
Chionanthus, **357**
Chionodoxa, **357**
Chive, *see Allium*
Chlidanthus, **357**
Chlorophytum, 245, **357–8**, *358*
Choisya, 151, *151*, **358**
Christmas rose, *see Helleborus*
Chrysanthemum, 41, 198, 235, **358–9**, *359*
Chrysogonum, **359**
Chufa, *see Cyperus*
Church, Thomas, 65, **592–3**, *593*
Cicer, **359–60**
Cicerbita, **360**
Cichorium, 226, **360**
Cimicifuga, 171, **360–1**
Cineraria, 169, **361**
Cinnamomum, **361**
Cirsium, **361**
Cissus, **362**, *362*
Cistus, 169, 170, **362**
Citron tree, *see Citrus*
Citrullus, **363**
Citrus, 130, 143, 253, 257, **363–5**, *363*
Clarkia, **365**
Clematis, 79, 97, 98, *98*, 99, 141, 170, 171, 221–2, *222*, 246, 247, 256, 287–8, **365–7**, *365*, 610, 611
Cleome, **367**
Clerodendrum, **367**, *367*
Clethra, 171, **367–8**
Clianthus, **368**, *368*
Climate, **188–92**, **583–5**
Climbing gazania, *see Mutisia*
Climbing plants, 79, **96–101**, 133, 221–2, **287–8**
Cloches, 228
Clover, *see Trifolium*
bush, *see Lespedeza*
Cobaea, 79, 97
Cockscomb, *see Celosia*
Codiaeum, **368**
Codonopsis, **368–9**, *369*
Coffee, 42, 605
Coix, **369**
Colchicum, 78, **369–70**, *369*, 596
Colden, Jane, **614**
Coleus, 86, 238, **370**
Colour, **74–6**
Columbine, *see Aquilegia*
Columnea, **370**
Colutea, 170, 171, **370–1**
Comfrey, *see Symphytum*
Commerson, Joseph-Philibert, 43, **607**
Compost, garden, 177–8, *177*
Comptonia, **371**
Cone flower, *see Echinacea*; *Rudbeckia*
Conservatories, 41, 52, 100–1, *100*, **143–6**, *143*, *192*
Convallaria, 172, **371**
Convolvulus, 79, 97, **371–2**, *371*
Cook, Captain James, 43, 607
Coral bells, *see Heuchera*
Coral berry, *see Ardisia*; *Symphoricarpos*
Coral tree, *see Erythrina*
Coralwort, *see Dentaria*
Coreopsis, **372**
Coriander, *see Coriandrum*
Coriandrum, **372**
Coriaria, **372**
Cornel, *see Cornus*
Cornflower, *see Centaurea*
Cornflower aster, *see Stokesia*
Corn salad mache, *see Valerianella*
Cornus, 102, 170, 171, 236, 246, 273, **372–3**, *373*
Cortaderia, 173, **373–4**
Corydalis, **374**, *374*
Corylopsis, **374**
Corylus, 130, *130*, 169, 170, 171, 247, 275, **374–5**
Cosmos, **375**
Cotinus, **375**
Cotoneaster, 52, 170, 171, **375–6**, 610
Courances, 62, *63*, 592
Courgette, *see Cucurbita*
Cowslip
giant, *see Primula*; Virginia, *see Mertensia*
Crambe, **376**
Cranesbill, *see Geranium*
Crape myrtle, *see Lagerstroemia*
Crassula, **376**
Crataegus, 41, *134*, 170, 171, 190, 226, **376–7**
Creeping Jenny, *see Lysimachia*
Creeping wintergreen, *see Gaultheria*
Creeping wire-vine, *see Muehlenbeckia*
Creeping zinnia, *see Sanvitalia*
Cress
blister, *see Erysimum*; chamois, *see Hutchinsia*; common white, common, *see Arabis*; garden, *see Barbarea*, *Lepidium*; land, *see Barbarea*; rock, *see Arabis*
Crinum, **377**, *377*
Crocosmia, 242, **377–8**
Crocus, 21, 42, 54, 140, **378–9**, *378*
Autumn, *see Colchicum*
Croton, *see Codiaeum*
Crown imperial, *see Fritillaria*
Crown of thorns, *see Euphorbia*
Cuckoo flower, *see Cardamine*
Cuckoo pint, *see Arum*
Cucumber, *see Cucumis*
Cucumis, 176, **379**
Cucurbita, 115, 116–17, 229, **379–80**
Cupid's dart, *see Catananche*
× *Cupressocyparis*, **380**
Cupressus, 72, 169, 190, 235, **380–1**
Currant, *see Ribes*, *Ribesodoratum*
flowering, *see Ribesodoratum*; Indian, *see Symphoricarpos*
Curry plant, *see Helichrysum*
Cuttings, **233–41**
Cycads, 263
Cyclamen, 21, **381–2**, *381*
Cydonia, 126–7, 130, 248, **382**
Cynara, 118, *190*, **382–3**, *383*
Cynoglossum, **383**
Cyperus, **383**
Cyphomandra, **383–4**
Cypress, *see Cupressus*
bald, *see Taxodium*; false, *see Chamaecyparis*; leyland, 235; summer, *see Kochia*; swamp, *see Taxodium*
Cypripedium, **384**, *384*
Cytisus, 171, 274, **384**

Daboecia, **385**
Daffodil, *see Narcissus*
sea, *see Pancratium*
Dahlia, 41, 43, 174, 235, 244, **385–6**, *385*
Daisen-in, 47–8, *47*
Daisy, *see Bellis*
African, *see Arctotis*; *Osteosperum*; Autumn, *see Chrysanthemum*; barberton, *see Gerbera*; blue, *see Felicia*; bush, *see Olearia*; everlasting, *see Helichrysum*; globe, *see Globularia*; Michaelmas, *see Aster*; Mount Atlas, *see Anacyclus*; shasta, *see Chrysanthemum*; Transvaal, *see Gerbera*; tree, *see Montanoa*; *Olearia*
Dame's violet, *see Hesperis*
Damson, *see Prunus*
Danae, **386**
Dandelion, *171*
Daphne, 171, **386–7**
Datura, **387**
Daucus, 116, 175, 227, **387–8**
Davallia, **388**
David, Jean-Pierre Armand, **610–11**
Davidia, **388**, *388*, 611, *611*
Decaisnea, **388–9**
De Jussieu family, **605–6**
Delavay, Jean-Marie, **611**
Delosperma, **389**
Delphinium, 77, 78, 104, 228, **389**
Dentaria, **389–90**
Desert de Retz, 40, *40*
Desfontainia, **390**, *390*
Deutzia, 171, 236, 273, **390**, 608
Devil's backbone, *see Kalanchoe*
Dianthus, 55, **390–1**, *391*
Diascia, **392**, *392*
Dicentra, **392**, *392*
Dictamnus, **392–3**
Dieffenbachia, **393**
Dierama, **393–4**, *394*
Diervilla, **394**; *see also Weigela*
Digitalis, **394**
Dill, *see Anethum*
Dioscordes, **595**
Diospyros, **394–5**
Dipelta, **395**
Dipladenia, 482
Disanthus, **395**
Diseases, **192–7**, **201–9**, 262
Distylium, **395**
Division, propagation by, 83, 108, **241–6**
Dodecatheon, *395*, **396**
Dogwood, *see Cornus*
Doronicum, 170, 172, **396**
Double digging, 111, 113, 216, *217*
Dove tree, *see Davidia*
Downing, A.J., 57, 617
Doxantha, **396**
Draba, **396–7**

Dracaena, 248, **397**, *397*
Dracocephalum, **397**
Dracunculus, **397–8**
Dragon arum, *see Dracunculus*
Dragon plant, *see Dracunculus*
Dragon's heads, *see Dracocephalum*
Dragon tree, *see Dracaena*
Drainage, 187–8, *187*
Drills, *228*, 229
Drimys, **398**
Dropwort, *see Filipendula*
Drosera, **398**, *398*
Dryas, **398–9**
Dryopteris, **399**, *399*
Drypis, **399**
du Cerceau family, 21
Duchêne, Achille, 62, **592**
Duchêne, Henri, 62, 592
Duke of Argyll's tea tree, *see Lycium*
Dumbarton Oaks, 58, *63*, *64*, 65, 592
Dumb cane, *see Dieffenbachia*
Duprat, Ferdinand, *29*
Dusty miller, *see Primula*; *Senecio*
Dutchman's breeches, *see Dicentra*
Dutchman's pipe, *see Aristolochia*
Dwarf bean, *see Phaseolus*
Dyer's greenwood, *see Genista*

Earth-nut pea, *see Lathyrus*
Eaton, Mary, **615**
Ebony wood, *see Bauhinia*
Eccremocarpus, **400**, *400*
Echinacea, **400**
Echinops, **400**, *401*
Echium, **401**
Eckbo, Garret, 617
Edelweiss, *see Leontopodium*
Edraianthus, **401**
Ehret, Georg Dionysius, **614**
Ehretia, **401**
Eichhornia, **402**, *402*
Elaeagnus, 134, 169, **402**
Elder, *see Sambucus*
Eleagnus, 236
Elephant ear, *see Bergenia*
Elm, *see Ulmus*
Elodea, **402–3**
Elsholtzia, **403**
Elymus, **403**
Embothrium, **403**
Endive, *see Cichorium*
Enkianthus, 171, **403–4**, *404*
Ephedra, **404**, 596
Epilobium, **404–5**, *404*
Epimedium, 172, **405**
Equisetum, **405**
Eranthis, **405–6**, *405*
Eremurus, 77, 78, **406**
Erica, *141*, **406–7**, *406*
Erigeron, 170, 171, **407**
Erinus, **407**
Ermenonville, 38–9, *38*, *39*
Erodium, **407**
Eryngium, **408**, *408*
Erysimum, **408**
Erythrina, **408–9**
Erythronium, **409**
Escallonia, 190, 270, **409**, *409*
Eschscholzia, 52, 54, 198, **410**
Eucalyptus, **410**
Eucomis, **410**, *411*
Eucryphia, **411**
Euonymus, 82, 170, 171, 235, 236, 270, 275, **411–12**
Eupatorium, **412**
Euphorbia, 105, 198, **412–13**, *412*
Evening primrose, *see Oenothera*
Everlasting flower, *see Helipterum*
Everlasting pea, *see Lathyrus*
Exacum, **413**
Exochorda, **413**

F1 hybrids, 226, 227
Fabiana, **414**
Fagus, 72, 132, *132*, 134, 141, 171, 253, *413*, **414**
Fairy moss, *see Azolla*
False dittany, *see Dictamnus*
False indigo, *see Baptisia*
False spikenard, *see Smilacina*
Farrand, Beatrix, 58, **592**
Fatsia, **415**, *415*
Fava, *see Vicia*
Featherfoil, *see Hottonia*
Feather grass, *see Stipa*
Felicia, **415**
Fennel, *see Foeniculum*
Fennel flower, *see Nigella*
Fern, 150, *168*, 263
buckler, *see Dryopteris*; deer, *see Blechnum*; hard, *see Blechnum*; hart's tongue, *see Phyllitis*; lady, *see Athyrium*; ostrich, *see Matteuccia*; royal, *see Osmunda*; rusty-back, *see Ceterach*; shield, *see Dryopteris*, *Polystichum*; sweet, *see Comptonia*
Fertilizers, 173–6, 178–82, *180*
Fescue grass, *see Festuca*
Festuca, **415**
Ficus, 130–1, *130*, 246, 248, **415–17**, *416*, *417*
Fig, *see Ficus*
Filipendula, 139, 171, **417**
Filoli, 58
Finnochio, *see Foeniculum*
Fir, *see Abies*
Colorado Douglas, *see Pseudotsuga*; Colorado white, *see Abies*; Douglas, *see Pseudotsuga*; Greek, *see Abies*; Korean, *see Abies*; silver, *see Abies*; Spanish, *see Abies*
Fire pink, *see Silene*
Firethorn, *see Pyracantha*
Fireweed, *see Epilobium*
Flame bush, *see Calliandra*
Flaming Katy, *see Kalanchoe*
Flax, *see Linum*
Fleabane, *see Erigeron*
Floss flower, *see Ageratum*
Flower gardens, **51–4**, **70–82**
cut flowers, **102–5**
Foam flower, *see Tiarella*
Foam of May, *see Spiraea*
Foeniculum, 115, **417–18**
Follies, **32**, 33, *33*, 39–40, *39*
Fontainebleau, 60, *60*
Fonthill Abbey, **37**, *37*
Forget-me-not, *see Myosotis*
Forsythia, 52, 102, 133, 169, 235, 236, 247, 272, 284, **418**, 608, 610
Fortune, Robert, **610**
Fothergilla, 171, **418**
Fountains, 19, 163, *163*
Four o'clock plant, *see Mirabilis*
Fox and cubs, *see Hieracium*
Foxglove, *see Digitalis*
Chinese, *see Rehmannia*; fairy, *see Erinus*
Fragaria, 119–20, *120*, 173, 174, 223, *224*, 245, 246, 262, **418–19**
Francini (Francine) family, 21, 23
Fraxinus, 134, 169, 170, 171, **419**, 606
Freckle face, *see Hypoestes*
Freesia, *414*, **419–20**, *420*
Fremontodendron, 169
French bean, *see Phaseolus*
Fringe tree, *see Chionanthus*
Fritillaria, **420–1**, *420*, *614*
Fritillary, *see Fritillaria*
Frost protection, *190*, 191–2
Fruit trees, 213, 214, 217, *218*, 219, 225
grafting, **249–57**; propagation, 226; pruning, **260–9**, 276–82; training, **263–9**
Fuchs, Leonard, 604
Fuchsia, 143, 233, 235, 273, **421**, *421*, 604
Fuchsia, California, *see Zauschneria*
Fungicides, 195–6
Furze, *see Ulex*

Gaillardia, 170, **422**
Galanthus, 140, **422**
Galega, **422–3**
Galingale, *see Cyperus*
Galtonia, **423**
Gardener's garters, *see Phalaris*
Gardenia, **423**
Garlic, *see Allium*
Garrya, 170, 247, **423**, *423*
Gaultheria, 171, **424**
Gaura, **424**
Gayfeather, *see Liatris*
Gazania, **424**
Genista, **424–5**
Gentiana, **425–6**, *425*, *613*
Geranium, 21, 79, *80*, 86, 170, 172, *210*, 233, 238, **426**, *426*
Geranium, *see Pelargonium*
Gerbera, **427**
Germander, *see Teucrium*
Geum, **427**
Gherkin, *see Cucumis*
Giant hogweed, *see Heracleum*
Giant hyssop, *see Agastache*
Gillenia, **427**
Ginger, wild, *see Asarum*
Ginkgo, 41, *41*, 169, **427–8**, *427*, 605
Girardin, Marquis de, 38, 59, **617–18**
Giverny, *51*, 53–4, *64*
Gladiolus, 104, **428–9**, *428*, *429*, 608
Glaucidium, **429**
Glaucium, **429**
Glechoma, **429–30**
Gleditsia, 169, 171, **430**
Globe amaranth, *see Gomphrena*
Globe flower, *see Trollius*
Globularia, **430**
Gloriosa, **430–1**, *430*
Glory flower, *see Eccremocarpus*
Glory-of-the-snow, *see Chionodoxa*
Glory pea, *see Clianthus*
Glyceria, **431**
Goat's beard, *see Aruncus*
Godetia, **431**, *431*
Goethe, Johann Wolfgang von, **597–8**, *598*, 601
Golden-chain tree, *see Laburnum*
Golden drop, *see Onosma*
Golden-eyed grass, *see Sisrinchium*
Golden Pavilion (*Kinkaku-ji*), *48*, 49
Golden-rain tree, *see Keolreuteria*
Golden rod, *see Solidago*
Golden shower, *see Cassia*
Goldfish plant, *see Columnea*
Gomphrena, **431**
Good King Henry, *see Chenopodium*
Good luck plant, *see Kalanchoe*
Gooseberry, *see Ribes*
Gorse, *see Ulex*
Gorse, Spanish, *see Genista*
Grafting, 15, 125, **249–59**
Granadilla, *see Passiflora*
Granny's bonnet, *see Aquilegia*
Grapefruit, *see Citrus*
Grape vine, *see Vitis*
Grassy-bells, *see Edraianthus*
Gray, Asa, **598**
Great Dixter, 53, 54, *54*, *100*
Great sallow, *see Salix*
Greengage, *see Prunus*
Greenhouses, 41, 52, 100–1, *100*, **143–6**, 183, 192, *192*, 228
Alpine, 95, *95*
Greub, Franz Joseph, 601
Grevillea, **431–2**, *431*
Grillet, 28
Grottoes, 32, 35, 40
Ground box, *see Polygala*
Ground-cover plants, **141–2**
Ground-nut, *see Apios*
Gum tree, *see Eucalyptus*
Gunnera, 54, 109, **432–3**
Gynerium, *190*
Gynura, *432*, **433**
Gypsophila, 170, **433**

Haberlea, **434**
Hackberry, *see Celtis*
Hacquetia, **434**
Hadrian's villa, 8, **10**, 32
Halesia, 169, 171, **434**
Halfpenny, William and John, 59
Halimodendron, **434**
Hall, George R., **610**
Hamamelis, 41, 169, 171, 275, **434–5**
Hamilton, Charles, 35
Handkerchief tree, *see Davidia*
Hare's ear, *see Bupleurum*
Hare's-tail grass, *see Lagurus*
Hawkweed, *see Hieracium*
Hawthorn, *see Crataegus*
water, *see Aponogeton*
Hazel/Hazelnut, *see Corylus*
corkscrew, *see Corylus*; winter, *see Corylopsis*
Heart's ease, *see Viola*
Heath, *see Erica*
mountain, *see Phyllodoce*; prickly, *see Acantholimon*; St Daboec's, *see Daboecia*
Heather, 169, 275, *see also Calluna*; *Daboecia*; *Erica*
Hebe, **435**, *435*
Hedera, 97, 98, 100, 141, 169, 170, 172, 238, 246, 247, 270, 287, **435–6**
Hedges, 70, 72, 102, 122, **132–4**, 189–90, *189*, *190*, 219–20, *219*
planting, 219–20, *219*; pruning and trimming, **269–71**
Hedychium, **436**
Helenium, 171, 243, **436**
Helianthemum, *77*, 169, 170, **436–7**
Helianthus, 243, **437**, *437*
Helichrysum, **437–8**, *438*
Helicorna, 593
Heliopsis, **438**
Heliotrope, *see Heliotropium*
Heliotropium, 235, **438**, 606
Helipterum, **438**
Helleborus, 21, 172, **439**, *439*
Helxine, **439**
Hemerocallis, 78, 170, **439–40**, *440*
Hepatica, **440**
Heracleum, **440**
Herbaceous borders, 21, 70
Herb Christopher, *see Actaea*
Herb gardens, 13, 123, *123*
Herbicides, 181, 197, 199–200
Hercules Club, *see Aralia*
Hesperis, **441**
Het Loo, 18, 22, *22*, 28, 62
Heuchera, **441**
Hevea, 606
Hibiscus, 169, **441**
Hickory, 171
Hidcote Manor, 53
Hieracium, **441–2**
Hippeastrum, **442**, *442*
Hippophae, **442–3**
Holboellia, **443**
Holly, *see Ilex*
sea, *see Eryngium*

Hollyhock, *see Althaea*
Honesty, *see Lunaria*
Honey locust, *see Gleditsia*; *Robinia*
Honeysuckle, *see Lonicera*
  bush, *see Diervilla*; Himalayan, *see Leycesteria*
Hooker, Sir Joseph Dalton, **611**
Hoop petticoat, *see Narcissus*
Hop, *see Humulus*
Horehound, *see Marrubium*
Hornbeam, *see Carpinus*
Horned rampions, *see Physoplexis*; *Phyteuma*
Hornwort, *see Ceratophyllum*
Horse chestnut, *see Aesculus*
Horseradish, *see Armoracia*
Horsetail, *see Equisetum*
Hosta, *80*, 171, 172, 244, **442**, *443*
Hottonia, **443–4**
Hound's tongue, *see Cynoglossum*
Houseleek, *see Sempervivum*
Houttuynia, **444**
Hoya, **444–5**, *444*
Humboldt, Alexander von, 43, 608–9
Humulus, **445**
Hutchinsia, **445**
Hyacinth, *see Hyacinthus*
  California, *see Brodiaea*; Cape *see Galtonia*; grape, *see Muscari*; summer, *see Galtonia*; tassel, *see Muscari*; water, *see Eichhornia*
Hyacinthoides, 445
Hyacinthus, 16, 220, **445**
Hydrangea, 41, 98, 171, 236, 246, 274, **446**, *446*, 605, 610, 612
Hypericum, 142, 169, 171, **446–7**, *447*
Hypoestes, **447**
Hyssopus, **447**

Iberis, 170
Ice plant, see *Mesembryantheum*; *Sedum*
Ilex, 169, 170, 171, 190, 214, **448**
Illicium, **448**
Impatiens, 86, 150, 238, **449**, *449*
Incarvillea, **449**
Indian bean, *see Catalpa*
Indian physic, *see Gillenia*
Indian shot, *see Canna*
Indigo, *see Indigofera*
Indigofera, **449–50**
Insecticides, 193–5
Inula, **450**
Ipecacuanha, 606
Ipomoea, **450**, *450*
Iresine, **450–1**
Iris, 55, 140, 169, 170, 171, 172, 174, 224–5, *225*, 242, **451–3**, *452*
Island flowerbeds, 80–1, *81*, 84
Isu tree, *see Distylium*
Ivy, *see Hedera*
  Boston, *see Parthenocissus*; German, *see Senecio*; grape, *see Cissus*; ground, *see Glechoma*; natal, *see Senecio*
Ixia, **453**
Ixiolirion, **453**

Jacaranda, **454**
Jack in the pulpit, *see Arisaema*
Jacob's ladder, *see Polemonium*
Jacob's rod, *see Asphodeline*
Jade plant, *see Crassula*
Japanese angelica tree, *see Aralia*
Japanese quince, *see Chaenomeles*
Japonica, *see Chaenomeles*
Jardin du Roi, 21
Jasione, **454**
Jasmine, *see Jasminum*
  Cape, *see Gardenia*; Chilean, *see Mandevilla*; jasmine nightshade, *see Solanum*; Madagascar, *see Stephanotis*; mountain, *166*; winter, 52
Jasminum, 58, 170, 171, 247, **454–5**, 610
Jefferson, Thomas, 57, *57*, **618**
Jeffersonia, **455**
Jekyll, Gertrude, 53, *53*, 54, 60, **591–2**, 617
Job's tears, *see Coix*
Joe-pye weed, *see Eupatorium*
Johnny-jump-up, *see Viola*
Jonquil, *see Narcissus*
Joseph's coat, *see Codiaeum*
Judas tree, *see Cercis*
Juglans, 130, 169, **455**
Jujube tree, *see Ziziphus*
Juncus, **456**
June berry, *see Amelanchier*
Juniper, *see Juniperus*
Juniperus, 134, 141, *142*, 171, 172, **456**, 610

Kaempfer, Engelbert, 43, **605**
Kaki, *see Diospyros*
Kalanchoe, **457**, *457*
Kale, *see Brassica*
Kalmia, 171, 220, **457–8**, *458*
Kalopanax, **458**
Katsura, 49–50, *50*
Kent, William, 33–4, **588–9**, *588*, 618
Keolreuteria, **459**
Kerria, 52, 169, 170, 171, **458**, 608
Kew, 33, *33*, 39–40, 52, *59*, 60, 599
Kingcup, *see Caltha*
Kingdon-Ward, Frank, **612**, *612*
King's spear, *see Asphodeline*
Kirengeshoma, **458**
Kiwi, *see Actinidia*
Knapweed, *see Centaurea*
Kniphofia, 41, *190*, **458–9**
Knotweed, *see Polygonum*
Kochia, **459**
Koeleria, **459**
Kohlrabi, *see Brassica*
Kolkwitzia, **459**

Labrador tea, *see Ledum*
Laburnum, *99*, 100, 169, 171, **460**
La Condamine, 43
Lactuca, 115, 173, 175, 223, *223*, 226, 227, 228, 230, **460–1**
Ladies fingers, *see Anthyllis*
Lad's love, *see Artemisia*
Ladybells, *see Adenophora*
Lady's slipper, *see Cypripedium*
Lady's smock, *see Cardamine*
Lagerstroemia, **461**
La Granja, 27
Lagurus, **461**
Lamb's lettuce, *see Valerianella*
Lamb's tongue, *see Stachys*
Lamium, 172, **461**
Lantana, 22, **461–2**
Lapageria, **462**
La Quintinie, J.-B. de, 23, *23*
Larch, *see Larix*
Larix, 169, **462**
La Roche-Courbon, *29*
Lathyrus, 104, 229, **462–3**, *462*
Laurel, 169, 272
  Alexandrian, *see Danae*; American, *see Kalmia*; common, *see Prunus*; mountain, *see Kalmia*; Portugal, *see Prunus*; rose, 134; sheep, *see Kalmia*; variegated, *see Codiaeum*
Laurus, 123, 149, **463**
Laurustinus, *see Viburnum*
Lavatera, 169, *188*, **464**, *464*
Lavender, *see Lavendula*
  lavender cotton, *see Santolina*; sea, *see Limonium*
Lavendula, 149, 169, 170, 275, **463**
Lawns, **135–40**, *156*, 173, 227, 230
  chamomile, 141; juniper, 141
Layering, propagation by, *191*, **246–9**
Leasowes, The 36, *36*
Le Brun, Charles, 23, 24, 586–7
l'Ecluse, Charles de, 600, **603–4**
Ledum, **464**
Leek, *see Allium*
Lemon, *see Citrus*
Le Notre, André, *20*, 22, 23–6, *23*, *24*, 59, 60, 62, *62*, **586–8**, *587*
Lens, 118, **464**
Lenten rose, *see Helleborus*
Lentil, *see Lens*
Leonotis, **464–5**
Leontopodium, **465**, *465*
Leopard flower, *see Belamcanda*
Leopard's bane, *see Doronicum*
Lepidium, **465**
Leptospermum, **465–6**
Lespedeza, **466**
Lettuce, *see Lactuca*
Leucojum, **466**
Leucothoe, 171, **466**
Levisticum, **467**
Lewisia, **467**, *467*
Leycesteria, **467**
Liatris, **467–8**
Life-everlasting, *see Anaphalis*
Ligularia, 171, 172, **468**, *468*
Ligustrum, 133, 169, 170, 171, 190, 233, 236, 270, **468–9**
Lilac, *see Syringa*
  Californian, *see Ceanothus*; Persian, *see Melia*
Lilium, 21, 55, 92, 103, 175, 241, **469–70**, *469*, 610, *611*, 612
Lily, *see Lilium*
  African blue, *see Agapanthus*; African corn, *see Ixia*; arum, *see Zantedeschia*; Aztec, *see Sprekelia*; belladonna, *see Amaryllis*; blackberry, *see Belamcanda*; boat, *see Tradescantia*; calla, *see Zantedeschia*; canna, *see Canna*; Cuban, *see Scilla*; day, *see Hemerocallis*; foxtail, *see Eremurus*; giant Himalayan, *see Cardiocrinum*; ginger, *see Hedychium*; Jacobean, *see Sprekelia*; kaffir, *see Schizostylis*; Lent, *see Narcissus*; leopard, *see Dieffenbachia*; lily of the Altai, *see Ixiolirion*; lily of the valley, *see Convallaria*; perfumed fairy, *see Chlidanthus*; Peruvian, *see Alstroemeria*; pineapple, *see Eucomis*; plantain, *see Hosta*; sea, *see Pancratium*; sword, *see Gladiolus*; torch, *see Kniphofia*; zephyr, *see Zephyranthes*
Lilyturf, *see Liriope*
Lime, *see Citrus*; *Tilia*
Limnanthes, **470**
Limoniastrum, **470**
Limonium, **470–1**
Linaria, **471**
Linden, *see Tilia*
Lindisfarne, 592
Ling, *see Calluna*
Linnaea, **471**
Linnaeus, *594*, **596**, 598, 600, 601, 605
Linum, **471–2**, *471*
Lion's heart, *see Physostegia*
Lion's tail, see *Leonotis leonurus*
Lippia, **472**
Liquidambar, 171, **472**
Liriodendron, 58, **472**
Liriope, **472–3**
Lithospermum, **473**
Lloyd family, 54, 617
Lobelia, 41, 171, 172, **473–4**, *473*, 604
Locust tree, 171
Lomatia, **474**
London pride, *see Saxifraga*
Longwood Gardens, 58, *58*
Lonicera, 79, 82, 98, 170, 171, 233, 236, 246, 247, **474–5**, *475*, 610, 612
Loosestrife
  false, *see Ludwigia*; purple, *see Lythrum*; yellow, *see Lysimachia*
Lopping, **275–6**
Loquat, 608
Lords and ladies, *see Arum*
Loropetalum, **475**
Lorrain, Claude, *30*, 31, *31*, 34, 35, 588
Lotus, **475**
Lotus, *see Nelumbo*
Loudon, Jane, 59–60
Lovage, *see Levisticum*
Love-in-a-mist, *see Nigella*
Love-lies-bleeding, *see Amaranthus*
Ludwigia, **475–6**, *476*
Lunaria, **476**
Lungwort, *see Pulmonaria*
Lupin, *see Lupinus*
Lupinus, **476**
Luzula, **476–7**
Lychnis, **477**
Lycium, **477**
Lycopersicon, 115, 117, *117*, 173, 174, 175, *195*, 223, 227, 228, **477–8**
Lyme grass, *see Elymus*
Lysichiton (Lysichitum), **478**
Lysichitum, *see Lysichiton*
Lysimachia, 172, **478**
Lythrum, 172, **478**

Maackia, **479**
Macleaya, *77*, *162*, **479**
Magic flower of the Incas, *see Cantua*
Magnol, Pierre, 601, 604
Magnolia, 41, 58, 169, 171, 221, 246, 248, 257, 275, **479–80**, *479*, 601, 604, 605, 606, 610
Mahonia, 52, **480–1**, *480*, 610
Maidenhair spleenwort, *see Asplenium*
Maidenhair tree, *see Ginkgo*
Maize, *see Zea*
Malcolmia, **481**
Mallow, *see Malva*
  chequer, *see Sidalcea*; Indian, *see Abutilon*; poppy, *see Callirhoe*; rose, see *Hibiscus*; tree see *Lavatera*
Malmaison, 43, *43*, 61, *61*, 609
Malope, **481**
Malus, 46, 68, 124, 126–7, 175, 248, 250, 255, 260, 263–8, 276, 278–80, **481**
Malva, 169, **481–2**, *481*
Mandarin, *see Citrus*
Mandevilla, **482**
Mange-tout, *see Pisum*
Manhattan, *see Euonymus*
Manna grass, *see Glyceria*
Manuka, *see Leptospermum*
Manure, 176, 178–9
Maple, *see Acer*
Maranta, 482–3
Marguerite, golden, *see Anthemis*
Marigold, 104, 169, 171, 198
  African, *see Tagetes*; French, *see Tagetes*; marsh, *see Caltha*; pot, *see Calendula*
Marjoram, sweet or knotted, *see Origanum*

Marly, 22, 25, 26, 29, 41
Marot, Daniel, 22, 28
Marrow, *see Cucurbita*
Marrubium, **483**
Marsh trefoil, *see Menyanthes*
Marvel of Peru, *see Mirabilis*
Mask flower, *see Alonsoa*
Masterwort, *see Astrantia*
Matteuccia, **483**
Matthiola, **483–4**
May, *see Crataegus*
Mazus, **484**
Meadow-grass, *see Poa*
Meadowsweet, *see Filipendula*
Meconopsis, **484**, *484*, *612*
Medicago, **484**
Medick, *see Medicago*
Medlar, *see Mespilus*
Melia, **484–5**
Melissa, **485**
Melon, 115, 176, 228, 229
Mentha, **485**
Menyanthes, **485**
Menziesia, **485–6**
Merian, Maria Sibylla, **613–14**, *614*
Merry bells, *see Uvularia*
Mertensia, **486**
Mesembryantheum, 41
Mespilus, **486**
Mezereon, *see Daphne*
Michaux, André *41*
Michaux, François-André, **608**
Middleton Place, *7*, 56, *56*
Mignonette, *see Reseda*
Milfoil, *see Achillea*
Milkweed, *see Asclepias*
Miller, Philip, 601
Milwort, *see Polygala*
Mimosa, *see Acacia*
Mimulus, 171, **486–7**, *486*
Mind-your-own-business, *see Helxine*
Mint, *see Mentha*
Minuartia, **487**
Mirabilis, **487**, *487*
Miscanthus, **487–8**
Mitella, **488**
Mitrewort, *see Mitella*
Mixed borders, **70–81**, 84, *84*, *157*
Molinia, **488**
Mollet, André, 18, 22, 59
Mollet, Claude, 20, 21, 22, 23
Mollet, Jacques, 20, 22
Moltkia, **488–9**
Moluccella, *488*, **489**
Monarda, 171, **489**, *489*
Monet, Claude, *51*, 53–4, *64*
Money flower plant, *see Lunaria*
Monkey flower, *see Mimulus*
Monkey musk, see *Mimulus*
Monkey puzzle, *see Araucaria*
Monk's hood, *see Aconitum*
Montanoa, **489**
Montbretia, *see Crocosmia*
Monticello, 36, 57, *57*, 618
Moon trefoil, *see Medicago*
Morina, **489–90**, *490*
Morning glory, 97; *see also Convolvulus*; *Ipomoea*
Morus, **490**
Mosaic flower gardens, 87, *87*
Moses-in-the-cradle, *see Tradescantia*
Moss rose, *see Portulaca*
Mother-of-thousands, *see Saxifraga*
Mountain avens, *see Dryas*
Mountain fleece, *see Polygonum*
Mountain gold, *see Alyssum*
Mouse plant, *see Arisarum*
Muehlenbeckia, **490–1**
Mulberry, *see Morus*
Mulching, 83–4, 105, 131, 187, 192, 221, 225
Mullein, *see Verbascum*
Musa, 263, **491**
Muscari, 54, 220, **491**
Mustard, *see Sinapis*
  buckler, *see Biscutella*
Mutisia, **491**
Myoporum, **492**
Myosotis, 86, 150, 228, **492**
Myriophyllum, **492**
Myrrh, *see Myrrhis*
Myrrhis, **492**
Myrsine, **492–3**
Myrtle, *see Myrtus*
  Cape, *see Myrsine*; myrtle grass, *see Acorus*
Myrtus, **493**

Nakai, *see Lespedeza*
Narcissus, 41, 54, 140, 220, **493–4**, *493*
Nasturtium, 229, **494**
Nasturtium, *see Tropaeolum*
Natal plum, *see Carissa*
Navelwort, *see Omphalodes*
Nectarine, *see Prunus*
Neillia, **495**
Nelumbo, **495**, *495*
Nemesia, **495**
Nepeta, **496**
Nerine, **496**
Nerium, **496**
Nettle
  dead, *see Lamium*; flame, *see Coleus*; nettle tree, *see Celtis*
New Zealand burr, *see Acaena*
New Zealand tea tree, *see Leptospermum*
Ngaio, *see Myoporum*
Nicandra, **496–7**
Nicotiana, **497**
Nigella, **497**
Nolina, **497**
North, Marianne, **615**
Nuphar, 108, 109, **497–8**
Nursery beds, 228
Nymphaea, **498**
Nyssa, 171

Oak, *see Quercus*
  silky, *see Grevillea*
Obedient plant, *see Physostegia*
Ocimum, 123, **498**
Oenothera, **499**
Old man, *see Artemisia*
Old man's beard, *see Clematis*
Olea, 130, **499**
Oleander, *see Nerium*
Olearia, 134, 190, **499–500**
Oleaster, *see Elaeagnus*
Olive, *see Olea*
  Russian, *see Eleagnus*, wild, *see Elaeagnus*
Olmsted, Frederick Law, 57–8, *57*, 63–4, **590–1**, *591*
Omphalodes, **500**
Onion, *see Allium*
Onoclea, **500**
Onopordum, **500**
Onosma, **500–1**, *501*
Opuntia, **501**
Orach, *see Atriplex*
Orange, *see Citrus*
  Mexican, *see Choisya*; mock, *see Philadelphus*
Orchards, **124–31**
Orchid
  lady, *see Orchis*; military, *see Orchis*; orchid tree, *see Bauhinia*; soldier, *see Orchis*; terrestrial, *see Orchis*
Orchis, **501–2**, *501*
Oregon grape, *see Mahonia*
Origano, *see Origanum*
Origanum, **502**
Ornamental gardens, **66–9**, 115, *116*
Ornithogalum, **502**
Osier, *see Salix*
Osmanthus, 169, 171, **502–3**
Osmunda, **503**
Osteospermum, **503**
Oswego tea, *see Monarda*
Othonna, **503–4**
Ourisia, **504**
Oxalis, **504**
Oyster plant, *see Mertensia*

Pachysandra, **505**
Paeonia, 41, 55, 171, **505–6**, *505*, 605, 611
Page, Russell, **593**
Pagoda tree, *see Sophora*
Painted tongue, *see Salpiglossis*
Palazzo Pfanner, *16*
Palm
  chusan, *see Trachycarpus*; date, *see Phoenix*; fan, *see Chamaerops*
Pampas grass, *see Cortaderia*
Pancratium, **506**
Panda plant, *see Kalanchoe*
Pansy, *see Viola*
Papaver, 21, 41, 42, 55, 58, 73, 104, 105, 169, *170*, 170, 241, 244, **506–7**, *506*
Papaya, *see Carica*
Paper flower, *see Bougainvillea*
Parks, public, 62–4
Parrot flower, *see Asclepias*
Parrot's feather, *see Myriophyllum*
Parry, Charles Christopher, **610**
Parsley, *see Petroselinum*
Parthenocissus, 170, 171, 237, 287, **507**
Partridge berry, *see Gaultheria*
Pasque flower, *see Pulsatilla*
Passiflora, 97, 101, 247, **507–8**
Passion flower/fruit, *see Passiflora*
Paths, *68*, 81, **155–8**
Patios, **147–54**, 161–2
Paulownia, **508**, *508*
Pawpaw, *see Carica*
Paxton, Joseph, 63, 590
Pea, *see Pisum*
  desert, *see Clianthus*; ornamental, *see Lathyrus*; pea shrub, *see* Caragana
Peach, *see Prunus*
Peacock flower, *see Tigridia*
Pear, *see Pyrus*
Pearl bush, *see Exochorda*
Pelargonium (geranium), 21, 41, 143, 150, 234, 235, **508–9**, *509*
Peltiphyllum, 172
Pennisetum, **509**
Penstemon, **509**
Peony, *see Paeonia*
  tree, *see Paeonia*
Peperomia, **510**
Pepper
  black, *see Poivrea*; Chilli, *see Capsicum*; mountain, *see Drimys*; pepper grass, *see Lepidium*; pepper tree, *see Schinus*; sweet, *see Capsicum*
Perilla, **510**
Periwinkle, *see Vinca*
Pernettya, 171, **510–11**
Persea, **511**
Persimmon, Chinese, *see Diospyros*
Pests, 84, **192–7**, **201–9**, 225
Petroselinum, 123, **511**
Pe-tsai, *see Brassica*
Petunia, 228, 229, **511–12**
Phalaris, **512**
Phaseolus, 115, 117, *117*, 229, **512**
Pheasant's eye, *see Narcissus*
Philadelphus, 41, 171, **512–13**
Phlomis, **513**
Phlox, 241, 243, **513–14**, *513*
Phoenix, **514**
Phragmites, **514**
pH scale, 165–6, *172*, 221
Phyllitis, **514**
Phyllodoce, **514–15**
Physalis, **515**, *515*
Physiological disorders, **202–9**
Physoplexis, **515**
Physostegia, **515–16**
Phyteuma, **516**
Phytolacca, **516**
Picea, **516–17**, 610
Pieris, 171, 220, **517–18**, *517*, 608
Pimento, *see Capsicum*
Pimpinella, **518**
Pinching out, 104–5, *104*
Pin cushion flower, *see Scabiosa*
Pine, *see Pinus*
  bungy bungy pine, *see Araucaria*; Chile, *see Araucaria*; Norfolk Island, *see Araucaria*
Pineapple, *see Ananas*
Pineapple flower, *see Eucomis*
Pinguicula, **518**, *518*
Pink, *see Dianthus*
  cushion, *see Silene*; sea, *see Armeria*
Pinus, *46*, 134, 169, 170, 172, **518–19**, 606
Pisum, 115, 117, 173, 175, 229, 230, **519–20**
Pitcher plant, *see Sarracenia*
Pitton de Tournefort, Joseph, **595–6**, *595*
Pittosporum, 134
Plane, *see Platanus*
Platanus, 171, **520**
Platycodon, 170, **520–1**, *520*
Pleione, **521**, *521*
Pliny the Elder, 10, **595**
Pliny the Younger, 10, **586**
Plum, *see Prunus*
Plumbago, hardy, *see Ceratostigma*
Plumier, Charles, **604**
Poa, **521**
Poached-egg flower, *see Limnanthes*
Poinsettia, *see Euphorbia*
Poivre, Pierre, 43, **606–7**
Poivrea, 607
Poke weed, *see Phytolacca*
Pole bean, *see Phaseolus*
Polemonium, 171, **521–2**
Polka dot plant, *see Hypoestes*
Polygala, **522**
Polygonatum, **522**
Polygonum, 52, 172, 522–3, *523*
Polypodium, **523**
Polypody, *see Polypodium*
Polystichum, **523–4**
Pomegranate, *see Punica*
Pomelo, *see Citrus*
Ponds, 106–10, *107*, *108*, *109*
Pope, Alexander, 32, 35
Poplar, *see Populus*
Poppy, *see Papaver*
  California, *see Eschscholzia*, *Romneya*; horned, *see Glaucium*; Iceland, *see Papaver*; Mexican, *see Argemone*; plume, *see Macleaya*; poppy mallow, *see Callirhoe*; prickly, *see Argemone*; sea, *see Glaucium*; Welsh, *see Meconopsis*
Populus, 41, 133, 170, 171, 238, **524**
Porcelin berry, *see Ampelopsis*
Portulaca, **524–5**
Potato, *see Solanum*
Potato bean, *see Apios*
Potato vine, *see Solanum*
Potentilla, 275, **525**
Poussin, Gaspard, *30*, 34, 35, 588
Powder-puffs, *see Calliandra*
Prayer plant, *see Maranta*
  Maranta
Pricking out seedlings, 231, *232*

Prickly pear, *see Opuntia*
Primrose, *see Primula*
evening, *see Oenothera*
Primula, 21, 86, 171, 241, **525–6**, *525*, 611
Prince's feather, *see Amaranthus*
Privet, desert, *see Peperomia*
Privet, *see Ligustrum*
Propagation, **226–59**
Prophet flower, *see Arnebia*
Protea, 608, *608*
Provence cane, *see Arundo*
Prunella, **526**
Pruning, 84, 125–6, 127, 128, **260–88**
Prunus, 42, 68, 124, *124*, *126*, 127–30, *128*, *129*, 131, 135, 169, 170, 171, 236, 250, 260, 264, 265, 270, 273–4, 281–2, *282*, **526–7**, *526*, 605, 610
Pseudotsuga, **527–8**
Pückler Muskau, Prince H.L.H., 616
Pulmonaria, 172, **528**
Pulsatilla, **528**
Pumpkin, *see Cucurbita*
Punica, **528**
Purple moorgrass, *see Molinia*
Purslane, *see Portulaca*
Pyracantha, 235, **528–9**
Pyrethrum, **529**
Pyrus, *23*, 126–7, 131, 175, *175*, 249, 250, 255, 260, 263–8, 276, 278–80, **529**

Quamash, *see Camassia*
Queen of the prairie, *see Filipendula*
Quercus, 99, 134, 171, **529–30**, 606
Quince, *see Cydonia*
Quinine, 42, 606

Rabbit foot/rabbit tracks, *see Maranta*
Radiator plant, *see Peperomia*
Radish, *see Raphanus*
Rafinesque, Constantine Samuel, **609**
Ragwort, *see Senecio*
Raised beds, 15, 85–7, *85*, *86*, 188
Raleigh, Sir Walter, 42, *42*
Rambling plants, 97–8
Ramonda, **530–1**, *530*
Ranunculus, 21, **531**
Raoulia, **531**
Raphanus, 115, 116, 227, **531–2**
Raspberry, *see Rubus*
Red buckeye, *see Aesculus*
Redbud, *see Cercis*
Redcurrant, *see Ribes*
Red-hot poker, *see Kniphofia*
Red ink plant, *see Phytolacca*
Redoul, *see Coriaria*
Redouté, Pierre-Joseph, *43*, *605*, *613*, **614–15**
Reed, *see Phragmites*
Reed grass, *see Glyceria*
Reedmace, *see Typha*
Rehmannia, **532**, *532*
Repton, Humphry, 59, **589–90**, *590*
Reseda, **532**
Rheum, 77, 118, 244, **532–3**
Rhododendron, *45*, 92, *148*, *159*, 171, 173, *179*, 220, 235, 246, 263, **533–6**, *533*, *534*, *535*, 596, 605, 610, 612
Rhubarb, *see Rheum*
Rhus, 170, 245, **536**
Ribbon grass, *see Phalaris*
Ribbon plant, *see Dracaena*
Ribes, 119, 121–2, *122*, 169, 170, 171, 236, 274, 284, **536–7**, *537*
Ricinus, **537**
Robin, Jean, 21
Robinia, 21, 41, 190, 291, **537–8**
Robinson, William, 53, 54, 60, **591**, 592
Rock cress, *see Arabis*
Rocket, *see Hesperis*
Rock gardens, **88–95**, *191*
Rock jessamine, *see Androsace*
Rock madwort, *see Alyssum*
Rock rose, *see Cistus*; *Helianthemum*
Rodgersia, 171, 172, **538**
Romneya, **538**
Rooting hormones, 234, 235
Roper, Lanning, 617
Rosa, 2, 13, 43, *43*, 55, *80*, 98, 103, 105, 133, 141, 151, 171, 173, *174*, 175, 182, *191*, 213, 214, 219, 225, 236, 249, 250, 252, 253, 256, 270, 285–7, *285*, *286*, *287*, **538–42**, *538*, *540*, *542*
Rose, *see Rosa*
Christmas, *see Helleborus*; guelder, *see Viburnum*; Lenten, *see Helleborus*; mallow, *see Hibiscus*; moss, *see Portulaca*; rock, *see Cistus*; *Helianthemum*; sun, *see Cistus*
Rosemarinus, 123, *150*, 169, 235, 236, 275, **542–3**
Rosemary, *see Rosemarinus*
Rose of Sharon, *see Hypericum*
Rotation of crops, 114–15, *115*
Rousseau, Jean-Jacques, 38–9, *38*, **597**, *597*, 617, *617*
Rowan, *see Sorbus*
Rubber, 42
Rubber plant, *see Ficus*
Rubus, 119, 120–21, *121*, 122, 133, 245, 246, 273, *282*, *285*, **543**
Rudbeckia, **543–4**
Rue, *see Ruta*
goat's, *see Galega*; meadow, *see Thalictrum*
Rumex **544**
Runner bean, *see Phaseolus*
Runners, 245–6, *245*
Ruscus, **544**
Rush, *see Juncus*
Ruta, **544**

Sackville-West, Vita, 75, 616
Saffron, *see Crocus*
Sage, *see Salvia*
Jerusalem, *see Phlomis*; white, *see Artemisia*
Sagittaria, **545**
St John's wort, *see Hypericum*
Saintpaulia, 239
Salix, 170, 171, 238, 247, 248, 273, **545–6**
Salpiglossis, **546**
Salsify, 115
Salt tree, *see Halimodendron*
Salvia, 86, 123, **546–7**
Sambucus, 171, **547**
Sandwort, *see Arenaria*
Sanguinaria, **547–8**, *547*
Sanguisorba, **548**
Sansevieria, 239
Santolina, 82, *83*, 169, **548**
Sanvitalia, **548**
Saponaria, **548–9**
Sargent, Charles Sprague, **598**
Sarracenia, **549**
Sasa, **549**
Satin flower, *see Godetia*
Satsuma, *see Citrus*
Satureja, 123, **549–50**
Savory, *see Satureja*
Saxifraga, 169, 171, 245, **550–1**
Saxifrage, *see Saxifraga*
Siberian, *see Bergenia*
Scabiosa, 170, **551**, *551*
Scabious, *see Scabiosa*
giant, *see Cephalaria*
Scarlet plume, *see Euphorbia*
Schinus, **551**
Schizostylis, **551–2**
Schwetzingen, *39*, 40
Scilla, 220, **552**
Scirpus, **552**
Scouring brush, common, *see Equisetum*
Scutellaria, **552**
Sea kale, *see Crambe*
Sea-kale beet, *see Beta*
Sea of Silver Sand (*Kogetsudai*), 49
Sedge, *see Carex*
Sedum, *141*, 169, **552–3**
Seeds, propagation from, **226–33**
Sempervivum, **553**, *553*
Senecio, **553–4**
Senna, *see Cassia*
Sequoia, 169, 170, **554–5**
Service tree, *see Sorbus*
Shad, 170, 171
Shadbush, *see Amelanchier*
Shaddock tree, *see Citrus*
Shallot, *see Allium*
Shell flower, *see Moluccella*
Shenstone, William, 36, 38, 616, 617
Shoo-fly plant, *see Nicandra*
Shooting star, *see Dodecatheon*
Shower tree, *see Cassia*
Shrubs, 213, 214, 219
pruning, 260, **271–6**, **284**
Sidalcea, 172, **555**
Siebold, Philipp Franz von, **609–10**
Silene, **555**
Silk-tassel bush, *see Garrya*
Silk tree, *see Albizia*
Silver-bell, *see Halesia*
Silver grass, *see Miscanthus*
Silver inch plant, *see Tradescantia*
Silver Pavilion (*Ginkaku-ji*), 48, 49
Sinapis, **555**
Sisrinchium, **556**
Sissinghurst Castle, *15*, 53, 75, *75*
Sitwell, Sir George, 53, 616
Skimmia, **556**, 605
Skull-cap, *see Scutellaria*
Smilacina, **556–7**
Smoke bush, *see Cotinus*
Snap bean, *see Phaseolus*
Snapdragon, common, *see Antirrhinum*
Sneezeweed, *see Helenium*
Snowberry, *see Symphoricarpos*
Snowdrop, *see Galanthus*
Snowdrop tree, *see Halesia*
Snowflake, *see Leucojum*
Snow-in-summer, *see Cerastium*
Snowy mespilus, *see Amelanchier*
Soapwort, *see Saponaria*
Soil, **164–78**
chemistry, 172–6; fertilizers, 173–6, 178–82, *180*; organic additives, 176–8; pH scale, 165–6, *172*, 221
Solander, Dr Daniel Carl, 43, **607**
Solanum, 42, *42*, 115, 117, 244, **557–8**, *557*
Soldanella. 558
Solidago, 171, **558**
Solomon's seal, *see Polygonatum*
Sophora, 41, **558–9**
Sorbaria, **559**
Sorbus, 68, 190, **559**
Sorrel, *see Rumex*
Southern cane, *see Arundinaria*
Southernwood, *see Artemisia*
Spanish dagger, *see Yucca*
Spartium, 170, **559–60**
Speedwell, *see Veronica*
Spider flower, *see Cleome*; *Grevillea*
Spider plant, *see Chlorophytum*
Spiderwort, *see Tradescantia*
Spinach, *see Spinacia*
Malabar, *see Basella*; mountain, *see Atriplex*
Spinacia, 115, 227, **560**
Spindle tree, *see Euonymus*
Spiraea, 169, 170, 171, **560–1**, 610
Spiraea, false, *see Sorbaria*
Sprekelia, **561**
Spruce, *see Picea*
Spurge, *see Euphorbia*
Squash, *see Cucurbita*
Stachys, **561**
Stag's antler, *see Aloe*
Staking plants, 84, *84*, 105, *105*
Star of Bethlehem, *see Ornithogalum*
Statice, *see Limonium*
Steele, Fletcher, **592**
Stephanandra, 172
Stephanotis, **562**
Sternbergia, 78, **562**, *562*
Stipa, **562**
Stock, *see Matthiola*
Virginia, *see Malcolmia*
Stokesia, **562–3**
Stonecress, *see Aethionema*
Stonecrop, *see Sedum*
Storksbill, *see Erodium*
Stourhead, *30*, 35, *35*
Stowe, 33–5, *34*, 588–9
Strabo, Walafrid, 13, 15
Stranvaesia, **563**
Strawberry, *see Fragaria*
Strawberry tree, *see Arbutus*
Strawflower, *see Helichrysum*
Streptocarpus, 239
String-of-beads, *see Senecio*
Suckers, 245, *245*, 275, *275*, 278, 282
Sumach, *see Rhus*
Summer sweet, *see Clethra*
Sundew, *see Drosera*
Sunflower, *see Helianthus*
Mexican, *see Tithonia*
Sun plant, *see Portulaca*
Swede, *see Brassica*
Sweet Cicely, *see Myrrhis*
Sweetcorn, *see Zea*
Sweet flag, *see Acorus*
Sweet gum, *see Liquidambar*
Sweet pea, *see Lathyrus*
Sweet pepper bush, *see Clethra*
Sweet sedge, *see Acorus*
Sweet shrub, *see Calycanthus*
Sweet William, *see Dianthus*
Swiss chard, *see Beta*
Sycamore (UK), *see Acer* (*Acer pseudoplatanus*)
Sycamore (US), *see Platanus* (*Platanus occidentalis*)
Symphoricarpos, 274, **563**
Symphytum, **563**
Syringa, 41, 151, 169, 170, 171, 236, 249, 273, 275, **563–4**
Syringa, *see Philadelphus*

Tagetes, 41, 58, 150, 228, 230, **564–5**, *564*
Tamarisk, *see Tamarix*
Tamarix, 134, 190, **565**
Tangerine, *see Citrus*
Tarragon, *see Artemisia*
Taxodium, **565**
Taxus, 14, 72, *271*, **565–6**, 610
Teucrium, **566**
Texas blue-bonnet, *see Lupinus*
Thalictrum, **566**
Theophrastus, **594–5**, 599
Thermopsis, **567**
Thinning seedlings, 231, *231*
Thistle, *see Cirsium*
blue sow, see *Cicerbita*; giant, **500**; globe, see *Echinops*; stemless carlina, *see Carlina*
Thorn-apple, *see Datura*
Thouin, Gabriel, 59, *60*
Thrift, *see Armeria*
Thrift, prickly, *see*

Acantholimon
Thunberg, Carl, **608**
Thunbergia, 608
Thuja, 72, 172, 190, 235, *270*, **567**
Thyme, *see Thymus*
Thymus, 78, 123, *141*, 169, **567–8**
Tiarella, 172
Tickseed, *see Coreopsis*
Tiger flower, *see Tigridia*
Tiger lily, 52
Tigernut, *see Cyperus*
Tigridia, **568**, *568*
Tilia, 41, *133*, 170, 171, 190, **568–9**
Tithonia, 104, **569**
Toad flax, *see Linaria*
Tobacco plant, *see Nicotiana*
Tobacco, 42, *42*
mountain, *see Arnica*
Tomato, *see Lycopersicon*
Tomato tree, *see Cyphomandra*
Toothwort, *see Dentaria*
Top and sub-soil, 68
Topiary, **14**, *14*, 52, 54, *54*, 100, *100*, 134, 271, *271*, 586, *586*
Touch-me-not, *see Impatiens*
Trachycarpus, **569**
Tradescant, John, the Elder, **604**
Tradescant, John, the Younger, **604**
Tradescantia, 171, 569–70, 604
Trapa, **570**
Traveller's joy, *see Clematis*
Treasure flower, *see Gazania*
Tree of heaven, *see Ailanthus*
Tree purslane, *see Atriplex*
Trees, 68, 111
buying and planting, **213–21**; climbing plants on, 98–100, *98*, *99*; fruit, *see* Fruit trees; lopping, 275–6; maidens, 215; planting, 217, *218*, 219; pruning, 125–6; tree structure, **277–8**; whips, 215
Trefoil, *see Trifolium*
Trianon, 22, 25, 26, 29, 32, 60, 61, 587
Trifolium, 173, **570**
Trinity flower, *see Tradescantia*
Trollius, 171, 172, **570**
Tropaeolum (nasturtium), 58, 79, 97, **570–1**, *605*, 606
Truffles, *see Tuber*
Trumpet creeper/vine, *see Campsis*
Tuber, 333
Tuberous pea, *see Lathyrus*
Tulip, *see Tulipa*
tree, *see Liriodendron*
Tulipa, 16, 21, 86, 92, 175, 220, **571**, *571*, 603, 604, *614*
Tupelo, *see Nyssa*
Turnip, *see Brassica*
Turtle-head, *see Chelone*
Twinflower, *see Linnaea*
Typha, **572**

Ulex, 169, 171, **573**
Ulmus, 41, 171, **573**, 606
Umbrella plant, *see Cyperus*
Ursinia, **573–4**
Uvularia, **574**, *574*

Vaccinium, 119, 122, 171, **574**
Valerian, *see Centranthus*
Valerianella, **575**
Vanda, 611
Vaux, Calvert, 57–8, *57*, 64, 590
Vaux-le-Vicomte, *20*, 22, 24, *24*, 25, 26, 62, *62*, *271*, 587, 592
Vegetable gardens, **111–23**
Velvet plant, *see Gynura*
Venetian sumach, *see Cotinus*
Verbascum, 77, **575**
Verbena, **575–6**
Verbena
lemon-scented, *see Lippia*; shrub, *see Lantana*
Veronica, 169, 170, **576**
Veronica, shrubby, *see Hebe*
Versailles, *6*, 10, 18, 21, 22, 23, *23*, 24, 25, 26, *27*, 28–9, *28*, 61, 587, *587*
Vervain, *see Verbena*
Viburnum, 151, 169, 171, 248, 275, **576–7**, *576*
Vicarage gardens, **81–3**
Vicia, 115, 117, *118*, 229, **577**
Villa Aldobrandini, *17*, 31
Villa d'Este, 10, *18*, 19, 31
Villa Gamberaia, *586*
Villandry, 19, *19*, 62, 115
Vinca, 142, **577–8**
Vine *see Vitis*
Cup-and-saucer, *see Cobaea*; flame, *see Senecio*; kangaroo, *see Cissus*; potato, *see Solanum*; rex-begonia, *see Cissus*; Russian, *see Polygonum*; trumpet, see *Camsis*; wax, *see Senecio*
Viola, 21, 86, 150, 228, **578**
Violet, *see Viola*
dog's-tooth, *see Erythronium*; Persian, *see Exacum*; water, *see Hottonia*; yellow dogtooth, *see Erythronium*
Violetta, *see Viola*
Viper's bugloss, *see Echium*
Virginia creeper, *see Parthenocissus*
Vitis, *96*, 98, 99, 101, 122, 131, 175, 237, 240, 247, 250, 256, 276, 282–4, *283*, **578**

Waldsteinia, 172
Wallflower, 228; *see also Cheiranthus*, *Erysimum*
Walls, 93–4, *93*, 96–8, 159, *159*, 160
Walnut, *see Juglans*
Walpole, Horace, 35, 59, **618**
Wandering Jew, *see Tradescantia*
Wand flower, *see Dierama*
Wardian case, 51–2, 610
Watercress, *see Nasturtium*
Water feather, *see Myriophyllum*
Water gardens, **106–10**
Watering, 68, 84, 104, 113, 146, **182–8**
Water-lily, *see Nymphaea*
yellow, *see Nuphar*
Water melon, *see Citrullus*
Watermelon begonia, *see Peperomia*
Water milfoil, *see Myriophyllum*
Water plantain, *see Alisma*
Wattle, *see Acacia*
Wax plant, *see Hoya*
Weedkillers, 181, 197, 199–200
Weeds and weeding, 83–4, *83*, 104, **198**
Weigela, 171, 235, **579**, 608, 610
Whitebeam, *see Sorbus*
White mugwort, *see Artemisia*
Whitlow grass, *see Draba*
Whorlflower, *see Morina*
Williamsburg, *55*, 56–7, 62
Willow, *see Salix*
Willowherb, *see Epilobium*
Wilson, Ernest Henry, *611*, **612**
Windbreaks, 113, 134, 189–90, *189*, *190*
Windflower, *see Anemone*
Window boxes, 147, 150–1
Wine berry, *see Rubus*
Winteraceae, *see Drimys*
Winter green, *see Gaultheria*
Winter's bark, *see Drimys*
Wintersweet, *see Chimonanthus*
Wistaria, 52, 79, 97, 98, *101*, 141, 172, 247, 253, *288*, **579–80**, *579*, 610
Witch hazel, *see Hamamelis*
Woodruff, *see Asperula*
Woodrush, *see Luzula*
Wood sorrel, *see Oxalis*
Woolflower, *see Celosia*
Wormwood, 596
Wrest House, *588*
Wulfenia, **580**

Yarrow, *see Achillea*
Yew, *see Taxus*
Yucca, 169, 248, **580**

Zantedeschia, **581**
Zauschneria, **581**
Zea, **581–2**
Zephyranthes, **582**
Zinnia, **582**
Ziziphus, **582**, 596
Zucchini, *see Cucurbita*

Picture Acknowledgements

Garden Picture Library/Derek Fell 7, 56, 57a, 58, 64a, 65, 593, 606; /Gary Rogers 46; /Lorna Rose 600. Ecole Normale Supérieure 8–9; Musée des Arts décoratifs 11; Giraudon 13, 27b, 43, 587; /Lauros 23r. Ronald Sheridan 12; Mary Evans Picture Library 14; M. Fleurent 15, 16, 17, 18, 21, 22, 23l, 24, 28a, 29, 30, 33, 34, 35, 38, 39, 40, 45, 47, 50, 53, 54, 60, 62, 63a, 64b, 75; J-C Mayer 19, 51, 81a, 116b; DIAF/B Régent 20, 189; /P Kerebel 48; /J-P Laugeland 167; /M Gyssels 169; ROGER-VIOLLET 27a; J de Givry 28b; BULLOZ 31, 61, 595, 596; Nigel Temple 36; Private Collection 37, 590, 599, 602, 614; A Descat 41, 59, 81b, 87, 95, 98, 100a, 116a, 117, 118, 120, 121, 124, 128, 136, 141, 144, 156, 173, 192; Mansell Collection 42; EXPLORER-Luc Girard 44; -F Huguler 49; Gerry Harpur 55; J-C Lamontagne 57b, 137, 199, 210, 211, 603, 608, 611r, 612; John Neubauer 63b; P Ferret 66, 76, 130a, 139, 142; C de Virieu 68, 91; G Lévêque 69, 70, 79, 80, 83, 84, 85, 88, 92, 93, 94, 96, 99, 101, 102, 106, 108, 109, 110, 123, 129, 130b, 131a, 131b, 132, 133, 134, 135, 143, 146, 147, 148, 150, 151, 155, 157, 159, 160, 161, 162, 163, 168, 179, 182, 183, 188, 190, 286, 611l; JACANA 122; A Faivre-Amiot 126; N et P Mioulane 166, 171, 174a, 174b, 175, 176, 184, 185, 186, 187, 190, 194, 195, 196, 198, 199, 212, 213, 214; SCOPE-M Guillard 170, 271; – D Faure 172; G Desnovers 586; Michael Holford 588; J d'Aguilar 193; Mansell Collection 591, 594, 609, 616; Christopher Thacker 597; Goethe Nationalmuseum 598; E T Archive 605, 613; Kew Gardens 615.